Federalism
and the
Charter

Federalism and the Charter

LEADING CONSTITUTIONAL DECISIONS
A NEW EDITION

Peter H. Russell
Rainer Knopff
Ted Morton

CARLETON UNIVERSITY PRESS
OTTAWA, CANADA
1993

© Carleton University Press Inc. 1989

ISBN 0-88629-087-2 (paperback)
      0-88629-096-1 (casebound)

Printed and bound in Canada

Carleton Library Series #155

Canadian Cataloguing in Publication Data

Main entry under title:

Federalism and the Charter

(The Carleton library ; 155)
New ed.
Previously published under title: Leading constitutional
    decisions.
ISBN 0-88629-096-1 (bound) -
ISBN 0-88629-087-2 (pbk.)

1. Canada—Constitutional law—Cases. I. Russell,
Peter H. II. Knopff, Rainer, 1948-   . III. Morton,
F. L. (Frederick Lee), 1949-   . IV. Title: Leading
constitutional decisions. V. Series.

KE4216.3.F34   1989   342.71   C89-090165-1

Distributed by: Oxford University Press Canada
                70 Wynford Drive,
                Don Mills, Ontario,
                Canada. M3C 1J9
                (416) 441-2941

Cover design: Robert Chitty

Cover photograph: Courtesy of The National

Acknowledgements: Archives of Canada, PA 130272

Carleton University Press gratefully acknowledges the support extended to its
publishing programme by the Canada Council and the Ontario Acts Council.

CONTENTS

PART TWO: **RIGHTS AND FREEDOMS**
A: FUNDAMENTAL RIGHTS AND FREEDOMS IN THE B.N.A. ACT

B: THE CANADIAN BILL OF RIGHTS

C: THE CHARTER OF RIGHTS AND FREEDOMS

PREFACE TO THE FIFTH EDITION

This edition of *Leading Constitutional Decisions* includes, for the first time, Supreme Court decisions interpreting the Charter of Rights and Freedoms. As we approached the task of adding the new Charter cases to the older material, thought was given to producing two volumes—one on federalism issues and the other on rights and freedoms. But this idea was discarded at least for now. The number of politically salient constitutional cases may some day become so large that two volumes will be necessary. Until then we think it will be in the interests of students and professors to have all the leading cases in a single volume.

There is a strong pedagogical reason for retaining the single volume format as long as possible. If the collection were divided into two volumes, one on federalism and the other on rights and freedoms, it is likely that some instructors would confine their coverage of judicial interpretation to the trendier volume on rights and freedoms. This would be a grave disservice to students. It would foster the false notion that Canada had followed the United States in abandoning federalism as a major basis for judicial review and blind students to the fact that in the Canadian constitutional system "provincial rights" continue to be an important rights issue.

Changes in the first part of the book show the continuing vitality of the division of powers as a basis for judicial review. One of the old Privy Council decisions (the 1916 *Insurance Reference*) has been dropped and several others shortened, but new Supreme Court decisions on the principal sources of federal legislative power, peace, order and good government, and trade and commerce, have been added. Also, for the first time, cases dealing with the judicial power are included. In the late 1970s and early 1980s the judicature sections of the Constitution generated more constitutional litigation than any other sections. The issues raised in these cases pertain both to federalism and to the separation of powers between the judiciary and the other branches of government.

In part two on rights and freedoms, the first two sections, as in previous editions, contain cases on implied rights in the Constitution Act, 1867 and on the statutory Canadian Bill of Rights. While several cases have been eliminated, most have been retained. Knowledge of these cases is essential for understanding the movement to add a comprehensive charter of rights to the Canadian Constitution. These cases also provide a bench-mark for assessing the significance of the Supreme Court's treatment of the Charter.

The third section of part two contains a selection of the Supreme Court's early Charter decisions. These cases deal with some of the more universal rights and freedoms in the Charter. The final section of this part contains both pre-Charter and Charter cases concerning language and education rights.

There are no cases on section 35 of the Constitution Act which recognizes and affirms "the existing aboriginal and treaty rights of the aboriginal peoples of Canada". At the time of writing the Supreme Court of Canada had rendered no decisions on this important addition to entrenched constitutional rights.

The only change in part three dealing with constitutional change is the addition of the Supreme Court's decision rejecting Quebec's claim to a constitutional veto.

The introductory essay at the beginning of the volume has been largely rewritten to incorporate references to the Constitution Act, 1982 and the important changes resulting from it in the significance and nature of constitutional interpretation in Canada. Similarly, the Suggestions for Further Reading at the end of the book have been up-dated to include some of the leading literature on the Charter. Small changes have been made to a number of the introductory notes to reflect recent constitutional developments. Appendices have been added setting out the principal provisions of the Constitution Act, 1867, the Constitution Act, 1982 and the Meech Lake Accord.

The other major change in this edition of *Leading Constitutional Decisions* is the help I have received from my colleagues, Rainer Knopff and Ted Morton. Our collaboration began in 1984 with the production of edited versions of the first Supreme Court decisions on the Charter of Rights. That series continues and now covers, on a case-by-case basis, Supreme Court decisions on all aspects of the Constitution. I was anxious to secure their collaboration in this volume not only to have the benefit of their insights in editing and discussing the cases but also to have some assurance that the collection will be carried on by two younger scholars active in this field of political science. I am most grateful to them for becoming partners in this enterprise.

Our purpose remains as it has been in earlier editions: to give those who are not legally trained convenient access to judicial decisions which have had an important bearing on Canada's political and constitutional history. This purpose continues to be the criterion for the selection of cases. The case commentaries are designed to put each case in its political setting, to identify interesting features of the judges' reasoning and to suggest the significance of the decision in the development of the constitution and for various policy issues.

As in earlier editions, the symbol ~ has been used to mark off the editors' words from those of the judges.

PETER H. RUSSELL
University of Toronto
November, 1988

Introduction

JUDICIAL REVIEW AND THE CANADIAN CONSTITUTION

Many Canadians expressed shock and surprise when the Supreme Court of Canada was called upon in the spring of 1981 to determine the constitutionality of the federal government's plan to proceed unilaterally with its proposed restructuring of Canada's Constitution. "Isn't it strange," they asked, "for the Court to be involved in such a *political* question?" This question reflects the fact that Canadians have little understanding of the political significance of judicial interpretation of the constitution. This is not surprising given the quiet, unheralded way in which judicial review became an important part of Canada's constitutional system.

It is in keeping with the nature of much of Canada's constitutional history that one of the most influential elements in its development—judicial interpretation of the British North America Act[1]—was accepted at the outset with little awareness of its full significance. The Fathers of Confederation were remarkably insensitive to the problems connected with judicial review under a federal constitution, despite the fact that American experience had, by 1867, shown the crucial importance of the Supreme Court in determining the extent of national and state powers. Section 101 of the B.N.A. Act granted to the federal Parliament the power to establish a "General Court of Appeal for Canada", but nowhere in the Constitution was there explicit recognition of the power of that court, nor of the Judicial Committee of the Privy Council (the English tribunal which was then the final court of appeal for British colonies), to determine the constitutional validity of federal or provincial legislation. Canadians never witnessed a case like *Marbury v. Madison*, in which Chief Justice Marshall successfully claimed for the United States' Supreme Court the role of constitutional arbiter with the power to strike down any act of government, national or local, which in the Court's view violated the terms of the constitution. Yet it was precisely that power which from the country's earliest days the Canadian judiciary, without explicit acknowledgment and despite the incompatibility of judicial review with the traditional British theory of parliamentary sovereignty, assumed with respect to the B.N.A. Act.

Canadians are apt to look upon judicial review as a necessary ingredient of a federal state. But to those who accepted judicial review so readily in the 1870s and 1880s, especially to the jurists who manned the Judicial Committee of the Privy Council, the courts' power to assess the constitutional validity of legislation was as much a corollary of imperialism as of federalism. The B.N.A. Act was, after all, an act of the Imperial Parliament, and according to the Colonial Laws Validity Act Dominion statutes were void if they conflicted with British statutes.

[1] In 1982, Canada's original Constitution, the British North America Act, 1867, was re-named the Constitution Act, 1867. Similarly, amendments to the Constitution, including the 1982 amendment, are now entitled the Constitution Act followed by the year of enactment.

However, over time, with the waning of the imperial connection and the experience of so many controversies associated with the division of powers between the federal and provincial legislatures, judicial review came to be seen as an imperative of federalism. Canadian judges in rejecting the few attempts by legislatures to evade judicial review reasoned that the federal division of powers could be effectively destroyed if a legislature could deny the right to challenge the constitutional validity of its actions in the courts.[2]

The patriation of the Constitution in 1982 significantly broadened the basis of judicial review in Canada. Section 52 of the Constitution Act, 1982[3] establishes, for the first time, an explicit basis for the judicial veto of unconstitutional laws by declaring that the Constitution of Canada is "the supreme law of Canada" and that "any law that is inconsistent with the provisions of the Constitution is, to the extent of the inconsistency, of no force or effect." More importantly, the addition of a charter of rights and freedoms to the constitution widens the focus of judicial review from a preoccupation with the powers of government to a concern for the rights of citizens. Until the advent of the Charter—despite the inclusion in the original constitution of clauses guaranteeing rights to denominational education (section 93), the use of English and French in certain institutions (section 133), as well as the implicit entrenchment of rights inherent in an independent judiciary (section 99) and parliamentary institutions (for example, section 17)—the prevailing theory was that the Constitution exhaustively distributes *all* the powers of self-government to the provincial and federal legislatures.[4] Under a constitution with a charter of rights and freedoms this so-called "exhaustion theory" must give way to a theory which acknowledges that the Constitution bestows rights on individuals and groups.

However, the shift away from a regime of legislative supremacy has not been unqualified. Section 33 of the Charter permits the federal Parliament and provincial legislatures to include clauses in their legislation which, for five years at a time, will enable the legislation to override designated sections of the Charter. The override can be applied to the political freedoms in section 2 of

---

[2] The fullest consideration of this issue was by Ontario's highest court in *Ottawa Valley Power Vo.* v. *A.G. Ontario* (1937) O.R. 297. The Supreme Court of Canada briefly considered the matter in *B.C. Power Corp.* v. *B.C. Electric Co.* [1962] S.C.R. 642.

[3] The Constitution Act, 1982 was made part of the Canadian Constitution by the Canada Act 1982, an Act of the United Kingdom Parliament. It is the Canada Act 1982 which patriated Canada's Constitution by establishing that it would no longer be amended in the United Kingdom. The Constitution Act, 1982 contains rules for amending the Constitution in Canada and the Canadian Charter of Rights and Freedoms. See case 62 below for the Supreme Court's decision concerning the validity of the federal government's attempt to accomplish these changes without the support of most of the provinces.

[4] For a classic statement of the theory see the opinion of Justice Kerwin in *Saumur*, case 33 below.

the Charter, the legal rights in sections 7 to 14 and the equality rights in section 15. Although the override clause has rarely been used as a deliberate means of insulating legislation from judicial review,[5] its existence removes much of the anti-democratic sting from judicial decisions vetoing the acts of the democratically accountable branches of government.[6]

These recent changes in the Canadian constitution—patriation, the addition of a supremacy clause and the Charter of Rights—complete the process of shifting the foundation of judicial review in Canada from imperialism to federalism to constitutionalism. From the perspective of constitutionalism, the role of the judiciary in exercising the power of judicial review is to enforce the constitution as a higher law on all who govern.

FROM THE JUDICIAL COMMITTEE TO THE SUPREME COURT

One reason Canadians were slow to realize the importance of judicial review is that until 1949 their highest court of appeal in constitutional matters was a foreign tribunal, the Judicial Committee of the Privy Council. When the Supreme Court of Canada was established in 1875, efforts were made, notably by the Liberal Minister of Justice, Edward Blake, to limit, if not abolish, appeals to the Judicial Committee. But these efforts came to naught before the determined opposition of the British law officers and Sir John A. Macdonald's Conservative party, both of whom looked upon the appeal as an essential link of imperial union. In the twentieth century the agitation to abolish appeals was rekindled, in part by growing nationalist sentiment, but also, with increasing urgency, by those Canadians who resented what they regarded as the unduly rigid and decentralizing tenor of the Judicial Committee's treatment of Canada's Constitution. The enactment of the Statute of Westminster in 1931 opened the way for the Canadian Parliament to abolish appeals to the Privy Council. Although the federal Parliament's power to do this was challenged in the courts, it was finally confirmed by the Judicial Committee itself in 1947.[7] When the Supreme Court Act was finally amended in 1949 to make the

---

[5] Saskatchewan used the override in legislation ordering striking civil servants back to work. Subsequently the Supreme Court ruled that ''freedom of association'' in the Charter does not embrace the right to strike. (See *Alberta Labour Reference*, case 49 below.) But at the time Saskatchewan was facing a Saskatchewan Court of Appeal decision which had come to the opposite conclusion. From 1982 to 1987, as a gesture of protest against the 1982 constitutional settlement which Quebec did not support, the Quebec National Assembly attached an override clause to all existing legislation. This blanket use of section 33 was found to be constitutional by the Supreme Court in its 1988 decision in the Quebec sign case (case 52 below). Following this case, the Bourassa Government used the override again to fend off any court challenges to new legislation requiring French only outdoor signs.

[6] For the theory behind the override, see Paul C. Weiler, ''Rights and Judges in a Democracy: A New Canadian Version,'' (1984) 18 *University of Michigan Journal of Law Reform*, 51.

[7] See case 17 below.

Supreme Court supreme in fact as well as in name, the most serious opposition came not from Anglo-Canadian imperial sentiment but from advocates of provincial interests, who by this time had come to believe that they had a vested interest in the Judicial Committee's line of constitutional interpretation.

There can be no doubt about the supremacy of the Judicial Committee up to the abolition of appeals in 1949. In some of its earliest constitutional decisions the Supreme Court exhibited considerable independence. The Court's first decision on the federal trade and commerce power in the *Severn* case[8] has been placed at the beginning of the first part of this book containing Privy Council decisions in order to display the sharp contrast between the early Supreme Court's very expansive interpretation of federal power and the Privy Council's concern for maintaining a balanced federal system. But within a decade the Supeme Court had succumbed to the reality of its subordinate position in the judicial hierarchy and remained, with few exceptions, a "captive court" until its emancipation in 1949. In the words of a scholar who was to become Chief Justice of the Court, "The task of the Supreme Court was not to interpret the constitution but rather to interpret what the Privy Council said the constitution meant."[9] The Court's recognition of its subservience to the Privy Council was reinforced by the tendency of Canadian litigants in some of the most important constitutional cases to by-pass the Supreme Court altogether. Nearly half of the Privy Council's decisions on the Canadian constitution (77 Out of 159) came in cases appealed directly from provincial courts of appeal.[10]

When the Supreme Court took over as Canada's highest court of appeal, in theory it was free to strike out on an independent course of constitutional interpretation.[11] But in practice there were powerful constraints limiting the Supreme Court's freedom to set aside the constitutional handiwork of the Privy Council. Supreme Court justices were aware of provincial anxieties that the Court might turn out to be dangerously centralist and of the federal government's promise in 1949 that the abolition of Privy Council appeals would not lead to the jettisoning of the Privy Council precedents. Further, the concern in our legal culture for consistency and predictability was too ingrained, and the Privy Council's decisions far too extensive and prescriptive, to leave much scope, at least in the short run, for judicial pioneering.[12] Still, over time, the

---

[8] See case 1.

[9] Bora Laskin, "The Supreme Court of Canada: A Final Court of Appeal of and for Canadians" (1951), 29 *Canadian Bar Review*, 1038, at p. 1069.

[10] This enumeration is based on the compilation of cases in *Decisions of the Judicial Committee of the Privy Council Relating to the British North America Act, 1867 and the Canadian Constitution 167-1954* arranged by Richard A. Olmsted.

[11] See Justice Rand's *dictum* in the *Ontario Farm Products Marketing Act Reference*, case 19 below.

[12] But the Liberal government rejected a proposal supported by the Canadian Bar Association and the Conservative opposition which would have made Privy Council decisions binding on the Supreme Court.

Supreme Court has given new shape and substance to Canada's constitutional law. It has done this not through dramatic overruling of Privy Council decisions but by choosing among competing lines of precedents (for instance, on the peace, order and good government power) and by applying established interpretative formulations to new fields of legislation (for instance wage and price controls). In the civil liberties field the Supreme Court has had virtually a free hand for the simple reason that the Privy Council never pronounced on most of the important issues in this area of constitutional adjudication.

We may now be at the point in the development of Canada's constitutional law where the Supreme Court's jurisprudence is surpassing in importance the work of the Judicial Committee. Still, the Privy Council's legacy will continue to be felt as an enduring ingredient of Canada's political culture. The core of that legacy is, above all, a tendency to look upon federalism as "a level of sovereign jurisdictional rivalry."[13] In endeavouring to preserve a division of powers appropriate for "classical federalism" and thereby resist the strongly centralizing tendencies of the constitutional text, the Judicial Committee developed an acute sensitivity to the competing claims of the provinces and the federal government. Despite periods of co-operative federalism, of province-building and of populist centralism, this atmosphere of competing jurisdictions is likely to remain a distinctive feature of the Canadian political system. If, in the future, the first question that Canadians can be counted on to ask of any new subject of legislation is, "Does it come under federal or provincial jurisdiction?", this will in large measure reflect the weight of the Privy Council's constitutional interpretation. Provincial rights remain an honourable part of Canada's constitutional tradition.[14]

The Judicial Committee's interpretation of the Canadian Constitution also generated a debate about the proper role of the courts in constitutional interpretation—a debate that has a timeless quality and that is highly relevant to the Charter of Rights.[15] This is another important reason for continuing to study the work of the Judicial Committee.

THE SUPREME COURT AS CONSTITUTIONAL ARBITER

The significant role the modern Supreme Court has come to play as the judicial arbiter of Canada's Constitution was not anticipated in the years immediately following World War II. Of course there was no constitutional

---

[13] F.E. Labrie, "Canadian Constitutional Interpretation and Legislative Review" (1949-50), 8 *University of Toronto Law Journal* 298.

[14] See Robert C. Vipond, "Constitutional Politics and the Legacy of the Provincial Rights Movement in Canada," (1985) 18 *Canadian Journal of Political Science*, 495.

[15] See, for example, Frederick Vaughan, "Critics of the Judicial Committee: The New Orthodoxy and an Alternative Explanation," and Replies by Alan Cairns and Peter Russell, (1986) 19 *Canadian Journal of Political Science*, 495.

bill of rights at that time and so far as federalism was concerned the emphasis was on instruments of "executive federalism" such as tax-sharing arrangements and shared-cost programs rather than judicial interpretation or constitutional amendment as the principal means of developing the constitution. Professor Donald Smiley expressed the prevailing view of constitutional observers in the 1950s and 1960s when he wrote that, "The federal aspects of the Canadian constitution, using the latter term in the broadest sense, have come to be less what the courts say they are than what the federal and provincial cabinets and bureaucracies in a continuous series of formal and informal relations determine them to be."[16]

Undoubtedly there was a great deal of truth in this thesis. Politicians and administrators certainly played a more prominent role than judges in the postwar evolution of Canadian federalism. Supreme Court decisions on the constitution in the two decades after 1949 were not as important as Privy Council decisions had been in the two decades before the war. Even so, the decline in the importance of judicial review tended to be exaggerated. Quantitatively there was virtually no change in the frequency with which Canada's highest court was called upon to decide constitutional issues: two to three constitutional cases a year continued to be the norm. Some of these decisions had a significant impact on developments in the federal system during these years. The Court's approval of a system of intergovernmental delegation to administrative agencies[17] contributed to the so-called "co-operative federalism" that flourished for a while. Its 1967 decision giving Ottawa jurisdiction over off-shore minerals[18] increased the federal government's bargaining power in a major field of federal-provincial combat and aroused provincial suspicions of the Supreme Court's fairness as a judicial umpire of Canadian federalism.

The veritable explosion of constitutional litigation which occurred in the 1970s demonstrated how wrong it was to write off the Supreme Court as an important element in the dynamics of Canadian federalism. Whereas the *Supreme Court Reports* for the first half of the 1970s contain only nine decisions on the division of powers, the *Reports* for the last five years of the decade record thirty-six decisions on constitutional issues—a fourfold increase. The trend continued into the 1980s. Forty-two constitutional decisions are reported for the four-year period from 1980 to 1983—the period preceding the Court's first decision on the Charter.

This sudden increase in constitutional litigation reflected a more combative period in federal-provincial relations. Instead of waiting to reach accommodations through intergovernmental negotiations, governments were often inclined to test the limits of their constitutional powers by taking unilateral

---

[16] D.V. Smiley, "The Rowell-Sirois Report and Provincial Autonomy," (1962), 28 *Canadian Journal of Political Science and Economics* 54, at p. 59.

[17] See case 60 below.

[18] See case 20 below.

policy initiatives hoping that they would withstand a court challenge. Provincial initiatives in the natural resource and cable TV areas[19] and the Trudeau government's attempts at unilateral constitutional reform are leading examples.[20]

In its treatment of the division of powers in the 1970s and 1980s, the Supreme Court adopted a remarkably balanced approach—perhaps not as solicitous of provincial rights as the Judicial Committee but certainly less centralist than the Court had been in its first two decades as Canada's highest court.[21] A clear indication of this shift is the *Anti-Inflation Reference*,[22] where the Court's majority rejected the national concern approach to peace, order and good government which it had embraced 14 years earlier in *Johannesson*.[23] In the 1970s for the first time since 1949, the Supreme Court overruled national legislation on federalism grounds.[24] True, there were some major provincial losses during this period—notably in the fields of natural resources and communications policy[25]—which generated public criticism of the Court by provincial premiers and demands for constitutional amendments to overcome the decisions. These provincial attacks on the Court put pressure on the justices to demonstrate their legitimacy as trustworthy arbiters of federal-provincial disputes. The fact that they were appointed by the federal government without any formal participation of the provinces in the appointment process probably added to this pressure. The balance the Court began to strike in adjudicating federalism issues—a balance highlighted in its decision in the *Patriation Reference*[26]—suggests that the justices were sensitive to their political environment.

The Supreme Court's very success in establishing its credibility as a federal umpire has encouraged constitutional litigation on issues of federalism. An umpire who is perceived to be reasonably balanced is much more likely to be resorted to than one who is demonstrably biased. In Canada "whatever side you are on in a constitutional dispute over the division of powers, the record of balance makes it reasonable to believe you might win."[27] The very opposite

---

[19] See cases 23, 24 and 25 below.

[20] See cases 61 and 62 below.

[21] For two scholarly analyses of the Court's balance, see Gilbert l'Ecuyer, *La Cour Supreme du Canada et la partage des Competences 1949-78* (Gouvernement du Quebec: Ministre des Affaires Intergouvernementales, 1978), and Peter W. Hogg, "Is the Supreme Court of Canada Biased in Constitutional Cases?" (1979), 57 *Canadian Bar Review* 721.

[22] See case 22 below.

[23] See case 18 below.

[24] *McDonald* v. *Vapor Canada Ltd.* [1977] 2 S.C.R. 655. For discussion and further examples, see case 28 below.

[25] See cases 23, 24 and 25 below.

[26] Case 62 below.

[27] Peter H. Russell, "The Supreme Court and Federal-Provincial Relations: The Political Use of Legal Resources," (1985), 11 *Canadian Public Policy* 161, at 164.

has been the case in the United States. In 1985, in *Garcia*, a majority of the United States Supreme Court took the position that challenges to Congressional legislation based on federalism grounds would no longer be dealt with by the courts; it would be the responsibility of the United States Senate to apply any states rights restrictions on Congress.[28]

At the same time that the Supreme Court was playing such an active role in deciding disputes over the powers of governments, its decisions were paving the way to a much larger judicial role in disputes about the constitutional rights of citizens. Its decision in *Dupond*[29] putting an end to the notion of an implied bill of rights in the Constitution Act, 1867 and its unwillingness to give much weight to the statutory Bill of Rights[30] gave added momentum to the movement in Canada to adopt a constitutional bill of rights. Yet, in its treatment of constitutionally entrenched language rights,[31] the Court was also indicating that it was prepared to be quite activist in giving a liberal interpretation of constitutional rights as restrictions on government power.

In the 1970s the Supreme Court's jurisdiction was changed in a way that greatly increased its exposure to issues of public law. Up until 1975 there was a right to appeal on a question of law from the highest court of a province or the Federal Court of Appeal to the Supreme Court in any suit involving $10,000 or more. Under this rule the Court was obliged to expend much of its energy on run-of-the-mill private suits. In 1975 this monetary criterion was abolished and the Court became its own gate-keeper with the opportunity to choose most of the cases it hears on the basis of their public importance.[32] Increasingly the Supreme Court of Canada has become primarily a public law forum. Most of its cases deal with administrative law, criminal law and constitutional law. The advent of the Charter of Rights has accelerated this trend. By the mid 1980s constitutional cases accounted for nearly a quarter of the Court's case-load.[33] While this means that the Canadian Supreme Court's docket has come to resemble more closely that of its American counterpart, it has a much wider range of responsibilities than the U.S. Supreme Court. As a "General Court of Appeal for Canada" the Supreme Court of Canada continues to serve as the final court of appeal in all matters of provincial law, which include judge-made common law and Quebec's Civil Code.

---

[28] *Garcia* v. *San Antonio Metropolitan Transit Authority* 105 S. Ct. 1005 (1985).

[29] Case 36 below.

[30] See cases 38 and 39 below.

[31] See case 54 below.

[32] There are still a few exceptional situations in which an appeal lies to the Supreme Court as of right without any need to seek the Court's leave. For details, see S.I. Bushnell, "Leave to Appeal Applications to the Supreme Court: A Matter of Public Importance" (1972), 1 *Supreme Court Review* 495.

[33] Patrick Monahan, *Politics and the Constitution: The Charter, Federalism and the Supreme Court of Canada* (Toronto, 1987), ch. 2.

Although the Charter of Rights came into force on April 17, 1982, it took two years for the first Charter cases to work their way up to the Supreme Court. From the very beginning the Court seems to have had no doubt about the judiciary's *general mandate* with respect to the Charter. In *Skapinker*,[34] its first Charter decision, Justice Estey, writing for a unanimous court, made it clear that the justices were prepared to take the Charter seriously, to avoid a narrow and overly technical interpretation of its terms and to strike down laws and practices of government found to be in conflict with it. In decisions which immediately followed, various members of the Court stated their conviction that the Charter brought with it, in the words of Justice LeDain, ''a new constitutional mandate for judicial review.''[35]

The Supreme Court certainly started off on an extremely activist note. In nine of the first fifteen Charter cases it decided, the Court upheld the Charter claim—a very high success rate of 60% for Charter claimants. In this early group of cases the Court struck down five pieces of legislation—two provincial laws (the section of Quebec's Charter of the French language restricting access to English schools[36] and a section of British Columbia's Motor Vehicle Act creating an absolute liability offence with a mandatory jail term for driving with a suspended license[37]) and three federal laws (the Lord's Day Act,[38] the search provisions of the Combines Investigation Act[39] and a section of the Narcotics Control Act reversing the onus of proof[40]). In this initial period of Charter interpretation, the Court also read onerous procedural requirements into the refugee provisions of the Immigration Act,[41] took a very liberal approach to the test for excluding evidence obtained in violation of an accused's Charter rights,[42] and made it clear that when a law is found to violate a Charter right the onus would be on the offending government to demonstrate that its law is ''justified in a free and democratic society.''[43]

But after this opening spurt, which ended in early 1986, the Court began to moderate its activism. Over the next two years, beginning in January 1986 with its rejection of language right claims in three cases[44] through to its decision in *Morgentaler*[45] at the end of January, 1988, the Charter claim was upheld in

---

[34] Case 40 below.
[35] *The Queen* v. *Therens*, case 44 below, at p. 430.
[36] *A.-G. Quebec* v. *Quebec Association of Protestant School Boards*, case 55 below.
[37] *Reference Re British Columbia Motor Vehicle Act*, case 45 below.
[38] *The Queen* v. *Big M Drug Mart*, case 42 below.
[39] *Hunter* v. *Southam* [1984] 2 S.C.R. 145.
[40] *The Queen* v. *Oakes*, case 46 below.
[41] *Singh* v. *Minister of Employment and Immigration*, case 41 below.
[42] *The Queen* v. *Therens*.
[43] *Hunter* v. *Southam*.
[44] See *Société des Acadiens* v. *Association of Parents*, case 56 below.
[45] Case 50 below.

only 8 of 32 cases. The Charter success rate had fallen from 60% to a much more modest 25%. While the Court's overruling of the abortion law (section 251 of the Criminal Code) in *Morgentaler* attracted a great deal of public attention, it was hardly typical of the Court's Charter decision-making during this period. Only two other laws were struck down during these two years—these too were pieces of federal criminal legislation.[46] Although the Court considered challenges to a number of important provincial laws—notably Alberta's and Saskatchewan's anti-strike legislation,[47] Ontario's Sunday-closing law[48] and a law extending full public funding to Ontario's Roman Catholic schools[49]—all were upheld. The Court sounded its loudest note of restraint in *Dolphin Delivery*[50] when it ruled, unanimously, that judge-made common law could not be challenged on Charter grounds when it is being applied in private litigation. This decision greatly limits the extent to which the Charter will penetrate private legal relationships in Canada.

In this second period of Charter decision-making important differences of constitutional philosophy began to emerge within the Supreme Court. Whereas all but two of the first fifteen decisions were unanimous, there were dissents in 16 of the next 32. Most of these have been solo dissents.[51] While we cannot talk about factions within the Court, it is possible to identify leaders of opposing tendencies. The two justices who have dissented most often, Wilson and McIntyre, stand at opposite ends of the Court. Justice Wilson is apt to give the broadest interpretation of the Charter's rights and freedoms and is the most difficult justice to persuade that limits on constitutional rights are justifiable, while Justice McIntyre is most deferential to the legislature's judgment on the scope of rights and freedoms.

This early experience with the Charter shows how dangerous it is to make categorical statements about the Supreme Court's orientation on the Charter. Judicial culture like political culture is apt to be dynamic. The one thing we can be sure about is that whatever approach the Court takes—restrained, activist or middle-of-the-road—it is bound to come in for some criticism. In applying the Charter it must deal with issues such as abortion, Sunday closing and public funding of religious education on which there are strongly opposed interest

---

[46] In *Smith* v. *The Queen* [1987] 1 S.C.R. 1045, the mandatory seven year sentence for importing illegal drugs was found to constitute cruel and unusual punishment, and in *The Queen* v. *Vaillancourt* [1987] 2 S.C.R. 631, the concept of "constructive murder" in section 213 of the Criminal Code was found to be fundamentally unjust and therefore in violation of section 7 of the Charter.

[47] Case 49 below and *Saskatchewan* v. *Retail, Wholesale and Department Store Union*, [1987] 1 S.C.R. 460.

[48] Case 48 below.

[49] Case 58 below.

[50] Case 47 below.

[51] Indeed, it was not until *Stevens* v. *The Queen* (ruling that the Charter can be applied retrospectively) decided on June 30, 1988 that as many as three justices dissented.

groups and no clear social consensus. Nor is there a consensus on the general approach judges should take to constitutional interpretation.

Thus in the Charter era the Supreme Court's political prominence continues to increase. With its activity in interpreting constitutional rights and freedoms (now virtually the only major judicial review function of the United States Supreme Court), added to its continuing role as a federal umpire. Canada's Supreme Court is now playing a larger role in exercising judicial review in Canada than its counterpart plays in the United States. In these circumstances, it is more anomalous than ever that this institution which has such a major responsibility in interpreting and applying the Constitution is not itself established by the Constitution but simply by an ordinary Act of Parliament. Moreover, increasing political awareness of the Court's role in shaping the powers of government and the rights of citizens should call into question the lack of any checks or balances on the federal government's appointment of its members.

This situation could be remedied by the Meech Lake Accord, the package of constitutional proposals negotiated by the federal and provincial first ministers to win Quebec's support for the constitutional changes effected in 1982.[52] One of the constitutional amendments contained in the Accord would, in effect, constitutionalize the Supreme Court. Adoption of this amendment will mean that the existence of the Court, the definition of its basic functions, the justices' security of tenure, the method of appointment and the number of justices (including the guarantee that three of the Court's nine judges must come from Quebec) are entrenched in the Constitution—and deeply entrenched at that, as changes will require the unanimous approval of the House of Commons and all provincial legislatures.

The Meech Lake Accord would make an important change in the appointing process.[53] The federal government would continue to exercise the final power of appointment but on the basis of nominations received from the provincial governments. In the case of Quebec places on the Court, the nominations would have to come from the Quebec government. The consequences of this change are apt to be less severe than its critics have claimed. The provincial and federal courts of appeal will in all likelihood continue to be the primary recruitment pools for the Supreme Court. It is here that opinion-writing ability and jurisprudential as well as ideological tendencies are most clearly displayed. The federal government has the exclusive control over appointments to

---

[52] See Peter W. Hogg, *Meech Lake Constitutional Accord Annotated* (Toronto, 1988). To be adopted the proposals must be approved by the federal House of Commons and all ten provincial legislatures. At the time of writing the Accord has the approval of all but Manitoba and New Brunswick.

[53] For a detailed analysis, see Peter H. Russell, "The Supreme Court Proposals in the Meech Lake Accord," (1988), 14 *Canadian Public Policy*, 161.

all of these intermediate appellate courts. In no instance could the federal government be forced to accept any particular federal nominee. Appointments will require a consensus of the federal government and at least one province. It could even turn out that with provincial participation built into the appointing process, Supreme Court justices might feel under less pressure to demonstrate their neutrality in adjudicating federal-provincial disputes.

APPROACHES TO CONSTITUTIONAL INTERPRETATION

Constitutional documents require interpretation. Many of the important rules and principles of a constitution are expressed in broad and abstract language. This is to be expected. As legal documents, constitutions cannot be drafted like private contracts designed to govern a very specific situation for a finite period of time. Constitutions are designed to endure, to provide a framework for the governance of a people into a future the framers of the constitution cannot foresee.[54] True, there are formal mechanisms for amending constitutions but they are ill-suited for the day-by-day, case-by-case application of the constitution to the circumstances which arise in the unfolding life of the nation. The mechanism for carrying out this function is constitutional interpretation through the exercise of judicial review.

Some of our Fathers of Confederation felt that they had been so detailed and thorough in drafting the Constitution that there would be little need for interpretation. "We have avoided all conflict of jurisdiction and authority," boasted John A. Macdonald.[55] How wrong he was! Consider the terms on which power is divided between federal and provincial legislatures. The federal parliament is to make laws for "the peace, order, and good government of Canada" in all matters except those assigned exclusively to the provincial legislature. The provincial legislatures have exclusive jurisdiction over "property and civil rights", while "the regulation of trade and commerce" is under exclusive federal jurisdiction. What do these phrases mean? More specifically, what do they mean when applied, say, to the regulation of industrial relations in an advanced industrial economy?

Consider, too, the terms of the Charter of Rights so recently added to the Canadian Constitution. That document, among other things, tells us, in section 7, that "Everyone has the right to life, liberty and security of the person and the right not to be deprived thereof except in accordance with the principles of fundamental justice." Now, just for starters, what does "everyone" embrace—a foetus? a person applying to enter Canada as a refugee? Does "liberty" cover anything and everything each of us wants to do? Are social and

---

[54] For a classic statement of this idea see the words of the American Chief Justice, John Marshall, adopted by the Supreme Court of Canada in *Skapinker*, case 40 below.

[55] *The Confederation Debates in the Province of Canada*, Carleton Library ed. (Toronto, 1963), p. 44.

economic security to be included under "security of the person"? And what on earth is "fundamental justice"? Philosophers have been wrestling with that question through the millenia. Then, bear in mind that whatever the rights in section 7 mean they, like all of the rights and freedoms set out in the Charter, are subject to "such reasonable limits prescribed by law as can be demonstrably justified in a free and democratic society." These words too will require more than a little interpretation.

These examples underline the fact that constitution-making is always incomplete. In applying the general terms of the constitutional text to specific disputes, the judiciary adds flesh and blood to the bare bones of the constitution. Judicial decisions, above all those of the final court of appeal, become part of the law of the constitution. But not a fixed and unmoving part. As interpretations accumulate, they too contain doctrines and statements of general principle which are interpreted and reinterpreted by ensuing generations of judges. Not that judges are the only participants in this on-going process of constitution-making. Occasionally their interpretations may generate so much political discontent that they are reversed by formal constitutional amendments. Such was the case with the Privy Council decision denying the federal parliament the power to establish a national unemployment scheme and the Supreme Court decisions denying the provinces the power to levy indirect taxes on their natural resources.[56]

The cases in this volume contain a number of different approaches to the task of constitutional interpretation. But one approach which will not be found is the so-called "literal interpretation". Sometimes the Judicial Committee's approach has been described as literalistic. This is a mistake. We can see this by examining its decision in *Citizens Insurance Co. v. Parsons*, its first constitutional interpretation reported in this volume.[57] The issue here was whether Ontario legislation regulating fire insurance contracts was a matter of "property and civil rights in the province" and thus within the province's constitutional powers or whether it was a "regulation of trade and commerce" and therefore beyond provincial powers. One will search the constitutional text in vain for a literal answer to this question. Literal interpretation was simply not a viable option.

The approach which the Judicial Committee took in *Parsons* and many other cases may more aptly be described as highly legalistic. Not surprisingly, the English judges who wrote these decisions applied to the B.N.A. Act the basic technique of interpretation they were accustomed to applying to any Act of Parliament. The key to this technique of statutory interpretation is to assume that the legislators were completely rational and logical (not always a very realistic assumption) and to adopt an interpretation that makes it possible to read the text in a logically coherent way. But this would only take the judges so

---

[56] See cases 12 and 24 below.
[57] Case 2 below.

far. They still had to go outside the text to obtain meanings for key terms such as "property and civil rights" and "trade and commerce". Consider where they went in *Parsons*. Not to the debates and discussions of the constitution drafters—English judges would never consider legislative debates in interpreting statutes. Instead they considered how these phrases had been used in other British statutes—the Act of Union (between England and Scotland) and the Quebec Act.

While the Judicial Committee's style of opinion-writing was exceptionally legalistic, it would be a mistake to believe that the members of the Judicial Committee had nothing but narrowly legal considerations on their minds when they interpreted the B.N.A. Act. Their commitment to the notion of classical federalism as a fundamental principle of the Canadian constitution underlies most of their opinions and occasionally breaks through the legalistic prose. An outstanding example occurred in *Local Prohibition* case where Lord Watson argued that the federal parliament's general power must be interpreted narrowly so as not to encroach on provincial powers because "To attach any other construction to the general power . . . would, in their Lordships' opinion, not only be contrary to the intendment of the Act, but would practically destroy the autonomy of the provinces."[58]

In marked contrast to the Judicial Committee's approach, the Canadian judges on the Supreme Court of Canada in their first encounters with constitutional interpretation resorted not to British legal history but to Canadian political history. In *Severn v. The Queen*[59] we can see how they derived a broad, virtually unlimited scope for the federal trade and commerce power from *their understanding* of the intentions of the Fathers of Confederation. A century later, the Supreme Court of Canada looked to the Confederation Debates for evidence of the Founding Fathers' intentions with regard to the Senate.[60]

Basing constitutional interpretation on the framers' intentions is an attractive approach. It would seem to conform with common sense for judges in determining the meaning of any legal document to consider evidence of the original intent of those who drafted it. The legitimacy of judges striking down laws passed by democratically elected legislatures on the grounds that they violate the constitution would certainly be enhanced if the judges could show that their reading of the constitution was based not on their own personal views but on the intentions of the founding fathers.[61] This has been a major reason for

---

[58] Case 5 below at p. ?.

[59] Case 1 below.

[60] Case 61 below.

[61] In the United States there is an important school of thought that believes this is the only legitimate approach to judicial review. For the leading exponent, see Raoul Berger, *Government By Judiciary* (Cambridge, Mass., 1977). For a critique of this theory, see Michael Perry, *The Constitution, The Courts and Human Rights* (New Haven, 1982).

the appeal of this so-called "interpretativist" approach. But one serious difficulty with this approach is that often it is very difficult to ascertain the intention of those who created the Constitution with regard to the question at issue in a constitutional case.[62] Consider again the issue in *Parsons*. Do the events and debates leading to Confederation make it clear what the original intent was concerning jurisdiction over the regulation of insurance contracts? Certainly we can tell from John A. Macdonald's speeches that he favoured the widest possible scope for Dominion powers and cared not a whit for "provincial autonomy". But Macdonald was not the only Father of Confederation. He had colleagues in the political coalition that put the constitution together, especially from the Maritimes and Quebec, who hoped that strong provincial governments with a significant role in economic regulation would develop under the new constitution.

Modern constitutions are not the product of a single mind or even a single, coherent political philosophy. Their key terms are usually the product of political compromise. That is certainly the case with the federal provisions of the B.N.A. Act. They were a compromise between political leaders like Macdonald who wanted a single, unitary government for the new Canada and other colonial politicians who wished to retain significant powers in provincial capitals.[63] Similarly, in the recent additions to the Canadian Constitution there was a compromise between those who favoured a very strong entrenchment of rights and freedoms and those who wanted the least possible restriction on legislative supremacy. Constitutional provisions resulting from such compromises gloss over important differences among the framers which will continue to be worked out in the political evolution of the nation—an evolution in which judicial interpretation will play a prominent role.

In interpreting the Charter of Rights, the Supreme Court has indicated that it will give "minimal weight" to the statements of any particular participants in the negotiating, drafting and adoption of the Charter, no matter how important or distinguished these individuals may be.[64] The history which the Supreme Court has considered in giving more precise meaning to the vague terms of the Charter has tended to be much broader and deeper than the discussion in Canada that preceded the Charter. The main thrust of the "purposive" approach to Charter interpretation, fashioned by Chief Justice Dickson in some early Charter cases,[65] is to inquire into the reasons a particular right or freedom

---

[62] For a discussion of these difficulties see Clifford Ian Kyer, "Has History a Role to Play in Constitutional Adjudication: Some Preliminary Considerations," (1981), 15 *Law Society Gazette* 135.

[63] For evidence that Quebec supporters of Confederation intended that provinces should have strong powers in the economic as well as the social and cultural spheres, see P.B. Waite, *The Life and Times of Confederation* (Toronto, 1962), ch. 10.

[64] See *References re B.C. Motor Vehicle Act*, case 45, at p. 446.

[65] See *Hunter* v. *Southam* and *The Queen* v. *Big M Drug Mart*, case 42 below.

came to be valued in the history of western civilization and thereby to identify the "interests" each right or freedom was meant to protect. While there would seem to be general agreement within the Court on this "purposive" approach, it is an approach which may not yield the same results for all who apply it.

Supreme Court of Canada judges have tended to be much more explicit than were the English Law Lords of the Privy Council in considering the policy consequences of constitutional interpretation. This is clearly one result of the Canadianization of judicial review. Frequently Supreme Court judges openly reflect on the possible effects of decisions on the capacity of government, national and local, for effectively handling a given problem. Good examples of this are Justice Locke's opinion in *Johannesson*[66] where he discusses how a local veto over the location of airports would impede the development of the country, and Justice Dickson's dissenting opinion in *Hauser*[67] elucidating the policy advantages of leaving the administration of criminal justice in provincial hands. Assessing the reasonableness of legislative limits on Charter rights and freedoms will provide many more occasions for such policy analysis. All of this increases the Court's political exposure and puts pressure on the Court to widen the kind of material it takes into account in considering the purposes and effects of challenged legislation.[68]

At one time it was fashionable for critics of the Privy Council to fault that body for failing "to adapt the constitution to the changing needs of the country."[69] The problem with that kind of thinking is its assumption that the changing needs of Canada are clear and self-evident, that there is some kind of sociological natural law which right-thinking judges need only find to give the constitution just the twist that all Canadians are looking for. But alas we know that such assumptions are simplistic. It is not self-evident that Canada needs unified national regulation of cable television or local censorship of the movies. We should not expect the Court to give us answers to these questions which in some objective sense are logically or legally necessary. All that we can reasonably expect is that the judges might persuade us that their decisions are based on principles which embody the wisdom of our collective experience.

The metaphor of treating the constitution as a "living tree" has come into vogue in Canada to justify a more creative, less history-bound approach to constitutional interpretation. The metaphor was coined in 1930 by a member of

---

[66] Case 18 below.

[67] Case 26 below.

[68] See Peter W. Hogg, "Proof of Facts in Constitutional Cases," (1977), 26 *University of Toronto Law Journal* 386. For a discussion of the Court's openness to the consideration of "extrinsic materials" in constitutional cases, see *Re Residential Tenancies Act*, case 27 below.

[69] See, Alan C. Cairns, "The Judicial Committee and Its Critics," (1971), 3 *Canadian Journal of Political Science* 301.

the Judicial Committee, Lord Sankey, in an appeal from a Supreme Court of Canada decision holding that women were ineligible for appointment to the Senate because they were not "Persons" according to the legal meaning of that word at the time of Confederation. Sankey rejected the Supreme Court's position. He justified moving beyond the historical meaning of constitutional language by comparing the B.N.A. Act to "a living tree capable of growth and expansion within its natural limits."[70] The "living tree" analogy was used by the Supreme Court in 1979 to justify a very expansive interpretation of the language guarantees in section 133.[71] The Supreme Court has continued to endorse "the living tree" approach in its interpretation of the Charter of Rights and Freedoms.[72] In the *B.C. Motor Vehicle Act Reference*, Justice Lamer, in explaining why the Court should give little weight to documentary evidence of the drafters intentions, stated that "If the newly planted 'living tree' which is the *Charter* is to have the possibility of growth and adjustment over time, care must be taken that historical materials . . . do not stunt its growth."[73]

The "living tree" approach appeals to those who are optimistic about the policy-making capabilities of courts. However, it is important to bear in mind that when applied to constitutional rights and freedoms, this approach is likely to have quite different results than when it is applied to government powers. A broad and liberal interpretation of rights and freedoms will constrain government power and serve as a basis on which an "activist" judiciary may frequently overturn legislation and executive acts. On the other hand, a flexible and generous interpretation of the terms defining legislative power may result in much more judicial "self-restraint" in dealing with challenges to legislation.

Thus, it should be recognized that "activism" and "self-restraint" are not to be confused with different modes of judicial reasoning. Activism refers to judicial vigour in enforcing constitutional limitations on the other branches of government and a readiness to veto the policies of those branches of government on constitutional grounds. Self-restraint connotes a judicial predisposition to find room within the constitution for the policies of democratically accountable decision-makers. The Judicial Committee of the Privy Council, although it tended to be relatively legalistic in its style of reasoning, became a fairly activist court under the leadership of Viscount Haldane, frequently striking down laws which violated its interpretation of the division of powers. By comparison, the Supreme Court, when it took over as Canada's highest court, was somewhat less legalistic in its reasoning and exercised more

---

[70] *Henrietta Muir Edwards* v. *A. G. Canada* (1930), A.C. 124, at p. 136.

[71] See *A.G. Quebec* v. *Blaikie*, case 54 below.

[72] See Justice Estey's reference to the "living tree" in *Skapinker*, case 40 below, the Court's first Charter decision.

[73] Case 45 below, at p. 446.

restraint with regard to enforcing the requirements of federalism on both levels of government.[74]

In cases involving the Charter of Rights, activism and self-restraint may come into play at two stages. The first step in every Charter case is to determine whether the challenged law or government action violates a right or freedom. If the Court finds no such violation then that is the end of the case. However, if the first stage yields the opposite result, the court must go on to consider whether the encroachment on the right can be upheld under section 1 of the Charter as a "reasonable limit prescribed by law . . . demonstrably justified in a free and democratic society." At this stage judges must openly assess the policy considerations behind the legislative or government initiative. In applying section 1 the Supreme Court has made it clear that the onus is on government to justify its limit.

Now the wider and more liberally rights and freedoms are interpreted at stage one, the more frequently stage two will be reached. This has been one fact inducing some members of the Supreme Court to limit the scope of broadly phrased rights and freedoms. A clear example is Justice McIntyre's opinion in the *Alberta Labour Reference* where he excludes the right to strike from the constitutionally protected "freedom of association" in part because he is reluctant to see the judiciary involved in reviewing the judgment of the legislature as to the circumstances which justify restricting the right to strike.[75]

Section 1 of the Charter creates jurisprudential options which are not available in interpreting constitutional guarantees in the American Constitution. The Bill of Rights in the Constitution of the United States does not contain any limiting clause so that constitutionally protected rights can be limited only by building limits into the way these rights and freedoms are defined— something the U.S. Supreme Court has frequently done. Under the Canadian Charter there is the option of treating the rights and freedoms as absolutes subject only to such limits as can be justified on a case by case basis under section 1. Such an approach would maximize judicial scrutiny of legislative decisions. If, for instance, no limits are attached to the "right to liberty" in section 7, then virtually every government restriction on anything any of us wants to do would be a violation of a constitutional right and could be saved only by convincing the judiciary that it was justifiable under section 1. It is doubtful that any judge would want to go this far. Thus we find that even the most activist judge currently on the Supreme Court, Justice Wilson, is inclined to build limits into the definition of some rights and freedoms.[76]

---

[74] This is particularly evident in its willingness to find new areas of concurrence in which both levels of government could operate. See W.R. Lederman, "The Concurrent Operation of Federal and Provincial Laws in Canada" (1963), 9 *McGill Law Journal* 185.

[75] Case 49 below, at pp. 504-6.

[76] See her opinion in *Operation Dismantle* limiting the meaning of "security of the person" in section 7. Case 43 below, at p. 424.

In these early Charter cases, the justices on the contemporary Supreme Court have more degrees of freedom than their successors will enjoy. They also must experience a greater burden of decision. For in these early cases they are dealing with constitutional concepts that are entirely novel to Canadian constitutional law. They will derive some guidance from the first approaches to these concepts in the lower court decisions which are appealed to the Court. Also they will consider how similar rights and freedoms have been dealt with in foreign jurisdictions—especially under the European Convention of Human Rights and by the United States Supreme Court, although with regard to the latter, the Court has shown more than a mild sense of Canadian nationalism. Justice LaForest expressed this well when he wrote that,

> Canadian legal thought has at many points in the past deferred to that of the British; the Charter will be no sign of our national maturity if it simply becomes an excuse for adopting another intellectual mentor. American jurisprudence, like the British, must be viewed as a tool, not as a master.[77]

As Supreme Court precedents accumulate, there will still be plenty of room for development. As befits the highest court of a sovereign nation the Supreme Court has relaxed the strict rule of *stare decisis* according to which it is bound to follow its own previous decisions. In *Paquette*,[78] decided in 1976 (a non-constitutional, criminal case) the Court for the first time explicitly departed from a position it had taken in an earlier case and, shortly afterwards, in *McNamara Construction v. The Queen*,[79] it reversed one of the Supreme Court's earlier constitutional decisions. The Court's repudiation of its Bill of Rights jurisprudence in the early Charter cases constitutes its most dramatic change of direction.[80]

Flexibility and change will come not nearly so much from the explicit overruling of earlier precedents as from the various ways judges work with previous decisions. Judges will sometimes "distinguish" previous decisions they do not wish to follow as turning on facts different from those in the case at hand. Alternatively, judges are adept at giving a new twist to the *ratio decidendi* (reason for decision) of an earlier decision. An instructive example in this volume is the *Crown Zellerbach* case where the majority opinion provides yet another way of interpreting previous decisions on peace, order and good government.[81] Already we can see how the test for meeting the

---

[77] *Rahey* v. *The Queen* [1987] 1 S.C.R. 588, at p. 639. See also the repudiation of American jurisprudence on "political questions" in *Operation Dismantle*, case 43 below, and on the distinction between substantive and procedural due process in the *B.C. Motor Vehicles Act Reference*, case 45 below.

[78] [1977] 2 S.C.R. 189.

[79] [1977] 2 S.C.R. 655.

[80] See *Big M Drug Mart* and *Therens*, cases 42 and 44 below.

[81] Case 31 below.

Charter's standard of a reasonable limit established in *Oakes* is being applied differently by different judges.[82]

The real effect of the application of *stare decisis* is not to freeze the law of the constitution in a fixed mould but to structure judicial discretion. Earlier precedents establish boundaries within which judges manoeuvre. On a given point there may be considerable room for choice between competing lines of cases. There are bound to be some ambiguities in the language of earlier decisions. But whatever course is taken, the reasoning of judges in Canada as in all common law countries will normally be developed by reference to the "authority" of previous cases.

The various approaches discussed above represent different tendencies, not mutually exclusive alternatives. Even the most creative, policy-oriented, activist judge will not be indifferent to the constitutional text, will wish to make some sense of its internal structure and the accumulation of precedents interpreting it, and will have some sense of the limits on the judiciary's mandate to strike down the policies of the "popular" branches of government. By the same token, it is unlikely that we will find today a judge whose approach to judicial review is so traditional as to preclude any inquiry into the underlying principles of the constitution and their practical implications for the governance of the country or to exude an unqualified deference for the legislature and executive.

We urge students using this text to be wary of simplistic labeling of courts or judges. Read the judges' reasons and conscientiously assess them as exercises in practical reasoning about how best to apply Canada's constituent political principles.

PROCEDURES OF JUDICIAL REVIEW

Most constitutional cases begin at the trial court level. Typically, constitutional issues are raised either by the defendant in a criminal case arguing that the police investigation or the law under which the accused is charged is unconstitutional, or by an individual or organization in a civil action claiming that a government regulation to which they are subject is unconstitutional. Most of the trial courts in which these cases originate are provincial or territorial courts; some begin in the smaller, more specialized Federal Court of Canada.[83] The losing party in the trial court has a right of appeal to the provincial or territorial court of appeal or from the trial to the appeal division of the Federal Court. A further appeal to the Supreme Court is possible only with the leave of the court appealed from or of the Supreme Court itself.[84]

---

[82] See cases 48 and 49 below.

[83] For a complete description of the Canadian court system, see Peter H. Russell, *The Judiciary in Canada: The Third Branch of Government* (Toronto, 1987).

[84] In practice lawyers seldom use the first option and almost always seek the Supreme Court's leave.

The one major exception to this way of bringing constitutional questions before the courts is reference cases. The reference case procedure enables governments in Canada to initiate and set the terms for constitutional adjudication. In 1875 the Supreme Court Act empowered the Governor in Council "to refer to the Supreme Court, for hearing and consideration, any matters whatsoever as he may think fit."[85] In practice, reference cases have been largely confined to assessing the constitutionality of statutes or proposed bills. Originally, the federal government's reference of provincial legislation to the Supreme Court was considered a means of obtaining judicial advice about whether or not provincial laws should be disallowed. However, this rationale has long be superseded. Frequently in this century, for instance in all of the "New Deal" references in the 1930s, the federal government has asked the Supreme Court to determine whether or not Parliament has exceeded its jurisdiction.[86] Moreover, the provinces have adopted their own reference case procedures under which they can refer their own or federal legislation to the provincial court of appeal. In these provincial reference cases there is a right of appeal to the Supreme Court. The importance of this procedure as a means of challenging federal initiatives was dramatically demonstrated by the decisions of three provinces to have their provincial courts of appeal pronounce upon the constitutionality of the Trudeau government's unilateral approach to constitutional change in 1980-81. This manoeuvre forced the Supreme Court to become a major player in the constitutional struggle.

The highest courts of both Australia and the United States have refused to answer questions put to them by governments on the grounds that to give advice outside of adjudicating issues raised in the regular process of litigation is incompatible with the judicial role. Although in theory opinions in reference cases are merely advisory, in practice they are treated as binding.[87] Indeed they have been frequently criticized as creating what Felix Frankfurter called "ghosts that slay" out of hypothetical situations in which judges do not have the facts necessary to ascertain the actual effects of challenged laws.[88] If reference questions are too abstract and hypothetical, judges may decline to answer them.[89]

Politicians have not shared the jurists' qualms about reference cases. They have found that the procedure has some practical advantages. When constitutional doubts are raised about an important legislative initiative, government

---

[85] *Statutes of Canada 1875*, c. 11, s. 52.

[86] See cases 12, 13 and 14 below.

[87] See Barry L. Strayer, *The Canadian Constitution and the Courts* (2nd ed.), (Toronto, 1983) chapter 9.

[88] See Justice Laskin's objection to this feature of reference cases in the *Chicken and Egg Reference*, case 21 below, at p. 156.

[89] See, for example, the Supreme Court's refusal to answer some of the questions put to it in the *Senate Reference*, case 61 below.

may be anxious to obtain an opinion on its constitutionality without waiting months or years for the constitutional question to be raised in an ordinary case and work its way up to the Supreme Court. When federal and provincial governments are trying to co-ordinate their programs and jointly maximize their regulatory power, a reference case opinion can serve as a judicious guide to those who must draft the federal and provincial legislation.[90] Where jurisdiction is much more an object of federal-provincial rivalry, the referring of a question to the courts undoubtedly has the effect of throwing sensitive political issues into the laps of the judges, but there may still be a real advantage in submitting the resolution of the political conflict to the relatively dispassionate ways of the judicial process. The *Patriation Reference* is surely a case in point. In the *Manitoba Language Rights Reference* the Supreme Court resolved an issue which the local politicians seemed incapable of handling through the legislative process.[91] Also, where there is serious doubt about the validity of major constitutional changes, as was the case before the 1980 *Senate Reference* and the 1981 *Patriation Reference*, it would seem wise to obtain a Supreme Court decision before they are put in place. Otherwise the legitimacy of the restructured institution and of the constitution itself would be in question.

Reference cases figured more prominently in constitutional adjudication in the past than they do today. One-third of all the constitutional cases decided by the Privy Council originated in questions referred to Canadian courts by federal or provincial governments. Among these were many of the most significant decisions concerning the division of legislative powers. Two-thirds of these cases were decided during the Privy Council's last three decades as Canada's final court of appeal. During this period, reference cases accounted for nearly all of its constitutional decisions. In the first decade after 1949 references continued to be a major source of constitutional cases: twelve of the thirty-six constitutional cases decided by the Supreme Court in the 1950s originated in references. Since then reference cases have become relatively infrequent: only 21 of the Supreme Court's constitutional decisions since 1960 originated as references. However, these include some of the Court's most important decisions, including some on the Charter of Rights.[92] Reference cases which give governments a privileged access to the courts and permit them to frame the terms on which constitutional questions are considered may seem less appropriate in Charter cases where the rights of citizens are pitted against the powers of government. In this regard it was interesting to observe the Supreme Court's refusal in the summer of 1988 to postpone hearing an appeal concerning the rights of the foetus brought by a citizen, Joe Borowski, until it had dealt with

---

[90] A good example is the *Ontario Farm Products Marketing Act Reference*, case 19 below.

[91] See case 56 below.

[92] See cases 45, 49 and 58 below.

the federal government's new abortion legislation in a reference case.[93]

In recent years constitutional litigation has become much more accessible to individual citizens. The Supreme Court has broadened the rules governing "standing"—that is the right to stand before the court and challenge legislation. In the *Thorson* and *McNeil* cases the Supreme Court recognized the right of individuals to challenge laws which affect them only as members of large sections of the general public (for example, as taxpayers or movie-goers) and not directly as individuals.[94] In 1981, the Court went even further and granted Joe Borowski standing to challenge federal legislation permitting abortions even though the legislation was totally inapplicable to him. In this case, Justice Martland on behalf of the majority set down the following rule on standing:

> To establish status as a plaintiff in a suit seeking a declaration that legislation is invalid, if there is a serious issue as to its validity, a person need only show that he is affected by it directly or that he has a genuine interest as a citizen in the validity of the legislation and that there is no other reasonable and effective manner in which the issue may be brought to the court.[95]

This rule, coming as it did just when the Charter of Rights was coming into force, makes it considerably easier for a Canadian citizen than it is for an American citizen to attack legislation in the courts. Still, as the decision in *Operation Dismantle* indicates, there are limits to the kinds of issues which the Court considers to be justiciable.[96]

Not only is constitutional litigation legally more accessible, but the rapid expansion of the legal profession, the development of legal aid and the increased resources and organizational skills of special interest groups have also made it more accessible in a practical sense. It costs many thousands of dollars to take a constitutional challenge through the courts. At least three-quarters of all Charter cases arise when an accused person challenges some aspect of the criminal justice system. Nearly all of these challenges have been supported through publicly funded legal aid. Challenges to non-criminal laws have been facilitated by pressure groups and advocacy organizations willing to back an individual's grievance as a test case.[97] The federal government itself has established funds for those claiming violations of language rights and equality rights.[98]

[93] See case 52 below.

[94] *Thorson* v. *A.G. Canada* [1975] 1 S.C.R. 138 and *Nova Scotia Board of Censors* v. *McNeil* [1978] 2 S.C.R. 662.

[95] *Minister of Justice (Canada)* v. *Borowski* (1982) 1 W.W.R. 97.

[96] Case 43 below and see the account of the hearing in the *Borowski* case before the Supreme Court in October, 1988, case 52 below.

[97] See F.L. Morton, "The Political Impact of The Canadian Charter of Rights and Freedoms" (1987), 20 *Canadian Journal of Political Science* 31.

[98] The challenge to Quebec's Bill 101 by the Association of Protestant School Boards, case 55 below, was facilitated by this federal funding.

Constitutional litigation in Canada, although it is usually initiated by private citizens, can quickly be transformed into an arena of political combat. In contrast to the United States where only the national government has the right to intervene in the federal courts, and then only when an act of Congress is challenged, in Canada, by legislation and custom, the provinces as well as the federal government are in most instances notified when their legislative powers are being tested in the courts and are given the right to become active parties in the case. It is not unusual to see the federal government and a number of provinces intervening to support one or other of the parties in a case raising a constitutional issue. Non-governmental organizations can also be given inter-venor status to argue points which may not be developed by the parties themselves.[99] In the Charter case reviewing the validity of the funding of Catholic schools in Ontario 24 such organizations were given intervenor status.[100] It may seem paradoxical that in Canada, while the style of constitu-tional jurisprudence has been more legalistic, the interventions of governments and pressure groups, coupled with the reference case, expose judicial review much more directly to the contention of major political forces in the country.

Since 1975 when the Supreme Court gained a real measure of control over its docket, one of the Court's most important functions is selecting the cases it will hear. It discharges this function through panels of three judges. Up until 1988 every request for leave to appeal required a hearing (which is sometimes conducted by long distance television). Now leave hearings occur only at the Court's discretion and are limited to the most difficult cases. For leave to be granted, two of the three judges on the panel must consider the issue raised in the case to be one that the court should decide. As the volume of litigation in the country increases, the Court has had to become much more selective in granting leave. It is difficult for the Court to handle much more than 100 cases a year. Indeed in the mid 1980s, when it has had the enormous responsibility of writing the first decisions on the Charter, the Court's annual case-load has been between 80 and 90. In these circumstances it has been refusing roughly 85% of requests for leave to appeal.[101]

This means that most cases, including most constitutional cases, go no higher than the intermediate appeal courts—the provincial courts of appeal and the Federal Court of Appeal. It is not the Supreme Court's function to correct mistakes made in the court of first instance. That is the primary purpose of the courts which hear the first appeal. The Supreme Court's function is to select those cases which raise difficult and contentious questions in all areas of law—

[99] For a discussion of recent changes in the rules governing private intervenors, see Kenneth B. Swan, "Intervention and Amicus Curiae Status in Charter Litigation," in Robert Sharpe (ed.), *Charter Litigation*, Toronto: Butterworths, 1987.

[100] Case 58 below.

[101] See, Russell, *The Judiciary in Canada*, ch. 14.

not just constitutional law—and to write opinions on these which will serve as principled guides to the lower courts and to the lawyers who advise citizens and governments on their legal rights and duties.

Thus with the Charter the Supreme Court has been dealing only with the tip of the iceberg. The fifty or so decisions the Supreme Court rendered on the Charter by 1988 represent only one to two per cent of the Charter cases reported in the lower courts during this period.[102] The Supreme Court has not been able to resolve the myriad of interpretative issues flowing from the Charter all at once. As a result, for some time the Charter may mean different things in different parts of Canada as differences among provincial courts of appeals remain unresolved by Supreme Court judgments.

After leave to appeal is granted there will be an interval of several weeks or months before the case is heard by the Court. A quorum for hearing a case is five judges. Under the leadership of both Chief Justice Laskin and Chief Justice Dickson an effort was made to have all nine judges sit for at least the major constitutional cases. But this goal has not been achieved and seven-judge panels have become the norm in constitutional cases. Even numbered panels are avoided to prevent ties, but occasionally an even number occurs when a justice who heard the appeal is forced by ill health to withdraw before a decision is reached. In the event of a tie vote the appeal from the decision below is dismissed.

Before the hearing the judges will have an opportunity to examine the parties' written submissions. Each party submits a "factum", which should be a succinct, carefully organized statement of their arguments with references to all the authorities they are using to buttress their points.[103] The interveners submit factums high-lighting the particular themes they wish to develop. The judges will also examine a record of the proceedings and opinions from the lower courts. Until recently there were virtually no limits on the time lawyers could take to make their oral arguments. Often cases were argued for many days, using up a lot of court time and contributing little to the lucidity or wisdom of the Court's decision-making. In the fall of 1987, the Court issued a notice stating that henceforth it would expect to hear two cases a day—one in the morning and one in the afternoon—giving each side an hour to make its case. This will make hearings more like seminars as they are in the U.S. Supreme Court, where the time allotted for each side is normally half an hour, and where the judges draw counsel out on the more problematic aspects of their arguments.

---

[102] See data on Charter litigation across Canada, see F.L. Morton, "Charting the Charter, 1982-1985: A Statistical Analysis," (1987), *Canadian Human Rights Yearbook*, 65.

[103] Prior to the Charter, there was no limit on the length of factums and they could run well over 100 pages. Beginning in the fall of 1987, the Court requested all parties coming before it to comply with a 40 page maximum.

After the hearing, the justices hold a brief conference. Each judge, in reverse order of seniority, gives his or her views on the case. This is the same order as is used in the English House of Lords but differs from the American Supreme Court where the Chief Justice speaks first. Justice Wilson has explained that the practice is designed to reduce the risk of junior members feeling pressure to side with more senior judges, a risk she assures us no longer exists.[104] In any event it does underline the fact that in the Court's decision-making all judges, including the Chief Justice, formally have equal power and status. The conference discussion will indicate whether the justices are all in agreement (as is most often the case) on the basic outcome. Often one member of the group will volunteer to draft the reasons for the decision. If not, the Chief Justice will ask someone to take this on. If the Court appears to be split, then writers for the majority and dissenting opinions will be designated.

Opinion-writing is the Supreme Court justice's most creative and challenging responsibility. Each justice will write only a handful of opinions each year but the reasons he or she articulates as the justification for the Court's decision add important propositions to Canadian law, including the law of the constitution. The judges will receive some research assistance and possibly even some drafting assistance from their "clerks", the bright young law graduates who spend a year or two at the Court. Also, at this stage there will be a fair amount of interaction among the judges as drafts are circulated and commented upon. When judges look at the reasons a colleague has drafted, the majority may begin to come apart or at least one or more justices may be moved to write a concurring opinion expressing their own reasons for supporting the majority position. The Supreme Court has become far more collegial than it was in the past and nowadays endeavours to produce a clear majority opinion. Indeed in cases which are extraordinarily political the authorship of the majority opinion is sometimes not disclosed and the opinion is simply attributed to "The Court".[105]

The Court's judgment will not be released to the parties and the public until months, sometimes many months, after the hearing. These judgments are the Court's final product. Each judgment ends by dismissing or granting the appeal or by giving simple one line or one word answers to reference questions. But these "bottom lines"—who wins and who loses—are not the important part of Supreme Court judgments. What warrants collecting the leading decisions together here and engaging the student's interest are the reasons for the decisions. At the heart of each is some principle or rule about the powers of government or the rights of citizens which plays its part in the evolution of one of the world's oldest constitutional democracies.

---

[104] Bertha Wilson, "Decision-Making in the Supreme Court" (1986), 26 *University of Toronto Law Journal* 236.

[105] The major examples are cases 20, 52, 54, 61, 62 and 63 below.

PART ONE
THE DIVISION OF POWERS

A: The Privy Council's Legacy

1. Severn v. The Queen, *1878*

~ This early Supreme Court of Canada decision is placed at the beginning of this series of Privy Council decisions to indicate the approach to constitutional interpretation taken by the Canadian Supreme Court judges *before* the Judicial Committee of the Privy Council began to shape Canada's constitutional jurisprudence.

The case provided the first opportunity for the Supreme Court of Canada to interpret the B.N.A. Act. The case arose out of charges brought against Severn, a liquor manufacturer who was licensed under federal customs legislation, for violating an Ontario act requiring brewers to purchase provincial licences before selling liquor by wholesale. Severn's refusal to pay the licence fee was based on his contention that the Ontario legislation establishing the licensing system was *ultra vires*. The Ontario Court of Appeal dismissed Severn's argument but this decision was reversed by the Supreme Court of Canada, which by a four-to-two majority found the provincial act invalid both on the ground that it provided for an indirect tax which could not be supported as a licence under head 9 of section 92 and also on the ground that it interfered with trade and commerce, a subject assigned exclusively to the national Parliament.

As a legal precedent this case is of little importance: the reasoning of the Supreme Court's majority on the "trade and commerce" power was overruled by later decisions of the Privy Council. The real significance of the case is the indication it provides of the basic attitudes of senior Canadian jurists to the division of powers in Canadian federalism at a time when the main issues and events of confederation must still have been fresh in their minds and when their interpretation of the B.N.A. Act was not yet fettered by Privy Council decisions. The remarkable feature of their general approach to the division of powers is their concern for upholding the national power. This is particularly marked in the opening paragraphs of the Chief Justice's judgment which echo the sentiments of those Fathers of Confederation who, like Sir John A. Macdonald, were anxious to eliminate from the Canadian federal system the centrifugal tendencies which in their view were inherent in the American system.

It is apparent that at this stage the Canadian Supreme Court in applying the federal terms of the Canadian constitution was inclined to look to American jurisprudence for guidance. As far as the federal commerce power was concerned American experience could only support a broad interpretation of the Canadian Parliament's power in relation to trade and commerce. The opinion of Justice Fournier points to the obvious conclusion that if in the

United States the central legislature's commerce power which is a limited one, restricted to foreign and interestate commerce, has been construed in broad enough terms to cut down local laws interfering with the flow of trade through the States, in Canada the national legislature's power over trade and commerce which is subject to no express limitations should be given an even more generous construction. Even the two dissenting judges (Justices Ritchie and Strong) while willing to support the Ontario Act under section 92(9), did not otherwise differ with the majority's view of the Dominion's trade and commerce power.

Two years later in *City of Fredericton* v. *The Queen*[1] the Supreme Court once again gave an extremely wide interpretation of Parliament's power in relation to trade and commerce when it upheld, by a five-to-one majority, the Canada Temperance Act under section 91(2). But this early treatment of the "trade and commerce" clause by the Supreme Court was to undergo a sharp reversal by the Judicial Committee of the Privy Council. In a series of cases the Privy Council evolved a number of implied limitations which had the effect of reducing the federal commerce power in Canada to a pale shadow of its counterpart in the United States' Constitution. ~

SEVERN v. THE QUEEN
In the Supreme Court of Canada. (1878), 2 S.C.R. 70

RICHARDS, C.J.C.: In deciding important questions arising under the Act passed by the Imperial Parliament for federally uniting the Provinces of Canada, Nova Scotia and New Brunswick, and forming the Dominion of Canada, we must consider the circumstances under which that Statute was passed, the condition of the different Provinces themselves, their relation to one another, to the Mother Country, and the state of things existing in the great country adjoining Canada, as well as the systems of government which prevailed in these Provinces and countries. The framers of the Statute knew the difficulties which had arisen in the great Federal Republic, and no doubt wished to avoid them in the new government which it was intended to create under that Statute. They knew that the question of State rights as opposed to the authority of the General Government under their constitution was frequently raised, aggravating, if not causing, the difficulties arising out of their system of government, and they evidently wished to

avoid these evils, under the new state of things about to be created here by the Confederation of the Provinces.

In distributing the Legislative powers, the British North America Act declares the Parliament of Canada shall, or, as the 91st section reads,

It shall be lawful for the Queen, by and with the advice and consent of the Senate and House of Commons, to make laws, for the peace, order and good government of Canada, in relation to all matters not coming within the classes of subjects assigned exclusively *to the Legislatures of the Provinces.*

And then, for greater certainty, that section defines certain subjects to which the exclusive legislative authority of the Parliament extends. Amongst other things are mentioned:

2. The regulation of trade and commerce.

3. The raising of money by any mode or system of taxation.

Certain other subjects of a general and quasi-national character are then referred to and mentioned, as coming within the powers of the Dominion Parliament.

The causing a brewer to take out a licence and pay a certain sum of money therefor, as required by the Ontario Statutes, is a means of raising money, and it, of course, is a tax. And there can be no doubt it is an indirect tax; and it is equally beyond a doubt that it is a means which may be resorted to by the Dominion Parliament for the raising of money. When, then, it is mentioned in the Statute under consideration that the Dominion Parliament may raise money under any mode or system of taxation, and when in the same Act, the taxing power of the Provincial Legislature is confined to *direct taxation* within the Province, in order to the raising of a revenue for provincial purposes, it seems to me beyond all doubt (except so far as the same may be qualified by No. 9 of section 92) that it was introduced not to allow the Provincial Legislature the right to impose indirect taxes for provincial or local purposes. . . .

The anomaly of allowing the Local Legislatures to compel a manufacturer to take out a licence from the Local Government to sell an article which has already paid a heavy excise duty to the Dominion Government, and after he has paid for and obtained a licence from the Dominion Government to do the very same thing, is obvious to every one. It is not doubted that the Dominion Legislature had a right to lay on this excise tax and to grant this licence, and the act of the Local Legislature forbids and punishes the brewer for doing that which the Dominion Statute permits and allows. Here surely is *what seems* a direct conflict and interference with the act of the Dominion Legislature, and such a conflict as the framers of the British North America Act never contemplated or intended. . . .

. . . I consider the power now claimed to interfere with the paramount authority of the Dominion Parliament in matters of trade and commerce and indirect taxation, so pregnant with evil, and so contrary to what appears to me to be the manifest intention of the framers of the British North America Act, that I cannot come to the conclusion that it is conferred by the language cited as giving that power. . . .

[Translated]

FOURNIER, J.: The only question to be decided in this case arises on the constitutionality of a law of the Province of Ontario, imposing upon brewers and distillers the obligation to taking out a licence of $50, in order that they may sell their products within the said Province.

The question we have therefore to consider is, whether the law in question is, or is not, in direct conflict with the British North America Act, and, more particularly, first, with No. 2 of section 91, relating to the ''regulation of trade and commerce,'' and, secondly, with section 122, which gives to the Parliament of Canada the control over the custom and excise laws, and, therefore, beyond the limits of the jurisdiction of the Ontario Legislature. . . .

The 91st section gives to the Federal Parliament the general power of taxation, a sovereignty over all subjects, except those specifically mentioned in section 92, as being subjects exclusively belonging to the Local Legislatures. We find, among the exclusive powers given to the Federal Parliament, the power of *regulating trade and commerce*.

This power, being full and complete, cannot be restricted, unless by some specific provision to be found in the British North America Act.

For this reason, the relative position of the Provinces towards the Federal Parliament is far different from that of the States towards the United States Congress. Here the power to regulate trade and commerce, without any distinction as to interior and exterior commerce, belongs *exclusively* to the Dominion Parliament, whilst, in the United States, Congress has power only to deal with exterior or foreign commerce, commerce between the different States and that with the Indian tribes. The States, not having delegated to Congress the power of regulating interior commerce, still have power to legislate on it as they please. We should not, therefore, look to the numerous decisions rendered on the laws relating to the interior commerce as precedents applicable to the present case, but rather to the decisions given on laws passed by the State Legislatures which happened to come in conflict with the power of Congress to deal with exterior commerce.

There is a decision, rendered as early as 1827, which has always been looked upon as being the true construction of that article of the Constitution of the United States which gives Congress power to regulate exterior commerce, and which is very applicable to the present case. It is that rendered in the case of *Brown* v. *State of Maryland* (12 Wheaton 419). In order to raise revenue to meet the expenses of the State, the Legislature of Maryland passed a law, by which, amongst other things, importers of foreign merchandise enumerated in the law, or such other persons as should sell by wholesale such merchandise, were directed to take out a licence, for which they were to pay $50, before selling any of the imported goods, subjecting them, in case of neglect or refusal, to forfeit the amount due for the licence and to a penalty of $100.

Brown, who was an importer residing in the city of Baltimore, refused to pay this tax, and an information was, in consequence, laid against him before the State Court, which declared the law to be valid and condemned him to pay the penalty prescribed.

This judgment was appealed by means of a writ of error to the Supreme Court, which Court, for the reasons so ably propounded by the learned Chief Justice Marshall, declared the law void as coming in conflict with the power of Congress to regulate exterior commerce.

The question here naturally arises, what was the extent of that power? This question was considered at great length in the case of *Gibbons* v. *Ogden* (9 Wheaton 231), by Chief Justice Marshall, who answered it as follows:

It is the power to regulate; that is, to prescribe the rule by which commerce is to be governed. This power, like all others vested in Congress, is complete in itself, may be exercised to its utmost extent, and acknowledges no limitations other than are prescribed by the Constitution.

Since this is the law in the United States, there is an additional reason why it should be so declared here, where our Constitution does not acknowledge, as in the United States, a division of power as to commerce. . . .

. . . I will add in support of my mode of reasoning, a passage of Chief Justice Marshall's opinion in the case of *Brown* v. *The State of Maryland* (12 Wheaton 448), and I also contend that in this case we should apply this ordinary rule of construction, that when a law is doubtful or ambiguous, it should be interpreted in such a way as to fulfil the intentions of the legislator, and attain the object for which it was passed. Marshall, C.J., says:

We admit this power to be sacred [the State power to tax its own citizens, on their property within its own territory]; *but cannot admit that it may be used so as to obstruct the free course of a power given to Congress. We cannot admit that it may be used so as to obstruct or defeat the power to regulate commerce. It has been observed, that the powers remaining with the States may be so exercised as to come in conflict with those vested in Congress. When this happens that which is not supreme must yield to that which is supreme. This great and universal truth is inseparable from the nature of things, and the constitution has applied it to the often interfering powers of the General and State Governments as a vital principle of perpetual operation. It results necessarily from this principle, that the taxing power of the State must have some limits. It cannot reach and restrain the action of the National Government within its proper sphere. It cannot reach the administration of justice in the Courts of the Union, or the collection of the taxes of the United States or restrain the operation of any law which Congress may constitutionally pass. It cannot interfere with any regulation of commerce. If the States may tax all persons and property found on their territory, what shall restrain them from taxing in their transit through the State from one port to another for the purpose of re-exportation? The laws of trade authorize this operation, and general convenience requires it. Or what should restrain a State from taxing any article passing from the State itself to another State, for commercial purposes? These are all within the sovereign power of taxation, but would obviously derange the measures of Congress to regulate commerce, and effect materially the purpose for which that power was given. We deem it unnecessary to press the argument further, or to give additional illustrations of it, because the subject was taken up, and considered with great attention in* McCulloch v. The State of Maryland (*4 Wheaton 316*), *the decision in which case is, we think, entirely applicable to this.*

This reasoning of the Supreme Court in that case, under a system of Government which left to the States the regulation of the interior commerce, is not only applicable to the present question, but should have more weight from the fact that under our system the Federal Government has the *exclusive* power over commerce. . . .

HENRY, J.: . . . The legislative power given to the Dominion Parliament is unlimited

To make laws for the peace, order and good government of Canada, in relation to all matters not coming within the classes of subjects by this Act assigned exclusively *to the Legislatures of the Provinces.*

and we need not necessarily consider the provisions of sub-sections 2 and 3 of section 91.

Everything in the shape of legislation for the peace, order and good government of Canada is embraced, except as before mentioned. But sub-section 29 goes further and provides for exceptions and reservations in regard to matters otherwise included in the power of legislation given to the Local Legislatures, and also provides that:

Any matter coming within any of the classes of subjects enumerated in this section shall not be deemed to come within the class of matters of a local or private nature comprised in the enumeration of the classes of subjects by this Act assigned exclusively to the Legislatures of the Provinces.

"The regulation of trade and commerce" and "the raising of money by any mode or system of taxation" is, however, specially mentioned, and both include the right to make and have carried out all the provisions in the Dominion Act. This position has not been, and cannot be, successfully assailed. The subjects in all their details of which trade and commerce are composed, and the regulation of them, and the raising of revenue by indirect taxation, must, therefore, be matters referred to and included in the latter clause of sub-section 29, before mentioned, and if so,

Shall not be deemed to come within the class of matters of a local or private nature comprised in the enumeration of the classes of subjects by this Act assigned exclusively to the Legislature of the Provinces.

Every constituent, therefore, of trade and commerce, and the subject of indirect taxation, is thus, as I submit, withdrawn from the consideration of the Local Legislatures, even if it should otherwise be *apparently* included. The Imperial Act fences in those twenty-eight subjects wholesale and in detail, and the Local Legislatures were intended to be, and are, kept out of the inclosure, and when authorized to deal with the subject of "direct taxation within the Province,'' as in sub-section 2 of section 92, and ''shop, saloon, tavern, auctioneer, and other licences,'' they are commanded, by the concluding clause of sub-section 29, sec. 91, not to interfere by measures for what they may call ''direct taxation,'' or in regard at least to ''other licences,'' or in reference to ''municipal institutions,'' with the prerogatives of the Dominion Parliament as to the ''regulation of trade and commerce,'' including ''Customs and Excise laws'' and ''the raising of money by any mode or system of taxation.'' I have already shown, that the exercise of the power contended for by the Legislature of Ontario is incompatible with the full exercise of that of the Dominion Parliament, and might be used to its total destruction. The object of the Imperial Act was clearly to give plenary powers of legislation to the Dominion Parliament with the exceptions before stated, and just as clearly to restrict local legislation so as to prevent any conflict with that of the former in regard to the subject with which it was given power to deal. . . .

~ Justice Taschereau also wrote an opinion in which he concluded that the Ontario legislation was *ultra vires*. Justices Ritchie and Strong wrote dissenting opinions. ~

2. Citizens Insurance Co. *v.* Parsons; Queen Insurance Co. *v.* Parsons, *1881*

~ The constitutional issue in this case concerned the validity of the Ontario Fire Insurance Policy Act which prescribed uniform conditions for all fire insurance contracts unless variations from the statutory conditions were properly indicated. Parsons, the respondent in the case, had taken actions against two fire insurance companies to obtain compensation for damages caused by fire in a warehouse insured by the companies. The companies' defence was that Parsons should not receive compensation because he had failed to observe conditions which had been written into the companies' policies or which were prescribed by the Ontario statute. Parson's reply was that he was not bound by the conditions written into the contracts because they were not written on the contracts as variations from the statutory conditions in the manner prescribed by the Ontario Fire Insurance Policy Act. The companies' counsel attempted to counter this contention by arguing that the Ontario statute was *ultra vires*. The judgments of the Ontario Court of Appeal and the Supreme Court of Canada were both in favour of Parsons.

The Privy Council's judgment, delivered by Sir Montague Smith, is important in terms of both the general approach to the interpretation of the B.N.A. Act and the construction of the federal trade and commerce power. The Judicial Committee treated the interpretation of the B.N.A. Act no differently than it would treat the interpretation of an ordinary statute. No reference was made to the historical context in which the constitution was drafted nor to the intentions of the Fathers of Confederation. Instead the English judges tried to interpret the words of the Act in a way which would make the Act internally consistent. This meant that they felt obliged to attach some limits to broad terms like "trade and commerce." If this were not done, then a broad general power as an exclusive field of jurisdiction for one level of government would render meaningless more specific subjects in that same field assigned exclusively to the other level of government.

In this case the Judicial Committee declined to stretch trade and commerce as an exclusive field of federal jurisdiction so far as to prevent the provinces from regulating the contracts of a particular trade, such as the business of fire insurance, in a province. On the other hand, the Committee refused to interpret provincial jurisdiction over property and civil rights so narrowly as to exclude rights arising from contract. As a result, the Ontario Act was found constitutional as a law relating to property and civil rights in the province.

At the end of this opinion Sir Montague Smith pointed to three kinds of laws which might be supported by the federal trade and commerce power: political arrangements in regard to trade requiring the sanction of Parliament (i.e., international trade arrangements); regulation of trade in matters of interprovincial concern; and general regulation of trade affecting the whole Dominion.

This definition of the parameters of the trade and commerce power, although not strictly necessary for the decision in this case, was returned to in many subsequent decisions. The consolidation in later cases of the doctrine that the trade and commerce power does not extend to intraprovincial, as distinguished from interprovincial, trade had the effect of excluding from the scope of that power all business or commercial transactions completed within a province. By thus excluding intra-provincial trade from federal jurisdiction, judicial review introduced into the Canadian constitution a restriction on the federal commerce power similar to that which the United States' constitution by express provision applies to the commerce power of its federal legislature. Although, ironically, the express restrictions in the American constitution have proved to be far less of a barrier to the development of national economic policies than have the judicially created restrictions in Canada. ~

CITIZENS INSURANCE CO. *v.* PARSONS;
QUEEN INSURANCE CO. *v.* PARSONS.
In the Privy Council. (1881), 7 App. Cas. 96; I Olmsted 94.

The judgment of their Lordships was delivered by

SIR MONTAGUE SMITH. The questions in these appeals arise in two actions brought by the same plaintiff (the respondent) upon contracts of insurance against fire of buildings situate in the province of Ontario, in the Dominion of Canada.

The most important question in both appeals is one of those, already numerous, which have arisen upon the provisions of the British North America Act, 1867, relating to the distribution of legislative powers between the parliament of Canada and the legislatures of the provinces, and, owing to the very general language in which some of these powers are described, the question is one of considerable difficulty. Their Lordships propose to deal with it before approaching the facts on which the particular questions in the actions depend. . . .

. . . The distribution of legislative powers is provided for by sects. 91 to 95 of the British North America Act, 1867; the most important of these being sect. 91, headed "Powers of the Parliament" and sect. 92, headed "Exclusive Powers of Provincial Legislatures.". . .

. . . The scheme of this legislation, as expressed in the first branch of sect. 91, is to give to the dominion parliament authority to make laws for the good government of Canada in all matters not coming within the classes of subjects assigned exclusively to the provincial legislature. If the 91st section had stopped here, and if the classes of subjects enumerated in sect. 92 had been altogether distinct and different from those in sect. 91, no conflict of legislative authority could have arisen. The provincial legislatures would have had exclusive power over the sixteen classes of subjects assigned to them, and the dominion parliament exclusive power over all other matters relating to the good government of Canada. But it must have been foreseen that this sharp and definite distinction had not been and could not be attained, and that some of the classes of subjects assigned to the provincial legislatures unavoidably ran into and were embraced by some of the enumerated classes of subjects in sect. 91; hence an endeavour appears to have been made to provide for cases of apparent conflict; and it would seem that with this object it was declared in the second branch of the 91st section, "for greater certainty, but not so as to restrict the generality of the foregoing terms of this section" that (notwithstanding anything in the Act) the exclusive legislative authority of the parliament of Canada should extend to all matters coming within the classes of subjects enumerated in that section. With the same object, apparently, the paragraph at the end of sect. 91 was introduced, though it may be observed that this paragraph applies in its grammatical construction only to No. 16 of sect. 92.

Notwithstanding this endeavour to give pre-eminence to the dominion parliament in cases of a conflict of powers, it is obvious that in some cases where this apparent conflict exists, the legislature could not have intended that the powers exclusively assigned to the provincial legislature should be absorbed in those given to the dominion parliament. Take as one instance the subject "marriage and divorce," contained in the enumeration of subjects in sect. 91; it is evident that solemnization of marriage would come within this general description; yet "solemnization of marriage in the province" is enumerated among the classes of subjects in sect. 92, and no one can doubt, notwithstanding the general language of sect. 91, that this subject is still within the exclusive authority of the legislatures of the provinces. So "the raising of money by any mode or system of taxation" is enumerated among the classes of subjects in sect. 91; but, though the description is sufficiently large and general to include "direct taxation within the province, in order to the raising of a revenue for provincial purposes," assigned to the provincial legislatures by sect. 92, it obviously could not have been intended that, in this instance also, the general power should override the particular one. With regard to certain classes of subjects, therefore, generally described in sect. 91, legislative power may reside as to some matters falling within the general description of these subjects in the legislatures of the provinces. In these cases it is the duty of the Courts, however difficult it may be, to ascertain in what degree, and to what extent, authority to deal with matters falling within these classes of subjects exists in each legislature and to define in the particular case before them the limits of their respective powers. It could not have

been the intention that a conflict should exist; and, in order to prevent such a result, the two sections must be read together, and the language of one interpreted, and, where necessary, modified, by that of the other. In this way it may, in most cases, be found possible to arrive at a reasonable and practical construction of the language of the sections, so as to reconcile the respective powers they contain, and give effect to all of them. In performing this difficult duty, it will be a wise course for those on whom it is thrown, to decide each case which arises as best they can, without entering more largely upon an interpretation of the statute than is necessary for the decision of the particular question in hand.

The first question to be decided is, whether the Act impeached in the present appeals falls within any of the classes of subjects enumerated in sect. 92, and assigned exclusively to the legislatures of the provinces; for if it does not, it can be of no validity, and no other question would then arise. It is only when an Act of the provincial legislature prima facie falls within one of these classes of subjects that the further questions arise, *viz.*, whether, notwithstanding this is so, the subject of the Act does not also fall within one of the enumerated classes of subjects in sect. 91, and whether the power of the provincial legislature is or is not thereby overborne.

The main contention on the part of the respondent was that the Ontario Act in question had relation to matters coming within the class of subjects described in No. 13 of sect. 92, *viz.*, "Property and civil rights in the province." The Act deals with policies of insurance entered into or in force in the province of Ontario for insuring property situate therein against fire, and prescribes certain conditions which are to form part of such contracts. These contracts, and the rights arising from them, it was argued, came legitimately within the class of subject, "Property and civil rights." The appellants, on the other hand, contended that civil rights meant only such rights as flowed from the law, and gave as an instance the status of persons. Their Lordships cannot think that the latter construction is the correct one. They find no sufficient reason in the language itself, nor in the other parts of the Act, for giving so narrow an interpretation to the words "civil rights." The words are sufficiently large to embrace, in their fair and ordinary meaning, rights arising from contract, and such rights are not included in express terms in any of the enumerated classes of subjects in sect. 91.

It becomes obvious, as soon as an attempt is made to construe the general terms in which the classes of subjects in sect. 91 and 92 are described, that both sections and the other parts of the Act must be looked at to ascertain whether language of a general nature must not by necessary implication or reasonable intendment be modified and limited. In looking at sect. 91, it will be found not only that there is no class including, generally, contracts and the rights arising from them, but that one class of contracts is mentioned and enumerated, *viz.*, "18, bills of exchange and promissory notes," which it would have been unnecessary to specify if authority over all contracts and the rights arising from them had belonged to the dominion parliament.

The provision found in sect. 94 of the British North America Act, which is one of the sections relating to the distribution of legislative powers, was referred to by the learned counsel on both sides as throwing light upon the sense in which the words "property and civil rights" are used. By that section the parliament of Canada is empowered to make provision for the uniformity of any laws relative to "property and civil rights" in Ontario, Nova Scotia, and New Brunswick, and to the procedure of the Courts in these three provinces, if the provincial legislatures choose to adopt the provision so made. The province of Quebec is omitted from this section for the obvious reason that the law which governs property and civil rights in Quebec is in the main the French law as it existed at the time of the cession

of Canada, and not the English law which prevails in the other provinces. The words "property and civil rights" are, obviously, used in the same sense in this section as in No. 13 of sect. 92, and there seems no reason for presuming that contracts and the rights arising from them were not intended to be included in this provision for uniformity. If, however, the narrow construction of the words "civil rights," contended for by the appellants were to prevail, the dominion parliament could, under its general power, legislate in regard to contracts in all and each of the provinces and as a consequence of this the province of Quebec, though now governed by its own Civil Code, founded on the French law, as regards contracts and their incidents, would be subject to have its law on that subject altered by the dominion legislature, and brought into uniformity with the English law prevailing in the other three provinces, notwithstanding that Quebec has been carefully left out of the uniformity section of the Act.

It is observed that the same words, "civil rights," are employed in the Act of 14 Geo. 3, c. 83, which made provision for the Government of the province of Quebec. Sect. 8 of that Act enacted that His Majesty's Canadian subjects within the province of Quebec should enjoy their property, usages, and other civil rights, as they had before done, and that in all matters of controversy relative to property and civil rights resort should be had to the laws of Canada, and be determined agreeably to the said laws. In this statute the words "property" and "civil rights" are plainly used in their largest sense; and there is no reason for holding that in the statute under discussion they are used in a different and narrower one.

The next question for consideration is whether, assuming the Ontario Act to relate to the subject of property and civil rights, its enactments and provisions come within any of the classes of subjects enumerated in sect. 91. The only one which the Appellants suggested as expressly including the subject of the

Ontario Act is No. 2, "the regulation of trade and commerce."

A question was raised which led to much discussion in the Courts below and this bar, *viz*, whether the business of insuring buildings against fire was a trade. This business, when carried on for the sake of profit, may, no doubt, in some sense of the word, be called a trade. But contracts of indemnity made by insurers can scarcely be considered trading contracts, nor were insurers who made them held to be "traders" under the English bankruptcy laws; they have been made subject to those laws by special description. Whether the business of fire insurance properly falls within the description of a "trade" must, in their Lordships' view, depend upon the sense in which that word is used in the particular statute to be construed; but in the present case their Lordships do not find it necessary to rest their decision on the narrow ground that the business of insurance is not a trade.

The words "regulation of trade and commerce," in their unlimited sense are sufficiently wide, if uncontrolled by the context and other parts of the Act, to include every regulation of trade ranging from political arrangements in regard to trade with foreign governments, requiring the sanction of parliament, down to minute rules for regulating particular trades. But a consideration of the Act shows that the words were not used in this unlimited sense. In the first place the collocation of No. 2 with classes of subjects of national and general concern affords an indication that regulations relating to general trade and commerce were in the mind of the legislature, when conferring this power on the dominion parliament. If the words had been intended to have the full scope of which in their literal meaning they are susceptible, the specific mention of several of the other classes of subjects enumerated in sect. 91 would have been unnecessary; as, 15, banking; 17, weights and measures; 18, bills of exchange and promissory notes; 19, interest; and even 21, bankruptcy and insolvency.

"Regulation of trade and commerce"

may have been used in some such sense as the words "regulations of trade" in the Act of Union between England and Scotland (6 Anne, c. 11), and as these words have been used in Acts of State relating to trade and commerce. Article V of the Act of Union enacted that all the subjects of the United Kingdom should have "full freedom and intercourse of trade and navigation" to and from all places in the United Kingdom and the colonies; and Article VI enacted that all parts of the United Kingdom from and after the Union should be under the *same* "prohibitions, restrictions, and *regulations of trade*." Parliament has at various times since the Union passed laws affecting and regulating specific trades in one part of the United Kingdom only, without its being supposed that it thereby infringed the Articles of Union. Thus the Acts for regulating the sale of intoxicating liquors notoriously vary in the two kingdoms. So with regard to Acts relating to bankruptcy, and various other matters.

Construing therefore the words "regulation of trade and commerce" by the various aids to their interpretation above suggested, they would include political arrangements in regard to trade requiring the sanction of parliament, regulation of trade in matters of interprovincial concern, and it may be that they would include general regulation of trade affecting the whole Dominion. Their Lordships abstain on the present occasion from any attempt to define the limits of the authority of the dominion parliament in this direction. It is enough for the decision of the present case to say that, in their view, its authority to legislate for the regulation of trade and commerce does not comprehend the power to regulate by legislation the contracts of a particular business or trade, such as the business of fire insurance in a single province, and therefore that its legislative authority does not in the present case conflict or compete with the power over property and civil rights assigned to the legislature of Ontario by No. 13 of sect. 92. . . .

. . . The opinions of the majority of the

Judges in Canada, as summed up by Ritchie, C.J., are in favour of the validity of the Ontario Act. In the present actions, the Court of Queen's Bench and the Court of Appeal of Ontario unanimously supported its legality; and the Supreme Court of Canada, by a majority of three Judges to two, have affirmed the judgments of the provincial Courts. The opinions of the learned Judges of the Supreme Court are stated with great fullness and ability, and clearly indicate the opposite views which may be taken of the Act, and the difficulties which surround any construction that may be given to it.

Taschereau, J., in the course of his vigorous judgment, seeks to place the plaintiff in the action against the Citizens Company in a dilemma. He thinks that the assertion of the right of the province to legislate with regard to the contracts of insurance companies amounts to a denial of the right of the dominion parliament to do so, and that this is, in effect, to deny the right of that parliament to incorporate the Citizens Company, so that the plaintiff was suing a non-existent defendant. Their Lordships cannot think that this dilemma is established. The learned Judge assumes that the power of the dominion parliament to incorporate companies to carry on business in the dominion is derived from one of the enumerated classes of subjects, *viz.*, "the regulation of trade and commerce," and then argues that if the authority to incorporate companies is given by this clause, the exclusive power of regulating them must also be given by it, so that the denial of one power involves the denial of the other. But, in the first place, it is not necessary to rest the authority of the dominion parliament to incorporate companies on this specific and enumerated power. The authority would belong to it by its general power over all matters not coming within the classes of subjects assigned exclusively to the legislatures of the provinces, and the only subject on this head assigned to the provincial legislature being "the incorporation of companies with provincial objects," it follows that the incorporation of companies for objects other than provincial falls within the general powers of the parliament of Canada. But it by no means follows (unless indeed the view of the learned judge is right as to the scope of the words "the regulation of trade and commerce") that because the dominion parliament has alone the right to create a corporation to carry on business throughout the dominion that it alone has the right to regulate its contracts in each of the provinces. Suppose the dominion parliament were to incorporate a company, with power, among other things, to purchase and hold lands throughout Canada in mortmain, it could scarcely be contended if such a company were to carry on business in a province where a law against holding land in mortmain prevailed (each province having exclusive legislative power over "property and civil rights in the province") that it could hold land in that province in contravention of the provincial legislation; and, if a company were incorporated for the sole purpose of purchasing and holding land in the Dominion, it might happen that it could do no business in any part of it, by reason of all the provinces having passed Mortmain Acts, though the corporation would still exist and preserve its status as a corporate body.

On the best consideration they have been able to give to the arguments addressed to them and to the judgments of the learned judges in Canada, their Lordships have come to the conclusion that the Act in question is valid. . . .

3. Russell *v.* The Queen, *1882*

~ In the case of *Russell* v. *The Queen* the Judicial Committee of the Privy Council was confronted for the first time with what has undoubtedly been the classic issue in the Canadian division of powers—the contest between the Dominion's "peace, order and good government" power and the provinces' power in relation to "property and civil rights" and "all matters of a merely local or private nature in the province." Here the Privy Council ruled the Dominion's temperance legislation *intra vires* on the grounds that since the subject matter of the legislation did not belong to any of the classes of subjects assigned exclusively to the provinces, it must fall under the central Parliament's residuary power.

The direct challenge to the Dominion's Temperance Act came from Charles Russell, who had been convicted under the Act of unlawfully selling liquor in Fredericton, New Brunswick. But the fate of Russell's appeal, the immediate issue of the case, was less important than the opportunity the case gave to the Privy Council to review the earlier decision of the Supreme Court of Canada in *City of Fredericton* v. *The Queen*[1] ruling the Canada Temperance Act *intra vires*. The Supreme Court majority in that case sustained the Act under the trade and commerce clause of section 91, giving a broad interpretation of that power. In *Russell* v. *The Queen* the Privy Council agreed with the Supreme Court of Canada that the Act was valid, but on the basis of Parliament's residuary power, not the trade and commerce power. While not repudiating the possibility of sustaining the legislation under section 91(2), Sir Montague Smith refused to endorse positively the Supreme Court's reasoning. This refusal was more in keeping with the narrower interpretation of section 91(2) which their Lordships had given the previous year in the *Parsons* case.

The Privy Council considered that the primary matter dealt with by the Canada Temperance Act was one relating to public order and safety and that any effect on property and civil rights was merely incidental. As in the *Parsons* case, the Judicial Committee was opposed to interpreting an exclusive power of one level of government (in this case, provincial jurisdiction over property and civil rights) so broadly as to sterilize a power assigned to the other level (the general authority of Parliament to make laws for the peace, order and good government of Canada and Parliament's jurisdiction in relation to criminal law).

The Privy Council's use of the peace, order and good government power in the *Russell* case as a constitutional basis for federal legislation proved to be highly exceptional as subsequent decisions considerably narrowed its scope. ~

---

[1] (1880), 3 S.C.R. 505.

RUSSELL v. THE QUEEN
In the Privy Council. (1882), 7 App. Cas. 829; 1 Olmsted 145.

The judgment of their Lordships was delivered by

SIR MONTAGUE E. SMITH. This is an appeal from an order of the Supreme Court of the Province of New Brunswick, discharging a rule nisi which had been granted on the application of the Appellant for a certiorari to remove a conviction made by the police magistrate of the city of Fredericton against him for unlawfully selling intoxicating liquors, contrary to the provisions of the Canada Temperance Act, 1878.

No question has been raised as to the sufficiency of the conviction, supposing the above-mentioned statute is a valid legislative Act of the Parliament of Canada. The only objection made to the conviction in the Supreme Court of New Brunswick, and in the appeal to Her Majesty in Council, is that, having regard to the provisions of the British North America Act, 1867, relating to the distribution of legislative powers, it was not competent for the Parliament of Canada to pass the Act in question.

The Supreme Court of New Brunswick made the order now appealed from in deference to a judgment of the Supreme Court of Canada in the case of the *City of Fredericton* v. *The Queen*. In that case the question of the validity of the Canada Temperance Act, 1878, though in another shape, directly arose, and the Supreme Court of New Brunswick, consisting of six Judges, then decided, Mr. Justice Palmer dissenting, that the Act was beyond the competency of the Dominion Parliament. On the appeal of the City of Fredericton, this judgment was reversed by the Supreme Court of Canada, which held, Mr. Justice Henry dissenting, that the Act was valid. (The case is reported in 3rd Supreme Court of Canada Reports, p. 505.) The present appeal to Her Majesty is brought, in effect, to review the last-mentioned decision.

The preamble of the Act in question states that "it is very desirable to promote temperance in the dominion, and that there should be uniform legislation in all the provinces respecting the traffic in intoxicating liquors." The Act is divided into three parts. The first relates to "proceedings for bringing the second part of this Act into force"; the second to "prohibition of traffic in intoxicating liquors"; and the third to "penalties and prosecution for offences against the second part."

The mode of bringing the second part of the Act into force, stating it succinctly, is as follows: On a petition to the Governor in Council, signed by not less than one fourth in number of the electors of any county or city in the Dominion qualified to vote at the election of a member of the House of Commons, praying that the second part of the Act should be in force and take effect in such county or city, and that the votes of all the electors be taken for or against the adoption of the petition, the Governor-General, after certain prescribed notices and evidence, may issue a proclamation, embodying such petition, with a view to a poll of the electors being taken for or against its adoption. When any petition has been adopted by the electors of the county or city named in it, the Governor-General in Council may, after the expiration of sixty days from the day on which the petition was adopted, by Order in Council published in the *Gazette*, declare that the second part of the Act shall be in force and take effect in such county or city, and the same is then to become of force and take effect accordingly. Such order in Council is not to be revoked for three years, and only on like petition and procedure.

The most important of the prohibitory enactments contained in the second part of the Act is s. 99, which enacts that, "from the day on which this part of this Act comes into force and takes effect in any county or city, and for so long thereafter as the same continues in force therein, no person, unless it be for exclusively sacramental or medicinal purposes, or for bona fide use in some art, trade, or manufacture, under the regulation contained in the fourth sub-section of this section, or as hereinafter authorized by one of the four next sub-sections of this section, shall, within such county or city, by himself, his clerk, servant, or agent, expose or keep for sale, or directly or indirectly, on any pretence or upon any device, sell or barter, or in consideration of the purchase of any other property give, to any other person, any spirituous or other intoxicating liquor, or any mixed liquor, capable of being used as a beverage and part of which is spirituous or otherwise intoxicating.''

Sub-sect. 2 provides that "neither any license issued to any distiller or brewer" (and after enumerating other licenses), "nor yet any other description of license whatever, shall in any wise avail to render legal any act done in violation of this section.''

Sub-sect. 3 provides for the sale of wine for sacramental purposes, and sub-sect. 4 for the sale of intoxicating liquors for medicinal and manufacturing purposes, these sales being made subject to prescribed conditions.

Other sub-sections provide that producers of cider, and distillers and brewers, may sell liquors of their own manufacture in certain quantities, which may be termed wholesale quantities, or for export, subject to prescribed conditions, and there are provisions of a like nature with respect to vine-growing companies and manufacturers of native wines.

The third part of the Act enacts (sect. 100) that whoever exposes for sale or sells intoxicating liquors in violation of the second part of the Act should be liable, on summary conviction, to a penalty of not less than fifty dollars for the first offence, and not less than one hundred dollars for the second offence, and to be imprisoned for a term not exceeding two months for the third and every subsequent offence; all intoxicating liquors in respect to which any such offence has been committed to be forfeited.

The effect of the Act when brought into force in any county or town within the Dominion is, describing it generally, to prohibit the sale of intoxicating liquors, except in wholesale quantities, or for certain specified purposes, to regulate the traffic in the excepted cases, and to make sales of liquors in violation of the prohibition and regulations contained in the Act criminal offences, punishable by fine, and for the third or subsequent offence by imprisonment.

It was in the first place contended, though not very strongly relied on, by the Appellant's counsel, that assuming the Parliament of Canada had authority to pass a law for prohibiting and regulating the sale of intoxicating liquors, it could not delegate its powers, and that it had done so by delegating the power to bring into force the prohibitory and penal provisions of the Act to a majority of the electors of counties and cities. The short answer to this objection is that the Act does not delegate any legislative powers whatever. It contains within itself the whole legislation on the matters with which it deals. The provision that certain parts of the Act shall come into operation only on the petition of a majority of electors does not confer on these persons power to legislate. Parliament itself enacts the condition and everything which is to follow upon the condition being fulfilled. Conditional legislation of this kind is in many cases convenient, and is certainly not unusual, and the power so to legislate cannot be denied to the Parliament of Canada, when the subject of legislation is within its competency. . . .

The general question of the competency of the Dominion Parliament to pass the Act depends on the construction of the 91st and 92nd sections of the British North America Act, 1867, which are found in Part VI of the statute under the heading, "Distribution of Legislative Powers.''

The 91st section enacts, "It shall be lawful for the Queen by and with the advice and consent of the Senate and House of Commons to make laws for the peace, order, and good government of Canada, in relation to all matters not coming within the classes of subjects by this Act assigned exclusively to the legislatures of the provinces; and for greater certainty, but not so as to restrict the generality of the foregoing terms of this section, it is hereby declared that (notwithstanding anything in this Act) the exclusive legislative authority of the Parliament of Canada extends to all matters coming within the classes of subject next hereinafter enumerated;'' then after the enumeration of twenty-nine classes of subjects, the section contains the following words: ''And any matter coming within any of the classes of subjects enumerated in this section shall not be deemed to come within the class of matters of a local or private nature comprised in the enumeration of the classes of subjects by this Act assigned exclusively to the Legislature of the province.''

The general scheme of the British North America Act with regard to the distribution of legislative powers, and the general scope and effect of sects. 91 and 92, and their relation to each other, were fully considered and commented on by this Board in the case of the *Citizens Insurance Company* v. *Parsons* (7 App. Cas. 96). According to the principle of construction there pointed out, the first question to be determined is, whether the Act now in question falls within any of the classes of subjects enumerated in sect. 92, and assigned exclusively to the Legislatures of the Provinces. If it does, then the further question would arise, *viz.*, whether the subject of the Act does not also fall within one of the enumerated classes of subjects in sect. 91, and so does not still belong to the Dominion Parliament. But if the Act does not fall within any of the classes of subjects in sect. 92, no further question will remain, for it cannot be contended, and indeed was not contended at their Lordships' bar, that, if the Act does not come within one of the classes of subjects assigned to the Provincial Legislatures, the Parliament of Canada had not, by its general power ''to

make laws for the peace, order, and good government of Canada,'' full legislative authority to pass it.

Three classes of subjects enumerated in sect. 92 were referred to, under each of which, it was contended by the appellant's counsel, the present legislation fell. These were:

9. Shop, saloon, tavern, auctioneer, and other licenses in order to the raising of a revenue for provincial, local, or municipal purposes.

13. Property and civil rights in the province.

16. Generally all matters of a merely local or private nature in the province.

With regard to the first of these classes, No. 9, it is to be observed that the power of granting licenses is not assigned to the Provincial Legislatures for the purpose of regulating trade, but ''in order to the raising of a revenue for provincial, local, or municipal purposes.''

The Act in question is not a fiscal law; it is not a law for raising revenue; on the contrary, the effect of it may be to destroy or diminish revenue; indeed it was a main objection to the Act that in the city of Fredericton it did in point of fact diminish the sources of municipal revenue. It is evident, therefore, that the matter of the Act is not within the class of subject No. 9, and consequently that it could not have been passed by the Provincial Legislature by virtue of any authority conferred upon it by that sub-section.

~ Sir Montague E. Smith then pointed out that while national legislation such as the Canada Temperance Act might affect the sale or use of an article covered by a license granted under sub-section 9 of section 92, this in itself was not grounds for bringing the legislation under that sub-section. ~

Next, their Lordships cannot think that the Temperance Act in question properly belongs to the class of subjects, ''Property and Civil Rights.'' It has in its legal aspect an obvious and close similarity to laws which place restrictions on the sale or custody of poisonous drugs, or of dangerously explosive substances. These things, as well as intoxicating liquors, can, of course, be held as property, but a law placing restrictions on their sale, custody, or removal, on the ground that the free sale or use of them is dangerous to public safety, and making it a criminal offence punishable by fine or imprisonment to violate these restrictions, cannot properly be deemed a law in relation to property in the sense in which those words are used in the 92nd section. What Parliament is dealing with in legislation of this kind is not a matter in relation to property and its rights, but one relating to public order and safety. That is the primary matter dealt with, and though incidentally the free use of things in which men may have property is interfered with, that incidental interference does not alter the character of the law. Upon the same considerations, the Act in question cannot be regarded as legislation in relation to civil rights. In however large a sense these words are used, it could not have been intended to prevent the Parliament of Canada from declaring and enacting certain uses of property, and certain acts in relation to property, to be criminal and wrongful. Laws which make it a criminal offence for a man wilfully to set fire to his own house on the ground that such an act endangers the public safety, or to overwork his horse on the ground of cruelty to the animal, though affecting in some sense property and the right of a man to do as he pleases with his own, cannot properly be regarded as legislation in relation to property or to civil rights. Nor could a law which prohibited or restricted the sale or exposure of cattle having a contagious disease be so regarded. Laws of this nature designed for the promotion of public order, safety, or morals, and which subject those who contravene them to criminal procedure and punishment, belong to the subject of public wrongs rather than to that of civil rights. They are of a nature which fall within the general authority of Parliament to make laws for the order and good government of Canada, and have direct relation to criminal law, which is one of the

enumerated classes of subjects assigned exclusively to the Parliament of Canada. It was said in the course of the judgment of this Board in the case of the *Citizens Insurance Company of Canada* v. *Parsons* that the two sections (91 and 92) must be read together, and the language of one interpreted, and, where necessary, modified by that of the other. Few, if any, laws could be made by Parliament for the peace, order, and good government of Canada which did not in some incidental way affect property and civil rights; and it could not have been intended, when assuring to the provinces exclusive legislative authority on the subjects of property and civil rights, to exclude the Parliament from the exercise of this general power whenever any such incidental interference would result from it. The true nature and character of the legislation in the particular instance under discussion must always be determined, in order to ascertain the class of subject to which it really belongs. In the present case it appears to their Lordships, for the reasons already given, that the matter of the Act in question does not properly belong to the class of subjects "Property and Civil Rights" within the meaning of sub-sect. 13. . . .

It was lastly contended that this Act fell within sub-sect. 16 of sect. 92—"Generally all matters of a merely local or personal nature in the province."

It was not, of course, contended for the appellant that the Legislature of New Brunswick could have passed the Act in question, which embraces in its enactments all the provinces; nor was it denied, with respect to this last contention, that the Parliament of Canada might have passed an Act of the nature of that under discussion to take effect at the same time throughout the whole Dominion. Their Lordships understand the contention to be that, at least in the absence of a general law of the Parliament of Canada, the provinces might have passed a local law of a like kind, each for its own province, and that, as the prohibitory and penal parts of the Act in question were to come into force in those counties and cities only in which it was adopted in the manner prescribed, or, as it was said, "by local option," the legislation was in effect, and on its face, upon a matter of a merely local nature. The judgment of Allen C.J., delivered in the Supreme Court of the Province of New Brunswick in the case of *Barker* v. *City of Fredericton* (3 Pugs & Burb. Sup. Ct. New Br. Rep. 139), which was adverse to the validity of the Act in question, appears to have been founded upon this view of its enactments. The learned Chief Justice says: "Had this Act prohibited the sale of liquor, instead of merely restricting and regulating it, I should have had no doubt about the power of the Parliament to pass such an Act; but I think an Act, which in effect authorizes the inhabitants of each town or parish to regulate the sale of liquor, and to direct for whom, for what purposes, and under what conditions spirituous liquors may be sold therein, deals with matters of a merely local nature, which, by terms of the 16th sub-section of sect. 92 of the British North America Act, are within the exclusive control of the local Legislature."

Their Lordships cannot concur in this view. The declared object of Parliament in passing the Act is that there should be uniform legislation in all the provinces respecting the traffic in intoxicating liquors, with a view to promote temperance in the Dominion. Parliament does not treat the promotion of temperance as desirable in one province more than in another, but as desirable everywhere throughout the Dominion. The Act as soon as it was passed became a law for the whole Dominion, and the enactments of the first part, relating to the machinery for bringing the second part into force, took effect and might be put in motion at once and everywhere within it. It is true that the prohibitory and penal parts of the Act are only to come into force in any county or city upon the adoption of a petition to that effect by a majority of electors, but this conditional application of these parts of the Act does not convert the Act itself into legislation in relation to a merely local

matter. The objects and scope of the legislation are still general, *viz.*, to promote temperance by means of a uniform law throughout the Dominion.

The manner of bringing the prohibitions and penalties of the Act into force, which Parliament has thought fit to adopt, does not alter its general and uniform character. Parliament deals with the subject as one of general concern to the Dominion, upon which uniformity of legislation is desirable, and the Parliament alone can so deal with it. There is no ground or pretence for saying that the evil or vice struck at by the Act in question is local or exists only in one province, and that Parliament, under colour of general legislation, is dealing with a provincial matter only. It is therefore unnecessary to discuss the considerations which a state of circumstances of this kind might present. The present legislation is clearly meant to apply a remedy to an evil which is assumed to exist throughout the Dominion, and the local option, as it is called, no more localizes the subject and scope of the Act than a provision in an Act for the prevention of contagious diseases in cattle that a public officer should proclaim in what districts it should come in effect, would make the statute itself a mere local law for each of these districts. In statutes of this kind the legislation is general, and the provision for the special application of it to particular places does not alter its character.

Their Lordships having come to the conclusion that the Act in question does not fall within any of the classes of subjects assigned exclusively to the Provincial Legislatures, it becomes unnecessary to discuss the further question whether its provisions also fall within any of the classes of subjects enumerated in sect. 91. In abstaining from this discussion, they must not be understood as intimating any dissent from the opinion of the Chief Justice of the Supreme Court of Canada and the other Judges, who held that the Act, as a general regulation of the traffic in intoxicating liquors throughout the Dominion, fell within the class of subject, "the regulation of trade and commerce," enumerated in that section, and was, on that ground, a valid exercise of the legislative power of the Parliament of Canada. . . .

4. Liquidators of the Maritime Bank of Canada *v.* Receiver General of New Brunswick, *1892*

~ While this case did not deal directly with the division of legislative powers, it did provide the occasion for Lord Watson to express a conception of Canadian federalism which underlies most of the Judicial Committee's decisions on the Canadian constitution.

The immediate issue in the case was whether the Government of New Brunswick could use Crown prerogative as a basis for claiming priority over other creditors seeking to recover funds from the liquidators of the Maritime Bank. The federal government endeavoured to deny New Brunswick's claim on the grounds that Confederation had severed any direct relationship between the Crown and a province and in this sense had made the provinces subordinate to the federal government.

Lord Watson, in dismissing this argument, denied that the B.N.A. Act was intended to produce a system in which provinces were subordinate to a central government. The conception of federalism he found in the B.N.A. Act was much closer to the definition of federalism found in classic constitutional texts than it was to Sir John A. Macdonald's conception of the purpose of Confederation. A.V. Dicey's *Introduction to the Law of the Constitution*, an influential English text which was first published in 1885, offered the following definition of federalism:

A federal state is a political contrivance intended to reconcile national unity and power with the maintenance of "state rights." The end aimed at fixes the essential character of federalism. For the method by which Federalism attempts to reconcile the apparently inconsistent claims of national sovereignty and of state sovereignty consists of the formation of a constitution under which the ordinary powers of sovereignty are elaborately divided between the common or national government and the separate states.[1]

Compare this with the following statement of Sir John A. Macdonald from the Confederation Debates:

The true principle of a Confederation lay in giving to the General Government all the principles and powers of sovereignty, and that the subordinate or individual states should have no powers but those expressly bestowed on them. We should thus have a powerful Central Government, a powerful Central Legislature, and a decentralized system of minor legislatures for local purposes.[2]

While the contrast between Macdonald's theory of confederation and the doctrine of classical federalism enunciated by the Privy Council is clear, it is

---

[1] *Introduction to the Law of the Constitution*, 10th ed. (London: Macmillan, 1961), p. 143.
[2] P.B. Waite, ed., *The Confederation Debates in the Province of Canada*, Carleton Library ed. (Toronto: McClelland and Stewart, 1963), p. 156.

important to bear in mind that Macdonald was only one of the Fathers of Confederation and he belonged to the group who were most sceptical about federalism. Other members of the political coalition which produced Confederation and forced Macdonald to accept federalism might not have been surprised or dismayed by the Privy Council's tendency to read classical federalism into the B.N.A. Act. ~

LIQUIDATORS OF THE MARITIME BANK OF CANADA
v. RECEIVER GENERAL OF NEW BRUNSWICK
In the Privy Council. (1892) A.C. 437; 1 Olmsted 263.

The judgment of their Lordships was delivered by

LORD WATSON. This appeal is brought by special leave in a suit which followed upon a case submitted for the opinion of the Supreme Court of the province of New Brunswick, by the appellants, the liquidators of the Maritime Bank of the Dominion of Canada, in the interest of unsecured creditors of the bank, on the one side, and by the Receiver-General of the Province, claiming to represent Her Majesty, on the other. The only facts which it is necessary to refer to are these: that the bank carried on its business in the city of St. John, New Brunswick; and that, at the time when it stopped payment in March, 1887, the provincial government was a simple contract creditor for a sum of $35,000, being public moneys of the province deposited in the name of the Receiver-General. The case, as originally framed, presented two questions for the decision of the Court; but, owing to the condition of the bank's assets, the first of these has ceased to be of practical importance, and it is only necessary to consider the second, which is in these terms: "Is the provincial government entitled to payment in full over the other depositors and simple contract creditors of the bank?"

The Supreme Court of New Brunswick unanimously, and, on appeal, the Supreme Court of Canada with a single dissentient voice, have held that the claim of the provincial government is for a Crown debt to which the prerogative attaches, and therefore answered the question in the affirmative.

The Supreme Court of Canada had previously ruled, in *Reg.* v. *Bank of Nova Scotia* (9 App. Cas. 117), that the Crown, as a simple contract creditor for public moneys of the Dominion deposited with a provincial bank, is entitled to priority over other creditors of equal degree. The decision appears to their Lordships to be in strict accordance with constitutional law. The property and revenues of the Dominion are vested in the Sovereign, subject to the disposal and appropriation of the legislature of Canada; and the prerogative of the Queen, when it has not been expressly limited by local law or statute, is as extensive in Her Majesty's colonial possessions as in Great Britain. In *Exchange Bank of Canada* v. *The Queen* (11 App. Cas. 157), this Board disposed of the appeal on that footing, although their Lordships reversed the judgment of the Court below, and negatived the preference claimed by the Dominion Government upon the ground that, by the law of the province of Quebec, the prerogative was limited to the case of the common debtor being an officer liable to account to the Crown for public moneys collected or held by him. The appellants did not impeach the authority of these cases, and they also conceded that, until the passing of the British North America Act, 1867, there was precisely the same relation between the Crown and the province which now subsists between the Crown and the Dominion. But they maintained that the effect of the statute has been to sever all connection between the Crown and the provinces; to make the government of the Dominion the only government of Her

Majesty in North America; and to reduce the provinces to the rank of independent municipal institutions. For these propositions, which contain the sum and substance of the arguments addressed to them in support of this appeal, their Lordships have been unable to find either principle or authority.

Their Lordships do not think it necessary to examine, in minute detail, the provisions of the Act of 1867, which nowhere profess to curtail in any respect the rights and privileges of the Crown, or to disturb the relations then subsisting between the Sovereign and the provinces. The object of the Act was neither to weld the provinces into one, nor to subordinate provincial governments to a central authority, but to create a federal government in which they should all be represented, entrusted with the exclusive administration of affairs in which they had a common interest, each province retaining its independence and autonomy. That object was accomplished by distributing, between the Dominion and the provinces, all powers executive and legislative, and all public property and revenues which had previously belonged to the provinces; so that the Dominion Government should be vested with such of these powers, property, and revenues as were necessary for the due performance of its constitutional functions, and that the remainder should be retained by the provinces for the purposes of provincial government. But, in so far as regards those matters which, by sect. 92, are specially reserved for provincial legislation, the legislation of each province continues to be free from the control of the Dominion, and as supreme as it was before the passing of the

Act. In *Hodge* v. *The Queen* (9 App. Cas. 117), Lord Fitzgerald delivering the opinion of this Board, said: "When the British North America Act enacted that there should be a legislature for Ontario, and that its legislative assembly should have exclusive authority to make laws for the province and for provincial purposes in relation to the matters enumerated in sect. 92, it conferred powers not in any sense to be exercised by delegation from or as agents of the Imperial Parliament, but authority as plenary and as ample within the limits prescribed by sect. 92 as the Imperial Parliament in the plenitude of its power possessed and could bestow. Within these limits of subject and area, the local legislature is supreme, and has the same authority as the Imperial Parliament, or the Parliament of the Dominion." The Act places the constitutions of all provinces within the Dominion on the same level; and what is true with respect to the legislature of Ontario has equal application to the legislature of New Brunswick.

It is clear, therefore, that the provincial legislature of New Brunswick does not occupy the subordinate position which was ascribed to it in the argument of the appellants. It derives no authority from the Government of Canada, and its status is in no way analogous to that of a municipal institution, which is an authority constituted for purposes of local administration. It possesses powers, not of administration merely, but of legislation, in the strictest sense of that word; and, within the limits assigned by sect. 92 of the Act of 1867, these powers are exclusive and supreme. . . .

5. Attorney General of Ontario v. Attorney General of Canada (Local Prohibition Case), 1896

~ Competition between Ontario and the federal government to regulate the consumption and sale of liquor was a major source of constitutional litigation in the last two decades of the nineteenth century. As we have seen a federal scheme for a system of local prohibition was upheld in the *Russell* case. In *Hodge* v. *The Queen*[1] the Judicial Committee upheld an Ontario scheme for licensing taverns and retail liquor outlets. But two years later, the Privy Council, without giving reasons, ruled *ultra vires* a federal law (the McCarthy Act) which provided a scheme for the appointment of local liquor licensing commissioners across Canada.[2] The *Local Prohibition* case of 1896 raised the question of whether a province could provide a system of local prohibition at least for those districts which had not availed themselves of the provisions of the Canada Temperance Act.

This question first arose in private litigation in *Huson* v. *South Norwich*.[3] In that case the Supreme Court by a three-to-two majority found Ontario's local prohibition scheme constitutional. But shortly after this decision the federal government referred the question of the validity of the Ontario law, along with six more hypothetical questions, to the Supreme Court. In the interval between the *Huson* case and the reference case Justice King replaced Justice Taschereau, with the result that the Supreme Court now found Ontario's local prohibition legislation unconstitutional. The Court's decision in the reference case represents the last manifestation of the early Supreme Court's allegiance to the centralist concepts of certain Fathers of Confederation. Justice Gwynne, for example, fortified his view that the prohibition of liquor sales fell under exclusive federal jurisdiction over trade and commerce by quoting George Brown in the Confederation Debates: "All matters of trade and commerce, banking and currency and all questions common to the whole people we have vested fully and unrestrictedly in the general government."[4]

On appeal, the Privy Council reversed the Supreme Court's decision in the reference case. The opinion written by Lord Watson had the effect of attenuating both the federal trade and commerce power and the federal Parliament's general power. By repudiating the Supreme Court's holding that the Canada Temperance Act was a proper exercise of the trade and commerce power, the Privy Council culminated its overruling of the early Supreme Court's tendency to assign virtually all aspects of trade and commerce exclusively to the federal Parliament. The Privy Council also held that the federal peace, order and good

---

[1] (1883), 9 App. Cas. 177.
[2] (1875-1893), Cassels, *Digest of Supreme Court Decisions*, p. 509.
[3] (1895), 24 S.C.R. 145.
[4] *Re Prohibitory Liquor Laws* (1895), 24 S.C.R. 170, at p. 207.

government power did not exclude the provinces from enacting their own local prohibition laws. In reaching this conclusion Lord Watson argued that the preservation of provincial autonomy required that Parliament's general power to legislate for the peace, order and good government of Canada not have the same capacity as the federal enumerated powers to override provincial jurisdiction over matters of a local or private nature.

This distinction between peace, order and good government and the enumerated powers (which are listed "for greater Certainty but not so as to restrict the Generality" of the general power) has been regarded as a serious diminution of the general power. Yet it should be noted that Lord Watson left what appears to be a potentially liberal test for the application of the general power when he stated that circumstances might transform local and private matters into matters of national concern and thus bring them under Parliament's power to make laws for the peace, order and good government of Canada. In succeeding decisions, however, this test was very restrictively applied by the Privy Council. ~

ATTORNEY GENERAL OF ONTARIO v. ATTORNEY GENERAL OF CANADA
In the Privy Council. [1896] A.C. 348; I Olmsted 343

~ The appeal was made by special leave from a judgment of the Supreme Court of Canada, 24 S.C.R. 170, on a reference to it of seven questions. ~

1. Has a provincial legislature jurisdiction to prohibit the sale within the province of spirituous, fermented, or other intoxicating liquors?

2. Or has the legislature such jurisdiction regarding such portions of the province as to which the Canada Temperance Act is not in operation?

3. Has a provincial legislature jurisdiction to prohibit the manufacture of such liquors within the province?

4. Has a provincial legislature jurisdiction to prohibit the importation of such liquors into the province?

5. If a provincial legislature has not jurisdiction to prohibit sales of such liquors, irrespective of quantity, has such legislature jurisdiction to prohibit the sale by retail, according to the definition of a sale by retail either in statutes in force in the province at the time of confederation, or any other definition thereof?

6. If a provincial legislature has a limited jurisdiction only as regards the prohibition of sales, has the legislature jurisdiction to prohibit sales subject to the limits provided by the several sub-sections of the 99th section of the Canada Temperance Act, or any of them (Revised Statutes of Canada, 49 Vict. c. 106, s. 99)?

7. Has the Ontario Legislature jurisdiction to enact s. 18 of Ontario Act, 53 Vict. c. 56, intituled "An Act to improve the Liquor Licence Acts," as said section is explained by Ontario Act, 54 Vict. c. 46, intituled "An Act respecting local option in the matter of liquor selling"?

Section 18, referred to in the last of the said questions, is as follows:

"18. Whereas the following provision of this section was at the date of confederation in force as a part of the Consolidated Municipal Act (29th and 30th Victoria, chapter 51, section 249, subsection 9), and was afterwards re-enacted as sub-section 7 of section 6 of 32nd Victoria, chapter 32, being the Tavern and Shop Licence Act of 1868, but was afterwards omitted in subsequent consolidations of the Municipal and the Liquor

Licence Acts, similar provisions as to local prohibitions being contained in the Temperance Act of 1864, 27th and 28th Victoria, chapter 18; and the said last-mentioned Act having been repealed in municipalities where not in force by the Canada Temperance Act, it is expedient that municipalities should have the powers by them formerly possessed; it is hereby enacted as follows:

"The council of every township, city, town, and incorporated village may pass by-laws for prohibiting the sale by retail of spirituous, fermented, or other manufactured liquors in any tavern, inn, or other house or place of public entertainment, and for prohibiting altogether the sale thereof in shops and places other than houses of public entertainment. Provided that the by-law before the final passing thereof has been duly approved of by the electors of the municipality in the manner provided by the sections in that behalf of the Municipal Act. Provided further that nothing in this section contained shall be construed into an exercise of jurisdiction by the Legislature of the province of Ontario beyond the revival of provisions of law which were in force at the date of the passing of the British North America Act, and which the subsequent legislation of this province purported to repeal."

Act 54 Vict. c. 46, referred to above, declares that s. 18 was not intended to affect the provisions of s. 252 of the Consolidated Municipal Act, being Canada Act, 29 & 30 Vict. c. 51.

A majority of the Supreme Court, after hearing counsel for the Dominion, the provinces of Ontario, Quebec, and Manitoba, and also, under s. 37, sub-s. 4, of the Supreme and Exchequer Courts Act for the Distillers and Brewers' Association of Ontario, answered all the questions in the negative. Strong C.J., and Fournier J., while agreeing in a negative answer to questions 3 and 4, answered the remainder in the affirmative.

The judgment of their Lordships was delivered by

LORD WATSON. Their Lordships think

it expedient to deal, in the first instance, with the seventh question, because it raises a practical issue, to which the able arguments of counsel on both sides of the Bar were chiefly directed, and also because it involves considerations which have a material bearing upon the answers to be given to the other six questions submitted in this appeal. In order to appreciate the merits of the controversy, it is necessary to refer to certain laws for the restriction or suppression of the liquor traffic which were passed by the Legislature of the old province of Canada before the Union, or have since been enacted by the Parliament of the Dominion, and by the Legislature of Ontario respectively.

~ Lord Watson then reviewed the history of liquor legislation in Ontario. He related how the Ontario legislature came to pass the Act referred to in the seventh question. This Act aimed at restoring to Ontario municipalities the power of making by-laws prohibiting the sale of liquor. The right had been bestowed upon them in 1864 but had later been allowed to lapse by the Ontario legislature and was not in force when the Canada Temperance Act of 1886, which provided for prohibition at the option of localities, purported to repeal it. ~

The seventh question raises the issue, whether, in the circumstances which have just been detailed, the provincial legislature had authority to enact s. 18. In order to determine that issue, it becomes necessary to consider, in the first place, whether the Parliament of Canada had jurisdiction to enact the Canada Temperance Act; and, if so, to consider in the second place, whether, after that Act became the law of each province of the Dominion, there yet remained power with the Legislature of Ontario to enact the provisions of s. 18.

The authority of the Dominion Parliament to make laws for the suppression of liquor traffic in the province is maintained, in the first place, upon the ground that such legislation deals with matters affecting "the peace, order, and good government of Canada,'' within the meaning of the introductory and general enactments of s. 91 of the British North America Act; and, in the second place, upon the ground that it concerns ''the regulation of trade and commerce,'' being No. 2 of the enumerated classes of subjects which are placed under the exclusive jurisdiction of the Federal Parliament by that section. These sources of jurisdiction are in themselves distinct, and are to be found in different enactments.

It was apparently contemplated by the framers of the Imperial Act of 1867 that the due exercise of the enumerated powers conferred upon the Parliament of Canada by s. 91 might, occasionally and incidentally, involve legislation upon matters which are prima facie committed exclusively to the provincial legislatures by s. 92. In order to provide against that contingency, the concluding part of s. 91 enacts that ''any matter coming within any of the classes of subjects enumerated in this section shall not be deemed to come within the class of matters of a local or private nature comprised in the enumeration of the classes of subjects by this Act assigned exclusively to the legislatures of the provinces.'' It was observed by this Board in *Citizens' Insurance Co. of Canada* v. *Parsons* (7 App. Cas. 108) that the paragraph just quoted ''applied in its grammatical construction only to No. 16 of s. 92.'' The observation was not material to the question arising in that case, and it does not appear to their Lordships to be strictly accurate. It appears to them that the language of the exception in s. 91 was meant to include and correctly describes all the matters enumerated in the sixteen heads of s. 92, as being, from a provincial point of view, of a local or private nature. It also appears to their Lordships that the exception was not meant to derogate from the legislative authority given to provincial legislatures by those sixteen subsections, save to the extent of enabling the Parliament of Canada to deal with matters local or private in those cases where such legislation is necessarily incidental to the exercise of the powers conferred upon it by the enumerative heads of clause 91. . . .

The general authority given to the Canadian Parliament by the introductory enactments of s. 91 is ''to make laws for the peace, order, and good government of Canada, in relation to all matters not coming within the classes of subjects by this Act assigned exclusively to the legislatures of the provinces''; and it is declared, but not so as to restrict the generality of these words, that the exclusive authority of the Canadian Parliament extends to all matters coming within the classes of subjects which are enumerated in the clause. There may, therefore, be matters not included in the enumeration, upon which the Parliament of Canada has power to legislate, because they concern the peace, order, and good government of the Dominion. But to those matters which are not specified among the enumerated subjects of legislation, the exception from s. 92, which is enacted by the concluding words of s. 91, has no application; and, in legislating with regard to such matters, the Dominion Parliament has no authority to encroach upon any class of subjects which is exclusively assigned to provincial legislatures by s. 92. These enactments appear to their Lordships to indicate that the exercise of legislative power by the Parliament of Canada, in regard to all matters not enumerated in s. 91, ought to be strictly confined to such matters as are unquestionably of Canadian interest and importance and ought not to trench upon provincial legislation with respect to any of the classes of subjects enumerated in s. 92. To attach any other construction to the general power which, in supplement of its enumerated powers, is conferred upon the Parliament of Canada by s. 91, would, in their Lordships' opinion, not only be contrary to the intendment of the Act, but would practically destroy the autonomy of the provinces. If it were once conceded that the Parliament of Canada has authority to make laws applicable to the whole Dominion, in relation to matters which in each province are substantially of local or private interest, upon the assumption that these matters also concern the peace, order, and good government of the Dominion, there is hardly a subject enumerated in s. 92 upon which it might not legislate, to the exclusion of the provincial legislatures.

In construing the introductory enactments of s. 91, with respect to matters other than those enumerated, which concern the peace, order, and good government of Canada, it must be kept in view that s. 94, which empowers the Parliament of Canada to make provision for the uniformity of the laws relative to property and civil rights in Ontario, Nova Scotia, and New Brunswick does not extend to the province of Quebec; and also that the Dominion legislation thereby authorized is expressly declared to be of no effect unless and until it has been adopted and enacted by the provincial legislature. These enactments would be idle and abortive, if it were held that the Parliament of Canada derives jurisdiction from the introductory provisions of s. 91, to deal with any matter which is in substance local or provincial, and does not truly affect the interest of the Dominion as a whole. Their Lordships do not doubt that some matters, in their origin local and provincial, might attain such dimensions as to affect the body politic of the Dominion, and to justify the Canadian Parliament in passing laws for their regulation or abolition in the interest of the Dominion. But great caution must be observed in distinguishing between that which is local and provincial, and therefore within the jurisdiction of the provincial legislatures, and that which has ceased to be merely local or provincial, and has become matter of national concern, in such sense to bring it within the jurisdiction of the Parliament of Canada. An Act restricting the right to carry weapons of offence, or their sale to young persons, within the province would be within the authority of the provincial legislature. But traffic in arms, or the possession of them under such circumstances as to raise a suspicion that they were to be used for seditious purposes, or against a foreign State, are matters which, their Lordships conceive, might be competently dealt with by the Parliament of the Dominion.

The judgment of this Board in *Russell* v. *Reg.* (7 App. Cas. 829) has relieved their Lordships from the difficult duty of considering whether the Canada Temperance Act of 1886 relates to the peace, order, and good government of Canada, in such sense as to bring its provisions within the competency of the Canadian Parliament. In that case the controversy related to the validity of the Canada Temperance Act of 1878; and neither the Dominion nor the Provinces were represented in the argument. It arose between a private prosecutor and a person who had been convicted, at his instance, of violating the provisions of the Canadian Act within a district of New Brunswick, in which the prohibitory clauses of the Act had been adopted. But the provisions of the Act of 1878 were in all material respects the same with those which are now embodied in the Canada Temperance Act of 1886; and the reasons which were assigned for sustaining the validity of the earlier, are, in their Lordships' opinion, equally applicable to the later Act. It therefore appears to them that the decision in *Russell* v. *Reg.* must be accepted as an authority to the extent to which it goes, namely, that the restrictive provisions of the Act of 1886, when they have been duly brought into operation in any provincial area within the Dominion, must receive effect as valid enactments relating to the peace, order and good government of Canada.

That point being settled by decision, it becomes necessary to consider whether the Parliament of Canada had authority to pass the Temperance Act of 1886 as being an Act for the "regulation of trade and commerce" within the meaning of No. 2 of s. 91. If it were so, the Parliament of Canada would, under the exception from s. 92 which has already been noticed, be at liberty to exercise its legislative authority, although in so doing it should interfere with the jurisdiction of the provinces. The scope and effect of No. 2

of s. 91 were discussed by this Board at some length in *Citizens' Insurance Co.* v. *Parsons* (7 App. Cas. 96), where it was decided that, in the absence of legislation upon the subject by the Canadian Parliament, the Legislature of Ontario had authority to impose conditions, as being matters of civil right, upon the business of fire insurance, which was admitted to be a trade, so long as those conditions only affected provincial trade. Their Lordships do not find it necessary to reopen that discussion in the present case. The object of the Canada Temperance Act of 1886 is, not to regulate retail transactions between those who trade in liquor and their customers, but to abolish all such transactions within every provincial area in which its enactments have been adopted by a majority of the local electors. A power to regulate, naturally, if not necessarily, assumes, unless it is enlarged by the context, the conservation of the thing which is to be made the subject of regulation. In that view, their Lordships are unable to regard the prohibitive enactments of the Canadian statute of 1886 as regulations of trade and commerce. . . .

The authority of the Legislature of Ontario to enact s. 18 of 53 Vict. c. 56, was asserted by the appellant on various grounds. The first of these, which was very strongly insisted on, was to the effect that the power given to each province by No. 8 of s. 92 to create municipal institutions in the province necessarily implied the right to endow these institutions with all the administrative functions which had been ordinarily possessed and exercised by them before the time of the Union. Their Lordships can find nothing to support that contention in the language of s. 92, No. 8, which, according to its natural meaning, simply gives provincial legislatures the right to create a legal body for the management of municipal affairs. Until confederation, the Legislature of each province as then constituted could, if it chose, and did in some cases, entrust to a municipality the execution of powers which now belong exclusively to the Parliament of Canada. Since its date a

provincial Legislature cannot delegate any power which it does not possess; and the extent and nature of the functions which it can commit to a municipal body of its own creation must depend upon the legislative authority which it derives from the provisions of s. 92 other than No. 8.

Their Lordships are likewise of opinion that s. 92, No. 9, does not give provincial legislatures any right to make laws for the abolition of the liquor traffic. It assigns to them "shop, saloon, tavern, auctioneer and other licences, in order to the raising, of a revenue for provincial, local or municipal purposes." It was held by this Board in *Hodge* v. *Reg.* (9 App. Cas. 117) to include the right to impose reasonable conditions upon the licencees which are in the nature of regulation; but it cannot, with any show of reason, be construed as authorizing the abolition of the sources from which revenue is to be raised.

The only enactments of s. 92 which appear to their Lordships to have any relation to the authority of provincial legislatures to make laws for the suppression of the liquor traffic are to be found in Nos. 13 and 16, which assign to their exclusive jurisdiction, (1) "property and civil rights in the province," and (2) "generally all matters of a merely local or private nature in the province." A law which prohibits retail transactions and restricts the consumption of liquor within the ambit of the province, and does not affect transactions in liquor between persons in the province and persons in other provinces or in foreign countries, concerns property in the province which would be the subject-matter of the transactions if they were not prohibited, and also the civil rights of persons in the province. It is not impossible that the vice of intemperance may prevail in particular localities within a province to such an extent as to constitute its cure by restricting or prohibiting the sale of liquor a matter of a merely local or private nature, and therefore falling prima facie within No. 16. In that state of matters, it is conceded that the Parliament of Canada could not imperatively enact a prohibitory law adapted and confined to the requirements of localities within the province where prohibition was urgently needed. . . .

The question must next be considered whether the provincial enactments of s. 18 to any, and if so to what, extent come into collision with the provisions of the Canadian Act of 1886. In so far as they do, provincial must yield to Dominion legislation, and must remain in abeyance unless and until the Act of 1886 is repealed by the parliament which passed it.

~ Lord Watson then examined the differences between the prohibitions authorized by section 18 of Ontario Act and the prohibitions of the Canada Temperance Act. ~

It thus appears that, in their local application within the province of Ontario, there would be considerable difference between the two laws; but it is obvious that their provisions could not be in force within the same district or province at one and the same time. . . .

If the prohibitions of the Canada Temperance Act had been made imperative throughout the Dominion, their Lordships might have been constrained by previous authority to hold that the jurisdiction of the Legislature of Ontario to pass s. 18 or any similar law had been superseded. In that case no provincial prohibitions such as are sanctioned by s. 18 could have been enforced by a municipality without coming into conflict with the paramount law of Canada. For the same reason, provincial prohibitions in force within a particular district will necessarily become inoperative whenever the prohibitory clauses of the Act of 1886 have been adopted by that district. But their Lordships can discover no adequate grounds for holding that there exists repugnancy between the two laws in districts of the province of Ontario where the prohibitions of the Canadian Act are not and may never be in force. . . .

Their Lordships, for these reasons, give a general answer to the seventh question in the affirmative. They are of opin-

ion that the Ontario Legislature had jurisdiction to enact s. 18, subject to this necessary qualification, that its provisions are or will become inoperative in any district of the province which has already adopted, or may subsequently adopt, the second part of the Canada Temperance Act of 1886.

Their Lordships will now answer briefly, in their order, the other questions submitted by the Governor-General of Canada. So far as they can ascertain from the record, these differ from the question which has already been answered in this respect, that they relate to matters which may possibly become litigious in the future, but have not as yet given rise to any real and present controversy. Their Lordships must further observe that these questions, being in their nature academic rather than judicial, are better fitted for the consideration of the officers of the Crown than of a court of law. The replies to be given to them will necessarily depend upon the circumstances in which they may arise for decision; and these circumstances are in this case left to speculation. It must, therefore, be understood that the answers which follow are not meant to have, and cannot have, the weight of a judicial determination, except in so far as their Lordships may have occasion to refer to the opinions which they have already expressed in discussing the seventh question.

Answers to questions 1 and 2—Their Lordships think it sufficient to refer to the opinions expressed by them in disposing of the seventh question.

Answer to question 3—In the absence of conflicting legislation by the Parliament of Canada, their Lordships are of opinion that the provincial legislatures would have jurisdiction to that effect if it were shown that the manufacture was carried on under such circumstances and conditions as to make its prohibition a merely local matter in the province.

Answer to question 4—Their Lordships answer this question in the negative. It appears to them that the exercise by the provincial legislature of such jurisdiction in the wide and general terms in which it is expressed would probably trench upon the exclusive authority of the Dominion Parliament.

Answers to questions 5 and 6—Their Lordships consider it unnecessary to give a categorical reply to either of these questions. Their opinion upon the points which the questions involve has been sufficiently explained in their answer to the seventh question.

6. In re Board of Commerce Act and Combines and Fair Prices Act, 1919, *1922*

~ The federal legislation reviewed in this case was introduced after World War One to break up business combines and monopolies and to prevent the hoarding of basic necessities. Although the legislation was prompted by profiteering in scarce commodities which had developed after the war, it was cast in the form of permanent legislation.

The Privy Council viewed legislation limiting the commercial liberty of entrepreneurs as essentially an interference with the property and civil rights of the inhabitants of the Provinces and hence subject to exclusive provincial jurisdiction. Viscount Haldane considered that the context in which the legislation was enacted did not amount to the "highly exceptional circumstances" which could transform such a subject into a matter of national concern thus bringing it under the federal peace, order and good government power. His reasoning amounted to the "emergency doctrine": only under special circumstances such as war or famine could a matter normally within section 92 become of such national importance as to be brought under the Dominion's general power. In this instance he reported that their Lordships could find no evidence to indicate that such a "standard of necessity" had been reached.

Nor could the Judicial Committee be persuaded that the challenged legislation was a valid exercise of Parliament's trade and commerce power. Under Viscount Haldane's leadership this power had reached its nadir. Sir Montague Smith's opinion in the *Parsons case* pointed to three kinds of trade which might be brought under the federal trade and commerce power-international, inter-provincial and general trade affecting the whole of Canada.[1] In 1915 in *John Deere Plow Co.* v. *Wharton*[2] Haldane invoked the general trade aspect of trade and commerce to uphold federal legislation defining the rights and capacities of companies which had been incorporated by Parliament. But a year later in the *Insurance Reference* he showed how limited this third aspect of trade and commerce would be by denying that it could be used as a basis for regulating an entire business such as insurance throughout the Dominion.[3] Now in the *Board of Commerce* case Haldane explains his use of the commerce power in *John Deere Plow* as supplementing Parliament's exercise of its general residual power. Thus, aside from its possible application to international and interprovincial trade, the trade and commerce power at this stage had been assigned by judicial interpretation to a position in the division of powers inferior to all other heads of power: it was now regarded as essentially an auxiliary power incapable of serving on its own as a primary source of legislative capacity.

---

[1] See above p. 41.

[2] (1915) A.C. 330.

[3] *Attorney General of Canada* v. *Attorney General of Alberta* (1916) 1 A.C. 589.

Viscount Haldane's opinion is also notable for the limit it imposed on federal jurisdiction in relation to criminal law. The criminal law power could be applied only to behaviour which "by its very nature belongs to the domain of criminal jurisprudence." While incest could meet this test, apparently postwar profiteering could not.

The six members of the Supreme Court of Canada had been evenly divided in this case. It is interesting to compare the opinion of Justice Anglin with that of the Judicial Committee. Justice Anglin found the federal legislation and the order authorized by it valid. Unlike the Privy Council, Justice Anglin relied on the "national dimensions" test of the peace, order and good government power set out in the *Local Prohibition* case. In the 1916 *Insurance Reference*, however, the Privy Council had struck down federal regulation despite acknowledging that "the business of insurance is a very important one, which has attained to great dimensions in Canada." Clearly, some kinds of national dimension would justify legislation under peace, order and good government and some would not. Justice Anglin could not have known that the Privy Council was about to make "special circumstances" of an emergency nature the test of the required degree of "national dimension." He found a plausible distinction between the Canada Temperance Act and the Insurance Act of 1910 in the fact that the former related to "public order, safety or morals" while the latter did not. In the case at hand, because he viewed profiteering as "an evil so prevalent and so insidious that . . . it threatens to-day the moral and social well-being of the Dominion,"[4] he could consider that the Board of Commerce Act dealt with a matter of national "public order," and on these grounds invoke Parliament's general power to sustain the legislation. He also thought that it could be supported by the trade and commerce power and, in part, by the criminal law power (section 91 [27]). Justice Duff, on the other hand, rejected what he regarded as the dangerous notion that the Dominion, simply in order to deal with vicissitudes of national trade, could, under its general power, legislate in relation to matters otherwise subject to provincial jurisdiction. Such reasoning would "justify Parliament in any conceivable circumstance forcing upon a province a system of nationalization of industry."[5] These disagreements between the two judges on the Supreme Court and between Justice Anglin and the Privy Council provide a good illustration of how extra-legal considerations can enter into the judiciary's determination of constitutional issues. ~

---

[4] (1920), 60 S.C.R. 456, at p. 467.

[5] *Ibid.*, p. 466.

IN RE THE BOARD OF COMMERCE ACT, 1919, AND
THE COMBINES AND FAIR PRICES ACT, 1919
In the Privy Council. [1922] 1 A.C. 191: II Olmsted 245

~ This Appeal was by special leave from the Supreme Court of Canada. The appeal related to the validity of two acts passed by the Parliament of Canada in 1919— namely, the Board of Commerce Act and the Combines and Fair Prices Act. ~

The judgment of their Lordships was delivered by

VISCOUNT HALDANE. This is an appeal from the Supreme Court of Canada, before which were brought, under statute, questions relating to the constitutional validity of the Acts above mentioned. As the six judges who sat in the Supreme Court were equally divided in opinion, no judgment was rendered. The Chief Justice and Anglin and Mignault JJ. considered that the questions raised should be answered in the affirmative, while Idington, Duff and Brodeur JJ. thought that the first question should be answered in the negative and that therefore the second question did not arise. These questions were raised for the opinion of the Supreme Court by a case stated under s. 32 of the Board of Commerce Act, 1919, and were: (1) whether the Board had lawful authority to make a certain order; and (2) whether the Board had lawful authority to require the Registrar, or other proper authority of the Supreme Court of Ontario, to cause the order, when issued, to be made a rule of that Court.

The order in question was to the effect that certain retail dealers in clothing in the City of Ottawa were prohibited from charging as profits on sales more than a certain percentage on cost, which was prescribed as being fair profit. The validity of this order depended on whether the Parliament of Canada had legislative capacity, under the British North America Act of 1867 to establish the Board and give it authority to make the order.

The statutes in question were enacted by the Parliament of Canada in 1919, and were to be read and construed as one Act. By the first of these statutes, the Board of Commerce Act, a Board was set up, consisting of three commissioners appointed by the Governor-General, which was to be a Court of Record. The duty of the Board was to be to administer the second of the two statutes in question, the Combines and Fair Prices Act, called the Special Act. It was to have power to state a case for the opinion of the Supreme Court of Canada upon any question which, in its own opinion, was one of law or jurisdiction. It was given the right to inquire into and determine the matters of law and fact entrusted to it, and to order the doing of any act, matter or thing required or authorized under either Act, and to forbid the doing or continuing of any act, matter or thing which, in its opinion, was contrary to either Act. The Board was also given authority to make orders and regulations with regard to these, and generally for carrying the Board of Commerce Act into effect. Its finding on any question of fact within its jurisdiction was to be binding and conclusive. Any of its decisions or order might be made a rule or order or decree of the Exchequer Court, or of any Superior Court of any Province of Canada.

The second statute, the Combines and Fair Prices Act, 1919, was directed to the investigation and restriction of combines, monopolies, trusts and mergers, and to the withholding and enhancement of the prices of commodities. By Part I, the Board of Commerce was empowered to prohibit the formation or operation of combines as defined, and, after investigation, was to be able to issue orders to that effect. A person so ordered to cease any act or practice in pursuance of the operations of a combine, was, in the event of failure to obey the order, to be guilty of an indictable offence, and the Board might remit to the Attorney-General of a

Province the duty of instituting the appropriate proceedings. By Part II, the necessaries of life were to include staple and ordinary articles of food, whether fresh, preserved, or otherwise treated, and clothing and fuel, including the materials from which these were manufactured or made, and such other articles as the Board might prescribe. No person was to accumulate or withhold from sale any necessary of life, beyond an amount reasonably required for the use or consumption of his household, or for the ordinary purposes of his business. Every person who held more, and every person who held a stock-in-trade of any such necessary of life, was to offer the excess amount for sale at reasonable and just prices. This, however, was not to apply to accumulating or withholding by farmers and certain other specified persons. The Board was empowered and directed to inquire into any breach or non-observance of any provision of the Act, and the making of such unfair profits as above referred to, and all such practices with respect to the holding or disposition of necessaries of life as, in the opinion of the Board, were calculated to enhance their cost or price. An unfair profit was to be deemed to have been made when the Board, after proper inquiry, so declared. It might call for returns and enter premises and inspect. It might remit what it considered to be offences against this part of the Act to the Attorney-General of the Province, or might declare the guilt of a person concerned, and issue to him orders or prohibitions, for breach of which he should be liable to punishment as for an indictable offence.

The above summary sufficiently sets out the substance of the two statutes in question for the present purpose.

In the first instance the Board stated, for the opinion of the Supreme Court of Canada, a case in which a number of general constitutional questions were submitted. That Court, however, took the view that the case was defective, inasmuch as it did not contain a statement of concrete facts, out of which such questions arose. Finally, a fresh case was stated containing a statement of the facts in certain matters pending before the Board, and formulating questions that had actually arisen. These related to the action of certain retail clothing dealers in the City of Ottawa. An order was framed by the Board which, after stating the facts found, gave directions as to the limits of profit, and a new case was stated which raised the questions already referred to.

In these circumstances the only substantial question which their Lordships have to determine is whether it was within the legislative capacity of the Parliament of Canada to enact the statutes in question.

The second of these statutes, the Combines and Fair Prices Act, enables the Board established by the first statute to restrain and prohibit the formation and operation of such trade combinations for production and distribution in the Provinces of Canada as the Board may consider to be detrimental to the public interest. The Board may also restrict, in the cases of food, clothing and fuel, accumulation of these necessaries of life beyond the amount reasonably required, in the case of a private person, for his household, not less than in the case of a trader for his business. The surplus is in such instances to be offered for sale at fair prices. Certain persons only, such as farmers and gardeners, are excepted. Into the prohibited cases the Board has power to inquire searchingly, and to attach what may be criminal consequences to any breach it determines to be improper. An addition of a consequential character is thus made to the criminal law of Canada.

The first question to be answered is whether the Dominion Parliament could validly enact such a law. Their Lordships observe that the law is not one enacted to meet special conditions in wartime. It was passed in 1919, after peace had been declared, and it is not confined to any temporary purpose, but is to continue without limit in time, and to apply throughout Canada. No doubt the initial words of s. 91 of the British North America Act confer on the Parliament of Canada power to deal with subjects which concern the Dominion generally, provided that they are not withheld from the powers of that Parliament to legislate, by any of the express heads in s. 92, untrammelled by the enumeration of special heads in s. 91. It may well be that the subjects of undue combination and hoarding are matters in which the Dominion has a great practical interest. In special circumstances, such as those of a great war, such an interest might conceivably become of such paramount and overriding importance as to amount to what lies outside the heads in s. 92, and is not covered by them. The decision in *Russell* v. *The Queen* ((1882) 7 App. Cas. 829) appears to recognize this as constitutionally possible, even in time of peace; but it is quite another matter to say that under normal circumstances general Canadian policy can justify interference, on such a scale as the statutes in controversy involve, with the property and civil rights of the inhabitants of the Provinces. It is to the Legislatures of the Provinces that the regulation and restriction of their civil rights have in general been exclusively confided, and as to these the Provincial Legislatures possess quasi-sovereign authority. It can, therefore, be only under necessity in highly exceptional circumstances, such as cannot be assumed to exist in the present case, that the liberty of the inhabitants of the Provinces may be restricted by the Parliament of Canada, and that the Dominion can intervene in the interests of Canada as a whole in questions such as the present one. For, normally, the subject-matter to be dealt with in the case would be one falling within s. 92. Nor do the words in s. 91, the "Regulation of trade and commerce," if taken by themselves, assist the present Dominion contention. It may well be, if the Parliament of Canada had, by reason of an altogether exceptional situation, capacity to interfere, that these words would apply so as to enable that Parliament to oust the exclusive character of the Provincial powers under s. 92.

In the case of Dominion companies their Lordships in deciding the case of *John Deere Plow Co.* v. *Wharton* ([1915] A.C. 330, 339, 340), expressed the opinion that the language of s. 91, head 2, could have the effect of aiding Dominion powers conferred by the general language of s. 91. But that was because the regulation of the trading of Dominion companies was sought to be invoked only on furtherance of a general power which the Dominion Parliament possessed independently of it. Where there was no such power in that Parliament, as in the case of the Dominion Insurance Act, it was held otherwise, and that the authority of the Dominion Parliament to legislate for the regulation of trade and commerce did not; by itself, enable interference with particular trades in which Canadians would, apart from any right of interference conferred by these words above, be free to engage in the Provinces ([1916] 1 A.C. 588). This result was the outcome of a series of well-known decisions of earlier dates, which are now so familiar that they need not be cited.

For analogous reasons the words of head 27 of s. 91 do not assist the argument for the Dominion. It is one thing to construe the words "the criminal law, except the constitution of courts of criminal jurisdiction, but including the procedure in criminal matters," as enabling the Dominion Parliament to exercise exclusive legislative power where the subject matter is one which by its very nature belongs to the domain of criminal jurisprudence. A general law, to take an example, making incest a crime, belongs to this class. It is quite another thing, first to attempt to interfere with a class of subject committed exclusively to the Provincial Legislature, and then to justify this by enacting ancillary provisions, designated as new phases of Dominion criminal law which require a title to so interfere as basis of their application. For analogous reasons their Lordships think that s. 101 of the British North America Act, which enables the Parliament of Canada, notwithstanding anything in the Act, to provide for the establishment of any additional Courts for the better administration of the laws of Canada, cannot be read as enabling that Parliament to trench on Provincial rights, such as the powers over property and civil rights in the Provinces exclusively conferred on their Legislatures. Full significance can be attached to the words in question without reading them as implying such capacity on the part of the Dominion Parliament. It is essential in such cases that the new judicial establishment should be a means to some end competent to the latter.

As their Lordships have already indicated, the jurisdiction attempted to be conferred on the new Board of Commerce appears to them to be ultra vires for the reasons now discussed. It implies a claim of title, in the cases of non-traders as well as of traders, to make orders prohibiting the accumulation of certain articles required for every-day life, and the withholding of such articles from sale at prices to be defined by the Board, whenever they exceed the amount of the material which appears to the Board to be required for domestic purposes or for the ordinary purposes of business. The Board is also given jurisdiction to regulate profits and dealings which may give rise to profit. The power sought to be given to the Board applies to articles produced for his own use by the householder himself, as well as to articles accumulated, not for the market but for the purposes of their own processes of manufacture by manufacturers. The Board is empowered to inquire into individual cases and to deal with them individually, and not merely as the result of applying principles to be laid down as of general application. This would cover such instances as those of coal mines and of local Provincial undertakings for meeting Provincial requirements of social life.

Legislation setting up a Board of Commerce with such powers appears to their Lordships to be beyond the powers conferred by s. 91. They find confirmation of this view in s. 41 of the Board of Commerce Act, which enables the Dominion Executive to review and alter the deci-

sions of the Board. It has already been observed that circumstances are conceivable, such as those of war or famine, when the peace, order and good Government of the Dominion might be imperilled under conditions so exceptional that they require legislation of a character in reality beyond anything provided for by the enumerated heads in either s. 92 or s. 91 itself. Such a case, if it were to arise would have to be considered closely before the conclusion could properly be reached that it was one which could not be treated as falling under any of the heads enumerated. Still, it is a conceivable case, and although great caution is required in referring to it, even in general terms, it ought not, in the view their Lordships take of the British North America Act, read as a whole, to be excluded from what is possible. For throughout the provisions of that Act there is apparent the recognition that subjects which would normally belong exclusively to a specifically assigned class of subject may, under different circumstances and in another aspect, assume a further significance. Such an aspect may conceivably become of paramount importance, and of dimensions that give rise to other aspects. This is a principle which, although recognized in earlier decisions, such as that of *Russell* v. *The Queen*, both here and in the Courts of Canada, has always been applied with reluctance, and its recognition as relevant can be justified only after scrutiny sufficient to render it clear that the circumstances are abnormal. In the case before them, however important it may seem to the Parliament of Canada that some such policy as that adopted in the two Acts in question should be made general throughout Canada, their Lordships do not find any evidence that the standard of necessity referred to has been reached, or that the attainment of the end sought is practicable, in view of the distribution of legislative powers enacted by the Constitution Act, without the cooperation of the Provincial Legislatures. It may well be that it is within the power of the Dominion Parliament to call, for example, for statistical and other information which may be valuable for guidance in questions affecting Canada as a whole. Such information may be required before any power to regulate trade and commerce can be properly exercised, even where such power is construed in a fashion much narrower than that in which it was sought to interpret it in the argument at the Bar for the Attorney-General for Canada. But even this consideration affords no justification for interpreting the words of s. 91, sub-s. 2, in a fashion which would, as was said in the argument on the other side, make them confer capacity to regulate particular trades and businesses.

For the reasons now given their Lordships are of opinion that the first of the questions brought before them must be answered in the negative. As a consequence the second question does not arise.

7. Fort Frances Pulp and Power Co. *v.* Manitoba Free Press, *1923*

~ The Privy Council in this case gave a positive application for the "emergency doctrine" which it had first enunciated in *the Board of Commerce Act* case. The outbreak of a great war was identified as one of those extraordinary contingencies in the life of the nation which could justify the national government's intervention in matters normally subject to provincial jurisdiction. It should be noted that the statutes and orders challenged in this case had been specifically designed to deal with the wartime and immediate postwar emergency. The Judicial Committee would ordinarily have characterized the laws controlling the price and supply of newsprint as relating to property and civil rights in the province but it was willing to recognize that under wartime conditions such laws took on a national aspect so that they could be brought under section 91.

Viscount Haldane, speaking for the Judicial Committee, went further and stated that with regard to war-related crises the judiciary would have to be presented with very clear evidence that the crisis had wholly passed away to justify overruling the federal government's decision that exceptional measures were necessary. This position should be compared with the position taken in the *Board of Commerce Act* case where the onus of proof seemed to be placed on the government to satisfy the judiciary that the standard of necessity had been reached.

The *Fort Frances* case was followed by the Privy Council after World War Two to sustain the national government's scheme for the deportation of Japanese Canadians.[1] The statutes under which the deportation orders were issued were the War Measures Act, 1914, and the National Emergency Transitional Powers Act, 1945. On this occasion the Privy Council declared its reluctance to question Parliament's judgment concerning both the existence and the continuation of a wartime emergency. In 1950 the Supreme Court of Canada followed a similar line of reasoning in ruling *intra vires* the Dominion Government's wartime rent control regulations.[2]

In so far as the peace, order and good government clause is concerned, the most important implication of this series of judgments is the view that the exercise of the central government's general power under emergency conditions entails a drastic departure from the normal practice of Canadian federalism. In the *Japanese Canadians* case Lord Wright pictured the invocation of the Dominion's emergency power as temporarily setting aside "the rule of law as to the distribution of powers between the . . . Dominion and the . . . Provinces."[3] Thus, during a great war and its immediate aftermath the normal working of the Canadian federal system is, at least potentially, in abeyance. ~

---

[1] *Co-operative Committee on Japanese Canadians* v. *A.-G. Canada*, [1947] A.C. 87.
[2] *Reference re Validity of Wartime Leasehold Regulations*, [1950] S.C.R. 124.
[3] [1947] A.C. 101.

FORT FRANCES PULP AND POWER CO. *v.* MANITOBA FREE PRESS
In the Privy Council. [1923] A.C. 695; II Olmsted 306

The judgment of their Lordships was delivered by

VISCOUNT HALDANE. This appeal raises questions of some novelty and delicacy.

The appellants are manufacturers of newsprint paper in Ontario, and the respondents are publishers of newspapers, carrying on business at various places in Canada. The action out of which the appeal arises was brought by the respondents against the appellants to recover sums the former had paid for paper delivered to them at controlled prices. These sums, which the respondents alleged to represent margins in excess of the prices regulated by law, they claimed to be repayable to them as the result of orders of the Paper Control Tribunal of Canada, the final order having been made on July 8, 1920. The sums represented the amounts due after an adjustment of accounts in accordance with the above-mentioned final order and previous orders which it modified. For the balance so arrived at the action was brought in the Supreme Court of Ontario. It was tried before Riddell J., who gave judgment for the plaintiffs, the respondents.

~ Viscount Haldane stated that the Judicial Committee would not follow the Appellate Division of the Supreme Court of Ontario which had ruled in favour of the respondents, the Manitoba Free Press, not on constitutional grounds but on the grounds that the appellants were bound by contract to accept the price set by the Paper Control Tribunal. The Privy Council considered that to decide the case it was necessary to determine the validity of the Dominion legislation and orders setting up the controlling tribunals.

Viscount Haldane then proceeded to examine the statutes and orders in question. The federal government's control over the supply and price of newsprint had

first been instituted in 1917 by Orders in Council under the War Measures Act, 1914. A Paper Commissioner and Controller was established with the power to fix quantities and set prices and, in 1918, a Paper Control Tribunal was set up to hear appeals from the orders of the Paper Commissioner. Another Act in 1919 confirmed both the Commissioner's and the Tribunal's power to settle any matters which were pending before the proclamation of peace. The Privy Council was of the opinion that the order challenged in this case had been made prior to any formal proclamation of peace. ~

It is clear that in normal circumstances the Dominion Parliament could not have so legislated as to set up the machinery of control over the paper manufacturers which is now in question. The recent decision of the Judicial Committee in the *Board of Commerce* case ([1922] 1 A.C. 191), as well as earlier decisions, show that as the Dominion Parliament cannot ordinarily legislate so as to interfere with property and civil rights in the Provinces, it could not have done what the two statutes under consideration purport to do had the situation been normal. But it does not follow that in a very different case, such as that of sudden danger to social order arising from the outbreak of a great war, the Parliament of the Dominion cannot act under other powers which may well be implied in the constitution. The reasons given in the *Board of Commerce* case recognize exceptional cases where such a power may be implied.

In the event of war, when the national life may require for its preservation the employment of very exceptional means, the provision of peace, order and good government for the country as a whole may involve effort on behalf of the whole nation, in which the interests of individuals may have to be subordinated to that of the community in a fashion which requires s. 91 to be interpreted as providing for such an emergency. The general control of property and civil rights for normal purposes remains with the Provincial Legislatures. But questions may arise by reason of the special circumstances of the national emergency which concern nothing short of the peace, order and good government of Canada as a whole.

The overriding powers enumerated in s. 91, as well as the general words at the commencement of the section, may then become applicable to new and special aspects which they cover of subjects assigned otherwise exclusively to the Provinces. It may be, for example, impossible to deal adequately with the new questions which arise without the imposition of special regulations on trade and commerce of a kind that only the situation created by the emergency places within the competency of the Dominion Parliament. It is proprietary and civil rights in new relations, which they do not present in normal times, that have to be dealt with; and these relations, which affect Canada as an entirety, fall within s. 91, because in their fullness they extend beyond what s. 92 can really cover. The kind of power adequate for dealing with them is only to be found in that part of the constitution which establishes power in the State as a whole. For it is not one that can be reliably provided for by depending on collective action of the Legislatures of the individual Provinces agreeing for the purpose. That the basic instrument on which the character of the entire constitution depends should be construed as providing for such centralised power in an emergency situation follows from the manifestation in the languages of the Act of the principle that the instrument has among its purposes to provide for the State regarded as a whole, and for the expression and influence of its public opinion as such. This principle of a power so implied has received effect also in countries with a written and apparently rigid constitution such as the United States, where the strictly federal character of the national basic agreement has retained the residuary powers not ex-

pressly conferred on the Federal Government for the component States. The operation of the scheme of interpretations is all the more to be looked for in a constitution such as that established by the British North America Act, where the residuary powers are given to the Dominion Central Government; and the preamble of the statute declares the intention to be that the Dominion should have a constitution similar in principle to that of the United Kingdom.

Their Lordships, therefore, entertain no doubt that however the wording of ss. 91 and 92 may have laid down a framework under which, as a general principle, the Dominion Parliament is to be excluded from trenching on property and civil rights in the Provinces of Canada, yet in a sufficiently great emergency such as that arising out of war, there is implied the power to deal adequately with that emergency for the safety of the Dominion as whole. The enumeration in s. 92 is not in any way repealed in the event of such an occurrence, but a new aspect of the business of Government is recognized as emerging, an aspect which is not covered or precluded by the general words in which powers are assigned to the Legislatures of the Provinces as individual units. Where an exact line of demarcation will lie in such cases it may not be easy to lay down a priori, nor is it necessary. For in the solution of the problem regard must be had to the broadened field covered, in case of exceptional necessity, by the language of s. 91, in which the interests of the Dominion generally are protected. As to these interests the Dominion Government, which in its Parliament represents the people as a whole, must be deemed to be left with considerable freedom to judge.

The other point which arises is whether such exceptional necessity as must be taken to have existed when the war broke out, and almost of necessity for some period subsequent to its outbreak, continued through the whole of the time within which the questions in the present case arose.

When the war has broken out it may be requisite to make special provision to ensure the maintenance of law and order in a country, even when it is in no immediate danger of invasion. Public opinion may become excitable, and one of the causes of this may conceivably be want of uninterrupted information in newspapers. Steps may have to be taken to ensure supplies of these and to avoid shortage, and the effect of the economic and other disturbance occasioned originally by the war may thus continue for some time after it is terminated. The question of the extent to which provision for circumstances such as these may have to be maintained is one on which a Court of law is loath to enter. No authority other than the central Government is in a position to deal with a problem which is essentially one of statesmanship. It may be that it has become clear that the crisis which arose is wholly at an end and that there is no justification for the continued exercise of an exceptional interference which becomes *ultra vires* when it is no longer called for. In such a case the law is laid down for distribution of powers in the ruling instrument would have to be invoked. But very clear evidence that the crisis has wholly passed away would be required to justify the judiciary, even when the question raised was one of *ultra vires* which it had to decide, in overruling the decision of the Government that exceptional measures were still requisite. In saying what is almost obvious, their Lordships observe themselves to be in accord with the view taken under analogous circumstances by the Supreme Court of the United States, and expressed in such decisions as that in October, 1919, in *Hamilton* v. *Kentucky Distilleries Co.* (251 U.S. 146).

When then, in the present instance, can it be said that the necessity altogether ceased for maintaining the exceptional measure of control over the newspaper print industry introduced while the war was at its height? At what date did the disturbed state of Canada which the war had produced so entirely pass away that the legislative measures relied on in the present case became *ultra vires*? It is enough to say that there is no clear and unmistakable evidence that the Government was in error in thinking that the necessity was still in existence at the dates on which the action in question was taken by the Paper Control Tribunal. No doubt late in 1919 statements were made to the effect that the war itself was at an end. For example, in the Order in Council made at Ottawa on December 20, 1919, it is stated that it must "be realised that although no proclamation has been issued declaring that the war no longer exists, actual war conditions have in fact long ago ceased to exist, and consequently existence of war can no longer be urged as a reason in fact for maintaining these extraordinary regulations as necessary or advisable for the security of Canada."

The Order in Council then goes on to say that in consequence of the armistice of November, 1918, the Expeditionary Force had since been withdrawn and demobilised, and the country generally is devoting its energies to re-establishment in the ordinary avocations of peace. In these circumstances, it states, the Minister of Justice considers that the time has arrived when the emergency Government legislation should cease to operate. This was in December, 1919. The Order then goes on to declare repealed all Orders and Regulations of the Governor in Council which depend for their sanction upon s. 6 of the War Measures Act, 1914, and repeals them as from January 1, 1920. But from this repeal it expressly excepts, among other Orders and Regulations specified, those relating to paper control, which are to remain in force until the end of another session of Parliament.

It will be observed that this Order in Council deals only with the results following from the cessation of actual war conditions. It excepts from repeal certain measures concerned with consequential conditions arising out of war, which may obviously continue to produce effects remaining in operation after war itself is over.

Their Lordships find themselves unable

to say that the Dominion Government had no good reason for thus temporarily continuing the paper control after actual war had ceased, but while the effects of war conditions might still be operative. They are, therefore, unable to accept the propositions submitted to them in the powerful argument for the appellants.

8. Toronto Electric Commissioners *v.* Snider, *1925*

~ In this case a major piece of national legislation, the Industrial Disputes Investigation Act, 1907, was cut down by the Privy Council's restrictive interpretation of the Dominion's peace, order and good government power. The subject matter of this statute—the establishment of national conciliation services to avoid work stoppages during labour disputes in some of the country's most vital industries such as mines, transportation and communication agencies and public service utilities—did not meet Viscount Haldane's "emergency" test. It should be noted that in this particular case the provisions of the Act were being applied not to an undertaking which was interprovincial or national in scope but to a municipal transportation agency.

As a result of this decision federal legislation providing for the settlement of labour disputes was confined to a much smaller field: industrial activities which are directly subject to federal jurisdiction, such as interprovincial railways or federal Crown agencies. National labour relations legislation limited to these areas was upheld in a reference to the Supreme Court of Canada in 1955.[1]

It would appear from the *Snider* case that the Judicial Committee, under Viscount Haldane's leadership, had come to look upon Parliament's general power almost exclusively as an emergency power. The least plausible, but perhaps most entertaining extension of this approach came in Viscount Haldane's attempt to reconcile the construction of the general power in earlier cases—in particular, in *Russell* v. *The Queen*—with the emergency doctrine. He was only able to do this by arguing that when the Privy Council decided *Russell* v. *The Queen* in 1882 it must have looked upon intemperance as a national menace serious enough to justify bringing the Canada Temperance Act under the peace, order and good government clause. ~

TORONTO ELECTRIC COMMISSIONERS *v.* SNIDER
In the Privy Council [1925] A.C. 396; II Olmsted 394.

The judgment of their Lordships was delivered by

VISCOUNT HALDANE. It is always with reluctance that their Lordships come to a conclusion adverse to the constitutional validity of any Canadian statute that has been before the public for years as having been validly enacted; but the duty encumbent on the Judicial Committee, now as always, is simply to interpret the British North America Act and to decide whether the statute in question has been within the competence of the Dominion Parliament under the terms of s. 91 of that Act. In this case the Judicial Committee have come to the conclusion that it was not. To that conclusion they find themselves compelled, alike by the structure of s. 91 and by the interpretation of its terms that has now been established by a series of authorities. They have had the advantage not only of hearing full arguments on the question, but of having before them judgments in the Courts of Ontario, from which this appeal to the Sovereign in Council came directly. Some of these judgments are against the view which they

[1] *Reference re Validity of Industrial Relations and Disputes Investigation Act* [1955] S.C.R. 529.

themselves take, others are in favour of it, but all of them are of a high degree of thoroughness and ability.

The particular exercise of legislative power with which their Lordships are concerned is contained in a well-known Act, passed by the Dominion Parliament in 1907, and known as the Industrial Disputes Investigation Act. As it now stands it has been amended by subsequent Acts, but nothing turns, for the purposes of the question now raised, on any of the amendments that have been introduced.

The primary object of the Act was to enable industrial disputes between any employer in Canada and any one or more of his employees, as to "matters or things affecting or relating to work done or to be done by him or them, or as to the privileges, rights and duties of employers or employees (not involving any such violation thereof as constitutes an indictable offence)," relating to wages or remuneration, or hours of employment; sex, age or qualifications of employees, and the mode, terms and conditions of employment; the employment of children or any person, or classes of persons; claims as to whether preference of employment should be given to members of labour or other organizations; materials supplied or damage done to work; customs or usages, either general or in particular districts; and the interpretation of agreements. Either of the parties to any such dispute was empowered by the Act to apply to the Minister of Labour for the Dominion for the appointment of a Board of Conciliation and Investigation, to which Board the dispute might be referred. The Act enabled the Governor in Council to appoint a Registrar of such Boards, with the duty of dealing with all applications for reference, bringing them to the notice of the Minister, and conducting the correspondence necessary for the constitution of the Boards. The Minister was empowered to establish a Board when he thought fit, and no question was to be raised in any Court interfering with his decision. Each Board was to consist of three members, to be appointed by the Minister, one on the recommendation of the employer, one on that of the employees, and the third, who was to be chairman, on the recommendation of the members so chosen. If any of them failed in this duty the Minister was to make the appointment. The department of the Minister of Labour was to provide the staffs required. The application for a Board was to be accompanied by a statutory declaration showing that, failing adjustment, a lock-out or strike would probably occur.

The Board so constituted was to make inquiry and to endeavour to effect a settlement. If the parties came to a settlement the Board was to embody it in a memorandum of recommendation which, if the parties had agreed to it in writing, was to have the effect of an award on a reference to arbitration or one made under the order of a Court of record. In such a case the recommendation could be constituted a rule of Court and enforced accordingly. If no such settlement was arrived at, then the Board was to make a full report and a recommendation for settlement to the Minister, who was to make it public.

The Boards set up were given powers to summon and to enforce the attendance of witnesses, to administer oaths and to call for business books and other documents, and also to order into custody or subject to fine, in case of disobedience or contempt. The Board was also empowered to enter any premises where anything was taking place which was the subject of the reference and to inspect. This power was also enforceable by penalty. The parties were to be represented before the Board, but no counsel or solicitors were to appear excepting by consent and subject to the sanction of the Board itself. The proceedings were normally to take place in public.

By s. 56 of the Act, in the event of a reference to a Board, it was made unlawful for the employer to lock-out or for the employees to strike on account of any dispute prior to or pending the reference, and any breach of this provision was made punishable by fine. By s. 57, employers and employed were both bound to give at least thirty days' notice of an intended change affecting conditions of employment with respect to wages or hours. In the event of a dispute arising over the intended change, until the dispute had been finally dealt with by a Board and a report had been made, neither employers nor employed were to alter the conditions, or lock-out or strike, or suspend employment or work, and the relationship of employer and employee was to continue uninterrupted. If, in the opinion of the Board, either party were to use this or any other provision of the Act for the purpose of unjustly maintaining a given condition of affairs through delay, and the Board were so to report to the Minister, such part was to be guilty of an offence and liable to penalties.

By s. 63(*a*), where a strike or lock-out had occurred or was threatened, the Minister was empowered, although neither of the parties to the dispute had applied for one, to set up a Board. He might also, under the next section, without any application, institute an inquiry.

Whatever else may be the effect of this enactment, it is clear that it is one which could have been passed, so far as any Province was concerned, by the Provincial Legislature under the powers conferred by s. 92 of the British North America Act. For its provisions were concerned directly with the civil rights of both employers and employed in the Province. It set up a Board of Inquiry which could summon them before it, administer to them oaths, call for their papers and enter their premises. It did not more than what a Provincial Legislature could have done under head 15 of s. 92, when it imposed punishment by way of penalty in order to enforce the new restrictions on civil rights. It interfered further with civil rights when, by s. 56, it suspended liberty to lock-out or strike during a reference to a Board. It does not appear that there is anything in the Dominion Act which could not have been enacted by the Legislature of Ontario, excepting one provision. The field for the operation of the Act was made the whole of Canada.

~ Viscount Haldane then pointed out the similarities between the provisions of Ontario Trade Disputes Act, 1914, and the Dominion's Industrial Disputes Investigation Act, 1907. ~

The primary respondents in this appeal are the members of a Board of Conciliation appointed by the Dominion Minister of Labour under the Act first referred to. There was a dispute in 1923 between the appellants and a number of the men whom they employed, which dispute was referred to the first respondents, who proceeded to exercise the powers given by the Dominion Act. The appellants then commenced an action in the Supreme Court of Ontario for an injunction to restrain these proceedings, on the allegation that the Dominion Act was ultra vires. The Attorneys-General of Canada and of Ontario were notified and made parties as intervenants.

There was a motion for an interim injunction, which was heard by Orde J., who after argument, granted an injunction till the trial. The action was tried by Mowat J., who intimated his dissent from the view of the British North America Act taken by Orde J., who was co-ordinate in authority with him, according to which view the Dominion Act was ultra vires. He, therefore, as he had power by the Provincial Judicature Act to do, directed the action to be heard by a Divisional Court, and it was ultimately heard by the Appellate Division of the Supreme Court of Ontario (Mulock C.J., Magee, Hodgins, Ferguson and Smith JJ.A.). The result was that by the majority (Hodgins J.A. dissenting) the action of the appellants was dismissed.

The broad grounds of the judgment of the majority, which will be referred to later on, was that the Dominion Act was not a law relating to matters as to which s. 92 conferred exclusive jurisdiction, but was a law within the competence of the Dominion Parliament, inasmuch as it was directed to the regulation of trade and commerce throughout Canada, and to the protection of the national peace, order and good government, by reason of (*a*) confining, within limits, a dispute which might spread over all the Provinces; (*b*) informing the general public in Canada of the nature of the dispute; and (*c*) bringing public opinion to bear on it. The power of the Dominion Parliament to legislate in relation to criminal law, under head 27 of s. 91, was also considered to apply.

Before referring to these grounds of judgment their Lordships, without repeating at length what has been laid down by them in earlier cases, desire to refer briefly to the construction which, in their opinion, has been authoritatively put on ss. 91 and 92 by the more recent decisions of the Judicial Committee. The Dominion Parliament has, under the initial words of s. 91, a general power to make laws for Canada. But these laws are not to relate to the classes of subjects assigned to the Provinces by s. 92, unless their enactment falls under heads specifically assigned to the Dominion Parliament by the enumeration in s. 91. When there is a question as to which legislative authority has the power to pass an Act, the first question must therefore be whether the subject falls within s. 92. Even if it does, the further question must be answered, whether it falls also under an enumerated head in s. 91. If so, the Dominion has the paramount power of legislating in relation to it. If the subject falls within neither of the sets of enumerated heads, then the Dominion may have power to legislate under the general words at the beginning of s. 91.

Applying this principle, does the subject of the legislation in controversy fall within s. 92? For the reasons already given their Lordships think that it clearly does. If so, is the exclusive power prima facie conferred on the Province trenched on by any of the overriding powers set out specifically in s. 91? It was, among other things, contended in the argument that the Dominion Act now challenged was authorized under head 27, "the Criminal Law, except the Constitution of Courts of Criminal Jurisdiction, but including the Procedure in Criminal Matters." It was

further suggested in the argument that the power so conferred is aided by the power conferred on the Parliament of Canada to establish additional Courts for the better administration of the laws of Canada.

But their Lordships are unable to accede to these contentions.

~ Viscount Haldane then advanced arguments and authorities rejecting the attempt to bring matters which would normally come under provincial jurisdiction under the criminal law power in section 91 merely by the insertion of penal sanctions in the legislation. ~

Nor does the invocation of the specific power in s. 91 to regulate trade and commerce assist the Dominion contention. In *Citizens Insurance Co.* v. *Parsons* (7 App. Cas. 96, 112) it was laid down that the collocation of this head (No. 2 of s. 91), with classes of subjects enumerated of national and general concern, indicates that what was in the mind of the Imperial Legislature when this power was conferred in 1867 was regulation relating to general trade and commerce. Any other construction would, it was pointed out, have rendered unnecessary the specific mention of certain other heads dealing with banking, bills of exchange and promissory notes, as to which it had been significantly deemed necessary to insert a specific mention. The contracts of a particular trade or business could not, therefore, be dealt with by Dominion legislation so as to conflict with the powers assigned to the Provinces over property and civil rights relating to the regulation of trade and commerce. The Dominion power has a really definite effect when applied in aid of what the Dominion Government are specifically enabled to do independently of the general regulation of trade and commerce, for instance, in the creation of Dominion companies with power to trade throughout the whole of Canada. This was shown in the decision in *John Deere Plow Co.* v. *Wharton* ([1915] A.C. 330, 340). The same thing is true of the exercise of an emergency power required, as on the occasion of war, in the interest of Canada as a whole, a power which may operate outside the specific enumerations in both ss. 91 and 92. And it was observed in *Attorney-General for Canada* v. *Attorney-General for Alberta* ([1916] 1 A.C. 588, 596), in reference to attempted Dominion legislation about insurance, that it must now be taken that the authority to legislate for the regulation of trade and commerce does not extend to the regulation, for instance, by a licensing system, of a particular trade in which Canadians would otherwise be free to engage in the Provinces ([1915] A.C. 330, 340). It is, in their Lordships' opinion, now clear that, excepting so far as the power can be invoked in aid of capacity conferred independently under other words in s. 91, the power to regulate trade and commerce cannot be relied on as enabling the Dominion Parliament to regulate civil rights in the Provinces.

A more difficult question arises with reference to the initial words of s. 91, which enable the Parliament of Canada to make laws for the peace, order and good government of Canada in matters falling outside the Provincial powers specifically conferred by s. 92. . . .

. . . It appears to their Lordships that it is not now open to them to treat *Russell* v. *The Queen* (7 App. Cas. 829) as having established the general principle that the mere fact that Dominion legislation is for the general advantage of Canada, or is such that it will meet a mere want which is felt throughout the Dominion, renders it competent if it cannot be brought within the heads enumerated specifically in s. 91. Unless this is so, if the subject matter falls within any of the enumerated heads in s. 92, such legislation belongs exclusively to Provincial competency. No doubt there may be cases arising out of some extraordinary peril to the national life of Canada, as a whole, such as the cases arising out of a war, where legisla-

tion is required of an order that passes beyond the heads of exclusive Provincial competency. Such cases may be dealt with under the words at the commencement of s. 91, conferring general powers in relation to peace, order, and good government, simply because such cases are not otherwise provided for. But instances of this, as was pointed out in the judgment in *Fort Frances Pulp and Power Co.* v. *Manitoba Free Press* ([1923] A.C. 695) are highly exceptional. Their Lordships think that the decision in *Russell* v. *The Queen* can only be supported today, not on the footing of having laid down an interpretation, such as has sometimes been invoked of the general words at the beginning of s. 91, but on the assumption of the Board, apparently made at the time of deciding the case of *Russell* v. *The Queen*, that the evil of intemperance at that time amounted in Canada to one so great and so general that at least for the period it was a menace to the national life of Canada so serious and pressing that the National Parliament was called on to intervene to protect the nation from disaster. An epidemic of pestilence might conceivably have been regarded as analogous. It is plain from the decision in the *Board of Commerce* case ([1922] 1 A.C. 191) that the evil of profiteering could not have been so invoked, for Provincial powers, if exercised, were adequate to it. Their Lordships find it difficult to explain the decision in *Russell* v. *The Queen* as more than a decision of this order upon facts, considered to have been established at its date rather than upon general law. . . .

. . . Their Lordships have examined the evidence produced at the trial. . . . They are of opinion that it does not prove any emergency putting the national life of Canada in unanticipated peril such as the Board which decided *Russell* v. *The Queen* may be considered to have had before their minds.

9. Proprietary Articles Trade Association v. Attorney General of Canada, *1931*

~ In 1929 the federal government referred to the Supreme Court of Canada the question of the validity of the Dominion's anti-combines legislation after doubts as to the constitutionality of the legislation had been raised by counsel and judges in the provincial courts. The Supreme Court unanimously declared the legislation *intra vires*. The Proprietary Articles of Trade Association which had been charged with an infraction of the anti-combines legislation appealed this decision to the Privy Council. It was joined in this appeal by the governments of Ontario and Quebec.

Although counsel for the Dominion had cited the federal commerce power as one of the possible constitutional supports for the legislation, this was not the grounds upon which the Privy Council rested its opinion that the legislation was valid. It was Parliament's power to legislate in relation to criminal law (section 91 [27]) which Lord Atkin used to sustain the main provisions of the legislation. To support those sections which could not be characterized as criminal law—the remedies which were designed to enforce the anti-combines policy through reductions of customs duty and revocation of patents—he cited the Dominion's taxation power (section 91 [3]), its power in relation to patents (section 21 [22]), and its power over customs and excise laws (section 122).

In this case Lord Atkin removed the limit which Viscount Haldane had imposed on the federal criminal law power in the *Board of Commerce Act* case. He denied that the criminal quality of an act can be discerned by intuition. The only test was whether penal consequences were attached to behaviour. This would seem to permit the federal Parliament under its criminal law power to prohibit any kind of activity. It remained for the Supreme Court of Canada in the *Margarine* case of 1949[1] to restore some limits to the scope of this power. In that case Justice Rand indicated that peace, order, security, health and morality were the public purposes normally served by criminal law as contrasted with a purely economic interest such as the protection of dairy farmers from competition with oleomargarine. Another notable feature of Lord Atkin's treatment of the criminal law power is the introduction of a "due process" requirement for the proper exercise of this power. He distinguished the anti-combines legislation condemned in the *Board of Commerce Act* case from the legislation upheld in this case on the grounds that the earlier legislation did not employ the traditional machinery of criminal justice whereby a conviction can be obtained only by producing evidence before the ordinary courts that the behaviour of the accused satisfies a statutory definition of criminal activity.

While the commerce power was not invoked in this case to sustain this extremely important piece of national economic legislation, Lord Atkin's references to section 91(2) indicated a considerable expansion in the Judicial

---

Canadian Federation of Agriculture v. *A.G. Que.* [1949] S.C.R. 1.

Committee's construction of that power. He took care to guard against the possibility of interpreting his judgment in this case as implying the elimination of the federal commerce power as a possible support for national anti-combines legislation. More positively, and most importantly, he discredited the notion put forward by Viscount Haldane in the *Board of Commerce* case[2] and repeated in the *Snider*[3] case that the power to regulate trade and commerce was a subordinate one which could only be invoked when used in support of some other federal power. He cautiously avoided, however, any attempts at defining the extent of the commerce power as an independent source of legislative authority.

This case also demonstrates how the failure of the trade and commerce power to develop as a significant source of national legislative capacity in the fields of economic management and regulation could be in large measure compensated by other elements in the division of powers. In this case the criminal law power emerged as the principal support for federal anti-combines measures. Parliament's power to incorporate national companies, as indicated in the *John Deere Plow*[4] case, is capable of providing the central government with some means of affecting the operations of national business agencies. Further, the exceptions to section 92(10) establish a broad field for federal control over interprovincial transportation and communications systems as well as public works, while the banking, currency, interest and taxation powers in section 91 arm the federal government, constitutionally, with the major instruments of monetary and fiscal management. Thus it would be wrong to attribute what some regard as the undue degree of decentralization in Canada's federal system solely to the effects of judicial review. It is necessary to look to extra-constitutional factors to explain the failure of federal authorities to exercise fully all the powers at their disposal. ~

PROPRIETARY ARTICLES TRADE ASSOCIATION *v.*
ATTORNEY GENERAL OF CANADA
In the Privy Council. [1931] A.C. 310; II Olmsted 668.

The judgment of their Lordships was delivered by

LORD ATKIN. This is an appeal from the Supreme Court of Canada on a reference by the Governor in Council under s. 55 of the Supreme Court Act. The questions submitted to the Court were:

1. Is the Combines Investigation Act, R.S. Can., 1927, c. 26, ultra vires the Parliament of Canada either in whole or in part, and if so, in what particular or particulars or to what extent?

2. Is s. 498 of the Criminal Code ultra vires the Parliament of Canada, and if so, in what particular or particulars or to what extent?

The Supreme Court answered both questions in the negative.

---

[2] See above p. 65.
[3] *Toronto Electric Commissioners* v. *Snider,* [1925] A.C. 409. See above p. 76.
[4] *John Deere Plow Co. Ltd.* v. *Wharton,* [1915] A.C. 330.

The appellants are the Proprietary Articles Trade Association, who had been found by a Commission appointed under the Combines Investigation Act to have been party to a combine as defined in the Act, and had been admitted to be heard on the reference under s. 55, sub-s. 4, of the Supreme Court Act. The other appellants are the Attorney General of the Province of Quebec and the Attorney General of the Province of Ontario. The reference involved important questions of constitutional law within the Dominion, and their Lordships have had the assistance of full and able argument in which all the numerous relevant authorities were brought to their notice. After careful consideration of the arguments and the authorities their Lordships are of opinion that the decision of the Supreme Court is right.

In determining judicially the distribution of legislative powers between the Dominion and the Provinces made by the two famous ss. 91 and 92 of the British North America Act two principles have to be observed. First, the accepted canon of construction as to the general effect of the sections must be maintained. This is that the general powers of legislation for the peace, order and good government of Canada are committed to the Dominion Parliament, though they are subject to the exclusive powers of legislation committed to the Provincial legislatures and enumerated in s. 92. But the Provincial powers are themselves qualified in respect of the classes of subjects enumerated in s. 91, as particular instances of the general powers assigned to the Dominion. Any matters coming within any of those particular classes of subjects is not to be deemed to come within the classes of matters assigned to the Provincial legislatures. This almost reproduces the express words of the sections, and this rule is well settled.

The second principle to be observed judicially was expressed by the Board in 1881, "it will be a wise course . . . to decide each case which arises as best they can, without entering more largely upon an interpretation of the statute than is necessary for the decision of the particular question in hand.": *Citizens Insurance Co. of Canada* v. *Parsons* ((1881) 7 App. Cas. 96, 109). It was restated in 1914: "The structure of ss. 91 and 92, and the degree to which the connotation of the expressions used overlaps, render it, in their Lordships' opinion, unwise on this or any other occasion to attempt exhaustive definitions of the meaning and scope of these expressions. Such definitions, in the case of language used under the conditions in which a constitution such as that under consideration was framed, must almost certainly miscarry"; *John Deere Plow Co.* v. *Wharton* ([1915] A.C. 330, 338). The object is as far as possible to prevent too rigid declarations of the Courts from interfering with such elasticity as is given in the written constitution.

With these two principles in mind the present task must be approached. The claim of the Dominion is that the Combines Act and s. 498 of the Criminal Code can be supported as falling within two of the enumerated classes in s. 91—namely, "(2) The regulation of trade and commerce," and "(27) The criminal law, except the constitution of courts of criminal jurisdiction, but including the procedure in criminal matters." Reliance is also placed on "(3) The raising of money by any mode or system of taxation," "(22) Patents of invention and discovery," and on the general power of legislating for peace, order and good government. The appellants, on the other hand, say that the Act and the section of the Code violate the exclusive right of the Provinces under s. 92 to make laws as to "(13) property and civil rights in the Province," and "(14) the administration of justice in the Province."

~ Lord Atkin then reviewed the legislative history of both the section in the Criminal Code which makes combinations in restraint of trade criminal offences and the legislation providing for the investigation and prosecution of trade combinations. He also set down the main provisions of the Board of Commerce and Fair Prices Acts of 1919 which had been ruled *ultra vires* by the Privy Council in the *Board of Commerce* case. ~

Their Lordships have dealt at some length with the provisions of the Acts of 1919 inasmuch as the appellants relied strongly on the judgment of the Board, in *In re Board of Commerce Act, 1919* ([1922] 1 A.C. 191), which held both Acts to be ultra vires. Unless there are material distinctions between those Acts and the present, it is plainly the duty of this Board to follow the previous decision. It is necessary therefore to contrast the provisions of the Acts of 1919 with the provisions of the Act now in dispute. The judgment above referred to was given in November, 1921, and in June 13, 1923, there was passed the Combines Investigation Act, 1923 (13 & 14 Geo. 5, c. 9), which repealed the two Acts of 1919 and enacted provisions which were substantially those of the present Act. The Act of 1923 was revised in 1927 and appears substantially in the original form in the revised Act—the Combines Investigation Act (R.S. Can., 1927, c. 26). By this Act "combines" are defined as combines "which have operated or are likely to operate to the detriment or against the interest of the public, whether consumers, producers or others," and which "are mergers, trusts or monopolies so-called" or result from the acquisition by any person of any control over the business of any other person or result from any agreement which has the effect of limiting facilities for production, manufacture or transport or of fixing a common price, or enhancing the price of articles or of preventing or lessening competition in or substantially controlling production or manufacture, or "otherwise restraining or injuring trade or commerce." By the Act the Governor in Council may name a Minister of the Crown to be charged with the administration of the Act, and must appoint a registrar of the Combines Investigation Act. The registrar is charged with the duty to inquire whether a combine exists, whenever an application is made for that purpose by six persons supported by evidence, or whenever he has reason to believe that a combine exists, or whenever he is directed by the Minister so to inquire. Provision is made for holding further inquiry by Commissioners appointed from time to time; and the registrar and a commissioner are armed with large powers of examining books and papers, demanding returns, and summoning witnesses. The proceedings are to take place in private unless the Minister directs that they should be public. The registrar is to report the result of any inquiry to the Minister, and every commissioner is to report to the registrar who is to transmit the report to the Minister. Any report of a commissioner is to be made public unless the commissioner reports that public interest requires publication to be withheld, in which case the Minister has a discretion as to publicity.

By s. 32 "Every one is guilty of an indictable offence and liable to a penalty not exceeding ten thousand dollars or to two years' imprisonment, or if a corporation to a penalty not exceeding twenty-five thousand dollars, who is a party or privy to or knowingly assists in the formation or operation of a combine within the meaning of this Act. (2) No prosecution for any offence under this section shall be commenced otherwise than at the instance of the Solicitor-General of Canada or of the Attorney-General of a Province." By subsequent sections, refusal to obey orders as to discovery and other interference with an investigation are made offences for the most part subject to summary conviction and appropriate penalties are imposed.

Under a group of ss. 29 to 31, entitled "Remedies" powers are given as in previous Acts for the Governor in Council to reduce customs duties, and for the Exchequer Court to revoke licences where the duties are used to facilitate a combine or when the holder of a patent uses it so as unduly to limit the manufacture, or enhance the price of any article. Power is given to the Minister to remit to the Attorney General of a Province any returns made in pursuance of the Act or any report of the registrar, or any commissioner; and if no action is taken thereon by the Attorney General of the Province, the Solicitor General (representing the Dominion) may take the appropriate action.

In their Lordships' opinion s. 498 of the Criminal Code and the greater part of the provisions of the Combines Investigation Act fall within the power of the Dominion Parliament to legislate as to matters falling within the class of subjects, "the criminal law including the procedure in criminal matters" (s. 91, head 27). The substance of the Act is by s. 2 to define, and by s. 32 to make criminal, combines which the legislature in the public interest intends to prohibit. The definition is wide, and may cover activities which have not hitherto been considered to be criminal. But only those combines are affected "which have operated or are likely to operate to the detriment or against the interest of the public, whether consumers, producers, or others"; and if Parliament genuinely determines that commercial activities which can be so described are to be suppressed in the public interest, their Lordships see no reason why Parliament should not make them crimes. "Criminal law" means "the criminal law in its widest sense": *Attorney-General for Ontario* v. *Hamilton Street Ry Co.* ([1903] A.C. 524). It certainly is not confined to what was criminal by the law of England or of any Province in 1867. The power must extend to legislation to make new crimes. Criminal law connotes only the quality of such acts or omissions as are prohibited under appropriate penal provisions by authority of the State. The criminal quality of an act cannot be discerned by intuition; nor can it be discovered by reference to any standard but one: Is the act prohibited with penal consequences? Morality and criminality are far from coextensive; nor is the sphere of criminality necessarily part of a more extensive field

covered by morality—unless the moral code necessarily disapproves all acts prohibited by the State, in which case the argument moves in a circle. It appears to their Lordships to be of little value to seek to confine crimes to a category of acts which by their very nature belong to the domain of "criminal jurisprudence"; for the domain of criminal jurisprudence can only be ascertained by examining what acts at any particular period are declared by the State to be crimes, and the only common nature they will be found to possess is that they are prohibited by the State and that those who commit them are punished. Their Lordships agree with the view expressed in the judgment of Newcombe J. ([1929] S.C.R. 409, 422) that the passage in the judgment of the Board in the *Board of Commerce* case ([1922] 1 A.C. 191, 198, 199) to which allusion has been made, was not intended as a definition. In that case their Lordships appear to have been contrasting two matters—one obviously within the line, the other obviously outside it. For this purpose it was clearly legitimate to point to matters which are such serious breaches of any accepted code of morality as to be obviously crimes when they are prohibited under penalties. The contrast is with matters which are merely attempts to interfere with Provincial rights, and are sought to be justified under the head of "criminal law" colourably and merely in aid of what is in substance an encroachment. The Board considered that the Combines and Fair Prices Act of 1919 came within the latter class, and was in substance an encroachment on the exclusive power of the Provinces to legislate on property and civil rights. The judgment of the Board arose in respect to an order under Part II of the Act. Their Lordships pointed out five respects in which the Act was subject to criticism. It empowered the Board of Commerce to prohibit accumulations in the case of non-traders; to compel surplus articles to be sold at prices fixed by the Board; to regulate profits; to exercise their powers over articles produced for his own use by the householder himself; to inquire into individual cases without applying any principles of general application. None of these powers exists in the provisions now under discussion. There is a general definition, and a general condemnation; and if penal consequences follow, they can only follow from the determination by existing courts of an issue of fact defined in express words by the statute. The greater part of the statute is occupied in setting up and directing machinery for making preliminary inquiries whether the alleged offence has been committed. It is noteworthy that no penal consequences follow directly from a report of either commissioner or registrar that a combine exists. It is not even made evidence. The offender, if he is to be punished, must be tried on indictment, and the offence proved in due course of law. Penal consequences, no doubt, follow the breach of orders made for the discovery of evidence; but if the main object be intra vires, the enforcement of orders genuinely authorized and genuinely made to secure that object are not open to attack.

It is, however, not enough for Parliament to rely solely on the powers to legislate as to the criminal law for support of the whole Act. The remedies given under ss. 29 and 30 reducing customs duty and revoking patents have no necessary connection with the criminal law and must be justified on other grounds. Their Lordships have no doubt that they can both be supported as being reasonably ancillary to the powers given respectively under s. 91, head 3, and affirmed by s. 122, "the raising of money by any mode or system of taxation," and under s. 91, head 22, "patents of invention and discovery." It is unfortunately beyond dispute that in a country where a general protective tariff exists persons may be found to take advantage of the protection, and within its walls form combinations that may work to the public disadvantage. It is an elementary point of self-preservation that the legislature which creates the protection should arm the executive with powers of withdrawing or relaxing the

protection if abused. The same reasoning applies to grants of monopolies under any system of patents.

The view that their Lordships have expressed makes it unnecessary to discuss the further ground upon which the legislation has been supported by reference to the power to legislate under s. 91, head 2, for "The regulation of trade and commerce." Their Lordships merely propose to disassociate themselves from the construction suggested in argument of a passage in the judgment in the *Board of Commerce* case under which it was contended that the power to regulate trade and commerce could be invoked only in furtherance of a general power which Parliament possessed independently of it. No such restriction is properly to be inferred from that judgment. The words of the statute must receive their proper construction where they stand as giving an independent authority to Parliament over the particular subject-matter. But following the second principle noticed in the beginning of this judgment their Lordships in the present case forbear from defining the extent of that authority. They desire, however, to guard themselves from being supposed to lay down that the present legislation could not be supported on that ground.

If then the legislation in question is authorized under one or other of the heads specifically enumerated in s. 91, it is not to the purpose to say that it affects property and civil rights in the Provinces. Most of the specific subjects in s. 91 do affect property and civil rights but so far as the legislation of parliament in pith and substance is operating within the enumerated powers there is constitutional authority to interfere with property and civil rights. The same principle would apply to s. 92, head 14, "the administration of justice in the Province," even if the legislation did, as in the present case it does not, in any way interfere with the administration of justice. Nor is there any ground for suggesting that the Dominion may not employ its own executive officers for the purpose of carrying out legislation which is within its constitutional authority, as it does regularly in the case of revenue officials and other matters which need not be enumerated.

10. In re Regulation and Control of Aeronautics in Canada, *1932*

~ An important issue in any federal system is the way in which the federal state's capacity for participating in international agreements is affected by its internal division of powers between national and local governments. Basic to this question is the distinction between the power of entering into treaties with other states and the power of implementing such treaties through changes in the domestic legal system. In Canada, as in the United States and Australia, the federal government has the power to sign treaties and enter into international agreements on all subjects. It is only in connection with the implementation or enforcement of such international undertakings that the division of legislative powers might impose limitations on the national legislature.

In Canada the only direct reference which the B.N.A. Act makes to the field of foreign affairs is section 132 which grants to the national Parliament and government all the powers necessary for carrying out obligations which Canada assumes as a result of treaties concluded between the British Empire and foreign states. Clearly when this section was draughted in 1867 there was no anticipation of a time when Canada would conduct her own external affairs. All that section 132 provided for was that the Canadian Parliament should have the power of enacting any legislation required in Canada for the implementation of treaties negotiated by the Imperial government. As long as Canada's relations with other states were carried on under the aegis of the Imperial government, the treaty-implementing power raised no serious constitutional problems. It would appear that under section 132 Parliament's power of enforcing British Empire treaties could even override the normal division of powers in sections 91 and 92 of the B.N.A. Act. For instance, a few years before this *Aeronautics Reference* both the Supreme Court and the Privy Council had ruled invalid a British Columbia Act which barred Japanese and Chinese from certain kinds of employment on the grounds that it violated an Act passed by the Dominion Parliament implementing a 1913 treaty made between Great Britain and Japan.[1] But in the 1920s and 1930s as Canada came to assume the status of an independent nation the question of treaty implementation emerged in an entirely different context: now that Canada entered into international agreements on her own as an autonomous nation and not as a subordinate part of the British Empire, would the national Parliament find adequate powers under the constitution for implementing such treaties?

The *Aeronautics Reference* did not force the courts to squarely face this issue. The questions submitted by the federal government to the Supreme Court concerned the validity of the Dominion's Aeronautics Act and Air Regulations establishing a comprehensive system of control over aerial naviga-

---

[1] *In re Employment of Aliens* (1922), 63 S.C.R. 293 and *A.-G., B.C.* v. *A.-G. Canada* [1924] A.C. 204.

85

tion in Canada. The main components of this scheme had been enacted with a view to performing Canada's obligations which arose out of a Convention ratified on behalf of the British Empire in 1922. Thus Lord Sankey had no difficulty in finding support in section 132 for the Dominion enactments. It should be noted, however, that the Canadian Supreme Court had not been willing to construe section 132 as granting to the Dominion *exclusively* the power of implementing British Empire treaties and was unanimous in giving a negative answer to the first question in the reference.

Although Lord Sankey did not deal directly with the effect of Dominion autonomy on the treaty enforcement power, the concluding words of his judgment did point to one possible solution to this problem. He applied the national aspect test to the question, suggesting that the regulation of aerial navigation, the subject matter of an international agreement, was a matter of such general concern to the whole body politic of Canada that it could be brought under Parliament's power of making laws for the peace, order and good government of Canada.

In a marked departure from the Privy Council's traditional style of constitutional interpretation, Lord Sankey's judgment includes reflections on the historic purposes which inspired the drafting of the B.N.A. Act. While acknowledging that one of those purposes was the preservation of the rights of minorities and describing the B.N.A. Act as "the charter of the Provinces," he emphasizes that its "real object" was to give the central government the "almost sovereign powers" required to provide legislation on matters of common concern to the whole country. Lord Sankey, who was appointed Lord Chancellor by the Labour government in 1929, introduced this approach to the B.N.A. Act in a decision in which the Privy Council reversed the Supreme Court of Canada and held that women were "persons" and hence eligible to serve in the Canadian Senate. On that occasion Lord Sankey referred to the constitution provided for Canada through the B.N.A. Act as "a living tree capable of growth and expansion within its natural limits." Their Lordships in interpreting this constitution should not, he cautioned, "cut down the provisions of the Act by a narrow and technical construction, but rather give it a large and liberal interpretation so that the Dominion to a great extent, but within certain fixed limits, may be mistress in her own house, as the Provinces to a great extent, but within certain fixed limits, are mistresses in theirs."[2] ~

IN RE REGULATION AND CONTROL OF AERONAUTICS IN CANADA
In the Privy Council. [1932] A.C. 54; II Olmsted 709.

The judgment of their Lordships was delivered by

LORD SANKEY L.C. This appeal raises an important question as between the

---

[2] *Henrietta Muir Edwards* v. *Attorney-General for Canada* [1930], A.C. 124, at p. 136.

Dominion and the Provinces of Canada regarding the right to control and regulate aeronautics, including the granting of certificates to persons to act as pilots, the inspection and licensing of aircraft, and the inspection and licensing of aerodromes and air-stations. The question is whether the subject is one on which the Dominion Parliament is alone competent to legislate, or whether it is in each Province so related to Provincial property and civil rights and local matters as to exclude the Dominion from any (or from more than a very limited) jurisdiction in respect of it.

The Supreme Court of Canada has decided the question in its several branches adversely to the claims of the Dominion, and has held in effect that while the Dominion has a considerable field of jurisdiction in the matter under various heads of s. 91 of the British North America Act, 1867, there is also a local field of jurisdiction for the Provinces, and that the Dominion jurisdiction does not extend so far as to permit it to deal with the subject in the broad way in which it has attempted to deal with it in the legislation under consideration.

During the sittings of the peace conference in Paris at the close of the European war, a convention relating to the regulation of aerial navigation, dated October 13, 1919, was drawn up by a Commission constituted by the Supreme Council of the peace conference. That convention was signed by the representatives of the allied and associated powers, including Canada, and was ratified by His Majesty on behalf of the British Empire on June 1, 1922. It is now in force between the British Empire and seventeen other States.

With a view to performing her obligations as part of the British Empire under this convention, which was then in course of preparation, the Parliament of Canada enacted the Air Board Act, c. 11 of the Statutes of Canada, 1919 (1st session), which with an amendment thereto, was consolidated in the Revised Statutes of Canada, 1927, as c. 43, under the title the

Aeronautics Act. It is to be noted, however, that the Act does not by reason of its reproduction in the Revised Statutes take effect as a new law. The Governor-General in Council, on December 31, 1919, pursuant to the Air Board Act, issued detailed "Air Regulations" which, with certain amendments, are now in force. By the National Defence Act, 1922, the Minister of National Defence thereafter exercised the duties and functions of the Air Board.

By these statutes and the Air Regulations, and the amendments thereto, provision is made for the regulation and control in a general and comprehensive way of aerial navigation in Canada, and over the territorial waters thereof. In particular, s. 4 of the Aeronautics Act purports to give the Minister of National Defence a general power to regulate and control, subject to approval by the Governor in Council (with statutory force and under the sanction of penalties on summary conviction), aerial navigation over Canada and her territorial waters, including power to regulate the licensing of pilots, aircraft, aerodromes and commercial services; the conditions under which aircraft may be used for goods, mails and passengers, or their carriage over any part of Canada; the prohibition (absolute or conditional) of flying over prescribed areas; aerial routes; and provision for safe and proper flying.

Their Lordships were told during the course of the argument that no Provincial Legislature had passed any such legislation, but that this had not prevented the progress of aeronautical development in the Provinces. It appears, for example, that in Ontario there has been established subject to these Regulations one of the most complete survey services in the Empire, and that it is working most harmoniously. Their Lordships are not aware that any practical difficulty has arisen in consequence of the general control of flying being in the hands of the Dominion, but at a conference at Ottawa between representatives of the Dominion Government and of the several Provincial Governments in November, 1927, a question was raised by the representatives of the Province of Quebec as to the legislative authority of the Parliament of Canada to sanction regulations for the control of aerial navigation generally within Canada—at all events in their application to flying operations carried on within a Province—and it was agreed that the question so raised was proper to be determined by the Supreme Court of Canada. Thereupon four questions were referred by His Excellency, the Governor-General in Council, under an Order dated April 15, 1929, to the Supreme Court for hearing and consideration, pursuant to s. 55 of the Supreme Court Act, R.S. Can., 1927, c. 35, touching the respective powers under the British North America Act, 1867, of the Parliament and Government of Canada and of the Legislatures of the Provinces in relation to the regulation and control of aeronautics in Canada.

The determination of these questions depends upon the true construction of ss. 91, 92 and 132 of the British North America Act, Sect. 132 provides as follows: "The Parliament and Government of Canada shall have all powers necessary or proper for performing the obligations of Canada or of any province thereof, as part of the British Empire, towards foreign countries, arising under treaties between the Empire and such foreign countries." It is not necessary to set out at length the familiar ss. 91 and 92 which deal with the distribution of legislative powers. Sect. 91 tabulates the subjects to be dealt with by the Dominion, and s. 92 the subjects to be dealt with exclusively by the Provincial legislatures, but it will not be forgotten that s. 91, in addition, authorizes the King by and with the advice and consent of the Senate and House of Commons of Canada to make laws for the peace, order and good government of Canada in relation to all matters not coming within the classes of subjects by this Act assigned exclusively to the legislatures of the Provinces, and further provides that any matter coming within any of the classes of subjects enumerated in the section shall not be deemed to come within the classes of matters of a local and private nature comprised in the enumeration of classes of subjects assigned by s. 92 exclusively to the legislatures of the Provinces.

The four questions addressed to the Court are as follows:

1. Have the Parliament and Government of Canada exclusive legislative and executive authority for performing the obligation entitled "Convention relating to the Regulation of Aerial Navigation?"

2. Is legislation of the Parliament of Canada providing for the regulation and control of aeronautics generally within Canada, including flying operations carried on entirely within the limits of a Province, necessary or proper for performing the obligations of Canada or of any Province thereof, under the convention aforementioned within the meaning of s. 132 of the British North America Act, 1867?

3. Has the Parliament of Canada legislative authority to enact, in whole or in part, the provisions of s. 4 of the Aeronautics Act, c. 3, Revised Statutes of Canada, 1927?

4. Has the Parliament of Canada legislative authority to sanction the making and enforcement, in whole or in part, of the regulations contained in the Air Regulations, 1920, respecting: (a) The granting of certificates or licences authorizing persons to act as pilots, navigators, engineers or inspectors of aircraft and the suspension or revocation of such licences; (b) the regulation, identification, inspection, certification, and licensing of all aircraft; and (c) the licensing, inspection and the regulation of all aerodromes and air stations? . . .

. . . To question 1, and retaining the word "exclusive," the Board's answer is "Yes."

~ The Judicial Committee was not asked to review the Supreme Court's answer to question 2. ~

To question 3, their answer is also "Yes."

To question 4, their answer is again "Yes."

Before discussing the several questions individually, it is desirable to make some general observations upon ss. 91 and 92, and 132.

With regard to ss. 91 and 92, the cases which have been decided on the provisions of these sections are legion. Many inquests have been held upon them, and many great lawyers have from time to time dissected them.

Under our system decided cases effectively construe the words of an Act of Parliament and establish principles and rules whereby its scope and effect may be interpreted. But there is always a danger that in the course of this process the terms of the statute may come to be unduly extended and attention may be diverted from what has been enacted to what has been judicially said about the enactment.

To borrow an analogy; there may be a range of sixty colours, each of which is so little different from its neighbour that it is difficult to make any distinction between the two, and yet at the one end of the range the colour may be white and at the other end of the range black. Great care must therefore be taken to consider each decision in the light of the circumstances of the case in view of which it was pronounced, especially in the interpretation of an Act such as the British North America Act, which was a great constitutional charter, and not to allow general phrases to obscure the underlying object of the Act, which was to establish a system of government upon essentially federal principles. Useful as decided cases are, it is always advisable to get back to the words of the Act itself and to remember the object with which it was passed.

Inasmuch as the Act embodies a compromise under which the original Provinces agreed to federate, it is important to keep in mind that the preservation of the rights of minorities was a condition on which such minorities entered into the federation, and the foundation upon which the whole structure was subsequently erected. The process of interpretation as the years go on ought not to be allowed to dim or to whittle down the provisions of the original contract upon which the federation was founded, nor is it legitimate that any judicial construction of the provisions of ss. 91 and 92 should impose a new and different contract upon the federating bodies.

But while the Courts should be jealous in upholding the charter of the Provinces as enacted in s. 92 it must no less be borne in mind that the real object of the Act was to give the central Government those high functions and almost sovereign powers by which uniformity of legislation might be secured on all questions which were of common concern to all the Provinces as members of a constituent whole.

While the decisions which the Board has pronounced in the many constitutional cases which have come under their consideration from the Dominion must each be regarded in the light of the facts involved in it, their Lordships recognize that there has grown up around the British North America Act a body of precedents of high authority and value as guides to its interpretation and application. The useful and essential task of taking stock of this body of authority and reviewing it in relation to the original text has been undertaken by this Board from time to time and notably, for example, in *Attorney-General for Ontario* v. *Attorney-General for Canada* ([1896] A.C. 348); *Attorney-General for Canada* v. *Attorney-General for Ontario* ([1898] A.C. 700); *City of Montreal* v. *Montreal Street Ry.* ([1912] A.C. 333); and in the same year *Attorney-General for Ontario* v. *Attorney-General for Canada* ([1912] A.C. 571). In all these four cases the scope of the two sections was carefully considered, but it is not necessary to cite them at length because so recently as last year this Board reviewed them in the case of *Attorney-General for Canada* v. *Attorney-General for British Columbia* ([1930] A.C. 111, 118), and laid down four propositions relative to the legislative competence of Canada and the Provinces respectively as established by the decisions of the Judicial

Committee. These propositions are as follows:

1. The legislation of the Parliament of the Dominion, so long as it strictly relates to subjects of legislation expressly enumerated in s. 91, is of paramount authority, even though it trenches upon matters assigned to the Provincial legislatures by s. 92.

2. The general power of legislation conferred upon the Parliament of the Dominion by s. 91 of the Act in supplement of the power to legislate upon the subjects expressly enumerated must be strictly confined to such matters as are unquestionably of national interest and importance, and must not trench on any of the subjects enumerated in s. 92, as within the scope of Provincial legislation, unless these matters have attained such dimensions as to affect the body politic of the Dominion.

3. It is within the competence of the Dominion Parliament to provide for matters which, though otherwise within the legislative competence of the Provincial legislature, are necessarily incidental to effective legislation by the Parliament of the Dominion upon a subject of legislation expressly enumerated in s. 91.

4. There can be a domain in which Provincial and Dominion legislation may overlap, in which case neither legislation will be ultra vires if the field is clear, but if the field is not clear and the two regulations meet the Dominion legislation must prevail.

Their Lordships particularly emphasize the second and third of these categories, and refer to the remarks made by Lord Watson in *Attorney-General for Ontario* v. *Attorney-General for Canada, supra,* p. 361, where he says: "Their Lordships do not doubt that some matters, in their origin local and provincial, might attain such dimensions as to affect the body politic of the Dominion, and to justify the Canadian Parliament in passing laws for their regulation or abolition in the interest of the Dominion. But great caution must be observed in distinguishing between that which is local and provincial, and therefore within the jurisdiction of the provincial legislatures, and that which has ceased to be merely local or provincial, and has become matter of national concern in such sense as to bring it within the jurisdiction of the Parliament of Canada." Further, their Lordships desire to refer to *Fort Frances Pulp and Power Co.* v. *Manitoba Free Press Co.* ([1923 A.C. 695, 704, 706), where it was held that the Canadian War Measures Act, 1914, and certain Orders in Council made thereunder during the War were intra vires of the Dominion. Lord Haldane there said: "The general control of property and civil rights for normal purposes remains with the Provincial Legislatures. But questions may arise by reason of the special circumstances of the national emergency which concern nothing short of the peace, order and good government of Canada as a whole." These remarks must again be taken subject to the situation then prevailing, for he adds later: "It may be that it has become clear that the crisis which arose is wholly at an end and that there is no justification for the continued exercise of an exceptional interference which becomes ultra vires when it is no longer called for. In such a case the law as laid down for the distribution of powers in the ruling instrument would have to be invoked."

It is obvious, therefore, that there may be cases of emergency where the Dominion is empowered to act for the whole. There may also be cases where the Dominion is entitled to speak for the whole, and this not because of any judicial interpretation of ss. 91 and 92, but by reason of the plain terms of s. 132, where Canada as a whole, having undertaken an obligation, is given the power necessary and proper for performing that obligation.

During the course of the argument, learned counsel on either side endeavoured respectively to bring the subject of aeronautics within s. 91 or s. 92. Thus, the appellant referred to s. 91, item 2 (the regulation of trade and commerce); item 5 (postal services); item 9 (beacons); item 10 (navigation and shipping). Their Lordships do not think that aeronautics can be brought within the subject navigation and shipping, although undoubtedly to a large extent, and in some respects, it might be brought under the regulation of trade and commerce, or the postal services. On the other hand, the respondents contended that aeronautics as a class of subject came within item 13 of s. 92 (property and civil rights in the Provinces) or item 16 (generally all matters of a merely local and private nature in the Provinces). Their Lordships do not think that aeronautics is a class of subject within property and civil rights in the Provinces, although here again, ingenious arguments may show that some small part of it might be so included.

In their Lordships' view, transport as a subject is dealt with in certain branches both of s. 91 and s. 92, but neither of those sections deals specially with that branch of transport which is concerned with aeronautics.

Their Lordships are of opinion that it is proper to take a broader view of the matter rather than to rely on forced analogies or piecemeal analysis. They consider the governing section to be s. 132, which gives to the Parliament and Government of Canada all powers necessary or proper for performing the obligations towards foreign countries arising under treaties between the Empire and such foreign countries. As far as s. 132 is concerned, their Lordships are not aware of any decided case which is of assistance on the present occasion. It will be observed, however, from the very definite words of the section, that it is the Parliament and Government of Canada who are to have all powers necessary or proper for performing the obligations of Canada, or any Province thereof. It would therefore appear to follow that any Convention of the character under discussion necessitates Dominion legislation in order that it may be carried out. It is only necessary to look at the Convention itself to see what wide powers are necessary for performing the obligations arising thereunder. By article 1 the high contracting parties rec-

ognize that every Power (which includes Canada) has complete and exclusive sovereignty over the air space above its territory; by article 40, the British Dominions and India are deemed to be States for the purpose of the Convention.

~ Lord Sankey then listed the principal obligations undertaken by Canada as part of the British Empire under the stipulations of the Convention. ~

It is therefore obvious that the Dominion Parliament, in order duly and fully to "perform the obligations of Canada or of any Province thereof" under the Convention, must make provision for a great variety of subjects. Indeed, the terms of the Convention include almost every conceivable matter relating to aerial navigation, and we think that the Dominion Parliament not only has the right, but also the obligation, to provide by statute and by regulation that the terms of the Convention shall be duly carried out. With regard to some of them, no doubt, it would appear to be clear that the Dominion has power to legislate, for example, under s. 91, item 2, for the regulation of trade and commerce, and under item 5 for the postal services, but it is not necessary for the Dominion to piece together its powers under s. 91 in an endeavour to render them co-extensive with its duty under the Convention when s. 132 confers upon it full power to do all that is legislatively necessary for the purpose.

To sum up, having regard (*a*) to the terms of s. 132, (*b*) to the terms of the Convention which covers almost every conceivable matter relating to aerial navigation; and (*c*) to the fact that further legislative powers in relation to aerial navigation reside in the Parliament of Canada by virtue of s. 91, items 2, 5 and 7, it would appear that substantially the whole field of legislation in regard to aerial navigation belongs to the Dominion. There may be a small portion of the field which is not by virtue of specific words in the British North America Act vested in the Dominion; but neither is it vested by specific words in the Provinces. As to that small portion it appears to the Board that it must necessarily belong to the Dominion under its power to make laws for the peace, order and good government of Canada. Further, their Lordships are influenced by the facts that the subject of aerial navigation and the fulfilment of Canadian obligations under s. 132 are matters of national interest and importance; and that aerial navigation is a class of subject which has attained such dimensions as to affect the body politic of the Dominion.

For these reasons their Lordships have come to the conclusion that it was competent for the Parliament of Canada to pass the Act and authorize the Regulations in question, and that questions 1, 3 and 4, which alone they are asked to answer, should be answered in the affirmative.

11. In re Regulation and Control of Radio Communication in Canada, *1932*

~ The question of Parliament's capacity to implement international agreements entered into by Canada as an independent nation was the central issue in the *Radio* case of 1932. In 1927, Canada with seventy-nine other countries had signed the international Radio Telegraph Convention. This Convention was ratified by the Canadian government without any reference to the British Empire. To implement its provisions Parliament subsequently enacted the Radio Telegraph Act. This reference initiated by the federal government was designed to test the Dominion's general capacity for regulating radio communications in Canada.

In the crucial paragraph of the Judicial Committee's judgment which refers to the treaty implementing power, Viscount Dunedin rejected the argument of Quebec's counsel that the power to implement international agreements such as the Radio Convention must be subject to the division of powers as provided for in sections 91 and 92 of the B.N.A. Act. In Lord Dunedin's view the power of ensuring that Canadian citizens do not violate undertakings which Canada has made with other states must be undivided and rests exclusively with the national Parliament. Further, he acknowledged that with the achievement of autonomy Canada's obligations to foreign states could no longer be construed in terms of the British Empire treaties envisaged by section 132. But the implementation of Canadian treaties must, in his view, be considered a new matter not explicitly provided for in either section 91 or 92 and therefore one that should be brought under Parliament's residual power.

Hence the outcome of Viscount Dunedin's decision was that the power of implementing treaties lay exclusively with Parliament and indeed the Dominion would acquire authority over a subject normally under provincial jurisdiction if legislation was required to carry out an international obligation dealing with that subject. This decision did much to encourage the Bennett government in the belief that Canada's participation in the conventions of the International Labour Organization could provide grounds for enacting a wide-sweeping program of labour legislation. It was this legislation which gave rise to the next major case dealing with the question of implementing treaties—a case which in effect cut in exactly the opposite direction from the *Radio Reference*.

It should be noted that the Privy Council's decision assigning jurisdiction over broadcasting to the federal Parliament does not rest solely on the treaty-implementing argument. Their Lordships also held that broadcasting (both the transmitting and receiving of radio waves) came under the power over lines of telegraphs and undertakings connecting the provinces or extending beyond a province which section 92(10)(a) of the B.N.A. Act assigns to the federal Parliament. ~

IN RE REGULATION AND CONTROL OF
RADIO COMMUNICATION IN CANADA
In the Privy Council [1932] A.C. 304; III Olmsted 18.

The judgment of their Lordships was delivered by

VISCOUNT DUNEDIN. This is an appeal from a judgment of the Supreme Court of Canada, answering questions referred to it by His Excellency the Governor-General in Council, for hearing and consideration, pursuant to the authority of s. 55 of the Supreme Court Act (R.S. Can., 1927, c. 35), touching the jurisdiction of the Parliament of Canada to regulate and control radio communication.

The questions so referred were as follows:

1. Has the Parliament of Canada jurisdiction to regulate and control radio communication, including the transmission and reception of signs, signals, pictures and sounds of all kinds by means of Hertzian waves, and including the right to determine the character, use and location of apparatus employed?

2. If not, in what particular or particulars or to what extent is the jurisdiction of Parliament limited?

The answers of the Chief Justice and the other judges of whom the Court was composed were as follows:

THE CHIEF JUSTICE: Question No. 1. In view of the present state of radio science as submitted. Yes. Question No. 2. No answer.

NEWCOMBE J.: Question No. 1. Should be answered in the affirmative. Question No. 2. No answer.

RINFRET J.: Question No. 1. Construing it as meaning "jurisdiction in every respect" the answer is in the negative. Question No. 2. The answer should be ascertained from the reasons certified by the learned judge.

LAMONT J.: Question No. 1. Not exclusive jurisdiction. Question No. 2. The jurisdiction of Parliament is limited as set out in the learned judge's reasons.

SMITH J.: Question No. 1. Should be answered in the affirmative. Question No. 2. No answer.

The learned Chief Justice and Rinfret J. expressed their regret that at the time of delivering judgment they had not had the advantage of knowing what was the conclusion reached by this Board on the question referred to as aviation. It is however unnecessary to speculate as to what would have been the result had the learned judges known as we know now that the judgment of this Board (*In re Regulation and Control of Aeronautics in Canada*, delivered on October 22, 1931) settled that the regulation of aviation was a matter for the Dominion. It would certainly only have confirmed the majority in their opinions. And as to the minority, though it is true that reference is made in their opinions to the fact that as the case then stood aviation had been decided not to fall within the exclusive jurisdiction of the Dominion, yet had they known the eventual judgment it is doubtful whether that fact would have altered their opinion. For this must at once be admitted; the leading consideration in the judgment of the Board was that the subject fell within the provisions of s. 132 of the British North America Act, 1867, which is as follows: "The Parliament and Government of Canada shall have all powers necessary or proper for performing the obligations of Canada or of any Province thereof as part of the British Empire towards foreign countries arising under treaties between the Empire and such foreign countries." And it is said with truth that, while as regards aviation there was a treaty, the convention here is not a treaty between the Empire as such and foreign countries, for Great Britain does not sign as representing the Colonies and Dominions. She only confirms the assent which had been signified by the Colonies and Dominions who were separately represented at the meetings which drafted the convention. But while this is so, the aviation case in their Lordships' judgment cannot be put on one side.

Counsel for the Province felt this and sought to avoid any general deduction by admitting that many of the things provided by the convention and the regulations thereof fell within various special heads of s. 91. For example, provisions as to beacon signals he would refer to head 10 of s. 91—navigation and shipping. It is unnecessary to multiply instances, because the real point to be considered is this manner of dealing with the subject. In other words the argument of the Province comes to this: Go through all the stipulations of the convention and each one you can pick out which fairly falls within one of the enumerated heads of s. 91, that can be held to be appropriate for Dominion legislation; but the residue belongs to the Province under the head either of head 13 of s. 92—property and civil rights, or head 16—matters of a merely local or private nature in the Province.

Their Lordships cannot agree that the matter should be so dealt with. Canada as a Dominion is one of the signatories to the convention. In a question with foreign powers the persons who might infringe some of the stipulations in the convention would not be the Dominion of Canada as a whole but would be individual persons residing in Canada. These persons must so to speak be kept in order by legislation and the only legislation that can deal with them all at once is Dominion legislation. This idea of Canada as a Dominion being bound by a convention equivalent to a treaty with foreign powers was quite unthought of in 1867. It is the outcome of the gradual development of the position of Canada *vis-à-vis* to the mother country, Great Britain, which is found in these later days expressed in the Statute of Westminster. It is not, therefore, to be expected that such a matter should be dealt with in explicit words in either s. 91 or s. 92. The only class of treaty which would bind Canada was thought of as a treaty by Great Britain, and that was provided for by s. 132. Being, therefore, not mentioned explicitly in either s. 91 or

s. 92, such legislation falls within the general words at the opening of s. 91 which assign to the Government of the Dominion the power to make laws "for the peace, order and good government of Canada in relation to all matters not coming within the classes of subjects by this Act assigned exclusively to the legislatures of the Provinces." In fine, though agreeing that the Convention was not such a treaty as is defined in s. 132, their Lordships think that it comes to the same thing. On August 11, 1927, the Privy Council of Canada with the approval of the Governor-General chose a body to attend the meeting of all the powers to settle international agreements as to wireless. The Canadian body attended and took part in deliberations. The deliberations ended in the convention with general regulations appended being signed at Washington on November 25, 1927, by the representatives of all the powers who had taken part in the conference, and this convention was ratified by the Canadian Government on July 12, 1928.

The result is in their Lordships' opinion clear. It is Canada as a whole which is amenable to the other powers for the proper carrying out of the convention; and to prevent individuals in Canada infringing the stipulations of the convention it is necessary that the Dominion should pass legislation which should apply to all the dwellers in Canada.

At the same time, while this view is destructive of the view urged by the Province as to how the observance of the international convention should be secured, it does not, they say, dispose of the whole of the question. They say it does not touch the consideration of inter-Provincial broadcasting. Now, much the same might have been said as to aeronautics. It is quite possible to fly without going outside the Province, yet that was not thought to disturb the general view, and once you come to the conclusion that the convention is binding on Canada as a Dominion, there are various sentences of the Board's judgment in the aviation case which might be literally transcribed to this. The idea pervading that judgment is that the whole subject of aeronautics is so completely covered by the treaty ratifying the convention between the nations, that there is not enough left to give a separate field to the Provinces as regards the subject. The same might at least very easily be said on this subject, but even supposing that it were possible to draw a rigid line between inter-Provincial and Dominion broadcasting, there is something more to be said. It will be found that the argument for the Provinces really depends on a complete difference being established between the operations of the transmitting and the receiving instruments. The Province admits that an improper use of a transmitting instrument could by invasion of a wave-length not assigned by international agreement to Canada bring into effect a breach of a clause of the convention. But it says this view does not apply to the operation of a receiving instrument. Now it is true that a dislocation of a receiving instrument will not in usual cases operate a disturbance beyond a comparatively limited circular area; although their Lordships understand that a receiving instrument could be so manipulated as to make its area of disturbance much larger than what is usually thought of.

But the question does not end with the consideration of the convention. Their Lordships draw special attention to the provisions of head 10 of s. 92. These provisions, as has been explained in several judgments of the Board, have the effect of reading the excepted matters into the preferential place enjoyed by the enumerated subjects of s. 91, and the exceptions run that the works or undertakings are to be other than such as are of the following classes:

(a) Lines of steam or other ships, railways, canals, telegraphs, and other works and undertakings connecting the Province with any other or others of the Provinces, or extending beyond the limits of the Province; (b) Lines of steamships between the Province and any British or foreign country; (c) Such works as, although wholly situate within the Province, are before or after their execution declared by the Parliament of Canada to be for the general advantage of Canada or for the advantage of two or more of the Provinces. Now, does broadcasting fall within the excepted matters? Their Lordships are of opinion that it does, falling in (a) within both the word "telegraphs" and the general words "undertakings connecting the Province with any other or others of the Provinces or extending beyond the limits of the Province."

The argument of the Province really depends on making, as already said, a sharp distinction between the transmitting and the receiving instrument. In their Lordships' opinion this cannot be done. Once it is conceded, as it must be, keeping in view the duties under the convention, that the transmitting instrument must be so to speak under the control of the Dominion, it follows in their Lordships' opinion that the receiving instrument must share its fate. Broadcasting as a system cannot exist without both a transmitter and a receiver. The receiver is indeed useless without a transmitter and can be reduced to a nonentity if the transmitter closes. The system cannot be divided into two parts, each independent of the other. . . . .

. . . Upon the whole matter, therefore, their Lordships have no hesitation in holding that the judgment of the majority of the Supreme Court was right, and their Lordships will therefore humbly advise His Majesty that the appeal should be dismissed. No costs will be awarded, this being a question to be decided between the Dominion and the Provinces.

Although the question had obviously to be decided on the terms of the statute, it is a matter of congratulation that the result arrived at seems consonant with common sense. A divided control between transmitter and receiver could only lead to confusion and inefficiency.

12. Attorney General of Canada *v.* Attorney General of Ontario (Employment and Social Insurance Act Reference), *1937*

~ The Employment and Social Insurance Act, 1935, which the Privy Council ruled *ultra vires* in this case, was the first measure of the Conservative government's social reform program (the so-called "New-Deal" legislation) which was introduced by Prime Minister R.B. Bennett at the beginning of the 1935 session of Parliament. The Liberal opposition under Mackenzie King's leadership, while approving the principle of the social legislation, contended that it was beyond Parliament's jurisdiction. Accordingly, following the defeat of the Bennett government in the general election of October, 1935, the King administration referred the question of the validity of eight of the reform measures of the 1935 session to the Supreme Court of Canada and then, on appeal to the Judicial Committee of the Privy Council. While the adversaries in all of these reference cases represented the two levels of government, in some of the cases provincial representatives supported the validity of the federal legislation. In this case, for instance, the Province of Ontario supported the federal government's side of the case, while New Brunswick was alone in maintaining the other side.

The Privy Council's decisions in these cases were a grave disappointment to those in Canada who had hoped that the powers assigned by the constitution to the central government would be sufficiently broad to enable it to deal effectively with the nation-wide consequence of a severe economic depression. The invalidation of five of the eight federal statutes submitted to the courts in this series of reference cases dashed the hopes raised by the Privy Council's recent decisions in the *Aeronautics* and *Radio* references, which had pointed to a much broader construction of the Dominion's legislative capacities. Among those who wished to strengthen the powers of the central government the immediate response was to turn to formal amendment of the B.N.A. Act to overcome what was regarded as the inappropriate division of powers being shaped by judicial review. The only real fruit of this renewal of interest in constitutional amendment was the amendment secured in 1940, which, with the unanimous consent of the provinces, assigned unemployment insurance to the exclusive jurisdiction of the federal Parliament.

Mr. Louis St. Laurent, who acted as legal counsel for the Dominion in this case, admitted that a scheme of unemployment insurance designed to have permanent effect could not be justified on emergency grounds. Instead, the case for bringing the legislation under the peace, order and good government power rested on both the residual aspect of that power and its application to matters of national concern. Council for the Dominion argued that the legislation attacked a problem which had not existed when the B.N.A. Act was drawn up and hence was not specifically provided for in any of the enumerated heads of sections 91 and 92. Further they urged that the problem of unemployment was one which threatened the well-being of the whole Dominion. Lord Atkin, speaking for the Judicial Committee, did not accept this reasoning. His reference to the lack of any special emergency sufficient to justify invoking the federal government's general power suggests an absorption of the residual and national importance phases of that power in the emergency power approach.

Lord Atkin also rejected the federal spending power as a constitutional basis for the unemployment insurance scheme. In doing so, he indicated one significant constitutional limit on the federal government's power to spend federal revenues. A federal spending program cannot take the form of a regulatory scheme which in pith and substance constitutes a regulation of civil rights in the province.

While the legislation considered in this case and in the two companion cases which follow was found unconstitutional, this was not the fate of all the New Deal legislation referred to the courts. A section of the Criminal Code prohibiting unfair competition, the Farmers' Creditors Arrangements Act reducing the mortgage liabilities of insolvent farmers, and legislation establishing a national trademark for products conforming to the requirements of government-established "Canada Standards," all survived judicial review. In upholding the last piece of legislation, the Judicial Committee reversed the Supreme Court of Canada and showed that some use could be made of the federal trade and commerce power as a basis for general regulations of trade affecting the whole Dominion. ~

ATTORNEY GENERAL OF CANADA v. ATTORNEY GENERAL OF ONTARIO
In the Privy Council. [1937] A.C. 355; III Olmsted 207

In the judgment of their Lordships was delivered by

LORD ATKIN. This is an appeal from the judgment of the Supreme Court, delivered on June 17, 1936, in the matter of a reference by the Governor-General in Council, dated November 5, 1935, asking whether the Employment and Social Insurance Act, 1935, was ultra vires of the Parliament of Canada. The majority of the Supreme Court, Rinfret, Cannon, Crocket, and Kerwin JJ., answered the question in the affirmative, the Chief Justice and Davis J. dissenting. The Act in its preamble recited art. 23 of the Treaty of Peace, by which in the Covenant of the League of Nations the members of the League agreed that they would endeavour to maintain fair and humane conditions of labour (omitting, however, in the recital that this agreement was subject to and in accordance with the provisions of international conventions existing or hereafter to be agreed), and art. 427 of the said treaty, by which it was declared that the well-being, physical, moral and intellectual, of industrial wage earners was of supreme international importance. It then recited that it was desirable to discharge the obligations to Canadian labour assumed under the provisions of the said treaty: and that it was essential for the peace, order and good government of Canada to provide for a national employment service and insurance against unemployment, etc. It consists of five Parts, Employment and Social Insurance Commission (ss. 4-9), Employment Service (ss. 10-14), Unemployment Insurance (ss. 15-38), National Health (ss. 39-41) and General (ss. 42-48). In substance the Act provides for a system of compulsory unemployment insurance. Part I sets up a commission charged with administering the Act and obtaining information and making proposals to the Governor in Council for making provision for the assistance of persons during unemployment who would not be entitled to unemployment insurance benefit under Part III. Part II provides for the organization by the commission of employment offices similar to the labour exchanges in the United Kingdom. Part III provides for unemployment insurance, while Part IV merely provides that the commission shall co-operate with other authorities in the Dominion or Provinces, and shall collect information concerning any plan for providing medical care or compensation in case of ill-health. Part V provides for regulations and reports. There are three schedules. The first defines employment within the meaning of Part III, and excepted employments, which include employment in agriculture and forestry, in fishing, and in lumbering and logging. The second enacts the weekly rates of contribution, and rules as to payment and recovery of contributions paid by employers on behalf of employed persons. The third enacts the rates of unemployment benefit, and supplementary provisions concerning the payment of unemployment benefit.

The substance of the Act is contained in the sections constituting Part III. They set up a now familiar system of unemployment insurance under which persons engaged in unemployment as defined in the Act are insured against unemployment. The funds required for making the necessary payments are to be provided partly from money provided by Parliament, partly from contributions by employed persons, and partly from contributions by the employers of those persons. The two sets of contributions are to be paid by revenue stamps. Every employed person and every employer is to be liable to pay contributions in accordance with the provisions of the second schedule, the employer being liable to pay both contributions in the first instance, recovering the employed person's share by deduction from his wages, or, if necessary, in certain cases by action.

There can be no doubt that, prima facie, provisions as to insurance of this kind, especially where they affect the contract of employment, fall within the class of property and civil rights in the Province, and would be within the exclusive competence of the Provincial Legislature. It was sought, however, to justify the validity of Dominion legislation on grounds which their Lordships on consideration feel compelled to reject. Counsel did not seek to uphold the legislation on the ground of the treaty-making power. There was no treaty or labour convention which imposed any obligation upon Canada to pass this legislation, and the decision on this question in the reference on the three labour Acts does not apply. A strong appeal, however, was made on the ground of the special importance of unemployment insurance in Canada at the time of, and for some time previous to, the passing of the Act. On this point it becomes unnecessary to do more than to refer to the judgment of this Board in the reference on the three labour Acts, and to the judgment of the Chief Justice in the Natural Products Marketing Act which, on this matter, the Board have approved and adopted. It is sufficient to say that the present Act does not purport to deal with any special emergency. It founds itself in the preamble on general world-wide conditions referred to in the Treaty of Peace: it is an Act whose operation is intended to be permanent: and there is agreement between all the members of the Supreme Court that it could not be supported upon the suggested existence of any special emergency. Their Lordships find themselves unable to differ from this view.

It only remains to deal with the argument which found favour with the Chief Justice and Davis J., that the legislation can be supported under the enumerated heads, 1 and 3 of s. 91 of the British North America Act, 1867: (1) The public debt and property, namely (3) The raising of money by any mode or system of taxation. Shortly stated, the argument is that the obligation imposed upon employers and persons employed is a mode of taxation: that the money so raised becomes public property, and that the Dominion have then complete legislative authority to direct that the money so raised, together with assistance from money raised by general taxation, shall be applied in forming an insurance fund and generally in accordance with the provisions of the Act.

That the Dominion may impose taxation for the purpose of creating a fund for special purposes, and may apply that fund for making contributions in the public interest to individuals, corporations or public authorities, could not as a general proposition be denied. Whether in such an Act as the present compulsion applied to an employed person to make a contribution to an insurance fund out of which he will receive benefit for a period proportionate to the number of his contributions is in fact taxation it is not necessary finally to decide. It might seem difficult to discern how it differs from a form of statutory obligation to pay insurance premiums to the State or to an insurance company. But assuming that the Dominion has collected by means of taxation a fund, it by no means follows that any legislation which disposes of it is necessarily within Dominion competence.

It may still be legislation affecting the classes of subjects enumerated in s. 92, and, if so, would be ultra vires. In other words, Dominion legislation, even though it deals with Dominion property, may yet be so framed as to invade civil rights within the Province, or encroach upon the classes of subjects which are reserved to Provincial competence. It is not necessary that it should be a colourable device, or a pretence. If on the true view of the legislation it is found that in reality in pith and substance the legislation invades civil rights within the Province, or in respect of other classes of subjects otherwise encroaches upon the provincial field, the legislation will be invalid. To hold otherwise would afford the Dominion an easy passage into the Provincial domain. In the present case, their Lordships agreed with the majority of the Supreme Court in holding that in pith and substance this Act is an insurance Act affecting the civil rights of employers and employed in each Province, and as such is invalid. The other parts of the Act are so inextricably mixed up with the insurance provisions of Part III that is impossible to sever them. It seems obvious, also, that in its truncated form, apart from Part III, the Act would never have come into existence. It follows that the whole Act must be pronounced ultra vires, and in accordance with the view of the majority of the Supreme Court their Lordships will humbly advise His Majesty that this appeal be dismissed.

13. Attorney General of British Columbia v. Attorney General of Canada (Natural Products Marketing Act Reference), *1937*

~ The Natural Products Marketing Act, 1934 (as amended in 1935) was another of the federal statutes submitted to the courts in the series of New Deal reference cases initiated by the King administration in 1935. This statute, provoked by the severe consequences of the worldwide depression in agricultural markets, was designed to provide orderly marketing arrangements for natural products. In framing the legislation the Dominion draughtsmen had been sensitive to the difficulties of divided jurisdiction in the field of marketing legislation and had included provisions which anticipated the need for co-operation between national and provincial marketing agencies. Indeed each of the nine provinces in 1934 had passed statutes designed to dovetail provincial coverage of marketing problems with Dominion legislation so that provincial and Dominion marketing boards could together deal completely with all the trade—domestic and foreign—in a given product. Despite this, Ontario, Quebec and New Brunswick before the Privy Council all supported the charge that the Dominion Act invaded provincial jurisdiction. British Columbia, however, argued in favour of upholding those parts of the federal Act relating to interprovincial and export trade.

Two earlier decisions of the Supreme Court had revealed the constraints which the application of a rigid constitution formula could impose upon effective government action in the field of marketing. In *The King* v. *Eastern Terminal Elevator Co.*,[1] a majority of the Court had thrown out the Canada Grain Act, 1912, which had provided a broad national scheme for regulating the marketing, grading, storing, and shipping of Canadian grain. The majority had reasoned that even though most of the grain affected by the Act was involved in export trade still the Act would also incidentally affect grain involved only in intra-provincial trade and hence it must be considered *ultra vires*. A few years later in *Lawson* v. *Interior Tree Fruit & Vegetable Committee of Direction*[2] the Supreme Court reversed its application of this rigid approach to marketing questions when it unanimously found the British Columbia Produce Marketing Act *ultra vires*. This Act provided for the regulation of marketing of all tree fruits and vegetables grown in a designated area in the province. Although the Act dealt with local trade, a substantial portion of the product subject to its provisions would be shipped outside the province. Because of its interference with interprovincial and export trade four of the five judges considered it infringed on Parliament's jurisdiction under section 91(2).

---

[1] [1925] S.C.R. 434.

[2] *Lawson* v. *Interior Tree Fruit & Vegetable Committee of Direction*, [1931] S.C.R. 357.

Coming after these decisions the Judicial Committee's (and the Supreme Court's) refusal to support the Dominion's Natural Products Marketing Act in this reference indicated that there were virtually insurmountable obstacles to the successful exercise of the federal commerce power in relation to export and interprovincial trade. Federal legislation designed to organize the export and interprovincial marketing of major crops or products to be valid could not touch any aspect of intra-provincial trade. But this line of cases also pointed to a possible no man's land where neither the Dominion nor the provinces could find constitutional support for effective marketing legislation. The fact that at the point where marketing legislation must take effect products often cannot be distinguished in terms of those destined for extra-provincial as opposed to those destined for intra-provincial markets made it doubtful whether Parliament or the provincial legislatures could regulate the marketing of products in which intra- and extra-provincial elements are inextricably combined. ~

ATTORNEY GENERAL OF BRITISH COLUMBIA v. ATTORNEY GENERAL OF CANADA
In the Privy Council. [1937] A.C. 377. III Olmsted 228.

The judgment of their Lordships was delivered by

LORD ATKIN. This is an appeal from the Supreme Court on a reference by the Governor-General in Council, dated November 5, 1935, raising the question whether the Natural Products Marketing Act, 1934, as amended by the Natural Products Marketing Act Amendment Act, 1935, is ultra vires of the Parliament of Canada. The Supreme Court unanimously answered the question in the affirmative.

The Act consists of two parts. The first provides for the establishment of a Dominion Marketing Board whose powers include powers to regulate the time and place at which, and the agency through which, natural products to which an approved scheme relates shall be marketed, and to determine the manner of distribution and the quantity, quality, grade or class of the product that shall be marketed by any person at any time, and to prohibit the marketing of any of the regulated products of any grade, quality or class.

There are other regulatory powers which need not be further specified. A scheme to regulate the marketing of a natural product is initiated by a representative number of persons engaged in the production or marketing of the natural product. It can be referred by the appropriate Minister to the Board, and if they approve the scheme as submitted or amended by them, and it is further approved by the Minister, the Governor-General in Council may approve the scheme. It is essential that the Governor-General in Council shall be satisfied either that the principal market for the natural product is outside the Province of production, or that some part of the product produced may be exported. The latter provision makes it clear that the regulation may apply to marketing transactions in natural products which have nothing to do with foreign export or inter-Provincial trade. If the Minister is satisfied that trade and commerce in a natural product are injuriously affected by the absence of a scheme prepared as above he may himself propose a scheme for approval of the Governor in Council. The Governor in Council is given power by order or regulation to regulate or restrict importation into Canada of a natural product which enters Canada in competition with a regulated product, and to regulate or restrict the exportation from Canada of any natural product. Part II contains provision for the appointment by the Minister of a Committee who may be entrusted with the duty of investigating all matters connected with the production or marketing of natural or regulated products for the purpose of ascertaining the charges made in distribution of a natural or regulated product. The receipt against the interest of the public of an excessive charge is made an indictable offence, and there are provisions for the trial of such offences.

There can be no doubt that the provisions of the Act cover transactions in any natural product which are completed within the Province, and have no connection with inter-Provincial or export trade. It is therefore plain that the Act purports to affect property and civil rights in the Province, and if not brought within one of the enumerated classes of subjects in s. 91 must be beyond the competence of the Dominion Legislature. It was sought to bring the Act within the class (2) of s. 91—namely, The Regulation of Trade and Commerce. Emphasis was laid upon those parts of the Act which deal with inter-Provincial and export trade. But the regulation of trade and commerce does not permit the regulation of individual forms of trade or commerce confined to the Province. In his judgment the Chief Justice says ([1936] Can. S.C.R. 412): "The enactments in question, therefore, in so far as they relate to matters which are in substance local and provincial are beyond the jurisdiction of Parliament. Parliament cannot acquire jurisdiction to deal in the sweeping way in which these enactments operate with such local and provincial matters by legislating at the same time respecting external and inter-provincial trade and committing the regulation of external and inter-provincial trade and the regulation of trade which is exclusively local and of traders and producers engaged in trade which is exclusively local to the same authority: *The King* v. *Eastern Terminal Elevator Co.* ([1925] Can. S.C.R. 434)."

Their Lordships agree with this, and find it unnecessary to add anything. There was a further attempt to support the Act upon the general powers to legislate for the peace, order and good government of Canada. Their Lordships have already dealt with this matter in their previous judgments in this series and need not repeat what is there said. The judgment of the Chief Justice in this case is conclusive against the claim for validity on this ground. In the result, therefore, there is no answer to the contention that the Act in substance invades the Provincial field and is invalid. . . .

~ Lord Atkin then dismissed the Dominion's request that the valid provisions of the Act be severed from the invalid provisions and allowed to stand alone. ~

The Board was given to understand that some of the Provinces attach much importance to the existence of marketing schemes such as might be set up under this legislation: and their attention was called to the existence of Provincial legislation setting up Provincial schemes for various Provincial products. It was said that as the Provinces and the Dominion between them possess a totality of complete legislative authority, it must be possible to combine Dominion and Provincial legislation so that each within its own sphere could in co-operation with the other achieve the complete power of regulation which is desired. Their Lordships appreciate the importance of the desired aim. Unless and until a change is made in the respective legislative functions of Dominion and Province it may well be that satisfactory results for both can only be obtained by co-operation. But the legislation will have to be carefully framed, and will not be achieved by either party leaving its own sphere and encroaching upon that of the other. In the present case their Lordships are unable to support the Dominion legislation as it stands. They will therefore humbly advise His Majesty that this appeal should be dismissed.

14. Attorney General of Canada *v.* Attorney General of Ontario (Labour Conventions Case), *1937*

~ The Canadian government first faced the question of whether it could "invade" provincial jurisdiction in order to carry out international labour conventions when Canada became a member of the International Labour Organization after World War I. At that time it took the cautious course and, following the advice of the federal Department of Justice, left the implementation of five of the six conventions adopted at the first session of the International Labour Conference to the provinces. This procedure was approved by the Supreme Court in 1925 when it was asked to review the proper method of implementing Canada's obligations as a participant in the International Labour Conference.[1] But in 1935 the Bennett government, emboldened by the outcome of the *Radio* case, tried to base an integral part of its New Deal program on the treaty implementing capacity of Parliament. Early in the 1935 session Parliament ratified Draft Conventions of the International Labour Organization dealing with hours of work, weekly rest and minimum wages and, later in the session, to give effect to these Conventions it passed the three Acts referred to in this case.

The Privy Council refused to accept the treaty implementing power as a constitutional support for the impugned labour legislation. Section 132 was ruled out on the grounds that even though the Treaty of Versailles was without question a British Empire treaty it had not obliged Canada to accede to the Conventions authorized by the labour part of the treaty. The Canadian government had acted on its own in deciding to ratify these Conventions. Lord Atkin who delivered the judgment also denied the interpretation of the *Radio* case that would justify characterizing the enforcement of independently negotiated treaties as a novel class of legislative matter and therefore subject to the Dominion's residual power. The regulation of radio communications as a new subject might rightly be regarded as falling under the residual power but legislation implementing Canadian treaties was not to be treated in the same way. On the contrary, the proper authority for enforcing a Canadian treaty would depend entirely on the subject matter of the treaty. If the treaty dealt with a subject that was normally under section 92, then legislation giving effect to it could be enacted only by the provincial legislatures.

Lord Atkin's judgment dealt a lethal blow to the doctrine that the national Parliament had a plenary power of implementing treaties. The federal legislature emerged from this decision subject to much more severe limitations on its power of performing international obligations than the federal constitutions of the United States or Austrialia impose on their central legislatures. Lord Atkin's approach in essence rendered the power of enforcing treaties thor-

---

[1] *In re Legislative Jurisdiction over Hours of Labour* [1925] S.C.R. 505.

oughly subject to the general division of powers in Canadian federalism. In effect this means that Canada cannot become a party to an international agreement which requires legislative action beyond the ambit of section 91 unless the prior approval of the provinces is first secured. While this has not prevented the Canadian government from participating in such important and extensive international undertakings as the United Nations Charter, still when an international arrangement such as the Universal Declaration of Rights has referred to matters which clearly come under section 92 of the B.N.A. Act, Canadian spokesmen have had to set appropriate qualifications to Canadian participation.

Most of those who have studied this area of Canadian constitutional law have found it difficult, if not impossible, to square Lord Atkin's judgment in the *Labour Conventions* case with Viscount Dunedin's in the *Radio* case. Certainly the fact that the composition of the Judicial Committee was completely different in the two cases did not contribute to continuity. Further, there is some evidence of a serious cleavage within the Judicial Committee on this case. In a speech published in 1955, Lord Wright, who had been a member of the Board which decided the *Labour Conventions* case, in a rare disclosure of dissent within the Privy Council, reported that there had been opposition to Lord Atkin's treatment of the treaty implementing power.[2] ~

ATTORNEY GENERAL OF CANADA *v.* ATTORNEY GENERAL OF ONTARIO
In the Privy Council. [1937] A.C. 327; III Olmsted 180.

The judgment of their Lordships was delivered by

LORD ATKIN. This is one of a series of cases brought before this Board on appeal from the Supreme Court of Canada on references by the Governor-General in Council to determine the validity of certain statutes of Canada passed in 1934 and 1935. Their Lordships will deal with all the appeals in due course, but they propose to begin with that involving The Weekly Rest in Industrial Undertakings Act, The Minimum Wages Act and The Limitation of Hours of Work Act, both because of the exceptional importance of the issues involved and because it affords them an opportunity of stating their opinion upon some matters which also arise in the other cases. At the outset they desire to express their appreciation of the valuable assistance which they have received from counsel, both for the Dominion and for the respective Provinces. No pains have been spared to place before the Board all the material both as to the facts and the law which could assist the Board in their responsible task. The arguments were cogent and not diffuse. The statutes in question in the present case were passed, as their titles recite, in accordance with conventions adopted by the International Labour Organization of the League of Nations in accordance with the Labour Part of the Treaty of Versailles of June 28, 1919. It was admitted at the bar that each statute affects property and civil rights within each Province; and that it was for the Dominion to establish that nevertheless the statute was validly enacted under

[2] (1955), 33 *Canadian Bar Review*, 1123.

the legislative powers given to the Dominion Parliament by the British North America Act, 1867. It was argued for the Dominion that the legislation could be justified either (1) under s. 132 of the British North America Act as being legislation "necessary or proper for performing the obligations of Canada, or of any Province thereof, as part of the British Empire, towards foreign countries, arising under treaties between the Empire and such foreign countries," or (2) under the general powers, sometimes called the residuary powers, given by s. 91 to the Dominion Parliament to make laws for the peace, order and good government of Canada in relation to all matters not coming within the classes of subjects by this Act assigned exclusively to the Legislatures of the Provinces.

The Provinces contended:

As to (1)—(a) That the obligations, if any, of Canada under the labour conventions did not arise under a treaty or treaties made between the Empire and foreign countries: and that therefore s. 132 did not apply. (b) That the Canadian Government had no executive authority to make any such treaty as was alleged. (c) That the obligations said to have been incurred, and the legislative powers sought to be exercised, by the Dominion were not incurred and exercised in accordance with the terms of the Treaty of Versailles.

As to (2), that if the Dominion had to rely only upon the powers given by s. 91, the legislation was invalid, for it related to matters which came within the classes of subjects exclusively assigned to the Legislatures of the Provinces—namely, property and civil rights in the Province.

In order to indicate the opinion of the Board upon these contentions it will be necessary briefly to refer to the Treaty of Versailles, Part XIII, Labour; to the procedure prescribed by it for bringing into existence labour conventions; and to the procedure adopted in Canada in respect thereto. The Treaty of Peace, signed at Versailles on June 28, 1919, was made between the Allied and Associated Powers of the one part and Germany of the other part. The British Empire was described as one of the Principal Allied and Associated Powers, and the High Contracting Party for the British Empire was His Majesty the King, represented generally by certain of his English Ministers, and represented for the Dominion of Canada by the Minister of Justice and the Minister of Customs, and for the other Dominions by their respective Ministers. The treaty began with Part I of the covenant of the League of Nations, by which the high contracting parties agreed to the covenant, the effect of which was that the signatories named in the annex to the covenant were to be the original members of the League of Nations. The Dominion of Canada was one of the signatories and so became an original member of the League. The treaty then proceeds in a succession of parts to deal with the agreed terms of peace, stipulations, of course, entered into not between members of the League, but between the high contracting parties, i.e., for the British Empire, His Majesty the King. Part XIII, entitled "Labour," after reciting that the object of the League of Nations is the establishment of universal peace, and that such a peace can only be established if it is based on social justice, and that social justice requires the improvement of conditions of labour throughout the world, provides that the high contracting parties agree to the establishment of a permanent organization for the promotion of the desired objects, and that the original and future members of the League of Nations shall be the members of this organization. The organization is to consist of a general conference of representatives of the members and an International Labour Office. After providing for meetings of the conference and for its procedure the treaty contains arts. 405 and 407:

~Lord Atkin then set out the two articles.~

In accordance with the provisions of Part XIII draft conventions were adopted by general conferences of the International Labour Organization as follows:

October 29—November 29, 1919, Conference.

Draft Convention limiting the hours of work in industrial undertakings.

October 25—November 19, 1921, Conference.

Draft Convention concerning the application of the weekly rest in industrial undertakings.

May 30—June 16, 1928. Conference.

Draft Convention concerning the creation of minimum wage-fixing machinery.

Each of the conventions included stipulations purporting to bind members who ratified it to carry out its provisions, the first two conventions by named dates—namely, July 1, 1921, and January 1, 1924, respectively. These three conventions were in fact ratified by the Dominion of Canada, Hours of Work on March 1, 1935, Weekly Rest on March 1, 1935, and Minimum Wages on April 12, 1935.

In each case in February and March, 1935, there had been passed resolutions of the Senate and House of Commons of Canada approving them. The ratification was approved by order of the Governor-General in Council, was recorded in an instrument of ratification executed by the Secretary of State for External Affairs for Canada, Mr. Bennett, and was duly communicated to the Secretary-General of the League of Nations. The statutes, which in substance give effect to the draft conventions, were passed by the Parliament of Canada and received the Royal Assent, "Hours of Work," on July 5, 1935, to come into force three months after assent; "Weekly Rest," on April 4, 1935, to come into force three months after assent; "Minimum Wage," on July 28, 1935, to come into force, so far as the convention provisions are concerned, when proclaimed by the Governor in Council, an event which has not yet happened. In 1925 the Governor-General in Council referred to the Supreme Court questions as to the obligations of Canada under the provisions of Part XIII of the Treaty of Versailles, and as to whether the Legislatures of the Provinces were the authorities

within whose competence the subject-matter of the conventions lay. The answers to the reference, which are to be found in *In re Legislative Jurisdiction over Hours of Labour* ([1925] Can. S.C.R. 505), were that the Legislatures of the Provinces were the competent authorities to deal with the subject-matter, save in respect of Dominion servants, and the parts of Canada not within the boundaries of any Province; and that the obligation of Canada was to bring the convention before the Lieutenant-Governor of each Province to enable him to bring the appropriate subject-matter before the Legislature of his Province, and to bring the matter before the Dominion Parliament in respect of so much of the convention as was within their competence. This advice appears to have been accepted, and no further steps were taken until those which took place as stated above in 1935.

Their Lordships, having stated the circumstances leading up to the reference in this case, are now in a position to discuss the contentions of the parties which were summarized earlier in this judgment. It will be essential to keep in mind the distinction between (1) the formation, and (2) the performance, of the obligations constituted by a treaty, using that word as comprising any agreement between two or more sovereign States. Within the British Empire there is a well-established rule that the making of a treaty is an executive act, while the performance of its obligations, if they entail alteration of the existing domestic law, requires legislative action. Unlike some other countries, the stipulations of a treaty duly ratified do not within the Empire, by virtue of the treaty alone, have the force of law. If the national executive, the government of the day, decide to incur the obligations of a treaty which involve alteration of law they have to run the risk of obtaining the assent of Parliament to the necessary statute or statutes. To make themselves as secure as possible they will often in such cases before final ratification seek to obtain from Parliament an expression of approval. But it has never been suggested, and it is not the law, that such an expression of approval operates as law, or that in law it precludes the assenting Parliament, or any subsequent Parliament, from refusing to give its sanction to any legislative proposals that may subsequently be brought before it. Parliament, no doubt, as the Chief Justice points out, has a constitutional control over the executive: but it cannot be disputed that the creation of the obligations undertaken in treaties and the assent to their form and quality are the function of the executive alone. Once they are created, while they bind the State as against the other contracting parties, Parliament may refuse to perform them and so leave the State in default. In a unitary State whose Legislature possesses unlimited powers the problem is simple. Parliament will either fulfil or not treaty obligations imposed upon the State by its executive. The nature of the obligations does not affect the complete authority of the Legislature to make them law if it so chooses. But in a State where the Legislature does not possess absolute authority, in a federal State where legislative authority is limited by a constitutional document, or is divided up between different Legislatures in accordance with the classes of subject matter submitted for legislation, the problem is complex. The obligations imposed by treaty may have to be performed, if at all, by several Legislatures; and the executive have the task of obtaining the legislative assent not of the one Parliament to whom they may be responsible, but possibly of several Parliaments to whom they stand in no direct relation. The question is not how is the obligation formed, that is the function of the executive; but how is the obligation to be performed, and that depends upon the authority of the competent Legislature or Legislatures. . . .

. . . The first ground upon which counsel for the Dominion sought to base the validity of the legislation was s. 132. So far as it is sought to apply this section to the conventions when ratified the answer is plain. The obligations are not obliga-

tions of Canada as part of the British Empire, but of Canada, by virtue of her new status as an international person, and do not arise under a treaty between the British Empire and foreign countries. This was clearly established by the decision in the *Radio* case ([1932] A.C. 304), and their Lordships do not think that the proposition admits of any doubt. It is unnecessary, therefore, to dwell upon the distinction between legislative powers given to the Dominion to perform obligations imposed upon Canada as part of the Empire by an Imperial executive responsible to and controlled by the Imperial Parliament, and the legislative power of the Dominion to perform obligations created by the Dominion executive responsible to and controlled by the Dominion Parliament. While it is true, as was pointed out in the *Radio* case, that it was not contemplated in 1867 that the Dominion would possess treaty-making powers, it is impossible to strain the section so as to cover the uncontemplated event. A further attempt to apply the section was made by the suggestion that while it does not apply to the conventions, yet it clearly applies to the Treaty of Versailles itself, and the obligations to perform the conventions arise "under" that treaty because of the stipulations in Part XIII. It is impossible to accept this view. No obligation to legislate in respect of any of the matters in question arose until the Canadian executive, left with an unfettered discretion, of their own volition acceded to the conventions, a novus actus not determined by the treaty. For the purposes of this legislation the obligation arose under the conventions alone. It appears that all the members of the Supreme Court rejected the contention based on s. 132, and their Lordships are in full agreement with them.

If, therefore, s. 132 is out of the way, the validity of the legislation can only depend upon ss. 91 and 92. Now it had to be admitted that normally this legislation came within the classes of subjects by s. 92 assigned exclusively to the Legislatures of the Provinces, namely—property and civil rights in the Province. This was in fact expressly decided in respect of these same conventions by the Supreme Court in 1925. How, then, can the legislation be within the legislative powers given by s. 91 to the Dominion Parliament? It is not within the enumerated classes of subjects in s. 91: and it appears to be expressly excluded from the general powers given by the first words of the section. It appears highly probable that some of the members of the Supreme Court would have departed from their decision in 1925 had it not been for the opinion of the Chief Justice that the judgments of the Judicial Committee in the *Aeronautics* case ([1932] A.C. 54) and the *Radio* case constrained them to hold that jurisdiction to legislate for the purpose of performing the obligation of a treaty resides exclusively in the Parliament of Canada. Their Lordships cannot take this view of those decisions. The *Aeronautics* case concerned legislation to perform obligations imposed by a treaty between the Empire and foreign countries. Sect. 132, therefore, clearly applied, and but for a remark at the end of the judgment, which in view of the stated ground of the decision was clearly obiter, the case could not be said to be an authority on the matter now under discussion. The judgment in the *Radio* case appears to present more difficulty. But when that case is examined it will be found that the true ground of the decision was that the convention in that case dealt with classes of matters which did not fall within the enumerated classes of subjects in s. 92, or even within the enumerated classes in s. 91. Part of the subject-matter of the convention, namely—broadcasting, might come under an enumerated class, but if so it was under a heading "Inter-provincial Telegraphs," expressly excluded from s. 92. Their Lordships are satisfied that neither case affords a warrant for holding that legislation to perform a Canadian treaty is exclusively within the Dominion legislative power.

For the purposes of ss. 91 and 92, i.e., the distribution of legislative powers between the Dominion and the Provinces, there is no such thing as treaty legislation as such. The distribution is based on classes of subjects; and as a treaty deals with a particular class of subjects so will the legislative power of performing it be ascertained. No one can doubt that this distribution is one of the most essential conditions, probably the most essential condition, in the inter-provincial compact to which the British North America Act gives effect. If the position of Lower Canada, now Quebec, alone were considered, the existence of her separate jurisprudence as to both property and civil rights might be said to depend upon loyal adherence to her constitutional right to the exclusive competence of her own Legislature in these matters. Nor is it of less importance for the other Provinces, though their law may be based on English jurisprudence, to preserve their own right to legislate for themselves in respect of local conditions which may vary by as great a distance as separates the Atlantic from the Pacific. It would be remarkable that while the Dominion could not initiate legislation, however desirable, which affected civil rights in the Provinces, yet its Government not responsible to the Provinces nor controlled by Provincial Parliaments need only agree with a foreign country to enact such legislation, and its Parliament would be forthwith clothed with authority to affect Provincial rights to the full extent of such agreement. Such a result would appear to undermine the constitutional safeguards of Provincial constitutional autonomy.

It follows from what has been said that no further legislative competence is obtained by the Dominion from its accession to international status, and the consequent increase in the scope of its executive functions. It is true, as pointed out in the judgment of the Chief Justice, that as the executive is now clothed with the powers of making treaties so the Parliament of Canada, to which the executive is responsible, has imposed upon it responsibilities in connection with such treaties, for if it were to disapprove of them they would either not be made or the Ministers would meet their constitutional fate. But this is true of all executive functions in their relation to Parliament. There is no existing constitutional ground for stretching the competence of the Dominion Parliament so that it becomes enlarged to keep pace with enlarged functions of the Dominion executive. If the new functions affect the classes of subjects enumerated in s. 92 legislation to support the new functions is in the competence of the Provincial Legislatures only. If they do not, the competence of the Dominion Legislature is declared by s. 91 and existed ab origine. In other words, the Dominion cannot, merely by making promises to foreign countries, clothe itself with legislative authority inconsistent with the constitution which gave it birth.

But the validity of the legislation under the general words of s. 91 was sought to be established not in relation to the treaty-making power alone, but also as being concerned with matters of such general importance as to have attained "such dimensions as to affect the body politic," and to have "ceased to be merely local or provincial," and to have "become matter of national concern.". . .

It is only necessary to call attention to the phrases in the various cases, "abnormal circumstances," "exceptional conditions," "standard of necessity" (*Board of Commerce* case ([1922] A.C. 191)), "some extraordinary peril to the national life of Canada," "highly exceptional," "epidemic of pestilence" (*Snider's* case ([1925] A.C. 396)), to show how far the present case is from the conditions which may override the normal distribution of powers in ss. 91 and 92. . . .

It must not be thought that the result of this decision is that Canada is incompetent to legislate in performance of treaty obligations. In totality of legislative powers, Dominion and Provincial together, she is fully equipped. But the legislative powers remain distributed, and if in the exercise of her new functions derived from her new international status Canada incurs obligations they must, so far as legislation be concerned, when they deal with Provincial classes of subjects, be dealt with by the totality of powers, in other words by co-operation between the Dominion and the Provinces. While the ship of state now sails on larger ventures and into foreign waters she still retains the watertight compartments which are an essential part of her original structure. The Supreme Court was equally divided and therefore the formal judgment could only state the opinions of the three judges on either side. Their Lordships are of opinion that the answer to the three questions should be that the Act in each case is ultra vires of the Parliament of Canada, and they will humbly advise His Majesty accordingly.

15. Atlantic Smoke Shops Limited *v.* Conlon, *1943*

~ There is one element in the division of powers about which the intentions of the framers of the constitution seem reasonably clear: in the allocation of financial powers the main sources of revenue were to be assigned to the federal government. While the B.N.A. Act restricts the provinces to "direct taxation within the province" (section 92[2]), it grants the central government the power to raise funds "by any mode or system of taxation" (section 91[3]). Section 122 explicitly brings customs and excise duties under the control of the Dominion. Thus, of the three main tax sources which existed in 1867, customs duties, excise duties and property taxes, the B.N.A. Act left only the latter field open to the provinces. However with the expansion of the role of government in general and of provincial responsibilities in particular there was increasing pressure on the provinces to develop new forms of taxation. This search for more revenue led provincial governments not only into such fields of taxation as income taxes and succession duties which were obviously direct but also into other areas of taxation such as corporation and sales taxes which were of more dubious constitutional propriety. These efforts gave rise to a series of challenges to the constitutional validity of provincial taxation measures. In most of these cases the question of whether or not the provincial tax was direct constituted the most serious test of its validity.

In *Bank of Toronto* v. *Lambe*,[1] decided in 1882, the Judicial Committee, in concluding that a Quebec tax on corporations was constitutional, adopted the distinction between direct and indirect taxation which is found in John Stuart Mill's classic work, *Principles of Political Economy*. According to Mill's definition a direct tax is one which is demanded from the very person who it is intended should pay it; whereas an indirect tax is one which is imposed on one person in the expectation that he will reimburse himself at the expense of another. But Lord Hobhouse stressed that the judiciary could not attempt to apply this economist's test of directness as an economist would by carefully tracing the real effects of the tax in order to ascertain its ultimate incidence. Instead, Mill's criterion was to be applied as a verbal formula to the language of taxing statutes. The mere possibility that someone subject to a tax might pass the burden on to someone else would in itself not constitute grounds for calling the tax indirect. A tax could be characterized as an indirect tax only if it had the general tendency of shifting the burden of taxation in an obviously traceable way to someone other than the actual taxpayer.

In succeeding cases Mill's definitions, offered at first with some diffidence as an indication of what the Fathers of Confederation must have had in mind in 1867, hardened into a firm principle of constitutional law. As a test of directness Mill's formula was qualified only by the rule that species of taxation which according to the common understanding in 1867 would obviously have been considered direct or indirect must continue to bear the same legal

---

[1] 12 App. Cas. 575.

character. It was on the basis of this principle that a local "business" tax was upheld as a direct tax by the Privy Council in 1928.[2]

As the provinces continued to seek new sources of revenue it became increasingly difficult to apply John Stuart Mill's distinction. For instance, in 1928 the Privy Council found that Alberta's mine owners tax was unconstitutional because it was imposed directly on producers and would most likely be passed on to consumers.[3] But six years later the Privy Council held that British Columbia's tax on consumers of fuel oil was direct and therefore constitutional because it was demanded from the very persons who the legislature intended should pay it.[4] The judges gave no weight to the tendency of consumers engaged in manufacturing, transportation or other service industries to pass the burden of the tax on to their customers.

The frequency with which the question of constitutional limitations on provincial taxation powers came up in cases before both the Supreme Court and the Privy Council reflected the continuing uncertainty in Canada over the financial powers of the provinces. In the 1930s the impact of the depression on traditional sources of revenue increased the provinces' interest in imposing retail sales taxes. But there were still grave doubts concerning the provinces' capacity under the B.N.A. Act for effectively entering the retail sales tax field. To remove these doubts the Dominion government, at the unanimous request of the provinces, agreed to seek an amendment to section 92(2) of the B.N.A. Act which would allow the provinces to impose a retail tax in the form of an indirect tax on the vendor. The resolution calling for this amendment was, however, defeated in the Senate. The attack on it was led by Arthur Meighen who argued that the power of imposing a sales tax would enable the provinces to erect what would amount to provincial tariff walls.

The Privy Council's decision in the *Atlantic Smoke Shops* case took a good deal of the steam out of the provinces' drive for a constitutional amendment. The New Brunswick tax challenged in this case was one imposed on anyone who purchased tobacco, by himself or through an agent, for his own consumption. It was also imposed on anyone who imported tobacco into New Brunswick for his own consumption. To obviate the charge that the burden of this tax, which was in effect a retail sales tax, would be shifted by the retailer to the purchaser, it had been so designed that the retailer became the tax-collector, collecting the tax directly from the consumer. A majority of the Supreme Court, while willing to uphold the tax as direct when levied on the actual consumer, ruled that it was indirect when imposed on the consumer's agent. The Privy Council denied the significance of this distinction and upheld the tax as direct and valid in all of its aspects.

---

[2] *Halifax* v. *Estate of Fairbanks* [1928] A.C. 117.

[3] *The King* v. *Caledonian Collieries Ltd.*, [1928] A.C. 358.

[4] *Attorney General of British Columbia* v. *Kingcome Navigation Co. Ltd.* [1934] A.C. 45.

Although this case had originated in private litigation between a retail tobacco company which had raised constitutional objections to the tax and the Tax Commissioner responsible for administering the tax, the federal government and most of the provinces intervened and supported their respective sides of the case before the Judicial Committee. The outcome was undoubtedly a victory for the provinces. In effect it reduced the provinces' difficulties in entering the retail sales tax field to one of shrewd draughtsmanship.

The result of this case which confirmed that it was possible to impose a tax on products imported into the province seemed, to some, to make a mockery of section 121 of the B.N.A. Act, which requires that the goods of any province be admitted free into each of the other provinces. But it should be noted that while, as a revenue-raising measure, a tax such as the one upheld in the *Atlantic Smoke Shops* case might perform the function of a customs duty, it could hardly perform the protective function of a tariff. ~

ATLANTIC SMOKE SHOPS LTD. *v.* CONLON
In the Privy Council. [1943] A.C. 550; III Olmsted 403.

The judgment of their Lordships was delivered by

VISCOUNT SIMON L.C. This appeal from a judgment of the Supreme Court of Canada raises the important and difficult question whether the Tobacco Act of New Brunswick, 1940 (4 Geo. 6, c. 44), and the regulations made thereunder are within the powers of the provincial legislature as constituting "direct taxation within the province," or whether, on the contrary, all or any part of these provisions must be held to be ultra vires having regard to the distribution of legislative powers effected by the British North America Act, 1867, and to the bearing of ss. 121 and 122 of the Act on provincial taxing powers.

The New Brunswick Tobacco Act is entitled "An Act to provide for imposing a tax on the consumption of tobacco." [His Lordship referred to ss. 2 to 10 of the Act and continued:] There are thus four applications of the tax provided for by ss. 4 and 5: (*a*) In its main and simplest form the tax is to be paid by anyone who purchases tobacco, as defined, for his own consumption (or for the consumption of other persons at his expense) from a retail vendor in the province. The tax amounts to ten per cent on the retail price charged on the sale. By regulations made under s. 20 of the Act it is to be collected by the retail vendor, who is constituted an agent of the minister for the collection of tax, and has to give a receipt for the tax to the customer and account to the Tobacco Tax Commissioner for the tax thus collected, subject to the allowance of three per cent as remuneration. (*b*) If the purchase from the retail vendor is made by an agent acting for a principal, who desires to acquire such tobacco for his own consumption (or for the consumption of other persons at his expense), the tax is payable by the agent. It is, however, clear that if the agent has not already been put in funds by his principal, he will be entitled to be indemnified by his principal for the tax, no less than for the purchase price. In both cases ((*a*) and (*b*)) the tax is payable at the time of making the purchase. (*c*) If a person residing or ordinarily resident or carrying on business in New Brunswick brings into the province such tobacco, or receives delivery of it in the province, for his own consumption (or for the consumption of other persons at his expense), he is to report the matter to the minister, with any invoice and other information required, and he becomes liable to pay the same tax as would have been payable if the tobacco had been purchased at a retail sale in the province. (*d*) Lastly, if such a person as is last described brings the tobacco into the province, or receives delivery there, as agent for a principal who desires to acquire it for his own consumption (or for the consumption of other persons at his expense), the agent is put under a similar obligation to report and to pay an equivalent tax. It may be noted that in this last case the principal is not in express terms limited to a prinicpal within the province. This is perhaps implied, but, in any event, the instance of an agent within the province acting for a principal outside can seldom occur.

A striking difference of opinion has disclosed itself in the Canadian courts as to the validity of this taxing legislation. In the Supreme Court of New Brunswick, Baxter C.J. and his two colleagues, Grimmer and Richards J.J., held that the tax was valid. Applying the definition of a direct tax which was used by Lord Hobhouse in *Bank of Toronto* v. *Lambe* (12 App. Cas. 575, 582), and which is derived from John Stuart Mill's "Principles of Political Economy" (bk. V. c. 3) as "one which is demanded from the very persons who it is intended or desired should pay it," they held that the tax in all its forms was a direct tax and within the power of the provincial legislature to impose. On appeal to the Supreme Court of Canada, conflicting views were expressed, and these need to be carefully analysed.

~ His Lordship then stated the conclusions reached by the individual judges. ~

. . . In the result, therefore, the majority of the Supreme Court of Canada decided that the tax in the forms (*a*) and (*c*) was valid, but that it was invalid in the forms (*b*) and (*d*), since these latter forms involved taxation of an agent, whereas the burden of the taxation would fall on his principal. The arguments addressed to the Board, which included arguments on behalf of the Attorney-General for Canada supporting the appellants, and of other interveners representing Quebec and five other provinces supporting the respondents, ranged over all aspects of the tax, and their Lordships are requested to reach a conclusion as to the validity or non-validity of the tax in all its forms.

Their Lordships must first consider whether the tax in the form (*a*) is a valid exercise of provincial legislative powers. It has been long and firmly established that, in interpreting the phrase "direct taxation" in head 2 of s. 92 of the Act of 1867, the guide to be followed is that provided by the distinction between direct and indirect taxes which is to be found in the treatise of John Stuart Mill. The question, of course, as Lord Herchell said in *Brewers and Maltsters' Association of Ontario* v. *Attorney-General for Ontario* ([1897] A.C. 231, 236), is not what is the distinction drawn by writers on political economy, but in what sense the words were employed in the British North America Act. Mill's *Political Economy* was first published in 1848, and appeared in a popular edition in 1865. Its author became a member of parliament in this latter year and commanded much attention in the British House of Commons. Having regard to his eminence as a political economist in the epoch when the Quebec Resolutions were being discussed and the Act of 1867 was being framed, the use of Mill's analysis and classification of taxes for the purpose of construing the expression now under review is fully justified. In addition to the definition from Mill's *Political Economy* already quoted, citations may be made of two other passages as follows: "Direct taxes are either on income or on expenditure. Most taxes on expenditure are indirect, but some are direct, being imposed not on the producer or seller of an article, but immediately on the consumer" (bk. V. ch. 3). And again, in ch. 6, in discussing the comparative merits of the two types of tax, he takes as the essential feature of direct taxation that "under it everyone knows how much he really pays.'' Their Lordships, therefore, consider that this tobacco tax in the form they have called (*a*) would fall within the conception of a ''direct'' tax, and ought so to be treated in applying the British North America Act. It is a tax which is to be paid by the last purchaser of the article, and, since there is no question of further re-sale, the tax cannot be passed on to any other person by subsequent dealing. The money for the tax is found by the individual who finally bears the burden of it. It is unnecessary to consider the refinement which might arise if the taxpayer who has purchased the tobacco for his own consumption subsequently changes his mind and in fact re-sells it. If so, he would, for one thing, require a retail vendor's licence. But the instance is exceptional and farfetched, while for the purpose of classifying the tax, it is the general tendency of the impost which has to be considered. So regarded, it completely satisfies Mill's test for direct taxation. Indeed, the present instance is a clearer case of direct taxation than the tax on the consumer of fuel oil in *Attorney-General for British Columbia* v. *Kingcome Navigation Co.* ([1934] A.C. 45), for fuel oil may be consumed for the purpose of manufacture and transport, and the tax on the consumption of fuel oil might, as one would suppose, be sometimes passed on in the price of the article manufactured or transported. Yet the Privy Council held that the tax was direct. In the case of tobacco, on the other hand, the consumer produces nothing but smoke. Mr. Pritt argued that the tax is a sales tax, and that a sales tax is indirect because it can be passed on. The ordinary forms of sales taxes are, undoubtedly, of this character, but it would be more accurate to say that a sales tax is indirect when in the normal course it can be passed on. If a tax is so devised that (as Mill expresses it) the taxing authority is not indifferent as to which of the parties to the transaction ultimately bears the burden, but intends it as a ''peculiar contribution'' on the particular party selected to pay the tax, such a tax is not proved to be indirect by calling it

a sales tax. Previous observation by this Board as to the general character of sales taxes, or of taxes on commercial dealings, ought not to be understood as denying the possibility of this exception.

There remains, on this first head, the question whether, notwithstanding that the tax in the form (*a*) is ''direct'' within Mill's test, it is none the less beyond the powers of the province to impose as being in the nature of ''excise'' in the sense that the attempted imposition would be an alteration of the ''excise laws'' of New Brunswick which the provincial legislature is debarred from affecting under s. 122 of the British North America Act. ''Excise'' is a word of vague and somewhat ambiguous meaning. Dr. Johnson's famous definition in his dictionary is distinguished by acerbity rather than precision. The word is usually (though by no means always) employed to indicate a duty imposed on home-manufactured articles in the course of manufacture before they reach the consumer. So regarded, an excise duty is plainly indirect. . . . Their Lordships do not find it necessary in the present case to determine whether this tobacco tax in the form (*a*) is for any purpose analogous to an excise duty, for it is enough to accept and apply the proposition laid down on behalf of this Board by Lord Thankerton in the *Kingcome* case, namely, ''that if the tax is demanded from the very persons who it is intended or desired should pay it, the taxation is direct, and that it is none the less direct, even if it might be described as an excise tax'' ([1934] A.C. 45, 55). . .

Next comes the question whether the tax, though ''direct'' when the principal deals personally with the retail vendor across the counter, ceases to be ''direct'' if the purchase is made by an agent acting for his principal. Their Lordships have already pointed out that in this case also the person who bears the tax is really the principal, either because he has already given his agent the money to pay it or because he is bound forthwith to repay his agent for the expense incurred with his authority and on his behalf. This indemnification does not follow because there is any fresh transaction analogous to re-sale after the purchase by the agent has been made. It is part and parcel of a single transaction. The agent pays the tax for and on behalf of his principal. If, indeed, the agent gave the name of his principal to the vendor the contract of sale would be with the principal. If there was anything to complain of in the quality of the article it would be the principal, whether named or not, who might have a remedy against the vendor. It is said that the tax in this second form is not direct because the agent, who is personally liable for the tax and has to pay it when receiving the tobacco, is distinct from the principal who bears the burden of the duty, but, in their Lordships' opinion, this circumstance does not, according to the distinction laid down by Mill, prevent the tax from being a direct tax. . . . Their Lordships find it impossible to suppose that, in applying the economic distinction which is at the bottom of Mill's contrast, it would be correct to call this tax "direct" if a man bought a packet of cigarettes over the counter by putting his hand in his pocket and paying price and tax himself to the vendor, but "indirect" if he stood outside the shop and gave his wife the necessary amount to get the cigarettes and pay the tax for him. . . . Their Lordships, therefore, take the view that the tax imposed by s. 4 of the Act is valid both in the form (a) and in the form (b).

For the same reasons, and apart from other considerations which apply only to s. 5, their Lordships are of opinion that the tax is valid in the forms (c) and (d), but the tax imposed by s. 5 raises difficulties of a different order. It is manifest that s. 5 is enacted merely as a supplementary provision, to guard against the methods of avoidance of s. 4 which might otherwise remain available. At the same time, the validity of s. 5 must be judged according to its terms, and, if its enactment by the provincial legislature be beyond the powers of that legislature, it cannot be justified on the ground that it is needed to make the whole scheme watertight.

Objection is taken to the validity of s. 5 on the alleged ground that it offends against ss. 121 and 122 of the British North America Act. When the scheme of Canadian federation is considered as a whole, the purpose and effect of these two sections seem plain enough. Previous to the date of federation, each province was a separate unit raising part of its revenue by customs duties on certain commodities imported from outside—it might even be from another province. One essential purpose of federating such units is that they should cease to maintain customs barriers against the produce of one another, and hence s. 121, supplemented by s. 123, established internal free trade from July 1, 1867, which was the date proclaimed for the Union. It was not, however, practicable to abolish provincial customs entirely on that date. Ordinary customs and excise are, as Mill's treatise shows, the classical examples of indirect taxation, and thus fell thenceforward within the exclusive legislative competence of the Dominion parliament. But until the Dominion had imposed and collected sufficient taxes on its own account, it was desirable to continue to gather in the revenue arising from the customs and excise laws of the provinces (with the exception of interprovincial import duties), though it would appear from the s. 102 of the British North America Act that after federation the proceeds passed into the consolidated revenue fund of the Dominion. A Dominion tariff has long since been enacted and the customs and excise laws of the different provinces have been brought to an end by Dominion legislation. The question, therefore, on this part of the case, which has to be determined is whether s. 5 of the New Brunswick Act is invalid as amounting to an attempt by the province to tax in disregard of the restrictions contained in ss. 121 and 122 of the constitution. If s. 5 purports to impose a duty of customs, it is wholly invalid, and, if it denies free admission of tobacco into New Brunswick, it is invalid so far as this refers to tobacco manufactured in another province of Canada. Their Lordships have reached the conclusion that s. 5 does not impose a customs duty, and they adopt the reasoning on this point of Rinfret J. and Crocket J. The argument to the contrary is the argument that failed in the *Kingcome* case. Lord Thankerton pointed out the distinction in his judgment in that case when he said: "Customs and excise duties are, in their essence, trading taxes, and may be said to be more concerned with the commodity in respect of which the taxation is imposed than with the particular person from whom the tax is exacted" (Ibid. 59 (A.C.)). Here the tax is not imposed on the commodity as such at all, and is not imposed on anyone as a condition of its lawful receipt. The "particular person" from whom the tax is exacted is the recipient in the province only if he is the prospective smoker, and, as Lord Hobhouse said in *Bank of Toronto* v. *Lambe*, "any person found within the province may legally be taxed there if taxed directly." Their Lordships agree with the majority of the Supreme Court that this is not a duty of customs.

Similar considerations dispose of the contention that, as applied to the recipient of tobacco manufactured in another province, the tax offends s. 121. Here again, it is important to remember the special feature of the tax that it is imposed as a direct tax on the consumer. Sect. 121 was the subject of full and careful exposition by the Supreme Court of Canada in *Gold Seal Ltd.* v. *Attorney-General for Alberta* ([1921] 62 S.C.R. [Can.] 424,

439), where the question arose whether the parliament of Canada could validly prohibit the importation of intoxicating liquor into those provinces where its sale for beverage purposes was forbidden by provincial law. The meaning of s. 121 cannot vary according as it is applied to dominion or to provincial legislation, and their Lordships agree with the interpretation put on the section in the *Gold Seal* case. Duff J. held that "the phraseology adopted, when the context is considered in which the section is found, shows, I think, that the real object of the clause is to prohibit the establishment of customs duties affecting interprovincial trade in the products of any province of the union" (Ibid. 456 (A.C.)). . . . These considerations make it clear that if s. 5 of the Tobacco Tax Act is not obnoxious to s. 122 of the British North America Act, it is also free from objection on the score of s. 121. That the tax is taxation within the province is, their Lordships think, clear for the reasons given by Taschereau J.

Their Lordships will humbly advise His Majesty that the appeal fails and that the Tobacco Tax Act, 1940, is in all respects a valid exercise of the powers of the legislature of the province of New Brunswick. The order of the Supreme Court must, therefore, be varied by omitting the words "with the exception of the provisions thereof making the agent liable for the tax."

16. Attorney General of Ontario v. Canada Temperance Federation, *1946*

~ This case originated in 1939 when the Government of Ontario referred the question of the validity of the Canada Temperance Act, 1927, to the Supreme Court of Ontario. As this Act had substantially the same provisions as the Act which had been upheld in 1882 by the Judicial Committee in *Russell* v. *The Queen*, the real object of the reference was to challenge that decision and consolidate the much narrower construction of the peace, order and good government clause which the Privy Council had been developing since 1882. This challenge to the central Parliament's legislative capacities brought about a major confrontation of the two levels of government. The Attorneys General of Alberta and New Brunswick intervened to support Ontario and received further support from both Nova Scotia and Saskatchewan.

The Board's judgment, delivered by Viscount Simon, constitutes a sharp break from the Privy Council's restrictive interpretation of Parliament's general power. Viscount Simon not only refuted the explanation of *Russell* v. *The Queen* which Viscount Haldane had provided in the *Snider* case[1] but also undermined the emergency doctrine as the proper test for determining whether legislation that affects a matter normally under provincial jurisdiction can be brought under the federal peace, order and good government power. According to his reasoning the validity of Dominion legislation does not depend on the existence of an emergency but on the subject matter of the legislation: "if it is such that it goes beyond local or provincial concern or interests and must from its inherent nature be the concern of the Dominion as a whole . . . then it will fall within the competence of the Dominion Parliament as a matter affecting the peace, order and good government of Canada, though it may in another aspect touch on matters specially reserved to the Provincial Legislatures." Despite Viscount Simon's disavowal of any intention of embarking on a fresh interpretation of the relationship between sections 91 and 92, his words in effect provided jurists in later cases with a method of constructing the peace, order and good government clause which is an important alternative to the emergency power conception.

In the Privy Council's few remaining years as Canada's final court of appeal there were only two more cases which tested their Lordship's approach to the opening words of Section 91. In neither of these did the Privy Council show any inclination to follow the path opened up by Viscount Simon's judgment in the *Canada Temperance Federation* case. On the contrary, its decision in both of these cases suggested a return to the emergency doctrine. The 1946 decision upholding the federal government's deportation of Japanese Canadians under the general power was based entirely on the grounds of wartime and postwar emergency.[2] In 1951 the Judicial Committee rejected the attempt to use

---

[1] See above p. 77.

[2] *Co-operative Comm. on Japanese Canadians* v. *A.-G. Canada*, [1947] A.C. 87.

Viscount Simon's reasoning as a means of bringing federal legislation prohibiting the sale of margarine in Canada under Parliament's general power. In dismissing this ground for validating the legislation the judgment referred to the absence of any conditions grave enough to justify invoking the Dominion's general power and implied that the exercise of that power entails an overriding of the normal distribution of powers in sections 91 and 92.[3] ~

ATTORNEY GENERAL OF ONTARIO *v.* CANADA TEMPERANCE FEDERATION
In the Privy Council. [1946] *A.C. 193; III Olmsted 424.*

The judgment of their Lordships was delivered by

VISCOUNT SIMON. On June 1, 1939, the Lieutenant-Governor of Ontario in Council referred to the Supreme Court of Ontario under the provisions of the Constitutional Questions Act, R.S.O., c. 130, the following question: "Are Parts I, II and III of the Canada Temperance Act, R.S.C. 1927, c. 196, constitutionally valid in whole or in part, and if in part, in what respect?" On September 26, 1939, the Supreme Court by a majority (Riddell, Fisher, McTague and Gillanders, JJ.A.) answered the question as follows: "This court is of opinion (Henderson J. dissenting) that Parts I, II and III of the Canada Temperance Act, R.S.C. 1927, c. 196, are within the legislative competence of the Parliament of Canada." Against this judgment the Attorney-General for Ontario and the Moderation League of Ontario have appealed to the Judicial Committee, and their appeal has been supported by the Attorneys-General for Alberta and New Brunswick, who were admitted as interveners and were represented on the hearing. The appeal was opposed by counsel appearing for the Attorney-General for Canada and for several Temperance Federations.

The object of the appeal is to challenge the decision of this Board in the case of *Russell* v. *The Queen* (7 App. Cas. 829),

or at any rate to deny its applicability to the Act now in question. The majority of the Supreme Court held that that decision governed the present case and obliged it to answer the question referred to it in the affirmative. The statute which was declared to be within the legislative competence of the Dominion Parliament in *Russell's* case was the Canada Temperance Act, 1878. That Act has been amended from time to time by the Dominion Parliament, and has been revised and re-enacted in a consolidated form on more than one occasion under the provisions of the Acts relating to the revision of Statutes of Canada. The last revision took place in 1927 under the provisions of the Dominion Act, 1924 (14 & 15 Geo 5, c. 65) and now appears on the Statute Roll as the Canada Temperance Act, R.S.C. of 1927, c. 196. The material provisions of the Act of 1927 are admittedly identical with those of the Act of 1878.

~ Viscount Simon then stated the main provisions of the Canada Temperance Act, 1878. Following this he stated the grounds of the Judicial Committee's decision in *Russell* v. *The Queen* and traced the citation of that case by the Privy Council in subsequent decisions. ~

But in 1925 *Russell's* case was commented on in a judgment of the Judicial Committee delivered by Lord Haldane in *Toronto Electric Commissioners* v.

---

[3] *Canadian Federation of Agriculture* v. *A.-G. Quebec.* [1951] A.C. 198.

Snider ([1925] A.C. 396), and it is on this comment that the present appellants largely rely in support of their contention that it was wrongly decided. After contrasting that case with other decisions of the Board already mentioned above, Lord Haldane said: "It appears to their Lordships that it is not now open to them to treat *Russell* v. *The Queen* as having established the general principle that the mere fact that Dominion legislation is for the general advantage of Canada, or is such that it will meet a mere want which is felt throughout the Dominion, renders it competent if it cannot be brought within the heads enumerated specifically in s. 91. . . . No doubt there may be cases arising out of some extraordinary peril to the national life of Canada, as a whole, such as the cases arising out of a war, where legislation is required of an order that passes beyond the heads of exclusive Provincial competency" ([1925] A.C. 412). And later he said "Their Lordships think that the decision in *Russell* v. *The Queen* can only be supported today, not on the footing of having laid down an interpretation, such as has sometimes been invoked, of the general words at the beginning of s. 91, but on the assumption of the Board, apparently made at the time of deciding the case of *Russell* v. *The Queen*, that the evil of intemperance at that time amounted in Canada to one so great and so general that at least for the period it was a menace to the national life of Canada so serious and pressing that the National Parliament was called on to intervene to protect the nation from disaster. An epidemic of pestilence might conceivably have been regarded as analogous" ([1937] A.C. 863).

The first observation which their Lordships would make on this explanation of *Russell's* case is that the British North America Act nowhere gives power to the Dominion Parliament to legislate in matters which are properly to be regarded as exclusively within the competence of the provincial legislatures merely because of the existence of an emergency. Secondly, they can find nothing in the judgment of the Board in 1882 which suggests that it proceeded on the ground of emergency; there was certainly no evidence before the Board that one existed. The Act of 1878 was a permanent, not a temporary, Act, and no objection was raised to it on that account. In their Lordships' opinion, the true test must be found in the real subject matter of the legislation: if it is such that it goes beyond local or provincial concern or interests and must from its inherent nature be the concern of the Dominion as a whole (as, for example, in the *Aeronautics* case ([1932] A.C. 54) and the *Radio* case ([1932] A.C. 304), then it will fall within the competence of the Dominion Parliament as a matter affecting the peace, order and good government of Canada, though it may in another aspect touch on matters specially reserved to the provincial legislatures. War and pestilence, no doubt, are instances; so, too, may be the drink or drug traffic, or the carrying of arms. In *Russell* v. *The Queen*, Sir Montague Smith gave as an instance of valid Dominion legislation a law which prohibited or restricted the sale or exposure of cattle having a contagious disease. Nor is the validity of the legislation, when due to its inherent nature, affected because there may still be room for enactments by a provincial legislature dealing with an aspect of the same subject in so far as it specially affects that province.

It is to be noticed that the Board in *Snider's* case nowhere said that *Russell* v. *The Queen* was wrongly decided. What it did was to put forward an explanation of what it considered was the ground of the decision, but in their Lordships' opinion the explanation is too narrowly expressed. True it is that an emergency may be the occasion which calls for the legislation, but it is the nature of the legislation itself, and not the existence of emergency, that must determine whether it is valid or not.

The appellants' first contention is that *Russell's* case was wrongly decided and ought to be overruled. Their Lordships do not doubt that in tendering humble advice to His Majesty they are not absolutely bound by previous decisions of the Board, as is the House of Lords by its own judgments. In ecclesiastical appeals, for instance, on more than one occasion, the Board has tendered advice contrary to that given in a previous case, which further historical research has shown to have been wrong. But on constitutional questions it must be seldom indeed that the Board would depart from a previous decision which it may be assumed will have been acted on both by governments and subjects. In the present case the decision now sought to be overruled has stood for over sixty years; the Act has been put into operation for varying periods in many places in the Dominion; under its provisions businesses must have been closed, fines and imprisonments for breaches of the Act have been imposed and suffered. Time and again the occasion has arisen when the Board could have overruled the decision had it thought it wrong. Accordingly, in the opinion of their Lordships, the decision must be regarded as firmly embedded in the constitutional law of Canada, and it is impossible now to depart from it. Their Lordships have no intention, in deciding the present appeal, of embarking on a fresh disquisition as to relations between ss. 91 and 92 of the British North America Act, which have been expounded in so many reported cases; so far as the Canada Temperance Act, 1878, is concerned the question must be considered as settled once and for all.

The second contention of the appellants was that in 1927, when the statute now in force was enacted, there were no circumstances which enabled the Parliament of the Dominion to legislate anew. As has already been said, the Act of 1927 is, in all respects material for this appeal, identical in its terms with the Act of 1878, and also with the Act of 1886, which itself was a revised edition of 1878 and was the Act in force in 1896 when the case of *Att.-Gen. for Ontario* v. *Att.-Gen. for the Dominion* ([1896] A.C. 348) was heard. It was not contended that if the Act of 1878 was valid when it was enacted it would have become invalid later on by a change of circumstances, but it was sub-

mitted that as that Act and the Act of 1886 have been repealed, the Act of 1927 was new legislation and consequently circumstances must exist in 1927 to support the new Act. Then it was said (and this, apparently, was the opinion of Henderson J.A., who dissented from the other members of the Supreme Court of Ontario) that no circumstances could exist in 1927 to support the Act, in view of the legislation that had been passed in the provinces, including Ontario, for the regulation of the liquor traffic. Their Lordships do not find it necessary to consider the true effect either of s. 5 or s. 8 of the Act of 1924 for the revision of the Statutes of Canada, for they cannot agree that if the Act of 1878 was constitutionally within the powers of the Dominion Parliament it could be successfully contended that the act of 1927 which replaced it was ultra vires. The same ground is not covered by provincial legislation setting up a licensing system and making the sale of a liquor a government monopoly. Moreover, if the subject-matter of the legislation is such that it comes within the province of the Dominion Parliament that legislature must, as it seems to their Lordships, have power to re-enact provisions with the object of preventing a recurrence of a state of affairs which was deemed to necessitate the earlier statute. To legislate for prevention appears to be on the same basis as legislation for cure. A pestilence has been given as an example of a subject so affecting, or which might so affect, the whole Dominion that it would justify legislation by the Parliament of Canada as a matter concerning the order and good government of the Dominion. It would seem to follow that if the Parliament could legislate when there was an actual epidemic it could do so to prevent one occurring and also to prevent it happening again. Once it has been decided that the Act of 1878 was constitutionally valid, it follows that an Act which replaces it and consolidates therewith the various amending Acts that have from time to time been enacted must be equally valid. . . .

17. Attorney General of Ontario *v.* Attorney General of Canada (References re Abolition of Privy Council Appeals), *1947*

~ In this decision the Judicial Committee of the Privy Council upheld the federal Parliament's power to abolish all Canadian appeals to the Privy Council and to make the Supreme Court Canada's highest court of appeal. Legislation to accomplish this purpose had been introduced in the House of Commons in 1939. The legislation took the form of an amendment to the Supreme Court Act under which the Supreme Court would exercise "exclusive ultimate appellate civil and criminal jurisdiction within and for Canada."

When the original Supreme Court Act was enacted in 1875, Sir John A. Macdonald's Conservatives had opposed severing Canada's judicial link with the Empire. But by the 1930s, with growth of Canadian nationalism and the acquisition of Dominion autonomy, the abolition of appeals was supported by all three national political parties. The antagonism aroused amongst English Canada's political and legal elite by the Privy Council's interpretation of the B.N.A. Act, especially its decisions on the New Deal legislation, further fuelled the fires of judicial nationalism. However, this factor was not publicly acknowledged as a reason for abolition by federal political leaders as they did not wish to arouse provincial sensitivities by implying that they hoped the Supreme Court of Canada would adopt a more centralist approach to constitutional interpretation.

The passage of the State of Westminster in 1931 meant that the power to abolish appeals to Britain now rested in Canada. The Privy Council's decision in the *British Coal Corporation*[1] case in 1935 upholding a section of the Criminal Code cutting off Privy Council appeals in criminal cases made it clear that Parliament could abolish appeals with respect to cases involving federal laws. The only major constitutional doubt that remained was whether the federal Parliament could also abolish appeals concerning provincial laws. This issue was referred to the Supreme Court in 1940 and, in a four-to-two decision, resolved in the federal Parliament's favour. This decision was appealed to the Privy Council by four provinces (British Columbia, New Brunswick, Ontario and Quebec), while two provinces (Manitoba and Saskatchewan) supported the federal government. The hearing of the appeal was postponed until after the war.

Lord Jowitt's opinion upholding federal power under section 101 of the B.N.A. Act to abolish appeals in all matters of law is remarkable for the connection it makes between Canada's becoming independent of Great Britain in 1931 and the powers of the federal level of government within Canada. One reason Jowitt advanced for holding that the federal Parliament should control

---

[1] [1935] A.C. 500.

appeals in cases relating to provincial laws as well as in cases relating to federal laws was that being able "to secure through its own courts of justice that the law should be one and the same for all citizens" is a "prime element in the self-government of the Dominion." This holding also indicates how far the Judicial Committee would go in attributing a unitary judicial structure to Canada in contrast to its solicitude for the division of legislative powers.

The amendment making the Supreme Court Canada's ultimate court of appeal was finally enacted in 1949. No cases instituted after that date could be appealed to the Privy Council. However, cases which had commenced prior to that date could be appealed so that nearly a decade elapsed before Canada's judicial self-government was in fact complete. ~

ATTORNEY GENERAL OF ONTARIO v. ATTORNEY GENERAL OF CANADA
In the Privy Council. [1947] A.C. 128; III Olmsted 508

The judgment of their Lordships was delivered by

LORD JOWITT, L.C. This appeal is brought from the judgment of the Supreme Court of Canada, given on January 19, 1940, on a question which was referred to that court under provisions of s. 55 of the Supreme Court Act, R.S.C. 1927, ch. 35. From the recitals contained in the order of reference, which was made by the Governor-General in Council on April 21, 1939, it appears that, at the Fourth Session of the Eighteenth Parliament of Canada, Bill 9, entitled "An Act to amend the Supreme Court Act," was introduced and received first reading in the House of Commons on January 23, 1939, and that on April 14 of the same year the debate on the motion for the second reading of the Bill was adjourned in order that steps might be taken to obtain a judicial determination of the legislative competence of the Parliament of Canada to enact the provisions of the said bill in whole or in part. The following question was accordingly referred to the Supreme Court of Canada for hearing and consideration:

Is said Bill 9, entitled "An Act to amend the Supreme Court Act," or any of the provisions thereof, and in what particular or particulars, or to what extent, intra vires of the Parliament of Canada?

The contents of the Bill, a short, but pregnant, one, must be stated in full. [His Lordship read the provisions of the Bill, and continued:] On January 19, 1940, the Supreme Court certified that the opinions in respect of the question referred to it were as follows: "By the court: The Parliament of Canada is competent to enact the Bill referred in its entirety. By Crocket J.: The Bill referred is wholly *ultra vires* of the Parliament of Canada. By Davis J.: The Bill referred if enacted would be within the authority of the Dominion Parliament if amended to provide that nothing therein contained shall alter or affect the rights of any province in respect of any action or other civil proceedings commenced in any of the provincial courts and solely concerned with some subject matter, legislation in relation to which is within the exclusive legislative competence of the legislature of such province."

From this judgment of the court the Attorneys General of Ontario, British Columbia and New Brunswick have by special leave brought this appeal, which the Attorney General of Quebec has intervened to support. The Attorneys General of Canada and of Manitoba and Saskatchewan are respondents to the appeal. The hearing of the appeal was postponed until the conclusion of the war. Their Lordships think it worth while to observe that H.M. Attorney General in

England took no part in the controversy, which has throughout been between the Dominion of Canada and certain of the provinces on the one hand and others of the provinces on the other hand. The single issue has been whether, as the appellants contend, the subject matter of Bill 9 falls within the exclusive powers committed to the provincial legislatures of the Provinces of Canada under s. 92 of the British North America Act, 1867, or, as the respondents contend, is within the powers of the Parliament of Canada under s. 101 or, alternatively, under s. 91 of that Act. An alternative argument was faintly addressed to their Lordships by counsel for the appellants, that the Bill lay within the powers of neither provinces nor Dominion, but H.M. Attorney General in England did not intervene to support this view and their Lordships see no valid reason for accepting it.

~ His Lordship then recited sections 91, 92, 101 and 129 of the B.N.A. Act. ~

It is convenient shortly to restate what at all times until the passing of the Statute of Westminster (to which reference will shortly be made) was the constitutional bar to legislation whether by Dominion or province in regard to appeals to His Majesty in Council. In the first place, it must be remembered that by the Colonial Laws Validity Act, 1865, any colonial law which was repugnant to the provisions of an Act of the United Kingdom extending to the colony either by express words or necessary intendment was void and inoperative to the extent of such repugnancy. It followed that neither Dominion nor province could then validly legislate so as to abolish a right of appeal to the King in Council which was provided by imperial Acts. In the second place, the doctrine which imposed a territorial limitation on the powers of colonial legislatures, might be regarded as a fetter on the legislative competence of Dominion or province to deal with the so-called "prerogative" right of appeal. In the third place, the express terms of the exception

in s. 129 of the Act, to which reference has been made, precluded any alteration of imperial Acts.

It is now necessary to return to s. 101 of the Act. Acting under its authority the Parliament of Canada in the year 1875 passed the Supreme Court of Canada Act, which has from time to time been amended and, as amended, is now R.S.C. 1927, ch. 35. Under the Act a Supreme Court of Appeal was established which, under s. 35, was to have, hold and exercise, an appellate civil and criminal jurisdiction within and throughout Canada. It prescribed the limits within, and the terms on which, an appeal might be brought from the courts of the provinces, and by s. 54 provided that the judgment of the court should in all cases be final and conclusive and that no appeal should be brought from any judgment or order of the court to any court of appeal established by the Parliament of Great Britain and Ireland by which appeals or petitions to His Majesty in Council might be ordered to be heard, saving any right which His Majesty might be graciously pleased to exercise by virtue of His royal prerogative. It is this s. 54 which the Bill now challenged seeks to amend, and two things may be noticed about the section as originally enacted. In the first place, it is silent, as is the whole Act, about appeals from the provincial courts to His Majesty in Council. In the second place, so far as appeals from the Supreme Court are concerned, it expressly saves the prerogative while denying any appeal as of right.

Such being the position before the year 1931, in that year was passed the Statute of Westminster, 1931, an Act of the Imperial Parliament, which has as its subtitle "An Act to give effect to certain resolutions passed by Imperial Conferences held in the years 1926 and 1930." The recitals in the preamble of this Act, after referring to the reports of the Conferences, affirm that it is proper to set out that, inasmuch as the Crown is the symbol of the free association of the members of the British Commonwealth of Nations, and as they are united by a common allegiance to the Crown, it would be in accord with the established constitutional position of all the members of the Commonwealth in relation to one another that any alteration in the law touching the succession to the Throne or the Royal Style and Titles should thenceforth require the assent as well of the Parliament of all the Dominions as of the Parliament of the United Kingdom, and that it is in accord with the established constitutional position that no law hereafter made by the Parliament of the United Kingdom shall extend to any of the said Dominions as part of the law of that Dominion otherwise than at the request and with the consent of that Dominion. By s. 2, sub-s. 1, it is provided that the Colonial Laws Validity Act, 1865, shall not apply to any law made after the commencement of the Act by the Parliament of a Dominion (which, by definition, includes the Dominion of Canada), and by s. 2, sub-s. 2, that no law and no provision of any law made after the commencement of the Act by the Parliament of a Dominion shall be void or inoperative on the ground that it is repugnant to the law of England, or to the provisions of any existing or future Act of Parliament of the United Kingdom, or to any order, rule or regulation made under any such Act, and the powers of the Parliament of a Dominion shall include the power to repeal or amend any such Act, order, rule or regulation in so far as the same is part of the law of the Dominion. By s. 3, it is declared and enacted that the Parliament of a Dominion has full power to make laws having extra-territorial operation. (It may be noticed that this power is not given to the legislature of a province.) By s. 4, it is provided that no Act of Parliament of the United Kingdom passed after the commencement of the Act shall extend or be deemed to extend to a Dominion as part of the law of that Dominion, unless it is expressly declared in that Act that that Dominion has requested, and consented to, the enactment thereof. It remains only to refer to s. 7, which deals with Canada only. By that section it is provided (by sub-s. 1)

that nothing in the Act shall be deemed to apply to the repeal, amendment or alteration of the British North America Acts, 1867 to 1930, or any order, rule or regulation made thereunder; (by sub-s. 2) that the provisions of s. 2 of the Act shall extend to laws made by any of the provinces of Canada and to the powers of the legislatures of such provinces, and (by sub-s. 3) that the powers conferred by the Act upon the Parliament of Canada or upon the legislatures of the provinces shall be restricted to the enactment of laws in relation to matters within the competence of the Parliament of Canada or of any of the legislatures of the provinces respectively.

It is in the light of this Act of transcendent constitutional importance that the question must now be considered whether it is competent for the Parliament of Canada to enact not only that the Supreme Court of the Dominion shall have appellate civil and criminal jurisdiction within and for Canada, but also that jurisdiction shall be "exclusive" and "ultimate." This question must be considered under two heads, first, in regard to appeals from the Supreme Court itself, and, secondly, in regard to appeals direct from the provincial courts to His Majesty in Council. First, then, as to appeals from the Supreme Court itself. Here the question is whether under sub-s. 1, of the substituted s. 54, the jurisdiction can validly be made "ultimate, by which, as the subsequent new sub-sections make clear, is intended the abolition of appeal from the Supreme Court to His Majesty in Council. On this question their Lordships can entertain no doubt. The power vested in the Dominion Parliament by s. 101 of the British North America Act to establish a general court of appeal for Canada was necessarily subject to the prerogative right of His Majesty, since that right was not expressly or by necessary intendment excluded, and this limitation was recognized in the first words of s. 54 of the Supreme Court Act. But that was a restriction or fetter on the legislative power of the Dominion which could be removed, and has been removed, by an Act of the Imperial Parliament, and, since it has been removed, it must be within the power of the Dominion Parliament to enact that the jurisdiction of its Supreme Court shall be ultimate. No other solution is consonant with the status of a self-governing Dominion.

Secondly, as to appeal direct from provincial courts to His Majesty in Council. It is in regard to these appeals that the validity of the Bill has been more strenuously challenged; and their Lordships have felt the familiar difficulty of determining which of two alternative meanings is to be given to an instrument, the authors of which did not contemplate the possibility of either meaning. For how could it be supposed in 1867, only two years after the passing of the Colonial Laws Validity Act, that the competence of either the Dominion or the provincial legislatures to pass laws directly repugnant to Acts of Parliament of the United Kingdom and to common law relating to the prerogative could be the subject of judicial determination? Yet this is the question which must now be decided. In its solution their Lordships have the advantage of two recent pronouncements of the Board, *Nadan* v. *The King* [1926] A.C. 482 and *British Coal Corporation* v. *The King* [1935] A.C. 500, the first before, the second after, the passing of the Statute of Westminster, and it will be convenient to see what these cases decided.

In *Nadan's* case, the question was as to the validity of s. 1025 of the Criminal Code of Canada if and so far as it purported to prevent the King in Council from giving effective leave to appeal against an order of a Canadian court in a criminal case. Criminal law, including the procedure in criminal matters, was, it will be remembered, one of the subjects to which, under s. 91 of the Act, the exclusive authority of the Parliament of Canada extended. It was argued that the legislative power so conferred was complete, and included power to limit the royal prerogative to entertain an appeal. The Board, after a review of the prerogative and of the manner in which the Judicial

Committee had been in effect established as a court of appellate jurisdiction, rejected the argument, holding that however widely the powers conferred by s. 91 were construed they were confined to action to be taken in the Dominion and did not authorize the Dominion Parliament to annul the prerogative right of the King in Council to grant special leave to appeal, and further holding that s. 1025 of the Criminal Code, if and so far as it was intended to have that effect, was repugnant to the Judicial Committee Acts and therefore void and inoperative by virtue of the Colonial Laws Validity Act, 1865.

In 1935 there came before the Board the *British Coal Corporation* case in which the same question was raised, but with this vital difference, that in the meantime the Statute of Westminster had been passed. The section of the Criminal Code then in force purported in unambiguous terms to abolish the appeal to His Majesty in Council; "Notwithstanding any royal prerogative or anything contained in the Interpretation Act or in the Supreme Court Act, no appeal shall be brought in any criminal case from any judgment or order of any court in Canada to any court of appeal or authority in which in the United Kingdom appeals or petitions to His Majesty may be heard." The validity of this provision was challenged by certain persons who sought leave to appeal in a criminal case from a judgment of the court of King's Bench (Appeal Side) of the Province of Quebec. But it was challenged in vain. The Board, after once more expounding the nature of appeals to His Majesty in Council, explained the decision in *Nadan's* case [1926] A.C. 482 thus: "Their Lordships are of opinion that the judgment was based on two grounds only: (1) that s. 1025 was repugnant to the Privy Council Acts of 1833 and 1844 and was therefore void under the Colonial Laws Validity Act, 1865; (2) that it could only be effective if construed as having an extra-territorial operation, whereas according to the law as it was in 1926 a Dominion statute could not have extra-territorial operation. These two difficulties as the law then stood could only be overcome by an Imperial Statute. . . . The Board proceeded to consider the question whether the difficulties had been overcome. Recalling the words used by Lord Loreburn L.C., in delivering the judgment of the Judicial Committee in *Attorney-General for Ontario* v. *Attorney-General for Canada* [1912] A.C. 571, 581: "Now, there can be no doubt that under this organic instrument the powers distributed between the Dominion on the one hand and the provinces on the other hand, cover the whole area of self-government within the whole area of Canada. It would be subversive of the entire scheme and policy of the Act to assume that any point of internal self-government was withheld from Canada" (words that their Lordships reiterate in regard to the present appeal), the Board concluded that both difficulties had been removed by the Statute of Westminster. "There now remain," it was said "only such limitations as flow from the Act itself, the operation of which as affecting the competence of Dominion legislation was saved by s. 7 of the statute, a section which excludes from the competence of the Dominion and provincial Parliaments any power of 'repeal, amendment or alteration' of the Act" [1935] A.C. 520. It has been properly urged on behalf of the appellants that at the conclusion of their judgment the Board observed that they were dealing only with the legal position in Canada in regard to that type of appeal in criminal matters, and that it was there neither necessary nor desirable to touch on the position as regards civil cases. It was this consideration that led Davis J. in the present case to give the qualified opinion already cited in regard to the validity of the referred Bill. This opinion rightly recognizes that whether or not the reasoning of the Board in the *British Coal Corporation* case [1935] A.C. 500 extends beyond the subject matter of legislation which was by s. 91 of the Act confided to the Dominion Parliament, at any rate it cannot be limited to one only of the twenty-nine classes of subject matter enumerated in that section, and that just as an appeal to His Majesty in Council may by Dominion legislation be abrogated in respect of "the criminal law . . . including the procedure in criminal matters," so it may be abrogated in respect of, e.g., class 21 "bankruptcy and insolvency" or class 22 "patents of invention and discovery."

But the conclusion reached by Davis J. involves a distinction which their Lordships would not willingly adopt. For if, as he holds, the subject matter provides the test whether the right of appeal may be abrogated by Dominion legislation so that it may not be abrogated in respect of classes of subjects assigned exclusively to the provinces under s. 92, a strange result would follow. It must be remembered that in the provincial courts the subject matter of litigation may arise as well under Dominion as under provincial legislation. The judicial and legislative spheres are not coterminous, provincial courts determining all questions except those for which a special court is set up under s. 101, whether the rights of the parties spring from the common law or Dominion or provincial statutes. Thus, if the right of the Dominion Parliament to prohibit appeals to His Majesty in Council from a provincial court depended on the subject matter in suit, the result would be that from the same court an appeal might lie in one suit to the Supreme Court of Canada only but in another to that court or to His Majesty in Council, nor is it impossible that in the same suit two or more questions might be raised in respect of which different rights of appeal would arise. This result is yet more remarkable when it is remembered how wide is the scope of those classes of subjects which, falling within s. 91 of the Act, can on this hypothesis be excluded from appeal to His Majesty in Council. Only the residue of civil cases, in which the rights of the parties were determinable by reference to other than Dominion legislation, would remain the subject of such appeal.

Therefore, while their Lordships give

full weight to the observation with which the judgment in the *British Coal Corporation* case [1935] A.C. 500 concluded and do not doubt that that case rightly decided that the Dominion Parliament was competent to exclude appeals in criminal cases for the reasons therein appearing, they must observe that that decision can be supported on wider grounds which cover not only criminal cases and not only civil cases falling within the subject matter of s. 91, but also every other case which can be brought before any provincial court in Canada. In coming to this conclusion their Lordships do not think it useful to embark on a nice discrimination between the legislative powers contained in ss. 91 and 92 respectively of the Act. Nor, as it appears to them, is it necessary to determine whether the words of head 14 of s. 92, "The administration of justice in the province" would, if they were disembarrassed of any context, be apt to embrace legislation in regard to appeals to His Majesty in Council. There appear to be cogent reasons for thinking that they would not. But their Lordships do not make this the ground of their decision; for it is elsewhere, it is in s. 101 of the Act that the solution lies.

In his judgment in the case under appeal the former Chief Justice of Canada, Sir Lyman Duff, used these words: "Assuming even that s. 92 gives some authority to the legislatures [of the provinces] in respect of appeals to the Privy Council, that cannot detract from the power of Parliament under s. 101. Whatever is granted by the words of the section, read and applied as prima facie intended to endow Parliament with power to effect high political objects concerning the self-government of the Dominion (s. 3 of the B.N.A. Act) in the matter of judicature, is to be held and exercised as a plenary power in that behalf with all ancillary powers necessary to enable Parliament to attain its objects fully and completely. So read it imports authority to establish a court having supreme and final appellate jurisdiction in Canada" [1940] S.C.R. (Can.) 63. The vital words in the passage cited, with which their Lordships are in full agreement, are the words in the last line "and final." But in the opinion of their Lordships the same considerations lead to the conclusion that the court so established must have not only "final," or "ultimate" but also exclusive appellate jurisdiction. They would emphasize that s. 101 confers a legislative power on the Dominion Parliament which by its terms overrides any power conferred by s. 92 on the provinces or preserved by s. 129. "Notwithstanding anything in this Act" are words in s. 101 which cannot be ignored. They vest in the Dominion a plenary authority to legislate in regard to appellate jurisdiction, which is qualified only by that which lies outside the Act, namely, the sovereign power of the Imperial Parliament. This was fully recognized in *Crown Grain Co.* v. *Day* [1908] A.C. 504.

What, then, is the power of the Dominion Parliament since the Statute of Westminster has come into operation? It is useful to examine what the position would be if now, for the first time, the Dominion legislature thought fit to exercise its power under s. 101. Nor is this a fanciful or inept mode of examination, for the power is to provide "from time to time" for a general court of appeal. To their Lordships it appears reasonably plain that, since, in the words used by Lord Robertson in delivering the opinion of the Board in the *Crown Grain Co.* case (ibid., 507 A.C.): "the subject in conflict belongs primarily to the subject matter committed to the Dominion Parliament, namely, the establishment of the Court of Appeal for Canada," to that Parliament also must belong the power not only to determine in what cases and under what conditions the appellate jurisdiction of that court may be invoked, but also to deny appellate jurisdiction to any other court. The natural attribute of sovereign power was no doubt qualified by an external constitutional limitation, namely, the existence of imperial statutes, but, given the power to abrogate such statutes, the authority conferred by s. 101 stands unqualified and absolute.

It is possible to regard this matter from a somewhat wider point of view. . . . The regulation of appeals is, to use the words of Lord Sankey in the *British Coal Corporation* case [1935] A.C. 500 a "prime element in Canadian sovereignty," which would be impaired if at the will of its citizens recourse could be had to a tribunal, in the constitution of which it had no voice. It is, as their Lordships think, irrelevant that the question is one that might have seemed unreal at the date of the British North America Act. To such an organic statute the flexible interpretation must be given which changing circumstances require, and it would be alien to the spirit, with which the preamble to the Statute of Westminster is instinct, to concede anything less than the widest amplitude of power to the Dominion legislature under s. 101 of the Act.

In this connection some argument was addressed to their Lordships on the importance of uniformity of legal decision, which, it was urged, could not be secured if appeal lay indifferently to the Supreme Court of Canada or to His Majesty in Council. For a decision of the Supreme Court would at least be final, though its jurisdiction would not on this hypothesis be exclusive. Against this it was contended that the British North America Act contained in s. 94 a provision whereby the postulated uniformity of law could be obtained. In their Lordships' opinion this section provides an imperfect remedy for a state of affairs in which an important Dominion Act might be finally interpreted in one way by the Supreme Court for a province which did not admit appeals to His Majesty in Council and in another way by the Judicial Committee for a province which did admit such appeals, neither tribunal admitting the authority of the other. But it is the possibility of such a conflict, creating a different law for different provinces out of the same Dominion Act, which points the way to a truer interpretation of the British North America Act in the light of the Statute of West-

minster. It is, in fact, a prime element in the self-government of the Dominion, that it should be able to secure through its own courts of justice that the law should be one and the same for all its citizens. This result is attainable only if s. 101 now authorizes the establishment of a court with final and exclusive appellate jurisdiction. . . .

It is right to conclude with some observations on s. 7 of the Statute of Westminster on which counsel for the appellants strongly relied. Subsection 1 of s. 7 is in general terms, and it was urged that to interpret the statute as vesting in the Dominion Parliament a power which it did not before possess was in effect to repeal or amend or, at least, to alter the British North America Act. But their Lordships cannot accept this reasoning. Necessarily the effect of the statute is to amend and alter the Act in so far as from the operation of the statute there arises a new power in the legislatures of both the Dominion and the provinces. The question is, in which legislature the power is vested in regard to this particular subject matter. That is a question of construction on which their Lordships have stated their opinion. Sub-section 2 does not call for further comment here. In regard to sub-s. 3 the same observations appear to apply as to sub-s. 1. If on the true construction of the British North America Act the conclusion had been that the power to legislate for the abrogation of appeals to His Majesty in Council was vested under s. 92 in a provincial legislature, that would have been an end of the matter. It is just because their Lordships have come to a different conclusion that sub-s. 3 does not assist the appellants.

Their Lordships are of opinion that this appeal fails, and that it ought to be declared that Bill 9 of the Fourth Session of the Eighteenth Parliament of Canada, entitled "An Act to amend the Supreme Court Act," is wholly *intra vires* of the Parliament of Canada, and they will humbly advise His Majesty accordingly.

B. The Supreme Court Since 1949

18. Johannesson *v*. West St. Paul, *1952*

~ This is the first case following the abolition of Privy Council appeals which provided an occasion for the Supreme Court to indicate the direction in which it might develop Canadian constitutional law in relation to two major issues: the peace, order and good government power and the power to implement Canadian treaties.

The case originated in private litigation between Johannesson, the operator of a commercial aviation enterprise in western Canada and the Manitoba town of West St. Paul which had passed a by-law preventing Johannesson from establishing an aerodrome in a location he had chosen in that municipality. Johannesson challenged the validity of the provincial Municipal Act which had delegated to the municipality the power to make the by-law in question. Both the trial judge and a majority of the Manitoba Court of Appeal had ruled the Manitoba legislation *intra vires*. On the appeal to the Supreme Court of Canada the Attorney General of Manitoba and the Attorney General of Canada intervened to support their respective sides of the case. The Supreme Court was unanimous in reversing the decision of the lower courts and finding that the Dominion's power in relation to aeronautics left no room for a province to regulate the location of aerodromes. Six of the seven judges who took part in the decision supported the validity of the federal Aeronautics Act and Air Regulations as an exercise of the peace, order and good government power. In doing so, it is significant that they used the test of "inherent national importance" from Viscount Simon's judgment in the *Canada Temperance Federation* case to determine whether the field of aeronautics was a matter affecting the peace, order and good government of Canada. Justice Locke's opinion demonstrates the policy considerations which judges might take into account in deciding whether legislation relates to a subject which from its inherent nature must be the concern of the Dominion as a whole.

While the decision in this case points to a more expansive treatment of Parliament's general power, its implications for the treaty-implementing power were less clear. The Court was divided on the question of whether section 132 which gives Parliament the power of implementing any obligations arising from treaties entered into by Canada as part of the British Empire, could be used, as it had been in the Aeronautics Reference,[1] to support the validity of the federal Aeronautics Act. The International Convention in support of which

---

[1] *In re Regulation and Control of Aeronautics in Canada*, [1932] A.C. 54. See case 10 above.

the Aeronautics Act had originally been enacted was ratified on behalf of the British Empire. But this Convention had been abrogated by the Civil Aviation Convention which Canada had signed in her own right at Chicago in 1944. In the light of these facts three of the judges were of the opinion that section 132 could no longer be used to sustain the Dominion's aeronautics legislation, while three others took the view that even though the Chicago Convention was not, strictly speaking, a British Empire treaty still "it comes to the same thing."[2] The seventh, Justice Locke, does not appear to have committed himself on this point. ~

JOHANNESSON v. WEST ST. PAUL
In the Supreme Court of Canada. [1952] 1 S.C.R. 292

KERWIN J.: This is an appeal by Mr. and Mrs. Johannesson against a judgment of the Court of Appeal for Manitoba affirming an order of Campbell J. dismissing their application for an order declaring that s. 921 of The Municipal Act, R.S.M. 1940, c. 141, was *ultra vires* as not being within the legislative competence of the Legislature, and that by-law 292 of the rural municipality of West St. Paul, passed May 27, 1948, in pursuance of such section, was, therefore, null and void.

Section 921 of The Municipal Act appears in Division II "Public Safety and Amenity" under the sub-head "Aerodromes" and reads as follows:

921. Any municipal corporation may pass by-laws for licensing, regulating, and, within certain defined areas, preventing the erection, maintenance and continuance of aerodromes or places where aeroplanes are kept for hire or gain.

~ Justice Kerwin then reviewed the history of this legislation. He also set out the provisions of the West St. Paul by-law 292, which banned aerodromes from the area in which Johannesson wished to locate his airport. This by-law was authorized by section 921 of Manitoba's Municipal Act. ~

The circumstances which give rise to the present dispute are important as showing the far-reaching effect of the provisions of the section. The appellant Johannesson had been engaged in commercial aviation since 1928 and held an air transport licence, issued by the Air Transport Board of Canada, to operate an air service at Winnipeg and Flin Flon. The charter service which he operated under this licence covers territory in central and northern Manitoba and northern Saskatchewan, and had substantially increased in volume over the years. This service was operated with light and medium weight planes, which in the main were equipped in summer with floats and in winter with skis in order to permit landing on the numerous lakes and rivers in this territory, and these planes had to be repaired and serviced in Winnipeg, which was the only place within the territory where the necessary supplies and any facilities were available for that purpose. The use by small planes of a large airfield, such as Stevenson Airport near Winnipeg which was maintained for the use of large transcontinental airplanes, was impractical and would eventually be prohibited. No facilities existed on the Red River in Winnipeg for the repairing and servicing of planes equipped with floats, and repairs could only be made to such planes by dismantling them at some private dock

---

[2] This was the phrase used by Viscount Dunedin in *In re Regulation and Control of Radio Communication in Canada*, [1932] A.C. 305, at p. 312. See above, p. 95.

and transporting them, by truck, through Winnipeg to Stevenson Airport. After a long search by Johannesson in the suburbs of Winnipeg for a site that would combine an area of level land of sufficient area and dimensions and location to comply with the regulations of the Civil Aviation Branch of the Canadian Department of Transport relating to a licensed air strip with access to a straight stretch of the Red River of sufficient length to be suitable for the landing of airplanes equipped with floats, he found such a location (but one only) in the rural municipality of West St. Paul and acquired an option to purchase it but, before the transaction was completed By-law 292 was passed. Title to the land was subsequently taken in the name of both appellants and these proceedings ensued. The Attorney General of Canada and the Attorney General of Manitoba were notified but only the latter was represented before the judge of first instance and the Court of Appeal. Leave to appeal to this Court was granted by the latter.

On behalf of the appellants and the Attorney General of Canada, reliance is placed upon the decision of the Judicial Committee in the *Aeronautics* case ([1932] A.C. 54). Irrespective of later judicial comments upon this case, in my view it is a decision based entirely upon the fact that the Dominion Aeronautics Act there in question had been enacted pursuant to an International Convention of 1919 to which the British Empire was a party and, therefore, within s. 132 of the British North America Act, 1867:

132. The Parliament and Government of Canada shall have all Powers necessary or proper for performing the obligations of Canada or of any Province thereof, as part of the British Empire, towards foreign countries arising under treaties between the Empire and such foreign countries.

However, in the subsequent decision in the *Labour Conventions* case (*A.-G. for Canada* v. *A.-G. for Ontario* ([1937] A.C. 326)), Lord Atkin, who had been a member of the Board in the *Aeronautics* case, said with reference to the judgment therein:

The Aeronautics *case ([1932] A.C. 54 at 351) concerned legislation to perform obligations imposed by a treaty between the Empire and foreign countries. Sect. 132, therefore, clearly applied, and but for a remark at the end of the judgment, which in view of the stated ground of the decision was clearly obiter, the case could not be said to be an authority on the matter now under discussion.*

The remarks of Viscount Simon in *A.-G. for Ontario* v. *Canada Temperance Federation* ([1946] A.C. 193), must be read when considering the words of Lord Sankey in the *Aeronautics* case in another connection. At the moment all I am concerned with emphasizing is that the *Aeronautics* case decided one thing, and one thing only, and that is that the matter there discussed fell within the ambit of s. 132 of the British North America Act.

At this stage it is necessary to refer to a matter that was not explained to the Courts below. According to a certificate from the Under-Secretary of State for Foreign Affairs, the Convention of 1919 was denounced by Canada, which denunciation became effective in 1947. This was done because on February 13, 1947, Canada had deposited its Instrument of Ratification of the Convention on International Civil Aviation signed at Chicago December 8, 1944, and which Convention came into force on April 4, 1947. With the exception of certain amendments that are not relevant to the present discussion, the Aeronautics Act remains on the statute books of Canada in the same terms as those considered by the Judicial Committee in the *Aeronautics* case. Section 132 of the B.N.A. Act, therefore ceased to have any efficacy to permit Parliament to legislate upon the subject of aeronautics.

Nevertheless the fact remains that the Convention of 1919 was a treaty between the Empire and foreign countries and that pursuant thereto the Aeronautics Act was enacted. It continues as c. 3 of the Revised Statutes of Canada, 1927, as amended. Under s. 4 of that Act, as it stood when these proceedings were commenced, the Minister, with the approval of the Governor in Council, had power to regulate and control aerial navigation over Canada and the territorial waters of Canada, and in particular but not to restrict the generality of the foregoing, he might make regulations with respect to . . . (c) the licensing, inspection and regulation of all aerodromes and air stations. Pursuant thereto regulations have been promulgated dealing with many of the matters mentioned in the section, including provisions for the licensing of air ports. If, therefore, the subject of aeronautics goes beyond local or provincial concern because it has attained such dimensions as to affect the body politic of Canada, it falls under the "peace, order and good government" clause of s. 91 of the B.N.A. Act since aeronautics is not a subject-matter confined to the provinces by s. 92. It does not fall within head 8, "Municipal Institutions," as that head "simply gives the provincial legislature the right to create a legal body for the management of municipal affairs. . . . The extent and nature of the functions" the provincial legislature "can commit to a municipal body of its own creation must depend upon the legislative authority which it derives from the provisions of s. 92 other than No. 8": *Attorney General for Ontario* v. *Attorney General for Canada* ([1896] A.C. 348 at 364). Nor, on the authority of the same decision is it within head 9: "shop, saloon, tavern, auctioneer, and other licences in order to the raising of a revenue for provincial, local, or municipal purposes." Once it is held that the subject-matter transcends "Property and Civil Rights in the Province" (head 13) or "Generally all matters of a merely local or private nature in the Province" (head 16), these two heads of s. 92 have no relevancy.

Now, even at the date of the *Aeronautics* case, the Judicial Committee was influenced (i.e. in the determination of the main point) by the fact that in their opinion the subject of air navigation was a matter of national interest and importance and had attained such dimensions. That that is so at the present time is shown by the terms of the Chicago Convention of 1944 and the provisions of the Dominion Aeronautics Act and the regulations thereunder referred to above. The affidavit of the appellant Johannesson, from which the statement of facts was culled, also shows the importance that the subject of air navigation has attained in Canada. To all of which may be added those matters of everyday knowledge of which the Court must be taken to be aware.

It is with reference to this phase of the matter that Viscount Simon's remarks in *A.G. for Canada* v. *Canada Temperance Federation* ([1946] A.C. 193 at 205), must be read. What was there under consideration was the Canada Temperance Act, originally enacted in 1878, and Viscount Simon stated: "In their Lordships' opinion, the true test must be found in the real subject-matter of the legislation: if it is such that it goes beyond local or provincial concern or interests and must from its inherent nature be the concern of the Dominion as a whole (as, for example, in the *Aeronautics* case and the *Radio* case ([1932] A.C. 304), then it will fall within the competence of the Dominion Parliament as a matter affecting the peace, order and good government of Canada, though it may in another aspect touch on matters specially reserved to the provincial legislatures." This statement is significant because, while not stating that the *Aeronautics* case was a decision on the point, it is a confirmation of the fact that the Board in the *Aeronautics* case considered that the subject of aeronautics transcended provincial legislative boundaries.

The appeal should be allowed, the orders below set aside, and judgment should be entered declaring s. 921 of the Act *Ultra vires* and By-law 292 of the rural municipality of West St. Paul null and void.

LOCKE, J.: . . . In my opinion, the

position taken by the province and by the municipality in this matter cannot be maintained. Whether control and direction of aeronautics in all its branches be one which lies within the exclusive jurisdiction of Parliament, and this I think to be the correct view, or whether it be a domain in which Provincial and Dominion legislation may overlap, I think the result must be the same. It has been said on behalf of the respondents that the by-law is merely a zoning regulation passed in exercise of the powers vested in the municipality elsewhere in the Municipal Act. . . . The by-law, in so far as it prohibits the erection, maintenance or continuation of aerodromes, must depend for its validity upon s. 921: subsec. 3 is apparently based upon subsec. (*h*) of s. 896. . . . The powers sought to be conferred upon the Municipal Council appear to me to be in direct conflict with those vested in the Minister of National Defence by the Aeronautics Act. Section 3(*a*) of that statute imposes upon the Minister the duty of supervising all matters connected with aeronautics and prescribing aerial routes and by s. 4 he is authorized, with the approval of the Governor in Council, to make regulations with respect to, *inter alia*, the areas within which aircraft coming from any place outside of Canada are to land and as to aerial routes, their use and control. The power to prescribe the aerial routes must include the right to designate where the terminus of any such route is to be maintained, and the power to designate the area within which foreign aricraft may land, of necessity includes the power to designate such area, whether of land or water, within any municipality in any province of Canada deemed suitable for such purpose.

If the validity of the Aeronautics Act and the Air Regulations be conceded, it appears to me that this matter must be determined contrary to the contentions of the respondent. It is, however, desirable, in my opinion, that some of the reasons for the conclusion that the field of aeronautics is one exclusively within federal jurisdiction should be stated. There has

been since the First World War an immense development in the use of aircraft flying between the various provinces of Canada and between Canada and other countries. There is a very large passenger traffic between the provinces and to and from foreign countries, and a very considerable volume of freight traffic not only between the settled portions of the country but between those areas and the northern part of Canada, and planes are extensively used in the carriage of mails. That this traffic will increase greatly in volume and extent is undoubted. While the largest activity in the carrying of passengers and mails east and west is in the hands of a government-controlled company, private companies carry on large operations, particularly between the settled parts of the country and the North and mails are carried by some of these lines. The maintenance and extension of this traffic, particularly to the North, is essential to the opening up of the country and the development of the resources of the nation. It requires merely a statement of these well-recognized facts to demonstrate that the field of aeronautics is one which concerns the country as a whole. It is an activity, which to adopt the language of Lord Simon in the *Attorney General for Ontario* v. *Canada Temperance Federation*, must from its inherent nature be a concern of the Dominion as a whole. The field of legislation is not, in my opinion, capable of division in any practical way. If, by way of illustration, it should be decided that it was in the interests of the inhabitants of some northerly part of the country to have airmail service with centres of population to the south and that for that purpose some private line, prepared to undertake such carriage, should be licensed to do so and to establish the southern terminus for their route at some suitable place in the Municipality of West St. Paul where, apparently, there is an available and suitable field and area of water where planes equipped in a manner enabling them to use the facilities of such an airport might land, it would be intolerable that such a national purpose might be defeated by a rural municipality, the Council of which decided that the noise attendant on the operation of airplanes was objectionable. Indeed, if the argument of the respondents be carried to its logical conclusion the rural municipalities of Manitoba through which the Red River passes between Emerson and Selkirk, and the City of Winnipeg and the Town of Selkirk might prevent the operation of any planes equipped for landing upon water by denying them the right to use the river for that purpose. . . .

While the statement of Lord Sankey in the *Aeronautics Reference* that aerial navigation is a class of subject which has attained such dimensions as to affect the body politic of the Dominion as a whole, and that of Lord Simon in the Canada Temperance matter in referring to that case and the *Radio* case, were perhaps unnecessary to the decision of those matters, they support what I consider to be the true view of this matter that the whole subject of aeronautics lies within the field

assigned to Parliament as a matter affecting the peace, order and good government of Canada. S. 921 of The Municipal Act (R.S.M. 1940 c. 141) clearly trespasses upon that field and must be declared *ultra vires* the province. As to the by-law I am unable, with respect, to agree with the contention that it is a mere zoning regulation or that, even if it were, it could be sustained. On the contrary, I consider it to be a clear attempt to prevent the carrying on of the operation of commercial aerodromes within the municipality. As the right to do this must depend upon s. 921, the by-law must also be declared *ultra vires*. . . .

~ Chief Justice Rinfret and Justices Kellock and Estey also wrote opinions in which they concluded that the provincial legislation in question was *ultra vires*. Justice Cartwright concurred with Justice Kellock and Justice Taschereau concurred with Justice Estey. ~

19. Reference re The Farm Products Marketing Act (Ontario), *1957*

~ In 1957 the federal government submitted to the Supreme Court of Canada eight questions which were designed to measure the extent to which a province could provide a comprehensive system of regulatory boards for organizing the marketing of farm products within the province. Three of the questions concerned the validity of two provisions of Ontario's Farm Products Marketing Act authorizing a system of marketing by means of a central pool and distribution of payments to producers and a proposed amendment which would enable local marketing boards to purchase and market the surplus of a regulated product using a system of licensing fees to recoup any losses suffered. The other five questions involved specific schemes and regulations passed under the Act dealing with the marketing of hogs, peaches and vegetables. A majority of the judges sitting found the impugned provisions of the Act and regulations *intra vires* with the qualification that they not affect extra-provincial trade. Only the proposed amendment to the Act was ruled invalid. But this latter decision was based not on considerations of extra-provincial versus intra-provincial trade but on the doctrine developed in earlier cases that an equalization scheme such as the one envisaged by the proposed amendment constituted an indirect tax and hence was beyond provincial jurisdiction.

The implications which this case has for the development of the federal commerce power have little to do with the specific answers which the Court gave to the questions posed by the reference. The most significant element in this decision is the pragmatic way in which a number of the judges tackled the task of drawing the boundary lines between national and provincial jurisdictions in regulating commercial activities. The order of reference had instructed the Court to assume that the statute and regulations extended only to intra-provincial transactions. A more cautious Court might have left the matter there. But more than half of the majority (Chief Justice Kerwin and Justices Rand, Locke and Nolan) took this as an invitation to abandon the mechanical, unreflective application of the categories of intra-provincial and extra-provincial trade and explore the realities of the movement of produce in trade with a view to describing in concrete terms the kind of economic activity which is inherently extra-provincial. This functional approach led this group of judges by rather different routes to the common conclusion that in business operations such as food-processing which involve a number of steps between the original producer and the final consumer even though some parts of the operation (or "transactions") might be completed within the province, the business as a whole might still be primarily extra-provincial in scope and hence subject to federal jurisdiction. Instead of simply taking all "intra-provincial transactions" to be coterminous with provincial authority these opinions in effect imply the application of the "aspect" doctrine to trading activities: looked at from the point of view of a regulation of marketing, a transaction might be one stage in the flow of interprovincial and international commerce and hence subject to the federal trade and commerce power, whereas from the point of view of the law of contracts it might be a matter of provincial concern.

All the members of the majority did not join this rather liberal exploration of the domain of extra-provincial trade and commerce. The judgment of Justice Fauteux (part of which is included below) indicates the more traditional and cautious approach to the issue. Also it should be noted that Justice Rand, towards the end of his opinion acknowledged that his own reasoning had not removed the barrier which would prevent either the Dominion or a province, acting alone, from regulating trade in a product before it can be identified as either extra-provincial or intra-provincial. But this does not detract from the general impression created by the judgments of Chief Justice Kerwin and Justices Locke and Rand that the Dominion's trade and commerce power could serve as a source of legislative authority for major economic policies in the field of international and interprovincial trade. This impression was given some further confirmation a year later in *Murphy* v. *C.P.R. and A.-G. Canada*[1] when both Justice Locke and Justice Rand, speaking for a unanimous Court, cited the federal trade and commerce power as the constitutional basis for the Canadian Wheat Board Act which provides for the regulation of the export trade in grains. ~

REFERENCE RE THE FARM PRODUCTS MARKETING ACT (ONTARIO)
In the Supreme Court of Canada. [1957] S.C.R. 198.

KERWIN, C.J.C.: This is a reference by His Excellency the Governor-General in Council as to the validity of one clause of one section of The Farm Products Marketing Act of the Province of Ontario, R.S.O. 1950, c. 131, of certain regulations made thereunder, of an order of The Ontario Hog Producers' Marketing Board, of a proposed amendment to the Act, and of a suggested authorization by the Farm Products Marketing Board if that amendment be held to be *intra vires*. On such a reference one cannot envisage all possible circumstances which might arise and it must also be taken that it is established that it is not to be presumed that a Provincial Legislature intended to exceed its legislative jurisdiction under the British North America Act, although the Court may, on what it considers the proper construction of a given enactment,

determine that the Legislature has gone beyond its authority.

Subsequent to the date of the order of reference, the Act was amended by c. 20 of the statutes of 1957, which came into force the day it received Royal Assent, s. 1 of which reads as follows:

1. The Farm Products Marketing Act is amended by adding thereto the following section:

1a. The purpose and intent of this Act is to provide for the control and regulation in any or all respects of the marketing within the Province of farm products including the prohibition of such marketing in whole or in part.

Without entering into discussion as to what is a declaratory law, since the term may have different connotations depend-

---

[1] [1958] S.C.R. 626.

ing upon the matter under review, it is arguable that, for the present purposes, this amendment should be read as part of The Farm Products Marketing Act, but in any event, the first question submitted to us directs us to assume that that Act as amended down to the date of the reference applies only in the case of "intra-provincial transactions." This term means "existing or occurring within a province"; see Shorter Oxford English Dictionary, including "intraparochial" as an example under the word "intra." As will appear later, the word "marketing" is defined in the Act, but, in accordance with what has already been stated, I take it as being confined to marketing within the Province.

Question 1 is as follows:

1. Assuming that the said Act applies only in the case of intra-provincial transactions, is clause (1) of subsection 1 of section 3 of The Farm Products Marketing Act, R.S.O. 1950, chapter 131 as amended by Ontario Statutes 1951, chapter 25, 1953, chapter 36, 1954, chapter 29, 1955, chapter 21, ultra vires the Ontario Legislature?

Clause (1) of subs. (1) of s. 3 referred to, as re-enacted by 1955, c. 21, s. 2, provides:

3. (1) The Board may, . . .
(1) authorize any marketing agency appointed under a scheme to conduct a pool or pools for the distribution of all moneys received from the sale of the regulated product and requiring any such marketing agency, after deducting all necessary and proper disbursements and expenses, to distribute the proceeds of sale in such manner that each person receives a share of the total proceeds in relation to the amount, variety, size, grade and class of the regulated product delivered by him and to make an initial payment, on delivery of the product and subsequent

payments until the total net proceeds are distributed.

For a proper understanding of the terms used in this clause and of the provisions of the Act it is necessary to refer to what is proposed by the latter.

The Board is the Farm Products Marketing Board and " 'farm products' includes animals, meats, eggs, poultry, wool, dairy products, grains, seeds, fruit, fruit products, vegetables, vegetable products, maple products, honey, tobacco and such articles of food or drink manufactured or derived in whole or in part from any such product and such other natural products of agriculture as may be designated by the regulations" (s. 1(b)). " 'Regulated product' means a farm product in respect of which a scheme is in force" (s. 1(g)). Provision is made for the formulation of a scheme for the marketing or regulating of any farm product upon the petition of at least 10 per cent of all producers engaged in the production of the farm product in Ontario, or in that part thereof to which the proposed scheme is to apply. " 'Marketing' means buying, selling and offering for sale and includes advertising, assembling, financing, packing and shipping for sale or storage and transporting in any manner by any person, and 'market' and 'marketed' have corresponding meanings" (s. 1(e), as re-enacted by 1955, c. 21, s. 1). The scheme may provide for a "marketing agency" designated by the Board in its regulations. Once the scheme is approved by the Board the latter's regulations will apply according to the farm products dealt with thereby.

It seems plain that the Province may regulate a transaction of sale and purchase in Ontario between a resident of the Province and one who resides outside its limits; that is, if an individual in Quebec comes to Ontario and there buys a hog, or vegetables, or peaches, the mere fact that he has the intention to take them from Ontario to Quebec does not deprive the Legislature of its power to regulate the transaction, as is evidenced by such enactments as The Sale of Goods Act, R.S.O. 1950, c. 345. That is a matter of the regulation of contracts and not of trade as trade and in that respect the intention of the purchaser is immaterial. However, if the hog be sold to a packing plant or the vegetables or peaches to a cannery, the products of those establishments in the course of trade may be dealt with by the Legislature or by Parliament depending, on the one hand, upon whether all the products are sold or intended for sale within the Province or, on the other, whether some of them are sold or intended for sale beyond Provincial limits. It is, I think, impossible to fix any minimum proportion of such last-mentioned sales or intended sales as determining the jurisdiction of Parliament. This applies to the sale by the original owner. Once a statute aims at "regulation of trade in matters of interprovincial concern" (*The Citizens Insurance Company of Canada* v. *Parsons; The Queen Insurance Company* v. *Parsons* ([1881], 7 App. Cas. 96 at 113), it is beyond the competence of a Provincial Legislature. The ambit of head 2 of s. 91 of the British North America Act, "The Regulation of Trade and Commerce" has been considerably enlarged by decisions of the Judicial Committee and expressions used in some of its earlier judgments must be read in the light of its later pronouncements, as is pointed out by Sir Lyman Duff in *Re Alberta Statutes* ([1938] S.C.R. 100 at 121). In fact, his judgment in *Re The Natural Products Marketing Act, 1934* ([1936] S.C.R. 398), which is justly considered as the *locus classicus*, must be read in conjunction with and subject to his remarks in the later case. The concept of trade and commerce, the regulation of which is confided to Parliament, is entirely separate and distinct from the regulation of mere sale and purchase agreements. Once an article enters into the flow of interprovincial or external trade, the subject matter and all its attendant circumstances cease to be a mere matter of local concern. No change has taken place in the theory underlying the construction of the British North America

Act that what is not within the legislative jurisdiction of Parliament must be within that of the Provincial Legislatures. This, of course, still leaves the question as to how far either may proceed, and, as Lord Atkin pointed out in the *Natural Products Marketing Act* case, *supra*, at p. 389, neither party may leave its own sphere and encroach upon that of another. . . .

. . . In view of the wording of question 1, I take clause (*l*) of subs. (1) of s. 3 of The Farm Products Marketing Act as being a successful endeavour on the part of the Ontario Legislature to fulfil its part while still keeping within the ambit of its powers. On the assumption directed to be made and reading the clause so as not to apply to transactions which I have indicated would be of a class beyond the powers of the Legislature, my answer to the first question is "No.". . .

RAND, J.: This reference raises questions going to the scope of Provincial authority over trade. They arise out of The Farm Products Marketing Act, R.S.O. 1950, c. 131, as amended, which deals comprehensively with the matter connoted by its name and out of certain schemes formed under it. Its object is to accord primary producers of farm products the advantages of various degrees of controlled marketing, for which it provides provincial and local machinery.

General jurisdiction over its administration is exercised by the Farm Products Marketing Board; regulation is by way of schemes for the marketing of any products; under a scheme, a local board, district committees and county groups are organized; and the marketing may be carried out exclusively by an agency designated by the Board upon the recommendation of the local board.

The questions put, which assume the Act to be limited in application to local trade, call for answers which make it necessary to examine and define the scope of local trade to the extent of the regulation provided. The enquiry must take into account regulatory power over acts and transactions which while objectively appearing to be consummated within the Province may involve or possess an interest of interprovincial or foreign trade, which for convenience I shall refer to as external trade. . . .

. . . Although not specifically mentioned in s. 92 of the British North America Act, there is admittedly a field of trade within provincial power, and the head or heads of s. 92 from which it is to be deduced will be considered later. The power is a subtraction from the scope of the language conferring on the Dominion by head 2 of s. 91 exclusive authority to make laws in relation to the regulation of trade and commerce, and was derived under an interpretation of the Act which was found necessary

in order to preserve from serious curtailment, if not from virtual extinction, the degree of autonomy which, as appears from the scheme of the Act as a whole, the provinces were intended to possess

(*per* Duff J. in *Lawson* v. *Interior Tree, Fruit and Vegetable Committee of Direction* ([1931] S.C.R. 357 at 366). In examining the legislation for the purpose mentioned we should bear in mind Lord Atkin's admonition in *Attorney-General for British Columbia* v. *Attorney-General for Canada et al* ([1937] A.C. 377 at 389), that

the legislation will have to be carefully framed, and will not be achieved by either party leaving its own sphere and encroaching upon that of the other.

The definitive statement of the scope of Dominion and Provincial jurisdiction was made by Duff C.J. in *Re The Natural Products Marketing Act, 1934* ([1936] S.C.R. 398 at 414 *et seq.*). The regulation of particular trades confined to the Province lies exclusively with the Legislature subject, it may be, to Dominion general regulation affecting all trade, and to such incidental intrusion by the Dominion as may be necessary to prevent the defeat of Dominion regulation; interprovincial and foreign trade are correspon-

dingly the exclusive concern of Parliament. That statement is to be read with the judgment of this Court in *The King* v. *Eastern Terminal Elevator Company* ([1925] S.C.R. 434), approved by the Judicial Committee in *Attorney-General for British Columbia* v. *Attorney-General for Canada, supra,* at p. 387, to the effect that Dominion regulation cannot embrace local trade merely because in undifferentiated subject matter the external interest is dominant. But neither the original statement nor its approval furnishes a clear guide to the demarcation of the two classes when we approach as here the origination, the first stages of trade, including certain aspects of manufacture and production.

That demarcation must observe this rule, that if in a trade activity, including manufacture or production, there is involved a matter of extraprovincial interest or concern its regulation thereafter in the aspect of trade is by that fact put beyond Provincial power. This is exemplified in *Lawson* v. *Interior Tree Fruit and Vegetable Committee of Direction, supra,* where the Province purported to regulate the time and quantity of shipment, the shippers, the price and the transportation of fruit and vegetables in both unsegregated and segregated local and interprovincial trade movements.

A producer is entitled to dispose of his products beyond the Province without reference to a provincial marketing agency or price, shipping or other trade regulation; and an outside purchaser is entitled with equal freedom to purchase and export. Processing is one of a number of trade services that may be given products in the course of reaching the consumer: milling (as of grain or lumber), sorting, packing, slaughtering, dressing, storing, transporting, etc. The producer or purchaser may desire to process the product either within or beyond the Province and if he engages for that with a local undertaking (using that expression in a non-technical sense), such as a packing plant—and it would apply to any sort of servicing—he takes that service as he finds it but free from such Provincial impositions as are strictly trade regulations such as prices or the specification of standards, which could no more be imposed than Provincial trade marks. Regulation of that nature could directly nullify external trade vital to the economy of the country. Trade arrangements reaching the dimensions of world agreements are now a commonplace; interprovincial trade, in which the Dominion is a single market, is of similar importance, and equally vital to the economic functioning of the country as a whole. The Dominion power implies responsibility for promoting and maintaining the vigour and growth of trade beyond Provincial confines, and the discharge of this duty must remain unembarrassed by local trade impediments. If the processing is restricted to external trade, it becomes an instrumentality of that trade and its single control as to prices, movements, standards, etc., by the Dominion follows: *Re The Industrial Relations and Disputes Investigation Act* ([1955] S.C.R. 529). The licensing of processing plants by the Province as a trade regulation is thus limited to their operations in local trade. Likewise the licensing of shippers, whether producers or purchasers, and the fixing of the terms and conditions of shipment, including prices, as trade regulation, where the goods are destined beyond the Province, would be beyond Provincial power.

Local trade has in some cases been classed as a matter of property and civil rights and related to head 13 of s. 92, and the propriety of that allocation was questioned. The production and exchange of goods as an economic activity does not take place by virtue of positive law or civil right; it is assumed as part of the residual free activity of men upon or around which law is imposed. It has an identity of its own recognized by head 2 of s. 91. I cannot agree that its regulation under that head was intended as a species of matter under head 13 from which by the language of s. 91 it has been withdrawn. It happened that in *The Citizens Insurance*

Company of Canada v. *Parsons; The Queen Insurance Company* v. *Parsons* ([1881], 7 App. Cas. 96), asuming insurance to be a trade, the commodity being dealt in was the making of contracts, and their relation to head 13 seemed obvious. But the true conception of trade (in contradistinction to the static nature of rights, civil or property) is that of a dynamic, the creation and flow of goods from production to consumption or utilization, as an individualized activity.

The conclusive answer to the question is furnished by a consideration of s. 94 which provides for the uniformity in Ontario, New Brunswick and Nova Scotia of "all or any of the laws relative to property and civil rights." It is, I think, quite impossible to include within this provision regulation of local trades; that appears to be one feature of the internal economy of each Province in which no such uniformity could ever be expected. What the language is directed to are laws relating to civil status and capacity, contracts, torts and real and personal property in the common law Provinces, jural constructs springing from the same roots, already more or less uniform, and lending themselves to more or less permanence. In some degree uniformity has been achieved by individual Provincial action in such legislation, for instance, as that of contributory negligence.

Head 16 contains what may be called the residuary power of the Province: *Attorney-General for Ontario* v. *Attorney-General for the Dominion et al.* ([1896] A.C. 348 at 365), and it is within that residue that the autonomy of the Province in local matters, so far as it might be affected by trade regulation, is to be preserved. As was recognized in the *Parsons* case, *supra*, this points up the underlying division of the matters of legislation into those which are primarily of national and those of local import. But this is not intended to derogate from regulation as well as taxation of local trade through licence under head 9 of s. 92, nor from its support under head 13.

It is important to keep in mind, as

already observed, that the broad language of head 2 of s. 91 has been curtailed not by any express language of the statute but as a necessary implication of the fundamental division of powers effected by it. The interpretation of this head has undergone a transformation. When it was first considered by this Court in *Severn* v. *The Queen* ([1878], 2 S.C.R. 70) and *The City of Fredericton* v. *The Queen* ([1880], 3 S.C.R. 505), the majority views did not envisage the limitation now established; that was introduced by the judgment in the *Parsons* case, *supra*. The nadir of its scope was reached in what seemed its restriction to a function ancillary to other Dominion powers; but that view has been irretrievably scotched.

The powers of this Court in the exercise of its jurisdiction are no less in scope than those formerly exercised in relation to Canada by the Judicial Committee. From time to time the Committee has modified the language used by it in the attribution of legislation to the various heads of ss. 91 and 92, and in its general interpretative formulations, and that incident of judicial power must, now, in the same manner and with the same authority, wherever deemed necessary, be exercised in revising or restating those formulations that have come down to us. This is a function inseparable from constitutional decision. It involves no departure from the basic principles of jurisdictional distribution; it is rather a refinement of interpretation in application to the particularized and evolving features and aspects of matters which the intensive and extensive expansion of the life of the country inevitably presents.

The reaches of trade may extend to aspects of manufacture. In *Attorney-General for Ontario* v. *Attorney-General for the Dominion et al.*, *supra*, the Judicial Committee dealt with the question whether the Provinces could prohibit the manufacture within the Province of intoxicating liquor, to which the answer was given that, in the absence of conflicting legislation of Parliament, there would be jurisdiction to that effect if it were shown that the manufacture was carried on under such circumstances and conditions as to make its prohibition a merely local matter in the Province. This involves a limitation of the power of the Province to interdict, as a trade matter, the manufacture or production of articles destined for external trade. Admittedly, however, local regulation may affect that trade: wages, workmen's compensation, insurance, taxes and other items that furnish what may be called the local conditions underlying economic activity leading to trade.

The federal character of our constitution places limits on legislative acts in relation to matters which as an entirety span, so to speak, the boundary between the two jurisdictions. In *The King* v. *Eastern Terminal Elevator Company, supra*, for example, there was a common storage of grain destined both to local and external trade. The situation in *City of Montreal* v. *Montreal Street Railway* ([1912] A.C. 333, 1 D.L.R. 681, 12 C.R.C. 541) was equally striking: there Parliament was held incapable of imposing through rates over a local railway on traffic passing between points on that line and points on a connecting Dominion railway; the only regulation open was declared to be parallel action by Legislature and Parliament, each operating only on its own instrumentality. Although by that means the substantial equivalent of a single administration may be attained, there is a constitutional difference between that co-operating action and action by an overriding jurisdiction.

It follows that trade regulation by a Province or the Dominion, acting alone, related to local or external trade respectively, before the segregation of products or manufacturers of each class is reached, is impracticable, with the only effective means open, apart from conditional regulation, being that of co-operative action; this, as in some situations already in effect, may take the form of a single board to administer regulations of both on agreed measures. . . .

FAUTEUX J.:

~ The learned Justice answered the first question in the negative but on grounds which did not depend on an analysis of the distinction between intra-provincial and external trade. He then addressed himself to questions 2, 3, and 4 which related to the Ontario hog-marketing scheme. ~

The first question related to this scheme is whether Regulation 104 of C.R.O. 1950, as amended by O. Reg. 100/55 and O. Reg. 104/55, is *ultra vires* the Lieutenant-Governor in council, either in whole or in part, and if so, in what particular or particulars and to what extent.

The main submission is that the scheme is applicable to the sale of hogs generally, for import and export as well, and as such regulates trade within the meaning of head 2 of s. 91 of the British North America Act and therefore is *ultra vires*. In support of this submission, reference was made to ss. 1*a* and 1*b* of sched. 1, reading:

Interpretation

1*a*. In this scheme
(a) *"hogs" means hogs produced in Ontario except that part thereof comprising the territorial districts and the Provincial County of Haliburton;*
(b) *"processing" means the slaughtering of hogs; and*
(c) *"producer" means a producer engaged in production of hogs.*

Application of Scheme

1*b*. *This scheme applies to hogs marketed either directly or indirectly for processing but does not apply to*
(a) *hogs sold by a producer*
    (i) *to a producer, or*
    (ii) *to a consumer, or*
    (iii) *to a retail butcher, and*
(b) *hogs resold by a processor who bought the hogs under this scheme.*

With respect to importation: It is clear from the above provisions that hogs produced elsewhere than in Ontario are not covered by the scheme. It is equally clear from s. 1*a*(c) read with the provisions of s. 4 of the scheme, which for the whole purpose thereof provides for the grouping of hog producers by districts within the Province, that producers beyond its boundaries are not affected either. In the result, anyone in Ontario is free to import therein and anyone beyond its boundaries to export thereto the regulated product.

Having reached the view that the transaction covered by the scheme is intraprovincial, I do not find it necessary or expedient to define in general terms what constitutes an intraprovincial transaction. The suggestion that to be intraprovincial a transaction must be completed within the Province, in the sense that the product, object of the transaction, must be ultimately and exclusively consumed or be sold for delivery therein for such consumption, is one which would, if carried to its logical conclusion, strip from a Province its recognized power to provide for the regulation of marketing within such Province in disregard of the decisions of the Judicial Committee in *Attorney-General for British Columbia* v. *Attorney-General for Canada et al.*, *supra*, and in *Shannon* v. *Lower Mainland Dairy Products Board*, *supra*.

That joint action of Parliament and of the Legislature may better solve the difficulties arising in particular cases is well known to those entrusted with the government of the nation and the Provinces but provides no answer to the questions here referred for consideration. . . .

20. Reference re Offshore Mineral Rights of British Columbia, *1967*

~ In 1965 the federal government referred to the Supreme Court the question of the ownership and control of the minerals in the seabed under Canadian waters off the British Columbia coast. The reference to the Court was made at a time when the question was at the centre of a hot political controversy between Ottawa and a number of provinces. Mr. Pearson's government referred this matter to the Court presumably because it hoped a favourable decision would strengthen its hand in negotiations with the provinces.

The joint opinion of the Court was totally favourable to the federal government. It held that ownership of the lands under the territorial sea immediately adjacent to the British Columbia coastline belonged to the Crown in the right of Canada not British Columbia and that legislative control over the development of natural resources in this sea-bed as well as in the continental shelf to a depth of 200 metres was under federal jurisdiction.

The Court reached this conclusion by two steps. The first step was to reject British Columbia's claim that the territorial sea was part of the colony when it joined Confederation and hence subject to sections 109 and 117 of the B.N.A. Act under which the provinces retained ownership of the lands and minerals they possessed at the time of union. Here the Court was confronted with competing lines of English judicial decisions and chose to follow those that denied the territorial sea was owned by the Crown when British Columbia joined Canada.

The second step was to find a positive basis for federal jurisdiction. Here the Court referred to section 91(1)(a) which gives the federal Parliament jurisdiction over the public debt and property as well as Parliament's residual power to make laws for the peace, order and good government of Canada in matters not assigned exclusively to the provinces. Land outside the boundaries of a province clearly did not come under any of the provincial powers. Further, the Court asserted that "the mineral resources of the lands underlying the territorial sea are of concern to Canada as a whole and go beyond local or provincial concern or interests." This, it should be noted, was the second time since the *Johannesson* case in 1952 that the Court had employed Viscount Simon's test of inherent national importance as a criterion for invoking peace, order and good government. A year earlier, in *Munro* v. *National Capital Commission*[1], the Court invoked the federal residual power to uphold federal legislation creating a National Capital Commission with zoning and expropriation powers in the Ottawa-Hull region. Justice Cartwright who wrote the Court's opinion in that case emphasized the national dimensions of the legislation. "I find it difficult," he said, "to suggest a subject matter of legislation which more clearly goes beyond local or provincial interests and is

---

[1] [1966] S.C.R. 663.

the common concern of Canada as a whole than the development, conservation and improvement of the National Capital Region. . . ."[2]

The Court's decision in the *Offshore Minerals Reference* also implies that Canada's attainment of national sovereignty has significantly expanded the powers of the federal government. Throughout the judgment it is assumed that "Canada" means the federal government. In the Court's view, rights which Canada enjoys through international recognition must be subject to the jurisdiction of Canada's national government. This line of reasoning should be compared with Lord Atkin's holding in the *Labour Conventions* case that an independent Canada might embark on larger ventures into foreign waters but she does so with her watertight compartments firmly intact.[3]

Several of the provincial premiers had strenuously opposed reference of this issue to the Supreme Court. Not surprisingly, the Court's decision provoked a sharp provincial reaction. Quebec's Premier Lesage for one stated that the decision showed that the Supreme Court of Canada would have to be changed if French-speaking Canadians' constitutional rights were to be protected. In 1968 Prime Minister Trudeau offered the eight provinces touching salt water more than half the revenues from minerals in the seabed off their coasts. This proposal was not accepted by the provinces. Prospects of enormous offshore oil and gas resources spurred Quebec and the four Atlantic provinces in 1972 to band together to press their claim to ownership of oil and other minerals in the Gulf of the St. Lawrence and the Atlantic seabed. At the constitutional conference of First Ministers in September 1980, the federal government offered the coastal provinces, until they become "have" provinces, the same revenues as are derived by provinces from onshore resources. However the provinces continued to press for a constitutional amendment confirming provincial ownership of offshore resources.

Several provinces also pressed their claims in the courts. In 1982, Newfoundland referred to its Court of Appeal the question of whether the province had ownership or control of the natural resources in the seabed from the province's shoreline to the seaward limit of the continental shelf. A few months later the federal government in a move which appeared designed to preempt the Newfoundland reference submitted to the Supreme Court of Canada the question of legislative control of the Hibernia oil fields 320 kilometres off the coast of Newfoundland. In 1983 Newfoundland's Court of Appeal rendered a split decision: finding in the province's favour with respect to the three mile territorial seabed (where there is no oil) but in favour of federal jurisdiction with respect to the continental shelf.[4] A year later the Supreme

---

[2] Ibid., at p. 671.

[3] See above, p. 110.

[4] *Reference Re Mineral and Other Natural Resources of the Continental Shelf* (1983), 145 D.L.R. (3d) 9.

Court came to the same conclusion in favour of federal jurisdiction over the development of the Hibernia field.[5] The Court rested its decision on narrower grounds than in the earlier B.C. case. It invoked the peace, order and good government power as the basis of federal jurisdiction not because of the inherent national importance of offshore mineral development but because the continental shelf was outside Canadian territory and legislation having extra-territorial effect fell under the federal parliament's general power as a residual matter not provided for in the list of provincial powers. Premier Peckford was able, in large measure, to reverse this loss in the courts by negotiating the Atlantic Accord with the Mulroney Government. Under this Accord, Newfoundland can collect royalties from offshore oil and gas and participates on the basis of equality of representation with the federal government in the Board responsible for regulating the development of these resources.[6]

In 1984 the Supreme Court rendered another decision on the offshore—this time in a province's favour. In a four-to-two decision, it awarded British Columbia ownership of the seabed under the waters between Vancouver Island and the mainland.[7] Justice Dickson who wrote the majority opinion based the decision on historical grounds finding that the waters in question (which had not been dealt with in the 1967 reference) were part of the colony of British Columbia when it entered Confederation and therefore were within the province's territory today. ~

REFERENCE RE THE OFFSHORE MINERAL RIGHTS OF
BRITISH COLUMBIA
In the Supreme Court of Canada. [1967] S.C.R. 792.

THE JOINT OPINION OF THE COURT: By Order in Council P.C. 1965-750 of April 26, 1965, the Governor in Council referred the following questions to this Court for hearing and consideration:

1. In respect of the lands, including the mineral and other natural resources, of the seabed and subsoil seaward from the ordinary low-water mark on the coast of the mainland and the several islands of British Columbia, outside the harbours,

bays, estuaries and other similar inland waters, to the outer limit of the territorial sea of Canada, as defined in the Territorial Sea and Fishing Zones Act, Statutes of Canada 1964, Chapter 22, as between Canada and British Columbia,
  (a) Are the said lands the property of Canada or British Columbia?
  (b) Has Canada or British Columbia the right to explore and exploit the said lands?

---

[5] *Reference Re Continental Shelf Offshore Newfoundland* (1984) 1 S.C.R. 86. The Court's decision did not deal with the territorial seabed question.

[6] Earlier, Nova Scotia and the Trudeau government negotiated a joint managment arrangement for the offshore. Under this agreement majority control is retained by the federal government.

[7] *Reference Re Ownership of the Bed of the Strait of Georgia and Related Areas* (1984) 1 S.C.R. 388.

(c) Has Canada or British Columbia legislative jurisdiction in relation to the said lands?

2. In respect of the mineral and other natural resources of the seabed and subsoil beyond that part of the territorial sea of Canada referred to in Question 1, to a depth of 200 metres or, beyond that limit, to where the depth of the superjacent waters admits of the exploitation of the mineral and other natural resources of the said areas, as between Canada and British Columbia,

(a) Has Canada or British Columbia the right to explore and exploit the said mineral and other natural resources?

(b) Has Canada or British Columbia legislative jurisdiction in relation to the said mineral and other natural resources?

Section 3 of the Territorial Sea and Fishing Zones Act, 1964 (Can.), c. 22, reads as follows:

3. (1) Subject to any exceptions under section 5, the territorial sea of Canada comprises those areas of the sea having, as their inner limits, the baselines described in section 5 and, as their outer limits, lines measured seaward and equidistant from such baselines so that each point of the outer limit line of the territorial sea is distant three nautical miles from the nearest point of the baseline.

(2) The internal waters of Canada include any areas of the sea that are on the landward side of the baselines of the territorial sea of Canada.

All the provinces of Canada, with the exception of Quebec, Manitoba, Saskatchewan and Alberta were represented on this Reference. Argument was heard from their counsel, who all supported the position taken by the Province of British Columbia. The Attorney General of Canada submitted that the answer to all the questions should be "Canada". British Columbia submitted it possesses exclusive proprietary rights and sole legislative jurisdiction in relation to the lands

in question and enjoys the sole right to exploration and exploitation within the limits defined by the terms of reference.

The Terms of Union whereby the Colony of British Columbia was admitted into and became part of the Dominion of Canada became effective on July 20, 1871. Paragraph 10 of the Terms of Union made the provisions of the British North America Act, 1867, applicable in the following language:

10. The provisions of the British North America Act, 1867, shall (except those parts thereof which are in terms made, or by reasonable intendment may be held to be specially applicable to and only affect one and not the whole of the Provinces now comprising the Dominion, and except so far as the same may be varied by this Minute) be applicable to British Columbia, in the same way and to the like extent as they apply to the other Provinces of the Dominion, and as if the Colony of British Columbia had been one of the Provinces originally united by the said Act.

Section 109 of the British North America Act, 1867 was thus made applicable to British Columbia. That section reads as follows:

109. All lands, mines, minerals, and royalties belonging to the several Provinces of Canada, Nova Scotia, and New Brunswick at the Union, and all sums then due or payable for such lands, mines, minerals, or royalties, shall belong to the several Provinces of Ontario, Quebec, Nova Scotia, and New Brunswick in which the same are situate or arise, subject to any trusts existing in respect thereof, and to any interest other than that of the Province in the same.

The Privy Council interpreted the above section and has held that whatever proprietary rights were vested in the provinces at the date of Confederation remain so vested unless by the express provisions of the Act transferred to the Dominion: *Attorney General of the*

Dominion of Canada v. *The Attorney General for the Provinces of Ontario, Quebec and Nova Scotia* ([1898] A.C. 700).

An example of the express transfers referred to above is contained in s. 108 of the Act, which provided that "The Public Works and Property of each Provinces enumerated in the Third Schedule to this Act, shall be the Property of Canada."

The judgment of Chief Justice Rinfret in *Attorney General of Canada* v. *Higbie et al* ([1945] S.C.R. 385 at 409, 3 D.L.R. 1) is to like effect:

Up to the time when British Columbia entered Confederation the title to public lands was in the Crown, and the latter's prerogative in respect thereof was in full effect. The Crown lands remained vested in His Majesty in right of the Province and His Royal prerogative to deal therewith remained unaltered, subject to any provincial statutory provisions binding the Crown, of which there were none.

This historical survey shows that:

1. Before Confederation all unalienated lands in British Columbia including minerals belonged to the Crown in right of the colony of British Columbia;

2. After union with Canada such lands remained vested in the Crown in right of the Province of British Columbia.

But it leaves untouched the problem that we have to face—whether the territorial sea was within the boundary of the Province of British Columbia at the time of Confederation.

QUESTION 1—THE TERRITORIAL SEA

It will be noted that question 1(a) asks whether the lands are the "property" of Canada or British Columbia. The word "property" is susceptible of two meanings here. Canada says that it means rights recognized by international law as described in the Geneva Convention of 1958. The alternative meaning is property in the common law sense, i.e., ownership. British Columbia can only succeed on this branch of the case if it is found that

the solum was situate in British Columbia in 1871 at the time of British Columbia's entry into Confederation. This is the whole purpose of the historical survey set out in the British Columbia factum. British Columbia takes the position that the Province of British Columbia included the territorial sea in 1871. Canada, on the other hand, argues that in 1871 at the time of British Columbia's entry into the Union, land below the low-water mark was regarded at common law as being outside the realm, that it was not part of the colony of British Columbia in 1871, and that at, or following Union, it did not become part of the Province of British Columbia. . . .

~ The Court then considered competing lines of English judicial decisions on whether the territorial sea was part of the realm when British Columbia joined Canada. Mainly on the basis of *Reg.* v. *Keyn*, (1876), 2 Ex.D. 63, it concluded that the territory of England and the sovereignty of the Queen stopped at low-water mark during British Columbia's colonial history. ~

So far, we are of the opinion that the territorial sea lay outside the limits of the Colony of British Columbia in 1871 and did not become part of British Columbia following union with Canada. We are also of the opinion that British Columbia did not acquire jurisdiction over the territorial sea following union with Canada.

After 1871, the extent of the jurisdiction of the Province of British Columbia is to be found in the British North America Act. The effect of the union was that the former colony of British Columbia became part of the larger Dominion of Canada. At that date Canada was not a sovereign state. . . .

The rights in the territorial sea formerly asserted by the British Crown in respect of the Colony of British Columbia were after 1871 asserted by the British Crown in respect of the Dominion of Canada. We have already dealt with the Territorial Waters Jurisdiction Act of the Imperial

Parliament in 1878. To summarize, its effect was that the United Kingdom clearly claimed jurisdiction over a territorial sea in respect of the Dominion of Canada. During the period prior to 1919, Canada had only limited rights to legislate in respect of the territorial sea. Legislation of the Dominion Parliament in 1867 and 1868, previously quoted, referred to these waters as "British waters." Not until 1928 did Canadian legislation refer to these waters as the "territorial waters of Canada."

There can be no doubt now that Canada has become a sovereign state. Its sovereignty was acquired in the period between its separate signature of the Treaty of Versailles in 1919 and the Statute of Westminster, 1931, 22 Geo. V., c. 4. Section 3 of the Statute of Westminster provides in an absolutely clear manner and without any restrictions that the Parliament of a Dominion has full power to make laws having extra-territorial operation.

It is Canada which is recognized by international law as having rights in the territorial sea adjacent to the Province of British Columbia. Canada signed and implemented by legislation the Pacific Salmon Fisheries Convention and the Pacific Fur Seals Convention, 1957 (Can.), c. 11 and c. 31. The first of these was between Canada and the United States in respect of the salmon fisheries in the Fraser River system, and the second was a convention among the governments of Canada, Japan, the Union of Soviet Socialist Republics and the United States of America.

Canada has now full constitutional capacity to acquire new areas of territory and new jurisdictional rights which may be available under international law. The territorial sea now claimed by Canada was defined in the Territorial Sea and Fishing Zones Act of 1964 referred to in Question 1 of the Order-in-Council. The effect of that Act, coupled with the Geneva Convention of 1958, is that Canada is recognized in international law as having sovereignty over a territorial sea three nautical miles wide. It is part of the territory of Canada.

The sovereign state which has the property in the bed of the territorial sea adjacent to British Columbia is Canada. At no time has British Columbia, either as a colony or a province, had property in these lands. It is the sovereign state of Canada that has the right as between Canada and British Columbia, to explore and exploit these lands, and Canada has exclusive legislative jurisdiction in respect of them either under s. 91(1)(a) of the British North America Act or under the residual power in s. 91: British Columbia has no legislative jurisdiction since the lands in question are outside its boundaries. The lands under the territorial sea do not fall within any of the enumerated heads of s. 92 since they are not within the province.

Legislative jurisdiction with respect to such lands must, therefore, belong exclusively to Canada, for the subject matter is one not coming within the classes of subjects assigned exclusively to the legislatures of the provinces within the meaning of the initial words of s. 91 and may, therefore, properly be regarded as a matter affecting Canada generally and covered by the expression "the peace, order and good government of Canada."

The mineral resources of the lands underlying the territorial sea are of concern to Canada as a whole and go beyond local or provincial concern or interests.

Moreover, the rights in the territorial sea arise by international law and depend upon recognition by other sovereign states. Legislative jurisdiction in relation to the lands in question belongs to Canada which is a sovereign state recognized by international law and thus able to enter into arrangements with other states respecting the rights in the territorial sea.

Canada is a signatory to the Convention on the Territorial Sea and Contiguous Zone and may become a party to other international treaties and conventions affecting rights in the territorial sea.

We answer questions 1(a), 1(b) and 1(c) in favour of Canada.

QUESTION 2—THE CONTINENTAL SHELF

International law in relation to the continental shelf is a recent development. . . .

The 1958 Geneva Convention on the Continental Shelf defines the rights that a coastal state may exercise over the continental shelf for the purpose of exploring and exploiting its natural resources. Articles 4 and 5 deal with the obligations and responsibilities which must be assumed. Article 6 deals with the problem of delimiting the boundaries of the shelf when it is adjacent to the territories of two or more states which are opposite or adjacent to each other. We set out Articles 1 to 5.

Article 1. For the purpose of these articles, the term "continental shelf" is used as referring (a) to the seabed and subsoil of the submarine areas adjacent to the coast but outside the area of the territorial sea, to a depth of 200 metres or, beyond that limit, to where the depth of the superjacent waters admits of the exploitation of the natural resources of the said areas; (b) to the seabed and subsoil of similar areas adjacent to the coasts of islands.

Article 2. 1. The coastal State exercises over the continental shelf sovereign rights for the purpose of exploring it and exploiting its natural resources.

The rights now recognized by international law to explore and exploit the natural resources of the continental shelf do not involve any extension of the territorial sea. The superadjacent waters continue to be recognized as high seas.

As with the territorial sea, so with the continental shelf. There are two reasons why British Columbia lacks the right to explore and exploit and lacks legislative jurisdiction:

1. The continental shelf is outside the boundaries of British Columbia, and

2. Canada is the sovereign state which will be recognized by international law as having the rights stated in the Convention of 1958, and it is Canada, not the Province of British Columbia, that will have to answer the claims of other members of the international community for breach of the obligations and responsibilities imposed by the Convention.

There is no historical, legal or constitutional basis upon which the Province of British Columbia could claim the right to explore and exploit or claim legislative jurisdiction over the resources of the continental shelf.

We answer questions 2(a) and 2(b) in favour of Canada.

21. Attorney General of Manitoba *v.* Manitoba Egg and Poultry Association (Chicken and Egg Reference), *1971*

~ The more pragmatic approach to the federal trade and commerce power exhibited by the Supreme Court in 1957 in the *Ontario Farm Products Marketing Reference* did not usher in a new era of federal intervention in the Canadian economy. The *Carnation*[1] case in 1968 provided the only occasion in the 1960s on which the Supreme Court was called upon to consider the scope of the trade and commerce power. But in this case, section 91(2), far from serving as a positive basis for federal power, was dismissed as grounds for objecting to provincial economic regulations which impinged on extra-provincial trade. The Quebec legislation in question authorized the province's Agricultural Marketing Board to fix the price of milk sold by Quebec dairy farmers to the Carnation Company, most of whose products were exported from the province. Justice Martland writing for a unanimous Court ruled that this indirect effect of the province's economic regulations on export trade did not constitute an invasion of federal jurisdiction over interprovincial and international trade.

But early in the 1970s the Supreme Court rendered two decisions, both of which expressed an inclination towards strengthening trade and commerce as a significant source of federal power. Both of these cases brought the Supreme Court as the nation's constitutional arbiter to the centre of major conflicts in federal-provincial politics.

At stake in the *Caloil*[2] case was a clash between a major element in the federal government's national energy policy and the economic development ambitions of Quebec. Caloil Inc. of Montreal had been importing petroleum from Algeria and Spain and selling its products through gasoline stations in Ontario and Quebec. But in May 1970, the National Energy Board, with the aim of preserving the key Ontario market for petroleum produced in Western Canada, moved to keep Caloil out of the Ontario market. Regulations were promulgated which would in effect have denied Caloil a licence to import petroleum if it sold *any* gasoline west of a line running down the Ontario-Quebec border and through the Ottawa valley. Caloil successfully challenged the constitutional validity of these regulations before the Exchequer Court. Immediately the federal authorities amended the regulations so that the conditions required for obtaining a licence to import petroleum were more explicitly stated and any restriction on selling oil within provincial markets applied only to imported petroleum. The Exchequer Court reviewed these amended regulations and found them valid. The Supreme Court "in view of the urgency of a matter involving an interference with important business operations"[3] heard

---

[1] *Carnation Co. Ltd.* v. *The Quebec Agricultural Marketing Board et al.* [1968] S.C.R. 238.

[2] *Caloil Inc.* v. *Attorney General of Canada*, [1971] S.C.R. 543.

[3] *Ibid.*, at p. 547.

the appeal from this judgment a few weeks later and also found the Energy Board regulations valid.

In the *Caloil* case the Supreme Court was again unanimous. Justice Pigeon, the newest Quebec appointee, wrote the principal opinion. He found the Supreme Court's earlier decision in the *Murphy* case[4] an apt precedent for bringing the impugned legislation within the federal trade and commerce power. In his view "the true character" of the enactment was the control of imports as part of the administration of an extra-provincial marketing scheme; in these circumstances the federal government could validly interfere with local trade in a province. Immediately following the decision, at a press conference in Montreal, Quebec economist Jacques Parizeau announced that some of Caloil's 1,200 workers might lose their jobs and the Montreal refinery close as a result of the Supreme Court decision.[5]

The second decision, the *"Chicken and Egg" Reference* which is reported below, was an episode in another economic struggle involving Quebec, this time with some of her sister provinces. Quebec, a major importer of eggs, had granted powers to FEDCO, the province's egg marketing agency, enabling it to restrict egg imports in order to protect Quebec producers. The major provinces affected by the regulations were Ontario and Manitoba which supply most of Quebec's egg imports. On the chicken side, the situation was reversed: here Quebec, a major exporter of broilers, soon found that a number of provinces were retaliating against her by restricting the importation of broilers into their provinces. Manitoba, the province most hurt by Quebec's restrictions on egg imports and least assisted by the retaliatory measures protecting broilers, propelled the Chicken and Egg War into the courts by initiating a reference case in its own Court of Appeal. The regulations referred to the Court were drawn up to resemble Quebec's egg marketing scheme. The question of their constitutional validity was hypothetical in the extreme: not only were they not put into force but Manitoba in fact is not an importer of eggs. Nonetheless, the Manitoba Court found the regulations beyond provincial competence and this decision was upheld on appeal by the Supreme Court of Canada.

Justice Martland, whose decision was supported by five other justices, considered that a scheme such as that drafted by Manitoba must be designed to protect Manitoba egg producers from imported eggs. Hence it could be characterized as legislation made primarily in relation to interprovincial trade, a field reserved to the federal legislature under the trade and commerce power in section 91. The case also provided the occasion for Justice Bora Laskin's first major decision on the Canadian constitution. Justice Laskin's concurring opinion carefully reviewed the recent tendency in judicial interpretation to overcome the earlier "attenuation of the federal power in relation to s. 91(2)"

---

[4] *Murphy* v. *C.P.R.* and *Attorney General of Canada* [1986] S.C.R. 626. See above p. 138.
[5] *Globe and Mail*, Nov. 26, 1970.

and establish a more balanced understanding of trade and commerce as a positive basis of federal power in regulating and integrating national economic life. Although Justice Laskin expressed his dismay at being asked to decide such a constitutional case without any of the relevant empirical data, still he was able to find that the Manitoba scheme was aimed primarily at the regulation of imports and as such constituted an invasion of the federal trade and commerce power. But he, like all the other judges who participated in the case, refused to answer the final part of the reference question which called upon the Court to define the degree to which a provincial marketing scheme could affect interprovincial trade without becoming unlawful.

This decision appeared to bolster the Canadian common market by preventing provinces from using marketing schemes to protect local producers from out-of-province competition. Subsequent developments, however, demonstrated that this policy outcome could be substantially reversed through the workings of co-operative federalism. In 1972 the two levels of government agreed to establish C.E.M.A. (the Canadian Egg Marketing Agency), a federal board to co-ordinate the activities of provincial boards. Under this arrangement each province was assigned a share of the national market and the quotas of producers in each province were adjusted to the provincial quotas. The constitutional validity of the federal and provincial legislation establishing this scheme was considered by the Supreme Court in 1978. Except for one provision, the Court upheld the legislative scheme which relied heavily on the interdelegation device approved by the Court in the 1952 *Willis* case.[6] The Court considered that federal legislation delegating to provincial boards the power to restrict imports from other provinces did not violate the requirement of section 121 of the B.N.A. Act that "All Articles of the Growth, Produce or Manufacture of anyone of the Provinces shall . . . be admitted free into each of the other Provinces." Chief Justice Laskin stated that the application of section 121 may differ according to whether it is provincial or federal legislation that is involved because "what may amount to a tariff or customs duty under a provincial regulatory statute may not have that character at all under a federal regulatory statute."[7] ~

ATTORNEY GENERAL OF MANITOBA *v.* MANITOBA EGG AND POULTRY ASSOCIATION ET AL.
In the Supreme Court of Canada [1971] S.C.R. 689.

The judgment of Fauteux C.J. and of Abbott, Martland, Judson, Ritchie and Spence J.J. was delivered by

MARTLAND J.: This is an appeal from

an opinion pronounced, unanimously, by the Court of Appeal for Manitoba ([1971] 18 D.L.R. (3d) 326) on a matter referred to it by an Order of the Lieutenant-Governor-in-Council, dated November 5, 1970,

---

[6] See case 60 below.

[7] *Reference re Agriculture Products Marketing* [1978] 2 S.C.R. 1198, at p. 1267.

as amended by a further Order-in-Council dated December 18, 1970. An appeal to this Court is permitted by s. 37 of the Supreme Court of Canada Act.

The Order-in-Council approved a recommendation of the Attorney-General for Manitoba for the submission to the Court of Appeal for its consideration of certain questions. The relevant portions of the Order-in-Council, as amended, as reproduced, as follows, with the answers given by the Court of Appeal to each of the questions:

~ The order-in-council refers to efforts by certain provinces to regulate the marketing of agricultural products imported from other provinces. It then asks the Court to consider the constitutional validity of Manitoba legislation authorizing a marketing scheme which would require all eggs s ᴧl in the province to be marketed through a Board elected by Manitoba producers. This Board could, among other things, establish quotas or prohibit the sale "of a particular regulated product." The Manitoba Court of Appeal held it was not within the legislative competence of Manitoba to authorize such a plan. ~

. . . The Plan . . . contemplates that it shall be applicable to all eggs marketed in Manitoba, whether or not they are produced in that province. While the provincial Legislature could not control, or permit the Producer Board (hereinafter referred to as "the Board") to control the production of eggs in another province, the terms of the Plan are applicable to the produce of another province once it is within Manitoba and available for marketing. . . .

We have, therefore, a Plan which is intended to govern the sale in Manitoba of all eggs, wherever produced, which is to be operated by and for the benefit of the egg producers of Manitoba, to be carried out by a Board armed with the power to control the sale of eggs in Manitoba, brought in from outside Manitoba, by means of quotas, or even outright prohibition.

The issue which has to be considered in this appeal is as to whether the Plan is *ultra vires* of the Manitoba Legislature because it trespasses upon the exclusive legislative authority of the Parliament of Canada to legislate on the matter of the regulation of trade and commerce conferred by s. 91(2) of the British North America Act.

When the Privy Council first addressed itself to the meaning of that provision it was stated that it included "regulation of trade in matters of interprovincial concern" (*Citizens Insurance Company of Canada* v. *Parsons*, [1881] 7 App. Cas. 96 at 113). That proposition has not since been challenged. However, the case went on to hold that the provision did not include the regulation of the contracts of a particular business or trade in a single province. . . .

The earlier authorities on the matter of provincial marketing regulation were considered by various members of this Court in the *Reference Respecting The Farm Products Marketing Act* ([1957] S.C.R. 198), which case, as well as some of those authorities, was reviewed in the judgment of this Court in *Carnation Company Limited* v. *The Quebec Agricultural Marketing Board* ([1968] S.C.R. 238). It was said, in that case, at p. 253:

While I agree with the view of the four judges in the Ontario Reference *that a trade transaction, completed in a province, is not necessarily, by that fact alone, subject only to provincial control, I also hold the view that the fact that such a transaction incidentally has some effect upon a company engaged in interprovincial trade does not necessarily prevent its being subject to such control.*

Our conclusion was that each transaction and regulation had to be examined in relation to its own facts, and that, in determining the validity of the regulatory legislation in issue in that appeal, the issue was not as to whether it might affect the inter-provincial trade of the appellant company, but whether it was made in relation to the regulation of inter-provincial trade and commerce. There was cited the following passage from the reasons of Kerwin C.J. in the *Ontario Reference* (at p. 204):

Once a statute aims at "regulation of trade in matters of interprovincial concern" it is beyond the competence of a Provincial Legislature.

It is my opinion that the Plan now in issue not only affects inter-provincial trade in eggs, but that it aims at the regulation of such trade. It is an essential part of this scheme, the purpose of which is to obtain for Manitoba producers the most advantageous marketing conditions for eggs, specifically to control and regulate the sale in Manitoba of imported eggs. It is designed to restrict or limit the free flow of trade between provinces as such. Because of that, it constitutes an invasion of the exclusive legislative authority of the Parliament of Canada over the matter of the regulation of trade and commerce.

That being so, I would hold that the Regulation and Order are not ones which are within the legislative competence of the Manitoba Legislature to authorize . . .

The judgment of Hall and Laskin JJ. was delivered by

LASKIN, J.: The utility of the Reference as a vehicle for determining whether actual or proposed legislation is competent under the allocations of power made by the British North America Act is seriously affected in the present case because there is no factual underpinning for the issues that are raised by the Order of Reference. Marketing data to illuminate those issues might have been set out in the Order itself (as was done, for example, in the *Margarine Reference* ([1949] S.C.R. 1), or in an agreed statement of facts, or, indeed, might have been offered to the court to indicate the circumstances which prompted the questions addressed to it.

As it is, I know nothing of the nature of the market for eggs in Manitoba or outside of it, nothing of the production of eggs in that province, nothing of the uses to which the production is put, nothing of the number of producers in Manitoba, nothing of any problems that may have been created in relation to quality, price or otherwise by the entry of out-of-province eggs. I know only, and then in the broad terms set out in the first two recitals in the Order of Reference (and of which matters I could, in any event, have taken judicial notice) that (to quote them) "many Provinces of Canada, including the Province of Manitoba, have enacted legislation pertaining to the regulation and control of marketing of agricultural products" and "certain of the marketing agencies established under the aforementioned legislation in some of the Provinces assert the right to prohibit, regulate and control the marketing within a Province of agricultural products produced outside that Province."

A knowledge of the market in Manitoba, the extent to which it is supplied by Manitoba producers, and of the competition among them as it is reflected in supply, quality and price, would be of assistance in determining the application of the proposed legislative scheme. Thus, if out-of-province eggs were, to put an example, insignificant in the Manitoba market, this would be a factor bearing on a construction of the scheme as operative only in respect of Manitoba producers, retailers and consumers in production, distribution and consumption in Manitoba. Conversely, if such eggs were significant in the Manitoba market, the legislative scheme, not being expressly confined to production distribution and consumption in Manitoba, could properly be regarded as directed to the out-of-province eggs. In this respect, the issue would be one of its validity or invalidity, and not one of construing it to be applicable only to the distribution and consumption within the province of eggs produced in the province.

The absence of what I regard as relevant data leaves the position as one where, on the face of the legislative scheme and in the light of the arguments thereon addressed to the court, the contemplated regulation and order purport to embrace out-of-province eggs sent or brought into the province. Moreover, the embrace would extend to out-of-province eggs of whatever quantity, and to whatever extent they might engulf the Manitoba retailer and consumer market. On this view of the situation, there is the naked constitutional question to be faced, namely; there being no federal regulatory legislation in force with the same thrust, is the proposed scheme offensive to the legislative power of Parliament in relation to "the regulation of trade and commerce" under s. 91(2) of the B.N.A. Act; and, if not or if so, is it, in any event offensive to the prescriptions of s. 121 of that Act?

Previous cases which have been concerned with the validity of provincial regulatory legislation as tested by the scope of s. 91(2) alone (and not also by the concurrent presence of federal regulatory legislation) cannot be dissociated from cases which have been concerned with the validity of federal regulatory legislation and which, accordingly, have dealt affirmatively with the scope of s. 91(2). These two classes are not necessarily opposite sides of the same coin, and hence, the frame of the legislation in each situation has central importance. On the provincial side, a comparison is apt of *Lawson* v. *Interior Tree Fruit and Vegetable Committee of Direction* ([1931] S.C.R. 357) with *Shannon* v. *Lower Mainland Dairy Products Board* ([1938] A.C. 708); and on the federal side, a comparison may be made of *Reference re Natural Products Marketing Act* ([1937] A.C. 377) with *Murphy* v. *C.P.R.* ([1958] S.C.R. 626).

I adopt the position put by Rand J. in *Reference re Ontario Farm Products Marketing Act* ([1957] S.C.R. 198 at 208-209), that there is a field of trade within provincial power, such power being a subtraction from that comprehended within s. 91(2). The subtraction is, to me, quite rational under the scheme of the B.N.A. Act, although stronger terms, referable to a necessary degree of

provincial autonomy, have been used in the cases to support it. That there is such subtraction if a provincial regulatory field is to be recognized was obvious to this court in its earliest years. In the very first reported case on the distribution of legislative power, *Severn* v. *The Queen* ([1878], 2 S.C.R. 70), Strong J., in a dissenting judgment which favoured the validity of the provincial statute that was successfully challenged, pointed out (at p. 104) that, literally, "the regulation of trade and commerce in the Provinces, domestic and internal, as well as foreign and external, [was] by the British North America Act exclusively conferred upon the Parliament of the Dominion." A reduction of this all-embracing authority was effected by this Court in *Citizens Insurance Co.* v. *Parsons* ([1880], 4 S.C.R. 215), a decision affirmed by the Privy Council ([1881], 7 App. Cas. 96) but with *obiter* remarks that led over the years to almost as much an attenuation of the federal power in relation to s. 91(2) as its literal construction would have led to its aggrandizement. A necessary balance has been coming into view over the past two decades, as is evident from the judgments of this court in *Murphy* v. *C.P.R.*, already cited (and emphasized by the refusal of leave to appeal in *Regina* v. *Klassen* ([1959], 20 D.L.R. (2d) 406, [1959] S.C.R. IX]) and *Carnation Company Ltd.* v. *Quebec Agricultural Marketing Board* ([1968] S.C.R. 238).

What this balance points to is a more particular understanding of the meaning of the terms "trade" and "trade and commerce" as they relate respectively to the areas of provincial and federal competence. In *Montreal* v. *Montreal Street Railway* ([1912] A.C. 333 at 344), the Judicial Committee referred to s. 91(2) as expressing "two of the matters enumerated in s. 91." That provision is perhaps better seen as specifying a single class of subject in words that indicate a stronger source of authority than would be found if "trade" alone was used or "commerce" alone. This view is strengthened by the fact that it is unnecessary here to rely on

s. 91(2) for transportation authority (having regard to ss. 92(10)(a)(b), 91(10) and 91(29), in contra-distinction to the judicial history of the commerce power in the United States under clause 3 of Article I of its Constitution and to the evolution of the power of the Commonwealth Parliament under s. 51(i) of the Australian Constitution to make laws with respect to "trade and commerce with other countries and among the States." Etymologically, commerce refers to the buying and selling of goods, and trade has among its meanings (other than commerce) that of mercantile occupation. Although literal application is unthinkable, these meanings do indicate the capacity which inheres in s. 91(2).

Not too often in the history of the interaction of provincial and federal legislation with s. 9(2) have there been attempts to define its terms. . . . It has been put beyond doubt that Parliament's power under s. 91(2) is exclusive so far as concerns the prohibition or regulation of exports to and imports from other countries, and that a province may not, as legislator, prohibit or regulate the export of goods therefrom. This last-mentioned proposition . . . does not, however, mean that, in the absence of federal legislation, a province is incompetent to impose any regulation upon transactions in goods produced therein and between persons therein simply because the regulation may have an effect upon ultimate export of the goods from the province, whether in their original or in some processed form.

The stage of dealing at which the regulation is imposed and its purpose, on which economic data would be relevant, are important considerations in assessing provincial competence. This emerges clearly from *Carnation Milk Company Ltd.* v. *Quebec Agricultural Marketing Board, supra,* where this court rejected a contention that the regulatory scheme, as reflected in three challenged orders, constituted an unlawful invasion of federal power in relation to export. What was there involved was the fixing of prices, by arbitration if agreement could not other-

wise be reached, at which milk and dairy products produced in the province were to be sold by provincial producers, operating under a joint marketing plan, to a distributor and processor in the province. The fact that the processed products were largely distributed and sold outside the province did not react upon the validity of the scheme whose purpose was to improve the bargaining position in the province of provincial producers in their dealings with manufacturers or processors in the province. The regulatory scheme under attack did not involve a marketing control which extended through the various stages of production, distribution and consumption.

What was raised in the *Carnation Milk* case was the meaning, for constitutional purposes, of an intraprovincial transaction where the issue was seen in the context of goods leaving the province. The present Reference raises this question in the context of goods entering the province and their subjection, in consequence, to the same regulatory scheme that operates upon like goods produced in the province. This was a matter which had been considered in the *Shannon* case, *supra,* and in *Home Oil Distributors Ltd.* v. *Attorney General of British Columbia* ([1940] S.C.R. 444), in both of which the impugned schemes were held to be within provincial legislative competence.

There is a passage in the reasons of the Judicial Committee in the *Shannon* case which has a bearing on this Reference. Lord Atkin said this (at pp. 718-719 of [1938] A.C.):

It is sufficient to say upon the first ground that it is apparent that the legislation in question is confined to regulating transactions that take place wholly within the Province, and are therefore within the sovereign powers granted to the Legislature in that respect by s. 92 of the British North America Act. Their Lordships do not accept the view that natural products as defined in the Act are confined to natural products produced in British Columbia. There is no such restriction in the

Act, and the limited construction would probably cause difficulty if it were sought at some future time to cooperate with a valid Dominion scheme. But the Act is clearly confined to dealings with such products as are situate within the Province.

The second sentence in this passage must be read in the light of the history of marketing legislation as it evolved in that period. Parliament and provincial legislatures had enacted what they thought was dovetailing legislation only to find that the central piece, the federal enactment, had over-reached in attempting to encompass purely intra-provincial transactions in products grown and marketed in the province, this element of the scheme being founded on the fact that some portion of the product might be exported: see *Attorney General of British Columbia* v. *Attorney General of Canada* ([1937] A.C. 377). The Privy Council appeared to think in the *Shannon* case that effective cooperation in marketing could better be ensured if the small extra-provincial element was an appendage of provincial legislation. The decision did not foresee the later developments in this area through such legislation as the Motor Vehicle Transport Act 1954 (Can.), c. 59 and the Agricultural Products Marketing Act, R.S.C. 1952, c. 6, as amended by 1957 (Can.), c. 15.

In my opinion, the *Shannon* case cannot today have the effect which a literal application of the second sentence of the quoted passage would suggest. Moreover, the fourth and last sentence indicates that the legislation did not purport to apply to out-of-province producers. However, I find this difficult to reconcile with the second sentence unless it be taken that the marketing scheme did not apply to out-of-province products on their mere entry into the province or that any such application was *de minimis* and not an aim of the scheme. If so, the scheme in the *Shannon* case differs from that involved in this Reference.

Home Oil Distributors Ltd. v. *Attorney*

General of British Columbia ([1940] S.C.R. 444) concerned not a marketing scheme of the type involved in the *Shannon* case or in the present case, but rather a price fixing scheme, embracing both maximum and minimum prices for coal and petroleum products sold at wholesale or retail in the province or for use in the province. It was urged that the legislation was intended to protect local industry from outside competition and, indeed, was aimed at extra-territorial sources of supply and at an integrated interprovincial and international industry. The challenge to the validity of the legislation was made by companies operating refineries in the province who sold to persons in the province, but whose raw supplies came from outside. There was no attempt to control the entry of their oil which, when refined in the province, was marketed therein, save as that control resulted from the price fixing authority. In these circumstances, the legislation was upheld on the principle of the *Shannon* case.

I cannot see in the *Home Oil* case any parallel with the marketing scheme which the Order of Reference put before the Manitoba Court of Appeal. In saying this, I reserve my opinion on a question not dealt with in the reasons of this court in the *Home Oil* case; that is, whether it would have made any difference if under the power given to "fix schedules of prices for different qualities, quantities, standards, grades and kinds of coal and petroleum products" imported goods were treated discriminatorily simply because they were imported. . . .

The Ontario Farm Products Marketing Act Reference, although refining the meaning of an intra-provincial transaction did not expressly address itself to the position of an extra-provincial producer, or a purchaser from him, seeking to bring his production into a province free of a regulatory scheme applicable to local produce. Fauteux J. as he then was, noted in that Reference that the hog marketing scheme which was the subject of the court's concern did not cover hogs produced outside the province nor were producers outside the province affected thereby. "In the result," he said, "any one in Ontario is free to import therein and one beyond its boundaries to export thereto the regulated product" (at p. 254 of [1957] S.C.R.). This is, however, precisely the issue that must be faced in the present Reference.

It must be faced under a scheme which, as set out in the proposed measures attached to the Order of Reference, has the following elements:

1. A Producer Board is established through which all eggs to be marketed in Manitoba must be sold.

2. All such eggs must go to grading and packing stations which are to be operated by persons under contract with the Board.

3. All such eggs must be graded, packed and marked in the grading and packing stations.

4. They are to be packed in containers provided by the Board which are to bear inscriptions of the grade, station number, grading date, place of origin of the eggs and the Board trade mark.

5. Only authorized collectors may take delivery of eggs from a producer.

6. Production and marketing quotas may be allotted to producers by the Board.

7. The Board may establish quotas for production and sale and also fix the time and place of marketing and, equally, may prohibit marketing otherwise or in violation of established quotas or standards.

8. The Board may contract with distributors as its intermediaries in sales to retailers.

9. Weekly prices for each grade of egg are to be set by the Board and distributors are entitled to buy at those prices.

Although the emphasis is on control of the Manitoba producers and distributors in order (as stated in the proposed measures) "to obtain for producers the most advantageous marketing conditions" and "to avoid overproduction", the scheme brings into its grasp "persons" as well as producers, that is, those outside the province who are either producers or dis-

tributors seeking to enter the Manitoba market or those inside the province who are not themselves producers but who bring in out-of-province eggs for disposition in Manitoba. This view is reinforced by the provision for indicating the origin of eggs, including eggs other than those produced in Manitoba.

There may be a variety of reasons which impel a province to enact regulatory legislation for the marketing of various products. For example, it may wish to secure the health of the inhabitants by establishing quality standards; it may wish to protect consumers against exorbitant prices; it may wish to equalize the bargaining or competitive position of producers or distributors or retailers, or all three classes; it may wish to ensure an adequate supply of certain products. These objects may not all nor always be realizable through legislation which fastens on the regulated product as being within the province. This is no longer, if it ever was, the test of validity. Just as the province may not, as a general rule, prohibit an owner of goods from sending them outside the province, so it may not be able to subject goods to a regulatory scheme upon their entry into the province. This is not to say that goods that have come into a province may not, thereafter, be subject to the same controls in, for example, retail distribution to consumers as apply to similar goods produced in the province.

Assuming such controls to be open to a province, the scheme before this court is not so limited. It embraces products which are in the current of interprovincial trade and, as noted at the beginning of these reasons, it embraces them in whatever degree they seek to enter the provincial market. It begs the question to say that out-of-province producers who come in voluntarily (certainly they cannot be compelled by Manitoba) must not expect to be treated differently from local producers. I do not reach the question of discriminatory standards applied to out-of-province producers or distributors (that is, the question of a possibly illegal administration of the scheme as bearing on its validity) because I am of opinion that the scheme is on its face an invasion of federal power in relation to s. 91(2).

There are several grounds upon which I base this conclusion. The proposed scheme has as a direct object the regulation of the importation of eggs, and it is not saved by the fact that the local market is under the same regime. Anglin J. said in *Gold Seal Ltd.* v. *Dominion Express Co.* ([1921], 62 S.C.R. 424 at 465) that "it is common ground that the prohibition of importation is beyond the legislative jurisdiction of the province". Conversely, the general limitation upon provincial authority to exercise of its powers within or in the provinces precludes it from intercepting either goods moving into the province or goods moving out, subject to possible exceptions, as in the case of danger to life or health. Again, the Manitoba scheme cannot be considered in isolation from similar schemes in other provinces; and to permit each province to seek its own advantage, so to speak, through a figurative sealing of its borders to entry of goods from others would be to deny one of the objects of Confederation, evidenced by the catalogue of federal powers and by s. 121, namely, to form an economic unit of the whole of Canada: see the *Lawson* case ([1931] S.C.R. 357 at 373). The existence of egg marketing schemes in more than one province, with objectives similar to the proposed Manitoba scheme, makes it clear that interprovincial trade in eggs is being struck at by the provincial barriers to their movement into various provincial markets. If it be thought necessary or desirable to arrest such movement at any provincial border then the aid of the Parliament of Canada must be sought, as was done through Part V of the Canada Temperance Act, R.S.C. 1952, c. 30, in respect of provincial regulation of the sale of intoxicating liquor.

I do not find it necessary in this case to invoke s. 121, and hence say nothing about its applicability to the marketing scheme under review. . . .

~ Justice Pigeon also wrote a brief concurring opinion and agreed with Justice Martland's opinion. ~

22. Reference re Anti-Inflation Act, *1976*

~ In the fall of 1975 the federal government launched a comprehensive programme of wage and price controls. The Anti-Inflation Act authorized the federal government to control the level of incomes, prices and profits in key sectors of the private sector (firms with five hundred or more employees, construction firms with twenty or more employees, and professionals). It applied directly to the federal public sector and to government employees of provinces which opted into the scheme. The authority could be exercised for up to three years and could be extended by Order-in-Council with the approval of both Houses of Parliament.

The scope of the legislation was not confined to interprovincial and international commerce. It regulated activities which the courts had long regarded as matters of property and civil rights in the province. In enacting the legislation the federal government was relying on its general power. It hoped that if there was a court challenge the Supreme Court would apply the national dimensions test and find that the national importance of combatting inflation made the subject of the legislation a matter concerning the peace, order and good government of Canada. The government was careful to refrain from declaring that inflation was an emergency and, in Parliament, denied that it was counting on the emergency doctrine as a basis for the legislation.

But the government did not rely solely on constitutional law. Before moving ahead with such a contentious economic policy, the government obtained the agreement of all the provinces that they would support the programme. Thus the provinces did not initiate a court challenge. However the programme was attacked in the courts by several Ontario public employees' unions. These groups were particularly concerned that Ontario had brought its public sector into the programme without having enabling legislation passed through the provincial legislature. To resolve legal doubts which had begun to be aired in the lower courts, the federal government decided in March 1976 to refer the question of the Anti-Inflation Act's constitutional validity as well as the question of the validity of Ontario's opting-in Agreement to the Supreme Court.

By a seven-to-two majority the Supreme Court upheld the Anti-Inflation Act as emergency legislation. But a majority of the judges rejected inherent national importance or national dimensions as the criterion for determining whether such a broad subject matter as combatting inflation can be brought under the peace, order and good government power. On this point, Justice Beetz's opinion was decisive. In his view the general power could be used in two ways. In extraordinary circumstances amounting to a national emergency it could be used even if it meant Parliament would be legislating on subjects normally falling under provincial jurisdiction. But the normal use of peace, order and good government was to legislate in relation to narrowly defined subject matters such as the incorporation of national companies, radio, aeronautics or the development of the national capital region which clearly constitute gaps in the distribution of powers and are matters of national concern. A subject such as combatting inflation did not qualify for this normal use because it was far too broad and encompassed matters clearly subject to provincial jurisdiction. This part of Justice Beetz's opinion was supported by five of the nine judges. It represented a victory for those provinces which, like Quebec, British Columbia and Saskatchewan, although willing to support the emergency doctrine, had opposed the national dimensions test.

On the other hand, the Court's willingness to sustain the Anti-Inflation Act as emergency legislation had frightening implications for the provinces. When the federal Parliament exercises its emergency powers, the normal rule of law governing the distribution of powers in Canadian federalism is set aside. This was the first time that the judiciary invoked the emergency doctrine as the constitutional basis for peacetime economic regulation.[1] The Court's decision indicated that the onus of proof as to the existence of an emergency lies with those who challenge the legislation. A brief before the Court supported by thirty-nine of the country's leading economists denying the existence of an emergency was given little weight by the judges. Nor was the majority impressed by the fact that the government had deliberately avoided declaring an emergency when the legislation was before Parliament. It was on this point that Justices Beetz and de Grandpré dissented. In their view a clear indication by Parliament that a national emergency existed was a necessary, although not sufficient, condition for the valid exercise of the emergency power. The ease with which the Court's decision suggested the federal government could have access to emergency powers stimulated provincial interest in giving a reformed federal Upper House representing provincial governments a veto over the exercise of federal emergency powers.

Although the Court ruled against the Ontario Agreement on the grounds that a change in provincial labour laws required an Act of the legislature, the practical import of this part of the decision was soon negated. The Liberal opposition party in the Ontario legislature withdrew its opposition to the anti-inflation programme, permitting the Ontario government, despite its minority position, to have retroactive enabling legislation enacted. ∼

REFERENCE RE ANTI-INFLATION ACT
In the Supreme Court of Canada. [1976] 2 S.C.R. 373.

The judgment of Laskin C.J. and of Judson, Spence and Dickson JJ. was delivered by

LASKIN C.J.: Although it is conceded that the Parliament of Canada could val-idly legislate as it has done if it had limited the legislation to the federal public service and to enterprises or undertakings which are within exclusive federal legislative authority, such as interprovincial trans-portation and communication services,

---

[1] For decisions rejecting the emergency argument as a basis for federal economic legislation in peacetime, see cases 6, 8 and 12 above. But note that the legislation in these earlier cases was not cast in the form of temporary legislation.

radio operations, aerial navigation, atomic energy enterprises, banks and works declared to be for the general advantage of Canada, the Anti-Inflation Act embraces sectors of industry and of services, including employers and employees therein, which are admittedly subject in respect of their intraprovincial operation to provincial regulatory authority. I take it as undeniable that it would have been open to each province to impose price and wage restraints in those sectors, to the extent to which there was no invasion of federal powers such as that in relation to the regulation of trade and commerce. It is equally undeniable that each province could have validly dealt with restraint of salaries and wages of persons in its public service. . . .

In founding himself upon the federal general power to make laws for the peace, order and good government of Canada, the Attorney General in his primary submission takes its scope to be that expounded by Viscount Simon in *Attorney General of Ontario* v. *Canada Temperance Federation*, [1946] A.C. 193. That case was a rerun, at a distance of more than sixty years, of the very issue brought before the Privy Council in *Russell* v. *The Queen* [1882], 7 App. Cas. 829.

~ The Chief Justice then reviewed the decisions of the Privy Council and the Supreme Court dealing with peace, order and good government from the *Russell* case to the *Snider* case in 1925. ~

What emerges from the lines of cases up to the *Snider* case are differences more of degree than of kind about the scope of the federal general power. It is true that neither the *Russell* case nor, indeed, Lord Watson's observations in the *Local Prohibition* case fitted into Viscount Haldane's emphasis on the need for exceptional circumstances, but even on that standard there was no preclusion against finding that a peacetime crisis would warrant resort to the general power in support of federal legislation.

Lord Watson's "national dimensions"

proposition, which appears to have been studiously ignored by the Privy Council through to the *Snider* case, was mentioned by it in the *Labour Conventions* case, [1937] A.C. 326, where Lord Atkin said of Lord Watson's words that "they laid down no principle of constitutional law, and were cautious words intended to safeguard possible eventualities which no one at the time had any interest or desire to define" (at p. 353). It is my view that a similar approach of caution is demanded even today, both against a loose and unrestricted scope of the general power and against a fixity of its scope that would preclude resort to it in circumstances now unforeseen. Indeed, I do not see how this Court can, consistently with its supervisory function in respect of the distribution of legislative power, preclude in advance and irrespective of any supervening situations a resort to the general power or, for that matter, to any other head of legislative authority. This is not to say that clear situations are to be unsettled, but only that a constitution designed to serve this country in years ahead ought to be regarded as a resilient instrument capable of adaptation to changing circumstances. . . .

Chief Justice Duff attempted in his extensive reasons in the *Natural Products Marketing Reference* a synthesis of the preceding case law touching the general power but, significantly, he began his discussion with the following prelude (at p. 416):

. . . *There is no dispute now that the exception which excludes from the ambit of the general power all matters assigned to the exclusive authority of the legislatures must be given its full effect. Nevertheless, it has been laid down that matters normally comprised within the subjects enumerated in section 92 may, in extraordinary circumstances, acquire aspects of such paramount significance as to take them outside the sphere of that section.*

What followed was a reconciliation of

Lord Watson's national dimensions approach with Viscount Haldane's notion of the extraordinary, by requiring that there be some crisis or peril to support federal legislation for the peace, order and good government of Canada, of which war, present or apprehended, was an example. This did not exclude peacetime crises. . . .

I come, finally, to the *Canada Temperance Federation* case. The Privy Council was fully entitled to overrule the *Russell* case and could have marshalled intervening observations in various cases to support it in doing so. But it felt, to use its own words, that "the decision now sought to be overruled has stood for over sixty years . . . and [it] must be regarded as firmly embedded in the constitutional law of Canada and it is impossible now to depart from it" (at p. 206). The importance of Viscount Simon's reasons in the *Canada Temperance Federation* case lies not only in his rejection of the explanation of the *Russell* case given in the *Snider* case but also in his restatement of the scope of the federal general power without advertence either to the *Board of Commerce* case or to the *Fort Frances* case and even without reference to Lord Watson's observations in the *Local Prohibitions* case. Of course, as I have already noted, general propositions must be viewed in the context of the facts and issues out of which they arise, and I emphasize again the point made earlier that it would be unwise to nail down any head of legislative power in such firm fashion as to make it incapable of application to situations as yet unforeseen.

The Attorney General of Canada, supported by the Attorney General of Ontario, put his position in support of the Anti-Inflation Act on alternative bases. He relied, primarily, on the *Canada Temperance Federation* case, contending that the Act, directed to containment and reduction of inflation, concerned a matter which went beyond local or private or provincial concern and was of a nature which engaged vital national interests, among them the integrity to the Canadian monetary system which was unchallengeably within exclusive federal protection and control. He urged, in the alternative, that there was an economic crisis amounting to an emergency or exceptional peril to economic stability sufficient to warrant federal intervention, and, if not an existing peril, there was a reasonable apprehension of an impending one that justified federal intervention through the legislation in question which was designed to support measures and politics of a fiscal and monetary character which were undoubtedly within Parliament's legislative authority. . . .

Since there was, in general, a concession by those opposing the legislation that it would be valid if it were what I may call crisis legislation, and since the proponents of the legislation urged this as an alternative ground on which its validity should be sustained, it appears to me to be the wise course to consider first whether the Anti-Inflation Act can be supported on that footing. If it is sustainable as crisis legislation, it becomes unnecessary to consider the broader ground advanced in its support, and this because, especially in constitutional cases, Courts should not, as a rule, go any further than is necessary to determine the main issue before them.

The competing arguments on the question whether the Act is supportable as crisis legislation raised four main issues: (1) Did the Anti-Inflation Act itself belie the federal contention because of the form of the Act and, in particular because of the exclusion of the provincial public sector from its imperative scope, notwithstanding that it is framed as a temporary measure albeit subject to extension of its operation? (2) Is the federal contention assisted by the preamble to the statute? (3) Does the extrinsic evidence put before the Court, and other matters of which the Court can take judicial notice without extrinsic material to back it up, show that there was a rational basis for the Act as a crisis measure? (4) Is it a tenable argument that exceptional character could be lent to the legislation as rising beyond local or provincial concerns because Parliament could reasonably take the view that it was a necessary measure to fortify action in other related areas of admittedly federal authority, such as that of monetary policy?

I have referred to the first of these issues earlier in these reasons. It goes to the form of the Anti-Inflation Act and to the question whether the scope of the compulsory application of the Anti-Inflation Act may be taken to indicate that the Parliament of Canada did not act through any sense of crisis or urgency in enacting it. I note that the federal public service, a very large public service, is governed by the Act and the Guidelines, that private employers of five hundred or more persons are subject to the Act and Guidelines, that the construction industry is particularly dealt with by making those who employ twenty or more persons in that industry subject to the Act and Guidelines and that the Act and Guidelines apply also to persons in various professions, including architects, accountants, dentists, engineers, lawyers, doctors and management consultants. Again, the Act provides for bringing within the Act and Guidelines businesses, irrespective of numbers employed, which are declared by Order-in-Council to be of strategic importance to the containment and reduction of inflation in Canada. Having regard to the enormous administrative problems which the programme entails, the coverage is comprehensive indeed in its immediately obligatory provisions. What is left out of compulsory coverage is the provincial public sector, including the municipal public sector, but provision is made for bringing this area into the programme under the Guidelines by agreements under s. 4(3) or s. 4(4) or s. 5.

I do not regard the provisions respecting the provincial public sector as an indicator that the Government and Parliament of Canada were not seized with urgency or manifested a lack of any sense of crisis in the establishment of the programme. Provincial governmental concern about rising inflation and concurrent unemployment was a matter of public

record prior to the inauguration of the programme, and this Court was provided with copies of agreements that eight of the ten provinces had made with the federal Government for the application therein of the federal Guidelines. Only British Columbia and Saskatchewan had not entered into agreements. With private industry and private services bound to the extent that they are, and with the federal public service also bound, I see it as a reasonable policy from the standpoint of administration to allow the Provinces to contract into the programme in respect of the provincial public sector under their own administration if this was their preference rather than by simply accepting, as they could, the federal administration. Since the "contracting in" is envisaged on the basis of the federal Guidelines the national character of the programme is underlined. . . .

The Attorney General of Canada relied upon the preamble to the Anti-Inflation Act both in respect of his primary argument and in respect of his alternative argument. He emphasized the words therein "that the containment and reduction of inflation has become a matter of *serious* national concern" and as well the following words that "to accomplish such containment and reduction of inflation it is *necessary* to restrain profit margins, prices, dividends and compensation" (the italicized words were especially emphasized). I do not regard it as telling against the Attorney General's alternative position that the very word "emergency" was not used. Forceful language would not carry the day for the Attorney General of Canada if the circumstances attending its use did not support the constitutional significance sought to be drawn from it. Of course, the absence of any preamble would weaken the assertion of crisis conditions, and I have already drawn attention to the fact that no preamble suggesting a critical economic situation, indeed no preamble at all was included in the legislation challenged in the *Board of Commerce* case.

The preamble in the present case is

sufficiently indicative that Parliament was introducing a far-reaching programme prompted by what in its view was a serious national condition. The validity of the Anti-Inflation Act does not, however, stand or fall on that preamble, but the preamble does provide a base for assessing the gravity of the circumstances which called forth the legislation.

This brings me to the third of the four issues above-mentioned, namely, the relevancy and weight of the extrinsic evidence and the assistance to be derived from judicial notice. When, as in this case, an issue is raised that exceptional circumstances underlie resort to a legislative power which may properly be invoked in such circumstances, the Court may be asked to consider extrinsic material bearing on the circumstances alleged, both in support of and in denial of the lawful exercise of legislative authority. In considering such material and assessing its weight, the Court does not look at it in terms of whether it provides proof of the exceptional circumstances as a matter of fact. The matter concerns social and economic policy and hence governmental and legislative judgment. It may be that the existence of exceptional circumstances is so notorious as to enable the Court, of its own motion, to take judicial notice of them without reliance on extrinsic material to inform it. Where this is not so evident, the extrinsic material need go only so far as to persuade the Court that there is a rational basis for the legislation which it is attributing to the head of power invoked in this case in support of its validity.

There is before this Court material from Statistics Canada, upon which the Court is justified in relying, which, proceeding from a base of 100 in 1971, shows that the purchasing power of the dollar dropped to 0.78 by September 1974 and to 0.71 in September 1975. On the same base, the cost of living index rose to 127.9 by September 1974 and to 141.5 by September 1975, with food, taken alone, and weighted at 28 per cent of all the items taken into calculation, showing a rise to

147.3 in September 1974 and 166.6 in September 1975. These are figures from the Consumer Price Index monitored by Statistics Canada. . . .

There have been inflationary periods before in our history but, again referring to Professor Lipsey's study, "the problem of the co-existence of high unemployment and high inflation rates was not, however, encountered before the late 1960's." These twin conditions continued to the time that the government and Parliament acted in establishing its prices and incomes policy under the Anti-Inflation Act and Guidelines, and were the prime reason for the policy. . . .

There is another consideration that arises from the submissions, particularly those of the Canadian Labour Congress, in opposition to the validity of the Anti-Inflation Act as a measure justified by crisis circumstances. The consideration I refer to is based on Professor Lipsey's study and on his conclusion that the policy adopted in the Anti-Inflation Act is not one that can, on the basis of experience elsewhere and on his appraisal as an economist, be expected to reduce the rate of inflation by more than one to two per cent. The answer to this submission is simple, and it is an answer that has been consistently given by the Courts, namely, that the wisdom or expediency or likely success of a particular policy expressed in legislation is not subject to judicial review. Hence, it is not for the Court to say in this case that because the means adopted to realize a desirable end, i.e., the containment and reduction of inflation in Canada, may not be effectual, those means are beyond the legislative power of Parliament.

I would not exclude the possibility that the means chosen to deal with an alleged evil may be some indicator of whether that evil exists as a foundation for legislation. Professor Lipsey is candid enough to say in his study that whether "a problem is serious enough to be described as a crisis must be partly a matter of judgment." The general question to which his study is directed is, to use his words, "could an economist say that the Canadian economy faced an economic crisis, or was in a critical situation, in October 1975?" He answers this question in the negative on the basis, *inter alia*, of comparative assessment of different periods, and he is supported in this view by many other economists. The Court cannot, however, be concluded by the judgment of an economist, distinguished as he is in the opinion of his peers, on a question of the validity of the exercise of the legislative power invoked in this case. The economic judgment can be taken into account as an element in arriving at an answer to the question whether there is a rational basis for the governmental and legislative judgment exercised in the enactment of the Anti-Inflation Act. It cannot determine the answer.

In my opinion, this Court would be unjustified in concluding, on the submissions in this case and on all the material put before it, that the Parliament of Canada did not have a rational basis for regarding the Anti-Inflation Act as a measure which, in its judgment, was temporarily necessary to meet a situation of economic crisis imperilling the well-being of the people of Canada as a whole and requiring Parliament's stern intervention in the interest of the country as a whole. That there may have been other periods of crisis in which no similar action was taken is beside the point.

The rationality of the judgment so exercised is, in my view, supported by a consideration of the fourth of the issues which I enumerated above. The fact that there had been rising inflation at the time federal action was taken, that inflation is regarded as a monetary phenomenon and that monetary policy is admittedly within exclusive federal jurisdiction persuades me that the Parliament of Canada was entitled, in the circumstances then prevailing and to which I have already referred, to act as it did from the springboard of its jurisdiction over monetary policy and, I venture to add, with additional support from its power in relation to the regulation of trade and commerce.

The Government White Paper refers to a prices and incomes policy as one element in a four-pronged programme of which the first engages its fiscal and monetary authority; and although the White Paper states that the Government rejects the use of severe monetary and fiscal restraints to stop inflation because of the alleged heavy immediate cost in unemployment and foregone output, it could seek to blend policies in those areas with a prices and incomes policy under the circumstances revealed by the extrinsic material.

Since no argument was addressed to the trade and commerce power I content myself with observing only that it provides the Parliament of Canada with a foothold in respect of "the general regulation of trade affecting the whole dominion," to use the words of the Privy Council in *Citizens Insurance Co.* v. *Parsons* (1881), 7 App. Cas. 96, at p. 113. The Anti-Inflation Act is not directed to any particular trade. It is directed to suppliers of commodities and services in general and to the public services of governments, and to the relationship of those suppliers and of the public services to those suppliers and of the public services to those employed by and in them, and to their overall relationship to the public. With respect to some of such suppliers and with respect to the federal public service, federal legislative power needs no support from the existence of exceptional circumstances to justify the introduction of a policy of restraint to combat inflation.

The economic interconnection with other suppliers and with provincial public services, underlined by collective bargaining conducted by, or under the policy umbrella of trade unions with Canada-wide operations and affiliations, is a matter of public general knowledge of which the Court can take judicial notice. The extrinsic material does not reveal any distinction in the operation and effect of inflation in respect of those economic areas which are ordinarily within and those ordinarily outside of effective federal regulatory control. In enacting the

Anti-Inflation Act as a measure for the peace, order and good government of Canada, Parliament is not opening an area of legislative authority which would otherwise have no anchorage at all in the federal catalogue of legislative powers but, rather, it is proceeding from legislative power bases which entitle it to wage war on inflation through monetary and fiscal policies and entitle it to embrace within the Anti-Inflation Act some of the sectors covered thereby but not all. The circumstances recounted above justify it in invoking its general power to extend its embrace as it has done.

For all the foregoing reasons, I would hold that the Anti-Inflation Act is valid legislation for the peace, order and good government of Canada and does not, in the circumstances under which it was enacted and having regard to its temporary character, invade provincial legislative jurisdiction. It is open to this Court to say, at some future time, as it in effect said in the *Margarine* case, [1949] S.C.R. 1, aff'd [1951] A.C. 179, that a statutory provision valid in its application under circumstances envisaged at the time of its enactment can no longer have a constitutional application to different circumstances under which it would, equally, not have been sustained had they existed at the time of its enactment.

~ On Question 2 Chief Justice Laskin found that the Agreement between the federal government and Ontario was not effective to render the Anti-Inflation Act and its Guidelines binding on the provincial public sector in Ontario. This part of the Chief Justices opinion was concurred in by the other eight judges. ~

The judgment of Martland, Ritchie and Pigeon JJ. was delivered by

RITCHIE, J.: I have had the privilege of reading the reasons for judgment of the Chief Justice and his comprehensive review of the authorities satisfies me that the answer to the question of whether or not the Anti-Inflation Act is *ultra vires* the Parliament of Canada, must depend upon whether or not the legislation was enacted to combat a national economic emergency. I use the phrase "national emergency" in the sense in which I take it to have been used by Lord Wright in *Co-operative Committee on Japanese Canadians* v. *Attorney General of Canada*, 1947 A.C. 87, and accepted by this Court in the *Reference as to the Validity of the Wartime Leasehold Regulations* (1950) S.C.R. 124. In those cases the "emergency" was occasioned by war and the aftermath of war, but I see nothing to exclude the application of the principles there enunciated from a situation created by highly exceptional economic conditions prevailing in times of peace.

In my opinion such conditions exist where there can be said to be an urgent and critical situation adversely affecting all Canadians and being of such proportions as to transcend the authority vested in the legislatures of the provinces and thus presenting an emergency which can only be effectively dealt with by Parliament in the exercise of the powers conferred upon it by s. 91 of the British North America Act "to make laws for the peace, order and good government of Canada." The authority of Parliament in this regard is, in my opinion, limited to dealing with critical conditions and the necessity to which they give rise and must perforce be confined to legislation of a temporary character.

I do not consider that the validity of the Act rests upon the constitutional doctrine exemplified in earlier decisions of the Privy Council, to all of which the Chief Justice has made reference, and generally known as the "national dimension" or "national concern" doctrine. It is not difficult to envisage many different circumstances which could give rise to national concern, but at least since the *Japanese Canadians* case, I take it to be established that unless such concern is made manifest by circumstances amounting to a national emergency, Parliament is not endowed under the cloak of the "peace, order and good government" clause with the authority to legislate in relation to matters reserved to the Provinces under s. 92 of the British North America Act. In this regard I am in full agreement with the reasons for judgment prepared for delivery by my brother Beetz which I have had the advantage of reading, and I have little to add to what he has said.

I should also say, however, that I cannot find that the authority of Parliament to pass legislation such as the present Act stems from any of the enumerated classes of subjects referred to in s. 91. The source of the federal power in relation to the Anti-Inflation Act must, in my opinion, be found in the peace, order and good government clause, and the aura of federal authority to which that clause relates can in my view only be extended so as to invade the provincial area when the legislation is directed to coping with a genuine emergency in the sense to which I have made reference.

In order to determine whether the legislation here in question was enacted to combat such an emergency, it is necessary to examine the legislation itself, but in so doing I think it not only permissible but essential to give consideration to the material which Parliament had before it at the time when the statute was enacted for the purpose of disclosing the circumstances which prompted its enactment. The most concrete source of this information is, in my opinion, the White Paper tabled in the House by the Minister of Finance and made a part of the case which was submitted on behalf of the Attorney General of Canada.

The preamble to the Anti-Inflation Act is quoted in full in the reasons for judgment of the Chief Justice and it is unnecessary for me to repeat it. It is enough to say that it manifests a recognition of the fact "that inflation in Canada at current levels is contrary to the interest of all Canadians" and that it has become a matter of such serious national concern as to make it necessary to enact this legislation. Neither the terms of the preamble nor any provisions of the Act specifically declare the existence of a national emergency, nor is there anything in the Act which could of itself be characterized as a proclamation that such a situation exists, but when the language of the preamble is read as I have suggested in conjunction with the White Paper, it does not appear to me that it was necessary for Parliament to use any particular form of words in order to disclose its belief that an emergency existed. The "Introduction" and "Conclusion" of the White Paper appear to me to be descriptive of the conditions with which Parliament purported to cope in enacting the legislation. The Introduction contains the following statement:

Canada is in the grip of serious inflation.

If this inflation continues or gets worse there is a grave danger that economic recovery will be stifled, unemployment increased and the nation subjected to mounting stresses and strains.

It has thus become absolutely essential to undertake a concerted national effort to bring inflation under control.

There are no simple or easy remedies for quickly resolving this critical problem. The inflationary process in Canada is so deeply entrenched that it can be brought under control only by a broad and comprehensive program of action on a national scale.

The Conclusion contains the following passage:

As a first essential, it is imperative that we take determined action as a nation to halt and reverse the spiral of costs and prices that jeopardizes the whole fabric of our economy and of our society.

When the words "serious national concern" are read against the background of these excerpts from the White Paper it becomes apparent that they were employed by Parliament in recognition of the existence of a national emergency.

The provisions of the Act quite clearly reveal the decision of Parliament that exceptional measures were considered to be required to combat this emergency and it has not been seriously suggested that these provisions were colourably enacted for any other purpose.

I am accordingly satisfied that the record discloses that in enacting the Anti-Inflation Act the Parliament of Canada was motivated by a sense of urgent necessity created by highly exceptional circumstances and that a judgment declaring the Act to be *ultra vires* could only be justified by reliance on very clear evidence that an emergency had not arisen when the statute was enacted. In this regard I reiterate what was said by Lord Wright in the *Japanese Canadians* case, supra, at page 101, in the following passage:

Again, if it be clear that an emergency has not arisen, or no longer exists, there can be no justification for the exercise or continued exercise of the exceptional powers. The rule of law as to the distribution of powers between the Parliaments of the Dominion and the Parliaments of the Provinces comes into play. But very clear evidence that an emergency has not arisen, or that the emergency no longer exists, is required to justify the judiciary, even though the question is one of ultra vires, in overruling the decision of the Parliament of the Dominion that exceptional measures were required or were still required. To this may be added as a corollary that it is not pertinent to the judiciary to consider the wisdom or the propriety of the particular policy which is embodied in the emergency legislation.

In my opinion, the evidence presented to the Court by those who opposed the validity of the legislation did not meet the requirements set by Lord Wright and I am unable to say that the exceptional measures contained in the Act were not required.

It is for these reasons I am in agreement with the Chief Justice that the first question posed by this Reference should be answered in the negative.

As to the second question posed by the Reference, I am in complete agreement with the reasons for judgment of the Chief Justice.

The judgment of Beetz and de Grandpré JJ. was delivered by

BEETZ J.: The Anti-Inflation Act authorizes the imposition of Guidelines for the restraint of prices, profit margins, dividends and compensation in those sectors of the economy which it specifies and which may be described as the federal public sector, the federal private sector and the provincial private sector. With provincial consent, the Guidelines can be extended, in whole or in part, to the provincial public sector. It is conceded that the Parliament of Canada has legislative competence to enact such legislation with respect to both the public and private federal sectors and to regulate prices, profit margins, dividends and compensation for commodities and services supplied by the federal government and its agencies or by private institutions or undertakings coming within exclusive federal jurisdiction such as banks, railways, bus lines and other transportation undertakings extending beyond the limits of a province, navigation and shipping undertakings and the like.

However, the Anti-Inflation Act is not confined to the federal public and private sectors. It extends compellingly to a substantial part of the provincial private sector, which is the most important one in quantitative terms and which comprises, for instance manufacturers of commodities such as automobiles and clothes, department stores and other large retailers, hotels, insurance companies, trust companies, all large suppliers of services, professionals such as doctors, dentists and lawyers.

The control and regulation of local trade and of commodity pricing and of profit margins in the provincial sectors have consistently been held to lie, short of a national emergency, within exclusive provincial jurisdiction. . . .

The Anti-Inflation Act, therefore, and the Guidelines directly and ostensibly interfere with classes of matters which have invariably been held to come within exclusive provincial jurisdiction, more particularly property and civil rights and the law of contract. . . .

Two submissions have been made in support of the validity of the Anti-Inflation Act. The first submission relates to a constitutional doctrine founded on judicial decisions and known as the national dimension or national concern doctrine. The second submission relates to another constitutional doctrine also founded on judicial decisions and known as the national emergency doctrine.

I

The first submission made by Counsel for Canada and for Ontario is that the subject matter of the Anti-Inflation Act is the containment and the reduction of inflation. This subject matter, it is argued, goes beyond local provincial concern or interest and is from its inherent nature the concern of Canada as a whole and falls within the competence of Parliament as a matter affecting the peace, order and good government of Canada. . . .

Some of the extremely far-reaching consequences of this submission must be underlined with respect to the so-called subject matter of inflation or its containment as well as in relation to the principles underlying the distribution of powers between Parliament and the Provincial Legislatures.

If the first submission is to be accepted, then it must be conceded that the Anti-Inflation Act could be compellingly extended to the provincial public sector. Parliament has not done so in this case as a matter of legislative policy but, it could decide to control and regulate at least the maximum salaries paid to all provincial public servants notwithstanding any provincial appropriations, budgets and laws. Parliament could also regulate wages paid by municipalities, educational institutions, hospitals and other provincial services as well as tuition or other fees charged by some of these institutions for their services. Parliament could occupy the whole field of rent controls. Since in time of inflation there can be a great deal

of speculation in certain precious possessions such as land or works of arts, Parliament could move to prevent or control that speculation not only in regulating the trade or the price of those possessions but by any other efficient method reasonably connected with the control of inflation. For example, Parliament could presumably enact legislation analogous to mortmain legislation and even extend it to individuals. Parliament could control all inventories in the largest as in the smallest undertakings, industries and trades. Parliament could ration not only food but practically everything else in order to prevent hoarding and unfair profits. One could even go further and argue that since inflation and productivity are greatly interdependent, Parliament could regulate productivity, establish quotas and impose the output of goods or services which corporations, industries, factories, groups, areas, villages, farmers, workers, should produce in any given period. Indeed, since practically any activity or lack of activity affects the gross national product, the value of the Canadian dollar and, therefore, inflation, it is difficult to see what would be beyond the reach of Parliament. Furthermore, all those powers would belong to Parliament permanently; only a constitutional amendment could reduce them. Finally, the power to regulate and control inflation as such would belong to Parliament to the exclusion of the Legislatures if, as is contended, that power were to vest in Parliament in the same manner as the power to control and regulate aeronautics or radio communication or the power to develop and conserve the national capital (*Aeronautics, Radio, Johannesson* and *Munro* cases) . . .

If the first submission is correct, then it could also be said that the promotion of economic growth or the limits to growth or the protection of the environment have become global problems and now constitute subject matters of national concern going beyond local provincial concern or interest and coming within the exclusive legislative authority of Parliament. It

could equally be argued that older subjects such as the business of insurance or
labour relations, which are not specifically listed in the enumeration of federal
and provincial powers and have been held
substantially to come within provincial
jurisdiction have outgrown provincial
authority whenever the business of insurance or labour have become national in
scope. It is not difficult to speculate as to
where this line of reasoning would lead: a
fundamental feature of the Constitution,
its federal nature, the distribution of
powers between Parliament and the
Provincial Legislatures, would disappear
not gradually but rapidly.

I cannot be persuaded that the first submission expresses the state of the law. It
goes against the persistent trend of the
authorities. It is founded upon an
erroneous characterization of the Anti-
Inflation Act. As for the cases relied upon
by Counsel to support the submission,
they are quite distinguishable and they do
not, in my view, stand for what they are
said to stand. . . .

~ Justice Beetz then reviews the major
cases dealing with peace, order and good
government. ~

This submission is predicated upon the
proposition that the subject matter of the
Anti-Inflation Act, its pith and substance,
is inflation or the containment and reduction of inflation.

To characterize a law is but to give a
name to its content or subject matter in
order to classify it into one or the other of
the classes of matters mentioned in s. 91
or s. 92 of the Constitution. These classes
of matters are themselves so many labels
bearing a more or less specific name,
except the general power of Parliament to
make laws in relation to matters not coming within the classes of matters
exclusively assigned to the Provinces—a
label specific only in a negative way—and
except the power of the Provinces in relation to all matters of a merely local or
private nature—a label unspecific except
mainly with regard to dimensions. This
leave some forty-six specific labels,

thirty-one of which are in the federal list
and fifteen of which are in the provincial
list.

But there are in language a great many
expressions other than those used for the
labels in the federal and the provincial
lists. Those innumerable other expressions, often broader and more extensive
than those of s. 91 and s. 92, may . . . be
employed in the title of a statute or to
describe a statute. The expression "inflation" or "the containment and reduction
of inflation" are of that nature. Needless
to say, their use in the title of a statute or
as an attempt to characterize a statute does
not suffice by far in disposing of the
characterization or in taking the matter
with which in fact they deal outside the
ambit of provincial jurisdiction. It is
necessary to look at the reality of the
matter or of the matters with which in
effect they deal.

*It is possible to invent such matters by
applying new names to old legislative purposes. There is an increasing tendency to
sum up a wide variety of legislative purposes in single, comprehensive designations. Control of inflation, environmental
protection, and preservation of the
national identity or independence are
examples.*

*Many matters within provincial juris-
diction can be transformed by being
treated as part of a larger subject or
concept for which no place can be found
within that jurisdiction. This perspective
has a close affinity to the notion that there
must be a single, plenary power to deal
effectively and completely with any problem. The future of the general power, in
the absence of emergency, will depend
very much on the approach that the courts
adopt to this issue of characterization.*

"Sir Lyman Duff and the Constitution" by Professor Gerald LeDain, Q.C.,
as he then was (1974), 12 *Osgoode Hall
Law Journal*, 261 at p. 293. See also
"Unity and Diversity in Canadian
Federalism" by Professor W.R. Lederman, Q.C., (1975), 53 *Canadian Bar*

Review, 596. I am much indebted to these two articles.

The "containment and reduction of inflation" can be achieved by various means including monetary policies—a federal field—the reduction of public expenditures—federal, provincial and municipal—and the restraint of profits, prices and wages—a federal or a provincial field depending on the sector.

I have no reason to doubt that the Anti-Inflation Act is part of a more general program aimed at inflation and which may include fiscal and monetary measures and government expenditure policies. I am prepared to accept that inflation was the occasion or the reason for its enactment. But I do not agree that inflation is the subject matter of the Act. In order to characterize an enactment, one must look at its operation, at its effects and at the scale of its effects rather than at its ultimate purpose where the purpose is practically all-embracing. If for instance Parliament is to enact a tax law or a monetary law as a part of an anti-inflation program no one will think that such laws have ceased to be a tax law or a monetary law and that they have become subsumed into their ultimate purpose so that they should rather be characterized as "anti-inflation laws," an expression which, in terms of actual content, is not meaningful. They plainly remain and continue to be called a tax law or a monetary law, although they have been enacted by reason of an inflationary situation. . . .

Similarly, the Anti-Inflation Act is, as its preamble states, clearly a law relating to the control of profit margins, prices, dividends and compensation, that is, with respect to the provincial private sector, a law relating to the regulation of local trade, to contract and to property and civil rights in the provinces, enacted as part of a program to combat inflation. Property and civil rights in the provinces are, for the greater part, the pith and substance or the subject matter of the Anti-Inflation Act. According to the Constitution, Parliament may fight inflation with the powers put at its disposal by the specific heads enumerated in s. 91 or by such powers as are outside of s. 92. But it cannot, apart from a declaration of national emergency or from a constitutional amendment, fight inflation with powers exclusively reserved to the provinces, such as the power to make laws in relation to property and civil rights. . . .

The authorities relied upon by Counsel for Canada and Ontario in support of the first submission are connected with the constitutional doctrine that became known as the national concern doctrine or national dimension doctrine.

In my view, the incorporation of companies for objects other than provincial, the regulation and control of aeronautics and of radio, the development, conservation and improvement of the National Capital Region are clear instances of distinct subject matters which do not fall within any of the enumerated heads of s. 92 and which, by nature, are of national concern.

I fail to see how the authorities which so decide lend support to the first submission. They had the effect of adding by judicial process new matters or classes of matters to the federal list of powers. However, this was done only in cases where a new matter was not an aggregate but had a degree of unity that made it indivisible, an identity which made it distinct from provincial matters and a sufficient consistence to retain the bounds of form. The scale upon which these new matters enabled Parliament to touch on provincial matters had also to be taken into consideration before they were recognized as federal matters: if an enumerated federal power designated in broad terms such as the trade and commerce power had to be construed so as not to embrace and smother provincial powers (*Parson's* case) and destroy the equilibrium of the Constitution, the Courts must be all the more careful not to add hitherto unnamed powers of a diffuse nature to the list of federal powers.

The "containment and reduction of inflation" does not pass muster as a new subject matter. It is an aggregate of several subjects some of which form a substantial part of provincial jurisdiction. It is totally lacking in specificity. It is so pervasive that it knows no bounds. Its recognition as a federal head of power would render most provincial powers nugatory.

I should add that inflation is a very ancient phenomenon, several thousands years old, as old probably as the history of currency. The Fathers of Confederation were quite aware of it.

It was argued that other heads of power enumerated in s. 91 of the Constitution and which relate for example to the regulation of trade and commerce, to currency and coinage, to banking, incorporation of banks and the issue of paper money may be indicative of the breadth of Parliament's jurisdiction in economic matters. They do not enable Parliament to legislate otherwise than in relation to their objects and it was not argued that the Anti-Inflation Act was in relation to their objects. The Act does not derive any assistance from those powers any more than the legislation found invalid in the *Board of Commerce* case.

For those reasons, the first submission fails.

The second submission made in support of the validity of the Anti-Inflation Act is that the inflationary situation was in October of 1975 and still is such as to constitute a national emergency of the same significance as war, pestilence or insurrection and then there is in Parliament an implied power to deal with the emergency for the safety of Canada as a whole.

Before I deal with this second submission I should state at the outset that I am prepared to assume the validity of the following propositions:

— the power of Parliament under the national emergency doctrine is not confined to war situations or to situations of transition from war to peace; an emergency of the nature contemplated by the doctrine may arise in peace time;

— inflation may constitute such an emergency;

— Parliament may validly exercise its national emergency powers before an emergency actually occurs; a state of apprehended emergency or crisis suffices to justify Parliament in taking preventive measures including measures to contain and reduce inflation where inflation amounts to state of apprehended crisis.

In order to decide whether the Anti-Inflation Act is valid as a national emergency measure, one must first consider the way in which the emergency doctrine operates in the Canadian Constitution; one must find, in the second place whether the Anti-Inflation Act was in fact enacted on the basis that it was a measure to deal with a national emergency in the constitutional sense.

In referring to the emergency doctrine, the Judicial Committee has sometimes used expressions which would at first appear to indicate that there is no difference between the national dimension or national concern doctrine and the emergency doctrine, the latter being but an instance of the first, or that the distribution of powers between Parliament and the provincial legislatures is not altered by a state of emergency, or again that when Parliament deals with a matter which in normal times would be an exclusively provincial matter, it does so under a federal aspect or in a new relation which lies outside of s. 92 of the Constitution.

Counsel for Canada and for Ontario have relied upon them for the proposition that the difference between the national concern doctrine and the emergency doctrine is one of semantics, which perhaps explains why the Ontario factum does not support the validity of the Anti-Inflation Act on the basis of an emergency although Counsel for Ontario said that his position did not, because of that reason of semantics, differ from that of Counsel for Canada. The latter insisted that the difference between the two doctrines is only one of form but made two separate submissions based on each of the two doctrines.

I disagree with the proposition that the national concern or national dimension doctrine and the emergency doctrine amount to the same. Even if it could be said that "where an emergency exists it is the emergency which gives the matter its dimension of national concern or interest" (LeDain, *op. cit.* p. 291), the emergency does not give the matter the same dimensions as the national concern doctrine applied for instance in the *Aeronautics* case, in the *Johannesson* case or in the *Munro* case. The national concern doctrine illustrated by these cases applies in practice as if certain heads such as aeronautics or the development and conservation of the national capital were added to the categories of subject matters enumerated in s. 91 of the Constitution when it is found by the Courts that, in substance, a class of subjects not enumerated in either s. 91 or s. 92 and is not of a merely local or private nature. Whenever the national concern theory is applied, the effect is permanent although it is limited by the identity of the subject newly recognized to be of national dimensions. By contrast, the power of Parliament to make laws in a great crisis knows no limits other than those which are dictated by the nature of the crisis. But one of those limits is the temporary nature of the crisis. . . .

In my view, the verbal precautions taken by the Judicial Committee in the *Fort Frances* case, pp. 704 to 706, and in other cases reflect its concern over the fact that a power of such magnitude as the national emergency power had to be inferred. But further passages, some of which are even to be found in the very judgments which in other parts appear to say the contrary, make clear that, in practice, the emergency doctrine operates as a partial and temporary alteration of the distribution of powers between Parliament and the Provincial Legislatures.

. . . If one looks at the practical effects of the exercise of the emergency power, one must conclude that it operates so as to give to Parliament for all purposes necessary to deal with the emergency, concurrent and paramount jurisdiction over matters which would normally fall within exclusive provincial jurisdiction. To that extent, the exercise of that power amounts to a temporary *pro tanto* amendment of a federal constitution by the unilateral action of Parliament. The legitimacy of that power is derived from the Constitution: when the security and the continuation of the Constitution and of the nation are at stake, the kind of power commensurate with the situation "is only to be found in that part of the Constitution which establishes power in the State as a whole" (Viscount Haldane in the *Fort Frances* case, p. 704).

The extraordinary nature and the constitutional features of the emergency power of Parliament dictate the manner and form in which it should be invoked and exercised. It should not be an ordinary manner and form. At the very least, it cannot be a manner and form which admits of the slightest degree of ambiguity to be resolved by interpretation. In cases where the existence of an emergency may be a matter of controversy, it is imperative that Parliament should not have recourse to its emergency power except in the most explicit terms indicating that it is acting on the basis of that power. Parliament cannot enter the normally forbidden area of provincial jurisdiction unless it gives an unmistakable signal that it is acting pursuant to its extraordinary power. Such a signal is not conclusive to support the legitimacy of the action of Parliament but its absence is fatal. It is the duty of the courts to uphold the Constitution, not to seal its suspension, and they cannot decide that a suspension is legitimate unless the highly exceptional power to suspend it has been expressly invoked by Parliament. Also, they cannot entertain a submission implicitly asking them to make findings of fact justifying even a temporary interference with the normal constitutional process unless Parliament has first assumed responsibility for affirming in plain words that the facts are such as to justify the interference. The responsibility of the Courts begins after the affirmation has been made. If there is no such affirmation, the Constitution receives its normal application. Otherwise, it is the Courts which are indirectly called upon to proclaim the state of emergency whereas it is essential that this be done by a politically responsible body.

We have not been referred to a single judicial decision, and I know of none, ratifying the exercise by Parliament of its national emergency power where the constitutional foundation for the exercise of that power had not been given clear utterance to. And, apart from judicial decisions, I know of no precedent where it could be said that Parliament had attempted to exercise such an extraordinary power by way of suggestion or innuendo. . . .

What is required from Parliament when it purports to exercise its extraordinary emergency power in any situation where a dispute could arise as to the existence of the emergency and as to the constitutional foundation of its action, is an indication, I would even say a proclamation, in the title, the preamble or the text of the instrument, which cannot possibly leave any doubt that, given the nature of the crisis, Parliament in fact purports to act on the basis of that power. The statutes of Canada and the *Canada Gazette* contain several examples of laws, proclamations and orders-in-council which leave room for no doubt that they have been enacted pursuant to the exceptional emergency power of Parliament. . . .

The preamble has been much relied upon:

WHEREAS the Parliament of Canada recognizes that inflation in Canada at current levels is contrary to the interests of all Canadians and that the containment and reduction of inflation has become a matter of serious national concern;

AND WHEREAS to accomplish such containment and reduction of inflation it is necessary to restrain profit margins, prices, dividends and compensation;

The words "a matter of serious national concern" have been emphasized.

I remain unimpressed.

The death penalty is a matter of national concern. So is abortion. So is the killing or maiming of innumerable people by impaired drivers. So is the traffic in narcotics and drugs. One can conceive of several drastic measures, all coming within the ordinary jurisdiction of the Parliament of Canada, and which could be preceded by a preamble reciting that a given situation had become a matter of serious national concern. I fail to see how the adding of the word "serious" can convey the meaning that Parliament has decided to embark upon an exercise of its extraordinary emergency power. The Canada Water Act, S.C. 1969-70 ch. 52 on the constitutionality of which, again, I refrain from expressing any view, contains a preamble where it is stated that pollution of the water resources of Canada has become "a matter of urgent national concern." Is the Canada Water Act an emergency measure in the constitutional sense? It does not seem to present itself as such. How is a matter of serious national concern to be distinguished from a matter of urgent national concern? I cannot read the preamble of the Anti-Inflation Act as indicating that the Act was passed to deal with a national emergency in the constitutional sense.

Counsel for Canada has also insisted upon the temporary nature of the Anti-Inflation Act. I note that the duration of the Act could, under s. 46, be extended by order-in-council with the approval of both Houses of Parliament, although I am not inclined to attach undue importance to this point. Nonetheless, while it would be essential to the validity of a measure enacted under the national emergency power of Parliament that it be not permanent, still the temporary character of an Act is hardly indicative and in no way conclusive that it constitutes a measure passed to deal with a national emergency: Parliament can and often does enact temporary measures relating to matters coming within its normal jurisdiction.

I have dealt with the arguments based on the preamble and the limited duration (s. 46) of the Anti-Inflation Act.

There is nothing in the rest of the Act and in the Guidelines to show that they have been passed to deal with a national emergency. There is much, on the other hand, within the Act and the Guidelines, in terms of actual or potential exemptions which is inconsistent with the nature of a global war launched on inflation considered as a great emergency. . . .

~ Justice Beetz noted that farmers and employers of less than five hundred persons are excluded and the provinces have the option of keeping their public sectors out of the scheme. ~

We were provided with a wealth of extrinsic material the consideration of which, it was expected, would enable us to make a finding of fact as to whether or not inflation had reached a level which justified Parliament's reliance on its extraordinary power or as to whether or not there was a rational basis for Parliament to judge that it could rely upon that power. I do not reach that point, of course, since I hold the view that Parliament did not rely upon its extraordinary power. It seems to me however that, if we are entitled to look at extrinsic material such as a policy statement tabled in the House of Commons by the Minister of Finance, statistics, an economic study, a speech delivered by the Governor of the Bank of Canada, it is not improper for us to read *Hansard* in this case, in order not to construe and apply the provisions of the Anti-Inflation Act, but to ascertain its constitutional pivot. A perusal of the debates reveals that between October 14, 1975, when the policy statement was tabled—the Anti-Inflation Bill C-73 was read for the first time in the Commons on October 16, 1975—and the third reading and the passing of the bill in the Senate on December 10, 1975, the question was raised repeatedly in both Houses and in committee as to what was the constitutional foundation of the bill and as to whether it was not necessary expressly to declare a state of emergency in order to insure its constitutionality. The replies vary but slightly; their general tenor is to the effect that Parliament has jurisdiction to pass the bill as drafted under the peace, order and good government power—which is rather unrevealing—in addition to other specific federal powers enumerated in s. 91 of the Constitution. . . .

Reliance upon those statements is not essential to my conclusions. However, they reinforce my opinion that the Anti-Inflation Act was enacted in this form because it was believed, erroneously, that Parliament had the ordinary power to enact it under the national concern or national dimension doctrine, that is, a basis which coincides identically with the first submission made to us by Counsel for Canada. Parliament did not purport to enact it under the extraordinary power which it possesses in time of national crisis.

The Anti-Inflation Act is in my opinion *ultra vires* of Parliament in so far at least as it applied to the provincial private sector; but severability having not been pleaded by Counsel for Canada, I would declare the Act *ultra vires* of Parliament in whole.

23. Public Service Board *v.* Dionne, *1978*

~ In 1978 the Supreme Court decided three cases dealing with legislative jurisdiction in relation to television broadcasting. In the first of these cases, *Capital Cities Communications* v. *C.R.T.C.*,[1] the Court dismissed a challenge to federal regulations authorizing cable television operators to delete and substitute commercials on programmes broadcast from U.S. stations. The majority decision was based primarily on the Privy Council's decision in the *Radio* case which assigned jurisdiction to the federal Parliament over the regulation of the transmission and reception of radio waves on the basis of both the treaty implementing power and section 92(10)(a). Chief Justice Laskin who wrote the majority opinion argued that from a functional point of view it would be a mistake to divide jurisdiction over broadcasting on the basis of whether programmes reach home television sets via Hertzian waves or via coaxial cable.

The issue in the *Dionne* case (which is reproduced below) concerned the constitutional validity of Quebec legislation providing a system for licensing cable T.V. operators in the province. These operators used coaxial cable on utility poles or underground to bring local communities in Quebec programmes they produced themselves and programmes picked up by the reception of broadcasts from within and from outside the province. The Court found the legislation *ultra vires*. As in the *Capital Cities* case, Chief Justice Laskin wrote the majority opinion and the three Quebec judges dissented. The Chief Justice again argued for unified federal control of broadcasting on the grounds that ''Divided constitutional control of what is functionally an interrelated system of transmitting and receiving television signals, whether directly through air waves or through intermediate cableline operations, not only invites confusion but is alien to the principle of exclusiveness of legislative authority''. Justice Pigeon's dissent focused on the point that section 92(10) establishes provincial jurisdiction over local works (including communications works such as telephone lines) as the basic rule of the constitution and federal jurisdiction over works extending beyond a province as the exception. In his view, the practical difficulties of divided jurisdiction over broadcasting were something that should be sorted out at the political level but should not stand as a legal bar to provincial jurisdiction over local works and undertakings.

In the third case, *Attorney General of Quebec* v. *Kellogg's Co.*,[2] the Court upheld the application to T.V. broadcasting of regulations passed under Quebec's Consumer Protection Act prohibiting certain kinds of advertising aimed at children. In this case the roles of Chief Justice Laskin and Justice Pigeon were reversed: Justice Pigeon wrote the majority opinion while the Chief Justice, with his two Ontario colleagues concurring, wrote a dissenting opinion.

[1] [1978] 2 S.C.R. 141.
[2] [1978] 2 S.C.R. 211.

The Supreme Court's decisions in these three cases stimulated interest in constitutional change, especially in Quebec, where broadcasting is widely regarded as an essential aspect of provincial control over cultural matters. Even at the federal level there was recognition of the merit of providing some scope for the provinces in the field of broadcasting. Immediately following this decision, the federal Communications Minister, Jeanne Sauvé, was reported in the press as stating that ''we have to find new ways of distributing power to the provinces''. Since then it has not been easy to reach agreement on new ways of dividing jurisdiction in this area. At the constitutional conference in September 1980 a federal proposal would have given the provinces jurisdiction over telecommunication carrier works in the province other than national, international, space and satellite carriers. A ''best efforts'' draft favoured by a number of provinces would have given the provinces a much larger measure of control especially in relation to programming. Perhaps the most imaginative proposals was that contained in the Beige Paper of the Quebec Liberal party. It would have given the federal government the power to allocate frequencies, confirmed the provinces' right to establish their own broadcasting stations, but denied both levels of government the power to control the content of broadcasting.

The Constitution Act, 1982 contained no provisions concerning jurisdiction over telecommunications. Nor did this matter figure in Quebec's proposals for accepting the 1982 constitutional changes. However, if the Meech Lake proposals are adopted, the issue dealt with in *Dionne* is one that might be affected by a new interpretation clause directing judges to interpret the Constitution ''in a manner consistent with the recognition that Quebec constitutes within Canada a distinct society''. It is possible that this interpretation clause might induce at least two more members of the Court to adopt the position taken by the dissenting Quebec justices in *Dionne*. ~

PUBLIC SERVICE BOARD *v*. DIONNE
In the Supreme Court of Canada. [1978] 2 S.C.R. 191.

The judgment of Laskin C.J. and Martland, Judson, Ritchie, Spence and Dickson JJ. was delivered by

THE CHIEF JUSTICE: This appeal raises a constitutional question which, by an order of March 16, 1977 was formulated as follows:

Are section 23 of the Public Service Board Act (R.S.Q. 1964, c. 229) and the ordinances rendered pursuant thereto unconstitutional, *ultra vires* or inoperative to the extent that they apply to a cable distribution public service as defined in

the Regulation respecting cable distribution public services (O.C. 3565-73 of the 25th of September, 1973) adopted pursuant to section 3a of the Communications Department Act (L.Q. 1969, c. 65).

The Quebec Court of Appeal in dealing with the issues raised by this question concluded unanimously, in reasons delivered by Tremblay C.J.Q., that it was beyond the competence of the Province of Quebec to regulate the operation of cable distribution systems through which television signals were captured and transmitted to subscribers. In the result, the Quebec Court of Appeal set aside three decisions of the Quebec Public Service Board which had authorized François Dionne, a respondent in this Court, and Raymond d'Auteuil, one of the appellants herein, to operate cable distribution enterprises in certain defined areas in the province and which had settled certain questions touching the carrying out of the authorizations. Dionne alone challenged the validity of the decisions of the Board, a challenge which required a consideration of the statutory authority exercised by the Board, and leave, as required by Quebec law, was obtained to bring the challenge before the Quebec Court of Appeal. . . .

. . . This Court concluded on the facts established in the *Capital Cities* case, that exclusive legislative authority in relation to the regulation of cablevision stations and their programming, at least where such programming involved the interception of television signals and their retransmission to cablevision subscribers, rested in the Parliament of Canada.

Since the matter was argued anew in the present case, and since other provinces intervened in support of the Quebec Attorney General's challenge to exclusive federal competence (they having also intervened in the *Capital Cities* case), I think it desirable that something more be said here, notwithstanding the extensive canvass that was made in the *Capital Cities* case. The two central strands of what I may call the provincial submissions were that (1) two enterprises, having no necessary connection with each other, were involved in television operations and in cablevision operations and (2) the fact that different controlling entities were involved in those operations emphasized the separateness of the enterprises, and since the cable distribution operation was locally situate and limited in its subscriber relations to persons in Quebec it was essentially a local work of undertaking within provincial competence under s. 92(10) of the British North America Act.

The fundamental question is not whether the service involved in cable distribution is limited to intraprovincial subscribers or that it is operated by a local concern but rather what the service consists of. This is the very question that was faced by the Privy Council in the *Radio* case, *supra* (in a different context, it is true) and which was also before that body in *Attorney General of Ontario* v. *Winner* ([1954] A.C. 541.) There is another element that must be noticed, and that is that where television broadcasting and receiving is concerned there can no more be a separation for constitutional purposes between the carrier system, the physical apparatus, and the signals that are received and carried over the system than there can be between railway tracks and the transportation service provided over them or between the roads and transport vehicles and the transportation service that they provide. In all these cases, the inquiry must be as to the service that is provided and not simply as to the means through which it is carried on. Divided constitutional control of what is functionally an interrelated system of transmitting and receiving television signals, whether directly through air waves or through intermediate cable line operations, not only invites confusion but is alien to the principle of exclusiveness of legislative authority, a principle which is as much fed by a sense of the constitution as a working and workable instrument as by a literal reading of its words. In the present case, both the relevant words and the view of the constitution as a pragmatic instrument come together to support the decision of the Quebec Court of Appeal.

I should emphasize that this is not a case where the cable distribution enterprises limit their operations to programmes locally produced by them for transmission over their lines to their local subscribers. Admittedly, they make use of television signals received at their antennae, both from within and without the province; and the fact that they may make changes or deletions in transmitting the off-air programmes to their subscribers does not affect their liability to federal regulatory control. The suggested analogy with a local telephone system fails on the facts because the very technology employed by the cable distribution enterprises in the present case establishes clearly their reliance on television signals and on their ability to receive and transmit such signals to their subscribers. In short, they rely on broadcasting stations, and their operations are merely a link in a chain which extends to subscribers who receive the programmes through their private receiving sets. . . .

For these reasons, as well as for those in the *Capital Cities* case, in which judgment is being given concurrently with the judgment herein, I would dismiss the appeal with costs.

The judgment of Pigeon, Beetz and de Grandpré JJ. was delivered by

PIGEON J. (*dissenting*). This is an appeal from three judgments of the Court of Appeal of the Province of Quebec setting aside three decisions of the Public Service Board and declaring *ultra vires* in so far as they apply to the cable distribution systems of François Dionne and Raymond d'Auteuil, the Communications Department Act, the Public Service Board Act, and the Cabledistribution Regulation. The decisions of the Public Service Board have authorized François Dionne and Raymond d'Auteuil respectively to establish and operate a cable distribution system in two specific areas, the first described as Matane and Matapedia Valley, the other as Mont-Joli and Rimouski. The Attorney General of Canada and the Attorney General of Quebec were parties to the case in the Court of Appeal, the former supporting the attack against provincial jurisdiction, the latter opposing it. On the appeal to this Court notice of the constitutional question was given to all the attorneys general and the attorneys general of Ontario, British Columbia, Saskatchewan, and Alberta, intervened in support of the appeal.

The facts are not in dispute, the parties having filed a declaration admitting for the purposes of the case that the facts are as stated in the orders of the Public Service Board. Those facts were summarized as follows in the unanimous opinion of the Court of Appeal written by Chief Justice Tremblay:

[TRANSLATION] *It is important . . . to describe the undertaking that appellant Dionne and respondent d'Auteuil were respectively authorized to set up and operate. The two undertakings are alike, differing only in the area they serve. I will describe them in layman's terms as I have understood them from studying the record. The purpose of these undertakings is to transmit sounds and pictures to specific receivers, using cables or other means. These sounds and pictures may come from one of the following two sources. They may be picked up from the air where they are present in a free state after being emitted by broadcasting stations located either outside or inside the province of Quebec. They may also be created by the undertaking itself when they represent either a programme produced by the undertaking in Quebec or another event occurring in Quebec.*

A large part of the argument of the appellants in this Court was devoted to the submission that a cable distribution such as those with which we are concerned in this case, was not to be considered as a single undertaking but as two separate undertakings. It was said that the antenna receiving signals transmitted by hertzian waves by TV stations was not a component part of the cable distribution system but a separate undertaking, that it was the only part that was involved in radio communication which is defined in the Radio Act (R.S.C. 1970, c. R-1, s. 2) as meaning:

. . . any transmission, emission or reception of signs, signals, writing, images, sounds or intelligence of any nature by means of electromagnetic waves of frequencies lower than 3,000 Gigacycles per second propagated in space without artificial guide;

On this view of the situation it was contended that only the antenna was a "broadcasting receiving undertaking" within the meaning of the Radio Act seeing that broadcasting is defined as:

. . . *any radiocommunication in which the transmissions are intended for direct reception by the general public; . . .*

In my view, the question in this case is whether the unchallengeable federal jurisdiction over radiocommunication involves exclusive legislative authority over all cable distribution systems making use of signals received by radio communication or whether such exclusive authority extends only to what I will call the radio communication aspect.

It is important at the outset to observe that federal jurisdiction over some activities or operations does not necessarily mean that any undertaking involved in such activities or operations automatically comes under federal jurisdiction. For instance, under head 10 of s. 91 of the B.N.A. Act "Navigation and Shipping" are enumerated among the classes of subjects coming within exclusive federal authority. It would, however, be wrong to conclude that this means that all navigation undertakings come under federal jurisdiction, because head 13 includes only "Ferries between a Province and any British or Foreign Country or between Two Provinces". A ferry operating within the limits of a single province is obviously a navigation operation. However, it is perfectly clear that, from a constitutional point of view, it is a "local", not a federal undertaking. This does not mean that it is not subject to federal jurisdiction but that it is subject to such jurisdiction only in respect of the navigation aspect. How far this may extend need not be considered, it is enough to say that it does not mean that the whole undertaking is subject to federal control. On the contrary, such an undertaking is subject to provincial control save in respect of what may properly be called the navigation aspect. It is equally clear

that the same is true of all shipping because in head 10 of s. 92 one finds that the following come under provincial legislative authority.

10. Local Works and Undertakings other than such as are of the following Classes:
 (a) Lines of Steam or other Ships, Railways, Canals, Telegraphs, and other Works and Undertakings connecting the Province with any other or others of the Provinces, or extending beyond the Limits of the Province;
 (b) Lines of Steam Ships between the Province and any British or Foreign Country; . . .

It must be stressed that by virtue of the above noted provisions, provincial jurisdiction over all undertakings is the rule, federal jurisdiction being the exception. With reference to undertakings of the kind with which we are presently concerned, it is to be noted that telegraph lines are specially included among the undertakings under provincial jurisdiction because exception is made only of those which connect the province with another or extend beyond its limits. At the time of Confederation, telegraph lines were the only known kind of lines used for communication at a distance by means of electrical impulses carried over wires. However in *Toronto* v. *Bell Telephone Co.* ([1905] A.C. 52), the Privy Council had no difficulty in coming to the conclusion that telephone lines should be considered as telegraph lines for constitutional purposes. . . .

It seems to me that the same should be said of coaxial cable lines as of telephone lines. Coaxial cables are nothing but a further development in the technology of using wires for the transmission of signals by means of electrical impulses. Morse telegraphy, as known in 1867, made use of long and short discrete impulses of direct current actuating a magnet at the receiving end. The telephone invented a few years later made use of an electrical current amplitude modulated at audio frequency by the human voice acting on a microphone at an end of the line. Instead of these low frequencies under 10 kilohertz, coaxial networks make use of very high frequencies in the range of 100 megahertz with a tremendous increase in the quantity of information that may be carried over a single cable, this is what makes it possible to transmit television images which, on the American standards require a band width of some 6 megahertz.

In support of federal jurisdiction over coaxial cable networks it is contended that the change of technology in transmission should make no difference. The fallacy of this argument is that it is inconsistent with the very basis of federal jurisdiction which is the use of hertzian waves. Let us not forget that the basic constitutional rule is provincial jurisdiction over local undertakings. Telegraph systems are specifically included in local undertakings. It is clear that these include all communication systems by electrical signals transmitted over wires as appears from the *Bell Telephone Co.* case. In the *Radio* case, the judgments of the majority in this Court which were affirmed by the Privy Council, make it abundantly clear that the very basis of federal jurisdiction was that hertzian waves, by their very nature, could not be confined within a province. . . .

. . . With respect to what was said by the Privy Council, it is important to bear in mind that the case was a reference dealing solely with "radio communications" that is transmissions by means of hertzian waves. The language used should be construed in the light of the question which was under consideration and should not be treated as applicable to an entirely different question.

I think it is of the utmost importance in this matter, to consider the tremendous extent to which communications transmitted by hertzian waves at one point or another are used by undertakings under provincial jurisdiction or conveyed by such undertakings. With the exception of the Bell Telephone Co. system which was established as an interprovincial undertaking and declared by Parliament to be a work for the general advantage of Canada, telephone companies generally come under provincial jurisdiction. It is a well-known fact of which we are entitled to take judicial notice, that they carry on their wires or cables not only telephone conversations but communications of all kinds, including radio network programs. No one has ever contended that, on that account, they have become undertakings subject to federal jurisdiction.

It appears from the record of the instant case that the provincial telephone company which provides the cables used for both Dionne's and d'Auteuil's systems does use for the transmission of communications several microwave links. It would not be reasonable for the federal authorities to claim jurisdiction over the whole undertaking because it is making use of radio communications. Of course, this telephone company has to comply with the Radio Act concerning the technical aspects of its microwave links, but it would, in my view, be an usurpation of power on the part of the federal authorities to claim to exercise control over the whole undertaking because of this use of radio communications.

It is equally obvious to me that the federal authorities could not by virtue of their jurisdiction over radio communications claim to exercise general control over all users of such communications like truckers, taxicabs, police forces, power companies, etc. In fact the use of radio communications, both sending and receiving, has become so much a feature of daily life that it has been made generally available to the public on what is known as citizens band recently expanded to forty channels. All those communications are undoubtedly subject to the federal licensing power and there is no specific limit to the possible extent of the conditions that may be appended to the licences. However, it seems clear to me that it would be an abuse of this licensing power to require that every undertaking obtaining a licence should become subject to federal jurisdiction. In so doing, the federal would exceed the limits of its authority over radio communications just as it would overstep the limits of its jurisdiction over navigation by requiring that all navigation undertakings, including ferries within a province and intraprovincial carriers, become subject to federal control over their whole operations rather than in respect of navigation only. That this is so, clearly appears from the unanimous opinion of the Court written by Duff J., as he then was, in the *Reference re: Waters and Water-Powers* ([1929] S.C.R. 200). In that case it was held that jurisdiction over navigation does not enable the federal authority to claim the benefit of water powers in navigable rivers, Duff J. said at p. 216:

There is nothing more clearly settled than the proposition that in construing section 91, its provisions must be read in light of the enactments of section 92, and of the other sections of the Act, and that where necessary, the prima facie *scope of the language may be modified to give effect to the Act as a whole.*

It was recognized at an early stage in the judicial elucidation of the Act that any other principle of construction might have the effect of frustrating the intention of its authors who could not have intended that the powers assigned exclusively to the provincial legislatures should be absorbed in those given to the Dominion Parliament.

As presently operated, the two cable distribution systems with which we are concerned distribute nothing but TV programmes broadcast by some four or five distant TV stations. These broadcasts are received over their aerials which are set up at a substantial distance from the area where the major part of their subscribers are residing. The distribution of locally produced programmes was initially contemplated and could be accomplished without any change in the distribution network but it remains as a future possibility only. In those circumstances it is contended that the cable networks are nothing but an adjunct of TV broadcasting, that they are nothing but a means of bringing to the subscribers programmes that the hertzian waves do not carry to them but that special antennae erected in favourable locations are able to receive and transmit to them in the form of electrical impulses carried over coaxial cable.

As against this, however, it must be considered that a cable distribution network has to be carried either in underground conduits, as is done only in some densely built urban areas, or, as in this case, carried over utility poles. Those utilities are, as a rule, under provincial jurisdiction as in these cases. In fact the cable networks are, in the main, the property of a provincial telephone company and the cable operators are only lessees. . . .

It will thus be seen that from a physical point of view, with respect to the material set-up which is the essential feature of a cable system, the provincial aspect is by far predominant. The distinctive feature of a cable system, as opposed to radio broadcasting, is that its channels of communication are carried over metal cables strung on poles throughout the area served instead of being carried over what is commonly called "airwaves". The importance of the provincial aspect is therefore undeniable. However, when an aerial is the sole source of signals to be distributed over the cable network, it cannot be denied that this part is also essential. Nevertheless, in view of the considerations previously developed, I cannot agree that "common sense" dictates that on that account the whole undertaking should be under federal jurisdiction. I have already shown by several illustrations how exorbitant it would be for the federal to claim jurisdiction over all undertakings which make use of radio communication and for many of which such use is essential under present conditions.

I cannot agree that the federal authority over radio broadcasting must extend to all undertakings receiving radio broadcasts. In the *Radio* case it was held that federal authority must extend to radio receivers but this does not mean or imply that it must extend to all undertakings operating receivers. Hotels often have aerials and cable distribution networks feeding more receiving sets than many cable distribution undertakings, could this put them under federal control? It is true that for them, it is accessory to their principal business. But cable distribution is a developing technology which may, in time, not only complement but even supplant radio broadcasting as a means of bringing television and some other programmes to the public. Those undertakings are essentially localized and as is properly stressed in the Public Service Board decisions, they should be specially controlled for the purpose of serving the local needs of the particular area for which they are licensed and must, on account of practical consideration, enjoy an exclusive franchise. In its order of September 13, 1974 the Board said:

[TRANSLATION] *Taken as a whole, the Regulation indicates that a primary objective to be attained is to give a voice to local communities; the organization and the laying out of the areas to be served must take this social and cultural objective into consideration. The Board should therefore promote the formation of public cable distribution companies whose owners, managers and organization are as closely related as possible to the communities they will be serving, so that on the one hand local vitality will be naturally led to express itself and on the other hand the company will always be sensitive to the social and cultural needs of the community and to the means of making cable distribution work to satisfy these needs.*

The Board chose to ignore the problem arising out of federal jurisdiction over the broadcast receiving antenna. It is however an issue that must be faced. I cannot agree that it should be solved by saying that the federal should have full control over the undertaking so as to avoid the difficulties of divided jurisdiction. Divided jurisdic-

tion is inherent in any federal system. Whatever may be the extent of the jurisdiction held to be included in the matters allocated to the federal, provincial powers will impinge at some point. Although an extensive view was adopted of the extent of federal power over interprovincial railways, these are far from being freed from any application of provincial legislation. As Lord Watson said in *C.P.R.* v. *Notre Dame de Bonsecours* [(1899] A.C. 367, at p. 372):

The British North America Act, whilst it gives the legislative control of the appellants' railway qua railway to the Parliament of the Dominion, does not declare that the railway shall cease to be part of the provinces in which it is situated, or that it shall, in other respects, be exempted from the jurisdiction of the provincial legislatures.

I have already pointed out that a great many undertakings and services under provincial authority require radio communication licences for a variety of purposes. There is no doubt that this implies complete federal control over technical aspects. In my view, it is equally clear that it does not involve control over economic aspects. This, I think, may be deduced from what was decided in the *Carnation Company Ltd.* case. Essentially, the decision was that extra-provincial economic repercussions would not remove a local matter from provincial authority. . . .

Policy statements of the Canadian Radio-Television Commission which were brought before us on appeal from the Federal Court of Appeal judgment in *Capital Cities Commission Inc., and others* ([1975] F.C. 18), show that the Commission was very much concerned with the economic repercussions of cable distribution on broadcasting station owners. . . . In my view, the principle adopted in the construction of the Canadian constitution is, as exemplified by the *Carnation Milk* case, to reject economic repercussions as a basis for the allocation of legislative jurisdiction apart from emergency conditions such as in the *Anti-Inflation Act Reference*.

In any event, even assuming that by virtue of its licensing authority over broadcasting receiving undertakings, the Canadian Radio-Television Commission could deny a licence to the operator of a cable distribution system licensed by the Public Service Board although his receiving antenna complied with all technical requirements prescribed under the Radio Act, I cannot agree that this possible conflict would justify the assumption by the Commission of full authority over the undertaking as it claims to exercise. Constitutionally, the situation would be no different from that which would obtain if the federal Parliament refused to provide salaries for as many judges on a particular superior, county or district court, as the constitution of that court called for under the law of the province. That court would

have to do without as many judges as the province considered necessary. There would be a political conflict not a legal conflict. In the particular field of radio and communication a similar conflict may arise whenever a federal licence is denied for the use of radio communication equipment which some provincial authority or provincially controlled undertaking considers necessary. At one time, the Canadian Radio-Television Commission was instructed by Orders-in-Council to deny broadcast licences to all provincial authorities. It resulted in sterilizing provincial legislation contemplating such operations. No one suggested it meant that such provincial legislation was *ultra vires*. . . .

I would therefore allow the appeal and set aside the three judgments of the Court of Appeal and restore the orders of the Public Service Board.

24. Canadian Industrial Gas & Oil Ltd. *v.* Government of Saskatchewan, *1978*

~ In the 1970s jurisdiction over natural resources became a focal point of constitutional conflict between Ottawa and provinces well endowed with natural resources, especially scarce energy resources such as oil and natural gas. The *C.I.G.O.L.* case in 1978 and the *Central Canada Potash* case the following year plunged the Supreme Court into this area of controversy. Both cases originated in private litigation between private companies and the Government of Saskatchewan, but, given the important constitutional issues involved, several provinces intervened on Saskatchewan's side while the federal government intervened to support the corporate challenge. The Supreme Court's decision in both cases went against the provinces and provoked demands from Alberta and Saskatchewan for changes in the structure of the Supreme Court as well as for constitutional amendments to strengthen provincial control over natural resources.

At issue in the *C.I.G.O.L.* case was legislation designed by Saskatchewan's N.D.P. government to capture for the provincial treasury 100% of the windfall gains resulting from the 1973 OPEC increases in the world price of oil. The legislation expropriated virtually all the petroleum and natural gas producing tracts in the province and imposed a royalty surcharge on production from Crown-owned land equal to the difference between the current international price for oil and the price before the OPEC increases.

In a seven-to-two decision the Court found the legislation unconstitutional. All nine judges agreed that the "royalty surcharge," because it lacked the voluntary character of royalty payments, was not a royalty (which under section 109 of the B.N.A. Act belong to the provinces) but a tax. Justice Martland (incidentally, an Albertan) writing for the majority held that the tax was indirect because the oil producers passed it on in the form of higher prices to their customers. The power which the legislation gave the Minister to specify the market price for the purpose of calculating the surcharge and to prevent producers from undercutting that price convinced the majority that the provincial tax could increase the price paid by the ultimate purchaser. They concluded that the tax in essence was an export tax, a category of taxation which in earlier cases had been considered unconstitutional. Further, because 98 per cent of Saskatchewan's crude oil is exported to the United States and Eastern Canada, they considered such an attempt to regulate the price of an export commodity to be an unconstitutional encroachment on exclusive federal jurisdiction over interprovincial and international trade and commerce.

Justice Dickson's dissenting opinion stressed the plenary power of the provinces over their natural resources "subject to limits imposed by the Canadian constitution". He contended that in terms of economic realities the surcharge would not determine the export price of oil nor require buyers of Saskatchewan crude to pay more than they would have paid without the surcharge. The Minister's price-setting powers were simply a device to ensure that companies did not evade the tax by selling oil to related international companies below fair market value. Justice Dickson insisted that "the tax does not set the price. Price sets the tax". Nor was there any evidence that the legislation was impeding the flow of interprovincial and international trade. On the contrary, export sales continued at their pre-tax level.

Although Premier Blakeney complained bitterly about this decision, he was able to overcome its immediate impact on the provincial budget by imposing an oil well income tax which presumably, as a direct tax, can survive constitutional challenge. This tax had retroactive effect and recovered for the province the half billion dollars (plus interest) raised by the unconstitutional royalty surcharge.

Soon after this decision, the Prime Minister agreed in principle to a constitutional amendment giving the provinces some capacity to apply indirect taxes to their natural resources. In 1981, the Trudeau government, in order to secure the support of the national New Democratic Party for its package of constitutional proposals which were then before Parliament, tacked onto the package a proposal to add section 92A to the B.N.A. Act confirming and expanding provincial jurisdiction in relation to natural resources. One part of this section, by giving the provinces the right to levy "any mode or system of taxation" on non-renewable natural resources, forestry resources and electrical energy "whether or not such production is exported in whole or in part from the province", would reverse the main implications of the Supreme Court's decision in the *C.I.G.O.L.* case. This natural resource amendment was included in the Constitution Act, 1982. ~

CANADIAN INDUSTRIAL GAS & OIL LTD. *v.*
GOVERNMENT OF SASKATCHEWAN
In the Supreme Court of Canada. [1978] 2 S.C.R. 545.

The judgment of Laskin C.J. and Martland, Judson, Ritchie, Spence, Pigeon and Beetz JJ. was delivered by

MARTLAND J. The question in issue in this appeal is as to the constitutional validity of certain statutes enacted by the Legislature of the Province of Saskatchewan and regulations enacted pursuant thereto, to which reference will be made hereafter. Their validity was challenged by the appellant, a corporation engaged in the exploration for, drilling for and production of oil and natural gas in Saskatchewan and owning freehold leases, Crown leases and royalty interests in that Province. The respondents are the Government of the Province of

Saskatchewan and the Attorney General of that Province. The appellant was unsuccessful in seeking to obtain a declaration of their invalidity, both at trial and on appeal to the Court of Appeal for Saskatchewan. It appeals, with leave, to this Court from the judgment of the Court of Appeal.

The legislation was enacted following the sharp rise in the price of oil on the world market which occurred in 1973. The effect of the legislation has been summarized in the reasons of my brother Dickson, which I have had the advantage of reading. For purposes of convenience I substantially repeat that summary here:

First, production revenues from free-

hold lands were subjected to what was called a "mineral income tax". The tax was one hundred per cent of the difference between the price received at the well-head and the "basic well-head price", a statutory figure approximately equal to the price per barrel received by producers prior to the energy crisis. The owner's interest in oil and gas rights in producing tracts of less than 1,280 acres were exempted from tax. Deductions approved by the Minister of Mineral Resources were allowed in respect of increases in production costs and extraordinary transportation costs. Provision was made for the Minister to determine the well-head value of the oil where he was of the opinion that oil had been disposed of at less than its fair value.

Secondly, all petroleum and natural gas in all producing tracts within the Province were expropriated and subjected to what was called a "royalty surcharge". Oil and gas rights owned by one person in producing tracts not exceeding 1,280 acres were exempted. Although introduced by regulation rather than statute, the royalty surcharge is calculated in the same manner as the mineral income tax. For all practical purposes they are the same, save one exception. The well-head value for the purposes of royalty surcharge is the higher of the price received at the well-head and the price per barrel listed in the Minister's order.

The statutes and regulations under consideration are:

1. The Oil and Gas Conservation, Stabilization and Development Act, 1973, S.S. 1973-74, hereinafter referred to as "Bill 42";
2. An Act to amend the foregoing Act, being Chapter 73, S.S. 1973-74, hereinafter referred to as "Bill 128";
3. An Act to amend the Mineral Resources Act, Chapter 64, S.S. 1973-74, hereinafter referred to as "Bill 127";
4. Amendments to the Petroleum and Natural Gas Regulations, 1969, made

under the Mineral Resources Act as made by:

(a) Order-in-Council 95/74, made pursuant to Section 18 of Bill 42 and confirmed by Section 1(a) of Bill 127;
(b) Order in Council 1238/74, made pursuant to Section 2 of Bill 127. . . .

In summary, Bill 42 imposes a mineral income tax on the income received on oil produced in Saskatchewan in respect to producing properties. The royalty surcharge is made applicable in respect to production from Crown lands. In each case the determination of the basic well-head price is the same; that is, by the Minister. In the case of the mineral income tax, the basic well-head price is set out in the schedules to the legislation. In the case of the royalty surcharge, the basic well-head price is set out in the regulations. The method of calculation is the same in each case. As the basic well-head price has been set at the same figure whether by statute or by regulation, and as the well-head value had been set by the Minister at the same figure for the purposes of both the mineral income tax and the royalty surcharge, the calculation of the mineral income tax and the royalty surcharge has been the same. When effect is given to the expropriation provision of Bill 42, the mineral income tax would apply only to those tracts exempted by s. 27(2) of Bill 42. The royalty surcharge applies both to Crown-owned land, owned by the Crown prior to the enactment of Bill 42, and to oil rights vested in the Crown under the expropriation provisions of Bill 42.

The practical consequence of the application of this legislation is that the Government of Saskatchewan will acquire the benefit of all increases in the value of oil produced in that province above the set basic well-head price fixed by the statute and regulations, which is approximately the same as that which existed in 1973 before the increase in world prices for oil. In this connection there is the important fact that 93 per cent of all crude oil produced in Saskatchewan is destined for export from the Province either to Eastern Canada or the United States of America.

The appellant's attack upon the legislation is made upon two grounds:

1. It is contended that both the mineral income tax and the royalty surcharge constitute indirect taxation, and are therefore beyond the power of the Province to impose, the provincial legislative powers being limited to direct taxation within the province under s. 92(2) of the British North America Act.

2. It is contended that the legislation relates to the regulation of interprovincial and international trade and commerce, a matter over which the Federal Parliament has exclusive legislative power under s. 91(2) of the British North America Act.

DIRECT OR INDIRECT TAXATION

My brother Dickson has reviewed the leading authorities dealing with the distinction between direct and indirect taxation. It is not necessary for me to repeat that review here. He has pointed out that it has been settled that:

The dividing line between a direct and an indirect tax is referable to and ascertainable by the "general tendencies of the tax and the common understanding of men as to those tendencies. The general tendency of a tax is the relevant criterion".

He has also pointed out that certain well understood categories of taxation have been generally established as falling within one or other of these classes. Thus custom levies are recognized as being indirect taxes, whereas income and property taxes have been recognized as being direct taxes. Similarly, a commodity tax has, as a general rule, been regarded as an indirect tax. The appellant submits that the levies here in question are commodity taxes, and refers to the Privy Council decision in *R.* v. *Caledonian Collieries, Limited* ([1928] A.C. 358), . . .

In that case the tax was imposed upon the gross revenue of every mine owner, at a rate not to exceed 2 per cent. The Privy Council considered that the general tendency of the tax would be for a mine owner to seek to recover the tax from his purchasers.

A sales tax, imposed upon vendors of goods, has been generally regarded as an indirect tax. On the other hand, where the tax, although collected through the vendor is actually paid by the ultimate consumer, the tax has been held to be direct. (*Atlantic Smoke Shops Ltd.* v. *Conlon* [1943] A.C. 550, *Cairns Construction Limited* v. *Government of Saskatchewan* [1960] S.C.R. 619.) However, in the present case the tax is imposed upon and payable by the producer in relation to the sale price of the oil which is produced. It is a sales tax, but the contention of the respondents is that it is not an indirect tax because the legislation does not contemplate and seeks to preclude the recovery of the tax from the purchaser.

The respondent contends that the mineral income tax is, as its name implies, an income tax, and so, a direct tax. I agree with the reasons of my brother Dickson for holding that that tax is not an income tax as that term is understood in the authorities which say that an income tax is a direct tax.

The respondent submits, with respect to the royalty surcharge, that it is not a tax, but that it is a genuine royalty payable to the Crown, as the owner of mineral rights, by its lessees, who have been authorized to extract minerals from Crown hands. To determine the validity of this contention it is necessary to consider the nature of the legal relationship between the Crown and the persons from whom payment of the royalty surcharge is demanded. . . .

~ Mr. Justice Martland found that, because producers on expropriated tracts were required to pay the royalty surcharge as a condition of preserving their leases, the levy imposed by the royalty surcharge was actually not a royalty but a tax. ~

In my opinion the royalty surcharge

made applicable to these Crown leases was not a royalty for which provision was made in the lease agreement. It was imposed as a levy upon the share of production to which, under the lease, the lessee was entitled, and was a tax upon production.

I agree with the reasons of my brother Dickson for concluding that the royalty surcharge is a tax imposed upon Crown lessees of the same nature as the mineral income tax imposed upon lessees holding leases from freehold owners. . . .

The reasons given by the Court of Appeal for concluding that the mineral income tax was a direct tax are summarized in the following extract from the judgment:

I think it must be concluded that the tax is one which is demanded from the very persons whom it is intended and desired should pay it. It is not one which is demanded from persons in the expectation and intent that they shall indemnify themselves at the expense of others. In my view, the language of the sections under which the tax is imposed, calculated and payment directed, leaves no doubt but the legislators intended the tax to be paid by the persons upon whom it was imposed and from whom payment is demanded.

If there were any doubt as to this view, I think that doubt would be resolved by an appreciation of the situation that would result if the persons taxed attempted to indemnify themselves at the expense of the purchasers of the oil. If the tax paid pursuant to Bill 42 was added to the sale price of the crude at the well-head, then to the extent it was so passed on, it would increase the well-head price. The effect, therefore, would simply be to increase the tax by the amount which the well-head price was so increased. In other words, such action by the taxpayers would result in no benefit to themselves, but could, if the selling price were increased by the total amount of the tax, substantially increase the tax collected by the Government. Surely such a result following from an attempt to pass on the tax clearly indicates that the Legislature intended the tax to be paid by those upon whom it was imposed and from whom payment was demanded.

With respect, my consideration of the real substance and intent of the legislation under review leads me to a different conclusion.

Both the mineral income tax and the royalty surcharge are taxes upon the production of oil virtually all of which is produced for export from the Province of Saskatchewan. Section 3 of Bill 42 imposes the mineral income tax upon every person having an interest in the oil produced from a well in a producing tract. Section 63(1) of The Petroleum and Natural Gas Regulations, 1969, requires payment of the royalty surcharge upon oil produced or deemed to be produced from Crown lands.

Section 4(1) of Bill 42 as originally enacted fixed the tax payable as being the amount of the difference between the basic well-head price and the international well-head price determined by the Minister. Bill 128 repealed that subsection and substituted the formula of the well-head price received for each barrel of oil produced and sold in each month less the basic well-head price. The operation of the new subsection was made subject to a new section, 4A.

Section 4A provides that where the Minister is of the opinion that oil, income from which is subject to tax, has been disposed of in any month at less than its fair value, he shall determine the well-head value of the oil sold, being the price which he determines should have been obtained, and it is that price, so determined by him, which governs in the computation of the tax and not the actual price received. The purpose of this important provision was twofold. First it enabled the Minister to prevent a reduction in the tax payable by reason of a sale at less than what he considered to be the fair value of the oil. Second it provided a basis for the computation of tax where oil produced from a Saskatchewan well had not been sold at the well-head but had been shipped out by the producer to be refined and sold.

Under this section it is the Minister who has power to determine what he considers to be the fair value of the oil produced, which figure will be applicable in the computation of the tax payable. His determination of fair value is final and conclusive. Section 11 of Bill 42 so provides and also states that his determination is not subject to review by any court of law or by any *certiorari, mandamus,* prohibition, injunction or other proceeding whatsoever.

With respect to the computation of royalty surcharge, I have referred earlier to s. 63(1) of The Petroleum and Natural Gas Regulations, as finally amended, which imposes a royalty surcharge calculated as follows:

(oil produced less Crown royalty oil, less Road Allowance Crown levy) times (well-head value, as established by the Minister less basic well-head price).

The effect of this provision is that the royalty surcharge is determined by subtracting from one figure (well-head value) established by the Minister, another figure (basic well-head price) established by the Crown in the regulations.

These taxing provisions, *i.e.,* both mineral income tax and royalty surcharge, have the following impact upon the Saskatchewan oil producer. In the first place he is effectively precluded from recovering in respect of the oil which he produces any return greater than the basic well-head price per barrel. He is subjected to an income freeze at that figure and can obtain no more than that. In the second place, he is compelled to sell his product at a price which will equal what the Minister determines to be the fair value of the oil which he produces. He must do this, because his production of oil is subject to a tax per barrel representing the difference between fair value and basic well-head price. If he is the lessee of mineral rights in lands in respect of which the mineral rights were expropriated by the Crown, he does not even have the option to discontinue production. Discontinuance of production without ministerial consent is subject to a heavy penalty.

The tax under consideration is essentially an export tax imposed upon oil production. In the past a tax of this nature has been considered to be an indirect tax. . . .

The mineral income tax and the royalty surcharge are taxes imposed in a somewhat unusual manner. The mineral income tax purports to be a direct tax upon income imposed upon the taxpayer, which he cannot pass on to his purchaser. The royalty surcharge, while carrying a different title, is the same in nature. What differentiates this legislation from other legislation imposing export taxes is that the true effect of the legislation is to impose a freeze upon the actual income which the producer exporter can derive from the sale of his product. All that he is permitted to retain on the sale of each barrel of oil is the basic well-head price. In addition to being subjected to an income freeze, he is compelled to sell his product at a price equivalent to what the Minister considers to be its fair value in order to obtain the funds necessary to meet the tax. This amount per barrel over and above the basic well-head price he must obtain from his purchaser as a part of the purchase price. In essence the producer is a conduit through which the increased value of each barrel of oil above the basic well-head price is channeled into the hand of the Crown by way of tax. The increase in value is itself the tax and it is paid by the purchaser of the oil.

It is contended that the imposition of these taxes will not result in an increase in the price paid by oil purchasers, who would have been required to pay the same market price even if the taxes had not been imposed, and so there could be no passing on of the tax by the Saskatchewan producer to his purchaser. On this premise, it is argued that the tax is not indirect. This, however, overlooks the all important fact that the scheme of the legislation under consideration involves the fixing of the maximum return of the Saskatchewan producers at the basic well-head price per barrel, while at the same time compelling him to sell at a higher price. There are two components in the sale price, first the basic well-head price and second the tax imposed. Both are intended by the legislation to be incorporated into the price payable by the purchaser. The purchaser pays the amount of the tax as a part of the purchase price.

For these reasons it is my opinion that the taxation scheme comprising the mineral income tax and the royalty surcharge does not constitute direct taxation within the province and is therefore outside the scope of the provincial power under s. 92(2) of the British North America Act.

REGULATION OF TRADE AND COMMERCE

In considering this issue the important fact is, of course, that practically all of the oil to which the mineral income tax or the royalty surcharge becomes applicable is destined for interprovincial or international trade. Some of this oil is sold by producers at the well-head and thereafter transported from the province by pipeline. Some of the oil is not sold at the well-head, but is produced by companies for their own purposes, and is likewise transported out of the province by pipeline. In either case the levy becomes applicable. The producer in the first case must, if he is to avoid pecuniary loss, sell at the well-head at the well-head value established. The company which has its own oil production transported from the province must, if it is to avoid pecuniary loss, ultimately dispose of the refined product at a price which will recoup the amount of the levy. Thus, the effect of the legislation is to set a floor price for Saskatchewan oil purchased for export by the appropriation of its potential incremental value in interprovincial and international markets, or to ensure that the incremental value is not appropriated by persons outside the province.

Chief Justice Kerwin in the *Reference re The Farm Products Marketing Act* ([1957] S.C.R. 198), said at p. 204:

Once a statute aims at "regulation of trade in matters of inter-provincial concern" it is beyond the competence of a Provincial Legislature.

At p. 205 he said:

The concept of trade and commerce, the regulation of which is confided to Parliament, is entirely separate and distinct from the regulation of mere sale and purchase agreements. Once an article enters into the flow of inter-provincial or external trade, the subject-matter and all its attendant circumstances cease to be a mere matter of local concern.

The purpose of the legislation under review was accurately defined by Chief Justice Culliton in the Court of Appeal:

There is no doubt in my mind that both the Mineral Income tax and the royalty surcharge were imposed for one purpose, and one purpose only—to drain off substantial benefits that would have accrued to the producers due to the sudden and unprecedented price of crude oil.

The means used to achieve this end are to compel a Saskatchewan oil producer to effect the sale of the oil at a price determined by the Minister. The mineral income tax is defined as the difference between the basic well-head price and the price at which the oil is sold, but with the important proviso that if the Minister is of the opinion that the oil has been sold at less than its fair value, he can determine the price at which it should have been sold, and that price governs in determining the amount of the tax. The royalty surcharge, as provided under the Regulations requires the payment of the surcharge on oil produced on the basis of the difference between its well-head value, as established by the Minister, less the basic well-head price. In either case the Minister is empowered to determine the well-head value of the oil which is produced which will govern the price at which the producer is compelled to sell the oil which he produces. In an effort to obtain for the provincial treasury the increases in the value of oil exported from Saskatchewan which began in 1973, in the form of a tax upon the production of oil in Saskatchewan, the legislation gave power to the Minister to fix the price receivable by Saskatchewan oil producers on their export sales of a commodity that has almost no local market in Saskatchewan. Provincial legislative authority does not extend to fixing the price to be charged or received in respect of the sale of goods in the export market. It involves the regulation of interprovincial trade and trenches upon s. 91(2) of the British North America Act.

This is not a case similar to *Carnation Co. Ltd.* v. *Quebec Agricultural Marketing Board* ([1968] S.C.R. 238), where the effect of the Regulations was to increase the cost of the milk purchased by Carnation in Quebec and processed there, mostly for sale outside Quebec. The legislation there indirectly affected Carnation's export trade in the sense that its costs of production were increased, but was designed to establish a method for determining the price of milk sold by Quebec milk producers, to a purchaser in Quebec, who processed it there. Here the legislation is directly aimed at the production of oil destined for export and has the effect of regulating the export price, since the producer is effectively compelled to obtain that price on the sale of his product.

For these reasons, in my opinion, the statutory provisions, and the Regulations and orders enacted and made relating to the imposition of the mineral income tax and the royalty surcharge, are *ultra vires* of the Legislature of the Province of Saskatchewan. . . .

The judgment of Dickson and de Grandpré JJ. was delivered by

DICKSON J. *(dissenting):* The question raised in this appeal is whether a complex of legislation, enacted by the Legislature of Saskatchewan, following the onset in late 1973 of what has been called the "energy crisis", is *intra vires* the Legislature of Saskatchewan. . . .

I

Virtually all of the crude oil produced in Saskatchewan is exported from the province. In 1973, only 1.8 per cent of Saskatchewan crude was used in Saskatchewan refineries; 43.9 per cent was used in provinces of Canada other than Saskatchewan; and 54.3 per cent was exported to the United States. This is attributable in part to the fact that most of the oil produced in the province is medium or heavy crude which, when refined, produces a heavy residue of bunker oil suitable only for use in heavy industry, which is not present in Saskatchewan. Another contributing factor is the fact that the flow of the pipeline through which the oil leaves the province is from west to east. Light and medium crudes, suitable for use in Saskatchewan, are produced in the southeastern part of the province, far from the refineries at Regina and Moose Jaw. These refineries are served by oil from the Province of Alberta.

The appellant, Canadian Industrial Gas & Oil Ltd., is a producer of crude oil in Saskatchewan and sells its entire production at the well site. Virtually all of its product leaves the province by pipeline for refining by others in more easterly provinces of Canada or in the United States. The appellant owns a variety of interests including freehold leases. Crown leases (granted to the appellant or to its predecessor in title, as lessee, subject to Crown royalty); non-operator interests under freehold leases and under Crown leases; royalty interests on freehold leases and on Crown leases; royalty trust certificates; freehold subject to leases to others. The total acreage involved for all types of interest is 156,011 acres, producing 46,000 to 51,000 barrels of oil per month. Prior to the enactment of the legislation, the validity of which is questioned in these proceedings, the appellant's weighted average receipt per barrel for the province amounted to $3.10, with direct field costs of 58 cents per barrel, exclusive of administrative overhead, depreciation, depletion and taxes.

Since the legislation came into force there have been no significant changes in the marketing of Saskatchewan crude oil. The levels of production and exports of oil have continued at a constant or slightly increased tempo, close to production capacity.

II

The appellant's attack upon the legislative scheme is made on two broad grounds. The first claim of invalidity rests on the submission that the mineral income tax and royalty surcharge are indirect taxes and hence beyond s. 92, head 2, of the British North America Act, 1867, which empowers a Legislature to "make laws in relation to matters coming within . . . direct taxation within the province in order to the raising of a revenue for provincial purposes". The second submission is that the legislation, as a whole, is in relation to the regulation of trade and commerce and thus within the exclusive jurisdiction of the federal Parliament under s. 91, head 2, of the Act. Section 121 is not relied upon.

Notwithstanding very able argument by Mr. Robinette, counsel for the appellant, and by Mr. Smith, counsel for the Attorney General of Canada. I have reached the conclusion that the appeal must fail. After reading and re-reading the legislation, the evidence and what appear to be the relevant authorities, I adjudge:

1. That the mineral income tax is not an income tax; it is, however, a direct tax, and therefore within provincial competence.

2. That the royalty surcharge is not a royalty; it too is a tax but also a direct tax.

3. That the entire legislative scheme is aimed at taxation and its effect, if any, upon extraprovincial trade and commerce is incidental and non-disabling.

III

Before considering in detail the legislation, one or two observations of a general nature are warranted. This Court is sensitive to the freedom of action which must be allowed to the Legislatures to safeguard their legitimate interests as in their wisdom they see fit. It presumes that they have acted constitutionally. The onus of rebutting that presumption is upon the appellant. Before the Court concludes that the province has transcended its constitutional powers the evidence must be clear and unmistakable; more than conjecture or speculation is needed to underpin a finding of constitutional incompetence.

On March 20, 1930, an agreement was entered into between the Government of Canada and the Government of Saskatchewan whereby the Government of Canada covenanted and agreed that the Province of Saskatchewan should own all public lands and mines and minerals and should administer and control natural resources within the province from its entry into Confederation in 1905 and should be placed in a position of equality with the other provinces of Confederation with respect to administration and control of its natural resources. The agreement effecting the natural resource transfer recited that:

[i] in order that the province may be in the same position as the original provinces of Confederation are in virtue of section one hundred and nine of the British North America Act 1867, the interest of the Crown in all Crown lands, mines, minerals (precious and base) and royalties derived therefrom within the province . . . shall . . . belong to the province . . . and the said lands shall be administered by the province for the purposes thereof. . . .

The agreement was confirmed by federal and provincial legislation as well as the B.N.A. Act, 1930, 21 Geo. V, c. 26 (Imp.).

Subject to the limits imposed by the Canadian Constitution, the power of the province to tax, control and manage its natural resources is plenary and absolute.

IV

~ In this portion of his opinion Mr. Justice Dickson reviewed the salient features of the legislation. ~

V

DIRECT OR INDIRECT TAXATION

The appellant claims that the mineral income tax and the royalty surcharge are indirect taxes and hence beyond the power of a provincial Legislature. The established guide for determining the validity of this submission is the classical formulation of John Stuart Mill (*Principles of Political Economy*, Book V, c. 3):

Taxes are either direct or indirect. A direct tax is one which is demanded from the very person who it is intended or desired should pay it. Indirect taxes are those which are demanded from one person in the expectation and intention that he shall indemnify himself at the expense of another; such are the excise or customs.

The producer or importer of a commodity is called upon to pay a tax on it not with the intention to levy a peculiar contribution upon him, but to tax through him the consumers of the commodity, from whom it is supposed that he shall recover the amount by means of an advance in price.

Mill's well-known writings appeared not long before the drafting of the British North America Act, 1867, and were presumed by the Privy Council to be familiar to the Fathers of Confederation. . . . Mill's test became firmly established in *Bank of Toronto* v. *Lambe* ([1887] 12 App. Cas. 575). In that case Lord Hobhouse said that while it was proper and, indeed, necessary to have regard to the opinion of economists, the question is a legal one, *viz.* what the words mean as used in the statute. The problem is primarily one of law rather than of refined economic analysis. The dividing line between a direct and an indirect tax is referable to and ascertainable by the "general tendencies of the tax and the common understanding of men as to those tendencies" . . .

There can be no doubt that by the words "direct and indirect taxation" the Fathers of Confederation contemplated certain distinct categories of taxation, as well as a general test of directness. Only certain of such categories, such as income and property taxes, were to be available to the Legislatures. There were two reasons for this. The first was based on arcane political economy. It was thought that a direct tax would be more perceived than an indirect tax. The effect was thought to provide for greater scrutiny and resistance by the electorate with a resulting parsimony in public expenditure. The second reason proved wrong from the start. It was thought that provincial activities would be limited and revenue needs would be slim; the Legislatures, therefore, would have no necessity to resort to most tax pools. . . .

Historically well-understood categories of taxation have a known jurisprudence fate. Thus, a customs levy cannot be made by the Legislature whereas a property tax or income tax falls unquestionably within their competence. Careful constitutional analysis is required in respect of any unusual or hybrid form of taxation. A hybrid form of taxation may well have aspects which are direct and others which are indirect. By nineteenth century political economy, any element of indirectness was a stigma as tending to obfuscate the actions of the Legislature. That consideration is of minor importance today. In assessing the policy of a new form of taxation the jurisprudence offers no certain guide. One begins with the British North America Act, 1867, in which there are two additional criteria: (1) that the taxation be within the province and (2) that it be in order to the raising of a revenue for provincial purposes. Implicit in this, and more important than a vestige of indirectness, is the prohibition of the imposition by a province of any tax upon citizens beyond its borders. Additionally, a province cannot, through the ostensible use of its power to tax, invade prohibited fields. It cannot by way of taxation regulate trade and commerce or prohibit the free admission of produce or manufactured goods from other provinces. It must confine itself to the raising of a revenue for provincial purposes.

VI

Argument was directed to the Court to the effect that the tax here in question is a commodity tax and, as such, the general tendency would be for the tax to be passed on and therefore categorized as indirect. It is true that a tax on any one commodity whether laid on its production, its importation, its carriage from place to place, or its sale will, as a general rule, raise the value and price of the commodity by at least the amount of the tax. Mill, Vol. II (1893 ed.) at p. 435. That is very old doctrine and for that reason a commodity tax is traditionally conceived as an indirect tax. The Courts have taken that as one criterion in characterizing the tax. . . .

It is hard to see that the mineral income tax fits snugly into the commodity tax category. There are several rough edges. First, the tax falls upon a holder of certain rights in respect of part of the amount received. Secondly, unlike a true commodity tax—*i.e.*, a fixed imposition or a percentage of the commodity—s. 6 of the Act contemplates an imposition varying with production costs. If production costs rise, the share of the province by taxation falls. Thirdly, the tax is not an "add-to-the-price" impost but rather a "take-from-the-owner" levy.

Finally, the tax does not fall on the product but only on certain entitled holders. Owners of rights having an aggregate area of less than 1,280 acres in producing tracts are exempted. For these reasons, the tax resists classification as a commodity tax in so far as constitutional jurisprudence knows that term. It must be subject, therefore, to further constitutional scrutiny. . . .

It should be clear from the foregoing that neat constitutional categories are of marginal assistance in the present case.

The tax resists such classification; it is a hybrid. It must be assessed in the light of constitutional analysis, keeping in mind the *indicia* to which I have above referred.

Can it be said, then, that the tax is one which is demanded from the very person who it is intended or desired should pay it, or can it be said, rather, that it is demanded from the oil producer in the expectation and intention that he shall indemnify himself at the expense of another? The question is not easily answered. An example might assist. If we assume a basic well-head price of $3 per barrel and a sale at $7 per barrel, the tax would amount to $4 per barrel. If basic well-head price and production costs remain constant but the selling price increases to $11 per barrel, the tax would amount to $8 per barrel. It is quite obvious that the oil producer will not be in a position to bear the tax of $4 or $8 out of the basic well-head price of $3 per barrel which he retains. On this view it is arguable that the tax is passed on to the purchaser as a component of price. I do not think, however, that this can be said to be the true view. An indirect tax is an amount which is added to what would otherwise be the price of the commodity or service. This appears from Mill's formulation. He says that tax is indirect when the producer is called upon to pay a tax not with the intention of levying a contribution upon him, but to tax through him the consumers of the commodity, from whom it is supposed that he will recover the amount "by means of an advance in price", *i.e.* as an "add-on". In *Attorney General of British Columbia* v. *Esquimalt and Nanaimo Railway Company* ([1950] A.C. 87 (P.C.)), Lord Greene pointed out that in order to constitute an indirect tax the *tax itself* must have a general tendency to be passed on. If an article selling for $10 is subjected to a ten per cent customs duty, the general tendency would be simply to add the amount of the tax or more to the price of the commodity. The purchaser would then pay one dollar or more in excess of the amount he would have paid in the absence of the tax. In *Security*

Export Co. v. *Hetherington* ([1923] S.C.R. 539), Duff J. adopted the following definition of a direct tax, taken from the *Oxford Dictionary:*

One levied immediately upon the persons who are to bear the burden, as opposed to indirect taxes levied upon commodities, of which the price is thereby increased so that the persons on whom the incidence ultimately falls pay indirectly a proportion of taxation included in the price of the article.

If the price is increased by reason of the tax, the tendency will be to have the consumer bear the increase. If the price is not increased, the tendency will be to have the producer bear the tax.

For myself, I can find nothing in the language of the Act nor in the oral or documentary evidence to suggest that the price of Saskatchewan oil was increased by the addition of the "mineral income tax" levied, or that the purchaser of Saskatchewan crude paid more per barrel than he would have paid in the absence of the tax. Nor can I discover anything which leads me to conclude that the Legislature of Saskatchewan acted on any view other than that of collecting maximum tax from the persons who are by the statute made liable to pay it, namely Saskatchewan oil producers.

There is a further consideration which should not be overlooked. If it had been intended that those subject to the tax would pass it on to others the inclusion of the "farmers' section", exempting tracts not exceeding 1,280 acres, would have been quite unnecessary.

The "farmers' section" highlights the essential axis on which the present litigation revolves. It is a dispute concerning who, as between the producers and the Government of Saskatchewan, will reap the benefit of a fortuitous rise in the price of oil. In the case of producers holding rights in producing tracts in excess of 1,280 acres, the Legislature has determined the benefit shall accrue to provincial coffers; in the case of a producer in a smaller tract, the Legislature has

abstained from imposition leaving the benefit in the producer's pocket. The ultimate position of the final consumer is unaffected. It is also patent that any attempt by an oil producer to pass on an amount additional to the selling price would be self-defeating. Every increase in selling price will be reflected by an equal increase in tax as, according to the formula, tax equals well-head price received minus basic well-head price.

Reference was made in the Saskatchewan Courts, and in argument in this Court, to the international or "world" price of oil and the effect of such upon the pricing of Saskatchewan crude. It has been contended on behalf of the province that the world price would place a ceiling on the price of Saskatchewan crude and, therefore, the Saskatchewan producer could not pass on the mineral income tax to the purchaser. Again, to take an example, if world price were $11 per barrel and basic well-head price $3 per barrel, the mineral income tax would amount to $8 per barrel. The producer could not recover this amount by increasing the price to $19 per barrel and for good reasons (i) his oil could not command that price in the market, and (ii) he would be deprived of the additional revenue by the mechanics of the Act. . . .

If Saskatchewan oil is sold in the market at prevailing market prices, as I understand to be the case, then I do not think it can properly be said that the Eastern Canadian oil consumer pays more by reason of imposition of the tax. There is no added "burden" to "cling" to the commodity unit. See Rand J. in *C.P.R.* v. *A.-G. Saskatchewan, supra.*

One of the cornerstones upon which appellant's case rests is the contention that there resides in the Minister a general power to fix the price at which oil is sold, and that the oil producer, if he is to avoid pecuniary loss, must sell at the ministerially pre-determined price. That is simply not the case. The power of the Minister to determine well-head value in respect of mineral income tax is not an unrestrained and unrestricted general power; it is exerciseable only when oil is disposed of at less than fair value, and then, only *after* the sale has taken place. The purpose of s. 4A of Bill 42 is obviously to prevent such practices as sale of oil between related companies at artificially low prices. Well-head value is not arbitrarily set by the Minister—it is set by world and national forces determining the market price at the well-head. No evidence was adduced that the Minister has ever set a figure above market price, thus forcing producers into a loss position if unable to sell at the artificially high figure set. In the normal course of events the tax is the difference between basic well-head price and the market price received by the producer in the course of trade. If the producer seeks to evade tax by undercutting the price his product would command at fair market value, then the possibility of ministerial determination arises, but only then. The tax does not set the price. Price sets the tax. . . .

I would hold that, in its true nature and effect, the mineral income tax constitutes direct taxation within the province in order to the raising of a revenue for provincial purposes.

IX

The Province seeks to sustain the constitutionality of the royalty surcharge imposed by The Oil and Natural Gas Regulations, 1969, on the basis that it is a "variable" royalty. The right of the Crown, in respect of Crown lands, to impose contractually a royalty and to vary such royalty is undisputed. . . .

The first question to be determined in respect of royalty surcharge, therefore, is whether the royalty surcharge is a royalty or a tax. The answer to that question turns on whether the province, in imposing royalty surcharge, was acting *qua* lessor or *qua* taxing authority. In other words, was the relationship of the Legislature *vis-à-vis* the oil producer that of lessor-lessee, or was the true character of the relationship that of sovereign taxing authority-taxpayer. . . .

In my view, although in name a royalty, the royalty surcharge is, in substance, a tax. Except as affecting lessees under pre-existing Crown leases, it is a levy compulsorily imposed on previously existing contractual rights by a public authority for public purposes. It is patent that the consensual agreement and mutuality ordinarily found in a lessor-lessee relationship is entirely absent in the relationship between the Crown and persons subjected to the royalty surcharge. Royalty surcharge is the same one hundred per cent levy as is imposed in other terms as mineral income tax. That it is a tax is not fatal. In object and purpose and mode of exaction it is congruent with mineral income tax. It is therefore direct and falls within provincial competence.

X

Counsel for appellant urged the Court to strike down the legislation as an infringement of Parliament's exclusive authority respecting the regulation of trade and commerce. Appellant says: "the tax and surcharge are established in a way which enables the Province of Saskatchewan to control the minimum price at which Saskatchewan crude oil is sold. This control is imposed on a commodity almost exclusively consumed outside of Saskatchewan, either in the Canadian or international marketplace. This imposition of a minimum price by the province to be passed on to consumers outside of the province is an interference with the free flow of trade between provinces . . . so as to prevent producers in Saskatchewan from dealing unhampered with purchasers outside of Saskatchewan."

Section 91, head 2 of the British North America Act, 1867, has undergone a jurisprudential renaissance during the past fifty years. Appellant asks the Court to extend that revivification to an unprecedented degree. . . .

The notion that a province may incidentally affect goods in interprovincial or international trade was developed in *Car-*

nation Company Ltd. v. *Quebec Agricultural Marketing Board* ([1968] S.C.R. 238). In that case it was held that a province could obliquely affect such goods by increasing their cost if the legislation in object and purpose was in relation to a valid head of provincial power. . . . The argument that the orders of the marketing board might have impact upon interprovincial trade was disposed of in these words, at p. 253.

I am not prepared to agree that, in determining that aim, the fact that these orders may have some impact upon the appellant's interprovincial trade necessarily means that they constitute a regulation of trade and commerce within s. 91(2) and thus renders them invalid. The fact of such impact is a matter which may be relevant in determining their true aim and purpose, but it is not conclusive.

It is now well established that incidental effect is not a quantum measurement. It is tested by the design or aim of the legislation. That was held in *Brant Dairy Company Limited* v. *Milk Commission of Ontario* ([1973] S.C.R. 131), where Mr. Justice Judson said, at p. 166:

The test that determines whether a marketing plan or its administration is ultra vires *the province is the test applied in the* Manitoba Reference *(Mr. Justice Martland at p. 703). Is it "designed to restrict or limit the free flow of trade between provinces as such"?* . . .

The conceptual tool of a "flow", or "current", or "stream" of commerce has been referred to by the Court in a number of subsequent cases, the most recent being *MacDonald* v. *Vapor Canada Ltd.* ([1976] 22 C.P.R. (2d) 1), at p. 27. The real question, unsettled in the jurisprudence, is the determination of when the product enters the export stream marking the start of the process of exportation. American jurisprudence has held that the distinguishing mark of an export product is shipment or entry with a common carrier for transportation to another jurisdiction: . . .

. . . Implicit in the argument of the appellant is the assumption that federal regulatory power pursuant to s. 91(2) follows the flow of oil backward across provincial boundaries, back through provincial gathering systems and finally to the well-head. A secondary assumption is that sale at the well-head marks the start of the process of exportation. In the view I take of the case it is unnecessary to reach any conclusion as to the validity of either of these assumptions. It is, however, worth noting that neither American nor Canadian jurisprudence has ever gone that far.

I can find nothing in the present case to lead me to conclude that the taxation measures imposed by the Province of Saskatchewan were merely a colourable device for assuming control of extraprovincial trade. The language of the impugned statutes does not disclose an intention on the part of the province to regulate, or control, or impede the marketing or export of oil from Saskatchewan. "Oil produced and sold" means produced and sold within the provinces. "Well-head price" by definition means the price at the well-head of a barrel of oil produced in Saskatchewan. The mineral income tax and the royalty surcharge relate only to oil produced within Saskatchewan. The transactions are well-head transactions. There are no impediments to the free movement of goods as were found objectionable in *Attorney General of Manitoba* v. *Manitoba Egg and Poultry Association* ([1971] S.C.R. 689), and in *Burns Foods Ltd.* v. *Attorney General of Manitoba* ([1975] 1 S.C.R. 494).

Nor is there anything in the extraneous evidence to form the basis of an argument that the impugned legislation in its *effect* regulated interprovincial or international trade. The evidence is all to the contrary and that evidence comes entirely from witnesses called on behalf of the appellant. Production and export of oil increased after the legislative scheme was implemented. Sales of oil by the appellant were continued in 1974 as in 1973 and previously.

The trial judge, Hughes J. made the following finding of fact:

I do emphasize that nothing has happened to suggest any intrusion or invasion on the part of the defendant with respect to the export of crude oil from this province unless it is to be suggested that it is to be found in price regulation.

Chief Justice Culliton, speaking for a unanimous Court of Appeal, made a further finding:

Neither of the charges [i.e. mineral income tax and royalty surcharge] have any effect on price. As a matter of fact, the true situation is that the tax does not influence the price but rather, the price determines the tax.

On the basis of such concurrent findings it is hard to say that the flow of commerce was in any way impeded, unless it can be said to relate to price.

It was contended in argument that the effect was to place a floor price under Saskatchewan oil and thereby interfere with interprovincial trade. So far as mineral income tax is concerned the incidence of taxation is pegged to the price received for the oil at the well-head. Section 4A is an "after-the-event" provision which comes into play only if there was a sale at less than fair value. The emphasis on fair value ensures that the tax will not change the export oil price. The price of oil subject to the tax and the price of oil free of the tax, *i.e.* from the exempted 1,280-acre tracts, will be the same as the product crosses the provincial border. The ultimate position of consumers is unaffected. The only way in which extraprovincial consumers could have benefited would have been in the event of the province freezing the price of oil, assuming constitutional competence to do so.

One is free to speculate that, to the extent producers would be prepared to undercut the fair market value of their oil,

the legislation discourages them from doing so by virtue of the constant tax liability. The possibility of price-cutting is highly theoretical, unsupported by evidence and in view of the inelasticity of demand for petroleum products, highly unlikely.

In *Burns Foods Limited* v. *Attorney General of Manitoba, supra,* in striking down a regulation under The Natural Products Marketing Act of Manitoba which required packers in Manitoba to buy hogs only from the Manitoba Hog Producers Marketing Board, Mr. Justice Pigeon said this, at pp. 504-5:

It is a case of directly regulating extra-provincial trade operations in their essential aspects namely, the price and all the other conditions of sale. . . . The situation here is totally unlike that which obtained in Brant Dairy Co. v. Milk Commission of Ontario, *([1973] S.C.R. 131, 30 D.L.R. (3d) 559). In that case, the challenge on constitutional grounds was dismissed because there was no evidence that the orders had any extra-provincial effect.*

The key word is "directly" for it leaves open the possibility for a scheme to affect incidentally interprovincial trade, so long as the scheme is not in pith and substance in relation to interprovincial trade. This last proposition, while obvious in other areas of constitutional law, was remarkably absent in the cases respecting trade and commerce decided in the first half of this century.

The Province of Saskatchewan had a *bona fide*, legitimate and reasonable interest of its own to advance in enacting the legislation in question, as related to taxation and natural resources, out of all proportion to the burden, if there can be said to be a burden, imposed on the Canadian free trade economic unit through the legislation. The effect, if any, on the extraprovincial trade in oil is merely indirectly and remotely incidental to the manifest revenue-producing object of the legislation under attack.

25. Central Canada Potash Co. Ltd. and Attorney General of Canada *v.* Government of Saskatchewan, *1979*

~ The background to this case involves a complex series of international negotiations between the Province of Saskatchewan, the State of New Mexico, trade officials in Washington and Ottawa and a number of multinational mining companies. These negotiations began in the 1960s when sales of Saskatchewan potash in the U.S. fertilizer market posed a severe threat to New Mexico based mines. By 1967 potash was selling in the United States at a price considerably below the break-even point for the older, less efficient New Mexico mines. This prompted the Governor of New Mexico to seek help from Washington in the form of anti-dumping sanctions and possibly a tariff on potash imports. The New Mexico companies, all but one of whom had a financial interest in Saskatchewan mines, while interested in the survival of their New Mexico operations, were not anxious to see the extra revenue created by a tariff flow to the government. Therefore they were not opposed to the government of New Mexico and Saskatchewan working out arrangements to restrict Saskatchewan production and restore the U.S. price to the break-even point. Saskatchewan established a pro-rationing scheme to achieve this purpose in 1969. Throughout these negotiations, the Liberal government of Ross Thatcher, aware that the province's participation in these international transactions might entail some constitutional difficulties, consulted with the Liberal government in Ottawa and obtained its somewhat reluctant acquiescence to these arrangements.

At first there was no constitutional challenge to Saskatchewan's pro-rationing regulations from either the corporations or Ottawa, both of whom in effect had given it their blessing. However, in 1971 the Blakeney NDP government changed the regulations so that production quotas were based more on the companies' productive capacity than on their market access. This system would have prevented Central Canada Potash from fully meeting its contractual commitment to the Chicago-based fertilizer company with which it was affiliated. Thus, the company initiated a constitutional challenge to the pro-rationing regulations, and, to Mr. Blakeney's horror, the federal government joined the litigation as a co-plaintiff.

The seven Supreme Court judges who heard the appeal unanimously found the regulations unconstitutional. Chief Justice Laskin's opinion acknowledged that ordinarily provinces have authority to control the production of natural resources. But the Court held that this authority does not go so far as to enable a province to pass legislation which in pith and substance is designed to control the marketing of products in interprovincial and international trade. The Chief Justice said that in so characterizing the Saskatchewan legislation the Court was influenced by the circumstances leading up to the introduction of the scheme.

The Court's decision in this case represents the culmination of a series of cases beginning with the *Ontario Farm Products Reference* in which the Supreme Court invoked the federal trade and commerce power as a constraint on the constitutional capacity of the provinces to control economic activities within the province that impinge on interprovincial or international trade and commerce. A more extreme example of this trend occurred four years earlier in the *Burns Food* case[1] when the Supreme Court overturned Manitoba regulations requiring the large meatpacking firms in the province to purchase all their hogs through a provincial marketing board. Although only 4 per cent of the hogs involved were imported from Saskatchewan, the Court found this sufficient to constitute an unconstitutional interference with the flow of interprovincial trade. In the *Potash* case, it should be noted, over 99 per cent of Saskatchewan's potash is exported from the province.

The limit these decisions impose on provincial power to regulate the production and pricing of export commodities has serious implications for a province like Alberta which may wish to prevent the sale of oil and gas at what it regards as less than economic prices. In the case of potash, the Saskatchewan government nationalized the industry in 1975, but this would not appear to alter the constitutional position. The limits set by section 91(2) of the B.N.A. Act on provincial regulatory power would seem to apply as much to a publicly owned as to a privately owned industry.[2]

The bar against provincial legislation aimed at regulating international trade was not removed by the new powers the provinces acquired when section 92A was added to the Constitution in 1982. This amendment gives the provinces the power to legislate in relation to "the export from the province to another part of Canada" of primary production in non-renewable natural resources, forestry resources and electrical energy providing such legislation does not discriminate against another part of Canada or conflict with overriding federal legislation on the same subject. However, there was no extension of provincial jurisdiction into the international trade field. The plenary federal power in this field would appear to provide a firm and broad basis for federal legislation implementing the Free Trade Agreement with the United States.

---

[1] *Burns Foods Ltd.* v. *Attorney General of Manitoba* [1975] 1 S.C.R. 494.

[2] However, section 125 of the B.N.A. Act, which prevents each level of government from taxing the other's property, does limit federal revenues obtainable from provincially owned enterprises. In the 1982 *Alberta Natural Gas Tax Reference*, a divided (6-3) Supreme Court ruled that a proposed federal tax on natural gas exported to the United States violated s. 125. The gas was derived from Alberta Crown land and was exported in a pipeline owned by the province.

CENTRAL CANADA POTASH CO. LTD. AND ATTORNEY GENERAL OF CANADA *v.* GOVERNMENT OF SASKATCHEWAN
In the Supreme Court of Canada. [1979] 1 S.C.R. 42.

Martland, Ritchie, Spence, Pigeon, Dickson and Pratte JJ. concurred with the judgment delivered by

THE CHIEF JUSTICE: This appeal, which is here by leave of this Court, concerns (1) the validity of what I may compendiously refer to as a potash prorationing scheme, established pursuant to the Mineral Resources Act, R.S.S. 1965, c. 50, as amended, and (2) a claim by the appellants for damages against the Government of Saskatchewan for the tort of intimidation by reason of certain circumstances connected with the establishment of the prorationing scheme.

The litigation was initiated by the appellant, which sought a declaration of the invalidity of the prorationing scheme and damages in tort. Disbery J. gave the relief sought, fixing the damages at $1.5 million. On appeal by the Government of Saskatchewan and a claim by the appellant for a variation in the judgment to increase the amount of damages, the Saskatchewan Court of Appeal, in a unanimous judgment delivered by Culliton C.J.S., set aside the judgment at trial in its entirety and, consequently, dismissed the notice to vary.

On leave being given to come here, an order was made for notice to be given of the following constitutional question and an associated evidentiary question:

1. Is the potash prorationing scheme constituted by the Province of Saskatchewan pursuant to the Potash Conservation Regulations 1969 numbered 287/69, and the Orders in Council O/C 1733/69 and O/C 404/70 enacting and amending them, and the Potash Allocation Formula effective January 1, 1970, and the Minister's Directive PCD-1, Potash Prorationing, effective July 1, 1972, enacted pursuant to the Mineral Resources Act, R.S.S., 1965, Chapter 50, and the various Notices,

Directives, Ministerial Orders and Licenses issued from time to time by the Minister of Mineral Resources for Saskatchewan and his Deputy implementing the schemes, ultra vires *the Province of Saskatchewan?*

2. Is extrinsic evidence admissible in this case in relation to the constitutional issue and, if so, to what extent and of what kind?

The Attorneys General of Quebec, New Brunswick, Manitoba, Alberta and Newfoundland intervened to support the judgment in appeal. The Attorney General of Canada had become a co-plaintiff at the trial in respect of the constitutional question raised by the action and remained a party to the proceedings in the Saskatchewan Court of Appeal and in this Court.

The Mineral Resources Act, R.S.S. 1965, as amended, through which the Potash Conservation Regulations, 287/69, were promulgated, is skeleton legislation, giving very wide authority to the responsible Minister and wide regulation-making power to the Lieutenant-Governor in Council. The Act itself is not challenged. It is common ground that at the time the 1969 Regulations were passed almost all of Saskatchewan-produced potash was sold outside the Province and that the larger part of the production, about 64 per cent, was marketed in the United States. Saskatchewan production, moreover, represented almost half, about 48 per cent, of the United States potash market. The appellant company itself had about 34 per cent of the Saskatchewan share of the United States market. So far as forecasts of future world consumption can be based on present knowledge and on scientific assessment of known or proven reserves, evidence was given that Saskatchewan could supply world demand for potash for almost 1,500 years or for even a longer period. The trial judge relied on this evidence for finding that the Potash Conservation Regulations could not be said to be a response to threatened shortages of the mineral or to conservation needs.

Potash is also produced in the State of New Mexico but production and quality, according to the evidence, did not match that of Saskatchewan and reserves were, apparently, minimal. There was concern about the penetration of Saskatchewan potash into the United States market, and a dumping inquiry was instituted in the United States not only in respect of Canadian exporters but as well in respect of French and West German exporters. A finding of dumping was made by the United States Bureau of Customs in August of 1969 and the matter was referred, as required by United States law, to the United States Tariff Commission, which fixed a hearing for October 7, 1969. Although the hearing commenced on that date and a determination was obligatory by the end of November 1969, in the events that happened the tariff inquiry did not prove damaging to Saskatchewan interests, although a determination of injury and the likelihood of continuing injury was made on November 21, 1969. The Government of Saskatchewan was aware of the course of proceedings in the United States affecting Saskatchewan potash, and was concerned about the damaging effect of a tariff levy on exports from Saskatchewan. Equally, the New Mexico authorities were concerned about loss of tax revenues from declining production and a federal tariff would not in itself be of any help to them. Both were concerned about overproduction and, in consequence, a drop in world price.

In the result, a meeting took place in Santa Fe, New Mexico, on October 6, 1969, between the then Governor of New Mexico and the then Premier of Saskatchewan and their respective associates, at which time a draft of proposed Saskatchewan potash regulations was produced and considered. A follow-up meeting took place in Regina, Saskatchewan, on October 17, 1969.

There is no doubt that the Potash Conservation Regulations, 1969, were the product of the two meetings and were prompted by the economic conditions that I have described. They were passed on November 17, 1969, under Order-in-Council 1733/69 and amended on March 8, 1970, under Order-in-Council 404/70. I will consider the proration scheme established by the Regulations and the amendment thereof after I deal with the position of the appellant Central Canada Potash Co. Limited in respect of its involvement in the potash industry.

The appellant was born of an agreement between Noranda Mines Limited and Central Farmers Fertilizer Company, a Chicago-based co-operative association which supplied large quantities of fertilizer to numerous co-operative associations and thus to farmer members thereof. Noranda had done exploration work in Saskatchewan in respect of potash mining and proposed to establish a mine if it could find a secure market for the production. It had extensive mineral rights in Saskatchewan under freehold interests and under Crown lease and held options to buy additional mineral lands. Its agreement with Central Farmers, dated July 1, 1965, provided that it would establish a mine with ancillary facilities, with a production capability of not less than one million tons of muriate of potash annually. Central Farmers agreed to buy half a million tons annually over a period of twenty years, with the right to increase its purchases to one and one-half million tons annually. The price fixed for the purchases was the prevailing commercial price less 15 per cent. Central Farmers was given the option of requiring that the mine and facilities be conveyed to a new company in which Noranda would have a controlling 51 per cent interest and Central Farmers the remaining 49 per cent. The option was exercised, and the appellant was incorporated and took a conveyance of the mine as a going concern at a price just short of $90 million. The Crown lease which Noranda held was assigned to the appellant on July 15,

1970, with the consent of the Saskatchewan government. The lease covered mineral rights under statutory road allowances and, overall, gave Noranda and later the appellant a continuous ore body running through and connected with its other holdings. . . .

The prorationing scheme first introduced under the Regulations, and known as the ABC scheme, is described in the reasons of the trial judge, as follows:

The ingredients of the formula for prorationing production among the producers were: (1) the productive capacity of each mining property; (2) the estimated demand for Saskatchewan potash or potash products for reasonable current requirements and consumption or use within and outside the province; and (3) the amounts of potash and potash products each producer reasonably required to keep in storage for working stock and for reserves. The ABC scheme allowed each producer to produce and sell 40% of its productive capacity and no more until every mine had produced and sold this basic quota. Producers holding orders in excess of this amount could purchase potash from mines that had not yet reached their 40% quota. After every producer in Saskatchewan had produced and sold its quota, then and only then, producers that still had unfilled orders could apply to the Minister for supplementary licences to produce and sell additional amounts. The Minister in his discretion could grant or refuse any such application. . . . The scheme allowed each producer additional production for storage and reserve purposes up to 55% of the producer's storage capacity. . . .

As of July 1, 1972, however, the ABC prorationing scheme was replaced by the so-called FP scheme, described as a flat prorationing scheme. Plans for the replacement were indicated in a program review dated March 2, 1972, sent to each producer. A directive of June 30, 1972, set up an allocation formula in these words:

Each producer's share of production to meet the market demand for Saskatchewan potash will be allocated according to a proration formula based solely on the productive capacity of each producing potash plant, except where the allocations are established by a production agreement approved by the Minister of Mineral Resources.

The allocation made thereunder of the productive capacity of each producer could be changed only with the approval of the responsible Minister. A control procedure was also set out. . . .

The appellant company, having regard to its supply commitments to Central Farmers, objected to the FP scheme which, based on productive capacities of the various producers and on allocation formulas involving market sharing, would prevent it from fulfilling its commitments unless it obtained supplementary licences. When its allocation for the 1972-1973 fertilizer year was short of its contractual obligation, it sought an increase and, on being refused, brought mandamus proceedings to compel the issue of a licence for a production quota that would enable it to meet its contractual commitment. It failed in those proceedings at first instance, in the Saskatchewan Court of Appeal and in this Court: see [1972] 6 W.W.R. 62; [1973] 1 W.W.R. 193; [1973] 2 W.W.R. 672. During those proceedings it was advised by a letter of September 20, 1972, from the Deputy Minister that its production schedule for the year commencing July 1, 1972, was out of line with governmental requirements and that it must reduce its monthly production to conform thereto. This the appellant did but on December 11, 1972, it instituted the action which gave rise to the appeal to this Court.

II

The trial judge came to the conclusion, upon his review of the evidence (and I should note here that he admitted a wide range of extrinsic evidence most of which the Court of Appeal held was inadmissible) and upon a lengthy examination of applicable case law (1) Orders-in-Council 1733/69 and 404/70, (2) the Potash Conservation Regulations, 1969, being Regulation 287/69, (3) the ABC and FP schemes, and (4) the directives and licences issued by the Minister and Deputy Minister for implementing the schemes were all *ultra vires* as an invasion of the exclusive federal power in relation to the regulation of trade and commerce. . . .

The declaration of unconstitutionality by the trial judge was founded upon the following considerations as expressed in his reasons:

A study of the regulations and a consideration of the extrinsic evidence relevant to the purposes for which they were passed establishes that the real aims and purposes of the [Executive] Council were as follows:

Firstly: *to restrict and limit the export of Saskatchewan potash into the United States.*

Secondly: *to control and impede the flow of trade in potash between Saskatchewan producers and the residents of other provinces of Canada unless they paid such price and obeyed such conditions as the Minister of Mineral Resources saw fit to demand and impose from time to time. Thus the Regulations and the ABC scheme were, in fact, designed to interfere with and to impede the free flow of trade in potash within Canada and to curtail the right of Canadians in other provinces to make their own contracts with Saskatchewan producers.*

Thirdly: *to control and impede the export trade in potash between Canada and other foreign nations in like manner.*

The mass of evidence before me irresistibly points to the conclusion that these aims and purposes of the Council constituted an intentional and deliberate invasion into "the exclusive legislative authority of the Parliament of Canada" over "The regulation of trade and commerce" assigned to it by Section 91(2) of

The British North America Act. It is completely beyond the competence of the provincial Legislature to legislate to impede or prohibit the export from Saskatchewan of products produced or manufactured in this province. . . .

In the Court of Appeal, Culliton C.J.S. took a different view. I think that he correctly assessed the trial judge's reasons on constitutionality as resting on the conclusion that what was before him was a marketing scheme. The learned Chief Justice was of another opinion, namely, that the scheme was directed to the conservation and orderly development of Saskatchewan's potash reserves; or, to put it in more specific terms, related to the authorization of the scheme under The Mineral Resources Act, it was a scheme for the management, utilization and conservation of the potash industry. Chief Justice Culliton appreciated that this view of the ABC and FP schemes did not *ipso facto* determine validity, but he also considered that the aforementioned objectives encompassed "the promotion and adoption of economic policies to assure a healthy and sound industry"; and he agreed with the trial judge that "the purposes as disclosed in the Regulations are to control the production and sale of potash, to determine fair prices and to prorate production when advisable".

Looking separately at the Regulations and at the directives issued thereunder, the Chief Justice had this to say about the Regulations:

. . . The Regulations, on their face, do not disclose any purpose or intent to interfere with the flow of interprovincial or international trade in potash. That being so, I am satisfied the Regulations are valid; they disclose neither an attempt to invade the field of trade and commerce nor are they inconsistent with the provisions of The Mineral Resources Act under which they were passed. . . .

III

In coming to his conclusion, the Chief

Justice rejected as inadmissible a good deal of the extrinsic evidence which the trial judge found relevant and admissible. He felt that the constitutional problems in the case "are so readily determinable from the impugned regulations, licences and directives that most of the extrinsic evidence which was admitted was inadmissible and unnecessary". What was admissible was summarized by the Chief Justice in these words:

Evidence as to the circumstances leading up to the adoption of the Regulations and evidence relating to the potash resources of the province, the history of the industry, its productive capacity, the demand for its production, the state of the market and the economic problems which it faced, were all properly admissible. Such evidence gave "the under-pinning for the issues" as Laskin J. (as he then was), stated in Attorney General of Manitoba v. Manitoba Egg and Poultry Association, et al, *[1971] S.C.R. 689. Too, such evidence sets out the evil sought to be remedied.*

However, he went on to say that there was no need for extrinsic evidence since ". . . the true nature and character of the Regulations as well as that of the programmes of prorationing and price stabilization and the effects resulting therefrom can be ascertained from a study of the Regulations and of the directives from time to time issued by the Minister and his departmental officials . . ." Nonetheless, he did refer to and quote some remarks of the then Premier of Saskatchewan, made on the day the Regulations were adopted, as showing the need for the Regulations under the prevailing circumstances; and he added that the Premier had correctly stated "the direct objectives of the Regulations, licences and schemes [to be] for the conservation and orderly development of Saskatchewan's potash reserves . . . through a licensing scheme or schemes to provide for controlled production and a minimum price, free on board, the mine".

It was the appellant who introduced the wide range of extrinsic evidence which was canvassed in the reasons of the trial judge. In its factum in this Court, this evidence was classified by it as (1) circumstantial and (2) direct, a classification which the respondent Government of Saskatchewan did not accept. The arguments of the parties in this Court did not, however, produce any division between them on whether or not it was necessary to go beyond what Chief Justice Culliton considered to be admissible.

Counsel for the appellant contended that it was not at all clear what was the evidence upon which the Court of Appeal acted. The Court did not detail it, but it did make findings upon which the constitutional question fell to be determined and, at the risk of some repetition of what has gone before in these reasons, I wish to reproduce those findings in the exact words of Chief Justice Culliton, and as well his prefatory remarks, as follows:

While I admire the industry of the learned trial Judge in his thorough and exhaustive review of virtually every piece of evidence, I do not think there is any real dispute as to the factual situation, in so far as it relates to the problems of constitutionality, validity and applicability. I think it can properly be said that the following statements of fact are fully and completely substantiated by the admissible evidence, and by the inferences which must necessarily be drawn from the schemes as established by minsterial and departmental directives and set out in the potash producing licences:

1. that in 1969, for all practical purposes, the entire potash production of Saskatchewan was sold and disposed of outside of the province; at that time 64% of the production was sold in the United States and the remainder in other parts of the world; Saskatchewan producers had captured 48% of the potash market in the United States;

2. that prior to the adoption of The Potash Conservation Regulations, 1969, as set out in Order-in-Council 1737/69 and amended by Order-in-Council

404/70, the potash industry of Saskatchewan was facing difficult economic conditions due to over-production and depressed market prices; conditions that were accentuated by the imposition of dumping duties by the United States Tariff Commission and by the threat of legislative action by the United States Congress to further protect the American potash industry by the imposition of import quotas and tariffs;

3. that the potash industry of the United States was situated primarily in the State of New Mexico, and that the industry was suffering the same economic problems as was the industry in Saskatchewan as a result of discussions between representatives of the Government of Saskatchewan and those of the State of New Mexico, it was agreed that each would do what it could to protect and conserve the potash industry, in their respective jurisdictions;

4. that the Potash Conservation Regulations were adopted for the purpose of conserving and maintaining the industry in Saskatchewan as a viable industry through a program of controlled production and price stabilization;

5. that both the ABC scheme and the FP scheme provided for strict prorationing of production as well as the establishment of a fixed minimum price, free on board at the mine; a price that could not be affected or reduced by discounts, commissions or other considerations or by loading costs incurred after loading at the plant gate—the licences were valid only as long as the producer complied with the price requirement;

6. that the prorationing and price stabilization schemes would result in a reduction of potash available on the international market but there was no evidence that at any time there was insufficient potash available to meet the market requirements;

7. that the prorationing and price stabilization schemes did result in benefit to the industry, both in New Mexico and in Saskatchewan; did forestall the imposition of import quotas and tariffs by the

United States Congress; did stabilize production and assist in the establishment of an economic price, and these schemes were supported by every potash producer in Saskatchewan except Central Canada Potash.

I am content to proceed on the basis of these findings and on an examination of the Regulations, directives and licences involved in the prorationing and price fixing scheme, without any further regard for any of the other extrinsic evidence adduced before the trial judge.

IV

What is evident from the circumstances under which the Potash Conservation Regulations were promulgated, and from the terms of the directives and licences through which the ABC and FP schemes were instituted and administered, is that the Government of Saskatchewan had in view the regulation of the marketing of potash through the fixing of a minimum selling price applicable to the permitted production quotas. The only market for which the schemes had any significance was the export market. There could be no suggestion that the schemes had any relation to the marketing of potash within the Province of Saskatchewan when there was hardly any Saskatchewan market for the mineral. There was no question here of any concluded transactions of sale and purchase in the province, as was the situation in the *Carnation* case. Out of province and offshore sales were the principal objects of the licences and directives.

The documentary evidence leaves no doubt about this. The first directive fixing the minimum floor price for potash to the producer, f.o.b. the potash plant, dated November 25, 1969, was stated to be for the purpose of determining the demand for it "for reasonable current requirements and current consumption or use within or without Saskatchewan". The first producing licence to Noranda, dated December 12, 1969, required the licensee to comply with "all applicable Acts, regulations, orders and directions governing production, conservation, processing, disposal, marketing, transporting. . . .'' The second producing licence conditioned its validity on observance of the minimum selling price, f.o.b. the producer's plant in Saskatchewan. Subsequent producing licences did not indicate any change of focus, although they fortified ministerial control.

A directive of August 24, 1971, to all producers fixed the minimum price f.o.b. vessel, Vancouver. On August 27, 1971, a letter to producers from the Deputy Minister advised of approval given, on certain conditions, to an agreement for delivery of potash to a business organization in France. One of the conditions required that ''all potash delivered to Europe from Saskatchewan pursuant to the agreement shall be for consumption in Europe''. The new allocation formula prescribed by the directive of June 30, 1972, from which I have already quoted, was concerned with the sharing of production ''to meet the market demand''. The purpose of Canpotex, to which I have also referred above, was to make it the instrument for offshore sales of Saskatchewan potash.

In all of the foregoing, the Government of Saskatchewan, and its responsible Ministers and their Deputies, were acting not under proprietary right but in pursuance of legislative and statutory authority directed to the proprietary rights of others, including the appellant. It was strenuously contended by the respondent Government (and in this they were supported by the intervening provinces) that the natural resources, the mineral wealth of the province was subject to provincial regulatory control alone, and that production controls or quotas were peculiarly matters within exclusive provincial legislative authority. Chief Justice Culliton gave force to this point in two concluding paragraphs of his reasons, which he prefaced by saying that ''courts must approach constitutional problems with a sense of realism and practicality.'' The two paragraphs read as follows:

It was admitted by all parties that the potash industry of Saskatchewan was facing difficult problems—problems which, if not solved, would have a most detrimental effect on the industry and on the province. In these circumstances, the potash industry had a right to seek assistance from whatever Government had the power to grant that assistance. Natural resources, being exclusively within provincial jurisdiction, the industry turned to the province. The province, to protect and conserve the potash industry, implemented controlled production and established minimum prices in the province. These programs did assist the industry, but at the same time, had some effect on areas within federal jurisdiction. However, in pith and substance, they were programmes directed to a matter within provincial jurisdiction and thus were valid notwithstanding such ultimate effects.

If I am not right in this conclusion, then it must be said the right to control production of potash within the province, and to establish a minimum price at the mine, rests with the Parliament of Canada, for the right to do so must rest somewhere. Clearly, in my opinion, the Parliament of Canada does not have the power to control the production of potash within the province, or to set a minimum price at the mine. Thus, in my opinion, to hold that the prorationing and price stabilization programs are ultra vires *the province, is to determine their validity by the ultimate effects of such programs and not by their true nature and character.*

It is, of course true, that production controls and conservation measures with respect to natural resources in a province are, ordinarily, matters within provincial legislative authority. This Court's reasons in its recent judgment in the Ontario Egg Reference (*Reference re Agricultural Products Marketing Act (Canada), Farm Products Marketing Agencies Act (Canada) and The Farm Products Marketing Act (Ontario)*), judgment delivered January 19, 1978, and as yet unreported, supports that view. The situation may be different, however, where a province establishes a marketing scheme with price fixing as its central feature. Indeed, it has been held that provincial legislative authority does not extend to the control or regulation of the marketing of provincial products, whether minerals or natural resources, in interprovincial or export trade. The Saskatchewan Courts recognized this almost fifty years ago in the judgment in *In re Grain Marketing Act*, 1931 ([1931] 2 W.W.R. 146). Legislation with this thrust in other provinces has likewise been struck down: see *Lawson* v. *Interior Tree Fruit & Vegetable Committee of Direction* ([1931] S.C.R. 357), *Re Sheep and Swine Marketing Scheme (P.E.I.)* ([1941] 3 D.L.R. 569).

The present case reduces itself therefore to a consideration of "the true nature and character" of the prorationing and price stabilization schemes which are before us. This Court cannot ignore the circumstances under which the Potash Conservation Regulations came into being, nor the market to which they were applied and in which they had their substantial operation. In *Canadian Industrial Gas & Oil Ltd.* v. *Government of Saskatchewan* [1978] 2 S.C.R. 545, this Court, speaking in its majority judgment through Martland J., said (at p. 568) that "provincial legislative authority does not extend to fixing the price to be charged or received in respect of the sale of goods in the export market". It may properly be said here of potash as it was said there of oil that "the legislation is directly aimed at the production of potash destined for export, and it has the effect of regulating the export price since the producer is effectively compelled to obtain that price on the sale of his product" (at p. 569).

I do not agree with Chief Justice Culliton that the consequence of invalidating the provincial scheme in this case is to move to the Parliament of Canada the power to control production of minerals in the province and the price to be charged at the mine. There is no accretion at all to

federal power in this case, which does not involve federal legislation, but simply a determination by this Court, in obedience to its duty, of a limitation on provincial legislative power. It is true, as he says that (with some exceptions, not relevant here) the British North America Act distributes all legislative power either to Parliament or to the provincial Legislatures, but it does not follow that legislation of a province held to be invalid may *ipso facto* be validly enacted by Parliament in its very terms. It is nothing new for this Court, or indeed, for any Court in this country seized of a constitutional issue, to go behind the words used by a Legislature and to see what it is that it is doing. It is especially important for Courts, called upon to interpret and apply a constitution which limits legislative power, to do so in a case where not only the authorizing legislation but regulations enacted pursuant thereto are themselves couched in generalities, and the bite of a scheme envisaged by the parent legislation and the delegated regulations is found in administrative directions.

Where governments in good faith, as in this case, invoke authority to realize desirable economic policies, they must know that they have no open-ended means of achieving their goals when there are constitutional limitations on the legislative power under which they purport to act. They are entitled to expect that the Courts, and especially this Court, will approach the task of appraisal of the constitutionality of social and economic programmes with sympathy and regard for the serious consequences of holding them *ultra vires*. Yet, if the appraisal results in a clash with the constitution, it is the latter which must govern. That is the situation here.

In my opinion, the judgment of the Saskatchewan Court of Appeal on the constitutional question posed for this Court should be set aside and the declaration of invalidity by the trial judge should be restored.

26. The Queen v. Hauser, 1979

~ The issue in the *Hauser* case concerns the division of powers in the general area of law enforcement. The fact that the Supreme Court has been called upon in recent years to adjudicate a number of disputes in this area shows how the climate of intense federal-provincial rivalry has spread from the economic and social policy areas to matters relating to the coercive police powers of the state.

Section 91(27) of the B.N.A. Act assigns jurisdiction over the substantive content of criminal law and the rules of criminal procedure to the federal Parliament. While Parliament has shaped much of Canada's criminal law and procedure through the Criminal Code and other federal statutes, the provinces have also played a significant role by exercising their power under section 92(15) to attach penal sanctions to provincial laws. In the 1960s and 1970s the Supreme Court permitted provincial legislative activity in this area to expand by dismissing challenges to provincial "criminal" law so long as the provincial law did not directly conflict with the federal Criminal Code. The Court's decisions in the *McNeil*[1] and *Dupond*[2] cases upholding provincial laws censoring movies and restricting the freedom of assembly in the streets are an indication of how far the Court's majority has been willing to go in making criminal law an area of concurrent jurisdiction.

But a different pattern developed in cases dealing not with the substance of criminal law but with the power to control the police and the machinery of criminal justice. In the *Keable*[3] case, decided just before *Hauser*, the Court ruled that the Keable Commission of Inquiry established by the Quebec government to investigate certain "illegal or reprehensible" acts allegedly carried out in Quebec by the R.C.M.P. Security Service in collaboration with provincial police forces could not investigate the internal management of the R.C.M.P. nor compel the federal minister responsible for the R.C.M.P. to testify or produce confidential documents. The Court's decision in the *Di Iorio*[4] case made it clear that a province, under its jurisdiction over the administration of justice in the province (section 92(14)), could direct an inquiry into the general extent of crime in the province (or into the operations of provincial and municipal police) providing it does not use this power to circumvent prescribed criminal justice procedures. But the Court's opinion in *Keable* turned on the proposition that neither level of government may investigate a validly established agency of the other. As for Parliament's authority to establish the R.C.M.P. and to provide for its management, Justice Pigeon, for the majority, stated that it was "unquestioned".

The immediate question in *Hauser* was whether the federal Attorney General could control prosecutions under the federal Narcotics Control Act. Up until 1969 the Criminal Code definition of the Attorney General with

[1] [1978] 2 S.C.R. 662.
[2] [1978] 2 S.C.R. 770, see case 36 below.
[3] [1979] 1 S.C.R. 218.
[4] [1978] 1 S.C.R. 152.

authority for directing prosecutions referred exclusively to provincial attorneys general. In practice, crimes created by federal statutes other than the Criminal Code were frequently prosecuted by agents of the federal Attorney General, subject to the supervision of the provincial Attorney General. However, in 1969 the federal Parliament amended the Criminal Code so that the Attorney General with authority to direct proceedings with respect to violations under Acts other than the Criminal Code would be the Attorney General of Canada. This was the legislation challenged in the *Hauser* case. The Attorney General powers at issue include the power to take over private prosecutions, to dispense with a preliminary inquiry, to control the mode of trial in certain cases and, perhaps most important, to prevent a prosecution from proceeding.

The seven judges who participated in this decision agreed that the federal Parliament had jurisdiction over proceedings in relation to the enforcement of federal laws whose constitutional basis is not the criminal law power. But they divided on the question of control of proceedings in relation to violations of offences based on the criminal law power. A bare majority managed to side-step this issue by finding that the Narcotic Control Act was not criminal law. Through an opinion written by Justice Pigeon, they came to the conclusion that, because this Act dealt with a genuinely new problem which did not exist at the time of Confederation and was not a matter of merely local or private nature, it fell under the federal residual power. This was a surprising conclusion given the number of earlier decisions characterizing the legislation as criminal law and the fact that these decisions were not seriously challenged before the Court. Justice Spence, on the other hand, on the basis that enforcement power must be coterminous with legislative power, was willing to accept the full federal argument that the federal power applied to all federally created crimes.

Justice Dickson wrote a lengthy dissent with which Justice Pratte concurred. He held that provincial jurisdiction over the administration of justice meant that constitutionally the provinces must have exclusive control over the prosecution of all offences based on the criminal law power. In Justice Dickson's view this outcome was supported both by the weight of legal authority and the historical wisdom of the "subtle balance" between national and local interests which was envisaged at the time of Confederation and had prevailed for a century thereafter. Under this balance, while the federal Parliament established a uniform national code of criminal law and procedure, the administration of criminal justice was left in provincial hands "where it could be more flexibly administered in response to local conditions".

Justice Dickson was the lone dissenter when the Court in 1981 decided in the *Putman*[5] case that provincial police review boards could not investigate complaints against the R.C.M.P. even in those provinces where the R.C.M.P. is engaged under contract to do provincial and municipal policing. ~

---

[5] *A.G. Alta.* v. *Putman and Cramer*, [1981] 2 S.C.R. 267.

THE QUEEN *v.* HAUSER
In the Supreme Court of Canada. [1979] 1 S.C.R. 984.

The judgment of Martland, Ritchie, Pigeon and Beetz JJ. was delivered by

PIGEON J.: The respondent was charged by indictment on two counts: 1) of possession of cannabis resin for the purpose of trafficking, 2) of possession of cannabis (marijuana) for the same purpose, contrary to s. 4(2) of the Narcotic Control Act. The indictment was signed by an agent of the Attorney General of Canada. Thereupon respondent moved for prohibition challenging the constitutional validity of para. (b) of the definition of "Attorney General" in s. 2 of the Criminal Code. The application for prohibition was dismissed in first instance but it was allowed by a majority decision in the Appellate Division of the Supreme Court of Alberta. On the appeal to this Court, the constitutional question was settled by the Chief Justice upon appellant's application in these terms:

Is it within the competence of the Parliament of Canada to enact legislation as in Section 2 of the Criminal Code to authorize the Attorney General of Canada or his Agent
1. to prefer indictments for an offence under the Narcotic Control Act,
2. to have the conduct of proceedings instituted at the instance of the Government of Canada in respect of a violation or conspiracy to violate any Act of the Parliament of Canada or regulations made thereunder other than the Criminal Code?

The relevant part of the definition in question reads:

"Attorney General" means the Attorney General . . . of a province in which proceedings to which this Act applies are taken and, with respect to

(b) proceedings instituted at the instance of the Government of Canada and conducted by or on behalf of that Government in

respect of a violation of or conspiracy to violate any Act of the Parliament of Canada or a regulation made thereunder other than this Act,

means the Attorney General of Canada. . . .

The Attorneys General of all provinces, except Manitoba, have intervened to support the judgment holding para. (b) invalid. However, the Attorneys General for Ontario, Quebec and British Columbia would restrict the invalidity to proceedings arising under an Act of the Parliament of Canada depending for its constitutional validity upon head 27 (*Criminal Law*) of s. 91 of the B.N.A. Act. . . .

In *Proprietary Articles Trade Association* v. *Attorney General of Canada* ([1931] A.C. 310), Lord Atkin said (at pp. 316-317):

The second principle to be observed judicially was expressed by the Board in 1881, "it will be a wise course . . . to decide each case which arises as best they can, without entering more largely upon an interpretation of the statute than is necessary for the decision of the particular question in hand": Citizens Insurance Co. of Canada v. Parsons (1881) 7 App. Cas. 96, 109. It was restated in 1914: "The structure of ss. 91 and 92, and the degree to which the connotation of the expressions used overlaps, render it, in their Lordships' opinion, unwise on this or any other occasion to attempt exhaustive definitions of the meaning and scope of these expressions. Such definitions, in the case of language used under the conditions in which a constitution such as that under consideration was framed, must almost certainly miscarry": John Deere Plow Co. v. Wharton [1915] A.C. 330, 338. . . .

In accordance with this principle I will

endeavour to express an opinion on the constitutional question without going any further than necessary. As worded, it does not put in issue what counsel for the appellant called the "broad proposition", namely, the assertion of complete federal legislative authority over the conduct of all criminal proceedings rather than only over criminal proceedings in respect of a violation or conspiracy to violate a federal enactment other than the Criminal Code. From a constitutional point of view, the distinction properly should be between enactments founded on the criminal law power and other enactments, as was pointed out on behalf of the three provinces which accept that, in legislating under any other head of power, the federal Parliament can completely provide for prosecutions by federal officials, although they deny such power for the enforcement of criminal law strictly so called.

In this connection it should be observed that, while under the B.N.A. Act the division of executive power generally follows the division of legislative authority, there are some exceptions, mainly in respect of judicial appointments. In order to avoid the inconveniences and difficulties of divided judicial jurisdiction, the Canadian constitution provides for one set of courts for the application of all laws federal and provincial, subject only to the federal power of creating additional courts for the better administration of federal laws. The ordinary courts are provincial only in the sense that they are established by the provinces. . . .

Furthermore, for all the higher degrees of jurisdiction, the power of appointment of the judges has been conferred to the federal executive by s. 96 of the B.N.A. Act, while the appointment of clerks and other officials forms parts of the provinces' executive duties.

With respect to the criminal law an unusual pattern was also adopted. While head 27 of s. 91 gives to the federal legislative authority over

27. The Criminal Law, except the Constitution of Courts of Criminal Juris-

diction, but including the Procedure in Criminal Matters,

head 14 of s. 92 gives to the provincial legislatures, not only the "Constitution of Courts of Criminal Jurisdiction", but all the "Administration of Justice":

14. The Administration of Justice in the province, including the Constitution, Maintenance and Organization of Provincial Courts, both of Civil and of Criminal Jurisdiction, and including Procedure in Civil Matters in those Courts.

That the Administration of Justice includes, to some extent at least, the powers traditionally exercised by the Attorney General and the Solicitor General is apparent from s. 135:

135. Until the Legislature of Ontario or Quebec otherwise provides, all Rights, Powers, Duties, Functions, Responsibilities, or Authorities at the passing of this Act vested in or imposed on the Attorney General, Solicitor General, Secretary and Registrar of the Province of Canada, Minister of Finance, Commissioner of Crown Lands, Commissioner of Public Works, and Minister of Agriculture and Receiver General, by any Law, Statute, or Ordinance of Upper Canada, Lower Canada, or Canada, and not repugnant to this Act, shall be vested in or imposed on any Officer to be appointed by the Lieutenant Governor for the Discharge of the same or any of them; . . .

In this respect it may be of some interest to see what were the views of the federal government shortly after Confederation. In *Lenoir v. Ritchie* ([1879], 3 S.C.R. 575), Fournier J. says (at p. 605):

[TRANSLATION] *After Confederation difficulties arose in the provinces of Ontario and Nova Scotia regarding the power of Lieutenant-Governors to appoint Queen's Counsel. As this question affected the royal prerogative, it was referred by the Privy Council of Canada to the Secretary of State for the Colonies, in order to obtain the opinion of the law officers of the Crown. The Privy Council submission, signed by Sir John Macdonald, after citing subsection 14 of section 92 regarding the organization of the courts, contains the following statement:*

Under this power, the undersigned is of opinion, that the legislature of a province, *being charged with the administration of justice and the organization of the Courts, may, by statute, provide for the general conduct of business before those Courts; and may make such provision with respect to the bar,* the management of criminal prosecution by counsel, *the selection of those Counsel, and the right of pre-audience, as it sees fit. Such enactment must, however, in the opinion of the undersigned, be subject to the exercise of the royal prerogative, which is paramount, and in no way diminished by the terms of the Act of Confederation.* (Emphasis added).

Whatever may be said as to the necessity of limiting the extent of the federal power over criminal procedure so as to preserve provincial jurisdiction over the administration of justice in criminal matters, it appears to me that one must accept, at least, what is conceded by three provinces: unrestricted federal legislative authority over prosecutions for violations or conspiracies for violations of federal enactments which do not depend for their constitutional validity on head 27 of s. 91 (Criminal Law). It appears to me that these provinces justly disclaim any constitutional power to subject the enforcement of federal statutes to their executive authority except in what may properly be considered as "criminal law".

There is in s. 91 no counterpart of head 15 of s. 92:

15. The Imposition of Punishment by Fine, Penalty, or Imprisonment for enforcing any Law of the Province made in relation to any Matter coming within any of the Classes of Subjects enumerated in this Section.

However, as is made abundantly clear by head 29 of s. 91, there can be no doubt

as to the existence of federal power to provide for the imposition of penalties for the violation of any federal legislation, entirely apart from the authority over criminal law. . . .

I will therefore proceed to consider whether the Narcotic Control Act is to be classified as legislation enacted under the Criminal Law power. I cannot accept as conclusive on this point the statements made in the judgment of this Court in *Industrial Acceptance Corporation Limited* v. *The Queen* ([1953] 2 S.C.R. 273). This was a private claim and it appears from what Locke J. (dissenting in part) said (at p. 280), that it was "conceded on behalf of the appellant that the Opium and Narcotic Drug Act 1929 is in pith and substance criminal law, within the meaning of that expression in s.-s. 27 of s. 91." That concession was effective towards the appellant who made it in that case and the Court could decide accordingly, but it would not result in a binding precedent on the point. Furthermore, it really made little difference in the case whether the Act was "criminal law" or not.

Drug abuse did not become a problem in this country during the last century. At the time of Confederation, there was concern only with alcohol. This was treated as a local matter, being dealt with only incidentally in head 9 of s. 92:

9. Shop, Saloon, Tavern, Auctioneer, and other Licenses in order to the raising of a Revenue for Provincial, Local, or Municipal Purposes.

When greater control was considered necessary by the federal Parliament, the legislation was not treated as criminal law. As is well known, it was supported under the general power to make laws for the peace, order and good government of Canada (*Russell* v. *The Queen, A.G. for Ontario* v. *Canada Temperance Federation*).

The history of the drug control legislation, as well as its general scheme, shows in my view that it is what the English title calls it: an act for the *control* of narcotic drugs.

The first statute was passed in 1908 (7-8 Edw. VII, c. 50). It prohibited the importation, manufacture and sale of opium for other than medicinal purposes. It was designed to put out of business a few opium merchants in British Columbia who were operating under municipal licences. A more elaborate act was adopted in 1911, the Opium Drug Act (1-2 Geo. V. c. 17). The schedule of this Act listed just four drugs: cocaine, morphine, opium and eucaine. Section 3 prohibited the possession of those drugs for other than scientific or medicinal purposes. The following year, an international convention was signed "for the progressive suppression of the abuse of opium, morphine, cocaine and derivative drugs". This treaty was executed on behalf of His Majesty as an imperial treaty for Great Britain and many dominions including Canada.

A new Act was passed in 1923 (13-14 Geo. V. c. 22). The title of this statute was: An Act to Prohibit the Improper Use of Opium and other Drugs. The schedule listed in addition to the four drugs previously covered: heroin, codeine, and "cannabis indica or hasheesh". The Act provided for the licensing of the distribution of any drug and prohibited any sale except on medical prescription.

A further international convention concerning dangerous drugs was executed in 1925. This convention included provisions respecting Indian hemp and the resins prepared from it. These stipulations were aimed at preventing the export of those substances to countries which prohibit their use. Canada was directly a party to this convention as well as to a later convention of 1931 and subsequent protocols. On March 30, 1961, Canada signed a new treaty entitled "Single Convention on Narcotic Control 1961". In this document cannabis and cannabis resin were put in a list of four specially dangerous drugs which includes heroin.

That same year, the previously existing Canadian Act, including many amendments made from time to time, was replaced by what is now in effect the present Act (1960-61 (Can.), c. 35). The schedule includes a great many drugs. The conditions under which narcotics may be sold, had in possession, or otherwise dealt in, are now determined by regulations. A large number of those drugs are authorized for sale or administration under medical prescription. . . .

It does not appear to me that the fact that the specific drugs with which we are concerned in this case are completely prohibited, alters the general character of the Act which is legislation for the proper control of narcotic drugs rather than a complete prohibition of such drugs. . . .

. . . The mere fact that severe penalties are provided for violations cannot of itself stamp out a federal statute as criminal law. Such is the case for most revenue Acts which are clearly a class of statutes founded on legislative authority other than head 27. . . .

I do not overlook what was said with respect to the distinctive features of criminal law in the *Margarine Reference* ([1949] S.C.R. 1). The Court was concerned in that case to ascertain whether the prohibitory legislation under consideration could be brought within the description of "criminal law". A negative conclusion was reached on the basis that the purpose of that prohibition was economic, this does not establish that all other prohibitions are "criminal law" and it should not be taken as decisive of the criterions accepted for so characterizing other prohibitions.

In my view, the most important consideration for classifying the Narcotic Control Act as legislation enacted under the general residual federal power, is that this is essentially legislation adopted to deal with a genuinely new problem which did not exist at the time of Confederation and clearly cannot be put in the class of "Matters of a merely local or private nature". The subject matter of this legislation is thus properly to be dealt with on the same footing as such other new developments as aviation (*Re Aeronautics*) and radio communications (*Re Radio Communication*).

I would therefore answer the constitutional question as follows:

As to para. 1: Yes.

As to para. 2: Yes, in respect of a violation or conspiracy to violate any Act of the Parliament of Canada or regulations made thereunder the constitutional validity of which does not depend upon head 27 of s. 91 of the British North America Act, no opinion being expressed whether the competence of the Parliament of Canada extends beyond that point.

I would accordingly allow the appeal, set aside the judgment of the Appellate Division and restore the judgment of Judge W. Stevenson. There should be no costs in any Court.

SPENCE J.: . . . I commence with what may well be regarded as a trite statement of a fundamental principle of Canadian constitutional law. Federal legislation powers under s. 91 of the British North America Act are conferred upon Parliament exclusively notwithstanding anything in that Act and particularly s. 92 thereof. The imposition of duties by Parliament and the conferring of powers of Parliament upon provincial courts and provincial officials comes from the exercise of federal legislative power and needs no enabling legislation or any type of permission from the provinces. . . .

Acting upon such a power Parliament has, throughout the Criminal Code, granted jurisdiction to various provincial courts and has imposed duties and has conferred powers on various provincial officials including of course the Attorneys General of the provinces. Those provincial courts in exercising such jurisdiction and those Attorneys General and other provincial officials in discharging their duties so imposed and exercising their powers so conferred do so by virtue of the federal legislation enacted under the enumerated head no. 27 of s. 91 of the British North America Act.

It is of course true that prior to Confederation the Attorneys General of the various colonies instituted prosecutions and still continue to do so in much the same fashion. Prior to Confederation, however, the Attorneys General acted under their common law jurisdiction or as directed by the valid legislation of the particular colony. After Confederation they do so as empowered and directed by valid federal legislation. I can see no bar to Parliament, in the discharge of its valid legislative power, providing that as to certain duties or procedures the provincial officials shall not be used exclusively but the power may also be exercised by a federal official who may be the Attorney General of Canada or any investigating or prosecuting agency designated by Parliament.

Indeed it is difficult to understand how much of the federal legislative field could be dealt with efficiently by other methods. Much of the legislation in such fields is in essence regulatory and concerns such typically federal matters as trade and commerce, importation and exportation and other like matters. The administration of such fields require decisions of policy and certainly would include the establishment of a policy as to the means of and methods of enforcement. It would be a denial of the basic concept of federalism to permit the provincial authorities to have exclusive control of the enforcement of such legislation and the sole determination as to how and when the legislation should be enforced by institution of prosecution or against whom such prosecution should be instituted. If the legislative field is within the enumerated heads in s. 91, then the final decision as to administrative policy, investigation and prosecution must be in federal hands. Perhaps the Narcotic Control Act is a prime example of this principle. The Act contains much which is purely prohibitive and many provisions creating and providing for the prosecution of offences. But much of the statute also deals with regulation of the trade in drugs, with the importation of them, with the use of them and with the detailed delineation of the various classes thereof. Trade in the drugs both legal and illicit constantly crosses national and provincial boundaries. It is apparent, in my opinion, that the regulation of the subject of narcotic drugs, the policy controlling their distribution, the investigation of breaches of the statute or regulations and the institution of prosecution must be carried out by federal officials.

The contention otherwise advanced by counsel for the various provinces is based on the provisions of s. 92(14) of the British North America Act. Such provision reads:

The Administration of Justice in the province, including the Constitution, Maintenance, and Organization of Provincial Courts, both of Civil and of Criminal Jurisdiction, and including Procedure in Civil Matters in those Courts.

It first must be noted that s. 91(27) grants to the federal Parliament jurisdiction in "the Procedure in Criminal Matters" and that power is, by virtue of the concluding sentence of s. 91, exclusive to Parliament. Secondly and most important, s. 92(14) is by its very words limited to administration of justice "in the Province". I do not contend that those words mean the administration of justice in civil matters only for, in the same enumerated head, both "civil" and "criminal" are expressly mentioned and contrasted and it would have been inevitable that the draftsman would have inserted the word "civil" in the phrase "in the Province" if such a limitation were intended. But I am of the opinion that the words "in the Province" indicate that the legislator was concerned with the operation of the judicial machinery within the confines of the province and not with the vital matter of who should enforce and prosecute breaches of federal statutes. . . .

For these reasons, I would answer "yes" to both parts of the question posed for the Court and therefore allow the appeal.

The judgment of Dickson and Pratte JJ. was delivered by

DICKSON J. (*dissenting*): Stated in narrow terms, the question raised in these proceedings is whether s. 2 of the Criminal Code, R.S.C. 1970, c. C-34, authorizes the Attorney General of Canada or his agent to prosecute offences under the Narcotic Control Act, R.S.C. 1970, c. N-1. It is apparent, however, from the amplitude of the factums and the breadth of argument in this Court, that the issues extend far beyond that simple question.

The Attorney General of Canada advances what was referred to by Mr. Robinette as the "broad proposition" that the British North America Act, 1867 gives the conduct of all criminal proceedings to the federal power. The provinces, who exclusively supervised criminal administration, unchallenged, for over a century prior to a 1968-69 amendment to the Criminal Code, hold a different view.

Prior to 1969, there would seem to have been an arrangement under which provincial Attorneys General, or their agents, prosecuted Criminal Code offences, while the agents of the federal Attorney General prosecuted narcotics and combines offences, but in the name of the provincial Attorneys General. The expansion of the definition of "Attorney General", operative in 1969, put an end to all of that and gave rise to the present constitutional controversy. . . .

The role of the Attorney General in criminal proceedings, as contrasted to the role of the "prosecutor", can best be defined in terms of three classifications of powers, unique to the Attorney General and his agents, or in some instances to the Attorney General alone.

1. *The Power to Intervene.* Under this heading fall two interrelated powers, the entry of a stay of proceedings, and a more general power of intervention. The Attorney General, or counsel instructed by him for the purpose, may direct that proceedings be stayed, whether the Attorney General or a private prosecutor has had the carriage of the prosecution up to that point. . . .

The Attorney General may also exercise a broader interventionist power, namely, the takeover of the conduct of proceedings from a private prosecutor, whatever the desire of that private prosecutor. . . .

2. *The Power to Prefer Indictments and to Control the Mode of Trial.* While the Attorney General has a broad power of intervention in any type of criminal proceeding, he also exercises certain specific powers in the Code in respect of more serious offences, *i.e.* indictable offences, in order to set the machinery of justice in motion. There are four ways in which an indictment can be preferred: (i) by the Attorney General or his agent; (ii) "by anyone who has the written consent of the Attorney General", and then two ways without intervention of the Attorney General; (iii) by anyone with the written consent of the judge, with or without grand jury; and (iv) by order of the court. It might be noted that the exceptional power of preferring an indictment in the absence of a preliminary inquiry, or upon the discharge of the accused on preliminary, is reserved to an individual with the written consent of a judge of the court, or to the Attorney General himself. All of the foregoing deals with *who* may prefer an indictment.

Another set of provisions relates to the control of *how* the accused is to be tried. . . .

The Attorney General—and only the Attorney General—has the right to override completely the election of the accused, and require the accused to be tried by a judge and jury.

3. *The Power to Control Appeals.* Broadly speaking, whatever the nature of the offence, one can characterize the Attorney General's control over appeals as being exclusive with respect to appeals to the court of appeal in the provinces and to this Court. . . . It must be noted that the Attorney General of Canada's rights of appeal are premised upon his power to institute and conduct proceedings, the precise issue in controversy in the present case. . . .

RESTATEMENT OF THE ISSUES

Now that the definition of "Attorney General" in s. 2 has been examined to determine those situations in which the Attorney General of Canada can become the "Attorney General" and the unique powers of the "Attorney General" have been touched upon, the real constitutional questions in this case can be more clearly delineated. Section 2(2) is not simply a law specifying who may prefer indictments. If it were so limited, no difficulty would be experienced. There is no question but that the Attorney General of Canada, if he wishes, like any other person, may prefer indictments and conduct proceedings with respect to offences under federal enactments other than the Criminal Code or, for that matter, under the Code itself, subject of course to the same limitations as those applying to any private prosecutor. The issues in this case, however, are broader and they can be more precisely put as follows:

1. Is it within the competence of the Parliament of Canada to enact legislation as in s. 2(2) of the Criminal Code to authorize the Attorney General of Canada, or his agent, to institute proceedings, to prefer indictments, and to conduct prosecutions in respect of an offence under the Narcotic Control Act as the "Attorney General" with all the powers of intervention, control and appeal attaching to that office?

2. Is it within the competence of the Parliament of Canada to enact legislation as in s. 2(2) of the Criminal Code to authorize the Attorney General of Canada, or his agent, to act as the "Attorney General" in respect of a violation or conspiracy to violate any Act of Parliament enacted under the "criminal law" power (head 91(27)), or an Act of Parliament enacted under any other head of federal power in s. 91 of the British North America Act? . . .

It has been argued that as a matter of statutory construction s. 2(2) does not act to exclude the provincial Attorney General, because its effect is to leave him with an exclusive role with respect to Code offences and a partial role with respect to non-Code offences. Accepting *arguendo* that to be the true construction of s. 2(2), two points of concern should here be emphasized.

First, there are a number of federal offences which rely for their constitutional validity upon s. 91(27), the criminal law power, which are not found in the Criminal Code. That is to say, there are a number of federal non-Code "criminal" offences. The effect of the last clause in s. 2(2), along with the Interpretation Act, is to extend the Attorney General of Canada's potential role as "Attorney General" to all federal offences whether found in the Criminal Code or not. For the purposes of the constitutional question, this has vital implications. If s. 2(2), as it now stands, is found within the powers of the federal government, then it is manifest that there is nothing to stop the federal government from similarly restricting the powers of the provincial Attorney General within the confines of the Criminal Code itself or, indeed, of stripping provincial Attorneys General of all Code powers. That is the "broad proposition" candidly advanced on behalf of the federal Crown in these proceedings. The constitutional issue does not respect the artificial barriers established by terming a piece of legislation "the Criminal Code", but directs the inquiry to the criminal law power of s. 91(27) of the British North America Act, 1867.

Second, a clear distinction must be drawn between statutory construction and constitutional competence. As a matter of statutory interpretation, s. 2(2) of the Code may have the effect of excluding the provincial Attorneys General only partially. It would be an error, in my view, to conclude from this that partial exclusion of the provincial Attorneys General would be constitutionally acceptable while complete exclusion would be beyond federal power. It cannot properly be said that because exclusion of the provincial Attorney General is only partial, the federal government is not claiming exclusive jurisdiction. If, as the provinces contend, the supervisory role of the Attorney General is exclusively within provincial jurisdiction, then *any* act, on the part of the federal government to exclude the provincial Attorney General, in whole or in part, would not be within federal constitutional competence.

In allocating the powers and functions of the office of Attorney General in criminal proceedings, the principal task is to construe two of the heads of power found in the British North America Act, 1867:

91(27) The Criminal Law, except the Constitution of Courts of Criminal Jurisdiction, but including the Procedure in Criminal Matters.

92(14) The Administration of Justice in the Province, including the Constitution, Maintenance, and Organization of Provincial Courts, both of Civil and of Criminal Jurisdiction, and including Procedure in Civil Matters in those Courts.

It is the position of the Attorney General of Canada that Parliament, and Parliament alone, has the *jurisdiction* to legislate with respect to the conduct of criminal proceedings. It is the position of the respondent and the provinces that the Attorney General's supervision over criminal proceedings is exclusively within provincial *jurisdiction* by reason of the Attorney General's role in the "administration of justice in the province". The constitutional question is not, therefore, whether the wording of s. 2(2) does, or does not, exclude the Attorney General of the province completely, but the constitutional basis upon which the jurisdiction is claimed. . . .

SUPPORTS FOR THE FEDERAL POSITION

Is s. 2(2) to be characterized as "criminal law" or "procedure in criminal matters" or as incidental thereto and, therefore, a valid exercise of federal legislative power, or is it to be characterized as "administration of justice within the province" and, therefore, *ultra vires* as an encroachment on an exclusive head of provincial power? The import of the federal case is to be found in para. 18 of the factum of the Attorney General of Canada and I cannot do better than to quote it:

> *18. By whom and in what circumstances proceedings for violations of the criminal law may be instituted, conducted, terminated, appealed, etc., are matters clearly relating to the criminal law and procedure in criminal matters within the meaning of Head 27 of Section 91 of the British North America Act. The authority to make laws in relation to classes of subject must be taken to carry with it the authority to determine the manner in which those laws shall be enforced and of the essence of enforcement is authority to prescribe the necessary rules pertaining to the initiating and conduct of any litigation required for the purposes of enforcement.*

In the absence of s. 92(14) I would agree with that submission. It seems reasonable that, unless a contrary intention appears in the British North America Act, authority to make laws in relation to a class of subject should carry with it the authority to enforce those laws. The difficulty facing the federal Crown, however, is that administration of justice is an exclusive provincial head of power and it includes the administration of criminal justice. That was decided in *Di Iorio and Fontaine* v. *The Warden of the Common Jail of Montreal and Brunet* ([1978] 1 S.C.R. 152). The power to administer criminal justice includes the power of enforcement. That has been demonstrated by a century of experience during which the provinces enforced the criminal laws. And the power of enforcement includes, in my view, the conduct of enforcement proceedings. Parliament has power to make criminal law and to define procedures, but the provinces are empowered under our Constitution to enforce those laws in a manner consistent with those procedures.

A case much relied upon by the federal Crown is *Regina* v. *Pelletier* ([1974], 18 C.C.C. (2d) 516 [Ont. C.A.]), (application for leave to appeal to this Court refused ([1974] S.C.R. x.). In that case, the accused was charged with conspiring to traffic in a narcotic contrary to the Narcotic Control Act thereby constituting the offence of conspiracy under the then s. 408 of the Criminal Code. On appeal, the appellant raised the issue as to whether or not the Attorney General of Canada can prosecute in one of the provinces of Canada an accused charged with that offence. In the course of a lengthy judgment, delivered on behalf of the Court, Mr. Justice Estey made the following observations, p. 542:

> *On the one hand, the province, under the guise of "administration of justice" or the included authority to "constitute criminal courts", has the authority to legislate (at least until Parliament expands the Criminal Code prosecutorial functions to exclude the provincial function), with reference to the appointment of a prosecutor in provincial criminal Courts.*
>
> *On the other hand, Parliament, by reason of the combination of exclusive sovereignty in criminal law and criminal procedure, and by its overriding authority in matters properly related to "peace, order and good government", has jurisdiction to legislate with reference to the prosecutorial function at least to the extent that a manifest national interest invokes its "Peace, Order and good Government" authority. In that event the inherent and heretofore largely somnambulant executive function lies in support of the enforcement of the Criminal Code by the Attorney General of Canada and his agents.*

If I understand correctly the foregoing passages, the right of Parliament "to legislate with reference to the prosecutorial function" is said to be grounded not only upon Parliament's exclusive sovereignty in criminal law and criminal procedure, but also upon "peace, order and good government" and the "inherent and heretofore largely somnambulant executive function". The challenge raised by the accused in *Pelletier* to the status of the Attorney General of Canada, as prosecutor, was resolved against the accused. . . .

I would like now to discuss the following matters which were relied upon in *Pelletier:* (1) Peace, order and good government; (2) Inherent executive power; (3) Concurrency; and to consider also one further matter (4) Characterization.

1. *Peace, order and good government.* With respect, I do not believe that the validity of para. (*b*) of the definition "Attorney General" in s. 2(2) of the Criminal Code can be buttressed by Parliament's general authority to legislate with respect to "peace, order and good government". Recourse may be had to Parliament's general power in respect of matters of "national concern" or of "national dimension" which are not enumerated in the specific heads of power. Equally, matters enumerated in s. 92 may temporarily reach "emergency" proportions, justifying federal intervention in what are normally matters of provincial jurisdiction. Before it can then be invoked, however, there must exist in Canada at the time a state of national emergency requiring the implementation of extraordinary measures of a temporary nature. Chief Justice Laskin in *Re Anti-Inflation Act*, at p. 426, was of the view that Parliament might be entitled to employ peace, order and good government to act from the "springboard" of its exclusive jurisdiction under some head of s. 91, (in that case, its jurisdiction over monetary policy and trade and commerce). But in situations other than the foregoing, the peace, order and good government power is not available, nor can it be invoked to strengthen a claim under a head of exclusive federal power.

2. *Inherent executive power.* In my view, an "inherent executive function" cannot be used to extend the ambit of legislative power of either government. Upon Confederation, the Crown was divided—of that, there is no doubt. But in that division, ss. 91 and 92 of the British

North America Act redistributed in an exhaustive fashion the legislative functions of a unitary state and the executive functions must have followed, of necessity, the distribution of legislative power. Executive power is nurtured by and is dependent upon legislative power. Executive functions, federal and provincial, must be exercised with due regard to, and within the limits prescribed by ss. 91 and 92 respectively. In short, the issue in this case is not one of executive power, but of legislative competence.

In *Pelletier*, the proposition was advanced that executive power to enforce the statutes of Parliament, and of the Legislatures, follows upon the legislative authority to enact those statutes. One could not question this as a broad and general statement, but it does little to assist in resolving the issue facing the Court in the present case, namely, which Legislature has authority to enact legislation in relation to the prosecution, conduct, and supervision of criminal proceedings. I am quite prepared to accept the proposition that, in respect of heads of federal power other than head 27, there may be implicit and inherent power residing in the federal executive to enforce the Acts validly enacted by Parliament, such as Revenue, Customs, Fisheries, and Bankruptcy statutes and regulations. . . . A different situation obtains with respect to s. 91(27) and s. 92(14) because of the specific conferral upon the provinces of the right and responsibility to administer justice, particularly criminal justice. The quarrel here is not over the right of Parliament to enforce its own enactments but rather, and this bears repeated emphasis, the attempt by Parliament to exclude the provinces from the right to supervise criminal prosecutions.

3. *Concurrency.* In *Pelletier*, the concept of concurrency was accepted. At the beginning of the judgment, the door is opened to this possibility, at p. 523:

At the same time it should be observed that the search for an answer to this question should not be restricted by an assumption that the appointment of a prosecutor in a criminal Court is necessarily the exclusive prerogative or duty of one or the other of the plenary authorities established under the British North America Act, 1867.

It will be observed that the issue is here cast in terms of the power to appoint a prosecutor in a criminal court, not the supervisory powers of the Attorney General. Subsequently, s. 2(2) is characterized in this manner, at p. 530:

for here the Criminal Code provision does not purport to establish exclusively on the Attorney General of Canada, and thus does not purport "to occupy the field" as against such statutes as the Crown Attorney Act of Ontario.

With respect, in my view the effect of s. 2(2) is to establish exclusively on the part of the federal Attorney General in the proceedings which he chooses to enter and, as to those proceedings, he does "occupy the field" as against the provincial Attorney General, and as against Crown Attorneys and all other persons. . . .

In *Di Iorio*, reference is made to the "aspect doctrine" at p. 207: "a matter which for some purpose may fall within the scope of the federal power over criminal law and procedure may also fall within the legitimate concern of the provinces as pertaining to the Administration of Justice"; and at pp. 225-6: "Given the ancillary powers of the Parliament of Canada and the interrelated aspects of criminal justice, one is likely to find room for overlapping legislation in this area". The general principle is accepted but the constitutional conflict engendered by s. 2(2) is too sharp and too complete to make this an appropriate case for an application of the "double-aspect" doctrine. It is difficult to perceive in what "aspect" and for what "purpose" the two governments can differentiate their claims to jurisdiction. Both claim jurisdiction over the powers of the Attorney General in criminal proceedings for the identical aspect and the identi-

cal purpose, namely, the prosecution and supervision of criminal offences. . . .

It should not be thought that the notion of concurrency offers an easy solution to the problem before the Court. Because of the effects of paramountcy, the result of declaring concurrent jurisdiction is, so far as the office of provincial Attorney General is concerned in relation to prosecution of criminal offences, the same as a declaration of exclusive federal power. Whether one speaks in terms of federal power, or of concurrency, the provincial power, being subservient, must give way. There can never be two Attorneys General in respect of the same proceeding. Acceptance of the notion of concurrency would have the effect of removing from the provincial Attorney General the primary right and duty to prosecute in the province.

4. *Characterization.* Characterization of para. (*b*) of the definition of "Attorney General" in the Criminal Code is not difficult. As the Attorney General of British Columbia submits, it is legislation encompassing who can set the criminal law in motion and who can have the carriage of the proceedings once they have been instituted. In my view, the pith and substance of s. 2(2), the dominant characteristic, is the enforcement of the criminal law. The effect of the section is to authorize the Attorney General of Canada, or his agent, to supplant the provincial Attorneys General in instituting proceedings, preferring indictments, and conducting proceedings in respect of offences under the Narcotic Control Act, and to deprive the Attorneys General of a province from having anything to do with a prosecution once it has been instituted at the instance of the Attorney General of Canada.

The federal position, the "broad proposition" advanced on behalf of the Attorney General of Canada, is that the powers exercised by the provinces in the prosecution of federal offences have been with the acquiescence of, and as a concession from, the federal Parliament, and that Parliament's jurisdiction over criminal law and procedure carries with it power over the manner of enforcement and prosecution. . . .

THE CONTENT OF THE COMPETING POWERS

. . . Criminal law is concerned with the statement of the legal principles which constitute the substance of the law. The criminal law gives or defines rights and obligations. Criminal procedure, on the other hand, in its broadest sense, comprehends the mode of proceeding by which those rights and obligations are enforced. In a more narrow sense "procedure" means the machinery of the Court by which the formal steps in a judicial proceeding are regulated. If one is to give meaning to, and reconcile, the federal power to legislate in respect of criminal procedure with the provincial power to administer justice, the former must, I think, be taken as limited to the right to define the form or manner of conducting criminal prosecutions, *i.e.* the rules according to which the substantive law is administered. The latter, the administration of justice, embodies the right to direct the judicial process by which are enforced, in accordance with prescribed federal procedures, the rights and duties recognized by validly enacted federal criminal law. It includes control over putting the machinery of the criminal courts in motion and taking the requisite steps to prosecute those accused of crime, as well as discretion exercised in terminating criminal process. . . .

HISTORICAL PERSPECTIVE

. . . The Attorney General of British Columbia submits that in enacting ss. 91(27) and 92(14) of the British North America Act, an attempt was made to achieve a "subtle balance" between national and local needs in the area of crime prevention and control. Constitutional authority to enact substantive criminal laws—the determination of what was a crime and how it should be punished—was vested in the federal government, but the administration of the criminal law remained in the local or provincial hands

where it could be more flexibly administered. This submission is well supported by the evidence. The position of decentralized control, which had obtained in England from time immemorial, and in Canada prior to Confederation, with local administration of justice, local police forces, local juries, and local prosecutors, was perpetuated and carried forward into the Constitution through s. 92(14). The administration of criminal justice was to be kept in local hands and out of the control of the central government.

It would seem to have been the view of the Fathers of Confederation that the countless decisions to be made in the course of administering criminal justice could best be made at the local level. Such decisions were made locally at the time of Confederation, and thereafter until 1969, by provincial Attorneys General and their agents in discharge of their significant constitutional responsibility. There is, I think, a certain unity and cohesion between the three aspects of law enforcement, namely, investigation, policing, and prosecution, which would be imperilled if the investigatory function were discharged at one level of government and the prosecutorial function at another level.

The enactment of s. 2(2) of the Criminal Code may be viewed as not only an attempt to intrude into matters traditionally reserved for the provincial Attorneys General, but also as a breach of the bargain struck at the time of Confederation. No practical reasons have been advanced for setting aside the practices and customs of one hundred years. It has not been suggested that authority to pass s. 2(2) is requisite to prevent the scheme of the Criminal Code or of non-Code "criminal" statutes from being frustrated or defeated. From the material before us, it would not appear that the arrangement existing between the federal and provincial authorities, to which I have referred earlier, had created any difficulties over the years. This, of course, does not decide the matter because we are dealing here essentially with constitutional power and not with the effect of alleged federal acquiescence, but the considerations I mention are by no means irrelevant. . . .

Procedural changes from time to time in the Criminal Code altered in minor detail the powers and privileges of the provincial Attorney General, but at no point did the federal government in the exercise of its "criminal procedure" powers purport to take away any of the powers of the provincial Attorneys General. Only in 1968-69 did Parliament take the step of, in effect, creating a second Attorney General, with competing claims to jurisdiction in respect of the control and supervision of the administration of criminal justice. . . .

RESOLUTION OF THE CONFLICT

The difficulty in resolving the conflict in this case stems from separate lines of authority which are brought into collision by the amendment to s. 2(2) of the Criminal Code:

1. cases such as *Niagara Falls Bridge* and *St. Louis* which clearly indicate that the supervision and control of criminal proceedings lies in the provincial Attorney General. These decisions are reinforced by a century of practice during which the provincial Attorneys General exercised that supervision and control with the concurrence of the federal Attorney General. The federal government has from time to time extended and altered the powers and privileges of the provincial Attorney General through amendments to the Criminal Code, but has never hitherto sought to exclude the provincial Attorney General from his supervisory role;

2. another line of cases, *e.g. Valin* v. *Langlois, Flint, Vancini, Smythe*, where the federal power to enforce its laws other than "criminal" laws has been supported, apparently without serious question;

3. a third line of cases, *e.g. In re McNutt; Simcovitch* v. *R.; The Margarine Reference*, where the unitary view of the criminal law was moderated for constitutional purposes, *i.e.* provincial offences are merely penal and federal offences are either penal or crimes in the true sense.

4. cases where various non-Code offences under other federal acts have been upheld on the basis of the criminal law power, *e.g.* the Combines Investigation Act in *Proprietary Articles Trade Association* v. *Attorney General of Canada, supra.*

There are these conflicts in the jurisprudence and some resolution of them must be found. A constitutional *modus vivendi* is necessary in order to accommodate both levels of government.

The inescapable conclusion to be drawn from the legislative history, governmental attitudes, and case law is that the supervisory functions of the Attorney General in the administration of criminal justice have been considered to fall to the provinces under s. 92(14), as opposed to the competing federal power under s. 91(27). Among the older cases, in particular *Niagara Falls Bridge* and *St. Louis*, there are clear statements to the effect that the provincial Attorney General is the representative of the Crown responsible for the conduct and supervision of criminal proceedings. In support of the federal position, one finds at best the *Proprietary Articles Trade Association* and *Dominion Trade and Industry Commission Act* cases, neither of which provides any basis for a claim to constitutional jurisdiction over the Attorney General's role.

If one follows the weight of judicial authority in (1) and (3), the provincial Attorney General would be the only Attorney General in criminal proceedings, since his role is in pith and substance one of administration of criminal justice. Historical analysis and an examination of the substance of his function support this view. The "broad proposition" maintained by the respondent and six of the provinces is that all federal offences are "crimes" and the federal government has no role to play in the administration and enforcement of criminal law beyond the creation of uniform offences, uniform punishments, and uniform procedures.

Alternatively, there is the "broad proposition" stated by the federal government which rests on the notion that the rights of the provincial Attorney General derive solely from the Criminal Code and hence can be removed, piecemeal, or at one fell swoop, from the Code. Undoubtedly, the federal Parliament has altered the details of the powers and privileges of the Attorney General in the Code. But it cannot be said that the Attorney General was a creation of the Code—for that office existed in the provinces prior to the introduction of the 1892 Code. Nor can the addition of powers to those possessed by the Attorney General at common law provide a basis for the converse proposition, that the federal Parliament can remove all of those powers from the provincial Attorney General, including whatever common law powers he might once have possessed. To accept the federal proposition would mean that the term "administration of justice" would become confined in an important respect to "the administration of civil justice". A finding that the federal government may legislate to exclude the provincial Attorney General under "criminal procedure" would make "criminal procedure" co-extensive with "criminal justice", a notion rejected in *Di Iorio*. There is a need, I think, to maintain the "subtle balance" between national and local interests envisaged in our Constitution, leaving the administration of criminal justice in provincial hands where it could be more flexibly administered in response to local conditions. If the present s. 2(2) were to be upheld in relation to all non-Code offences, owing to the line of decisions mentioned in (4), and more broadly (3), such a conclusion on the narrow facts of this case would expose the whole of the Code to similar treatment by the federal government. The end result would be one Attorney General for the whole of Canada and that Attorney General would be the federal Attorney General.

A finding of *concurrent* jurisdiction with respect to the office of the Attorney General could obviate these constitutional problems. The provincial Attorney General would thus constitutionally be permitted to prosecute and supervise any offence, Code or non-Code. No accused could object to his jurisdiction. Alternatively, in respect of non-Code offences, the Attorney General of Canada could prosecute and supervise those proceedings, again without constitutional complaint from the accused, since in the concurrent field, the federal Attorney General is paramount in the event of a conflict. In effect, this would resolve the constitutional problem by ignoring it, since to find concurrent jurisdiction would run counter to (1) above, counter to the notion of divided jurisdiction implicit in ss. 91(27) and 92(14), counter to the accepted view of the aspect doctrine and counter to this Court's traditional reluctance to find concurrency and its corollary of paramountcy. Much as one might wish to find in a case such as this some constitutional compromise permitting both levels of government to operate validly in a given field, there is the overriding need to maintain the integrity of the criminal justice system. In criminal matters, and more precisely in criminal prosecutions, a powerful argument can be made for the drawing of firm lines not dependent upon the vagaries of the institution of proceedings in the individual case. The words of Chief Justice Laskin in *Di Iorio* bear repeating, pp. 181-2:

Moreover, if governmental powers are to be exercised coercively against individuals, the latter are entitled to have at least such protection as is provided by the distribution of legislative power under the British North America Act, in the sense that the Act should be construed as far as possible to preclude both levels of governmental authority from being entitled to converge on an individual for the same purpose and possibly even at the same time. . . .

Broadly speaking, then, the division of authority would be as follows:

1. The Attorney General of the province would have exclusive authority in respect of provincial penal offences.

2. The Attorney General of Canada would have exclusive authority in respect of federal offences found in statutes, the pith and substance of which is other than criminal law.

3. The Attorney General of the province would have exclusive authority in respect of federal statutes, the pith and substance of which is criminal law.

NARCOTIC CONTROL ACT AS CRIMINAL LAW

It is contended by the Attorney General of Canada that the Narcotic Control Act is not legislation enacted under the "criminal law" power and therefore, as I understand the argument, proceedings instituted under that Act are free of any supervisory power of the provincial Attorneys General. . . .

In the face of the structure of the Narcotic Control Act and Regulations, the terms of the 1961 Single Convention and the decided cases, the Narcotic Control Act cannot be characterized as being anything other than criminal law in pith and substance. That was the view of this Court in *Industrial Acceptance Corporation Ltd.* v. *The Queen* and I see no reason to reconsider the correctness of that decision.

To revert to the "peace, order and good government" power to support the validity of the Narcotic Control Act in the wake of this Court's decision in *Re Anti-Inflation Act*, would represent an unwarranted expansion of the general power and run counter to the opinions expressed in that case with reference to the "temperance" cases. Drug abuse is a very ancient phenomenon. While not a pressing problem at the time of Confederation, it was not than an unknown danger in North America: see Trasov, "History of the Opium and Narcotic Drug Legislation in Canada" (1962), 4 Crim. L.Q. 274.

While similarities certainly do exist between the Canada Temperance Act of 1878 and the present day Narcotic Control Act, I do not think one should press those similarities to the extent of supporting the latter legislation upon the basis of *Russell* v. *The Queen*. As Mr. Justice Beetz put it in the *Anti-Inflation Act Reference*, "the *Russell* case is a special case" (p. 453) and "It is perhaps unfortunate that a case with a history as chequered as *Russell* be sometimes regarded as the authority which gave birth to the national concern doctrine" (p. 454). Given the expansive view taken of the interpretation of s. 91 in *Russell*, Sir Montague Smith simply held that the subject of the Act did not fall within any of the classes of subjects assigned to the provinces. As Beetz J. observed in the *Anti-Inflation* case at p. 454, "The Judicial Committee came close to characterizing the Act as relating to criminal law; however it found it unnecessary to classify its provision in the classes of subjects enumerated in s. 91 of the Constitution". . . .

Many courts have struggled to rationalize *Russell*, the best known effort being that of Viscount Simon in *Attorney General of Ontario* v. *Canada Temperance Federation*. In the recent *Anti-Inflation Act* reference, Mr. Justice Beetz (with whom a majority of the Court agreed on the national dimensions doctrine) indicated a desire to restrict the scope of that doctrine to new matters, "distinct subject matters which do not fall within any of the enumerated heads of s. 92 and which, by nature are of national concern" (p. 457). In my view, the signal restraint in the application of the general power ought to extend to a case such as this, where it would seem clear that the Narcotic Control Act can be easily and properly characterized as falling within one of the enumerated heads of federal power, namely, head 27 of s. 91.

Accepting, as I think one must, that the Narcotic Control Act is criminal legislation, it follows from what has gone before that provincial supervisory power is maintained in respect of prosecution of offences under that Act.

CONCLUSION

In the result, I would answer the restated constitutional questions:

1. It is not within the competence of the Parliament of Canada to enact legislation, as in s. 2 of the Criminal Code, to authorize the Attorney General of Canada, or his agent, to institute proceedings, to prefer indictments, and to conduct prosecutions in respect of an offence under the Narcotic Control Act as the "Attorney General" with all the powers of intervention, control and appeal attaching to that office.

2. It is within the competence of the Parliament of Canada to enact legislation, as in s. 2 of the Criminal Code, to authorize the Attorney General of Canada, or his agent, to act as the "Attorney General", and indeed the "*only* Attorney General", in respect of a violation or conspiracy to violate an Act of Parliament enacted under any head of power in s. 91 of the British North America Act, *other than* head 27 relating to the criminal law power.

The appeal should be dismissed.

27. Residential Tenancies Reference, *1979*

~ In the immediate pre-Charter era when constitutional litigation was very much on the rise, no section of the Constitution generated as many cases as section 96 of the B.N.A. Act. Section 96 gives the federal government the power to appoint the judges of the superior, district and county courts of the provinces. It would seem an odd section to serve as a basis for judicial review of legislation for, on its face, it does not deal with legislative power. However, the courts have reasoned that if provinces were free to pass legislation restructuring their courts and transfer the traditional functions of section 96 courts to tribunals presided over by provincially appointed judges then section 96 could be rendered an empty shell. Thus, from the earliest days, the courts enforced section 96 as a limit on the legislative power of the provinces over "The Administration of Justice in the Province".[1]

Section 96, the federal appointing power, was not the only basis for restricting provincial jurisdiction in this field. Section 99 of the B.N.A. Act secures the tenure of the judges of the superior courts of the provinces (but not the judges of their lower courts) and section 100 provides that the remuneration of section 96 judges will be fixed by Parliament. Judges have seen in these sections some constitutional protection of judicial independence. Lord Atkin referred to sections 96, 99 and 100 as the "three principle pillars in the temple of justice".[2] By the 1930s the Judicial Committee had become so activist in enforcing the judicature sections of the Constitution as to virtually preclude further development of provincial lower courts or administrative tribunals.

But both the Supreme Court and the Privy Council soon began to soften this approach. In the *Adoption Reference* case the Supreme Court made room for considerable growth in the lower provincial courts by ruling that these courts could exercise jurisdiction in new fields of adjudication, unheard of at the time of Confederation, providing it "broadly conforms" to that "generally exercisable by courts of summary jurisdiction."[3] Also the courts began to develop a very policy-oriented test of the adjudicative functions which could be constitutionally assigned to administrative tribunals. Some of these modern administrative agencies integrate traditional judicial functions into broad regulatory schemes. It was recognized that in these new institutional settings traditional judicial functions might be transformed and no longer be appropriate for superior courts to perform. Thus, legislation establishing labour relations boards was upheld even though these boards settled disputes about labour contracts—something which section 96 courts had done before the era of collective bargaining.[4]

---

[1] For an account, see Peter H. Russell, *The Judiciary in Canada*, ch. 3 (Toronto, 1987).

[2] *Toronto* v. *York* (1938) A.C. 415, at p. 426.

[3] (1938) S.C.R. 398.

[4] *Labour Relations Bd. of Sask.* v. *John East Ironworks* (1949) A.C. 134 and *Tomko* v. *Labour Relations Bd. (N.S.)* 1 S.C.R. 112.

However the decision in the reference concerning Ontario's Residential Tenancies Act shows that there are real limits to how far the Supreme Court would go in permitting traditional functions of the superior courts to be subsumed by a modern regulatory agency. The legislation had been enacted in 1979 to bring together all aspects of landlord-tenant relations and put them under the aegis of a single administrative agency. Thus the Act gave the Ontario Residential Tenancy Commission not only the modern functions of education and mediation and of administering a system of rent controls but also the responsibility for deciding disputes about leases and issuing compliance orders, functions which up to then had been performed by section 96 courts. It was the transfer of these traditional judicial functions to an administrative agency which the Supreme Court found to be unconstitutional. In Chief Justice Dickson's view, these functions were 1) traditionally performed by section 96 courts, 2) inherently judicial, even in their new institutional setting and 3) at the very centre of the Commission's work. On the basis of this three-fold test, the Supreme Court ruled that these functions could not be transferred to the Residential Tenancy Commission. Although Ontario went ahead with the establishment of the Commission and a system of rent review, it did not put into force those parts of the Act giving the Commission the power to determine the rights and obligations of landlords and tenants.

In the *Residential Tenancies Reference* we find the Chief Justice speaking with some feeling of how the judicature sections of the Constitution were "conceived as a strong constitutional basis for national unity." Perhaps this concern for national unity has something to do with the Court's vigour in enforcing the judicature sections of the Constitution as limitations on provincial power in several other cases at this time. In the *B.C. Family Relations Act Reference*,[5] the Court ruled that certain kinds of family law disputes—those concerning the custody of children and the family home—could be dealt with only by section 96 courts, thus preventing the provinces from unifying all family law jurisdiction in courts presided over by provincially appointed judges. In the *Crevier* case[6] the Supreme Court struck down Quebec legislation establishing a Professions Tribunal, consisting of provincially appointed judges, which was to serve as a final court of appeal from the discipline committees of professional groups in the province. This decision made it clear that the power of the federally appointed judges of the provincial superior courts to review the decisions of provincial administrative tribunals on matters of law and jurisdiction was entrenched in the Constitution.

This series of cases did not sit well with provincial governments. The provinces, particularly Quebec, were coming to regard section 96 as an unacceptable constraint on their freedom to develop a modern, integrated

[5] (1982) 1 S.C.R. 62.
[6] *Crevier* v. *A.G. Quebec* (1981) 2 S.C.R. 220.

provincial justice system. This constraint was all the more unacceptable in that it did not appear at this time to apply to the federal Parliament. By 1980 nine of the ten provinces were calling for the complete dismantling of section 96 and acquisition by the provinces of the power to appoint the judges of all provincial courts. In 1983 the federal government went so far as to propose an amendment to section 96 which would permit the provinces to confer judicial functions on any board, commission or administrative authority subject to review by a superior court for want or excess of jurisdiction.[7] But this proposal met a rough reception when it was unveiled to gatherings of judges and lawyers who were fiercely opposed to this invitation to transfer adjudicative functions away from the formal court system. It was quietly withdrawn. ~

RE RESIDENTIAL TENANCIES ACT, 1979
In the Supreme Court of Canada, (1981) 1 S.C.R. 714.

The judgment of Laskin C.J. and Martland, Ritchie, Dickson, Estey, McIntyre and Lamer JJ. was delivered by

DICKSON J.—The resolution of disputes between landlords and tenants has long been a central preoccupation of the common law courts. As early as 1587, Lord Coke observed that the law of landlord and tenant was vital since, "for the most part, every man is a lessor or a lessee". (*Walker's Case* ((1587), 76 E.R. 676, at p. 680.)

Within the past few years the Province of Ontario, in common with a number of other provinces, has enacted legislation to redress what was perceived to be an imbalance, in favour of landlords, in the landlord and tenant relationship. On June 21, 1979, the Legislative Assembly of Ontario enacted *The Residential Tenancies Act, 1979*, 1979 (Ont.), c. 78, to come into effect on proclamation. The Act contains a detailed legislative code to govern landlords and tenants and establishes a tribunal, bearing the name the Residential Tenancy Commission, to oversee and enforce the newly enunciated rights and obligations. Questions having been raised as to the authority of the Legislative Assembly of Ontario to empower the Commission to make orders evicting tenants from residential premises and to require landlords and tenants to comply with obligations imposed under the Act, the Executive Council of the Province, pursuant to s. 1 of *The Constitutional Questions Act*, R.S.O. 1970, c. 79, referred the following questions to the Court of Appeal of Ontario for hearing and consideration:

1. Is it within the legislative authority of the Legislative Assembly of Ontario to empower the Residential Tenancy Commission to make an order evicting a tenant as provided in *The Residential Tenancies Act, 1979*?
2. Is it within the legislative authority of the Legislative Assembly of Ontario as provided in *The Residential Tenancies Act, 1979* to empower the Residential Tenancy Commission to make orders requiring landlords and tenants to comply with obligations imposed under that Act?

The Court of Appeal delivered a careful and scholarly unanimous judgment in which each of these questions was answered in the negative. . . .

---

[7] The Hon. Mark MacGuigan, Minister of Justice, *A Suggested Amendment Relating to Provincial Administrative Tribunal*, (Ottawa, 1983).

I

In advance of the hearing before the Ontario Court of Appeal, the Attorney General of Ontario filed with the court the 1968 report of the Ontario Law Reform Commission entitled "Interim Report on Landlord and Tenant Law Applicable to Residential Tenancies"; the 1972 report of the Commission on Part IV of *The Landlord and Tenant Act*; the 1976 report of the Commission entitled "Report on Landlord and Tenant Law"; and a Green Paper published in 1978 by the Ministry of Consumer and Commercial Relations entitled "Policy Options for Continuing Tenant Protection". In the Court of Appeal, a question was raised as to whether, and the extent to which, this material was properly before the court. Although there was some argument, it was not pressed to the point where the Court of Appeal felt called upon to rule on it. . . .

The same four documents were before us, and it seems appropriate at this time to rule whether properly so. There is little authority to guide decision.

Professors Whyte and Lederman correctly point out in chapter 4 of their work on *Canadian Constitutional Law* that a classification process is at the heart of judicial determination of the distribution or limitation of primary legislative powers. That process joins logic with social fact, value decisions and the authority of precedents. A court faces particular difficulty in a constitutional reference when only the bare bones of the statute arrive for consideration. The Chief Justice of this Court made this point in the "chicken and egg" reference, *Attorney-General for Manitoba* v. *Manitoba Egg and Poultry Association*. There is normally a dearth of relevant facts from which to draw logical inferences, determine social impact, make value decisions and select governing precedents. As Whyte and Lederman note, p. 229, ". . . the challenge of *ultra vires* raises a need for evidence of facts of social context and legislative effect . . ."

In my view a court may, in a proper case, require to be informed as to what the effect of the legislation will be. The object or purpose of the Act in question may also call for consideration though, generally speaking, speeches made in the Legislature at the time of enactment of the measure are inadmissible as having little evidential weight.

It now seems reasonably clear that Royal Commission Reports and the Reports of the Parliamentary committees made prior to the passing of a statute are admissible to show the factual context and purpose of the legislation. . . .

. . . We should be loathe, it seems to me, to enunciate any inflexible rule governing the admissibility of extrinsic materials in constitutional references. The effect of such a rule might well be to exclude logically relevant and highly probative evidence. It is preferable, I think, to follow the practice adopted in the *Anti-Inflation Reference* and give timely directions establishing the evidence or extraneous materials to be admitted to serve the ends of the Court in the particular reference.

Generally speaking, for the purpose of constitutional characterization of an act we should not deny ourselves such assistance as Royal Commission reports or Law Reform Commission reports underlying and forming the basis of the legislation under study, may afford. The weight to be given such reports is, of course, an entirely different matter. They may carry great, little, or no weight, but at least they should, in my view, generally be admitted as an aid in determining the social and economic conditions under which the Act was enacted. . . .

A constitutional reference is not a barren exercise in statutory interpretation. What is involved is an attempt to determine and give effect to the broad objectives and purpose of the Constitution, viewed as a "living tree", in the expressive words of Lord Sankey in *Edwards and Others* v. *Attorney-General for Canada and Others* ([1930] A.C. 124). Material relevant to the issues before the court, and not inherently unreliable or offending against public policy should be admissible, subject to the proviso that such extrinsic materials are not available for the purpose of aiding in statutory construction. . . .

II

~ Justice Dickson traced reform of Ontario's landlord and tenant law up to 1975. ~

In 1975 the Legislature of Ontario introduced *The Residential Premises Rent Review Act, 1975*, 1975 (Ont.), c. 12, to establish rent control. The ability of the province to administer a rent review system, of course, in no way encroached on the traditional jurisdiction of the s. 96 courts to order termination, eviction and compliance. A companion Act, 1975, (Ont.), c. 13, amended *The Landlord and Tenant Act* to make substantial changes in the substantive law of landlord and tenant. This latter Act established security of tenure for tenants by providing for automatic renewal of tenancy agreements upon expiration of the term, unless the agreement had been lawfully terminated in accordance with the Act. A tenant might terminate it by agreement or by giving notice in the form and at the time prescribed by the statute. A landlord might terminate only for specified causes and at specified times. The rules for proceedings by the county or district court judge were relaxed and simplified. The powers of these judges were expanded to cover most of the issues that might arise between a landlord and a tenant, including power to declare a tenancy agreement terminated.

After the 1975 statutes were passed the courts continued to exercise the functions traditionally performed by s. 96 courts since Confederation, and to the present time, to order termination of leases, make eviction orders and compel compliance with the provisions of a lease of residential premises. . . .

On February 10, 1978 a Government Green Paper was released relating to policy options for continuing tenant protection. The Green Paper made reference to the very large number of Ontario citizens whose lives are governed in part by the law of landlord and tenant. From 1961 to 1971 the number of tenants grew by 70 per cent from 483,500 to 825,000. It was estimated that there were more than one million rental households in Ontario constituting about 36 per cent of all households.

A reading of the Green Paper would suggest that at least three factors led to the establishment of the Residential Tenancy Commission. First, the legislature had removed the landlord's traditional right to employ 'self-help' remedies (*i.e.* repossession) and now required a landlord to apply for an order of eviction. It was felt that the demands of this "new business" would clog an already over-burdened court system. A specialized Commission was seen as a convenient method for ensuring prompt and efficient resolution of landlord-tenant disputes. A second major factor was the belief that the regular court system was too formal in structure for the resolution of landlord and tenant disputes; that such disputes could best be adjudicated in an informal, summary proceeding before a tribunal where individual complainants would feel less inhibited in presenting their own cases. Third, the Green Paper saw the creation of a Tenancy Commission as a convenient method of consolidating functions which had previously been performed by different organizations. The new tribunal would be a centralized body which could provide authoritative advice to landlords and tenants. By combining administrative functions with judicial functions, the tribunal would be able to offer a wider range of remedies to individuals than the regular court system. The Paper noted that while many had hailed the development of tenancy boards and tribunals as an effective means of realizing the rights embodied in the residential tenancy legislation, others had pointed out that such "rough justice" might run counter to well-established principles of procedure. The Green Paper recommended a "mediation-adjudication" approach under which authority to mediate would be combined with jurisdiction to adjudicate a dispute. In this approach, an official would listen to both sides of the case and attempt to guide the parties toward a mutually agreeable solution. If agreement could not be reached, the official would convene a hearing with the parties present, hear evidence and arrive at a determination according to the law. The decision would be legally enforceable.

The Residential Tenancies Act was enacted to implement the recommendations of the Green Paper. As I have said, the Act set up a new tribunal, the Residential Tenancy Commission, to oversee and enforce the obligations of landlords and tenants in Ontario. The tribunal is given wide-ranging powers and functions. Some of these are purely administrative in nature, for example, the Commission is charged with the obligation of informing members of the public as to their rights under the legislation. But by far the most significant role to be played is in the resolution of disputes between landlords and tenants. The mechanism for dispute resolution is triggered 'upon application' by either the landlord or the tenant. In one or two circumstances the process is put in motion by application by a third party— *e.g.* a neighbouring tenant.

The Residential Tenancies Act is not directed solely to low rental housing. It applies to every residential tenancy, including the most expensive housing, and leases of great value, and any length of term, in city or country.

III

As Professor Hogg has noted in his work on *Constitutional Law of Canada* (1977), p. 129, there is no general "separation of powers" in the *British North America Act, 1867*. Our Constitution does not separate the legislative, executive, and judicial functions and insist that each branch of government exercise only its own function. Thus it is clear that the Legislature of Ontario may confer non-judicial functions on the courts of Ontario and, subject to s. 96 of the *B.N.A. Act*, which lies at the heart of the present appeal, confer judicial functions on a body which is not a court.

Under s. 92(14) of the *B.N.A. Act* the provincial legislatures have the legislative power in relation to the administration of justice in the province. This is a wide power but subject to subtraction of ss. 96 to 100 in favour of the federal authority. Under s. 96 the Governor General has the sole power to appoint the judges of the Superior, District and County Courts in each province. Under s. 97 the judges who are to be appointed to the Superior, District and County Courts are to be selected from the respective bars of each province. Under s. 100 the Parliament of Canada is obliged to fix and provide for their salaries. Section 92(14) and ss. 96 to 100 represent one of the important compromises of the Fathers of Confederation. It is plain that what was sought to be achieved through this compromise, and the intended effect of s. 96, would be destroyed if a province could pass legislation creating a tribunal, appoint members thereto, and then confer on the tribunal the jurisdiction of the superior courts. What was conceived as a strong constitutional base for national unity, through a unitary judicial system, would be gravely undermined. Section 96 has thus come to be regarded as limiting provincial competence to make appointments to a tribunal exercising s. 96 judicial powers and therefore as implicitly limiting provincial competence to endow a provincial tribunal with such powers.

IV

The belief that any function which in 1867 had been vested in a s. 96 court must forever remain in that court reached its apogee in the judgment of Lord Atkin in *Toronto Corporation* v. *York Corporation* (1938) A.C. 415. Describing s. 96 as one of the "three principal pillars in the temple of justice . . . not to be undermined", Lord Atkin held that the Ontario Municipal Board could not validly receive "judicial authority". At the same time, he held that the Municipal Board was in 'pith and substance' an administrative body, and the impugned 'judicial functions' were severable from the administrative powers given to the Board under its enabling legislation. There was no analysis of the inter-relationship between the judicial and administrative features of the legislative scheme; the assumption was that any attempt to confer a s. 96 function on a provincially-appointed tribunal was *ultra vires* the legislature.

This sweeping interpretation of s. 96, with its accompanying restrictive view of provincial legislative authority under s. 92, was limited almost immediately by the judgment of this Court in the *Reference re Adoption Act and Other Acts* [1938] S.C.R. 398. Chief Justice Duff held that the jurisdiction of inferior courts was not "fixed forever as it stood at the date of Confederation". On his view, it was quite possible to remove jurisdiction from a Superior Court and vest it in a court of summary jurisdiction. The question which must be asked was whether "the jurisdiction conferred upon magistrates under these statutes broadly conform[s] to a type of jurisdiction generally exercisable by courts of summary jurisdiction rather than the jurisdiction exercised by courts within the purview of s. 96". . . .

The same process of liberalization, this time in the context of a transfer of jurisdiction from a Superior Court to an administrative tribunal, was initiated by the Privy Council in *Labour Relations Board of Saskatchewan* v. *John East Iron Works, Limited* [1949] A.C. 134. Lord Simonds proposed a two-fold test. The first limb of the test is to ask whether the board or tribunal exercises "judicial power". Lord Simonds did not propose a 'final' answer to the definition of "judicial power", but he suggested that,

. . . *the conception of the judicial function is inseparably bound up with the idea of a suit between parties, whether between Crown and subject or between subject and subject, and that it is the duty of the court to decide the issue between those parties, with whom alone it rests to initiate or defend or compromise the proceedings. [p. 149]*

If the answer to the initial question as to "judicial power" is in the negative, then that concludes the matter in favour of the provincial board. If, however, the power is in fact a judicial power, then it becomes necessary to ask a second question: in the exercise of that power, is the tribunal analogous to a superior, district or county court?

This formulation represented a subtle modification of the test proposed by Duff C.J. in the *Adoption Reference*. Duff C.J. had suggested it was necessary to determine whether the impugned jurisdiction was more analogous to a summary type of jurisdiction exercised at the time of Confederation rather than to a jurisdiction traditionally exercised by s. 96 courts. The formulation of Duff C.J. froze the provincial jurisdiction to that of summary courts. Lord Simonds in *John East* suggested that it was not absolutely necessary to consider whether there was a true analogy between the impugned jurisdiction and the jurisdiction of summary courts; it would be sufficient, for constitutional purposes, to establish that the power or jurisdiction was not one traditionally falling within s. 96. . . .

It is apparent that *John East* represented a break with the line of jurisprudence developed in *Toronto* v. *York*. The approach of *Toronto* v. *York*, in which the sole issue was whether the tribunal was being clothed with a s. 96 'judicial power', had been effectively, though not expressly, repudiated.

In *Tomko* v. *Labour Relations Board (Nova Scotia) et al.* [1977] 1 S.C.R. 112, the issue was the validity of the Nova Scotia Labour Relations Board's authority to issue a "cease and desist" order. It was argued that this jurisdiction was analogous to the jurisdiction of s. 96

courts to issue mandatory injunctions to halt illegal activity. The Chief Justice, speaking for eight members of the Court, held that this consideration was not conclusive, since ". . . it is not the detached jurisdiction or power alone that is to be considered but rather its setting in the institutional arrangements in which it appears and is exercisable, under the provincial legislation". A consideration of the 'institutional setting' indicated that the power to make cease and desist orders was merely one aspect of a broad legislative scheme for the peaceful regulation of collective bargaining, an area which the courts had not entered. Thus, the Labour Board had been validly clothed with the power impugned.

The recent decision of this Court, *The Corporation of the City of Mississauga* v. *The Regional Municipality of Peel et al.* [1979] 2 S.C.R. 244, is, in the words of the Chief Justice in that case, ". . . a prime illustration of the proposition laid down in *Tomko*". In *Mississauga*, the Ontario Municipal Board had been given certain powers to resolve disputes over assets between amalgamating municipalities. Noting that *Toronto* v. *York* must be viewed with 'considerable qualification', it was stated that the power to adjudicate was merely one ". . . incident . . . in the over-all picture of the general restructuring of the municipalities in which the Municipal Board is given an important part to play . . .". Viewed in their "institutional setting, the 'judicial powers' to determine rights and liabilities under provincial legislation had been validly granted to the Municipal Board".

I do not think it can be doubted that the courts have applied an increasingly broad test of constitutional validity in upholding the establishment of administrative tribunals within provincial jurisdiction. In general terms it may be said that it is now open to the provinces to invest administrative bodies with 'judicial functions' as part of a broader policy scheme. . . .

The teaching of *John East, Tomko* and *Mississauga* is that one must look to the 'institutional setting' in order to determine whether a particular power or jurisdiction can validly be conferred on a provincial body. . . .

. . . An administrative tribunal may be clothed with power formerly exercised by s. 96 courts, so long as that power is merely an adjunct of, or ancillary to, a broader administrative or regulatory structure. If, however, the impugned power forms a dominant aspect of the function of the tribunal, such that the tribunal itself must be considered to be acting 'like a court', then the conferral of the power is *ultra vires*.

The jurisprudence since *John East* leads one to conclude that the test must now be formulated in three steps. The first involves consideration, in the light of the historical conditions existing in 1867, of the particular power or jurisdiction conferred upon the tribunal. The question here is whether the power or jurisdiction conforms to the power or jurisdiction exercised by superior, district or county courts at the time of Confederation. . . .

If the historical inquiry leads to the conclusion that the power or jurisdiction is not broadly conformable to jurisdiction formerly exercised by s. 96 courts, that is the end of the matter. . . . If, however, the historical evidence indicates that the impugned power is identical or analogous to a power exercised by s. 96 courts at Confederation, then one must proceed to the second step of the inquiry.

Step two involves consideration of the function within its institutional setting to determine whether the function itself is different when viewed in that setting. In particular, can the function still be considered to be a 'judicial' function? In addressing the issue it is important to keep in mind the further statement by Rand J. in *Dupont* v. *Inglis* that ". . . it is the subject-matter rather than the apparatus of adjudication that is determinative". Thus the question of whether any particular function is 'judicial' is not to be determined simply on the basis of procedural trappings. The primary issue is the nature of the question which the tribunal is called upon to decide. Where the tribunal is faced with a private dispute between parties, and is called upon to adjudicate through the application of a recognized body of rules in a manner consistent with fairness and impartiality, then, normally, it is acting in a 'judicial capacity'. . . .

If, after examining the institutional context, it becomes apparent that the power is not being exercised as a "judicial power" then the inquiry need go no further for the power, within its institutional context, no longer conforms to a power or jurisdiction exercisable by a s. 96 court and the provincial scheme is valid. On the other hand, if the power or jurisdiction is exercised in a judicial manner, then it becomes necessary to proceed to the third and final step in the analysis and review the tribunal's function as a whole in order to appraise the impugned function in its entire institutional context. . . . It may be that the impugned 'judicial powers' are merely subsidiary or ancillary to general administrative functions assigned to the tribunal (*John East; Tomko*) or the powers may be necessarily incidental to the achievement of a broader policy goal of the legislature (*Mississauga*). In such a situation, the grant of judicial power to provincial appointees is valid. The scheme is only invalid when the adjudicative function is a sole or central function of the tribunal. . . .

V

Step one, the historical inquiry. The Residential Tenancy Commission is given a broad range of powers under the Act: in this reference, as I have noted, we are concerned with only two, power to make an eviction order and power to make a 'compliance' order. These powers recur constantly throughout the Act; there are nineteen separate provisions which empower the Commission to make an eviction order seventeen separate provisions empowering the Commission to make a compliance order. . . .

The Ontario Court of Appeal held that the power to order eviction was analogous to the traditional power of the courts to order the ejectment of a tenant, while the power to order compliance was analogous to the power of the courts to award damages or specific performance or to grant injunctive relief. This finding was not challenged on the hearing of this appeal. The Attorney General for Ontario conceded that the powers given to the Residential Tenancy Commission "... are not merely analogous to those [pre-1867] powers but are the same powers".

We start therefore with the proposition that the power to order eviction in the 1979 Act is broadly conformable to pre-1867 jurisdiction in ejectment, and the power to order compliance is broadly conformable to the pre-1867 jurisdiction to award damages or specific performance.

The question whether the powers or jurisdiction conferred by the statute are analogous to, in broad conformity with, the kind of powers or jurisdiction historically exercised by the superior, county or district courts admits of only one answer—yes.

... It is urged that the powers conferred on the Residential Tenancy Commission conform to a type of jurisdiction generally exercisable by courts of summary jurisdiction. As to the question of subject matter, the appellant relies on the form and language in which the statute is enacted. The statute contains non-technical language and its application involves questions of fact or involves the exercise of discretionary factual judgments expressed in ordinary language. It is submitted that no significant jurisprudential questions are involved. As to pecuniary limits, the Residential Tenancy Commission is empowered to make an order for the payment of money only where the amount claimed does not exceed $3,000. The suggestion seems to be that, since the Residential Tenancy Commission proceeds in a summary manner under a statute drafted in 'layman's' language, its jurisdiction is, for constitutional purposes, analogous to the jurisdiction of a summary court. This submission misconceives the import of the reasoning in the *Adoption Reference*. Provinces cannot avoid the limitations of s. 96 simply by taking a traditional s. 96 function, simplifying procedural matters, and then transferring the jurisdiction to a non-section-96 tribunal. If this could be done, s. 96 would be stripped of all force and effect.

VI

We pass now to the second step of the inquiry, to consideration of the impugned powers within their institutional setting. Is the power to order eviction or compliance when so viewed still a 'judicial power'? I have already indicated that the hallmark of a judicial power is a *lis* between parties in which a tribunal is called upon to apply a recognized body of rules in a manner consistent with fairness and impartiality. The adjudication deals primarily with the rights of the parties to the dispute, rather than considerations of the collective good of the community as a whole.

With very few exceptions, the Residential Tenancy Commission is not free to intervene of its own motion in disputes between landlords and tenants. Virtually all of the provisions of the Act require that either a landlord or a tenant apply to the Commission before any action be taken. Moreover, the power to order eviction or compliance will, in all case, be exercised in the context of a *lis* between parties. This is so even where a third party may invoke the Commission's intervention. Under s. 29, for example, a Public Utility may notify the Commission that its service has been or is likely to be stopped, and the Commission may intervene. But s. 29 goes on to provide that the Commission shall determine whether a particular landlord is breaching his obligation to supply vital services to his tenants. Thus there will clearly be a *lis* between parties and an issue to be resolved.

When confronted with a *lis*, the task of the Commission will be to determine the respective rights and obligations of the parties according to the terms of the legislation. The Commission does not have an untrammelled discretion to 'set matters right'. The powers which it may invoke and the remedies which it may award are circumscribed by the terms of the Act. At no point is the individual's right at law surrendered for the benefit of a common group or policy. The Commission deals exclusively with matters of contract and land law as they arise between landlords and tenants. . . .

The Commission has authority to hear and determine disputes in accordance with rules of law, and by the authority of the law. It authorizes actions for which application is made. It has the power to impose penalties and sanctions and to award remedies for the infringement of rights. Disobedience of an order of the Commission is a penal offence. The Commission decides contractual and property rights between individual landlords and tenants and in so doing determines not only the right to land and property, but also other rights. In each case, there is an analysis of the law, an application of the applicable law to the particular facts, and then a judicial decision and a consequent order. It is difficult to conceive that when so acting the Commission acts otherwise than as a curial tribunal. In substance the tribunal is exercising judicial powers roughly in the same way as they are exercised by the courts. . . .

I conclude that the impugned powers, when viewed in their institutional setting, remain essentially 'judicial powers'.

VII

We now face the most difficult aspect of this appeal—an examination of the inter-relationship between the Commission's impugned 'judicial powers' and the other powers and jurisdiction conferred under the Act.

Prior to 1979, three broad functions were exercised by three separate bodies. The function of giving advice, mediating and educating was handled by the Landlord and Tenant Advisory Bureau. The function of administering rent review was handled by the Residential Premises Rent Review Board. The function of adjudicating disputes between landlords and tenants was handled by s. 96 courts. The 1979 Act effected relatively minor changes in the substantive law of landlord and tenant. The primary change introduced in 1979 was to transfer the separate and distinct functions of the Advisory Bureau, the Rent Review Board and the courts to the Residential Tenancy Commission.

The Attorney General for Ontario argues that the Commission is essentially an administrative body charged with "supervising and regulating" the relationship of landlord and tenant in the Province of Ontario. The function of adjudicating disputes, it is contended, is merely a subsidiary or ancillary aspect of the Commission's role. . . .

It appears upon reading the Act as a whole that the central function of the Commission is that of resolving disputes, in the final resort by a judicial form of hearing between landlords and tenants. The bulk of the Act is taken up with defining the rights and obligations of landlords and tenants and with prescribing a method for resolving disputes over those obligations. Dispute resolution is achieved through application to the Commission. It is true that the Commission is granted the power to mediate the dispute before it is obliged to hold a hearing, but the Commission will ordinarily have no right or duty to act as mediator unless invited to do so by one of the parties. If one party does not wish to settle, then a judicial hearing must be held and a judgment rendered. The other functions of the Commission are either ancillary to this function (*i.e.* the power to recommend policy or to advise the parties) or are separate and distinct from this core power, and bear no relation to it (*i.e.* the power over rent review).

There is no broad legislative scheme as there was in *Mississauga, supra*, to subsume the judicial functions of the Commission. It was argued that the powers

vested in the Residential Tenancy Commission were merely incidental or ancillary to the policy of "security of tenure" for tenants. This submission is unconvincing. The primary purpose and effect of the 1979 Act was to transfer jurisdiction over a large and important body of law, affecting landlords and tenants of one million rental units, from the s. 96 courts where it has been administered since Confederation to a provincially appointed tribunal.

Here the chief role of the Commission is not to administer a policy or to carry out an administrative function. Its primary role is to adjudicate. The administrative features of the legislation can be characterized as ancillary to the main adjudicative function. The power of the Commission to mediate disputes is aimed at the speedy resolution of differences between the parties. So too is the informal nature of the proceedings. The goal of these provisions is to enable the Commission to 'process' controversies in an expeditious manner. As such, they are merely incidental to the main purpose of the legislation.

In the case at bar, as the Court of Appeal observed, powers until now exercised by the courts have simply been transferred to the Commission as the "chosen vehicle for their exercise". In the instant case the impugned powers are the nuclear core around which other powers and functions are collected. In *Tomko* the tribunal was composed of persons familiar with labour relations matters and presumably better able than the courts to weigh the interests involved and to assess the implications of cease and desist orders upon the parties. In the present case the Act imposes no particular qualifications or experience as essential to appointment to the Commission. There is no requirement of legal training or occupational experience for any member of the Commission and the process of selection is not based on any bipartite or tripartite principle. The Commission is in no way a specialized agency. In the instant case the whole of a s. 96 court's jurisdiction in a certain area, however limited, has been transferred to provincially appointed officials. The provincial legislature has sought to withdraw historically entrenched and important judicial functions from the superior court and vest them in one of its own tribunals. Although the legislature may undoubtedly contract, as well as enlarge, court jurisdiction it cannot lift wholesale from the superior courts and bestow on a tribunal of its own making the resolution of disputes theretofore handled by superior courts in respect of rights and obligations in the nature of eviction orders and orders for compliance with contractual mandates. . . .

Implicit throughout the argument advanced on behalf of the Attorney General of Ontario is the assumption that the court system is too formal, too cumbersome, too expensive and therefore unable to respond properly to the social needs which *The Residential Tenancies Act* is intended to meet. All statutes respond to social needs. The courts are not unfamiliar with equity and the concepts of fairness, justice, convenience, reasonableness. Since the enactment in 1976 of the legislation assuring "security of tenure" the County Court judges of Ontario have been dealing with matters arising out of that legislation, apparently with reasonable despatch, as both landlords and tenants in the present proceedings have spoken clearly against transfer of jurisdiction in respect of eviction and compliance orders from the courts to a special commission. It is perhaps also of interest that there is no suggestion in the material filed with us that the Law Reform Commission favoured removal from the courts of the historic functions performed for over one hundred years by the courts.

I am neither unaware of, nor unsympathetic to, the arguments advanced in support of a view that s. 96 should not be interpreted so as to thwart or unduly restrict the future growth of provincial administrative tribunals. Yet, however worthy the policy objectives, it must be recognized that we, as a Court, are not given the freedom to choose whether the problem is such that provincial, rather than federal, authority should deal with it. We must seek to give effect to the Constitution as we understand it and with due regard for the manner in which it has been judicially interpreted in the past. If the impugned power is violative of s. 96 it must be struck down. . . .

In the result, I would dismiss the appeal, and answer in the negative the constitutional questions which have been posted by the Executive Council of the Province of Ontario. No question of costs arises.

28. Labatt v. Attorney General of Canada, *1980*

~ In the *Labatt* case the Supreme Court rejected the trade and commerce power as a basis for federal consumer protection legislation. This decision indicated that the Court's majority was inclined to set very tight limits on exercises of federal regulatory power not aimed primarily at interprovincial or international trade.

Back in 1881 in the *Parsons*[1] case, Sir Montague Smith referred to "general regulation of trade affecting the whole Dominion" as another possible application of the trade and commerce power in addition to the regulation of interprovincial and international activities. The modern Supreme Court's reluctance to give much scope to this "general regulation of trade" dimension of trade and commerce first became evident in the Court's 1977 decision in *MacDonald* v. *Vapor Canada Ltd.*[2] There the Court unanimously ruled that a part of the federal Trade Marks Act establishing a national code of fair business practice was *ultra vires*. The application of the legislation to business throughout the Dominion did not, in the Court's view, justify federal legislation which, by embracing civil wrongs covered by the law of torts, encroached on provincial jurisdiction over property and civil rights. This was the first time since the abolition of Privy Council appeals in 1949 that the Supreme Court had found federal legislation unconstitutional.

The *Vapor Canada* case was followed by some further federal losses and provincial gains. In two cases decided shortly after *Vapor Canada* the Court held that federal legislation giving the Federal Court of Canada jurisdiction to try suits in which the federal government is a plaintiff exceeded Parliament's power under section 101 of the B.N.A. Act to establish courts "for the better Administration of the Laws of Canada."[3] In one of these cases, *McNamara Construction* v. *The Queen*, the Court explicitly overruled an earlier Supreme Court decision made in 1894. In the same year, in *Canada Indemnity Co.* v. *The Queen*,[4] the Court found that the interprovincial effects of British Columbia legislation giving a provincial corporation a monopoly of the automobile insurance business in the province did not constitute grounds for holding the legislation *ultra vires*. In *Dominion Stores Ltd.* v. *The Queen*[5], decided immediately before the *Labatt* case, the Supreme Court, in a five-to-four decision, held that federal legislation establishing a grading system for apples could not validly apply to transactions which are entirely intraprovincial.

The cases cited above, taken together with the cases in which the Court has upheld provincial incursions into the domain of criminal law, demonstrate a

---

[1] See case 2 above.
[2] [1977] 2 S.C.R. 134.
[3] *McNamara Construction* v. *The Queen*, [1977] 2 S.C.R. 655, and *Quebec Northshore Ltd.* v. *C.P. Ltd.*, [1977] 2 S.C.R. 1054.
[4] [1977] 2 S.C.R. 504.
[5] [1980] 1 S.C.R. 139.

considerable balance in the Supreme Court's approach to the division of powers. These cases have not, however, attracted nearly as much political attention as those favouring the federal government.

At issue in the *Labatt* case were regulations passed under the federal Food and Drugs Act requiring brewers using the generic term ''light beer'' to meet certain prescribed standards (e.g., an alcoholic content of 1.2 to 2.5 per cent). The Court decided, six to three, that the legislation was unconstitutional. None of the judges considered that the legislation could be based on the criminal law or the peace, order and good government powers. Justice Estey's majority opinion focused on his finding that the legislation did not in its pith and substance apply to international and interprovincial trade but to a particular industry which appeared to be essentially local in character. Justice Pigeon's dissent, concurred in by Justice McIntyre, was based primarily on the Privy Council's decision in one of the 1937 New Deal references which upheld federal legislation permitting the use of a national trademark for products meeting the requirements of a Canada Standard.[6] Chief Justice Laskin's dissent went further. He defended Parliament's power to equalize competitive advantages in the national market by enforcing commodity standards. In his view section 121's prohibition of interprovincial trade barriers provided a constitutional ''reinforcement'' of such a power by indicating a constitutional intention of ''marking Canada as a whole as an economic union.''

The aftermath of *Labatt* shows how limited the practical impact of a ruling of *ultra vires* can be. Observers originally thought this decision, along with *Dominion Stores*, would undermine a coherent system of national product standards to the detriment of the consumer, but this has not happened. The food industry has an interest in maintaining such standards because common standards facilitate a differential price structure for degrees of quality that are not evident to visual inspection. The industry has thus continued to support the standards. In addition, the impulse to cheat has been kept in check by alternative enforcement possibilities. *Labatt* struck down section 6 of the Act, which enforced the product standards directly, but left in place prohibitions of ''false, misleading or deceptive'' packaging and labelling. The latter prohibitions have been used to enforce the standards indirectly.[7]~

LABATT *v.* ATTORNEY GENERAL OF CANADA
In the Supreme Court of Canada. [1980] 1 S.C.R. 914.

THE CHIEF JUSTICE (*dissenting*): I agree with Mr. Justice Pigeon that the appeal should be dismissed with costs to the respondent. . . . The constitutional issue which Justice Pigeon resolved in favour of federal power, raises for me

---

[6] *Dominion Trade and Industry Reference*, [1937] A.C. 405.

[7] See Patrick Monahan, *Politics and the Constitution: The Charter, Federalism and the Supreme Court of Canada* (Toronto: Carswell/Methuen, 1987), 228-234.

more extended considerations than those on which he was content to proceed and I wish to state my position briefly on what I regard as a highly important issue.

I do not think that the *Dominion Trade and Industry Commission* ([1937] A.C. 405) is conclusive here. That was a case involving non-compulsory regulation whereas the Food and Drugs Act and the relevant Regulations thereunder operate compulsorily. I do not think that anything is added by reference to *Dominion Stores Limited* v. *The Queen* in which judgment was handed down by this Court on December 13, 1979. Insofar as it turned on dealing with local marketing it does not touch the present case . . .

The matter therefore comes down to whether this Court views the federal trade and commerce power as a sufficient support for the legislation and Regulations which are attacked in the present case. I would hold that it does, and, in so doing I would adopt the statement in the *Parsons* case, at p. 113, which envisages competent federal legislation by way of "general regulation of trade affecting the whole Dominion." . . .

In the *Board of Commerce* case, at p. 201, the Privy Council indicated that it might be open to Parliament "to call . . . for statistical and other information which may be valuable for guidance in questions affecting Canada as a whole. Such information may be required before any power to regulate trade and commerce can be properly exercised. . . ." I do not press any perfect analogy to the prescription of common standards for an article of food which is produced throughout the country and which is also imported from abroad, but it does appear to me that if Parliament can set up standards for required returns for statistical purposes, it should be able to fix standards that are common to all manufacturers of foods, including beer, drugs, cosmetics and therapeutic devices, at least to equalize competitive advantages in the carrying on of businesses concerned with such products. I find some reinforcement in this view of the scope of the federal trade and commerce power in

s. 121 of the British North America Act which precluded interprovincial tariffs, marking Canada as a whole as an economic union.

The operations of Labatt Breweries and of other brewers of beer extend throughout Canada, and I would not attenuate the federal trade and commerce power any further than has already been manifested in judicial decisions by denying Parliament authority to address itself to uniform prescriptions for the manufacture of food, drugs, cosmetics, therapeutic devices in the way, in the case of beer, of standards for its production and distribution according to various alcoholic strengths under labels appropriate to the governing regulations.

The judgment of Martland, Dickson, Beetz and Estey JJ. was delivered by

ESTEY J.: The appellant seeks a declaration that its product "Labatt's Special Lite" as labelled, packaged and sold "is not likely to be mistaken for a 'light beer' within the standards set out . . ." in the regulations under the Food and Drugs Act, R.S.C. 1970, c. F-27 . . .

Two issues arise by reason of the marketing of this product under the label set out above. Firstly, the appellant takes the position that this product when so advertised is not likely to be mistaken for a light beer within the applicable regulation. This regulation, being s. B.02.134 of the Food and Drug Regulations, C.R.C., c. 870, was enacted pursuant to s. 25(1) of the Act to which I will return shortly. Section 6 of the Act states as follows:

Where a standard has been prescribed for a food, no person shall label, package, sell or advertise any article in such a manner that it is likely to be mistaken for such food, unless the article complies with the prescribed standard.

The second position taken by the appellant is that s. 6 of the Act and regulation B.02.134 are *ultra vires* the Parliament of Canada, and to the extent that it authorizes such regulation, s. 25 is likewise *ultra vires*.

~ Justice Estey found that Labatt's "Special Lite" could be mistaken for light beer and therefore had to meet the light beer standards set out in the regulations if the regulations were constitutionally valid. ~

I turn now to the constitutional issue. The appellant challenges the constitutional validity of s. 6 and s. 25(1)(c) of the Food and Drugs Act and the regulations promulgated thereunder with reference to the production and sale of beer. Before embarking on a discussion of the constitutional considerations, let us examine the form and thrust of the Act and its regulations.

Part I of the Act is entitled "Foods, Drugs, Cosmetics and Devices." Under the heading "Food" we find four sections creating offences such as the sale of harmful substances, adulterated food and food unfit for human consumption and food manufactured under unsanitary conditions. There is a prohibition against the labelling, packaging, selling or advertising of food in any manner that is false and misleading or deceptive; and there is a general provision applicable to the whole of Part I making it an offence to advertise food, drugs, cosmetics or devices to the general public as a treatment, preventative or cure for any disease. Then we come to s. 6 in the "Food" portion of Part I of the Act which has already been set out above . . .

. . . In Part II of the statute, provision is made for the "administration and enforcement" of the Act, including the powers of inspectors, the power of forfeiture, the right to make analysis of substances. Section 25(1)(c) appears in this part and establishes the authority in the Governor-in-Council to pass regulations under the statute

. . . for carrying the purposes and provisions of this Act into effect, and, in particular, but not so as to restrict the generality of the foregoing . . .
   (c) prescribing standards of composition, strength, potency, purity, quality or other property of any article of food, drug, cosmetic or device;

The regulatory authority under subs. (c) appears to extend to the four classes of goods or articles regulated under Part I which include "foods" with which we are here concerned.

Under the authority of s. 25(1)(c), there has been produced an elaborate set of regulations dealing with the preparation, manufacture and sale of the four articles or commodities dealt with in Part I of the Act . . . The part of the regulations pertaining to alcoholic beverages with which this proceeding is concerned commences under the heading "Malt Liquors" with regulation B.02.130, already reproduced above, which prescribes the nature of "beer," its alcoholic content, and permitted additives. The other malt liquors described by these regulations are ale, stout, porter, light beer, and malt liquor. The only difference between these various malt liquors appears to be the alcoholic content, and "the aroma, taste and character commonly attributed to" them. As we have seen, the alcoholic content for beer shall be not less than 2.6 per cent and not more than 5.5 per cent by volume, and in the case of light beer shall be not less than 1.2 per cent and not more than 2.5 per cent alcohol by volume. It may be observed that s. 6 was introduced into the Act in 1953 and s. 25(1)(c) was expanded at the same time to its present form . . .

What then is the constitutional basis for the enactment of the contested portions of this statute by Parliament? The possible origins of this sovereign power include the federal authority under s. 91 of the British North America Act in respect of criminal law, trade and commerce, and peace, order and good government. I turn first to the criminal jurisdiction . . .

That there are limits to the extent of the criminal authority is obvious and these limits were pointed out by this Court in *The Reference as to the Validity of Section 5(a) of the Dairy Industry Act (Margarine Reference)*, where Rand J. looked to the object of the statute to find whether or not it related to the traditional field of criminal law, namely public peace, order, security, health and morality. In that case, the Court found that the object of the statute was economic:

. . . to give trade protection to the dairy industry in the production and sale of butter; to benefit one group of persons as against competitors in business in which, in the absence of the legislation, the latter would be free to engage in the province. To forbid manufacture and sale for such an end is prima facie *to deal directly with the civil rights of individuals in relation to particular trade within the provinces.*

(*per* Rand J., at p. 50)

The test is one of substance, not form, and excludes from the criminal jurisdiction legislative activity not having the prescribed characteristics of criminal law.

A crime is an act which the law, with appropriate penal sanctions, forbids; but as prohibitions are not enacted in a vacuum, we can properly look for some evil or injurious or undesirable effect upon the public against which the law is directed. That effect may be in relation to social, economic or political interests; and the legislature has had in mind to suppress the evil or to safeguard the interests threatened.

(*per* Rand J., at p. 49.)

This approach to the federal authority in the field of criminal law was relied upon by this Court in *Dominion Stores* v. *The Queen* (judgment rendered December 13, 1979). That there is an area of legitimate regulations in respect of trade practices contrary to the interest of the community such as misleading, false or deceptive advertising and misbranding, is not under debate. In the statute now before us, the question of mislabelling arises only after the category of "light beer" is created and the specifications for its production are assigned. When all this has been obtained, the use of the words "Special Lite" by the appellant may be said to be misleading to the beer-buying public. The contest, however, is not in respect of this second stage, but rather the first stage, that is the right in the federal Parliament and the federal government to establish the standards of production and content of this product. In any case, the first stage of the process does not come within the criminal law reach as traditionally described in the authorities. I can find no basis, therefore, for this detailed regulation of the brewing industry in the production and sale of its product as a proper exercise of the federal authority in criminal law.

The jurisdiction of Parliament in matters related to health similarly has no application here. Parliament may make laws in relation to health for the peace, order and good government of Canada: quarantine laws come to mind as one example. The Privy Council hinted that legislation enacted by Parliament to deal with an "epidemic of pestilence" would be valid in *Toronto Electric Commissioners* v. *Snider*. But we are not concerned with such matters here. Where health is an aspect of criminal law, as in the case of adulteration provisions in the statute, the answer is clear but here not helpful. The appellant discussed succinctly in its submissions to this Court another aspect of the "health" jurisdiction.

Furthermore the regulations under consideration do not on their face purport to be, nor can they be, connected or related to the protection of health since any such beverage regardless of its name having an alcoholic content by volume of not less than 1.2% and not more than 8.5% and otherwise brewed in accordance with the process common to all "Malt Liquors" is presumptively not a hazard to health.

One cannot successfully ground the contested elements of this legislation in the field of the federal health power.

By s. 91(2) of the British North America Act, authority with reference to "the regulation of Trade and Commerce" was assigned without qualification or explanation to Parliament. Without judicial restraint in the interpretation of this provision, the provincial areas of jurisdiction would be seriously truncated. It is not surprising, therefore, to find the Privy Council stating within fifteen years of Confederation:

The words "regulation of trade and commerce," in their unlimited sense are sufficiently wide, if uncontrolled by the context and other parts of the Act, to include every regulation of trade ranging from political arrangements in regard to trade with foreign governments, requiring the sanction of parliament, down to minute rules for regulating particular trades.But a consideration of the Act shews that the words were not used in this unlimited sense. In the first place the collocation of No. 2 with classes of subjects of national and general concern affords an indication that regulations relating to general trade and commerce were in the mind of the legislature, when conferring this power on the dominion parliament. If the words had been intended to have the full scope of which in their literal meaning they are susceptible, the specific mention of several of the other classes of subjects enumerated in sect. 91 would have been unnecessary; as, 15, banking; 17, weights and measures; 18, bills of exchange and promissory notes; 19, interest; and even 21, bankruptcy and insolvency.
per Sir Montague Smith at p. 112 in *Citizens Insurance Company of Canada* v. *Parsons*. (Emphasis added.)

Thus it is clear that "minute rules for regulating particular trades" are not within the trade and commerce competence. The statute and regulation with which we are here concerned purport to establish such a detailed single industry regulatory pattern. The judgment of the Privy Council continues:

Construing therefore the words "regulation of trade and commerce" by the various aids to their interpretation above

suggested, they would include political arrangements in regard to trade requiring the sanction of parliament, regulation of trade in matters of interprovincial concern, and it may be that they would include general regulation of trade affecting the whole dominion. Their Lordships abstain on the present occasion from any attempt to define the limits of the authority of the dominion parliament in this direction. It is enough for the decision of the present case to say that, in their view, its authority to legislate for the regulation of trade and commerce does not comprehend the power to regulate by legislation the contracts of a particular business or trade, such as the business of fire insurance in a single province, and therefore that its legislative authority does not in the present case conflict or compete with the power over property and civil rights assigned to the legislature of Ontario by No. 13 of sect. 92.

Reverting to the *Parsons* case, *supra*, the trade and commerce head was there described as consisting of two branches. The first in the words of the judgment includes "political arrangements in regard to trade requiring the sanction of Parliament, regulation of trade in matters of interprovincial concern. . . ." The second branch is said to ". . . include general regulation of trade affecting the whole Dominion." The first branch is illustrated in the succession of cases dealing with the marketing of natural products commencing with *R.* v. *Eastern Terminal Elevator Co.* ([1925] S.C.R. 434), and continuing to the recent egg marketing judgment in *Reference Re Agricultural Products Marketing Act* ([1978] 2 S.C.R. 1198). . . .

The principles developed in the natural products marketing judgments only obliquely deal with the second branch of the *Parsons* description of trade and commerce, *supra*, and hence are not of direct application here. The impugned regulations in and under the Food and Drugs Act are not concerned with the control and guidance of the flow of articles of commerce through the distribution channels, but rather with the production and local sale of the specified products of the brewing industry. There is no demonstration by the proponent of these isolated provisions in the Food and Drugs Act and its regulations of any interprovincial aspect of this industry. The labels in the record reveal that the appellant produces these beverages in all provinces but Quebec and Prince Edward Island. From the nature of the beverage, it is apparent, without demonstration, that transportation to distant markets would be expensive, and hence the local nature of the production operation . . .

The first successful attempt to breathe life into the second branch of the *Parsons* trade and commerce description, *supra*, is found in *John Deere Plow Co.* v. *Wharton* ([1915] A.C. 330). The provincial legislature had attempted to establish regulation in a limited sense of federally incorporated companies within the provincial boundaries. The Court determined that such provincial action was *ultra vires* as being an invasion of the power of Parliament to regulate the exercise by federal companies of their powers throughout the Dominion. This subject should not be left without adding that the Court there found the constitutional basis for legislation authorizing the establishment of federal incorporations in the peace, order and good government clause while the regulation of their activities fell into the trade and commerce category. Viscount Haldane speaking in the *Wharton* case, *supra*, stated at p. 340:

. . . *the power to regulate trade and commerce at all events enables the Parliament of Canada to prescribe to what extent the powers of companies the objects of which extend to the entire Dominion should be exercisable, and what limitations should be placed on such powers. For if it be established that the Dominion Parliament can create such companies, then it becomes* <u>a question of general interest throughout the Dominion</u> *in what fashion they should be permitted to trade.* (Emphasis Added.)

To this date this is still the test in determining whether the second branch of the trade and commerce power applies; *vide* Laskin C.J. in *Reference re the Anti-Inflation Act*, at p. 426.

What clearly is not of general national concern is the regulation of a single trade or industry. *Vide In Re Insurance Act, 1910,* at pp. 308-9; *Eastern Terminal Elevator Co.*, *supra*.

The section of the Act before the Court in *In Re Insurance Act 1910* provided:

3. The provisions of this Act shall not apply—

. . .

(b) to any company incorporated by an Act of the legislature of the late province of Canada, or by an Act of the legislature of any province now forming part of Canada, which carries on the business of insurance wholly within the limits of the province by the legislature of which it was incorporated, and which is within the exclusive control of the legislature of such province;

Nevertheless the statute was struck down as an attempt to regulate a trade within a particular province whether or not the trade was also carried on in all the provinces. The businesses before the Court were national concerns operating in several provinces under a statute which exempted from its application wholly intraprovincial businesses. Thus it is clear that neither national ownership of a trade or undertaking or even national advertising of its products will alone suffice to authorize the imposition of federal trade and commerce regulation.

In more modern times, this Court in *MacDonald* v. *Vapor Canada Ltd.* struck down that part of the Trade Marks Act of Canada purporting to create a cause of action in connection with "any business practice contrary to honest industrial or commercial usage in Canada." Unrestricted geographic play of the provision was not sufficient to find legislative authority under the trade and commerce heading. *Vide* Chief Justice Laskin at pp. 156 and 159. . . .

. . . As we have seen, the trade and commerce head cannot be applied to the regulation of a single trade, even though it be on a national basis, and in the *Board of Commerce* disposition, *supra*, the invocation of the trade and commerce head of federal jurisdiction is forbidden in the regulation of elements of commerce such as contracts, in an individual trade or concern even though the control was imposed in a series of separate regulatory codes each purporting to regulate a separate trade or industry. . . .

In the result, the trade and commerce power has been rescued from near oblivion following the *Citizens Insurance* case, *supra*, by the extention or development of the *obiter* or afterthought of Sir Montague Smith in that case. The application of the power to this stage in our constitutional development finds illustration firstly in general regulation of an element of trade such as the regulation of federal incorporations. With respect to legislation relating to the support, control or regulation of the various levels or components in the marketing cycle of natural products, the provincial authority is *prima facie* qualified to legislate with reference to production (*vide* Pigeon J. in the *Reference Re Agricultural Products Marketing Act, supra*, at p. 1296), and the federal Parliament with reference to marketing in the international and interprovincial levels of trade. In between, the success or failure of the legislator depends upon whether the pith and substance or primary objective of the statute or regulation is related to the heads of power of the legislative authority in question. Incidental effect on the other legislative sphere will no longer necessarily doom the statute to failure. Several indicia of the proper tests have evolved. For example, if contractual rights within the province are the object of the proposed regulation, the province has the authority. On the other hand, if regulation of the flow in extraprovincial channels of trade is the object, then the federal statute will be valid. Between

these spectrum ends, the shadings cannot be foretold in anything approaching a constitutional formula. The majority of the illustrated tests thus far encountered are largely in the distribution, and not the production, of farm products. Here, however, we are concerned with the proper regulatory authority in connection with the production process of a single industry and, to some extent, with the sale of its products, the latter being concerned largely with the use of labels or identification. Nowhere are the impugned statutory regulations or provisions concerned with the control or regulation of the extraprovincial distribution of these products or their movement through any channels of trade. On the contrary, their main purpose is the regulation of the brewing process itself by means of a "legal recipe," as counsel for the appellant put it. Indeed, if the industry is substantially local in character, as seems to be the case from the sparse record before the court (as noted above), the regulations are, in fact, confined to the regulation of a trade within a province.

In the end, the effort of the respondent here is simply to build into these regulations a validity essentially founded upon the embryonic definition of the application of the trade and commerce heading in the *Citizens Insurance* case, *supra*. That observation and the subsequent references thereto are all predicated upon the requirement that the purported trade and commerce legislation affected industry and commerce at large or in a sweeping, general sense. In the context of the Food and Drugs Act, it follows that even if this statute were to cover a substantial portion of Canadian economic activity, one industry or trade at a time, by a varying array of regulations or trade codes applicable to each individual sector, there would not, in the result, be at law a regulation of trade and commerce in the sweeping general sense contemplated in the *Citizens Insurance* case, *supra*. That, in my view, is the heart and core of the problem confronting the respondent in this appeal. Thus the provisions regulating malt liquors relate either to a single industry or a sector thereof, while other regulations appear to concern themselves in a similar way with other individual industries; the former being condemned by the *Citizens Insurance* case, *supra*, and the latter does not rescue the malt liquor regulations by reason of the *Board of Commerce* case, *supra*.

I conclude, therefore, in this part, that the impugned sections as they relate to malt liquors cannot be founded in the trade and commerce head of jurisdiction.

There remains to be examined the peace, order and good government clause in s. 91 as the basis for these federal regulations. This subject has already been adverted to above in connection with the health aspect of this statute. The principal authorities dealing with the range of the federal jurisdiction under this heading are illustrated by:

1. *Fort Frances Pulp and Paper Co.* v. *Manitoba Free Press*, basing the federal competence on the existence of a national emergency;

2. The *Radio Reference* and the *Aeronautics Reference*, wherein the federal competence arose because the subject matter did not exist at the time of Confederation and clearly cannot be put into the class of matters of merely local or private nature; and

3. Where the subject matter "goes beyond local or provincial concern or interest and must, from its inherent nature, be the concern of the Dominion as a whole." *Attorney General of Ontario* v. *Canada Temperance Federation per* Viscount Simon, at p. 205.

The brewing and labelling of beer and light beer has not been said to have given rise either to a national emergency or a new problem not existing at the time of Confederation, nor to a matter of national concern transcending the local authorities' power to meet and solve it by legislation. This latter concept is the subject of analysis and review by P. W. Hogg, *Constitutional Law of Canada*, 1977 at pp. 259-261. That learned author concludes at p. 261:

These cases suggest that the most important element of national dimension or national concern is a need for one national law which cannot realistically be satisfied by cooperative provincial action because the failure of one province to cooperate would carry with it grave consequences for the residents of other provinces. A subject matter of legislation which has this characteristic has the necessary national dimension or concern to justify invocation of the p.o.g.g. power.

I see no basis for advancing the proposition that the impugned statutory provisions and regulations as they relate to malt liquor find their basis in law in the peace, order and good government clause of s. 91.

For these reasons, I would therefore answer the following question in the negative:

Is it within the competence of the Parliament of Canada to enact sections 6 and 25(1)(c) of the Food and Drugs Act R.S.C. 1970, c. F-27, and are regulations B.02-130 to B.02-135 inclusive thereunder validly made?

The reasons of Pigeon and McIntyre JJ. were delivered by

PIGEON J. (*dissenting*) . . . in a reference concerning the validity of the Dominion Trade and Industry Commission Act 1935, Lord Atkin said (at pp. 417-418):

Sect. 18, sub-s. 1 provides that "the words 'Canada Standard' or the initials 'C.S.' shall be a national trademark and the exclusive property in and the right to the use of such trade-mark is thereby declared to be vested in His Majesty in the right of the Dominion. . . ." By sub-s. 2 such national trade mark as applied to any commodity pursuant to the provisions of that Act or any other Act of the Parliament of Canada is to constitute a representation that such commodity conforms to the requirements of a specification of a commodity standard established under the provisions of any Dominion Act. . . .

There exists in Canada a well established code relating to trade marks created by the Dominion statutes, to be found now in Trade Marks and Designs Act, R.S.C., 1927, c. 201, amended by S.C. 1928, c. 10. It gives to the proprietor of a registered trade mark the exclusive right to use the trade mark to designate articles manufactured or sold by him. It creates, therefore, a form of property in each Province and the rights that flow therefrom. No one has challenged the competence of the Dominion to pass such legislation. If challenged one obvious source of authority would appear to be the class of subjects enumerated in s. 91(2), the Regulation of trade and commerce, referred to by the Chief Justice. There could hardly be a more appropriate form of the exercise of this power than the creation and regulation of a uniform law of trade marks. But if the Dominion has power to create trade mark rights for individual traders, it is difficult to see why the power should not extend to that which is now a usual feature of national and international commerce—a national mark. . . .

In my view, the enactments and regulations under attack in the present case are essentially for the same legislative purpose as the sections considered by Lord Atkin. This purpose is to provide that some specific trade designations will guarantee compliance with what the 1935 statute called a "commodity standard" and is known in the present statute and regulations as a "specification" for a "food." The 1935 statute would have such effect only if the producer, manufacturer or merchant chose to apply the trade mark "Canada Standard" or the initials "C.S.". The present scheme controls whenever a defined designation is applied to a food for which a specification has been established. I fail to see how this difference can be significant from a constitutional point of view. . . .

In my view, the federal enactments under attack provide for no more than what might be called "labelling regulations." These state what specifications must be met if some specific designations are used on food labels. In my view this does not go beyond a proper concept of trade mark legislation and I fail to see any invasion of provincial jurisdiction as was found in *Macdonald* v. *Vapor Canada Ltd.* in respect of s. 7(e) of the *Trade Marks Act.*

I would, therefore, answer the constitutional question in the affirmative . . .

~ Justice Ritchie wrote a short opinion concurring with Justice Estey. Justice Pratte also held that the appeal should be allowed. ~

29. McEvoy v. Attorney General of New Brunswick, *1983*

~ In *McEvoy* the Supreme Court held for the first time that section 96 and those other sections of the Constitution providing for the qualifications, tenure and remuneration of section 96 judges restrict not only provincial legislative power but federal legislative power as well. This case makes it clear that the Canadian Constitution does contain a separation of powers doctrine so far as the judiciary is concerned. Neither the federal or provincial legislatures can strip the provincial superior courts of their essential functions.

This case has an interesting background. Legislative jurisdiction over criminal trials rests exclusively with the federal Parliament. Through the Criminal Code Parliament designates the courts in which the various offences are to be tried. Over the years amendments to the Code greatly increased the offences which could be tried, either exclusively or at the option of the accused, in the lower courts of the provinces. Only a core of the most serious offences—murder and treason are the main ones—were reserved exclusively for trial in a superior court. A number of provinces became interested in completing this process and eliminating the distinction between superior and inferior courts by giving one court jurisdiction to try all offences.[1] In the 1980s New Brunswick was looking into the possibility of making its Provincial Court, presided over by provincially appointed judges, the single criminal trial court for the province. Such a unification scheme would require that Parliament transfer all of the remaining criminal jurisdiction of New Brunswick's superior court (the Court of Queen's Bench) to the Provincial Court. Approached about this scheme, federal officials said they would first like to test the constitutional waters. Perhaps the Constitution prevented Parliament— even if it were willing—from passing this judicial power over to the Provincial Court. This, essentially, was the question referred to the New Brunswick Court of Appeal. Joseph McEvoy was retained to argue against the unification scheme and, although he lost in the New Brunswick Court of Appeal, he was successful before the Supreme Court of Canada.

At the outset, the Court expresses displeasure at being asked to consider the constitutional validity of such a hypothetical plan. Nonetheless, the Court goes on in an unsigned institutional opinion to answer the questions with a resounding "no". "Parliament," says the Court, "can no more give away federal constitutional powers than a province can usurp them." It is beyond the powers of the federal Parliament to transfer the entire criminal law jurisdiction of the superior court, on either a concurrent or exclusive basis, to Provincial Court judges lacking the constitutional qualities of section 96 judges. Parliament is not free to alter the basic scheme built into the judicature sections of the

---

[1] For a discussion of these proposals, see Perry Millar and Carl Baar, *Judicial Administration in Canada*, ch. 4 (Montreal and Toronto, 1981).

B.N.A. Act. For the Court what seems most important in this scheme is the independence of the judiciary which is referred to as "a fundamental principle of our federal system".

The Court's decision in *McEvoy* inspired a Provincial Court judge in Toronto, Maurice Charles, to challenge his constitutional capacity to try the cases which the Criminal Code in the past had put under the jurisdiction of provincially appointed magistrates and Provincial Court judges. By questioning his own jurisdiction Judge Charles hoped that he (and presumably judges of the Provincial and Territorial Courts all across Canada) would have to be elevated to superior court status. But this gambit failed. The Ontario Court of Appeal ruled that this piecemeal transfer of superior court criminal jurisdiction was not unconstitutional.[2] The Supreme Court of Canada refused to grant leave to appeal.

A practical consequence of the *McEvoy* decision is that criminal court unification in Canada can only be achieved at the higher, superior court level. The Supreme Court's decision in the *B.C. Family Relations Act Reference*[3] had a similar consequence for unification of family courts. Thus the Supreme Court's activism in enforcing the judicature sections of the Constitution has preserved a key role for the court which was given pride of place in the original Constitution—the provincial superior court. A further manifestation of the Supreme Court's solicitude for this court has been its decisions tightly restricting the civil jurisdiction of the Federal Court of Canada.[4] While these decisions certainly put a crimp in certain approaches to court reform, they entrench at the center of Canada's justice system a court which is neither all federal or all provincial but is a provincial court with federally appointed judges. By so doing they may well contribute to national integration. ~

McEVOY *v.* ATTORNEY GENERAL OF NEW BRUNSWICK
In the Supreme Court of Canada, [1983] 1 S.C.R. 704.

THE COURT—This is an appeal from a unanimous judgment of the New Brunswick Court of Appeal, delivered by Hughes C.J.N.B., answering in the affirmative three questions put before that Court on a reference by the provincial Lieutenant-Governor in Council pursuant to s. 23(1) of the *Judicature Act*, R.S.N.B. 1973, c. J-2, as amended. The questions, attached as a schedule to the reference Order, are stated to be draft questions directed to determine the constitutional validity of a proposed course of action with respect to the establishment of a unified criminal court in New Brunswick.

The three questions posed to the Court in New Brunswick, and the very same questions are now before this Court on appeal, read as follows:

---

[2] *The Queen* v. *Trimarchi* (judgment rendered Dec. 18, 1987 but not yet reported).

[3] Discussed above at p. 232.

[4] For a discussion of these cases, see Russell, *The Judiciary in Canada*, ch. 13.

1. Is it *intra vires* the Parliament of Canada to amend the *Criminal Code* to confer upon a court constituted by the legislature of a province, the judges of which are appointed by the Lieutenant-Governor in Council, exclusive jurisdiction to try all indictable offences under that Act?

2. Is it *intra vires* the Parliament of Canada to amend the *Criminal Code* to confer upon a court constituted by the legislature of a province, the judges of which are appointed by the Lieutenant-Governor in Council, jurisdiction to try all indictable offences under that Act, if that jurisdiction is concurrent with that of courts whose judges are appointed pursuant to section 96 of the *British North America Act*?

3. Is it *intra vires* the legislature of a province to constitute a court, the judges of which are appointed by the Lieutenant-Governor in Council, to exercise such jurisdiction in criminal law matters as is conferred upon it by the Parliament of Canada, if the jurisdiction conferred by Parliament is to try all indictable offences under the *Criminal Code*, and is either

(a) exclusive; or
(b) concurrent with that of courts whose judges are appointed pursuant to section 96 of the *British North America Act*?

It will be noted that Questions 1 and 2 relate to the constitutional power of the Parliament of Canada. Only Question 3 relates to the powers of the Provincial Legislature. The New Brunswick Court of Appeal answered all three questions in the affirmative.

In general terms the issue is whether s. 96 of the *Constitution Act, 1867* is a bar to a plan whereby the federal government and a provincial government would by conjoint action transfer the criminal jurisdiction of Provincial Superior Courts to a new court to be called the "unified criminal court" the judges of which would be provincially appointed.

1) Should this Court answer the Questions?

There is no draft legislation nor even any draft proposals to infuse the three questions which, in our view, suffer from excessive abstractness. There is no explanatory material, no supplementary notes, no draft report which would give concreteness to what is proposed. We are left to speculate as to the form the legislative schemes contemplated by the questions might take. When one realizes that what is intended is a drastic realignment of criminal law authority, an intended transfer, either exclusively or concurrently with existing provincial Superior Courts, to a new provincial Court in which judges appointed by the Province will sit to try all indictable offences, and that serious questions arise whether the proposed provincial Court is to have unreviewable jurisdiction subject perhaps to statutory rights of appeal, it will be seen how necessary or at least advantageous it would have been to have some direction as to the thrust of the proposed legislation under New Brunswick law and under federal law.

The Government of Canada has not adopted any policy for establishing a unified criminal Court nor, it appears, has the Government of New Brunswick, although the Attorney General of the Province is a proponent.

This Court is entitled to exercise its judgment on whether it should answer referred questions if it concludes that they do not exhibit sufficient precision to permit cogent answers. This is irrespective of the fact that the reference power is couched in broad terms, as it is here. Section 23(1) of the *Judicature Act* of New Brunswick provides:

23. (1) Important questions of law or fact touching

(a) the interpretation of The British North America Acts,
(b) the constitutionality or interpretation of any Canadian or Provincial legislation,

(c) the powers of the Legislature of the Province, or the Government thereof, whether or not the particular power in question has been or is proposed to be exercised, or

(d) any other matter, whether or not in the opinion of the Court ejusdem generis with the foregoing enumeration, with reference to which the Lieutenant-Governor in Council sees fit to submit any such question,

may be referred by the Lieutenant-Governor in Council to the Court of Appeal for hearing and consideration, and any question touching any of the matters aforesaid, so referred by the Lieutenant-Governor in Council, shall be conclusively deemed to be an important question.

It will be observed that the Lieutenant-Governor in Council may refer questions touching the powers of the Legislature of the Province or the Government thereof "whether or not the particular power in question has been or is proposed to be exercised".

Section 23(1) empowers a reference on the constitutionality or interpretation of any Canadian or provincial legislation. There is, however, no such legislation here, and it is a nice question whether proposed legislation of Parliament can be embraced unless it is subsumed under one of the other powers in s. 23(1), for example the intrepretation of the *British North America Act*, now the *Constitution Act, 1867*. The constitutional propriety of provincial legislation which invites the placing before the provincial courts of questions concerning the constitutionality of existing or pending federal legislation was not argued by any counsel before this Court and we expressly refrain from comment on such issue.

The first thing the Court has to decide then is whether we have been provided with an adequate base on which to answer the Lieutenant Governor's questions. . . .

This Court has from time to time refused to answer reference questions when it considered them lacking in specificity. . . .

In two instances, the *Senate Reference* and the *Water-Powers* case, the Court refused to answer questions referred by the federal government; in one instance, the *Montreal Schools* case, the Court refused to answer a question referred by a provincial government to the provincial court of appeal; in the fourth example the Court refused to answer a question referred by the Board of Railway Commissioners.

While we deprecate the practice of bringing before the Court as important constitutional questions as are raised in this case on extremely flimsy material, we would not abort the appeal on this ground. We believe for the reasons which follow that the Court has enough of the essential features of the proposed scheme to be compelled to the conclusion that all three questions must be answered in the negative.

2) The Reasons of the New Brunswick Court of Appeal

The Attorney General of New Brunswick outlined the proposed scheme for the New Brunswick Court of Appeal as follows:

The proposal envisages a new court constituted to accept and to exercise complete criminal jurisdiction: Dealing exclusively with all criminal law matters, including criminal code offences, other federal offences and provincial offences. This court would replace the present Provincial Court and its judges would be appointed by the Lieutenant-Governor in Council. It would not be constituted by the Legislature as a superior court and it would exercise statutory jurisdiction only.

Amendments to the Criminal Code and other federal statutes would be requested of the Parliament of Canada to confer jurisdiction in criminal matters upon the new court. The implementation of the pro-

posal thus is conceived as a blending of the authority of the two legislative bodies.

The New Brunswick Court of Appeal had no difficulty in concluding that because the Parliament of Canada had plenary authority in relation to the criminal law under s. 91(27) of the *Constitution Act, 1867* it was fully empowered to endow a provincially-established provincial Court presided over by a provincial appointee with power to administer the federal criminal law and to do so exclusively as well as concurrently with existing s. 96 provincial Superior Courts. . . .

The New Brunswick Court of Appeal also rejected an argument (one that was repeated in this Court) that there was a core of exclusive criminal jurisdiction inherent in Superior Courts by virtue of s. 96, jurisdiction which cannot be conferred upon an inferior court administered by provincial appointees. . . .

3) The Other Side of the Issue

There is no doubt that jurisdiction to try indictable offences was part of the Superior Court's jurisdiction in 1867; none of the parties suggests otherwise. Nor does anyone argue that inferior courts had concurrent jurisdiction to try indictable offences in 1867. Although this fact is not conclusive (see *Re Residential Tenancies Act, 1979,* [1981] 1 S.C.R. 714) none of the other considerations which might save the scheme from the force of s. 96 apply here. The proposed court is obviously a judicial body; its judicial aspect does not change colour when considered in the factual setting in which the court will operate; nor will the court exercise administrative powers to which its adjudicative functions are incidental. The proposed body is clearly and only a criminal court. . . .

. . . It has long been the rule that s. 96, although in terms an appointing power, must be addressed in functional terms lest its application be eroded. What then, is the relation between the proposed new

statutory Court and s. 96? This is the key constitutional issue in the present case and, as we view the matter, the result is to defeat the new statutory Court because it will effectively be a s. 96 Court.

Sections 96, 97, 98, 99 and 100 are couched in mandatory terms. They do not rest merely on federal statutory powers as does s. 91(27). This is how they read:

VII. JUDICATURE

96. The Governor General shall appoint the Judges of the Superior, District, and County Courts in each Province, except those on the Courts of Probate in Nova Scotia and New Brunswick.

97. Until the laws relative to Property and Civil Rights in Ontario, Nova Scotia, and New Brunswick, and the Procedure of the Courts in those Provinces, are made uniform, the Judges of the Courts of those Provinces appointed by the Governor General shall be selected from the respective Bars of those Provinces.

98. The Judges of the Courts of Quebec shall be selected from the Bar of that Province.

99. (1) Subject to subsection (2) of this section, the judges of the superior courts shall hold office during good behaviour, but shall be removable by the Governor General on address of the Senate and House of Commons.

(2) A judge of a superior court, whether appointed before or after the coming into force of this section, shall cease to hold office upon attaining the age of the seventy-five years, or upon the coming into force of this section if at that time he has already attained that age.

100. The Salaries, Allowances, and Pensions of the Judges of the Superior, District, and County Courts (except the Courts of Probate in Nova Scotia and New Brunswick), and of the Admiralty Courts in Cases where the Judges thereof are for the Time being paid by Salary, shall be fixed and provided by the Parliament of Canada.

What is being contemplated here is not one or a few transfers of criminal law power, such as has already been accomplished under the *Criminal Code*, but a complete obliteration of Superior Court criminal law jurisdiction. Sections 96 to 100 do not distinguish between courts of civil jurisdiction and courts of criminal jurisdiction. They should not be read as permitting the Parliament of Canada through use of its criminal law power to destroy Superior Courts and to deprive the Governor General of appointing power and to exclude members of the Bar from preferment for Superior Court appointments.

Parliament can no more give away federal constitutional powers than a province can usurp them. Section 96 provides that "The Governor General shall appoint the Judges of the Superior, District, and County Courts in each Province". The proposal here is that Parliament transfer the present Superior Courts' jurisdiction to try indictable offences to a provincial court. The effect of this proposal would be to deprive the Governor General of his power under s. 96 to appoint the judges who try indictable offences in New Brunswick. That is contrary to s. 96. Section 96 bars Parliament from altering the constitutional scheme envisaged by the judicature sections of the *Constitution Act, 1867* just as it does the provinces from doing so.

The traditional independence of English Superior Court judges has been raised to the level of a fundamental principle of our federal system by the *Constitution Act, 1867* and cannot have less importance and force in the administration of criminal law than in the case of civil matters. Under the Canadian constitution the Superior Courts are independent of both levels of government. The provinces constitute, maintain and organize the Superior Courts; the federal authority appoints the judges. The judicature sections of the *Constitution Act, 1867* guarantee the independence of the Superior Courts; they apply to Parliament as well as to the Provincial Legislatures.

Both sides of the proposal under review are flawed. Parliament cannot in effect give away the Governor General's s. 96 appointing power under colour of legislation vesting jurisdiction to try all indictable offences in a provincial court. New Brunswick cannot exercise an appointing power in respect of courts with s. 96 jurisdiction under colour of legislation in relation to the constitution, maintenance and organization of courts with criminal jurisdiction.

Nor is much gained for the proposed new provincial statutory Court by providing for concurrent Superior Court jurisdiction. The theory behind the concurrency proposals is presumably that a Provincial court with concurrent rather than exclusive powers would not oust the Superior Courts' jurisdiction, at least not to the same extent; since the Superior Courts' jurisdiction was not frozen as of 1867, it would be permissible to alter that jurisdiction so long as the essential core of the Superior Courts' jurisdiction remained; s. 96 would be no obstacle because the Superior Court would retain jurisdiction to try indictable offences. With respect, we think this overlooks the fact that what is being attempted here is the transformation by conjoint action of an inferior court into a superior court. Section 96 is, in our view, an insuperable obstacle to any such endeavour. . . .

It is hardly necessary to say that the proposed provincial scheme is not saved by preserving civil jurisdiction for the provincial Superior Courts.

We have taken perhaps a limited view of the important issues that are thrown up by the three referred questions but, having decided to address them, we felt it best to consider only those provisions of the Constitution which we think are beyond conjoint provincial and federal action.

We would, therefore, allow the appeal and answer all three questions in the negative. There will be no order as to costs.

30. Attorney General of Canada v. Canadian National Transportation, *1983*

~ The political importance of *C.N. Transportation* may be overlooked because the case appears to deal with the rather technical question of jurisdiction over the prosecution of criminal offences. But the case's real significance lies in the opinion of Justice Brian Dickson—soon to become Chief Justice of the Supreme Court. Dickson's treatment of the trade and commerce power could pave the way to a considerable expansion of the federal parliament's powers of economic regulation.

The immediate issue in the case was whether the section of the federal Combines Investigation Act giving the federal Attorney General control of prosecutions under the Act was within federal jurisdiction. In *Hauser*,[1] the Court upheld similar provisions of the Narcotic Controls Act giving the federal Attorney General control of prosecutions under that Act. But the majority in *Hauser* considered that the Narcotics Control Act had not been passed under section 91(27), the federal criminal law power, but under the peace, order and good government power. Only Justice Spence took the position that federal control over the prosecution of offences extended to all offences created by federal legislation. Justice Dickson, in dissent, took a much narrower view of federal power, holding that where offences are created by legislation enacted under the criminal law power legislative power to control prosecutions lies with the provinces under section 92(14), the Administration of Justice in the Province.

In *C.N. Transportation* Justice Spence's position is endorsed by the majority. Chief Justice Laskin, who had not participated in *Hauser*, finds that there is no basis for provincial legislative control over the prosecution of *any* federal offences. The Administration of Justice in the Province does not embrace criminal prosecutions. Any powers exercised by provincial attorneys general and crown prosecutors with regard to Criminal Code offences are delegated to them by federal legislation. In Laskin's view it is well within the federal parliament's jurisdiction to retain control over the prosecution of criminal offences in the hands of federal authorities, as it has done in enacting the Combines Investigation Act, and not delegate it to the provincial attorneys general. For the Chief Justice and the three justices who concurred with him it did not matter whether the Combines Act rested on the criminal law power or some other head of power. Thus they were willing to assume, without further analysis, that the Combines Act might rest solely on the criminal law power.

But this question was crucial to Justice Dickson for he continued to adhere to the position he had taken in *Hauser* that legislative power over the prosecution of offences depending entirely on the criminal law power lies with the provinces. He did not dispute the majority finding that the Combines Act can be upheld under the federal criminal law power. Indeed there is a long line of

---

[1] Case 26 above.

cases taking that position.[2] But Dickson argues that this legislation can also be upheld as a valid exercise of Parliament's power over the regulation of trade and commerce. This enables him to conclude that there is a concurrent prosecutorial authority with respect to offences under the Combines Act.[3]

The Combines Act applied to many industries which were not interprovincial or international. Thus to view the Act as a valid exercise of the trade and commerce power, Dickson had to breathe new life into that branch of trade and commerce—the general regulation of trade affecting the whole Dominion—which in the past the courts had been most reluctant to invoke.[4] He develops an interpretation of this general trade power which, while precluding regulations of particular industries within a province, would support federal legislation aimed at the national economy as a whole especially where the ends in view are ones that the provinces individually could not achieve on their own. It is remarkable that this very functional test of federal economic power was endorsed by two Quebec justices, Beetz and Lamer, and was not repudiated by the majority.

The Court's decision in this case had little practical effect on the conduct of criminal prosecutions in Canada. The federal Attorney General maintained responsibility for offences under federal statutes other than the Criminal Code and provincial attorneys general continued to exercise their considerable responsibilities for the prosecution of Criminal Code offences. Except now, in theory, the provincial officials are acting entirely as administrative agents of the federal government. It may be only the shift from the combative federal provincial relations of the Trudeau era to the more conciliatory style of the Mulroney government which kept the provinces from pressing their case to be fiscally compensated for carrying out what the Supreme Court now deemed to be an exclusive federal responsibility.

Justice Dickson's holding that federal anti-monopoly legislation could find a constitutional foundation in the trade and commerce power was soon given legislative effect. In 1986 Parliament replaced the Combines Investigation Act with a new Competition Act. The new legislation no longer employs the traditional machinery of criminal justice. A Competition Tribunal made up of judges and economists can issue directives aimed at solving the economic problem at issue. In enacting this legislation, the government openly relied on

[2] See especially *Proprietary Articles of Trade Association* v. *A.G. of Canada*, case 9 above.
[3] In a companion case, *The Queen* v. *Wetmore* (1983) 2 S.C.R. 284, where the majority upheld federal prosecutorial authority under the Food and Drugs Act, Dickson dissented on the grounds that this legislation depended entirely on the criminal law power and therefore prosecutorial authority was under provincial jurisdiction.
[4] See especially the Court's decision in *Labatt*, case 28 above.

Dickson's opinion in *C.N. Transportation*.[5] Here we can see how a shift in constitutional jurisprudence can provide a basis for a change of policy instruments. A challenge to the new Competition Act may soon tell us whether this shift has the support of a clear majority on the Supreme Court. ~

ATTORNEY GENERAL OF CANADA *v.* CANADIAN NATIONAL
TRANSPORTATION
In the Supreme Court of Canada [1983] 2 S.C.R. 206.

The judgment of Laskin C.J. and Ritchie, Estey and McIntyre JJ. was delivered by

THE CHIEF JUSTICE—The issue in this appeal engages the constitutional power of the provincial legislatures to control through their own officers the prosecution in the provincial courts of offences validly created by legislation of the Parliament of Canada. Although the constitutional questions posed in this appeal have a narrower compass by being limited to the preferring of indictments and the conduct of prosecutions under the *Combines Investigation Act*, R.S.C. 1970, c. C-23, as amended, it became obvious during the course of the argument in this Court that the constitutional issues require a broader and principled canvass of the scope of provincial power under s. 92(14) of the former *British North America Act*, now the *Constitution Act, 1867*, and its relation to the federal power under s. 91(27).

Confining myself for the time being to the particular questions raised in this appeal, they read as follows:

1. Does the constitutional validity of Section 32(1)(c) of the Combines Investigation Act, *S.C. 1970, c. C-23, depend upon Section 91(27) of the* British North America Act?

2. If so, is it within the competence of the Parliament of Canada to enact legislation as in Section 2 of the Criminal Code, *and Section 15(2) of the* Combines Investigation Act, *to authorize the*

Attorney General of Canada or his agents to prefer indictments and conduct proceedings in respect of alleged violations of the aforementioned provision?

They require fleshing out to show how they arose and I turn to the relevant facts.

II

An officer under the federal *Combines Investigation Act* swore an information against the respondents, charging them and other corporations and individuals with unlawful conspiracy to prevent or lessen unduly competition in the interprovincial transportation of general merchandise in shipments weighing up to and including ten thousand pounds from points in Alberta to points in British Columbia, Saskatchewan and Manitoba to points in Alberta. The charge alleged a violation of s. 32(1)(c) of the *Combines Investigation Act* which is in the following terms:

32. (1) Every one who conspires, combines, agrees or arranges with another person

. . .

(c) to prevent, or lessen, unduly, competition in the production, manufacture, purchase, barter, sale, storage, rental, transportation or supply of a product, or in the price of insurance upon persons or property, . . .

. . .

[5] See *Minutes of Proceedings of Legislative Committee on Bill C-91*, April 23, 1986, p. 9.

is guilty of an indictable offence and is liable to imprisonment for five years or a fine of one million dollars or to both.

The conduct of the proceedings was put in the hands of counsel authorized by the Attorney General of Canada. Prohibition was thereupon sought by various of those charged with the offence to restrain the Alberta Provincial Court, before which the information was brought, from proceeding thereon so long as the prosecution was to be conducted by counsel for the federal Attorney General. Medhurst J. of the Alberta Court of Queen's Bench dismissed the application brought by the respondents herein, Canadian Pacific Transport Company Limited and Kenneth G. Paulley and by Canadian National Transportation, Limited. . . .

On appeal to the Alberta Court of Appeal, Prowse J.A., speaking for the Court consisting of himself, Haddad and Laycraft JJ.A., held that s. 32(1)(c) of the *Combines Investigation Act* does not depend for its validity in whole or in part on the federal trade and commerce power. Indeed, if it was to be viewed as a regulatory scheme and not as criminal law under s. 91(27) it would be *ultra vires* as beyond federal competence. Viewed as an exercise of the federal criminal law power under s. 91(27), he concluded that the *Hauser* case applied to preclude the federal conduct of the prosecution under s. 32(1)(c) of the *Combines Investigation Act*. . . .

III

Implicit in the first of the two questions raised in this appeal was the contention, pursued by the Attorney General of Canada, that if the *Combines Investigation Act*, and especially s. 32(1)(c) thereof, was supportable under the federal trade and commerce power, the assertion of exclusive provincial prosecutorial authority would be precluded even if (and this was also contested) it was sustainable in relation to the prosecution of criminal offences. I may say that I find it impos-

sible to separate prosecution for offences resting on a violation of valid trade and commerce legislation and those resting on a violation of the federal criminal law. If exclusive provincial authority rests in the latter, it must equally rest in the former. Indeed, counsel for the respondent Canadian National Transportation, Limited was bold enough—and I think he was logically right—to sweep all offences under federal legislation, enacted pursuant to federal enumerated power under s. 91, into the exclusive care and authority of provincial prosecuting officers. In short, if the provinces are constitutionally in control of criminal prosecutions, they must equally be in control of other prosecutions resting on violation of federal legislation other than under the criminal law, at least so far as the prosecutions are brought in provincial courts. Any reading of s. 92(14) of the provincial catalogue of powers does not exhibit any special mention, indeed there is no mention, of criminal offences.

I am content, however, to limit my examination of the constitutional submissions in this appeal to the question whether, assuming that the *Combines Investigation Act* rests only on the criminal law power (as distinguished from a *Criminal Code* offence, an important distinction in my opinion), the federal Attorney General is not entitled to prosecute offences under the Act and, as was alleged in argument for the respondents and for the intervening provinces, may only intrude to enforce federal criminal legislation by permission or delegation or nomination of a province.

IV

Until the *Criminal Code* was amended by 1968-69 (Can.), c. 38, s. 2(1), the federal Attorney General, his lawful deputy and the Solicitor General were excluded from the general definition of Attorney General in that section, although there are references elsewhere to provisions requiring the federal Attorney General's consent to prosecute, as for example, in ss. 592 and 593 of the *Criminal Code*, R.S.C. 1906, c. 146. This was not, however, the first time in federal legislation that the federal Attorney General was given prosecutorial authority. It was given under the *Combines Investigation Act* by 1960 (Can.), c. 45, ss. 6, 11, 12 and 16 under which the then Exchequer Court of Canada was given a limited jurisdiction over criminal prosecutions under that Act. . . .

There were even earlier instances of federal prosecutorial authority under the federal *Dominion Trade and Industry Commission Act*, 1935 (Can.), c. 59, s. 22. There the Attorney General of Canada was authorized in certain circumstances to institute criminal proceedings for violation of federal laws prohibiting unfair trade practices and this authority was held to be validly conferred: see *Reference re Dominion Trade and Industry Commission Act*, [1936] S.C.R. 379, aff'd [1937] A.C. 405. . . .

The constitutional question which is raised as a result of the foregoing decisions is whether provincial prosecutorial power rested and has rested only on the abstention of the federal authorities from intervening in the prosecution of federal offences. I start at the beginning in the consideration of this question, namely, the initial creation of the Canadian federation in 1867 under the then *British North America Act.*

V

When the Canadian federation came into being, it was obvious that existing laws of the confederating provinces and existing courts, powers and authorities had to be continued subject to being altered in accordance with the distribution of legislative power under the federating Act. Section 129 covered the matter in these words.

129. Except as otherwise provided by this Act, all Laws in force in Canada, Nova Scotia, or New Brunswick at the Union, and all Courts of Civil and Criminal Jurisdiction, and all legal Commissions, Powers, and Authorities, and all Officers, Judicial, Administrative, and Ministerial, existing therein at the Union, shall continue in Ontario, Quebec, Nova Scotia, and New Brunswick respectively, as if the Union had not been made; subject nevertheless (except with respect to such as are enacted by or exist under Acts of the Parliament of Great Britain or of the Parliament of the United Kingdom of Great Britain and Ireland), to be repealed, abolished, or altered by the Parliament of Canada, or by the Legislature of the respective Province, according to the Authority of the Parliament or of that Legislature under this Act.

The Parliament of Canada moved, soon after Confederation, to exercise the new federal legislative power conferred upon it under s. 91. One of its early exercises of power was in relation to the substantive criminal law and this was almost coincident with a statute, 1869 (Can.), c. 29, respecting procedure in criminal matters. . . . The 1869 Act dealt with the prosecution of indictable offences and it defined indictment widely to include information, inquisition and presentment. Section 28 treated the role of the provincial Attorney General or Solicitor General as coming under the scope of the federal Act. . . .

In this and related legislation, prosecutors or complainants had standing to invoke the criminal law, in broader compass than was later permitted. . . .

I am not aware that during this period there was any attempt by a province to enact legislation that would limit prosecution for federal criminal offences, let alone any other types of offences, to a provincial Attorney General or prosecutor. Nor did the provinces purport to enact post-Confederation legislation of their own to command prosecutorial authority in respect of federal criminal law offences. Until federal legislation embraced the provincial Attorney General and Solicitor General within the scope of its criminal enactments, those officers exercised their prosecutorial authority pursuant to pre-Confederation legislation as continued under s. 129, which I have previously quoted.

The generalized definition of provincial Attorney General or Solicitor General appeared in the original *Criminal Code*, 1892 (Can.), c. 29. Section 3(*b*) of the *Code* was as follows:

3. In this Act the following expressions have the meanings assigned to them in this section unless the context requires otherwise:

. . .

(b) The expression "Attorney-General" means the Attorney-General or Solicitor-General of any province in Canada in which any proceedings are taken under this Act, and, with respect to the North-west Territories and the district of Keewatin, the Attorney-General of Canada; . . .

This limited reference to the Attorney General of Canada remained unaltered until the *Criminal Law Amendment Act, 1968-69*, 1968-69 (Can.), c. 38, introduced a major change under s. 2, which I have already quoted. In the meantime, the definition and reference to provincial Attorney General remained the same. It appears that it was this introduction of a generalized prosecutorial authority in the Attorney General of Canada that brought about the provincial claim that criminal procedure under s. 91(27) of the then *British North America Act* did not give legislative authority to Parliament against the mandate of s. 92(14) so as to empower the federal Attorney General to prosecute offences engaging the violation of validly enacted federal criminal law.

VI

Language and logic inform constitutional interpretation, and they are applicable in considering the alleged reach of s. 92(14) and the allegedly correlative limitation of criminal procedure in s. 91(27). I find it difficult, indeed impos-

sible, to read s. 92(14) as not only embracing prosecutorial authority respecting the enforcement of federal criminal law but diminishing the *ex facie* impact of s. 91(27) which includes procedure in criminal matters. As a matter of language, there is nothing in s. 92(14) which embraces prosecutorial authority in respect of federal criminal matters. Section 92(14) grants jurisdiction over the administration of justice, including procedure in civil matters and including also the constitution, maintenance and organization of civil and criminal provincial courts. The section thus narrows the scope of the criminal law power under s. 91, but only with respect to what is embraced within "the Constitution, Maintenance, and Organization of Provincial Courts . . . of Criminal Jurisdiction". By no stretch of language can these words be construed to include jurisdiction over the conduct of criminal prosecutions. Moreover, as a matter of conjunctive assessment of the two constitutional provisions, the express inclusion of procedure in civil matters in provincial Courts points to an express provincial exclusion of procedure in criminal matters specified in s. 91(27). . . .

It must be remembered, at the risk of undue repetition, that the practice of provincial prosecution was continued after 1867 into post-1867 by virtue of s. 129. It was a practical accommodation to allow this to continue, and the affirmation of this practice under the 1892 *Criminal Code* and in ensuing years did not, as I read the authorities, cast any doubt on federal authority to invest and regulate provincial prosecutorial power to enforce the federal criminal law. . . .

It must be remembered that s. 92(14) is a grant of legislative power and if it gave the provinces legislative authority over the conduct of criminal prosecutions, then federal legislation conferring prosecutorial authority on either provincial or federal Attorneys General would be *ultra vires*. It cannot be argued that Parliament confers prosecutorial authority only with the consent of the provinces, for this would involve an unconstitutional delegation of legislative power: see *Attorney General of Nova Scotia* v. *Attorney General of Canada*, [1951] S.C.R. 31. The provincial position appears to blur legislative and executive power and to treat s. 92(14) as if it were a grant of executive power to which the legislative power of Parliament under s. 91(27) was subordinate.

I have examined the pre-Confederation debates in the then provincial Parliament of Canada. The resolutions introduced on February 3, 1865 into the Legislative Council were in pursuance of those that were adopted at the Charlottetown Conference of 1864 and included what were and what remained the terms included in s. 92(14) (it was originally s. 43(17)) and s. 91(27) (it was originally s. 29(32)).

There are, at best, general observations in the Confederation Debates respecting criminal law and procedure. John A. Macdonald referred (at p. 41) to the principle that the determination of what is a crime and how crime shall be punished is to be left to the general government. References to the administration of justice were in such general terms (see pp. 69, 215, 248) as to be of no particular significance. Mr. Hector Langevin, then Solicitor General East, viewed what is now s. 92(14) as providing protection to Quebec civil law. Mr. Christopher Dunkin raised the question (at p. 508) that there is a special refinement of confusion as to criminal matters. He put the matter as follows (at p. 508 bottom):

. . . Criminal procedure is to be federal; civil procedure, provincial; criminal legislation, proper, is to be federal; but with a most uncertain quantity of what one may call legislation about penalties, provincial; civil rights, in the main, provincial; but with no one can tell how much of federal interference and over-ruling, and all with courts provincial in constitution, but whose judges hold by federal tenure and under federal pay. I pity the poor man who is at once a criminal judge and a civil judge.

Nothing in these observations touches the issue now before us, nor is there any basis for any special reading of the Charlottetown or the subsequent London Palace Hotel resolutions to gloss the present s. 92(14) and s. 91(27) in the way proposed by the respondents and their supporting interveners.

VII

It is patent that neither the respondents nor their supporting interveners view the present case as pointing to possible concurrency. Since Parliament has in fact legislated, that would defeat their contention without more. Yet there is good reason to say that even if there is merit in the respondents' position, there is at least equal merit in the assertion of parliamentary authority to control prosecution for violation of the federal criminal law.

VIII

I come now, at long last, to consider the case law which has developed around s. 92(14) and s. 91(27) since the introduction of federal prosecution of criminal law offences under the amendment of the *Criminal Code* by 1968-69 (Can.), c. 38, s. 2(1). There are four cases to be considered, apart from the present one, the first in time being *R.* v. *Pelletier, supra,* (leave to appeal here refused: see [1974] S.C.R. x); the second in time being *Re Hauser and The Queen* (1977), 37 C.C.C. (2d) 129, rev'd here on other grounds, [1979] 1 S.C.R. 984; the third being *R.* v. *Pontbriand* (1978), 1 C.R. (3d) 97, [1978] C.S. 134 and the fourth, *R.* v. *Hoffman-LaRoche Ltd.* (1980), 14 C.R. (3d) 289, aff'd on appeal (1981), 24 C.R. (3d) 193. . . .

What then does the *Hauser* case in this Court say about the matter? . . . Pigeon J., speaking for the majority of the Court (Martland, Ritchie and Beetz JJ.) held that the *Narcotic Control Act* was properly classifiable under the federal general residual power, dealing as it did with a new problem which did not exist at Confederation. Accordingly, he did not have to go beyond recognition of the authority of the federal Attorney General to prosecute for an offence which did not depend upon s. 91(27). Pigeon J. made it clear that no opinion was being expressed of any federal prosecutorial competence beyond that point. In the result, the appeal was allowed and Spence J. joined in that result but on a different plane than that of the majority, exhibiting in this respect a difference of opinion from Dickson J., with whom Pratte J. concurred. . . .

I turn now to say a word about the recent judgment of the Ontario Court of Appeal in *Hoffman-LaRoche*. Martin J.A., speaking for the Court in that case, found himself substantially in agreement with *Pelletier* and with Spence J. in *Hauser*, as well as with the views expressed by Linden J. at trial. I have referred earlier to these reasons to Linden J. and need not recanvass his reasons. There are a number of passages in the reasons of Martin J.A. which I fully endorse and they are as follows. Thus, he said (at p. 225):

I am satisfied that, at the least, Parliament has concurrent jurisdiction with the provinces to enforce federal legislation validly enacted under head 27 of s. 91 which, like the Combines Investigation Act, is mainly directed at suppressing in the national interest, conduct which is essentially trans-provincial in its nature, operation and effects, and in respect of which the investigative function is performed by federal officials pursuant to powers validly conferred on them and using procedure which only Parliament can constitutionally provide. . . .

IX

Apart from the reasons in this Court which I have produced, it is sufficient in my view to rely on the *Pelletier* case, the reasons of Justice Spence in *Hauser* and the reasons of the Ontario Court of Appeal in the *Hoffman-LaRoche* case. The reasons and decisions to which I refer lead to

the conclusion that this appeal should be allowed, the judgment of the Alberta Court of Appeal set aside and the questions posed for decisions should be answered in the affirmative.

DICKSON J.—Is the Attorney General of Canada constitutionally competent to prefer indictments and conduct proceedings in respect of alleged violations of the *Combines Investigation Act*, R.S.C. 1970, c. C-23, as amended? That is the narrow question raised by this appeal. Behind it, however, much broader questions are put in issue, touching on the fundamental principles that govern the division of powers between the federal and provincial authorities in the areas of criminal justice and economic regulation. . . .

The *Combines Investigation Act* as Criminal Law

There is a long history of Canadian anti-combines legislation being sustained as criminal law. The original statute, passed in 1889, was entitled *An Act for the Prevention and Suppression of Combinations formed in restraint of Trade*, 1889 (Can.), c. 41. The statute was motivated by concern over the emergence in Canada of smaller versions of the huge trusts in the United States, through which a few personalities could control enormous financial empires. The combines problem was seen as one with strong moral overtones and criminal sanctions were selected as the appropriate means for its control: see McDonald, *Criminality and the Canadian Anti-Combines Laws* (1965), 4 Alta. L.R. 67, at pp. 69-71. When the first Canadian *Criminal Code* was enacted in 1892, the prohibitions in the 1889 statute were included therein as 1892 (Can.), c. 29, s. 520. In 1910 Parliament enacted *The Combines Investigation Act*, 1910 (Can.), c. 9, which provided investigative machinery and empowered a board appointed by the Minister to levy fines against individuals and companies whom the Board found guilty of combines offences, and who "continue[d] so to offend" (s. 23). None of these early statutes was challenged in the courts: see Hogg, *Constitutional Law of Canada*, p. 282, and Hogg and Grover, *The Constitutionality of the Competition Bill* (1975-76), 1 *Can. Bus. L.J.* 197, at p. 202.

In 1919 a more ambitious scheme was enacted by *The Combines and Fair Prices Act, 1919*, 1919 (Can.), c. 45, and *The Board of Commerce Act*, 1919 (Can.), c. 37. These statutes prohibited combinations which in the opinion of the Board of Commerce were detrimental to the public interest, and also included provisions directed at hoarding and unduly profiting from the necessities of life, which were defined as food, clothing and fuel. The Board was empowered to determine when undue profits were being made, and could issue cease and desist orders which in effect fixed maximum prices. In *Re Board of Commerce Act, 1919, and the Combines and Fair Prices Act, 1919*, [1922] 1 A.C. 191, these statutes were declared unconstitutional. . . .

The year after the *Board of Commerce* decision Parliament enacted *The Combines Investigation Act*, 1923 (Can.), c. 9, which repealed the two 1919 statutes, and replaced them with a more modest scheme that prohibited combines in restraint of trade, but went no further. The new Act gave investigatory power to a registrar and commissioners, but did not confer authority to issue cease and desist orders. In *Proprietary Articles Trade Associations* v. *Attorney-General for Canada* (the *P.A.T.A.* case), [1931] A.C. 310, the Privy Council, now speaking through Lord Atkin, repudiated Viscount Haldane's "domain of criminal jurisprudence" theory, saying that federal criminal law jurisdiction was "not confined to what was criminal by the law of England or of any Province in 1867", and that "the power must extend to legislation to make new crimes" (p. 324). Lord Atkin also said that their Lordships wished to "dissociate themselves" from the *Board of Commerce* proposition that the trade

and commerce power "could be invoked only in furtherance of a general power which Parliament possessed independently of it" (p. 326). Having found the new *Combines Investigation Act* valid under the criminal law power, Lord Atkin did not find it necessary to consider whether it could also be supported under the trade and commerce jurisdiction. He did say, however, that their Lordships wished to "guard themselves from being supposed to lay down that the present legislation could not be supported on that ground" (p. 326).

In 1935 *The Dominion Trade and Industry Commission Act*, 1935 (Can.), c. 59, was enacted. This Act established a new Commission which was "charged with the administration of the *Combines Investigation Act*" (s. 13). The Commission was also given "responsibility to recommend the prosecution of offences against acts of the Parliament of Canada . . . relating to commodity standards" (s. 15(1)). The Commission received investigatory powers relating to both combines and commodity standards (ss. 15(2), 20). Section 14 gave the Governor in Council, on the advice of the Commission, power to give advance clearance to agreements among businessmen regulating prices or production in any particular industry when the arrangement was not "detrimental" to the public interest.

In *Reference re Dominion Trade and Industry Commission Act*, [1936] S.C.R. 379, this Court upheld the Commission's investigatory powers relating to commodity standards under both the criminal law and trade and commerce powers (p. 382), and its investigatory powers in the combines field as criminal law (p. 383). The Court held, however, that s. 14, which conferred the advance clearance powers, was *ultra vires*. Duff C.J. said, for the Court, that an advance clearance power was not "necessarily incidental" to the criminal law aspect of the statute, and they could not be upheld under the trade and commerce head because it was not "in substance" confined to interprovincial trade (p. 381-82). In *Attorney-General for Ontario* v. *Attorney-General for Canada (Canada Standard Trade Mark Case)*, [1937] A.C. 405, the Privy Council upheld the judgment of this Court, except on a point not relevant here. The Judicial Committee expressly agreed with the reasoning of Duff C.J., (at p. 416) saying the investigatory powers sections were "legitimate provisions for ascertaining whether criminal acts have been committed". The decision of this Court with respect to the advance clearance powers was not appealed to the Privy Council. . . .

In 1951 Parliament prohibited resale price maintenance and, again, this Court upheld the new provision as criminal law: *R.* v. *Campbell* (1965), 58 D.L.R. (2d) 673, affirming the judgment and reasons of the Ontario Court of Appeal reported at (1964), 46 D.L.R. (2d) 83. In 1952 Parliament added new sections to the *Combines Investigation Act* permitting courts hearing combines charges to make orders prohibiting the continuation of combines, or orders dissolving mergers, trusts or monopolies, such orders to be in addition to any other penalty the court might impose upon conviction: 1952 (Can.), c. 39, s. 3. These sections were upheld by this Court under the criminal law power in *Goodyear Tire and Rubber Co.* v. *The Queen*, [1956] S.C.R. 303.

The foregoing survey shows that both this Court and the Privy Council have consistently sustained anti-combines legislation as criminal law. The same may be said about the specific section in issue in the first constitutional question. . . . Indeed all parties in this appeal agree that s. 32(1)(c) is *intra vires* as criminal law and I see no reason to disagree.

That, however, does not end the matter. There is no reason why an enactment which is valid as coming within one of the federal heads of power in s. 91 of the *Constitution Act, 1867* cannot also be valid by virtue of one or more additional federal heads of power. In most constitutional cases involving federal legislation, the issue is whether the impugned enact-ment is properly within federal or provincial law-making authority. Once federal competence has been established under one s. 91 power, it is little to the point whether the enactment might also have been supported under another federal head. In most cases to speculate about such further possible justifications would be to ignore the venerable principle of constitutional interpretation contained in Sir Montague Smith's admonition in *Citizens Insurance Company of Canada* v. *Parsons* (1881), 7 App. Cas. 96, at p. 109, to judges attempting to construe the limits of ss. 91 and 92:

In performing this difficult duty, it will be a wise course for those on whom it is thrown, to decide each case which arises as best they can, without entering more largely upon an interpretation of the statute than is necessary for the decision of the particular question in hand. . . .

In view of this established policy of minimizing unnecessary constitutional pronouncements I attach little significance to the fact that in most cases courts have simply endorsed the *P.A.T.A.* decision that the *Combines Investigation Act* could be justified as criminal law.

The Trade and Commerce Power

Any consideration of the federal Parliament's s. 91(2) power to regulate trade and commerce must begin with the Privy Council decision in the *Parsons* case.

. . . passages from Parsons *establish three important propositions with regard to the federal trade and commerce power: (i) it does not correspond to the literal meaning of the words "regulation of trade and commerce"; (ii) it includes not only arrangements with regard to international and interprovincial trade but "it may be that . . . [it] would include general regulation of trade affecting the whole dominion"; (iii) it does not extend to regulating the contracts of a particular business or trade. Subsequent jurisprudence on the meaning and extent of*

s. 91(2) is to a large extent an expansion and an explication of these three interrelated propositions.

(ii) General Regulation of Trade
    Affecting the Whole Dominion

One possible indication of federal competence over economic regulation is its operation across and beyond provincial borders. In *Parsons* the Privy Council identified international and interprovincial trade as coming within the ambit of s. 91(2) and much of the subsequent jurisprudence on the federal trade and commerce power has been devoted to a consideration of just how much or how little intraprovincial commerce could be validly swept into the flow of the interprovincial trade affected by a given enactment. In the present case, however, even on the most generous definition, s. 32(1)(c) of the *Combines Investigation Act* cannot be seen as a regulation of interprovincial trade and commerce. The appellant Attorney General of Canada concedes that if it is to be justified under s. 91(2), this enactment must fall within what has been called the "second branch" of the *Parsons* classification, namely the "general regulation of trade affecting the whole dominion".

Although in *Parsons* this second branch is presented as merely a possibility ("and it may be that they would include . . ."), the existence of a "general trade and commerce" power seems to have been widely assumed in subsequent cases. In *John Deere Plow Co.* v. *Wharton, supra*, the Privy Council held that the limits of the powers of federally-incorporated companies was "a question of general interest throughout the Dominion" and hence under federal competence pursuant to s. 91(2). In *Attorney-General for Ontario* v. *Attorney-General for Canada (Canada Standard Trade Mark Case), supra*, at p. 417, the Privy Council held that the creation of a national trade mark was within "the class of subjects enumerated in s. 91(2)". Even in cases where the

impugned legislation was held to fall outside of the ambit of s. 91(2), the existence of such a "general" power seems not to have been put in doubt. See *Toronto Electric Commissioners* v. *Snider*, [1925] A.C. 396, [1925] 2 D.L.R. 5, at p. 13; *Reference re Natural Products Marketing Act, supra*, at p. 629. In more recent cases, the existence of a "general" trade and commerce power has been affirmed by the Chief Justice in *MacDonald* v. *Vapor Canada Ltd.*, [1977] 2 S.C.R. 134, at p. 167, and by Estey J. in *Labatt Breweries of Canada Ltd.* v. *Attorney General of Canada*, [1980] 1 S.C.R. 914, at p. 936. Yet, despite all these affirmations, the *Wharton* and *Canada Standard Trade Mark* cases remain the only ones in which a final appellate court has actually applied the general trade and commerce power to validate federal legislation and the correctness of even these decisions has been widely doubted. See, Smith, *The Commerce Power in Canada and the United States* (1963), pp. 96-99. With these exceptions, the potential applicability of the general trade and commerce power has been considered and rejected in a string of final appellate court decisions beginning the year after *Wharton's* case with *Attorney-General for Canada* v. *Attorney-General for Alberta (Insurance Reference)*, [1916] 1 A.C. 588, through to and including both the *Vapor Canada* and *Labatt* cases.

One reason for this conspicuous lack of success is doubtless to be found in the test for the general trade and commerce power implicit in *Wharton*. If every economic issue that could be characterized as a "question of general interest throughout the Dominion" were to fall under federal competence by virtue of s. 91(2), then the extent of the power would hardly be narrower than it would on a literal reading of the words "regulation of trade and commerce" alone. There is hardly an economic issue which, if only by virtue of its recurrence in locations around the country, could not be characterized as a matter of general interest throughout the Dominion.

In the *Labatt* case, *supra*, at p. 940, Estey J. states that the criterion of constituting a question of general interest throughout the Dominion is still the correct test in determining whether the second branch of the trade and commerce power applies. I agree with this statement, just as I am of opinion that the long disuse of this second branch does not impugn its constitutional validity. But I am also of the view—as Estey J.'s treatment of the issue in *Labatt* confirms—that the same considerations which led Sir Montague Smith to limit the scope of the words "regulation of trade and commerce" in *Parsons'* case also necessitate a restrictive reading of the *Wharton* test of "general interest throughout the Dominion". The question, of course, is how much is to be subtracted from these words, and on what basis?

iii) Regulating the Contracts of a Particular Business or Trade

Although the Privy Council in *Parsons* was unwilling to consider in detail the boundary between ss. 91(2) and 92(13) it did go as far as holding that "regulation of trade and commerce" could not include "the power to regulate by legislation the contracts of a particular business or trade". . . .

The reason why the regulation of a single trade or business in the province cannot be a question of general interest throughout the Dominion, is that it lies at the very heart of the local autonomy envisaged in the *Constitution Act, 1867*. That a federal enactment purports to carry out such regulation in the same way in all the provinces or in association with other regulatory codes dealing with other trades or businesses does not change the fact that what is being created is an exact overlapping and hence a nullification of a jurisdiction conceded to the provinces by the Constitution. A different situation obtains, however, when what is at issue is general legislation aimed at the economy as a single integrated national unit rather than as a collection of separate local enter-

prises. Such legislation is qualitatively different from anything that could practically or constitutionally be enacted by the individual provinces either separately or in combination. The focus of such legislation is on the general, though its results will obviously be manifested in particular local effects any one of which may touch upon "Property and Civil Rights in the Province". Nevertheless, in pith and substance such legislation will be addressed to questions of general interest throughout the Dominion. The line of demarcation is clear between measures validly directed at a general regulation of the national economy and those merely aimed at centralized control over a large number of local economic entities. The regulations in the *Labatt's* case were probably close to the line. It may also well be that, given the state of the economy in 1920 and the actual mechanics of the legislation, *The Board of Commerce Act* and *The Combines and Fair Prices Act, 1919*, amounted simply to an attempt to authorize the issuance of an uncoordinated series of local orders and prohibitions.

In approaching this difficult problem of characterization it is useful to note the remarks of the Chief Justice in *MacDonald v. Vapor Canada Ltd., supra*, at p. 165, in which he cites as possible *indicia* for a valid exercise of the general trade and commerce power the presence of a national regulatory scheme, the oversight of a regulatory agency and a concern with trade in general rather than with an aspect of a particular business. To this list I would add what to my mind would be even stronger indications of valid general regulation of trade and commerce, namely (i) that the provinces jointly or severally would be constitutionally incapable of passing such an enactment and (ii) that failure to include one or more provinces or localities would jeopardize successful operation in other parts of the country.

The above does not purport to be an exhaustive list, nor is the presence of any or all of these *indicia* necessarily decisive.

The proper approach to the characterization is still the one suggested in *Parsons*, a careful case by case assessment. Nevertheless, the presence of such factors does at least make it far more probable that what is being addressed in a federal enactment is genuinely a national economic concern and not just a collection of local ones.

It is with these considerations in mind that I turn to the question of whether s. 32(1)(c) can be said validly to depend on the federal trade and commerce power.

Section 32(1)(c) as Trade and Commerce

The first question is how much of the *Combines Investigation Act* is relevant for purposes of deciding whether s. 32(1)(c) is authorized by the federal trade and commerce power. . . .

Having found that s. 32(1)(c) is not an isolated provision, but rather part of a regulatory scheme, it still remains to assess whether this scheme is valid under the second branch of s. 91(2). The fact of forming part of such a scheme is but one *indicium* of validity and not in itself determinative. A number of cases have found that the scheme embodied by the Act also displays such additional *indicia* as a national scope, a general application and a concern with the trade as a whole rather than with a single business . . . it is still necessary even in the face of all these factors to consider the issue of constitutional balance, and whether a finding of validity under the trade and commerce power might not erode the local autonomy in economic regulation contemplated by the Constitution. This was the fear voiced by Marceau J. in *Rocois Construction Inc.* v. *Quebec Ready Mix Inc.*, [1980] 1 F.C. 184 (T.D.), at p. 203:

It is because a general statute on competition as such, that is a statute regulating competition beyond the detection, prevention and penalization of disapproved and proscribed acts, may make such an encroachment [on provincial powers] possible that I do not think that it *can be based on the power of Parliament over trade and commerce. As the prime mover in our system of production and exchange of goods and services, competition depends on so many factors and takes on so many aspects that it may give rise to legislation as far-reaching as it is diversified. To admit that, as such, it is covered by Parliament's power pursuant to subsection (2) of section 91 would be to open the door to a potential trenching on the powers of the provinces which, in my view, the courts have definitively rejected, despite their persistent hesitation.*

For the reasons cited earlier I would in any event be inclined to reject this contention. To give it heed would amount to a denial of the possibility of Parliament ever validly exercising its general trade and commerce power, a power which if properly understood and properly constrained does not erode local autonomy but rather complements it. I would also, however, mention an additional factor. A scheme aimed at the regulation of competition is in my view an example of the *genre* of legislation that could not practically or constitutionally be enacted by a provincial government. Given the free flow of trade across provincial borders guaranteed by s. 121 of the *Constitution Act, 1867* Canada is, for economic purposes, a single huge marketplace. If competition is to be regulated at all it must be regulated federally. . . .

All these considerations lead to the conclusion that s. 32(1)(c) is valid federal legislation under s. 91(2) of the *Constitution Act, 1867* as well as s. 91(27). The Attorney General of Canada also contends that s. 32(1)(c) is valid under the peace, order and good government power, but in view of the finding of validity under s. 91(2) it is unnecessary to pursue this contention.

Authority to Prosecute under s. 32(1)(c)

The result of holding s. 32(1)(c) to be valid under both the criminal law and the trade and commerce power is in my view a finding of concurrent federal and provincial prosecutorial authority. The majority in *Hauser* held that the authority to prefer indictments and conduct prosecutions with reference to legislation other than that enacted under s. 91(27) was validly vested in the Attorney General of Canada. Therefore, in so far as s. 32(1)(*c*) depends on the trade and commerce power, the federal Attorney General is the proper prosecutor. As to prosecutorial authority by virtue of the characterization of s. 32(1)(*c*) as criminal law, I am still of the opinion that only the provincial Attorney General can validly prosecute criminal enactments. See my reasons, *R. v. Wetmore* [[1983] 2 S.C.R. 284], judgment which is being delivered concurrently herewith. . . .

Conclusion

I would answer the questions in the following manner:

Question 1:"Yes" in the sense that s. 32(1)(*c*) of the *Combines Investigation Act* is supportable under s. 91(27) and also supportable under s. 91(2). If the meaning of the question is whether s. 32(1)(*c*) is supportable solely under s. 91(27) I would answer "No".

Question 2:"Yes" as to s. 15(2) of the *Combines Investigation Act*, and "yes" as to s. 2(2) of the *Criminal Code* in so far as they relate to s. 32(1) of the *Combines Investigation Act*.

However in so far as s. 2(2) of the *Criminal Code* generally gives the Attorney General of Canada authority to initiate and conduct prosecutions resting on offences created under federal legislation enacted solely under s. 91(27) of the *Constitution Act, 1867*, it is *ultra vires*. . . .

I would allow the appeal and vary the judgment of the Alberta Court of Appeal by answering the questions posed for decision in the manner above set forth.

BEETZ AND LAMER JJ.—We have had the considerable advantage of reading the reasons for judgment of the Chief Justice and of our brother Dickson and we find ourselves in substantial agreement with those of our brother Dickson to the effect that s. 32(1)(*c*) of the *Combines Investigation Act*, R.S.C. 1970, c. C-23, as amended by 1974-75-76 (Can.), c. 76, s. 14(1), has been validly enacted by the Parliament of Canada under its authority to make laws in relation to trade and commerce, pursuant to s. 91(2) of the *Constitution Act, 1867*.

It follows that the constitutional validity of s. 32(1)(*c*) does not depend upon s. 91(27) of the *Constitution Act, 1867*, the criminal law power of Parliament, whether or not it can also be supported under this section.

We would accordingly answer "No" to the first question stated by the Chief Justice and we do not find it necessary to answer the second question. . . .

31. The Queen *v.* Crown Zellerbach Canada Ltd., *1988*

~ Constitutional interpretation never stands still—for long. In the *Anti-Inflation Reference* the Court's majority supported Justice Beetz's view that the peace, order and good government power could serve as a constitutional basis only for (i) temporary legislation dealing with a national emergency, or (ii) legislation dealing with "distinct subject matters which do not fall within any of the enumerated heads of s. 92 and which, by nature, are of national concern".[1] Subsequent decisions indicated that this second use of peace, order and good government might be wide enough to accommodate a "provincial inability" test which would justify federal legislation if it could be established that a particular problem required national treatment unobtainable through provincial co-operation.[2] In *Crown Zellerbach*, the Court, for the first time, used this test to uphold federal legislation.

The issue in the case was whether federal legislation regulating dumping in the sea could apply to waters well within provincial territory. In defending this application of the legislation the federal government relied primarily not on specific heads of power dealing with matters such as navigation and fisheries but on its general power to legislate for the peace, order and good government of Canada. The federal government was successful in persuading a plurality of judges (four out of seven) that controlling marine pollution is one of those problems which from a functional point of view is indivisible and therefore a justifiable use of the peace, order and good government power. The dissenting judges saw no evidence that in order to deal effectively with ocean pollution Parliament had to claim a plenary power to control the dumping of any substance in provincial waters. They are clearly much more cautious about employing a functional test to justify the use of peace, order and good government in areas normally under provincial jurisdiction.

If the plurality position articulated by Justice LeDain prevails, the legislative capacity of the national government will be significantly widened. Changes in court personnel will, as they have in the past, have a critical bearing on the outcome. By the time of the *Crown Zellerbach* case only two of the judges who had participated in the *Anti-Inflation Reference*—Chief Justice Dickson and Justice Beetz—were still on the Court. Chief Justice Dickson who had been with the minority on the interpretation of peace, order and good government in the *Anti-Inflation* case is now with the majority in *Crown Zellerbach*, while Justice Beetz dissents from the expansive interpretation of his majority opinion in the *Anti-Inflation Reference*. Which view will prevail in the future depends very much on the constitutional philosophies of the newest appointees to the Supreme Court—Justice L'Heureux-Dube from Quebec and Justice Sopinka from Ontario. ~

---

[1] See above p. 174.

[2] See, for example, Justice Estey's opinion in the *Labatt* case above at p. 251.

THE QUEEN v. CROWN ZELLERBACH CANADA LTD.
In the Supreme Court of Canada. [1988] 1 S.C.R. 401.

The judgment of Dickson C.J. and McIntyre, Wilson and Le Dain JJ. was delivered by

LE DAIN J.—The question raised by this appeal is whether federal legislative jurisdiction to regulate the dumping of substances at sea, as a measure for the prevention of marine pollution, extends to the regulation of dumping in provincial marine waters. In issue is the validity of s. 4(1) of the *Ocean Dumping Control Act*, S.C. 1974-75-76, c. 55, which prohibits the dumping of any substance at sea except in accordance with the terms and conditions of a permit, the sea being defined for the purposes of the Act as including the internal waters of Canada other than fresh waters.

The appeal is by leave of this Court from the judgment on January 26, 1984 of the British Columbia Court of Appeal (1984), 51 B.C.L.R. 32, 7 D.L.R. (4th) 449, [1984] 2 W.W.R. 714, 11 C.C.C. (3d) 113, 13 C.E.L.R. 29, dismissing an appeal by way of stated case from the judgment on May 26, 1982 of Schmidt Prov. Ct. J. (1982), 11 C.E.L.R. 151, who dismissed charges against the respondent of unlawfully dumping in the waters of Johnstone Strait near Beaver Cove in the province of British Columbia on the ground that s. 4(1) of the *Ocean Dumping Control Act* is *ultra vires* the Parliament of Canada.

I

The general purpose of the *Ocean Dumping Control Act* is to regulate the dumping of substances at sea in order to prevent various kinds of harm to the marine environment. The Act would appear to have been enacted in fulfilment of Canada's obligations under the *Convention on the Prevention of Marine Pollution by Dumping of Wastes and other Matter*, which was signed by Canada on December 29, 1972. . . .

The concerns of the Act are reflected in

the nature of the prohibited and restricted substances in Schedules I and II and in the factors to be taken into account by the Minister of the Environment in granting permits to dump, which are set out in ss. 9 and 10 of the Act and in Schedule III. What these provisions indicate is that the Act is concerned with marine pollution and its effect on marine life, human health and the amenities of the marine environment. There is also reference to the effect of dumping on navigation and shipping and other legitimate uses of the sea.

Section 4(1) of the Act, with the contravention of which the respondent was charged, reads as follows:

4. (1) No person shall dump except in accordance with the terms and conditions of a permit.

"Dumping" is defined by s. 2(1) of the Act as follows:

2. (1) In this Act,

"dumping" means any deliberate disposal from ships, aircraft, platforms or other man-made structures at sea of any substance but does not include

(a) any disposal that is incidental to or derived from the normal operations of a ship or an aircraft or of any equipment thereof other than the disposal of substances from a ship or aircraft operated for the purpose of disposing of such substances at sea, and

(b) any discharge that is incidental to or derived from the exploration for, exploitation of and associated off-shore processing of sea bed mineral resources;

"The sea" is defined, for the purposes of the Act, by s. 2(2) and (3) as follows:

2. . . .
(2) For the purposes of this Act, "the sea" means

(a) the territorial sea of Canada;

(b) the internal waters of Canada other than inland waters;

(c) any fishing zones prescribed pursuant to the Territorial Sea and Fishing Zones Act;

(d) the arctic waters within the meaning of the Arctic Waters Pollution Prevention Act;

(e) any area of the sea adjacent to the areas referred to in paragraphs (a) to (d) as may be prescribed;

(f) any area of the sea, under the jurisdiction of a foreign state, other than internal waters; and

(g) any area of the sea, other than the internal waters of a foreign state, not included in the areas of the sea referred to in paragraphs (a) to (f).

(3) For the purposes of paragraph (2)(b), "inland waters" means all the rivers, lakes and other fresh waters in Canada and includes the St. Lawrence River as far seaward as the straight lines drawn.

(a) from Cap des Rosiers to the western-most point of Anticosti Island; and

(b) from Anticosti Island to the north shore of the St. Lawrence River along the meridian of longitude sixty-three degrees west. . . .

The respondent was charged, in an information consisting of two counts, with contravening s. 4(1) of the Act, and thereby committing an offence under s. 13(1)(c) as follows:

Count 1: On or about the 16th day of August, A.D. 1980, in the waters of Johnstone Strait near Beaver Cove, Province of British Columbia, did unlawfully dump except in accordance with the terms and conditions of a permit in contravention of Section 4 of the Ocean Dumping Control Act, thereby committing an offence under Section 13(1)(c) of the said Act.

Count 2: On or about the 17th day of August, A.D. 1980, in the waters of Johnstone Strait near Beaver Cove, Province of British Columbia, did unlawfully dump except in accordance with the terms and conditions of a permit in contravention of Section 4 of the Ocean Dumping Control Act, thereby committing an offence under Section 13(1)(c) of the said Act.

The admitted facts concerning the location and nature of the dumping with which the respondent was charged are as follows. The respondent carries on logging operations on Vancouver Island in connection with its forest products business in British Columbia and maintains a log dump on a water lot leased from the provincial Crown for the purpose of log booming and storage in Beaver Cove, off Johnstone Strait, on the northeast side of Vancouver Island. The waters of Beaver Cove are *inter fauces terrae*, or as put in the stated case, "Beaver Cove is of such size that a person standing on the shoreline of either side of Beaver Cove can easily and reasonably discern between shore and shore of Beaver Cove." On August 16 and 17, 1980 the respondent, using an 80-foot crane operating from a moored scow, dredged woodwaste from the ocean floor immediately adjacent to the shoreline at the site of its log dump in Beaver Cove and deposited it in the deeper waters of the cove approximately 60 to 80 feet seaward of where the woodwaste had been dredged. The purpose of the dredging and dumping was to allow a new A-frame structure for log dumping to be floated on a barge to the shoreline for installation there and to give clearance for the dumping of bundled logs from the A-frame structure into the waters of the log dump area. The woodwaste consisted of waterlogged logging debris such as bark, wood and slabs. There is no evidence of any dispersal of the woodwaste or any effect on navigation or marine life.

At the relevant time the only permit held by the respondent under the Act was one issued on or about July 28, 1980, effective until July 25, 1981, to dump at a site in Johnstone Strait some 2.2 nautical miles from the place where the woodwaste was dumped.

In the Provincial Court of British Columbia, Schmidt Prov. Ct. J. found that the waters of Beaver Cove in which the woodwaste was dumped are within the province of British Columbia. In support of this finding he referred to the judgment of the British Columbia Court of Appeal in *Reference re Ownership of the Bed of the Strait of Georgia and Related Areas* (1976), 1 B.C.L.R. 97, in which a majority of the Court held that the waters of Johnstone Strait, of which Beaver Cove forms part, are within British Columbia. (An appeal from this judgment was subsequently dismissed by this Court in *Reference re Ownership of the Bed of the Strait of Georgia and Related Areas,* [1984] 1 S.C.R. 388.) Schmidt Prov. Ct. J. held that the regulation of the dumping of woodwaste in the respondent's log dump area in Beaver Cove, as part of the respondent's logging operations, fell within provincial legislative jurisdiction under head 92(5) of the *Constitution Act, 1867*—"The Management and Sale of Public Lands belonging to the Province and of the Timber and Wood thereon". He further held that the regulation of such dumping did not fall within federal legislative jurisdiction under head 91(10)— "Navigation and Shipping"—or under head 91(12)—"Sea Coast and Inland Fisheries". Applying this Court's judgment in *Fowler* v. *The Queen,* [1980] 2 S.C.R. 213, he concluded that s. 4(1) of the Act "makes no attempt to link the proscribed conduct to actual or potential harm to fisheries or to interference with navigation or shipping. . . .

II

As the constitutional question indicates, the issue raised by the appeal is the constitutionality of the application of s. 4(1) of the Act to the dumping of waste in waters, other than fresh waters, within a province. The respondent concedes, as it must, that Parliament has jurisdiction to regulate dumping in waters lying outside the territorial limits of any province. It also concedes that Parliament has jurisdiction to regulate the dumping of substances in provincial waters to prevent pollution of those waters that is harmful to fisheries, if the federal legislation meets the test laid down in the *Fowler* and *Northwest Falling* cases. It further concedes, in view of the opinion expressed in this Court in *Interprovincial Co-operatives Ltd.* v. *The Queen,* [1976] 1 S.C.R. 477, that Parliament has jurisdiction to regulate the dumping in provincial waters of substances that can be shown to cause pollution in extra-provincial waters. What the respondent challenges is federal jurisdiction to control the dumping in provincial waters of substances that are not shown to have a pollutant effect in extra-provincial waters. The respondent contends that on the admitted facts that is precisely the present case. The respondent submits that in so far as s. 4(1) of the Act can only be read as purporting to apply to such dumping it is *ultra vires* and, alternatively, that it should be read, if possible, so as not to apply to such dumping. In either case the appeal must fail. The Attorney General of British Columbia, who supported the attack on s. 4(1), as applied to the dumping of waste in Beaver Cove, and with whom the Attorney General of Quebec agreed, made a similar submission that s. 4(1) should be read down so as not to apply to dumping in provincial waters. . . .

In this Court the Attorney General of Canada did not contend that there was a sufficient connection between the Act and navigation to support the validity of s. 4(1) on the basis of federal jurisdiction with respect to navigation and shipping. He did submit, as I understood his argument, that there was a sufficient connection between the Act and the protection of fisheries to meet the test laid down in *Fowler* and *Northwest Falling,* but I did not understand him to place very great reliance on this submission. His principal submission in this Court was that the control of dumping in provincial marine waters, for the reasons indicated in the Act, was part of a single matter of national concern or dimension which fell within the federal peace, order and good government power. . . .

Before considering the relationship of the subject-matter of the Act to the possible bases of federal legislative jurisdiction something more should be said about the characterization of that subject-matter, according to the respective contentions of the parties. As I have indicated, the appellant contends that the Act is directed to the control or regulation of marine pollution, the subject-matter of the *Convention on the Prevention of Marine Pollution by Dumping of Wastes and other Matter*. The respondent, on the other hand, contends that by its terms the Act is directed at dumping which need not necessarily have a pollution effect. It prohibits the dumping of *any* substance, including a substance not specified in Schedule I or Schedule II, except in accordance with the terms and conditions of a permit. In my opinion, despite this apparent scope, the Act, viewed as a whole, may be properly characterized as directed to the control or regulation of marine pollution, in so far as that may be relevant to the question of legislative jurisdiction. The chosen, and perhaps only effective, regulatory model makes it necessary, in order to prevent marine pollution, to prohibit the dumping of any substance without a permit. Its purpose is to require a permit so that the regulatory authority may determine before the proposed dumping has occurred whether it may be permitted upon certain terms and conditions. The Act is concerned with the dumping of substances which may be shown or presumed to have an adverse effect on the marine environment. The Minister and not the person proposing to do the dumping must be the judge of this, acting in accordance with the criteria or factors indicated in ss. 9 and 10 and

Schedule III of the Act. There is no suggestion that the Act purports to authorize the prohibition of dumping without regard to perceived adverse effect or the likelihood of such effect on the marine environment. The nature of the marine environment and its protection from adverse effect from dumping is a complex matter which must be left to expert judgment.

III

~ Justice LeDain after reviewing the Court's decisions in *Fowler* and *Northwest Falling* holding that for legislation to be upheld under the fisheries power there must be a direct connection between the prohibited conduct and harm to fish concludes that ~

I agree with Schmidt Prov. Ct. J. and the British Columbia Court of Appeal that federal legislative jurisdiction with respect to seacoast and inland fisheries is not sufficient by itself to support the constitutional validity of s. 4(1) of the Act because that section, viewed in the context of the Act as a whole, fails to meet the test laid down in *Fowler* and *Northwest Falling*. While the effect on fisheries of marine pollution caused by the dumping of waste is clearly one of the concerns of the Act it is not the only effect of such pollution with which the Act is concerned. A basis for federal legislative jurisdiction to control marine pollution generally in provincial waters cannot be found in any of the specified heads of federal jurisdiction in s. 91 of the *Constitution Act, 1867*, whether taken individually or collectively.

IV

It is necessary then to consider the national dimensions or national concern doctrine (as it is now generally referred to) of the federal peace, order and good government power as a possible basis for the constitutional validity of s. 4(1) of the Act, as applied to the control of dumping in provincial marine waters.

The national concern doctrine was suggested by Lord Watson in the *Local Pro-hibition* case (*Attorney-General for Ontario* v. *Attorney-General for the Dominion*, [1896] A.C. 348) and given its modern formulation by Viscount Simon in *Attorney-General for Ontario* v. *Canada Temperance Federation*, [1946] A.C. 193. In *Local Prohibition*, Lord Watson said at p. 361:

Their Lordships do not doubt that some matters, in their origin local and provincial, might attain such dimensions as to affect the body politic of the Dominion, and to justify the Canadian Parliament in passing laws for their regulation or abolition in the interest of the Dominion. But great caution must be observed in distinguishing between that which is local or provincial, and therefore within the jurisdiction of the provincial legislatures, and that which has ceased to be merely local or provincial, and has become matter of national concern, in such sense as to bring it within the jurisdiction of the Parliament of Canada.

In *Canada Temperance Federation*, Viscount Simon said at pp. 205-6:

In their Lordships' opinion, the true test must be found in the real subject matter of the legislation: if it is such that it goes beyond local or provincial concern or interests and must from its inherent nature be the concern of the Dominion as a whole (as, for example, in the Aeronautics *case and the* Radio *case), then it will fall within the competence of the Dominion Parliament as a matter affecting the peace, order and good government of Canada, though it may in another aspect touch on matters specially reserved to the provincial legislatures. . . .*

This Court's conception of the national concern doctrine of the federal peace, order and good government power, as enunciated in *Canada Temperance Federation*, is to be derived from the consideration or application given to the doctrine in the following cases: *Johannesson* v. *Municipality of West St. Paul*, [1952] 1

S.C.R. 292; *Munro* v. *National Capital Commission*, [1966] S.C.R. 663; *Re: Anti-Inflation Act*, [1976] 2 S.C.R. 373; *R.* v. *Hauser, supra; Labatt Breweries of Canada Ltd.* v. *Attorney General of Canada*, [1980] 1 S.C.R. 914; *Schneider* v. *The Queen*, [1982] 2 S.C.R. 112; and *R* v. *Wetmore*, [1983] 2 S.C.R. 284.

The national concern doctrine, as enunciated in *Canada Temperance Federation*, was referred to with approval by a majority of this Court in *Johannesson* as supporting exclusive federal legislative jurisdiction with respect to the whole field of aeronautics. In *Munro*, where the *National Capital Act* was upheld on the basis of the federal peace, order and good government power, Cartwright J., delivering the unanimous judgment of the Court said that the national concern doctrine had been adopted by this Court in *Johannesson* and that the development of the National Capital Region was "a single matter of national concern" (p. 671).

The national concern doctrine was the subject of important commentary in this Court in the *Anti-Inflation Act* reference. A majority of the Court (Laskin C.J. and Martland, Judson, Ritchie, Spence, Pigeon and Dickson JJ.) upheld the Act on the basis of the emergency doctrine of the federal peace, order and good government power as legislation required to meet a "crisis" (the word used by Laskin C.J.) or "national emergency" (the words used by Ritchie J.). In the course of a comprehensive review of the judicial decision with respect to the federal peace, order and good government power, Laskin C.J., with whom Judson, Spence and Dickson JJ. concurred, referred, with implicit approval, to the dictum of Viscount Simon in *Canada Temperance Federation*, but indicated that if he found, as he did, that the Act was valid on the basis of the emergency doctrine, as "crisis" legislation, he did not intend to express an opinion as to its possible validity on the basis of the national concern doctrine, on which the Attorney General of Canada had principally relied. . . . He indicated, however, that he did not think it wise to attempt to define the scope of the federal peace, order and good government power in such precise or fixed terms as to make it incapable of application to changing or unforeseen circumstances. There is, moreover, a hint that he was disposed to seek a unified theory of the peace, order and good government power and that he regarded the emergency doctrine as a particular application of the national concern doctrine. . . .

Ritchie J., with whom Martland and Pigeon JJ. concurred, held that the validity of the Act could rest only on the emergency doctrine of the peace, order and good government power and that the national concern doctrine, in the absence of national emergency, could not give Parliament jurisdiction with respect to matters which would otherwise fall within provincial legislative jurisdiction. He said that he was in agreement with what was said by Beetz J. with reference to the national concern doctrine. Beetz J., with whom de Grandprè J. concurred, was obliged to consider the contention based on the national concern doctrine because he was of the view that the validity of the *Anti-Inflation Act* could not be supported on the basis of national emergency. He held that the national concern doctrine applied, in the absence of national emergency, to single, indivisible matters which did not fall within any of the specified heads of provincial or federal legislative jurisdiction. He held that the containment and reduction of inflation did not meet the test of singleness or indivisibility. . . .

In *Hauser*, a majority of the Court (Martland, Ritchie, Pigeon and Beetz JJ.) held that the constitutional validity of the *Narcotic Control Act* rested on the peace, order and good government power of Parliament rather than on its jurisdiction with respect to criminal law. Pigeon J., who delivered the judgment of the majority, said that the principal consideration in support of this view was that the abuse of narcotic drugs, with which the Act dealt, was a new problem which did not exist at the time of Confederation, and that since

it did not come within matters of a merely local or private nature in the province it fell within the "general residual power" in the same manner as aeronautics and radio.

In *Labatt Breweries*, in which a majority of the full Court held that certain provisions of the *Food and Drugs Act* and regulations thereunder were *ultra vires*, Estey J., with whom Martland, Dickson and Beetz JJ. concurred, had occasion to consider the peace, order and good government power as a possible basis of validity. He summed up the doctrine with respect to that basis of federal legislative jurisdiction as falling into three categories: (a) the cases "basing the federal competence on the existence of a national emergency"; (b) the cases in which "federal competence arose because the subject matter did not exist at the time of Confederation and clearly cannot be put into the class of matters of a merely local or private nature", of which aeronautics and radio were cited as examples; and (c) the cases in which "the subject matter 'goes beyond local or provincial concern or interest and must, from its inherent nature, be the concern of the Dominion as a whole' ", citing *Canada Temperance Federation*. Thus Estey J. saw the national concern doctrine enunciated in *Canada Temperance Federation* as covering the case, not of a new subject matter which did not exist at Confederation, but of one that may have begun as a matter of a local or provincial concern but had become one of national concern. He referred to that category as "a matter of national concern transcending the local authorities' power to meet and solve it by legislation", and quoted in support of this statement of the test a passage from Professor Hogg's *Constitutional Law of Canada* (1977), at p. 261, in which it was said that "the most important element of national dimension or national concern is a need for one national law which cannot realistically be satisfied by cooperative provincial action because the failure of one province to cooperate would carry with it grave consequences for the residents of other provinces."

In *Schneider*, in which the Court unanimously held that the *Heroin Treatment Act* of British Columbia was *intra vires*, Dickson J. (as he then was), with whom Martland, Ritchie, Beetz, McIntyre, Chouinard and Lamer JJ. concurred, indicated, with particular reference to the national concern doctrine and what has come to be known as the "provincial inability" test, why he was of the view that the treatment of heroin dependency, as distinct from the traffic in narcotic drugs, was not a matter falling within the federal peace, order and good government power. He referred to the problem of heroin dependency as follows at pp. 131-32:

It is largely a local or provincial problem and not one which has become a matter of national concern, so as to bring it within the jurisdiction of the Parliament of Canada under the residuary power contained in the opening words of the B.N.A. *Act (now, Constitution Act, 1867).*

There is no material before the Court leading one to conclude that the problem of heroin dependency as distinguished from illegal trade in drugs is a matter of national interest and dimension transcending the power of each province to meet and solve its own way. . . .

In *Wetmore*, where the issue was whether the federal Attorney General was entitled to conduct the prosecution of charges for violation of the *Food and Drugs Act*, Dickson J., dissenting, considered whether the applicable provisions of the *Food and Drugs Act* had their constitutional foundation in the federal criminal law power, or as was held in *Hauser* with respect to the *Narcotic Control Act*, in the peace, order and good government power. In rejecting the latter basis of jurisdiction, he referred to what was said concerning the national concern doctrine of the peace, order and good government power in the *Anti-Inflation Act* reference, *Labatt* and *Hauser* as follows at pp. 294-95:

In the Reference re Anti-Inflation Act, *[1976] 2 S.C.R. 373, Beetz J., whose judgment on this point commanded majority support, reviewed the extensive jurisprudence on the subject and concluded that the peace, order and good government power should be confined to justifying (i) temporary legislation dealing with a national emergency (p. 459) and (ii) legislation dealing with "distinct subject matters which do not fall within any of the enumerated heads of s. 92 and which, by nature, are of national concern" (p. 457). In the* Labatt *case, supra, at pp. 944-45, Estey J. divided this second heading into (i) areas in which the federal competence arises because the subject matter did not exist at the time of Confederation and cannot be classified as of a merely local and private nature and (ii) areas where the subject matter "goes beyond local or provincial concern or interests and must from its inherent nature be the concern of the Dominion as a whole". This last category is the one enunciated by Viscount Simon in* Attorney-General for Ontario v.Canada Temperance Federation, *[1946] A.C. 193, at p. 205. The one preceding it formed the basis of the majority decision in* Hauser *that the* Narcotic Control Act, *R.S.C. 1970, c. N-1, came under the peace, order and good government power as dealing with "a genuinely new problem which did not exist at the time of Confederation".*

Applying these principles to the subject matter of the *Food and Drugs Act*, Dickson J. noted that there was no question of emergency or of a new matter that did not exist at Confederation and rejected the national concern doctrine of the peace, order and good government as a basis for the constitutional validity of the provisions in question . . .

From this survey of the opinion expressed in this Court concerning the national concern doctrine of the federal peace, order and good government power I draw the following conclusions as to what now appears to be firmly established:

1. The national concern doctrine is separate and distinct from the national emergency doctrine of the peace, order and good government power, which is chiefly distinguishable by the fact that it provides a constitutional basis for what is necessarily legislation of a temporary nature;

2. The national concern doctrine applies to both new matters which did not exist at Confederation and to matters which, although originally matters of a local or private nature in a province, have since, in the absence of national emergency, become matters of national concern;

3. For a matter to qualify as a matter of national concern in either sense it must have a singleness, distinctiveness and indivisibility that clearly distinguishes it from matters of provincial concern and a scale of impact on provincial jurisdiction that is reconcilable with the fundamental distribution of legislative power under the Constitution;

4. In determining whether a matter has attained the required degree of singleness, distinctiveness and indivisibility that clearly distinguishes it from matters of provincial concern it is relevant to consider what would be the effect on extra-provincial interests of a provincial failure to deal effectively with the control or regulation of the intra-provincial aspects of the matter.

This last factor, generally referred to as the "provincial inability" test and noted with apparent approval in this Court in *Labatt, Schneider* and *Wetmore*, was suggested, as Professor Hogg acknowledges, by Professor Gibson in his article, "Measuring 'National Dimensions' " (1976), 7 *Man. L.J.* 15, as the most satisfactory rationale of the cases in which the national concern doctrine of the peace, order and good government power has been applied as a basis of federal jurisdiction. As expounded by Professor Gibson, the test would appear to involve a limited or

qualified application of federal jurisdiction. As put by Professor Gibson at pp. 34-35, "By this approach, a national dimension would exist whenever a significant aspect of a problem is beyond provincial reach because it falls within the jurisdiction of another province or of the federal Parliament. It is important to emphasize however that the entire problem would not fall within federal competence in such circumstances. Only that aspect of the problem that is beyond provincial control would do so. Since the "P.O. & G.G." clause bestows only residual powers, the existence of a national dimension justifies no more federal legislation than is necessary to fill the gap in provincial powers. For example, federal jurisdiction to legislate for pollution of interprovincial waterways or to control "pollution price-wars" would (in the absence of other independent sources of federal competence) extend only to measures to reduce the risk that citizens of one province would be harmed by the non-co-operation of another province or provinces." To similar effect, he said in his conclusion at p. 36: "Having regard to the residual nature of the power, it is the writer's thesis that 'national dimensions' are possessed by only those aspects of legislative problems which are beyond the ability of the provincial legislatures to deal because they involve either federal competence or that of another province. Where it would be possible to deal fully with the problem by co-operative action of two or more legislatures, the "national dimension" concerns only the risk of non-co-operation, and justifies only federal legislation addressed to that risk." This would appear to contemplate a concurrent or overlapping federal jurisdiction which, I must observe, is in conflict with what was emphasized by Beetz J. in the *Anti-Inflation Act* reference—that where a matter falls within the national concern doctrine of the peace, order and good government power, as distinct from the emergency doctrine, Parliament has an exclusive jurisdiction of a plenary nature to legislate in relation to that matter, including its intra-provincial aspects.

As expressed by Professor Hogg in the first and second edition of his *Constitutional Law of Canada*, the "provincial inability" test would appear to be adopted simply as a reason for finding that a particular matter is one of national concern falling within the peace, order and good government power: that provincial failure to deal effectively with the intra-provincial aspects of the matter could have an adverse effect on extra-provincial interests. In this sense, the "provincial inability" test is one of the indicia for determining whether a matter has that character of singleness or indivisibility required to bring it within the national concern doctrine. It is because of the interrelatedness of the intra-provincial and extra-provincial aspects of the matter that it requires a single or uniform legislative treatment. The "provincial inability" test must not, however, go so far as to provide a rationale for the general notion, hitherto rejected in the cases, that there must be a plenary jurisdiction in one order of government or the other to deal with any legislative problem. In the context of the national concern doctrine of the peace, order and good government power, its utility lies, in my opinion, in assisting in the determination whether a matter has the requisite singleness or indivisibility from a functional as well as a conceptual point of view. . . .

V

Marine pollution, because of its predominantly extra-provincial as well as international character and implications, is clearly a matter of concern to Canada as a whole. The question is whether the control of pollution by the dumping of substances in marine waters, including provincial marine waters, is a single, indivisible matter, distinct from the control of pollution by the dumping of substances in other provincial waters. The *Ocean Dumping Control Act* reflects a distinction between the pollution of salt water and the

pollution of fresh water. The question, as I conceive it, is whether that distinction is sufficient to make the control of marine pollution by the dumping of substances a single, indivisible matter falling within the national concern doctrine of the peace, order and good government power.

Marine pollution by the dumping of substances is clearly treated by the *Convention on the Prevention of Marine Pollution by Dumping of Wastes and other Matter* as a distinct and separate form of water pollution having its own characteristics and scientific considerations. This impression is reinforced by the United Nations Report of the Joint Group of Experts on the Scientific Aspects of Marine Pollution, Reports and Studies No. 15, *The Review of the Health of the Oceans* (UNESCO 1982) (hereinafter referred to as the "U.N. Report"), which forms part of the materials placed before the Court in the argument. It is to be noted, however, that, unlike the *Ocean Dumping Control Act*, the Convention does not require regulation of pollution by the dumping of waste in the internal marine waters of a state. Article III, para. 3, of the Convention defines the "sea" as "all marine waters other than the internal waters of the States." The internal marine waters of a state are those which lie landward of the baseline of the territorial sea, which is determined in accordance with the rules laid down in the United Nations *Convention on the Law of the Sea* (1982). The limitation of the undertaking in the Convention, presumably for reasons of state policy, to the control of dumping in the territorial sea and the open sea cannot, in my opinion, obscure the obviously close relationship, which is emphasized in the U.N. Report, between pollution in coastal waters, including the internal marine waters of a state, and pollution in the territorial sea. Moreover, there is much force, in my opinion, in the appellant's contention that the difficulty of ascertaining by visual observation the boundary between the territorial sea and the internal marine waters of a state creates an unacceptable degree of uncertainty for the application of regulatory and penal provisions. This, and not simply the possibility or likelihood of the movement of pollutants across that line, is what constitutes the essential indivisibility of the matter of marine pollution by the dumping of substances.

There remains the question whether the pollution of marine waters by the dumping of substances is sufficiently distinguishable from the pollution of fresh waters by such dumping to meet the requirement of singleness or indivisibility. In many cases the pollution of fresh waters will have a pollutant effect in the marine waters into which they flow, and this is noted by the U.N. Report, but that report, as I have suggested, emphasizes that marine pollution, because of the differences in the composition and action of marine waters and fresh waters, has its own characteristics and scientific considerations that distinguish it from fresh water pollution. Moreover, the distinction between salt water and fresh water as limiting the application of the *Ocean Dumping Control Act* meets the consideration emphasized by a majority of this Court in the *Anti-Inflation Act* reference—that in order for a matter to qualify as one of national concern falling within the federal peace, order and good government power it must have ascertainable and reasonable limits, in so far as its impact on provincial jurisdiction is concerned.

For these reasons I am of the opinion that s. 4(1) of the *Ocean Dumping Control Act* is constitutionally valid as enacted in relation to a matter falling within the national concern doctrine of the peace, order and good government power of the Parliament of Canada, and, in particular, that it is constitutional in its application to the dumping of waste in the waters of Beaver Cove. I would accordingly allow the appeal, set aside the judgments of the Court of Appeal and Schmidt Prov. Ct. J. and refer the matter back to the Provincial Court judge. The constitutional question should be answered as follows:

Is section 4(1) of the Ocean Dumping Control Act, *S.C. 1974-75-76, c. 55,* ultra vires *of the Parliament of Canada, and, in particular, is it* ultra vires *of the Parliament of Canada in its application to the dumping of waste in the waters of Beaver Cove, an area within the province of British Columbia?*

Answer: No.

The reasons of Beetz, Lamer and La Forest JJ. were delivered by

LA FOREST J. (dissenting)—The issue raised in this appeal involves the extent to which the federal Parliament may constitutionally prohibit the disposal of substances not shown to have a pollutant effect in marine waters beyond the coast but within the limits of a province. . . .

I start with the proposition that what is sought to be regulated in the present case is an activity wholly within the province, taking place on provincially owned land. Only local works and undertakings are involved, and there is no evidence that the substance made subject to the prohibition in s. 4(1) is either deleterious in any way or has any impact beyond the limits of the province. It is not difficult, on this basis, to conclude that the matter is one that falls within provincial legislative power unless it can somenow be established that it falls within Parliament's general power to legislate for the peace, order and good government of Canada.

Peace, Order and Good Government

There are several applications of the peace, order and good government power that may have relevance to the control of ocean pollution. One is its application in times of emergency. The federal Parliament clearly has power to deal with a grave emergency without regard to the ordinary division of legislative power under the Constitution. The most obvious manifestation of this power is in times of war or civil insurrection, but it has in recent years also been applied in peacetime to justify the control of rampant inflation; see *Re: Anti-Inflation Act, supra*. But while there can be no doubt that the control of ocean pollution poses a serious problem, no one has argued that it has reached such grave proportions as to require the displacement of the ordinary division of legislative power under the Constitution.

A second manner in which the power to legislate respecting peace, order and good goverment may be invoked in the present context is to control that area of the sea lying beyond the limits of the provinces. The federal government may not only regulate the territorial sea and other areas over which Canada exercises sovereignty, either under its power to legislate respecting its public property, or under the general power respecting peace, order and good government under s. 91 (*Reference re Offshore Mineral Rights of British Columbia*, [1967] S.C.R. 792) or under s. 4 of the *Constitution Act, 1871* (U.K.) 34 & 35 Vict., c. 28. I have no doubt that it may also, as an aspect of its international sovereignty, exercise legislative jurisdiction for the control of pollution beyond its borders; see *Reference re Newfoundland Continental Shelf*, [1984] 1 S.C.R. 86.

In legislating under its general power for the control of pollution in areas of the ocean falling outside provincial jurisdiction, the federal Parliament is not confined to regulating activities taking place within those areas. It may take steps to prevent activities in a province, such as dumping substances in provincial waters that pollute or have the potential to pollute the sea outside the province. Indeed, the exercise of such jurisdiction, it would seem to me, is not limited to coastal and internal waters but extends to the control of deposits in fresh water that have the effect of polluting outside a province. Reference may be made here to *Interprovincial Co-operatives Ltd.* v. *The Queen*, [1976] 1 S.C.R. 477, where a majority of this Court upheld the view that the federal Parliament had exclusive legislative jurisdiction to deal with a problem that resulted from the depositing of a pollutant in a river in one province that had injurious effects in another province. This is but an application of the doctrine of national dimensions triggering the operation of the peace, order and good government clause.

It should require no demonstration that water moves in hydrologic cycles and that effective pollution control requires regulating pollution at its source. That source may, in fact, be situated outside the waters themselves. It is significant that the provision of the *Fisheries Act* upheld by this Court in *Northwest Falling Contractors Ltd.* v. *The Queen, supra*, as a valid means of protecting the fisheries not only prohibited the depositing of a deleterious substance in water, but in any place where it might enter waters frequented by fish. Given the way substances seep into the ground and the movement of surface and ground waters into rivers and ultimately into the sea, this can potentially cover a very large area. Indeed, since the pollution of the ocean in an important measure results from aerial pollution rather than from substances deposited in waters, similar regulations could be made in respect of substances that so pollute the air as to cause damage to the ocean or generally outside the provinces. . . .

In fact, as I see it, the potential breadth of federal power to control pollution by use of its general power is so great that, even without resort to the specific argument made by the appellant, the constitutional challenge in the end may be the development of judicial strategies to confine its ambit. It must be remembered that the peace, order and good government clause may comprise not only prohibitions, like criminal law, but regulation. Regulation to control pollution, which is incidentally only part of the even larger global problem of managing the environment, could arguably include not only emission standards but the control of the substances used in manufacture, as well as the techniques of production generally, in so far as these may have an impact on pollution. This has profound implications for the federal-provincial balance mandated by the Constitution. The challenge for the courts, as in the past, will be to allow the federal Parliament sufficient scope to acquit itself of its duties to deal with national and international problems while respecting the scheme of federalism provided by the Constitution.

These considerations underline the importance of linking the prohibition to the purpose sought to be achieved. At times, that link can readily be inferred, for example in the case of dumping noxious fluid into coastal waters. In other cases, such as the depositing of noxious solid material inland, cogent proof will be required. . . .

However widely one interprets the federal power to control ocean pollution along the preceding line of analysis, it will not serve to support the provision impugned here, one that, as in the *Fowler* case, *supra*, is a blanket prohibition against depositing any substance in waters without regard to its nature or amount, and one moreover where there is, in Martland J.'s words, at p. 226 of that case, "no attempt to link the proscribed conduct to actual or potential harm" to what is sought to be protected; in *Fowler*, the fisheries, here, the ocean. As in *Fowler*, too, there is no evidence to indicate that the full range of activities caught by the provision cause the harm sought to be prevented. . . .

Why Parliament should have chosen to enact a prohibition in such broad terms is a matter upon which one is left to speculate. It may be that, in view of the lack of knowledge about the effects of various substances deposited in water, it may be necessary to monitor all such deposits. We have no evidence on the extent to which it is necessary to monitor all deposits into the sea to develop an effective regime for the prevention of ocean pollution. A system of monitoring that was necessarily incidental to an effective legislative scheme for the control of ocean pollution could constitutionally be justified. But here not only was no material advanced to establish the need for such a system, the Act goes much further and prohibits the deposit of any substance in

the sea, including provincial internal waters. If such a provision were held valid, why would a federal provision prohibiting the emission of any substance in any quantity into the air, except as permitted by federal authorities, not be constitutionally justifiable as a measure for the control of ocean pollution, it now being known that deposits from the air are a serious source of ocean pollution? . . .

Counsel for the appellant did not, of course, frame the issue in the manner in which I have thus far discussed it. I have examined it in this way, however, to show that on a more traditional approach to the underlying issues than he suggests Parliament has very wide powers to deal with ocean pollution, whether within or outside the limits of the province, but that even if one stretches this traditional approach to its limits, the impugned provision cannot constitutionally be justified. It requires a quantum leap to find constitutional justification for the provision, one, it seems to me, that would create considerable stress on Canadian federalism as it has developed over the years. What he argues for, we saw, is that the dumping of any substance in the sea beginning, apparently, from the coasts of the provinces and the mouths of provincial rivers falls exclusively within the legislative jurisdiction of Parliament as being a matter of national concern or dimension even though the sea-bed is within the province and whether or not the substance is noxious or potentially so.

Le Dain J. has in the course of his judgment discussed the cases relating to the development of the "national concern or dimension" aspect of the peace, order and good government clause, and I find it unnecessary to review that development in any detail. It is sufficient for my purpose to say that this development has since the 1930s particularly been resorted to from time to time to bring into the ambit of federal power a number of matters, such as radio (*In re Regulation and Control of Radio Cummunication in Canada*, [1932] A.C. 304), aeronautics (*Johannesson* v. *Municipality of West St. Paul*,

[1952] 1 S.C.R. 292), and the national capital region (*Munro* v. *National Capital Commission*, [1966] S.C.R. 663), that are clearly of national importance. They do not fit comfortably within provincial power. Both in their workings and in their practical implications they have predominantly national dimensions. Many of these subjects are new and are obviously of extra-provincial concern. They are thus appropriate for assignment to the general federal legislative power. They are often related to matters intimately tied to federal jurisdiction. Radio (which is relevant to the power to regulate interprovincial undertakings) is an example. The closely contested issue of narcotics control (cf. *R.* v. *Hauser*, [1979] 1 S.C.R. 984, and *Schneider* v. *The Queen*, [1982] 2 S.C.R. 112, *per* Laskin C.J.) is intimately related to criminal law and international trade.

The need to make such characterizations from time to time is readily apparent. From this necessary function, however, it is easy but, I say it with respect, fallacious to go further, and, taking a number of quite separate areas of activity, some under accepted constitutional values within federal, and some within provincial legislative capacity, consider them to be a single indivisible matter of national interest and concern lying outside the specific heads of power assigned under the Constitution. By conceptualizing broad social, economic and political issues in that way, one can effectively invent new heads of federal power under the national dimensions doctrine, thereby incidentally removing them from provincial jurisdiction or at least abridging the provinces' freedom of operation. This, as I see it, is the implication of the statement made by my colleague, then Professor Le Dain, in his article, "Sir Lyman Duff and the Constitution" (1974), 12 *Osgoode Hall L.J.* 261. He states, at p. 293:

As reflected in the Munro *case, the issue with respect to the general power, where reliance cannot be placed on the notion of emergency, is to determine what are to be considered to be single, indivis-ible matters of national interest and concern lying outside the specific heads of jurisdiction in sections 91 and 92. It is possible to invent such matters by applying new names to old legislative purposes. There is an increasing tendency to sum up a wide variety of legislative purposes in single, comprehensive designations. Control of inflation, environmental protection, and preservation of the national identity or independence are examples.*

Professor Le Dain was there merely posing the problem; he did not attempt to answer it. It seems to me, however, that some of the examples he gives, notably the control of inflation and environmental protection, are all-pervasive, and if accepted as items falling within the general power of Parliament, would radically alter the division of legislative power in Canada. The attempt to include them in the federal general power seems to me to involve fighting on another plane the war that was lost on the economic plane in the Canadian new deal cases. My colleague Beetz J. has, in *Re: Anti-Inflation Act, supra*, fully supported this way of viewing things in rejecting the control of inflation as a proper subject for incorporation into the peace, order and good government clause under the national dimension doctrine. (His was, we saw, a dissenting judgment, but on this issue too, his views were shared by a majority of the Court.) . . .

What was there said by Beetz J. seems to me to apply, *a fortiori*, to the control of the environment, a subject more germane to the present issue. All physical activities have some environmental impact. Possible legislative responses to such activities cover a large number of the enumerated legislative powers, federal and provincial. To allocate the broad subject-matter of environmental control to the federal government under its general power would effectively gut provincial legislative jurisdiction. As I mentioned before, environment protection, of course, encompasses far more than environmental pollution, which is what we are principally concerned with here. To take an example from the present context, woodwaste in some circumstances undoubtedly pollutes the environment, but the very depletion of forests itself affects the ecological balance and, as such, constitutes an environmental problem. But environmental pollution alone is itself all-pervasive. It is a by-product of everything we do. In man's relationship with his environment, waste is unavoidable. The problem is thus not new, although it is only recently that the vast amount of waste products emitted into the atmosphere or dumped in water has begun to exceed the ability of the atmosphere and water to absorb and assimilate it on a global scale. There is thus cause for concern and governments at every level have begun to deal with the many activities giving rise to problems of pollution. In Canada, both federal and provincial levels of government have extensive powers to deal with these matters. Both have enacted comprehensive and specific schemes for the control of pollution and the protection of the environment. Some environmental pollution problems are of more direct concern to the federal government, some to the provincial government. But a vast number are interrelated, and all levels of government actively co-operate to deal with problems of mutual concern; . . .

It is true, of course, that we are not invited to create a general environmental pollution power but one restricted to ocean pollution. But it seems to me that the same considerations apply. I shall, however, attempt to look at it in terms of the qualities or attributes that are said to mark the subjects that have been held to fall within the peace, order and good government clause as being matters of national concern. Such a subject, it has been said, must be marked by a singleness, distinctiveness and indivisibility that clearly distinguishes if from matters of provincial concern. In my view, ocean pollution fails to meet this test for a variety of reasons. In addition to those applicable to environmental pollution generally, the following specific difficulties may be noted. First of all, marine waters are not wholly bounded by the coast; in many areas, they extend upstream into rivers for many miles. The application of the Act appears to be restricted to waters beyond the mouths of rivers (and so intrude less on provincial powers), but this is not entirely clear, and if it is so restricted, it is not clear whether this distinction is based on convenience or constitutional imperative. Apart from this, the line between salt and fresh water cannot be demarcated clearly; it is different at different depths of water, changes with the season and shifts constantly . . . There is a constant intermixture of waters; fresh waters flow into the sea and marine waters penetrate deeply inland at high tide only to return to the sea laden with pollutants collected during their incursion inland. Nor is the pollution of the ocean confined to pollution emanating from substances deposited in water. In important respects, the pollution of the sea results from emissions into the air, which are then transported over many miles and deposited into the sea . . . I cannot, therefore, see ocean pollution as a sufficiently discrete subject upon which to found the kind of legislative power sought here. It is an attempt to create a federal pollution control power on unclear geographical grounds and limited to part only of the causes of ocean pollution. Such a power then simply amounts to a truncated federal pollution control power only partially effective to meet its supposed necessary purpose, unless of course one is willing to extend it to pollution emanating from fresh water and the air, when for reasons already given such an extension could completely swallow up provincial power, no link being necessary to establish the federal purpose.

To allocate environmental pollution exclusively to the federal Parliament would, it seems to me, involve sacrificing the principles of federalism enshrined in the Constitution. . . .

This leads me to another factor considered in identifying a subject as falling within the general federal power as a matter of national domain: its impact on provincial legislative power. Here, it must be remembered that in its supposed application within the province the provision virtually prevents a province from dealing with certain of its own public property without federal consent. A wide variety of activities along the coast or in the adjoining sea involves the deposit of some substances in the sea. In fact, where large cities like Vancouver are situated by the sea, this has substantial relevance to recreational, industrial and municipal concerns of all kinds. As a matter of fact, the most polluted areas of the sea adjoin the coast. . . . Among the major causes of this are various types of construction, such as hotels and harbours, the development of mineral resources and recreational activities. . . . These are matters of immediate concern to the province. They necessarily affect activities over which the provinces have exercised some kind of jurisdiction over the years. Whether or not the ''newness'' of the subject is a necessary criterion for inventing new areas of jurisdiction under the peace, order and good government clause, it is certainly a relevant consideration if it means removing from the provinces areas of jurisdiction which they previously exercised. As I mentioned, pollution, including coastal pollution, is no new phenomenon, and neither are many of the kinds of activities that result in pollution.

A further relevant matter, it is said, is the effect on extra-provincial interests of a provincial failure to deal effectively with the control of intra-provincial aspects of the matter. I have some difficulty following all the implications of this, but taking it at face value, we are dealing here with a situation where, as we saw earlier, Parliament has extensive powers to deal with conditions that lead to ocean pollution wherever they occur. The difficulty with the impugned provision is that it seeks to deal with activities that cannot be demonstrated either to pollute or to have a reasonable potential of polluting the ocean. The prohibition applies to an inert substance regarding which there is no proof that it either moves or pollutes. The prohibition in fact would apply to the moving of rock from one area of provincial property to another. I cannot accept that the federal Parliament has such wide legislative power over local matters having local import taking place on provincially owned property. . . .

Disposition

I would dismiss the appeal with costs and reply to the constitutional question in the affirmative.

PART TWO
RIGHTS AND FREEDOMS

A. Fundamental Rights and Freedoms in the B.N.A. Act

32. The Alberta Press Case, *1938*

~ Until 1982, the Canadian Constitution, unlike that of the United States, did not contain a comprehensive Bill of Rights protecting a list of fundamental civil liberties from legislative encroachment. The enactment of the Canadian Bill of Rights in 1960 did not change that situation. The Canadian Bill of Rights was simply a federal statute, not an amendment to the B.N.A. Act. As such, it did not apply to the provinces and even at the federal level could be set aside by ordinary federal legislation. Besides, as the cases in section B below show, the Supreme Court has been reluctant to give much weight to its provisions even when they have not been explicitly overridden by Parliament.

But the absence of a comprehensive charter of rights from the B.N.A. Act did not mean that no entrenched constitutional rights could be found in the B.N.A. Act. The mistake is often made of stating that the powers of self-government have been exhaustively distributed between the two levels of government provided for in the B.N.A. Act. According to this "exhaustion theory," the only constitutional limitation on legislative supremacy in Canada is the division of legislative powers. But this theory is a slight exaggeration. There are a few quite specific cultural rights relating to education and language which it would appear cannot be diminished by either federal or provincial legislation without a constitutional amendment. Judicial decisions interpreting these rights are included in section D below. In addition, constitutional safeguards of more fundamental rights may be implied by some of the institutional provisions of the B.N.A. Act. For instance, Section 99 providing security of tenure for the judges of Superior Courts (Canada's trial courts for the most serious civil and criminal cases) restricts the legislative powers not only of the provinces but of the federal Parliament as well.[1]

In the *Alberta Press* case, constitutional protection of another cluster of rights of fundamental importance to the practice of liberal democracy was first suggested in the reasons given by Chief Justice Duff and Justice Cannon for declaring Alberta's Accurate News and Information Act unconstitutional. The federal government had asked the Supreme Court to examine the constitutional validity of this Act along with two other Social Credit Bills enacted by the Alberta Legislature in 1937. The other two Acts concerned some of the regulations and institutions required for a Social Credit system of credit and

---

[1] See *McEvoy* v. *A.-G. New Brunswick*, Case 29 above.

exchange. The Accurate News and Information Act was designed to ensure that newspaper presentation of Social Credit policy satisfied the government's criterion of accuracy. The Supreme Court unanimously found all three Acts *ultra vires*. Only its decision on the Bank Taxation Act was appealed to the Privy Council.

Chief Justice Duff's opinion, with which Justice Davis concurred, characterized the Accurate News and Information Act as legislation affecting the "right of free public discussion of public affairs." This right, he maintained, is essential for the proper working of the parliamentary system of government called for by those sections of the B.N.A. Act vesting legislative power at the national level in a federal parliament and by the reference in the B.N.A. Act's preamble to "a constitution similar in Principle to that of the United Kingdom." He considered provincial legislation abrogating this right to be unconstitutional. He stated that the federal Parliament was empowered to protect this right, but he did not suggest that it was beyond the federal Parliament's power to restrict this right. While Justice Cannon also held that the Alberta legislation should be struck down because it interfered with the freedom of discussion essential to a democratic state, he based his opinion on more conventional division of powers grounds. Legislation curtailing freedom of the press was traditionally part of the criminal law and therefore could be enacted only by the federal Parliament under its exclusive criminal law power.

If one looks only at the Court's prior decisions, the invocation of an implied bill of rights by three of its members is somewhat surprising, especially since it was unnecessary to invalidating the legislation. As Carl Baar notes, "The Court had no record of support for civil liberties," and Justice Duff himself, a British Columbian, "had written opinions in previous years that reflected the anti-oriental sentiments of the Canadian west coast."[2] The answer to this riddle appears to lie in the political context in which the decision was made. The federal government had already disallowed earlier Social Credit legislation in Alberta and disallowance was seriously considered in this case. One argument in favour of disallowance was that it could be justified on the broad ground of protecting freedom of speech and press, while judicial invalidation was likely to focus on narrow jurisdictional considerations. On the other hand, too frequent resort to disallowance could be seen as an attack on the province by a heavy-handed central government. Ottawa chose a legal reference, but its own factum clearly invited an implied-bill-of-rights interpretation. In addition, most of the public criticism of the Press Bill was based on civil libertarian considerations. Given the widespread consensus on the importance of a free press, "it was both politically safe and politically heroic for the Supreme Court to defend civil liberties."[3] It was an inviting context for a new departure. ~

[2] Carl Baar, "Using Process Theory to Explain Judicial Decision Making," (1986), 1 *Canadian Journal of Law and Society*, 73.
[3] Ibid. p. 74.

REFERENCE RE ALBERTA STATUTES
In the Supreme Court of Canada, [1938] 2 S.C.R. 100.

DUFF C.J.:

~The Chief Justice first examined the constitutional validity of The Bank Taxation Act and the Credit of Alberta Regulation Act and concluded that both of these bills were *ultra vires*. ~

We now turn to Bill No. 9.

This Bill contains two substantive provisions. Both of them impose duties upon newspapers published in Alberta which they are required to perform on the demand of "the Chairman," who is, by the interpretation clause, the Chairman of "the Board constituted by section 3 of The Alberta Social Credit Act."

The Board, upon the acts of whose Chairman the operation of this statute depends, is, in point of law, a non-existent body (there is, in a word, no "board" in existence "constituted by section 3 of The Alberta Social Credit Act") and both of the substantive sections, sections 3 and 4, are, therefore, inoperative. The same, indeed, may be said of sections 6 and 7 which are the enactments creating sanctions. It appears to us, furthermore, that this Bill is part of the general scheme of Social Credit legislation, the basis of which is the Alberta Social Credit Act; the Bill presupposes, as a condition of its operation, that the Alberta Social Credit Act is validly enacted; and, since that Act is *ultra vires*, the ancillary and dependent legislation must fall with it.

This is sufficent for disposing of the question referred to us but, we think, there are some further observations upon the Bill which may properly be made. Under the constitution established by the British North America Act, legislative power for Canada is vested in one Parliament consisting of the Sovereign, an upper house styled the Senate, and the House of Commons. Without entering in detail upon an examination of the enactments of the Act relating to the House of Commons, it can be said that these provisions manifestly contemplate a House of Commons which is to be, as the name itself implies, a representative body; constituted, that is to say, by members elected by such of the population of the united provinces as may be qualified to vote. The preamble of the statute, moreover, shows plainly enough that the constitution of the Dominion is to be similar in principle to that of the United Kingdom. The statute contemplates a parliament working under the influence of public opinion and public discussion. There can be no controversy that such institutions derive their efficacy from the free public discussion of affairs, from criticism and answer and counter-criticism, from attack upon policy and administration and defence and counter-attack; from the freest and fullest analysis and examination from every point of view of political proposals. This is signally true in respect of the discharge by Ministers of the Crown of their responsibility to Parliament, by members of Parliament of their duty to the electors, and by the electors themselves of their responsibilities in the election of their representatives.

The right of public discussion is, of course, subject to legal restrictions; those based upon considerations of decency and public order, and others conceived for the protection of various private and public interests with which, for example, the laws of defamation and sedition are concerned. In a word, freedom of discussion means, to quote the words of Lord Wright in *James* v. *Commonwealth* ([1936] A.C. 578, at 627), "freedom governed by law."

Even within its legal limits, it is liable to abuse and grave abuse, and such abuse is constantly exemplified before our eyes; but it is axiomatic that the practice of this right of free public discussion of public affairs, notwithstanding its incidental mischiefs, is the breath of life for parliamentary institutions.

We do not doubt that (in addition to the

power of disallowance vested in the Governor-General) the Parliament of Canada possesses authority to legislate for the protection of this right. That authority rests upon the principle that the powers requisite for the protection of the constitution itself arise by necessary implication from the British North America Act as a whole (*Fort Frances Pulp & Power Co. Ltd.* v. *Manitoba Free Press Co. Ltd.* ([1923] A.C. 695)); and since the subject matter in relation to which the power is exercised is not exclusively a provincial matter, it is necessarily vested in Parliament.

But this by no means exhausts the matter. Any attempt to abrogate this right of public debate or to suppress the traditional forms of the exercise of the right (in public meeting and through the press) would, in our opinion, be incompetent to the legislatures of the provinces, or to the legislature of any one of the provinces, as repugnant to the provisions of the British North America Act, by which the Parliament of Canada is established as the legislative organ of the people of Canada under the Crown, and Dominion legislation enacted pursuant to the legislative authority given by those provisions. The subject matter of such legislation could not be described as a provincial matter purely; as in substance exclusively a matter of property and civil rights within the province, or a matter private or local within the province. It would not be, to quote the words of the judgment of the Judicial Committee in *Great West Saddlery Co.* v. *The King* ([1921] 2 A.C. 91, at 122), "legislation directed solely to the purposes specified in section 92"; and it would be invalid on the principles enunciated in that judgment and adopted in *Caron* v. *The King* ([1924] A.C. 999, at 1005-6).

The question, discussed in argument, of the validity of the legislation before us, considered as a wholly independent enactment having no relation to the Alberta Social Credit Act, present no little difficulty. Some degree of regulation of newspapers everybody would concede to the provinces. Indeed, there is a very wide field in which the provinces undoubtedly are invested with legislative authority over newspapers; but the limit, in our opinion, is reached when the legislation effects such a curtailment of the exercise of the right of public discusssion as substantially to interfere with the working of the parliamentary institutions of Canada as contemplated by the provisions of the British North America Act and the statutes of the Dominion of Canada. Such a limitation is necessary, in our opinion, "in order," to adapt the words quoted above from the judgment in *Bank of Toronto* v. *Lambe* ((1887) 12 A.C. 575), "to afford scope" for the working of such parliamentary institutions. In this region of constitutional practice, it is not permitted to a provincial legislature to do indirectly what cannot be done directly (*Great West Saddlery Co.* v. *The King*).

Section 129 of the British North America Act is in these words:

129. Except as otherwise provided by this Act, all Laws in force in Canada, Nova Scotia or New Brunswick, at the Union, and all Courts of Civil and Criminal Jurisdiction, and all legal Commissions, Powers, and Authorities, and all Officers, Judicial, Administrative, and Ministerial, existing therein at the Union, shall continue in Ontario, Quebec, Nova Scotia, and New Brunswick respectively, as if the Union had not been made; subject nevertheless (except with respect to such as are enacted by or exist under Acts of the Parliament of Great Britain or of the Parliament of the United Kingdom of Great Britain and Ireland), to be repealed, abolished, or altered by the Parliament of Canada, or by the Legislature of the respective Province, according to the Authority of the Parliament or of that Legislature under this Act.

The law by which the right of public discussion is protected existed at the time of the enactment of the British North America Act and, as far as Alberta is concerned, at the date on which the Alberta Act came into force, the 1st of

September, 1905. In our opinion (on the broad principle of the cases mentioned which has been recognized as limiting the scope of general words defining the legislative authority of the Dominion) the Legislature of Alberta has not the capacity under section 129 to alter that law by legislation obnoxious to the principle stated.

The legislation now under consideration manifestly places in the hands of the Chairman of the Social Credit Commission autocratic powers which, it may well be thought, could, if arbitrarily wielded, be employed to frustrate in Alberta these rights of the Crown and the people of Canada as a whole. We do not, however, find it necessary to express an opinion upon the concrete question whether or not this particular measure is invalid as exceeding the limits indicated above.

The answer to the question concerning this Bill is that it is *ultra vires*.

CANNON J.:

~The learned judge first examined the Bank Taxation Act and the Credit of Alberta Regulation Act and concluded that both were *ultra vires*.~

The third question put to us is the following:

Is Bill No. 9 entitled "An Act to ensure the Publication of Accurate News and Information," or any of the provisions thereof in what particular or particulars or to what extent intra vires *of the legislature of the province of Alberta? . . .*

The preamble of the bill, which I will hereafter call the "Press bill" recites that it is

expedient and in the public interest that the newspapers published in the Province should furnish to the people of the Province statements made by the authority of the Government of the Province as to the true and exact objects of the policy of the Government and as to the hindrances to or difficulties in achieving such objects to the end that the people may be informed with respect thereto.

Section 3 provides that any proprietor, editor, publisher or manager of any newspaper published in the province shall, when required to do so by the Chairman of the Board constituted by section 3 of the Alberta Social Credit Act, publish in that newspaper any statement furnished by the Chairman which has for its object the correction or amplification of any statement relating to any policy or activity of the government of the province published by that newspaper within the next preceding thirty-one days.

And section 4 provides that the proprietor, etc., of any newspaper upon being required by the Chairman in writing shall within twenty-four hours after the delivery of the requirement

make a return in writing setting out every source from which any information emanated, as to any statement contained in any issue of the newspaper published within sixty days of the making of the requirement and the names, addresses and occupations of all persons by whom such information was furnished to the newspaper and the name and address of the writer of any editorial, article or news item contained in any such issue of the newspaper.

Section 5 denies any action for libel on account of the publication of any statement pursuant to the Act.

Section 6 enacts that in the event of a proprietor, etc., of any newspaper being guilty of any contravention of any of the provisions of the Act, the Lieutenant-Governor-in-Council, upon a recommendation of the Chairman, may by order prohibit,

(a) *the publication of such newspaper either for a definite time or until further order;*

(b) *the publication in any newspaper of anything written by any person specified in the order;*

(c) *the publication of any information emanating from any person or source specified in the order.*

Section 7 provides for penalties for contraventions or defaults in complying with any requirement of the Act.

The policy referred to in the preamble of the Press bill regarding which the people of the province are to be informed from the government standpoint, is undoubtedly the Social Credit policy of the government. The administration of the bill is in the hands of the Chairman of the Social Credit Board who is given complete and discretionary power by the bill. "Social Credit," according to sec. 2(*b*) of ch. 3, 1937, second session, of the Alberta Social Credit Amendment Act is

the power resulting from the belief inherent within society that its individual members in association can gain the objectives they desire;

and the objectives in which the people of Alberta must have a firm and unshaken belief are the monetization of credit and the creation of a provincial medium of exchange instead of money to be used for the purposes of distributing to Albertans loans without interest, per capita dividends and discount rates to purchase goods from retailers. This free distribution would be based on the unused capacity of the industries and people of the province of Alberta to produce goods and services, which capacity remains unused on account of the lack or absence of purchasing power in the consumers in the province. The purchasing power would equal or absorb this hitherto unused capacity to produce goods and services by the issue of Treasury Credit certificates against a Credit Fund or Provincial credit account established by the Commission each year representing the monetary value of this "unused capacity"—which is also called "Alberta credit."

It seems obvious that this kind of credit cannot succeed unless every one should be induced to believe in it and help it along. The word "credit" comes from the latin: *credere*, to believe. It is, therefore, essential to control the sources of information of the people of Alberta, in order to keep them immune from any vacillation in their absolute faith in the plan of the government. The Social Credit doctrine must become, for the people of Alberta, a sort of religious dogma of which a free and uncontrolled discussion is not permissible. The bill aims to control any statement relating to any policy or activity of the government of the province and declares this object to be a matter of public interest. The bill does not regulate the relations of the newspapers' owners with private individual members of the public, but deals exclusively with expressions of opinion by the newspapers concerning government policies and activities. The pith and substance of the bill is to regulate the press of Alberta from the viewpoint of public policy by preventing the public from being misled or deceived as to any policy or activity of the Social Credit Government and by reducing any opposition or bring upon it ridicule and public contempt.

I agree with the submission of the Attorney General of Canada that this bill deals with the regulation of the press of Alberta, not from the viewpoint of private wrongs or civil injuries resulting from any alleged infringement or privation of civil rights which belong to individuals, considered as individuals, but from the viewpoint of public wrongs or crimes, i.e., involving a violation of the public rights and duties to the whole community, considered as a community, in its social aggregate capacity.

Do the provisions of this bill, as alleged by the Attorney General of Canada, invade the domain of criminal law and trench upon the exclusive legislative jurisdiction of the Dominion in this regard?

The object of an amendment of the criminal law, as a rule, is to deprive the citizen of the right to do that, apart from the amendment, he could lawfully do. Sections 130 to 136 of the Criminal Code deal with seditious words and seditious publications; and sect. 133(*a*) reads as follows:

No one shall be deemed to have a sedi-

tious intention only because he intends in good faith,—

> (a) *to show that His Majesty has been misled or mistaken in his measures; or*
> (b) *to point out errors or defects in the* government *or constitution of the United Kingdom, or of any part of it, or of Canada or any province* thereof, *or in either House of Parliament of the United Kingdom or of Canada, or in any legislature, or in the administration of justice; or to excite His Majesty's subjects to attempt to procure, by lawful means, the alteration of any matter of state; or*
> (c) *to point out, in order to their removal, matters which are producing or have a tendency to produce feelings of hatred and ill-will between different classes of His Majesty's subjects.*

It appears that in England, at first, criticism of any government policy was regarded as a crime involving severe penalties and punishable as such; but since the passing of Fox's Libel Act in 1792, the considerations now found in the above article of our criminal code that it is not criminal to point out errors in the Government of the country and to urge their removal by lawful means have been admitted as a valid defence in a trial for libel.

Now, it seems to me that the Alberta legislature by this retrograde Bill is attempting to revive the old theory of the crime of seditious libel by enacting penalties, confiscation of space in newspaper and prohibitions for actions which, after due consideration by the Dominion Parliament, have been declared innocuous and which, therefore, every citizen of Canada can do lawfully and without hindrance or fear of punishment. It is an attempt by the legislature to amend the Criminal Code in this respect and to deny the advantage of sect. 133(a) to the Alberta newspaper publishers.

Under the British system, which is ours, no political party can erect a prohibitory barrier to prevent the electors from getting information concerning the policy of the government. Freedom of discussion is essential to enlighten public opinion in a democratic State; it cannot be curtailed without affecting the right of the people to be informed through sources independent of the government concerning matters of public interest. There must be an untrammelled publication of the news and political opinions of the political parties contending for ascendancy. As stated in the preamble of the British North America Act, our constitution is and will remain, unless radically changed, "similar in principle to that of the United Kingdom." At the time of Confederation, the United Kingdom was a democracy. Democracy cannot be maintained without its foundation: free public opinion and free discussion throughout the nation of all matters affecting the State within the limits set by the criminal code and the common law. Every inhabitant in Alberta is also a citizen of the Dominion. The province may deal with his property and civil rights of a local and private nature within the province; but the province cannot interfere with his status as a Canadian citizen and his fundamental right to express freely his untrammelled opinion about government policies and discuss matters of public concern. The mandatory and prohibitory provisions of the Press Bill are, in my opinion, *ultra vires* of the provincial legislature. They interfere with the free working of the political organization of the Dominion. They have a tendency to nullify the political rights of the inhabitants of Alberta, as citizens of Canada, and cannot be considered as dealing with matters purely private and local in that province. The federal parliament is the sole authority to curtail, if deemed expedient and in the public interest, the freedom of the press in discussing public affairs and the equal rights in that respect of all citizens throughout the Dominion. These subjects were matters of criminal law before Confederation, have been recognized by Parliament as criminal matters and have been expressly dealt with by the criminal code. No province has the power to reduce in that province the political rights of its citizens as compared with those enjoyed by the citizens of other provinces of Canada. Moreover, citizens outside the province of Alberta have a vital interest in having full information and comment, favourable and unfavourable, regarding the policy of the Alberta government and concerning events in that province which would, in the ordinary course, be the subject of Alberta newspapers' news items and articles.

I would, therefore, answer the question as to Bill No. 9 in the negative.

~Justice Davis concurred with Chief Justice Duff. Justices Kerwin, Crocket, and Hudson all concluded that the three bills were *ultra vires*. However their conclusion that the Press Bill was *ultra vires* was based not on the considerations regarding freedom of the press advanced by Chief Justice Duff and Justice Cannon, but on the much narrower grounds that the Act was ancillary to and dependent upon the Alberta Social Credit Act which was itself *ultra vires*.~

33. Saumur *v.* Quebec and Attorney General of Quebec, *1953*

~ In the 1950s the Supreme Court decided seven Quebec appeals which raised important civil liberties issues. All involved policies of the Quebec government directed against political or religious minorities in the Province of Quebec. In all seven the Supreme Court reversed the Quebec Court of Appeal and upheld the claim of the political or religious minority against the Quebec government. Only three of the cases involved a constitutional challenge based on the B.N.A. Act.[1] The cases indicated that despite the absence of either a constitutional or statutory Bill of Rights the Canadian legal system provided considerable protection for the communicative freedoms of unpopular minorities at least from attacks by oppressive provincial governments.

In the *Saumur* case, a Jehovah's Witness challenged the constitutional validity of a Quebec City by-law passed under the Charter of the City of Quebec, prohibiting the distribution in the streets of any book, pamphlet or tract without the permission of the Chief of Police. But the significance of this case went far beyond the immediate question of the validity of the Quebec City by-law. As far as the Jehovah's Witnesses were concerned it was designed to test the general competence of the provinces to restrict a Canadian citizen's rights to freedom of expression and freedom of religious practice. Saumur claimed that these rights were guaranteed by the constitution, referring in particular to the preamble of the B.N.A. Act, and also by statute, referring here to a number of Acts including the Freedom of Worship Act, a pre-Confederation Canadian statute which had been re-enacted by the Quebec Legislature in 1941. Saumur's action was rejected in the Superior Court of Quebec and his appeal against this judgment had been dismissed by the Quebec Court of Queen's Bench.

Before the Supreme Court of Canada Saumur was more successful—at least on the immediate issue. By a five-to-four majority the Supreme Court ruled that the by-law did not operate so as to prevent Saumur from distributing his tracts. Four of the five judges who made up the majority (Justices Rand, Locke, Kellock, and Estey) rested their conclusion on the broad grounds that it was beyond the jurisdiction of a province to restrict freedom of religious expression. But the deciding vote was cast by Justice Kerwin and his decision was based on the very different grounds that the by-law, although *intra vires*, must not conflict with the Freedom of Worship Act. Contrary to the view of the other

---

[1] Two of the constitutional cases, *Saumur* and *Switzman*, are reproduced here (cases 30 and 31) and the third, *Birks*, is discussed in the introduction to the *Switzman* case. The other four cases were *Boucher* v. *The King*, [1951] S.C.R. 265 (interpretation of the seditious libel section of the Criminal Code), *Chaput* v. *Romain*, [1955] S.C.R. 834 (police powers to break up religious meetings) *Roncarelli* v. *Duplessis*, [1959] S.C.R. 121 (the Premier of Quebec's power to remove a restaurant liquor license because of his disapproval of the proprietor's political activities), and *Lamb* v. *Benoit*, [1959] S.C.R. 321 (police power to detain persons for distributing pamphlets considered by the police to be seditious).

members of the majority, Justice Kerwin held that the matter of religious freedom (as well as freedom of the press) was subject to provincial jurisdiction. His opinion would consequently entitle the Quebec Legislature to amend the Freedom of Worship Act so as to exclude sects like the Jehovah's Witnesses from its protection. Indeed under the leadership of Premier Duplessis the Quebec Legislature lost little time in taking advantage of the loop-hole created by Justice Kerwin's opinion and shortly after this decision amended the Freedom of Worship Act so that it would not apply to the distribution of Jehovah's Witness literature. Saumur initiated action to have this amendment declared unconstitutional. But the Supreme Court of Canada upheld a decision of the Quebec Court of Appeal dismissing the action on the grounds that, since the new legislation had not actually been applied against the Jehovah's Witnesses, the case did not involve a real dispute or *lis* but only an academic question.

On the larger issue of the constitutional status of civil liberties, the Supreme Court's decision in the *Saumur* case was inconclusive and confusing. Three sharply contrasting views were expressed on the general relationship of civil liberties to the divison of powers and not one of these views could command the support of a majority. At one extreme, three judges (Chief Justice Rinfret and Justices Taschereau and Kerwin) adopted the completely novel position that freedom of religious practice was subject to provincial jurisdiction, holding that religious freedom was a "civil right in the province" and hence as a subject matter of legislation fell under 92(13). In direct contradiction of this, four judges (Justices Rand, Locke, Kellock, and Estey) denied that the phrase "civil rights" in 92(13) embraced such rights as the right to the free exercise of one's religion. On a number of grounds they held that the B.N.A. Act removed from the provinces the power of legislating for the purpose of curtailing religious freedom. All four of these judges cited the preamble of the B.N.A. Act in support of their conclusion and two (Justices Rand and Locke) explicitly associated freedom of religious expression with the rights which Chief Justice Duff in *Reference re Alberta Statutes* had deduced from the preamble. Justices Locke and Estey considered that the power of limiting religious freedom lay exclusively with Parliament under its "criminal law" power. Three members of this group also cited the safeguards provided by section 93 of the B.N.A. Act against provincial infringement of the educational rights of religious denominations as implying that the provinces have no jurisdiction in relation to religious freedom. Finally an intermediate position adopted by Justices Cartwright and Fauteux would deny that a question of civil liberties might be considered to be the main ingredient of a piece of legislation for the purpose of bringing it under one of the heads of power in the B.N.A. Act. Restrictions on civil liberties might be incidental effects of laws but not their pith and substance. Thus both Parliament and the provinces could validly limit freedom of worship providing they did so in the course of legislating on some other subject which lay within their respective powers. ~

SAUMUR *v.* QUEBEC AND ATTORNEY GENERAL OF QUEBEC
In the Supreme Court of Canada, [1953] 2 S.C.R. 299.

RINFRET C.J. (*dissenting*): Dépouillée de son extravagante mise-en-scène et réduit à sa véritable dimension, cette cause, à mon avis, est vraiment très simple. Elle n'a sûrement pas l'ampleur et l'importance qu'ont tenté de lui donner les Témoins de Jéhovah par le truchement de M. Laurier Saumur, l'appelant, se désignant comme un missionnaire-évangéliste.

Il s'agit de la validité d'un règlement municipal et il y a probablement eu des centaines et des centaines de causes de ce genre depuis la Confédération. Si, par contre, cette catégorie de causes n'a pas été soumise trés fréquemment à la Cour Suprème du Canada, c'est uniquement à raison de son peu d'importance relative et de son application restreinte, dans chaque cas, au territoire de la municipalité concernée.

Voice le texte du règlement attaqué:

Règlement n° 184

1° Il est, par le présent règlement, défendu de distribuer dans les rues de la Cité de Québec, aucun livre, pamphlet, brochure, circulaire, fascicule quelconque sans avoir au préalable obtenu pour ce faire la permission par écrit du Chef de Police.

2° Toute personne qui contreviendra au présent règlement sera passible d'une amende avec ou sans les frais, et à défaut du paiement immédiat de ladite amende avec ou sans les frais, selon le cas, d'un emprisonnement, le montant de ladite amende et le terme d'emprisonnement à être fixé par la Cour du Recorder de la Cité de Québec, à sa discrétion; mais ladite amende ne dépassera pas cent dollars, et l'emprisonnement n'excédera pas trois mois de calendrier; ledit emprisonnement cependant, devant cesser en tout temps avant l'expiration du terme fixé par le paiement de ladite amende et des frais, selon le cas; et si l'infraction est réitérée, cette récidive constituera, jour par jour, après sommation ou arrestation, une offense séparée.

L'appelant, invoquant sa qualité de sujet de Sa Majesté le Roi et de résident dans la Cité de Québec, alléguant en outre qu'il est un missionnaire-évangéliste et l'un des Témoins de Jéhovah, déclare qu'il considère de son devoir de prêcher la Bible, soit oralement, soit en distribuant des publications sous forme de livres, opuscules, périodiques, feuillets, etc., de maison en maison et dans les rues.

Il prétend que le règlement n° 184, reproduit plus haut, a pour effet de rendre illégale cette distribution de littérature sans l'approbation écrite du Chef de Police de la Cité de Québec. Il ajoute qu'en sa qualité de citoyen canadien il a un droit absolu à l'expression de ses opinions et que cela découle de son droit à la liberté de parole, la liberté de la presse et le libre exercice de son culte envers Dieu, tel que garanti par la Constitution britannique non écrite, par l'Acte de l'Amérique britannique du Nord généralement, et également par les Statuts de la province de Québec, spécialement la "Loi concernant la liberté des cultes et le bon ordre dans les églises et leurs alentours" (S.R.Q. 1941, c. 307).

Il allègue que la Cité de Québec et la province de Québec n'ont aucune juridiction, soit en loi, soit constitutionnellement, pour adopter un règlement tel que ci-dessus, et que ce dernier est *ultra vires*, inconstitutionnel, illégal et nul. . . .

. . . L'intimée, la Cité de Québec, a plaidé que le règlement n° 184 était une loi municipale légalement passée dans l'exercice des pouvoirs de règlementation de la Cité et conforme à son acte d'incorporation; que la loi de la province, en vertu de laquelle le règlement a été adopté, est constitutionnelle, légale et valide; que le règlement concerne la propreté, le bon ordre, la paix et la sécurité publiques, la prévention de troubles et émeutes et se rapporte à l'économie intérieure et au bon gouvernement local de la ville; que le demandeur a systématiquement contrevenu à ce règlement de façon délibérée et s'est obstinément refusé à s'y soumettre; qu'il n'a jamais demandé et, par conséquent, n'a pu obtenir de permis pour distribuer ses pamphlets dans la ville de Québec et qu'il a ignoré d'une manière absolue si le règlement est susceptible de le priver d'aucun de ses droits, ayant préféré y désobéir de son plein gré. . . .

La plaidoirie écrite allègue, en outre, que l'appelant n'est pas un ministre du culte et que l'organisation dont il fait partie n'est pas une église ni une religion. Au contraire, les pamphlets ou tracts qu'il insiste à distribuer sans autorisation ont caractère provocateur et injurieux, ne sont pas des gestes religieux mais des actes anti-sociaux qui étaient et sont de nature à troubler la paix publique et la tranquillité et la sécurité des paisibles citoyens dans la Cité de Québec, où ils risquent de provoquer des désordres. Il est malvenu en fait et en droit d'invoquer des libertés de parole, de presse et de culte, qui ne sont aucunement concernées en l'occurrence; il n'a jamais été persécuté et, si la Cité de Québec a mis en vigueur son règlement, ce ne fut que pour remplir ses obligations envers le bien commun, l'ordre public exigeant que le règlement soit dûment appliqué dans la Cité.

Après une longue enquête et la production de quelque chose comme soixante-quinze exhibits, avec en plus des mémoires rédigés par l'abbé Gagné, le très révérend Doyen Evans, le rabbin Frank et M. Damien Jasmin, le juge de première instance a maintenu la défense et rejeté l'action de l'appelant. Ce jugement a été confirmé dans son intégrité par la Cour du Banc de la Reine (en appel). . . .

~The Chief Justice then listed the powers asserted in the Cities and Towns Act. These included the power of regulating the distribution of literature in the streets.~

Il est non moins clair que l'Acte de l'Amérique britannique du Nord 1867, dans la distribution qu'elle fait des pouvoirs législatifs, aux paragraphes 91 et 92 attribue, dans chaque province, à la Législature, le pouvoir exclusif de faire des lois relatives aux institutions municipales dans la province (par. 8), à la propriété et les droits civils dans la province (par. 13) et généralement à toutes les matières d'une nature purement locale et privée dans la province (par. 16).

Il serait vraiment fantastique de prétendre que quelques-uns des pouvoirs ci-dessus mentionnés et que l'on trouve dans la "Loi des Cités et Villes" de la province de Québec, pourraient relever du domaine fédéral. Je ne me représente pas facilement le Parlement fédéral entreprenant d'adopter des lois sur aucune de ces matières (Voir le jugement du Conseil Privé dans *Hodge* v. *The Queen* ((1883) 9 App. Cas. 117, 131, 133, 134)).

Je ne comprends pas, d'ailleurs, que le procureur de l'appelant dirige son argumentation à l'encontre de ce principe général. Il demande à la Cour de s'écarter du texte du règlement et il cherche à y trouver un motif qui serait celui, qu'il avait déjà allégué dans sa déclaration, "que ce règlement avait été passé spécialement dans le but de limiter les activités du demandeur et des Témoins de Jéhovah."

Il est à remarquer que le règlement lui-même ne dit rien de tel; il s'applique à tous, quelle que soit leur nationalité, leur doctrine ou leur religion. Mais, en plus, le juge de première instance a décidé en fait qu'il "n'a pas été prouvé que ce règlement avait été passé spécialement dans ce but." D'autre part, en matière d'excès de pouvoirs, c'est toujours au mérite ("pith and substance") de la législation qu'il faut s'arrêter. Ce que le règlement vise est uniquement l'usage des rues pour fins de distribution. En outre que, ainsi que l'a décidé le juge de la Cour Supérieure, aucun motif, aucune arrière-pensée n'a été dévoilée par la preuve faite à l'enquête, c'est une idée erronée que de chercher à attribuer un motif à une loi qui n'en mentionne pas. Un règlement peut être valide même si le but du conseil municipal est mauvais. . . .

. . . La seule question que les tribunaux ont à examiner est celle de savoir si la Cité de Québec avait le pouvoir d'adopter ce règlement. Nous n'avons pas à chercher derrière le texte qu'elle a adopté pour voir quel a pu être son but en ce faisant. J'irai même plus loin et je dirai que l'usage des rues d'une municipalité est indiscutablement une question du domaine municipal et une question locale. Je cherche encore en vertu de quoi on pourrait prétendre que cette matière ne tombe pas exclusivement dans la catégorie des sujets attribués aux provinces en vertu de l'article 92 de l'Acte de l'Amérique britannique du Nord; et, dans ce cas, même s'il est admis que le droit de culte est du domaine fédéral, le pouvoir de contrôle des rues municipales, étant un sujet spécifiquement attribué aux provinces, il aurait préséance sur le pouvoir supposé du Parlement fédéral de légiférer en matière de culte. Il est de jurisprudence constante que du moment qu'un sujet est spécialement attribué au domaine provincial par l'article 92, il a préséance et priorité sur tout pouvoir que prétendrait exercer le fédéral, en vertu des pouvoirs généraux mentionnés dans l'article 91. . . .

. . . Ironie du sort, les Témoins de Jéhovah qui, dans leurs publications, affirment catégoriquement non seulement qu'ils ne constituent pas une religion, mais qu'ils sont opposés à toute religion et que les religions sont une invention du démon, sont maintenant devant les tribunaux du Canada pour demander protection au nom de la religion; et, à cette fin, à l'encontre de la constitutionnalité des lois municipales de la province de Québec, ils sont contraints d'invoquer une loi de la province de Québec, à savoir: la Loi concernant la liberté des cultes et du bon ordre dans les églises et leurs alentours (c. 307, S.R.Q. 1941).

Cette loi, invoquée par eux, contient l'article suivant:

2. La jouissance et le libre exercice du culte de toute profession religieuse, sans distinction ni préférence, mais de manière à ne pas servir d'excuse à la licence ni à autoriser des pratiques incompatibles avec la paix et la sûreté de la province, sont permis par la constitution et les lois

de cette province à tous les sujets de Sa Majesté qui y vivent. S.R. 1925, c. 198, a.2.

C'est bien ainsi que l'appelant a posé le problème dans sa déclaration:

. . . his unqualified right as a Canadian citizen to the expression of his views on the issues of the day and in employing thereby his right of freedom of speech, freedom of the press and free exercise of worship of Almighty God as guaranteed by the unwritten British Constitution, by the provisions of the British North America Act generally and, in particular, in its preamble and sections 91, 92 and 129, as well as by the statute of the Province of Quebec generally and in particular, by "An Act Respecting Peddlers," (R.S.Q. 1941, Chapter 230, especially section 8 thereof); and by "An Act Respecting Licences," (R.S.Q. 1941, Chapter 76, especially section 82 thereof); and by "An Act Respecting Freedom of Worship and the Maintenance of Good Order In and Near Places of Public Worship," (R.S.Q. 1941, Chapter 307, especially section 2 thereof);

Il n'y a pas lieu de s'arrêter à la référence à la Loi concernant les colporteurs et à la Loi des licences.

Le procureur de l'appelant ne s'est pas non plus expliqué sur ce qu'il entend par "the unwritten British Constitution" comme gouvernant les pouvoirs respectifs du Parlement canadien et des Législatures provinciales (tels qu'ils sont définis dans les articles 91 et 92 de l'Acte de l'Amérique britannique du Nord). C'est cette loi qui contient la Constitution du Canada et le Conseil Privé, à plusieurs reprises, a déclaré que les pouvoirs ainsi distribués entre le Parlement et les législatures couvraient absolument tous les pouvoirs que pouvait exercer le Canada comme entité politique. Mais l'appelant prétend que la question de l'exercice du culte est exclusivement de la juridiction du Parlement fédéral et, en particulier, que les prescriptions du règlement attaqué seraient couvertes par le début de l'article

91 qui autorise l'adoption de "lois pour la paix, l'ordre et le bon gouvernement du Canada," ou la "Loi criminelle."

Au sujet de la première prétention, il suffit de poursuivre la lecture de l'article 91 pour constater que le pouvoir du Parlement fédéral relativement à la paix, l'ordre et le bon gouvernement du Canada se bornent à toutes les matières ne tombant pas dans les "catégories de sujets exclusivement assignés par le présent acte aux Législatures des provinces." Comme il a été invariablement décidé par le Conseil Privé et conformément, d'ailleurs, au texte précis que nous venons de citer, dès que la matière est couverte par l'un des paragraphes de l'article 92, elle devient du domaine exclusif des législatures de chaque province et elle est soustraite à juridiction du Parlement fédéral. Naturellement, nous ne parlons plus ici du contrôle des rues municipales, car il est évident que, dans ce cas, les paragraphes 8, 13 et 16 de l'article 92 (comme d'ailleurs nous l'avons vu plus haut) attribuent cette juridiction exclusivement aux législatures. Mais, si nous comprenons bien la prétention, c'est que la garantie de l'exercice du culte doit venir du Parlement fédéral et n'appartient pas aux législatures. Nous disons bien qu'elle doit venir, car il est très certain que, pour le moment, elle n'existe pas ailleurs que dans la "Loi concernant la liberté des cultes" invoquée par l'appelant dans sa déclaration (S.R.Q. 1941, c. 307).

La difficulté qu'éprouve ici l'appelant résulte de plusiers raisons:

Premièrement:—Son droit de distribuer des pamphlets religieux ne constitue pas l'exercice d'un culte d'une profession religieuse.

Deuxièmement:—A tout événement, la jouissance et le libre exercice du culte d'une profession religieuse ne jouit pas, en vertu du chapitre 307, S.R.Q. 1941, d'une autorisation absolue, mais il faut que ce culte s'exerce "de manière à ne pas servir d'excuse à la licence, ni à autoriser des pratiques incompatibles avec la paix et la sûreté de la province."

Troisièmement:—L'exercice du culte est un droit civil et, par conséquent, tombe sous le paragraphe 13 de l'article 92 de l'Acte de l'Amérique britannique du Nord. Il est donc du domaine provincial.

Le premier point ci-dessus depend d'une question de fait. Or, l'appelant a fait entendre comme témoin un monsieur Hayden C. Covington, qui s'est décrit comme "ordained minister of the gospel, and lawyer, 124 Columbia Heights, Brooklyn, New York." Au cours de ce témoignage, ce témoin a identifié un nombre considérable de publications dont il a déclaré qu'elles contenaient la doctrine des Témoins de Jéhovah, en ajoutant: "They comprise the official view, doctrines and principles advocated and taught by Jehovah's Witnesses at the date of publication of each of such books." Or, dans toutes ces publications, il est affirmé que les Témoins de Jéhovah ne sont pas une religion; que, au contraire, leur but est de combattre toutes les religions et que la religion est une invention du démon. . . .

. . . Pour ce qui est du deuxième point ci-dessus mentionné, il faut réitérer que l'article 2 du chapitre 307 ne permet pas la jouissance et le libre exercice du culte d'une profession religieuse d'une façon absolue. Il faut que cela ne "serve pas d'excuse à la licence, ni à des pratiques incompatibles avec la paix et la sûreté de la province." C'est le texte même de la loi.

Si donc, à l'encontre de la preuve, il fallait décider que les Témoins de Jéhovah pratiquent un culte, il n'en faudrait pas moins, en vertu du texte de la Loi concernant la liberté des cultes, que la province ou la municipalité ait le droit de contrôler cet exercice "de mainère à ne pas servir d'excuse à la licence, ni à autoriser des pratiques incompatibles avec la paix et la sûreté de la province."

Puisque les Témoins de Jéhovah prétendent que leur profession religieuse consiste à distribuer des tracts religieux, il s'ensuit que la province ou la municipalité, à laquelle la province délègue ce pouvoir, a le droit d'examiner les pamphlets religieux que l'on entend distribuer, de façon á en autoriser ou non la distribution.

A cet égard, je le répète, les Témoins de Jéhovah, ayant pris la position qu'ils ne demanderaient pas l'autorisation et qu'ils ne soumettraient pas la littérature qu'ils voulaient distribuer, nous n'avons aucune preuve au dossier susceptible de nous permettre de savoir si cette littérature tombait ou non dans les exceptions prévues par l'article 2 du chapitre 307. Mais, si nous nous croyions justifiés de prendre pour acquit que cette littérature serait de la même nature que les livres et les tracts qui ont été produits au dossier, ou encore qu'elle contiendrait les déclarations faites par le vice-président Covington, il serait inconcevable qu'une municipalité ne put empêcher la circulation dans ses rues de cette littérature que son conseil pourrait certainement considérer comme constituant de la licence ou des pratiques incompatibles avec la paix et la sûreté de la province; et, dès lors, comme tombant dans l'exception exprimée dans l'article 2.

Voice, en effet, ce qu'on trouve dans le témoignage de M. Covington:

Q. Are you informed that the religion of a greater part of the people in this province and in this city is Roman Catholic?—A. Yes, I have that information.

En fait, il est notoire que 90 pour cent de la population de la Cité de Québec est catholique romaine et 45 pour cent de la population du Canada appartient à la même religion.

On lui demande alors de lire les passages suivants des publications des Témoins de Jéhovah:

. . . Religion is the adulteress and idolatress that befriends and commits religious fornication with the political and commercial elements. She is the lover of this world and blesses the world from the balcony of the Vatican and in the pulpits. Religion, whose most powerful representative has ruled from Rome for sixteen centuries, traces her origin all the way back to Babylon of Nimrod's found-

ing, and organized religion deservedly bears the name Babylon. . . . I will shew unto thee the judgment of the great whore (or idolatress) that sitteth upon many waters: with whom the kings of the earth have committed fornication, and the inhabitants of the earth have been made drunk with the wine of her fornication . . . full of abominations and filthiness of her fornication; and upon her forehead was a name written, MYSTERY, BABYLON THE GREAT, THE MOTHER OF HARLOTS AND ABOMINATIONS OF THE EARTH.

Les citations qui précèdent sont tirées de l'exhibit D-49, aux pages 345 et 346.

Après avoir mis le témoin Covington en présence des extraits ci-dessus, l'avocat de la Cité de Québec lui demande:

Q. Do you consider that writing such books with such insults against another religion, in fact the religion practised by the people of this province or city, a proper means of preaching the gospel?— A. I do.

Et au cours de cette réponse, il dit:

. . . history abundantly attests to the fact that the Roman Catholic Hierarchy has had relationship with the world and has had part tacitly in the wars between the nations and the destruction of nations.

Un peu plus loin:

Q. Do you consider it necessary for your organization to attack the other religions, in fact, the Catholic, the Protestant and the Jews? —A. Indeed. The reason for that is because the Almighty God commands that error shall be exposed and not persons or nations. . . .

Qui oserait prétendre que des pamphlets contenant les déclarations qui précèdent, distribués dans une cité comme celle de Québec, ne constitueraient pas une pratique incompatible avec la paix et la sûreté de la Cité ou de la province? Quel tribunal condamnerait un conseil municipal qui empêcherait la circulation de pareilles déclarations? Et je n'ai choisi que quelques passages dans des livres et des tracts qui fourmillent de semblables affirmations. La décence, d'ailleurs, me commanderait de ne pas en citer davantage. Et cela ne me paraît pas nécessaire pour démontrer qu'une municipalité, dont 90 pour cent de la population est catholique, a non seulement le droit, mais le devoir, d'empêcher la dissémination de pareilles infamies.

Enfin, le dernier point c'est la question que l'exercice des cultes est un droit civil qui relève de la juridiction des législatures provinciales. C'est ainsi que l'ont considéré les provinces de la Saskatchewan et de l'Alberta, qui ont adopté des lois intitulées: An Act to Protect Certain Civil Rights (1947, 11 Geo. VI, c. 35). L'objet de la loi est déclaré dans le préambule comme étant "to protect certain civil rights" et l'article 3 de la Loi stipule:

. . . Every person and every class of persons shall enjoy the right to freedom of conscience, opinion and belief, and freedom of religious association, teaching, practice and worship.

La province de l'Alberta a un statut semblable:

Il est intéressant, sur ce point, de référer á l'interprétation donnée par le Conseil Privé de l'expression "civil rights" dans l'Acte de Québec de 1774, dans la cause de Citizens Insurance Company of Canada v. Parsons ((1881) 7 App. Cas. 96):

. . . It is to be observed that the same words, "Civil rights" are employed in the Act of 14 Geo. 3, c. 83, which made provision for the Government of the province of Quebec, Sect. 8 of that Act enacted that His Majesty's Canadian subjects within the province of Quebec should enjoy their property, usages, and other civil rights, as they had before done, and that in all matters of controversy relative to property and civil rights resort should be had to the laws of Canada, and be determined agreeably to the said laws. In this statute the words "property" and "civil rights" are plainly used in their largest sense; and there is no reason for holding that in the statute under discussion they are used in a different and narrower one.

Il suffit de signaler la contradiction de l'argumentation du procureur de l'appelant qui, d'une part, allègue l'inconstitutionnalité de la Charte de Québec, en invoquant, d'autre part, qu'elle est en conflit avec la "Loi concernant la liberté des cultes" (S.R.Q. 1941, c. 307) de cette même province de Québec. Il est indiscutable que la législature qui a adopté le chapitre 307 avait la compétence voulue pour adopter la Charte de la Cité de Québec, en vertu de laquelle le règlement 184 a été édicté. . . .

. . . Sur le tout, je n'ai donc aucune hésitation á dire que le règlement attaqué est légal, valide et constitutionnel et que les jugements qui l'ont déclaré tel doivent être confirmés, avec dépens.

KERWIN J.: . . . Counsel for the appellant declined to contend that the by-law was invalid because a discretion was delegated to the Chief of Police. Counsel for the respondent, the City of Quebec, and for the intervenant, the Attorney General of Quebec, did not deal with the point and nothing is therefore said about it. However, an argument was advanced based upon a pre-Confederation statute of 1852 of the old Province of Canada, 14-15 Vict. c. 175, the relevant part of which provides:

the free exercise and enjoyment of Religious Profession and Worship, without discrimination or preference, so as the same be not made an excuse for acts of licentiousness, or a justification of practices inconsistent with the peace and safety of the Province, is by the constitution and law as of this Province allowed to all Her Majesty's subjects within the same.

Section 129 of the British North America Act, 1867, enacts:

129. Except as otherwise provided by this Act, all Laws in force in Canada,

Nova Scotia, or New Brunswick at the Union, and all Courts of Civil and Criminal Jurisdiction, and all legal Commissions, Powers, and Authorities, and all Officers, Judicial, Administrative and Ministerial, existing therein at the Union, shall continue in Ontario, Quebec, Nova Scotia, and New Brunswick respectively, as if the Union had not been made; subject nevertheless (except with respect to such as are enacted by or exist under Acts of the Parliament of Great Britain or of the Parliament of the United Kingdom of Great Britain and Ireland) to be repealed, abolished, or altered by the Parliament of Canada, or by the Legislature of the respective Province, according to the Authority of the Parliament or of that Legislature under this Act.

By virtue of this section that part of the pre-Confederation statute extracted above continued to operate in the Province of Quebec at the time of the coming into force of the British North America Act. Since then the Quebec Legislature enacted legislation practically in the same words, and certainly to the same effect, which legislation has been continued from time to time and is now found in section 2 of R.S.Q. 1941, c. 307, the Freedom of Worship Act. Whether or not such legislation be taken to supersede the pre-Conference enactment, no statutes such as the Quebec City Charter, in the general terms in which they are expressed, and whenever originally enacted, have the effect of abrogating the specific terms of the enactment providing for freedom of worship.

It appears from the material filed on behalf of the appellant that Jehovah's Witnesses not only do not consider themselves as belonging to a religion but vehemently attack anything that may ordinarily be so termed but in my view they are entitled to "the free exercise and enjoyment of (their) Religious Profession and Worship." The Witnesses attempt to spread their views by way of the printed and written word as well as orally and state that such attempts are part of their belief. Their attacks on religion generally,

or on one in particular, do not bring them within the exception "so as the same be not made an excuse for licentiousness or a justification of practices inconsistent with the peace and safety of the Province." While several definitions of "licentious" appear in standard dictionaries, the prevailing sense of that term is said to be "libertine, lascivious, lewd." To certain biblical expressions the pamphlets, etc., of Jehovah's Witnesses which they desire to distribute attach a meaning which is offensive to a great majority of the inhabitants of the Province of Quebec. But, if they have a legal right to attempt to spread their beliefs, as I think they have, the expressions used by them in so doing, as exemplified in the exhibits filed, do not fall within the first part of the exception. Nor in my opinion are their attacks "inconsistent with the peace and safety of the Province" even where they are directed particularly against the religion of most of the Province's residents. The peace and safety of the Province will not be endangered if that majority do not use the attacks as a foundation for breaches of the peace.

Confined to the argument now under consideration, the above reasons do not justify a declaration that the by-law is *ultra vires* the City of Quebec since, if not otherwise objectionable, the by-law may have its effect in other cases and under other circumstances; but they do warrant a declaration that the by-law does not extend so as to prohibit the appellant as a member of Jehovah's Witnesses from distributing in the streets of Quebec any book, pamphlet, booklet, circular or tract of Jehovah's Witnesses included in the exhibits and an injunction restraining the City, its officers and agents from in any way interfering with such actions of the appellant.

The appellant further contended that the by-law should be declared illegal on the ground that the Provincial Legislature has no power to authorize the Council of the City of Quebec to pass a general by-law prohibiting the distribution of books, pamphlets, etc., in the City streets. At first he argued that the subject-matter of any such legislation and by-law falls under section 91 of the British North America Act and not section 92, but later changed his position by arguing that neither Parliament nor the Provincial Legislatures possessed the requisite power. I am unable to agree with either of these submissions. I do not find it helpful to refer to rights conferred by early treaties or sanctioned by Imperial statutes dealing with the old colonies and subdivisions of what is now Canada since it is well-settled that the British North America Act has conferred all powers of legislation either upon Parliament or the Legislatures of the Provinces and that there is no field in which the one or the others may operate. . . .

. . . In my view the right to practise one's religion is a civil right in the Province under head 13 of section 92 of the British North America Act just as much as the right to strike or lockout dealt with by the Judicial Committee in *Toronto Electric Commission* v. *Snider* ([1925] A.C. 396). . . .

. . . For the same reason I also think that freedom of the press is a civil right in the Province. In *Re Alberta Information Act* ([1938] S.C.R. 100), Sir Lyman Duff stated a short ground considered by him (and Davis J.) sufficient to dispose of the question as to whether Bill No. 9 of the Legislative Assembly of Alberta, "An Act to Ensure the Publication of Accurate News and Information" was *intra vires* the Legislature of that Province. With the greatest respect I am unable to agree with that part of his ensuing reasons for judgment commencing at the foot of page 132 and continuing to the end of page 135, and particularly the following statement: "Any attempt to abrogate this right of public debate or to express the traditional forms of the exercise of the right (in public meeting and through the press), would, in our opinion be incompetent to the Legislature of the Province." Also, with respect, I must dissent from the views of Cannon J. upon this topic as expressed in the same report.

We have not a Bill of Rights such as is contained in the United States Constitution and decisions on that part of the latter are of no assistance. While it is true that, as recited in the preamble to the British North America Act the three Provinces expressed a desire to be federally united with a constitution similar in principle to that of the United Kingdom, a complete division of legislative powers being effected by the Act, I assume as it was assumed in *Re Adoption Act* ([1938] S.C.R. 398), (with reference, it is true, to entirely different matters) that Provincial Legislatures are willing and able to deal with matters of importance and substance that are within their legislative jurisdiction. It is perhaps needless to say that nothing in the foregoing has reference to matters that are confined to Parliament. . . .

RAND J: . . . As in all controversies of this nature, the first enquiry goes to the real nature and character of the by-law; in what substance and aspect of legislative matter is it enacted? and we must take its objects and purposes to be what its language fairly embraces. The by-law places no restriction on the discretion of the officer and none has been suggested. If, under cover of such a blanket authority, action may be taken which directly deals with matters beyond provincial powers, can the fact that the language may, at the same time, encompass action on matters within provincial authority preserve it from the taint of *ultra vires*? May a court enter upon a delineation of the limits and contours of the valid and invalid areas within it? Must the provision stand or fall as one or can it be severed or otherwise dealt with? These are the subsidiary questions to be answered.

What the practice under the by-law demonstrates is that the language comprehends the power of censorship. From its inception, printing has been recognized as an agency of tremendous possibilities, and virtually upon its introduction into Western Europe it was brought under the control and licence of government. At that time, as now in despotisms, authority viewed with fear and wrath the uncensored printed word: it is and has been the *bête noire* of dogmatists in every field of thought; and the seat of its legislative control in this country becomes a matter of the highest moment.

The Christian religion, its practices and profession, exhibiting in Europe and America an organic continuity, stands in the first rank of social, political and juristic importance. The Articles of Capitulation in 1760, the Treaty of Paris in 1763, and the Quebec Act of 1774, all contain special provisions placing safeguards against restrictions upon its freedom, which were in fact liberations from the law in force at the time in England. The Quebec Act, by sec. 5, declared that His Majesty's subjects,

professing the religion of the Church of Rome of and in the said Province of Quebec, may have, hold and enjoy, the free exercise of the religion of the Church of Rome, subject to the King's supremacy. . . .

and, by sec. 15, that

no ordnance touching religion . . . shall be of any force or effect until the same shall have received His Majesty's approbation.

This latter provision, in modified form, was continued by sec. 42 of the Constitutional Act of 1791:

whenever any act or acts shall . . . in any manner relate to or affect the enjoyment of or exercise of any religious form or mode of worship

the proposed Act was to be laid before both Houses of Parliament and the assent of the Sovereign could be given only if within thirty days thereafter no address from either House to withhold assent had been presented. The Union Act of 1840, sec. 42, contained a like provision. In each of the latter Acts existing laws were continued by secs. 33 and 46 respectively. From 1760, therefore, to the present

moment religious freedom has, in our legal system, been recognized as a principle of fundamental character; and although we have nothing in the nature of an established church, that the untrammelled affirmations of religious belief and its propagation, personal or institutional, remain as of the greatest constitutional significance throughout the Dominion is unquestionable. . . .

. . . The only powers given by sec. 92 of the Confederation Act which have been suggested to extend to legislation in relation to religion are nos. 13, Property and Civil Rights, and 16, Matters of a merely local or private nature in the province. The statutory history of the expression "Property and Civil Rights" already given exhibiting its parallel enactment with special provisions relating to religion shows indubitably that such matters as religious belief, duty and observances were never intended to be included within that collocation of powers. If it had not been so, the exceptional safeguards to Roman Catholics would have been redundant.

Strictly speaking, civil rights arise from positive law; but freedom of speech, religion and the inviolability of the person, are original freedoms which are at once the necessary attributes and modes of self-expression of human beings and the primary conditions of their community life within a legal order. It is in the circumscription of these liberties by the creation of civil rights in persons who may be injured by their exercise, and by the sanctions of public law, that the positive law operates. What we realize is the residue inside that periphery. Their significant relation to our law lies in this, that under its principles to which there are only minor exceptions, there is no prior or antecedent restraint placed upon them: the penalties, civil or criminal, attach to results which their exercise may bring about, and apply as consequential incidents. So we have the civil rights against defamation, assault, false imprisonment and the like, and the punishments of the criminal law; but the sanctions of the latter lie within the exclusive jurisdiction of the Dominion. Civil rights of the same nature arise also as protection against infringements of these freedoms.

That legislation "in relation" to religion and its profession is not a local or private matter would seem to me to be self-evident: the dimensions of this interest are nationwide; it is even today embodied in the highest level of the constitutionalism of Great Britain; it appertains to a boundless field of ideas, beliefs and faiths with the deepest roots and loyalties; a religious incident reverberates from one end of this country to the other, and there is nothing to which the "body politic of the Dominion" is more sensitive.

There is, finally, the implication of sec. 93 of the Confederation Act which deals with education. In this section appear the only references in the statute to religion. Subsec. (i) speaks of "Denominational Schools" and preserves their existing rights and privileges. Subsec. (ii) extends to the separate schools "of the Queen's Protestant and Roman Catholic subjects" in Quebec the same "powers, privileges and duties" then conferred and imposed upon the separate schools of the "Queen's Roman Catholic subjects" in Upper Canada. Subsec. (iii) provides for an appeal to the Governor-General in Council from any act or decision of a provincial authority "affecting any right or privilege of the Protestant or Roman Catholic minority of the Queen's subjects in relation to education." Subsec. (iv) declares that in the event of any failure on the part of the provincial authority to observe or enforce the provincial laws contemplated by the section, Parliament may provide for the execution of the provisions of the section. On the argument advanced, and apart from the question of criminal law, these vital constitutional provisions could be written off by the simple expedient of abolishing, as civil rights and by provincial legislation, the religious freedoms of minorities, and so, in legal contemplation, the minorities themselves.

So is it with freedom of speech. The Confederation Act recites the desire of the three provinces to be federally united into one Dominion "with a constitution similar in principle to that of the United Kingdom." Under that constitution, government is by parliamentary institutions, including popular assemblies elected by the people at large in both provinces and Dominion: government resting ultimately on public opinion reached by discussion and the interplay of ideas. If that discussion is placed under licence, its basic condition is destroyed: the government, as licensor, becomes disjoined from the citizenry. The only security is steadily advancing enlightenment, for which the widest range of controversy is the sine qua non.

In the *Reference re The Accurate News and Information Act of Alberta* ([1938] S.C.R. 100), Sir Lyman Duff deals with this matter. The proposed legislation did not attempt to prevent discussion of affairs in newspapers but rather to compel the publication of statements as to the true and exact objects of governmental policy and as to the difficulties of achieving them.

~The learned Judge then quoted the reasons given by Chief Justice Duff and Justice Cannon in *Reference re Alberta Statutes* for ruling that the provinces cannot abrogate the right of public debate.~

What is proposed before us is that a newspaper, just as a religious, political or other tract or handbill, for the purposes of sale or distribution through use of streets, can be placed under the uncontrolled discretion of a municipal officer; that is, that the province, while permitting all others, could forbid a newspaper or any writing of a particular colour from being so disposed of. That public ways, in some circumstances the only practical means available for any appeal to the community generally, have from the most ancient times been the avenues for such communications, is demonstrated by the Bible itself: in the 6th verse of ch. xi of Jeremiah these words appear: "Proclaim all these words in the cities of Judah, and in the streets of Jerusalem''; and a more objectionable interference, short of complete suppression, with that dissemination which is the "breath of life" of the political institutions of this country than that made possible by the by-law can scarcely be imagined.

But it is argued that the by-law relates not to religion or free speech at all but to the administration of streets. Undoubtedly the city may pass regulations for that purpose but within the general and neutral requirement of licence by the by-law a number of equally plausible objects may be conjectured. No purpose whatever is indicated much less specified by the language; its sole effect is to create and vest in a functionary a power, to be exercised for any purpose or reason he sees fit, disclosed or undisclosed. . . .

. . . It was argued by Mr. Beaulieu that the city as proprietor of the streets has authority to forbid or permit as it chooses, in the most unlimited and arbitrary manner, any action or conduct that takes place on them. The possibilities of such a proposition can be easily imagined. But it misconceives the relation of the province to the public highways. The public entitled to use them is that of the Dominion, whose citizens are not of this or that province but of Canada. What has been confided to the provinces is the regulation of their use by that public.

Conceding, as in the Alberta Reference, that aspects of the activities of religion and free speech may be affected by provincial legislation, such legislation, as in all other fields, must be sufficiently definite amd precise to indicate its subject matter. . . . Where the language is sufficiently specific and can fairly be interpreted as applying only to matter within the enacting jurisdiction, that attribution will be made; and where the requisite elements are present, there is the rule of severability. But to authorize action which may be related indifferently to a variety of incompatible matters by means of the device of a discretionary licence cannot be brought within either of these mechanisms; and the Court is powerless,

under general language that overlaps exclusive jurisdictions, to delineate and preserve valid power in a segregated form. If the purpose is street regulation, taxation, registration or other local object, the language must, with sufficient precision, define the matter and mode of administration; and by no expedient which ignores that requirement can constitutional limitations be circumvented.

I would, therefore, allow the appeal, direct judgment declaring the by-law invalid, and enjoin the respondent City from acting upon it.

LOCKE J.: The preamble to chapter 175 of the Statutes of the Province of Canada for the year 1851 reads as follows:

Whereas the recognition of legal equality amongst all Religious Denominations is an admitted principle of Colonial Legislation: And whereas in the state and condition of this Province, to which such a principle is peculiarly applicable, it is desirable that the same should receive the sanction of direct Legislative Authority recognizing and declaring the same as a fundamental principle of our civil polity: Be it therefore declared and enacted by the Queen's Most Excellent Majesty, by and with the advice and consent of the Legislative Council and of the Legislative Assembly of the Province of Canada constituted and assembled by virtue of and under the authority of an Act passed in the Parliament of the United Kingdom of Great Britain and Ireland, and intituled, An Act to re-unite the Provinces of Upper and Lower Canada, and for the Government of Canada, and it is hereby declared and enacted by the authority of the same. That the free exercise and enjoyment of Religious Profession and Worship, without discrimination or preference, so as the same be not made an excuse for acts of licentiousness, or a justification of practices inconsistent with the peace and safety of the Province, is by constitution and laws of this Province allowed to all Her Majesty's subjects within the same.

The statute was reserved for the signification of Her Majesty's pleasure and the Royal assent given by Her Majesty in Council on May 15th, 1852.

This statute was in force when the British North America Act of 1867 was passed by the Imperial Parliament. It could not, in my opinion, be repealed by the Province of Quebec or by the Legislature of any other province of Canada (*Dobie* v. *Temporalities Board* ((1882) 7 App. Cas. 136)). Whether it would be *intra vires* Parliament to repeal the Act, in view of the language of the preamble to the British North America Act, is a matter to be decided when that question arises. It does not arise in the present case. Parliament has passed no legislation purporting to repeal the Act. . . .

. . . On behalf of the intervenant it has been contended before us that, assuming the belief of the Jehovah's Witnesses is one entitled otherwise to the protection of the Statute of 1852 or the Provincial Statute, he may be deprived of that right by or under the authority of a statute of the Provincial Legislature. The argument is based on the contention that the rights so given to the people of Canada to complete freedom in these matters is a civil right of which they may be deprived by appropriate legislation by the Province. It is further contended, though rather faintly, that the legislation may be justified under head 16 as being a matter of a merely local or private nature in the province.

In the factum of the intervenant the matter is thus expressed:

Under our constitution there is no religious freedom except within the limits determined by the competent legislative authority. No such authority is known other than the provincial authority; religious teaching as a matter of fact is part of the realm of education reserved to the provinces; besides, religious freedom is one of the civil rights also reserved to the provinces.

The reference to rights reserved to the provinces in respect of religious teaching refers, of course, to the provisions of section 93 of the British North America Act. If the argument is sound, then the holding of religious services by the adherents of any faith designated by the Legislature may be prohibited.

This argument put forward, so far as I am aware, for the first time in any reported case in Canada since Confederation, raises questions which are of profound importance to all of the people of this country. Not only the right of freedom of worship would be affected but the exercise of other fundamental rights, such as that of free speech on matters of public interest and to publicly disseminate news, subject only to the restraints imposed by the Criminal Code and to such civil liability as may attach to the publication of libelous matters, might be restrained or prohibited. The language of the by-law is perfectly general and if this contention of the intervenants be right the Chief of Police might forbid the distribution in the streets of circulars or pamphlets published by the one political party while allowing such distribution by that party which he personally favoured. It is well, in my opinion, that it be made clear that this right is involved in the decision of this case. Once a right of censorship of the contents of religious publications is established, the dissemination of the political views of writers by circulars or pamphlets delivered on the streets may equally be prohibited or restrained. . . .

. . . The purpose of this by-law is to establish a censorship upon the distribution of written publications in the City of Quebec. It is not the distribution of all pamphlets, circulars or other publications in the streets which is prohibited but of those in respect of which the written permission of the Chief of Police has not been obtained.

In the preamble to the British North America Act the opening paragraph says:

Whereas the Provinces of Canada, Nova Scotia and New Brunswick have expressed their desire to be federally united into one Dominion under the

Crown of the United Kingdom of Great Britain and Ireland with a constitution similar in principle to that of the United Kingdom

and, after reciting that such a nation would conduce to the welfare of the provinces, it is said that it is expedient not only that the constitution of the legislative authority in the Dominion be provided for but also that the nature of the Executive Government therein be declared. At the time this Act was passed, the Act of 1852 declaring the right to freedom of religious belief and worship was in force in Canada and gave to the inhabitants of the provinces the same rights in that respect as were then enjoyed by the people of the United Kingdom.

It has, I think, always been accepted throughout Canada that, while the exercise of this right might be restained under the provisions of the saving clause of the statute of 1852 by criminal legislation passed by Parliament under head 27 of section 91, it was otherwise a constitutional right of all the inhabitants of this country. . . .

. . . Whether the right to religious freedom and the right to free public discussion of matters of public interest and the right to disseminate news, subject to the restrictions to which I have above referred to, differ in their nature, it is unnecessary to decide. The former of these rights is, however, certainly not the lesser of them in Canada. Unless they differ, had the powers of censorship vested by the by-law in the Chief of Police of the City of Quebec been exercised by preventing the distribution of the written views of a political party (and they may be so used) rather than the religious views of Saumur, the opinion of Sir Lyman Duff, C.J. in the *Reference* as to *The Accurate News and Information Act of the Province of Alberta* ([1938] S.C.R. 100 at 132), would be directly to the contrary of the argument advanced on behalf of the intervenant.

~The learned Judge then quoted at length Chief Justice Duff's reasons for ruling the

Accurate News and Information Act invalid.~

With this opinion in its entirety I respectfully agree and I have heard no reasoned argument against any of its conclusions. It may be said, with at least equal and I think greater force, that the right to the free exercise and enjoyment of religious profession and worship without discrimination or preference, subject to the limitations expressed in the concluding words of the first paragraph of the Statute of 1852, existed at the time of the enactment of the British North America Act and was not a civil right of the nature referred to under head 13 of section 92 of the British North America Act. . . .

CARTWRIGHT J. (*dissenting*): . . . It is first necessary to determine the proper construction of the by-law. In doing so we must give to the words used their plain meaning in everyday language and when this is done I think it clear that what is prohibited is the distribution, without the permission of the Chief of Police, of printed matter of the kind described in the by-law in the streets of the City. The distribution of such matter anywhere else, as for example in private houses is not affected by the by-law. There is evidence in the record to indicate that the officials charged with the enforcement of the by-law have not so construed it and have instituted proceedings against persons, as for an infraction of the by-law, on the ground that such persons had distributed written matter at private residences in the City. Such evidence does not seem to me to be relevant to the proper construction of the by-law. It is only if the words of the by-law are ambiguous that we may resort to extraneous aids in its interpretation and the words used appear to me to be clear and unambiguous. The fact, if be the fact, that the by-law has been misinterpreted, can affect neither its proper construction nor the question of its validity.

In my view, legislation authorizing the city to pass this by-law is *prima facie*, in relation to either or both of two subjects within the provincial power which may be conveniently described as (i) the use of highways, and (ii) police regulations and the suppression of conditions likely to cause disorder.

~The learned Judge then cited a number of cases which in his view supported both grounds (i) and (ii) for finding the by-law valid. ~

It follows from these authorities that it is within the competence of the Legislature of the Province to prohibit or regulate the distribution, in the streets of the municipalities in the Province, of written matter having a tendency to insult or annoy the recipients thereof with the possible result of giving rise to disorder, and perhaps violence, in the streets.

It is said, however, if I have correctly apprehended the argument for the appellant, that even if the legislation in question appears *prima facie* to fall within the powers of the Provincial Legislature under the two heads with which I have dealt above it is in reality an enactment destructive of the freedom of the press and the freedom of religion both of which are submitted to be matters as to which the Province has no power to legislate. In support of such submission counsel referred to a large number of cases decided in the Courts of the United States of America but I am unable to derive any assistance from them as they appear to be founded on provisions in the Constitution limiting the power to make laws in relation to such matters. Under the British North America Act, on the other hand, the whole range of legislative power is committed either to Parliament or the Provincial Legislatures and competence to deal with any subject matter must exist in one or other of such bodies. There are thus no rights possessed by the citizens of Canada which cannot be modified by either Parliament or the Legislature, but it may often be a matter of difficulty to decide which of such bodies has the legislative power in a particular case.

It will be convenient to first examine the appellant's argument in so far as it deals with the freedom of the press. In Blackstone's *Commentaries* (1769) Vol. 4, at pages 151 and 152 it is said:

The liberty of the press is indeed essential to the nature of a a free state: but this consists in laying no previous restraints upon publications, and not in freedom from censure for criminal matter when published. Every free-man has an undoubted right to lay what sentiments he pleases before the public: to forbid this, is to destroy the freedom of the press: but if he publishes what is improper, mischievous, or illegal, he must take the consequence of his own temerity. To subject the press to the restrictive power of a licenser, as was formerly done, both before and since the revolution, is to subject all freedom of sentiment to the prejudices of one man and make him the arbitrary and infallible judge of all controverted points in learning, religion, and government. But to punish (as the law does at present) any dangerous or offensive writings, which, when published, shall on a fair and impartial trial be adjudged of a pernicious tendency, is necessary for the preservation of peace and good order, of government and religion, the only solid foundations of civil liberty.

Accepting this as an accurate description of what is commonly understood by the expression "the liberty of the press," as heretofore enjoyed by the inhabitants of Canada, it is clear that By-law No. 184 does infringe such liberty to a limited extent. It does, to adapt the words of Blackstone, lay some previous restraint upon publication. So far as the by-law is concerned every individual is left free to print and publish any matter he pleases except that one particular method of publication is conditionally denied to him. He is forbidden to publish such matter by distributing it in the streets of the City of Quebec without having previously obtained for so doing the written permission of the Chief of Police. I will assume, as is argued for the appellant, that the by-law contemplates that the Chief of Police will examine the written matter in respect of which he is asked to grant a permit and that his decision, whether to grant or refuse it, will be based on the view which he takes of the contents of such matter; that if he regards it as harmless, he will grant the permit, and that if he thinks it is calculated to provoke disorder by annoying or insulting those to whom it is distributed he will refuse the permit. It is urged that power to restrict the liberty of the press even to the limited extent provided in the by-law, is committed exclusively to Parliament under the opening words of section 91 or under head 27 of that section and further that Parliament has fully occupied the field by enacting those provisions of the Criminal Code which deal with blasphemous libel, seditious libel, speaking seditious words, spreading false news, defamatory libel, and publishing obscene matter. If I have followed the argument correctly, it is that as Parliament has enacted that certain publications are to be deemed criminal it has by implication declared that all other publications are lawful and that consequently the Legislature has no power to deal with any other type of publication. I am unable to accept this conclusion.

In my view, freedom of the press is not a separate subject matter committed exclusively to either Parliament or the Legislatures. In some respects, Parliament, and in others, the Legislatures may validly deal with it. In some aspects it falls within the field of criminal law, but in others it has been dealt with by Provincial legislation, the validity of which is not open to question, as for example The Libel and Slander Act R.S.O. 1950 Cap. 204, and the similar Acts in the other provinces. If the subject matter of a Provincial enactment falls within the class of subjects enumerated in section 92 of the British North America Act such enactment does not, in my opinion, cease to be *intra vires* of the legislature by reason of the fact that it has the effect of cutting down the fredom of the press. . . .

It is next necessary to consider the argument that the by-law is invalid because, as it is alleged, it interferes with freedom of religion. While it was questioned before us, I will, for the purposes of this argument, assume that the system of faith and worship professed by the body to which the plaintiff belongs is a religion, and that the distribution of printed matter in the streets is a practice directed by its teachings.

It may well be that Parliament alone has power to make laws in relation to the subject of religion as such, that that subject is, in its nature, one which concerns Canada as a whole and so cannot be regarded as of a merely local or private nature in any province or as a civil right in any province; but we are not called upon to decide that question in this appeal and I express no opinion upon it. I think it clear that the provinces, legislating within their allotted sphere, may affect the carrying on of activities connected with the practice of religion. For example, there are many municipal by-laws in force in cities in Ontario, passed pursuant to powers conferred by the Provincial Legislature, which provide that no buildings other than private residences shall be erected on certain streets. Such by-laws are, in my opinion, clearly valid although they prevent any religious body from building a church or similar edifice on such streets. Another example of Provincial Legislation which might be said to interfere directly with the free exercise of religious profession is that under which the by-law considered in *Re Cribbin* v. *The City of Toronto* ((1891) 21 O.R. 325) was passed. That was a by-law of the City of Toronto which provided in part:

No person shall on the Sabbath-day, in any public park, square, garden, or place for exhibition in the city of Toronto, publicly preach lecture or declaim.

The by-law was attacked on the ground, *inter alia*, that it was unconstitutional but it was upheld by Galt C.J. and in my opinion, his decision was right. No useful purpose would be served by endeavouring to define the limits of the provincial power to pass legislation affecting the carrying on of activities connected with the practice of religion. The better course is, I think, to deal only with the particular legislation now before us.

For the appellant, reliance was placed upon the Statute of Canada (1851) 14-15 Victoria, Chapter 175, re-enacted in substantially identical terms as R.S.Q. 1941 Cap. 307. I will assume, for the purposes of the argument, that counsel for the appellant is right in his submission that it is to the pre-Confederation Statute that we should look. In the relevant portion of that Statute it is enacted:

That the free exercise and enjoyment of Religious Profession and Worship, without discrimination or preference, so as the same be not made an excuse for acts of licentiousness, or a justification of practices inconsistent with the peace and safety of the Province, is by the constitution and laws of this Province allowed to all Her Majesty's subjects within the same.

I do not think that, on a proper construction, this statute absolves a religious body or an individual member thereof from obedience to any Act of Parliament or of the Legislature which happens to conflict with the teachings of such body.

. . . To summarize, I am of the opinion that it was within the competence of the Legislature to authorize the passing of the by-law in question under its power to legislate in relation to (i) the use of highways, and (ii) police regulations and the suppression of conditions likely to cause disorder; and that such legislation is not rendered invalid because it interferes to the limited extents indicated above with either the freedom of the press or the freedom of religion. It follows that I would dismiss the appeal. . . .

~Justices Kellock and Estey gave reasons similar to those advanced by Justices Rand and Locke for finding the by-law *ultra vires*. Justice Taschereau concurred with Chief Justice Rinfret, and Justice Fauteux concurred with Justice Cartwright. ~

34. Switzman v. Elbling and Attorney General of Quebec, 1957

~ The legislation challenged before the Supreme Court of Canada in this case was the Act Respecting Communistic Propaganda, the so-called Padlock Law, which the Quebec Legislature had passed in 1937. As its title implies, the object of this Act was to prohibit the propagation of communist ideology in the Province of Quebec. The litigation which led to this appeal began in 1949 when Switzman, the tenant of premises in Montreal, was sued by his landlord, Freda Elbling, for cancellation of the lease and damages on the grounds that the premises had been used by Switzman for the illegal purpose of propagating communism. In his defence Switzman pleaded that the Padlock Act was unconstitutional. The Attorney General of Quebec intervened to defend the Act. Both the trial judge and the Quebec Court of Queen's Bench (Appeal Side) found the Act *intra vires*.

The Supreme Court of Canada with only Justice Taschereau dissenting declared the Act *ultra vires*. Among the eight Judges who made up the majority five, Chief Justice Kerwin and Justices Locke, Cartwright, Fauteux, and Nolan based their conclusion on the grounds that the Act by making the propagation of communism a crime was in pith and substance legislation in respect of criminal law and hence an invasion of Parliament's criminal law power. This invocation of the federal criminal law power to invalidate a provincial Act regulating the expression of political ideas followed a similar decision by the Court two years earlier in *Birks and Sons (Montreal) Ltd.* v. *Montreal.*[1] In the *Birks* case the Supreme Court unanimously ruled that a Quebec statute authorizing municipal by-laws for closing stores on Roman Catholic holy days was unconstitutional. Here too, the decision of six of the nine Judges was based on their view that legislation compelling the observance of religious practices was criminal law under Section 91(27).

In the *Padlock Law* case as in the *Birks* case only three judges (Justices Rand, Kellock and Abbott)[2] looked upon the provincial Act as constituting a restriction of a fundamental civil liberty. Justice Rand in his judgment returned again to the theme that the B.N.A. Act, as is indicated by its preamble, requires that Canadian citizens enjoy the free circulation of opinions without which the parliamentary system of government contemplated by the Act would be impossible. While Justice Rand cited this doctrine here as grounds for invalidating a provincial statute restricting freedom of speech there is nothing in his judgment to suggest that he would not also apply it to a federal statute which attempted to do the same thing. Justice Abbott went even further and for the first time explicitly stated that the prescriptions of an open society implied by the preamble to the B.N.A. Act put the power of abrogating the right of

---

[1] [1955] S.C.R. 799.
[2] In the *Birks* case Justices Rand, Kellock, and Locke construed the issue in terms of a restriction of civil liberties.

discussion and debate beyond the federal Parliament as well as the provincial legislatures.

Switzman, like the other cases in this series of Quebec appeals, benefitted the immediate interests of civil liberties claimants but left the Canadian constitutional jurisprudence in relation to civil liberties in a confused state. The only clear conclusion that could be drawn from these cases was that a province cannot use what in pith and substance is criminal law to restrict freedom of speech or religion. But beyond this, the Court remained badly divided on whether fundamental civil liberties constitute a distinct subject matter of legislation and on whether the B.N.A Act protects rights essential to the working of a parliamentary system of government from legislative encroachment by the provinces or the federal Parliament. The failure of the Supreme Court to establish clear, majority support for the jurisprudence of an implied bill of rights in the B.N.A. Act was an important contributing factor in the movement to establish a formal bill of rights in Canada.

In the 1960's only one member of the Supreme Court, Justice Abbott, returned to Chief Justice Duff's doctrine of constitutional protection for the political freedoms necessary for the functioning of parliamentary institutions. But this was a dissenting decision in a case involving a union challenge to legislation introduced by W.A.C. Bennett's Social Credit administration in British Columbia.[3] The legislation in question aimed at preventing unions from using funds collected through a mandatory check-off for political purposes. The majority upheld the legislation as in pith and substance dealing with labour relations in the province. Two justices, Cartwright and Judson, joined Abbott in dissent but based their opinion on federalism not constitutionally protected civil liberties. In their view the legislation dealt with federal electoral activity, a subject under exclusive federal jurisdiction. It was on these grounds that a majority of the Court in 1965 ruled that local zoning laws could not prohibit lawn-signs in federal elections.[4]

A further attempt to invoke the implied bill of rights was turned aside by the Supreme Court at the end of the decade in *Walter* v. *A.-G. Alberta*.[5] In this case a Hutterite community in Alberta challenged provincial legislation restricting the amount of land religious communities could purchase in each part of the province. Relying mainly on dicta from *Saumur*, *Switzman* and Birks, the Hutterites contended that the legislation was an unconstitutional restriction on their freedom of religion. The Supreme Court gave this argument the back of its hand and found that the legislation in pith and substance dealt not with civil liberties but with the management of provincial lands, a subject well within provincial authority. ∼

[3] *Oil, Chemical and Atomic Workers International Union* v. *Imperial Oil Ltd. and A.G. B.C.* (1963) S.C.R. 584.

[4] *McKay et al.* v. *The Queen* [1965] S.C.R. 789.

[5] [1969] S.C.R. 383.

SWITZMAN *v.* ELBLING AND ATTORNEY GENERAL OF QUEBEC
In the Supreme Court of Canada, [1957] S.C.R. 285.

KERWIN C.J.: This Act may be cited as Act Respecting Communistic Propaganda.

Sections 3 and 12 read:

3. It shall be illegal for any person, who possesses or occupies a house within the Province, to use it or allow any person to make use of it to propagate communism or bolshevism by any means whatsoever.

12. It shall be unlawful to print, to publish in any manner whatsoever or to distribute in the Province any newspaper, periodical, pamphlet, circular, document or writing whatsoever propagating or tending to propagate communism or bolshevism.

Sections 4 to 11 provide that the Attorney General, upon satisfactory proof that an infringement of s. 3 has been committed, may order the closing of the house; authorize any peace officer to execute such order, and provide a procedure by which the owner may apply by petition to a judge of the Superior Court to have the order revised. Section 13 provides for imprisonment of anyone infringing or participating in the infringement of s. 12. In my opinion it is impossible to separate the provisions of ss. 3 and 12.

The validity of the statute was attacked upon a number of grounds, but, in cases where constitutional issues are involved, it is important that nothing be said that is unnecessary. In my view it is sufficient to declare that the Act is legislation in relation to the criminal law over which, by virtue of head 27 of s. 91 of the British North America Act, the Parliament of Canada has exclusive legislative authority. The decision of this Court in *Bédard* v. *Dawson et al* ([1923] S.C.R. 681) is clearly distinguishable. As Mr. Justice Barclay points out, the real object of the Act here under consideration is to prevent propagation of communism within the Province and to punish anyone who does so — with provisions authorizing

steps for the closing of premises used for such object. The *Bédard* case was concerned with the control and enjoyment of property. . . . It is not necessary to refer to other authorities, because, once the conclusion is reached that the pith and substance of the impugned Act is in relation to criminal law, the conclusion is inevitable that the Act is unconstitutional. . . .

TASCHEREAU J. (*dissenting*): . . . Il ne fait pas de doute qu'en vertu de l'art. 91 de l'Acte de l'Amérique britannique du Nord (s. 27), le droit criminel est une matière qui relève, exclusivement de l'autorité fédérale, sur laquelle cette dernière seule a le pouvoir de légiférer. Et dans un cas comme celui-là, la théorie dite de l'"unoccupied field" ne peut trouver son application, et ne peut justifier une législation provinciale de s'arroger un pouvoir que la constitution lui refuse. . . .

. . . Le loi dite "Loi protégeant la province contre la propagande communiste" stipule qu'il est illégal pour toute personne qui possède ou occupe une maison dans la province, de l'utiliser ou de permettre à une personne d'en faire usage pour propager le communisme ou bolchévisme par quelque moyen que ce soit. La loi autorise le procureur général, sur preuve satisfaisante d'une infraction, d'ordonner la fermeture de la maison pour une période n'excédant pas une année. Le recours conféré par la loi au propriétaire de la maison, est de présenter une requête à la Cour pour faire réviser l'ordonnance, en prouvant qu'il était de bonne foi, qu'il ignorait que la maison fût employée en contravention à la loi, ou que la maison n'a pas été employée pour les fins qu'on lui reproche.

L'appelant prétend que cette législation relève exclusivement du droit criminel, et qu'en conséquence, elle dépasse la compétence législative de l'autorité provinciale. Je m'accorderais volontiers avec lui; si la législature avait décrété que le communisme était un crime punissable par la loi, car il y aurait là clairement un empiétement dans le domaine fédéral, qui frapperait la législation d'illégalité et la rendrait *ultra vires* de la province. Mais tel n'est pas le cas qui se présente à nous. La législature, en effet, n'a érigé aucun acte au niveau d'un crime, et elle n'a nullement donné le caractère de criminalité à la doctrine communiste. Si la législature n'a pas le droit de créer des offenses criminelles, elle a le droit de légiférer pour prévenir les crimes, les désordres, comme la trahison, la sédition, les attroupements illégaux, déclarés des crimes par l'autorité fédérale, et pour faire disparaître les conditions qui sont de nature à favoriser le développement du crime. Pour atteindre ces buts, je n'entretiens pas de doute qu'elle peut validement légiférer sur la possession et l'usage d'un immeuble, car ceci est exclusivement du domaine du droit civil, et relève en vertu de l'art. 92 de l'Acte de l'Amérique britannique du Nord (s. 13) de l'autorité provinciale.

La cause de *Bédard* v. *Dawson et al.*, *supra*, présente beaucoup de similitude avec le litige actuel. Là encore la validité d'une loi provinciale intitulée "Loi concernant les propriétaires de maisons employées comme maisons de désordre," 10 Geo. V (1920), c. 18, a été attaquée. Cette loi déclarait qu'il était illégal pour toute personne qui possède ou occupe une maison ou bâtisse de quelque nature que ce soit, de l'utiliser ou de permettre à une personne d'en faire usage comme maison de désordre. . . .

La Cour Suprême du Canada, confirmant la Cour d'Appel de la province de Québec ((1921), 33 Que. K.B. 246), a décidé que cette loi était constitutionnelle, et bien que la loi criminelle et les règles de procédure qui s'y rapportent soient du ressort exclusif du Parlement fédéral, le Parlement provincial avait droit de légiférer sur toutes les matières civiles en rapport avec le droit criminel, et de sanctionner ses lois par une pénalité. Le jugé ([1923] S.C.R. at 681) de cette cause est le suivant:

The Quebec statute entitled "An Act respecting the owners of houses used as disorderly houses," 10 Geo. V. c. 81, authorizing a judge to order the closing of a disorderly house, is intra vires *the provincial legislature, as it deals with a matter of property and civil rights by providing for the suppression of a nuisance and not with criminal law by aiming at the punishment of a crime.* . . .

. . . Je suis clairement d'opinion que si une province peut validement légiférer sur toutes les matières civiles en rapport avec le droit criminel, si elle peut *adopter des lois destinées à supprimer les conditions qui favorisent le crime*, et contrôler les propriétés afin de protéger la société contre tout usage illégal qu'on peut en faire, si elle a le pouvoir incontestable de réglementer les courtiers dans leurs transactions financières pour protéger le public contre la fraude, si, enfin, elle a le droit d'imposer des incapacités civiles comme conséquence d'une offense criminelle, je ne vois pas pourquoi elle n'aurait pas également le pouvoir de décréter que ceux qui prêchent et écrivent des doctrines de nature à favoriser la trahison, la violation des secrets officiels, la sédition, etc., . . . soient privés de la jouissance des immeubles d'où se propagent ces théories destinées à saper à ses bases, et renverser l'ordre établi.

On a aussi prétendu que cette legislation constituait une entrave à la liberté de la presse et à la liberté de parole. Je crois à ces libertés: ce sont des droits indéniables dont bénéficient heureusement les gens de ce pays, mais ces libertés ne seraient plus un droit, et deviendraient un privilège, si on permettait à certains individus d'en abuser et de s'en servir pour diffuser des doctrines malsaines, qui conduisent nécessairement à de flagrantes violations des lois établies. Ces libertés, dont jouissent les citoyens et la presse, d'exprimer leurs croyances, leurs pensées et leurs doctrines, sans autorisation ou censure préalables, ne sont pas des droits absolus. Elles sont nécessairement limitées, et doivent s'exercer dans le cadre de la légalité.

Quand les bornes sont dépassées, elles deviennent abusives, et la loi doit alors intervenir pour exercer une action répressive, et protéger les citoyens et la société.

La même raisonnement doit nécessairement servir à rencontrer l'objection soulevée par l'appelant à l'effet que la loi attaquée, est une entrave à la libre expression de pensée de tout individu, candidat à une élection. Les idées destructives de l'ordre social et de l'autorité établie, par des méthodes dictatoriales, n'ont pas plus de droits en temps électoraux qu'en aucun autre temps. Cette loi, dans l'esprit de certains, peut paraître sévère, il ne m'appartient pas d'en juger la sagesse, mais la sévérité d'une loi adoptée par le pouvoir compétent ne la marque pas du caractère d'inconstitutionnalité.

Pour toutes ces raisons, je suis d'avis que le présent appel doit être rejeté. . . .

RAND J.: By 1 Geo. VI, c. 11, passed by the Legislature of the Province of Quebec and entitled "An Act to Protect the Province against Communistic Propaganda" (now R.S.Q. 1941, c. 52), the following provisions are enacted:

3. *It shall be illegal for any person, who possesses or occupies a house within the Province, to use it or allow any person to make use of it to propagate communism or bolshevism by any means whatsoever.*
. . .
12. *It shall be unlawful to print, to publish in any manner whatsoever or to distribute in the Province any newspaper, periodical, pamphlet, circular, document or writing whatsoever propagating or tending to propagate communism or bolshevism.*

The word "house" is defined to extend to any building or other construction whatever. By s. 4 the Attorney General,

. . . *upon satisfactory proof that an infringement of section 3 has been committed, may order the closing of the house against its use for any purpose whatsoever for a period of not more than one year; the closing order shall be registered*

at the registry office of the registration division wherein is situated such house, upon production of a copy of such order certified by the Attorney General.

When a house is closed, an owner who has not been in possession may apply to the Superior Court to have the order revised upon proving that in good faith he was ignorant of the use being made in contravention of the Act or that the house has not been so used during the twelve months preceding the order. Conversely, after an order has been so modified or terminated, the Attorney General may, on application to the same Court, obtain a decree reviving it. No remedy by resort to a Court is extended to the person in possession against whom the order has become effective. The Attorney General may at any time permit reoccupation on any conditions thought proper for the protection of the property and its contents or he may revoke the order.

The action in this appeal was brought by an owner against a tenant to have a lease set aside and for damages on the ground of the use of the leased premises for the illegal purpose so defined and their closure under such an order. As the validity of the Act was challenged by the defence, the Attorney General intervened and that issue became the substantial question in the proceedings. . . .

. . . The first ground on which the validity of s. 3 is supported is head 13 of s. 92 of the British North America Act, "Property in the Province," and Mr. Beaulieu's contention goes in this manner: by that head the Province is vested with unlimited legislative power over property; it may, for instance, take land without compensation and generally may act as amply as if it were a sovereign state, untrammelled by constitutional limitation. The power being absolute can be used as an instrument or means to effect any purpose or object. Since the objective accomplishment under the statute here is an Act on property, its validity is self-evident and the question is concluded.

I am unable to agree that in our federal

organization power absolute in such a sense resides in either legislature. The detailed distribution made by ss. 91 and 92 places limits to direct and immediate purposes of provincial action. Under head 13 the purpose would, in general, be a "property" purpose either primary or subsidiary to another head of the same section. If such a purpose is foreign to powers vested in the Province by the Act, it will invade the field of the Dominion. For example, land could not be declared forfeited or descent destroyed by attainder on conviction of a crime, nor could the convicted person's right of access to provincial Courts be destroyed. These would trench upon both criminal law and citizenship status. The settled principle that calls for a determination of the "real character", the "pith and substance," of what purports to be enacted and whether it is "colourable" or is intended to effect its ostensible object, means that the true nature of the legislative act, its substance in purpose, must lie within s. 92 or some other endowment of provincial power. . . . The heads of ss. 91 and 92 are to be read and interpreted with each other and with the provisions of the statute as a whole; and what is then exhibited is a pattern of limitations, curtailments and modifications of legislative scope within a texture of interwoven and interacting powers.

In support of the legislation on this ground, *Bédard* v. *Dawson et al.* ([1923] S.C.R. 681) was relied on. In that case the statute provided that it should be illegal for the owner or occupier of any house or building to use it or allow it to be used as a disorderly house; and procedure was provided by which the Superior Court could, after a conviction under the Criminal Code, grant an injunction against the owner restraining that use of it. If the use continued, the Court could order the building to be closed for a period of not more than one year.

This power is seen to have been based upon a conviction for maintaining a public nuisance. Under the public law of England which underlies that of all the Provinces, such an act was not only a matter for indictment but in a civil aspect the Court could enjoin its continuance. The essence of this aspect is its repugnant or prejudicial effect upon the neighbouring inhabitants and properties.

On that view this Court proceeded in *Bédard*. . . .

. . . That the scene of study, discussion or dissemination of views or opinions on any matter has ever been brought under legal sanction in terms of nuisance is not suggested. For the past century and a half in both the United Kingdom and Canada, there has been a steady removal of restraints on this freedom, stopping only at perimeters where the foundation of the freedom itself is threatened. Apart from sedition, obscene writings and criminal libels, the public law leaves the literary, discursive and polemic use of language, in the broadest sense, free.

The object of the legislation here, as expressed by the title, is admittedly to prevent the propagation of communism and bolshevism, but it could just as properly have been the suppression of any other political, economic or social doctrine or theory; and the issue is whether that object is a matter "in relation to which" under s. 92 the Province may exclusively make laws. Two heads of the section are claimed to authorize it: head 13, as a matter of "Civil Rights," and head 16, "Local and Private Matters." . . .

There is nothing of civil rights in this; it is to curtail or proscribe those freedoms which the majority so far consider to be the condition of social cohesion and its ultimate stabilizing force.

. . .

Indicated by the opening words of the preamble in the Act of 1867, reciting the desire of the four Provinces to be united in a federal union with a constitution "similar in principle to that of the United Kingdom," the political theory which the Act embodies is that of parliamentary government, with all its social implications, and the provisions of the statute elaborate that principle in the institutional apparatus which they create or contemplate. Whatever the deficiencies in its workings, Canadian government is in substance the will of the majority expressed directly or indirectly through popular assemblies. This means ultimately government by the free public opinion of an open society, the effectiveness of which, as events have not infrequently demonstrated, is undoubted.

But public opinion, in order to meet such a responsibility, demands the condition of a virtually unobstructed access to and diffusion of ideas. Parliamentary government postulates a capacity in men, acting freely and under self-restraints, to govern themselves; and that advance is best served in the degree achieved of individual liberation from subjective as well as objective shackles. Under that government, the freedom of discussion in Canada, as a subject matter of legislation, has a unity of interest and significance extending equally to every part of the Dominion. With such dimensions it is *ipso facto* excluded from head 16 as a local matter.

This constitutional fact is the political expression of the primary condition of social life, thought and its communication by language. Liberty in this is little less vital to man's mind and spirit than breathing is to his physical existence. As such an inherence in the individual it is embodied in his status of citizenship. . . . Of the fitness of this order of government to the Canadian organization, the words of Taschereau J. in *Brassard et al.* v. *Langevin* ([1877], 1 S.C.R. 145 at p. 195) should be recalled:

The object of the electoral law was to promote, by means of the ballot, and with the absence of all undue influence, the free and sincere expression of public opinion in the choice of members of the Parliament of Canada. This law is the just sequence to the excellent institutions which we have borrowed from England, institutions which, as regards civil and religious liberty, leave to Canadians nothing to envy in other countries.

Prohibition of any part of this activity as an evil would be within the scope of criminal law, as ss. 60, 61 and 62 of the Criminal Code dealing with sedition exemplify. Bearing in mind that the endowment of parliamentary institutions is one and entire for the Dominion, that Legislatures and Parliament are permanent features of our constitutional structure, and that the body of discussion is indivisible, apart from the incidence of criminal law and civil rights, and incidental effects of legislation in relation to other matters, the degree and nature of its regulation must await future consideration; for the purposes here it is sufficient to say that it is not a matter within the regulation of a Province. . . .

. . . I would, therefore, allow the appeal, set aside the judgments below, dismiss the action and direct a declaration on the intervention that the statute in its entirety is *ultra vires* of the Province. . . .

ABBOTT J.: The first question to be determined is whether the impugned legislation, in pith and substance, deals with the use of real property or with the propagation of ideas. As Mr. Scott put it to us in his very able argument: (1) the *motive* of this legislation is dislike of communism as being an evil and subversive doctrine, motive, of course, being something with which the Courts are not concerned; (2) the *purpose* is clearly the suppression of the propagation of communism in the Province, and (3) one *means* provided for effecting such suppression is denial of the use of a house.

In my opinion the act does not create two illegalities which are separate and independent, as was suggested to us by Mr. Beaulieu, it creates only one namely, the propagation of communism in the Province. Both s. 3 and s. 12 are directed to the same purpose, namely, the suppression of communism, although different means are provided to achieve that end. The whole Act constitutes one legislative scheme and in my opinion its provisions are not severable.

Since in my view the true nature and purpose of the Padlock Act is to suppress the propagation of communism in the Province, the next question which must be answered is whether such a measure, aimed at suppressing the propagation of ideas within a Province, is within the legislative competence of such Province.

The right of free expression of opinion and of criticism, upon matters of public policy and public administration, and the right to discuss and debate such matters, whether they be social, economic or political, are essential to the working of a parliamentary democracy such as ours. Moreover, it is not necessary to prohibit the discussion of such matters, in order to protect the personal reputation or the private rights of the citizen. That view was clearly expressed by Duff C.J. in *Re Alberta Statutes* ([1938] S.C.R. 100 at pp. 132-34) . . .

. . . The Canada Elections Act, the provisions of the British North America Act which provide for Parliament meeting at least once a year and for the election of a new parliament at least every five years, and the Senate and House of Commons Act, are examples of enactments which make specific statutory provision for ensuring the exercise of this right of public debate and public discussion. Implicit in all such legislation is the right of candidates for Parliament or for a Legislature, and of citizens generally, to explain, criticize, debate and discuss in the freest possible manner such matters as the qualifications, the policies, and the political, economic and social principles advocated by such candidates or by the political parties or groups of which they may be members.

This right cannot be abrogated by a Provincial Legislature, and the power of such Legislature to limit it, is restricted to what may be necessary to protect purely private rights, such as for example provincial laws of defamation. It is obvious that the impugned statute does not fall within that category. It does not, in substance, deal with matters of property and civil rights or with a local or private matter within the Province and in my opinion is clearly *ultra vires*. Although it is not necessary, of course, to determine this question for the purposes of the present appeal, the Canadian constitution being declared to be similar in principle to that of the United Kingdom, I am also of opinion that as our constitutional Act now stands, Parliament itself could not abrogate this right of discussion and debate. The power of Parliament to limit it is, in my view, restricted to such powers as may be exercisable under its exclusive legislative jurisdiction with respect to criminal law and to make laws for the peace, order and good government of the nation.

For the reasons which I have given, I would allow the appeal. . . .

~Justices Cartwright, Fauteux and Nolan wrote judgments in which they held the Act *ultra vires* on the grounds that it was legislation in relation to criminal law and hence fell under head 27 of Section 91. Justice Locke concurred with Justice Nolan. Justice Kellock wrote a short judgment concurring with Justice Rand.~

35. Morgan *v.* Attorney General of P.E.I., *1976*

~ The *Morgan* case concerned the extent to which elements of a common Canadian citizenship might provide another possible basis for constitutional protection of some basic rights and freedoms at least from provincial encroachments. This possibility was originally opened up by the *Union Colliery*[1] case of 1899 in which the Privy Council overruled British Columbia legislation prohibiting persons of Chinese descent, whether foreigners or citizens, from being employed in mines. The Privy Council found that the legislation invaded the exclusive jurisdiction over "Nationalization and Aliens" which section 91(25) assigns to the federal Parliament. The Privy Council's decision extended that power to cover the consequences of naturalization including "the rights and privileges pertaining to residents of Canada after they have been naturalized." The implications of this holding appeared to be considerably narrowed a few years later in the *Tomey Homma*[2] case, when the Privy Council upheld provincial legislation denying the right to vote in provincial elections to Japanese persons, including naturalized citizens of Japanese descent. But the opinion of Justice Ivan Rand of the Supreme Court in the *Winner*[3] case in 1951 raised some considerations about the meaning of Canadian citizenship which might be used to reinforce the orientation of the *Union Colliery* case. Justice Rand stated that the institution of a common Canadian citizenship was a fundamental accomplishment of Confederation and that this concept meant that Canadian citizens should be able to move freely from one province to another for otherwise "the country could be converted into a number of enclaves and the 'union' which the original provinces sought and obtained disrupted."

The *Morgan* case indicated that the Supreme Court was not inclined to give a broad interpretation to the rights of Canadian citizenship which are constitutionally protected from provincial legislation. The case arose out of legislation introduced by Prince Edward Island in 1972 requiring non-residents of the Island to obtain the approval of the provincial cabinet for land purchases exceeding ten acres or five chains of shoreline. Although the constitutional challenge was initiated by two Americans, the legislation in question applied to non-resident Canadians as much as to non-resident foreigners. The strength of the feelings aroused by the constitutional issues at stake in this case is evidenced by the fact that this was one of those rare cases when the federal government and all ten of the provincial governments made submission to the Supreme Court.

The Supreme Court unanimously upheld the Prince Edward Island law. Chief Justice Laskin who wrote the opinion of the Court found that the

---

[1] *Union Colliery Co.* v. *Bryden*, [1899] A.C. 580.

[2] *Cunningham* v. *Tomey Homma*, [1903] A.C. 151.

[3] *Winner* v. *S.M.T. (Eastern) Ltd.* and *Attorney General of New Brunswick*, [1951] S.C.R. 887.

jurisprudence which had developed since the *Union Colliery* case permitted the provinces to pass legislation affecting the rights of aliens and naturalized persons providing the legislation was not directed primarily at defining the rights of aliens or naturalized persons and was in relation to a subject within provincial jurisdiction. He noted that the legislation did not conflict with any of the provisions of the federal Citizenship Act nor did it prevent any one from entering or residing in the province. The legislation was essentially a regulation of land ownership within the province — a subject of legitimate provincial concern, especially in Prince Edward Island's case with its long historical struggle against absentee landownership.

The provincial victory in the *Morgan* case was one of the factors which stimulated federal government interest in constitutional reforms directed towards strengthening the "economic union" aspects of Confederation. The federal government's Constitutional Amendment Bill of June 1978 included a section on mobility rights which would have entrenched the right to acquire property or gain a livelihood in any province. However, the right to own property in any province was dropped from the mobility rights in section 6 of the Charter of Rights. Section 6 of the Charter refers only to the right to reside or gain a livelihood in any province. Thus the Charter, probably would not affect the outcome of the *Morgan* case unless legislation restricting the property ownership rights of non-residents was considered to be a violation of section 15, the anti-discrimination section of the Charter. Section 15 includes national origin but not province of origin among the explicitly prohibited categories of discrimination. ~

MORGAN *v.* ATTORNEY GENERAL OF P.E.I.
In the Supreme Court of Canada, [1976] 2 S.C.R. 349.

The judgment of the Court was delivered by

THE CHIEF JUSTICE: This appeal arises out of a declaratory action by two citizens of the United States, who are also resident there, challenging the validity of s. 3 of the Real Property Act, R.S.P.E.I. 1951, c. 138, as enacted by 1972 (P.E.I.), c. 40, s. 1. By order of Bell J. the question of the constitutionality of this provision was referred to the Supreme Court of Prince Edward Island *in banco*, and that Court, in reasons for judgment delivered by Trainor C.J. on November 19, 1973, rejected the attack on the re-enacted s. 3 on all the grounds urged against it. In substance, that Court's view was that s. 3 was legislation in relation to property and

civil rights in the Province, it did not invade the exclusive authority of Parliament in relation to naturalization and aliens, it did not conflict with s. 24(1) of the Canadian Citizenship Act, R.S.C. 1970, c. C-19, and it was not in conflict with the Real and Personal Property Convention, 1899, between Her Majesty and the United States, made applicable to Canada by a convention of October 21, 1921.

This last point was not pressed on the appeal to this Court which proceeded on the other grounds taken by the Court below. On the appeal here the appellants were supported by the Attorney General of Canada as an intervenant, and the respondent Attorney General of Prince Edward Island was supported by the

Attorneys General of all the other provinces as intervenants.

The challenged s. 3 reads as follows:

3. (1) Persons who are not Canadian citizens may take, acquire, hold, convey, transmit, or otherwise dispose of, real property in the Province of Prince Edward Island subject to the provisions of sub-section two (2) here next following.

(2) Unless he receives permission so to do from the Lieutenant-Governor-in-Council, no person who is not a resident of the Province of Prince Edward Island shall take, acquire, hold or in any other manner receive, either himself, or through a trustee, corporation, or any such the like, title to any real property in the Province of Prince Edward Island the aggregate total of which exceeds ten (10) acres, nor to any real property in the Province of Prince Edward Island the aggregate total of which has a shore frontage in excess of five (5) chains.

(3) The grant of any such permission shall be at the discretion of the Lieutenant-Governor-in-Council, who shall notify the applicant in writing by means of a certified copy of an Order-in-Council of his decision within a reasonable time.

(4) An application for any such permission shall be in the form prescribed, from time to time, by the Lieutenant-Governor-in-Council.

(5)(a) For the purposes of this section, "Canadian citizen" means persons defined as Canadian citizens by the Canadian Citizenship Act (R.S.C. 1970, Vol. 1, Cap. C-19).

   (b) For the purposes of this section "resident of the Province of Prince Edward Island" means a bona fide resident, animus et factum of the Province of Prince Edward Island.

   (c) For the purpose of this section "corporation" means any company, corporation or other body corporate and politic, and any association, syndicate or other body, and any such the like, and the heirs, executors, administrators and curators, or other legal

representatives of such person, as such is defined and included by The Domiciled Companies Act (Laws of Prince Edward Island 1962).

It replaced pre-Confederation legislation of 1859 (P.E.I.), c. 4 under which the common law disability of aliens to hold land was abolished but aliens, or persons holding for them, were limited to a maximum of two hundred acres. In 1939, this limitation to two hundred acres was qualified by the words "except with the consent of the Lieutenant Governor in Council": see 1939 (P.E.I.), c. 44; and by 1964 (P.E.I.), c. 27, s. 1 the limitation to two hundred acres was reduced to ten acres. So the law stood in Prince Edward Island until the enactment in 1972 of the provision now under challenge.

Of the earlier legislation to which I have referred, the Supreme Court of Prince Edward Island *in banco* said this:

There can be no doubt that the statute of 1859 and the amendment of 1939 were, in pith and substance, legislation respecting aliens. The former, being a pre-Confederation enactment was unquestionably valid legislation, while the latter as post-Confederation legislation was probably invalid as being beyond the powers of the Province under the British North America Act, 1867. However, its validity was never questioned in the Courts and it remained until 1972. As the national park was developed and numerous provincial parks were set up, the island's beauty as a tourist resort gained such status that many non-residents were rapidly acquiring large portions of island lands, and so great was the alarm as to the possibililty of the island once more falling under the control of absentee owners that in 1972 the Legislature repealed the 1939 legislation and enacted the impugned provisions above set forth.

I take the Court below to have based the distinction between the former legislation and that now under review on the ground that the province had made residence rather than alienage *per se* the touch-stone of the limitation on the holding of land in the province, and it followed in the view of that Court that federal power was not invaded by giving such a preference in the holding of land, as s. 3 provided in favour of residents. . . .

I view s. 3 as applying to Canadian citizens who reside outside of Prince Edward Island, whether elsewhere in Canada or outside of Canada and to aliens who reside outside of Prince Edward Island, whether elsewhere in Canada or, as here, outside of Canada. This being so, the attack on this provision was based initially on an allegedly unconstitutional discrimination between resident and non-resident Canadian citizens, at least those residing elsewhere in Canada. Citizenship, it was urged, involved being at home in every province, it was a status that was under exclusive federal definition and protection, and it followed that a residential qualification for holding land in any province offended against the equality of status and capacity that arose from citizenship and, indeed, inhered in it. This submission was fortified by reliance on s. 24 of the Canadian Citizenship Act which is in the following terms:

24.(1) Real and personal property of every description may be taken, acquired, held and disposed of by an alien in the same manner in all respects as by a natural-born Canadian citizen; and a title to real and personal property of every description may be derived through, from or in succession to an alien in the same manner in all respects as through, from or in succession to a natural-born Canadian citizen. . . .

Section 3 which is under challenge here does not distinguish between natural-born and naturalized Canadian citizens in making provincial residence the relevant factor for holding land. If it did, a different question would be presented, and account would have to be taken of the effect of s. 22 of the Canadian Citizenship Act which prescribes equality of status and equality of rights and obligations for all citizens, whether natural-born or naturalized.

Although citizenship as such is not mentioned in the British North America Act, it was not doubted by anyone on this appeal that, whether by implication from s. 91(25) thereof or under the opening words thereof, it was for Parliament alone to define citizenship and to define how it may be acquired and lost. How far beyond this Parliament may go in investing citizenship with attributes that carry against provincial legislation has not been much canvassed in this Court; nor, on the other hand, is there any large body of case law dwelling on the limitation on provincial legislative power arising from a grant of citizenship or the recognition thereof in a natural-born citizen or arising from federal power in relation to naturalization and aliens under s. 91(25) of the British North America Act.

The well-known dictum by Rand J. in Winner v. S.M.T. (Eastern) Ltd., at p. 920 that "a province cannot prevent a Canadian from entering it except, conceivably, in temporary circumstances, for some local reason, as for example health," was preceded by some observations upon which stress was laid by the appellants and by the Attorney General of Canada. These observations engaged the decisions of the Privy Council in Union Colliery Co. v. Bryden, and Cunningham v. Tomey Homma, and they are as follows at (pp. 918-920):

Citizenship is membership in a state; and in the citizen inhere those rights and duties, the correlatives of allegiance and protection, which are basic to that status.
. . .

But incidents of status must be distinguished from elements or attributes necessarily involved in status itself. British subjects have never enjoyed an equality in all civil or political privileges or immunities as is illustrated in Cunningham v. Tomey Homma, in which the Judicial Committee maintained the right of British Columbia to exclude a naturalized person from the electoral fran-

chise. On the other hand, in Bryden's *case, a statute of the same province that forbade the employment of Chinamen, aliens or naturalized, in underground mining operations, was found to be incompetent. As explained in* Homma's *case, that decision is to be taken as determining,*

"that the regulations there impeached were not really aimed at the regulation of metal mines at all, but were in truth devised to deprive the Chinese, naturalized or not, of the ordinary rights of the inhabitants of British Columbia and, in effect, to prohibit their continued residence in that province, since it prohibited their earning their living in that province."

What this implies is that a province cannot, by depriving a Canadian of the means of working, force him to leave it: it cannot divest him of his right or capacity to remain and to engage in work there: that capacity inhering as a constituent element of his citizenship status is beyond nullification by provincial action. The contrary view would involve the anomaly that although British Columbia could not by mere prohibition deprive a naturalized foreigner of his means of livelihood, it could do so to a native-born Canadian. He may, of course, disable himself from exercising his capacity or he may be regulated in it by valid provincial law in other aspects. But that attribute of citizenship lies outside of those civil rights committed to the province, and is analogous to the capacity of a Dominion corporation which the province cannot sterilize.

These passages from the reasons of Rand J. in the *Winner* case raise, by and large, the issues upon which the parties and the intervenants have made their various submissions, both in respect of the scope of the federal citizenship power and the federal power in relation to aliens. Rand J. recognized that even a native-born citizen (to use his words) "may . . . disable himself from exercising his capacity or he may be regulated in it by valid

provincial law in other aspects."

The power of a provincial legislature to regulate the way in which land in the province may be held, how it may be transferred, how it may be used (and this, whether the land be privately owned or be land held by the Crown in right of the province) is not contested. Nor, as I understand the submissions that were made, is it doubted that the provincial legislature may limit the amount of land that may be held by any person, assuming equal opportunity to anyone to purchase. The contention is, however, that as soon as the province moves to differentiate in this respect between classes of persons the legislation becomes suspect, and if it turns out that some citizens, and indeed some aliens, are disadvantaged as against others, that is as against those who are resident in the province, the legislation must be regarded as in pith and substance in relation to citizenship and in relation to aliens and hence *ultra vires*.

I do not agree with this characterization, and I do not think it is supportable either in principle or under any case law. No one is prevented by Prince Edward Island legislation from entering the province and from taking up residence there. Absentee ownership of land in a province is a matter of legitimate provincial concern and, in the case of Prince Edward Island, history adds force to this aspect of its authority over its territory. In *Walter* v. *Attorney General of Alberta*, this Court concluded that it was open to the Province of Alberta to control the extent to which groups of persons could hold land on a communal basis, and the legislation that was unsuccessfully challenged in that case flatly prohibited the acquisition of land in the province by "colonies" outside the province, without the consent of the Lieutenant-Governor-in-Council. It is true that no differentiation was expressly made on the basis of residence or citizenship or alienage, and that all who fell within the regulated groups were treated alike. Yet, it is also clear that the definition of the regulated bodies of persons was for the province and if the province could determine who could hold or the extent to which land could be held according to whether a communal property regime was observed, it is difficult to see why the province could not equally determine the extent of permitted holdings on the basis of residence. In neither case is this Court concerned with the wisdom or utility of the provincial land policy but only with whether the province has transgressed the limits of its legislative authority. I recognize, of course, that there may be cases where the line between wisdom and validity may be difficult to draw, but I find no such difficulty here. . . .

The Naturalization and Aliens Act, 1881 (Can.), c. 13, s. 4 was the first federal provision removing the common law disability of aliens to hold land. It was preceded however by certain pre-Confederation legislation such as that of 1859 in Prince Edward Island, already mentioned, and by earlier legislation such as that of the Province of Canada, being 1849 (Can.), c. 197, s. 12. It appears to me that it was open to a province after Confederation to remove the disability of an alien to hold land in the province without the need of prior or supporting federal legislation unless, of course, the Parliament of Canada, having legislative jurisdiction in relation to aliens, had expressly retained or imposed the disability. Legislation of a province dealing with the capacity of a person, whether alien or infant or other, to hold land in the province is legislation in an aspect open to the province because it is directly concerned with a matter in relation to which the province has competence. Simply because it is for Parliament to legislate in relation to aliens does not mean that it alone can give an alien capacity to buy or hold land in a province or take it by devise or by descent.

It is urged, here, however, that the qualified recognition given to the capacity of a non-resident alien by s. 3(2) of the challenged legislation is in the teeth of the general and unqualified recognition of the capacity of an alien to hold land given by s. 24(1) of the Canadian Citizenship Act. . . . Whatever be the proper characterization of the limitations in s. 3(2) the question is whether s. 24(1) of the Canadian Citizenship Act, as an affirmative exercise of the power of Parliament in relation to aliens, obliges a province to treat nonresident aliens (and citizens can surely be on no worse footing) on a basis of equality with resident aliens. . . .

The *Union Colliery Co.* case involved a preliminary question of the construction of the challenged s. 4 of the British Columbia Coal Mines Regulation Act, 1890 in its reference to "Chinaman" in that provision, which was as follows:

No boy under the age of twelve years, and no woman or girl of any age, and no Chinaman, shall be employed in or allowed to be for the purpose of employment in any mine to which the Act applies, below ground.

The Privy Council construed the term "Chinaman" as embracing Chinese who were aliens or naturalized persons, and it went on from there to assess the scope of the exclusive federal power in relation to "naturalization and aliens" under s. 91(25) of the British North America Act. It said of this power that (1) "The subject of 'naturalization' seems *prima facie* to include the power of enacting what shall be the consequences of naturalization; or, in other words, what shall be the rights and privileges pertaining to residents of Canada after they have been naturalized" (at p. 586); and (2) it invested the Parliament of Canada "with exclusive authority in all matters which directly concern the rights, privileges and disabilities of the class of Chinamen who are resident in the provinces of Canada" (at p. 587). In the result, the challenged legislation which, in the words of the Privy Council, consisted in pith and substance "in establishing a statutory prohibition which affects aliens or naturalized subjects" was *ultra vires* as invading exclusive federal authority.

. . . It is plain to me that the Privy Council receded from the literal effect of its language in the *Union Colliery Co.* case when it decided *Cunningham* v. *Tomey Homma*. It was said flatly in this last-mentioned case that "the truth is that the language of [s. 91(25)] does not purport to deal with the consequences of either alienage or naturalization" (at p. 156), and hence it was open to a province to deny the provincial franchise to Japanese persons, whether naturalized or not, and this notwithstanding that so far as naturalized Japanese persons were concerned federal legislation put them on a basis of equality with natural-born persons. But even natural-born persons of Japanese descent were excluded from the franchise, and this too was held to be within provincial competence. The Privy Council stated that while it was for the Parliament of Canada to determine what constitutes alienage or naturalization, "the question as to what consequences shall follow from either is not touched. The right of protection and the obligations of allegiance are necessarily involved in the nationality conferred by naturalization but the privileges attached to it, where these depend upon residence, are quite independent of nationality" (at p. 157).

The Privy Council regarded the electoral legislation in *Cunningham* v. *Tomey Homma* as validly enacted under s. 92(1) of the British North America Act, which authorizes legislation in relation to "the amendment from time to time, notwithstanding anything in this Act, of the Constitution of the Province, except as regards the office of Lieutenant-Governor." . . .

I do not think that federal power as exercised in ss. 22 and 24 of the Citizenship Act, or as it may be exercised beyond those provisions, may be invoked to give aliens, naturalized persons or natural-born citizens any immunity from provincial regulatory legislation, otherwise within its constitutional competence, simply because it may affect one class more than another or may affect all of them alike by what may be thought to be undue stringency. The question that would have to be answered is whether the provincial

legislation, though apparently or avowedly related to an object within provincial competence, is not in truth directed to, say, aliens or naturalized persons so as to make it legislation striking at their general capacity or legislation so discriminatory against them as in effect to amount to the same thing.

The issue here is not unlike that which has governed the determination of the validity of provincial legislation embracing federally incorporated companies. The case law, dependent so largely on the judicial appraisal of the thrust of the particular legislation, has established, in my view, that federally incorporated companies are not constitutionally entitled, by virtue of their federal incorporation, to any advantage, as against provincial regulatory legislation, over provincial corporations or over extra-provincial or foreign corporations, so long as their capacity to establish themselves as viable corporate entities (beyond the mere fact of their incorporation), as by raising capital through issue of shares and debentures, is not precluded by the provincial legislation. Beyond this, they are subject to competent provincial regulations in respect of businesses or activities which fall within provincial legislative power.

In the present case, the residency requirement affecting both aliens and citizens alike and related to a competent provincial object, namely, the holding of land in the province and limitations on the size of the holdings (relating as it does to a limited resource), can in no way be regarded as a sterilization of the general capacity of an alien or citizen who is a non-resident, especially when there is no attempt to seal off provincial borders against entry. Since, in my view, s. 3(2) is valid provincial legislation in its application to aliens or citizens who reside elsewhere in Canada than in Prince Edward Island, and hence is a *fortiori* valid in respect of persons resident outside of Canada I need not consider whether the appellants would be subject to the limitations of s. 3(2) even if persons resident elsewhere in Canada would constitutionally be free of them.

I would dismiss the appeal with costs, and would make no order as to costs by or against the intervenants.

36. Attorney General of Canada and Dupond v. Montreal, *1978*

~The Supreme Court rendered two judgments in 1978 in appeals involving constitutional challenges to provincial laws allegedly infringing fundamental rights and freedoms. In these two cases, *McNeil* and *Dupond*, the Court upheld the provincial legislation. The opinions of the Court's majority indicated that the contemporary Supreme Court was not inclined to give much weight to those constitutional constraints on provincial legislation affecting civil liberties which had been elucidated by Supreme Court judges in the 1950s. These decisions provided additional ammunition for advocates of a Constitutional Bill of Rights.

The *McNeil*[1] case was initiated by a journalist who was prevented from seeing *Last Tango in Paris* by Nova Scotia's film censorship laws. McNeil's effort to challenge provincial film censorship laws on constitutional grounds involved two trips to the Supreme Court of Canada. First, because courts have traditionally confined their adjudicative activities to disputes in which laws are applied to particular parties, McNeil had to establish his right as a member of the general film-viewing public to raise the constitutional issue in court. The Supreme Court agreed with the Nova Scotia courts that McNeil should be granted "standing" to raise the constitutional question.[2] This decision, following a similar decision permitting a disgruntled taxpayer to challenge the validity of the Official Languages Act,[3] was a significant step in making the judicial process more accessible to private citizens who wish to bring constitutional issues before the courts.[4]

McNeil, after succeeding on the procedural question of standing, lost when he brought the substantive issue before the Supreme Court. The Court was narrowly split, five to four, but the majority held that Nova Scotia's Theatre and Amusement Act and all but one of the regulations passed under it were constitutional. The one exception was a regulation prohibiting indecent performances which was virtually identical to a section of the federal Criminal Code. Justice Martland's majority opinion characterized the subject matter of the Act as the regulation of a local trade. He reasoned that "In a country as vast and diverse as Canada, where tastes and standards may vary from one area to another, the determination of what is and what is not acceptable for public exhibition on moral grounds may be viewed as a matter of a 'local and private nature in the Province' within the meaning of s. 92(16) of the B.N.A. Act." Chief Justice Laskin's dissenting opinion, on the other hand, emphasized the development of provincial film censorship across Canada, including legislative schemes with extremely vague standards delegating nearly arbitrary powers to

---

[1] *Nova Soctia Board of Censors* v. *McNeil*, [1978] 2 S.C.R. 662.
[2] *Nova Scotia Board of Censors* v. *McNeil*, [1976] 2 S.C.R. 265.
[3] *Thorson* v. *Attorney General of Canada*, [1975] 1 S.C.R. 138.
[4] For further developments on "standing", see p. 25 above.

Boards of Censors. In his view, the power to decide what is obscene lies exclusively with the federal Parliament under its criminal law power.

The *Dupond* case which is reproduced below concerned a Montreal by-law and ordinance used in 1969 during a period of continuing terrorist incidents to prevent gatherings and demonstrations of all kinds in public places. Justice Beetz for the majority held that it is within the constitutional authority of a province to empower a municipality to adopt such a measure. He distinguished legislation of this kind from Criminal Code provisions relating to unlawful assembly and disturbing the peace on the grounds that it was designed to prevent disorder rather than to punish it after it has broken out. His dismissal of the implied Bill of Rights argument was categorical. "None of the freedoms (speech, assembly and association, press and religion)," he said, "is enshrined in the constitution as to be above the reach of competent legislation."

Again, Chief Justice Laskin wrote the dissent. He was joined by Justices Spence and Dickson who had also concurred with him in *McNeil*. But Justice Judson, the fourth dissenting judge in McNeil, this time shifted to the majority position. The Chief Justice's opinion, it should be noted, focused on the criminal law power not the implied Bill of Rights. He regarded the Montreal regulations as a "mini-Criminal Code" which, in effect, would permit a municipal authority to legislate for the "peace, order and good government" of the City of Montreal.

The outcome of the *McNeil* and *Dupond* cases might not be different under the Charter. Much would depend on whether the Court found the laws in question to be "reasonable limits" on freedom of expression or assembly "such as can be demonstrably justified in a free and democratic society."[5]

Although *Dupond* appears to be virtually the final nail in the coffin of the implied bill of rights, the Duff doctrine and some of the Supreme Court's 1950's civil liberties jurisprudence retain a residual significance in the Charter era. The federal division of powers will continue to be a constitutional restriction on provincial legislation creating offences which restrict freedom of religion or speech. In *Westendorp* v. *The Queen*,[6] for instance, the appellant's counsel abandoned a Charter of Rights challenge to Calgary's by-law prohibiting street soliciting and won the case on division of powers grounds. The essential core of the Duff doctrine may also survive. Justice Beetz in *Dupond* did distinguish freedom to demonstrate from the communicative freedoms considered by Chief Justice Duff in the *Alberta Press* case as the life blood of parliamentary democracy. Such freedoms may continue to enjoy the constitutional protection of those sections of Canada's original Constitution establish-

---

[5] See *Oakes*, case 46 below, for the Supreme Court's formulation of its approach to section 1, the Charter's reasonable limits clause.

[6] [1983] 1 S.C.R. 43.

ing parliamentary institutions. This argument might be used against legislation based on the override section of the Charter which aimed at restricting political debate or discussion. A 1987 *obiter dictum* of Justice Beetz in which he recognized that the "basic structural imperatives . . . of free Parliamentary institutions" impose restrictions on legislatures "quite apart from the Charter" demonstrates that the nub of the Duff doctrine is still alive.[7]

ATTORNEY GENERAL OF CANADA AND DUPOND *v.* MONTREAL
In the Supreme Court of Canada, [1978] 2 S.C.R. 770.

The judgment of Martland, Judson, Ritchie, Pigeon, Beetz, Grandpré JJ. was delivered by

BEETZ J.: Appellant Claire Dupond has attacked the constitutional validity of the City of Montreal By-law 3926 and of Ordinance no. 1 passed by the Executive Committee of the City pursuant to s. 5 of that by-law. She did so under s. 515 of the Charter of the City of Montreal (Q.S. 1959-60, c. 102) which provides that any ratepayer, by petition in his own name presented to the Superior Court, may demand the annulment of any by-law on the ground of illegality. The Attorney General of Quebec and the Attorney General of Canada were impleaded as third parties and participated in the proceedings throughout, the first to support the validity of the By-law and of the Ordinance and the second to oppose it. The trial judge having declared the By-law and the Ordinance unconstitutional, the City of Montreal and the Attorney General of Quebec both appealed to the Quebec Court of Appeal. In separate judgments on each appeal, the Court of Appeal set aside the judgment at trial and dismissed Claire Dupond's petition. These are the judgments separately appealed from by the Attorney General of Canada and Claire Dupond. The Attorney General of Ontario and the Attorney General of Alberta were granted leave to intervene but only the Attorney General of Alberta did in fact intervene; he supported the

validity of the By-law and of the Ordinance.

By-law 3926 reads as follows:

By-law relating to exceptional measures to safeguard the free exercise of civil liberties, to regulate the use of the public domain and to prevent riots and other violations of order, peace and public safety.

At the meeting of the Council of the City of Montreal held on November 12, 1969, Council ordained:

WHEREAS it is imperative to provide for the protection of citizens in the exercise of their liberties, safeguard public peace and prevent violence against persons and property:

WHEREAS violence, armed robberies and other criminal acts often accompany certain demonstrations;

WHEREAS it is in order to enact exceptional emergency measures for the protection of citizens and the maintenance of peace and public order;

WHEREAS it is in order to regulate the use of the public domain and safeguard the right of citizens to the peaceful enjoyment of the public domain of the City;

1.—Anyone is entitled to the use and enjoyment of the streets, public places and public domain of the City of Montreal untroubled and in peace and public order.

2.—Assemblies, parades or other

[7] SEFPO v. Ontario [1987] 2 S.C.R. 2, at p. 57.

gatherings that endanger tranquility, safety, peace or public order are prohibited in public places and thoroughfares, parks or other areas of the City's public domain.

3.—No person participating in or present at an assembly, parade or other gathering on the public domain of the City shall molest or jostle anyone, or act in any way so as to hamper the movement, progress or presence of other citizens also using the public domain of the City on that occasion.

4.—Any assembly, parade or gathering on the public domain which gives rise to the violation against any article of this by-law, or to any acts, behaviour or utterances which disturb the peace or public order shall ipso facto be an assembly, parade or gathering which endangers tranquility, safety, peace or public order under the terms of Article 2 of this by-law, and shall disperse forthwith.

5.—When there are reasonable grounds to believe that the holding of assemblies, parades or gatherings will cause tumult, endanger safety, peace or public order or give rise to such acts, on report of the Directors of the Police Department and of the Law Department of the City that an exceptional situation warrants preventive measures to safeguard peace or public order, the Executive Committee may, by ordinance, take measures to prevent or suppress such danger by prohibiting for the period that it shall determine, at all times or at the hours it shall set, on all or part of the public domain of the City, the holding of any or all assemblies, parades or gatherings.

6.—All persons shall immediately obey the order of a peace officer to leave the scene of any assembly, parade or gathering held on violation of this by-law.

7.—Whoever participates in an assembly, parade or gathering held in violation of this by-law or otherwise contravenes, in any way, any provision of this by-law, shall be liable to either imprisonment or a

fine, with or without costs, for the term or the amount that the Municipal Court of Montreal will determine, at its discretion, and failing the immediate payment of such fine, or such fine and costs, as the case may be, to imprisonment for a term to be determined by the said Municipal Court, at its discretion; the imprisonment for failure to pay the fine or costs shall cease at any time before expiry of the term determined by the Court, upon payment of the fine or of the fine and costs, as the case may be.

Such imprisonment shall not exceed sixty (60) days nor such fine one hundred (100) dollars.

The Ordinance passed by the Executive Committee of the City pursuant to s. 5 of the By-law reads as follows:

Under by-law 3926 relating to exceptional measures to safeguard the free exercise of civil liberties, to regulate the use of the public domain and to prevent riots and other violations of order, peace and public safety.

At the meeting of the Executive Committee of the City of Montreal held on November 12, 1969 (no. 38961)

The Executive Committee ordained:

ORDINANCE TO PROHIBIT THE HOLDING OF ANY ASSEMBLY, PARADE OR GATHERING ON THE PUBLIC DOMAIN OF THE CITY OF MONTREAL FOR A TIME-PERIOD OF 30 DAYS.

CONSIDERING the reports from the Directors of the Police Department and of the Law Department of the City of Montreal attached hereto as an integral part of these presents;

CONSIDERING there are reasonable grounds to believe that the holding of assemblies, parades or gatherings on the public domain of the City would endanger the safety, peace or public order might give rise to such danger;

CONSIDERING the exceptional situation prevailing in the City of Montreal and the need to take preventive measures to safeguard peace and public order.

The holding of any assembly, parade or gathering anywhere and at any time on the public domain of the City is prohibited for a time-period of thirty (30) days to end the thirteenth (13) day of December 1969 at midnight, except for the parades already authorized by the Director of the Police Department under By-law 1319 dealing with traffic, before the adoption of this ordinance, and provided such parades do not endanger tranquility, peace and public order.

~ The reports of the Police Department and Law Department read as follows. ~

Date: November 12, 1969
To: Mr. Lucien Saulnier
Chairman of the Executive Committee
City of Montreal
From: Mr. J.-P Gilbert
Director of the Police Department
City of Montreal
Subject:
demonstrations and parades

1. Since the beginning of 1969, 97 demonstrations have been held in Montreal, 21 of which have taken place from early October up to this date.

2. Some of these demonstrations have drawn several thousand demonstrators which we have had to control.

3. It should be noted that the demonstrations mentioned above do not include parades held for religious, ethnic, commercial or sports purposes, where we are called upon to maintain order.

4. On four occasions, since October 1, 1969, we have had to call on duty more than eight hundred (800) policemen on the occasion of demonstrations.

5. Demonstrations for all types of causes or purposes have increased to such an extent that, on an average yearly basis, we set at 20% the number of Montreal Police Department men/day needed to control such demonstrations.

6. In determining the cost of these demonstrations in terms of salaries paid to policemen on duty on such occasions, we have set an estimate of approximately $3,000 per hour in over-time pay.

7. In determining the cost at regular rates of the police forces assigned to the setting up of crowd-control systems and the carrying out of police operations at the time of the demonstrations, we have arrived at an estimated yearly cost of approximately $7,000,000 for the City.

8. Attention should be drawn to the fact that, when a demonstration occurs, we must perforce reduce the normal amount of protection extended by us to other areas, so as to concentrate most of our forces at the site of the demonstration. This can only benefit crime throughout the metropolis.

9. Moreover, in the past two months, demonstrations have increased both in frequency and in the number of participants involved.

10. We note that such demonstrations are accompanied increasingly by violence, vandalism and looting.

11. Considerable damage has been inflicted on a great number of commercial establishments in the course of such demonstrations.

12. The experience of recent demonstrations has shown that many agitators, usually the same ones, infiltrate a large crowd in order to throw various missiles — Molotov cocktails, for instance — from within such crowds, or otherwise to disturb the peace or endanger persons or property, while it is extremely difficult to identify and restrain such agitators soon enough.

13. The present climate of social unrest and the frequency of demonstrations, as characterized above, make it impossible to guarantee within reasonable limits that the holding of assemblies, parades or gatherings within the City of Montreal can take place at this time without the occurrence of violence against either persons or property or without an increase in the number of armed robberies and major crimes when police personnel is assigned to demonstration duty;

14. We therefore have reasonable ground to believe that within the next 30 days, the holding of assemblies, parades or gatherings can only endanger public safety, peace and order and provide

opportunities for the perpetration of serious criminal offences or of acts seriously disturbing public safety, peace and order;

15. We therefore feel it our duty to recommend that preventive steps be taken to protect civil liberties and safeguard public peace and order and, consequently, we recommend that the Executive Committee, pursuant to the powers it holds under the by-law prohibiting demonstrations on the City's public domain, forbid for 30 days the holding of any and all assemblies, parades or gatherings, of any type whatsoever everywhere on the City's public domain, excepting those events already authorized by the Director of the Police Department of the City of Montreal.

We recommend that our report be submitted to the Chief Attorney for the drafting of the required ordinance and of any report he must make pursuant to the provisions of the by-law referred to above.

Law Office
Date: November 12, 1969
To: Chairman and Members of the Executive Committee City Hall

and

Mr. Maurice Farley,
Executive Secretary of the City City Hall
From: Mr. Michel Côté,
Chief Attorney,
Law Office.
Subject:
Recommendation for the adoption of an ordinance prohibiting any demonstrations for thirty days on the public domain — By-law concerning demonstrations on the public domain.

Gentlemen:

Following the adoption of the by-law concerning demonstrations on the City's public domain, we have received and examined a report dated November 12, 1969, from the Director of the Police Department, Mr. Jean-Paul Gilbert, rec-

ommending that, pursuant to the above-mentioned by-law, an ordinance be adopted prohibiting for thirty (30) days all demonstrations on the public domain.

In view of the many demonstrations which are expected to take place or have been publicly announced for the coming days, and in view of the facts set forth in the report of the Director of the Police Department, Mr. Jean-Paul Gilbert, we find that we must concur with his conclusion that a special situation exists in Montreal, that there is reasonable ground to believe that the holding of assemblies, parades and gatherings will endanger public safety, peace and order, cause tumult or give rise to such acts, and that it is therefore in order to take preventive steps to safeguard public peace and order. We therefore recommend jointly with the Director of the Police Department, Mr. Jean-Paul Gilbert, that the Executive Committee prohibit, by ordinance, the holding of any and all assemblies, parades or gatherings, anywhere and all times on the public domain of the City of Montreal, for a thirty (30) day period to end on the thirteenth (13th) day of December 1969, at midnight, excepting those parades which had already been authorized in accordance with By-law 1319 concerning traffic by the Director of the Police Department, Mr. Jean-Paul Gilbert, prior to the adoption of this ordinance and providing that they take place in tranquility, peace and public order.

We recommend that the form and wording of the said ordinance be the same as those of the draft ordinance attached hereto.

Hoping that you will find the whole in order, we remain.

Sincerely yours,
Chief Attorney,
Michel Côté.

The only evidence tendered at trial was the brief testimony of Claire Dupond that she is a ratepayer of the City of Montreal and a Canadian citizen.

There is in the case no factual background except what is mentioned in the reports of the Directors of the Police Department and of the Law Department of the City of Montreal attached to Ordinance no. 1 and quoted above. The facts recited in those reports have not been disputed. They must be taken to be true. It was conceded at the hearing that Ordinance no. 1 was enacted on account of those facts.

The submissions made against the constitutional validity of the By-law and of the Ordinance may be summarized as follows:

1. They are in relation to criminal law and *ultra vires* of the City of Montreal and of the provincial legislature;
2. They are in relation to and in conflict with the fundamental freedoms of speech, of assembly and association, of the press and of religion which are made part of the constitution by the preamble of the British North America Act, 1867, or which come under federal jurisdiction and are protected by the Canadian Bill of Rights. . . .

The trial judge, Trépanier J., whose judgment is unreported, found some overlapping between s. 2, 3 and 5 of the By-law and several provisions of the Criminal Code. He came to the conclusion that s. 5 of the By-law creates a new offense intended to supplement the Criminal Code and was accordingly *ultra vires* as being in relation to criminal law. Since it was unlikely in his view that the City Council would have enacted the By-law without s. 5, he declared the By-law entirely void, together with the Ordinance. . . .

The Court of Appeal (Lajoie J.A. speaking for himself and for Owen, Brossard, Turgeon and Bélanger JJ.A.) unanimously held that the By-law and the Ordinance were *intra vires*: it characterized the By-law and the Ordinance as local police regulations the essential purpose of which was to secure to the inhabitants of the City the free and peaceful enjoyment of the municipal public domain; as to the Canadian Bill of Rights it was pointed out that it does not apply to provincial and municipal legislation: [1974] C.A. 402.

II

In *Hodge* v. *The Queen*, the Judicial Committee of the Privy Council upheld the constitutional validity of the Ontario Liquor Licence Act of 1877 and of regulations enacted pursuant to that Act. At page 131, the Judicial Committee referred to those regulations as

regulations in the nature of police or municipal regulations of a merely local character . . . and such as are calculated to preserve in the municipality, peace . . . and repress . . . disorderly and riotous conduct.

I could not find a better description to characterize s. 5 of the By-law and the Ordinance. They are on their face regulations of a merely local character. The Ordinance was passed for reasons peculiar to the City of Montreal at the relevant time. Both s. 5 and the Ordinance relate to the use of the municipal public domain in exceptional circumstances when there are reasonable grounds to believe that the holding of assemblies, parades or gatherings in the streets, parks and other parts of the public domain will endanger safety, peace or public order. These are not punitive but essentially preventive measures, the purpose and effect of which is the prevention of conditions conducive to breaches of the peace and detrimental to the administration of justice. This preventive character is illustrated by the fact that the Ordinance prohibits the holding on the public domain of *any* assembly, parade or gathering, including those of the most innocent and innocuous kind. The temporary nature of the Ordinance and of any ordinance which could be passed pursuant to s. 5 is also indicative of the preventive aspect of this legislative scheme.

In *Reference re the Adoption Act* ([1938] S.C.R. 398), Sir Lyman Duff wrote, at p. 403:

. . . while as subject matter of legislation, the criminal law is entrusted to the Dominion Parliament, responsibility for the administration of justice and, broadly speaking, for the policing of the country, the execution of the criminal law, the suppression of crime and disorder, has from the beginning of Confederation been recognized as the responsibility of the provinces and has been discharged at great cost to the people; so also, the provinces, sometimes acting directly, sometimes through the municipalities, have assumed responsibility for controlling social conditions having a tendency to encourage vice and crime.

It is now well established that the suppression of conditions likely to favour the commission of crimes falls within provincial competence: *Bédard* v. *Dawson* ([1923] S.C.R. 681) *Di Iorio* v. *Warden of the Montreal Jail* ([1978] 1 S.C.R. 15).

It would be an over-simplification to say that ordinances which may be passed under s. 5 are purely prohibitory: demonstrations can be restricted to certain areas of the municipal public domain, to certain times of the day or the night, to certain types of assemblies, parades or gatherings; that is why, in spite of the prohibitory form of the ordinances, s. 5 can be said to be in substances, regulatory of the use of the public domain as the by-law held *intra vires* by McRuer C.J.H.C. in *R.* v. *Campbell* ([1962] O.R. 1134).

However, I would not hesitate to uphold the validity of ordinances contemplated by s. 5 even if they were strictly prohibitory:

A provincial enactment does not become a matter of criminal law merely because it consists of a prohibition and makes it an offense for failure to observe the prohibition; . . .

(per Judson J. in *O'Grady* v. *Sparling* ([1960] S.C.R. 804), at p. 810).

In my view, the impugned enactments relate to a matter of a merely local nature in the Province within the meaning of s. 92(16) of the constitution. Bearing in mind that the other heads of power enumerated in s. 92 are illustrative of the general power of the Province to make laws in relation to all matters of a merely local or private nature in the Province, I am of the opinion that the impugned enactments also derive constitutional validity from heads (8), (13), (14) and (15) of s. 92. . . .

III

When an enactment is in itself of a local or private nature, the *onus* of showing that it otherwise comes within one or more of the classes of subjects enumerated in s. 91 falls upon the party so asserting: *L'Union St-Jacques de Montréal* v. *Bélisle* ([1874], L.R. 6 P.C. 31), at p. 36. Appellants have tried to discharge the *onus* by submitting that s. 5 of the By-law and the Ordinance relate to criminal law.

One line of argument was that the impugned enactments are anti-riot measures dealing with a field already covered by ss. 64 to 70 of the *Criminal Code* and that their essential purpose is to supplement what was thought to be a lacuna in the Code.

I do not agree that s. 5 and the Ordinance deal with the same subject matter as the Code, under the same aspect and for the same purpose. They differ in more than one way but the main difference is as follows: the *Criminal Code* forbids unlawful assemblies and riots and provides for the punishment of these offenses once they have been committed; it also compels a justice, mayor or sheriff to command, in Her Majesty's name, the dispersion of an unlawful assembly which has already begun to disturb the peace tumultuously; s. 5 and the Ordinance on the other hand are aimed at preventing assemblies, parades and gatherings which have not yet taken place. There are in the Code no preventive measures similar to s. 5 of the By-law. Counsel for the Attorney General of Canada readily conceded this; his point was that Parliament could enact a measure such as s. 5 of the

By-law, and moreover, that only Parliament could do so.

It may be that Parliament could enact measures of a preventive nature under its ancillary powers. But we are not concerned in this case with the outer limits of federal jurisdiction over criminal law and I fail to see how the fact that Parliament has not exercised a possible incidental power should sterilize provincial legislative competence and prevent a province or a city from exercising their own powers. And, in the exercise of their own powers, the provinces may constitutionally complement federal legislation. The reports are replete with cases where provincial legislation complementary to federal legislation was upheld as long as it did not collide with the latter. . . .

This part of appellants' first submission must fail.

The second line of argument with respect to appellants' first submission is that s. 5 of the by-law and the ordinance are *ultra vires* under the doctrine of *Saumur* v. *City of Quebec, Henry Birks and Sons Ltd.* v. *City of Montreal* and *Switzman* v. *Elbling*.

I cannot see anything in the Ordinance which interferes with freedom of religion, of the press or of speech, or which imposes religious observances, in such a way as to bring the matter within the criminal law power of Parliament. The Ordinance prohibits the holding of *all* assemblies, parades or gatherings for a time period of thirty days, irrespective of religion, ideology or political views. It does so for the reasons given in the reports of the Director of the Police Department and of the Chief Attorney of the City; the reasons have nothing to do with those for which provincial enactments were invalidated in the *Saumur, Birks* and *Switzman* cases.

Furthermore, the discretionary power to pass an Ordinance under s. 5 of the By-law is not an uncontrollable discretion given to a municipal officer, as was the case in *Saumur*: it is vested in the Executive Committee of the City; it cannot be

exercised except on report of the Directors of the Police Department and of the Law Department of the City; this report must give reasons why an ordinance should be passed; these reasons must be up to the standard contemplated in the preamble of the By-law and in s. 5, that is, an exceptional emergency situation must have arisen which warrants the enactment of preventive measures; finally, the prohibition must be limited in time to the period determined by the Executive Committee; it must be temporary for by their very nature exceptional emergency measures cannot be permanent.

Should the discretionary power vested in the Executive Committee by s. 5 be exercised for unconstitutional purposes, or should it simply be exercised unreasonably, judicial review would be available.

IV

The second submission against the constitutionality of s. 5 and of the Ordinance was that they are in relation to and in conflict with the fundamental freedoms of speech, of assembly and association, of the press and of religion which were inherited from the United Kingdom and made part of the Constitution by the preamble of the *British North America Act, 1867*, or which come under federal jurisdiction and are protected by the *Canadian Bill of Rights*. The *Reference* re *Alberta Statutes* was relied upon.

I find it exceedingly difficult to deal with a submission couched in such general terms. What is it that distinguishes a right from a freedom and a fundamental freedom from a freedom which is not fundamental? Is there a correlation between freedom of speech and freedom of assembly on the one hand and, on the other, the right, if any, to hold a public meeting on a highway or in a park as opposed to a meeting open to the public on private land? How like or unlike each other are an assembly, a parade, a gathering, a demonstration, a procession? Modern parlance has fostered loose language upon lawyers. As was said by Sir Ivor

Jennings, the English at least have no written constitution and so they may divide their law logically. (W. Ivor Jennings, ''The Right of Assembly in England'', (1931-32), 9 *New York University Law Quarterly Review*, 217.)

I am afraid I cannot avoid answering in kind appellants' submissions. I believe I can state my position in a relatively small number of propositions which require little or no development for, difficult as it is at this level of abstraction, I must try not to say more than is necessary to dispose of the submission:

1. None of the freedoms referred to is so enshrined in the constitution as to be above the reach of competent legislation.

2. None of those freedoms is a single matter coming within exclusive federal or provincial competence. Each of them is an aggregate of several matters which, depending on the aspect, come within federal or provincial competence.

(This proposition is postulated in s. 5(3) of An Act for the Recognition and Protection of Human Rights and Fundamental Freedoms of which the Canadian Bill of Rights constitutes Part 1.)

3. Freedoms of speech, of assembly and association, of the press and of religion are distinct and independent of the faculty of holding assemblies, parades, gatherings, demonstrations or processions on the public domain of a city. This is particularly so with respect to freedom of speech and freedom of the press as considered in the *Reference re Alberta Statutes (supra)*. Demonstrations are not a form of speech but of collective action. They are of the nature of a display of force rather than of that of an appeal to reason; their inarticulateness prevents them from becoming part of language and from reaching the level of discourse.

4. The right to hold public meetings on a highway or in a park is unknown to English law. Far from being the object of a right, the holding of a public meeting on a street or in a park may constitute a trespass against the urban authority in whom the ownership of the street is vested even though no one is obstructed and no injury is done; it may also amount to a nuisance. . . .

Being unknown to English law, the right to hold public meetings on the public domain of a city did not become part of the Canadian constitution under the preamble of the *British North America Act, 1867*.

5. The holding of assemblies, parades or gatherings on the public domain is a matter which, depending on the aspect, comes under federal or provincial competence and falls to be governed by federal and provincial legislation such as the *Criminal Code*, laws relating to picketing, civil laws, municipal regulations and the like including s. 5 of the impugned By-law and the Ordinance passed pursuant to it.

6. The *Canadian Bill of Rights*, assuming it has anything to do with the holding of assemblies, parades or gatherings on the public domain, does not apply to provincial and municipal legislation.

Appellants' second submission must also fail.

I would therefore dismiss both appeals.

The judgment of Laskin C.J. and of Spence and Dickson JJ. was delivered by

THE CHIEF JUSTICE (*dissenting*): The terms of the impugned By-law and of the Ordinance, passed pursuant to s. 5 thereof, are set out in the reasons of my brother Beetz which I have had the advantage of reading, and I shall not repeat them. It is obvious from the recitals as well as from the terms of the key s. 5 that the City of Montreal has enacted a mini-Criminal Code, dealing with apprehended breach of the peace, apprehended violence and the maintenance of public order, and we are urged to sustain this incursion into the field of criminal law—a matter exclusively for the Parliament of Canada—because it is a matter of a local or private nature in the Province.

The only local or private aspect is, in my opinion, the territorial ambit of the By-law and of the Ordinance, and this has never been a test of constitutional validity. My brother Beetz has referred to the challenged provisions as regulatory of the public domain, the reference being to public streets and parks. It is not, however, directed to that end as the recitals and central terms clearly indicate. What it does, plainly and without reference to any regulatory consideration, is to make it a punishable offence—a crime— to breach s. 5 of the By-law and the Ordinance. Sections 1 and 3 of the By-law do have a relationship to traffic regulation and may be justified in themselves on that basis as provisions which may competently be authorized by provincial legislation. They are, however, integrated in other provisions which are in no sense directed to traffic considerations or to any regulatory use of public parks and, indeed, as my brother Beetz has noted, the focus is on s. 5 of the By-law and on the Ordinance passed in implementation thereof. That provision is so explicitly directed to breach of the peace and to the maintenance of public order as to fall squarely within exclusive federal authority in relation to the criminal law.

The very title of the By-law, as one "relating to exceptional measures to safeguard the free exercise of civil liberties, to regulate the use of the public domain and to prevent riots and other violations of order, peace and public safety" shows its character. The references to safeguarding the free exercise of civil liberties and to regulation of the use of the public domain are hollow references, not in any way fulfilled by the substantive terms of the By-law as are the references to riots, breach of the peace and public order. Moreover, the enactment of the By-law as an exceptional measure is itself an indicator of how far removed it is from any concern, except a consequential one, with regulation of the use of streets and public parks. The enactment of the By-law smacks of an assertion of municipality

authority to legislate for the "peace, order and good government" of the City of Montreal, an authority which I do not find in the catalogue of provincial powers under the *British North America Act.*

The central s. 5 of the By-law and the Ordinance are a long way from *Hodge* v. *The Queen.* That case was concerned with provincial liquor licensing legislation and hence had a constitutional foundation in the local regulation of a trade or business in the Province. The legislation was, therefore, substainable either under s. 92(13) or under s. 92(16) of the *British North America Act,* although it will be recalled that in *Attorney General of Manitoba* v. *Manitoba Licence Holders' Association* ([1902] A.C. 73), the Privy Council preferred to assign provincial regulatory liquor legislation to s. 92(16). There is no similar foundation for the By-law and especially for s. 5 thereof, which is enacted as a strict prohibitory provision unredeemed by any regulatory aspect.

No doubt a prohibition, as a matter of its impact, is regulatory but, for constitutional purposes, provincial prohibitions to be valid have to be associated with a valid scheme of regulation as enforcement or reinforcements thereof, and are not sustainable as preemptory directions against forbidden conduct or behaviour. . . .

Two other points are made by the proponents of the By-law. One is that it was called forth by exceptional conditions in Montreal, an assertion which in itself makes the By-law suspect. There is no accretion to provincial legislative authority to enable it to deal with apprehended riots or public disorder merely because the provincial government or delegated municipal authorities are of the opinion that preventive measures must be taken. They may be taken under ordinary police powers and in accordance with the federal *Criminal Code,* to which I will refer later in these reasons. The second point is that there is no constitutional bar to provincial (or validly authorized municipal) legislation which complements the federal *Criminal Code.* This is a proposition which flies in the face of the scheme of distribution of legislative power; it is destructive of the principle of exclusiveness as expressed in *Union Colliery Co.* v. *Bryden* ([1899] A.C. 580), at p. 588; and it is not supported by any authorities. Cases such as *O'Grady* v. *Sparling* ([1960] R.C.S. 804) and *Mann* v. *The Queen* ([1966] R.C.S. 238), to take two of those relied upon by the proponents of the By-law, turn on a conclusion that the enactments challenged therein were independently valid as being in relation to a matter within provincial competence. Judson J., speaking for the majority in *O'Grady* v. *Sparling*, at p. 810, said that "The power of a provincial legislature to enact legislation for the regulation of highway traffic is undoubted . . . [and] the legislation under attack here is part and parcel of this regulation." It cannot be said of the challenged s. 5 of the By-law in this case that it has any such anchorage.

Whether the apt term be "complementary" or "supplementary," it has hitherto been a mark of our constitutional jurisprudence that a Province cannot legislate to reinforce the federal criminal law: *Johnson* v. *Attorney General of Alberta* ([1954] S.C.R. 127). The fact that it might seek to foreclose a breach of the criminal law by preventive measures did not relieve against this provincial disability: see *Attorney General of Ontario* v. *Koynok* ([1941] 1 D.L.R. 548). There may, of course, be differences as to the appropriateness of the application of this principle in particular cases but the principle itself has not, as I read the case law, been heretofore doubted.

If any reported case in the Canadian Courts has an affinity to the one now before us it is *District of Kent* v. *Storgoff* ([1962] 38 D.L.R. (2d) 362). It is very much in point, and on this I differ from my brother Beetz. That case also involved a municipal by-law which was likewise passed as an exceptional measure; and the same expediency that is invoked here to support the By-law and s. 5 thereof was invoked there. Whittaker J. of the British Columbia Supreme Court did not yield to the expediency reflected in the by-law, although he sympathized with the municipality in its problem; and he pointed out, quite properly, that preventive measures were open under provisions of the *Criminal Code* relating to unlawful assemblies, to prevention of use of force and to power to arrest without warrant.

The by-law in the *District of Kent* case purported to prohibit members of a Doukhobor sect from entering the municipality which contained a prison where a large number of members were serving sentences. Fellow members, numbering about 1,000, were intending to march on the prison and had begun to do so from their homes about 400 miles away, and the by-law was passed as an emergency measure because of concern that the facilities of the municipality, with a population of 2,200, would be overtaxed so far at least as housing and sanitation were concerned, and there was also an apprehension of a breakdown of law and order. The by-law made it an offence punishable by a fine or imprisonment or both for a member of the sect to enter the municipality during the continuance of the emergency and they were liable, if they did so, to arrest without warrant.

Two passages from the reasons of Whittaker J. invalidating the by-law are so apposite here that I quote them, as follows, at p. 367 of the D.L.R. report:

It is true that in the preamble the by-law refers to anticipated problems of housing, education and health. Those are local problems, but the penalties imposed are not for the breach of any law relating to those subjects. The by-law is designed to prevent conditions arising which may lead to their breach. This is a laudable object, if it could be achieved by the exercise of powers within the jurisdiction of the municipality or the Province, but Kent has sought to meet the situation by the creation of a new crime. This is clearly beyond its powers.

The by-law is also designed to prevent conditions arising which may lead to a breach of the peace or unlawful assembly.

These are matters relating to the criminal law and as such are within the exclusive legislative jurisdiction of the Parliament of Canada. Both are covered by the Criminal Code, *1953-54 (Can.), c. 51; breach of the peace by ss. 30 and 31, and unlawful assembly by s. 64.*

There is more to be said for the validity of the by-law in the *District of Kent* case than there is for the validity of the one in the present case. There are here no considerations of health or sanitation or education but a naked concern for the public peace and about anticipated violence. The by-law is directed to these considerations and they are matters of criminal law alone. Of course, there can be only sympathetic regard for the ability of the police to handle violent demonstrators. I should have thought, however, that an internal instruction or memorandum of procedures to this end would have sufficed in invocation of the extensive police powers of arrest without warrant given by ss. 449 and 450 of the Criminal Code and of the power to deal with and disperse unlawful assemblies, given by ss. 64 to 69 of the Criminal Code. There are express supporting provisions in ss. 32 and 33 as well as general support in ss. 27 and 30. Any doubt about the actual encroachment of the By-law into the field of criminal law may easily be resolved by comparing s. 5 of the By-law with ss. 27 and 68 of the Criminal Code, s. 6 of the By-law with s. 69(b)(c) of the Criminal Code, and s. 7 of the By-law with ss. 66 and 67 of the Criminal Code.

There is a distasteful part of the challenged By-law and Ordinance which, surprisingly, appears to be relied on to support their validity. The prohibition of assemblies or gatherings is not limited to those from which disorder or violence is anticipated but extends to all assemblies, all gatherings for the prescribed thirty-day period. I am unable to appreciate how this gives credence to the By-law as a local measure. We are left in no doubt here as to the scope of operation of the By-law. In *Saumur* v. *City of Quebec*, Kellock J. noted that the challenged by-law there

was "not to be judged from the standpoint of matters to which it might be limited but upon the completely general terms in which it in fact is couched" (at p. 339). Here, persons who might seek to associate or gather for innocent purposes are to be barred, not because of any problem as to whether certain public areas should be open at certain times or on certain days or occasions—all of which go to their ordinary regulation—but because of a desire to forestall the violent or the likely violent. This is the invocation of a doctrine which should alarm free citizens even if it were invoked and applied under the authority of the Parliament of Canada, which has very wide power to enact criminal law. To find it invoked by a delegated authority like a municipality, which is limited at the outside to those powers that are open to a Province, appears to me to be an aggravation of its intrusion into the field of criminal law.

Certainly, enforcement of the criminal law is often difficult, and where large numbers of persons may be involved the difficulties are compounded. Yet it has always been central to our criminal law that the police are expected to enforce it against violators and not against innocents, and to exercise a reasonable and honest judgment as to those who are in each of these classifications. What can be more draconian than for a municipality to ignore the distinction and then to insist that it is not legislating in relation to crime or criminal law when its prime purpose is to forestall anticipated breaches of the peace and to deal with unlawful assemblies and riots!

The By-law goes much beyond what was invalidated in *Henry Birks & Sons Ltd.* v. *City of Montreal* and in *Switzman* v. *Elbling*. Of course, those cases relate to other factual issues but they reflect the scope of the federal criminal law power even in situations where there is a connection—found there to be too tenuous to support the challenged provisions—with the regulation of commercial establishments and the use of private premises.

I see nothing in *Bédard* v. *Dawson*, to

give any support to the By-law. It has been overtaken by later cases such as *Johnson* v. *Attorney General of Alberta, supra*, and *Switzman* v. *Elbling, supra*, and even if it still has any vitality, its rationale relates to the suppression of a nuisance, a matter pertaining to the enjoyment of private premises. The By-law here has nothing to do with private nuisances but only with conduct and antici-pated conduct of persons in streets and public parks.

I would allow the appeal, set aside the judgment below and restore the order at trial declaring the By-law and the Ordinance ultra vires. It is clear that if s. 5 goes, ss. 6 and 7 of the By-law must also fall, and so too must s. 4. This effectively denudes the By-law of any substance.

B. The Canadian Bill of Rights

37. The Queen v. Drybones, *1970*

~ A new chapter in Canadian civil liberties was inaugurated in 1960 with the enactment of the Canadian Bill of Rights. Technically the new Bill of Rights was not an addition to Canada's formal Constitution. It was passed as an ordinary Act of the federal Parliament. As such it did not apply to the provinces and could be set aside by subsequent federal legislation. The Act had two main clauses. Section 1 declared that in Canada certain fundamental rights and freedoms "have existed and shall continue to exist without discrimination by reason of race, national origin, colour, religion or sex." It listed as such fundamental rights the right to life, liberty, security of the person and property and the right not to be deprived thereof except by due process of law, the individual's right to equality before the law and protection of the law, freedom of religion, speech, assembly, association and the press. Section 2 provided that unless the Bill of Rights was explicitly set aside, every federal law shall "be so construed and applied as not to abrogate, abridge or infringe" the rights and freedoms set out in the Bill. It added to the rights listed in section 1 a list of procedural rights, including the right of arrested persons to legal counsel, habeas corpus, the presumption of innocence, the right to an interpreter and the right to a fair hearing when a person's rights or duties are being determined. The final section of the Bill provided that the Bill of Rights would not apply to anything done under the War Measures Act.

Following the passage of the Bill of Rights, there was a spate of cases in the lower courts of Canada testing the scope and meaning of the Act. But very few of these filtered up to the Supreme Court. The first two to do so elicited a very terse response from the Court.[1] They both involved appeals against deportation orders issued under the Immigration Act, and in both cases the Court considered that because the immigration officials had not exceeded their authority in issuing the deportation orders, the appellants had not been deprived of their liberty "except by due process of law."

The first real test of the Supreme Court's treatment of the Bill of Rights came in 1963 in the *Robertson and Rosetanni* case.[2] Robertson and Rosetanni had been charged with an offence under the federal Lord's Day Act, namely operating a bowling alley on Sunday. On appeal their main defence was that the Lord's Day Act conflicted with the Canadian Bill of Rights and was

---

[1] *Rebrin* v. *Bird and the Minister of Citizenship and Immigration et. al.*, [1961] S.C.R. 376 and *Louie Yuet Sun* v. *The Queen*, [1961] S.C.R. 70.
[2] [1963] S.C.R. 652.

therefore inoperative. Justice Ritchie (supported by the three Quebec justices, Taschereau, Fauteux and Abbott) wrote the majority's opinion, dismissing the appeal. His approach to the Bill of Rights was basically conservative. He interpreted it not as a charter designed to enlarge the fundamental rights and freedoms of Canadians but as a means of conserving these rights in their 1960 form. The Canadian Bill of Rights, he argued, "is not concerned with 'human rights and fundamental freedoms' in any abstract sense, but rather with such 'rights and freedoms' as they existed in Canada immediately before the statute was enacted." His review of Canadian history and jurisprudence revealed that the concept of religious freedom was well enshrined in Canadian law as was Lord's Day observance legislation long before 1960. Thus he concluded that the freedom of religion guaranteed by the Bill of Rights was not infringed by the Lord's Day Act. Justice Cartwright, the sole dissenter, rejected the implication in the majority's position that the Bill of Rights could have no effect on laws enacted before the Bill of Rights. In his view section 5 made it clear that the Bill was "to apply to all laws of Canada already in existence at the time it came into force as well as those thereafter enacted."

If Canadian civil libertarians were dismayed by the Court's decision in *Robertson and Rosetanni* they found new grounds for hope in the Court's next major decision on the Bill of Rights. This did not occur until 1970 in the *Drybones* decision which concerned the compatibility of provisions in the Indian Act restricting the drinking rights of Indians with the egalitarian provisions of the Bill of Rights. Ironically, on this occasion the positions of Cartwright and Ritchie were completely reversed. Justice Ritchie still spoke for the majority, but this time it was an "activist" majority willing to use the Bill of Rights to invalidate a long-established piece of federal legislation. Cartwright, now Chief Justice, along with Justices Abbott and Pigeon, refused to give the Bill such a wide-reaching effect.

Justice Ritchie's opinion removed the most conservative meaning of his judgment in the *Robertson and Rosetanni* case: the Bill of Rights could expand rights and freedoms beyond legislative restrictions which existed at the time of its enactment. But it is still not entirely clear what in his view is the precise role of historical data in interpreting the meaning of the rights and freedoms inscribed in the Bill. Still it is notable that a majority of the Court rejected the position adopted by a number of lower court judges that the Bill of Rights was nothing more than an interpretation Act. According to this view, the Bill simply sets out some guidelines for the interpretation of statutes; statutes should be interpreted so far as possible in a manner consistent with the Bill of Rights but where no such interpretation is possible the Bill of Rights must be ignored. This was the most conservative approach the courts could have taken to the Bill. The three justices (Abbott, Pigeon and Chief Justice Cartwright) who did accept this conservative approach were clearly troubled by the implications of a more activist approach and did not want to enlarge the judiciary's opportunities for overruling Parliament. The Chief Justice frankly acknowledged that he had arrived at this position after a reconsideration of the position he had taken in *Robertson and Rosetanni*.

The majority's position on the meaning of "equality before the law" was also much more liberal than the understanding of this concept which had prevailed in some of the lower courts. Justice Tysoe of British Columbia had advanced the view that this egalitarian ideal simply required that there must be no discrimination amongst the particular category of people to whom a law applies. This would mean that it would be perfectly in accord with equality before the law to have laws restricting the rights of women, or Indians, or Catholics, so long as all who belong to a particular category were equally discriminated against. The six judge majority (and the three dissenters did not dissent on this point) rejected this view and held that equality before the law meant at least that the criminal law should not treat one racial group more harshly than other Canadians.

Since *Drybones* the Court has not reversed the position that legislation is inoperative to the extent that it conflicts with the Canadian Bill of Rights unless Parliament has expressly declared that the legislation shall operate notwithstanding the Canadian Bill of Rights. However, a majority of judges have interpreted the rights and freedoms in the Bill so narrowly that the Court has not ruled legislation inoperative since *Drybones*. This narrow construction of the rights and freedoms in the Bill is particularly evident in the cases dealing with equality before the law.

In *Miller and Cockerill* v. *The Queen*,[3] Justice Ritchie came close to returning to a pre-Drybones position. The case raised the question of whether capital punishment contravened the protection against "cruel and unusual punishment" in section 2(b) of the Bill of Rights. In Justice Ritchie's view "the fact that Parliament had retained the death penalty as part of the Criminal Code after the enactment of the Canadian Bill of Rights constitutes strong evidence of the fact that it had never been intended that the word 'punishment' as employed in s. 2(b) should preclude punishment by death in the case of an individual who has been duly convicted of murder." But it must be noted that this was only one of the reasons advanced by Justice Ritchie for concluding that capital punishment did not constitute a violation of the protection against cruel and unusual punishment. Chief Justice Laskin wrote a concurring opinion carefully examining U.S. constitutional jurisprudence on this issue and concluded that there were reasonable grounds for Parliament's believing that a valid social purpose could be served by retaining the death penalty for the murder of policemen and prison guards. (Parliament subsequently abolished the death penalty even for these cases.) ~

---

[3] [1977] 2 S.C.R. 680.

THE QUEEN v. DRYBONES
In the Supreme Court of Canada [1970] S.C.R. 282.

CHIEF JUSTICE CARTWRIGHT (dissenting) . . .

In approaching this question I will assume the correctness of the view that s. 94(b) infringes the right of the respondent to equality before the law declared by clause (b) of s. 1 of the Bill, in that because he is an Indian it renders him guilty of a punishable offence by reason of conduct which would not have been punishable if indulged in by any person who was not an Indian. . . .

In *Robertson and Rosetanni* v. *The Queen, supra,* I had to deal with a similar question as in my view The Lord's Day Act did infringe the freedom of religion. At pages 661 and 662 I used the following words:

It remains to consider the reasons for judgment of Davey J.A. in Regina v. Gonzales *(1962) 32 D.L.R. (2d) 290. At page 239 of the C.C.C. Reports the learned Justice of Appeal says:*

In so far as existing legislation does not offend against any of the matters specifically mentioned in clauses (a) to (g) of s. 2, but is said to otherwise infringe upon some of the human rights and fundamental freedoms declared in s. 1, in my opinion the section does not repeal such legislation either expressly or by implication. On the contrary, it expressly recognizes the continued existence of such legislation, but provides that it shall be construed and applied so as not to derogate from those rights and freedoms. By that it seems merely to provide a canon or rule of interpretation for such legislation. The very language of s. 2 "be so construed and applied as not to abrogate" assumes that the prior Act may be sensibly construed and applied in a way that will avoid derogating from the rights and freedoms declared in s. 1. If the prior legislation cannot be so construed and applied sensibly, then the effect of s. 2 is exhausted, and the prior legislation must prevail according to its plain meaning.

With the greatest respect I find myself unable to agree with this view. The imperative words of s. 2 of the Canadian Bill of Rights, quoted above, appear to me to require the courts to refuse to apply any law, coming within the legislative authority of Parliament, which infringes freedom of religion unless it is expressly declared by an Act of Parliament that the law which does so infringe shall operate notwithstanding the Canadian Bill of Rights. As already pointed out s. 5(2), quoted above, makes it plain that the Canadian Bill of Rights is to apply to all laws of Canada already in existence at the time it came into force as well as to those thereafter enacted. In my opinion where there is irreconcilable conflict between another Act of Parliament and the Canadian Bill of Rights the latter must prevail. . . .

After a most anxious reconsideration of the whole question, in the light of the able arguments addressed to us by counsel, I have reached the conclusion that the view expressed by Davey J.A., as he then was, in the words quoted above is the better one.

The question is whether or not it is the intention of Parliament to confer the power and impose the responsibility upon the courts of declaring inoperative any provisions in a Statute of Canada although expressed in clear and unequivocal terms, the meaning of which after calling in aid every rule of construction including that prescribed by s. 2 of the Bill is perfectly plain, if in the view of the court it infringes any of the rights or freedoms declared by s. 1 of the Bill.

In approaching this question it must not be forgotten that the responsibility mentioned above, if imposed at all, is imposed upon every justice of the peace, magistrate and judge or any court in the country who is called upon to apply a Statute of Canada or any order, rule or regulation made thereunder.

If it were intended that the question should be answered in the affirmative there would, in my opinion, have been added after the word "declared" in the seventh line of the opening paragraph of s. 2 of the Bill some such words as the following "and if any law of Canada cannot be so construed and applied it shall be regarded as inoperative or *pro tanto* repealed".

What now appears to me to have been the error in my reasoning in the passage from *Robertson and Rosetanni* v. *The Queen* quoted above is found in the statement that the Bill requires the courts to refuse to apply any law of Canada which is successfully impugned as infringing one of the declared rights or freedoms whereas on the contrary, as Davey J.A. had pointed out, the Bill directs the courts to apply such a law not to refuse to apply it.

For these reasons I would dispose of the appeal as proposed by my brother Pigeon.

The judgment of Fauteux, Martland, Judson, Ritchie and Spence JJ. was delivered by

RITCHIE J.: This is an appeal brought with leave of this Court from a judgment of the Court of Appeal for the Northwest Territories ([1967], 61 W.W.R. 370) dismissing an appeal by the Crown from a judgment of Mr. Justice W.G. Morrow of the Territorial Court of the Northwest Territories by which he had acquitted Joseph Drybones of being "unlawfully intoxicated off a reserve" contrary to s. 94(*b*) of the Indian Act, R.S.C. 1952, c. 149, after having heard an appeal by way of trial *de novo* from a judgment of Magistrate Anderson-Thompson who had convicted the respondent of this offence and sentenced him to be fined $10 and costs and in default to spend three days in custody. The full charge against Drybones was that he, *On or about the 8th day of April, 1967 at Yellowknife in the Northwest Territories, being an Indian, was unlawfully intoxicated off a reserve, contrary to s. 94(b) of the Indian Act.*

The respondent is an Indian and he was indeed intoxicated on the evening of April 8, 1967, on the premises of the Old Stope Hotel in Yellowknife in the Northwest Territories where there is no "reserve" within the meaning of the Indian Act.

When he was first arraigned before Magistrate Anderson-Thompson, Drybones, who spoke no English, pleaded guilty to this offence, but on appeal to the Territorial Court, Mr. Justice Morrow found that there was some serious doubt as to whether he fully appreciated his plea in the lower court and he was allowed to withdraw that plea whereafter the appeal proceeded as a trial *de novo* with a plea of not guilty. Section 94 of the Indian Act reads as follows:

> *94. An Indian who*
> *(a) has intoxicants in his possession,*
> *(b) is intoxicated, or*
> *(c) makes or manufactures intoxicants off a reserve, is guilty of an offence and is liable on summary conviction to a fine of not less than ten dollars and not more than fifty dollars or to imprisonment for a term not exceeding three months or to both fine and imprisonment.*

I agree with the Court of Appeal that the use of the words "off a reserve" creates

> . . . *an essential element to be proved in any charge laid under section 94. But once it is proved, as it was in the present case, that the offence was not committed upon a reserve, the requirement of the section was satisfied. The fact that there are no reserves in the Territories is quite irrelevant.*

The important question raised by this appeal has its origin in the fact that in the Northwest Territories it is not an offence for anyone except an Indian to be intoxicated otherwise than in a public place. The Liquor Ordinance which is of general application in the Territories, (R.O.N.W.T. 1957, c. 60, s. 19(1)) provides that: *No person shall be in an intoxicated condition in a public place*

. . . but unlike s. 94 of the Indian Act, there is no provision for a minimum fine and the maximum term of imprisonment is only 30 days as opposed to three months under the Indian Act.

The result is that an Indian who is intoxicated in his own home "off a reserve" is guilty of an offence and subject to a minimum fine of not less than $10 or a term of imprisonment not exceeding three months or both, whereas all other citizens in the Territories may, if they see fit, become intoxicated otherwise than in a public place without committing any offence at all. And even if any such other citizen is convicted of being intoxicated in a public place, the only penalty provided by the Ordinance is "a fine not exceeding $50 or . . . imprisonment for a term not exceeding 30 days or . . . both fine and imprisonment."

The argument which was successfully advanced by the respondent before Mr. Justice Morrow and before the Court of Appeal was that because of this legislation, Indians in the Northwest Territories, by reason of their race, are denied "equality before the law" with their fellow Canadians, and that s. 94(b) of the Indian Act therefore authorizes the abrogation, abridgement or infringement of one of the human rights and fundamental freedoms recognized and declared as existing in Canada without discrimination by reason of race, pursuant to the provisions of the Canadian Bill of Rights . . . which provides, *inter alia:*

1. It is hereby recognized and declared that in Canada there have existed and shall continue to exist without discrimination by reason of race, national origin, colour, religion or sex, the following human rights and fundamental freedoms, namely

. . .

(b) the right of the individual to equality before the law and the protection of the law;

. . .

2. Every law of Canada shall, unless it
is expressly declared by an Act of the Parliament of Canada that it shall operate notwithstanding the Canadian Bill of Rights, be so construed and applied as not to abrogate, abridge or infringe, or to authorize the abrogation, abridgement or infringement of any of the rights or freedoms herein recognized and declared.

5.(2) The expression "law of Canada" in Part I means an Act of the Parliament of Canada enacted before or after the coming into force of this Act, any order, rule or regulation thereunder, and any law in force in Canada or in any part of Canada at the commencement of this Act that is subject to be repealed, abolished or altered by the Parliament of Canada.

The Court of Appeal agreed with Mr. Justice Morrow that s. 94(b) of the Indian Act is rendered inoperative by reason of this legislation and the Notice of appeal to this Court is limited to the single ground

That the Court of Appeal in the Northwest Territories in upholding the decision of the Territorial Court of the Northwest Territories erred in acquitting the respondent of "an offence contrary to s. 94(b) of the Indian Act, R.S.C. 1952 Ch. 149 on the ground that s. 94 of the Indian Act is rendered inoperative by reason of the Canadian Bill of Rights, Stat. Can. 1960 Ch. 44".

It was contended on behalf of the appellant that the reasoning and conclusion of the courts below make the question of whether s. 94 has been rendered inoperative by the Bill of Rights dependent upon whether or not the law of any province or territory makes it an offence to be intoxicated otherwise than in a public place and that its operation could therefore not only vary from place to place in Canada but also from time to time, depending upon amendments which might be made to the provincial or territorial legislation. I can, however, find no room for the application of this argument in the present case as the ordinance in question is a law of Canada within the meaning of s. 5(2) of the Bill of Rights (see Northwest Territories Act, R.S.C. 1952, c. 195, s. 17) and it is a law of general application in the Territories, whereas the Indian Act is, of course, also a law of Canada although it has special application to Indians alone.

The question of whether s. 94 of the Indian Act is rendered inoperative by reason of the provisions of the Bill of Rights on the ground that it abrogates, abridges or infringes the right of Canadians of the Indian race to "equality before the law" was considered by the Court of Appeal of British Columbia in *Regina* v. *Gonzales* ([1962], 37 W.W.R. 257) where Tysoe J.A., speaking for the majority of the Court, concluded that:

Sec. 94(a) of the Indian Act does not abrogate or infringe the right of the appellant to 'equality before the law' as I understand it. Sec. 2 of the Canadian Bill of Rights does not therefore affect it.

In reaching the same conclusion, Davey J.A., (as he then was) who wrote separate reasons for judgment from the other two members of the Court, took the view that s. 1 of the Bill of Rights should be treated as merely providing a canon of construction for the interpretation of legislation existing at the time when the statute was enacted.

~ Justice Ritchie then quotes at length from the same judgment quoted by the Chief Justice above. ~

This proposition appears to me to strike at the very foundation of the Bill of Rights and to convert it from its apparent character as a statutory declaration of the fundamental human rights and freedoms which it recognizes, into being little more than a rule for the construction of federal statutes, but as this approach has found favour with some eminent legal commentators, it seems to me to be important that priority should be given to a consideration of it.

I will hereafter refer to the case of *Robertson and Rosetanni* v. *The Queen*

([1963] S.C.R. 652), but in the present context I mention it only to say that like the courts below I agree with what was said by the present Chief Justice in his dissenting reasons for judgment when commenting on the above view expressed by Mr. Justice Davey. . . . I do not find that this expression of opinion in any way conflicts with the reasoning of the majority of this Court in *Robertson and Rosetanni* v. *The Queen, supra*, which held that there was no conflict between the impugned section of the Lord's Day Act and the Bill of Rights.

I am, however, with respect, of the opinion that Mr. Justice Davey's reasoning is untenable on another ground. The result of that reasoning is to conclude that any law of Canada which can only be "construed and applied sensibly" so that it offends against the Bill of Rights, is to operate notwithstanding the provisions of the Bill. I am unable to reconcile this interpretation with the opening words of s. 2 where it is provided that: "Every law of Canada shall, *unless it is expressly declared by an Act of the Parliament of Canada that it shall operate notwithstanding the Canadian Bill of Rights*, be so construed and applied as not to abrogate . . ." (The italics are my own.)

If Mr. Justice Davey's reasoning were correct and the Bill of Rights were to be construed as meaning that all laws of Canada which clearly offend the Bill were to operate notwithstanding its provisions, then the words which I have italicized in s. 2 would be superfluous unless it be suggested that Parliament intended to reserve unto itself the right to exclude from the effect of the Bill of Rights only such statutes as are unclear in their meaning.

It seems to me that a more realistic meaning must be given to the words in question and they afford, in my view, the clearest indication that s. 2 is intended to mean and does mean that if a law of Canada cannot be "sensibly construed and applied" so that it does not abrogate, abridge or infringe one of the rights and freedoms recognized and declared by the

Bill, then such law is inoperative "unless it is expressly declared by an Act of the Parliament of Canada that it shall operate notwithstanding the Canadian Bill of Rights".

I think a declaration by the courts that a section or portion of a section of a statute is inoperative is to be distinguished from the repeal of such a section and is to be confined to the particular circumstances of the case in which the declaration is made. The situation appears to me to be somewhat analogous to a case where valid provincial legislation in an otherwise unoccupied field ceases to be operative by reason of conflicting federal legislation.

I think it is desirable at this stage to deal with the submission made on behalf of the appellant to the effect that the rights and freedoms recognized and declared by the Bill of Rights must have reference to *and be circumscribed by* the laws of Canada as they existed on the 10th of August, 1960, when the Bill was passed, which laws included s. 94 of the Indian Act. This submission is based in large measure on the following paragraph from the reasons for judgment of this Court in *Robertson and Rosetanni* v. *The Queen, supra,* where it said:

It is to be noted at the outset that the Canadian Bill of Rights is not concerned with "human rights and fundamental freedoms" in any abstract sense but rather with such rights and freedoms as existed in Canada immediately before the statute was enacted (see also s. 5(1)). It is therefore the "religious freedom" then existing in this country that is safeguarded by the provisions of s. 2. . . .

What was at issue in that case was whether the Lord's Day Act, in providing that "it shall be unlawful for any person on the Lord's Day . . . to carry on or transact any business of his ordinary calling . . ." abrogated, abridged or infringed the right to "freedom of religion", and it was contended on behalf of the appellant that the phrase "freedom of religion" as used in the Bill of Rights meant "freedom to enjoy the freedom

which my own religion allows without being confined by restrictions imposed by Parliament for the purpose of enforcing the tenets of a faith to which I do not subscribe". In considering the contention, it became necessary to examine the decided cases in order to determine what was the accepted meaning of "freedom of religion" as it existed in Canada immediately before the Bill of Rights was enacted and the last-quoted excerpt from the reasons for justment must, in my view, be read in this sense. This appears to me to be confirmed by the succeeding paragraph of these reasons where it is said:

It is accordingly of first importance to understand the concept of religious freedom which was recognized in this country before the enactment of the Bill of Rights and after the enactment of the Lord's Day Act in its present form.

If it had been accepted that the right to "freedom of religion" as declared in the Bill of Rights was circumscribed by the provisions of the Canadian statutes in force at the date of its enactment, there would have been no need, in determining the validity of the Lord's Day Act to consider the authorities in order to examine the situation in light of the concept of religious freedom which was recognized in Canada at the time of the enactment of the Bill of Rights. It would have been enough to say that "freedom of religion" as used in the Bill must mean freedom of religion subject to the provisions of the Lord's Day Act. This construction would, however, have run contrary to the provisions of s. 5(2) of the Bill which makes it applicable to every "Act of Parliament of Canada enacted before or after the coming into force of this Act".

In any event, it was not necessary to decide this question in *Robertson and Rosetanni* because it was found that the impugned provisions of the Lord's Day Act and the Bill of Rights were not in conflict, and I accordingly do not consider that case to be any authority for the suggestion that the Bill of Rights is to be treated as being subject to federal legislation existing at the time of its enactment, and more particularly I, do not consider that the provisions of s. 1(*b*) of the Bill of Rights are to be treated as being in any way limited or affected by the terms of s. 94(*b*) of the Indian Act.

The right which is here at issue is "the right of the individual to equality before the law and the protection of the law". Mr. Justice Tysoe, who wrote the reasons for judgment on behalf of the majority of the Court of Appeal of British Columbia in the *Gonzales* case, *supra*, expressed the opinion that as these words occur in the Bill of Rights they mean: "A right of every person to *whom a particular law relates or extends*, no matter what may be a person's race, national origin, colour, religion or sex, to stand on an equal footing with every other person to whom a particular law relates or extends and a right to the protection of the law." (The italics are Mr. Justice Tysoe's.)

Like the members of the courts below, I cannot agree with this interpretation pursuant to which it seems to me that the most glaring discriminatory legislation against a racial group would have to be construed as recognizing the right of each of its individual members "to equality before the law", so long as all the other members are being discriminated against in the same way.

I think that the word "law" as used in s. 1(*b*) of the Bill of Rights is to be construed as meaning "the law of Canada" as defined in s. 5(2) (i.e. Acts of the Parliament of Canada and any orders, rules or regulations thereunder) and without attempting any exhaustive definition of "equality before the law" I think that s. 1(*b*) means at least that no individual or group of individuals is to be treated more harshly than another under that law, and I am therefore of the opinion that an individual is denied equality before the law if it is made an offence punishable at law, on account of his race, for him to do something which his fellow Canadians are free to do without having committed any

offence or having been made subject to any penalty.

It is only necessary for the purpose of deciding this case for me to say that in my opinion s. 94(*b*) of the Indian Act is a law of Canada which creates such an off offence and that it can only be construed in such manner that its application would operate so as to abrogate, abridge or infringe one of the rights declared and recognized by the Bill of Rights. For the reasons which I have indicated, I am therefore of opinion that s. 94(*b*) is inoperative. . . .

It may well be that the implementation of the Canadian Bill of Rights by the courts can give rise to great difficulties, but in my view full effect must be given to the terms of s. 2 thereof.

The present case discloses laws of Canada which abrogate, abridge and infringe the right of an individual Indian to equality before the law and in my opinion if those laws are to be applied in accordance with the express language used by Parliament in s. 2 of the Bill of Rights, then s. 94(*b*) of the Indian Act must be declared to be inoperative.

It appears to me to be desirable to make it plain that these reasons for judgment are limited to a situation in which, under the laws of Canada, it is made an offence punishable at law on account of race; for a person to do something which all Canadians who are not members of that race may do with impunity; in my opinion the same considerations do not by any means apply to all the provisions of the Indian Act.

HALL J.: I agree with the reasons of my brother Ritchie and wish only to add some observations regarding the decision in *Regina* v. *Gonzales* ([1962], 37 W.W.R. 257).

The concept that the Canadian Bill of Rights is operative in the face of a law of Canada only when that law does not give equality to all persons within the class to whom that particular law extends or relates, as it was expressed by Tysoe J.A. at p. 264:

Coming now to sec. 1(b) of the Canadian Bill of Rights. The meaning of the word "equality" is well known. In my opinion, the word "before" in the expression "equality before the law", in the sense in which that expression is used in sec. 1(b) means "in the presence of". It seems to me this is the key to the correct interpretation of the expression and makes it clear that "equality before the law" has nothing to do with the application of the law equally to everyone and equal laws for everyone in the sense for which appellant's counsel contends, namely, the same laws for all persons, but to the position occupied by persons to whom a law relates or extends. They shall be entitled to have the law as it exists applied equally and without fear or favour to all persons to whom it relates or extends.

is analogous to the position taken by the Supreme Court of the United States in *Plessy* v. *Ferguson* ([1896], 163 U.S. 537) and which was wholly rejected by the same Court in its historic desegregation judgment *Brown* v. *Board of Education* ([1954], 347 U.S. 483).

In *Plessy* v. *Ferguson*, the Court had held that under the "separate but equal" doctrine equality of treatment is accorded when the races are provided substantially equal facilities even though these facilities be separate. In *Brown* v. *Board of Education*, the Court held the "separate but equal" doctrine to be totally invalid.

The social situations in *Brown* v. *Board of Education* and in the instant case are, of course, very different, but the basic philosophic concept is the same. The Canadian Bill of Rights is not fulfilled if it merely equates Indians with Indians in terms of equality before the law, but can have validity and meaning only when subject to the single exception set out in s. 2 it is seen to repudiate discrimination in every law of Canada by reason of race, national origin, colour, religion or sex in respect of human rights and fundamental freedoms set out in s. 1 in whatever way that discrimination may manifest itself not

only as between Indian and Indian but as between all Canadians whether Indian or non-Indian.

PIGEON J. (*dissenting*): . . . one must observe that the Bill itself begins by a solemn declaration by Parliament in the form of an enactment that, in Canada, the enumerated rights and freedoms "have existed and shall continue to exist. . . ." This statement is the essential element of the very first provision of the Bill and it is absolutely unqualified. It is the starting point of that legislation and I have great difficulty in reconciling it with the contention that in fact those rights and freedoms were not wholly and completely existing but were restricted by any number of statutory and other provisions infringing thereon. . . .

In the instant case, the question whether all existing legislation should be considered as in accordance with the non-discrimination principle cannot fail to come immediately to mind seeing that it arises directly out of head 24 of s. 91 of the B.N.A. Act whereby Parliament has exclusive legislative authority over "Indians, and Lands reserved for Indians". As was pointed out by Riddell J. in *Rex* v. *Martin* ([1917], 29 C.C.C. 189 at 192), this provision confers legislative authority over the Indians *qua* Indians and not otherwise. Its very object in so far as it relates to Indians, as opposed to Lands reserved for the Indians, is to enable the Parliament of Canada to make legislation applicable only to Indians as such and therefore not applicable to Canadian citizens generally. This legislative authority is obviously intended to be exercised over matters that are, as regards persons other than Indians, within the exclusive authority of the provinces. Complete uniformity in provincial legislation is clearly not to be expected, not to mention the fact that further diversity must also result from special legislation for the territories. Equality before the law in the sense in which it was understood in the Courts below would require the Indians to be subject in every province to the same rules of law as all others in every particular not merely on the question of drunkenness. Outside the territories, provincial jurisdiction over education and health facilities would make it very difficult for federal authorities to provide such facilities to Indians without "discrimination" as understood in the Courts below.

If one of the effects of the Canadian Bill of Rights is to render inoperative all legal provisions whereby Indians as such are not dealt with in the same way as the general public, the conclusion is inescapable that Parliament, by the enactment of the Bill, has not only fundamentally altered the status of the Indians in that indirect fashion but has also made any future use of federal legislative authority over them subject to the requirement of expressly declaring every time "that the law shall operate notwithstanding the Canadian Bill of Rights". I find it very difficult to believe that Parliament so intended when enacting the Bill. If a virtual suppression of federal legislation over Indians as such was meant, one would have expected this important change to be made explicitly not surreptitiously so to speak.

In s. 2, the crucial words are that every law of Canada shall, subject to the exception just noted, "be so construed and applied as not to abrogate, abridge or infringe" any of the rights and freedoms recognized and declared in the Bill. The question is whether those words enact something more than a rule of construction. Of themselves, it seems to me that they do not. Certainly the word "construed" implies nothing else. Does the word "applied" express a different intention? I do not think so and, even if this may appear a trite saying, I must point out that what respondent asks the Court to do and what the Courts below have effectively done is not to apply the statute, the Indian Act, but to decline to apply it.

The strongest argument against viewing s. 2 as a canon of construction is undoubtedly that the exception "unless it is expressly declared by an Act of Parliament of Canada that it shall operate notwithstanding the Canadian Bill of Rights" is thereby deprived of any practical meaning. It cannot be denied that the operation of a rule of construction is not normally subject to such a qualification. On the contrary, that principle is that it has no effect against the clearly expressed will of Parliament in whatever form it is put.

On the other hand, in seeking to give effect to some words in s. 2 that cannot for obvious reasons be applicable to any existing law, one must always bear in mind the very starting point of the Bill, namely that the rights and freedoms therein recognized are declared as existing, not as being introduced or expanded. If in s. 1 the Act means what it says and recognizes and declares *existing* rights and freedoms only, nothing more than proper construction of existing laws in accordance with the Bill is required to accomplish the intended result. There can never be any necessity for declaring any of them inoperative as coming in conflict with the rights and freedoms defined in the Bill seeing that these are declared as existing in them. Thus, it appears to me that s. 2 cannot be construed as suggested by respondent without coming in conflict with s. 1.

If, with respect to existing legislation, we had to choose between reading s. 1 as written and failing to adopt a construction of s. 2 that gives some meaningful effect to the exception, it seems to me that the choice should be in favour of giving paramount effect to s. 1. It is the provision establishing the principle on which the whole Act rests.

Another compelling reason is the presumption against implicit alteration of the law, Parliament must not be presumed to have intended to depart from the existing law any further than expressly stated Maxwell, *On Interpretation of Statutes*, 9th ed., p. 84, cited in *Duchesneau* v. *Cook* ([1955] S.C.R. 207 at 215). . . .

The meaning of such expressions as "due process of law", "equality before the law", "freedom of religion", "freedom of speech", is in truth largely unlimited and undefined. According to individual views and the evolution of current ideas, the actual content of such legal concepts is apt to expand and to vary as is strikingly apparent in other countries. In the traditional British system that is our own by virtue of the B.N.A. Act, the responsibility for updating the statutes in this changing world rests exclusively upon Parliament. If the Parliament of Canada intended to depart from that principle in enacting the Bill, one would expect to find clear language expressing that intention. On the contrary, what do we find in s. 1 but an apparent desire to adhere to the traditional principle and to avoid the uncertainties inherent in broadly worded enactments by tying the broad words to the large body of existing law and in effect declaring the recognized human rights and fundamental freedoms to be as existing in the laws of Canada.

~ Justice Abbott also wrote a short dissenting opinion. ~

38. Attorney General of Canada v. Lavell and Bédard, *1974*

~ The Supreme Court's decision in the *Lavell* case indicates that a majority of the judges felt the Court had gone too far in an "activist" direction in *Drybones*. The majority opinion does not retreat from the position established in *Drybones* that the Bill of Rights can render inoperative legislation which clearly violates rights enshrined in the Bill, but it did considerably water down the significance of the right to equality before the law.

The decision dealt with appeals in two cases involving Indian women who claimed that section 12(1)(b) of the Indian Act infringed their right to equality before the law under the Bill of Rights. Section 12(1)(b) denied an Indian woman who married a non-Indian her Indian status, including her right to hold property and live on an Indian reserve. A male Indian who married a non-Indian could retain his Indian status. Thus, Mrs. Lavell and Mrs. Bédard argued that section 12(1)(b) constituted discrimination by reason of sex. While they were supported by the Native Council of Canada representing non-status Indians and by several non-Indian women's organizations, most of the organizations representing status Indians, including eight provincial and two territorial organizations and the National Indian Brotherhood, intervened to oppose Mrs. Lavell and Mrs. Bédard.

The Supreme Court decided, five to four, that section 12(1)(b) did not constitute a violation of equality before the law. Again Justice Ritchie wrote the majority opinion. Just as it is difficult to reconcile his opinion in *Drybones* with the position he had taken earlier in *Robertson and Rosetanni*, it is a daunting task to trace a thread of consistency between his approach to equality before the law in *Lavell* and his treatment of that concept in *Drybones*. Citing A.V. Dicey, the nineteenth-century English constitutional writer, as his authority, Justice Ritchie now defined equality before the law not as a substantive requirement of the law itself, but a requirement of the way in which laws are administered. The Indian Act might well discriminate against women but so long as it was applied equally to all whom it affected there would be no violation of equality before the law. To this argument Justice Ritchie added the concern expressed by Justice Pigeon in his dissenting opinion in *Drybones*: it would be unreasonable to extend the Bill of Rights so far as to make it impossible for Parliament to enact special legislation concerning the property and civil rights of Indians.

Justice Laskin, as has so often been the case in civil liberties cases, wrote a vigorous dissent. He could not reconcile the majority's interpretation of equality before the law with the Court's decision in *Drybones*. The opening paragraph of section 1 of the Canadian Bill of Rights, in his view, amounted to a prohibition of legal classifications based on race, national origin, colour, religion or sex. In this sense the Canadian Bill of Rights was more specific and categorical than the equal protection of laws clause in the American Constitution which did not prohibit any specific form of discrimination, leaving it to the judiciary to distinguish reasonable and unreasonable forms of discrimination. Laskin could not see why laws based on Parliament's power under section 91(24) of the B.N.A. Act to legislate in relation to Indians should enjoy any special immunity from the Bill of Rights. To decide otherwise in this case would, in his view, compound racial inequality with sexual inequality. Justice Laskin's dissent was supported by Justices Spence, Hall and Abbott. Justice Abbott had dissented in *Drybones* but regarded that decision as now requiring him to support Justice Laskin's dissent. Justice Pigeon, on the other hand, who also dissented in *Drybones*, this time joined the majority and appeared to regard the results of this case as supportive of the position he had taken in *Drybones*.

The most promising explanation for the logical difficulties posed by the majority opinion is political, not jurisprudential. The judges had been made aware that ruling section 12(1)(b) inoperative would cause political and policy difficulties not posed by the *Drybones* decision, and they drew back in an attempt to avoid the political thicket Justice Cartwright had warned them about in *Drybones*.

The central question was whether a broad interpretation of the Bill of Rights equality guarantee would undermine the entire Indian Act. This concern had been expressed by Justice Pigeon in his dissenting opinion in *Drybones*. His argument had not then impressed the majority of the Court, but by the time the *Lavell* and *Bedard* cases reached them it had become a pressing concern. In a number of cases in the lower courts various sections of the Indian Act had been successfully challenged on the basis of *Drybones*, including section 12(1)(b), which had been invalidated by the Federal Court of Canada in *Lavell*. Furthermore, arguments alleging the invalidation of the entire Indian Act had been respectfully considered in some courts. Finally, in July of 1973, Justice Osler of the Ontario High Court accepted the latter argument in *Isaac* v. *Davey*.[1]

By the time this decision was rendered, the Indian community had become alerted to the threat posed to the Indian Act by this jurisprudence and had mobilized to oppose it. Although Indians were not happy with all aspects of the Act and its administration, they were not prepared to abandon the idea of special status as such. Not long before, they had successfully resisted the Trudeau government's 1969 proposal to dismantle the Indian Act in favour of an individualized concept of equal Canadian citizenship, and they worried that their political victory might now be judicially undone.

In addition to the implicit challenge to the idea of special status, serious

---

[1] [1973] 3 O.R. 677. For an account of these events see Douglas Sanders, "The Bill of Rights and the Indian Act," in Anne Bayefsky and Mary Eberts (eds.), *Equality Rights and the Charter* (Toronto: Carswell, 1985), 534-7.

political problems were raised by the possible invalidation of s. 12(1)(b) itself. The liquor provisions of the Indian Act struck down in *Drybones* were relatively unimportant parts of the Indian Act, with few implications for the system of special status established by the Act. Their invalidation really did not change anything. To the contrary, in most of the country they had already been repealed under local option provisions of the Indian Act, and they were nowhere actively supported. Thus, in *Drybones* the "Supreme Court was invited to strike down the feeble remnants of 19th century Indian liquor laws."[2] To do so, moreover, would create no legal gap and pose no policy dilemmas; the relevant laws for the rest of the population would now simply apply to Indians as well.

The same could not be said of the status-defining provisions of s. 12(1)(b). Some way of determining status was required, and if these rules were invalidated what would replace them? The Court, which could invalidate them, could not itself fill the legal gap that would ensue. Furthermore, what would be the practical, particularly the financial, implications of returning status to women who had lost it? Through the Minister of Indian Affairs, the National Indian Brotherhood expressed strong opposition "to the principles contained in the Lavell decision [in the Federal Court] and, in particular, to the effects which they fear it will have on their already overcrowded reserves and their already overcrowded schools." For example, the Minister estimated that it would cost one million dollars to reimburse women like Lavell for the share of band funds they did not receive following their marriages to non-Indians, "even if the principle of the Lavell case only applies to marriages which have taken place since the Canadian Bill of Rights was enacted."[3]

The existence of major political problems and the extent of the opposition to the invalidation of s. 12(1)(b) was underlined for the Supreme Court by the number of aspiring intervenors clamouring at its door. Whereas in *Drybones* the judges were faced by an antiquated and insignificant section of the Act, which nobody was willing to defend, in *Lavell* and *Bedard* they saw the Federal Government and all of the status Indian organizations lining up in vigorous support of the status quo. Indeed, "the provincial Indian Associations, along with the National Indian Brotherhood, joined together in support of a single submission to the Court in support of section 12(1)(b), a rare show of unity and organization."[4] In this context, the concerns Justice Cartwright expressed in *Drybones* about the dangers of the political thicket must have loomed much larger for the Court as a whole.

Since *Lavell and Bédard* the Supreme Court has rejected a series of attacks

---

[2] Ibid., p. 539.

[3] Ibid., p. 543.

[4] Baar, "Using Process Theory to Explain Judicial Decision Making," (1986), 1 *Canadian Journal of Law and Society*, 86.

on discriminatory provisions in federal legislation. In *Burnshine*[5] the Court dismissed an attack on provisions of the Prisons and Reformatories Act under which young offenders in British Columbia and Ontario may serve longer periods of detention than adults or youths in other provinces. In the *Canard*[6] case the Court held that provisions of the Indian Act giving a federal Minister the power to administer the estates of Indians did not infringe the right of Indians to equality before the law. Justice Laskin (who between these two cases had been elevated to the Chief Justiceship) wrote dissents in both cases.

The *Bliss*[7] case concerned amendments to the Unemployment Insurance Act which created a special pregnancy benefit but made it conditional on serving a much longer employment period than required for other benefits and denied a woman who left the work force because of pregnancy access to the ordinary benefits. The Court unanimously (Chief Justice Laskin did not participate in this decision) held that these provisions involved no denial of equality before the law. Justice Ritchie who authored the Court's opinion contended that they were "an integral part of a legislative scheme enacted for valid federal objectives and they are concerned with conditions from which men are excluded. Any inequality between the sexes in this area is not created by legislation but by nature." The idea that so long as legislation serves "a valid federal objective" it is a justifiable discrimination was enunciated three years earlier in the *Prata*[8] case in which the Court unanimously rejected the contention that provisions of the Immigration Act restricting the rights of persons deemed to be security risks constituted a denial of equality before the law.

However, there is still no clear consensus amongst the members of the Supreme Court as to whether the test of "serving a valid federal objective" means more than that legislation should be in relation to a matter constitutionally within the federal Parliament's jurisdiction. The *MacKay* case, decided in 1980, provided a good test of the justices' position on this question. The case concerned provisions of the National Defence Act under which a member of the armed forces had been convicted by a court martial for a number of drug offences committed at a military base. While the Court decided, seven to two, that in these circumstances there was no denial of equality before the law, two of the judges who supported the majority (Justices McIntyre and Dickson) took the position that equality before the law would be violated by the broad provisions of the Act that subjected members of the armed forces to military trials for *all* criminal offences even those having no relationship to a military context. In reaching this conclusion, Justice McIntyre held that in

---

[5] [1975] 1 S.C.R. 693.
[6] [1976] 1 S.C.R. 170.
[7] [1979] 1 S.C.R. 183.
[8] [1976] 1 S.C.R. 376.

determining whether a discriminatory classification in federal legislation served a valid federal objective and therefore did not violate equality before the law, the Court must decide whether the inequality "has been created rationally in the sense that it is not arbitrary or capricious and not based upon any ulterior motive . . . and whether it is a necessary departure from the general principle of universal application of the law for the attainment of some necessary and desirable social objective.''⁹ The two dissenting judges, Chief Justice Laskin and Justice Estey, also appeared to accept the view that discriminatory laws must be based on reasonable classifications. Still, this test of the rationality of legislative classifications, borrowed from American constitutional law, has not been endorsed by a majority of Supreme Court judges.

The equality clause of the Charter of Rights, section 15, is certainly meant to have a more significant effect than the equality provisions in the Canadian Bill of Rights. Indeed, the section contains wording explicitly intended to counteract the *Lavell* and *Bliss* cases. In addition to "equality before the law and the equal protection of the law," section 15 protects "equality under the law" (to overrule *Lavell*) and "equal benefit of the law" (to overrule *Bliss*). The section stipulates that these rights are to be enjoyed "without discrimination and, in particular, without discrimination based on race, national or ethnic origin, colour, religion, sex, age or mental or physical disability." An interpretation imposed on the equal protection of laws by the U.S. Supreme Court is explicitly overcome by providing that affirmative action laws which discriminate in order to improve the condition of disadvantaged individuals or groups shall not be regarded as violating the equality rights.

Despite these efforts to provide a clearer definition of a constitutional right to equality, section 15 is likely to be a fertile source of litigation. Indeed, the complexities posed by section 15 are such that its applicability was delayed until three years after the rest of the Charter came into force so that the provincial and federal governments could have a breathing period in which to bring their laws in practices into line with its requirements. The section almost certainly goes beyond Justice Ritchie's procedural definition of equality in *Lavell* and makes equality a substantive requirement of the law itself, but this does not mean that the Court will overrule all laws which discriminate. Redistributive laws and laws rationing access to scarce goods, opportunities, or public services are bound to discriminate in favour of some and against others. Amongst the prohibited forms of discrimination are age and mental and physical disability, which are frequently employed as legislative criteria. The application of the equality provisions of the Charter challenges the Supreme Court to take on the important policy-making task of deciding what kinds of discrimination are reasonable. Because the "notwithstanding" clause in the

⁹ [1980] 2 S.C.R. 370, at 407.

Charter applies to Section 15, judicial determination of these issues need not be final. This feature of the Charter will likely generate an important process of interaction between courts and legislatures in settling a wide range of social policy issues.

Although the wording of section 15 was designed to overrule *Lavell*, the precise issue in that case was resolved politically rather than judicially when Parliament, in 1985, ended the sexual discrimination of s. 12(1)(b) and restored the status of an estimated 22,000 individuals who had lost it under that provision. The status of the children of these women was left to be determined by Indian bands, who were given power to determine their own membership systems.[10] ~

ATTORNEY GENERAL OF CANADA *v*. LAVELL AND BEDARD
In the Supreme Court of Canada, [1974] S.C.R. 1349.

The judgment of Fauteux C.J., and Martland, Judson and Ritchie was delivered by

RITCHIE J.: . . . These appeals, which were heard together, are from two judgments holding that the provisions of s. 12(1)(*b*) of the Indian Act, R.S.C. 1970, c. I-6, are rendered inoperative by s. 1(*b*) of the Canadian Bill of Rights, 1960 (Can.), c. 44, as denying equality before the law to the two respondents.

Both respondents were registered Indians and Band members within the meaning of s. 11(*b*) of the Indian Act when they elected to marry non-Indians and thereby relinquished their status as Indians in conformity with the said s. 12(1)(*b*) which read as follows:

12.(1) The following persons are not entitled to be registered, namely, (b) a woman who married a person who is not an Indian, unless that woman is subsequently the wife or widow of a person described in section 11.

It is contended on behalf of both respondents that s. 12(1)(*b*) of the Act should be held to be inoperative as discriminating between Indian men and women and as

being in conflict with the provisions of the Canadian Bill of Rights and particularly s. 1 thereof which provides:

1. It is hereby recognized and declared that in Canada there have existed and shall continue to exist without discrimination by reason of race, national origin, colour, religion or sex, the following human rights and fundamental freedoms, namely, . . .

(b) the right of the individual to equality before the law and the protection of the law; . . .

. . . The contention which formed the basis of the argument submitted by both respondents was that they had been denied equality before the law *by reason of sex*, and I propose to deal with the matter on this basis. . . .

In my opinion the exclusive legislative authority vested in Parliament under s. 91(24) could not have been effectively exercised without enacting laws establishing the qualifications required to entitle persons to status as Indians and to the use and benefit of Crown "lands reserved for Indians". The legislation enacted to this end was, in my view, necessary for the implementation of the authority so vested

---

[10] Sanders, op. cit., p. 550.

in Parliament under the constitution.

To suggest that the provisions of the Bill of Rights have the effect of making the whole Indian Act inoperative as discriminatory is to assert that the Bill has rendered Parliament powerless to exercise the authority entrusted to it under the constitution of enacting legislation which treats Indians living on reserves differently from other Canadians in relation to their property and civil rights. The proposition that such a wide effect is to be given to the Bill of Rights was expressly reserved by the majority of this Court in the case of *The Queen* v. *Drybones*, at 298, to which reference will hereafter be made, and I do not think that it can be sustained.

What is at issue here is whether the Bill of Rights is to be construed as rendering inoperative one of the conditions imposed by Parliament for the use and occupation of Crown lands reserved for Indians. These conditions were imposed as a necessary part of the structure created by Parliament for the internal administration of the life of Indians on reserves and their entitlement to the use and benefit of Crown lands situated thereon, they were thus imposed in discharge of Parliament's constitutional function under s. 91(24) and in my view can only be changed by plain statutory language expressly enacted for the purpose. It does not appear to me that Parliament can be taken to have made or intended to make such a change by the use of broad general language directed at the statutory proclamation of the fundamental rights and freedoms enjoyed by all Canadians, and I am therefore of opinion that the Bill of Rights had no such effect. . . .

The contention that the Bill of Rights is to be construed as overriding all of the special legislation imposed by Parliament under the Indian Act is, in my view, fully answered by Pigeon J. in his dissenting opinion in the *Drybones* case where he said, at p. 304:

If one of the effects of the Canadian Bill of Rights is to render inoperative all legal provisions whereby Indians as such are not dealt with in the same way as the general public, the conclusion is inescapable that Parliament, by the enactment of the Bill, has not only fundamentally altered the status of the Indians in that indirect fashion but has also made any future use of federal legislative authority over them subject to the requirement of expressly declaring every time "that the law shall operate notwithstanding the Canadian Bill of Rights". I find it very difficult to believe that Parliament so intended when enacting the Bill. If a virtual suppression of federal legislation over Indians as such was meant, one would have expected this important change to be made explicitly not surreptitiously so to speak. . . .

In considering the meaning to be given to section 1(b) of the Bill of Rights, regard must of course be had to what was said by Mr. Justice Laskin, speaking in this regard for the whole of the Court in *Curr* v. *The Queen* ([1972] S.C.R. 889), at pp. 896 and 897, where he interpreted sections 1(a) and 1(b) of the Bill in the following passage:

In considering the reach of s. 1(a) and s. 1(b), and, indeed, of s. 1 as a whole, I would observe, first, that the section is given its controlling force over federal law by its referential incorporation into s. 2; and, second, that I do not read it as making the existence of any of the forms of prohibited discrimination, a sine qua non of its operation. Rather, the prohibited discrimination is an additional lever to which federal legislation must respond. Putting the matter another way, federal legislation which does not offend s. 1 in respect of any of the prohibited kinds of discrimination may nonetheless be offensive to s. 1 if it is violative of what is specified in any of the clauses (a) to (f) of s. 1. It is, a fortiori, offensive if there is discrimination by reason of race so as to deny equality before the law. That is what this Court decided in Regina v. Drybones, *and I need say no more on this point.*

It is, therefore, not an answer to reliance by the appellant on s. 1(a) and s. 1(b) of the Canadian Bill of Rights that s. 223 does not discriminate against any person by reason of race, national origin, colour, religion or sex. The absence of such discrimination still leaves open the question whether s. 223 can be construed and applied without abrogating, abridging or infringing the rights of the individual listed in s. 1(a) and s. 1(b).

My understanding of this passage is that the effect of s. 1 of the Bill of Rights is to guarantee to all Canadians the rights specified in paragraphs (*a*) to (*f*) of that section, irrespective of race, national origin, colour or sex. This interpretation appears to me to be borne out by the French version which reads:

1. Il est par les présentes reconnu et déclaré que les droits de l'homme et les libertés fondamentales ci-après énoncés ont existé et continueront à exister pour tout individu au Canada quels que soient sa race, son origine nationale, sa couleur, sa religion ou son sexe: . . .

It was stressed on behalf of the respondents that the provisions of s. 12(1)(*b*) of the Indian Act constituted "discrimination by reason of sex" and that the section could be declared inoperative on this ground alone even if such discrimination did not result in the infringement of any of the rights and freedoms specifically guaranteed by s. 1 of the Bill.

I can find no support for such a contention in the *Curr* case in which, in any event, no question of any kind of discrimination was either directly or indirectly involved. My own understanding of the passage which I have quoted from that case was that it recognized the fact that the primary concern evidenced by the first two sections of the Bill of Rights is to ensure that the rights and freedoms thereby recognized and declared shall continue to exist for all Canadians, and it follows, in my view, that those sections cannot be invoked unless one of the enumerated rights and freedoms has been denied to an individual Canadian or group of Canadians. Section 2 of the Bill of Rights provides for the manner in which the rights and freedoms which are recognized and declared by s. 1 are to be enforced and the effect of this section is that every law of Canada shall "be so construed and applied as not to abrogate, abridge or infringe or authorize the abrogation, abridgment or infringement of any of the rights and freedoms herein recognized and declared . . ." (i.e. by s. 1). There is no language anywhere in the Bill of Rights stipulating that the laws of Canada are to be construed without discrimination unless that discrimination involves the denial of one of the guaranteed rights and freedoms, but when, as in the case of *The Queen* v. *Drybones, supra*, denial of one of the enumerated rights is occasioned by reason of discrimination, then, as Mr. Justice Laskin has said, the discrimination affords an "additional lever to which federal legislation must respond".

The opening words of s. 2 of the Bill of Rights are, in my view, determinative of the test to be applied in deciding whether the section here impugned is to be declared inoperative. The words to which I refer are:

2. Every law of Canada shall, unless it is expressly declared by an act of the Parliament of Canada that it shall operate notwithstanding the Canadian Bill of Rights, be so construed and applied as not to abrogate, abridge or infringe or authorize the abrogation, abridgement or infringement of the freedoms herein recognized and declared . . .

In the course of the reasons for judgment rendered on behalf of the majority of this Court in *The Queen* v. *Drybones, supra*, this language was interpreted in the following passage at p. 294:

It seems to me that a more realistic meaning must be given to the words in question and they afford, in my view, the clearest indication that s. 2 is intended to mean and does mean that if a law of

Canada cannot be "*sensibly construed and applied*" so that it does not abrogate, abridge or infringe one of the rights and freedoms, recognized and declared by the Bill, then such law is inoperative "*unless it is expressly declared by an Act of the Parliament of Canada that it shall operate notwithstanding the Canadian Bill of Rights.*"

Accordingly, in my opinion, the question to be determined in these appeals is confined to deciding whether the Parliament of Canada in defining the prerequisites of Indian status so as not to include women of Indian birth who have chosen to marry non-Indians, enacted a law which cannot be sensibly construed and applied without abrogating, abridging or infringing the rights of such women to equality before the law.

In my view the meaning to be given to the language employed in the Bill of Rights is the meaning which it bore in Canada at the time when the Bill was enacted, and it follows that the phrase "equality before the law" is to be construed in light of the law existing in Canada at that time.

In considering the meaning to be attached to "equality before the law" as those words occur in section 1(*b*) of the Bill, I think it important to point out that in my opinion this phrase is not effective to invoke the egalitarian concept exemplified by the 14th Amendment of the U.S. Constitution as interpreted by the courts of that country. (See *Smythe* v. *The Queen* ([1971] S.C.R. 680 per Fauteux C.J. at pp. 683 and 686). I think rather that, having regard to the language employed in the second paragraph of the preamble to the Bill of Rights, the phrase "equality before the law" as used in s. 1 is to be read in its context as a part of "the rule of law" to which overriding authority is accorded by the terms of that paragraph.

In this connection I refer to *Stephens Commentaries on the Laws of England*, 21st Ed. 1950, where it is said in Vol. III at p. 337:

Now the great constitutional lawyer Dicey writing in 1885 was so deeply impressed by the absence of arbitrary governments present and past, that he coined the phrase "the rule of law" to express the regime under which Englishmen lived; and he tried to give precision to it in the following words which have exercised a profound influence on all subsequent thought and conduct.

"*That the rule of law which forms a fundamental principle of the constitution has three meanings or may be regarded from three different points of view . . .*"

The second meaning proposed by Dicey is the one with which we are here concerned and it was stated in the following terms:

It means again equality before the law or the equal subjection of all classes to the ordinary law of the land administered by the ordinary courts; the "rule of law" in this sense excludes the idea of any exemption of officials or others from the duty of obedience to the law which governs other citizens or from the jurisdiction of the ordinary courts.

"Equality before the law" in this sense is frequently invoked to demonstrate that the same law applies to the highest official of government as to any other ordinary citizen, and in this regard Professor F.R. Scott, in delivering the Plaunt Memorial Lectures on Civil Liberties and Canadian Federalism in 1959, speaking of the case of *Roncarelli* v. *Duplessis* ([1959] S.C.R. 121), had occasion to say:

It is always a triumph for the law to show that it is applied equally to all without fear or favour. This is what we mean when we say that all are equal before the law.

The relevance of these quotations to the present circumstances is that "equality before the law" as recognized by Dicey as a segment of the rule of law, carries the meaning of equal subjection of all classes to the ordinary law of the land *as administered by the ordinary courts*, and in my opinion the phrase "equally before the law" as employed in section 1(*b*) of the

Bill of Rights is to be treated as meaning equality in the administration or application of the law by the law enforcement authorities and the ordinary courts of the land. This construction is, in my view, supported by the provisions of subsections (a) to (g) of s. 2 of the Bill which clearly indicate to me that it was equality in the administration and enforcement of the law with which Parliament was concerned when it guaranteed the continued existence of "equality before the law".

Turning to the Indian Act itself, it should first be observed that by far the greater part of that Act is concerned with the internal regulation of the lives of Indians on reserves and that the exceptional provisions dealing with the conduct of Indians off reserves and their contacts with other Canadian citizens fall into an entirely different category. . . .

A careful reading of the Act discloses that section 95 (formerly 94) is the only provision therein made which creates an offence for any behaviour of an Indian *off* a reserve and it will be plain that there is a wide difference between legislation such as s. 12(1)(b) governing the civil rights of designated persons living on Indian reserves to the use and benefit of Crown lands, and criminal legislation such as s. 95 which creates an offence punishable at law for Indians to act in a certain fashion when *off* a reserve. The former legislation is enacted as a part of the plan devised by Parliament, under s. 91(24) for the regulation of the internal domestic life of Indians on reserves. The latter is criminal legislation exclusively concerned with behaviour of Indians *off* a reserve. . . .

The *Drybones* case can, in my opinion, have no application to the present appeals as it was in no way concerned with the internal regulation of the lives of Indians *on* reserves or their right to the use and benefit of Crown lands thereon, but rather deals exclusively with the effect of the Bill of Rights on a section of the Indian Act creating a crime with attendant penalties for the conduct by Indians *off* a reserve in an area where non-Indians, who

were also governed by federal law, were not subject to any such restriction.

The fundamental distinction between the present case and that of *Drybones*, however, appears to me to be that the impugned section in the latter case could not be enforced without denying equality of treatment in the administration and enforcement of the law before the ordinary courts of the land to a racial group, whereas no such inequality of treatment between Indian men and women flows as a necessary result of the application of s. 12(1)(b) of the Indian Act.

To summarize the above, I am of opinion:

1. That the Bill of Rights is not effective to render inoperative legislation, such as s. 12(1)(b) of the Indian Act, passed by the Parliament of Canada in discharge of its constitutional function under s. 91(24) of the B.N.A. Act, to specify how and by whom Crown lands reserved for Indians are to be used;

2. that the Bill of Rights does not require federal legislation to be declared inoperative unless it offends against one of the rights specifically guaranteed by section 1, but where legislation is found to be discriminatory, this affords an added reason for rendering it ineffective;

3. that equality before the law under the Bill of Rights means equality of treatment in the enforcement and application of the laws of Canada before the law enforcement authorities and the ordinary courts of the land, and no such inequality is necessarily entailed in the construction and application of s. 12(1)(b).

I would allow the appeal of the *Attorney General of Canada against J.V. Corbiere Lavell*, reverse the judgment of the Federal Court of Appeal and restore the decision of Judge B. W. Grossberg.

ABBOTT J. (*dissenting*): The facts which are not in dispute are set out in the reasons of Ritchie and Laskin JJ. which I have had the advantage of reading. I am in agreement with the reasons of Laskin J. and wish to add only a few observations.

I share this view that the decision of this

Court in *The Queen* v. *Drybones* cannot be distinguished from the two cases under appeal although in these two appeals the consequences of the discrimination by reason of sex under s. 12(1)(*b*) of the Indian Act are more serious than the relatively minor penalty for the drinking offence under s. 94 of the Act which was in issue in *Drybones*.

In that case, this Court rejected the contention that s. 1 of the Canadian Bill of Rights provided merely a canon of construction for the interpretation of legislation existing when the Bill was passed. With respect I cannot interpret "equality before the law" as used in s. 1(*b*) of the Bill as meaning simply "the equal subjection of all classes to the ordinary law of the land as administered by the ordinary courts" to use the language of Dicey which is quoted in the reasons of Ritchie J.

Unless the words "without discrimination by reason of race, national origin, colour, religion or sex" used in s. 1 are to be treated as mere rhetorical window dressing, effect must be given to them in interpreting the section. I agree with Laskin J. that s. 1(*b*) must be read as if those words were recited therein.

In my view the Canadian Bill of Rights has substantially affected the doctrine of the supremacy of Parliament. Like any other statute it can of course be repealed or amended, or a particular law declared to be applicable notwithstanding the provisions of the Bill. In form the supremacy of Parliament is maintained but in practice I think that it has been substantially curtailed. In my opinion that result is undesirable, but that is a matter for consideration by Parliament not the courts.

Ritchie J. said in his reasons for judgment in *Drybones* that the implementation of the Bill of Rights by the courts can give rise to great difficulties and that statement has been borne out in subsequent litigation. Of one thing I am certain, the Bill will continue to supply ample grist to the judicial mills for some time to come.

The Judgment of Hall, Spence and Laskin JJ. was delivered by

LASKIN J. (*dissenting*): . . . In my opinion, unless we are to depart from what was said in *Drybones*, both appeals now before us must be dismissed. I have no disposition to reject what was decided in *Drybones*; and on the central issue of prohibited discrimination as catalogued in s. 1 of the Canadian Bill of Rights, it is, in my opinion, impossible to distinguish *Drybones* from the two cases in appeal. If, as in *Drybones*, discrimination by reason of race makes certain statutory provisions inoperative, the same result must follow as to statutory provisions which exhibit discrimination by reason of sex. . . .

In both cases, which were argued together, leave was given to various bodies and organizations and to a number of individuals to intervene by representation and by submissions to this Court. The position of the Attorney General of Canada in the *Lavell* case was supported by counsel appearing on behalf of the Indian Association of Alberta, the Union of British Columbia Indian Chiefs, the Manitoba Indian Brotherhood Inc., the Union of New Brunswick Indians, the Indian Brotherhood of the Northwest Territories, the Union of Nova Scotia Indians, the Union of Ontario Indians, the Federation of Saskatchewan Indians, the Indian Association of Quebec, the Yukon Native Brotherhood and the National Indian Brotherhood, by counsel appearing on behalf of the Six Nations Band and by counsel appearing on behalf of the Treaty Voice of Alberta Association. The position of the respondent was supported by counsel appearing for the Native Council of Canada, by counsel appearing for Rose Wilhelm, Alberta Committee on Indian Rights for Indian Women Inc., Viola Shannacappo, University Women's Club of Toronto and University Women Graduates Limited, the North Toronto Business and Professional Women's Club Inc. and Monica Agnes Turner and by counsel for Anishnawbekwek of Ontario Incorporated. There was the same division of support for the appellants and the respondent in the *Bédard* case, in which the Attorney General of Canada also intervened to support the position of the appellants. . . .

The contentions of the appellants in both cases in appeal, stripped of their detail, amount to a submission that the Canadian Bill of Rights does not apply to Indians on a reserve, nor to Indians in their relations to one another whether or not on a reserve. This submission does not deny that the effect of s. 12(1)(*b*) of the Indian Act is to prescribe substantive discrimination by reason of sex, a differentiation in the treatment of Indian men and Indian women when they marry non-Indians, this differentiation being exhibited in the loss by the women of their status as Indians under the Act. It does, however, involve the assertion that the particular discrimination upon which the two appeals are focussed is not offensive to the relevant provisions of the Canadian Bill of Rights, and it also involves the assertion that the *Drybones* case is distinguishable or, if not, that it has been overcome by the re-enactment of the Indian Act in the Revised Statutes of Canada, 1970, including the then s. 94 (now s. 95) which was in issue in that case. I regard this last-mentioned assertion, which is posited on the fact that the Canadian Bill of Rights was not so re-enacted, as simply an oblique appeal for the overruling of the *Drybones* case.

The *Drybones* case decided two things. It decided first—and this decision was a necessary basis for the second point in it—that the Canadian Bill of Rights was more than a mere interpretation statute whose terms would yield to a contrary intention; it had paramount force when a federal enactment conflicted with its terms, and it was the incompatible federal enactment which had to give way. This was the issue upon which the then Chief Justice of this Court, Chief Justice Cartwright, and Justices Abbott and Pigeon, dissented. Pigeon J. fortified his view on

this main point by additional observations, bringing into consideration, *inter alia*, s. 91(24) of the British North America Act. The second thing decided by *Drybones* was that the accused in that case, an Indian under the Indian Act, was denied equality before the law, under s. 1(*b*) of the Canadian Bill of Rights, when it was made a punishable offence for him, on account of his race, to do something which his fellow Canadians were free to do without being liable to punishment for an offence. Ritchie J., who delivered the majority opinion of the Court, reiterated this basis of decision by concluding his reasons as follows:

It appears to me to be desirable to make it plain that these reasons for judgment are limited to a situation in which, under the laws of Canada, it is made an offence punishable at law on account of race, for a person to do something which all Canadians who are not members of that race may do with impunity.

It would be unsupportable in principle to view the *Drybones* case as turning on the fact that the challenged s. 94 of the Indian Act created an offence visited by punishment. The gist of the judgment lay in the legal disability imposed upon a person by reason of his race when other persons were under no similar restraint. If for the words "on account of race" there are substituted the words "on account of sex" the result must surely be the same where a federal enactment imposes disabilities or prescribes disqualifications for members of the female sex which are not imposed upon members of the male sex in the same circumstances.

It is said, however, that although this may be so as between males and females in general, it does not follow where the distinction on the basis of sex is limited as here to members of the Indian race. This, it is said further, does not offend the guarantee of "equality before the law" upon which the *Drybones* case proceeded. I wish to deal with these two points in turn and to review, in connection with the first point, the legal consequences for an Indian woman under the Indian Act when she marries a non-Indian.

It appears to me that the contention that a differentiation on the basis of sex is not offensive to the Canadian Bill of Rights where that differentiation operates only among Indians under the Indian Act is one that compounds racial inequality even beyond the point that the *Drybones* case found unacceptable. In any event, taking the Indian Act as it stands, as a law of Canada whose various provisions fall to be assessed under the Canadian Bill of Rights, I am unable to appreciate upon what basis the command of the Canadian Bill of Rights, that laws of Canada shall operate without discrimination by reason of sex, can be ignored in the operation of the Indian Act.

The Indian Act defines an Indian as a person who is registered as an Indian pursuant to the Act or is entitled to be so registered. It is registration or registrability upon a Band list or upon a general list that is the key to the scheme and application of the Act. The Registrar, charged with keeping the membership records, is the person to whom protests may be made by a Band Council or by an affected person respecting the inclusion or deletion of a name from the Indian Register. By s. 9(2) his decision on a protest is final subject to a reference to a judge under s. 9(3). The *Lavell* case arose in this way: Section 11 of the Act enumerates the persons entitled to be registered, and it is common ground that both Mrs. Lavell and Mrs. Bédard were so entitled prior to their respective marriages. Section 12 lists the classes of persons not entitled to be registered, and the only clause thereof relevant here is subsection 1(*b*) which I have already quoted. Section 14 has a peripheral relevance to the present case in its provision that a woman member of a Band who marries a person outside that Band ceases to be a member thereof but becomes a member of the Band of which her husband is a member. There is no absolute disqualification of an Indian woman from registrability on the Indian Register (that is, as a member on the general list) by marrying outside a Band unless the marriage is to a non-Indian.

Registration or registrability entitles an Indian as a member of a Band (and that was the status of both Mrs. Lavell and Mrs. Bédard prior to their respective marriages) to the use and benefit of the reserve set aside for the Band. This may take the form of possession or occupation of particular land in the reserve under an allotment by the Council of the Band with the approval of the responsible Minister, and it may be evidenced by a certificate of possession or a certificate of occupation, the latter representing possession for a limited period only. Indians may make wills disposing of their property, and it may also pass on intestacy, in either case subject to approval or control of the Minister or of a competent court; and in the case of a device or descent of land in a reserve the claimant's possession must be approved by the Minister under s. 49. Section 50 has only a remote bearing on the *Bédard* case in providing that a person who is not entitled to reside on a reserve does not by devise or descent acquire a right to possession or occupation of land in that reserve. It begs the question in that the issue here is whether or not Mrs. Bédard became disentitled to reside on the land in the reserve which was left to her by her mother upon the latter's death in 1969. The fact that the respondent's brother now holds a certificate of possession of all the land formerly possessed by the mother, that certificate having been issued after the respondent transferred her interest to her brother in February 1971, does not affect the overriding question of the respondent's right to reside on the land, having her brother's consent to residence thereon.

Indians entitled to be registered and to live on a reserve are members of a society in which, through Band Councils, they share in the administration of the reserve subject to overriding governmental authority. There is provision for election of councillors by Band members residing on a reserve, and I note that there is no statutory discrimination between Indian men and women either as qualified electors or as qualified candidates for election as councillors. Other advantages that come from membership in the social unit relate to farm operations and to eligibility for governmental loans for various enumerated purposes.

Section 12(1)(b) effects a statutory excommunication of Indian women from this society but not of Indian men. Indeed, as was pointed out by counsel for the Native Council of Canada, the effect of ss. 11 and 12(1)(b) is to excommunicate the children of a union of an Indian woman with a non-Indian. There is also the invidious distinction, invidious at least in the light of the Canadian Bill of Rights, that the Indian Act creates between brothers and sisters who are Indians and who respectively marry non-Indians. The statutory banishment directed by s. 12(1)(b) is not qualified by the provision in s. 109(2) for a governmental order declaring an Indian woman who has married a non-Indian to be enfranchised. Such an order is not automatic and no such order was made in relation to Mrs. Bédard; but when made the woman affected is, by s. 110, deemed not to be an Indian within the Indian Act or any other statute or law. It is, if anything, an additional legal instrument of separation of an Indian woman from her native society and from her kin, a separation to which no Indian man who marries a non-Indian is exposed.

It was urged, in reliance in part on history, that the discrimination embodied in the Indian Act under s. 12(1)(b) is based upon a reasonable classification of Indians as a race, that the Indian Act reflects this classification and that the paramount purpose of the Act to preserve and protect the members of the race is promoted by the statutory preference for Indian men. Reference was made in this connection to various judgments of the Supreme Court of the United States to illustrate the adoption by that Court of reasonable classifications to square with

the due process clause of the Fifth Amendment and with due process and equal protection under the Fourteenth Amendment. Those cases have at best a marginal relevance because the Canadian Bill of Rights itself enumerates prohibited classifications which the judiciary is bound to respect; and, moreover, I doubt whether discrimination on account of sex, where as here it has no biological or physiological rationale, could be sustained as a reasonable classification even if the direction against it was not as explicit as it is in the Canadian Bill of Rights.

I do not think it is possible to leap over the telling words of s. 1, "without discrimination by reason of race, national origin, colour, religion or sex," in order to explain away any such discrimination by invoking the words "equality before the law" in clause (b) and attempting to make them alone the touchstone of reasonable classification. That was not done in the Drybones case; and this Court made it clear in Curr v. The Queen, that federal legislation, which might be compatible with the command of "equality before the law" taken alone, may nonetheless be inoperative if it manifests any of the prohibited forms of discrimination. In short, the proscribed discriminations in s. 1 have a force either independent of the subsequently enumerated clauses (a) to (f) or, if they are found in any federal legislation, they offend those clauses because each must be read as if the prohibited forms of discrimination were recited therein as a part thereof.

This seems to me an obvious construction of s. 1 of the Canadian Bill of Rights. When that provision states that the enumerated human rights and fundamental freedoms shall continue to exist "without discrimination by reason of race, national origin, colour, religion or sex," it is expressly adding these words to clauses (a) to (f). Section 1(b) must read therefore as "the right of the individual to equality before the law and the protection of the law without discrimination by reason of race, national origin, colour, religion or sex." It is worth repeating that this is what emerges from the *Drybones* case and what is found in the *Curr* case.

There is no clear historical basis for the position taken by the appellants, certainly not in relation to Indians in Canada as a whole, and this was in effect conceded during the hearing in this Court. In any event, history cannot avail against the clear words of ss. 1 and 2 of the Canadian Bill of Rights. It is s. 2 that gives this enactment its effective voice, because without it s. 1 would remain a purely declaratory provision. Section 2 brings the terms of s. 1 into its orbit, and its reference to "every law of Canada" is a reference, as set out in s. 5(2), to any Act of the Parliament of Canada enacted before or after the effective date of the Canadian Bill of Rights. Pre-existing Canadian legislation as well as subsequent Canadian legislation is expressly made subject to the commands of the Canadian Bill of Rights, and those commands, where they are as clear as the one which is relevant here, cannot be diluted by appeals to history. Ritchie J. in his reasons in the *Drybones* case touched on this very point when he rejected the contention that the terms of s. 1 of the Canadian Bill of Rights must be circumscribed by the provisions of Canadian statutes in force at the date of the enactment of the Canadian Bill of Rights: see [1970] S.C.R. 282, at pp. 295-296. I subscribe fully to the rejection of that contention. Clarity here is emphasized by looking at the French version of the Canadian Bill of Rights which speaks in s. 1 of the enumerated human rights and fundamental freedoms "pour tout individu au Canada quels que soient sa race, son origine nationale, sa couleur, sa réligion ou son sexe."

In my opinion, the appellants' contentions gain no additional force because the Indian Act, including the challenged s. 12(1)(*b*) thereof, is a fruit of the exercise of Parliament's exclusive legislative power in relation to "Indians, and Lands reserved for the Indians" under s. 91(24) of the British North America Act. Discriminatory treatment on the basis of race or colour or sex does not inhere in that grant of legislative power. The fact that its exercise may be attended by forms of discrimination prohibited by the Canadian Bill of Rights is no more a justification for a breach of the Canadian Bill of Rights than there would be in the case of the exercise of any other head of federal legislative power involving provisions offensive to the Canadian Bill of Rights. The majority opinion in the *Drybones* case dispels any attempt to rely on the grant of legislative power as a ground for escaping from the force of the Canadian Bill of Rights. The latter does not differentiate among the various heads of legislative power; it embraces all exercises under whatever head or heads they arise. Section 3 which directs the Minister of Justice to scrutinize every Bill to ascertain whether any of its provisions are inconsistent with ss. 1 and 2 is simply an affirmation of this fact which is evident enough from ss. 1 and 2.

There was an intimation during the argument of these appeals that the Canadian Bill of Rights is properly invoked only to resolve a clash under its terms between two federal statutes, and the *Drybones* case was relied on in that connection. It is a spurious contention, if seriously advanced, because the Canadian Bill of Rights is itself the indicator to which any Canadian statute or any provision thereof must yield unless Parliament has declared that the statute or the particular provision is to operate notwithstanding the Canadian Bill of Rights. A statute may in itself be offensive to the Canadian Bill of Rights, or it may be by relation to another statute that it is so offensive.

I would dismiss both appeals with costs.

PIGEON J.: I agree in the result with Ritchie J. I certainly cannot disagree with the view I did express in *The Queen* v. *Drybones* (at p. 304) that the enactment of the Canadian Bill of Rights was not intended to effect a virtual suppression of federal legislation over Indians. My difficulty is Laskin J.'s strongly reasoned opinion that, unless we are to depart from what was said by the majority in *Drybones*, these appeals should be dismissed because, if discrimination by reason of race makes certain statutory provisions inoperative, the same result must follow as to statutory provisions which exhibit discrimination by reason of sex. In the end, it appears to me that, in the circumstances, I need not reach a firm conclusion on that point. Assuming the situation is such as Laskin J. says, it cannot be improper for me to adhere to what was my dissenting view, when a majority of those who did not agree with it in respect of a particular section of the Indian Act, now adopt it for the main body of this important statute.

I would observe that this result does not conflict with any of our decisions subsequent to *Drybones*. In no case was the Canadian Bill of Rights given an invalidating effect over prior legislation.

In *Lowry and Lepper* v. *The Queen* ((1972) 26 D.L.R. (3d) 224) and in *Brownridge* v. *The Queen* ([1972] S.C.R. 926), the application of criminal legislation, past and subsequent, was held to be subject to provisions respecting a "fair hearing" and "the right to retain and instruct counsel." These decisions are important illustrations of the effectiveness of the Bill without any invalidating effect.

In *Smythe* v. *The Queen* it was held that provisions for stiffer penalties depending on the method of prosecution were not rendered inoperative by the Canadian Bill of Rights as infringing equality before the law, although the choice of the method of prosecution always depends on executive discretion.

In *Curr* v. *The Queen* recent Criminal Code provisions for compulsory breath analysis were held not to infringe the right to the "protection of the law" any more than the right to the "protection against self-crimination."

Finally, in *Duke* v. *The Queen* ([1972] S.C.R. 917) these same provisions were said not to deprive the accused of a "fair trial" although proclaimed without some paragraphs contemplating a specimen being offered and given on request to the suspect.

39. Hogan v. The Queen, *1975*

~ Rendering conflicting legislation inoperative is not the only way in which the courts can give effect to a Bill of Rights. A bill may also serve as a set of interpretative guidelines directing the judiciary to read the rights it enshrines into the law where the law is silent or ambiguous. The Canadian Bill of Rights has been given effect in this way in several decisions of the Supreme Court. For instance, in *Lowry and Lepper*[1] the Court ruled that the right to a fair hearing in section 2(e) of the Bill of Rights gave an accused the right to make a submission to the court before sentencing, and in the case of *Cosimo Reale*[2] the Court set aside a conviction because the trial judge had not permitted his charge to the jury to be translated into Italian, thus denying Mr. Reale his right to the assistance of an interpreter under section 2(g) of the Bill of Rights. In a series of cases concerning legislation requiring persons suspected of impaired driving to take a breathalyzer test, while the Court found that the legislation did not violate the protection against self-incrimination[3] or the right to a fair hearing,[4] it held in the *Brownridge case*[5] that a person may not be convicted of the offence of refusing to take a breathalyzer test if the reason for the refusal is police denial of the right in section 2(c) of persons arrested or detained to retain and instruct counsel without delay.

But the Court's decision in the *Hogan* case demonstrated the limited extent to which the majority was willing to apply the Canadian Bill of Rights as a rule of interpretation. This case involved a classic issue in the administration of criminal justice: should courts exclude evidence if it has been obtained by the police in a manifestly illegal or improper manner? In the common law world courts themselves have played a major role in developing the rules of evidence. Canadian judges, following English precedents, have taken the position they have no discretion to exclude evidence which is relevant and probative on the grounds that the police may have broken the law or used highly questionable methods to obtain the evidence. In the case at hand, Hogan had asked to see his lawyer before taking the breathalyzer test. The police refused his request. He took the test anyway and the results were used to obtain his conviction for impaired driving. If the normal Canadian common law rule of evidence were followed, the Court would not exclude the evidence. The question was: Should the right to counsel in the Bill of Rights be read into the common law to modify the normal rule against the exclusion of illegally or improperly obtained evidence?

The Court's majority answered this question in the negative. They rejected Chief Justice Laskin's view that the Bill of Rights should be treated as a

---

[1] [1974] S.C.R. 195.
[2] [1975] 2 S.C.R. 624.
[3] *Curr* v. *The Queen*, [1972] S.C.R. 889.
[4] *Duke* v. *The Queen*, [1972] S.C.R. 917.
[5] [1972] S.C.R. 926.

"quasi-constitutional instrument" and given sufficient weight to require the courts to adopt a policy at variance with common law. Chief Justice Laskin, on the other hand, once again in dissent, urged that Canadian courts should adopt the doctrine of the U.S. Supreme Court and exclude evidence obtained by practices that infringe constitutional rights.

Hogan underlined the low status accorded the Canadian Bill of Rights by a majority of Supreme Court judges. For most of them it did not possess even quasi-constitutional status. When the Court turned to the interpretation of the Canadian Charter of Rights and Freedoms in the 1980's, it emphasized the Charter's constitutional status. On a number of occasions it has rejected precedents based on the Bill of Rights as inappropriate for the interpretation of the Charter precisely because of the Charter's status as a constitutional instrument.[6]

One section of the Charter was designed specifically to prevent the possibility of a *Hogan* approach to the Charter. Section 24(2) of the Charter requires judges to exclude evidence obtained in violation of the accused's constitutional rights if, having regard to all the circumstances, its admission "would bring the administration of justice into disrepute."[7]

HOGAN v. THE QUEEN
In the Supreme Court of Canada, [1975] 2 S.C.R. 574.

The judgment of Fauteux C.J. and Abbott, Martland, Judson, Ritchie and Dickson JJ. was delivered by

RITCHIE J.: This is an appeal brought, with leave of this Court, from a judgment of the Appeal Division of the Supreme Court of Nova Scotia, which affirmed the judgment of Anderson Co. Ct. J., rendered after a trial *de novo* whereby he had affirmed the appellant's conviction entered in the provincial magistrate's court before M.D. Haley, a judge of that court, on an information charging that he "did unlawfully have the control of a motor vehicle having consumed alcohol in such a quantity that the proportion thereof in his blood exceeded 80 milligrams of alcohol in 100 millilitres of blood, contrary to s. 236 of the Criminal Code."

The case presented by the Crown rested on the evidence of the result of a chemical analysis of the breath of the accused made in purported compliance with s. 237 of the Criminal Code. . . .

Having regard to the arguments presented in this appeal, I think it desirable at the outset to reproduce section 235 of the Criminal Code which reads as follows:

235. (1) Where a peace officer on reasonable and probable grounds believes that a person is committing, or at any time within the preceding two hours has committed, an offence under section 234, he may, by demand made to that person forthwith or as soon as practicable, require him to provide then or as soon thereafter as is practicable a sample of his breath suitable to enable an analysis to be made in order to determine the propor-

---

[6] For the first instance, see *Big M Drug Mart*, case 42 below.
[7] For the Supreme Court's treatment of this section, see *Therens*, case 44 below.

tion, if any, of alcohol in his blood, and to accompany the peace officer for the purpose of enabling such a sample to be taken.

(2) Every one who, without reasonable excuse, fails or refuses to comply with a demand made to him by a peace officer under subsection (1) is guilty of an offence punishable on summary conviction and is liable to a fine of not less than fifty dollars and not more than one thousand dollars or to imprisonment for not more than six months, or both.

The evidence discloses that at about 1:30 a.m. on June 3, 1972, a constable of the Dartmouth Police Force stopped a car being driven by the appellant because he noticed that it had swerved over the sidewalk. The constable had some conversation with the appellant through the window of the car and he gave the following evidence of his actions and observations:

Q. Now tell me what observations you made of the accused, please?

A. First of all I smelled a strong smell of alcohol on the accused's breath. Secondly, I noticed the accused had bloodshot eyes and a flushed face.

Q. Did you have any opinion after making your observation as to his condition of sobriety?

A. Yes, I did.

Q. What was your opinion?

A. I . . . my own opinion he was intoxicated so I gave him a demand regarding the breathalyzer.

Q. Now what demand did you give him?

A. I demand you accompany me to the Dartmouth Police Station to provide a sample of your breath suitable to be analyzed to determine the amount of alcohol if any in your blood.

Q. Did you tell him anything else?

A. Yes. If he refused this demand he would be charged with refusal.

Q. Now what time was it that you gave him this demand?

A. 1:35 a.m. I looked at my watch at the time.

Q. I take it it was only a matter of a few minutes before that you had seen the car?

A. Yes, it was, sir.

Q. All right, did you go directly back to the station?

A. Yes. I did.

Q. And what happened back there? Very briefly, now.

A. I turned the accused Mr. Hogan over to Constable Gary Mac-Donald, our qualified breathalyzer operator.

THE COURT: *Apparently Mr. Hogan returned to the station with you?*

A. Yes, he did.

In describing his actions after the "demand" had been made, the appellant said:

My girlfriend and I both got out of the car and we got in the back of Constable Rafuse's car and we proceeded to the Dartmouth police station. Upon arrival I asked my girlfriend to call my counsel.

No charge had been laid against the appellant at this stage and he had accordingly not been formally arrested, but he gave the following account of what transpired after his arrival at the police station:

Q. What happened then?

A. I was taken into the breathalyzer room and introduced to Constable MacDonald and I was sitting waiting for the test when I heard my counsel.

Q. What do you mean you heard your counsel?

A. I could hear him through the door my counsel asking if I was at the police station, my counsel was present.

Q. I see, you recognize your counsel's voice?

A. Yes, I do.

Q. You know it well?

A. Yes.

Q. So you heard his voice asking to see

you, before the test was completed?
A. *This was before the first test was given, yes.*
Q. *I see and what did you do at that point?*
A. *I requested to Constable MacDonald to see my counsel before taking the test and I was told that I didn't have any right to see anyone until after the test and if I refused the test I would be charged with refusal of the breathalyzer.*
Q. *I see, so he told you no when you asked to see your counsel?*
A. *That's right.*
Q. *Why did you want to see counsel?*
A. *I wanted to see counsel to see whether I had to take the test or not.*
Q. *And then I gather the test was given to you?*
A. *Yes. I took the test rather than be nailed with refusal.*
Q. *I see, in other words you took the alternative?*
A. *Yes.*
Q. *It was offered to you by Constable MacDonald?*
A. *Yes.*
Q. *And that alternative was offered to you in reply to your request for counsel?*
A. *Yes, it was.*
Q. *Was counsel present when your test was finished?*
A. *After I left the room I saw my counsel.*
Q. *I see and where was he?*
A. *Counsel was just outside the door to the breathalyzer room.*
Q. *At any time was he present during the test?*
A. *No, he wasn't.*

The result of the breathalyzer test was a finding of 230 milligrams of alcohol per 100 millilitres of blood and in the course of his cross-examination the appellant agreed that he had been drinking rum and could have had "a good pint."

It was contended on behalf of the appellant that the evidence of the result of the chemical analysis of his breath taken by Constable MacDonald, who was a qualified technician was inadmissible because it was obtained in violation of s. 2(c)(ii) of the Canadian Bill of Rights which provides, in part, that:

. . . no law of Canada shall be construed or applied so as to . . .
   (c) deprive a person who has been arrested or detained . . .
     (ii) of the right to retain and instruct counsel without delay

  . . .

Counsel for the appellant relied on the case of *Brownridge* v. *The Queen*, in support of his contention that the evidence of the result of the breathalyzer test should have been excluded.

In the *Brownridge* case it was held that the denial of the right to retain and instruct counsel without delay to an accused person who was under arrest, afforded that person "reasonable excuse" for refusing to comply with the demand pursuant to s. 223(2) (now 235(2)), *supra*. In considering whether the *Brownridge* case can be said to govern the circumstances disclosed in the present case, it is to be remembered that Brownridge had refused to comply with a demand made under the purported authority of s. 235(1), and the only question to be determined was whether his having been denied the right to retain and instruct counsel constituted a "reasonable excuse" for such refusal. . . .

In the *Brownridge* case it was the denial of his right to "retain and instruct counsel without delay" which caused the accused to refuse to comply with the demand to provide a sample of his breath for analysis, whereas in the present case the appellant complied with the demand, albeit reluctantly, and there is no causal connection between the denial of the right to counsel and the obtaining of the certificate of the breathalyzer test which led to his conviction.

In my opinion the excerpts from the evidence which I have reproduced above clearly indicate that the initial demand to provide a sample of the breath for analysis was legally made by the constable on the highway in accordance with s. 235(1) at a time when the appellant was neither "arrested" nor "detained" and he appears to me to have complied with that demand without hesitation at least to the extent of agreeing "to accompany the peace officer for the purpose of enabling such a sample to be taken." There was no request for counsel at this stage, and it was only after he had reached the police station and was sitting waiting for the test that he heard the voice of the lawyer whom he had retained through the agency of his girlfriend and requested to see him in order to find out whether he had to take the test or not. It was then that Constable MacDonald told him that he "didn't have any right to see anyone until after the test and if I refused the test I would be charged with refusal of the breathalyzer." The appellant then took the test.

I have had the advantage of reading the reasons for judgment prepared for delivery by the present Chief Justice and I agree with him that the fact that the appellant could have refused the breathalyzer test unless he first consulted counsel does not mean that the breath test evidence was procured by illegal means or trickery and I agree with him also that the common law rule of admissibility of illegally or improperly obtained evidence rests primarily on the relevancy of that evidence subject only to the discretion of the trial judge to exclude it on the ground of unfairness as that word was interpreted in this Court in *The Queen* v. *Wray* ([1971] S.C.R. 272).

The result of the breathalyzer test in the present case was not only relevant, it was in fact of itself the only evidence upon which the appellant could have been convicted of the offence of which he was charged and it therefore constitutes proof of "the main issue before the court." Even if this evidence had been improperly or illegally obtained, there were therefore no grounds for excluding it at common law. In the case of an accused who the police considered to be intoxicated before the test was taken and who himself agreed that he could have had "a good pint of rum," it can hardly be characterized as unfair to accept evidence in proof of the exact quantity of alcohol that he had absorbed into his blood stream. Apart from the result of the test constituting proof of an offence under s. 236, it also afforded confirmation of the diagnosis made by the police officer and served to corroborate the appellant's own estimate of the amount of rum which he had consumed.

As the technician's certificate was both relevant and cogent it was, in my opinion, clearly admissible at common law and the courts at first instance and on appeal were correct in accepting it in accordance with the rules of evidence governing the trial of criminal cases as they presently exist in this country.

Laskin C.J., however, characterizes the Canadian Bill of Rights as a "quasi constitutional instrument" by which I take him to mean that its provisions are to be construed and applied as if they were constitutional provisions, and in so doing he would adopt as a matter of policy for Canada, apart from and at variance with the common law position, the rule of absolute exclusion of all evidence obtained under circumstances where one of the provisions of the Canadian Bill of Rights has been violated. This approach stems from an acceptance of the reasoning of the Supreme Court of the United States in such cases as *Mapp* v. *Ohio* ((1961), 367 U.S. 643), where that rule was accepted in relation to evidence obtained after the violation of a right guaranteed by the American Constitution. These American cases, however, turn on the interpretation of a Constitution basically different from our own and particularly on the effect to be given to the "due process of law" provision of the 14th Amendment of that Constitution for which I am unable to find any counterpart in the British North America Act, which is the source of the legislative authority of the Parliament of Canada and is characterized in the British North America Act (No. 2) 1949 (13

Geo. VI Ch. 81) as "the Constitution of Canada."

The case of *The Queen* v. *Drybones*, is authority for the proposition that any law of Canada which abrogates, abridges or infringes any of the rights guaranteed by the Canadian Bill of Rights should be declared inoperative and to this extent it accorded a degree of paramountcy to the provisions of that statute, but whatever view may be taken of the constitutional impact of the Bill of Rights, and with all respect for those who may have a different opinion, I cannot agree that, wherever there has been a breach of one of the provisions of that Bill, it justifies the adoption of the rule of "absolute exclusion" on the American model which is in derogation of the common law rule long accepted in this country. . . .

It follows from all the above that I am of opinion that the evidence of the result of the breathalyzer test in the present case was properly admitted in evidence and I would accordingly dismiss this appeal.

LASKIN J. (*dissenting*): The issue in this appeal may be formulated as follows. What is the effect of a denial by a police officer of a right to counsel under s. 2(*c*)(ii) of the Canadian Bill of Rights, 1960 (Can.), c. 44 upon the admissibility of subsequently obtained breathalyzer evidence by which the appellant accused may be convicted of an offence under Criminal Code s. 236? Under s. 2(*c*)(ii), no law of Canada shall be construed or applied so as to deprive a person, who has been arrested or detained, of the right to retain and instruct counsel without delay. The offence under s. 236 is driving or having care or control of a motor vehicle while having a reading of alcohol in the blood exceeding 0.08.

In *Brownridge* v. *The Queen*, this Court decided that an arrested person who refused to submit to a breath test when he was denied an opportunity to consult counsel before taking the test could not be found guilty of an offence under what is now Criminal Code s. 235(2) That provision, so far as material, makes it an offence for a person without reasonable excuse to fail or refuse to comply with a demand by a peace officer under s. 235(1) to take a breath test. The case now in appeal to this Court involves an accused who, similarly, was denied an opportunity to consult counsel before submitting to a demand that he take a breath test but who, unlike Brownridge, did not continue to insist that he must first consult his counsel. He yielded to the demand and took the test. His conviction under s. 236 was founded upon the evidence of the breathalyzer technician obtained in accordance with Criminal Code s. 237. It was conceded that without this evidence, obtained following denial of the accused's request to see his counsel (who was then in the police station to attend upon the accused), the conviction cannot stand.

It is common both to *Brownridge* and to the present case that access to counsel was not for the purpose nor would it have had the effect of delaying the taking of the breath sample beyond the two hour period specified in s. 237(1)(*c*)(ii). In this case, the accused was confronted by a police officer at about 1:35 a.m., and then asked to go to the police station, and they arrived there at 1:55 a.m., whereupon steps were taken to administer a breath test. The accused had asked his female companion to get in touch with his lawyer, and the latter had come immediately to the police station and the accused heard his voice in an adjoining room. The record is clear that he asked to see and consult with the lawyer but was categorically refused an opportunity to do so. The demand that he submit to a breath test was renewed and the accused submitted to it.

It is not disputed that the peace officer who conducted the accused to the police station had at the time reasonable and probable cause, within s. 235(1), to make the demand that the accused take a breath test and accompany the peace officer for that purpose. There is no doubt, therefore, that the accused was "detained" within the meaning of s. 2(*c*)(ii) of the Canadian Bill of Rights; he risked prosecution under s. 235(2) if, without reasonable excuse, he refused the demand which involved accompanying the peace officer to fulfil it.

Counsel for the appellant urged that the demand must be a lawful one, and contended that it could not be when it was supported by an unlawful denial of right to counsel. In my opinion, what is involved in this submission, if it is not to be treated as an effort to invalidate retroactively a demand that was properly made in the first place, is an allegation that the demand, being a continuing one to the time when the breathalyzer test is given, may justifiably be resisted at the point where the right to consult counsel is denied before the test is taken. This, however, is the *Brownridge* case, and turns on whether a charge under s. 235(2) will succeed. In the present case, the issue goes a little deeper, and the question is not the lawfulness of a resistance to the continuing demand but whether, failing resistance, an accused, who has wrongfully been denied counsel before taking the test, may successfully contest the admissibility of the breathalyzer evidence which, taken under the special provisions for its use prescribed by s. 237, is tendered in support of a charge under s. 236.

In my opinion, the accused appellant is entitled to succeed in this contention. I do not find it necessary to gloss the word "demand" in s. 237(1)(*c*) and (*f*) to mean "lawful demand," consonant with the Canadian Bill of Rights, in order to qualify the breathalzyer evidence as receivable, with all the statutory advantages for its reception provided by s. 237. Strictly speaking, if the demand is made in conformity with s. 235(1) this satisfies s. 237(1)(*c*) and (*f*). The more relevant consideration is the relationship between the Canadian Bill of Rights and the resort to special statutory methods of proof where there is previous denial to an accused of a related guarantee of the Canadian Bill of Rights. In this connection, I point out that there was in the present case no incompatibility between recognition of the particular guarantee of access to counsel and resort to the special mode of proof; and it was clearly the right

of the accused to have access to counsel before the authorities proceeded to administer the breathalyzer test.

The question that arises, therefore, is whether the vindication of this right should depend only on the fortitude or resoluteness of an accused so as to give rise to a *Brownridge* situation, or whether there is not also an available sanction of a ruling of inadmissibility where the police authorities are able to overcome an accused's resistance to a breathalyzer test without prior access to counsel. Nothing short of this would give reasonable assurance of respect of an individual's right to counsel by police authorities whose duty to enforce the law goes hand in hand with a duty to obey it.

There is no suggestion here of any physical force in the ultimate submission of the accused without having had his right to counsel recognized, but I do not think that any distinction should be drawn in the establishment of principle according to whether an accused yields through fear or a feeling of helplessness or as a result of polite or firm importuning or aggressive badgering. I should note also that there was no contention of waiver by the accused of his right to counsel, assuming that would be an answer to an alleged breach of any of his rights as an individual under the Canadian Bill of Rights.

The present case does not involve this Court in any reassessment of the principles underlying the admissibility of illegally obtained evidence as they developed at common law. We have a statutory policy to administer, one which this Court has properly recognized as giving primacy to the guarantees of the Canadian Bill of Rights by way of a positive suppressive effect upon the operation and application of federal legislation: see *The Queen* v. *Drybones*. The result may be, as in *Drybones*, to render federal legislation inoperative or, as in *Brownridge*, federal legislation may become inapplicable in the particular situation while otherwise remaining operative. The sanction in the present case would be to preclude use against a person or a special form of proof when it is obtained following a deliberate violation of a right of that person under the Canadian Bill of Rights. If, as the Bill enjoins, s. 237 of the Criminal Code is not to be applied so as to deprive a detained person of access to counsel, I do not see how its provisions can be utilized against a detained person in any case where that person's right of access to counsel has been denied in the course of that utilization. Moreover, it cannot matter that resort to s. 237 is the only way in which proof can be made of the main element of the offence defined in s. 236. . . .

Although it appears to me to be enough to rest my decision in this appeal on the operative view of the Canadian Bill of Rights taken in *Drybones*, I feel constrained to elaborate on the considerations which move me to allow this appeal. I do this because otherwise a comparison will inevitably be drawn between the policy underlying the admissibility of relevant evidence, no matter how obtained (unless it falls within the involuntary confession category) and the contrary policy which I would enforce here, and an explanation should be offered for preferring the latter. . . .

The common law rule of admissibility of illegally or improperly obtained evidence rests simply on the relevancy of the evidence to issues on which it is adduced, without regard to the means by which it was procured (confessions or out-of-court statements by an accused aside). The rule in Canada goes back to *Regina* v. *Doyle*, ((1886) 12 O.R. 347), where it was said, at p. 353, in respect of evidence obtained by execution of an illegal search warrant, that "the evidence is admissible so long as the fact so wrongly discovered is a fact—apart from the manner in which it was discovered—admissible against the party." There is no thought that the criminal should go free because the constable has blundered, (to use the words of Judge Cardozo in *People* v. *Defore* ((1926), 242 N.Y. 13), at p. 21), subject only to a discretion in the trial judge to exclude the

evidence on the ground of unfairness. In this Court, the discretion has been very narrowly confined: see *The Queen* v. *Wray* ([1971] S.C.R. 272). . . .

The choice of policy here is to favour the social interest in the repression of crime despite the unlawful invasion of individual interests and despite the fact that the invasion is by public officers charged with law enforcement. Short of legislative direction, it might have been expected that the common law would seek to balance the competing interests by weighing the social interest in the particular case against the gravity or character of the invasion, leaving it to the discretion of the trial judge whether the balance should be struck in favour of reception or exclusion of particular evidence. I have already indicated that the discretion has been narrowed, and, I would add, to an extent that underlines a wide preference for admissibility. It appears that only in a line of Scottish and Irish cases has there been any consideration of striking a balance between the competing interests involved where there is a challenge to admissibility because of illegality or impropriety: . . . Relevant to that consideration would be, of course, the trustworthiness of the tendered evidence.

Opposed to the dominant common law position is that at which the Supreme Court of the United States has arrived in enforcing the guarantees of the Fourth Amendment of the Constitution, applicable to the central authorities, against unreasonable searches and seizures, and, through it, those of the Fourteenth Amendment enjoining the States not to "deprive any person of life, liberty or property without due process of law." In general, a rule of exclusion of illegally obtained evidence, tendered to show the guilt of an accused, is enforced both in federal and state prosecutions: see *Weeks* v. *U.S.* ((1914), 232 U.S. 383). *Mapp* v. *Ohio*.

The American exclusionary rule, in enforcement of constitutional guarantees, is as much a judicial creation as was the common law of admissibility. It is not dictated by the Constitution, but its rationale appears to be that the constitutional guarantees cannot be adequately served if their vindication is left to civil actions in tort or criminal prosecutions, and that a check rein on illegal police activity which invades constitutional rights can best be held by excluding evidence obtained through such invasions. Whether this has resulted or can result in securing or improving respect for constitutional guarantees is not an easy question to answer, although attempts are being made to do so through empirical studies: see Spiotto, "Search and Seizure: An Empirical Study of the Exclusionary Rule and Its Alternative" (1973), 1 *Jo.Leg.S. 243.*

It may be said that the exclusion of relevant evidence is no way to control illegal police practices and that such exclusion merely allows a wrongdoer to escape conviction. Yet where constitutional guarantees are concerned, the more pertinent consideration is whether those guarantees, as fundamentals of the particular society, should be at the mercy of law enforcement officers and a blind eye turned to their invasion because it is more important to secure a conviction. The contention that it is the duty of the Courts to get at the truth has in it too much of the philosophy of the end justifying the means; it would equally challenge the present law as to confessions and other out-of-court statements by an accused. In the United States, its Supreme Court, after weighing over many years whether other methods than exclusion of evidence should be invoked to deter illegal searches and seizures in state as well as in federal prosecutions, concluded that the constitu-

tional guarantees could best be upheld by a rule of exclusion.

The Canadian Bill of Rights is a half-way house between a purely common law regime and a constitutional one; it may aptly be described as a quasi-constitutional instrument. It does not embody any sanctions for the enforcement of its terms, but it must be the function of the Courts to provide them in the light of the judicial view of the impact of that enactment. The *Drybones* case has established what the impact is, and I have no reason to depart from the position there taken. In the light of that position, it is to me entirely consistent, and appropriate, that the prosecution in the present case should not be permitted to invoke the special evidentiary provisions of s. 237 of the Criminal Code when they have been resorted to after denial of access to counsel in violation of s. 2(*c*)(ii) of the Canadian Bill of Rights. There being no doubt as to such denial and violation, the Courts must apply a sanction. We would not be justified in simply ignoring the breach of a declared fundamental right or in letting it go merely with words of reprobation. Moreover, so far as denial of access to counsel is concerned, I see no practical alternative to a rule of exclusion if any serious view at all is to be taken, as I think it should be, of this breach of the Canadian Bill of Rights. . . .

I would, therefore, allow this appeal, set aside the judgments below and quash the conviction.

~ Pigeon J. wrote a short opinion concurring with Ritchie J. ~

~ Spence J. wrote a short opinion concurring with Laskin J. ~

C.   The Charter of Rights and Freedoms

40.   Law Society of Upper Canada *v*. Skapinker, *1984*

~ The Canadian Charter of Rights and Freedoms came into force on April 17, 1982. Immediately there was a rush of Charter litigation in the lower courts but it took many months for the first cases to work their way up through the trial courts and intermediate courts of appeal to the Supreme Court of Canada.[1]

In *Skapinker* we have the Supreme Court's first Charter decision, rendered May 3, 1984. With a roll of drums and a blast of trumpets, the Court's opinion, written by Justice Estey, heralds the arrival of a new era in Canadian judicial review. Justice Estey employs the words of the great American Chief Justice, John Marshall, to expound on the power and responsibility which the application of constitutional guarantees confers on the judiciary.

In *Skapinker*, as in *Marbury* v. *Madison*, Marshall's landmark decision of 1803, the assertion of judicial power to overturn unconstitutional legislation comes in a rather inconsequential case. The immediate issue in the case was whether Ontario legislation requiring all members of the provincial bar to be Canadian citizens violated rights in section 6, the mobility rights clause in the Charter. By the time the case reached the Supreme Court, Skapinker had become a citizen and was practicing law in Ontario. But the Court heard the case anyway by permitting Richardson, an American law graduate of Queen's University who had intervened in support of Skapinker and who did not intend to become a Canadian citizen, to replace Skapinker.

Justice Estey's reasons for rejecting the challenge to Ontario's legislation are extremely technical. The interpretative question he must answer is whether the right "to pursue the gaining of a livelihood in any province" in section 6(2)(b) is a free standing right or a right associated with movement across provincial boundaries. In opting for the latter interpretation, Estey eschews any reference to the broad historical purpose of section 6 or to the policy consequences of finding a right to work in the Constitution. He sticks to traditional techniques for interpreting ordinary statutes, concentrating on the logical structure of section 6 and its heading. This interpretative technique very much resembles that of the Privy Council in its first decisions on the B.N.A. Act.

Estey's opinion in *Skapinker* like Marshalls's in *Marbury* v. *Madison* will not be remembered for what it says on the particular issues in the case but for its

---

[1] The procedures of constitutional litigation are described above in the Introduction, at pp. 22 to 28.

general propositions about judicial review. Here two points stand out. First, Estey senses that the Charter brings with it a clear mandate for the judiciary to overturn legislation which is found to contravene its terms. He does not base this mandate on the mechanisms of constitution-making (which was scarcely a popular process) but on a broad conception of the written Constitution as supreme law.

But this power of judicial review must be exercised with great sensitivity to its implications for the nation's future. This is Estey's second general point— and it is very general indeed. The "living tree" metaphor is trotted out: the Constitution must have an organic growth; it is very difficult to amend; narrow and technical interpretations by the judiciary must not stunt its growth. This organic approach, it should be noted, is not a recipe for extreme activism. Estey cites with approval Marshall's recognition that in construing the terms of a constitution the judiciary must leave room for the legislative branch to function effectively for the benefit of the people.

Although these general propositions are very vague as to how they might apply to any particular case, they did indicate to the legal community that the Court was prepared to take the Charter seriously. This was the very opposite message to that conveyed by the Court in 1963 in *Robertson and Rosetanni*, its first major decision on the Canadian Bill of Rights.[2] In marked contrast to that case, Estey's general sense of enthusiasm and excitement about the Charter, supported as it was by the other six justices participating in the case, could not help but encourage lawyers to raise Charter issues in the courts.

Why the Court inaugurated its Charter jurisprudence with this case and with an opinion written by Justice Estey remains something of a mystery. Estey himself appears not to have been overly impressed with the challenge to judicial statecraft flowing from the Charter. In 1985 he took off to head a Royal Commission on insolvent western banks leaving the Court short handed at a critical time in its history. Shortly after returning to the Court he opted for an early retirement and in his farewell message belittled the Court's work. A John Marshall he was not. ~

LAW SOCIETY OF UPPER CANADA *v.* SKAPINKER
In the Supreme Court of Canada. [1984] 1 S.C.R. 357.

The judgment of Dickson C.J.C., Ritchie, Beetz, Estey, McIntyre, Lamer and Wilson JJ. was delivered by

ESTEY, J.: By s. 28(c) of The Law Society Act, R.S.O. 1980, chapt. 233, the legislature of Ontario required all members of the bar of the province to be Canadian citizens. At the outset, let it be emphasized in the clearest possible language that the issue before this Court in this appeal is not whether it is or is not in the interest of this community to require Canadian citizenship as a precondition to

---

[2] This case is discussed above at p. 347.

membership in the bar. Rather, the only issue is whether s. 28(c) of the Law Society Act, *supra*, is inconsistent with s. 6(2)(b) of the Charter of Rights and Freedoms.

The intervener Richardson is an American citizen and a member of the bar of the State of Massachusetts. As we shall see, these proceedings were commenced by the respondent, Skapinker, who later was, for all practical purposes, replaced (when he became a member of the Law Society) by Richardson who was labelled an intervener when he joined the proceedings. Richardson, by the time the appeal came on for hearing in this Court, was the only person who actually had the status of a respondent in the Law Society appeal. In these reasons, it is convenient simply to identify him as Richardson. He is also a permanent resident of Canada, received his LL.B. from Queen's University, Kingston, Ontario in 1980, articled in a law firm in the province for the year ending June 1981 and has now successfully completed the Bar Admission Course of the Law Society of Upper Canada. He has candidly expressed his intention not to become a citizen of Canada. As a result, the appellant has advised Richardson that he will not be accepted as a member of the Law Society. The respondent Skapinker was in the same position but became a Canadian citizen in the course of these proceedings and has been admitted to the bar of Ontario. . . .

The originating Notice of Motion initiating this matter sought a declaration that s. 28(c) of the Law Society Act, *supra*, is "inoperative and of no force and effect to the extent that it discriminates between Canadian citizens and permanent residents of Canada and, in particular, because this is inconsistent with s. 6(2)(b) of the Constitution Act, 1982." The Judge of First Instance, the Honourable Mr. Justice Carruthers, dismissed the application, finding that s. 28(c) of the Law Society Act, *supra*, was not inconsistent with the Charter of Rights, s. 6(2)(b), and therefore was not rendered inoperative by s. 52(1) of the Constitution Act, 1982. . . .

In the Court of Appeal, the majority, speaking through Grange J.A. (Weatherston J.A. concurring), reversed the decision below and declared (Arnup J.A. dissenting) that "s. 28(c) of the Law Society Act, insofar as it excludes from its benefits persons having the status of permanent residents of Canada, is inoperative by reasons of the Canadian Charter of Rights and Freedoms.". . .

The respondent submits that clauses (a) and (b) are two separate rights and that the heading "Mobility Rights" does not dictate a narrow interpretation of the clause (b) right. The appellant and all interveners, including The Attorney General of Canada, The Attorney General of Ontario, The Attorney General of Quebec, The Attorney General of Saskatchewan and the Federation of Law Societies of Canada, take the position that clause (b) is not simply a "right to work" clause but is predicated on a mobility element. Within the group espousing this view, there are some differences as to the meaning properly to be attributed to clause (b). . . .

We are here engaged in a new task, the interpretation and application of the Canadian Charter of Rights and Freedoms as adopted first as an appendage to the Resolution of Parliament on 8 December 1981 and then as an appendix to the Canada Act 1982, Statutes of the United Kingdom, 1982; c. 11. This is not a statute or even a statute of the extraordinary nature of the Canadian Bill of Rights, R.S.C. 1970, Appendix III. It is a part of the constitution of a nation adopted by constitutional process which, in the case of Canada in 1982, took the form of a statute of the Parliament of the United Kingdom. The adoptive mechanisms may vary from nation to nation. They lose their relevancy or shrink to mere historical curiosity value on the ultimate adoption of the instrument as the Constitution. The British North America Act of 1867 was such a law, albeit but a statute of the Parliament of the

United Kingdom and albeit incomplete in the absence of an intra-national amending mechanism. In the interpretation and application of this document the Judicial Committee of the Privy Council of the United Kingdom, which until 1949 was the highest level of the judicial branch engaged in resolving constitutional issues, said: "The British North America Act planted in Canada a living tree capable of growth and expansion within its natural limits": Edwards v. Attorney-General for Canada, [1930] A.C. 124 per Lord Sankey at p. 136, who reiterated this judicial attitude towards a "constituent or organic statute such as the (B.N.A.) Act" in British Coal Corporation v. The King, [1935] A.C. 500 at 518. This Court recognized the distinction between simple 'statutory interpretation' and 'a constitutional role' when the Court was called upon to determine the effect of the Canadian Bill of Rights: Curr v. The Queen, [1972] S.C.R. 889 at 899 per Laskin J. as he then was. The Canadian Bill of Rights is, of course, in form, the same as any other statute of Parliament. It was designed and adopted to perform a more fundamental role than ordinary statutes in this country. It is, however, not a part of the Constitution of the country. It stands, perhaps, somewhere between a statute and a constitutional instrument. Nevertheless, it attracted the principles of interpretation developed by the courts in the constitutional process of interpreting and applying the Constitution itself.

There are some simple but important considerations which guide a Court in construing the Charter, and which are more sharply focussed and discernible than in the case of the federal Bill of Rights. The Charter comes from neither level of the legislative branches of government but from the Constitution itself. It is part of the fabric of Canadian law. Indeed, it "is the supreme law of Canada": s. 52, Constitution Act 1982. It cannot be readily amended. The fine and constant adjustment process of these constitutional provisions is left by a tradition of necessity to the judicial branch. Flex-

ibility must be balanced with certainty. The future must, to the extent foreseeably possible, be accommodated in the present. The Charter is designed and adopted to guide and serve the Canadian community for a long time. Narrow and technical interpretation, if not modulated by a sense of the unknowns of the future, can stunt the growth of the law and hence the community it serves. All this has long been with us in the process of developing the institutions of government under the B.N.A. Act, 1867 (now the Constitution Act). With the Constitution Act 1982 comes a new dimension, a new yardstick of reconciliation between the individual and the community and their respective rights, a dimension which, like the balance of the Constitution, remains to be interpreted and applied by the Court.

The courts in the United States have had almost 200 years experience at this task and it is of more than passing interest to those concerned with these new developments in Canada to study the experience of the United States courts. When the United States Supreme Court was first concerned with the supervision of constitutional development through the application of the recently adopted Constitution of the United States, the Supreme Court of the United States speaking through Chief Justice Marshall stated:

The question, whether an act, repugnant to the constitution, can become the law of the land, is a question deeply interesting to the United States; but, happily, not of an intricacy proportioned to its interest. It seems only necessary to recognise certain principles, supposed to have been long and well established, to decide it. Marbury v. Madison (1803) 5 U.S. (1 Cranch) 173.

As to the nature of a written constitution in relation to the component governments, the Chief Justice continued:

Certainly all those who have framed written constitutions contemplate them as forming the fundamental and paramount law of the nation, and, consequently, the *theory of every such government must be, that an act of the legislature, repugnant to the constitution, is void.*

This theory is essentially attached to a written constitution, and, is consequently, to be considered, by this court, as one of the fundamental principles of our society. It is not therefore to be lost sight of in the further consideration of this subject.

The Court then turned to the role of the court:

It is emphatically the province and duty of the judicial department to say what the law is. Those who apply the rule to particular cases, must of necessity expound and interpret that rule. If two laws conflict with each other, the courts must decide on the operation of each.

So if a law be in opposition to the constitution; if both the law and the constitution apply to a particular case, so that the court must either decide that case conformably to the law, disregarding the constitution; or conformably to the constitution, disregarding the law; the court must determine which of these conflicting rules governs the case. This is of the very essence of judicial duty. (at p. 177)

The Court having staked out its constitutional ground then moved on in *M'Culloch* v. *State of Maryland* (1819), 17 U.S. (4 Wheaton) 316, to consider the techniques of interpretation to be applied in construing a constitution. Again speaking through Chief Justice Marshall:

A constitution, to contain an accurate detail of all the subdivisions of which its great powers will admit, and of all the means by which they may be carried into execution, would partake of the prolixity of a legal code, and could scarcely be embraced by the human mind. It would probably never be understood by the public. Its nature, therefore, requires, that only its great outlines should be marked, its important objects designated, and the minor ingredients which compose these objects be deduced from the nature of the

objects themselves. . . . In considering this question, then, we must never forget, that it is a constitution *we are expounding. (at p. 407)*

In recognizing that both legislative and judicial power under the Constitution is limited, the Chief Justice observed that the Court must allow the legislative branch to exercise that discretion authorized by the Constitution which will:

. . . enable that body to perform the high duties assigned to it, in the manner most beneficial to the people. Let the end be legitimate, let it be within the scope of the constitution, and all means which are appropriate, which are plainly adapted to that end, which are not prohibited, but consist with the letter and spirit of the constitution, are constitutional. (at p. 421)

I come back to the key in this appeal, the meaning of clause (b) in s. 6(2) of the Charter. There are at least three arguably applicable readings of subs. (2) of s. 6 of the Canadian Charter of Rights and Freedoms as adopted in the Constitution Act 1982, and as now incorporated in the Constitution Act 1867 to 1982.

1. The conjunction "and" appearing between clauses (a) and (b) in the English version (absent in the French version), and the heading "Mobility Rights" over the whole of s. 6, enable one to read the subsection with the word "then" understood to follow the conjunction "and" so that (a) and (b) would read as follows: Every citizen . . . and . . . permanent resident has the right (a) to move and take up residence in any province; and [then] (b) to pursue the gaining of a livelihood in any province.

2. A disjunctive reading may be given to subs. (2) by deleting the conjunction "and" between (a) and (b) and by assigning no interpretive value to the heading "Mobility Rights"; and further by taking into account the presence of subs. (4) which may indicate that "mobility" is not a necessary element in each segment of s. 6. Such an approach may be said to lead

to a recognition of two unrelated 'free standing' rights in clauses (a) and (b), the first being a right to move and to reside in any province; the second being the right of a permanent resident to work in any province unrestricted by any law of that province which, in effect, is directed to restricting the right of the permanent resident to do so.

3. The third approach to the reading of clause 2(b) is to separate the two clauses (a) and (b) as though the conjunction "and" were absent, but to read (b) as requiring a mobility aspect. Clause (b) would then assure to the permanent resident the right to work "in any province" whether or not he has exercised the right under (a) to move and to take up residence "in any province". It may be said that such a reading separates but does not divorce the two clauses one from the other or from the balance of the section. This is the view advanced by Mr. MacPherson on behalf of the Attorney General for Saskatchewan. The clause would cover the additional circumstance of transborder commuting to perform work in the province adjoining the province of residence whether or not the permanent resident has previously or subsequently moved to the second province for the purpose of undertaking or continuing to undertake the work in question.

A great deal of argument was devoted to the use of headings as an aid to interpretation of substantive sections of the Charter. Like many provisions in Part I of the Constitution Act, 1982, s. 6 is preceded by a heading "Mobility Rights." Twelve such headings in fact appear in Part I which itself is headed "Canadian Charter of Rights and Freedoms". Apart from headings or titles to the Part itself, the other six parts of the Constitution have no headings of the character found in Part I, except Part VI which introduces an amendment to the Constitution Act, 1867, but which has no headings comparable to those found in Part I. These headings in Part I appear to be integral to the Charter provisions and hence of more significance than the marginal notes and chapter headings sometimes appearing in the statutes. . . .

~ Justice Estey then reviewed Canadian, English and U.S. decisions on the use of headings. ~

The question of the role of the heading in the interpretation of statutes appears to be open. The same must, of course, be true where the Court is engaged in the analysis of a constitutional provision. Here we have a Charter of individual rights incorporated in the broader expanse of the Constitution. . . .

It can be safely concluded that the Charter of Rights will be read by more members of the Canadian community than any other part of the Constitution, 1867 to 1982. It is clear that these headings were systematically and deliberately included as an integral part of the Charter for whatever purpose. At the very minimum, the Court must taken them into consideration when engaged in the process of discerning the meaning and application of the provisions of the Charter. . . .

At a minimum the heading must be examined and some attempt made to discern the intent of the makers of the document from the language of the heading. It is at best one step in the constitutional interpretation process. It is difficult to foresee a situation where the heading will be of controlling importance. It is, on the other hand, almost as difficult to contemplate a situation where the heading could be cursorily rejected. . . .

I return, therefore, to the words of the section itself. "Mobility Rights" has a common meaning until one attempts to seek its outer limits. In a constitutional document relating to personal rights and freedoms, the expression "Mobility Rights" must mean rights of the person to move about, within and outside the national boundaries. . . .

. . . I return to subs. (2) itself. Subclause (a) is pure mobility. It speaks of moving to any province and of residing in any province. If (b) is caught up with (a), it is likewise a mobility provision. If it is separate when properly construed, then it may, as the respondent urges, be a ''right to work'' clause without reference to movement as a prerequisite or otherwise. The presence of the conjunction ''and'' in the English version is not sufficient, in my view, to link (a) to (b) so as to create a single right. Conversely, the absence of the conjunctive link in the French language version is not sufficient to separate the two clauses completely. In the first alternative interpretation, *supra*, if only one right is created by subs. (2), then a division into clauses (a) and (b) is superfluous. Moreover, this suggested interpretation of s. 6(2) is inconsistent with s. 6(3) which subjects the *''rights* specified in subsection (2)'' to certain limitations (my emphasis).

In the second alternative meaning, *supra*, the complete isolation of the two clauses (a) and (b), which is necessary to create a free standing ''right to work'' provision out of clause (b), fails to account for the presence of the phrase ''in any province'' in clause (b). That clause, subject to one further consideration, would announce such a right if these words were omitted. Such a reading out of the phrase ''in any province'' from clause (b) creates a result verging on the absurd. Clause (b) would, alone amongst its neighbours, be out of context under the heading ''Mobility Rights''. . . .

It is reasonable to conclude, therefore, that s. 6(2)(b) should not be read in isolation from the nature and character of the rights granted in subs. (1) and subs. (2)(a). Indeed, the repeated appearance of the expression ''in any province'' in each of the subprovisions of subs. (2) would appear to make relevant the heading ''Mobility Rights.'' The phrase ''in any province'' would appear to be one more link between the heading and the right granted in subs. (2) read as a whole. Nor should s. 6(2) be construed as a discrete section entirely separate from s. 6(3). As I have already mentioned, s. 6(3) refers to the ''rights,'' plural, granted in s. 6(2) and provides an exception to the paramountcy of those rights. In

my opinion, s. 6(3)(a) further evinces the intention to guarantee the opportunity to move freely within Canada unimpeded by laws that ''discriminate primarily . . . on the basis of province of present or previous residence.''

There are many considerations which lead one to adopt the third interpretation of clause (b), *supra*. Clause (b) is thereby accorded a meaning consistent with the heading of s. 6. The transprovincial border commuter is accorded the right to work under (b) without the need of establishing residence in the province of employment in exercise of the right under clause (a). There is a separation of function and purpose between (a) and (b), and the need for separate clauses is demonstrated.

This conclusion as to the meaning and purposes of s. 6(2)(b) finds further support in the writings of all the authors whose works were brought to the attention of the Court: see ''Mobility Rights under the Charter,'' Professor John Laskin, (1982), 4 *Supreme Court Law Review* 89 and pp. 97-8; *Canadian Charter of Rights and Freedoms*, Tarnopolsky and Beaudoin, 1982, in particular Pierre Blache at p. 247; *Canada Act 1982, Annotated,* Peter Hogg, at p. 25.

Much argument by all counsel was devoted to the history of s. 6 as the Charter of Rights was developed and incorporated into the constitutional process, culminating in the Resolution of the Parliament of Canada passed in 1981. Presentations in the House of Commons in 1980-81 by the Minister of Justice of the day were cited. The Court was also referred to the statements by the Premier of the Province of Quebec. . . .

The earlier practice in constitutional fields before this Court and before the Privy Council where historical matter was excluded, has been disapproved in constitutional writings: see, for example, *Constitution of Canada*, Hogg, p. 97. The Court on this appeal received this historical material. I have not found it necessary to take recourse to it in construing s. 6, and therefore, I do not wish to be taken in this appeal as determining, one way or the other, the propriety in the constitutional interpretative process of the admission of such material to the record.

I conclude, for these reasons, that clause (b) of subs. (2) of s. 6 does not establish a separate and distinct right to work divorced from the mobility provisions in which it is found. The two rights (in clause (a) and in clause (b)) both relate to movement into another province, either for the taking up of residence, or to work without establishing residence. Clause (b), therefore, does not avail Richardson of an independent constitutional right to work as a lawyer in the province of residence so as to override the provincial legislation, The Law Society Act, s. 28(c), through s. 52 of the Constitution Act 1981.

Having reached this conclusion, it is not necessary to examine the submissions made by all parties and interveners with reference to s. 6(3) and s. 1 of the Charter of Rights. Richardson has failed to demonstrate that s. 28(c) of The Law Society Act is inconsistent with s. 6(2)(b) of the Charter. Consequently, I need not determine whether the Act is nonetheless saved by s. 6(3) or s. 1 of the Charter.

The development of the Charter as it takes its place in our constitutional law, must necessarily be a careful process. Where issues do not compel commentary on these new Charter provisions, none should be undertaken. There will be occasion when guidance by *obiter* or anticipation of issues will serve the Canadian community, and particularly the evolving constitutional process. On such occasions, the Court might well enlarge its reasons for judgment beyond that required to dispose of the issues raised. Such an instance might, in a small way, arise here. The appellant has, from the outset of these proceedings, relied upon s. 1 of the Charter as the final constitutional test supporting the validity of s. 28(c) of The Law Society Act, *supra*. To that end, a minimal record was established to demonstrate the justification of the citizenship requirement as a "reasonable limit" on the rights granted by the Charter. . . .

As experience accumulates, the law profession and the courts will develop standards and practices which will enable the parties to demonstrate their position under s. 1 and the courts to decide issues arising under that provision. May it only be said here, in the cause of being helpful to those who come forward in similar proceedings, that the record on the s. 1 issue was indeed minimal, and without more, would have made it difficult for a court to determine the issue as to whether a reasonable limit on a prescribed right has been demonstrably justified. Such are the problems of the pioneer and such is the clarity of hindsight.

41. Singh *v*. Minister of Employment and Immigration, *1985*

~ The Supreme Court's decision in *Singh* shows that not all members of the Court share the same degree of enthusiasm for the Charter. The original claim that gave rise to the case was that the absence of a right to a hearing in the procedures under the Immigration Act for determining whether a person is entitled to stay in Canada as a political refugee violated section 7 of the Charter of Rights. But when the matter came before the Supreme Court the parties were asked to make submissions on how the Canadian Bill of Rights should apply to the legislation. In the result, three of the six judges who participated in the decision—Beetz, Estey and McIntyre—based their judgment in favour of the refugees' on the Canadian Bill of Rights. The other three—Dickson, Lamer and Wilson—also found in the refugees' favour but on the basis of the Charter.

Justice Beetz points to the "right to a fair hearing" in section 2(e) of the Canadian Bill of Rights which deals more specifically with the claim made in this case than does anything in the Charter. The statutory Bill of Rights, he emphasizes, along with its provincial counterparts, have not been rendered totally redundant and can usefully complement the Charter. Therefore, he and the two judges who concur with him, prefer to ground their decision on the "tailor-made" provision of this quasi-constitutional instrument. The other three justices opt for the heavier, constitutional artillery of the Charter.

Justice Wilson uses the occasion to write the Court's first opinion on the most broadly phrased right in the Charter: "the right to life, liberty and security of the person and the right not to be deprived thereof except in accordance with the principles of fundamental justice." Understandably, she is careful not to commit herself to a full definition of what section 7 entails. She does establish, however, that section 7, *as a minimum*, requires that government procedures depriving persons of their life, liberty or security of the person, be procedurally fair and that "security of the person" encompasses freedom from the threat of physical suffering or imprisonment apt to be incurred by a deported refugee claimant. More remarkable is her holding that the protection afforded by section 7 (and presumably by other Charter rights which apply to "everyone" or to "every individual" rather than to "citizens" or "permanent residents") extends to "every human being who is physically present in Canada".

The most activist aspect of Justice Wilson's opinion is her response to the government's attempt to save its legislation by arguing that the cost of providing a hearing to determine refugee status constitutes a reasonable justification under section 1 for limiting the Charter right. In Justice Wilson's and her concurring colleagues' view, administrative convenience cannot justify overriding a Charter right. In support of this view she points to statements of a senior immigration official and a ministerial task calling for reform of refugee procedures.

---

[1] "Law expected to halve refugee entries," *Toronto Globe & Mail*, June 14, 1988.

As a consequence of the Court's decision in *Singh*, the personnel of the Immigration Appeal Board had to be greatly expanded to hear the appeals of persons denied refugee status. An enormous backlog of cases began to accumulate as thousands of foreigners who had arrived in Canada by one means or another claimed to be political refugees. This prompted the introduction of Bill C-55, An Act to Amend the Immigration Act, providing for a summary hearing at the point of entry to determine whether a person's claim for refugee status is sufficiently credible to warrant a full hearing before the Immigration Department's Refugee Division.[1] It remains to be seen whether this new legislation will meet the Charter's standard of fundamental justice. ~

SATNAM SINGH ET AL. *v.* MINISTER OF EMPLOYMENT
AND IMMIGRATION
In the Supreme Court of Canada. [1985] 1 S.C.R. 177.

The judgment of Beetz, Estey and McIntyre JJ. was delivered by

BEETZ J.: The main issue which was argued when these appeals were heard on April 30 and May 1, 1984, was whether the procedures set out in the Immigration Act, 1976, S.C. 1976-77, c. 52 as amended, for the adjudication of the claims of persons claiming refugee status in Canada, deny such claimants rights they are entitled to assert under s. 7 of the Canadian Charter of Rights and Freedoms. No submissions were made at that time as to the possible application of the Canadian Bill of Rights to these appeals.

On December 7, 1984, the Deputy Registrar wrote to counsel to inform them that the members of the Court would like to have their submissions in writing on the application of the Canadian Bill of Rights. Counsel for all the parties and the interveners complied and counsel for the appellants replied, also in writing.

Like my colleague, Madame Justice Wilson, whose reasons for judgment I have had the advantage of reading, I conclude that these appeals ought to be allowed. But I do so on the basis of the Canadian Bill of Rights. I refrain from expressing any views on the question whether the Canadian Charter of Rights and Freedoms is applicable at all to the circumstances of these cases and more particularly, on the important question whether the claim affords any protection against a deprivation or the threat of a deprivation of the right to life, liberty or security of the person by foreign governments.

Section 26 of the Canadian Charter of Rights and Freedoms should be kept in mind. It provides:

26. *The guarantee in this Charter of certain rights and freedoms shall not be construed as denying the existence of any other rights or freedoms that exist in Canada.*

Thus, the Canadian Bill of Rights retains all its force and effect, together with the various provincial charters of rights. Because these constitutional or quasi-constitutional instruments are drafted differently, they are susceptible of producing cumulative effects for the better protection of rights and freedoms. But this beneficial result will be lost if these instruments fall into neglect. It is particularly so where they contain provisions not to be found in the Canadian Charter of Rights and Freedoms and almost tailormade for certain factual situations such as those in the case at bar. . . .

The main issue, as I see it, is whether the procedures followed in these cases for the determination of Convention refugee status are in conflict with the Canadian Bill of Rights and more particularly with s. 2(3) thereof. . . .

2. Every law of Canada shall, unless it is expressly declared by an Act of the Parliament of Canada that it shall operate notwithstanding the Canadian Bill of Rights, *be so construed and applied as not to abrogate, abridge or infringe, or to authorize the abrogation, abridgment or infringement of any of the rights or freedoms herein recognized and declared, and in particular, no law of Canada shall be construed or applied so as to . . .*

(e) deprive a person of the right to have a fair hearing in accordance with the principles of fundamental justice for the determination of his rights and obligations.

. . . the process of determining and redetermining Appellant's refugee claims involves the determination of rights and obligations for which the Appellants have, under s. 2(e) of the Canadian Bill of Rights, the right to a fair hearing in accordance with the principles of fundamental justice. . . .

What remains to be decided is whether in the cases at bar, the Appellants were afforded "a fair hearing in accordance with the principles of fundamental justice."

I have no doubt that they were not.

What the Appellants are mainly justified of complaining about in my view is that their claims to refugee status have been finally denied without their having been afforded a full oral hearing at a single stage of the proceedings before any of the bodies or officials empowered to adjudicate upon their claim on the merits. They have actually been heard by the one official who has nothing to say in the matter, a senior immigration officer. But they have been heard neither by the Refugee Status Advisory Committee, who could advise the Minister, neither by the Minister, who had the power to decide and who dismissed their claim, nor by the Immigration Appeal Board which did not allow their application to proceed and which determined, finally, that they are not Convention refugees. . . .

Again, I express no views as to the

applicability of the Canadian Charter of Rights and Freedoms, but I otherwise agree with these submissions: threats to life or liberty by a foreign power are relevant, not with respect to the applicability of the Canadian Bill of Rights, but with respect to the type of hearing which is warranted in the circumstances. In my opinion, nothing will pass muster short of at least one full oral hearing before adjudication on the merits. . . .

For the purposes of these seven cases, I would declare inoperative all the words of section 71(1) of the Immigration Act, 1976, following the words: "Where the Board receives an application referred to in subsection 70(2), it shall forthwith consider the application.". . .

The judgment of Dickson C.J.C., Wilson and Lamer J. was delivered by

WILSON J.: The issue raised by these appeals is whether the procedures set out in the Immigration Act, 1976, S.C. 1976-77, c. 52 as amended, for the adjudication of the claims of persons claiming refugee status in Canada deny such claimants rights they are entitled to assert under s. 7 of the Canadian Charter of Rights and Freedoms. . . .

In the written submissions presented in December 1984 counsel considered whether the procedures for the adjudication of refugee status claims violated the Canadian Bill of Rights, in particular s. 2(e). There can be no doubt that this statute continues in full force and effect and that the rights conferred in it are expressly preserved by s. 26 of the Charter. However, since I believe that the present situation falls within the constitutional protection afforded by the Canadian Charter of Rights and Freedoms, I prefer to base my decision upon the Charter. . . .

As noted above, the procedures for determination of whether an individual is a Convention refugee and for redetermination of claims by the Immigration Appeal Board are set out in ss. 45 to 48 and 70 to 71 respectively. Focussing first on the initial determination, s. 45 provides as follows:

45. (1) Where, at any time during an inquiry, the person who is the subject of the inquiry claims that he is a Convention refugee, the inquiry shall be continued and, if it is determined that, but for the person's claim that he is a Convention refugee, a removal order or a departure notice would be made or issued with respect to that person, the inquiry shall be adjourned and that person shall be examined under oath by a senior immigration officer respecting his claim.

(2) Where a person who claims that he is a Convention refugee is examined under oath pursuant to subsection (1), his claim, together with a transcript of the examination with respect thereto, shall be referred to the Minister for determination.

(3) A copy of the transcript of an examination under oath referred to in subsection (1) shall be forwarded to the person who claims that he is a Convention refugee.

(4) Where a person's claim is referred to the Minister pursuant to subsection (2), the Minister shall refer the claim and the transcript of the examination under oath with respect thereto to the Refugee Status Advisory Committee established pursuant to section 48 for consideration and, after having obtained the advice of that Committee, shall determine whether or not the person is a Convention refugee.

(5) When the Minister makes a determination with respect to a person's claim that he is a Convention refugee, the Minister shall thereupon in writing inform the senior immigration officer who conducted the examination under oath respecting the claim and the person who claimed to be a Convention refugee of his determination.

(6) Every person with respect to whom an examination under oath is to be held pursuant to subsection (1) shall be informed that he has the right to obtain the services of a barrister or solicitor or other counsel and to be represented by any such counsel at his examination and shall be given a reasonable opportunity, if he so desires and at his own expense, to obtain such counsel.

Counsel for the respondent in this case submitted that the Act did not contemplate an oral hearing before the Minister or the Refugee Status Advisory Committee and that the Minister and the Committee were entitled to rely upon what he described as "the government's knowledge of world affairs" in rendering a decision. As I read s. 45, and in particular s. 45(4), these submissions appear to be correct. It is clear from s. 45(4) that the Act does not envisage an opportunity for the refugee claimant to be heard other than through his claim and the transcript of his examination under oath. Nor does the Act appear to envisage the refugee claimant's being given an opportunity to comment on the advice the Refugee Status Advisory Committee has given to the Minister. The insulation of the process is reinforced by the fact that the Minister is entitled under s. 123 of the Act to delegate his powers under s. 45 and in fact these powers are customarily delegated to the Registrar of the Refugee Status Advisory Committee: see *Wieckowska* v. *Lanthier* [1980] 1 F.C. 655 at p. 656. In substance, therefore, it would appear that the Refugee Status Advisory Committee acts as a decision-making body isolated from the persons whose status it is adjudicating and that it applies policies and makes use of information to which the refugee claimants themselves have no access. . . .

The refugee claimant's status, however, need not be conclusively determined by the Minister's decision on the advice of the Refugee Status Advisory Committee made pursuant to s. 45. Under s. 70(1) of the Act a person whose refugee claim has been refused by the Minister may, within a period prescribed in Regulation 40(1) as fifteen days from the time he is so informed, apply for a redetermination of his claim by the Immigration Appeal Board. Section 70(2) requires the refugee claimant to submit with such an application a copy of the transcript of the examination under oath which was conducted pursuant to s. 45(1) and a declaration under oath setting out the basis of the application, the facts upon which the appellant relies and the information and evidence the applicant intends to offer at a redetermination hearing. The applicant is also permitted pursuant to s. 70(2)(d) to set out in his declaration such other representations as he deems relevant to his application.

The Immigration Appeal Board's duties in considering an application for redetermination of a refugee status claim are set out in s. 71 which reads as follows:

71. (1) Where the Board receives an application referred to in subsection 70(2), it shall forthwith consider the application and if, on the basis of such consideration, it is of the opinion that there are reasonable grounds to believe that a claim could, upon the hearing of the application, be established, it shall allow the application to proceed, and in any other case it shall refuse to allow the application to proceed and shall thereupon determine that the person is not a Convention refugee.

(2) Where pursuant to subsection (1) the Board allows an application to proceed, it shall notify the Minister of the time and place where the application is to be heard and afford the Minister a reasonable opportunity to be heard.

(3) Where the Board has made its determination as to whether or not a person is a Convention refugee, it shall, in writing, inform the Minister and the applicant of its decision.

(4) The Board may, and at the request of the applicant or the Minister shall, give reasons for its determination.

If the Board were to determine pursuant to s. 71(1) that the application should be allowed to proceed, the parties are all agreed that the hearing which would take place pursuant to s. 71(2) would be a quasi-judicial one to which full natural justice would apply. The Board is not, however, empowered by the terms of the statute to allow a redetermination hearing to proceed in every case. It may only do so if "it is of the opinion that there are reasonable grounds to believe that a claim could, upon the hearing of the applica-

tion, be established...." In *Kwiatkowsky* v. *Minister of Employment and Immigration* [1982] 2 S.C.R. 856, this Court interpreted those words as requiring the Board to allow the claim to proceed only if it is of the view that "it is more likely than not" that the applicant will be able to establish his claim at the hearing, following the test laid down by Urie J. in *Lugano* v. *Minister of Manpower and Immigration* [1976] 2 F.C. 438. . . .

ARE THE APPELLANTS ENTITLED TO THE PROTECTION OF S. 7 OF THE CHARTER?

Section 7 of the Charter states that "Everyone has the right to life, liberty and security of the person and the right not to be deprived thereof except in accordance with the principles of fundamental justice." Counsel for the appellants contrasts the use of the word "Everyone" in s. 7 with the language used in other sections, for example, "Every citizen of Canada" in s. 3, "Every citizen of Canada and every person who has the status of a permanent resident of Canada" in s. 6(2) and "Citizens of Canada" in s. 23. He concludes that "Everyone" in s. 7 is intended to encompass a broader class of persons than citizens and permanent residents. Counsel for the Minister concedes that "everyone" is sufficiently broad to include the appellants in its compass and I am prepared to accept that the term includes every human being who is physically present in Canada and by virtue of such presence amenable to Canadian law. . . .

It seems to me that in attempting to decide whether the appellants have been deprived of the right to life, liberty and security of the person within the meaning of s. 7 of the Charter, we must begin by determining what rights the appellants have under the Immigration Act. As noted earlier, s. 5(1) of the Act excludes from persons other than those described in s. 4 the right to come into or remain in Canada. The appellants therefore do not have such a right. However, the Act does accord a Convention refugee certain rights which it does not provide to others, namely the right to a determination from the Minister based on proper principles as to whether a permit should issue entitling him to enter and remain in Canada (ss. 4(2) and 37); the right not to be returned to a country where his life or freedom would be threatened (s. 55); and the right to appeal a removal order or a deportation order made against him (ss. 72(2)(a), 72(2)(b) and 72(3)).

We must therefore ask ourselves whether the deprivation of these rights constitutes a deprivation of the right to life, liberty and security of the person within the meaning of s. 7 of the Charter. Even if we accept the "single right" theory advanced by counsel for the Minister in interpreting s. 7, I think we must recognize that the "right" which is articulated in s. 7 has three elements: life, liberty and security of the person. As I understand the "single right" theory, it is not suggested that there must be a deprivation of all three of these elements before an individual is deprived of his "right" under s. 7. In other words, I believe that it is consistent with the "single right" theory advanced by counsel to suggest that a deprivation of the appellants' "security of the person," for example, would constitute a deprivation of their "right" under s. 7, whether or not it can also be said that they have been deprived of their lives or liberty. Rather, as I understand it, the "single right" theory is advanced in support of a narrow construction of the words "life," "liberty" and "security of the person" as different aspects of a single concept rather than as separate concepts each of which must be construed independently.

Certainly, it is true that the concepts of the right to life, the right to liberty, and the right to security of the person are capable of a broad range of meaning. The Fourteenth Amendment to the United States Constitution provides in part ". . . nor shall any State deprive any person of life, liberty, or property, without the due process of law. . . ." In *Board of Regents*

of State Colleges v. *Roth* (1972) 408 U.S. 546 at p. 572, Steward J. articulated the notion of liberty as embodied in the Fourteenth Amendment in the following way:

While this Court has not attempted to define with exactness the liberty . . . guaranteed (by the Fourteenth Amendment), the term has received much consideration and some of the included things have been definitely stated. Without doubt, it denotes not merely freedom from bodily restraint but also the right of the individual to contract, to engage in any of the common occupations of life, to acquire useful knowledge, to marry, establish a home and bring up children, to worship God according to the dictates of his own conscience, and generally to enjoy those privileges long recognized . . . as essential to the orderly pursuit of happiness by free men. Meyer v. Nebraska, 262 U.S. 390, 399. In a Constitution for a free people, there can be no doubt that the meaning of "liberty" must be broad indeed. See, e.g., Bolling v. Sharpe, 347 U.S. 497, 499-500; Stanley v. Illinois, 405 U.S. 645.

The "single right" theory advanced by counsel for the Minister would suggest that this conception of "liberty" is too broad to be employed in our interpretation of s. 7 of the Charter. Even if this submission is sound, however, it seems to me that it is incumbent upon the Court to give meaning to each of the elements, life, liberty and security of the person, which make up the "right" contained in s. 7.

To return to the facts before the Court, it will be recalled that a Convention refugee is by definition a person who has a well-founded fear of prosecution in the country from which he is fleeing. In my view, to deprive him of the avenues open to him under the Act to escape from that fear of persecution must, at least, *impair* his right to life, liberty and security of the person in the narrow sense advanced by the counsel for the Minister. The question, however, is whether such an impairment constitutes a "deprivation" under s. 7.

It must be acknowledged, for example, that even if a Convention refugee's fear of persecution is a well-founded one, it does not automatically follow that he will be deprived of his life or his liberty if he is returned to his homeland. Can it be said that Canadian officials have deprived a Convention refugee of his right to life, liberty and security of the person if he is wrongfully returned to a country where death, imprisonment or another form of persecution *may* await him? . . .

I cannot, however, accept the submission of counsel for the Minister that the denial of the rights possessed by a Convention refugee under the Act does not constitute a deprivation of his security of the person. Like "liberty," the phrase "security of the person" is capable of a broad range of meaning. The phrase "security of the person" is found in s. 1(a) of the Canadian Bill of Rights and its interpretation in that context might have assisted us in its proper interpretation under the Charter. Unfortunately no clear meaning of the words emerges from the case law. . . .

The Law Reform Commission, in its Working Paper No. 26 Medical Treatment and Criminal Law (1980) suggested at p. 6 that:

The right to security of the person means not only protection of one's physical integrity, but the provision of necessaries for its support.

The Commission went on to describe the provision of necessaries in terms of Art. 25, para. 1 of the Universal Declaration of Human Rights (1948) which reads:

Every one has the right to a standard of living adequate for the health and well-being of himself and of his family, including food, clothing, housing and medical care and necessary social services, and the right to security in the event of unemployment, sickness, disability, widowhood, old age, or other lack of livelihood in circumstances beyond his control.

Commentators have advocated the adoption of a similarly broad conception of "security of the person" in the interpretation of s. 7 of the Charter: see Garant "Fundamental Freedoms and Natural Justice" in Tarnopolsky and Beaudoin (eds.), *The Canadian Charter of Rights and Freedoms* (1982) at pp. 264-65, 271-74; Manning, *Rights, Freedoms and the Courts: A Practical Analysis of the Constitution Act, 1982* (1983) at pp. 249-54.

For purposes of the present appeal it is not necessary, in my opinion, to consider whether such an expansive approach to "security of the person" in s. 7 of the Charter should be taken. It seems to me that even if one adopts the narrow approach advocated by the counsel for the Minister, "security of the person" must encompass freedom from the threat of physical punishment or suffering as well as freedom from such punishment itself. I note particularly that a Convention refugee has the right under s. 55 of the Act not to ". . . be removed from Canada to a country where his life or freedom would be threatened. . . ." In my view, the denial of such a right must amount to a deprivation of security of the person within the meaning of s. 7. . . .

The creation of a dichotomy between privileges and rights played a significant role in narrowing the scope of the application of the *Canadian Bill of Rights*, as is apparent from the judgment of Martland J. in *Mitchell* v. *The Queen* [1976] 2 S.C.R. 570. At p 588 Martland J. said:

The appellant also relies upon s. 2(e) of the Bill of Rights, which provides that no law of Canada shall be construed or applied so as to deprive a person of the right to a fair hearing in accordance with the principles of fundamental justice for the determination of his rights and obligations. In the McCaud *case [[1965] 1 C.C.C. 168 Spence J., whose view was adopted unanimously on appeal, held that the provisions of s. 2(e) do not apply to the question of the revocation of parole under the provisions of the Parole Act.*

The appellant had no right to parole.

He was granted parole as a matter of discretion by the Parole Board. He has no right to remain on parole. His parole was subject to revocation at the absolute discretion of the Board.

I do not think this kind of analysis is acceptable in relation to the Charter. It seems to me rather that the recent adoption of the Charter by Parliament and nine of the ten provinces as part of the Canadian constitutional framework has sent a clear message to the courts that the restrictive attitude which at times characterized their approach to the Canadian Bill of Rights ought to be re-examined. I am accordingly of the view that the approach taken by Laskin C.J.C. dissenting in *Mitchell* is to be preferred to that of the majority as we examine the question whether the Charter has any application to the adjudication of rights granted to an individual by statute. . . .

IS FUNDAMENTAL JUSTICE DENIED BY THE PROCEDURES FOR THE DETERMINATION OF CONVENTION REFUGEE STATUS SET OUT IN THE ACT?

All counsel were agreed that at a minimum the concept of "fundamental justice" as it appears is s. 7 of the Charter includes the notion of procedural fairness articulated by Fauteux C.J. in *Duke* v. *the Queen* [1972] S.C.R. 917. At p. 923 he said:

Under s. 2(e) of the Bill of Rights no law of Canada shall be construed or applied so as to deprive him of "a fair hearing in accordance with the principles of fundamental justice." Without attempting to formulate any final definition of those words, I would take them to mean, generally, that the tribunal which adjudicates upon his rights must act fairly, in good faith, without bias and in a judicial temper, and must give to him the opportunity adequately to state his case.

Do the procedures set out in the Act for the adjudication of refugee status claims meet this test of procedural fairness? Do they provide an adequate opportunity for a refugee claimant to state his case and know the case he has to meet? This seems to be the question we have to answer and, in approaching it, I am prepared to accept Mr. Bowie's submission that procedural fairness may demand different things in different contexts: see *Martineau No. 2 (supra)* at p. 630. Thus it is possible that an oral hearing before the decision-maker is not required in every case in which s. 7 of the Charter is called into play. . . .

I should note, however, that even if hearings based on written submissions are consistent with the principles of fundamental justice for some purposes, they will not be satisfactory for all purposes. In particular, I am of the view that where a serious issue of credibility is involved, fundamental justice requires that credibility be determined on the basis of an oral hearing. . . .

As I have suggested, the absence of an oral hearing need not be inconsistent with fundamental justice in every case. My greatest concern about the procedural scheme envisaged by ss. 45 to 58 and 70 and 71 of the Immigration Act is not, therefore, with the absence of an oral hearing in and of itself, but with the inadequacy of the opportunity the scheme provides for a refugee claimant to state his case and know the case he has to meet. Mr. Bowie argued that since the procedure under s. 45 was an administrative one, it was quite proper for the Minister and the Refugee Status Advisory Committee to take into account policy considerations and information about world affairs to which the refugee claimant had no opportunity to respond. . . .

It seems to me that the basic flaw in Mr. Bowie's characterization of the procedure under ss. 70 and 71 is his description of the procedure as non-adversarial. It is in fact highly adversarial but the adversary, the Minister, is waiting in the wings. What the Board has before it is a determination by the Minister based in part on information and policies to which the applicant has no means of access that the applicant for redetermination is not a Convention refugee. The applicant is entitled to submit whatever relevant material he wishes to the Board but he still faces the hurdle of having to establish to the Board that on the balance of probabilities the Minister was wrong. Moreover, he must do this without any knowledge of the Minister's case beyond the rudimentary reasons which the Minister has decided to give him in rejecting his claim. It is this aspect of the procedures set out in the Act which I find impossible to reconcile with the requirements of "fundamental justice" as set out in s. 7 of the Charter. . . .

CAN THE PROCEDURES BE SAVED UNDER S. 1 OF THE CHARTER?

The question of the standards which the Court should use in applying s. 1 is, without a doubt, a question of enormous significance for the operation of the Charter. If too low a threshold is set, the courts run the risk of emasculating the Charter. If too high a threshold is set, the courts run the risk of unjustifiably restricting government action. It is not a task to be entered upon lightly.

Unfortunately, counsel devoted relatively little time in the course of argument to the principles the Court should espouse in applying s. 1. This is certainly understandable given the complexity of the other issues which are in one sense preliminary to the application of s. 1. It is nevertheless to be regretted. A particular disappointment is the limited scope of the factual material brought forward by the respondent in support of the proposition that the Immigration Act's provisions constitute a "reasonable limit" on the appellant's rights. It must be acknowledged that counsel operated under considerable time pressure in the preparation of these appeals and I do not intend these remarks as a criticism of the presentation made to the Court by counsel which was, indeed, extremely valuable. On the other hand, I feel constrained to echo the observations made by Estey J. in *The Law Society of Upper Canada* v. *Skapinker* [1984] 1 S.C.R. 357 at p. 384 where he said:

As experience accumulates, the law

profession and the courts will develop standards and practices which will enable the parties to demonstrate their position under s. 1 and the courts to decide issues arising under that provision. May it only be said here, in the cause of being helpful to those who come forward in similar proceedings, that the record on the s. 1 issue was indeed minimal, and without more, would have made it difficult for a court to determine the issue as to whether a reasonable limit on a prescribed right has been demonstrably justified.

Mr. Bowie's submissions on behalf of the Minister with respect to s. 1 were that Canadian procedures with respect to the adjudication of refugee claims had received the approbation of the office of the United Nations High Commissioner for Refugees and it was not uncommon in the Commonwealth and Western European countries for refugee claims to be adjudicated administratively without a right to appeal. He further argued that the Immigration Appeal Board was already subjected to a considerable strain in terms of the volume of cases which it was required to hear and that a requirement of an oral hearing in every case where an application for redetermination of a refugee claim has been made would constitute an unreasonable burden on the Board's resources.

One or two comments are in order respecting this approach to s. 1. It seems to me that it is important to bear in mind that the rights and freedoms set out in the Charter are fundamental to the political structure of Canada and are guaranteed by the Charter as part of the supreme law of our nation. I think that in determining whether a particular limitation is a reasonable limit prescribed by law which can be "demonstrably justified in a free and democratic society," it is important to remember that the courts are conducting this inquiry in light of a commitment to uphold the rights and freedoms set out in the other sections of the Charter. The issue in the present case is not simply whether the procedures set out in the

Immigration Act for the adjudication of refugee claims are reasonable; it is whether it is reasonable to deprive the appellants of the right to life, liberty and security of the person by adopting a system for the adjudication of refugee status claims which does not accord with the principles of fundamental justice.

Seen in this light I have considerable doubt that the type of utilitarian consideration brought forward by Mr. Bowie can constitute a justification for a limitation on the rights set out in the Charter. Certainly the guarantees of the Charter would be illusory if they could be ignored because it was administratively convenient to do so. No doubt considerable time and money can be saved by adopting administrative procedures which ignore the principles of fundamental justice but such an argument, in my view, misses the point of the exercise under s. 1. The principles of natural justice and procedural fairness which have long been espoused by our courts, and the constitutional entrenchment of the principles of fundamental justice in s. 7, implicity recognize that a balance of administrative convenience does not override the need to adhere to these principles. Whatever standard of review eventually emerges under s. 1, it seems to me that the basis of the justification for the limitation of rights under s. 7 must be more compelling than any advanced in these appeals.

Moreover, I am not convinced in light of the submissions made by appellants that the limitations on the rights of refugees claimants which are imposed by the adjudication procedures of the Immigration Act are reasonable even on the respondent's own terms. It is obvious that there is a considerable degree of dissatisfaction with the present system even on the part of those administer it. In an address given in Toronto on October 25, 1980 Janet Scott, Q.C., the Chairman of the Immigration Appeal Board made the following remarks:

There is no blinking at the fact that the sections dealing with the Board's juris-diction in refugee redetermination are highly unsatisfactory. Leaving aside any consideration of natural justice, the system is extremely cumbersome and when we enter into the sphere of natural justice, open to criticism as unjust.

In September 1980 the Minister of Employment and Immigration established a Task Force on Immigration Practices and Procedures and in November 1981 the Task Force issued a report entitled "The Refugee Determination Process." The Task Force recommended wholesale changes in the procedures employed in the determination of refugee claims, including a recommendation that "A refugee claimant should be entitled to a hearing in every case where the [Refugee Status Advisory Committee] is not prepared to make a positive recommendation on the basis of the transcript" (Report p. xvi). In its conclusion, the Task Force discussed the impact of its recommendation that an oral hearing be given in each case. At p. 103 the Report states:

In the end, then, the question is one of resources. Would the additional expenditures be warranted? How does one do a cost-benefit analysis where the "benefit" is to be found in vague concepts, such as "fairness" and "justice"? One approach may be to canvass other forms of adjudication by federal tribunals and compare the significance of their decisions and the kinds of hearings which they offer with those of the refugee determination process. Without referring to specific bodies or in any way denigrating the importance of their work, the impact of their decisions often pales in comparison to refugee determination. Yet they generally offer far more in the way of procedural fairness.

Even if the cost of compliance with fundamental justice is a factor to which the courts would give considerable weight, I am not satisfied that the Minister has demonstrated that this cost would be so prohibitive as to constitute a justification within the meaning of s. 1.

To recapitulate, I am persuaded that the appellants are entitled to assert the protection of s. 7 of the Charter in the determination of their claims to Convention refugee status under the Immigration Act. I am further persuaded that the procedures under the Act as they were applied in these cases do not meet the requirements of fundamental justice under s. 7 and that accordingly the appellants' rights under s. 7 were violated. Finally, I believe that the respondent has failed to demonstrate that the procedures set out in the Act constitute a reasonable limit on the appellants' rights within the meaning of s. 1 of the Charter. I would accordingly allow the appeals. In so doing I should, however, observe that the acceptance of certain submissions, particularly concerning the scope of s. 7 of the Charter in the context of these appeals, is not intended to be definitive of the scope of the section in other contexts. I do not by any means foreclose the possibility that s. 7 protects a wider range of interests than those involved in these appeals.

42. The Queen *v.* Big M Drug Mart Ltd., *1985*

~ *Big M Drug Mart* clearly demonstrates the contrast between the Supreme Court's treatment of the Charter of Rights and Freedoms and its treatment two decades earlier of the Canadian Bill of Rights. In 1963 in *Robertson and Rosetanni*[1] the Court, with only one dissent, found that the federal Lord's Day Act did not contravene the right to freedom of religion in the Canadian Bill of Rights. Now in *Big M* the Court strikes down the federal Lord's Day Act on the grounds that it violates the right to freedom of conscience and religion in section 2 of the Charter.

In their initial approach to the Bill of Rights the Court had adopted the view that the rights and freedoms in that document must be no wider than what was provided for under Canadian law at the time the Bill was adopted. There is no trace of that "frozen rights" thesis in the Court's early treatment of the Charter. The fact that the Lord's Day Act had been on the statute book since 1906 has no bearing on whether or not it violates the Charter's guarantee of religious freedom. In *Robertson and Rosetanni* the majority considered the effect not the purpose of the legislation and held that because compulsory Sunday closing does not actually force anyone to worship in a Christian manner it does not affect freedom of religion. In *Big M*, for all of the justices except Justice Wilson, analysis of the challenged legislation begins with the purpose behind the legislation at the time of its enactment. In the Court's view that purpose, back in 1906, was clearly religious—to secure the observance by all of the Christian sabbath. Legislation passed for such a purpose, in the Court's view, clearly violates the right to freedom of religion.

The difference between the majority and Justice Wilson on whether the assessment of challenged legislation should begin with its purpose or effect is not likely to be of great importance. All the justices agree that if either the purpose or effect of legislation violates the Charter the legislation must be considered unconstitutional. Perhaps the majority's preference for beginning with the purpose of legislation is to avoid, if possible, the extensive examination of the practical consequences of legislation. Justice Wilson is less diffident about the judiciary's capacity for this kind of policy analysis.

Far more essential to the Court's "purposive" approach to Charter interpretation is Chief Justice Dickson's inquiry into the meaning of "freedom of religion". The purpose he looks for here is not the stated intent of the Charter's drafters but the broad historical reasons for this freedom becoming a cherished ideal in western civilization. While this "purposive" approach may yield a fairly generous interpretation of Charter rights and freedoms, the Chief Justice is careful to point out that it must not be pushed so far as to "overshoot the actual purpose of the right or freedom in question". The Chief Justice is laying the groundwork for a moderate activism.

The Court's decision in *Big M* by no means settled the Sunday closing issue

---

[1] (1963) S.C.R. 651. For a discussion of this case see p. 347 above.

in Canada. By ruling out a religious or moral rationale for Sunday Closing legislation it eliminated the criminal law power, the only basis for federal legislation, thereby leaving this controversial policy issue to the provinces. All of the provinces had developed more contemporary and secular legislation regulating commercial activities on Sundays. The constitutionality of this legislation remained to be determined, a year and a half later, in the *Edwards Books* case.[2]

The Supreme Court's decision in this case recognizes that a major transformation has taken place in Canadian society. Canada is no longer to be considered, in any official or legal sense, a Christian society. Chief Justice Dickson's opinion brings into play, for the first time, section 27 of the Charter directing the courts to interpret the Charter "in a manner consistent with the preservation and enhancement of the multicultural heritage of Canadians". The Chief Justice cites this section as a further reason for interpreting the right to freedom of religion as excluding laws enacted for the purpose of enforcing the precepts of the Christian religion. Religious pluralism is to be an essential ingredient of the cultural pluralism of the modern Canadian state. ~

HER MAJESTY THE QUEEN *v.* BIG M DRUG MART LTD.
In the Supreme Court of Canada. [1985] 1 S.C.R. 295.

The judgment of Dickson C.J.C., Beetz, McIntyre, Chouinard and Lamer JJ. was delivered by

DICKSON C.J.C.: Big M Drug Mart Ltd. was charged with unlawfully carrying on the sale of goods, on Sunday, May 30, 1982 in the City of Calgary, Alberta, contrary to the Lord's Day Act, R.S.C. 1970, c. L-13.

Big M has challenged the constitutionality of the Lord's Day Act, both in terms of the division of powers and the Canadian Charter of Rights and Freedoms. Such challenge places in issue before this Court, for the first time, one of the fundamental freedoms protected by the Charter, the guarantee of "freedom of conscience and religion" entrenched in s. 2.

The constitutional validity of Sunday observance legislation has in the past been tested largely through the division of powers provided in sections 91 and 92 of the Constitution Act, 1867. Freedom of religion has been seen to be a matter falling within federal legislative competence. Today, following the advent of the Constitution Act, 1982, we must address squarely the fundamental issues raised by individual rights and freedoms enshrined in the Charter, as well as those concerned with legislative powers. . . .

THE CHARACTERIZATION OF THE LORD'S DAY ACT

There are obviously two possible ways to characterize the purpose of Lord's Day legislation, the one religious, namely securing public observance of the Christian institution of the Sabbath and the other secular, namely providing for a uniform day of rest from labour. It is undoubtedly true that both elements may be present in any given enactment, indeed it is almost inevitable that they will be, considering that such laws combine a prohibition of ordinary employment for one

---

[2] See case 48 below.

day out of seven with a specification that this day of rest shall be the Christian sabbath—Sunday. In the Anglo-Canadian tradition this intertwining is to be seen as far back as early Saxon times in such laws as that promulgated by Ine, King of Wessex from 688-725. . . .

Historically, there seems little doubt that it was religious purpose which underlay the enactment of English Lord's Day legislation. From early times the moral exhortation found in the Fourth Commandment (Exodus 20: 8-11) "Remember the Sabbath day, to keep it holy" increasingly became a legislative imperative. The first major piece of legislation, The Sunday Fairs Act, 1448, 27 Hen.VI, c. 5, prefaced its prohibition of fairs and markets on Sunday with a recital of "abomenable injuries and offences done to Almighty God and to his Saints" because of bodily labour, deceitful bargaining, drunkenness and religious non-observance associated with fairs. Following the Reformation under Henry VIII, religious observance acquired an added political significance and a number of statutes aimed at securing religious conformity were promulgated. . . .

Under Charles I the first modern Sunday observance statutes were enacted and their religious purpose is reflected in their titles, An Act for Punishing Divers Abuses Committed on the Lord's Day called Sunday, 1625, 1 Car. I, c. 1 and An Act for the Further Reformation of Sundry Abuses Committed on the Lord's Day Commonly called Sunday, 1627, 3 Car. I, c. 2. During the Commonwealth or Interregnum period, the Puritan Parliament passed strict laws prohibiting the profanation of the Lord's Day by any form of marketing, travel, worldly labour, sports or recourse to taverns, tobacco shops or restaurants. With the Restoration came An Act for the Better Observation of the Lord's Day Commonly Called Sunday, 1677, 26 Car. II, c. 7, also known as the Sunday Observance Act. As its full title indicates, the primary object of this legislation, like that of its predecessors, was clearly religious

rather than secular. . . .

The Sunday Observance Act of 1677 served as a model for Canadian pre-Confederation legislation, especially An Act to Prevent the Profanation of the Lord's Day, commonly called Sunday, 1845, 8 Vict. c. 45 (U.C.), which substantially re-enacted the English law with only minor alterations designed to suit it to the specific conditions and activities of Upper Canada. It was this statute, as re-enacted by the post-Confederation legislature of Ontario (R.S.O. 1897, c. 246), that the Privy Council found to be beyond the competence of the province to enact in *Attorney General for Ontario* v. *Hamilton Street Railway Company, supra,* a decision which lay behind the passage in 1906 of the federal Lord's Day Act. Like the Ontario *Act,* the federal *Act,* embodied the basic framework and much of the language of the English Sunday Observance Act of 1667. After four consolidations, it still exhibits these same essential characteristics in its present form.

From the time of Confederation until the Privy Council decision in 1903 in *Hamilton Street Railway, supra,* it was the widely-held view that Sunday observance legislation fell within provincial purview under the Constitution Act, 1867 as being a matter falling under either s. 92(13), property and civil rights within the province, or s. 92(16), a matter of merely local or private nature in the Province. Several of the provinces passed laws prohibiting Sunday activities. In the *Hamilton Street Railway* case the Ontario statute fell to be considered. Aylesworth K.C. argued before the Privy Council that the primary object of the *Act* under consideration was the promotion of public order, safety and morals, and not the regulation of civil rights as between subject and subject. That view would seem to have prevailed, as their Lordships held that the Act as a whole was beyond the competence of the Ontario Legislature to enact. . . .

The Parliament of Canada passed the federal Lord's Day Act S.C. 1906, c. 27, with what would appear to have been some degree of reluctance because, firstly, s. 14 provided that nothing in the Act should be construed to repeal or in any way affect "any provisions of any Act or law relating in any way to the observance of the Lord's day in force in any province of Canada when this Act comes into force." Sunday observance legislation in force in a province at the time it entered Confederation was expressly preserved. Secondly, while the *Act* prohibited a very few activities unconditionally, such as shooting in such a manner as to disturb public worship or observance of the day, or selling foreign newspapers, the most important sections of the *Act* made other activities unlawful only to the extent that provincial legislation did not provide otherwise.

Acting under the authority of the federal Lord's Day Act, the provinces have enacted legislation such as the Lord's Day (Ontario) Act, R.S.O. 1980, c. 253 and the Lord's Day (Saskatchewan) Act, R.S.S. 1978, c. L-34. Provincial legislation of this nature was upheld by the Judicial Committee of the Privy Council in *Lord's Day Alliance* v. *Attorney General of Manitoba et al.*, [1925] A.C. 384, and more recently by this Court in *Lord's Day Alliance* v. *Attorney General of British Columbia et al.*, [1959] S.C.R. 497. . . .

We come now to the case of *Robertson and Rosetanni* v. *the Queen, supra*, to which much attention was directed during argument. The appellants were convicted on a charge of operating a bowling alley on a Sunday, contrary to the Lord's Day Act. They contended that the Canadian Bill of Rights, R.S.C. 1970, App. III, had in effect repealed s. 4 of the Lord's Day Act, or, in any event, rendered it inoperative. The Court, Cartwright J. dissenting, rejected the contention and dismissed the appeal. . . .

The United States Supreme Court has sustained the constitutionality of Sunday observance legislation against First Amendment challenges: *McGowan* v. *Maryland* (1961), 366 U.S. 420; *Braunfeld* v. *Brown* (1961), 366 U.S. 599, *Gal-lagher* v. *Crownkosher Supermarkets of Massachussetts* (1961), 366 U.S. 617, and *Two Guys from Harrison-Allentown* v. *McGinley* (1961) 366 U.S. 582. Despite the undoubted religious motivation of the state laws in question at the time of their passage and their clear origin in the religiously coercive statutes of Stuart England, Chief Justice Warren, writing for the majority, found that those statutes had evolved to become purely secular labour regulation. In his view, none of the impugned state statutes violated the First Amendment guarantee of freedom of religion. Whatever religious terminology still appeared in the legislation (such as the use of the term "Lord's Day" in the Maryland statute) was to be seen simply as a historical curiosity. . . .

It is somewhat ironic that the United States courts upheld the validity of Sunday observance laws, characterizing them as secular in order not to run afoul of the religion clauses of the First Amendment, while in contrast, in *Robertson and Rosetanni, supra*, the Court found in the same type of legislation, a religious purpose in order to sustain its *vires* as criminal law. At the same time it accorded to the legislation a secular effect in order not to bring it into conflict with the religious freedom recognized and declared in the Canadian Bill of Rights.

PURPOSE AND EFFECT OF LEGISLATION

A finding that the Lord's Day Act has a secular purpose is, on the authorities, simply not possible. Its religious purpose, in compelling sabbatical observance, has been long-established and consistently maintained by the courts of this country.

The Attorney-General for Alberta concedes that the *Act* is characterized by this religious purpose. He contends, however, that it is not the purpose but the effects of the *Act* which are relevant. In his submission, *Robertson and Rosetanni, supra*, is support for the proposition that it is effects alone which must be assessed in determining whether legislation violates a constitutional guarantee of freedom of religion.

I cannot agree. In my view, both purpose and effect are relevant in determining constitutionality; either an unconstitutional purpose or an unconstitutional effect can invalidate legislation. All legislation is animated by an object the legislature intends to achieve. This object is realized through the impact produced by the operation and application of the legislation. Purpose and effect respectively, in the sense of the legislation's object and its ultimate impact, are clearly linked, if not indivisible. Intended and actual effects have often been looked to for guidance in assessing the legislation's object and thus, its validity.

Moreover, consideration of the object of legislation is vital if rights are to be fully protected. The assessment by the courts of legislative purpose focuses scrutiny upon the aims and objectives of the legislature and ensures they are consonant with the guarantees enshrined in the Charter. The declaration that certain objects lie outside the legislature's power checks governmental action at the first stage of unconstitutional conduct. Further, it will provide more ready and more vigorous protection of constitutional rights by obviating the individual litigant's need to prove effects violative of Charter rights. It will also allow courts to dispose of cases where the object is clearly improper, without inquiring into the legislation's actual impact.

In short, I agree with the respondent that the legislation's purpose is the initial test of constitutional validity and its effects are to be considered when the law under review has passed or, at least, has purportedly passed the purpose test. If the legislation fails the purpose test, there is no need to consider further its effects, since it has already been demonstrated to be invalid. Thus, if a law with a valid purpose interferes by its impact, with rights or freedoms, a litigant could still argue the effects of the legislation as a means to defeat its applicability and possibly its validity. In short, the effects test will only be necessary to defeat legislation with a valid purpose; effects can never be relied upon to save legislation with an invalid purpose.

A second related submission is made by the Attorney-General of Saskatchewan with respect to the characterization of the Lord's Day Act. Both Stevenson, Prov. Ct. J., at trial, and the American Supreme Court, in its quartet on Sunday observance legislation, suggest that the purpose of legislation may shift, or be transformed over time by changing social conditions. . . . A number of objections can be advanced to this "shifting purpose" argument.

First, there are the practical difficulties. No legislation would be safe from a revised judicial assessment of purpose. Laws assumed valid on the basis of persuasive and powerful authority could, at any time, be struck down as invalid. Not only would this create uncertainty in the law, but it would encourage re-litigation of the same issues and, it could be argued, provide the courts with a means by which to arrive at a result dictated by other than legal considerations. . . .

Furthermore, the theory of a shifting purpose stands in stark contrast to fundamental notions developed in our law concerning the nature of "Parliamentary intention." Purpose is a function of the intent of those who drafted and enacted the legislation at the time, and not of any shifting variable. . . .

While the effect of such legislation as the Lord's Day Act may be more secular today than it was in 1677 or in 1906, such a finding cannot justify a conclusion that its purpose has similarly changed. In result, therefore, the Lord's Day Act must be characterized as it has always been, a law the primary purpose of which is the compulsion of sabbatical observance.

FREEDOM OF RELIGION

A truly free society is one which can accommodate a wide variety of beliefs, diversity of tastes and pursuits, customs and codes of conduct. A free society is one which aims at equality with respect to the enjoyment of fundamental freedoms and I say this without any reliance on

s. 15 of the Charter. Freedom must surely be founded in respect for the inherent dignity and the inviolable rights of the human person. The essence of the concept of freedom of religion is the right to entertain such religious beliefs as a person chooses, the right to declare religious beliefs openly and without fear of hindrance or reprisal, and the right to manifest religious belief by worship and practice or by teaching and dissemination. But the concept means more than that.

Freedom can primarily be characterized by the absence of coercion or restraint. If a person is compelled by the state or the will of another to a course of action or inaction which he would not otherwise have chosen, he is not acting of his own volition and he cannot be said to be truly free. One of the major purposes of the Charter is to protect, within reason, from compulsion or restraint. Coercion includes not only such blatant forms of compulsion as direct commands to act or refrain from acting on pain of sanction, coercion includes indirect forms of control which determine or limit alternative courses of conduct available to others. Freedom in a broad sense embraces both the absence of coercion and constraint, and the right to manifest beliefs and practices. Freedom means that, subject to such limitations as are necessary to protect public safety, order, health, or morals or the fundamental rights and freedoms of others, no one is to be forced to act in a way contrary to his beliefs or conscience.

What may appear good and true to a majoritarian religious group, or to the state acting at their behest, may not, for religious reasons, be imposed upon citizens who take a contrary view. The Charter safeguards religious minorities from the threat of "the tyranny of the majority."

To the extent that it binds all to a sectarian Christian ideal, the Lord's Day Act works a form of coercion inimical to the spirit of the Charter and the dignity of all non-Christians. In proclaiming the standards of the Christian faith, the Act creates a climate hostile to, and gives the appearance of discrimination against, non-Christian Canadians. It takes religious values rooted in Christian morality and, using the force of the state, translates them into a positive law binding on believers and non-believers alike. The theological content of the legislation remains as a subtle and constant reminder to religious minorities within the country of their differences with, and alienation from, the dominant religious culture.

Non-Christians are prohibited for religious reasons from carrying out activities which are otherwise lawful, moral and normal. The arm of the state requires all to remember the Lord's day of the Christians and to keep it holy. The protection of one religion and the concomitant non-protection of others imports disparate impact destructive of the religious freedom of the collectivity. I agree with the submission of the respondent that to accept that Parliament retains the right to compel universal observance of the day of rest preferred by one religion is not consistent with the preservation and enhancement of the multicultural heritage of Canadians. To do so is contrary to the expressed provisions of s. 27. . . .

If I am a Jew or a Sabbatarian or a Muslim, the practice of my religion at least implies my right to work on a Sunday if I wish. It seems to me that any law purely religious in purpose, which denies me that right, must surely infringe my religious freedom. . . .

Much of the argument before this Court on the issue of the meaning of freedom of conscience and religion was in terms of "free exercise" and "establishment." These categories derive from the guarantee of freedom of religion in the First Amendment to the Constitution of the United States. The relevant part of the First Amendment reads: "Congress shall make no law respecting an establishment of religion, or prohibiting the free exercise thereof. . .". It is the appellant's argument that unlike the American Bill of Rights, the Canadian Charter of Rights and Freedoms does not include an "establishment clause." He urged therefore that the protection of freedom of conscience and religion extends only to the "free exercise" of religion. . . .

In my view this recourse to categories from the American jurisprudence is not particularly helpful in defining the meaning of freedom of conscience and religion under the Charter. The adoption in the United States of the categories "establishment" and "free exercise" is perhaps an inevitable consequence of the wording of the First Amendment. The cases illustrate, however, that these are not two totally separate and distinct categories, but rather, as the Supreme Court of the United States has frequently recognized, in specific instances "the two clauses may overlap". . . .

Thus while it is true that in its four Sunday closing cases the United States Supreme Court does categorize compulsory religious observance as a potential violation of the "anti-establishment" principle, more frequently and more typically these same words signify the very different principle of the prohibition of preferential treatment of, or state financial support to, particular religions or religious institutions.

In further support for this line of argument the appellant cites s. 29 of the Charter quoted earlier, and s. 93 of the Constitution Act, 1867. These provisions were cited as proof of the non-existence of an anti-establishment principle because they guarantee existing rights to financial support from the state for denominational schools. The respondent replies that these express provisions constitute specific and limited exceptions to the general principle of religious freedom which would otherwise prohibit any support or preference to denominational schools. Subsequent cases will decide the extent to which the Charter allows for state financial support for, or preferential treatment of, particular religions or religious institutions. That is not before us in the present case.

It is not necessary to reopen the issue of the meaning of freedom of religion under the Canadian Bill of Rights, because whatever the situation under that document, it is certain that the Canadian Charter of Rights and Freedoms does not simply "recognize and declare" existing rights as they were circumscribed by legislation current at the time of the Charter's entrenchment. The language of the Charter is imperative. It avoids any reference to existing or continuing rights but rather proclaims in the ringing terms of s. 2 that: "Everyone has the following fundamental freedoms: (a) Freedom of conscience and religion."

I agree with the submission of the respondent that the Charter is intended to set a standard upon which *present as well as future* legislation is to be tested. . . .

This Court has already, in some measure, set out the basic approach to be taken in interpreting the Charter. In *Lawson A.W. Hunter* v. *Southam Inc.* (1984) . . . this Court expressed the view that the proper approach to the definition of the rights and freedoms guaranteed by the Charter was a purposive one. The meaning of a right or freedom guaranteed by the Charter was to be ascertained by an analysis of the *purpose* of such a guarantee; it was to be understood, in other words, in the light of the interests it was meant to protect.

In my view this analysis is to be undertaken, and the purpose of the right or freedom in question is to be sought by reference to the character and the larger objects of the Charter itself, to the language chosen to articulate the specific right or freedom, to the historical origins of the concepts enshrined, and where applicable, to the meaning and purpose of the other specific rights and freedoms with which it is associated within the text of the Charter. The interpretation should be, as the judgment in *Southam* emphasizes, a generous rather than a legalistic one, aimed at fulfilling the purpose of the guarantee and securing for individuals the full benefit of the Charter's protection. At the same time it is important not to overshoot the actual purpose of the right or freedom in question, but to recall that the Charter was not enacted in a vacuum, and must therefore, as this Court's decision in *Law*

Society of Upper Canada v. *Skapinker* (1984), 9 D.L.R. (4th) 161, illustrates, be placed in its proper linguistic, philosophic and historical contexts.

With regard to freedom of conscience and religion, the historical context is clear. As they are relevant to the Charter, the origins of the demand for such freedom are to be found in the religious struggles in post-Reformation Europe. The spread of new beliefs, the changing religious allegiance of kings and princes, the shifting military fortunes of their armies and the consequent repeated redrawing of national and imperial frontiers led to situations in which large numbers of people—sometimes even the majority in a given territory—found themselves living under rules who professed faiths different from, and often hostile to, their own and subject to laws aimed at enforcing conformity to religious beliefs and practices they did not share.

English examples of such laws, passed during the Tudor and Stuart periods have been alluded to in the discussion above of the criminal law character of Sunday observance legislation. Opposition to such laws was confined at first to those who upheld the prohibited faiths and practices, and was designed primarily to avoid the disabilities and penalties to which these specific adherents were subject. As a consequence, when history or geography put power into the hands of these erstwhile victims of religious oppression the persecuted all too often became the persecutors.

Beginning, however, with the Independent faction within the parliamentary party during the Commonwealth or Interregnum, many, even among those who shared the basic beliefs of the ascendent religion, came to voice opposition to the use of the State's coercive power to secure obedience to religious precepts and to extirpate non-conforming beliefs. The basis of this opposition was no longer simply a conviction that the State was enforcing the wrong set of beliefs and practices but rather the perception that belief itself was not amenable to compulsion. Attempts to compel belief or practice denied the reality of individual conscience and dishonoured the God that had planted it in His creatures. It is from these antecedents that the concepts of freedom of religion and freedom of conscience became associated, to form as they do in s. 2(a) of our Charter, the single integrated concept of "freedom of conscience and religion."

What unites enunciated freedoms in the American First Amendment, s. 2(a) of the Charter and in the provisions of other human rights documents in which they are associated is the notion of the centrality of individual conscience and the inappropriateness of governmental intervention to compel or to constrain its manifestation. In *Hunter* v. *Southam, supra,* the purpose of the Charter was identified, at p. 13, as "the unremitting protection of individual rights and liberties." It is easy to see the relationship between respect for individual conscience and the valuation of human dignity that motivates such unremitting protection.

It should also be noted, however, that an emphasis on individual conscience and individual judgment also lies at the heart of our democratic political tradition. The ability of each citizen to make free and informed decisions is the absolute prerequisite for the legitimacy, acceptability, and efficacy of our system of self-government. It is because of the centrality of the rights associated with freedom of individual conscience both to basic beliefs about human worth and dignity and to a free and democratic political system that American jurisprudence has emphasized the primacy or "firstness" of the First Amendment. It is this same centrality that in my view underlies their designation in the Canadian Charter of Rights and Freedoms as "fundamental." They are the *sine qua non* of the political tradition underlying the Charter.

Viewed in this context, the purpose of freedom of conscience and religion becomes clear. The values that underlie our political and philosophic traditions demand that every individual be free to hold and to manifest whatever beliefs and opinions his or her conscience dictates, provided *inter alia* only that such manifestations do not injure his or her neighbours or their parallel rights to hold and manifest beliefs and opinions of their own. Religious belief and practice are historically prototypical and, in many ways, paradigmatic of conscientiously-held beliefs and manifestations and are therefore protected by the Charter. Equally protected, and for the same reasons, are expressions and manifestations of religious non-belief and refusals to participate in religious practice. It may perhaps be that freedom of conscience and religion extends beyond these principles to prohibit other sorts of governmental involvement in matters having to do with religion. For the present case it is sufficient in my opinion to say that whatever else freedom of conscience and religion may mean, it must at the very least mean this: government may not coerce individuals to affirm a specific religious belief or to manifest a specific religious practice for a sectarian purpose. . . .

In my view, the guarantee of freedom of conscience and religion prevents the government from compelling individuals to perform or abstain from performing otherwise harmless acts because of the religious significance of those acts to others. The element of religious compulsion is perhaps somewhat more difficult to perceive (especially for those whose beliefs are being enforced) when, as here, it is non-action rather than action that is being decreed, but in my view compulsion is nevertheless what it amounts to.

I would like to stress that nothing in these reasons should be read as suggesting any opposition to Sunday being spent as a religious day; quite the contrary. It is recognized that for a great number of Canadians, Sunday is the day when their souls rest in God, when the spiritual takes priority over the material, a day which, to them, gives security and meaning because it is linked to Creation and the Creator. It is a day which brings a balanced perspective to life, an opportunity for man to be in

communion with man and with God. In my view, however, as I read the Charter, it mandates that the legislative preservation of a Sunday day of rest should be secular, diversity of belief and non-belief, the diverse socio-cultural backgrounds of Canadians make it constitutionally incompetent for the federal Parliament to provide legislative preference for any one religion at the expense of those of another religious persuasion.

In an earlier time, when people believed in the collective responsibility of the community toward some duty, the enforcement of religious conformity may have been a legitimate object of government, but since the Charter, it has become the right of every Canadian to work out for himself or herself what his or her religious obligations, if any, should be and it is not for the state to dictate otherwise. The state shall not use the criminal sanctions at its disposal to achieve a religious purpose, namely, the uniform observance of the day chosen by the Christian religion as its day of rest.

On the authorities and for the reasons outlined, the true purpose of the Lord's Day Act is to compel the observance of the Christian Sabbath and I find the *Act*, and especially s. 4 thereof, infringes upon the freedom of conscience and religion guaranteed in s. 2(a) of the Charter. . . .

SECTION 1 OF THE CHARTER

. . . The appellant submits that even if the Lord's Day Act does not involve a violation of freedom of conscience and religion as guaranteed by s. 2(a) of the Charter, the provisions of the *Act* constitute a reasonable limit, demonstrably justifiable in a free and democratic society on that right and that therefore the *Act* can be saved pursuant to s. 1 of the Charter. . . .

Two reasons have been advanced to justify the legislation here in issue as a reasonable limit. It can be urged that the choice of the day of rest adhered to by the Christian majority is the most practical. This submission is really no more than an argument of convenience and expedience and is fundamentally repugnant because it would justify the law upon the very basis upon which it is attacked for violating s. 2(a).

The other more plausible argument is that everyone accepts the need and value of a universal day of rest from all work, business and labour and it may as well be the day traditionally observed in our society. I accept the secular justification for a day of rest in a Canadian context and the reasonableness of a day of rest has been clearly enunciated by the courts in the United States of America. The first and fatal difficulty with this argument is, as I have said, that it asserts an objective which has never been found by this Court to be the motivation for the legislation. It seems disingenuous to say that the legislation is valid criminal law and offends s. 2(a) because it compels the observance of a Christian religious duty, yet is still a reasonable limit demonstrably justifiable because it achieves the secular objective the legislators did not primarily intend. The appellant can no more assert under s. 1 a secular objective to validate legislation which in pith and substance involves a religious matter than it could assert a secular objective as the basis for the argument that the legislation does not offend s. 2(a). While there is no authority on this point, it seems clear that Parliament cannot rely upon an *ultra vires* purpose under s. 1 of the Charter. This use of s. 1 would invite colourability, allowing Parliament to do indirectly what it could not do directly. . . .

CLASSIFICATION

The third question put in issue by this Court is this: Is the Lord's Day Act R.S.C. 1970 c. L-13, and especially s. 4 thereof enacted pursuant to the criminal law power under s. 91(27) of the Constitution Act, 1867.

All members of the Alberta Court of Appeal agreed that settled authority compelled the conclusion that the Lord's Day Act was competent to Parliament pursuant to its power to legislate in relation to criminal law under s. 91(27). The

appellant and his supporting interveners submit that the Court of Appeal was correct in their conclusion and the respondent concedes the point. . . .

It should be noted, however, that this conclusion as to the federal Parliament's legislative competence to enact the Lord's Day Act depends on the identification of the purpose of the Act as compelling observance of Sunday by virtue of its religious significance. Were its purpose not religious but rather the secular goal of enforcing a uniform day of rest from labour, the Act would come under s. 92(13), property and civil rights in the province and, hence, fall under provincial rather than federal competence. . . .

WILSON J.: . . . In his reasons for judgment the Chief Justice (Dickson J. at the date of the hearing) has canvassed in a most thorough fashion all the substantive questions entailed in the analysis of constitutionality and has come to the conclusion that the Lord's Day Act is validly enacted pursuant to the federal criminal law power under s. 91(27) of the Constitution Act, 1867. He has concluded, however, that it infringes upon the right to freedom of religion in s. 2(a) of the Charter and that such infringement cannot be justified under s. 1 of the Charter. I agree with those conclusions and the only issue I wish to address in these reasons is the appropriate analytic approach to a Charter case, in a word, the distinction between the analysis demanded by the Charter and the analysis traditionally pursued in resolving division of powers litigation under ss. 91 and 92 of the Constitution Act, 1867.

It is, of course, trite law that the analytic starting point in a division of powers case is the determination of the "pith and substance" of the challenged enactment. In the words of Professor Bora Laskin (as he then was) the Court endeavours to achieve a "distillation of the constitutional value represented by the challenged legislation . . . and its attribution to a head of power. . . .''

The division of powers jurisprudence is

repleat with instances where the analytic focal point in determining whether a given piece of legislation is *ultra vires* the enacting legislature is the purpose or primary function of the legislation. Only when the effects of the legislation so directly impinge on some other subject matter as to reflect some alternative or ulterior purpose do the effects themselves take on analytic significance. . . .

In my view, the constitutional entrenchment of civil liberties in the Canadian Charter of Rights and Freedoms necessarily changes the analytic approach the courts must adopt in such cases. As Chief Justice Burger indicated in the celebrated anti-discrimination case of *Griggs* v. *Duke Power Co.* 401 U.S. 424, 432 (1970), the starting point for any analysis of a civil rights violation is "the *consequences* of the [discriminatory] practices, not simply the motivation." Speaking in the context of equality rights as they pertain to employment, Burger C.J. stated at p. 432:

> . . . *good intent or absence of discriminatory intent does not redeem employment procedures or testing mechanisms that operate as "built-in headwinds" for minority groups.* . . .

While it remains perfectly valid to evaluate the purpose underlying a particular enactment in order to determine whether the legislature has acted within its constitutional authority in division of powers terms, the Charter demands an evaluation of the impingement of even *intra vires* legislation on the fundamental rights and freedoms of the individual. It asks not whether the legislature has acted for a purpose that is within the scope of the authority of that tier of government, but rather whether in so acting it has had the effect of violating an entrenched individual right. It is in other words, first and foremost an effects-oriented document. . . .

Applying such reasoning to the case at bar, one can agree with the Chief Justice that in enacting the Lord's Day Act "[t]he arm of the state requires all to remember the Lord's day of the Christians and to keep it holy," and that "[t]he protection of one religion and the concomitant non-protection of others imports disparate impact destructive of the religious freedom of the collectivity." Accordingly, the Act infringes upon the freedom of conscience and religion guaranteed in s. 2(a) of the Charter. This is not, however, because the statute was enacted for this *purpose* but because it has this *effect*. In my view, so long as a statute has such an actual or potential effect on an entrenched right, it does not matter what the purpose behind the enactment was. . . .

Accordingly, I agree with Chief Justice that the appeal in this case must be dismissed. The Lord's Day Act is in pith and substance legislation with a criminal law purpose and is therefore enacted by Parliament pursuant to the federal criminal law power in s. 91(27) of the Constitution Act, 1867. In so far as the Charter of Rights is concerned, however, I believe that the appropriate analytic starting point is the effect rather than the purpose of the enactment. . . .

43. Operation Dismantle Inc. *v.* the Queen, *1985*

~ Operation Dismantle was a coalition of "peace" and anti-nuclear groups opposed to the government's decision to allow the U.S. to test unarmed cruise missiles over northern and western Canada. Having failed in the political arena, the coalition turned to the courts and challenged the legality of the Cabinet's decision. Their statement of claim alleged that the Cruise Missile testing violated Canadians' rights to life and security of the person protected by section 7 of the Charter. For a remedy, they asked the court to issue an injunction to stop the testing. In effect they were asking the courts to reverse one of the government's more important national defense policy decisions.

The Supreme Court unanimously rejected Operation Dismantle's claim, but not on the substantive, section 7 issues. Rather, from start to finish, *Operation Dismantle* was fought and decided on the threshold issues of jurisdiction and justiciability. The government had argued that the ancient convention of "Crown prerogative" prohibited judicial review of Cabinet decisions. ("Crown prerogative" is the traditional source of the government's authority to make decisions with respect to national security and foreign policy matters.) The Court rejected this claim, stating that section 32 of the Charter applied to all government actions, whether pursuant to legislation or royal prerogative. This aspect of the case—that there is no automatic shield against Charter challenges to foreign policy/national security decisions—makes *Operation Dismantle* an important precedent.

The government also advanced a second argument against the courts' even hearing the case: that it presented a "non-justiciable" issue and a "political question." In this instance, non-justiciability denotes the lack of "judicially managable standards" by which to decide the case. The "political questions" doctrine comes from U.S. jurisprudence, and discourages courts from hearing constitutional challenges to foreign policy or defense issues. It is based on an ill-defined combination of considerations of justiciability and the "separation of powers" doctrine. The latter holds that for the court to hear certain cases would be judicial encroachment on responsibilities constitutionally vested with Congress or the President.

The majority opinion written by Chief Justice Dickson sidestepped these arguments. He argued that there is no reasonable cause of action because it is impossible to prove "the facts" on which the claim rests—the increased risk of nuclear war resulting from Cruise testing. The "facts" in this case are merely speculations about what might happen in the future and could never be proven. The statement of claim, concluded the Chief Justice, must be struck out, and the case dismissed.

In a concurring opinion that initiated her reputation as the most activist judge on the Court, Justice Wilson met the justiciability/"political questions" arguments head on. She pointedly rejected both. The main issue, declared Justice Wilson, is "whether the courts *should* or *must* rather than . . . whether they *can* deal with such matters." "The question before us," she continued, "is not whether the government's defense policy is sound but whether or not it violates the appellants' rights under s. 7 of the Charter. This is a totally different question.''

This reasoning has been subject to question. Patrick Monahan has suggested that Justice Wilson's ''statement is only meaningful if the issue of legality can be determined without recourse to questions of 'wisdom.' Madam Justice Wilson's confident assertion that the issues are 'totally different' seems based on the fact that the Court is being called on to interpret and to apply a specific 'legal' standard, in this case s. 7. But the mere fact that statutory language is involved does not, in itself, provide a distinction between legal and political questions. The issue is whether it is possible to apply the statutory language without an inquiry into the 'wisdom' of the legislation under review.''[1] Monahan (and others) believe that *Operation Dismantle* presents a good example of an instance when it is not.

While Justice Wilson did not find Operation Dismantle's claim non-justiciable for evidentiary reasons (like the majority), she went on to rule that it was non-justiciable on legal grounds; that is, that it had no basis in law. Justice Wilson based this conclusion on her finding that section 7 was intended to protect the rights of individual citizens. It did not extend to government action or inaction that may threaten the security or lives of citizens in general. Justice Wilson's narrowing of the scope of section 7 suggests an element of judicial self-restraint.[2] This stands in ironic contrast to her very activist handling of the evidentiary issues.

Operation Dismantle also illustrates one of the most significant impacts of the Charter—the creation of a new forum for interest group activity. Historically Canadian interest groups have concentrated their lobbying activities at the cabinet and senior levels of the bureaucracy. Unlike their American counterparts, they avoided using litigation as a political tactic. The Charter is changing this, and *Operation Dismantle* is an example of this change. While the litigation ultimately failed to stop the Cruise Missile testing, it did achieve considerable publicity for the ''peace movement.'' Each of three judicial rulings (trial, appeal, second appeal) was reported on the front page of newspapers across Canada. Also, their principal argument was never actually rejected on its merits by any court. Such publicity and the legitimacy that it can confer was probably the realistic objective of Operation Dismantle all along. In this sense it may have been a victory of sorts. ~

---

[1] Patrick Monahan, *Politics and the Constitution: The Charter, Federalism, and the Supreme Court of Canada*, pp. 52-53.

[2] See Introduction, pp. 20-21.

OPERATION DISMANTLE, INC. *v.* THE QUEEN
In the Supreme Court of Canada. [1985] 1 S.C.R. 441.

The judgment of Dickson C.J.C., Estey, McIntyre, Chouinard, and Lamer, JJ. was delivered by

DICKSON C.J.C.: This case arises out of the appellants' challenge under s. 7 of the Canadian Charter of Rights and Freedoms to the decision of the Federal Cabinet to permit the testing of the cruise missile by the United State of America in Canadian territory. The issue that must be addressed is whether the appellants' Statement of Claim should be struck out, before the trial, as disclosing no reasonable cause of action. In their Statement of Claim, the appellants seek: (i) a declaration that the decision to permit the testing of the cruise missile is unconstitutional; (ii) injunctive relief to prohibit the testing; and (iii) damages. Cattanach J. of the Federal Court, Trial Division, refused the respondents' motion to strike. The Federal Court of Appeal unanimously allowed the respondents' appeal, struck out the Statement of Claim and dismissed the appellants' action.

The facts and procedural history of this case are fully set out and discussed in the reasons for judgment of Madame Justice Wilson. I agree with Madame Justice Wilson that the appellants' Statement of Claim should be struck out and this appeal dismissed. I have reached this conclusion, however, on the basis of reasons which differ somewhat from those of Madame Justice Wilson.

In my opinion, if the appellants are to be entitled to proceed to trial, their Statement of Claim must disclose facts, which, if taken as true, would show that the action of the Canadian Government could cause an infringement of their rights under s. 7 of the Charter. I have concluded that the causal link between the actions of the Canadian Government, and the alleged violation of appellants' rights under the Charter is simply too uncertain, speculative and hypothetical to sustain a cause of action. Thus, although decisions of the Federal Cabinet are reviewable by the courts under the Charter and the government bears a general duty to act in accordance with the Charter's dictates, no duty is imposed on the Canadian Government by s. 7 of the Charter to refrain from permitting the testing of the cruise missile.

I

The relevant portion of the appellants' Statement of Claim is found in paragraph 7 thereof. The deprivation of s. 7 Charter rights alleged by the appellants and the facts they advance to support this deprivation are described as follows:

The plaintiffs state and the fact is that the testing of the cruise missile in Canada is a violation of the collective rights of the plaintiffs and their members and all Canadians, specifically their right to security of the person and life in that:

(a) *the size and eventual dispersion of the air-launched cruise missile is such that the missile cannot be detected by surveillance satellites, thus making verification of the extent of this nuclear weapons system impossible;*

(b) *with the impossibility of verification, the future of nuclear weapons' control and limitations agreements is completely undermined as any such agreements become practically unenforceable;*

(c) *the testing of the air-launched cruise missiles would result in an increased American military presence and interest in Canada which would result in making Canada more likely to be the target of a nuclear attack;*

(d) *as the cruise missile cannot be detected until approximately eight minutes before it reaches its target, a "Launch on Warning" system would be necessary in order to*

*respond to the cruise missile
thereby eliminating the effective
human discretion and increasing
the likelihood of either a pre-emptive strike or an accidental firing,
or both;*

*(e) the cruise missile is a military
weapon, the development of which
will have the effect of a needless
and dangerous escalation of the
nuclear arms race, thus endanger-
ing the security and lives of all
people. . . .*

Before turning to an examination of the
appellants' allegations concerning the
results of the decision to permit testing
and its consequences on their rights under
s. 7, I think it would be useful to examine
the principles governing the striking out
of a Statement of Claim and dismissal of a
cause of action.

The respondents, by a motion pursuant
to Rule 419(1)(a) of the Rules of the
Federal Court, moved for an order to
strike out the appellants' Statement of
Claim as disclosing no reasonable cause
of action. Rule 419(1)(a) reads as follows:

*Rule 419(1) The Court may at any stage
of an action order any pleading to be
struck out, with or without leave to
amend, on the ground that*

*(a) it discloses no reasonable cause of
action or defence, as the case may
be . . .*

I agree with Madame Justice Wilson
that, regardless of the basis upon which
the appellants advance their claim for
declaratory relief—whether it be s. 24(1)
of the Charter, s. 52 of the Constitution
Act, 1982, or the common law—they
must at least be able to establish a threat of
violation, if not an actual violation, of
their rights under the Charter.

In short then, for the appellants to succeed on this appeal, they must show that
they have some chance of proving that the
action of the Canadian Government has
caused a violation or a threat of violation
of their rights under the Charter.

The principal allegation of the State-

ment of Claim is that the testing of the
cruise missile in Canada poses a threat to
the lives and security of Canadians by
increasing the risk of nuclear conflict, and
thus violates the right to life, liberty and
security of the person guaranteed by s. 7
of the Charter. . . . Thus, to succeed at
trial, the appellants would have to demonstrate, *inter alia*, that the testing of the
cruise missile would cause an increase in
the risk of nuclear war. It is precisely this
link between the Cabinet decision to permit the testing of the cruise and the
increased risk of nuclear war which, in
my opinion, they cannot establish. It will
not be necessary therefore to address the
issue of whether the deprivations of life
and security of the person advanced by the
appellants could constitute violations of
s. 7. . . .

The Statement of Claim speaks of
weapons control agreements being "practically unenforceable," Canada being
"more likely to be the target of a nuclear
attack," "increasing the likelihood of
either a pre-emptive strike or an accidental firing, or both," and "escalation of the
nuclear arms race." All of these eventualities, culminating in the increased risk
of nuclear war, are alleged to flow from
the Canadian Government's single act of
allowing the United States to test the
cruise missile in Canada.

Since the foreign policy decisions of
independent and sovereign nations are not
capable of prediction, on the basis of
evidence, to any degree of certainty
approaching probability, the nature of
such reactions can only be a matter of
speculation; the causal link between the
decision of the Canadian Government to
permit the testing of the cruise and the
results that the appellant alleges could
never be proven.

An analysis of the specific allegations
of the Statement of Claim reveals that
they are all contingent upon the possible
reactions of the nuclear powers to the
testing of the cruise missile in Canada.
The gist of paragraphs (a) and (b) of the
Statement of Claim is that verification of
the cruise missile system is impossible

because the missile cannot be detected by surveillance satellites, and that, therefore, arms control agreements will be unenforceable. This is based on two major assumptions as to how foreign powers will react to the development of the cruise missile: first, that they will not develop new types of surveillance satellites or new methods of verification, and second, that foreign powers will not establish new modes of cooperation for dealing with the problem of enforcement. With respect to the latter of these points, it is just as plausible that lack of verification would have the effect of enhancing enforceability than of undermining it, since an inability on the part of nuclear powers to verify systems like the cruise could precipitate a system of enforcement based on cooperation rather than surveillance.

As for paragraph (c), even if it were the case that the testing of the air-launched cruise missile would result in an increased American military presence and interest in Canada, to say that this would make Canada more likely to be the target of a nuclear attack is to assume certain reactions of hostile foreign powers to such an increased American presence. . . .

Paragraph (d) assumes that foreign states will not develop their technology in such a way as to meet the requirements of effective detection of the cruise and that there will therefore be an increased likelihood of pre-emptive strike or an accidental firing, or both. Again, this assumption concerns how foreign powers are likely to act in response to the development of the cruise. It would be just as plausible to argue that foreign states would improve their technology with respect to detection of missiles, thereby decreasing the likelihood of accidental firing or pre-emptive strike.

Finally, paragraph (e) asserts that the development of the cruise will lead to an escalation of the nuclear arms race. This again involves speculation based on assumptions as to how foreign powers will react. One could equally argue that the cruise would be the precipitating factor in compelling the nuclear powers to negotiate agreements that would lead to a de-escalation of the nuclear arms race. . . .

What can be concluded from this analysis of the Statement of Claim is that all of its allegations, including the ultimate assertion of an increased likelihood of nuclear war, are premised on assumptions and hypotheses about how independent and sovereign nations operating in an international arena of radical uncertainty, and continually changing circumstances, will react to the Canadian Government's decision to permit the testing of the cruise missile.

The point of this review is not to quarrel with the allegations made by the appellants about the results of cruise missile testing. They are, of course, entitled to their opinion and belief. Rather, I wish to highlight that they are raising matters that, in my opinion, lie in the realm of conjecture, rather than fact. In brief, it is simply not possible for a court, even with best available evidence, to do more than speculate upon the likelihood of the Federal Cabinet's decision to test the cruise missile resulting in an increased threat of nuclear war.

II

I agree with Madame Justice Wilson that Cabinet decisions fall under s. 32(1)(a) of the Charter and are therefore reviewable in the courts and subject to judicial scrutiny for compatability with the Constitution. I have no doubt that the executive branch of the Canadian Government is duty bound to act in accordance with the dictates of the Charter. Specifically, the Cabinet has a duty to act in a manner consistent with the right to life, liberty and security of the person and the right not to be deprived thereof except in accordance with the principles of fundamental justice.

I do not believe the action impugned in the present case can be characterized as contrary to the duties of the executive under the Charter. Section 7 of the Charter cannot reasonably be read as imposing a duty on the government to refrain from those acts which *might* lead to consequences that deprive or threaten to deprive individuals of their life and security of the person. A duty of the Federal Cabinet cannot arise on the basis of speculation and hypothesis about possible effects of government action. Such a duty only arises in my view, where it can be said that a deprivation of life and security of the person could be proven to result from the impugned government act.

III

The approach which I have taken is not based on the concept of justiciability. I agree in substance with Madame Justice Wilson's discussion of justiciability and her conclusion that the doctrine is founded upon a concern with the appropriate role of the courts as the forum for the resolution of different types of disputes. I have no doubt that disputes of a political or foreign policy nature may be properly cognizable by the courts. My concerns in the present case focus on the impossibility of the Court finding, on the basis of evidence, the connection, alleged by the appellants, between the duty of the government to act in accordance with the Charter of Rights and Freedoms and the violation of their rights under s. 7. As stated above, I do not believe the alleged violation—namely, the increased threat of nuclear war—could ever be sufficiently linked as a factual matter to the acknowledged duty of the government to respect s. 7 of the Charter.

IV

I would like to note that nothing in these reasons should be taken as the adoption of the view that the reference to "laws" in s. 52 of the Charter is confined to statutes, regulations and the common law. It may well be that if the supremacy of the Constitution expressed in s. 52 is to be meaningful, then all acts taken pursuant to powers granted by law will fall within s. 52. . . .

I would accordingly dismiss the appeal with costs.

WILSON J.:

IS THE GOVERNMENT'S DECISION REVIEWABLE?

The royal prerogative. The respondents submit that at common law the authority to make international agreements (such as the one made with the United States to permit the testing) is a matter which falls within the prerogative power of the Crown and that both at common law and by s. 15 of the Constitution Act, 1867 the same is true of decisions relating to national defence. They further submit that since by s. 32(1)(a) the Charter applies "to the Parliament and government of Canada in respect of all matters within the authority of Parliament," the Charter's application must, so far as the government is concerned, be restricted to the exercise of powers which derive directly from statute. It cannot, therefore, apply to an exercise of the royal prerogative which is a source of power existing independently of Parliament; . . . Since there is no reason in principle to distinguish between Cabinet decisions made pursuant to statutory authority and those made in the exercise of the royal prerogative, and since the former clearly fall within the ambit of the Charter, I conclude that the latter do so also.

Non-justiciability. Le Dain and Ryan JJ. in the Federal Court of Appeal were of the opinion that the issues involved in this case are inherently non-justiciable, either because the question whether testing the cruise missile increases the risk of nuclear war is not susceptible of proof and hence is not triable (per Ryan J.) or because answering that question involves factors which are either inaccessible to a court or are of a nature which a court is incapable of evaluating (*per* Le Dain J.). To the extent that this objection to the appellants' case rests on the inherent evidentiary difficulties which would obviously confront any attempt to prove the appellants' allegations of fact, I do not think it can be sustained. It might well be that, if the issues were allowed to go to trial, the appellants would lose simply by reason of their not having been able to establish the factual basis of their claim but that does not seem to me to be a reason for striking the case out at this preliminary stage. It is trite law that on a motion to strike out a Statement of Claim the plaintiff's allegations of fact are to be taken as having been proved. Accordingly, it is arguable that by dealing with the case as they have done Le Dain and Ryan JJ. have, in effect, made a presumption against the appellants which they are not entitled, on a preliminary motion of this kind, to make.

I am not convinced, however, that Le Dain and Ryan JJ. were restricting the concept of non-justiciability to difficulties of evidence and proof. Both rely on Lord Radcliffe's judgment in *Chandler* v. *Director of Public Prosecutions* [1962] 3 All E.R. 142 (H.L.), and especially on the following passage at p. 151:

The disposition and equipment of the forces and the facilities afforded to allied forces for defence purposes constitute a given fact and it cannot be a matter of proof or finding that the decisions of policy on which they rest are or are not in the country's best interests. I may add that I can think of few issues which represent themselves in less triable form. It would be ingenuous to suppose that the kind of evidence that the appellants wanted to call could make more than a small contribution to its final solution. The facts which they wished to establish might well be admitted: even so, throughout history men have had to run great risk for themselves and others in the hope of attaining objectives which they prize for all. The more one looks at it, the plainer it becomes, I think, that the question whether it is in the true interests of this country to acquire, retain or house nuclear armaments depends on an infinity of considerations, military and diplomatic, technical, psychological and moral, and of decisions, tentative or final, which are themselves part assessments of fact and part expectations and hopes.I do not think that there is anything amiss with a legal ruling that does not make this issue a matter for judge or jury. (Emphasis added)

In my opinion, this passage makes clear that in Lord Radcliffe's view these kinds of issues are to be treated as non-justiciable not simply because of evidentiary difficulties but because they involve moral and political considerations which it is not within the province of the courts to assess. . . .

I cannot accept the proposition that difficulties of evidence or proof absolve the Court from making a certain kind of decision if it can be established on other grounds that it has a duty to do so. I think we should focus our attention on whether the courts *should* or *must* rather than on whether they *can* deal with such matters. We should put difficulties of evidence and proof aside and consider whether as a constitutional matter it is appropriate or obligatory for the courts to decide the issue before us. I will return to this question later.

The Political Question Doctrine. It is a well established principle of American constitutional law that there are certain kinds of "political questions" that a court ought to refuse to decide. In *Baker* v. *Carr* 369 U.S. 186 (1962) at pp. 210-11 Brennan J. discussed the nature of the doctrine in the following terms:

We have said that 'In determining whether a question falls within [the political question] category, the appropriateness under our system of government of attributing finality to the action of the political departments and also the lack of satisfactory criteria for a judicial determination are dominant considerations.' Coleman v. Miller, 307 U.S. 433, 454-455. The non-justiciability of a political question is primarily a function of the separation of powers. Much confusion results from the capacity of the 'political question' label to obscure the need for case-by-case inquiry. Deciding whether a matter has in any measure been committed by the Constitution to another branch of government, or whether the action of that branch exceeds whatever authority has been committed, is itself a delicate exercise in constitutional interpretation, and is a responsibility of this

Court as ultimate interpreter of a Constitution.

At p. 217 he said:

It is apparent that several formulations which vary slightly according to the settings in which the questions arise may describe a political question, although each has one or more elements which identify it as essentially a function of the separation of powers. Prominent on the surface of any case held to involve a political question is found a textually demonstrable constitutional commitment of the issue to a coordinate political department; or a lack of judicially discoverable and manageable standards for resolving it; or the impossibility of deciding without an initial policy determination of a kind clearly for nonjudicial discretion; or the impossibility of a court's undertaking independent resolution without expressing lack of the respect due coordinate branches of government; or an unusual need for unquestioning adherence to a political decision already made; or the potentiality of embarrassment from multifarious pronouncements by various departments on one question.

While one or two of the categories of political question referred to by Brennan J. raise the issue of judicial or institutional competence already referred to, the underlying theme is the separation of powers in the sense of the proper role of the courts vis-a-vis the other branches of government. In this regard it is perhaps noteworthy that a distinction is drawn in the American case law between matters internal to the United States on the one hand and foreign affairs on the other. In the area of foreign affairs the courts are especially deferential to the executive branch of government. . . .

While Brennan J.'s statement, in my view, accurately sums up the reasoning American courts have used in deciding that specific cases did not present questions which were judicially cognizable, I do not think it is particularly helpful in determining when American courts will

find that those factors come into play. In cases from *Marbury* v. *Madison*, 5 U.S. (1 Cranch) 137 (1803) to *United States* v. *Nixon*, 418 U.S. 683 (1974) the Court has not allowed the "respect due coordinate branches of government" to prevent it from rendering decisions highly embarrassing to those holding executive or legislative office. . . . More recently, commentators such as Tigar ("Judicial Power, the 'Political Question Doctrine' and Foreign Relations," 17 *U.C.L.A. L.R.* 1135 (1970)) and Henkin ("Is there a 'Political Question' Doctrine?", 85 *Yale L.J.* 597 (1976)) have doubted the need for a political questions doctrine at all, arguing that all the cases which were correctly decided can be accounted for in terms of orthodox separation of powers doctrine.

Professor Tigar in his article suggests that the political questions doctrine is not really a doctrine at all but simply "a group of quite different legal rules and principles, each resting in part upon deference to the political branches of government" (p. 1163). He sees Justice Brennan's formulation of the doctrine in *Baker* v. *Carr* (*supra*) as an "unsatisfactionary effort to rationalize a collection of disparate precedent" (p. 1163).

In the House of Lords in *Chandler* (*supra*), Lord Devlin expressed a similar reluctance to retreat from traditional techniques in the interpretation of the phrase "purpose prejudicial to the safety or interest of the State . . ." in the Official Secrets Act, 1911. . . .

It seems to me that the point being made by Lord Devlin, as well as by Tigar and Henkin in their writings, is that the courts should not be too eager to relinquish their judicial review function simply because they are called upon to exercise it in relation to weighty matters of state. Equally, however, it is important to realize that judicial review is not the same thing as substitution of the court's opinion on the merits for the opinion of the person or the body to whom discretionary decision-making power has been committed. . . . The question before us is not whether the government's defence policy is sound but whether or not it violates the appellants' rights under s. 7 of the Charter of Rights and Freedoms. This is a totally different question. I do not think there can be any doubt that this is a question for the courts. Indeed, s. 24(1) of the Charter, also part of the Constitution, makes it clear that the adjudication of that question is the responsibility of "a court of competent jurisdiction." While the court is entitled to grant such remedy as it "considers appropriate and just in the circumstances," I do not think it is open to it to relinquish its jurisdiction either on the basis that the issue is inherently nonjusticiable or that it raises a so-called "political question": see Martin H. Redish, "Abstention, Separation of Powers, and the Limits of the Judicial Function" 94 *Yale L.J.* 71 (1984).

I would conclude, therefore, that if we are to look at the Constitution for the answer to the question whether it is appropriate for the courts to "second guess" the executive on matters of defence, we would conclude that it is not appropriate. However, if what we are being asked to do is to decide whether any particular act of the executive violates the rights of the citizens, then it is not only appropriate that we answer the question; it is our obligation under the Charter to do so.

One or two hypothetical situations will, I believe, illustrate the point. Let us take the case of a person who is being conscripted for service during wartime and has been ordered into battle overseas, all of this pursuant to appropriate legislative and executive authorization. He wishes to challenge his being conscripted and sent overseas as an infringement of his rights under s. 7. It is apparent that his liberty has been constrained and if he is sent into battle, his security of the person and, indeed, his life are put in jeopardy. It seems to me that it would afford the conscriptee a somewhat illusory protection if the validity of his challenge is to be determined by the executive. On the other hand, it does not follow from these facts that the individual's rights under the Char-

ter have been violated. Even if an individual's rights to life and liberty under s. 7 are interpreted at their broadest, it is clear from s. 1 that they are subject to "such reasonable limits prescribed by law as can be demonstrably justified in a free and democratic society." If the Court were of the opinion that conscription during wartime was a "reasonable limit" within the meaning of s. 1, the conscriptee's challenge on the facts as presented would necessarily fail.

By way of contrast, one can envisage a situation in which the government decided to force a particular group to participate in experimental testing of a deadly nerve gas. Although the government might argue that such experiments were an important part of our defence effort, I find it hard to believe that they would survive judicial review under the Charter. . . .

IN WHAT CIRCUMSTANCES MAY A STATEMENT OF CLAIM SEEKING DECLARATORY RELIEF BE STRUCK OUT?

. . . In my view, several of the allegations contained in the Statement of Claim are statements of intangible fact. Some of them invite inferences; others anticipate probable consequences. They may be susceptible to proof by inference from real facts or by expert testimony or "through the application of common sense principles": see *Leyland Shipping Co.* v. *Norwich Union Fire Insurance Society* [1918] A.C. 350 at p. 363 per Lord Dunedin. We may entertain serious doubts that the plaintiff's will be able to prove them by any of these means. It is not, however, the function of the Court at this stage to prejudice that question. I agree with Cattanach J. that the Statement of Claim contains sufficient allegations to raise a justiciable issue. . . .

The law then would appear to be clear. The facts pleaded are to be taken as proved. When so taken, the question is do they disclose a reasonable cause of action, i.e. a cause of action "with some chance of success". . . .

COULD THE FACTS AS ALLEGED CONSTITUTE A VIOLATION OF S. 7 OF THE CHARTER?

Whether or not the facts that are alleged in the appellants' Statement of Claim could constitute a violation of s. 7 is, of course, the question that lies at the heart of this case. If they could not, then the appellants' Statement of Claim discloses no reasonable cause of action and the appeal must be dismissed. The appellants submit that on its proper construction s. 7 gives rise to two separate and presumably independent rights, namely the right to life, liberty and security of the person, and the right not to be deprived of such life, liberty and security of the person except in accordance with the principles of fundamental justice. In their submission, therefore, a violation of the principles of fundamental justice would only have to be alleged in relation to a claim based on a violation of the second right. . . .

The appellants' submission, however, touches upon a number of important issues regarding the proper interpretation of s. 7. Even if the section gives rise to a single unequivocal right not to be deprived of life, liberty or security of the person except in accordance with the principles of fundamental justice, there nonetheless remains the question whether fundamental justice is entirely procedural in nature or whether it has a substantive aspect as well. This, in turn, leads to the related question whether there might not be certain deprivations of life, liberty or personal security which could not be justified no matter what procedure was employed to effect them. These are among the most important and difficult questions of interpretation arising under the Charter, but I do not think it is necessary to deal with them in this case. It can, in my opinion, be disposed of without reaching these issues.

In my view, even an independent, substantive right to life, liberty and security of the person cannot be absolute. For example, the right to liberty, which I take to be the right to pursue one's goals free of

governmental constraint, must accommodate the corresponding rights of others. The concept of "right" as used in the Charter postulates the inter-relation of individuals in society all of whom have the same right. The aphorism that "A hermit has no need of rights" makes the point. . . .

The concept of "right" as used in the Charter must also, I believe, recognize and take account of the political reality of the modern state. Action by the state or, conversely, inaction by the state will frequently have the effect of decreasing or increasing the risk to the lives or security of its citizens. It may be argued, for example, that the failure of government to limit significantly the speed of traffic on the highways threatens our right to life and security in that it increases the risk of highway accidents. Such conduct, however, would not, in my view, fall within the scope of the right protected by s. 7 of the Charter.

In the same way, the concept of "right" as used in the Charter must take account of the fact that the self-contained political community which comprises the state is faced with at least the possibility, if not the reality, of external threats to both its collective well-being and to the individual well-being of its citizens. In order to protect the community against such threats it may well be necessary for the state to take steps which incidentally increase the risk to the lives or personal security of some or all of the state's citizens. Such steps, it seems to me, cannot have been contemplated by the draftsman of the Charter as giving rise to violations of s. 7. As John Rawls states in *A Theory of Justice* (1971) at p. 213:

> *The government's right to maintain public order and security is . . . a right which the government must have if it is to carry out its duty of impartially supporting the conditions necessary for everyone's pursuit of his interests and living up to his obligations as he understands them.*

The rights under the Charter not being absolute, their content or scope must be discerned quite apart from any limitation sought to be imposed upon them by the government under s. 1. . . .

It is not necessary to accept the restrictive interpretation advanced by Pratte J., which would limit s. 7 to protection against arbitrary arrest or detention, in order to agree that the central concern of the section is direct impingement by government upon the life, liberty and personal security of individual citizens. At the very least, it seems to me, there must be a strong presumption that governmental action which concerns the relations of the state with other states, and which is therefore not directed at any member of the immediate political community, was never intended to be caught by s. 7 even though such action may have the incidental effect of increasing the risk of death or injury that individuals generally have to face.

I agree with Le Dain J. that the essence of the appellants' case is the claim that permitting the cruise missile to be tested in Canada will increase the risk of nuclear war. But even accepting this allegation of fact as true, which as I have already said I think we must do on a motion to strike, it is my opinion for the reasons given above that this state of affairs could not constitute a breach of s. 7. Moreover, I do not see how one can distinguish in a principled way between this particular risk and any other danger to which the government's action vis-a-vis other states might incidentally subject its citizens. A declaration of war, for example, almost certainly increases the risk to most citizens of death or injury. Acceptance of the appellants' submissions, it seems to me, would mean that any such declaration would also have to be regarded as a violation of s. 7. I cannot think that that could be a proper interpretation of the Charter.

This is not to say that every governmental action that is purportedly taken in furtherance of national defence would be beyond the reach of s. 7. If, for example, testing the cruise missile posed a direct threat to some specific segment of the populace—as, for example, if it were

being tested with live warheads—I think that might well raise different considerations. A court might find that that constituted a violation of s. 7 and it might then be up to the government to try to establish that testing the cruise with live warheads was justified under s. 1 of the Charter. Section 1, in my opinion, is the uniquely Canadian mechanism through which the courts are to determine the justiciability of particular issues that come before it. It embodies through its reference to a free and democratic society the essential features of our constitution including the separation of powers, responsible government and the rule of law. It obviates the need for a "political questions" doctrine and permits the court to deal with what might be termed "prudential" considerations in a principled way without renouncing its constitutional and mandated responsibility for judicial review. It is not, however, called into operation here since the facts alleged in the Statement of Claim, even if they could be shown to be true, could not in my opinion constitute a violation of s. 7. . . .

In summary, it seems to me that the issues raised on the appeal are to be disposed of as follows: 1) The government's decision to permit testing of the cruise missile in Canada cannot escape judicial review on any of the grounds advanced; 2) The Statement of Claim may be struck out if the facts as alleged do not disclose a reasonable cause of action. . . . 3) Taking the facts alleged as proven, they could not constitute a violation of s. 7 of the *Charter* so as to give rise to a cause of action under s. 24(1); 4) The appellants could not establish their status to sue at common law for declaratory relief for the same reason that they could not establish a cause of action under s. 24(1); and 5) The appellants could not establish a cause of action for declaratory relief under s. 52(1) since the facts as alleged could not constitute a violation of s. 7 and therefore no inconsistency with the provisions of the Constitution could be established.

I would accordingly dismiss the appeal with costs.

44. The Queen *v.* Therens, *1985*

~ *Therens* is the first Supreme Court decision dealing with section 24, the remedy section of the Charter. Experience with the Canadian Bill of Rights demonstrated the truth of the old adage that "there is no right without a remedy". Section 24(1) permits anyone whose rights or freedoms, as guaranteed in the Charter, have been infringed to "apply to a court of competent jurisdiction to obtain such remedy as the court considers appropriate and just in the circumstances." Remedies available under 24(1) cover all the traditional judicial remedies ranging from monetary compensation to declaring a law unconstitutional. Section 24(2) adds a special remedy which, as the *Hogan* case shows so clearly, was not part of the Canadian judicial tradition.[1] This remedy is aimed at police violations of the Charter and directs judges to exclude evidence if (1) it was obtained in a manner that infringed any rights or freedoms guaranteed by the Charter, and (2) "having regard to all the circumstances, the admission of it in the proceedings would bring the administration of justice into disrepute."

This provision of the Charter was designed as a compromise between traditional Anglo-Canadian common law under which judges admitted evidence if it was relevant regardless of how the police had obtained it and American law which excluded evidence because of very minor infractions of constitutional rights by the police. The new Canadian exclusionary rule gives judges the responsibility of weighing the danger of having police misconduct result in the acquittal of persons guilty of serious crimes against the danger to the administration of justice in having courts condone police lawlessness.[2] In *Therens*, the Court established that this balanced rule is to be the only basis for excluding evidence obtained through unconstitutional means and that an easier test for excluding evidence would not be available through section 24(1), the general remedies clause.

The first issue to be decided in *Therens* was whether the police had violated a motorist's rights under the Charter when they administered a breathalyzer test at the police station without first informing him of his right to consult a lawyer. Section 10(b) establishes a right—new to Canadian law—not only to retain and instruct counsel without delay but to be informed of that right. This right comes into play "on arrest or detention". Was Therens "detained" when he complied with the police request that he accompany them to the police station and submit to a breathalyzer test? In giving an affirmative answer to this question, Justice LeDain's opinion (and all the other justices agree with him on this point) repudiates the narrow view of detention the Court had taken in interpreting the Canadian Bill of Rights. The constitutional protection of section 10 applies not only when a person is physically confined but also when subjected

---

[1] See case 39 above.
[2] For a discussion, see *Freedom and Security Under the Law*. Part 10 (Report of the Commission of Inquiry on Certain Activities of the R.C.M.P., Ottawa, 1981).

to psychological pressure to comply with police requests.

Because the section of the Criminal Code authorizing the police to take motorists suspected of impaired driving to the police station for a breathalyzer test did not expressly or by necessary implication compel the police to deny a detained person's section 10(b) rights, the Court held that section 1, the Charter's reasonable limits clause, did not apply. The executive branch of government could invoke section 1 only when its actions are "prescribed by law". But the law may prescribe explicitly or implicitly. This point is crucial in understanding the Court's subsequent decision in *Thomsen*[3] permitting the police to administer road-side breathalyzer tests without advising motorists of their right to counsel. In the Court's view, an operational necessity of the road-side tests was that they be administered "forthwith" without the delay which would result if motorists were allowed to contact a lawyer. So the section of the Criminal Code authorizing road-side screening mechanisms, in contrast to the section providing for breathalyzer tests at the police station, was held to prescribe implicitly that a motorist's right to counsel be limited and this limit was held to be justifiable because the Court regarded it as essential to the effective deterrence of drunk driving. In *Hufsky*[4], a companion case of *Thomsen*, the Court further indicated its support for the collective interest in safe conditions on the roads. It upheld Ontario legislation authorizing random road-side inspections which might, among other things, result in the administration of a breathalyzer test. This encroachment on the right under section 9 of the Charter "not to be arbitrarily detained or imprisoned" was also justified as a necessary element in the legislative campaign against drunk driving.[5]

The other issue in *Therens* was whether the breathalyzer evidence obtained in violation of a Charter right should be excluded. This issue produced the first dissent in a Supreme Court decision on the Charter. For Justice LeDain a critical factor was that the police, on the basis of the law as it stood at the time, were entitled to assume that they were not detaining Therens. Thus, in LeDain's view, they had not willfully denied Therens his constitutional rights. Under this circumstance he thought admitting the evidence would not bring the administration of justice into disrepute. Only Justice McIntyre agreed with him. Indeed, in McIntyre's view, excluding the evidence would bring the administration of justice into disrepute. The six other justices, however, took the opposite view and supported Justice Estey's assertion that the violation of the Charter right was so flagrant the evidence must be excluded.

The application of section 24(2) frequently arises in the trial courts as it has given defence lawyers an opportunity they did not have in the past to call upon

---

[3] *The Queen* v. *Thomsen* [1988] 1 S.C.R. 640.

[4] *The Queen* v. *Hufsky* [1988] 1 S.C.R. 621.

[5] Justice LeDain wrote the opinions in *Thomsen* and in *Hufsky* for a unanimous seven-judge panel which included Chief Justice Dickson and Justice Wilson.

the judiciary to review police investigatory techniques. In the cases which have reached the Supreme Court there is further evidence of the Court's moderate activism. In *Clarkson*[6], the Court decided that a murder confession must be excluded when it was given after the accused in an intoxicated state had waived her right to counsel. But in *Tremblay*,[7] although the Court found that the right to counsel had been infringed when the police administered a breathalyzer test before Tremblay's lawyer arrived at the police station, nevertheless it held that the resulting evidence should not be excluded because "(f)rom the moment the accused was intercepted on the road to the moment he was asked to give his first sample of breath his behaviour was violent, vulgar and obnoxious." While the Supreme Court's treatment of Canada's new exclusionary rule may not be easy to predict, it can also be said that it has not yet become politically controversial. ~

THE QUEEN *v.* PAUL MATHEW THERENS
In the Supreme Court of Canada. [1985] 1 S.C.R. 613.

LE DAIN J. (dissenting): The appeal is by leave of this Court from the judgment of the Saskatchewan Court of Appeal on April 15, 1983 (now reported at (1983), 5 C.C.C. (3d) 409) dismissing an appeal by way of stated case from a judgment of Judge Alastair J. Muir of the Provincial Court of Saskatchewan on July 30, 1982, which dismissed a charge that the respondent "on or about the 25th day of April A.D. 1982 at the City of Moose Jaw, in the Province of Saskatchewan, did unlawfully drive a motor vehicle while having consumed alcohol in such quantity that the proportion thereof in his blood exceeds 80 milligrams of alcohol in 100 millilitres of blood, contrary to Section 236(1) of the Criminal Code."

The facts found by Judge Muir at the trial of the respondent are set out in the stated case as follows:

(a) On April 24th, 1982, at approximately 10:30 P.M., the accused was operating a motor vehicle in a street in the City of Moose Jaw at which time he lost control of the vehicle and it collided with a tree at the side of the street.

(b) Very shortly thereafter, Constable Measner of the Moose Jaw City Police Department arrived at the scene and conducted an investigation. Constable Measner, having reasonable and probable grounds for doing so, made a demand on the accused under the provisions of Section 235(1) of the Criminal Code requiring the accused to accompany him for the purpose of obtaining samples of the accused's breath for analysis. The accused accompanied the officer and supplied samples of his breath in compliance with the demand.

(c) The accused was at no time informed of any rights to retain and instruct counsel.

(d) The accused was co-operative throughout the investigation and was at no time placed under arrest.

In the reasons which he delivered on behalf of the majority for the Saskatchewan Court of Appeal Tallis J.A. said at p. 420: "It is common ground between counsel that after a demand was made under Section 235(1) of the Criminal Code, the respondent accompanied

---

[6] *Clarkson* v. *The Queen* [1986] 1 S.C.R. 383.
[7] *Tremblay* v. *The Queen* [1987] 2 S.C.R. 435.

the officer in a patrol car to the City Police Station in Moose Jaw, where the breathalyzer tests were subsequently conducted.'' There was no evidence that the accused, of his own knowledge, was aware of his right to retain and instruct counsel.

At the trial of the respondent the Crown sought to tender in evidence the certificate of analysis prepared, pursuant to s. 237 of the Criminal Code, by the technician who conducted the breathalyzer test. Counsel for the respondent objected to the admission of the certificate and applied, pursuant to s. 24 of the Charter, for its exclusion on the ground that the respondent had been denied the right, guaranteed by s. 10 of the Charter, to be informed, upon arrest or detention, of his right to retain and instruct counsel without delay. The trial judge allowed the application, ordered the exclusion of the certificate, and for lack of other evidence of the respondent's blood alcohol level dismissed the charge. He held that the respondent had been detained within the meaning of s. 10 of the Charter and that the court was empowered by s. 24(1) thereof to exclude the certificate if it considered such exclusion to be appropriate and just in the circumstances, and that it was not confined to the test laid down in s. 24(2)—that the admission of the evidence would bring the admission of justice into disrepute. . . .

II

In both the trial court and the Court of Appeal the issue as to whether there had been a detention turned essentially, as it has in the judgments of other courts of appeal, on the effect to be given to the decision of this Court in *Chromiak* v. *The Queen*, [1980] 1 S.C.R. 471, which dealt with a demand under s. 234.1(1) of the Criminal Code to provide a sample of breath into a roadside screening device and with the right to counsel guaranteed by s. 2(c) of the Canadian Bill of Rights. These provisions are as follows:

234.1(1) Where a peace officer rea-sonably suspects that a person who is driving a motor vehicle or who has the care or control of a motor vehicle, whether it is in motion or not, has alcohol in his body, he may, by demand made to that person, require him to provide forth-with such a sample of his breath as in the opinion of the peace officer is necessary to enable a proper analysis of his breath to be made by means of an approved road-side screening device and, where neces-sary, to accompany the peace officer for the purpose of enabling such a sample of his breath to be taken.

2. Every law of Canada shall, unless it is expressly declared by an Act of the Parliament of Canada that it shall operate notwithstanding the Canadian Bill of Rights, be so construed and applied as not to abrogate, abridge or infringe or to authorize the abrogation, abridgment of infringement of any of the rights or free-doms herein recognized and declared, and in particular, no law of Canada shall be construed or applied so as to . . .

(c) deprive a person who has been arrested or detained

> *(i) of the right to be informed promptly of the reason for his arrest or detention,*
> *(ii) of the right to retain and instruct counsel without delay, or*
> *(iii) of the remedy by way of habeas corpus for the deter-mination of the validity of his detention and for his release if the detention is now lawful;*
> . . .

In this appeal the appellant contends that the decision of this Court in *Chro-miak* determined, in effect, that a person upon whom a demand is made pursuant to s. 235(1) of the Criminal Code is not detained within the meaning of s. 2(c) of the Canadian Bill of Rights and that the same conclusion should be applied to s. 10 of the Charter because of the similar wording of the two provisions guarantee-ing the right to counsel. . . .

I agree with the contention that *Chromiak* is not distinguishable on the basis of a significant difference between the power conferred by s. 234.1(1) and that conferred by s. 235(1), in so far as the interference with liberty or freedom of action is concerned. Both provisions empower a police officer to require a person to accompany him or her and to provide a breath sample. It has been suggested that the difference in practice in the nature and duration of the interference with liberty effected by a s. 235(1) demand and that effected by a s. 234.1(1) demand constitutes a sufficient basis for distinguishing the two provisions in respect of the question of detention. . . . The fact that a roadside screening test under a s. 234.1(1) demand is generally administered in the back of a police car, whereas the breathalyzer test under a s. 235(1) demand is generally administered in a police station, amounts to a mere difference of degree in so far as the question of detention is concerned. This difference does not in my opinion afford a principled basis for holding that a s. 235(1) demand amounts to a detention if a s. 234.1(1) demand does not.

Other courts of appeal, which have come to a conclusion contrary to that of the Saskatchewan Court of Appeal in the present case on the issue of detention, have held that, notwithstanding the difference in the constitutional nature or status of the Charter and the Canadian Bill of Rights, the word "detention" in s. 10 of the Charter should be given the same meaning as it was given by this Court in *Chromiak* because of the essential similarity in the wording of the two provisions guaranteeing the right to counsel. They have reasoned that had the framers of the Charter found the meaning and effect given to the word "detention" in *Chromiak* unacceptable they could easily have adopted different language as a criterion of the right to counsel. . . .

In my opinion the premise that the framers of the Charter must be presumed to have intended that the words used by it should be given the meaning which had been given to them by judicial decisions at the time the Charter was enacted is not a reliable guide to its interpretation and application. By its very nature a constitutional charter of rights and freedoms must use general language which is capable of development and adaptation by the courts. As Dickson J. (as he then was) said in *Hunter* v. *Southam Inc.*, [1984] 2 S.C.R. 145 at p. 155: "The task of expounding a constitution is crucially different from that of construing a statute." Even if the framers of the Charter had reservations about the meaning given by this Court in *Chromiak* to the word "detained" in s. 2(c) of the Canadian Bill of Rights, assuming they gave consideration to it at all, it would be quite inappropriate, and indeed impracticable, in a constitutional document of this kind, to make detailed qualifications to provide for issues such as that which arises in the present appeal. Cf. the distinction between "concepts" and "conceptions" in Dworkin, *Taking Rights Seriously* (1977), pp. 132-137. That process of reconsideration must of necessity be left to the courts. Although it is clear that in several instances, as in the case of s. 10, the framers of the Charter adopted the wording of the Bill of Rights, it is also clear that the Charter must be regarded, because of its constitutional character, as a new affirmation of rights and freedoms and of judicial power and responsibility in relation to their protection. . . . In considering the relationship of a decision under the Canadian Bill of Rights to an issue arising under the Charter, a court cannot, in my respectful opinion, avoid bearing in mind an evident fact of Canadian judicial history, which must be squarely and frankly faced: that on the whole, with some notable exceptions, the courts have felt some uncertainty or ambivalence in the application of the Canadian Bill of Rights because it did not reflect a clear constitutional mandate to make judicial decisions having the effect of limiting or qualifying the traditional sovereignty of Parliament. The significance of the new constitutional mandate for judicial review provided by the Charter was emphasized by this Court in its recent decisions in *Law Society of Upper Canada* v. *Skapinker* [1984] 1 S.C.R. 357 and *Hunter* v. *Southam Inc., supra.*

Moreover, despite the similarity in the wording of s. 2(c) of the Canadian Bill of Rights and s. 10 of the Charter, there is a difference under the Charter in the scope or content of the right to counsel and in the approach to the qualification or limitation of the right that must, I think, have an influence on the interpretation and application given to it. Section 10(b) of the Charter guarantees not only the right to retain and instruct counsel without delay, as under s. 2(c)(ii) of the Canadian Bill of Rights, but also the right to be informed of that right. This, in my opinion, shows the additional importance which the Charter attaches to the right to counsel. . . .

In determining the meaning that should be given to the word "detention" in s. 10 of the Charter it is necessary to consider the purpose of the section. This is the approach to the interpretation and application of the Charter that was affirmed by this Court in *Hunter* v. *Southam Inc.* . . .

The purpose of s. 10 of the Charter is to ensure that in certain situations a person is made aware of the right to counsel and is permitted to retain and instruct counsel without delay. . . . In its use of the word "detention," s. 10 of the Charter is directed to a restraint of liberty other than arrest in which a person may reasonably require the assistance of counsel but might be prevented or impeded from retaining and instructing counsel without delay but for the constitutional guarantee.

In addition to the case of deprivation of liberty by physical constraint, there is in my opinion a detention with s. 10 of the Charter when a police officer or other agent of the state assumes control over the movement of a person by a demand or direction which may have significant legal consequence and which prevents or impedes access to counsel.

In *Chromiak* this Court held that detention connotes "some form of compulsory constraint." There can be no doubt that there must be some form of compulsion or coercion to constitute an interference with liberty or freedom of action that amounts to a detention within the meaning of s. 10 of the Charter. The issue, as I see it, is whether that compulsion need be of a physical character, or whether it may also be a compulsion of a psychological or mental nature which inhibits the will as effectively as the application, or threat of application, of physical force. . . .

A refusal to comply with a s. 235(1) demand without reasonable excuse is, under s. 235(2), a criminal offence. It is not realistic to speak of a person who is liable to arrest and prosecution for refusal to comply with a demand which a peace officer is empowered by statute to make as being free to refuse to comply. The criminal liability for refusal to comply constitutes effective compulsion. This psychological compulsion or coercion effected by the consequence of a refusal to comply with a s. 235(1) demand appears to be what Laskin J. (as he then was) had in mind in *Hogan* v. *The Queen* [1975] 2 S.C.R. 574 at p. 587, where he said: "There is no doubt, therefore, that the accused was 'detained' within the meaning of s. 2(c)(ii) of the Canadian Bill of Rights; he risked prosecution under s. 235(2) if, without reasonable excuse, he refused the demand which involved accompanying the peace officer to fulfill it." Any criminal liability for failure to comply with a demand or direction of a police officer must be sufficient to make compliance involuntary. . . .

Although it is not strictly necessary for purposes of this case, I would go further. In my opinion, it is not realistic, as a general rule, to regard compliance with a demand or direction by a police officer as truly voluntary, in the sense that the citizen feels that he or she has the choice to obey or not, even where there is in fact a lack of statutory or common law authority for the demand or direction and therefore an absence of criminal liability for failure to comply with it. Most citizens are not aware of the precise legal limits of police authority. Rather than risk the application of physical force or prosecution for wilful obstruction, the reasonable person is likely to err on the side of caution, assume lawful authority and comply with the demand. The element of psychological compulsion, in the form of a reasonable perception of suspension of freedom of choice, is enough to make the restraint of liberty involuntary. . . .

For these reasons I am of the opinion that the s. 235(1) demand to accompany the police officer to a police station and to submit to a breathalyzer test resulted in the detention of the respondent within the meaning of s. 10 of the Charter.

The respondent was accordingly entitled at the time of his detention to be informed of his right to retain and instruct counsel without delay, and there was an infringement or denial of this right, unless it can be shown that the right to retain and instruct counsel (and consequently the right to be informed of such right) does not exist in the context of a s. 235(1) demand by reason of a limit which meets the requirements of s. 1 of the Charter. . . .

Section 1 requires that the limit be prescribed by law, that it be reasonable, and that it be demonstrably justified in a free and democratic society. . . .

Section 235(1) and the related breathalyzer provisions of the *Criminal Code* do not expressly purport to limit the right to counsel. . . . A s. 235(1) demand must be made "forthwith or as soon as practicable" and the person upon whom the demand is made is required to provide a sample of breath "then or as soon thereafter as is practicable". Such samples can be used in evidence as proof of an offence under s. 234 or s. 236 of the *Criminal Code* only if "each sample was taken as soon as practicable after the time when the offence was alleged to have been committed and in any event not later than two hours after that time, with an interval of at least fifteen minutes between the times when the samples were taken" (s. 237(1)(c)(ii)). This two-hour operating requirement does not, as in the case of

the "forthwith" requirement of a s. 234.1(1) demand, preclude any contact at all with counsel prior to the breathalyzer test. The right, at the time of the detention effected by a s. 235(1) demand, to be informed of the right to retain and instruct counsel without delay is not, therefore, subject to a limit prescribed by law within the meaning of s. 1 of the Charter. . . .

III

It is necessary now to consider whether the evidence provided by the breathalyzer test should have been excluded, pursuant to s. 24 of the Charter, because of this infringement or denial of the right to counsel. . . .

As indicated earlier in these reasons, the first issue under s. 24 is whether, as was held by the majority of the Saskatchewan Court of Appeal, evidence may be excluded pursuant to s. 24(1) on the ground that it is appropriate and just in the circumstances to do so, or whether it may be excluded pursuant only to s. 24(2) on the ground that, having regard to all the circumstances, the admission of it in the proceedings would bring the administration of justice into disrepute. . . .

The trial judge and the majority of the Court of Appeal held that while s. 24(2) imposed a *duty* to exclude evidence if its admission would bring the administration of justice into disrepute, s. 24(1) conferred a *discretion* to exclude it if such exclusion appeared to the court to be appropriate and just in the circumstances. It would appear that this distinction between duty and discretion was the principal rationale for the majority view that the framers of the Charter intended to provide two different bases for the exclusion of evidence where there has been an infringement or a denial of a guaranteed right or freedom.

I do not find it necessary to consider whether we should look, as was suggested by counsel for the appellant, at the legislative history of s. 24 as an aid to the determination of this issue. I am satisfied from the words of s. 24 that s. 24(2) was intended to be the sole basis for the exclusion of evidence because of an infringement or a denial of a right or freedom guaranteed by the Charter. It is clear, in my opinion, that in making explicit provision for the remedy of exclusion of evidence in s. 24(2), following the general terms of s. 24(1), the framers of the Charter intended that this particular remedy should be governed entirely by the terms of s. 24(2). It is not reasonable to ascribe to the framers of the Charter an intention that the courts should address two tests or standards on an application for the exclusion of evidence—first, whether the admission of the evidence would bring the administration of justice into disrepute, and if not, secondly, whether its exclusion would nevertheless be appropriate and just in the circumstances. . . . I conclude, therefore, that the Saskatchewan Court of Appeal erred in law in affirming the exclusion of the evidence provided by the breathalyzer test on the ground that it was appropriate and just in the circumstances, within the meaning of s. 24(1) of the Charter.

It is necessary, then, to consider the meaning of the test or standard prescribed by s. 24(2) and its application to the facts as established by the record in this case. There are two requirements for the exclusion of evidence pursuant to s. 24(2): (a) that the evidence has been obtained in a manner that infringed or denied a right or freedom guaranteed by the Charter; and (b) that, having regard to all the circumstances, the admission of the evidence would bring the administration of justice into disrepute. The first requirement suggests that there must be some connection or relationship between the infringement or denial of the right or freedom in question and the obtaining of the evidence the exclusion of which is sought by the application. Some courts have held, or appear to have assumed, that the relationship must be one of causation, similar to the "but for" causation requirement of tort law. . . .

In my opinion the words "obtained in a manner that infringed or denied any rights or freedoms guaranteed by this Charter," particularly when they are read with the French version, "obtenus dans des conditions qui portent atteinte aux droits et libertés garantis par la presente charte", do not connote or require a relationship of causation. It is sufficient if the infringement or denial of the right or freedom has preceded, or occurred in the course of, the obtaining of the evidence. It is not necessary to establish that the evidence would not have been obtained but for the violation of the Charter. . . .

In the result, I am of the opinion that the evidence represented by the certificate of analysis in this case was obtained in a manner that infringed or denied the respondent's right to be informed of his right to retain and instruct counsel without delay and thus meets the first requirement under s. 24(2).

The meaning and application of the words in s. 24(2), "if it is established that, having regard to all the circumstances, the admission of it in the proceedings would bring the administration of justice into disrepute", has been the subject of considerable judicial and academic commentary. . . .

On the whole, courts of appeal have adopted, in some cases with certain reservations, what has come to be known as the "community shock" test suggested by Lamer J. in *Rothman*. . . .

In *Manninen, Chapin*, and *Simmons, supra*, the Ontario Court of Appeal, while acknowledging that what would shock the community would clearly bring the administration of justice into disrepute, indicated that it did not think the application of the words in s. 24(2) should be limited to this test. . . .

I agree, with respect, that we should not substitute for the words of s. 24(2) another expression of the standard, drawn from a different jurisprudential context. The values which must be balanced in making the determination required by s. 24(2) have been placed in a new relationship of relative importance by the constitutional status given to guaranteed rights and freedoms by the Charter. . . . In this context the two principal considerations in the balancing which must be undertaken are the relative seriousness of the constitutional violation and the relative seriousness of the criminal charge. The relative seriousness of the constitutional violation has been assessed in the light of whether it was committed in good faith, or was inadvertent or of a merely technical nature, or whether it was deliberate, wilful or flagrant. Another relevant consideration is whether the action which constituted the constitutional violation was motivated by urgency or necessity to prevent the loss or destruction of the evidence.

The application of these factors to a denial of the right to counsel involves, in my view, a different balance because of the importance of that right in the administration of criminal justice. In my opinion, the right to counsel is of such fundamental importance that its denial in a criminal law context must *prima facie* discredit the administration of justice. That effect is not diminished but, if anything, increased by the relative seriousness of the possible criminal law liability. In view, however, of the judgement of this Court in *Chromiak*, the police officer in this case was in my opinion entitled to assume in good faith that the respondent did not have a right to counsel on a demand under s. 235(1) of the *Criminal Code*. Because of this good faith reliance, I am unable to conclude, having regard to all the circumstances, as required by s. 24(2) of the Charter, that the admission of the evidence of the breathalyzer test in this particular case would bring the administration of justice into disrepute. See Tarnopolsky J.A. in *Simmons, supra*, at pp. 228-9. The evidence cannot, therefore, be excluded.

As this conclusion indicates, I am also of the opinion that the question whether evidence must be excluded because, having regard to all the circumstances, its admission would bring the administration of justice into disrepute is a question of law which may be determined by a court without evidence of the actual or likely effect of such admission on public opinion. . . . There is no reliable evidentiary basis for determining what the actual effect on public opinion would be of the admission of evidence in the circumstances of a particular case. The suggestion of opinion polls (see D. Gibson, "Determining Disrepute: Opinion Polls and the Canadian Charter of Rights and Freedoms," (1983), 61 *Can. Bar Rev.* 377) encounters, in my opinion, two fatal objections. The first is the requirement which Professor Gibson refes to as "specificity". How could "all the circumstances" of a case and the necessary balancing exercise be conveyed in an opinion poll or survey? The second objection is the cost of requiring such evidence, which, since it would have to be borne by the person whose constitutional right or freedom had been violated, would surely be a further factor reducing availability of the remedy provided by s. 24(2). . . .

I would accordingly allow the appeal, set aside the judgments of the Saskatchewan Court of Appeal and Judge Muir, and order a new trial.

McINTYRE J. (dissenting): I am in full agreement with the Reasons for Judgment of Le Dain J. I would add that to exclude the questioned evidence in this case solely on a finding that a Charter right was breached in obtaining it would be to disregard the provisions of s. 24(2) of the Canadian Charter of Rights and Freedoms. In my view, this section must have its effect. The exclusion of such evidence is not automatic. It must be excluded only where it is established that its admission, having regard to all the circumstances, would bring the administration of justice into disrepute. In my view, that is not established here. The exclusion of the evidence in the circumstances of this case would itself go far to bring the administration of justice into disrepute.

The Judgment of Beetz, Estey, Chouinard and Wilson JJ. was delivered by

ESTEY J.: I have had the benefit of reading the judgement of my colleague Le Dain J. in this appeal and while I am in agreement, as shall be seen below, with much of what has been there written, I am in respectful disagreement as to the disposition. I would dismiss the appeal for these reasons.

I am in agreement that the respondent-defendant was "detained" within the meaning of s. 10 of the Charter of Rights when the police officers administered the breathalyzer test under s. 235 of the *Criminal Code*. . . .

Because Parliament has not purported to place a limitation on the right of the respondent under s. 10(b) of the Charter, in s. 235(1), the Court is not here concerned with s. 1 of the Charter. That section subjects all Charter rights, including s. 10, "only to such reasonable limits prescribed by law. . . ." Here Parliament has not purported to prescribe any such limit and hence s. 1 of the Charter does not come into play. The limit on the respondent's right to consult counsel was imposed by the conduct of the police officers and not by Parliament.

This brings one to the core issue in this appeal, namely the admissibility of the evidence as to the alcohol content in the respondent's blood as determined by the test taken under s. 235(1) of the Code. The admissibility of this evidence in my view, and again I am in respectful agreement with my colleague Le Dain J., falls to be determined by s. 24(2) of the Charter and not by reason of subs. (1) of that section, as was the view of the Court of Appeal below. Subsection (2) alone in the Charter of Rights empowers a court to exclude evidence where "that evidence was obtained in a manner that infringed or denied any rights or freedoms guaranteed by this Charter. . . ." Here the police authority has flagrantly violated a Charter right without any statutory authority for so doing. Such an overt violation as occurred here must, in my view, result in the rejection of the evidence thereby obtained. We are here dealing only with direct evidence or evidence thereby obtained directly and

I leave to another day any consideration of evidence thereby indirectly obtained. To do otherwise than reject this evidence on the facts and circumstances in this appeal would be to invite police officers to disregard Charter rights of the citizen and to do so with an assurance of impunity. If s. 10(b) of the Charter of Rights can be offended without any statutory authority for the police conduct here in question and without the loss of admissibility of evidence obtained by such a breach then s. 10(b) would be stripped of any meaning and would have no place in the catalogue of "legal rights" found in the Charter.

The violation by the policy authority of a fundamental Charter right, which transpired here, will render this evidence inadmissible. Admitting this evidence under these circumstances would clearly "bring the administration of justice into disrepute". I am strongly of the view that it would be most improvident for this Court to expatiate, in these early days of life with the Charter of Rights, upon the meaning of the expression 'administration of justice' and particularly its outer limits. There will no doubt be, over the years to come, a gradual build-up in delineation and definition of the words used in the Charter in s. 24(1).

For these reasons, I would therefore dismiss this appeal.

LAMER J.: I agree with my brother Le Dain for the reasons set out in his judgment that the respondent was detained. I also agree with Le Dain J. that there was here a violation of the respondent's rights under s. 10(b). . . .

At first blush, there would appear not to be any need to expand upon the content of s. 10(b) given that the facts of this case indicate a clear violation of the section whatever be that content. However, in order to meet the requirements for exclusion of evidence under s. 24(2) there must not only exist a violation of a Charter right, but there must also be, as was said by Le Dain J., "some connection or relationship between the infringement or denial of the right or freedom in question and the obtaining of the evidence the exclusion of which is sought by the application''.

With respect, however, I cannot subscribe to the proposition later advanced by Le Dain J. that this requirement is met by the simple fact that the infringement or denial of the right has preceded the obtaining of the evidence. Indeed, if there is no relationship other than a temporal one, the evidence was not *"obtained* in a manner that infringed'' the Charter.

Thus, when one addresses the consequences that should flow under s. 24 as a result of the violation in this case, one has to go back and give some content to s. 10(b) if one is to consider whether, under s. 24(2), the ''breathalyzer evidence'' was obtained in a manner that infringed or denied that right. . . .

I do not want to be taken here as giving an exhaustive definition of the s. 10(b) rights and will limit my comments in that respect to what is strictly required for the disposition of this case. In my view, s. 10(b) requires at least that the authorities inform the detainee of his rights, not prevent him in any way from exercising them and, where a detainee is required to provide evidence which may be incriminating and refusal to comply is punishable as a criminal offence, as is the case under s. 235 of the Code, s. 10(b) also imposes a duty not to call upon the detainee to provide that evidence without first informing him of his s. 10(b) rights and providing him with a reasonable opportunity and time to retain and instruct counsel. Failure to abide by that duty will lead to the obtainment of evidence in a manner which infringes or denies the detainee's s. 10(b) rights. Short of that, s. 10(b) would be a near empty right, as remedies could seldom affect the admissibility of evidence obtained through the accused.

Whether s. 10(b) extends any further, so as to encompass, for example, the principle of *Miranda* v. *Arizona* (1966), 384 U.S. 436 (USSC), and apply to matters such as interrogation and police line-ups, need not be decided in this case and I

shall refrain from so doing.

Whether s. 235(1) of the Code in general, and its two hour limitation in particular, are in conflict with s. 10(b), especially that aspect of being given a reasonable time to speak to counsel, does not arise in this case and I would choose not to address that question for the following reason. Were we to find that s. 235(1) does impose a limit on the amount of time the peace officer can give a detainee to exercise his rights under s. 10(b) before requiring a breath sample, we would in my view be faced with a very incomplete file when called upon to determine whether the limitation is one that is reasonable under the test set out in s. 1 of the Charter. I think that question, if it is to be addressed, will be more properly considered in a case where there will have been adduced evidence in support of the demonstration the authorities have the burden to make under s. 1. As an example, why is there a two hour limit? Is it for scientific reasons related to reliability? I suspect so but do not find any evidence in the record.

In this case, the test was required by the peace officer and then given to the detainee prior to his being informed of his right to counsel. By so doing, the police officer violated the accused's rights under s. 10(b) and obtained the ''breathalyzer evidence'' in a manner which infringed and denied those rights.

I would decide the disposition of this case as does Estey J., and for the reasons he sets out in his judgment. Indeed, I am of the view that admitting the breathalyzer evidence in this case would bring the administration of justice into disrepute. Having so concluded, I need not express any views as regards the exclusion of evidence under s. 24(1).

DICKSON C.J.C.: I agree with Mr. Justice Le Dain, for the reasons he has given in his judgment, that the respondent was detained within the meaning of s. 10 of the Charter, and that his rights under subsection (b) were violated. I also agree with Mr. Justice Le Dain that s. 235(1) does not create a limit, prescribed by law, under s. 1 of the Charter, on a detained person's right to be informed of the right to retain and instruct counsel. Subsection 235(1) does not expressly or by necessary implication compel the police to deny a detained person's right to be informed of his s. 10(b) rights.

I agree with Mr. Justice Lamer, for the reasons he has given, that the breathalyzer evidence tendered in this case was obtained in a manner which infringed and denied the respondent's rights under s. 10(b) and that it has been established that, having regard to all the circumstances, the admission of this evidence in the proceedings would bring the administration of justice into disrepute. Accordingly, the certificate of analysis prepared pursuant to s. 237 of the Criminal Code should be excluded under s. 24(2) of the Charter.

Since this evidence may properly be excluded by the operation of s. 24(2) of the Charter, I do not wish to be taken as expressing any view on the availability of the exclusion of evidence as an appropriate and just remedy under s. 24(1) of the Charter.

I would accordingly dismiss this appeal.

45. Reference re B.C. Motor Vehicle Act, 1985

~ The B.C. Motor Vehicle Reference is an example of a case that is relatively unimportant with respect to the policy issue at stake but very significant in terms of its impact on constitutional interpretation and development. While the fate of s. 94(2) of British Columbia's Motor Vehicle Act will soon be forgotten, the Supreme Court's decision in this case has gone on to be one of the Court's most frequently cited judgements.

Section 94(1) of British Columbia's Motor Vehicle Act made it an offense for a person to drive if his license had been revoked or he had been legally prohibited from driving. Section 94(2) made it an absolute liability offense; that is, guilt was established by proof of driving, whether or not the driver knew of the prohibition or suspension. The offense was punishable by a fine and a minimum term of imprisonment. Shortly after the adoption of the Charter, the British Columbia government had doubts about the compatibility of s. 94(2) with the Charter, and so referred the question to the provincial Court of Appeal. The latter found that the provision violated the Charter, and there was an automatic appeal to the Supreme Court of Canada.

At issue was whether the absolute liability provision violated the "principles of fundamental justice" set forth in section 7 of the Charter. The Attorney-General of British Columbia argued that the meaning of section 7 was limited to "procedural fairness" alone, and that section 7 did not authorize judges to pass judgement on the fairness of the "substance" of impugned legislation.

The notion of "substantive due process" had a long and checkered history in American constitutional law. Between 1900 and 1937, the American Supreme Court had used the Due Process Clause of the American Constitution to strike down numerous progressive laws that imposed new social and economic regulations on American business. In effect, the American Court had used "substantive due process" to protect the laissez-faire economic system and conservative economic interests from the emerging welfare state. This culminated in the New Deal "court crisis" of 1937, after which the substantive due process precedents were abandoned and discredited. However, substantive due process re-emerged in American jurisprudence in the 1970s, most notably in the Abortion Decision.[1] As the Charter was being drafted, the term "fundamental justice" replaced "due process" in order to avoid the substantive connotations the latter term had acquired in American law.

Speaking for a unanimous court, Justice Lamer rejected a strict dichotomy between "substantive" and "procedural" interpretations of section 7. The two could not be so easily separated. The entire array of procedural safeguards enumerated in sections 8 through 14 of the Charter constitute the substance of "principles of fundamental justice" articulated in section 7. More to the point, Lamer wrote, "A law that has the potential to convict a person who has not

---

[1] Roe v. Wade, 410 U.S. 113 (1973). See introduction to *Morgentaler* v. *the Queen*, case 50, below.

really done anything wrong offends the principles of fundamental justice. . . . In other words, absolute liability and imprisonment cannot be combined.''

Justice Lamer was well aware that attributing substantive meaning to the concept of ''principles of fundamental justice'' could unduly widen the scope of judicial review under section 7, resulting in what he called a ''super judicial legislature.'' To discourage this, he stressed that a substantive interpretation of section 7 was limited to the field of criminal law and legal rights, ''the inherent domain of the judiciary,'' and would not be applied ''in the realm of general public policy.'' However, several subsequent decisions by lower courts have extended this doctrine to areas of economic and social policy. If this becomes a trend, the scope of the Charter—and thus the power of the judges—will expand considerably.

Of equal significance was Justice Lamer's handling of the historical evidence of the ''framers' intent'' to limit section 7 to a narrow procedural meaning. While conceding the admissability of the ''framers' intent'' as relevant to determining the proper interpretation of Charter rights, Justice Lamer cautioned against granting such extrinsic evidence anything more than ''minimal weight.'' To attach any more significance to the ''original understanding'' of Charter rights, he cautioned, ''would in effect be assuming a fact which is nearly impossible of proof, i.e., the intention of the legislative bodies which adopted the Charter.'' Moreover, it would re-introduce the much criticized ''frozen concepts'' doctrine, rather than a ''large and liberal'' interpretation of the Charter mandated by the frequently cited ''living tree'' approach.[2]

By freeing constitutional law from the drafters' intentions, the Court has granted itself and all other Canadian judges the discretion to read new meaning into the Charter sections other than what the framers' understood and intended those sections to mean. Future litigants can now invoke the symbol of the Charter as a ''living tree'' and argue that even if the meaning they attribute to a Charter right was not part of its original meaning, the judge is still free to add the new meaning.

This aspect of the *B.C. Motor Vehicle Reference* is best illustrated by an anecdote from the Borowski anti-abortion case.[3] The very day the Supreme Court handed down its decision in the *Motor Vehicle Reference*—December 17, 1985—pro-life crusader Joe Borowski began his hearing before the Court of Appeal of Saskatchewan. Borowski's lawyer, Morris Schumiatcher, argued that the sections of the Criminal Code allowing therapeutic abortions violate the ''right to life'' of the unborn child/foetus as protected by section 7 of the Charter. The history of the drafting of the Charter clearly indicates that the government rejected requests to include either a right to abortion for women or

[2] See Introduction, pp. 18-19.
[3] See case no. 51.

a right to life for the unborn. The Crown attorney had effectively used this evidence of the ''framers' intent'' to rebut Schumiatcher's arguments. The court would be unjustified, the Crown argued, to give a meaning to the Charter that had been explicitly rejected by the people who wrote it.

On the third and last day of the hearing, Schumiatcher was making his closing statement when one of his assistants hurriedly arrived clutching a document. After a brief huddle, Schumiatcher excitedly announced to the Court that he had just received a copy of a Supreme Court decision handed down in Ottawa the previous day. The case was the *B.C. Motor Vehicle Reference*. Schumiatcher triumphantly quoted Justice Lamer's comments about the non-binding character of the ''original intent.'' The three judges were now free, Schumiatcher exhorted them, to adopt the ''living tree'' approach and to expand the meaning of section 7 to include the unborn. Ironically but not surprisingly, Dr. Henry Morgentaler, Borowski's counterpart in the legal battle over Canada's abortion law, subsequently made extensive use of the *B.C. Motor Vehicle* precedent but for the opposite purpose—to urge the Supreme Court to find a right to abortion in section 7 of the Charter.[4]

It should be noted that the Supreme Court has not been consistent on this matter. In other cases it has relied heavily on the use of the ''original understanding'' of Charter text to bolster the authority of its decisions. A majority of the Court relied on the ''framers' intent'' in the *Alberta Labour Reference*.[5] In the *Morgentaler* decision, the two dissenting judges attached great importance to the historical evidence that the Charter was intentionally silent on abortion. (The three opinions that constituted the majority simply avoided it.)

The most important judicial use of ''original understanding'' was the *Quebec Protestant School Board* decision striking down the education provisions of Bill 101.[6] Referring to the ''Canada clause'' of section 23 of the Charter, the Court declared: ''This set of constitutional provisions was not enacted by the legislator in a vacuum . . . the legislator knew, and clearly had in mind the regimes governing Anglophone and Francophone linguistic minorities in various provinces in Canada . . . and their intention was to remedy the perceived defects of these regimes by uniform corrective measures, namely those contained in s. 23 of the Charter.'' ~

---

[4] See case 50 below.

[5] See case 49 below.

[6] See case 55 below.

REFERENCE RE BRITISH COLUMBIA MOTOR VEHICLE ACT
In the Supreme Court of Canada. [1985] 2 S.C.R. 486.

The judgement of Dickson, Beetz, Chouinard, Le Dain and Lamer JJ. was delivered by

LAMER J.: A law that has the potential to convict a person who has not really done anything wrong offends the principles of fundamental justice and, if imprisonment is available as a penalty, such a law then violates a person's right to liberty under s. 7 of the Charter of Rights and Freedoms (Constitution Act, 1982, as enacted by the Canada Act, 1982, c, 11 (U.K.)). In other words, absolute liability and imprisonment cannot be combined.

On August 16, 1982, the Lieutenant-Governor in Council of British Columbia referred the following question to the Court of Appeal of that province, by virtue of s. 1 of the Constitutional Question Act R.S.B.C. 1979, c. 63:

Is s. 94(2) of the Motor Vehicle Act, R.S.B.C. 1979, as amended by the Motor Vehicle Amendment Act, 1982, consistent with the Canadian Charter of Rights and Freedoms?

On February 3, 1983, the Court of Appeal handed down reasons in answer to the question in which it stated that s. 94(2) of the Act is inconsistent with the Canadian Charter of Rights and Freedoms. . . .

Motor Vehicle Act, R.S.B.C. 1979, c. 288, s. 94, as amended by the Motor Vehicle Amendment Act 1982, S.B.C. 1982 c. 36, s. 19:

94.(1) A person who drives a motor vehicle on a highway or industrial road while

(a) he is prohibited from driving a motor vehicle under sections 90, 91, 92, or 92.1, or

(b) his driver's licence or his right to apply for or obtain a driver's licence is suspended under s. 82 or 92 as it was before its repeal and replacement came into force pursuant to the Motor Vehicle Amendment Act, 1982,

commits an offence and is liable,

(c) on a first conviction, to a fine of not less than $300 and not more than $2000 and to imprisonment for not less than 7 days and not more than 6 months, and

(d) on a subsequent conviction, regardless of when the contravention occurred, to a fine of not less than $300 and not more than $2000 and to imprisonment for not less than 14 days and not more than one year.

(2) Subsection (1) creates an absolute liability offence in which guilt is established by proof of driving, whether or not the defendant knew of the prohibition or suspension. . . .

SECTION 7

The issue in this case raises fundamental questions of constitutional theory, including the nature and the very legitimacy of constitutional adjudication under the Charter as well as the appropriateness of various techniques of constitutional interpretation. . . .

The novel feature of the Constitution Act . . . is not that it has suddenly empowered courts to consider the content of legislation. This the courts have done for a good many years when adjudicating upon the *vires* of legislation. . . .

The truly novel features of the Constitution Act, 1982 are that it has sanctioned the process of constitutional adjudication and has extended its scope so as to encompass a broader range of values. Content of legislation has always been considered in constitutional adjudication. Content is now to be equally considered as regards new constitutional issues. Indeed, the values subject to constitutional adjudication now pertain to the rights of individuals as well as the distribution of governmental powers. In short, it is the scope of constitutional adjudication which has been altered rather than its nature, at least, as regards the right to consider the content of legislation.

In neither case, be it before or after the Charter, have the courts been enabled to decide upon the appropriateness of policies underlying legislative enactments. In both instances, however, the courts are empowered, indeed required, to measure the content of legislation against the guarantees of the Constitution. . . .

In this respect, s. 7 is no different than other Charter provisions. As the Attorney General for Ontario has noted in his factum:

Section 7, like most of the other sections in the Charter, limits the bounds of legislative action. It is the function of the Court to determine whether the challenged legislation has honoured those boundaries. This process necessitates judicial review of the content of the legislation.

Yet, in the context of s. 7, and in particular of the interpretation of "principles of fundamental justice," there has prevailed in certain quarters an assumption that all but a narrow construction of s. 7 will inexorably lead the courts to "question the wisdom of enactments," to adjudicate upon the merits of public policy.

From this have sprung warnings of the dangers of a judicial "super-legislature" beyond the reach of Parliament, the provincial legislatures and the electorate. The Attorney General for Ontario, in his written argument, stated that,

. . . *the judiciary is neither representative of, nor responsive to the electorate on whose behalf, and under whose authority policies are selected and given effect in the laws of the land.*

This is an argument which was heard countless times prior to the entrenchment of the Charter but which has in truth, for better or for worse, been settled by the very coming into force of the Constitution Act, 1982. It ought not to be forgotten that the historic decision to entrench the Charter in our Constitution was taken not by the courts but by the elected representatives of the people of Canada. It was those representatives who extended the scope of constitutional adjudication and entrusted the courts with this new and onerous responsibility. Adjudication under the Charter must be approached free of any lingering doubts as to its legitimacy.

The concerns with the bounds of constitutional adjudication explain the characterization of the issue in a narrow and restrictive fashion, i.e., whether the terms "principles of fundamental justice" have a substantive or merely procedural content. In my view, the characterization of the issue in such fashion preempts an open-minded approach to determining the meaning of "principles of fundamental justice."

The substantive/procedural dichotomy narrows the issue almost to an all-or-nothing proposition. Moreover, it is largely bound up in the American experience with substantive and procedural due process. It imports into the Canadian context American concepts, terminology and jurisprudence, all of which are inextricably linked to problems concerning the nature and legitimacy of adjudication under the U.S. Constitution. That Constitution, it must be remembered, has no s. 52 nor has it the internal checks and balances of sections 1 and 33. We would, in my view, do our own Constitution a disservice to simply allow the American debate to define the issue for us, all the while ignoring the truly fundamental structural differences between the two constitutions. Finally, the dichotomy creates its own set of difficulties by the attempt to distinguish between two concepts whose outer boundaries are not always clear and often tend to overlap. Such difficulties can and should, when possible, be avoided.

The overriding and legitimate concern that courts ought not to question the wisdom of enactments, and the presumption that the Legislator could not have intended same, have to some extent distorted the discussion surrounding the meaning of "principles of fundamental justice." This has led to the spectre of a judicial "super-legislature" without a full consideration of the process of constitutional adjudication and the significance of sections 1, 33 and 52 of the Constitution Act, 1982. This in turn has also led to a narrow characterization of the issue and to the assumption that only a procedural content to "principles of fundamental justice" can prevent the courts from adjudicating upon the merits or wisdom of enactments. If this assumption is accepted, the inevitable corollary, with which I would have to then agree, is that the Legislator intended that the words "principles of fundamental justice" refer to procedure only.

But I do not share that assumption. Since way back in time and even recently the courts have developed the common law beyond procedural safeguards without interfering with the "merits or wisdom" of enactments. . . .

The task of the Court is not to choose between substantive or procedural content *per se* but to secure for persons "the full benefit of the Charter's protection" (Dickson C.J.C. in *R.* v. *Big M Drug Mart Ltd.*, [1985] 1 S.C.R. 295 at 344), under s. 7, while avoiding adjudication of the merits of public policy. This can only be accomplished by a purposive analysis. . . .

I propose therefore to approach the interpretation of s. 7 in the manner set forth by Dickson C.J.C. . . . [I]n *Big M Drug Mart Ltd.*, Dickson C.J.C. wrote at p. 344:

In Hunter v. Southam Inc., *[1984] 2 S.C.R. 145, this Court expressed the view that the proper approach to the definition of the rights and freedoms guaranteed by the Charter was a purposive one. The meaning of a right or freedom guaranteed by the Charter was to be ascertained by an analysis of the* purpose *of such a guarantee; it was to be understood, in other words, in the light of the interests it was meant to protect.* . . .

[Section 7] states "and the right not to be deprived thereof except in accordance with the principles of fundamental justice." On the facts of this case it is not necessary to decide whether the section gives any greater protection, such as deciding whether, absent a breach of the principles of fundamental justice, there still can be, given the way the section is structured, a violation of one's rights to life, liberty and security of the person under s. 7. Furthermore, because of the fact that only deprivation of liberty was considered in these proceedings and that no one took issue with the fact that imprisonment is a deprivation of liberty, my analysis of s. 7 will be limited, as was the course taken by all, below and in this Court, to determining the scope of the words "principles of fundamental justice." I will not attempt to give any further content to liberty nor address that of the words life or security of the person.

In the framework of a purposive analysis, designed to ascertain the purpose of the s. 7 guarantee and "the interests it was meant to protect" (*R.* v. *Big M Drug Mart Ltd., supra*), it is clear to me that the interests which are meant to be protected by the words "and the right not to be deprived thereof except in accordance with the principles of fundamental justice" of s. 7 are the life, liberty and security of the person. The principles of fundamental justice, on the other hand, are not a protected interest, but rather a qualifier of the right not to be deprived of life, liberty and security of the person. . . .

As a qualifier, the phrase serves to establish the parameters of the interests but it cannot be interpreted so narrowly as to frustrate or stultify them. For the narrower the meaning given to "principles of fundamental justice" the greater will be the possibility that individuals may be deprived of these most basic rights.

For these reasons, I am of the view that it would be wrong to interpret the term "fundamental justice" as being synonymous with natural justice as the Attorney General of British Columbia and others have suggested. To do so would strip the protected interests of much, if not most, of their content and leave the "right" to life, liberty and security of the person in a sorely emaciated state. . . .

Sections 8 to 14 . . . address specific deprivations of the "right" to life, liberty and security of the person in breach of the principles of fundamental justice, and as such, violations of s. 7. They are designed to protect, in a specific manner and setting, the right to life, liberty and security of the person set forth in s. 7. It would be incongruous to interpret s. 7 more narrowly than the rights in sections 8 to 14. . . .

Clearly, some of those sections embody principles that are beyond what could be characterized as "procedural."

Thus, sections 8 to 14 provide an invaluable key to the meaning of "principles of fundamental justice." Many have been developed over time as presumptions of the common law, others have found expression in the international conventions on human rights. All have been recognized as essential elements of a system for the administration of justice which is founded upon a belief in "the dignity and worth of the human person" (preamble to the Canadian Bill of Rights, R.S.C. 1970, app. III) and on "The Rule of Law" (preamble to the Canadian Charter of Rights and Freedoms).

It is this common thread which, in my view, must guide us in determining the scope and content of "principles of fundamental justice." In other words, the principles of fundamental justice are to be found in the basic tenets of our legal system. They do not lie in the realm of general public policy but in the inherent domain of the judiciary as guardian of the justice system. . . .

Thus, it seems to me that to replace "fundamental justice" with the term "natural justice" misses the mark entirely. It was, after all, clearly open to the Legislator to use the term natural justice, a known term of art, but such was not done. We must, as a general rule, be loath to exchange the terms actually used with terms so obviously avoided.

Whatever may have been the degree of synonymy between the two expressions in the past . . . as of the last few decades this

country has given a precise meaning to the words natural justice for the purpose of delineating the responsibility of adjudicators (in the wide sense of the word) in the field of administrative law.

It is, in my view, that precise and somewhat narrow meaning that the Legislator avoided, clearly indicating thereby a will to give greater content to the words "principles of fundamental justice" . . .

A number of courts have placed emphasis upon the minutes of the Proceedings and Evidence of the Special Joint Committee of the Senate and of the House of Commons on the Constitution in the interpretation of "principles of fundamental justice" . . .

In particular, the following passages dealing with the testimony of federal civil servants from the Department of Justice, have been relied upon:

Mr. Strayer (Assistant Deputy Minister, Public Law):

> *Mr. Chairman, it was our belief that the words "fundamental justice" would cover the same thing as what is called procedural due process, that is the meaning of due process in relation to requiring fair procedure. However, it in our view does not cover the concept of what is called substantive due process, which would impose substantive requirements as to policy of the law in question.*
>
> *This has been most clearly demonstrated in the United States in the area of property, but also in other areas such as the right to life. The term due process has been given the broader concept of meaning both the procedure and substance. Natural justice or fundamental justice in our view does not go beyond the procedural requirements of fairness. . . .*
>
> *The term "fundamental justice" appears to us to be essentially the same thing as natural justice.*

Mr. Tasse (Deputy Minister) also said of the phrase "principles of fundamental justice" in testimony before the Committee: "We assume that the Court would look at that much like a Court would look at the requirements of natural justice. . . .''

The Honourable Jean Chretien, then federal Minister of Justice, also indicated to the Committee that, while he thought "fundamental justice marginally more appropriate than natural justice" in s. 7, either term was acceptable to the Government.

The first issue which arises is whether the Minutes of the Proceedings and Evidence of the Joint Committee may even be considered admissible as extrinsic aids to the interpretation of Charter provisions. Such extrinsic materials were traditionally excluded from consideration in constitutional adjudication. . . . .

In Reference re Upper Churchill Water Rights Reversion Act, [1984] 1 S.C.R. 297 at p. 317, however, McIntyre J. stated that,

The general exclusionary rule formerly considered to be applicable in dealing with the admissibility of extrinsic evidence in constitutional cases has been set aside or at least greatly modified and relaxed.

Indeed, in the Reference re Anti-inflation Act, [1976] 2 S.C.R. 373, Laskin C.J.C. stated, at p. 389:

. . . no general principle of admissibility or inadmissibility can or ought to be propounded by this Court, and . . . the questions of resort to extrinsic evidence and what kind of extrinsic evidence may be admitted must depend on the constitutional issues on which it is sought to adduce such evidence.

This approach was adopted by Dickson J. (as he then was) in Reference re The Residential Tenancies Act 1979 . . . .

It is to be noted, however, that McIntyre J.'s remarks are in relation to the interpretation of the challenged statutory enactment rather than the interpretation of the Constitution itself. The same is true of the remarks of Laskin C.J.C. and Dickson J. (as he then was).

With respect to the interpretation of the

Constitution, however, such extrinsic materials were considered, in at least two cases, by this Court.

In the Re Authority of Parliament in relation to the Upper House Reference, [1980] 1 S.C.R. 54, the Court stated, at p. 66:

It is, we think, proper to consider the historical background which led to the provision which was made in the Act for the creation of the Senate as a part of the apparatus for the enactment of federal legislation. In the debates which occurred at the Quebec Conference in 1864, considerable time was occupied in discussing the provisions respecting the Senate. Its important purpose is stated in the following passages in speeches delivered in the debates on Confederation in the parliament of the province of Canada: . . .

The other case is *A.G. Canada v. Canadian National Transportation Ltd.*, [1983] 2 S.C.R. 206. Laskin C.J.C., in that case, referred to the pre-Confederation debates in the course of interpreting sections 91(27) and 92(14) of the Constitution Act, 1867 (at p. 225).

I would adopt this approach when interpreting the Charter. Consequently, the Minutes of the Proceedings and Evidence of the Special Joint Committee on the Constitution should, in my view, be considered.

Having said that, however, I nonetheless believe that the logic underlying the reluctance to allow the use of materials such as speeches in Parliament carries considerable force with respect to the Minutes of the Committee as well.

In Reference re Upper Churchill Water Rights Reversion Act, *supra*, McIntyre J. wrote at p. 319:

. . . I would say that the speeches and public declarations by prominent figures in the public and political life of Newfoundland on this question should not be received as evidence. They represent, no doubt, the considered views of the speakers at the time they were made, but cannot be said to be expressions of the

intent of the Legislative Assembly. . . .

If speeches and declarations by prominent figures are inherently unreliable (*per* McIntyre J. in Reference re Upper Churchill Water Rights Reversion Act, *supra*, at p. 319) and "speeches made in the Legislature at the time of enactment of the measures are inadmissible as having little evidential weight" (*per* Dickson J. (as he then was) in Reference re Residential Tenancies Act 1979, *supra*, at p. 721), the Minutes of the Proceedings of the Special Joint Committee, though admissible, and granted somewhat more weight than speeches, should not be given too much weight. The inherent unreliability of such statements and speeches is not altered by the mere fact that they pertain to the Charter of Rights rather than a statute.

Moreover, the simple fact remains that the Charter is not the product of a few individual public servants, however distinguished, but of a multiplicity of individuals who played major roles in the negotiating, drafting and adoption of the Charter. How can one say with any confidence that within this enormous multiplicity of actors, without forgetting the role of the provinces, the comments of a few federal civil servants can in any way be determinative?

Were this Court to accord any significant weight to this testimony, it would in effect be assuming a fact which is nearly impossible of proof, i.e., the intention of the legislative bodies which adopted the Charter. In view of the indeterminate nature of the data, it would in my view be erroneous to give these materials anything but minimal weight.

Another danger with casting the interpretation of s. 7 in terms of the comments made by those heard at the Joint Committee Proceedings is that, in so doing, the rights, freedoms and values embodied in the Charter in effect becomes frozen in time to the moment of adoption with little or no possibility of growth, development and adjustment to changing societal needs. . . . If the newly planted "living tree" which is the Charter is to have the possibility of growth and adjustment over time, care must be taken to ensure that historical materials, such as the Minutes of Proceedings and Evidence of the Special Joint committee, do not stunt its growth. . . .

The appellant states that s. 7 "is a blend of s. 1(a) and s. 2(e) of the Canadian Bill of Rights. Considerable emphasis is then placed upon the case of *Duke* v. *The Queen*, [1972] S.C.R. 917 in which this Court interpreted the words "principles of fundamental justice" in s. 2(e) of the Bill. Fauteux C.J.C. noted, at p. 923:

Without attempting to formulate any final definition of those words, I would take them to mean, generally, that the tribunal which adjudicates upon his rights must act fairly, in good faith, without bias, and in a judicial temper, and must give to him the opportunity adequately to state his case.

However, as Le Dain J. has written in *R.* v. *Therens, supra*, with the implicit support of the majority. . . .

In considering the relationship of a decision under the Canadian Bill of Rights to an issue arising under the Charter, a court cannot, in my respectful opinion, avoid bearing in mind an evident fact of Canadian judicial history, which must be squarely and frankly faced: that on the whole, with some notable exceptions, the courts have felt some uncertainty or ambivalence in the application of the Canadian Bill of Rights because it did not reflect a clear constitutional mandate to make judicial decisions having the effect of limiting or qualifying the traditional sovereignty of Parliament. . . .

In section 2(e) of the Bill of Rights, the words "principles of fundamental justice" were placed explicitly in the context of, and qualify a "right to a fair hearing." Section 7 of the Charter does not create the same context. In s. 7, the words "principles of fundamental justice" are placed in the context of, and qualify much more fundamental rights, the "right to life, liberty and security of the person." The distinction is important. . . .

Whether any given principle may be said to be a principle of fundamental justice within the meaning of s. 7 will rest upon an analysis of the nature, sources, rationale and essential role of that principle within the judicial process and in our legal system, as it evolves.

Consequently, those words cannot be given any exhaustive content or simple enumerative definition, but will take on concrete meaning as the courts address alleged violations of s. 7.

I now turn to such an analysis of the principle of *mens rea* and absolute liability offences in order to determine the question which has been put to the Court in the present Reference.

ABSOLUTE LIABILITY AND FUNDAMENTAL JUSTICE IN PENAL LAW

It has from time immemorial been part of our system of laws that the innocent not be punished. This principle has long been recognized as an essential element of a system for the administration of justice which is founded upon a belief in the dignity and worth of the human person and on the rule of law. It is so old that its first enunciation was in latin *actus non facit reum nisi mens sit rea*.

As Glanville Williams said:

There is no need here to go into the remote history of mens rea; *suffice . . . it to say that the requirement of a guilty state of mind (at least for the more serious crimes) had been developed by the time of Coke, which is as far back as the modern lawyer needs to go. " 'If one shoot at any wild fowl upon a tree, and the arrow killeth any reasonable creature afar off, without any evil intent in him, this is per infortunium.' . . .*

This view has been adopted by this Court in unmistakable terms in many cases, amongst which the better known are *Beaver* v. *the Queen*, [1957] S.C.R.

531, and the most recent and often quoted judgment of Dickson J. (as he then was), writing for the Court in *R.* v. *City of Sault Ste. Marie, supra*.

This Court's decision in the latter case is predicated upon a certain number of postulates one of which, given the nature of the rules it elaborates, has to be to the effect that absolute liability in penal law offends the principles of fundamental justice. Those principles are, to use the words of Dickson J., to the effect that "there is a generally held revulsion against punishment of the morally innocent." He also stated that the argument that absolute liability "violates fundamental principles of penal liability" was the most telling argument against absolute liability and one of greater force than those advanced in support thereof. . . .

A law enacting an absolute liability offence will violate s. 7 of the Charter only if and to the extent that it has the potential of depriving of life, liberty, or security of the person.

Obviously, imprisonment (including probation orders) deprives persons of their liberty. An offence has that potential as of the moment it is open to the judge to impose imprisonment. There is no need that imprisonment, as in s. 94(2), be made mandatory.

I am therefore of the view that the combination of imprisonment and of absolute liability violates s. 7 of the Charter and can only be salvaged if the authorities demonstrate under s. 1 that such a deprivation of liberty in breach of those principles of fundamental justice is, in a free and democratic society, under the circumstances, a justified reasonable limit to one's rights under s. 7. . . .

I would not want us to be taken by this conclusion as having inferentially decided that absolute liability may not offend s. 7 as long as imprisonment or probation orders are not available as a sentence. The answer to that question is dependent upon the content given to the words "security of the person." That issue was and is a live one . . . [I]n penal law, absolute liability always offends the principles of fundamental justice irrespective of the nature of the offence; it offends s. 7 of the Charter if as a result, anyone is deprived of their life, liberty or security of the person, irrespective of the requirement of public interest. In such cases it might only be salvaged for reasons of public interest under s. 1.

In this latter regard, something might be added. Administrative expediency, absolute liability's main supportive argument, will undoubtedly under s. 1 be invoked and occasionally succeed. Indeed, administrative expediency certainly has its place in administrative law. But when administrative law chooses to call in aid imprisonment through penal law, indeed sometimes criminal law and the added stigma attached to a conviction, exceptional, in my view, will be the case where the liberty or even the security of the person guaranteed under s. 7 should be sacrificed to administrative expediency. Section 1 may, for reasons of administrative expediency, successfully come to the rescue of an otherwise violation of s. 7, but only in cases arising out of exceptional conditions, such as natural disasters, the outbreak of war, epidemics, and the like.

Of course I understand the concern of many as regards corporate offences, specially, as was mentioned by the Court of Appeal, in certain sensitive areas such as the preservation of our vital environment and our natural resources. This concern might well be dispelled were it to be decided, given the proper case, that s. 7 affords protection to human persons only and does not extend to corporations.

Even if it be decided that s. 7 does extend to corporations, I think the balancing under s. 1 of the public interest against the financial interests of a corporation would give very different results from that of balancing public interest and the liberty or security of the person of a human being.

Indeed, the public interest as regards "air and water pollution offences" requires that the guilty be dealt with firmly, but the seriousness of the offence does not in my respectful view support the proposition that the innocent *human* person be open to conviction, quite the contrary. . . .

SECTION 1

Having found that s. 94(2) offends s. 7 of the Charter there remains the question as to whether the appellants have demonstrated that the section is salvaged by the operation of s. 1 of the Charter. No evidence was adduced in the court of Appeal or in this Court. . . .

I do not take issue with the fact that it is highly desirable that "bad drivers" be kept off the road. I do not take issue either with the desirability of punishing severely bad drivers who are in contempt of prohibitions against driving. The bottom line of the question to be addressed here is: whether the Government of British Columbia has demonstrated as justifiable that the risk of imprisonment of a few innocents is, given the desirability of ridding the roads of British Columbia of bad drivers, a reasonable limit in a free and democratic society. That result is to be measured against the offence being one of strict liability open to a defence of due diligence, the success of which does nothing more than let those few who did nothing wrong remain free.

As did the Court of Appeal, I find that this demonstration has not been satisfied, indeed, not in the least.

In the result, I would dismiss the appeal and answer the question in the negative, as did the Court of Appeal, albeit for somewhat different reasons, and declare s. 94(2) of the Motor Vehicle Act, R.S.B.C. 1979, as amended by the Motor Vehicle Amendment Act, 1982, inconsistent with s. 7 of the Canadian Charter of Rights and Freedoms. Having come to this conclusion, I choose as did the Court of Appeal, not to address whether the section violates the rights guaranteed under ss. 11(d) and 12 of the Charter.

McINTYRE, J. wrote a short concurring opinion.

WILSON, J. (concurring): I agree with my colleague, Mr. Justice Lamer, that s. 94(2) of the Motor Vehicle Act violates s. 7 of the Charter and is not saved by s. 1. I reach that result, however, by a somewhat different route.

I start with a consideration of statutory "offences." These are divisible into offences for which *mens rea* is required and those for which it is not. Statutory offences are subject to a presumption in favour of a *mens rea* requirement as a matter of interpretation, but the courts have increasingly come to accept the proposition that legislatures may create non *mens rea* offences provided they make it clear that the *actus reus* itself is prohibited. This is typically so in the case of the so-called "regulatory" or "public welfare" offences. There is no moral delinquency involved in these offences. They are simply designed to regulate conduct in the public interest.

Two questions, therefore, have to be answered on this appeal. The first is do absolute liability offences created by statute *per se* offend the Charter? The second is, assuming they do not, can they be attended by mandatory imprisonment or can such a sanction only be attached to true *mens rea* offences? Certainly, in the absence of the Charter, legislatures are free to create absolute liability offences and to attach to them any sanctions they please. Does s. 7 of the Charter circumscribe their power in this regard?

ABSOLUTE LIABILITY OFFENCES

Section 7 affirms the right to life, liberty and security of the person while at the same time indicating that a person may be deprived of such a right if the deprivation is effected "in accordance with the principles of fundamental justice." I do not view the latter part of the section as a qualification on the right to life, liberty and security of the person in the sense that it limits or modifies that right or defines its parameters. Its purpose seems to me to be the very opposite, namely to protect the right against deprivation or impairment unless such deprivation of impairment is effected in accordance with the principles of fundamental justice.

Section 7 does not, however, affirm a right to the principles of fundamental justice *per se*. There must first be found an impairment of the right to life, liberty or security of the person. It must then be determined whether that impairment has been effected in accordance with the principles of fundamental justice. If it has, it passes the threshold test in s. 7 itself but the Court must go on to consider whether it can be sustained under s. 1 as a limit prescribed by law on the s. 7 right which is both reasonable and justified in a free and democratic society. If, however, the limit on the s. 7 right has been effected through a violation of the principles of fundamental justice, the enquiry, in my view, ends there and the limit cannot be sustained under s. 1. I say this because I do not believe that a limit on the s. 7 right which has been imposed in violation of the principles of fundamental justice can be either "reasonable" or "demonstrably justified in a free and democratic society." . . .

Assuming that I am correct in my analysis of s. 7 and its relationship to s. 1, an absolute liability offence cannot violate s. 7 unless it impairs the right to life, liberty or security of the person. It cannot violate s. 7 because it offends the principles of fundamental justice because they are not protected by s. 7 absent an impairment of the s. 7 right. Leaving aside for the moment the mandatory imprisonment sanction, I cannot find an interference with life, liberty or security of the person in s. 94 of the Motor Vehicle Act. It is true that the section prevents citizens from driving their vehicles when their licenses are suspended. Citizens are also prevented from driving on the wrong side of the road. Indeed, all regulatory offences impose some restriction on liberty broadly construed. But I think it would trivialize the Charter to sweep all those offences into s. 7 as violations of the right to life, liberty and security of the person even if they can be sustained under s. 1. It would be my view, therefore, that absolute liability offences of this type do not *per se* offend s. 7 of the Charter.

ABSOLUTE LIABILITY PLUS MANDATORY IMPRISONMENT

The real question, as I see it, is whether s. 7 of the Charter is violated by the attachment of a mandatory imprisonment sanction to an absolute liability offence. Clearly a s. 7 right is interfered with here in that a person convicted of such an offence automatically loses his liberty. . . . Given that we can have statutory non *mens rea* offences, what is repugnant to fundamental justice in imprisoning someone for their commission? . . . I believe we must turn to the theory of punishment for the answer.

PUNISHMENT AND FUNDAMENTAL JUSTICE

It is now generally accepted among penologists that there are five main objectives of a penal system: see Nigal Walker, *Sentencing in a Rational Society*, 1969. They are 1) to protect offenders and suspected offenders against unofficial retaliation; 2) to reduce the incidence of crime; 3) to ensure that offenders atone for their offences; 4) to keep punishment to the minimum necessary to achieve the objectives of the system; and 5) to express society's abhorrence of crime. Apart from death, imprisonment is the most severe sentence imposed by the law and is generally viewed as a last resort i.e., as appropriate only when it can be shown that no other sanction can achieve the objectives of the system.

The Law Reform Commission of Canada in its Working Paper 11 - Imprisonment and Release (*Studies on Imprisonment*, 1976) states at p. 10: "Justice requires that the sanction of imprisonment not be disproportionate to the offence, and humanity dictates that it must not be heavier than necessary to achieve its objective." Because of the absolute liability nature of the offence created by s. 94(2) of the Motor Vehicle Act a person can be convicted under the section even though he was unaware at the time he was driving that his licence was

suspended and was unable to find this out despite the exercise of due diligence. While the legislature may as a matter of government policy make this an offence, and we cannot question its wisdom in this regard, the question is whether it can make it mandatory for the courts to deprive a person convicted of it of his liberty without violating s. 7. This, in turn, depends on whether attaching a mandatory term of imprisonment to an absolute liability offence such as this violates the principles of fundamental justice. I believe that it does. I think the conscience of the court would be shocked and the administration of justice brought into disrepute by such an unreasonable and extravagant penalty. It is totally disproportionate to the offence and quite incompatible with the objective of a penal system referred to in paragraph (4) above.

It is basic to any theory of punishment that the sentence imposed bear some relationship to the offence; it must be a "fit" sentence proportionate to the seriousness of the offence. Only if this is so can the public be satisfied that the offender "deserved" the punishment he received and feel a confidence in the fairness and rationality of the system. This is not to say that there is an inherently appropriate relationship between a particular offence and its punishment but rather that there is a scale of offences and punishments into which the particular offence and punishment must fit. Obviously this cannot be done with mathematical precision and many different factors will go into the assessment of the seriousness of a particular offence for purposes of determining the appropriate punishment but it does provide a workable conventional framework for sentencing. Indeed, judges in the exercise of their sentencing discretion have been employing such a scale for over a hundred years.

I believe that a mandatory term of imprisonment for an offence committed unknowingly and unwittingly and after the exercise of due diligence is grossly excessive and inhumane. It is not required to reduce the incidence of the offence. It is beyond anything required to satisfy the needs for ''atonement.'' And society, in my opinion, would not be abhorred by an unintentional and unknowing violation of the section. I believe, therefore, that such a sanction offends the principles of funda-mental justice embodied in our penal system. Section 94(2) is accordingly inconsistent with s. 7 of the Charter and must, to the extent of the inconsistency, be declared of no force and effect under s. 52.

46. The Queen *v*. Oakes, *1986*

~ The Charter will "judicialize politics and politicize the judiciary" in part because interpretive controversies over the meaning of vaguely formulated rights are political as well as legal controversies, with policy consequences extending well beyond the confines of the particular case. Giving concrete meaning to broad constitutional standards, however, does not exhaust the political aspects of the judicial task. If a right, having been defined, is found to be violated, the court must ask whether the violation is saved by section 1 of the Charter, which permits such "reasonable limits prescribed by law as are demonstrably justified in a free and democratic society." This question makes the political nature of Charter jurisprudence even more transparent; it is clearly not a traditionally legal question, as the Supreme Court has itself admitted.[1] Despite the ritual judicial denial of the claim that constitutional review involves second-guessing the wisdom of legislative choices, many observers think that this is precisely what section 1 requires.

In the *Oakes* case, the Supreme Court attempts a comprehensive articulation of the standards it will use in addressing the section 1 question. The case involved a "reverse onus" provision in the Narcotic Control Act, under which someone found guilty of "possession" was deemed also to be guilty of "trafficking" unless he could prove otherwise. Having been found guilty of the first charge, Oakes claimed that the reverse onus violated his section 11(d) right to be presumed innocent (of trafficking) until proven guilty. The Court agreed, and thereby set aside the established interpretation of a similar guarantee of the presumption of innocence in the Canadian Bill of Rights. The fact that there might be a "rational connection" between the "basic fact" (possession) and the "presumed fact" (trafficking) was considered irrelevant to establishing the violation because "a basic fact may rationally tend to prove a presumed fact, but not prove its existence beyond a reasonable doubt," as required in criminal cases. Justice Dickson was careful to add, however, that such a rational connection could be used as part of a section 1 defence.

To establish a section 1 defence, the onus is on the state to demonstrate to a "very high degree of probability" that the Charter violation is justified by a "pressing and substantial" objective, and that the means used are "proportional" to that objective. Proportional means have three characteristics: 1) they are not arbitrary and thus actually achieve the objective, 2) they impair the right as little as possible, and 3) their costs are proportional to their benefits—i.e. "the more severe the deleterious effects, the more [pressing and substantial] the objective must be."

The Court readily conceded that controlling drug trafficking was a sufficiently compelling purpose to justify a violation of Charter rights. The means, however, were not proportional to this end because the reverse onus applied to

---

[1] See Justice Estey's remarks on the novelty of section one in *Skapinker*, case 40 above.

all cases of possession and there was no "rational connection" between trafficking and possession of small quantities of illegal drugs.

The Court's deference regarding the objective of the policy characterizes all subsequent forays by the Court into section 1 analysis.[2] This is perhaps not surprising. Challenging the very purpose of a policy would most obviously place the Court in a naked political confrontation with the legislature. If the Court accepts the purpose of the law, on the other hand, and limits its scrutiny to the means chosen to achieve that purpose, it might be easier to sustain the claim that it is not second-guessing the wisdom of legislative policy.[3] In *Oakes*, for example, the Court's judgment may be read as saying no more than that the legislature had been somewhat insensitive or careless in determining how to achieve its legitimate end. Indeed, having conceded the legitimacy of *some* violation of Charter rights to control trafficking, the Court implied that more carefully tailored and hence less intrusive means were possible—perhaps a reverse onus that applied only to possession of sufficently "large" quantities.

As subsequent cases will show,[4] however, the Court cannot consistently hide the political nature of section 1 jurisprudence by concentrating on the question of means. To reject legislative means, it must compare them, more or less explicitly, to "better" alternatives. But political controversy is as often about means as it is about ends, and the legislative choice of means may be carefully deliberated rather than careless. In such cases, some will consider the judicial evaluation of alternative means to be no less a matter of second-guessing policy wisdom than is the evaluation of objectives. ~

THE QUEEN *v*. DAVID EDWIN OAKES
In the Supreme Court of Canada. [1986] 1 S.C.R. 103.

The judgment of Dickson, Chouinard, Lamer, Wilson and Le Dain JJ. was delivered by

DICKSON C.J.C.: This appeal concerns the constitutionality of s. 8 of the Narcotic Control Act, R.S.C. 1970, c. N-1. The section provides, in brief, that if the Court finds the accused in possession of a narcotic, he is presumed to be in possession for the purpose of trafficking. Unless the accused can establish the contrary, he must be convicted of trafficking. The

Ontario Court of Appeal held that this provision constitutes a "reverse onus" clause and is unconstitutional because it violates one of the core values of our criminal justice system, the presumption of innocence, now entrenched in s. 11(d) of the Canadian Charter of Rights and Freedoms. The Crown has appealed. . . .

The respondent, David Edwin Oakes, was charged with unlawful possession of a narcotic for the purpose of trafficking, contrary to s. 4(2) of the Narcotic Control Act. At trial, the Crown adduced evidence

---

[2] See, for example, *Edwards Books* and the *Alberta Labour Reference*, cases 48 and 49 below.

[3] See Patrick Monahan, *Politics and the Constitution: The Charter, Federalism and the Supreme Court of Canada* (Toronto: Carswell/Methuen, 1987), 67-68.

[4] See, for example, *Edwards Books*, case 48 below.

to establish that Mr. Oakes was found in possession of eight one gram vials of *cannabis* resin in the form of hashish oil. Upon a further search conducted at the police station, $619.45 was located. Mr. Oakes told the police that he had bought ten vials of hashish oil for $150 for his own use, and that the $619.45 was from a workers' compensation cheque. He elected not to call evidence as to possession of the narcotic. Pursuant to the procedural provisions of s. 8 of the Narcotic Control Act, the trial judge proceeded to make a finding that it was beyond a reasonable doubt that Mr. Oakes was in possession of the narcotic.

Following this finding, Mr. Oakes brought a motion to challenge the constitutional validity of s. 8 of the Narcotic Control Act, which he maintained imposes a burden on an accused to prove that he or she was not in possession for the purpose of trafficking. He argued that s. 8 violates the presumption of innocence in s. 11(d) of the Charter. . . .

Before examining the presumption of innocence contained in s. 11(d) of the Charter, it is necessary to clarify the meaning of s. 8 of the Narcotic Control Act. The procedural steps contemplated by s. 8 were clearly outlined by Branca J.A. in *R. v. Babcock and Auld.*

~ Justice Branca observed that the trial of an accused charged with trafficking was divided into parts. First, the trial "proceeds as if it was a prosecution . . . on a simple charge of possession," with the burden of proof resting with the crown. Second, if simple possession is proven, the onus shifts to the accused to prove that he was not in possession for purposes of trafficking. ~

I conclude that s. 8 of the Narcotic Control Act contains a reverse onus provision imposing a legal burden on an accused to prove on a balance of probabilities that he or she was not in possession of a narcotic for the purpose of trafficking. It is therefore necessary to determine whether s. 8 of the Narcotic

Control Act offends the right to be "presumed innocent until proven guilty" as guaranteed by s. 11(d) of the Charter. . . .

To interpret the meaning of s. 11(d), it is important to adopt a purposive approach. . . .

To identify the underlying purpose of the Charter right in question . . . it is important to begin by understanding the cardinal values it embodies.

The presumption of innocence is a hallowed principle lying at the very heart of criminal law. Although protected expressly in s. 11(d) of the Charter, the presumption of innocence is referable and integral to the general protection of life, liberty and security of the person contained in s. 7 of the Charter (see Reference re s. 92(2) of the Motor Vehicle Act . . .). The presumption of innocence protects the fundamental liberty and human dignity of any and every person accused by the State of criminal conduct. An individual charged with a criminal offence faces grave social and personal consequences, including potential loss of physical liberty, subjection to social stigma and ostracism from the community, as well as other social, psychological and economic harms. In light of the gravity of these consequences, the presumption of innocence is crucial. It ensures that until the State proves an accused's guilt beyond all reasonable doubt, he or she is innocent. This is essential in a society committed to fairness and social justice. The presumption of innocence confirms our faith in humankind; it reflects our belief that individuals are decent and law-abiding members of the community until proven otherwise.

The presumption of innocence has enjoyed longstanding recognition at common law. In the leading case, *Woolmington* v. *Director of Public Prosecution*, [1935], Viscount Sankey wrote:

Throughout the web of the English Criminal Law one golden thread is always to be seen, that it is the duty of the pros-

ecution to prove the prisoner's guilt subject to what I have already said as to the defence of insanity and subject also to any statutory exception. If, at the end of and on the whole of the case, there is a reasonable doubt, created by the evidence given by either the prosecution or the prisoner, as to whether the prisoner killed the deceased with a malicious intention, the prosecution has not made out the case and the prisoner is entitled to an acquittal. No matter what the charge or where the trial, the principle that the prosecution must prove the guilt of the prisoner is part of the common law of England and no attempt to whittle it down can be entertained. . . .

In light of the above, the right to be presumed innocent until proven guilty requires that s. 11(d) have, at a minimum, the following content. First, an individual must be proven guilty beyond a reasonable doubt. Second, it is the State which must bear the burden of proof. . . . Third, criminal prosecutions must be carried out in accordance with lawful procedures and fairness. The latter part of s. 11(d), which requires the proof of guilt "according to law in a fair and public hearing by an independent and impartial tribunal," underlines the importance of this procedural requirement.

Having considered the general meaning of the presumption of innocence, it is now, I think, desirable to review briefly the authorities on reverse onus clauses in Canada and other jurisdictions.

Section 2(f) of the Canadian Bill of Rights, which safeguards the presumption of innocence, provides:

No law of Canada shall be construed or applied so as to . . . (f) deprive a person charged with a criminal offence of the right to be presumed innocent until proven guilty according to law in a fair and public hearing by an independent and impartial tribunal.

The wording of this section closely parallels that of s. 11(d). For this reason, one of the Crown's primary contentions is that the Canadian Bill of Rights jurisprudence should be determinative of the outcome of the present appeal.

The leading case decided under s. 2(f) of the Canadian Bill of Rights and relied on by the Crown, is *R. v. Appleby.* In that case, the accused had challenged s. 224A(1)(a) (now s. 237(1)(a)) of the Criminal Code, R.S.C. 1970, c. C-24, which imposes a burden upon an accused to prove that he or she, though occupying the driver's seat, did not enter the vehicle for the purpose of setting it in motion and did not, therefore, have care and control. This Court rejected the arguments of the accused that s. 2(f) had been violated; it relied on the *Woolmington* case which held that the presumption of innocence was subject to "statutory exceptions". As Ritchie J. stated in his judgment for the majority at pp. 315-316:

It seems to me, therefore, that if Woolmington's *case is to be accepted, the words "presumed innocent until proven guilty according to law . . ." as they appear in s. 2(f) of the Bill of Rights, must be taken to envisage a law which recognizes the existence of statutory exceptions reversing the onus of proof with respect to one or more ingredients of an offence in cases where certain specific facts have been proved by the Crown in relation to such ingredients.*

Although there are important lessons to be learned from the Canadian Bill of Rights jurisprudence, it does not constitute binding authority in relation to the constitutional interpretation of the Charter. As this Court held in *R. v. Big M Drug Mart Ltd., supra,* the Charter, as a constitutional document, is fundamentally different from the statutory Canadian Bill of Rights, which was interpreted as simply recognizing and declaring existing rights. (See also *Singh, et al. v. Minister of Employment and Immigration,* [1985] 1 S.C.R. 177 *per* Wilson J.: *R. v. Therens,* [1985] 1 S.C.R. 613, *per* Le Dain J.). . . .

With this in mind, one cannot but question the appropriateness of reading into the phrase "according to law" in s. 11(d) of the Charter the statutory exceptions acknowledged in *Woolmington* and in *Appleby*. The *Woolmington* case was decided in the context of a legal system with no constitutionally entrenched human rights document. In Canada, we have tempered parliamentary supremacy by entrenching important rights and freedoms in the Constitution. Viscount Sankey's statutory exception proviso is clearly not applicable in this context and would subvert the very purpose of the entrenchment of the presumption of innocence in the Charter. I do not, therefore, feel constrained in this case by the interpretation of s. 2(f) of the Canadian Bill of Rights presented in the majority judgment in *Appleby*. Section 8 of the Narcotic Control Act is not rendered constitutionally valid simply by virtue of the fact that it is a statutory provision. . . .

As we have seen, the potential for a rational connection between the basic fact and the presumed fact to justify a reverse onus provision has been elaborated in some of the cases discussed above and is now known as the "rational connection test." In the context of s. 11(d), however, the following question arises: if we apply the rational connection test to the consideration of whether s. 11(d) has been violated, are we adequately protecting the constitutional principle of the presumption of innocence? . . . A basic fact may rationally tend to prove a presumed fact, but not prove its existence beyond a reasonable doubt. An accused person could thereby be convicted despite the presence of a reasonable doubt. This would violate the presumption of innocence.

I should add that this questioning of the constitutionality of the "rational connection test" as a guide to interpreting s. 11(d) does not minimize its importance. The appropriate stage for invoking the rational connection test, however, is under s. 1 of the Charter. This consideration did not arise under the Canadian Bill of Rights because of the absence of an equivalent to s. 1. At the Court of Appeal level in the present case, Martin J.A.

sought to combine the analysis of s. 11(d) and s. 1 to overcome the limitations of the Canadian Bill of Rights jurisprudence. To my mind, it is highly desirable to keep s. 1 and s. 11(d) analytically distinct. Separating the analysis into two components is consistent with the approach this Court has taken to the Charter to date.

To return to s. 8 of the Narcotic Control Act, I am in no doubt whatsoever that it violates s. 11(d) of the Charter by requiring the accused to prove on a balance of probabilities that he was not in possession of the narcotic for the purpose of trafficking. Mr. Oakes is compelled by s. 8 to prove he is *not* guilty of the offence of trafficking. He is thus denied his right to be presumed innocent and subjected to the potential penalty of life imprisonment unless he can rebut the presumption. This is radically and fundamentally inconsistent with the societal values of human dignity and liberty which we espouse, and is directly contrary to the presumption of innocence enshrined in s. 11(d). Let us turn now to s. 1 of the Charter. . . .

It is important to observe at the outset that s. 1 has two functions: first, it constitutionally guarantees the rights and freedoms set out in the provisions which follow; and, second, it states explicitly the exclusive justificatory criteria (outside of s. 33 of the Constitution Act, 1982) against which limitations on those rights and freedoms must be measured. Accordingly, any s. 1 inquiry must be premised on an understanding that the impugned limit violates constitutional rights and freedoms—rights and freedoms which are part of the supreme law of Canada. . . .

A second contextual element of interpretation of s. 1 is provided by the words "free and democratic society." Inclusion of these words as the final standard of justification for limits on rights and freedoms refers the Court to the very purpose for which the Charter was originally entrenched in the Constitution: Canadian society is to be free and democratic. The Court must be guided by the values and principles essential to a free and democratic society which I believe embody, to name but a few, respect for the inherent dignity of the human person, commitment to social justice and equality, accommodation of a wide variety of beliefs, respect for cultural and group identity, and faith in social and political institutions which enhance the participation of individuals and groups in society. The underlying values and principles of a free and democratic society are the genesis for the rights and freedoms guaranteed by the Charter and the ultimate standard against which a limit on a right or freedom must be shown, despite its effect, to be reasonable and demonstrably justified.

The rights and freedoms guaranteed by the Charter are not, however, absolute. It may become necessary to limit rights and freedoms in circumstances where their exercise would be inimical to the realization of collective goals of fundamental importance. For this reason, s. 1 provides criteria of justification for limits on the rights and freedoms guaranteed by the Charter. These criteria impose a stringent standard of justification, especially when understood in terms of the two contextual considerations discussed above, namely, the violation of a constitutionally guaranteed right or freedom and the fundamental principles of a free and democratic society.

The onus of proving that a limit on a right or freedom guaranteed by the Charter is reasonable and demonstrably justified in a free and democratic society rests upon the party seeking to uphold the limitation. It is clear from the text of s. 1 that limits on the rights and freedoms enumerated in the Charter are exceptions to their general guarantee. The presumption is that the rights and freedoms are guaranteed unless the party invoking s. 1 can bring itself within the exceptional criteria which justify their being limited. This is further substantiated by the use of the word "demonstrably" which clearly indicates that the onus of justification is on the party seeking to limit. . . .

The standard of proof under s. 1 is the civil standard, namely, proof by a preponderance of probability. The alternative criminal standard, proof beyond a reasonable doubt, would, in my view, be unduly onerous on the party seeking to limit. Concepts such as "reasonableness," "justifiability" and "free and democratic society" are simply not amenable to such a standard. Nevertheless, the preponderance of probability test must be applied rigorously. Indeed, the phrase "demonstrably justified" in s. 1 of the Charter supports this conclusion. Within the broad category of the civil standard, there exist different degrees of probability depending on the nature of the case. . . .

Having regard to the fact that s. 1 is being invoked for the purpose of justifying a violation of the constitutional rights and freedoms the Charter was designed to protect, a very high degree of probability will be, in the words of Lord Denning, "commensurate with the occasion." Where evidence is required in order to prove the constituent elements of a s. 1 inquiry, and this will generally be the case, it should be cogent and persuasive and make clear to the Court the consequences of imposing or not imposing the limit. . . . A court will also need to know what alternative measures for implementing the objective were available to the legislators when they made their decisions. I should add, however, that there may be cases where certain elements of the s. 1 analysis are obvious or self-evident.

To establish that a limit is reasonable and demonstrably justified in a free and democratic society, two central criteria must be satisfied. First, the objective, which the measures responsible for a limit on a Charter right or freedom are designed to serve, must be "of sufficient importance to warrant overriding a constitutionally protected right or freedom": *R.* v. *Big M Drug Mart Ltd.* The standard must be high in order to ensure that objectives which are trivial or discordant with the principles integral to a free and democratic society do not gain s. 1 protection. It is necessary, at a minimum, that an objective relate to concerns which are pressing and substantial in a free and democratic society before it can be characterized as sufficiently important.

Second, once a sufficiently significant objective is recognized, then the party invoking s. 1 must show that the means chosen are reasonable and demonstrably justified. This involves "a form of proportionality test": *R. v. Big M Drug Mart Ltd, supra.* Although the nature of the proportionality test will vary depending on the circumstances, in each case courts will be required to balance the interests of society with those of individuals and groups. There are, in my view, three important components of a proportionality test. First, the measures adopted must be carefully designed to achieve the objective in question. They must not be arbitrary, unfair or based on irrational considerations. In short, they must be rationally connected to the objective. Second, the means, even if rationally connected to the objective in this first sense, should impair "as little as possible" the right or freedom in question: *R. v. Big M Drug Mart Ltd.* Third, there must be a proportionality between the *effects* of the measures which are responsible for limiting the Charter right or freedom, and the objective which has been identified as of "sufficient importance."

With respect to the third component, it is clear that the general effect of any measure impugned under s. 1 will be the infringement of a right or freedom guaranteed by the Charter; this is the reason why resort to s. 1 is necessary. The inquiry into effects must, however, go further. A wide range of rights and freedoms are guaranteed by the Charter, and an almost infinite number of factual situations may arise in respect of these. Some limits on rights and freedoms protected by the Charter will be more serious than others in terms of the nature of the right or freedom violated, the extent of the violation, and the degree to which the measures which impose the limit trench upon the integral principles of a free and democratic society. Even if an objective is of sufficient importance, and the first two elements of the proportionality test are

satisfied, it is still possible that, because of the severity of the deleterious effects of a measure on individuals or groups, the measure will not be justified by the purposes it is intended to serve. The more severe the deleterious effects of a measure, the more important the objective must be if the measure is to be reasonable and demonstrably justified in a free and democratic society.

Having outlined the general principles of a s. 1 inquiry, we must apply them to s. 8 of the Narcotic Control Act. Is the reverse onus provision in s. 8 a reasonable limit on the right to be presumed innocent until proven guilty beyond a reasonable doubt as can be demonstrably justified in a free and democratic society?

The starting point for formulating a response to this question is, as stated above, the nature of Parliament's interest or objective which accounts for the passage of s. 8 of the Narcotic Control Act. According to the Crown, s. 8 of the Narcotic Control Act is aimed at curbing drug trafficking by facilitating the conviction of drug traffickers. In my opinion, Parliament's concern with decreasing drug trafficking can be characterized as substantial and pressing. The problem of drug trafficking has been increasing since the 1950s at which time there was already considerable concern. . . . Throughout this period, numerous measures were adopted by free and democratic societies, at both the international and national levels.

The objective of protecting our society from the grave ills associated with drug trafficking, is, in my view, one of sufficient importance to warrant overriding a constitutionally protected right or freedom in certain cases. Moreover, the degree of seriousness of drug trafficking makes its acknowledgement as a sufficiently important objective for the purposes of s. 1, to a large extent, self-evident. The first criterion of a s. 1 inquiry, therefore, has been satisfied by the Crown.

The next stage of inquiry is a consideration of the means chosen by Parliament to achieve its objective. The means must be reasonable and demonstrably justified in a free and democratic society. As outlined above, this proportionality test should begin with a consideration of the rationality of the provision: is the reverse onus clause in s. 8 rationally related to the objective of curbing drug trafficking? At a minimum, this requires that s. 8 be internally rational; there must be a rational connection between the basic fact of possession and the presumed fact of possession for the purpose of trafficking. Otherwise, the reverse onus clause could give rise to unjustified and erroneous convictions for drug trafficking of persons guilty only of possession of narcotics.

In my view, s. 8 does not survive this rational connection test. As Martin J.A. of the Ontario Court of Appeal concluded, possession of a small or negligible quantity of narcotics does not support the inference of trafficking. In other words, it would be irrational to infer that a person had an intent to traffic on the basis of his or her possession of a very small quantity of narcotics. The presumption required under s. 8 of the Narcotic Control Act is overinclusive and could lead to results in certain cases which would defy both rationality and fairness. In light of the seriousness of the offence in question, which carries with it the possibility of imprisonment for life, I am further convinced that the first component of the proportionality test has not been satisfied by the Crown.

Having concluded that s. 8 does not satisfy this first component of proportionality, it is unnecessary to consider the other two components. . . .

~ Estey and McIntyre JJ. concurred in the reasons of Dickson C.J.C. with respect to the relationship of s. 11(d) and s. 1 of the Charter but adopted the reasons of Martin J.A. in the court below for the disposition of all other issues. ~

47. Retail, Wholesale and Department Store Union v. Dolphin Delivery, *1986*

~ The Charter raises questions concerning not only the meaning of its various rights but also the scope of their application. Such questions are raised particularly by section 52, which applies the Charter to "any law of Canada," and section 32, which applies it to "the Parliament and government of Canada" and "the legislature and government of each province." The latter section would appear to limit the Charter's applicability to what the Americans in similar circumstances call "state action." On this interpretation, which the Court accepts in the *Dolphin Delivery* case, the Charter would not apply to purely private violation of Charter rights, such as racial discrimination by private landlords against tenants. The problem is that private action often relies on "state action" of some sort. Private contracts, for example, depend for their efficacy on the law of contracts, which is enforced by agencies of the state. *Dolphin Delivery* addresses the question of whether and to what extent private activity becomes subject to the Charter when it relies on state action.

The question arose out of a labour dispute between Purolator Courier and the union representing its employees, both "private" parties. On strike against Purolator, the union also wanted to picket Dolphin Delivery, a company to which Purolator sub-contracted some of its Vancouver-area business. The union claimed that Purolator was avoiding the strike by continuing, indirectly, to give business to Dolphin. Dolphin prevented this "secondary picketing" by successfully applying for an injunction based on the common law tort of inducing a breach of contract. Contracts would have been breached to the extent that employees of Dolphin, who were not legally on strike, honoured the picket line. The Court found that picketing was a form of "expression" within the meaning of the Charter's section 2(b) guarantee of "freedom of expression." Thus one of the parties in a private dispute had relied on a court order to limit the other party's freedom of expression. Was there a sufficient degree of "government" action within the meaning of section 32 to bring the Charter into effect? Because the court order was based on the common law, the case also raised the question of whether the common law was included in the term "law" in section 52.

Justice McIntyre interprets the term "government" in section 32 narrowly. In his view, it refers only to the executive, not to the courts. When the executive violation of a Charter right is authorized by law, he continues, the law itself is subject to the Charter, and this is true whether it is legislation or common law. Thus, in answer to the section 52 question, the Charter applies to common law, at least when it forms the basis of executive action.

The two kinds of law fare differently, however, when they form the basis of private action. In such circumstances, legislation is covered because it is the act of the legislature, one of the entities specified by section 32. As an example of legislation authorizing the private violation of Charter rights, Justice McIntyre refers to section 19(2) of the *Ontario Human Rights Code*, which exempts private sports from a general prohibition of sex discrimination. Common law, on the other hand, is not the act of either a "government" or a "legislature"; thus, when private actors rely on the common law to violate a Charter right, no section 32 entity is involved and the Charter does not apply. Nor does a court order enforcing the common law in private litigation represent the requisite state action because, again, courts are not part of the "government." Justice McIntyre concedes that it "is probably acceptable" for political scientists "to treat the courts as one of the three fundamental branches of Government," but declines to treat a court order as governmental action "for the purposes of Charter application." To do so, he argues, would "widen the scope of Charter application to virtually all private litigation."[1]

This judgment means that the Charter would have applied had the restriction on picketing in this case been based on legislation rather than on the common law. In *obiter*, however, Justice McIntyre suggests (with Justice Wilson objecting to his mode of analysis) that such legislation would be saved by section 1. ~

RETAIL, WHOLESALE AND DEPARTMENT STORE UNION v. DOLPHIN DELIVERY LTD.
In the Supreme Court of Canada. [1986] 2 S.C.R. 573.

The judgment of Dickson C.J.C., Estey, McIntyre, Chouinard and Le Dain JJ. was delivered by

McINTYRE J.: This appeal raises the question of whether secondary picketing by members of a trade union in a labour dispute is a protected activity under s. 2(b) of the Canadian Charter of Rights and Freedoms and, accordingly, not the proper subject of an injunction to restrain it. In reaching the answer, consideration must be given to the application of the Charter to the common law and as well to its application in private litigation.

The respondent, Dolphin Delivery Ltd. ("Dolphin"), is a company engaged in the courier business in Vancouver and the surrounding area. Its employees are represented by a trade union, not the appellant. A collective agreement is in effect between Dolphin and the union represent-

ing its employees, which provides in clause 8: "it shall not be a violation of this agreement or cause for discipline or discharge if an employee refuses to cross a picket line which has been established in full compliance with the British Columbia Labour Code." The appellant trade union is the bargaining agent under a federal certification for the employees of Purolator Courier Incorporated ("Purolator"). That company has a principal place of operations in Ontario but, prior to the month of June, 1981 when it locked out its employees in a labour dispute, it had a place of operations in Vancouver. That dispute is as yet unresolved. Prior to the lock-out, Dolphin did business with Purolator making deliveries within its area for Purolator. Since the lock-out, Dolphin has done business in a similar manner with another company, known as Supercourier Ltd. ("Supercourier"), which is

---

This decision provoked one of the toughest criticism's the Supreme Court has received for its interpretation of the Charter—see David Beatty, "Constitutional Conceits: The Coercive Authority of Courts," (1987) 37 *University of Toronto Law Journal*, 183.

incorporated in Ontario. There is a connection between Supercourier and Purolator, the exact particulars of which are not clearly established in the evidence, but it appears that Dolphin carries on in roughly the same manner with Supercourier as it had formerly done with Purolator and about twenty per cent of its total volume of business originates with Supercourier. This about the same percentage of business as was done with Purolator before the lock-out.

In October of 1982 the appellant applied to the British Columbia Labour Relations Board for a declaration that Dolphin and Supercourier were allies of Purolator in their dispute with the appellant. A declaration to this effect would have rendered lawful the picketing of the place of business of Dolphin under British Columbia legislation. The Board, however, declined to make the declaration sought, on the basis that it had no jurisdiction because the union's collective bargaining relationship with Purolator and any picketing which might be done was governed by the Canada Labour Code, R.S.C. 1970, c. L-1. In the face of this finding it became common ground between the parties that where the Labour Code of British Columbia, R.S.B.C. 1979, c. 212, does not apply, the legality of picketing falls for determination under the common law because the Canada Labour Code is silent on the question. In November of 1982 the individual appellants, on behalf of the appellant union, advised Dolphin that its place of business in Vancouver would be picketed unless it agreed to cease doing business with Supercourier. An application was made at once for a *quia timet* injunction to restrain the threatened picketing. No picketing occurred, the application being made before its commencement.

The matter came before Sheppard L.J.S.C. and on November 30 he granted the injunction. . . .

The task of the Court in dealing with this case is made difficult by the way it developed in the courts below. The application for the injunction was made before any picketing occurred. The evidence was limited to affidavits, and some cross-examination upon them. Findings of fact on the crucial question of the nature of the apprehended picketing are limited. Ordinarily, the Court would not entertain constitutional questions without a more secure factual basis upon which to rest the argument. Because of the nature of this case, however, the Court has felt obliged to do so. I refer below to the findings of fact and to certain assumptions upon which the Court's judgment will rest. . . .

Hutcheon J.A. in the Court of Appeal also seems to have recognized the difficulty regarding the factual underpinning. He said [at p. 484]:

The interim injunction was granted before any picketing took place. The proper assumptions to be made are that the picketing would be peaceful, that some employees of Dolphin Delivery and other trade union members of customers would not cross the picket line, and that the daily business of Dolphin Delivery would be disrupted to a considerable extent.

These assumptions are reasonable and I adopt them. In summary then, it has been found that the respondent was a third party, that the anticipated picketing would be tortious, that the purpose was to injure the plaintiff. It was assumed that the picketing would be peaceful, that some employees of the respondent and other trade union members of customers would decline to cross the picket lines, and that the business of the respondent would be disrupted to a considerable extent. . . .

FREEDOM OF EXPRESSION

As has been noted above, the only basis on which the picketing in question was defended by the appellants was under the provisions of s. 2(b) of the Charter which guarantees the freedom of expression as a fundamental freedom. Freedom of expression is not, however, a creature of the Charter. It is one of the fundamental concepts that has formed the basis for the historical development of the political, social and educational institutions of western society. Representative democracy, as we know it today, which is in great part the product of free expression and discussion of varying ideas, depends upon its maintenance and protection.

The importance of freedom of expression has been recognized since early times: see John Milton, *Areopagitica; A Speech for the Liberty of Unlicenc'd Printing, to the Parliament of England* (1644), and as well John Stuart Mill, "On Liberty" in *On Liberty and Considerations on Representative Government* (Oxford, 1946), at p. 14:

If all mankind minus one were of one opinion, and only one person were of the contrary opinion, mankind would be no more justified in silencing that one person, than he, if he had the power, would be justified in silencing mankind.

And, after stating that "All silencing of discussion is an assumption of infallibility," he said, at p. 16:

Yet it is as evident in itself, as any amount of argument can make it, that ages are no more infallible than individuals; every age having held many opinions which subsequent ages have deemed not only false but absurd; and it is as certain that many opinions now general will be rejected by future ages, as it is that many, once general, are rejected by the present.

Nothing in the vast literature on this subject reduces the importance of Mill's words. The principle of freedom of speech and expression has been firmly accepted as a necessary feature of modern democracy. The courts have recognized this fact. For an American example, see the words of Holmes J. in his dissent in *Abrams* v. *United States*, 250 U.S. 616 (1919), at p. 630:

Persecution for the expression of opinions seems to me perfectly logical. If you have no doubt of your premises or your power and want a certain result with all your heart you naturally express your wishes in law and sweep away all opposition. . . . But when men have realized that time has upset many fighting faiths, they may come to believe even more than they believe the very foundations of their own conduct that the ultimate good desired is better reached by free trade in ideas—that the best test of truth is the power of the thought to get itself accepted in the competition of the market, and that truth is the only ground upon which their wishes safely can be carried out.

Prior to the adoption of the Charter, freedom of speech and expression had been recognized as an essential feature of Canadian parliamentary democracy. Indeed, this Court may be said to have given it constitutional status. In *Boucher* v. *The King*, [1951] S.C.R. 265, Rand J., who formed a part of the majority which narrowed the scope of the crime of sedition, said, at p. 288:

There is no modern authority which holds that the mere effect of tending to create discontent or disaffection among His Majesty's subjects or ill-will or hostility between groups of them, but not tending to issue in illegal conduct, constitutes the crime, and this for obvious reasons. Freedom in thought and speech and disagreement in ideas and beliefs, on every conceivable subject, are of the essence of our life. The clash of critical discussion on political, social and religious subjects has too deeply become the stuff of daily experience to suggest that mere ill-will as a product of controversy can strike down the latter with illegality. A superficial examination of the word shows its insufficiency: what is the degree necessary to criminality? Can it ever, as mere subjective condition, be so? Controversial fury is aroused constantly by differences in abstract conceptions; heresy in some fields is again a mortal sin; there can be fanatical puritanism in ideas as well as in morals; but our compact of free society accepts and absorbs these differences and they are exercised at large within the framework of freedom

and order on broader and deeper unifor-
mities as bases of social stability. Sim-
ilarly in discontent, affection and
hostility: as subjective incidents of con-
troversy, they and the ideas which arouse
them are part of our living which
ultimately serve us in stimulation, in the
clarification of thought and, as we
believe, in the search for the constitution
and truth of things generally.

~ Justice McIntyre then reviewed the discussions of freedom of speech in the Alberta Press Case and in *Switzman* v. *Elbling.* ~

The Charter has now in s. 2(b) declared freedom of expression to be a fundamental freedom and any questions as to its constitutional status have therefore been settled.

The question now arises: Is freedom of expression involved in this case? In seeking an answer to this question, it must be observed at once that in any form of picketing there is involved at least some element of expression. The picketers would be conveying a message which at the very minimum would be classified as persuasion, aimed at deterring customers and prospective customers from doing business with the respondent. The question then arises. Does this expression in the circumstances of this case have Charter protection under the provisions of s. 2(b), and if it does, then does the injunction abridge or infringe such freedom?

The appellants argue strongly that picketing is a form of expression fully entitled to Charter protection and rely on various authorities to support the proposition, including Reference re Alberta Statutes, *supra*; *Switzman* v. *Elbling, supra,* the American cases of *Thornhill* v. *Alabama,* 310 U.S. 88 (1940) (*per* Murphy J., at p. 95); *Milk Wagon Drivers Union* v. *Meadowmoor Dairies,* 312 U.S. 298 (1941), (*per* Black J., at p. 302), and various other Canadian authorities. They reject the American distinction between the concept of speech and that of conduct made in picketing cases, and they accept the view of Hutcheon J.A. in the Court of

Appeal, in adopting the words of Freedman C.J.M. in *Channel Seven Television Ltd.* v. *National Association of Broadcast Employees and Technicians,* [1971] 5 W.W.R. 328, that ''Peaceful picketing falls within freedom of speech.''

The respondent contends for a narrower approach to the concept of freedom of expression. The position is summarized in the respondent's factum:

4. We submit that constitutional protection under section 2(b) should only be given to those forms of expression that warrant such protection. To do otherwise would trivialize freedom of expression generally and lead to a downgrading or dilution of this freedom.

Reliance is placed on the view of the majority in the Court of Appeal that picketing in a labour dispute is more than mere communication of information. It is also a signal to trade unionists not to cross the picket line. The respect accorded to picket lines by trade unionists is such that the result of the picketing would be to damage seriously the operation of the employer, not to communicate any information. Therefore, it is argued, since the picket line was not intended to promote dialogue or discourse (as would be the case where its purpose was the exercise of freedom of expression), it cannot qualify for protection under the Charter.

On the basis of the finding of fact that I have referred to above, it is evident that the purpose of the picketing in this case was to induce a breach of contract between the respondent and Supercourier and thus to exert economic pressure to force it to cease doing business with Supercourier. It is equally evident that, if successful, the picketing would have done serious injury to the respondent. There is nothing remarkable about this, however, because all picketing is designed to bring economic pressure on the person picketed and to cause economic loss for so long as the object of the picketing remains unfulfilled. There is, as I have earlier said, always some element of expression in picketing. The union is making a statement to the general public that it is involved in a dispute, that it is seeking to impose its will on the object of the picketing, and that it solicits the assistance of the public in honouring the picket line. Action on the part of the picketers will, of course, always accompany the expression, but not every action on the part of the picketers will be such as to alter the nature of the whole transaction and remove it from Charter protection for freedom of expression. That freedom, of course, would not extend to protect threats of violence or acts of violence. It would not protect the destruction of property, or assaults, or other clearly unlawful conduct. We need not, however, be concerned with such matters here because the picketing would have been peaceful. I am therefore of the view that the picketing sought to be restrained would have involved the exercise of the right of freedom of expression.

SECTION 1 OF THE CHARTER

It is not necessary, in view of the disposition of this appeal that I propose, to deal with the application of s. 1 of the Charter. It was, however, referred to in the Court of Appeal and I will deal with it here. It will be recalled that the Chambers judge in granting the injunction did so on the basis that the picketing involved the commission of two common law torts, that of civil conspiracy to injure and that of inducing a breach of contract. . . . It should be noted that in British Columbia the common law tort of conspiracy to injure, as employed in labour disputes, has been abolished by statute and it would not be available as a support for an injunction. I am aware that the labour relations of the appellants are governed by the Canada Labour Code. However, since the Canada Labour Code is silent on the question of picketing, the common law applies, in this case the common law of British Columbia from which the tort of conspiracy has been expunged in labour disputes. In my view then the tort of civil conspiracy to injure may not be relied upon to support the injunction, which therefore must find its sole support from

the tort of inducing a breach of contract.

The question then is: Can an injunction based on the common law tort of inducing a breach of contract, which has the effect of limiting the Charter right to freedom of expression, be sustained as a reasonable limit imposed by law in the peculiar facts of this case. . . . Ordinarily, some evidence will be necessary to enable the Court to decide whether s. 1 should be applied to preserve a limitation on a right, and the burden of proof will lie upon the party supporting the limitation. Dickson C.J. in the *Oakes* case, however, at p. 138, remarked concerning the need for evidence:

I should add, however, that there may be cases where certain elements of the s. 1 analysis are obvious or self-evident.

This, in my view, is such a case in so far as the need for evidence is concerned. The evidence before the Chambers judge, together with the assumptions and findings referred to above, provide a sufficient basis for the consideration of this question.

From the evidence, it may well be said that the concern of the respondent is pressing and substantial. It will suffer economically in the absence of an injunction to restrain picketing. On the other hand, the injunction has imposed a limitation upon a Charter freedom. A balance between the two competing concerns must be found. It may be argued that the concern of the respondent regarding economic loss would not be sufficient to constitute a reasonable limitation on the right of freedom of expression, but there is another basis upon which the respondent's position may be supported. This case involves secondary picketing—picketing of a third party not concerned in the dispute which underlies the picketing. The basis of our system of collective bargaining is the proposition that the parties themselves should, wherever possible, work out their own agreement. . . . When the parties do exercise the right to disagree, picketing and other forms of industrial conflict are likely to follow. The social cost is great, man-hours and wages are lost, production and services will be disrupted, and general tensions within the community may be heightened. Such industrial conflict may be tolerated by society but only as an inevitable corollary to the collective bargaining process. It is therefore necessary in the general social interest that picketing be regulated and sometimes limited. It is reasonable to restrain picketing so that the conflict will not escalate beyond the actual parties. While picketing is, no doubt, a legislative weapon to be employed in a labour dispute by the employees against their employer, it should not be permitted to harm others. . . .

It should be noted here that in the Province of British Columbia, secondary picketing of the nature involved in this case, save for the picketing of allies of the employer, has been made unlawful by the combined effect of ss. 85(3) and 88 of the British Columbia Labour Code, R.S.B.C. 1979, c. 212, as amended. This statute, of course, does not apply in this case, but it is indicative of the legislative policy in respect of the regulation of picketing in that Province. It shows that the application of s. 1 of the Charter to sustain the limitation imposed by the common law would be consistent with legislative policy in British Columbia. I would say that the requirement of proportionality is also met, particularly when it is recalled that this is an interim injunction effective only until trial when the issues may be more fully canvassed on fuller evidence. It is my opinion then that a limitation on secondary picketing against a third party, that is, a non-ally, would be a reasonable limit in the facts of this case. I would therefore conclude that the injunction is "a reasonable limit prescribed by law which can be demonstrably justified in a free and democratic society."

DOES THE CHARTER APPLY TO THE COMMON LAW?

In my view, there can be no doubt that it does apply. . . . The English text [of s. 52(1) of the Constitution Act] provides that "any law that is inconsistent with the provisions of the Constitution is, to the extent of the inconsistency, of no force or effect." If this language is not broad enough to include the common law, it should be observed as well that the French text adds strong support to this conclusion in its employment of the words "*elle rend inopérantes les dispositions incompatibles de tout autre règle de droit*." (Emphasis added.) To adopt a construction of s. 52(1) which would exclude from Charter application the whole body of the common law which in great part governs the rights and obligations of the individuals in society, would be wholly unrealistic and contrary to the clear language employed in s. 52(1) of the Act.

DOES THE CHARTER APPLY TO PRIVATE LITIGATION?

This question involves consideration of whether or not an individual may found a cause of action or defence against another individual on the basis of a breach of a Charter right. In other words, does the Charter apply to private litigation divorced completely from any connection with Government? This is a subject of controversy in legal circles and the question has not been dealt with in this Court. One view of the matter rests on the proposition that the Charter, like most written constitutions, was set up to regulate the relationship between the individual and the Government. It was intended to restrain government action and to protect the individual. It was not intended in the absence of some governmental action to be applied in private litigation. . . .

I am in agreement with the view that the Charter does not apply to private litigation. It is evident from the authorities and articles cited above that that approach has been adopted by most judges and commentators who have dealt with this question. In my view, s. 32 of the Charter, specifically dealing with the question of Charter application, is conclusive on this issue. . . . Section 32(1) refers to the Parliament and Government of Canada and to the legislatures and governments of the

Provinces in respect of all matters within their respective authorities. In this, it may be seen that Parliament and the Legislatures are treated as separate or specific branches of government, distinct from the executive branch of government, and therefore where the word 'government' is used in s. 32 it refers not to government in its generic sense—meaning the whole of the governmental apparatus of the state—but to a branch of government. The word 'government' following as it does the words 'Parliament' and 'Legislature,' must then, it would seem, refer to the executive or administrative branch of government. This is the sense in which one generally speaks of the Government of Canada or of a province. I am of the opinion that the word 'government' is used in s. 32 of the Charter in the sense of the executive government of Canada and the Provinces. This is the sense in which the words 'Government of Canada' are ordinarily employed in other sections of the Constitution Act, 1867. Sections 12, 16, and 132 all refer to the Parliament and the Government of Canada as separate entities. The words 'Government of Canada,' particularly where they follow a reference to the word 'Parliament,' almost always refer to the executive government.

It is my view that s. 32 of the Charter specifies the actors to whom the Charter will apply. They are the legislative, executive and administrative branches of government. It will apply to those branches of government whether or not their action is invoked in public or private litigation. It would seem that legislation is the only way in which a legislature may infringe a guaranteed right or freedom. Action by the executive or administrative branches of government will generally depend upon legislation, that is, statutory authority. Such action may also depend, however, on the common law, as in the case of the prerogative. To the extent that it relies on statutory authority which constitutes or results in an infringement of a guaranteed right or freedom, the Charter will apply and it will be unconstitutional.

The action will also be unconstitutional to the extent that it relies for authority or justification on a rule of the common law which constitutes or creates an infringement of a Charter right or freedom. In this way the Charter will apply to the common law, whether in public or private litigation. It will apply to the common law, however, only in so far as the common law is the basis of some governmental action which, it is alleged, infringes a guaranteed right or freedom.

The element of governmental intervention necessary to make the Charter applicable in an otherwise private action is difficult to define. We have concluded that the Charter applies to the common law but not between private parties. The problem here is that this is an action between private parties in which the appellant resists the common law claim of the respondent on the basis of a Charter infringement. The argument is made that the common law, which is itself subject to the Charter, creates the tort of civil conspiracy and that of inducing a breach of contract. The respondent has sued and has procured the injunction which has enjoined the picketing on the basis of the commission of these torts. The appellants say the injunction infringes their Charter right of freedom of expression under s. 2(b). Professor Hogg meets this problem when he suggests, at p. 677 of his text, after concluding that the Charter does not apply to private litigation, that:

Private action is, however, a residual category from which it is necessary to subtract those kinds of action to which s. 32 does make the Charter applicable.

He added:

The Charter will apply to any rule of the common law that specifically authorizes or directs an abridgement of a guaranteed right.

and he concluded by saying, at p. 678:

The fact that a court order is governmental action means that the Charter will apply to a purely private arrangement, such as a contract or proprietary interest, but only to the extent that the Charter will preclude judicial enforcement of any arrangement in derogation of a guaranteed right.

Professor Hogg, at p. 678, rationalized his position in these words:

In a sense, the common law authorizes any private action that is not prohibited by a positive rule of law. If the Charter applied to the common law in that attenuated sense, it would apply to all private activity. But it seems more reasonable to say that the common law offends the Charter only when it crystallizes into a rule that can be enforced by the courts. Then, if an enforcement order would infringe a Charter right, the Charter will apply to preclude the order, and, by necessary implication, to modify the common law rule.

I find the position thus adopted troublesome and, in my view, it should not be accepted as an approach to this problem. While in political science terms it is probably acceptable to treat the courts as one of the three fundamental branches of Government, that is, legislative, executive, and judicial, I cannot equate for the purposes of Charter application the order of a court with an element of governmental action. This is not to say that the courts are not bound by the Charter. The courts are, of course, bound by the Charter as they are bound by all law. It is their duty to apply the law, but in doing so they act as neutral arbiters, not as contending parties involved in a dispute. To regard a court order an an element of governmental intervention necessary to invoke the Charter would, it seems to me, widen the scope of Charter application to virtually all private litigation. All cases must end, if carried to completion, with an enforcement order and if the Charter precludes the making of the order, where a Charter right would be infringed, it would seem that all private litigation would be subject to the Charter. In my view, this approach will not provide the answer to the ques-

tion. A more direct and a more precisely-defined connection between the element of government action and the claim advanced must be present before the Charter applies.

An example of such a direct and close connection is to be found in Re Blainey and Ontario Hockey Association, *supra*. In that case, proceedings were brought against the hockey association in the Supreme Court of Ontario on behalf of a twelve year old girl who had been refused permission to play hockey as a member of a boys' team competing under the auspices of the Association. A complaint against the exclusion of the girl on the basis of her sex alone had been made under the provisions of the Human Rights Code, 1981, S.O. 1981, c. 53, to the Ontario Human Rights Commission. It was argued that the hockey association provided a service ordinarily available to members of the public without discrimination because of sex, and therefore that the discrimination against the girl contravened this legislation. The Commission considered that it could not act in the matter because of the provisions of s. 19(2) of the Human Rights Code, which are set out hereunder:

19.—(1) . . .
(2) The right under section 1 to equal treatment with respect to services and facilities is not infringed where membership in an athletic organization or participation in an athletic activity is restricted to persons of the same sex.

In the Supreme Court of Ontario it was claimed that s. 19(2) of the Human Rights Code was contrary to s. 15(1) of the Charter and that it was accordingly void. The application was dismissed. In the Court of Appeal, the appeal was allowed (Dubin, Morden JJ.A., Finlayson J.A. dissenting). Dubin J.A., writing for the majority, stated the issue in these terms at [D.L.R., p. 735]:

Indeed it was on the premise that the ruling of the Ontario Human Rights Commission was correct that these proceed-

ings were launched and which afforded the status to the applicant to complain now that, by reason of s. 19(2) of the Human Rights Code she is being denied the equal protection and equal benefit of the Human Rights Code by reason of her sex, contrary to the provisions of s. 15(1) of the Canadian Charter of Rights and Freedoms (the "Charter").

He concluded that the provisions of s. 19(2) were in contradiction of the Charter and hence of no force or effect. In the *Blainey* case, a law suit between private parties, the Charter was applied because one of the parties acted on the authority of a statute, i.e., s. 19(2) of the Ontario Human Rights Code, which infringed the Charter rights of another. *Blainey* then affords an illustration of the manner in which Charter rights of private individuals may be enforced and protected by the courts, that is, by measuring legislation—government action—against the Charter.

As has been noted above, it is difficult and probably dangerous to attempt to define with narrow precision that element of governmental intervention which will suffice to permit reliance on the Charter by private litigants in private litigation. Professor Hogg has dealt with this question, at p. 677, *supra*, where he said:

. . . the Charter would apply to a private person exercising the power of arrest that is granted to "any one" by the Criminal Code, and to a private railway company exercising the power to make by-laws (and impose penalties for their breach) that is granted to a "railway company" by the Railway Act; all action taken in exercise of a statutory power is covered by the Charter by virtue of the references to "Parliament" and "legislature" in s. 32. The Charter would also apply to the action of a commercial corporation that was an agent of the Crown, by virtue of the reference to "government" in s. 32.

It would also seem that the Charter would apply to many forms of delegated legislation, regulations, orders in council,

possibly municipal by-laws, and by-laws and regulations of other creatures of Parliament and the Legislatures. It is not suggested that this list is exhaustive. Where such exercise of, or reliance upon, governmental action is present and where one private party invokes or relies upon it to produce an infringement of the Charter rights of another, the Charter will be applicable. Where, however, private party "A" sues private party "B" relying on the common law and where no act of government is relied upon to support the action, the Charter will not apply. I should make it clear, however, that this is a distinct issue from the question whether the judiciary ought to apply and develop the principles of the common law in a manner consistent with the fundamental values enshrined in the Constitution. The answer to this question must be in the affirmative. In this sense, then, the Charter is far from irrelevant to private litigants whose disputes fall to be decided at common law. But this is different from the proposition that one private party owes a constitutional duty to another, which proposition underlies the purported assertion of Charter causes of action or Charter defences between individuals.

Can it be said in the case at bar that the required element of government intervention or intrusion may be found? In *Blainey*, s. 19(2) of the Ontario Human Rights Code, an Act of a legislature, was the factor which removed the case from the private sphere. If in our case one could point to a statutory provision specifically outlawing secondary picketing of the nature contemplated by the appellants, the case—assuming for the moment an infringement of the Charter—would be on all fours with *Blainey* and, subject to s. 1 of the Charter, the statutory provisions could be struck down. In neither case, would it be, as Professor Hogg would have it, the order of a court which would remove the case from the private sphere. It would be the result of one party's reliance on a statutory provision violative of the Charter.

In the case at bar, however, we have no

offending statute. We have a rule of the common law which renders secondary picketing tortious and subject to injunctive restraint, on the basis that it induces a breach of contract. While, as we have found, the Charter applies to the common law, we do not have in this litigation between purely private parties any exercise of or reliance upon governmental action which would invoke the Charter. It follows then that the appeal must fail. The appeal is dismissed. The respondent is entitled to its costs. In the circumstances of this case, it becomes unnecessary to answer the constitutional question framed by the Chief Justice on September 5, 1984.

BEETZ J.: I agree with the reasons of the majority in the British Columbia Court of Appeal for holding that in the circumstances and on the evidence of this case, the picketing which has been enjoined would not have been a form of expression and that no question of infringement of s. 2(b) of the Canadian Charter of Rights and Freedoms could accordingly arise. This reason suffices for the dismissal of the appeal with costs.

It is unnecessary for me to express any view on other issues in order to reach this conclusion. However, given the importance of these issues, I wish to state that I otherwise agree with the reasons for judgment written by my brother McIntyre.

WILSON J. (dissenting in part): I agree with the reasons of my colleague, McIntyre J., with the exception of his reasons dealing with the application of s. 1 of the Charter.

The search under s. 1 is, I believe, for the appropriate test to apply when weighing a principle of the common law against a fundamental freedom protected by the Charter. On a s. 1 analysis the purposes and objectives of a piece of impugned legislation are ascertained through an objective approach: see, for example, the

approach taken by this Court in *R.* v. *Big M Drug Mart Ltd.*, [1985] 1 S.C.R. 295 and *R.* v. *Oakes*, [1986] 1 S.C.R. 103. It seems to me that the same objective approach must be taken when weighing a principle of the common law against a fundamental freedom.

There are, as I see it, two distinct questions which must be answered, namely: (1) Does the tort of inducing breach of contract represent a reasonable limit under s. 1 on freedom of expression in the labour relations context? and (2) If the tort does represent a reasonable limit under s. 1, should injunctive relief be granted in this particular case?

The first question requires the application of the objective approach mentioned above. If the tort does not survive the first question then, of course the conduct is not wrongful and no injunction can issue. If, however, it does survive the first question, then the facts of this particular case (including the subjective impact on the employer) must be considered in order to see whether the other requirements for the award of an interlocutory injunction are present, i.e., does the balance of convenience favour the plaintiff? However, even on this question it seems to me that some weight must be given to the freedom of speech of the picketers.

My difficulty with my colleague's approach to s. 1 is twofold. First, he has used the subjective impact on the employer on the first question. It is, on his analysis, the "pressing and substantial concern." And second, he has given no consideration to the origin and historical development of the tort and its role in relation to labour disputes. I would have thought that this was crucial on the s. 1 inquiry. As a consequence the two questions referred to above have been merged into one and no objective criteria for the s. 1 inquiry have been identified.

I nevertheless agree with McIntyre J.'s proposed disposition of the appeal.

48. Edwards Books and Art Ltd. *v.* The Queen, *1986*

~ The *Edwards* case involved a challenge to Ontario's Retail Business Holidays Act, which, like the Federal Lord's Day Act, prohibited Sunday shopping. The judges unanimously concluded, however, that the Ontario Act was not intended to establish a particular religious faith, but had the secular purpose of promoting a common day of rest. If this Act infringed section 2 of the Charter, it was because of its effect, not its purpose.

Ontario's prohibition of Sunday retailing was subject to exceptions for such businesses as corner stores, pharmacies and gas stations, as well as for educational and recreational services. It also included a "Saturday exception," under which relatively small retailers selling goods of any description, whether or not they came within the other exceptions, could open on Sunday if they had closed the previous Saturday. Although it was framed in religiously neutral terms, this exception was clearly intended to accommodate the interests of Saturday sabbatarians, such as Jews and Seventh Day Adventists. It was available, however, only to businesses under a certain size and thus did not cover all businesses operated by Saturday sabbatarians.

The case combined the challenges of four retailers who had been charged under the law's provisions. Three of these retailers did not claim an effect that made it more difficult for them to practice their religion. They argued that the Act forced them to comply with a religious practice they did not subscribe to, that it was their "freedom *from*" religion that was being infringed. The fourth retailer, Nortown Foods, was a kosher store that closed on Saturdays but that was too large to qualify for the Saturday exemption. To obey both the law and the tenets of their faith, Nortown's owners would have to close the store for two days a week, while their Christian or irreligious competitors would close for only one day. Nortown claimed that this competitive disadvantage infringed the freedom "affirmatively to practise one's religious beliefs."

The "freedom-from" argument of the first three retailers was quickly disposed of. "[L]egislation with a secular inspiration," said Justice Dickson, "does not abridge the freedom from conformity to religious dogma merely because statutory provisions coincide with the tenets of a religion." He could not accept, for example, "that a legislative prohibition of criminal conduct such as theft and murder is a state-enforced compulsion to conform to religious practices merely because some religions enjoin their members not to steal or kill."

More contentious was the question whether the Act infringed the affirmative religious freedom of Saturday sabbatarians like Nortown who could not avail themselves of the "Saturday exemption." Justices Beetz and McIntyre found no such infringement because they thought the economic disadvantage suffered by Saturday sabbatarians was caused by their religious conscience, not by the law. The remaining five judges thought that the law contributed to the disadvantage and that it thus had an unconstitutional effect. These judges then asked whether this violation of section 2 was a "reasonable limit" under section one.

Under the test established by *Oakes*, a Charter violation is saved by section 1 if it has a sufficiently compelling purpose and if the means are proportionate to that purpose. As might be expected, the first of these questions raised little controversy.[1] Justice Dickson regarded as simply "self-evident" the desirability of enabling parents to have regular days off from work in common with their child's day off from school, and a day off enjoyed by most other family and community members." He concluded that "the Act is aimed at a pressing and substantial concern." None of the other judges who reached the section 1 question disagreed with this. Serious controversy emerged, however, when the judges turned to the question of proportionate means.

For Justices Dickson and Wilson, proportionate means had to include some attempt to accommodate the religious needs of Saturday sabbatarians, and the important question was whether Ontario's Saturday exemption went far enough in this regard. This involved comparing the exemption to possible alternatives to determine whether more accommodation could be made without unduly undermining the purpose of a common day of rest. For Justice Dickson, Ontario's Saturday exemption emerged unscathed from this comparison; for Justice Wilson, it did not.

Justice La Forest objected to this judicial comparison of alternative legislative schemes. "[A]ttempts to protect the rights of one group," he argued, "will inevitably impose burdens on the rights of other groups. There is no perfect scenario in which the rights of all can be equally protected." He argued that just as Sunday closing imposes disadvantages on retailers who observe a Saturday sabbath, so an exemption for such retailers may impose similar burdens on their Sunday-observing employees. "How," asked Justice La Forest, "is a court able to second-guess the Legislature on such issues?" He added that employers faced with this problem "might seek to avoid infringing other people's religious beliefs by hiring only their co-religionists but this, too, is a result a legislature might not wish to encourage."

Justice La Forest opposed not only the judicial weighing of alternative accommodations, but also the constitutional requirement of accommodation itself. This was because the latter inevitably led to the former. If an exemption was required, the courts would eventually be called on to second guess legislatures on the appropriateness of particular exemptions. Having upheld Ontario's scheme, for example, the courts would have to determine whether Quebec's narrower exemption, "limited as it is to establishments that are operated by no more than three persons at any one time (and then subject to Ministerial approval and conditions), is sufficient to pass constitutional muster?" This would be inappropriate, said Justice La Forest, because "what

---

[1] See introduction to *Oakes*, case 46 above.

may work effectively in one province (or in a part of it) may simply not work in another without unduly interfering with the legislative scheme. And a compromise adopted at a particular time may not be possible at another.'' In other words, everything depended on various and changing circumstances, which the courts were not well equipped to judge and monitor. Thus, while he personally favoured exemptions, Justice La Forest was ''of the view that the nature of the choices and compromises that must be made in relation to Sunday closing are essentially legislative in nature. In the absence of unreasonableness or discrimination, courts are simply not in a position to substitute their judgment for that of the Legislature.''

By contrast, Justice Dickson concluded his review of alternatives by emphasizing ''that it is not the role of this Court to devise legislation that is constitutionally valid, or to pass on the validity of schemes which are not directly before it, or to consider what legislation might be the most desirable. The discussion of alternative legislative schemes that I have undertaken is directed to one end only, that is, to address the issue whether the existing scheme meets the requirements of the second limb of the test for the application of s. 1 of the Charter as set down in *Oakes*.'' He thus rejected Justice La Forest's contention that such evaluation of alternative exemptions is inevitably to second guess the legislature on the question of ''what legislation might be the most desirable.'' It is an illuminating exercise to consider the various alternatives from these opposing perspectives.

Although Justice Dickson adopted a more activist procedure than did Justice La Forest, it should be noted that his application of this procedure showed considerable deference to legislative judgments. For example, among Justice Dickson's reasons for upholding the size limit on the Saturday exemption was the fact that a store over the limit was a ''substantial retail operation,'' and ''not, by any stretch, a mere corner store staffed by the family.'' This meant that the interests of employees in a common day of rest had to be balanced against the religious interests of employers who tend to ''have available to them options flowing from the resources at their disposal which are foreclosed to their employees.'' Justice Dickson concluded that ''in interpreting and applying the Charter . . . the courts must be cautious to ensure that it does not simply become an instrument of better situated individuals to roll back legislation which has as its object the improvement of the condition of less advantaged persons.'' Legislatures were not constitutionally required to strike the balance between the competing interests in favour of the employees, but neither were they constitutionally prohibited from doing so. Justice Dickson's restrained application of an activist rhetoric and methodology typifies the ''moderate activism'' of the Court in this early period of Charter jurisprudence.[2]

---

[2] See Introduction, pp. 11-12.

In the result, the law was upheld in its totality by six of the seven judges. Two of the judges found no violation of section 2, and all of the others agreed that the law satisfied the compelling purpose part of the *Oakes* test. Only Justice Wilson found that the Saturday exemption did not meet the proportionate means test. This high degree of judicial support, however, settled neither the legal nor the political issue. Paul Magder, one of the appellants in the case, lost little time in launching a new challenge under section 15 of the Charter.[3] Shortly thereafter, Ontario's Attorney-General announced that the province would abandon the legislation and leave the issue to the municipalities.[4] ~

EDWARDS BOOKS AND ART LTD. *v.* THE QUEEN
In the Supreme Court of Canada. [1986] 2 S.C.R. 713.

The judgment of Dickson C.J.C., Chouinard and Le Dain JJ. was delivered by

DICKSON C.J.C.: In this appeal the Court is called upon to consider the constitutional validity of Sunday closing legislation enacted by the Province of Ontario *sub nom.* Retail Business Holidays Act, R.S.O. 1980, c. 453. Four Ontario retailers were charged in 1983 with failing to ensure that no goods were sold or offered for sale by retail on a holiday, contrary to s. 2 of the Retail Business Holidays Act. Each of the retailers admits that his store was open for business on a Sunday. In the Ontario Court of Appeal, in a decision reported *sub nom. R.* v. *Videoflicks Ltd. et al.* (1984), 48 O.R. (2d), 395 three of the retailers, the appellants, Edwards Books and Art Ltd., Longo Brothers Fruit Markets Ltd. et al., and Paul Magder, were convicted. In their appeals to this Court they challenge the constitutional validity of the Retail Business Holidays Act. The fourth, the respondent Nortown Foods Ltd., was acquitted. In answer to a Crown appeal, Nortown questions on constitutional grounds the applicability of the Act to its particular business. Nortown Foods

Ltd. asks to be exempted from the Act, saying that otherwise its freedom of religion, or that of its owners, would be violated.

The Attorneys General of each of the provinces except Prince Edward Island have intervened in support of Ontario. The Ontario Conference Corporation of the Seventh-Day Adventist Church lends its voice to that of the retailers. The Attorney General of Canada has intervened to question the manner in which the Ontario Court of Appeal purported to apply s. 52 of the Constitution Act, 1982 to acquit Nortown.

The scheme of the Retail Business Holidays Act is simple. Section 1 defines "holiday" to include Sundays and various other days, including some days which are of special significance to Christian denominations, and some which are clearly secular in nature. . . .

Sections 2 and 7 make it an offence to carry on a retail business on a holiday, punishable by a maximum fine of $10,000. . . .

Sections 3 and 4 contain a diverse array of exceptions. Most "corner store" operations are exempted by subs. 3(1). Pharmacies, gas stations, flower stores, and, during the summer months, fresh fruit and

---

[3] "Ontario furrier wins battle to stay open," *Calgary Herald*, July 24, 1987.
[4] "Ontario to permit Sunday shopping," *Calgary Herald*, December 3, 1987.

vegetable stores or stands are excluded by subss. 3(2) and 3(3). Subsection 3(6) exempts educational, recreational or amusement services. Prepared meals, laundromat services, boat and vehicle rentals and service are permitted under subs. 3(7). Subsection 3(8) and s. 4 allow a municipality to create its own scheme of exemptions where necessary for the promotion of the tourist industry.

A particularly controversial exemption is contained in subs. 3(4). It applies to businesses which, on Sundays, have seven or fewer employees engaged in the service of the public and less than 5,000 square feet used for such service. Its effect is to exempt these businesses from having to close on Sunday if they closed on the previous Saturday:

3(4) Section 2 does not apply in respect of the carrying on of a retail business in a retail business establishment on a Sunday where,

(a) *the retail business establishment was closed to the public and no goods or services were sold or offered for sale therein during a period of twenty-four consecutive hours in the period of thirty-two hours immediately preceding the Sunday; and*

(b) *the number of persons engaged in the service of the public in the establishment on the Sunday does not at any time exceed seven; and*

(c) *the total area used for serving the public or for selling or displaying to the public in the establishment on the Sunday is less than 5,000 square feet.*

~ Justice Dickson then discusses the circumstances that led the four retailers to be charged under the Act. The three appellant retailers, Edward Books and Art Ltd., Longo Brothers Fruit Markets Ltd., and Paul Magder, had been open on a Sunday without having closed on the preceding Saturday. The respondent retailer, Nortown Foods Ltd., was a kosher grocery that closed every Saturday, but that opened on Sundays with more than the

seven employees permitted by s. 3(4) of the Act. ~

THE DISTRIBUTION OF POWERS UNDER ss. 91-92 OF THE CONSTITUTION ACT, 1867

I observe at the outset that counsel for Nortown was prepared to assume that the legislation was *intra vires* the province. Many of the arguments propounded by the appellant retailers in an effort to have this Court declare the Act *ultra vires* would also serve to impugn the legislation for the purposes of s. 2(a) of the Charter. For if the Retail Business Holidays Act were intended by the legislators to promote or prefer certain Christian faiths, it would not only be *ultra vires* but would also be inconsistent with the Charter guarantee of freedom of religion, for the reasons given by this Court in the *Big M Drug Mart* case. . . .

I agree with Mr. Justice Tarnopolsky that the Retail Business Holidays Act was enacted with the intent of providing uniform holidays to retail workers. I am unable to conclude that the Act was a surreptitious attempt to encourage religious worship. The title and text of the Act, the legislative debates and the Ontario Law Reform Commission's Report on Sunday Observance Legislation (1970), all point to the secular purposes underlying the Act. . . .

There was considerable argument regarding the motives of the legislature in enacting subs. 3(4) until Mr. Robinette drew our attention to the Legislative Debates of Ontario for December 17, 1975. The debates clearly indicate that the exemption was inspired by concerns about the effect of the Act on Saturday observers. . . . In any event, the religious purpose of the exemption is plainly revealed by the timing of the exemption to coincide with a Sabbath beginning at sundown on Friday evening. . . .

Never has a majority of this Court held that Parliament (or indeed the provincial legislatures) has exclusive jurisdiction in respect of religion or freedom of religion. The question remains an open one. There are, undoubtedly, religious matters within exclusive federal competence, most notably prohibitions against the profanation of the Sabbath. As I have already observed, however, the characterization of Sabbath observance legislation as criminal law has its roots not in any general or inherent connection between religion and criminal law, but in the history of the specific criminal offence of profaning the Sabbath. In my view there exist religious matters which must similarly fall within provincial competence. Section 92(12) expressly allocates the solemnization of marriages, a class of subjects with important historical or traditional religious dimensions, to the provincial legislatures. Section 93 imposes restrictions on provincial competence with respect to denominational schools which would be unnecessary if religion as a whole were beyond the sphere of provincial jurisdiction. It would seem, therefore, that the Constitution does not contemplate religion as a discrete constitutional "matter" falling exclusively within either a federal or provincial class of subjects. Legislation concerning religion or religious freedom ought to be characterized, I believe, in light of its context, according to the particular religious matter upon which the legislation is focussed. . . .

Applying the above principles to the appeals at bar, it is, in my opinion, open to a provincial legislature to attempt to neutralize or minimize the adverse effects of otherwise valid provincial legislation on human rights such as freedom of religion. All that is achieved by subs. 3(4) of the Retail Business Holidays Act is the subtraction of a duty imposed elsewhere in the Act. Subsection 3(4) cannot be divorced from its context in valid provincial legislation in relation to property and civil rights: an exemption must be read in light of the affirmative provision to which it relates. I might add that it would be a peculiar result indeed if the federal Parliament and not the provincial legislature were the competent body to create exemptions from provincial legislation, whether motivated by religious or other concerns.

Consequently, neither the Act nor the exemption is, in my opinion, *ultra vires* the province. . . .

FREEDOM OF CONSCIENCE AND RELIGION UNDER S. 2(a)

. . . The Court held, in the *Big M Drug Mart* case, at pp. 331-334, that both the purposes and effects of legislation are relevant to determining its constitutionality. Even if a law has a valid purpose, it is still open to a litigant to argue that it interferes by its effects with a right or freedom guaranteed by the Charter. It will therefore be necessary to consider in some detail the impact of the Retail Business Holidays Act. . . .

The first question is whether indirect burdens on religious practice are prohibited by the constitutional guarantee of freedom of religion. In my opinion indirect coercion by the state is comprehended within the evils from which s. 2(a) may afford protection. The Court said as much in the *Big M Drug Mart* case and any more restrictive interpretation would, in my opinion, be inconsistent with the Court's obligation under s. 27 to preserve and enhance the multicultural heritage of Canadians. . . . It matters not, I believe, whether a coercive burden is direct or indirect, intentional or unintentional, foreseeable or unforseeable. All coercive burdens on the exercise of religious beliefs are potentially within the ambit of s. 2(a).

This does not mean, however, that every burden on religious practices is offensive to the constitutional guarantee of freedom of religion. It means only that indirect or unintentional burdens will not be held to be outside the scope of Charter protection on that account alone. Section 2(a) does not require the legislatures to eliminate every miniscule state-imposed cost associated with the practice of religion. Otherwise the Charter would offer protection from innocuous secular legislation such as a taxation act that imposed a modest sales tax extending to all products, including those used in the course of religious worship. In my opinion, it is unnecessary to turn to s. 1 in order to justify legislation of that sort. The purpose of s. 2(a) is to ensure that society does not interfere with profoundly personal beliefs that govern one's perception of oneself, humankind, nature, and, in some cases, a higher or different order of being. These beliefs in turn govern one's conduct and practices. The Constitution shelters individuals and groups only to the extent that religious beliefs or conduct might reasonably or actually be threatened. For a state-imposed cost or burden to be proscribed by s. 2(a) it must be capable of interfering with religious belief or practice. In short, legislative or administrative action which increases the cost of practising or otherwise manifesting religious beliefs is not prohibited if the burden is trivial or insubstantial: see, on this point, *Jones* v. *The Queen*, [1986] 2 S.C.R. 284 *per* Wilson J. at p. 314.

. . . [T]he second form of religious coercion allegedly flowing from the Act. . . . is of a different nature entirely since it involves not the freedom affirmatively to practise one's religious beliefs, but rather the freedom to abstain from the religious practices of others. The Retail Business Holidays Act prevents some retailers from selling their products on Sundays. Longo Brothers submits that these effects are identical to those which flow from any other form of Sunday closing legislation, including the Lord's Day Act, and submits that the Act thereby requires retailers to conform to the religious practices of dominant Christian sects.

In *Big M Drug Mart* this Court acknowledged that freedom of conscience and religion included the freedom to express and manifest religious non-belief and the freedom to refuse to participate in religious practice: p. 346. These freedoms, which may compendiously be referred to as the freedom from conformity to religious dogma, are governed by somewhat different considerations than the freedom to manifest one's own religious beliefs. Religious freedom is inevitably abridged by legislation which

has the effect of impeding conduct integral to the practice of a person's religion. But it is not necessarily impaired by legislation which requires conduct consistent with the religious beliefs of another person. One is not being compelled to engage in religious practices merely because a statutory obligation coincides with the dictates of a particular religion. I cannot accept, for example, that a legislative prohibition of criminal conduct such as theft and murder is a state-enforced compulsion to conform to religious practices, merely because some religions enjoin their members not to steal or kill. Reasonable citizens do not perceive the legislation as requiring them to pay homage to religious doctrine. . . .

The majority judgment of the Court in *Big M Drug Mart* was careful, in defining the freedom from conformity to religious dogma, to restrict its applicability to circumstances when the impugned legislation was motivated by a religious purpose. . . .

In my view, legislation with a secular inspiration does not abridge the freedom from conformity to religious dogma merely because statutory provisions coincide with the tenets of a religion. I leave open the possibility, however, that such legislation might limit the freedom of conscience and religion of persons whose conduct is governed by an intention to express or manifest his or her non-conformity with religious doctrine. None of the retail stores involved in the present appeals has established that it was open on Sunday for any purpose other than to make money. Accordingly, there is no evidentiary foundation to substantiate the contention of some of the retailers that their freedom from conforming to religious doctrine has been abridged. . . .

It therefore remains only to consider the impact of the Act with a view to determining whether it significantly impinges on the freedom to manifest or practise religious beliefs.

The Act has a different impact on persons with different religious beliefs. Four classes of persons might be differently affected: those not observing any religious day of rest, those observing Sundays, those observing Saturdays and those observing some other day of the week. . . .

~ Chief Justice Dickson decides that the effect on non-observing retailers is "generally secular in nature," that the Act "has a favourable impact on Sunday observers," and that the Court has too little evidence about those observing days other than Saturday or Sunday to decide that issue. He then turns to the question of Saturday observers. ~

The Attorney General of Ontario submits that any disability suffered by Saturday-observing retailers is a consequence of their religious beliefs, and not of the Act. . . . Professor Petter expressed the argument thusly in his critique of the Ontario Court of Appeal's decision in the present cases, "Not 'Never on a Sunday': R. v. Videoflicks Ltd. et al.," (1984), 49 Sask. L.R. 96 at 99:

It is not the legislation which causes the financial burden; it is the religion itself. Consider the following example. Suppose that all Sunday closing legislation, provincial and federal, were repealed tomorrow. Would the repeal of this legislation eliminate the financial burden suffered by persons who observe a Friday or Saturday Sabbath? Clearly it would not: while persons who do not observe a Sabbath would be able to open their stores seven days a week, persons who observe a Friday or Saturday Sabbath would be able to open their stores only six days a week. What is the cause of this burden? Clearly the cause is the religious requirement that one abstain from work on one's Sabbath. To suggest otherwise would be to imply a positive obligation upon the state to protect persons from any economic hardship which might arise as a result of their religious practices. Yet this is an untenable position which goes far beyond even the broad definition of freedom of religion adopted by the Court of Appeal. It would mean that if just one

person could demonstrate that her sincere religious beliefs required her to close her store for five days each week, the state would be required to compel all others to close their stores for five days each week.

Professor Petter then explains that the true effect of the Act is only to confer a benefit on Sunday observers.

In view of the characteristics of the retail industry described in the Report on Sunday Observance Legislation, I find myself unable to draw such a neat distinction between benefits accruing to Sunday-observing retailers and burdens imposed on Saturday observers. The Report refers on numerous occasions to the highly competitive nature of the retail industry, such that an increase in sales by one individual retailer occasioned by that retailer's marketing practices tends to result in significant decreases in the sales of other retailers. It follows that if the Act confers an advantage on Sunday-observing retailers relative to Saturday-observing retailers, the latter are burdened by the legislation.

A careful comparison of the effects of Sunday closing legislation on different religious groups clearly demonstrates the manner in which the burden flows from the legislation. In the absence of legislative intervention, the Saturday observer and the Sunday observer would be on a roughly equal footing in competing for shares of the available consumer buying power. Both might operate for a maximum of six days each week. Both would be disadvantaged relative to non-observing retailers who would have the option of a seven day week. On this account, however, they would have no complaint cognizable in law since the disability would be one flowing exclusively from their religious tenets: I agree with Professor Petter that the state is normally under no duty under s. 2(a) to take affirmative action to eliminate the natural costs of religious practices. But, exemptions aside, the Retail Business Holidays Act has the effect of leaving the Saturday observer at the same natural disadvantage relative to the non-observer and adding the new, purely statutory disadvantage of being closed an extra day relative to the Sunday observer. Just as the Act makes it less costly for Sunday observers to practise their religious beliefs, it thereby makes it more expensive for some Jewish and Seventh Day Adventist retailers to practise theirs.

It is apparent from the above analysis that the competitive disadvantage experienced by non-exempt Saturday-observing retailers as a result of the Act is at the hands of Sunday-observing retailers. The *Report on Sunday Observance Legislation*, at p. 269, refers to persons attending church on Sundays as "a substantial minority of the population." On the only evidence before the Court, I therefore do not think that the competitive pressure on non-exempt retailers to abandon the observance of a Saturday Sabbath can be characterized as insubstantial or trivial. It follows that their freedom of religion is abridged by the Act.

It is important to recognize, however, that not all Saturday-observing retailers are detrimentally affected. The Act is not merely neutral in its impact on those Jewish and Seventh Day Adventist retailers who can practically comply with the employee and square-footage limits of subs. 3(4). It confers a benefit by placing them on a roughly equal competitive footing with non-observing retailers, who, in the absence of legislative intervention, would be free to transact business seven days per week. The effect of the Act, far from producing a systematic discriminatory burden on all retailers of a particular faith, is to benefit some while burdening others.

Finally, I note that the Act also imposes a burden on Saturday-observing consumers. For single parent families or two-parent families with both spouses working from Monday to Friday, the weekend is a time to do the things one did not have time to do during the week. The Act does not impair the ability of Sunday-observers to go shopping or seek professional services on Saturdays, but it does circumscribe that of the Saturday-observer on Sundays. Although there is no evidence before the Court of the degree to which shopping variety is restricted on Sundays I am prepared to assume for the purposes of these appeals that the burden on Saturday-observing consumers is substantial and constitutes an abridgment of their religious freedom. I note that the burden may be particularly onerous on Jewish consumers who rely on retailers such as Nortown Foods Ltd. to supply them with foodstuffs that conform to religious dietary laws, although, once again, I must observe that there is no evidence regarding the degree to which Kosher foods can be purchased from smaller retailers on Sundays. . . .

SECTION 1 OF THE CHARTER

The reasons of the majority of this Court in *The Queen* v. *Oakes*, [1986] 1 S.C.R. 103, summarized and expanded upon the earlier cases (*Law Society of Upper Canada* v. *Skapinker*, [1984] 1 S.C.R. 357, *Hunter* v. *Southam Inc.*, [1984] 2 S.C.R. 145, *Singh* v. *Minister of Employment and Immigration*, [1985] 1 S.C.R. 177, *R.* v. *Big M Drug Mart Ltd.*) in respect of the criteria which must be addressed by the proponent of a limitation on a right or freedom guaranteed by the Charter. It has been held that the onus of proof is on the party seeking the limitation, and the standard of proof is the civil standard, proof by a preponderance of probabilities.

Two requirements must be satisfied to establish that a limit is reasonable and demonstrably justified in a free and democratic society. First, the legislative objective which the limitation is designed to promote must be of sufficient importance to warrant overriding a constitutional right. It must bear on a "pressing and substantial concern." Second, the means chosen to attain those objectives must be proportional or appropriate to the ends. The proportionality requirement, in turn, normally has three aspects: the limiting measures must be carefully designed, or rationally connected, to the objective;

they must impair the right as little as possible; and their effects must not so severely trench on individual or group rights that the legislative objective, albeit important, is nevertheless outweighed by the abridgment of rights. The Court stated that the nature of the proportionality test would vary depending on the circumstances. Both in articulating the standard of proof and in describing the criteria comprising the proportionality requirement the Court has been careful to avoid rigid and inflexible standards.

In the present appeals, the only evidence available to the Court which relates to s. 1 of the Charter is the Report on Sunday Observance Legislation (1970). . . .

I am conscious of the possibility that some of the statistical evidence contained in the Report has been rendered less helpful by the passage of time. Nevertheless, it is the only evidence before the Court and I have considered the age of the materials in assessing its weight. . . .

A family visit to an uncle or a grandmother, the attendance of a parent at a child's sports tournament, a picnic, a swim, or a hike in the park on a summer day, or a family expedition to a zoo, circus, or exhibition—these, and hundreds of other leisure activities with family and friends are amongst the simplest but most profound joys that any of us can know. The aim of protecting workers, families and communities from a diminution of opportunity to experience the fulfilment offered by these activities, and from the alienation of the individual from his or her closest social bonds, is not one which I regard as unimportant or trivial. In the context of the "fast-growing trend toward wide-scale store openings" (Report, p. 267), I am satisfied that the Act is aimed at a pressing and substantial concern. It therefore survives the first part of the inquiry under s. 1.

The requirement of rational connection calls for an assessment of how well the legislative garment has been tailored to suit its purpose. In the context of the Retail Business Holidays Act two questions are raised. First, is it acceptable for the legislature to have focused exclusively on the retail industry? Second, is the scheme of exemptions within the Act, as between types of retail business, justifiable?

I have already referred to the perception of the Law Reform Commission that the retail industry presented a particularly pressing problem. It was in this industry that the Report told of competitive pressures forcing individual operators to extend their hours of business, largely against their wishes. The Report also documented the characteristics of the retail trade's labour force, including its low level of unionization, its high proportion of women, and its generally heterogeneous composition: p. 103. The Commission's conclusion that this labour force was especially vulnerable to subtle and overt pressure from its employers amply justified on the evidence the legislature's decision to single out the retail industry for special and immediate attention.

The exemptions for various types of business are also justifiable. The Report describes at pp. 271-272 the tensions between the two objectives of protecting as many employees as possible from having to work on Sundays and providing a "quality environment" permitting the fulfillment of family and community recreational pursuits:

For the most part, these two secular objectives are consistent with each other, i.e., to engage in leisure pursuits with family and friends on the pause day, a person must be free from work. Where the two conflict, however, is in respect of leisure activities which require substantial employment of people on the pause day in order to make leisure facilities available. Professional sports, libraries and symphony concerts are three cases in point. If we were to propose that the sole objective of Sunday laws was to free persons from work on that day, then this well might deprive thousands of people of any leisure activities whatsoever on Sundays.

With the exception of subs. 3(4), the

exemptions in ss. 3 and 4 closely parallel the recommendations of the Report. . . . I might add that in regulating industry or business it is open to the legislature to restrict its legislative reforms to sectors in which there appear to be particularly urgent concerns or to constituencies that seem especially needy. . . . In drafting its statute, the legislature can, if it wishes, create categories of retail business which are exempted, even though some unexempted businesses may sell some of the same products. Legislative choices regarding alternative forms of business regulation do not generally impinge on the values and provisions of the Charter of Rights, and the resultant legislation need not be tuned with great precision in order to withstand judicial scrutiny. Simplicity and administrative convenience are legitimate concerns for the drafters of such legislation.

A more difficult question—and one which goes to the heart of this litigation—is whether the Retail Business Holidays Act abridges the freedom of religion of Saturday observers as little as is reasonably possible. Subsection 3(4) has the effect, and was intended to have the effect, of very substantially reducing the impact of the Act on those religious groups for whom Saturday is a Sabbath. What must be decided, however, is whether there is some reasonable alternative scheme which would allow the province to achieve its objective with fewer detrimental effects on religious freedom.

One suggestion was that the objective of protecting workers from involuntary Sunday labour could be achieved by legislation which focused on the employee rather than the employer. There could, for example, be an enactment conferring on workers a right to refuse Sunday work. But such a scheme would in my view fall far short of achieving the objectives of the Retail Business Holidays Act. It would fail to recognize the subtle coercive pressure which an employer can exert on an employee. The vulnerability of retail employees makes them an improbable

group to resist such pressures. A scheme which requires an employee to assert his or her rights before a tribunal in order to obtain a Sunday holiday is an inadequate substitute for the regime selected by the Ontario legislature. Also a bilateral decision of individual retailers and employees to stay open and work on Sunday would pressure others to a similar decision and would, as the Report observes at p. 267, place increased demands on ancillary services required to keep the stores open, such as wholesalers, truckers and public transportation.

The other alternative would be to retain the basic format of the Retail Business Holidays Act, but to replace subs. 3(4) with a complete exemption from s. 2 for those retailers who have a sincerely held religious belief requiring them to close their stores on a day other than Sunday. The Province of New Brunswick has such an exemption in subs. 7(1) of its Days of Rest Act, S.N.B. 1985, c. D-4.2. The New Brunswick exemption is administered by a Board which is authorized to issue permits exempting [observers of days other than Sundays].

Such an exemption has advantages and disadvantages relative to subs. 3(4) of the Ontario Act. From the perspective of the Saturday-observing consumer the New Brunswick exemption is more beneficial than Ontario's in including within its ambit large stores with more than 7 employees or 5,000 square feet of floor space, but less beneficial in the restriction of its availability to retailers with a specified religious or conscientous belief. I am unable to say whether one scheme results in a greater availability of Sunday shopping services to the Jewish or Seventh-Day Adventist consumer than the other. In this context, I note that the Report on Sunday Observance Legislation (1970) at p. 98, Table V, discloses that only 8.1% of retail stores had 10 or more employees at the time of the previous Census in 1961. Since, subject to the square footage requirement, the exemption in subs. 3(4) is available to any store provided that at any given time on Sunday the number of persons engaged in serving the public is fewer than eight, it appears that a very substantial variety of products, including specialty products such as Kosher foods, is available to Sunday shoppers, even if the proportion of large stores were to have doubled since 1961.

The most difficult questions stem from the different impacts of these exemptions on Saturday-observing retailers. It is interesting to consider how the United States Supreme Court dealt with some of the same issues in its 1961 quartet of Sunday closing cases. I repeat that the legislation before that Court in *Braunfeld* v. *Brown* contained no exemption clause of any kind aimed at alleviating its deleterious impact on Saturday observing retailers. Nevertheless, the majority upheld the legislation. Chief Justice Warren considered, at pp. 608-09, whether a Sabbatarian exemption ought to have been provided:

A number of States provide such an exemption, and this may well be the wiser solution to the problem. But our concern is not with the wisdom of legislation but with its constitutional limitation. Thus, reason and experience teach that to permit the exemption might well undermine the State's goal of providing a day that, as best possible, eliminates the atmosphere of commercial noise and activity. Although not dispositive of the issue, enforcement problems would be more difficult since there would be two or more days to police rather than one and it would be more difficult to observe whether violations were occurring.

Additional problems might also be presented by a regulation of this sort. To allow only people who rest on a day other than Sunday to keep their businesses open on that day might well provide these people with an economic advantage over their competitors who must remain closed on that day; this might cause the Sunday observers to complain that their religions are being discriminated against. With this competitive advantage existing, there could well be the temptation for some, in

order to keep their businesses open on Sunday, to assert that they have religious convictions which compel them to close their businesses on what had formerly been their least profitable day. This might make necessary a state-conducted inquiry into the sincerity of the individual's religious beliefs, a practice which a State might believe would itself run afoul of the spirit of constitutionally protected religious guarantees. Finally, in order to keep the disruption of the day at a minimum, exempted employers would probably have to hire employees who themselves qualified for the exemption because of their own religious beliefs, a practice which a State might feel to be opposed to its general policy prohibiting religious discrimination in hiring. For all of these reasons, we cannot say that the Pennsylvania statute before us is invalid, either on its face or as applied.

. . . In my view, the enforcement problems which might be created by a full Sabbatarian exemption do not constitute a sufficiently compelling reason to reject it as an alternative to the Ontario scheme. Nor do I see merit to the contention that a Sabbatarian exemption would discriminate against retailers who do not observe Saturday as a religious day of rest. There is no evidence before this Court to suggest that Sunday is generally a preferable day for retailers to do business. Undoubtedly, some retailers selling particular products in particular areas would find Sundays more profitable than Saturdays, but other retailers would find the converse to be true. In the absence of convincing evidence to the contrary, the Court must presume that one day is on average as good as another. By its nature, legislation must, to some degree, cut across individual circumstances in order to establish general rules. Alleged discrimination flowing from one day of the weekend being more profitable for particular retailers than the other day of the weekend would be of an entirely different order of magnitude from the disadvantage experienced by retailers who cannot open their stores on a weekend at all.

I am impressed . . . with the concerns of the majority of the United States Supreme Court in two respects. The first relates to the balancing of an indirect burden on the religious freedom of a retail store owner against the interests of his or her perhaps sometimes numerous employees. The second relates to the undesirability of state-sponsored inquiries into religous beliefs.

With respect to the first concern, I agree with the majority of the United States Supreme Court that it is legitimate for legislatures to be concerned with minimizing the disruptive effect of any exemption on the scope and quality of the pause day, and that it would be highly undesirable for such concern to find expression in a rule conditioning the availability of an exemption on the hiring by retailers of co-religionists. Because of their substantial share of total sales volume (the Report at p. 98, Table V, indicates that stores with 10 or more employees accounted for 53.3% of retail sales in Canada according to the Census of 1961) and their numerous employees, the operation of large retail outlets on Sundays would entail a substantial disruption of the quality of the pause day. It is, however, not so much the disruption of the quality of the pause day in terms of commercial activity that concerns me. What concerns me, rather, is the limitation of its scope in terms of the employees who would be denied the benefits which the Act was designed to provide them.

What cannot be forgotten is that the object of the legislation is to benefit retail employees by making available to them a weekly holiday which coincides with that enjoyed by most of the community. These employees do not constitute a powerful group in society. . . .

The economic position of these employees affords them few choices in respect of their conditions of employment. It would ignore the realities faced by these workers to suggest that they stand up to their employer or seek a job elsewhere if they wish to enjoy a common day of rest with their families and friends.

Although I have acknowledged that the legislation under review burdens the freedoms of Saturday-observing retailers, it must also be recognized that larger retailers have available to them options flowing from the resources at their disposal which are foreclosed to their employees. It is, perhaps, worth stating the obvious: a store with eight or more employees serving the public at any one time or with 5,000 square feet of retail space indeed constitutes a substantial retail operation. Such a store is not, by any stretch, a mere corner store staffed by the family. In interpreting and applying the Charter I believe that the courts must be cautious to ensure that it does not simply become an instrument of better situated individuals to roll back legislation which has as its object the improvement of the condition of less advantaged persons. When the interests of more than seven vulnerable employees in securing a Sunday holiday are weighed against the interests of their employer in transacting business on a Sunday, I cannot fault the legislature for determining that the protection of the employees ought to prevail. This is not to say that the legislature is constitutionally obligated to give effect to employee interests in preference to the interests of the store owner for large retail operations, but only that it may do so if it wishes.

I turn now to the second factor which, in my opinion, contributes to the justification of the legislation under review. In discussing the possibility of a Sabbatarian exemption as a means of reducing the burdens of Sunday closing laws on religious freedom, the majority of the United States Supreme Court had occasion to express concern about state-conducted inquiries into religious beliefs. The striking advantage of the Ontario Act is that it makes available an exemption to the small and mid-size retailer without the indignity of having to submit to such an inquiry. In my view, state-sponsored inquiries into any person's religion should be avoided wherever reasonably possible, since they expose an individual's most personal and private beliefs to public airing and testing in a judicial or quasi-judicial setting. The inquiry is all the worse when it is demanded only of members of a non-majoritarian faith, who may have good reason for reluctance about so exposing and articulating their non-conformity.

I do not mean to suggest that a judicial inquiry into the sincerity of religious beliefs is unconstitutional. To so hold would mean that the courts could never grant constitutional exemptions from legislation which impinged on the free exercise of religious beliefs. Judicial inquiries into religious beliefs are largely unavoidable if the constitutional freedoms guaranteed by s. 2(a) are to be asserted before the courts. We must live with the reality that such an inquiry is necessary in order for the same values to be given effect by the judicial system. Inquiries which are genuinely designed as a means of giving effect to religious freedoms will not therefore generally be unconstitutional. There will, however, be occasions when a substantial measure of religious freedom can be achieved without mandating a state-conducted inquiry into personal religious convictions and the legislatures ought to be encouraged to do so, if a fair balance is struck.

I do not, of course, suggest that to a person whose religious freedom would otherwise be impaired, a voluntary inquiry into religion is worse than the original impairment of freedom of religion. Clearly that is not the case, since the person need not submit to the inquiry. It is worth reiterating, however, that the evidence indicates that the overwhelming majority of Saturday-observing retailers are capable of complying with the requirements of subs. 3(4). It is these retailers who benefit from the adoption of a scheme such as that selected by the Ontario legislature in preference to a scheme involving an inquiry into religious beliefs. In my view, there exists to some degree a trade-off between a scheme which provides complete relief from burdens on religious freedom to most Saturday-observing retailers by avoiding a distasteful inquiry, and, on the other hand, an alternative scheme which provides substantial relief from burdens on religious freedom to all Saturday-observing retailers. Both schemes provide incomplete relief for the class of Saturday-observing retailers as a whole, but the incompleteness is a necessary consequence of ensuring that as many employees as possible will realize the benefits of the common pause day legislation. Both schemes represent genuine and serious attempts to minimize the adverse effects of pause day legislation on Saturday-observers. It is far from clear that one scheme is intrinsically better than the other.

In this context, I note that freedom of religion, perhaps unlike freedom of conscience has both individual and collective aspects. Legislatures are justified in being conscious of the effects of legislation on religious groups as a whole, as well as on individuals. In some circumstances, it is open to balance the religious freedoms of the many members of any particular relgious group against those of the few when differential treatment is based on a criterion, such as the size of one's retail business, which is not in itself offensive to constitutional provisions, principles, and purposes.

Nevertheless, while the number of detrimentally affected retailers may be small, no legislature in Canada is entitled to do away with any of the religious freedoms to which these or any other individuals are entitled without strong reason. In my view, the balancing of the interests of more than 7 employees to a common pause day against the freedom of religion of those affected constitutes justification for the exemption scheme selected by the Province of Ontario, at least in a context wherein any satisfactory alternative scheme involves an inquiry into religious beliefs.

I might add that I do not believe there is any magic in the number seven as distinct from, say, five, ten, or fifteen employees as the cut-off point for eligibility for the exemption. In balancing the interests of retail employees to a holiday in common with their family and friends against the s. 2(a) interests of those affected the legislature engaged in the process envisaged by s. 1 of the Charter. A ''reasonable limit'' is one which, having regard to the principles enunciated in *Oakes*, it was reasonable for the legislature to impose. The courts are not called upon to substitute judicial opinions for legislative ones as to the place at which to draw a precise line.

Having said this, however, I do not share the views of the majority of the United States Supreme Court that no legislative effort need be made to accommodate the interests of any Saturday-observing retailers. In particular, I would be hard pressed to conceive of any justification for insisting that a small, family store which operates without any employees remain closed on Sundays when the tenets of the retailer's religion requires closing on Saturdays. In my view, the principles articulated in *Oakes* make it incumbent on a legislature which enacts Sunday closing laws to attempt very seriously to alleviate the effects of those laws on Saturday-observers. The exemption in subs. 3(4) of the Act under review in these appeals represents a satisfactory effort on the part of the legislature of Ontario to that end and is, accordingly, permissible.

Arguably, the legislature might have retained the desirable qualities of subs. 3(4) and added thereto a special exemption for those with sincerely held Sabbatarian beliefs who cannot bring themselves within paragraphs (b) and (c) of subs. 3(4). In my view, there was no constitutional duty on the Ontario legislature to do so. To insist that the only acceptable scheme of exemptions would have the attributes of s. 3(4) in respect of small to mid-size employers, but the attributes of s. 7(1) of the New Brunswick Act in respect of larger employers, would be to impose an excessively high standard on the legislators in view of the nature and extent of the abridgment of rights and the complexity of balancing against one another the constitutional and statutory interests of consumers, retailers and employees. Such a hybrid scheme would entail a greater disruption of the pause day than either scheme standing on its own. It would, in any event, fail to recognize that there is a point at which the size of retail business makes permissible a legislative decision to favour the employees' interests over those of the store owner.

I should emphasize that it is not the role of this Court to devise legislation that is constitutionally valid, or to pass on the validity of schemes which are not directly before it, or to consider what legislation might be the most desirable. The discussion of alternative legislative schemes that I have undertaken is directed to one end only, that is, to address the issue whether the existing scheme meets the requirements of the second limb of the test for the application of s. 1 of the Charter as set down in *Oakes*.

In view of the extent and quality of the abridgment of rights flowing from the legislation, I have little difficulty in applying the third element of the proportionality test. The infringement is not disproportionate to the legislative objectives. A serious effort has been made to accommodate the freedom of religion of Saturday-observers, in so far as that is possible without undue damage to the scope and quality of the pause day objective. It follows that I would uphold the Act under s. 1.

REMEDIAL ISSUES

In *Big M Drug Mart Ltd.* at p. 315, the majority of the Court left open the possibility that in certain circumstances a ''constitutional exemption'' might be granted from otherwise valid legislation to particular individuals whose religious freedom was adversely affected by the legislation. Such a remedy would, of course, not be available where the limitation of those individuals' religious freedom had been addressed by the legislature by means of a statutory exemption and was held to be reasonable and demonstrably justified. Subs. 3(4) of the legislation under review in these appeals demonstrates that the Ontario Legislature has carefully considered the effects of the Act on Jewish retailers such as the owners of Nortown Foods Ltd. The legislature consciously chose to alleviate the burdens on those Jewish retailers who can comply with the requirement that seven or fewer employees serve the public at any given time on Sundays. At the same time, however, it chose to subordinate the interests of larger retailers to the interests of their employees. As I have concluded that the legislature's decision in this respect was permissible under s. 1, there is no basis upon which to grant a constitutional exemption to Nortown Foods Ltd. which was operating with nine rather than seven employees serving the public on January 16, 1983.

In view of the above conclusions, it is unnecessary to decide on the remedial issues presented by this case. I note, however, that if I had reached a different conclusion under s. 1 regarding the justifiability of the limitation on the freedom of religion of large Saturday-observing retailers, a number of issues would arise:

1. Would the inadequacy of the exemption result in a declaration that s. 2 (or alternatively s. 3(4)(b) and (c)) of the Act was universally of no force or effect, or, on the contrary, would the Act be rendered ineffective or inapplicable with respect to a limited class of persons?

2. If a remedy ought to be granted to a limited class of persons, such as observers of a day of rest other than Sunday, should such a remedy flow from s. 24 or s. 52 of the Constitution Act 1982?

3. If a remedy ought to be granted to a limited class of persons, is the respondent Nortown Foods Ltd. within that class having regard to the question whether (and if so, in what circumstances) a corporation can be attributed religious beliefs, or alternatively can be given standing to seek a constitutional exemption from legislation which abridges the freedom of religion of the corporation's principals? I have no hesitation in remarking that a

business corporation cannot possess religious beliefs: see, in this respect Andrew Petter, Not "Never on a Sunday," at p. 101 and Wallace Rozefort, "Are Corporations Entitled to Freedom of Religion Under the Canadian Charter of Rights and Freedoms?" (1986), 15 Man. L.J. 199. A more difficult question is whether a corporate entity ought to be deemed in certain circumstances to possess the religious values of specified natural persons. If so, should the religion of the directors or shareholders or even employees be adopted as the appropriate test? What if there is a divergence of religious beliefs within the corporation?

The remedy granted to Nortown Foods Ltd. by the Ontario Court of Appeal implies answers to the above questions upon which I wish to express no further opinion in the present appeals.

~ Justice Dickson C.J.C. then rejects a s. 7 argument because whatever "liberty" may mean in that section, it does not extend "to an unrestrained right to transact business whenever one wishes." He also disposes of a s. 15 argument because that section has no bearing on convictions prior to April 17, 1985. ~

The appeals of Edwards Books and Art Ltd., Longo Brothers et al, and Paul Magder ought to be dismissed without costs. The Crown appeal in the Nortown Foods Ltd. case ought to be allowed without costs and the respondent convicted.

LA FOREST J. (Concurring in part): I have had the advantage of reading the judgment of the Chief Justice and while I agree with his disposition of the case and with most of his supporting reasons, we have significant differences of views regarding the Sabbatarian exemption that impel me to write a separate judgment. Essentially, what we differ about is whether the Legislature is by s. 2(a) of the Canadian Charter of Rights and Freedoms constitutionally required to provide a Sabbatarian exemption in order to relieve those who worship on Saturday from the economic burden they may suffer because of the existence of the Act. . . .

In several cases decided by the Court . . . in particular, *R*. v. *Oakes*, [1986] 1 S.C.R. 103, this Court has expressed the view that the means chosen by the legislature must be proportionate to the ends sought to be achieved. Having examined and disposed of other possible courses that might have been taken to provide a weekly day of rest, the Chief Justice concludes that the means adopted by the Legislature meets the test of proportionality, but that it would not if a Sabbatarian exemption had not been provided. . . .

The Act, in my view, would be valid even if it did not contain this exemption. Indeed, as I will attempt to demonstrate, the exemption may be subject to constitutional weaknesses, though I do not think these jeopardize the validity of the Act itself. Our difference of opinion is important. A determination that such an exemption is necessary may raise serious issues regarding the constitutionality of Sunday closing laws in several provinces. . . .

Let me first underline what is mentioned in the Chief Justice's judgment, that in describing the criteria comprising the proportionality requirement, the Court has been careful to avoid rigid and inflexible standards. That seems to me to be essential. Given that the objective is of pressing and substantial concern, the Legislature must be allowed adequate scope to achieve that objective. It must be remembered that the business of government is a practical one. The Constitution must be applied on a realistic basis having regard to the nature of the particular area sought to be regulated and not on an abstract theoretical plane. In interpreting the Constitution, courts must be sensitive to what Frankfurter J. in *McGowan, supra*, at p. 524 calls "the practical living facts" to which a legislature must respond. That is especially so in a field of so many competing pressures as the one here in question.

By the foregoing, I do not mean to suggest that this Court should, as a general rule, defer to legislative judgments when those judgments trench upon rights considered fundamental in a free and democratic society. Quite the contrary, I would have thought the Charter established the opposite regime. On the other hand, having accepted the importance of the legislative objective, one must in the present context recognize that if the legislative goal is to be achieved, it will inevitably be achieved to the detriment of some. Moreover, attempts to protect the rights of one group will also inevitably impose burdens on the rights of other groups. There is no perfect scenario in which the rights of all can be equally protected.

In seeking to achieve a goal that is demonstrably justified in a free and democratic society, therefore, a legislature must be given reasonable room to manoeuvre to meet these conflicting pressures. Of course, what is reasonable will vary with the context. Regard must be had to the nature of the interest infringed and to the legislative scheme sought to be implemented. In a case like the present, it seems to me, the Legislature is caught between having to let the legislation place a burden on people who observe a day of worship other than Sunday or create exemptions which in their practical workings may substantially interfere with the goal the Legislature seeks to advance and which themselves result in imposing burdens on Sunday observers and possibly on others as well. That being so, it seems to me that the choice of having or not having an exemption for those who observe a day other than Sunday must remain, in essence, a legislative choice. That, barring equality considerations, is true as well of the compromises that must be made in creating religious exemptions. These choices require an in-depth knowledge of all the circumstances. They are choices a court is not in a position to make.

To begin with, a Sabbatarian exemption always involves defining the nature of the day of rest. The extent to which it does so depends on the kind of day of rest the Legislature seeks to achieve and the breadth of the exemption. Here the Legislature has sought to have, as much as possible, a uniform weekly day of rest and recreation with only such exemptions as it, on sufficient grounds, considers essential. All exempted activities tend to disturb the relaxed atmosphere sought to be achieved by a uniform weekly day of rest. In addition to the disruption from the exempted activities themselves, these activities inevitably result in others, such as increased traffic and the like, that further disturb the atmosphere sought to be achieved. They also create competitive pressures on others to remain open, which makes enforcement more difficult and, indeed, can ultimately threaten the viability of the legislative goal; see in this context the debate regarding the British Shops (Sunday Trading Restriction) Act, 6 Geo. 5, 1 Edw. 8, c. 53, referred to by Frankfurter J. in *McGowan* v. *State of Maryland, supra*, pp. 480 *et seq.*

Through the operation of sociological and economic forces, an exemption of this kind also puts pressure on Sunday observers to work on Sunday. The Ontario Law Reform Commission's Report, pp. 103-4 referred to the special vulnerability of retail workers to such pressures. . . . Sunday observers, no less than other people in that group, would tend to respond to those pressures. Thus a legislative attempt to avoid economic coercion of one religious group may result in economic coercion of another religious group. How is a court able to second-guess the Legislature on such issues? Of course, employers might seek to avoid infringing other people's religious beliefs by hiring only their co-religionists but this, too, is a result a legislature might not wish to encourage.

The Legislature in this case has attempted to avoid obvious differentiation on religious grounds by making the Sabbatarian exemption open to anyone falling within the requirements regarding the number of employees and the amount of space mentioned in s. 3(4) of the Act. This exemption could, of course, interfere with the atmosphere of repose and recrea-

tion it seeks to create, and impose an economic burden on some Sunday observers. That is, of course, a legislative choice, but I simply refer to it to underline that such choices inevitably define the nature of the day of rest sought to be created and detrimentally affect other religious groups. What is more, the provision hardly disguises the fact that differentiation is being made on the ground of religion. For my part, I do not think it is much of an improvement over being expressly exempted on the ground of religion. In any event, the choice is one that another legislature might reasonably wish to avoid. . . .

My conclusion may also be supported by a close consideration of how a Sabbatarian exemption must be framed. If such exemptions are to operate without placing the whole Sunday closing scheme in jeopardy, judgments have to be made in context about the kinds of establishments that may be excepted, whether in terms of numbers of employees or the spatial dimensions of these establishments or otherwise. For this type of decision one must necessarily rely on legislative judgment. In terms of intrusion on religion, there can be no difference, as Wilson J. demonstrates, between the owner of a large or small establishment. Indeed, the owner of the larger establishment is likely to suffer a greater economic loss than the owner of the smaller one.

As I mentioned, decisions of this kind call for informed legislative judgment. Judges do not have the specific information necessary to decide where the line is to be drawn. Thus can we say, by the mere fact that Ontario exempts establishments having up to seven workers at a time and up to 5,000 square feet of space, that Quebec's Sabbatarian exception for retail establishments, limited as it is to establishments that are operated by no more than three persons at any one time (and then only subject to Ministerial approval and conditions), is insufficient to pass constitutional muster? See *An Act Respecting Commercial Establishments Business Hours, supra*, s. 5.3. The

Quebec Sunday Observance Act, *supra*, which prohibits industrial work in any business or calling, as well as retail sales, contains no Sabbatarian exemption, a fact that indicates that the Legislature perceives different requirements in different contexts. (I leave out of consideration the general provision in these Acts restricting the application of the Charter.)

What is more are both the Ontario and Quebec Acts to be measured against the broad exemptions present in the Manitoba Act (The Retail Businesses Holiday Closing Act, S.M. 1977, c. 26) and the Prince Edward Island Act (the Day of Rest Act, S.P.E.I. 1985, c. 12, s. 4(3)) which are not qualified by the size of the establishment or the number of persons employed? The New Brunswick Act (the Days of Rest Act, R.S.N.B., 1970, c. D. 4.2, s. 7(1)(c)) also contains a similar broad exemption but it is subject to specific approval by a Board, which may attach conditions to an exemption. The Alberta Act, Municipal Government Amendment Act, S.A. 1985, c. 43, s. 31 (enacting s. 241) contains enabling provisions whose practical workings cannot be determined in the abstract. The simple fact is that what may work effectively in one province (or in a part of it) may simply not work in another without unduly interfering with the legislative scheme. And a compromise adopted at a particular time may not be possible at another; one cannot be bound constitutionally to facts found to exist when the studies preparatory to legislation were made.

The foregoing is sufficient to dispose of the issue with which I am particularly concerned but I would draw attention to the fact that the New Brunswick and Prince Edward Island statutes raise a further dimension which tends to show how difficult the legislative task of framing adequate religious exemptions may be. The religious exemptions in those statutes are not limited to those who worship on Saturday, but are open to anyone who worships on any other day of the week.

. . . [I]t is not at first sight easy to see why an exemption is not constitutionally required for Moslems, if it is required for Jews and other Saturday observers. The provision of the Charter, s. 27, favouring multiculturalism would reinforce this way of looking at things.

Indeed, the more serious long term question may be whether an exemption restricted to Saturday can meet the demands of the equality provision, s. 15, rather than whether the Act is valid without that exemption; see Cihlar, Cook, Martori, Jr. and Meyer, ''State-Religious Institutions and Values: A Legal Survey—1964-66,'' 41 Notre Dame Lawyer, at pp. 739 *et seq.* (1966); R.A. Spellman, ''A New Look at Sunday Closing Legislation,'' 45 Nebraska Law Rev. 775 (1966). Section 15, however, was not in force at the time the offences charged here took place and I need not enter further into the matter.

I have not mentioned other religious groups, many of which, I gather, do not have a specific weekly holy day as opposed to periodic religious holidays, though some have quite a number of these and may be subject to varying pressures from the requirements of Sunday closing laws. What exemptions are to be made for these groups, and what are the implications of such exemptions for the requirements of equality and the viability of the legislative scheme? From some laws it is possible to make exemptions on the ground of religion, without undermining the legislative scheme or affecting the religious and other rights of others. But this is not possible for other laws. Sunday closing laws appear to me to fall within the latter category.

The likelihood is that the burden on minority religious groups results less from Sunday closing than from other laws and social customs; see The Canadian Encyclopedia, vol. 2, p. 907. Though an effort must be made to avoid imposing majority views on minority groups so far as this is reasonably possible, in the end in the particular area with which we are concerned here, Sunday closing laws, the nature of the choices and compromises to be made are matters that must be left to the legislatures. There has, in fact, been a growing legislative recognition of the desirability of making accommodations for minority religious groups in this area. When the Ontario Law Reform Commission Report was published in 1970 (see p. 350), there were no religious exemptions in any province of Canada. Today four of the provinces have enacted such exemptions. A similar pattern has prevailed in the United States. Of the thirty-four more or less comprehensive State Sunday closing laws in force when *McGowan*, was decided, twenty-one had some form of Sabbatarian exemption, *supra* at pp. 496, 517. While, like the Chief Justice, I favour the making of whatever exemptions are possible to accommodate minority groups, I am of the view that the nature of the choices and compromises that must be made in relation to Sunday closing are essentially legislative in nature. In the absence of unreasonableness or discrimination, courts are simply not in a position to substitute their judgment for that of the Legislature. . . .

WILSON J. (concurring in part): I agree with Dickson C.J.C. that the Retail Business Holidays Act, R.S.O. 1980, c. 453, is *intra vires* the Province of Ontario because its purpose is to establish a common pause day for those employed in retail business. I also agree with the Chief Justice that s. 2 of the statute infringes the freedom of religion of those who close on Saturdays for religious reasons because it attaches an economic penalty to their religious observance. It requires them to be closed two days in the week instead of one.

I part company with the Chief Justice, however, on the application of s. 1 of the Charter to the "Saturday exemption" contained in s. 3(4) of the Act. It seems to me that once it is accepted that s. 2 infringes the freedom of religion of those who close on Saturdays for religious reasons, the question becomes whether that infringement can be justified under s. 1 in order that a common pause day be established for retail workers. The Chief Justice finds that it can be justified in the case of large retailers but not in the case of small. He does so, as I understand his reasons, by reference to the number of persons the larger retailer employs on the basis that a decision made by that retailer to stay open on Sundays would deprive a larger number of employees of their common pause day than would the same decision made by a smaller retailer. The Chief Justice finds that this disparate treatment of the members of the group whose religious freedom has been infringed can be justified on the basis that they are being differentiated on the ground of size which is not a prohibited ground of discrimination.

With respect, I do not think that a limit on freedom of religion which recognizes the freedom of some members of the group but not of other members of the same group can be reasonable and justified in a free and democratic society. The effect of the disparate treatment, characterized by the Chief Justice as being based on size, is that the religious freedom of some is respected by the legislation and the religious freedom of others is not. It is this effect which, in my view, makes the legislation vulnerable to attack on constitutional grounds.

In his commentary on the Canadian Charter of Rights and Freedoms Professor Tarnopolsky (as he then was) points out that the Charter protects group rights as well as individual rights. He distinguishes between individual and group rights on the basis that the assertion of an individual right emphasises the proposition that everyone is to be treated the same regardless of his or her membership in a particular identifiable group whereas the assertion of a group right is based on the claim of an individual or group of individuals because of membership in a particular identifiable group: see "The Equality Rights," The Canadian Charter of Rights and Freedoms: Commentary (1982), at p. 437.

It seems to me that s. 3(4) of the Retail Business Holidays Act purports to recognize a group right, namely the right of those who close on Saturdays on religious grounds to stay open on Sundays because otherwise their s. 2(a) right would be violated. But it does not recognize the group right of all members of the group, only of some. Accordingly, the violation of the s. 2(a) right of the others has legislative sanction. Yet it seems to me that when the Charter protects group rights such as freedom of religion, it protects the rights of all members of the group. It does not make fish of some and fowl of the others. For, quite apart from considerations of equality, to do so is to introduce an invidious distinction into the group and sever the religious and cultural tie that binds them together. It is, in my opinion, an interpretation of the Charter expressly precluded by s. 27 which requires the Charter to be interpreted "in a manner consistent with the preservation and enhancement of the multicultural heritage of Canadians." Can it then be a reasonable limit under s. 1? In my opinion, it cannot.

To approach the matter from a different vantage point, I think that what the legislature has attempted to do in the Retail Business Holidays Act is effect a compromise between the government's objective of a common pause day and the freedom of religion of those who close on Saturdays for religious reasons. The problem is that the compromise it has effected is, in Professor Dworkin's terms, an "internal compromise": see Ronald Dworkin, *Law's Empire* (1986), c. 6, p. 178 *et seq.* Dworkin believes that a legal system must be animated by "integrity." Accordingly, when a government legislates on an issue on which people hold widely divergent views, it must do so on the basis of principle. Dworkin states at p. 179:

If there must be compromise because people are divided about justice, then the compromise must be external, not internal; it must be compromise about which scheme of justice to adopt rather than a compromised scheme of justice.

Applying that to the present case, the legislature must decide whether to subordinate freedom of religion to the objective of a common pause day, one scheme of justice, or subordinate the common pause day to freedom of religion, the competing scheme of justice, and, having decided which scheme of justice to adopt, it must then apply it in all cases. It cannot decide to subordinate the freedom of religion of some members of the group to the objective of a common pause day and subordinate the common pause day to the freedom of religion of other members of the same group. Yet this is the effect of the distinction between the large and small retailer adopted by the legislature in this legislation. It is, in my view, "a compromised scheme of justice." It does not affirm a principle which is applicable to all. It reflects rather a failure on the part of the legislature to make up its mind which scheme of justice to adopt. The result is, in my opinion, what Professor Dworkin refers to as "checkerboard" legislation.

It follows from what I have said that, in my view, s. 3(4) cannot constitute a reasonable limit under s. 1 of the Charter or be justified in a free and democratic society. However, if I am wrong in this and disparate treatment of this kind can be justified under s. 1, it would, in my view, require much more compelling evidence than was adduced by the Crown in order to establish that the government objective of a common pause day required it. The Crown adduced no evidence to establish that permitting all retailers who close on Saturdays on religious grounds to stay open on Sundays would cause a substantial disruption of the common pause day. Nor was it established that retailers who were not motivated to close on Saturdays by religious considerations would elect under s. 3(4)(a) to close on Saturdays for the sole purpose of being open on Sundays. Economic considerations may well make such a choice unlikely. We simply do not know. I agree, therefore, with Tarnopolsky J. that the Crown failed totally to discharge its burden under s. 1 of the Charter.

The fault with s. 3(4) is, I believe, that

it does not go far enough. It does not protect the freedom of religion of all those who close on Saturdays for religious reasons. Section 3(4)(a) standing by itself is, in my view, a perfectly valid exemption from the operation of s. 2 of the Act because it recognizes and accommodates the s. 2(a) right protected by the Charter but paras. (b) and (c) of subs. (4) impose a limit on that exemption (and therefore on the freedom of religion of those who close on Saturdays on religious grounds) which is neither reasonable nor justified in a free and democratic society. These paragraphs are accordingly not saved by s. 1. However, they seem to me to be clearly severable from s. (4)(a). I would accordingly hold them to be of no force and effect under s. 52(1) of the Charter. . . .

I take no issue with the course followed by Tarnopolsky J. in granting a s. 24(1) remedy to the appellant Nortown Foods Limited on the basis that s. 2 of the Act is of no force and effect vis-a-vis it. It appears to me, however, that where the impugned legislation is capable of severance, severance is the preferable route to follow. It avoids isolating the remedy to the particular litigant and provides relief to all those adversely affected by the unconstitutional provision. In a word, it preserves rather than fractures the integrity of the group.

I have one or two comments to add. The first is that when the court is called upon to balance under s. 1 of the Charter a fundamental value such as freedom of religion against the admittedly desirable legislative objective of a common pause day, it has to keep in mind that the legislature, inasmuch as it has provided the common pause day for only a small proportion of the populace, namely certain classes of retail workers, and has not seen fit to provide a common pause day for the great masses of people involved in industry, has put its own value on the common pause day. It has not made it generally available to workers in the Province. I express no view as to whether this is a good thing or a bad thing—that is not the Court's business—I simply say that it is some evidence of the importance attached to the concept of a common pause day by the legislators themselves.

The second comment I would make addresses the concern expressed by the Chief Justice that the effect of extending the exemption to all Saturday observers would be that some Sunday observers might be compelled to work on Sundays if they are employed by employers who close on Saturdays for religious reasons. This Court held in Ontario Human Rights Commission and O'Malley v. Simpsons-Sears Ltd., [1985] 2 S.C.R. 536, that under the Ontario Human Rights Code employers were under a duty to accommodate employees who found themselves in this position. If an employee objects on religious grounds to working on a particular day, the employer must take reasonable steps, short of undue hardship, to make alternate arrangements for that employee. The Sunday-observing employee is therefore not without a remedy although the remedy is not provided in this legislation but in the Ontario Human Rights Code. . . .

Since none of Edwards Books and Art Limited, Longo Brothers Fruit Markets Limited or Paul Magder were closed on the Saturday preceding the laying of the charges against them, their appeals must be dismissed. They do not qualify for an exemption under s. 3(4)(a) of the Act. Nortown Foods Limited does, however, qualify for the exemption under s. 3(4)(a) and the appeal of the Crown must therefore be dismissed with costs. I would not award costs against the three unsuccessful appellants. . . .

~ On behalf of himself and Justice McIntyre, Justice Beetz wrote an opinion agreeing with Justice Dickson in most respects but rejecting the latter's conclusion that the legislation infringed religious freedom. Following Professor A. Petter, whose article is discussed in Justice Dickson's opinion above, Beetz contends that the economic harm suffered by a Saturday-observing retailer flows not from the Act but from his "deliberate choice'' to ''give priority to the tenets of his religion over his financial benefit.'' Because s. 2 of the Charter is not violated, the legislation ''is of full force and effect without any need to rely on s. 1.'' ~

49. Alberta Labour Reference *(1987)*

~ Alberta had enacted legislation that prohibited strikes and lockouts for three classes of public service employees: firemen, policemen, and hospital workers. The government maintained that the no-strike laws were necessary to insure the continued provision of essential services. The legislation provided for compulsory arbitration and also limited the matters that could be considered by an arbitration board. The Alberta Union of Public Employees had always opposed the legislation. In 1983, the Union announced that it was planning to challenge the constitutionality of the laws as a violation of the freedom of association provision of the recently adopted Charter of Rights. The Alberta government promptly preempted the Union by referring the legislation to the Alberta Court of Appeal.

The reference was unusual in that it was accompanied by public statements by the Attorney General of Alberta that the provincial government would not hesitate to use the section 33 ''legislative override'' power to protect the legislation if the Court declared it invalid. The threatened use of section 33 provoked widespread criticism by the opposition and local newspaper editorials.[1] Alberta Premier Peter Lougheed, one of the original ''gang of eight'' provincial leaders who had opposed the Charter during 1980-81, responded by publicly defending his Attorney General's threatened use of section 33. The U.S. constitutional experience which allows judges to make public policy, said Lougheed, ''is not one that has a happy result or that we want to duplicate in Canada.'' Lougheed continued, ''It is our view that . . . much more important is the question that elected legislators within provinces can make public policy.''[2] The Court of Appeal of Alberta upheld the legislation, and this decision was appealed to the Supreme Court of Canada by the Alberta Union of Provincial Employees.

The central question posed by the reference was whether the right to freedom of association declared in section 2(d) of the Charter included the right to strike. If it did, then Alberta's ''no strike'' laws would be invalid, unless they could be ''saved'' by a section 1 ''reasonable limits'' defense. Seven other provinces and the government of Canada intervened before the Supreme Court of Canada to support Alberta's argument that the freedom of association did not extend the right to strike to labour unions. Three labour unions and the NDP government of Manitoba intervened on the opposing side.

In a 4-2 ruling, the Supreme Court upheld the legislation. Justice McIntyre's majority opinion held that the actions of an association do not enjoy any more constitutional protection than the sum of the rights enjoyed by its members individually. While individual workers have a right to quit work, this was not deemed analogous to the right of a union to strike. Justice McIntyre reinforced

---

[1] See ''Opting out is overkill,'' Calgary Herald, Nov. 21, 1983, p. A5. Also ''The weasel words have trapped us,'' Calgary Herald, Nov. 24, 1983, p. A6.

[2] ''Premier defends opting out,'' Calgary Herald, Nov. 22, 1983, p. A3.

his interpretation of section 2(d) with an appeal to the intention of the framers of the Charter not to include the right to strike. He also cited social policy reasons as to why courts should resist invitations to become involved in labour law disputes. Last but not least, McIntyre cited lack of institutional competence as militating against judicial involvement. "Judges do not have the expert knowledge . . . ," he concluded, and "specialized labour tribunals are better suited than courts for resolving labour problems." This concern with institutional competence—or the lack thereof—explains in part McIntyre's preference to giving a narrower interpretation to "freedom of association" and thereby avoiding any resort to the section 1 "balancing" test.[3] All told, the McIntyre judgement presents a classic example of judicial self-restraint and the "interpretivist" approach to Charter interpretation.[4]

A very different approach and a different result was reached by Chief Justice Dickson, joined by Justice Wilson, dissenting. The Chief Justice chastised the majority for apparently taking the position that the Charter only protects rights already in place at the time of its adoption. He characterized this approach as "legalistic, ungenerous, [and] indeed vapid." The freedom of workers to associate and to bargain collectively as a union, Dickson declared, would be ineffective without a corresponding right to strike. Having found Alberta's legislation in violation of s. 2(d), Dickson then applied the "Oakes" test. While some of the provisions met the s. 1 "reasonable limitations" test, others did not, and should be declared invalid.

The key to understanding the Chief Justice's judgment may be his view that an important part of the purpose of the Charter in general and "freedom of association" in particular is to help social and economic "underdogs." This view of the Charter as a "progressive" document is found in his obiter dicta in *Edwards Books*, and is repeated here. Freedom of association, Dickson writes, "has enabled those who would otherwise be vulnerable and ineffective to meet on more equal terms the power and strength of those with whom their interests interact, and perhaps, conflict." Madame Justice Wilson appears to share the Chief Justice's "underdog" approach to Charter interpretation.

The Alberta Labour Reference provided an interesting preview of the Court's *Morgentaler* abortion decision handed down nine months later.[5] In terms of issues, both cases represent invitations to the Court to "find" an implied right that is not explicitly enumerated in the text of the Charter. Justice McIntyre's caveat—that "the Charter should not be regarded as an empty vessel to be filled with whatever meaning we might wish from time to time"—

---

[3] For a discussion of section 1, see Introduction, p. 20.

[4] For a discussion of the "interpretivist" approach to constitutional interpretation, see Introduction, pp. 16-17.

[5] See case no. 50 below.

turned out to be an accurate indicator of his similarly unreceptive response to Morgentaler's argument that the "liberty" and "security of the person" provisions of section 7 of the Charter contained a right to abortion. By contrast, Dickson and Wilson, the two dissenters in the Alberta Labour Reference, subsequently wrote the two most activist opinions for the majority in the Morgentaler case. Both cases illustrate how different theories of proper judicial role and different approaches to Charter interpretation can lead to very different results.

It merits notice that this case is just one of a string of Charter defeats for organized labour. In two similar decisions announced the same day as the Alberta Labour Reference, the Court rejected similar claims of a constitutionally protected "right to strike" (*Public Service Alliance of Canada* v. *the Queen*, [1986] 1 S.C.R. 424 and *Saskatchewan* v. *Retail, Wholesale and Department Store Union*, [1987] 1 S.C.R. 460). A labour union also lost in the *Dolphin Delivery* case, when the Supreme Court refused to confer Charter protection (freedom of expression) on secondary picketing.[6] This trend seems to vindicate Premier Blakeney's (NDP Saskatchewan) fear that the Charter would provide little benefit to organized labour. ∼

REFERENCE RE PUBLIC SERVICE EMPLOYEE RELATIONS ACT, LABOR RELATIONS ACT, AND POLICE OFFICERS COLLECTIVE BARGAINING ACT OF ALBERTA
In the Supreme Court of Canada. [1987] 1 S.C.R. 313.

The judgment of Beetz, Le Dain and La Forest JJ. was delivered by

LE DAIN, J.: The background, the issues and the relevant authority and considerations in this appeal are fully set out in the reasons for judgment of the Chief Justice and Mr. Justice McIntyre. I agree with Mr. Justice McIntyre that the constitutional guarantee of freedom of association in s. 2(d) of the Canadian Charter of Rights and Freedoms does not include, in the case of a trade union, a guarantee of the right to bargain collectively and the right to strike, and accordingly I would dismiss the appeal and answer the constitutional questions in the manner proposed by him. I wish to indicate, if only briefly, the general considerations that lead me to this conclusion.

In considering the meaning that must be given to freedom of association in s. 2(d) of the Charter it is essential to keep in mind that this concept must be applied to a wide range of associations or organizations of a political, religious, social or economic nature, with a wide variety of objects, as well as activity by which the objects may be pursued. It is in this larger perspective, and not simply with regard to the perceived requirements of a trade union, however important they may be, that one must consider the implications of extending a constitutional guarantee, under the concept of freedom of association, to the right to engage in particular activity on the ground that the activity is essential to give an association meaningful existence.

In considering whether it is reasonable

---

[6] See case 47 above.

to ascribe such a sweeping intention to the Charter I reject the premise that without such additional constitutional protection the guarantee of freedom of association would be a meaningless and empty one. Freedom of association is particularly important for the exercise of other fundamental freedoms, such as freedom of expression and freedom of conscience and religion. These afford a wide scope for protected activity in association. Moreover, the freedom to work for the establishment of an association, to belong to an association, to maintain it, and to participate in its lawful activity without penalty or reprisal is not to be taken for granted. That is indicated by its express recognition and protection in labour relations legislation. It is a freedom that has been suppressed in varying degrees from time to time by totalitarian regimes.

What is in issue here is not the importance of freedom of association in this sense, which is the one I ascribe to s. 2(d) of the Charter, but whether particular activity of an association in pursuit of its objects is to be constitutionally protected or left to be regulated by legislative policy. The rights for which constitutional protection is sought—the modern rights to bargain collectively and to strike, involving correlative duties or obligations resting on an employer—are not fundamental rights or freedoms. They are the creation of legislation, involving a balance of competing interests in a field which has been recognized by the courts as requiring a specialized expertise. It is suprising that in an area in which this Court has affirmed a principle of judicial restraint in the review of administrative action we should be considering the substitution of our judgment for that of the legislature by constitutionalizing in general and abstract terms rights which the legislature has found it necessary to define and qualify in various ways according to the particular field of labour relations involved. The resulting necessity of applying s. 1 of the Charter to a review of particular legislation in this field demonstrates in my respectful opinion the extent to which the

Court becomes involved in a review of legislative policy for which it is really not fitted.

McINTYRE J.: . . . The question raised in this appeal, stated in its simplest terms, is whether the Canadian Charter of Rights and Freedoms gives constitutional protection to the right of a trade union to strike as an incident to collective bargaining. The issue is not whether strike action is an important activity, nor whether it should be protected at law. The importance of strikes in our present system of labour relations is beyond question and each provincial legislature and the federal Parliament has enacted legislation which recognizes a general right to strike. The question for resolution in this appeal is whether such a right is guaranteed by the Charter. If this right is found in the Charter, a subsidiary question must be addressed: is the legislation in issue nevertheless "demonstrably justified" under s. 1 of the Charter? Since it is my conclusion that the Charter does not guarantee the right to strike, I need not consider this subsidiary question. . . .

FREEDOM OF ASSOCIATION AND S. 2(d) OF THE CHARTER

Freedom of association is one of the most fundamental rights in a free society. The freedom to mingle, live and work with others gives meaning and value to the lives of individuals and makes organized society possible. The value of freedom of association as a unifying and liberating force can be seen in the fact that historically the conqueror, seeking to control foreign peoples, invariably strikes first at freedom of association in order to eliminate effective opposition. Meetings are forbidden, curfews are enforced, trade and commerce is suppressed, and rigid controls are imposed to isolate and thus debilitate the individual. Conversely, with the restoration of national sovereignty the democratic state moves at once to remove restrictions on freedom of association.

It is clear that the importance of freedom of association was recognized by

Canadian law prior to the Charter. It is equally clear that prior to the Charter a provincial legislature or Parliament acting within its jurisdiction could regulate and control strikes and collective bargaining. The Charter has reaffirmed the historical importance of freedom of association and guaranteed it as an independent right. The courts must now define the range or scope of this right and its relation to other rights, both those grounded in the Charter and those existing at law without Charter protection. . . .

While a liberal and not overly legalistic approach should be taken to constitutional interpretation, the Charter should not be regarded as an empty vessel to be filled with whatever meaning we might wish from time to time. The interpretation of the Charter, as of all constitutional documents, is constrained by the language, structure, and history of the constitutional text, by constitutional tradition, and by the history, traditions, and underlying philosophies of our society.

THE VALUE OF FREEDOM
OF ASSOCIATION

The starting point of the process of interpretation is an inquiry into the purpose or value of the right at issue. While freedom of association like most other fundamental rights has no single purpose or value, at its core rests a rather simple proposition: the attainment of individual goals, through the exercise of individual rights, is generally impossible without the aid and cooperation of others. "Man, as Aristotle observed, is a 'social animal, formed by nature for living with others', associating with his fellows both to satisfy his desire for social intercourse and to realize common purposes." (L. J. Mac-Farlane, *The Theory and Practice of Human Rights* (1985), p. 82.) This thought was echoed in the familiar words of Alexis de Tocqueville:

The most natural privilege of man, next to the right of acting for himself, is that of combining his exertions with those of his fellow creatures and of acting in common with them. The right of association there-

fore appears to me almost as inalienable in its nature as the right of personal liberty. No legislator can attack it without impairing the foundations of society." (Democracy in America, *P. Bradley, ed., 1945, vol. 1, p. 196).*

The increasing complexity of modern society, which has diminished the power of the individual to act alone, has greatly increased the importance of freedom of association. In the words of Professor T. I. Emerson, ("Freedom of Association and Freedom of Expression," 74 Yale L.J. 1, 1 (1964)):

Freedom of association has always been a vital feature of American society. In modern times it has assumed even greater importance. More and more the individual, in order to realize his own capacities or to stand up to the institutionalized forces that surround him, has found it imperative to join with others of like mind in pursuit of common objectives.

. . . Our society supports a multiplicity of organized groups, clubs and associations which further many different objectives, religious, political, educational, scientific, recreational, and charitable. This exercise of freedom of association serves more than the individual interest, advances more than the individual cause; it promotes general social goals. Of particular importance is the indispensable role played by freedom of association in the functioning of democracy. Paul Cavalluzzo said, (in "Freedom of Association and the Right to Bargain Collectively" in *Litigating the Values of a Nation: The Canadian Charter of Rights and Freedoms* (1986), Weiler and Elliot, eds., at pp. 199-200):

Secondly, it [freedom of association] is an effective check on state action and power. In many ways freedom of association is the most important fundamental freedom because it is the one human right which clearly distinguishes a totalitarian state from a democratic one. In a totalitarian system, the state cannot tolerate group activity because of the powerful check it might have on state power.

Associations serve to educate their members in the operation of democratic institutions. As Tocqueville noted, *supra*, vol. II, at p. 116:

[Individuals] cannot belong to these associations for any length of time without finding out how order is maintained among a large number of men and by what contrivance they are made to advance, harmoniously and methodically, to the same object. Thus they learn to surrender their own will to that of all the rest and to make their own exertions subordinate to the common impulse, things which it is not less necessary to know in civil than in political associations. Political associations may therefore be considered as large free schools, where all the members of the community go to learn the general theory of association.

Associations also make possible the effective expression of political views and thus influence the formation of governmental and social policy. . . . Freedom of association then serves the interest of the individual, strengthens the general social order, and supports the healthy functioning of democratic government.

In considering the constitutional position of freedom of association, it must be recognized that while it advances many group interests and, of course, cannot be exercised alone, it is nonetheless a freedom belonging to the individual and not to the group formed through its exercise. While some provisions in the Constitution involve groups, such as s. 93 of the Constitution Act, 1867 protecting denominational schools, and s. 25 of the Charter referring to existing aboriginal rights, the remaining rights and freedoms are individual rights; they are not concerned with the group as distinct from its members. The group or organization is simply a device adopted by individuals to achieve a fuller realization of individual rights and aspirations. People, by merely combining together, cannot create an entity which has greater constitutional rights and freedoms than they, as individuals, possess. Freedom of association cannot therefore vest independent rights in the group. . . .

The recognition of this principle in the case at bar is of great significance. The only basis on which it is contended that the Charter enshrines a right to strike is that of freedom of association. Collective bargaining is a group concern, a group activity, but the group can exercise only the constitutional rights of its individual members on behalf of those members. If the right asserted is not found in the Charter for the individual, it cannot be implied for the group merely by the fact of association. It follows as well that the rights of the individual members of the group cannot be enlarged merely by the fact of association.

THE SCOPE OF FREEDOM OF ASSOCIATION IN S. 2(d)

Various theories have been advanced to define freedom of association guaranteed by the Constitution. They range from the very restrictive to the virtually unlimited. To begin with, it has been said that freedom of association is limited to a right to associate with others in common pursuits or for certain purposes. Neither the objects nor the actions of the group are protected by freedom of association. . . .

A second approach provides that freedom of association guarantees the collective exercise of constitutional rights or, in other words, the freedom to engage collectively in those activities which are constitutionally protected for each individual. . . .

It will be seen that this approach guarantees not only the right to associate but as well the right to pursue those objects of association which by their nature have constitutional protection.

A third approach postulates that freedom of association stands for the principle that an individual is entitled to do in concert with others that which he may lawfully do alone, and conversely, that individuals and organizations have no right to do in concert what is unlawful when done individually. . . .

A fourth approach would constitutionally protect collective activities which may be said to be fundamental to our culture and traditions and which by common assent are deserving of protection. . . .

A fifth approach rests on the proposition that freedom of association, under s. 2(d) of the Charter, extends constitutional protection to all activities which are essential to the lawful goals of an association. . . .

The sixth and final approach so far isolated in the cases, and by far the most sweeping, would extend the protection of s. 2(d) of the Charter to all acts done in association, subject only to limitation under s. 1 of the Charter. . . .

Turning to the various approaches which have been briefly described above, I would conclude that both the fifth approach (which postulates that freedom of association constitutionally protects all activities which are essential to the lawful goals of an association) and the sixth (which postulates that freedom of association constitutionally protects all activities carried out in association, subject only to reasonable limitation under s. 1 of the Charter) are unacceptable definitions of freedom of association.

The fifth approach rejects the individual nature of freedom of association. To accept it would be to accord an independent constitutional status to the aims, purposes, and activities of the association, and thereby confer greater constitutional rights upon members of the association than upon non-members. It would extend Charter protection to all the activities of an association which are essential to its lawful objects or goals, but, it would not extend an equivalent right to individuals. The Charter does not give, nor was it ever intended to give, constitutional protection to all the acts of an individual which are essential to his or her personal goals or objectives. If Charter protection is given to an association for its lawful acts and objects, then the Charter-protected rights of the association would exceed those of the individual merely by virtue of the fact of association. The unacceptability of such an approach is clearly demonstrated by Peter Gall in "Freedom of Association and Trade Unions: A Double-Edged Constitutional Sword" in *Litigating the Values of a Nation: The Canadian Charter of Rights and Freedoms* (1986) Weiler and Elliot, eds., at p. 247:

A brief example illustrates this point. One of our levels of government may decide to ban the ownership of guns. This would not infringe any individual right under the Charter. But if some individuals have combined to form a gun club, does the Charter's protection of freedom of association mean that the principal activity of the gun club, namely the ownership and use of guns, is now constitutionally protected? One is quickly forced to the conclusion that it does not. The Charter does not protect the right to bear arms, regardless of whether that activity is carried out by an individual or by an association. The mere fact that it is the principal activity of the gun club does not give it a constitutional status. I doubt whether there would be much, if any, disagreement on this point. Thus, by referring to this hypothetical situation we see that the principal activities of associations are not necessarily protected under the concept of freedom of association.

The sixth approach, in my opinion, must be rejected as well, for the reasons expressed in respect of the fifth. It would in even more sweeping terms elevate activities to constitutional status merely because they were performed in association. For obvious reasons, the Charter does not give constitutional protection to all activities performed by individuals. There is, for instance, no Charter protection for the ownership of property, for general commercial activity, or for a host of other lawful activities. And yet, if the sixth approach were adopted, these same activities would receive protection if they were performed by a group rather than by an individual. In my view, such a proposition cannot be accepted. There is simply no justification for according Charter protection to an activity merely because it is performed by more than one person. . . .

I am also of the view that the fourth approach, which postulates that freedom of association embraces those collective activities which have attained a fundamental status in our society because they are deeply rooted in our culture, traditions and history, is an unacceptable definition. By focusing on the activity or the conduct itself, this fourth approach ignores the fundamental purpose of the right. The purpose of freedom of association is to ensure that various goals may be pursued in common as well as individually. Freedom of association is not concerned with the particular activities or goals themselves; it is concerned with how activities or goals may be pursued. While activities such as establishing a home, pursuing an education, or gaining a livelihood are important if not fundamental activities, their importance is not a consequence of their potential collective nature. Their importance flows from the structure and organization of our society and they are as important when pursued individually as they are when pursued collectively. Even institutions such as marriage and the family, which by their nature are collective, do not fall easily or completely under the rubric of freedom of association. For instance, freedom of association would have no bearing on the legal consequences of marriage, such as the control or ownership of matrimonial property. This is not to say that fundamental institutions, such as marriage, will never receive the protection of the Charter. The institution of marriage, for example, might well be protected by freedom of association in combination with other rights and freedoms. Freedom of association alone, however, is not concerned with conduct; its purpose is to guarantee that activities and goals may be pursued in common. When this purpose is considered, it is clear that s. 2(d) of the Charter cannot be interpreted as guaranteeing specific acts or goals, whether or not they are fundamental in our society.

Of the remaining approaches, it must surely be accepted that the concept of freedom of association includes at least the right to join with others in lawful, common pursuits and to establish and maintain organizations and associations as set out in the first approach. This is essentially the freedom of association enjoyed prior to the adoption of the Charter. It is, I believe, equally clear that, in accordance with the second approach, freedom of association should guarantee the collective exercise of constitutional rights. Individual rights protected by the Constitution do not lose that protection when exercised in common with others. People must be free to engage collectively in those activities which are constitutionally protected for each individual. This second definition of freedom of association embraces the purposes and values of the freedoms which were identified earlier. For instance, the indispensable role played by freedom of association in the democratic process is fully protected by guaranteeing the collective exercise of freedom of expression. Group advocacy, which is at the heart of all political parties and special interest groups, would be protected under this definition. As well, group expression directed at educating or informing the public would be protected from government interference (see the judgment of this Court in *Dolphin Delivery, supra*). Indeed, virtually every group activity which is important to the functioning of democracy would be protected by guaranteeing that freedom of expression can be exercised in association with others. Furthermore, religious groups would receive protection if their activities constituted the collective exercise of freedom of religion. Thus, the principal purposes or values of freedom of association would be realized by interpreting s. 2(d) as protecting the collective exercise of the rights enumerated in the Charter.

One enters upon more controversial ground when considering the third approach which provides that whatever action an individual can lawfully pursue as an individual, freedom of association ensures he can pursue with others. Conversely, individuals and organizations have no constitutional right to do in concert what is unlawful when done alone. This approach is broader than the second, since constitutional protection attaches to all group acts which can be lawfully performed by an individual, whether or not the individual has a constitutional right to perform them. It is true, of course, that in this approach the range of Charter-protected activity could be reduced by legislation, because the Legislature has the power to declare what is and what is not lawful activity for the individual. The Legislature, however, would not be able to attack directly the associational character of the activity, since it would be constitutionally bound to treat groups and individuals alike. A simple example illustrates this point: golf is a lawful but not constitutionally protected activity. Under the third approach, the Legislature could prohibit golf entirely. However, the Legislature could not constitutionally provide that golf could be played in pairs but in no greater number, for this would infringe the Charter guarantee of freedom of association. This contrasts with the second approach, which would provide no protection against such legislation, because golf is not a constitutionally protected activity for the individual. Thus, the range of group activity protected by the third approach is greater than that of the second, but the greater range is to some extent illusory because of the power of the Legislature to say what is and what is not lawful activity for the individual. This approach, in my view, is an acceptable interpretation of freedom of association under the Charter. It is clear that, unlike the fifth and sixth approaches, this definition of freedom of association does not provide greater constitutional rights for groups than for individuals; it simply ensures that they are treated alike. If the state chooses to prohibit everyone from engaging in an activity and that activity is not protected under the Constitution, freedom of association will not afford any

protection to groups engaging in the activity. Freedom of association as an independent right comes into play under this formulation when the state has permitted an individual to engage in an activity and yet forbidden the group from doing so. . . .

It follows from this discussion that I interpret freedom of association in s. (d) of the Charter to mean that Charter protection will attach to exercise in association of such rights as have Charter protection when exercised by the individual. Furthermore, freedom of association means the freedom to associate for the purposes of activities which are lawful when performed alone. But, since the fact of association will not by itself confer additional rights on individuals, the association does not acquire a constitutionally guaranteed freedom to do what is unlawful for the individual.

When this definition of freedom of association is applied, it is clear that it does not guarantee the right to strike. Since the right to strike is not independently protected under the Charter, it can receive protection under freedom of association only if it is an activity which is permitted by law to an individual. Accepting this conclusion, the appellants argue that freedom of association must guarantee the right to strike because individuals may lawfully refuse to work. This position, however, is untenable for two reasons. First, it is not correct to say that it is lawful for an individual employee to cease work during the currency of his contract of employment. . . . The second reason is simply that there is no analogy whatever between the cessation of work by a single employee and a strike conducted in accordance with modern labour legislation. The individual has, by reason of the cessation of work, either breached or terminated his contract of employment. It is true that the law will not compel the specific performance of the contract by ordering him back to work as this would reduce "the employee to a state tantamount to slavery" (I. Christie, *Employment Law in Canada* (1980), p. 268). But, this is markedly different from a lawful strike.

An employee who ceases work does not contemplate a return to work, while employees on strike always contemplate a return to work. In recognition of this fact, the law does not regard a strike as either a breach of contract or a termination of employment. Every province and the federal Parliament has enacted legislation which preserves the employer-employee relationship during a strike. . . .

Modern labour relations legislation has so radically altered the legal relationship between employees and employers in unionized industries that no analogy may be drawn between the lawful actions of individual employees in ceasing to work and the lawful actions of union members in engaging in a strike. . . . It is apparent, in my view, that interpreting freedom of association to mean that every individual is free to do with others that which he is lawfully entitled to do alone would not entail guaranteeing the right to strike. I am supported in this conclusion by the Chief Justice, who states at p. 46 in his judgment, "There is no individual equivalent to a strike. The refusal to work by one individual does not parallel a collective refusal to work. The latter is qualitatively rather than quantitatively different." Restrictions on strikes are not aimed at and do not interfere with the collective or associational character of trade unions. It is therefore my conclusion that the concept of freedom of association does not extend to the constitutional guarantee of a right to strike. This conclusion is entirely consistent with the general approach of the Charter which accords rights and freedoms to the individual but, with a few exceptions noted earlier, does not confer group rights. It is also to be observed that the Charter, with the possible exception of s. 6(2)(b) (right to earn a livelihood in any province) and s. 6(4), does not concern itself with economic rights. Since trade unions are not one of the groups specifically mentioned by the Charter, and are overwhelmingly, though not exclusively, concerned with the economic interests of their members, it would run counter to the overall structure and approach of the Charter to accord by implication special constitutional rights to trade unions.

Labour relations and the development of the body of law which has grown up around that subject have been for many years one of the major preoccupations of legislators, economic and social writers, and the general public. Strikes are commonplace in Canada and have been for many years. The framers of the Constitution must be presumed to have been aware of these facts. Indeed, questions of collective bargaining and a right to strike were discussed in the Minutes of Proceedings and Evidence of the Special Joint Committee of the Senate and of the House of Commons on the Constitution of Canada (Issue No. 43, pp. 68-79, January 22, 1981). It is apparent from the deliberations of the Committee that the right to strike was understood to be separate and distinct from the right to bargain collectively. And, while a resolution was proposed for the inclusion of a specific right to bargain collectively, no resolution was proposed for the inclusion of the right to strike. This affords strong support for the proposition that the inclusion of a right to strike was not intended.

Specific reference to the right to strike appears in the constitutions of France (in the preamble of the Constitution of the Vth Republic of 1958) and Italy (Art. 40). Further, in Japan (Art. 28) the rights of trade unions are specifically guaranteed. The framers of the Constitution must be presumed to have been aware of these constitutional provisions. The omission of similar provisions in the Charter, taken with the fact that the overwhelming preoccupation of the Charter is with individual, political, and democratic rights with conspicuous inattention to economic and property rights, speaks strongly against any implication of a right to strike. Accordingly, if s. 2(d) is read in the context of the whole Charter, it cannot, in my opinion, support an interpretation of freedom of association which could include a right to strike.

Furthermore, it must be recognized that

the right to strike accorded by legislation throughout Canada is of relatively recent vintage. It is truly the product of this century and, in its modern form, is in reality the product of the latter half of this century. It cannot be said that it has become so much a part of our social and historical traditions that it has acquired the status of an immutable, fundamental right, firmly embedded in our traditions, our political and social philosophy. There is then no basis, as suggested in the fourth approach to freedom of association, for implying a constitutional right to strike. It may well be said that labour relations have become a matter of fundamental importance in our society, but every incident of that general topic has not. The right to strike as an element of labour relations has always been the subject of legislative control. It has been abrogated from time to time in special circumstances and is the subject of legal regulation and control in all Canadian jurisdictions. In my view, it cannot be said that at this time it has achieved status as a fundamental right which should be implied in the absence of specific reference in the Charter.

While I have reached a conclusion and expressed the view that the Charter upon its face cannot support an implication of a right to strike, there is as well, in my view, a sound reason grounded in social policy against any such implication. Labour law, as we have seen, is a fundamentally important as well as an extremely sensitive subject. It is based upon a political and economic compromise between organized labour—a very powerful socio-economic force—on the one hand, and the employers of labour—an equally powerful socio-economic force—on the other. The balance between the two forces is delicate and the public-at-large depends for its security and welfare upon the maintenance of that balance. One group concedes certain interests in exchange for concessions from the other. There is clearly no correct balance which may be struck giving permanent satisfaction to the two groups, as well as securing

the public interest. The whole process is inherently dynamic and unstable. Care must be taken then in considering whether constitutional protection should be given to one aspect of this dynamic and evolving process while leaving the others subject to the social pressures of the day. Great changes—economic, social, and industrial—are afoot, not only in Canada and in North America, but as well in other parts of the world. Changes in the Canadian national economy, the decline in resource-based as well as heavy industries, the changing patterns of international trade and industry, have resulted in great pressure to reassess the traditional approaches to economic and industrial questions, including questions of labour law and policy. In such countries as Sweden (Prof. Dr. Axel Adlercreutz, Sweden, in *International Encyclopaedia for Labour Law and Industrial Relations* (1985), vol. 9, ed.-in-chief Prof. Dr. R. Blanpain) and West Germany (Prof. Dr. Th. Ramm, Federal Republic of Germany in *International Encyclopaedia for Labour Law and Industrial Relations* (1979), vol. 5) different directions in labour relations have been taken. It has been said that these changes have led to increased efficiency and job satisfaction. Whatever the result of such steps, however, it is obvious that the immediate direction of labour policy is unclear. It is, however, clear that labour policy can only be developed step by step with, in this country, the Provinces playing their "classic federal role as laboratories for legal experimentation with our industrial relations ailments" (Paul Weiler, *Reconcilable Differences* (1980), p. 11). The fulfilment of this role in the past has resulted in the growth and development of the body of labour law which now prevails in Canada. The fluid and constantly changing conditions of modern society demand that it continue. To intervene in that dynamic process at this early stage of Charter development by implying constitutional protection for a right to strike would, in my view, give to one of the contending forces an economic weapon removed from and made immune, subject to s. 1, to legislative control which could go far towards freezing the development of labour relations and curtailing that process of evolution necessary to meet the changing circumstances of a modern society in a modern world. This, I repeat, is not to say that a right to strike does not exist at law or that it should be abolished. It merely means that at this stage of our Charter development such a right should not have constitutional status which would impair the process of future development in legislative hands. . . .

To constitutionalize a particular feature of labour relations by entrenching a right to strike would have other adverse effects. Our experience with labour relations has shown that the courts, as a general rule, are not the best arbiters of disputes which arise from time to time. Labour legislation has recognized this fact and has created other procedures and other tribunals for the more expeditious and efficient settlements of labour problems. Problems arising in labour matters frequently involve more than legal questions. Political, social, and economic questions frequently dominate in labour disputes. The legislative creation of conciliation officers, conciliation boards, labour relations boards, and labour dispute-resolving tribunals, has gone far in meeting needs not attainable in the court system. The nature of labour disputes and grievances and the other problems arising in labour matters dictates that special procedures outside the ordinary court system must be employed in their resolution. Judges do not have the expert knowledge always helpful and sometimes necessary in the resolution of labour problems. The courts will generally not be furnished in labour cases, if past experience is to guide us, with an evidentiary base upon which full resolution of the dispute may be made. In my view, it is scarcely contested that specialized labour tribunals are better suited than courts for resolving labour problems, except for the resolution of purely legal questions. If the right to strike is constitutionalized, then its application, its extent, and any questions of its legality, become matters of law. This would inevitably throw the courts back into the field of labour relations and much of the value of specialized labour tribunals would be lost. . . .

A further problem will arise from constitutionalizing the right to strike. In every case where a strike occurs and relief is sought in the courts, the question of the application of s. 1 of the Charter may be raised to determine whether some attempt to control the right may be permitted. This has occurred in the case at bar. The section 1 inquiry involves the reconsideration by a court of the balance struck by the Legislature in the development of labour policy. The court is called upon to determine, as a matter of constitutional law, which government services are essential and whether the alternative of arbitration is adequate compensation for the loss of a right to strike. In the Public Service Alliance Case, the Court must decide whether mere postponement of collective bargaining is a reasonable limit, given the Government's substantial interest in reducing inflation and the growth in government expenses. In the *Dairy Workers* case, the Court is asked to decide whether the harm caused to dairy farmers through a closure of the dairies is of sufficient importance to justify prohibiting strike action and lockouts. None of these issues is amenable to principled resolution. There are no clearly correct answers to these questions. They are of a nature peculiarly apposite to the functions of the Legislature. However, if the right to strike is found in the Charter, it will be the courts which time and time again will have to resolve these questions, relying only on the evidence and arguments presented by the parties, despite the social implications of each decision. This is a legislative function into which the courts should not intrude. It has been said that the courts, because of the Charter, will have to enter the legislative sphere. Where rights are specifically guaranteed in the Charter, this may on occasion be true. But where no specific right is found in the Charter and the only support for its constitutional guarantee is an implication, the courts should refrain from intrusion into the field of legislation. That is the function of the freely-elected Legislatures and Parliament.

The Judgement of Dickson, C.J. and Wilson, J. was delivered by

DICKSON, C.J. (dissenting): . . . Freedom of association is the freedom to combine together for the pursuit of common purposes or the advancement of common causes. It is one of the fundamental freedoms guaranteed by the Charter, a *sine qua non* of any free and democratic society, protecting individuals from the vulnerability of isolation and ensuring the potential of effective participation in society. In every area of human endeavour and throughout history individuals have formed associations for the pursuit of common interests and aspirations. Through association individuals are able to ensure that they have a voice in shaping the circumstances integral to their needs, rights and freedoms.

Freedom of association is the cornerstone of modern labour relations. Historically, workers have combined to overcome the inherent inequalities of bargaining power in the employment relationship and to protect themselves from unfair, unsafe, or exploitative working conditions. . . .

THE MEANING OF S. 2(d)

At the outset, it should be noted that, contrary to submissions by the respondent and some of the intervenors in support, the purpose of s. 2 of the Charter must extend beyond merely protecting rights which already existed at the time of the Charter's entrenchment. . . .

Similarly, the scope of the Charter's provisions is not to be confined by the fact of legislative regulation in a particular subject area. In argument, counsel for the respondent seemed to suggest that if freedom of association were interpreted to include strike activity, this would "constitutionalize" a statutory right. His argument appeared to be premised on the proposition that, because the "right to strike" was a subject of legislative regulation prior to the Charter's entrenchment, it followed that strike activity could not be a matter for constitutional protection after entrenchment of the Charter. While it may be true that the Charter was not framed for the purpose of guaranteeing rights conferred by legislative enactment, the view that certain rights and freedoms cannot be protected by the Charter's provisions because they are subject of statutory regulation is premised on a fundamental misconception about the nature of judicial review under a written constitution.

The Constitution is supreme law. Its provisions are not to be circumscribed by what the legislature has done in the past, but, rather, the activities of the legislature—past, present and future—must be consistent with the principles set down in the Constitution. . . .

This is not to say, however, that the legislative regulation of collective bargaining and strikes is entirely irrelevant to the manner in which a constitutional freedom to strike may be given effect in particular circumstances: see, on this point, my reasons in the *Dairy Workers* case, released concurrently. But the present case does not involve a challenge to the general labour law of Alberta which permits strike activity, subject to regulation. This appeal concerns the substitution of an entirely different mechanism for resolving labour disputes for particular employees, and one which does not merely regulate the freedom to strike but abrogates it entirely. . . .

A wide variety of alternative interpretations of freedom of association has been advanced in the jurisprudence summarized above and in argument before this Court.

At one extreme is a purely constitutive definition whereby freedom of association entails only a freedom to belong to or form an association. On this view, the constitutional guarantee does not extend beyond protecting the individual's status as a member of an association. It would not protect his or her associational actions.

In the trade union context, then, a constitutive definition would find a *prima facie* violation of s. 2(d) of the Charter in legislation such as s. 2(1) of the Police Officers Act which prohibits membership in any organization affiliated with a trade union. But it could find no violation of s. 2(d) in respect of legislation which prohibited a concerted refusal to work. Indeed, a wide variety of trade union activities, ranging from the organization of social activities for its members, to the establishment of union pension plans, to the discussion of collective bargaining strategy, could be prohibited by the state without infringing s. 2(d).

The essentially formal nature of a constitutive approach to freedom of association is equally apparent when one considers other types of associational activity in our society. While the constitutive approach might find a possible violation of s. 2(d) in a legislative enactment which prohibited marriage for certain classes of people, it would hold inoffensive an enactment which precluded the same people from engaging in the activities integral to a marriage, such as cohabiting and raising children together. If freedom of association only protects the joining together of persons for common purposes, but not the pursuit of the very activities for which the association was formed, then the freedom is indeed legalistic, ungenerous, indeed vapid.

In my view, while it is unquestionable that s. 2(d), at a minimum, guarantees the liberty of persons to be in association or belong to an organization, it must extend beyond a concern for associational status to give effective protection to the interests to which the constitutional guarantee is directed. . . .

A second approach, the derivative approach, prevalent in the United States, embodies a somewhat more generous definition of freedom of association than the formal, constitutive approach. In the Canadian context, it is suggested by some that associational action which relates specifically to one of the other freedoms enumerated in s. 2 is constitutionally protected, but other associational activity is not.

I am unable, however, to accept that freedom of association should be interpreted so restrictively. Section 2(d) of the Charter provides an explicit and independent guarantee of freedom of association. In this respect it stands in marked contrast to the First Amendment to the American Constitution. The derivative approach would, in my view, largely make surplusage of s. 2(d). The associational or collective dimensions of s. 2(a) and (b) have already been recognized by this Court in *R. v. Big M Drug Mart Ltd.* without resort to s. 2(d). The associational aspect of s. 2(c) clearly finds adequate protection in the very expression of a freedom of peaceful assembly. What is to be learnt from the United States jurisprudence is not that freedom of association must be restricted to associational activities involving independent constitutional rights, but rather, that the express conferral of a freedom of association is unnecessary if all that is intended is to give effect to the collective enjoyment of other individual freedoms.

I am also unimpressed with the argument that the inclusion of s. 2(d) with freedoms of a "political" nature requires a narrow or restrictive interpretation of freedom of association. I am unable to regard s. 2 as embodying purely political freedoms. Paragraph (a), which protects freedom of conscience and religion is quite clearly not exclusively political in nature. It would, moreover, be unsatisfactory to overlook our Constitution's history of giving special recognition to collectivities or communities of interest other than the government and political parties. Sections 93 and 133 of the Constitution Act, 1867 and sections 16-24, 25, 27 and 29 of the Charter, dealing variously with denominational schools, language rights, aboriginal rights, and our multicultural heritage implicitly embody an awareness of the importance of various collectivities in the pursuit of educational, linguistic, cultural and social as well as political ends. Just as the individual is incapable of resisting political domination without the support of persons with similar values, so too is he or she, in isolation, incapable of resisting domination, over the long term, in many other aspects of life.

Freedom of association is protected in s. 2(d) under the rubric of "fundamental" freedoms. In my view, the "fundamental" nature of freedom of association relates to the central importance to the individual of his or her interaction with fellow human beings. The purpose of the constitutional guarantee of freedom of association is, I believe, to recognize the profoundly social nature of human endeavours and to protect the individual from state-enforced isolation in the pursuit of his or her ends. In the famous words of Alexis de Tocqueville in *Democracy in America*, vol. 1, (P. Bradley, ed. 1945) at p. 196:

The most natural privilege of man, next to the right of acting for himself, is that of combining his exertions with those of his fellow creatures and of acting in common with them. The right of association therefore appears . . . almost as inalienable in its nature as the right of personal liberty. No legislator can attack it without impairing the foundations of society.

As social beings, our freedom to act with others is a primary condition of community life, human progress and civilized society. Through association, individuals have been able to participate in determining and controlling the immediate circumstances of their lives, and the rules, mores and principles which govern the communities in which they live. As John Stuart Mill stated, "if public spirit, generous sentiments, or true justice and equality are desired, association, not isolation, of interests, is the school in which these excellences are nurtured" (*Principles of Political Economy* (1893), vol. 2, at p. 352).

Freedom of association is most essential in those circumstances where the individual is liable to be prejudiced by the actions of some larger and more powerful entity, like the government or an employer. Association has always been the means through which political, cultural and racial minorities, religious groups and workers have sought to attain their purposes and fulfil their aspirations; it has enabled those who would otherwise be vulnerable and ineffective to meet on more equal terms the power and strength of those with whom their interests interact and, perhaps, conflict. Emerson, "Freedom of Association and Freedom of Expression," (1964) 74 Yale L.J. 1 at p. 1, states that:

More and more the individual, in order to realize his own capacities or to stand up to the institutionalized forces that surround him, has found it imperative to join with others of like mind in pursuit of common objectives.

What freedom of association seeks to protect is not associational activities *qua* particular activities, but the freedom of individuals to interact with, support, and be supported by, their fellow humans in the varied activities in which they choose to engage. But this is not an unlimited constitutional license for all group activity. The mere fact that an activity is capable of being carried out by several people together, as well as individually, does not mean that the activity acquires constitutional protection from legislative prohibition or regulation.

I believe that . . . s. 2(d) normally embraces the liberty to do collectively that which one is permitted to do as an individual. . . . However, it is not in my view correct to regard this proposition as the exclusive touchstone for determining the presence or absence of a violation of s. 2(d). Certainly, if a legislature permits an individual to enjoy an activity which it forecloses to a collectivity, it may properly be inferred that the legislature intended to prohibit the collective activity because of its collective or associational aspect. Conversely, one may infer from a legislative proscription which applies equally to individuals and groups that the purpose of the legislation was a *bona fide* prohibition of a particular activity because of detrimental qualities inhering in the activity (e.g. criminal conduct), and not merely because of the fact that the activity might sometimes be done in association. . . . There will, however, be occasions when no analogy involving individuals can be found for associational activity, or when a comparison between groups and individuals fails to capture the essence of a possible violation of associational rights. This is precisely the situation in this case. There is no individual equivalent to a strike. The refusal to work by one individual does not parallel a collective refusal to work. The latter is qualitatively rather than quantitatively different. The overarching consideration remains whether a legislative enactment or administrative action interferes with the freedom of persons to join and act with others in common pursuits. The legislative purpose which will render legislation invalid is the attempt to preclude associational conduct because of its concerted or associational nature.

I wish to refer to one further concern. It has been suggested that associational activity for the pursuit of economic ends should not be accorded constitutional protection. If by this it is meant that something as fundamental as a person's livelihood or dignity in the workplace is beyond the scope of constitutional protection, I cannot agree. If, on the other hand, it is meant that concerns of an exclusively pecuniary nature are excluded from such protection, such an argument would merit careful consideration. In the present case, however, we are concerned with interests which go far beyond those of a merely pecuniary nature.

Work is one of the most fundamental aspects in a person's life, providing the individual with a means of financial support and, as importantly, a contributory role in society. A person's employment is an essential component of his or her sense of identity, self worth and emotional well-being. Accordingly, the conditions in which a person works are highly significant in shaping the whole compendium of psychological, emotional and physical elements of a person's dignity and self respect. . . .

The role of association has always been vital as a means of protecting the essential needs and interest of working people. Throughout history, workers have associated to overcome their vulnerability as individuals to the strength of their employers. The capacity to bargain collectively has long been recognized as one of the integral and primary functions of associations of working people. While trade unions also fulfil other important social, political and charitable functions, collective bargaining remains vital to the capacity of individual employees to participate in ensuring fair wages, health and safety protections, and equitable and humane working conditions. As Professor Paul Weiler explains in *Reconcilable Differences: New Directions in Canadian Labour Law* (1980), at p. 31:

An apt way of putting it is to say that good collective bargaining tries to subject the employment relationship and the work environment to the "rule of law." Many theorists of industrial relations believe that this function of protecting the employee from the abuse of managerial power, thereby enhancing the dignity of the worker as a person, is the primary value of collective bargaining, one which entitles the institution to positive encouragement from the law.

Professor Weiler goes on to characterize collective bargaining as "intrinsically valuable as an experience in self-government" (p. 33), and writes at p. 32:

. . . collective bargaining is the most significant occasion upon which most of these workers ever participate in making social decisions about matters that are salient to their daily lives. That is the essence of collective bargaining.

A similar rationale for endorsing collective bargaining was advanced in the Woods Task Force Report on Canadian Industrial Relations (1968), at p. 96:

One of the most cherished hopes of those who originally championed the concept of collective bargaining was that it would introduce into the work place some of the basic features of the political democracy that was becoming the hallmark of most of the western world. Traditionally referred to as industrial democracy, it can be described as the substitution of the rule of law for the rule of men in the work place.

Closely related to collective bargaining, at least in our existing industrial relations context, is the freedom to strike. . . .

I am satisfied, in sum, that whether or not freedom of association generally extends to protecting associational activity for the pursuit of exclusively pecuniary ends—a question on which I express no opinion—collective bargaining protects important employee interests which cannot be characterized as merely pecuniary in nature. Under our existing system of industrial relations, effective constitutional protection of the associational interests of employees in the collective bargaining process requires concomitant protection of their freedom to withdraw collectively their services, subject to s. 1 of the Charter. . . .

SECTION 1

The respondent submits that even if any of the legislative provisions at issue in this appeal violates freedom of association as guaranteed by s. 2(d) of the Charter, it can be upheld under s. 1 of the Charter. . . .

The onus of demonstrating that a limit on a right or freedom should be upheld under s. 1 is on the party seeking to uphold the limit. The standard of proof is the preponderance of probabilities and, as a general rule, evidence is required to meet this standard: see *R. v. Oakes*, [1986] 1 S.C.R. 103, and authorities therein.

The constituent elements of any s. 1 inquiry are as follows. First, the legislative objective, in pursuit of which the measures in question are implemented, must be sufficiently significant to warrant overriding a constitutionally guaranteed right: it must be related to social concerns which are pressing and substantial in a free and democratic society. Second, the means chosen to advance such an objective must be reasonable and demonstrably justified in a free and democratic society. This requirement of proportionality of means to ends normally has three aspects: a) there must be a rational connection between the measures and the objective they are to serve; b) the measures should impair as little as possible the right or freedom in question; and, c) the deleterious effects of the measures must be justifiable in light of the objective which they are to serve. See *Oakes*, and authorities cited therein.

As I understand the respondent's submissions, there are two objectives which the legislation in issue in this Reference is designed to achieve: 1) protection of essential services and 2) protection of government from political pressure through strike action. The question is whether either or both of these are "of sufficient importance to warrant overriding a constitutionally guaranteed right or freedom" (*Big M Drug Mart Ltd.*), or, in other words, whether they relate to "pressing and substantial social concerns" (*Oakes*). The proportionality of the measures in relation to the objectives must then be assessed.

I observe at the outset that the analysis below is limited to assessing the justifications advanced by the province for its legislative action. It is the actual objectives of the Alberta Legislature and not some other legitimate but hypothetical objectives for passing the particular statutes in question that must be scrutinized. It may be that other rationales will be advanced in future cases. The Court has not been asked, in this case, to determine whether economic harm to third parties can justify the abrogation of the freedom to strike. Nor has it been asked to determine whether a universally applicable substitute for the confrontational strike/lockout paradigm of present-day industrial relations would be acceptable. It might be that some alternative scheme, be it a novel one of worker participation in employer decisions through ownership or otherwise, or a more familiar one, such as arbitration, would be acceptable. The Constitution does not freeze into place an existing formula of industrial relations.

The Protection of Essential Services. The protection of services which are truly essential is in my view a legislative objective of sufficient importance for the purpose of s. 1 of the Charter. It is, however, necessary to define "essential services' in a manner consistent with the justificatory standards set out in s. 1. The logic of s. 1 in the present circumstances requires that an essential service be one the interruption of which would threaten serious harm to the general public or to a part of the population. In the context of an argument relating to harm of a non-economic nature I find the decisions of the Freedom of Association Committee of the I.L.O. to be helpful and persuasive. These decisions have consistently defined an essential service as a service ''whose interruption would endanger the life, personal safety or health of the whole or part of the population'' (Freedom of Association and Collective Bargaining: General Survey by the Committee of Experts on the Application of Conventions and Recommendations, Report III (Part 4B), I.L.O. Geneva, 1983). In my view, and without attempting an exhaustive list, persons essential to the maintenance and administration of the rule of law and national security would also be included within the ambit of essential services. Mere inconvenience to members of the public does not fall within the ambit of the essential services justification for abrogating the freedom to strike.

Having decided that the protection of essential services is an objective of sufficient importance, it is necessary for the respondent to demonstrate proportionality between the measures adopted and the objective. Four classes of employees are covered by the Acts: public service employees (Public Service Act); firefighters and employees of employers who operate approved hospitals under the Hospitals Act (Labour Relations Act); and police officers (Police Officers Act). The government must, as a first step, prove, on a balance of probabilities, that these employees are "essential"; otherwise the abrogation of their freedom to strike would be over-inclusive and unjustified under s. 1.

Counsel for the Attorney General of Alberta did not adduce any evidence on this point. He submitted only that essential services must not be interrupted and that, though some of the employees covered by the Acts are not essential, "they are so closely linked to those providing essential services as to make it reasonable that they should be treated in the same way." In *Oakes*, this Court acknowledged that the extent of evidentiary submissions required under s. 1 would vary according to the nature of the case. . . .

The essentiality of police officers and firefighters is, in my view, obvious and self-evident, and does not have to be proven by evidence. Interruption in police protection and firefighting would clearly endanger life, personal safety and health. Therefore, I believe the legislature's decision to prevent such interruptions is rationally connected to the objective of protecting essential services.

The situation with respect to employees of employers who operate approved hospitals under the Hospitals Act is quite different. Prohibiting the right to strike across the board in hospital employment is too drastic a measure for achieving the object of protecting essential services. It is neither obvious nor self-evident that all bargaining units in hospitals represent workers who provide essential services, or that those who do not provide essential services are "so closely linked" to those who do as to justify similar treatment. . . .

Counsel for the Attorney-General has

not provided any evidence or information from which it can be concluded on a preponderance of probabilities that services will be interrupted whenever strike activity is undertaken by any of the bargaining units in a hospital. While it may be obvious or self-evident that strikes by certain hospital employees, such as nurses or doctors, would be inimical to the hospital's ability to dispense proper health care, the same cannot be said for all hospital workers without some evidentiary basis. For this reason, I do not believe it can be maintained that the employees covered by s. 117.1 of the Labour Relations Act are all "essential." The provision is too wide to be justified as relating to essential services for the purpose of s. 1.

The Public Service Act is, in my opinion, a victim of the same defect. . . .

Protection of the Government From Political Pressure. As mentioned above, the respondent advances a second argument for justification under s. 1, namely, that the legislation is necessary to protect the government from the political pressure of strike action by its employees. In other words, even if public servants are not truly essential, the fact they are employees of the government is sufficient reason for denying them the freedom to strike. I do not find this argument convincing. The respondent has not submitted any evidence from which it can be concluded that collective bargaining and strike activity in the public sector have or will cause undue political pressure on government. Indeed, all across Canada, collective bargaining and freedom to strike have played an important role in public sector labour relations. . . .

In my opinion the fact of government employment is not a sufficient reason for the purpose of s. 1 for limiting freedom of association through legislative prohibition of freedom to strike. It has not been shown that all public service employees have a substantial bargaining advantage on account of their employer's governmental status. Nor has it been shown that any political pressure exerted on the government during strikes is of an unusual or peculiarly detrimental nature.

Arbitration as a Substitute for Freedom to Strike. As noted above the provisions relating to police officers and firefighters meet the first test of proportionality: there is a rational connection between prohibiting freedom to strike in these services and the legislative objective of protecting essential services. It is helpful to consider, therefore, whether the measures adopted impair as little as possible the freedom of association of those affected. Clearly, if the freedom to strike were denied and no effective and fair means for resolving bargaining disputes were put in its place, employees would be denied any input at all in ensuring fair and decent working conditions, and labour relations law would be skewed entirely to the advantage of the employer. It is for this reason that legislative prohibition of freedom to strike must be accompanied by a mechanism for dispute resolution by a third party. I agree with the Alberta International Fire Fighters Association at p. 22 of its factum that "it is generally accepted that employers and employees should be on an equal footing in terms of their positions in strike situations or at compulsory arbitration where the right to strike is withdrawn." The purpose of such a mechanism is to ensure that the loss in bargaining power through legislative prohibition of strikes is balanced by access to a system which is capable of resolving in a fair, effective and expeditious manner disputes which arise between employees and employers.

As noted above, the purpose of the prohibitions of strike activity of police officers and firefighters is to prevent interruptions in essential services. If prohibition of strikes is to be the least drastic means of achieving this purpose it must, in my view, be accompanied by adequate guarantees for safeguarding workers' interests. Any system of conciliation or arbitration must be fair and effective or, in the words of the I.L.O. Committee on Freedom of Association "adequate, impartial and speedy . . . in which the parties can take part at every stage'': Case No. 1247, I.L.O. Official Bulletin, vol. LXVIII, Series B., No. 3, 1985, p. 36.

The contentious issues in respect to the legislative provisions concerning arbitration are as follows: (i) they require the arbitrator to consider certain items; (ii) they limit the arbitrability of certain items; and (iii) they place discretion in the hands of a minister or agency of the government to decide whether or not a dispute will go to arbitration. I will deal with each of these in turn.

(i) *Arbitrator Must Consider Certain Items*. Under the Labour Relations Act and the Police Officers Act arbitrators are required to consider (i) the fiscal policies of the government as declared by the Provincial Treasurer in writing (s. 117.8(a)(iii) Labour Relations Act; s. 15(a)(iii) Police Officers Act); and (ii) wages and benefits in private and public unionized and non-unionized employment (117.8(a)(i) Labour Relations Act; s. 15(a)(i) Police Officers Act). . . .

In my view the fiscal policy of the government is a measure of the employer's ability to pay, and there is nothing improper in requiring the arbitrator to consider it. The arbitrator is not bound by the statute to take the stated fiscal policy as the conclusive measure of the employer's ability to pay, and it would be open to the unions to make submissions requesting that the arbitrator depart from the fiscal policy.

Turning to s. 117.8(a)(i) of the Labour Relations Act, and s. 15(a)(i) of the Police Officers Act, which require that arbitrators consider the wages and benefits of private and public unionized and non-unionized employees, I do not believe these sections compromise the adequacy of the arbitration system. As Professor Swan has stated (in The Search for Meaningful Criteria in Interest Arbitration, Reprint Series No. 41, Industrial Relations Centre, Queen's University, 1978) at p. 11: ''Fairness remains an essentially relative concept, and it there-

fore depends directly upon the identification of fair comparisons if it is to be meaningful.'' Under s. 117.8(a)(i) and s. 15(a)(i) the arbitrator is required to consider, presumably for the sake of comparison, the wages of unionized, non-unionized, public sector and private sector employees. The appellant, Alberta International Fire Fighter Association, implies that s. 117.8(a)(i) and s. 15(a)(i) mandate an unfair comparison; one that ''is bound to result in lowering the wages of the unionized employees.'' I do not agree. A requirement to establish as broad a comparative base as possible does not, in my view, compromise the fairness of the arbitration, or disadvantage the employees concerned.

(ii) *Limiting the Arbitrability of Certain Items*. Section 48(2) of the Public Service Act establishes that certain matters cannot be referred to arbitration or contained in an arbitral award. These matters are generally arbitrable in other labour relations contexts. . . .

As noted above, an arbitration system must be fair and effective if it is to be adequate in restoring to employees the bargaining power they are denied through prohibition of strike activity. In my opinion, the exclusion of these subjects from the arbitration process compromises the effectiveness of the process as a means of ensuring equal bargaining power in the absence of freedom to strike. Serious doubt is cast upon the fairness and effectiveness of an arbitration scheme where matters which would normally be bargainable are excluded from arbitration. ''Given that without some binding mechanism for dispute resolution, meaningful collective bargaining is very unlikely, it seems more reasonable to ensure that the scope of arbitrability is as wide as the scope of bargainability if the bargaining process is to work at all'': Swan, ''Safety Belt or Strait-Jacket? Restrictions on the Scope of Public Sector Collective Bargaining,'' in *Essays in Collective Bargaining and Industrial Democracy*, 20 at p. 36.

It may be necessary in some circumstances for a government employer to maintain absolute control over aspects of employment through exclusion of certain subjects from arbitration. The presumption, however, must be against such exclusion to ensure the effectiveness of an arbitration scheme as a substitute for freedom to strike is not compromised. In the present case, the government has not satisfied the onus upon it to demonstrate such necessity.

(iii) *The Absence of a Right to go to Arbitration.* None of the arbitration schemes in the Acts in question in this Reference provides a right to refer a dispute to arbitration. Rather, a discretionary power is placed in a Minister or an administrative board to establish an arbitration board if deemed appropriate: see above, s. 50 of the Public Service Act, s. 117.3 of the Labour Relations Act, and s. 10 of the Police Officers Act. Under s. 50 of the Public Service Act the Public Service Employees Relations Board can direct the parties to continue collective bargaining or appoint a mediator instead of establishing an arbitration board. Under s. 117.3 of the Labour Relations Act and s. 10 of the Police Officers Act the Minister can direct the parties to continue collective bargaining and can prescribe the procedures or conditions under which it is to take place.

The respondent makes no submissions in respect of these provisions. In the absence of argument or evidence demonstrative of why such government involvement is necessary in the arbitration process, I believe the legal capacity of a Minister or administrative board to determine when and under what circumstances a dispute is to reach arbitration compromises the fairness and effectiveness of compulsory arbitration as a substitute for the freedom to strike. In effect, under the Labour Relations Act and Police Officers Act the employer—i.e. the executive branch of government—has absolute authority to determine at what point a dispute should go to arbitration. Such authority considerably undermines the balance of power between employer and employee which the arbitration scheme is designed to promote. Under previous legislation either party had an absolute right to remit the matter to an arbitration board. In the present legislation they do not, and counsel for the respondent has not provided any reasons for this alteration. The discretionary power of a Minister or administrative board to determine whether or not a dispute goes to arbitration is, in my view, an unjustified compromise of the effectiveness of the arbitration procedure in promoting equality of bargaining power between the parties. . . .

50. Morgentaler *v.* the Queen *(1988)*

~ The *Morgentaler* decision has been the most publicized and most controversial Charter decision to date. This is due in part to the emotional and divisive character of its subject matter—abortion. It also relects the flamboyant personality of the appellant. Pro-choice crusader Dr. Henry Morgentaler's victory culminated almost twenty years of civil disobedience in protest of Canada's abortion law. In the early seventies Morgentaler openly defied the abortion law by performing unauthorized abortions in his Montreal clinic. In three successive trials, juries refused to convict him. However, the Quebec Court of Appeal (1974) overturned his first jury acquittal and took the unprecedented step of directly convicting him rather than remanding the case back for re-trial. The Supreme Court of Canada rejected Morgentaler's appeal (1975), and he was sentenced to eighteen months in prison.

Ironically, Morgentaler's legal defeat laid the basis for a subsequent political victory. In response to protests, Parliament amended the Criminal Code to withdraw the power to convict from appeal courts. In light of what was immediately dubbed "the Morgentaler amendment," the federal Attorney-General granted Morgentaler a new trial. After his third jury acquittal, Morgentaler was released from prison. The newly elected Parti Quebecois government of René Levesque dropped outstanding charges against Morgentaler, and announced they would no longer enforce section 251 (the abortion section) of the Criminal Code in Quebec. The Levesque government subsequently supported the creation of community health clinics that included abortion services. By 1980, Morgentaler had achieved his objective of easy and inexpensive access to abortion services in Quebec. In the rest of Canada, however, the section 251 regime was still in effect.

In 1983, Morgentaler renewed his campaign of civil disobedience. With financial backing from the Canadian Abortion Rights Action League (CARAL), he opened abortion clinics in Toronto and Winnipeg. Once again he was acquitted by a jury, and once again he saw his acquittal overturned by a court of appeal. The time, however, armed with the new Charter of Rights, Morgentaler prevailed in the Supreme Court of Canada.

The contrast between the Supreme Court's handling of the first *Morgentaler* appeal and its 1988 decision reveals just how much the Charter has changed the Court's willingness to use the power of judicial review. In his 1975 appeal, Morgentaler used the 1960 Bill of Rights to challenge the validity of the abortion section (s. 251) of the Criminal Code. At oral argument before the Supreme Court, Morgentaler's lawyer's argued that section 251 violated women's right to liberty and also "equality before the law." After hearing these arguments, the Court recessed briefly and then announced that section 251 did not violate the Bill of Rights. The Crown was told it need not even argue the Bill of Rights issues.

In its written judgement six months later, the six judge majority did not even address the Bill of Rights issues. Chief Justice Laskin dissented for other reasons, but explained why the Court was unwilling to accept Morgentaler's

Bill of Rights arguments. In distinguishing the *Morgentaler* case from the then recently decided American abortion decision, *Roe* v. *Wade* (1973), the Chief Justice observed, "how foreign to our constitutional traditions, to our constitutional law and to our conceptions of judicial review was any interference by a Court with the substantive content of legislation." This difference, Laskin explained, stemmed from the fact that the Canadian Bill of Rights was not constitutionally-entrenched.[1]

> *It cannot be forgotten that it is a statutory instrument, illustrative of Parliament's primacy within the limits of its assigned legislative authority, and this is a relative consideration in determining how far the language of the Canadian Bill of Rights should be taken in assessing the quality of federal enactments which are challenged under s. 1(a).*

The constitutional status of the Charter appears to have erased whatever doubts the Court had about the legitimacy of its power to review and nullify Parliament's laws. However, the *Morgentaler* decision was much narrower than was generally reported. The Supreme Court did not declare a constitutional right to abortion or "freedom of choice." Only Justice Wilson took this position, and even she acknowledged a legitimate state interest in protecting the life of the foetus/unborn child at some point in the second trimester of a pregnancy. The other six carefully and explicitly avoided this "substantive" policy issue.

The two dissenters, McIntyre and LaForest, looked behind the text of the Charter to the framers' understanding of its meaning. They found that the legislative history of the Charter in 1980-81 indicated that it was intentionally neutral on the abortion issue. They concluded that when the Charter is purposely silent on an issue, so too must be the judges.

The other four judges who ruled against the abortion law did so because they said that it violated the *procedural fairness* required by section 7, not because there is any independant right to abortion. These four further disagreed amongst themselves on just how serious even the procedural violations were. Two, Dickson and Lamer, suggested that certain elements of the current law— such as removal of the decision-making power for the abortion decision from the pregnant woman—violated the "security of the person." The other two judges—Beetz and Estey—defined the procedural problems more narrowly and thus as remediable. While certain requirements *as currently written*—such as approval by a Therapeutic Abortion Committee (TAC)—created unfair delays and burdens, a revised version of the TAC might be acceptable. Unlike Dickson and Lamer, Beetz and Estey ruled that in principle there was no legal problem with the requirement of the current law that abortions be permitted

---

[1] *Morgentaler v. The Queen* [1976] 1 S.C.R. 616, at p. 632.

only when the continuation of a pregnancy "would threaten the life or health of the mother"; or with the requirement that an independent and impartial third-party be the judge of this issue.

A significant aspect of the three plurality opinions was their extensive reliance on "social facts" or "extrinsic evidence." In 1975 Chief Justice Laskin rejected similar evidence that indicated unequal access to abortion services across the country. "This is a reach for equality by judicially unmanageable standards," declared Laskin. "It would mean that the Court would have to come to . . . decide how large or small an area must be within which an acceptable distribution of physicians and hospitals must be found."[2] Thirteen years later, in the second *Morgentaler* appeal, the dissenters, McIntyre and LaForest, were still sceptical about the use of extrinsic evidence to support the "unequal access" argument. McIntyre declared that he would prefer to rely on "evidence given under oath in my consideration of factual matters." He also noted that there had been no first-hand testimony by doctors or patients that supported the lack of access argument.

Justices Wilson, Dickson, and Beetz had no such qualms. They cited at length from the Badgley Report to support the lack of access claim. The Badgley Report had been commissioned in 1976 by the Trudeau government in response to the first *Morgentaler* case. It was intended to serve as the basis for possible legislative reform of the abortion law, but Parliament had never acted on it. Now, ten years later, the Badgley Report was being used by judges to strike down the same abortion law. This extensive use of and reliance on extrinsic evidence is a clear indicator of the greater policy-making role the Court has accepted under the Charter.

Despite similarities, the *Morgentaler* decision differs significantly from the American abortion decision (1973). In *Roe* v. *Wade*, the American Supreme Court declared that there was an implied "right to privacy" in the American constitution and that it included a woman's right to determine for herself whether to continue or terminate a pregnancy. The Court effectively precluded any legislative response to protect the interests of the unborn or the father except in the last trimester (three months) of a pregnancy. By contrast, in the *Morgentaler* decision, by limiting their ruling to procedural requirements of the criminal law, the majority left the door open for Parliament to respond with an amended abortion law.

Six months later, in July, 1988, the Mulroney government introduced a motion in the House of Commons for a reformed abortion law. The motion proposed easy access to abortions during the "early stages" of a pregnancy, but an abortion in "subsequent stages" would only be permitted if two doctors found that continuation of the pregnancy would "endanger the woman's life or

---

[2] *Ibid.*, p. 635.

seriously endanger her health.'' After two days of almost around-the-clock debate, the government motion was defeated in a ''free vote'' (147-76). Both ''prolife'' and ''prochoice'' MP's voted against the compromise measure. Both sides offered their own amendments that would have greatly eased or restricted access to abortion, but these too were defeated. The ''prolife'' amendment came closest to adoption, losing 118-105. The government subsequently announced that it would postpone further action on the abortion issue, presumably until after the federal election expected in the Fall of 1988.

Thus while the Supreme Court's decision marked the end of the *Morgentaler* case, it has not marked the end of the abortion issue. The Court's decision will become an important factor—but not a conclusive factor—in the ongoing debate in the larger political arena. Just as a loss in court does not always mean a political loss, so a legal victory does not automatically translate into a political victory. As indicated by the strong pro-life and pro-choice voting blocks during the free vote in the House of Commons in July, 1988, the abortion issue seems far from settled. ~

DR. HENRY MORGENTALER, ET AL. *v.* THE QUEEN
In the Supreme Court of Canada. [1988] 1 S.C.R. 30

The judgement of Dickson C.J.C. and Lamer J. was delivered by

DICKSON C.J.C.: The principal issue raised by this appeal is whether the abortion provisions of the Criminal Code infringe the ''right to life, liberty and security of the person and the right not to be deprived thereof except in accordance with the principles of fundamental justice'' as formulated in s. 7 of the Canadian Charter of Rights and Freedoms. The appellants, Dr. Henry Morgentaler, Dr. Leslie Frank Smoling and Dr. Robert Scott, have raised thirteen distinct grounds of appeal. During oral submissions, however, it became apparent that the primary focus of the case was upon the s. 7 argument. It is submitted by the appellants that s. 251 of the Criminal Code, R.S.C. 1970, c. C-34, contravenes s. 7 of the Canadian Charter of Rights and Freedoms and that s. 251 should be struck down. Counsel for the Crown admitted during the course of her submissions that s. 7 of the Charter was indeed ''the key'' to the entire appeal. . . . In view of my resolution of the s. 7 issue, it will not be necessary for me to address the appellants' other Charter arguments and I expressly refrain from commenting upon their merits.

During argument before this Court, counsel for the Crown emphasized repeatedly that it is not the role of the judiciary in Canada to evaluate the wisdom of legislation enacted by our democratically elected representatives, or to second-guess difficult policy choices that confront all governments. In *Morgentaler* v. *The Queen*, [1976] 1 S.C.R. 616, at p. 671, [hereinafter *Morgentaler (1975)*] I stressed that the Court had ''not been called upon to decide, or even to enter, the loud and continuous public debate on abortion.'' Eleven years later, the controversy persists, and it remains true that this Court cannot presume to resolve all of the competing claims advanced in vigorous and healthy public debate. Courts and legislators in other democratic societies have reached completely contradictory decisions when asked to weigh the competing values relevant to the abortion question. . . .

But since 1975, and the first *Morgentaler* decision, the Court has been given added responsibilities, I stated in *Morgentaler* (1975), at p. 671, that

> The values we must accept for the purposes of this appeal are those expressed by Parliament which holds the view that the desire of a woman to be relieved of her pregnancy is not, of itself, justification for performing an abortion.

Although no doubt it is still fair to say that courts are not the appropriate forum for articulating complex and controversial programmes of public policy, Canadian courts are now charged with the crucial obligation of ensuring that the legislative initiatives pursued by our Parliament and legislatures conform to the democratic values expressed in the Canadian Charter of Rights and Freedoms. As Justice McIntyre states in his reasons for judgment, ". . . the task of the Court in this case is not to solve nor seek to solve what might be called the abortion issue, but simply to measure the content of s. 251 against the Charter." It is in this latter sense that the current Morgentaler appeal differs from the one we heard a decade ago. . . .

THE CRIMINAL CODE
251.(1) Every one who, with intent to procure the miscarriage of a female person, whether or not she is pregnant, uses any means of the purpose of carrying out his intention is guilty of an indictable offence and is liable to imprisonment for life.

(2) Every female person who, being pregnant, with intent to procure her own miscarriage, uses any means or permits any means to be used for the purpose of carrying out her intention is guilty of an indictable offence and is liable to imprisonment for two years.

(3) In this section, "means" includes

(a) the administration of a drug or other noxious thing,

(b) the use of an instrument, and

(c) manipulation of any kind.

(4) Subsections (1) and (2) do not apply to

(a) a qualified medical practitioner, other than a member of a therapeutic abortion committee for any hospital, who in good faith uses in an accredited or approved hospital any means for the purpose of carrying out his intention to procure the miscarriage of a female person, or

(b) a female person who, being pregnant, permits a qualified medical practitioner to use in an accredited or approved hospital any means described in paragraph (a) for the purpose of carrying out her intention to procure her own miscarriage, if, before the use of those means, the therapeutic abortion committee for that accredited or approved hospital, by a majority of the members of the committee and at a meeting of the committee at which the case of such female person has been reviewed,

(c) has by certificate in writing stated that in its opinion the continuation of the pregnancy of such female person would or would be likely to endanger her life or health, and

(d) has caused a copy of such certificate to be given to the qualified medical practitioner.

. . .

SECTION 7 OF THE CHARTER
In his submissions, counsel for the appellants argued that the Court should recognize a very wide ambit for the rights protected under s. 7 of the Charter. Basing his argument largely on American constitutional theories and authorities, Mr. Manning submitted that the right to "life, liberty and security of the person" is a wide-ranging right to control one's own life and to promote one's individual autonomy. The right would therefore include a right to privacy and a right to make unfettered decisions about one's own life.

In my opinion, it is neither necessary nor wise in this appeal to explore the broadest implications of s. 7 as counsel would wish us to do. I prefer to rest my conclusions on a narrower analysis than that put forward on behalf of the appellants. I do not think it would be appropriate to attempt an all-encompassing explication of so important a provision as s. 7 so early in the history of Charter interpretation. The Court should be presented with a wide variety of claims and factual situations before articulating the full range of s. 7 rights. I will therefore limit my comments to some interpretive principles already set down by the Court and to an analysis of only two aspects of s. 7, the right to "security of the person" and "the principles of fundamental justice."

The goal of Charter interpretation is to secure for all people "the full benefit of the Charter's protection": *R.* v. *Big M Drug Mart Ltd.*, [1985] 1 S.C.R. 295, at p. 344. To attain that goal, this Court has held consistently that the proper technique for the interpretation of Charter provisions is to pursue a "purposive" analysis of the right guaranteed. A right recognized in the Charter is "to be understood, in other words, in the light of the interests it was meant to protect": *R.* v. *Big M Drug Mart Ltd.*, at p. 344. (See also *Hunter* v. *Southam Inc.*, [1984] 2 S.C.R. 145; and *R.* v. *Therens*, [1985] 1 S.C.R. 613.)

In *Singh* v. *Minister of Employment and Immigration*, [1985] 1 S.C.R. 177, at p. 204, Justice Wilson emphasized that there are three distinct elements to the s. 7 right, that "life, liberty, and security of the person" are independent interests, each of which must be given independent significance by the Court (p. 205). This interpretation was adopted by a majority of the Court, per Lamer J., in *Re B.C. Motor Vehicle Act*, [1985] 2 S.C.R. 486, at p. 500. It is therefore possible to treat only one aspect of the first part of s. 7 before determining whether any infringement of that interest accords with the principles of fundamental justice. (See *Singh, Re B.C. Motor Vehicle Act*, and *R.* v. *Jones*, [1986] 2 S.C.R. 284.)

With respect to the second part of s. 7, in early academic commentary one of the principal concerns was whether the refer-ence to "principles of fundamental justice" enables the courts to review the substance of legislation. . . . In *Re B.C. Motor Vehicle Act*, Lamer J. noted at p. 497 that any attempt to draw a sharp line between procedure and substance would be ill-conceived. He suggested further that it would not be beneficial in Canada to allow a debate which is rooted in United States constitutional dilemmas to shape our interpretation of s. 7. . . . Lamer J. went on to hold that the principles of fundamental justice referred to in s. 7 can relate both to procedure and to substance, depending upon the circumstances presented before the Court.

I have no doubt that s. 7 does impose upon courts the duty to review the substance of legislation once it has been determined that the legislation infringes an individual's right to "life, liberty and security of the person." The section states clearly that those interests may only be impaired if the principles of fundamental justice are respected. Lamer J. emphasized, however, that the courts should avoid "adjudication of the merits of public policy" (p. 499). In the present case, I do not believe that it is necessary for the Court to tread the fine line between substantive review and the adjudication of public policy. As in the *Singh* case, it will be sufficient to investigate whether or not the impugned legislative provisions meet the procedural standards of fundamental justice. First it is necessary to determine whether s. 251 of the Criminal Code impairs the security of the person.

The law has long recognized that the human body ought to be protected from interference by others. At common law, for example, any medical procedure carried out on a person without that person's consent is an assault. Only in emergency circumstances does the law allow others to make decisions of this nature. Similarly, art. 19 of the Civil Code of Lower Canada provides that "[t]he human person is inviolable" and that "[n]o person may cause harm to the person of another without his consent or without being authorized by law to do so." "Security of the person,'' in other words, is not a value alien to our legal landscape. With the advent of the Charter, security of the person has been elevated to the status of a constitutional norm. This is not to say that the various forms of protection accorded to the human body by the common and civil law occupy a similar status. ''Security of the person'' must be given content in a manner sensitive to its constitutional position. The above examples are simply illustrative of our respect for individual physical integrity. . . . Nor is it to say that the state can never impair personal securities interests. There may well be valid reasons for interfering with security of the person. It is to say, however, that if the state does interfere with security of the person, the Charter requires such interference to conform with the principles of fundamental justice.

The appellants submitted that the ''security of the person'' protected by the Charter is an explicit right to control one's body and to make fundamental decisions about one's life. The Crown contended that ''security of the person'' is a more circumscribed interest and that, like all of the elements of s. 7, it at most relates to the concept of physical control, simply protecting the individual's interest in his or her bodily integrity. . . .

The case law leads me to the conclusion that state interference with bodily integrity and serious state-imposed psychological stress, at least in the criminal law context, constitute a breach of security of the person. It is not necessary in this case to determine whether the right extends further, to protect either interests central to personal autonomy, such as a right to privacy, or interests unrelated to criminal justice. . . .

At the most basic, physical and emotional level, every pregnant woman is told by the section that she cannot submit to a generally safe medical procedure that might be of clear benefit to her unless she meets criteria entirely unrelated to her own priorities and aspirations. Not only does the removal of decision making power threaten women in a physical

sense; the indecision of knowing whether an abortion will be granted inflicts emotional stress. Section 251 clearly interferes with a woman's bodily integrity in both a physical and emotional sense. Forcing a woman, by threat of criminal sanction, to carry a foetus to term unless she meets certain criteria unrelated to her own priorities and aspirations, is a profound interference with a woman's body and thus a violation of security of the person. Section 251, therefore, is required by the Charter to comport with the principles of fundamental justice.

Although this interference with physical and emotional integrity is sufficient in itself to trigger a review of s. 251 against the principles of fundamental justice, the operation of the decision making mechanism set out in s. 251 creates additional glaring breaches of security of the person. The evidence indicates that s. 251 causes a certain amount of delay for women who are successful in meeting its criteria. In the context of abortion, any unnecessary delay can have profound consequences on the woman's physical and emotional well-being. . . .

~ Chief Justice Dickson here quotes relevant findings of the 1977 Badgley Report. The Badgley Report was commissioned by the Federal Government in the wake of the first Morgentaler case (1973-75). It found uneven access to and delays in access to abortion since the 1969 reforms. The delays were linked to increased threat to the health of the mother in later stage abortions. ~

The above physical interference caused by the delays created by s. 251, involving a clear risk of damage to the physical well-being of a woman, is sufficient, in my view, to warrant inquiring whether s. 251 comports with the principles of fundamental justice. However, there is yet another infringement of security of the person. It is clear from the evidence that s. 251 harms the psychological integrity of women seeking abortions. A 1985 report of the Canadian Medical Association, discussed in the Powell Report, at

p. 15, emphasized that the procedure involved in s. 251, with the concomitant delays, greatly increases the stress levels of patients and that this can lead to more physical complications associated with abortion. . . .

In its supplementary factum and in oral submissions, the Crown argued that evidence of what could be termed "administrative inefficiency" is not relevant to the evaluation of legislation for the purposes of s. 7 of the Charter. The Crown argued that only evidence regarding the purpose of legislation is relevant. The assumption, of course, is that any impairment to the physical or psychological interests of individuals caused by s. 251 of the Criminal Code does not amount to an infringement of security of the person because the injury is caused by practical difficulties and is not intended by the legislator.

The submission is faulty on two counts. First, as a practical matter it is not possible in the case of s. 251 to erect a rigid barrier between the purposes of the section and the administrative procedures established to carry those purposes into effect. . . .

Secondly, were it nevertheless possible in this case to dissociate purpose and administration, this Court has already held as a matter of law that purpose is not the only appropriate criterion in evaluating the constitutionality of legislation under the Charter. . . . Even if the purpose of legislation is unobjectionable, the administrative procedures to bring that purpose into operation may produce unconstitutional effects, and the legislation should then be struck down. . . .

In summary, s. 251 is a law which forces women to carry a foetus to term contrary to their own priorities and aspirations and which imposes serious delay causing increased physical and psychological trauma to those women who meet its criteria. It must, therefore, be determined whether that infringement is accomplished in accordance with the principles of fundamental justice, thereby saving s. 251 under the second part of s. 7. . . .

My discussion will . . . be limited to various aspects of the administrative structure and procedure set down in s. 251 for access to therapeutic abortions. . . .

The procedure surrounding the defence is rather complex. A pregnant woman who desires to have an abortion must apply to the "therapeutic abortion committee" of an "accredited or approved hospital." Such a committee is empowered to issue a certificate in writing stating that in the opinion of a majority of the committee, the continuation of the pregnancy would be likely to endanger the pregnant woman's life or health. Once a copy of the certificate is given to a qualified medical practitioner who is not a member of the therapeutic abortion committee, he or she is permitted to perform an abortion on the pregnant woman and both the doctor and the woman are freed from any criminal liability. . . .

As is so often the case in matters of interpretation, however, the straightforward reading of this statutory scheme is not fully revealing. In order to understand the true nature and scope of s. 251, it is necessary to investigate the practical operation of the provisions. The Court has been provided with a myriad of factual submissions in this area. One of the most useful sources of information is the Badgley Report. . . .

The Badgley Report contains a wealth of detailed information which demonstrates, however, that many of the most serious problems with the functioning of s. 251 are created by procedural and administrative requirements established in the law. . . . [For example], the seemingly neutral requirement of s. 251(4) that at least four physicians be available to authorize and to perform an abortion meant in practice that abortions would be absolutely unavailable in almost one quarter of all hospitals in Canada.

Other administrative and procedural requirements of s. 251(4) reduce the availability of therapeutic abortions even further. For the purposes of s. 251, therapeutic abortions can only be performed in "accredited" or "approved" hospitals. As noted above, an "approved" hospital is one which a provincial minister of health has designated as such for the purpose of performing therapeutic abortions. The minister is under no obligation to grant any such approval. Furthermore, an "accredited" hospital must not only be accredited by the Canadian Council on Hospital Accreditation, it must also provide specified services. Many Canadian hospitals do not provide all of the required services, thereby being automatically disqualified from undertaking therapeutic abortions. The Badgley Report stressed the remarkable limitations created by these requirements, especially when linked with the four-physician rule discussed above:

Of the total of 1,348 non-military hospitals in Canada in 1976, 789 hospitals, or 58.5 percent, were ineligible in terms of their major treatment functions, the size of their medical staff, or their type of facility to establish therapeutic abortion committees.

Moreover, even if a hospital is eligible to create a therapeutic abortion committee, there is no requirement in s. 251 that the hospital need do so. The Badgley Committee discovered that in 1976, of the 559 general hospitals which met the procedural requirements of s. 251, only 271 hospitals in Canada, or only 20.1 per cent of the total, had actually established a therapeutic abortion committee.

Even though the Badgley Report was issued ten years ago, the relevant statistics do not appear to be out of date. Indeed, Statistics Canada reported that in 1982 the number of hospitals with therapeutic abortion committees had actually fallen to 261.

A further flaw with the administrative system established in s. 251(4) is the failure to provide an adequate standard for therapeutic abortion committees which must determine when a therapeutic abortion should, as a matter of law, be granted. Subsection (4) states simply that a therapeutic abortion committee may grant a certificate when it determines that a continuation of a pregnancy would be likely to endanger the "life or health" of the pregnant woman. It was noted above that "health" is not defined for the purposes of the section. . . .

Various expert doctors testified at trial that therapeutic abortion committees apply widely differing definitions of health. For some committees, psychological health is a justification for therapeutic abortion; for others it is not. Some committees routinely refuse abortions to married women unless they are in physical danger, while for other committees it is possible for a married woman to show that she would suffer psychological harm if she continued with a pregnancy, thereby justifying an abortion. It is not typically possible for women to known in advance what standard of health will be applied by any given committee. . . .

It is no answer to say that "health" is a medical term and that doctors who sit on therapeutic abortion committees must simply exercise their professional judgment. A therapeutic abortion committee is a strange hybrid, part medical committee and part legal committee [in the words of Parker A.C.J.H.C.]. . . .

When the decision of the therapeutic abortion committee is so directly laden [with] consequences, the absence of any clear legal standard to be applied by the committee in reaching its decision is a serious procedural flaw.

The combined effect of all of these problems with the procedure stipulated in s. 251 for access to therapeutic abortions is a failure to comply with the principles of fundamental justice. In *Re B.C. Motor Vehicle Act*, Lamer J. held, at p. 503, that "the principles of fundamental justice are to be found in the basic tenets of our legal system." One of the basic tenets of our system of criminal justice is that when Parliament creates a defence to a criminal charge, the defence should not be illusory or so difficult to attain as to be practically illusory. The criminal law is a very special form of governmental regulation, for it seeks to express our society's collective disapprobation of certain acts and omissions. When a defence is provided, especially a specifically-tailored defence to a particular charge, it is because the legislator has determined that the disapprobation of society is not warranted when the conditions of the defence are met.

Consider then the case of a pregnant married woman who wishes to apply for a therapeutic abortion certificate because she fears that her psychological health would be impaired seriously if she carried the foetus to term. The uncontroverted evidence reveals that there are many areas in Canada where such a woman would simply not have access to a therapeutic abortion. . . .

The Crown argues in its supplementary factum that women who face difficulties in obtaining abortions at home can simply travel elsewhere in Canada to procure a therapeutic abortion. That submission would not be especially troubling if the difficulties facing women were not in large measure created by the procedural requirements of s. 251 itself. If women were seeking anonymity outside their home town or were simply confronting the reality that it is often difficult to obtain medical services in rural areas, it might be appropriate to say "let them travel." But the evidence establishes convincingly that it is the law itself which in many ways prevents access to local therapeutic abortion facilities. . . . Parliament must be given room to design an appropriate administrative and procedural structure for bringing into operation a particular defence to criminal liability. But if that structure is "so manifestly unfair, having regard to the decisions it is called upon to make, as to violate the principles of fundamental justice," that structure must be struck down. In the present case, the structure—the system regulating access to therapeutic abortions—is manifestly unfair. It contains so many potential barriers to its own operation that the defence

it creates will in many circumstances be practically unavailable to women who would prima facie qualify for the defence, or at least would force such women to travel great distances at substantial expense and inconvenience in order to benefit from a defence that is held out to be generally available.

I conclude that the procedures created in s. 251 of the Criminal Code for obtaining a therapeutic abortion do not comport with the principles of fundamental justice. It is not necessary to determine whether s. 7 also contains a substantive content leading to the conclusion that, in some circumstances at least, the deprivation of a pregnant woman's right to security of the person can never comport with fundamental justice. Simply put, assuming Parliament can act, it must do so properly. . . .

SECTION 1 ANALYSIS

Section 1 of the Charter can potentially be used to "salvage" a legislative provision which breaches s. 7. . . . A statutory provision which infringes any section of the Charter can only be saved under s. 1 if the party seeking to uphold the provision can demonstrate first, that the objective of the provision is "of sufficient importance to warrant overriding a constitutionally protected right or freedom" (*R. v. Big M Drug Mart Ltd.*, at p. 352) and second, that the means chosen in overriding the right or freedom are reasonable and demonstrably justified in a free and democratic society. This second aspect ensures that the legislative means are proportional to the legislative ends (*Oakes*, at pp. 139-40). In *Oakes*, at p. 139, the Court referred to three considerations which are typically useful in assessing the proportionality of means to ends. First, the means chosen to achieve an important objective should be rational, fair and not arbitrary. Second, the legislative means should impair as little as possible the right or freedom under consideration. Third, the effects of the limitation upon the relevant right or freedom should not be out of proportion to the objective sought to be achieved.

The appellants contended that the sole purpose of s. 251 of the Criminal Code is to protect the life and health of pregnant women. The respondent Crown submitted that s. 251 seeks to protect not only the life and health of pregnant women, but also the interests of the foetus. On the other hand, the Crown conceded that the Court is not called upon in this appeal to evaluate any claim to ''foetal rights'' or to assess the meaning of ''the right to life.'' I expressly refrain from so doing. In my view, it is unnecessary for the purpose of deciding this appeal to evaluate or assess ''foetal rights'' as an independent constitutional value. Nor are we required to measure the full extent of the state's interest in establishing criteria unrelated to the pregnant woman's own priorities and aspirations. What we must do is evaluate the particular balance struck by Parliament in s. 251, as it relates to the priorities and aspirations of pregnant women and the government's interests in the protection of the foetus.

Section 251 provides that foetal interests are not to be protected where the ''life or health'' of the woman is threatened. Thus, Parliament itself has expressly stated in s. 251 that the ''life or health'' of pregnant women is paramount. The procedures of s. 251(4) are clearly related to the pregnant woman's ''life or health'' for that is the very phrase used by the subsection. As McIntyre J. states in his reasons, the aim of s. 251(4) is ''to restrict abortion to cases where the continuation of the pregnancy would, or would likely, be injurious to the life or health of the woman concerned, not to provide unrestricted access to abortion.'' I have no difficulty in concluding that the objective of s. 251 as a whole, namely, to balance the competing interests identified by Parliament, is sufficiently important to meet the requirements of the first step in the *Oakes* inquiry under s. 1. I think the protection of the interests of pregnant women is a valid governmental objective, where life and health can be jeopardized by criminal sanctions. Like Beetz and Wilson JJ., I agree that protection of foetal interests by

Parliament is also a valid governmental objective. It follows that balancing these interests, with the lives and health of women a major factor, is clearly an important governmental objective. As the Court of Appeal stated, ''the contemporary view [is] that abortion is not always socially undesirable behavior.''

I am equally convinced, however, that the means chosen to advance the legislative objectives of s. 251 do not satisfy any of the three elements of the proportionality component of *R. v. Oakes*. The evidence has led me to conclude that the infringement of the security of the person of pregnant women caused by s. 251 is not accomplished in accordance with the principles of fundamental justice. It has been demonstrated that the procedures and administrative structures created by s. 251 are often arbitrary and unfair. The procedures established to implement the policy of s. 251 impair s. 7 rights far more than is necessary because they hold out an illusory defence to many women who would *prima facie* qualify under the exculpatory provisions of s. 251(4). In other words, many women whom Parliament professes not to wish to subject to criminal liability will nevertheless be forced by the practical unavailability of the supposed defence to risk liability or to suffer other harm such as a traumatic late abortion caused by the delay inherent in the s. 251 system. Finally, the effects of the limitation upon the s. 7 rights of many pregnant women are out of proportion to the objective sought to be achieved. Indeed, to the extent that s. 251(4) is designed to protect the life and health of women, the procedures it establishes may actually defeat that objective. The administrative structures of s. 251(4) are so cumbersome that women whose health is endangered by pregnancy may not be able to gain a therapeutic abortion, at least without great trauma, expense and inconvenience.

I conclude, therefore, that the cumbersome structure of subs. (4) not only unduly subordinates the s. 7 rights of pregnant women but may also defeat the value Parliament itself has established as paramount, namely, the life and health of the mother. As I have noted, counsel for the Crown did not contend that one purpose of the procedures required by subs. (4) is to protect the interests of the foetus. State protection of foetal interests may well be deserving of constitutional recognition under s. 1. Still, there can be no escape from the fact that Parliament has failed to establish either a standard or a procedure whereby any such interests might prevail over those of the woman in a fair and non-arbitrary fashion.

Section 251 of the Criminal Code cannot be saved, therefore, under s. 1 of the Charter. . . .

Section 251 of the Criminal Code infringes the right to security of the person of many pregnant women. The procedures and administrative structures established in the section to provide for therapeutic abortions do not comply with the principles of fundamental justice. Section 7 of the Charter is infringed and that infringement cannot be saved under s. 1. . . .

The judgement of Estey and Beetz, JJ. was delivered by

BEETZ J.: . . . Access to abortion without risk of criminal penalty under the Criminal Code is expressed by Parliament in subs. 251(4), (5), (6) and (7) as relieving provisions in respect of the indictable offences defined at subsections 251(1) and (2). According to Laskin C.J. (dissenting) in *Morgentaler* v. *The Queen*, [1976] . . . these relieving provisions "simply permit a person to make conduct lawful which would otherwise be unlawful" (at 631). In the same case, Pigeon J. said that in 1969 "an explicit and specific definition was made of the circumstances under which an abortion could lawfully be performed" (at 660). . . .

Given that it appears in a criminal law statute, subs. 251(4) cannot be said to create a "right," much less a constitutional right, but it does represent an exception decreed by Parliament pursuant to what the Court of Appeal aptly called

"the contemporary view that abortion is not always socially undesirable behaviour." Examining the content of the rule by which Parliament decriminalizes abortion is the most appropriate first step in considering the validity of s. 251 as against the constitutional right to abortion alleged by the appellants in argument. . . .

That abortions are recognized as lawful by Parliament based on a specific standard under its ordinary laws is important, I think, to a proper understanding of the existence of a right of access to abortion founded on rights guaranteed by s. 7 of the Charter. The constitutional right does not have its source in the Criminal Code, but, in my view, the content of the standard in subs. 251(4) that Parliament recognized in the Criminal Law Amendment Act, 1969 was for all intents and purposes entrenched at least as a minimum in 1982 when a distinct right in s. 7 became part of Canadian constitutional law.

THE RIGHT TO SECURITY OF THE PERSON IN S. 7

. . . A pregnant woman's person cannot be said to be secure if, when her life or health is in danger, she is faced with a rule of criminal law which precludes her from obtaining effective and timely medical treatment. . . .

If a rule of criminal law precludes a person from obtaining appropriate medical treatment when his or her life or health is in danger, then the state has intervened and this intervention constitutes a violation of that man's or that woman's security of the person. "Security of the person" must include a right of access to medical treatment for a condition representing a danger to life or health without fear of criminal sanction. If an act of Parliament forces a person whose life or health is in danger to choose between, on the one hand, the commission of a crime to obtain effective and timely medical treatment and, on the other hand, inadequate treatment or no treatment at all, the right to security of the person has been violated.

This interpretation of s. 7 of the Charter is sufficient to measure the content of s. 251 of the Criminal Code against that of the Charter in order to dispose of this appeal. While I agree with McIntyre J. that a breach of a right to security must be "based upon an infringement of some interest which would be of such nature and such importance as to warrant constitutional protection," I am of the view that the protection of life or health is an interest of sufficient importance in this regard. Under the Criminal Code, the only way in which a pregnant woman can legally secure an abortion when the continuation of the pregnancy would or would be likely to endanger her life or health is to comply with the procedure set forth at subs. 251(4). Where the continued pregnancy does constitute a danger to life or health, the pregnant woman faces a choice: (1) she can endeavour to follow the subs. 251(4) procedure, which, as we shall see, creates an additional medical risk given its inherent delays and the possibility that the danger will not be recognized by the state-imposed therapeutic abortion committee; or (2) she can secure medical treatment without respecting subs. 251(4) and subject herself to criminal sanction under subs. 251(2).

DELAYS CAUSED BY S. 251 PROCEDURE

~ Justice Beetz's treatment of the causes of delay is similar to that of Chief Justice Dickson. He then goes on to consider whether the delays violate the s. 7 right to security of the person. ~

The delays which a pregnant woman may have to suffer as a result of the requirements of subs. 251(4) must undermine the security of her person in order that there be a violation of this element of s. 7 of the Charter. As I said earlier, s. 7 cannot be invoked simply because a woman's pregnancy amounts to a medically dangerous condition. If, however, the delays occasioned by subs. 251(4) of the Criminal Code result in an additional danger to the pregnant woman's health, then the state has intervened and this

intervention constitutes a violation of that woman's security of the person. By creating this additional risk, s. 251 prevents access to effective and timely medical treatment for the continued pregnancy which would or would be likely to endanger her life or health. If an effective and timely therapeutic abortion may only be obtained by committing a crime, then s. 251 violates the pregnant woman's right to security of the person.

The evidence reveals that the delays caused by subs. 251(4) result in at least three broad types of additional medical risks. The risk of postoperative complications increases with delay. Secondly, there is a risk that the pregnant woman require a more dangerous means of procuring a miscarriage because of the delay. Finally, since a pregnant woman knows her life or health is in danger, the delay created by the subs. 251(4) procedure may result in an additional psychological trauma. . . .

The delays mean therefore that the state has intervened in such a manner as to create an additional risk to health, and consequently this intervention constitutes a violation of the woman's security of the person.

THE PRINCIPLES OF FUNDAMENTAL JUSTICE

I turn now to a consideration of the manner in which pregnant women are deprived of their right to security of the person by s. 251. Section 7 of the Charter states that everyone has the right not to be deprived of security of the person except in accordance with the principles of fundamental justice. As I will endeavour to demonstrate, subs. 251(4) does not accord with the principles of fundamental justice.

I am of the view, however, that certain elements of the procedure for obtaining a therapeutic abortion which counsel for the appellants argued could not be saved by the second part of s. 7 are in fact in accordance with the principles of fundamental justice. The expression of the standard in para. 251(4)(c), and the requirement for some independent medical opinion to ascertain that the standard has been met as well as the consequential necessity of some period of delay to ascertain the standard are not in breach of s. 7 of the Charter.

Counsel for the appellants argued that the expression of the standard in para. 251(4)(c) is so imprecise that it offends the principles of fundamental justice. He submits that pregnant women are arbitrarily deprived of their s. 7 right by reason of the different meanings that can be given to the word ''health'' in para. 251(4)(c) by therapeutic abortion committees.

I agree with Mr. Justice McIntyre and the Ontario Court of Appeal that the expression ''the continuation of the pregnancy of such female person would or would be likely to endanger her life or health'' found in para. 251(4)(c) does provide, as a matter of law, a sufficiently precise standard by which therapeutic abortion committees can determine when therapeutic abortions should be granted. . . .

Chief Justice Laskin held in *Morgentaler, 1975* that para. 251(4)(c) was not so vague as to constitute a violation of ''security of the person'' without due process of law under s. 1(a) of the Canadian Bill of Rights. . . . I agree with Laskin C.J. that the standard is manageable because it is addressed to a panel of doctors exercising medical judgment on a medical question. This being the case, the standard must necessarily be flexible. Flexibility and vagueness are not synonymous. Parliament has set a medical standard to be determined over a limited range of circumstances. With the greatest of respect, I cannot agree with the view that the therapeutic abortion committee is a ''strange hybrid, part medical committee and part legal committee'' as the Chief Justice characterizes it. In sub. 251(4) Parliament has only given the committee the authority to make a medical determination regarding the pregnant woman's life or health. The committee is not called upon to evaluate the sufficiency of the

state interest in the foetus as against the woman's health. This evaluation of the state interest is a question of law already decided by Parliament in its formulation of subs. 251(4). Evidence has been submitted that many committees fail to apply the standard set by Parliament by requiring the consent of the pregnant woman's spouse, by refusing to authorize second abortions or by refusing all abortions to married women. Insofar as these and other requirements fall outside para. 251(4)(c), they constitute an unfounded interpretation of the plain terms of the Criminal Code. These patent excesses of authority do not, however, mean that the standard of s. 251 is vague. . . .

Just as the expression of the standard in para. 251(4)(c) does not offend the principles of fundamental justice, the requirement that an independent medical opinion be obtained for a therapeutic abortion to be lawful also cannot be said to constitute a violation of these principles when considered in the context of pregnant women's right to security of the person. . . .

As I noted in my analysis of subs. 251(4), by requiring that a committee state that the medical standard has been met for the criminal sanction to be lifted, Parliament seeks to assure that there is a reliable, independent and medically sound opinion that the continuation of the pregnancy would or would be likely to endanger the woman's life or health. Whatever the failings of the current system, I believe that the purpose pursuant to which it was adopted does not offend the principles of fundamental justice. As I shall endeavour to explain, the current mechanism in the Criminal Code does not accord with the principles of fundamental justice. This does not preclude, in my view, Parliament from adopting another system, free of the failings of subs. 251(4), in order to ascertain that the life or health of the pregnant woman is in danger, by way of a reliable, independent and medically sound opinion.

Parliament is justified in requiring a

reliable, independent and medically sound opinion in order to protect the state interest in the foetus. This is undoubtedly the objective of a rule which requires an independent verification of the practising physician's opinion that the life or health of the pregnant woman is in danger. It cannot be said to be simply a mechanism designed to protect the health of the pregnant woman. While this latter objective clearly explains the requirement that the practising physician be a "qualified medical practitioner" and that the abortion take place in a safe place, it cannot explain the necessary intercession of an in-hospital committee of three physicians from which is excluded the practising physician.

While a second medical opinion is very often seen as necessary in medical circles when difficult questions as to a patient's life or health are at issue, the independent opinion called for by the Criminal Code has a different purpose. Parliament requires this independent opinion because it is not only the woman's interest that is at stake in a decision to authorize an abortion. The Ontario Court of Appeal alluded to this at pp. 377-78 when it stated that "[o]ne cannot overlook the fact that the situation respecting a woman's right to control her own person becomes more complex when she becomes pregnant and that some statutory control may be appropriate." The presence of the foetus accounts for this complexity. By requiring an independent medical opinion that the pregnant woman's life or health is in fact endangered, Parliament seeks to ensure that, in any given case, only therapeutic reasons will justify the decision to abort. The amendments to the Criminal Code in 1969 amounted to a recognition by Parliament, as I have said, that the interest in the life or health of the pregnant woman takes precedence over the interest of the state in the protection of the foetus when the continuation of the pregnancy would or would be likely to endanger the pregnant woman's life or health. Parliament decided that it was necessary to ascertain this from a medical

point of view before the law would allow the interest of the pregnant woman to indeed take precedence over that of the foetus and permit an abortion to be performed without criminal sanction.

I do not believe it to be unreasonable to seek independent medical confirmation of the threat to the woman's life or health when such an important and distinct interest hangs in the balance. I note with interest that in a number of foreign jurisdictions, laws which decriminalize abortions require an opinion as to the state of health of the woman independent from the opinion of her own physician. . . . This said, the practising physician must, according to para. 251(4)(a), be in "good faith" and, consequently, have no reason to believe that the standard in para. 251(4)(c) has not been met. The practising physician is, however, properly excluded from the body giving the independent opinion. I believe that Parliament is justified in requiring what is no doubt an extraordinary medical practice in its regulation of the criminal law of abortion in accordance with the various interests at stake.

The assertion that an independent medical opinion, distinct from that of the pregnant woman and her practising physician, does not offend the principles of fundamental justice would need to be reevaluated if a right of access to abortion is founded upon the right to "liberty" in s. 7 of the Charter. I am of the view that there would still be circumstances in which the state interest in the protection of the foetus would require an independent medical opinion as to the danger to the life or health of the pregnant woman. Assuming without deciding that a right of access to abortion can be founded upon the right to "liberty," there would be a point in time at which the state interest in the foetus would become compelling. From this point in time, Parliament would be entitled to limit abortions to those required by therapeutic reasons and therefore require an independent opinion as to the health exception. The case law reveals a substantial difference of opinion as to the state interest in the protection of the foetus as against the pregnant woman's right to liberty. Madame Justice Wilson, for example, in her discussion of s. 1 of the Charter in the case at bar, notes the following:

The precise point in the development of the foetus at which the state's interest in its protection becomes "compelling" I leave to the informed judgment of the legislature which is in a position to receive guidance on the subject from all the relevant disciplines. It seems to me, however, that it would fall somewhere in the second trimester.

This view as to when the state interest becomes compelling may be compared with that of Justice O'Connor of the United States Supreme Court in her dissenting opinion in *City of Akron* v. *Akron Center for Reproductive Health, Inc.*, 103 S.Ct. 2481 at 2509 (1983):

In Roe v. Wade 410 U.S. 113 (1973)], the Court held that although the State had an important and legitimate interest in protecting potential life, that interest could not become compelling until the point at which the foetus was viable. The difficulty with this analysis is clear: potential life is no less potential in the first weeks of pregnancy than it is at viability or afterward. At any stage in pregnancy, there is the potential for human life. Although the court refused to "resolve the difficult question of when life begins", the Court chose the point of viability—when the foetus is capable of life independent of its mother—to permit the complete proscription of abortion. The choice of viability as the point at which state interest in potential life becomes compelling is no less arbitrary than choosing any point before viability or any point afterward. Accordingly, I believe that the State's interest in protecting potential human life exists throughout the pregnancy.

As I indicated at the outset of my reasons, it is nevertheless possible to resolve this appeal without attempting to delineate the right to "liberty" in s. 7 of the Charter. The violation of the right to "security of the person" and the relevant principles of fundamental justice are sufficient to invalidate s. 251 of the Criminal Code.

Some delay is inevitable in connection with any system which purports to limit to therapeutic reasons the grounds upon which an abortion can be performed lawfully. . . .

One . . . example of a rule which is unnecessary is the requirement in subs. 251(4) that therapeutic abortions must take place in an eligible hospital to be lawful. I have observed that subs. 251(4) directs that therapeutic abortions take place in accredited or approved hospitals, with at least four physicians, and that, because of the lack of such hospitals in many parts of Canada, this often causes delay for women seeking treatment. . . .

Experts testified at trial that the principal justification for the inhospital rule is the problem of post-operative complications. There are of course instances in which the danger to life or health observed by the therapeutic abortion committee will constitute sufficient grounds for the procedure to take place in a hospital. There are other instances in which the circumstances of the procedure itself requires that it be performed in hospital, such as certain abortions performed at an advanced gestational age or cases in which the patient is particularly vulnerable to what might otherwise be a simple procedure.

In many cases, however, there is no medical justification that the therapeutic abortion take place in a hospital. Experts testified at trial, that many first trimester therapeutic abortions may be safely performed in specialized clinics outside of hospitals because the possible complications can be handled, and in some cases better handled, by the facilities of a specialized clinic. . . .

The substantial increase in the percentage of abortions performed on an outpatient basis since 1975 underscores the view that the in-hospital requirement, which may have been justified when it was first adopted, has become exorbitant. . . .

Although the protection of health of the woman is the objective which the in-hospital rule is intended to serve, the requirements that all therapeutic abortions be performed in eligible hospitals is unnecessary to meet that objective in all cases. In this sense, the rule is manifestly unfair and offends the principles of fundamental justice. I appreciate that the precise nature of the administrative solution may be complicated by the constitutional division of powers between Parliament and the provinces. There is no doubt that Parliament could allow the criminal law exception to operate in all hospitals, for example, though the provinces retain the power to establish these hospitals under s. 92(7) of the Constitution Act, 1867. On the other hand, if Parliament decided to allow therapeutic abortions to be performed in provincially licensed clinics, it is possible that both Parliament and the provinces would be called upon to collaborate in the implementation of the plan.

An objection can also be raised in respect of the requirement that the committee come from the accredited or approved hospital in which the abortion is to be performed. It is difficult to see a connection between this requirement and any of the practical purposes for which subs. 251(4) was enacted. It cannot be said to have been adopted in order to promote the safety of therapeutic abortions or the safety of the pregnant woman. Nor is the rule designed to preserve the state interest in the foetus. The integrity of the independent medical opinion is no better served by a committee within the hospital than a committee from outside the hospital as long as the practising physician remains excluded in both circumstances as part of a proper state participation in the choice of the procedure necessary to secure an independent opinion. . . .

[I]t is plain that the requirement that the therapeutic abortion committee come from the hospital in which the abortion will be performed serves no real purpose. The risk resulting from the delay caused by subs. 251(4) in this respect is unnecessary. Consequently, this requirement violates the principles of fundamental justice.

Other aspects of the committee requirement in subs. 251(4) add to the manifest unfairness of the administrative structure. These include requirements which are at best only tenuously connected to the purpose of obtaining independent confirmation that the standard, in para. 251(4)(c) has been met and which do not usefully contribute to the realization of that purpose. Hospital boards are entitled to appoint committees made up of three or more qualified medical practitioners. As I observed earlier, if more than three members are appointed, precious time can be lost when quorum cannot be established because members are absent. . . .

Similarly, the exclusion of all physicians who practise therapeutic abortions from the committees is exorbitant. This rule was no doubt included in subs. 251(4) to promote the independence of the therapeutic abortion committees' appreciation of the standard. As I have said, the exclusion of the practising physician, although it diverges from usual medical practice, is appropriate in the criminal context to ensure the independent opinion with respect to the life or health of that physician's patient. The exclusion of all physicians who perform therapeutic abortions from committees, when they have no connection with the patient in question, is not only unnecessary but potentially counterproductive. There are no reasonable grounds to suspect bias from a physician who has no connection with the patient simply because, in the course of his or her medical practice, he or she performs lawful abortions. Furthermore, physicians who perform therapeutic abortions have useful expertise which would add to the precision and the integrity of the independent opinion itself. Some state control is appropriate to ensure the independence of the opinion. However, this rule as it now stands is excessive and can increase the risk of delay because fewer physicians are qualified to serve on the committees.

The foregoing analysis of the administrative structure of subs. 251(4) is by no means a complete catalogue of all the current systems' strengths and failings. It demonstrates, however, that the administrative structure put in place by Parliament has enough shortcomings so that subs. 251(4), when considered as a whole, violates the principles of fundamental justice. These shortcomings stem from rules which are not necessary to the purposes for which subs. 251(4) was established. These unnecessary rules, because they impose delays which result in an additional risk to women's health, are manifestly unfair.

SECTION 1 OF THE CHARTER
. . . I agree with Madame Justice Wilson's characterization of s. 251, explained in the following terms:

In my view, the primary objective of the impugned legislation must be seen as the protection of the foetus. It undoubtedly has other ancillary objectives, such as the protection of the life and health of pregnant women, but I believe that the main objective advanced to justify a restriction on the pregnant woman's s. 7 right is the protection of the foetus.

The primary objective of the protection of the foetus is the main objective relevant to the analysis of s. 251 under the first test of *Oakes*. With the greatest respect, I believe the Chief Justice incorrectly identifies the objective of balancing foetal interests and those of pregnant women, "with the lives and health of women as a major factor," as "sufficiently important to meet the requirements of the first step of the *Oakes* inquiry under s. 1."

The focus in *Oakes* is the objective "which the measures responsible for a limit on a Charter right or freedom are designed to serve." In the context of the criminal law of abortion, the objective which the measures in s. 251 responsible for a limit on the s. 7 Charter right are

designed to serve is the protection of the foetus. The narrow aim of subs. 251(4) should not be confused with the primary objective of s. 251 as a whole. . . .

Does the objective of protecting the foetus in s. 251 relate to concerns which are pressing and substantial in a free and democratic society? The answer to the first step of the *Oakes* test is yes. I am of the view that the protection of the foetus is and, as the Court of Appeal observed, always has been, a valid objective in Canadian criminal law. . . . I think s. 1 of the Charter authorizes reasonable limits to be put on a woman's right having regard to the state interest in the protection of the foetus.

I turn now to the second test in *Oakes*. The Crown must show that the means chosen in s. 251 are reasonable and demonstrably justified. In *Oakes, supra*, at p. 139, the Chief Justice outlined three components of the proportionality test. . . .

For the purposes of the first component of proportionality, I observe that it was necessary, in my discussion of subs. 251(4) and the principles of fundamental justice, to explain my view that certain of the rules governing access to therapeutic abortions free from criminal sanction are unnecessary in respect of the objectives which s. 251 is designed to serve. A rule which is unnecessary in respect of Parliament's objectives cannot be said to be "rationally connected" thereto or to be "carefully designed to achieve the objective in question." Furthermore, not only are some of the rules in s. 251 unnecessary to the primary objective of the protection of the foetus and the ancillary objective of the protection of the pregnant woman's life or health, but their practical effect is to undermine the health of the woman which Parliament purports to consider so important. Consequently, s. 251 does not meet the proportionality test in *Oakes*.

There is no saving s. 251 by simply severing the offending portions of subs. 251(4). The current rule expressed in s. 251, which articulates both Parliament's principal and ancillary objectives, cannot stand without the exception in subs. 251(4). The violation of pregnant women's security of the person would be greater, not lesser, if subs. 251(4) was severed leaving the remaining subsections of s. 251 as they are in the Criminal Code.

Given my conclusion in respect of the first component of the proportionality test, it is not necessary to address the questions as to whether the means in s. 251 "impair as little as possible" the s. 7 Charter right and whether there is a proportionality between the effects of s. 251 and the objective of protecting the foetus. Thus, I am not required to answer the difficult question concerning the circumstances in which there is a proportionality between the effects of s. 251 which limit the right of pregnant women to security of the person and the objective of the protection of the foetus. I do feel bound, however, to comment upon the balance which Parliament sought to achieve between the interest in the protection of the foetus and the interest in the life or health of the pregnant woman in adopting the amendments to the Criminal Code in 1969. . . .

The gist of subs. 251(4) is, as I have said, that the objective of protecting the foetus is not of sufficient importance to defeat the interest in protecting pregnant women from pregnancies which represent a danger to life or health. I take this parliamentary enactment in 1969 as an indication that, in a free and democratic society, it would be unreasonable to limit the pregnant woman's right to security of the person by a rule prohibiting abortions in all circumstances when her life or health would or would likely be in danger. This decision of the Canadian Parliament to the effect that the life or health of the pregnant woman takes precedence over the state interest in the foetus is also reflected in legislation in other free and democratic societies. . . .

I note that the laws in some of these foreign jurisdictions, unlike s. 251 of the Criminal Code, require a higher standard of danger to health in the latter months of pregnancy, as opposed to the early months, for an abortion to be lawful. Would such a rule, if it was adopted in Canada, constitute a reasonable limit on the right to security of the person under s. 1 of the Charter? As I have said, given the actual wording of s. 251, pursuant to which the standard necessary for a lawful abortion does not vary according to the stage of pregnancy, this Court is not required to consider this question under s. 1 of the Charter. It is possible that a future enactment by Parliament along the lines of the laws adopted in these jurisdictions could achieve a proportionality which is acceptable under s. 1. As I have stated, however, I am of the view that the objective of protecting the foetus would not justify the complete removal of the exculpatory provisions from the Criminal Code.

Finally, I wish to stress that we have not been asked to decide nor is it necessary, given my own conclusion that s. 251 contains rules unnecessary to the protection of the foetus, to decide whether a foetus is included in the word "everyone" in s. 7 so as to have a right to "life, liberty and security of the person" under the Charter. . . .

WILSON J.:

. . . My colleagues, the Chief Justice and Beetz J., have attacked those requirements in reasons which I have had the privilege of reading. They have found that the requirements do not comport with the principles of fundamental justice in the procedural sense and have concluded that, since they cannot be severed from the provisions creating the substantive offence, the whole of s. 251 must fall.

With all due respect, I think that the Court must tackle the primary issue first. A consideration as to whether or not the procedural requirements for obtaining or performing an abortion comport with fundamental justice is purely academic if such requirements cannot as a constitutional matter be imposed at all. . . . Moreover, it would, in my opinion, be an exercise in futility for the legislature to expend its time and energy in attempting to remedy the defects in the procedural requirements unless it has some assurance that this process will, at the end of the day, result in the creation of a valid criminal offence. I turn, therefore, to what I believe is the central issue that must be addressed. . . .

It seems to me, therefore, that to commence the analysis with the premise that the s. 7 right encompasses only a right to physical and psychological security and to fail to deal with the right to liberty in the context of "life, liberty and security of the person" begs the central issue in the case. If either the right to liberty or the right to security of the person or a combination of both confers on the pregnant woman the right to decide for herself (with the guidance of her physician) whether or not to have an abortion, then we have to examine the legislative scheme not only from the point of view of fundamental justice in the procedural sense but in the substantive sense as well. I think, therefore, that we must answer the question: what is meant by the right to liberty in the context of the abortion issue? Does it, as Mr. Manning suggests, give the pregnant woman control over decisions affecting her own body? . . .

In order to ascertain the content of the right to liberty we must . . . commence with an analysis of the purpose of the right. . . .

The Charter is predicated on a particular conception of the place of the individual in society. An individual is not a totally independent entity disconnected from the society in which he or she lives. Neither, however, is the individual a mere cog in an impersonal machine in which his or her values, goals and aspirations are subordinated to those of the collectivity. The individual is a bit of both. The Charter reflects this reality by leaving a wide range of activities and decisions open to legitimate government control while at the same time placing limits on the proper scope of that control. Thus, the rights guaranteed in the Charter erect around each individual, metaphorically speaking,

an invisible fence over which the state will not be allowed to trespass. The role of the courts is to map out, piece by piece, the parameters of the fence.

The Charter and the right to individual liberty guaranteed under it are inextricably tied to the concept of human dignity. . . .

The idea of human dignity finds expression in almost every right and freedom guaranteed in the Charter. Individuals are afforded the right to choose their own religion and their own philosophy of life, the right to choose with whom they will associate and how they will express themselves, the right to choose where they will live and what occupation they will pursue. These are all examples of the basic theory underlying the Charter, namely that the state will respect choices made by individuals and, to the greatest extent possible, will avoid subordinating these choices to any one conception of the good life.

Thus, an aspect of the respect for human dignity on which the Charter is founded is the right to make fundamental personal decisions without interference from the state. This right is a critical component of the right to liberty. Liberty, as was noted in *Singh*, is a phrase capable of a broad range of meaning. In my view, this right, properly construed, grants the individual a degree of autonomy in making decisions of fundamental personal importance.

This view is consistent with the position I took in the case of *R*. v. *Jones*, [1986] 2 S.C.R. 284. One issue raised in that case was whether the right to liberty in s. 7 of the Charter included a parent's right to bring up his children in accordance with his conscientious beliefs. In concluding that it did I stated at pp. 318-319:

I believe that the framers of the Constitution in guaranteeing liberty as a fundamental value in a free and democratic society had in mind the freedom of the individual to develop and realize his potential to the full, to plan his own life to suit his own character, to make his own choices for good or ill, to be non-conformist, idiosyncratic and even eccentric—to be, in today's parlance, 'his own person' and accountable as such. John Stuart Mill described it as "pursuing our own good in our own way." This, he believed, we should be free to do "so long as we do not attempt to deprive others of theirs or impede their efforts to obtain it." He added: "Each is the proper guardian of his own health, whether bodily or mental and spiritual. Mankind are greater gainers by suffering each other to live as seems good to themselves than by compelling each to live as seems good to the rest."

Liberty in a free and democratic society does not require the state to approve the personal decisions made by its citizens; it does, however, require the state to respect them.

This conception of the proper ambit of the right to liberty under our Charter is consistent with the American jurisprudence on the subject. . . .

For our purposes the most interesting development in this area of American law are the decisions of the Supreme Court in *Roe* v. *Wade*, 410 U.S. 113 (1973), and its sister case *Doe* v. *Bolton*, 410 U.S. 179 (1973). In *Roe* v. *Wade* the Court held that a pregnant woman has the right to decide whether or not to terminate her pregnancy. This conclusion, the majority stated, was mandated by the body of existing law ensuring that the state would not be allowed to interfere with certain fundamental personal decisions such as education, child-rearing, procreation, marriage and contraception. The Court concluded that the right to privacy found in the Fourteenth Amendment guarantee of liberty ". . . is broad enough to encompass a woman's decision whether or not to terminate her pregnancy.". . .

This right was not, however, to be taken as absolute. At some point the legitimate state interests in the protection of health, proper medical standards, and prenatal life would justify its qualification. Professor Tribe (Professor of Law, Har-

vard University): American Constitutional Law (1978), conveniently summarizes the limits the Court found to be inherent in the woman's right. I quote from pp. 924-25:

Specifically, the Court held that, because the woman's right to decide whether or not to end a pregnancy is fundamental, only a compelling interest can justify state regulation impinging in any way upon that right. During the first trimester of pregnancy, when abortion is less hazardous in terms of the woman's life than carrying the child to term would be, the state may require only that the abortion be performed by a licensed physician; no further regulations peculiar to abortion as such are compellingly justified in that period.

After the first trimester, the compelling state interest in the mother's health permits it to adopt reasonable regulations in order to promote safe abortions—but requiring abortions to be performed in hospitals, or only after approval of another doctor or committee in addition to the woman's physician, is impermissible, as is requiring that the abortion procedure employ a technique that, however preferable from a medical perspective, is not widely available.

Once the fetus is viable, in the sense that it is capable of survival outside the uterus with artificial aid, the state interest in preserving the fetus becomes compelling, and the state may thus proscribe its premature removal (i.e., its abortion) except to preserve the mother's life or health.

. . . In my opinion, the respect for individual decision-making in matters of fundamental personal importance reflected in the American jurisprudence also informs the Canadian Charter. Indeed, as the Chief Justice pointed out in *R.* v. *Big M Drug Mart Ltd.*, beliefs about human worth and dignity "are the *sine qua non* of the political tradition underlying the Charter." I would conclude, therefore, that the right to liberty contained in s. 7 guarantees to every individual a degree of personal autonomy over important decisions intimately affecting their private lives.

The question then becomes whether the decision of a woman to terminate her pregnancy falls within this class of protected decisions. I have no doubt that it does. This decision is one that will have profound psychological, economic and social consequences for the pregnant woman. The circumstances giving rise to it can be complex and varied and there may be, and usually are, powerful considerations militating in opposite directions. It is a decision that deeply reflects the way the woman thinks about herself and her relationship to others and to society at large. It is not just a medical decision; it is a profound social and ethical one as well. Her response to it will be the response of the whole person. . . .

Given then that the right to liberty guaranteed by s. 7 of the Charter gives a woman the right to decide for herself whether or not to terminate her pregnancy, does s. 251 of the Criminal Code violate this right? Clearly it does. The purpose of the section is to take the decision away from the woman and give it to a committee. Furthermore, as the Chief Justice correctly points out, the committee bases its decision on "criteria entirely unrelated to [the pregnant woman's] priorities and aspirations." The fact that the decision whether a woman will be allowed to terminate her pregnancy is in the hands of a committee is just as great a violation of the woman's right to personal autonomy in decisions of an intimate and private nature as it would be if a committee were established to decide whether a woman should be allowed to continue her pregnancy. Both these arrangements violate the woman's right to liberty by deciding for her something that she has the right to decide for herself.

Section 7 of the Charter also guarantees everyone the right to security of the person. Does this, as Mr. Manning suggests, extend to the right of control over their own bodies?

I agree with the Chief Justice and with Beetz J. that the right to "security of the person" under s. 7 of the Charter protects both the physical and psychological integrity of the individual. . . . I agree with my colleague and I think that his comments are very germane to the instant case because, as the Chief Justice and Beetz J. point out, the present legislative scheme for the obtaining of an abortion clearly subjects pregnant women to considerable emotional stress as well as to unnecessary physical risk. I believe, however, that the flaw in the present legislative scheme goes much deeper than that. In essence, what it does is assert that the woman's capacity to reproduce is not to be subject to her own control. It is to be subject to the control of the state. She may not choose whether to exercise her existing capacity or not to exercise it. This is not, in my view, just a matter of interfering with her right to liberty in the sense (already discussed) of her right to personal autonomy in decision-making, it is a direct interference with her physical "person" as well. She is truly being treated as a means—a means to an end which she does not desire but over which she has no control. She is the passive recipient of a decision made by others as to whether her body is to be used to nurture a new life. Can there be anything that comports less with human dignity and self-respect? How can a woman in this position have any sense of security with respect to her person? I believe that s. 251 of the Criminal Code deprives the pregnant woman of her right to security of the person as well as her right to liberty.

THE SCOPE OF THE RIGHT UNDER S. 7

I turn now to a consideration of the degree of personal autonomy the pregnant woman has under s. 7 of the Charter when faced with a decision whether or not to have an abortion or, to put it into the legislative context, the degree to which the legislature can deny the pregnant woman access to abortion without violating her s. 7 right. This involves a consideration of the extent to which the legislature can "deprive" her of it under the second part of s. 7 and the extent to which it can put "limits" on it under s. 1. . . .

The Principles of Fundamental Justice. I believe . . . that a deprivation of the s. 7 right which has the effect of infringing a right guaranteed elsewhere in the Charter cannot be in accordance with the principles of fundamental justice.

In my view, the deprivation of the s. 7 right with which we are concerned in this case offends s. 2(a) of the Charter. I say this because I believe that the decision whether or not to terminate a pregnancy is essentially a moral decision, a matter of conscience. I do not think there is or can be any dispute about that. The question is: whose conscience? Is the conscience of the woman to be paramount or the conscience of the state? I believe, for the reasons I gave in discussing the right to liberty, that in a free and democratic society it must be the conscience of the individual. Indeed, s. 2(a) makes it clear that this freedom belongs to "everyone," i.e., to each of us individually. . . .

In *R.* v. *Big M Drug Mart Ltd., supra,* Dickson C.J. made some very insightful comments about the nature of the right enshrined in s. 2(a) of the Charter at pp. 345-47:

 . . . *It should also be noted, however, that an emphasis on individual conscience and individual judgment also lies at the heart of our democratic political tradition. The ability of each citizen to make free and informed decisions is the absolute prerequisite for the legitimacy, acceptability, and efficacy of our system of self-government. It is because of the centrality of the rights associated with freedom of individual conscience both to basic beliefs about human worth and dignity and to a free and democratic political system that American jurisprudence has emphasized the primacy or "firstness" of the First Amendment. It is this same centrality that in my view underlies their designation in the Canadian Charter of Rights and Freedoms as "fundamental." They are the sine qua non of the political tradition underlying the Charter.*

Viewed in this context, the purpose of freedom of conscience and religion

becomes clear. The values that underlie our political and philosophic traditions demand that every individual be free to hold and to manifest whatever beliefs and opinions his or her conscience dictates, provided inter alia only that such manifestations do not injure his or her neighbours or their parallel rights to hold and manifest beliefs and opinions of their own. . . .

The Chief Justice sees religious belief and practice as the paradigmatic example of conscientiously-held beliefs and manifestations and as such protected by the Charter. But I do not think he is saying that a personal morality which is not founded in religion is outside the protection of s. 2(a). Certainly, it would be my view that conscientious beliefs which are not religiously motivated are equally protected by freedom of conscience in s. 2(a). In so saying I am not unmindful of the fact that the Charter opens with an affirmation that "Canada is founded upon principles that recognize the supremacy of God. . . ." But I am also mindful that the values entrenched in the Charter are those which characterize a free and democratic society. . . .

It seems to me, therefore, that in a free and democratic society "freedom of conscience and religion" should be broadly construed to extend to conscientiously-held beliefs, whether grounded in religion or in a secular morality. Indeed, as a matter of statutory interpretation, "conscience" and "religion" should not be treated as tautologous if capable of independent, although related, meaning. Accordingly, for the state to take sides on the issue of abortion, as it does in the impugned legislation by making it a criminal offence for the pregnant woman to exercise one of her options, is not only to endorse but also to enforce, on pain of a further loss of liberty through actual imprisonment, one conscientiously-held view at the expense of another. It is to deny freedom of conscience to some, to treat them as means to an end, to deprive them, as Professor MacCormick puts it, of their "essential humanity.". . .

Legislation which violates freedom of conscience in this manner cannot, in my view, be in accordance with the principles of fundamental justice within the meaning of s. 7.

Section 1 of the Charter. . . . In my view, the primary objective of the impugned legislation must be seen as the protection of the foetus. It undoubtedly has other ancillary objectives, such as the protection of the life and health of pregnant women, but I believe that the main objective advanced to justify a restriction on the pregnant woman's s. 7 right is the protection of the foetus. I think this is a perfectly valid legislative objective.

Miss Wein submitted on behalf of the Crown that the Court of Appeal was correct in concluding that "the situation respecting a woman's right to control her own person becomes more complex when she becomes pregnant, and that some statutory control may be appropriate." I agree. I think s. 1 of the Charter authorizes reasonable limits to be put upon the woman's right having regard to the fact of the developing foetus within her body. The question is: at what point in the pregnancy does the protection of the foetus become such a pressing and substantial concern as to outweigh the fundamental right of the woman to decide whether or not to carry the foetus to term? At what point does the state's interest in the protection of the foetus become "compelling" and justify state intervention in what is otherwise a matter of purely personal and private concern? . . .

It would be my view, and I think it is consistent with the position taken by the United States Supreme Court in *Roe* v. *Wade*, that the value to be placed on the foetus as potential life is directly related to the stage of its development during gestation. The undeveloped foetus starts out as a newly fertilized ovum; the fully developed foetus emerges ultimately as an infant. A developmental progression takes place in between these two extremes and, in my opinion, this progression has a

direct bearing on the value of the foetus as potential life. It is a fact of human experience that a miscarriage or spontaneous abortion of the foetus at six months is attended by far greater sorrow and sense of loss than a miscarriage or spontaneous abortion at six days or even six weeks. This is not, of course, to deny that the foetus is potential life from the moment of conception. Indeed, I agree with the observation of O'Connor J. dissenting in *City of Akron* v. *Akron Center for Reproductive Health Inc., supra,* at p. 461, . . . that the foetus is potential life from the moment of conception. It is simply to say that in balancing the state's interest in the protection of the foetus as potential life under s. 1 of the Charter against the right of the pregnant woman under s. 7 greater weight should be given to the state's interest in the later stages of pregnancy than in the earlier. The foetus should accordingly, for purposes of s. 1, be viewed in differential and developmental terms. . . .

A developmental view of the foetus, on the other hand, supports a permissive approach to abortion in the early stages of pregnancy and a restrictive approach in the later stages. In the early stages the woman's autonomy would be absolute; her decision, reached in consultation with her physician, not to carry the foetus to term would be conclusive. The state would have no business inquiring into her reasons. Her reasons for having an abortion would, however, be the proper subject of inquiry at the later stages of her pregnancy when the state's compelling interest in the protection of the foetus would justify it in prescribing conditions. The precise point in the development of the foetus at which the state's interest in its protection becomes "compelling" I leave to the informed judgment of the legislature which is in a position to receive guidance on the subject from all the relevant disciplines. It seems to me, however, that it might fall somewhere in the second trimester. Indeed, . . . a differential abortion policy with a time limit in the second trimester is already in operation in the United States, Great Britain, France, Italy, Sweden, the Soviet Union, China, India, Japan and most of the countries of Eastern Europe although the time limits vary in these countries from the beginning to the end of the second trimester. . . .

Section 251 of the Criminal Code takes the decision away from the woman at all stages of her pregnancy. It is a complete denial of the woman's constitutionally protected right under s. 7, not merely a limitation on it. It cannot, in my opinion, meet the proportionality test in *Oakes*. It is not sufficiently tailored to the legislative objective and does not impair the woman's right "as little as possible." It cannot be saved under s. 1. Accordingly, even if the section were to be amended to remedy the purely procedural defects in the legislative scheme referred to by the Chief Justice and Beetz J. it would, in my opinion, still not be constitutionally valid. . . .

The judgement of McIntyre and LaForest, JJ. was delivered by

McINTYRE J. (dissenting): . . . I would say at the outset that it may be thought that this case does not raise the Charter issues which were argued and which have been addressed in the reasons of my colleagues. The charge here is one of conspiracy to breach the provisions of s. 251 of the Criminal Code. There is no doubt, and it has never been questioned, that the appellants adopted a course which was clearly in defiance of the provisions of the Code and it is difficult to see where any infringement of their rights, under s. 7 of the Charter, could have occurred. There is no female person involved in the case who has been denied a therapeutic abortion and, as a result, the whole argument on the right to security of the person, under s. 7 of the Charter, has been on a hypothetical basis. The case, however, was addressed by all the parties on that basis and the Court has accepted that position.

Sections 251(1) and (2) of the Criminal Code make it an indictable offence for a person to use any means to procure the

miscarriage of a female person. . . . Subsection (4) provides that subss. (1) and (2) shall not apply where an abortion is performed in accordance with subss. (4)(a), (b), (c) and (d). . . . It is clear from the foregoing that abortion is prohibited and that subs. (4) provides relieving provisions allowing an abortion in certain limited circumstances. It cannot be said that s. 251 of the Criminal Code confers any general right to have or to procure an abortion. On the contrary, the provision is aimed at protecting the interests of the unborn child and only lifts the criminal sanction where an abortion is necessary to protect the life or health of the mother.

In considering the constitutionality of s. 251 of the Criminal Code, it is first necessary to understand the background of this litigation and some of the problems which it raises. Section 251 of the Code has been denounced as ill-conceived and inadequate by those at one extreme of the abortion debate and as immoral and unacceptable by those at the opposite extreme. There are those, like the appellants, who assert that on moral and ethical grounds there is a simple solution to the problem: the inherent "right of women to control their own bodies" requires the repeal of s. 251 in favour of the principle of "abortion on demand." Opposing this view are those who contend with equal vigour, and also on moral and ethical grounds, for a clear and simple solution: the inherent "right to life of the unborn child" requires the repeal of s. 251(4), (5), (6) and (7) in order to leave an absolute ban on abortions. The battle lines so drawn are firmly held and the attitudes of the opposing parties admit of no compromise. From the submission of the Attorney General of Canada (as set out in his factum at para. 6), however, it may appear that a majority in Canada do not see the issue in such black and white terms. Paragraph 6 is in these words:

The evidence of opinion surveys indicates that there is a surprising consistency over the years and in different survey groups in the spectrum of opinions on the issue of abortion. Roughly 21 to 23% of people at one end of the spectrum are of the view, on the one hand, that abortion is a matter solely for the decision of the pregnant woman and that any legislation on this subject is an unwarranted interference with a woman's right to deal with her own body, while about 19 to 20% are of the view, on the other hand, that destruction of the living fetus is the killing of human life and tantamount to murder. The remainder of the population (about 60%) are of the view that abortion should be prohibited in some circumstances.

Parliament has heeded neither extreme. Instead, an attempt has been made to balance the competing interests of the unborn child and the pregnant woman. Where the provisions of s. 251(4) are met, the abortion may be performed without legal sanctions. Where they are not, abortion is deemed to be socially undesirable and is punished as a crime. In *Morgentaler* v. *The Queen*, [1976] 1 S.C.R. 616 [hereinafter *Morgentaler (1975)*], Laskin C.J. said (in dissent, but not on this point), at p. 627:

What is patent on the face of the prohibiting portion of s. 251 is that Parliament has in its judgment decreed that interference by another, or even by the pregnant woman herself, with the ordinary course of conception is undesirable conduct subject to punishment. That was a judgment open to Parliament in the exercise of its plenary criminal law power, and the fact that there may be safe ways of terminating a pregnancy or that any woman or women claim a personal privilege to that end, becomes immaterial. I need cite no authority or position that Parliament may determine what is not criminal as well as what is, and may hence introduce dispensations or exemptions in its criminal legislation.

Parliament's view that abortion is, in its nature, "socially undesirably conduct" is not new. Parliament's policy, as expressed in s. 251 of the Code, is consistent with that which has governed Canadian criminal law since Confederation and before. . . .

SCOPE OF JUDICIAL REVIEW UNDER THE CHARTER

Before the adoption of the Charter, there was little question of the limits of judicial review of the criminal law. For all practical purposes it was limited to a determination of whether the impugned enactment dealt with a subject which could fall within the criminal law power in s. 91(27) of the Constitution Act, 1867. There was no doubt of the power of Parliament to say what was and what was not criminal and to prohibit criminal conduct with penal sanctions, although from 1960 onwards legislation was subject to review under the Canadian Bill of Rights. . . . The adoption of the Charter brought a significant change. The power of judicial review of legislation acquired greater scope but, in my view, that scope is not unlimited and should be carefully confined to that which is ordained by the Charter. I am well aware that there will be disagreement about what was ordained by the Charter and, of course, a measure of interpretation of the Charter will be required in order to give substance and reality to its provisions. But the courts must not, in the guise of interpretation, postulate rights and freedoms which do not have a firm and a reasonably identifiable base in the Charter. . . . While I differ with the Chief Justice in the disposition of this appeal, I would accept his words, referred to above, which describe the role of the Court, but I would suggest that in "ensuring that the legislative initiatives pursued by our Parliament and legislatures conform to the democratic values expressed in the Canadian Charter of Rights and Freedoms" the courts must confine themselves to such democratic values as are clearly found and expressed in the Charter and refrain from imposing or creating other values not so based.

It follows, then, in my view, that the task of the Court in this case is not to solve nor seek to solve what might be called the abortion issue, but simply to measure the content of s. 251 against the Charter. While this may appear to be self-evident, the distinction is of vital importance. If a particular interpretation enjoys no support, express or reasonably implied, from the Charter, then the Court is without power to clothe such an interpretation with constitutional status. It is not for the Court to substitute its own views on the merits of a given question for those of Parliament. The Court must consider not what is, in its view, the best solution to the problems posed; its role is confined to deciding whether the solution enacted by Parliament offends the Charter. If it does, the provision must be struck down or declared inoperative, and Parliament may then enact such different provisions as it may decide. I adopt the words of Holmes J., which were referred to in *Ferguson* v. *Skrupka*, 372 U.S. 726 (1963), at pp. 729-30:

There was a time when the Due Process Clause was used by this Court to strike down laws which were thought unreasonable, that is, unwise or incompatible with some particular economic or social philosophy. In this manner the Due Process Clause was used, for example, to nullify laws prescribing maximum hours for work in bakeries, Lochner v. New York, *. . . outlawing "yellow dogs" contracts,* Coppage v. Kansas, *. . . setting minimum wages for women,* Adkins v. Children's Hospital, *. . . and fixing the weight of loaves of bread,* Jay Burns Baking Co. v. Bryan, *. . . .*

This intrusion by the judiciary into the realm of legislative value judgments was strongly objected to at the time, particularly by Mr. Justice Holmes and Mr. Justice Brandeis. Dissenting from the Court's invalidating a state statute which regulated the resale price of theatre and other tickets, Mr. Justice Holmes said: "I think the proper course is to recognize that a state legislature can do whatever it sees fit to do unless it is restrained by some express prohibition in the Constitution of the United States or of the State, and that Courts should be careful not to extend

such prohibitions beyond their obvious meaning by reading into them conceptions of public policy that the particular Court may happen to entertain."

And in an earlier case he had emphasized that,

The criterion of constitutionality is not whether we believe the law to be for the public good. The doctrine that prevailed in Lochner, Coppage, Adkins, Burns, *and like cases—that due process authorizes courts to hold laws unconstitutional when they believe the legislature has acted unwisely—has long since been discarded. We have returned to the original constitutional proposition that courts do not substitute their social and economic beliefs for the judgment of legislative bodies, who are elected to pass laws.*

Holmes J. wrote in 1927, but his words have retained their force in American jurisprudence. . . . In my view, although written in the American context, the principle stated is equally applicable in Canada.

It is essential that this principle be maintained in a constitutional democracy. The Court must not resolve an issue such as that of abortion on the basis of how many judges may favour "pro-choice" or "pro-life." To do so would be contrary to sound principle and the rule of law affirmed in the preamble to the Charter which must mean that no discretion, including a judicial discretion, can be unlimited. But there is a problem, for the Court must clothe the general expression of rights and freedoms contained in the Charter with real substance and vitality. How can the courts go about this task without imposing at least some of their views and predilections upon the law? This question has been the subject of much discussion and comment. Many theories have been postulated but few have had direct reference to the problem in the Canadian context. In my view, this Court has offered guidance in this matter. In such cases as *Hunter* v. *Southam Inc.*, [1984] 2 S.C.R. 145, at pp. 155-56, and

R. v. Big M Drug Mart Ltd., [1985] 1 S.C.R. 295, at p. 344, it has enjoined what has been termed a "purposive approach" in applying the Charter and its provisions. I take this to mean that the Courts should interpret the Charter in a manner calculated to give effect to its provisions, not to the idiosyncratic view of the judge who is writing. This approach marks out the limits of appropriate Charter adjudication. It confines the content of Charter guaranteed rights and freedoms to the purposes given expression in the Charter. Consequently, while the courts must continue to give a fair, large and liberal construction to the Charter provisions, this approach prevents the Court from abandoning its traditional adjudicatory function in order to formulate its own conclusions on questions of public policy, a step which this Court has said on numerous occasions it must not take. That Charter interpretation is to be purposive necessarily implies the converse: it is not to be "non-purposive." A court is not entitled to define a right in a manner unrelated to the interest which the right in question was meant to protect. I endeavoured to formulate an approach to the problem in *Reference Re Public Service Employee Relations Act*, [1987] 1 S.C.R. 313, in these words, at p. 394:

It follows that while a liberal and not overly legalistic approach should be taken to constitutional interpretation, the Charter should not be regarded as an empty vessel to be filled with whatever meaning we might wish from time to time. The interpretation of the Charter, as of all constitutional documents, is constrained by the language, structure and history of the constitutional text, by constitutional tradition, and by the history, traditions, and underlying philosophies of our society.

The approach, as I understand it, does not mean that judges may not make some policy choices when confronted with competing conceptions of the extent of rights or freedoms. Difficult choices must be made and the personal views of judges will unavoidably be engaged from time to time. The decision made by judges, however, and the interpretations that they advance or accept must be plausibly inferable from something in the Charter. It is not for the courts to manufacture a constitutional right out of whole cloth. I conclude on this question by citing and adopting the following words, although spoken in dissent, from the judgment of Harlan J. in *Reynolds* v. *Sims*, 377 U.S. 533 (1964), which, in my view, while stemming from the American experience, are equally applicable in a consideration of the Canadian position. Harlan J. commented, at pp. 624-25, on the:

. . . current mistaken view of the Constitution and the constitutional function of this Court. This view, in a nutshell, is that every major social ill in this country can find its cure in some constitutional "principle," and that this Court should "take the lead" in promoting reform when other branches of government fail to act. The Constitution is not a panacea for every blot upon the public welfare, nor should this Court, ordained as a judicial body, be thought of as a general haven for reform movements. The Constitution is an instrument of government, fundamental to which is the premise that in a diffusion of governmental authority lies the greatest promise that this Nation will realize liberty for all its citizens. This Court, limited in function in accordance with that premise, does not serve its high purpose when it exceeds its authority, even to satisfy justified impatience with the slow workings of the political process. For when, in the name of constitutional interpretation, the Court adds something to the Constitution that was deliberately excluded from it, the Court in reality substitutes its view of what should be so for the amending process.

THE RIGHT TO ABORTION AND S. 7 OF THE CHARTER

The judgment of my colleague, Wilson J., is based upon the proposition that a pregnant woman has a right, under s. 7 of the Charter, to have an abortion. The same concept underlies the judgment of the Chief Justice. . . .

All laws, it must be noted, have the potential for interference with individual priorities and aspirations. In fact, the very purpose of most legislation is to cause such interference. It is only when such legislation goes beyond interfering with priorities and aspirations, and abridges rights, that courts may intervene. If a law prohibited membership in a lawful association it would be unconstitutional, not because it would interfere with priorities and aspirations, but because of its interference with the guaranteed right of freedom of association under s. 2(d) of the Charter. Compliance with the Income Tax Act has, no doubt, frequently interfered with priorities and aspirations. The taxing provisions are not, however, on that basis unconstitutional, because the ordinary taxpayer enjoys no right to be tax free. Other illustrations may be found. In my view, it is clear that before it could be concluded that any enactment infringed the concept of security of the person, it would have to infringe some underlying right included in or protected by the concept. For the appellants to succeed here, then, they must show more than an interference with priorities and aspirations; they must show the infringement of a right which is included in the concept of security of the person.

The proposition that women enjoy a constitutional right to have an abortion is devoid of support in the language of s. 7 of the Charter or any other section. While some human rights documents, . . . expressly address the question of abortion, the Charter is entirely silent on the point. It may be of some significance that the Charter uses specific language in dealing with other topics, such as voting rights, religion, expression and such controversial matters as mobility rights, language rights and minority rights, but remains silent on the question of abortion which, at the time the Charter was under consideration, was as much a subject of public controversy as it is today. Furthermore, it would appear that the history of

the constitutional text of the Charter affords no support for the appellants' proposition. A reference to the *Minutes of the Special Joint Committee of Senate and House of Commons on the Constitution of Canada* (Proceedings 32nd. Parl. Sess. 1 (1981), vol. 46, p. 43) reveals the following exchange:

Mr. Crombie: . . . And I ask you then finally, what effect will the inclusion of the due process clause have on the question of marriage, procreation, or the parental care of children?

Mr. Chretien: The point, Mr. Crombie, that it is important to understand the difference is that we [pass] legislation here on abortion, criminal code, and we pass legislation on capital punishment; parliament has the authority to do that, and the court at this moment, because we do not have the due process of law written there, cannot go and see whether we made the right decision or the wrong decision in Parliament.

If you write down the words, "due process of law" here, the advice I am receiving is the court could go behind our decision and say that their decision on abortion was not the right one, their decision on capital punishment was not the right one, and it is a danger, according to legal advice I am receiving that it will very much limit the scope of the power of legislation by the Parliament and we do not want that; and it is why we do not want the words "due process of law." These are the two main examples that we should keep in mind.

You can keep speculating on all the things that have never been touched, but these are two very sensitive areas that we have to cope with as legislators and my view is that Parliament has decided a certain law on abortion and a certain law on capital punishment, and it should prevail and we do not want the courts to say that the judgment of Parliament was wrong in using the constitution.

This passage, of course, revolves around the second and not the first limb of s. 7, but it offers no support for the suggestion that it was intended to bring the question of abortion into the Charter.

It cannot be said that the history, traditions and underlying philosophies of our society would support the proposition that a right to abortion could be implied in the Charter. . . .

HISTORY OF THE LAW OF ABORTION
~ At English common law, abortion before quickening was not a criminal offence. Quickening occurred when the pregnant woman could feel the foetus move in her womb—usually around four months. In 1803, the law of criminal abortion was codified in England. In 1861, the distinction between pre- and post-quickening was abolished. All abortions were treated as felony offences. In *R*. v. *Bourne* (1939), the crime of abortion was held to be subject to the defence of necessity—viz. saving the mother's life. In Canada, abortion was first made a statutory crime in 1869, and has continued to be so under the various revisions of the Criminal Code. In 1969, Parliament significantly reformed the abortion law by adding the exculpatory provisions of s. 251(4). ~

. . . The historical review of the legal approach in Canada taken from the judgment of the Court of Appeal serves, as well, to cast light on the underlying philosophies of our society and establishes that there has never been a general right to abortion in Canada. There has always been clear recognition of a public interest in the protection of the unborn and there has been no evidence or indication of any general acceptance of the concept of abortion at will in our society. It is to be observed as well that at the time of adoption of the Charter the sole provision for an abortion in Canadian law was that to be found in s. 251 of the Criminal Code. It follows then, in my view, that the interpretive approach to the Charter, which has been accepted in this Court, affords no support for the entrenchment of a constitutional right of abortion.

As to an asserted right to be free from any state interference with bodily integrity and serious state-imposed psychological stress, I would say that to be accepted, as a constitutional right, it would have to be based on something more than the mere imposition, by the State, of such stress and anxiety. It must, surely, be evident that many forms of government action deemed to be reasonable, and even necessary in our society, will cause stress and anxiety to many, while at the same time being acceptable exercises of government power in pursuit of socially desirable goals. The very facts of life in a modern society would preclude the entrenchment of such a constitutional right. . . .

To invade the s. 7 right of security of the person, there would have to be more than state-imposed stress or strain. A breach of the right would have to be based upon an infringement of some interest which would be of such nature and such importance as to warrant constitutional protection. This, it would seem to me, would be limited to cases where the state-action complained of, in addition to imposing stress and strain, also infringed another right, freedom or interest which was deserving of protection under the concept of security of the person. For the reasons outlined above, the right to have an abortion—given the language, structure and history of the Charter and given the history, traditions and underlying philosophies of our society—is not such an interest. . . .

It is for these reasons I would conclude, that save for the provisions of the Criminal Code, which permit abortion where the life or health of the woman is at risk, no right of abortion can be found in Canadian law, custom or tradition, and that the Charter, including s. 7, creates no further right. Accordingly, it is my view that s. 251 of the Code does not in its terms violate s. 7 of the Charter. Even accepting the assumption that the concept of security of the person would extend to vitiating a law which would require a woman to carry a child to the completion of her pregnancy at the risk of her life or health, it must be observed that this is not our case. As has been pointed out, s. 251 of the Code already provides for abortion in such circumstances.

PROCEDURAL FAIRNESS

I now turn to the appellant's argument regarding the procedural fairness of s. 251 of the Criminal Code. . . . Because abortions are not generally available to all women who seek them, the argument goes, the defence is illusory, or practically so, and the section therefore fails to comport with the principles of fundamental justice.

Precise evidence on the questions raised is, of course, difficult to obtain and subject to subjective interpretation depending upon the views of those adducing it. Much evidence was led at trial based largely on the Ontario experience. Additional material in the form of articles, reports and studies was adduced, from which the Court was invited to conclude that access to abortion is not evenly provided across the country and that this could be the source of much dissatisfaction. While I recognize that in constitutional cases a greater latitude has been allowed concerning the reception of such material, I would prefer to place principal reliance upon the evidence given under oath in court in my considerations of the factual matters. Evidence was adduced from the chairman of a therapeutic abortion committee at a hospital in Hamilton, where in 1982 eleven hundred and eighty-seven abortions were performed, who testified that of all applications received by his committee in that year less than a dozen were ultimately refused. Refusal in each case was based upon the fact that a majority of the committee was not convinced that "the continuation of the pregnancy would be detrimental to the woman's health." All physicians who performed abortions under the Criminal Code provisions admitted in cross-examination that they had never had an application for a therapeutic abortion on behalf of the patient ultimately refused by an abortion committee. No woman testified that she personally had applied for an abortion

anywhere in Canada and had been refused, and no physician testified to his participation in such an application. . . . In all, the extent to which the statutory procedure contributes to the problems connected with procuring an abortion is anything but clear. Accordingly, even if one accepts that it would be contrary to the principles of fundamental justice for Parliament to make available a defence which, by reason of its terms, is illusory or practically so, it cannot, in my view, be said that s. 251 of the Code has had that effect.

It would seem to me that a defence created by Parliament could only be said to be illusory or practically so when the defence is not available in the circumstances in which it is held out as being available. The very nature of the test assumes, of course, that it is for Parliament to define the defence and, in so doing, to designate the terms and conditions upon which it may be available. . . . I would suggest it is apparent that the Court's role is not to second-guess Parliament's policy choice as to how broad or how narrow the defence should be. The determination of when "the disapprobation of society is not warranted" is in Parliament's hands. . . .

It was further argued that the defence in s. 251(4) is procedurally unfair in that it fails to provide an adequate standard of "health" to guide the abortion committees which are charged with the responsibility for approving or disapproving applications for abortions. It is argued that the meaning of the word "health" in s. 251(4) is so vague as to render the subsection unconstitutional. . . . This argument was dealt with fully and effectively in the Court of Appeal:

In this case, however, from a reading of s. 251 with its exception, there is no difficulty in determining what is proscribed and what is permitted. It cannot be said that no sensible meaning can be given to the words of the section. Thus, it is for the courts to say what meaning the statute will bear. Counsel was unable to give the Court any authority for holding a statute void for uncertainty. In any event, there is no doubt the respondents knew that the acts they proposed and carried out were in breach of the section. The fact that they did not approve of the law in this regard does not make it "uncertain." . . .

Finally, this Court has dealt with the matter. Dickson J. (as he then was), speaking for the majority in *Morgentaler (1975), supra,* in concluding a discussion of s. 251(4) of the Criminal Code, said, at p. 675:

Whether one agrees with the Canadian legislation or not is quite beside the point. Parliament has spoken unmistakably in clear and unambiguous language.

In the same case, Laskin C.J., while dissenting on other grounds, said at p. 634:

The contention under point 2 is equally untenable as an attempt to limit the substance of legislation in a situation which does not admit of it. In submitting that the standard upon which therapeutic abortion committees must act is uncertain and subjective, counsel who make the submission cannot find nourishment for it even in Doe v. Bolton. There it was held that the prohibition of abortion by a physician except when "based upon his best clinical judgment that an abortion is necessary" did not prescribe a standard so vague as to be constitutionally vulnerable. A fortiori, under the approach taken here to substantive due process, the argument of uncertainty and subjectivity fails. It is enough to say that Parliament has fixed a manageable standard because it is addressed to a professional panel, the members of which would be expected to bring a practised judgment to the question whether 'continuation of the pregnancy

. . . would or would be likely to endanger . . . life or health.'

In my opinion, then, the contention that the defence provided in s. 251(4) of the Criminal Code is illusory cannot be supported. . . .

CONCLUSION

Before leaving this case, I wish to make it clear that I express no opinion on the question of whether, or upon what conditions, there should be a right for a pregnant woman to have an abortion free of legal sanction. No valid constitutional objection to s. 251 of the Criminal Code has, in my view, been raised and, consequently, if there is to be a change in the law concerning this question it will be for Parliament to make. Questions of public policy touching on this controversial and divisive matter must be resolved by the elected Parliament. It does not fall within the proper jurisdiction of the courts. Parliamentary action on this matter is subject to judicial review but, in my view, nothing in the Canadian Charter of Rights and Freedoms gives the Court the power or duty to displace Parliament in this matter involving, as it does, general matters of public policy. . . .

The solution to this question in this country must be left to Parliament. It is for Parliament to pronounce on and to direct social policy. This is not because Parliament can claim all wisdom and knowledge but simply because Parliament is elected for that purpose in a free democracy and, in addition, has the facilities—the exposure to public opinion and information—as well as the political power to make effective its decisions. . . .

For all of these reasons, I would dismiss the appeal. . . .

51. Borowski *v*. Minister of Justice of Canada, *1988*

An Account of the Hearing before the Supreme Court of Canada, October 3 and 4, 1988

~ On September 8, 1978, in a Regina Court of Queen's Bench, Joe Borowski filed his statement of claim challenging the constitutionality of Canada's abortion law. On October 3 and 4, 1988, the Supreme Court finally heard his case. In the interim, Borowski has become to Canada's pro-life movement what Henry Morgentaler is to the pro-choice camp—a hero, a symbol, an opportunity to win in the courts what they could not win in Parliament.

Like Morgentaler, Borowski based his challenge on the new Charter of Rights. He was represented by Regina lawyer Morris Schumiatcher, one of the living legends of the Canadian bar, a veteran of forty years before the bar of the Supreme Court. Schumiatcher's legal argument was deceptively simple. Section 7 of the Charter declares that "everyone has the right to life, liberty, and security of the person." The unborn child, Schumiatcher argued, is included in the concept "everyone."

If the legal question seemed simple and narrow, its potential policy consequences were anything but. This explained the packed courtroom. In addition to Schumiatcher and Crown counsel, Ed Sojonky, there were counsel for three "intervenors"—groups with an interest in the case who had been given permission to participate in the hearing. Supporting the Crown's position was the Legal Education and Action Fund, or LEAF, an organization that litigates issues of concern to feminists. LEAF was represented by Mary Eberts, one of its founders and most able advocates. Supporting Borowski were REAL Women, a conservative women's group; and the Interfaith Coalition, a diverse alliance of Catholic, protestant, Jewish, Islamic, Hindu, evangelical and native Indian groups.

The supporting casts for both sides were duly assembled in the public benches at the rear. Top brass from LEAF, the National Advisory Committee on the Status of Women (NACSW), and the Canadian Abortion Rights Action League (CARAL) on one side; their counterparts from REAL Women, Alliance for Life, and Toronto Right to Life, on the other. Both groups were symbolically seated on opposing sides of the centre aisle: the Borowski supporters behind their champion, to the right of the judges; the anti-Borowski camp to the left. Students and other curious onlookers grabbed seats on whichever side they could find them. Reporters had filled all the side seats reserved for the press, and the media overflowed into the adjacent, closed circuit, press room.

When Joe Borowski began his case back in 1978, the government had argued that he had no business being in the courts at all. Borowski's claim was alleged to lack the threshold legal requirement of "standing"—that there be an actual dispute between the government and a private citizen before any court can hear the case. Mere dislike of a government policy does not create a right to challenge its constitutional validity. To be able to challenge a law in court, an individual must first demonstrate a personal stake in the application of the law—that the law actually harms him in an individual and concrete way. Mr. Borowski, not pregnant and with no prospect of becoming so, could not claim that the law either prevented him or forced him to have an abortion.

It took Borowski three years and $150,000 to defeat the government's claim. Even then, only a precedent-setting Supreme Court decision that dramatically expanded the law of standing allowed Borowski to begin his abortion challenge.[1] The Chief Justice, Bora Laskin, dissented. He warned that if Borowski were granted standing, "other persons with an opposite point of view might seek to intervene and would be allowed to do so, [and] the result would be to set up a battle between parties who do not have a direct interest, to wage it in a judicial arena." In October, 1988, after two more trials, seven more years and another $200,000—Joe Borowski was back in the Supreme Court. With the full array of interest group intervenors, Laskin's fears seemed to be realized.

Once again, however, the government was arguing that Borowski had no business being there. The new problem for Mr. Borowski was the Supreme Court victory of his longtime abortion adversary, Dr. Henry Morgentaler. Morgentaler had also challenged section 251 of the Criminal Code, although for the opposite reason. When the Court accepted Dr. Morgentaler's contention that the abortion law violated the Charter of Rights and declared section 251 invalid, it pulled the legal rug out from under Borowski's claim. How could he challenge the constitutionality of a law that no longer exists? In legal parlance, Borowski's case became "moot"—no longer a live controversy— with the death of section 251.

From a legal perspective, Borowski barely had a leg to stand on. But in a broader sense, he would certainly seemed to have earned a right to a hearing by the Court. Borowski has paid his dues and then some. When he began his fight against the then new (1969) abortion law, he was riding the crest of the biggest political success story in the Prairies. In 1968 the 36 year old, former nickel miner and union firebrand was elected as the NDP MLA from Thompson. Later that year when Ed Schreyer formed the first NDP government in the history of Manitoba, he appointed the popular Borowski as Minister of Transport. Soon he was given a second portfolio—Public Works—which together meant that he administered the largest annual budgets in the Cabinet— over $60 million dollars. A 1970 *Maclean's* article observed that Joe's humorous malapropisms and uncompromising honesty had made him the most popular politician in Manitoba and the favourite of the local press. Joe's political future seemed unlimited. Then came the abortion issue.

---

[1] For discussion of this case, see Introduction, p. 37.

In 1971 Joe resigned from Schreyer's Cabinet to protest continued government funding of abortions. Two years later, running as an independent, he lost
his seat in the Legislature. Over the next seven years, Joe went to jail three
times for refusing to pay his income taxes—his way of protesting public
funding of abortions. In 1978, Revenue Canada confiscated his car (the first
new one he had ever owned) and also the $32,000 he had raised for his court
challenge. In 1982 he nearly killed himself with a 78 day hunger strike to
protest the absence of a right to life for the unborn in the proposed new Charter
of Rights. In 1978 Joe had hired Morris Schumiatcher to turn his cause into a
case. Now after 10 years of litigation and $350,000 in expenses, Joe was back
in the Supreme Court. How, Schumiatcher implored the Court, could the seven
justices tell Borowski that they would not even hear his case?

All this is of course legally irrelevant. As Justice Lamer reminded
Schumiatcher, "It's not just a question of pleasing or displeasing Mr. Borowski. It's a question of this Court taking a very big step as regards its
jurisdiction in relation to Parliament. . . . I am very concerned about judges
gnawing away at Parliament's jurisdiction. . . ."[2] If the Supreme Court
functioned strictly as a court of law, the jurisdictional issue would probably
have disposed of the Borowski case at the outset. But the justices knew that
they were not just dealing with Borowski the individual, but with Borowski the
symbol—the symbol of the prolife cause and the tens of thousands of Canadians who actively support it. Borowski was the symbolic counterpart to
Morgentaler. To hear one but not the other might give the appearance of bias.
The modern Supreme Court has become sensitive to the political environment
in which it works. In its role as umpire of Canadian federalism, the Court has
gone out of its way to appear evenhanded in its treatment of competing federal
and provincial claims. Dr. Morgentaler had had his day in Court. Should not
Joe have his?

The Court spent almost the entire first day on this issue—trying to decide
whether to decide. The justices took turns pressing Schumiatcher with jurisdictional questions. In the absence of any law, began the Chief Justice, wouldn't
any answer by the Court be a case of "blatant legal legislation?"[3] Justice
Antonio Lamer elaborated:[4]

> *There is no law prohibiting abortions and there is no law prohibiting*
> *pregnancy and ordering abortions as in some countries. Where are we*
> *going to latch onto . . . a proper judicial function as distinct from a policy*
> *pronouncement? . . . I can't relate to a law, I can't apply a law, I can't*
> *strike a law down, I can't uphold it, I can only express an opinion as to what*
> *maybe the law should say.*

---

[2] Transcript of Appeal Proceedings on October 3, 1988; Supreme Court of Canada; vol. I,
    page 25. (Hereafter cited as I,25).
[3] I,10.
[4] I,17.

Schumiatcher, a veteran of forty years of legal sparring, tried to deflect the question.

> *My Lord, with all respect, I don't think that Your Lordship should have difficulty. What is the law that bears upon this case? I'm not looking to a statute. . . . I've got something much better before the Court and that's the supreme law of Canada, I've got the Charter of Rights and Freedoms.*[5]

Sensing the vulnerability of this position, Schumiatcher quickly mounted a second line of defense. "No law is a kind of law," he countered. "To fail to hear this [case] now is to make a decision. It is to make a decision against Mr. Borowski."[6]

Schumiatcher alternated his legal arguments with pleas for moral leadership from the Court. "[T]he situation here is a desperate and urgent one," he told the Court. "[T]he people of Canada are looking to this Court as never before, not just for guidance in respect of legal matters, but in respect of moral conduct."[7]

This tack met with only limited success. Madame Justice l'Heureux-Dubé countered:

> *An easy answer to your query would be that it is up to the state to decide rather than the courts. You say [the foetus] has no rights. Well, it is up to the state to decide, the legislators, is it not?*[8]

Schumiatcher refused to retreat. The legislators had acted, he reminded the Court, and they had given some protection to the unborn until, that is, the *Morgentaler* decision in January of this year. "I put it to you that the responsibility for there being no abortion laws in Canada to protect the unborn is the result of a decision of this Court,"[9] declared Schumiatcher. His implication was clear: You created this problem. Now it's your responsibility to fix it.

Still, Schumiatcher had not met head on the central concern of the Court. It was best articulated by Justice Lamer:

> *"[I]f this Court [proceeds with the case], then it is an acknowledgement . . . that it has the power to tell Parliament that it should enact a law, and that if it doesn't, Parliament is in violation of the Charter of Rights."*[10]

Schumiatcher initially responded with a discourse on how with the adoption of the Charter "the whole jurisdiction of this Court has expanded enormously"

[5] I,17.
[6] I,21.
[7] I,20-21.
[8] I,94.
[9] I,94.
[10] I,18.

and created "new perceptions in the relationship between" courts and legislatures.[11] But these theoretical reflections tailed off into a dangerously frank and perhaps ill-advised conclusion: "[L]et's face it, this Court is telling the legislature what to do or what not to do all the time."[12]

While there was some truth in Schumiatcher's assessment, his timing could hardly have been worse. In its eighty-plus Charter decisions to date, the Court has repeatedly denied that its role is to make public policy—especially in cases where it clearly is. Schumiatcher's candor had touched a raw nerve.

Sensing the potential damage, Claude Thomson, counsel for one of the pro-life intervenors, tried to narrow the scope of the case. "This is not a case in which the Court is being asked to direct Parliament to pass a law," Thomson reassured the justices. The Court, he continued, is merely being asked to clarify the meaning of section 7 of the Charter: Is the unborn child included in the concept of "everyone" used in section 7? The Court, he concluded, is not being asked "to strike down in advance any proposed legislation [or] to get into the difficult question of balancing whatever rights the unborn may have against the rights of women. . . . [W]hat we have here is [only] . . . a question of declaratory relief."[13]

Mary Eberts, the counsel for LEAF, urged the justices not to be fooled by Thomson's narrowing of the issue.

The Charter may have circumscribed the doctrine of parliamentary supremacy, but it did not create an environment where there are no guidelines about the proper relations between this Honourable Court and Parliament. . . . [T]his Court . . . is not an actor of first instance, but . . . a reviewing actor, and what Mr. Borowski asks you to do in this Court today is to be an actor of first instance. . . . The proper role for this Court under the Charter . . . is to review legislation and not to be a pronouncer in the first instance.[14]

The Court clearly was uncomfortable with Borowski's request, but it soon became apparent that they were not too happy with the Crown either. In July, the Mulroney government had requested the Court to postpone the *Borowski* hearing until it had enacted new abortion legislation. The Chief Justice had flatly refused. Judicial independence, Dickson declared, protected the Court's agenda from being rearranged to suit the political convenience of the government.

Crown counsel Ed Sojonky began by renewing his request that the case be postponed. He had just begun his attack on the mootness issue—that the Court

[11] I,31.
[12] I,31.
[13] I,34,35.
[14] I,86-87.

should not hear the case until there was a law—when Justice Heureux-Dubé interrupted him. "Counsel, I am surprised [by your] stand," she observed dryly. "I would have suspected that since you did not ask for quashing that you would be happy that we hear it."[15]

Sojonky backpedalled. It is true, he conceded, that the Crown had not asked that the appeal be quashed, but his authorities "could well be used in support of such a motion."[16] Justice LaForest shot back impatiently: "[But] none was made, and in the meantime, the parties on all sides have prepared for a question that was at least part of the original question."

Sojonky politely conceded the point and quickly tried to steer the Court back to the issue of mootness. He was cut off again, this time by Justice Lamer. "Mr. Sojonky, I realize that you follow instructions," Lamer observed causticly. "I understand the position. . . . In other words, you would like us to quash it, but you do not want to ask for it."[17] Muffled laughter rippled across the previously somber courtroom. Sojonky replied somewhat meekly: "With the greatest of deference, My Lord, the word 'quash' does not appear in the factum."[18]

The exchange continued, but it was now clear that the Court was exasperated with the government's tactics. The Mulroney government did not want the Court to hear the Borowski case—at least not before the November 21 election—but it did not have the political courage to say so. In May, Morris Manning, representing the Canadian Abortion Rights Action League (CARAL), had written the Attorney-General requesting that he move to quash the appeal on the grounds that it was moot. No doubt this was discussed at the highest levels—probably Cabinet—and rejected. The government recognized the symbolic meaning of Borowski. They did not want to alienate the prolife vote—or the substantial number of pro-life Tory backbenchers—by asking the Court to close its doors to Borowski. Sojonky had indeed been given instructions—try to persuade the Court to quash the appeal but do not ask for it directly. The government was trying to have the Court do its dirty work—and take the political heat that went with it.

The Court took the unusual step of recessing not once but twice to decide whether to continue. At 3:00 o'clock the Court returned, and the Chief Justice rose to announce their decision: "We will reserve decision on these matters [of jurisdiction]," and continue to hear the remainder of the case.[19] There was an audible sigh of relief from the Borowski side of the courtroom.

Schumiatcher picked up where he had left off. The most important aspect of

[15] I,43.
[16] I,44.
[17] I,54.
[18] I,54.
[19] I,101.

his case, he reminded the Court, was the evidence—the evidence that the unborn child is a human being. He summarized the evidence given by the fifteen "expert witnesses" whom he had brought from around the world to Regina in 1983 for the initial trial. These experts in genetics, prenatal and neonatal medecine, testified to the "individuality, the separateness, and the uniqueness" of the human qualities and characteristics of the unborn. Their testimony ranged from the technical—30 divisions, or two-thirds, of the 45 cell divisions that occur in a lifetime take place in the first 8 weeks after fertilization—to the homely:

"[E]ach of us may say and none of us may deny that I am the fetus that was. There has never been a time when I was not the same individual. . . . There was a time when I couldn't walk and a time when I couldn't speak and a time when I couldn't articulate my claim upon you as my brother, but there has never been a time when I was not the same individual."[20]

In an unusual move for a court whose function is to review questions of law not questions of fact, Schumiatcher was then granted permission to show a series of ultrasound videotapes of life in the womb. The tapes showed the development and activities of the foetus/unborn child from six to fifteen weeks after gestation. For most right-to-lifers, these videos are the ultimate rejoinder—the proof of just how human-like the foetus is. At first all seven justices paid rapt attention to the television screens in front of them. But the flickering images were hard on the eyes, and soon the justices'—and the audience's—attention wained. They ended at 4:00 o'clock, and the Chief— somewhat sleepily—suggested that this had been enough for one day and adjourned the Court until the next morning.

Schumiatcher completed his presentation Tuesday morning. His strategy was evident. On top of the factual base already constructed, he now added a long string of legal precedents. Criminal law, property law, torts, family law, and the civil law have all recognized rights in the unborn child. How unfair it is, Schumiatcher declared, that the unborn child is now deprived of the one right that is a prerequisite for the enjoyment of all the others—the right to be born alive. And how ironic, Schumiatcher continued, that society took away this right just at a time when modern medical science was discovering how distinctively human the unborn child really is. A "primitive society," Schumiatcher observed, lacks this knowledge and "cannot be expected to accord to the unborn the care and concern that are bestowed upon children once they are born."[21]

Schumiatcher concluded with an emotional appeal for the Court to temper

---

[20] Dr. Harley Smyth, Factum of the Appellant, p. 6.
[21] Factum of the Appellant, p. 36.

the administration of the law with compassion. "In our advanced society," observed Schumiatcher, "it is both the mother and the unborn child within her who are deserving of the compassion of which Chief Justice Dickson [recently] spoke . . . ." Using a favourite tactic of lawyers appearing before the Supreme Court, Schumiatcher quoted the Chief Justice back to himself:[22]

> *It is common now for individuals to assert their rights and liberties [under] the Charter. But we all must recognize that there is another side of the coin . . . that we must have . . . a sense of obligation [and] responsibility . . . ; [that] we must retain a profound respect for the rights of others. . . . compassion is not some extralegal factor. . . . Rather, compassion is part and parcel of the nature and content of that which we call 'law'.*

Schumiatcher was followed by counsel for the intervenors who supported the Borowski motion, REAL Women and the Interfaith Coalition. They had been allotted 15 minutes each, and the Court held them to it. After a brief lunch recess, the Court reconvened to hear Sojonsky's presentation of the Crown's position. The justices listened intently but asked few questions. Sojonky was finished in less than an hour. There was a growing impression that—unlike the day before—the justices were more interested with finishing the case than in the issues it raised.

The Crown's position was predictable and prosaic. Sojonky repeated the government's preference that the Court postpone any decision on the merits pending new abortion legislation. If, however, the Court insisted on proceeding, there were sound legal arguments for rejecting Borowski's claims. Sojonky plodded through a careful, point by point rebuttal of Schumiatcher's legal arguments. There had never been an absolute foetal right to life in English or Canadian criminal law. The interests of both the mother and the foetus had always been recognized. Canada's 1969 abortion law reform was consistent with this tradition—continuing the criminal prohibition on abortion per se, but allowing it for therapeutic reasons under specified circumstances. As for the various legal rights vested in the foetus by tort, property, and family law—these had always been understood as depending on live birth, and in no way implied such a right. Sojonky reminded the justices that the framers of the Charter had been asked to include the right to life for the unborn and had refused. Surely the Court would not be justified in adding to the Charter what its authors had rejected. Sojonky finished with a flourish and appeared to brace himself for an onslaught of questions from the bench. Instead, the Chief Justice quietly asked Ms. Eberts to make LEAF's presentation.

Ebert's opened with an impassioned plea for the justices not to be seduced into thinking that the only issue before them was the rights of the fetus. Mr. Borowski and Mr. Schumiatcher like to show films of the foetus happily

---

[22] Factum of the Appellant, p. 37.

bouncing around, she began. "But where is that fetus?" she demanded. "It is in a grainy blur. That grainy blur is a woman. . . ." "Broaden your focus," Eberts implored the Court. The woman is there and she is not just a "grainy blur." You cannot and must not separate the foetus from the mother, or the discussion of a right to life from abortion.

LEAF had been allocated 20 minutes. Eberts used most of the remainder of this time to reinforce some of the legal arguments advanced by the Crown. She ended with a caution that the Court should refrain from changing the status quo. Parliament is now trying to frame a law that balances the "rights" of the mother with the "interests" of the foetus. An affirmative answer to the Borowski case would change the equation from an issue of "rights versus interest" to "rights versus rights." "The legislative context must be free from judicial interference," she admonished.

Eberts' plea may have been good law under the 1960 Bill of Rights, but it was hardly an accurate description of legislative-judicial relations since 1982. It was also quite hypocritical coming from LEAF, the leading example of a new breed of interest groups that frequently ask courts to overrule legislative policy choices. More importantly, however, Eberts' remarks reveal more clearly what really is at stake in the *Borowski* case—the battle for public opinion.

Supreme Court decisions may settle legal cases but they rarely "solve" political issues. Just as the abortion issue survived the *Morgentaler* decision, so it will outlive whatever the Court decides in *Borowski*. Pro-choicers are no more likely to pack up their bags and go home if Borowski wins, than the pro-lifers did after Morgentaler's victory in January. This is not to say that the Court's decisions have no consequences. They do. But the nature of that consequence is to create a new political resource for the winning side. The victor in the judicial arena returns to the larger political arena armed with a new weapon—the favorable judgement of the Court and the moral authority that it carries. In the abortion policy debate in the wake of *Morgentaler*, pro-choice advocates have had the considerable advantage of being able to claim that the Charter protects a woman's right to abortion. While such claims are typically overstated, legislators and other public office-holders cannot safely ignore them. Borowski has the potential to give to prolifers a similar "moral club."

This is what Borowski, Schumiatcher, and their prolife supporters want from the Court—a declaration that the unborn child is indeed a human person and thus entitled to the protection granted by section 7 of the Charter. Armed with such a statement, they would return to Parliament and aggressively lobby for a much more restrictive abortion law. It is most unlikely that they could persuade Parliament to outlaw all abortions. But it is undeniable that a favourable ruling in *Borowski* would strengthen their position. At a minimum, it would allow them to argue that a just abortion policy must balance "rights against rights."

This is what Eberts, LEAF, and their pro-choice supporters obviously want to prevent. While the legal basis of *Morgentaler* was a narrow, procedural ruling, its practical consequence was to suspend the enforcement of the law until Parliament fixed it. Symbolically, it also defined the abortion issue as a conflict of ''rights versus interests.'' The ensuing political paralysis in the House of Commons has produced a policy of ''no law.'' From the pro-choice perspective, ''no law'' is a good law as far as abortion goes, thus the defense of the status quo.

Whatever and whenever the Court decides, it will mark the end of another round, but hardly the end of the fight. ~

NOTE: On March 9, 1989, the Supreme Court dismissed the Borowski appeal. Justice Sopinka, writing for a unanimous court, ruled that in the wake of the *Morgentaler* decision, the case had become moot and that Borowski had lost standing. To answer the Borowski challenge, wrote Justice Sopinka, would be to create a new kind of ''private reference,'' a procedure that would intrude on the prerogative of the executive and possibly pre-empt Parliament's policy options on the abortion issue.

52. Quebec *v.* Ford et al (Quebec Sign Case), *1988*

~ The decision which the Supreme Court of Canada rendered on December 15, 1988 striking down Quebec's French only sign law is one of the Court's most important Charter decisions. The decision moves constitutional jurisprudence in two different directions simultaneously: while it embraces a very wide interpretation of ''freedom of expression'' as a constitutional right, it also establishes a very broad basis for legislatures to use the power they have under section 33 of the Charter to override constitutional rights and freedoms. In addition to these important developments in the interpretation of the Charter, the decision had a major impact on constitutional politics in Canada.

This was by no means the first Supreme Court decision overturning sections of Bill 101, the Charter of The French Language introduced by the PQ Government in 1977. In 1979 the Court struck down provisions of Bill 101 making French the official language of the province's legislature and courts. Another decision in 1984 forced Quebec to open its English schools to Canadians moving to Quebec from other provinces.[1] Both of these decisions were based on entrenched constitutional language rights to which the legislative override in the Charter did not apply. But the attack on sections of Bill 101 making French the exclusive language for commercial signs and firm names was based not on specific language rights but on the right to freedom of expression—a right found in section 2(b) of the Canadian Charter (a section to which the override does apply) as well as in Quebec's Charter of Human Rights and Freedoms.

In June 1982, just two months after the Charter was proclaimed, Quebec's National Assembly, in a defiant gesture against the constitutional settlement of 1982 to which Quebec had not consented, passed a law re-enacting all laws passed prior to the Charter but adding to each a section invoking the override.[2] After five years, in 1987, this omnibus use of the override lapsed and was not renewed. However, Quebec had used the override a second time: in February 1984 a law came into force applying the override just to the French only sign provision of Bill 101. This override, if valid, was still in force when the Supreme Court was deciding the sign case. But the section of Bill 101 requiring French only firm names had not been protected from judicial review by the override clause. Also the Quebec Charter of Rights contained a right to freedom of expression and it had not been overridden. Thus, whether or not an override was still in force, the Supreme Court had to consider the compatibility of French only commercial regulations with the right to freedom of expression.

In the 1985 election campaign in which the Liberals led by Robert Bourassa threw the Parti Quebecois out of office, the Liberals indicated that they would lift restrictions on the use of bilingual commercial signs. This promise was

---

[1] These cases are included in Part 2(D) below dealing with Language and Education Rights. See cases 54 and 55 (Blaikie & Que. Prot. Sch. Bd.).

[2] For a discussion of the override or ''notwithstanding clause'', as it is often called, see pp. 4-5 above.

important in attracting some outstanding representatives of the Quebec's English-speaking minority to the Liberal team. On the other hand it threatened to alienate many Quebec Francophones who regarded the French only sign policy as essential for insuring that the public face of Quebec would be French.

After the election, Premier Bourassa decided not to act on this controversial issue until the constitutional litigation under way had run its course. A number of firms had challenged provisions of Bill 101 requiring French only commercial signs and firm names.[3] A challenge had also been brought by Alan Singer, the owner of a stationary shop in an English-speaking district of Montreal, against provisions of Bill 101 which for some commercial activities—for instance the publication of catalogues and the signs of firms employing less than four persons or specializing in foreign products—required the use of French but also permitted the use of another language.[4] Like other politicians in Charterland, Bourassa hoped that the Court might take a deeply divisive issue off his hands.

The litigation may have given the Premier a temporary reprieve but when the Court's decision finally came down it did not make his political burden any lighter. On the contrary, the Supreme Court's finding that laws prohibiting the use of any language other than French violated the right to freedom of expression in both the Canadian Charter and the Quebec Charter deepened the resentment of the English-speaking community. The right to advertise in the language of one's choice could now be referred to as ''a fundamental right''. On the other hand, the Court's argument that a French only policy was not necessary to preserve the French face of Quebec failed to make much impression on the Francophone majority.

The Court took a remarkably liberal approach to the concept of ''freedom of expression''. It built into this freedom a new, universal language right—a right to communicate in one's own language, a right, it argued, which is essential to personal identity. The Court rejected arguments that commercial speech should be excluded from freedom of expression. It recognized that when consumer-protection regulations of advertising are under review consideration would have to be given to competing policy interests. But the Court took the position that this kind of balancing was to be done not by narrowly defining freedom of expression but by considering the justification for limits on the right under section 1 of the Charter. Applying section 1 to the cases at hand, the Court felt that the objective of maintaining the predominantly French character of Quebec could justify requiring the use of French on a joint use basis and even a law requiring the ''marked predominance'' of the French language.

---

[3] Only one of the five businesses raising the challenge—Valerie Ford's wool shop—was not incorporated. Her name appears to have been used for the citation in this case because equality right arguments were also made in the case and the Supreme Court had not yet decided whether equality rights extend to corporations.

[4] The citation for the Supreme Court decision in this case is *Devine* v. *Quebec*.

However, it saw no evidence justifying the exclusive use of French. Hence it struck down the French only provisions attacked in *Ford* but upheld bilingual requirements attacked by Singer.

While the Court's expansive interpretation of freedom of expression expanded the basis for judicial review, the Court in this same decision made it easier for legislatures to use section 33 of the Charter, the override clause, to immunize their laws from judicial review. Quebec's Court of Appeal had found Quebec's broad-brush use of the override to be unconstitutional, insisting that to fulfill its democratic purpose the override must be used in an accountable way with the legislature indicating precisely which rights and freedoms it was overriding. But here in *Ford* the Supreme Court rejected this argument: it would come too close to requiring "a prima facie justification of the decision to exercise the override". The Supreme Court made it clear that it wished to minimize judicial review of the use of the override.

And use the override is exactly what Premier Bourassa did in response to the Court's decision. After agonizing for 48 hours, Bourassa announced his decision to bring in legislation permitting bilingual signs indoors but requiring French only signs outside. To fend off a court challenge the override clause was applied to this legislation. The new law, Bill 178, cost Bourassa the services of three of his Anglophone Ministers and aroused the ire of English-speaking Quebecers. From the other side it was attacked by the opposition PQ Party and by many Quebec francophones who resented compromising the French-only program of Bill 101.

In the arena of constitutional politics Bourassa's action was a bombshell. By December 1988, there remained only two provinces, Manitoba and New Brunswick, whose legislatures had not approved the Meech Lake package of constitutional amendments. On the day after the Supreme Court decision, the Premier of Manitoba, Gary Filmon, introduced the Meech Lake Accord in the Manitoba legislature. But a few days later, following Premier Bourassa's decision to use the override and restore a unilingual French policy for outdoor signs, Filmon announced that he was suspending legislative consideration of the Meech Lake Accord. Legislative hearings, he said, "may invite a very negative anti-Quebec backlash."[5]

So at this stage the Meech Lake Accord, with its controversial clause recognizing Quebec as a "distinct society", was stalled if not dead. Although this meant that the prospects of a constitutional reconciliation with Quebec were dimmed, the French majority in Quebec learned through these events that the 1982 constitutional changes had left them with considerable power to protect their distinctive culture. For all Canadians the really ominous implication of these events was that they pointed to a deep gulf between the French majority in Quebec and the non-French majority in Canada over what should be regarded as fundamental in Canadian constitutionalism. ~

[5] *Toronto Globe & Mail*, December 20, 1988.

QUEBEC *v.* FORD et al.
In the Supreme Court of Canada. Judgment rendered Dec. 15, 1988.

THE COURT*: The principal issue in this appeal is whether ss. 58 and 69 of the Quebec Charter of the French Language, R.S.Q., c. C-11, which require that public signs and posters and commercial advertising shall be in the French language only and that only the French version of a firm name may be used, infringe the freedom of expression guaranteed by s. 2(b) of the Canadian Charter of Rights and Freedoms and s. 3 of the Quebec Charter of Human Rights and Freedoms, R.S.Q., c. C-12. There is also an issue as to whether ss. 58 and 69 of the Charter of the French Language infringe the guarantee against discrimination based on language in s. 10 of the Quebec Charter of Human Rights and Freedoms. The application of the Canadian Charter of Rights and Freedoms turns initially on whether there is a valid and applicable override provision, enacted pursuant to s. 33 of the Canadian Charter, that s. 58 and s. 69 of the Charter of the French Language shall operate notwithstanding s. 2(b) of the Canadian Charter.

The appeal is by leave of this Court from the judgment of the Quebec Court of Appeal on December 22, 1986, [1987] R.J.Q. 80, 5 Q.A.C. 119, 36 D.L.R. (4th) 374, dismissing the appeal of the Attorney General of Quebec from the judgment of Boudreault J. in the Superior Court for the District of Montreal on December 28, 1984, [1985] C.S. 147, 18 D.L.R. (4th) 711, which, on an application for a declaratory judgment, declared s. 58 of the Charter of the French Language to be inoperative to the extent that it prescribes that public signs and posters and commercial advertising shall be solely in the French language. The appeal is

also from the judgment of the Court of Appeal insofar as it allowed the incidental appeal of the respondents from the judgment of Boudreault J. and declared s. 69 of the Charter of the French Language to be inoperative to the extent that it prescribes that only the French version of a firm name may be used. In allowing the incidental appeal the Court of Appeal also declared ss. 205 to 208 of the Charter of the French Language respecting offences, penalties and other sanctions for a contravention of any of its provisions to be inoperative in so far as they apply to ss. 58 and 69.

The Respondents' Application for a Declaratory Judgment

On February 15, 1984 the respondents brought a motion for a declaratory judgment pursuant to art. 454 of the Quebec Code of Civil Procedure and s. 24(1) of the Canadian Charter of Rights and Freedoms. The commercial advertising and signs displayed by the five respondents are described in paragraphs 1 to 5 of their petition as follows:

1. La Chaussure Brown's Inc. ("Brown's") operates a business of retail shoe stores throughout the Province of Quebec, and since at least September 1, 1981, it has used and displayed within and on its premises of its store situated in the Fairview Shopping Centre, 6801 Trans-Canada Highway, Pointe-Claire, commercial advertising containing the following words:

---

* Chief Justice Dickson and Justices Beetz, Estey, McIntyre, Lamer, Wilson and LeDain heard the case when it was argued in November, 1987. But Estey and LeDain did not participate in the decision—Estey because he resigned soon after the hearing and LeDain because he was too ill.

BRAVO
"Brown's quality.

Bravo's price."

BRAVO
"La qualite a tout prix"

2. *Valerie Ford, carrying on business under the firm name and style of Les Lainages du Petit Mouton Enr. ("Ford"), operates a retail store selling, inter alia, wool, and since at least September 1, 1981, she has used and displayed on her premises at 311 St. Johns Boulevard, Pointe-Claire, an exterior sign containing the following words:*

"LAINE   WOOL"

3. *Nettoyeur et Tailleur Masson Inc. ("Nettoyeur Masson") carries on the business of a tailor and dry cleaner, and since at least September 1, 1981, it has used and displayed on its premises at 3259 Masson Street, Montreal an exterior sign containing the following words:*

NETTOYEURS
TAILLEUR
SERVICE
1 HEURE

*Masson
inc.*

CLEANERS
TAILOR
ALTERATIONS
REPAIRS
1 HOUR

4. *McKenna Inc. ("McKenna") carries on business as a florist in the City of Montreal and since at least September 1, 1981, it has used and displayed on its premises at 4509 Cote Des Neiges Road, Montreal, an exterior sign containing the following words:*

"Fleurs McKENNA Flowers"

5. *La Compagnie de Fromage Nationale Ltée ("Fromage Nationale")*

carries on the business of a cheese distributor and since at least September 1, 1981, it has used and displayed on its premises at 9001 Salley Street, Ville LaSalle, exterior signs containing the following words:

"NATIONAL CHEESE Co Ltd La Cie de FROMAGE NATIONALE Ltée"

The petition further alleges that the respondents La Chaussure Brown's Inc., Valerie Ford and La Compagnie de Fromage Nationale Ltée received a *mise en demeure* from the Commission de surveillance de la langue française advising them that their signs were not in conformity with the provisions of the Charter of the French Language and calling on them to conform to such provisions and that the respondents McKenna Inc. and Nettoyeur et Tailleur Masson Inc. were charged with violation of the Charter of the French Language.

The respondents conclude in their petition for a declaration that they have the right, notwithstanding ss. 58, 69 and 205 to 208 of the Charter of the French Language, to use the signs, posters and commercial advertising described in their petition and a declaration that ss. 58 and 69 and ss. 205 to 208, as they apply to ss. 58 and 69 of the Charter of the French Language, are inoperative and of no force or effect.

The Relevant Legislative and Constitutional Provisions

To facilitate an understanding of the issues in the appeal, as they are reflected in the reasons for judgment of the Superior Court and the Court of Appeal and in the constitutional questions and submissions of the parties in this Court, it is desirable at this point to set out the relevant legislative and constitutional provisions.

A. The Charter of the French Language

Sections 1, 58, 69, 89, 205, 206 . . . of

the Charter of the French Language, R.S.Q., c. C-11, provide:

1. French is the official language of Quebec.

58. Public signs and posters and commercial advertising shall be solely in the official language.

Notwithstanding the foregoing, in the cases and under the conditions or circumstances prescribed by regulation of the Office de la langue française, public signs and posters and commercial advertising may be both in French and in another language or solely in another language.

69. Subject to section 68, only the French version of a firm name may be used in Quebec.

89. Where this act does not require the use of the official language exclusively, the official language and another language may be used together.

205. Every person who contravenes a provision of this act other than section 136 or of a regulation made under this act by the Government or by the Office de la langue française is guilty of an offence and liable, in addition to costs,
   (a) for each offence, to a fine of $30 to $575 in the case of a natural person, and of $60 to $1150 in the case of an artificial person.
   (b) for any subsequent offence within two years of a first offence, to a fine of $60 to $1150 in the case of a natural person, and of $575 to $5750 in the case of an artificial person.

206. A business firm guilty of an offence contemplated in section 136 is liable, in addition to costs, to a fine of $125 to $2300 for each day during which it carries on its business without a certificate.

. . .

B. The Quebec Charter of Human Rights and Freedoms

Sections 3, 9.1 and 10 of the Quebec Charter of Human Rights and Freedoms, R.S.Q. c. C-12, provide:

3. Every person is the possessor of the fundamental freedoms, including freedom of conscience, freedom of religion, freedom of opinion, freedom of expression, freedom of peaceful assembly and freedom of association.

9.1 In exercising his fundamental freedoms and rights, a person shall maintain a proper regard for democratic values, public order and the general well-being of the citizens of Quebec.

In this respect, the scope of the freedoms and rights, and limits to their exercise, may be fixed by law.

10. Every person has a right to full and equal recognition and exercise of his human rights and freedoms, without distinction, exclusion or preference based on race, colour, sex, pregnancy, sexual orientation, civil status, age except as provided by law, religion, political convictions, language, ethnic or national origin, social condition, a handicap or the use of any means to palliate a handicap.

Discrimination exists where such a distinction, exclusion or preference has the effect of nullifying or impairing such right.

Sections 51 and 52 of the Quebec Charter of Human Rights and Freedoms, R.S.Q., c. C-12, provide:

51. The Charter shall not be so interpreted as to extend, limit or amend the scope of a provision of law except to the extent provided in section 52.

52. No provision of any Act, even subsequent to the Charter, may derogate from sections 1 to 38, except so far as provided by those sections, unless such Act expressly states that it applies despite the Charter.

Prior to its amendment by s. 16 of an Act to amend the Charter of Human Rights and Freedoms, S.Q. 1982, c. 61, s. 52 of the Quebec Charter read as follows:

52. Sections 9 to 38 prevail over any provision of any subsequent act which may be inconsistent therewith unless such act expressly states that it applies despite the Charter.

. . .

The Constitutional Questions and the Issues in the Appeal

On the appeal to this Court the following constitutional questions were stated by Lamer J. in his order of May 11, 1987:

1. Are section 214 of the Charter of the French Language, R.S.Q. 1977, c. C-11, as enacted by S.Q. 1982, c. 21, s. 1, and section 52 of An Act to Amend the Charter of the French Language, S.Q. 1983, c. 56, inconsistent with section 33(1) of the Constitution Act, 1982 and therefore inoperative and of no force or effect under section 52(1) of the latter Act?

2. If the answer to question 1 is affirmative, to the extent that they require the exclusive use of the French language, are sections 58 and 69, and sections 205 to 208 to the extent they apply thereto, of the Charter of the French Language, R.S.Q. 1977, c. C-11, as amended by S.Q. 1983, c. 56, inconsistent with the guarantee of freedom of expression under section 2(b) of the Canadian Charter of Rights and Freedoms?

3. If the answer to question 2 is affirmative in whole or in part, are sections 58 and 69, and sections 205 to 208 to the extent they apply thereto, of the Charter of the French Language, R.S.Q. 1977, c. C-11, as amended by S.Q. 1983, c. 56 justified by the application of section 1 of the Canadian Charter of Rights and Freedoms and therefore not inconsistent with the Constitution Act, 1982?

The issues in the appeal, as reflected in the above constitutional questions, the reasons for judgment of the Superior Court and the Court of Appeal and the submissions in this Court, may be summarized as follows:

1. Is s. 58 or s. 69 of the Charter of the French Language protected from the application of s. 2(b) of the Canadian Charter of Rights and Freedoms by a valid and applicable override provision enacted in conformity with s. 33 of the Canadian Charter?

2. What are the dates from which s. 3 of the Quebec Charter of Human Rights and Freedoms took precedence, in case of conflict, over ss. 58 and 69 of the Charter of the French Language?

3. Does the freedom of expression guaranteed by s. 2(b) of the Canadian Charter and by s. 3 of the Quebec Charter include the freedom to express oneself in the language of one's choice?

4. Does the freedom of expression guaranteed by s. 2(b) of the Canadian Charter and s. 3 of the Quebec Charter extend to commercial expression?

5. If the requirement of the exclusive use of French by ss. 58 and 69 of the Charter of the French Language infringes the freedom of expression guaranteed by s. 2(b) of the Canadian Charter and s. 3 of the Quebec Charter, is the limit on freedom of expression imposed by ss. 58 and 69 justified under s. 1 of the Canadian Charter and s. 9.1 of the Quebec Charter?

6. Do ss. 58 and 69 of the Charter of the French Language infringe the guarantee against discrimination based on language in s. 10 of the Quebec Charter of Human Rights and Freedoms?

Submissions with respect to the validity and application of the override provisions in issue, as well as the content of freedom of expression and the effect of s. 1 of the Canadian Charter and s. 9.1 of the

Quebec Charter, were also made in the appeals in *Devine* v. *Quebec (Attorney General)* and *Irwin Toy Ltd.* v. *Quebec (Attorney General)*, which were heard at the same time as this appeal. They will necessarily be taken into consideration in disposing of the issues in this appeal.

Is s. 58 or s. 69 of the Charter of the French Language Protected from the Application of s. 2(b) of the Canadian Charter of Rights and Freedoms by a valid and applicable override provision enacted in conformity with s. 33 of the Canadian Charter?

There are two override provisions in issue: (a) s. 214 of the Charter of the French Language, which was enacted by s. 1 of An Act respecting the Constitution Act, 1982, S.Q. 1982, c. 21; and (b) s. 52 of An Act to amend the Charter of the French Language, S.Q. 1983, c. 56. The two override provisions are in identical terms, reading as follows: "This Act shall operate notwithstanding the provisions of sections 2 and 7 to 15 of the Constitution Act, 1982 (Schedule B of the Canada Act, chapter 11 in the 1982 volume of Acts of Parliament of the United Kingdom)." The issue of validity that is common to both s. 214 and s. 52 is whether a declaration in this form is one that is made in conformity with the override authority conferred by s. 33 of the Canadian Charter of Rights and Freedoms. There are additional issues of validity applicable to s. 214 of the Charter of the French Language arising from the manner of its enactment, that is, the "omnibus" character of the Act which enacted it, and from the retrospective effect given to s. 214 by s. 7 of the Act, which has been quoted above.

Section 214 of the Charter of the French Language ceased to have effect by operation of s. 33(3) of the Canadian Charter of Rights and Freedoms five years after it came into force, and it was not re-enacted pursuant to ss. 33(4) of the Charter. If the retrospective effect to April 17,

1982 given to s. 214 by s. 7 of An Act respecting the Constitution Act, 1982, was valid, s. 214 ceased to have effect on April 17, 1987. If not, it ceased to have effect on June 23, 1987, which was five years after the enacting Act came into force on the day of its sanction. In either case the question of the validity of s. 214 is moot, on the assumption, which was the one on which the appeal was argued, that on an application for a declaratory judgment in a case of this kind the Court should declare the law as it exists at the time of its judgment. We were, nevertheless, invited by the parties in this appeal and the appeals that were heard at the same time to rule on the validity of the standard override provision as enacted by An Act respecting the Constitution Act, 1982, because of the possible significance of that issue in cases pending before other tribunals. Before considering how the Court should respond to that invitation we propose to consider the other override provision in issue which, as we have said, raises a common question of validity.

Section 52 of An Act to amend Charter of the French Language, which was proclaimed in force on February 1, 1984, will not cease to have effect by operation of s. 33(3) of the Canadian Charter of Rights and Freedoms until February 1, 1989. It is therefore necessary to consider its validity since the Attorney General of Quebec contends that it protects s. 58 of the Charter of the French Language from the application of s. 2(b) of the Canadian Charter of Rights and Freedoms. . . .

Those who challenged the constitutionality of the override provisions in s. 214 of the Charter of the French Language and s. 52 of An Act to amend Charter of the French Language placed particular reliance on the judgment of the Quebec Court of Appeal in *Alliance des professeurs de Montréal* v. *Procureur général du Québec*, *supra*, in which the Court of Appeal held that the standard override provision was *ultra vires* and null as not being in conformity with the authority conferred by s. 33 of the Canadian Charter of Rights and Freedoms. . . .

In that case the petitioners, Alliance des professeurs de Montréal, sought declarations that s. 1 and other provisions of An Act respecting the Constitution Act, 1982, which purported to add the standard override provision to all provincial legislation enacted up to June 23, 1982, and the standard override provisions enacted in some forty-nine statutes after that date were *ultra vires* and null as not being in conformity with s. 33 of the Canadian Charter of Rights and Freedoms. Thus the petitioners put in issue not only the validity of the standard override provision as enacted by the "omnibus" Act respecting the Constitution Act, 1982, but also its validity as separately enacted in particular statutes. . . .

The essential contention in *Alliance des professeurs*, as in the present appeals, against the validity of the standard override provision, which was rejected by the Superior Court but upheld by the Court of Appeal, was that the provision did not sufficiently specify the guaranteed rights or freedoms which the legislation intended to override. In support of this contention reliance was placed not only on the wording of s. 33(1) and s. 33(2) of the Charter but on general considerations concerning the effectiveness of the democratic process. For convenience the standard override provision that is in issue, as well as ss. 33(1) and 33(2) of the Charter, are quoted again:

This Act shall operate notwithstanding the provisions of sections 2 and 7 to 15 of the Constitution Act, 1982 (Schedule B of the Canada Act, chapter 11 in the 1982 volume of the Acts of the Parliament of the United Kingdom).

33.(1) Parliament or the legislature of a province may expressly declare in an Act of Parliament or of the legislature, as the case may be, that the Act or a provision thereof shall operate notwithstanding a provision included in section 2 or sections 7 to 15 of this Charter.

(2) An Act or a provision of an Act in respect of which a declaration made

under this section is in effect shall have such operation as it would have but for the provision of this Charter referred to in the declaration.

It was contended that the words "a provision included in section 2 or sections 7 to 15 of this Charter" in s. 33(1) and the words "but for the provision of this Charter referred to in the declaration" in s. 33(2) indicate that in order to be valid, a declaration pursuant to s. 33 must specify the particular provision within a section of the Charter which Parliament or the legislature of a province intends to override. That is, the specific guaranteed right or freedom to be overridden must be referred to in the words of the Charter and not merely by the number of the section or paragraph in which it appears. The rationale underlying this contention is that the nature of the guaranteed right or freedom must be sufficiently drawn to the attention of the members of the legislature and of the public so that the relative seriousness of what is proposed may be perceived and reacted to through the democratic process. As the Attorney General for Ontario, who argued against the constitutionality of the standard override provision, put it, there must be a "political cost" for overriding a guaranteed right or freedom. . . .

In the course of argument different views were expressed as to the constitutional perspective from which the meaning and application of s. 33 of the Canadian Charter of Rights and Freedoms should be approached: the one suggesting that it reflects the continuing importance of legislative supremacy, the other suggesting the seriousness of a legislative decision to override guaranteed rights and freedoms and the importance that such a decision be taken only as a result of a fully informed democratic process. These two perspectives are not, however, particularly relevant or helpful in construing the requirements of s. 33. Section 33 lays down requirements of form only, and there is no warrant for importing into it grounds for substantive review of the legislative policy in exercising the override authority in a particular case. The requirement of an apparent link or relationship between the overriding Act and the guaranteed rights or freedoms to be overridden seems to be a substantive ground of review. It appears to require that the legislature identify the provisions of the Act in question which might otherwise infringe specified guaranteed rights or freedoms. That would seem to require a *prima facie* justification of the decision to exercise the override authority rather than merely a certain formal expression of it. There is, however, no warrant in the terms of s. 33 for such a requirement. A legislature may not be in a position to judge with any degree of certainty what provisions of the Canadian Charter of Rights and Freedoms might be successfully invoked against various aspects of the Act in question. For this reason it must be permitted in a particular case to override more than one provision of the Charter and indeed all of the provisions which it is permitted to override by the terms of s. 33. The standard override provision in issue in this appeal is, therefore, a valid exercise of the authority conferred by s. 33 insofar as it purports to override all of the provisions in s. 2 and ss. 7 to 15 of the Charter. The essential requirement of form laid down by s. 33 is that the override declaration must be an express declaration that an Act or a provision of an Act shall operate notwithstanding a provision included in s. 2 or ss. 7 to 15 of the Charter. With great respect for the contrary view, this Court is of the opinion that a s. 33 declaration is sufficiently express if it refers to the number of the section, subsection or paragraph of the Charter which contains the provision or provisions to be overridden. Of course, if it is intended to override only a part of the provision or provisions contained in a section, subsection or paragraph then there would have to be a sufficient reference in words to the part to be overridden. . . .

Therefore, s. 52 of An Act to amend the Charter of the French Language is a valid and subsisting exercise of the override authority conferred by s. 33 of the Canadian Charter of Rights and Freedoms that protects s. 58 of the Charter of the French Language from the application of s. 2(b) of the Canadian Charter. Section 69 of the Charter of the French Language is not so protected since it was not affected by An Act to amend the Charter of the French Language. In the result, as indicated in the following Part VI of these reasons, s. 58 is subject to s. 3 of the Quebec Charter of Human Rights and Freedoms while s. 69 is subject to both s. 2(b) of the Canadian Charter and s. 3 of the Quebec Charter.

Before leaving Part V of these reasons, it remains to be considered whether the Court should exercise its discretion to rule on the other aspects of the validity of the standard override provision as enacted by An Act respecting the Constitution Act, 1982: the "omnibus" character of the enactment; and the retrospective effect given to the override provision. These issues affect both s. 214 of the Charter of the French Language, which is in issue in this appeal and in the Devine appeal and s. 364 of the Consumer Protection Act, R.S.Q., c. P-40.1, in the *Irwin Toy* appeal. The Court has concluded that although both of these provisions have ceased to have effect it is better that all questions concerning their validity should be settled in these appeals because of their possible continuing importance in other cases. Given the conclusion that the enactment of the standard override provision in the form indicated above is a valid exercise of the authority conferred by s. 33 of the Canadian Charter of Rights and Freedoms, this Court is of the opinion that the validity of its enactment is not affected by the fact that it was introduced into all Quebec statutes enacted prior to a certain date by a single enactment. That was an effective exercise of legislative authority that did not prevent the override declaration so enacted in each statute from being an express declaration within the meaning of s. 33 of the Canadian Charter. Counsel referred to this form of enactment as reflecting an impermissibly "routine" exercise of the override authority or even a "perversion" of it. It was even suggested that it amounted to an attempted amendment of the Charter. These are once again essentially submissions concerning permissible legislative policy in the exercise of the override authority rather than what constitutes a sufficiently express declaration of override. As has been stated, there is no warrant in s. 33 for such considerations as a basis of judicial review of a particular exercise of the authority conferred by s. 33. The Court is of a different view, however, concerning the retrospective effect given to the standard override provision by s. 7 of An Act respecting the Constitution Act, 1982. . . . In providing that s. 1, which re-enacted all of the Quebec statutes adopted before April 17, 1982 with the addition in each of the standard override provision, should have effect from that date, s. 7 purported to give retrospective effect to the override provision. . . .

In *Gustavson Drilling (1964) Ltd.* v. *Minister of National Revenue*, [1977] 1 S.C.R. 271, Dickson J. (as he then was) wrote, for the majority (at p. 279):

The general rule is that statutes are not to be construed as having retrospective operation unless such a construction is expressly or by necessary implication required by the language of the Act.

Where, as here, an enabling provision is ambiguous as to whether it allows for retroactive legislation, the same rule of construction applies. In this case, s. 33(1) admits of two interpretations; one that allows Parliament or a legislature to enact retroactive override provisions, the other that permits prospective derogation only. We conclude that the latter and narrower interpretation is the proper one, and that s. 7 cannot give retrospective effect to the override provision. Section 7 of An Act respecting the Constitution Act, 1982, is to the extent of this inconsistency with s. 33 of the Canadian Charter, of no force or effect, with the result that the standard override provisions enacted by s. 1 of that Act came into force on June 23, 1982 in accordance with the first paragraph of s. 7. . . .

~Editor's Note: In the next section the Court concluded that as of February 1, 1984, section 3 of, Quebec's Charter of Human Rights and Freedoms took precedence over its Charter of the French Language.~

Whether the freedom of expression guaranteed by s. 2(b) of the Canadian Charter of Rights and Freedoms and by s. 3 of the Quebec Charter of Human Rights and Freedoms includes the freedom to express oneself in the language of one's choice

Insofar as this issue is concerned, the words "freedom of expression" in s. 2(b) of the Canadian Charter and s. 3 of the Quebec Charter should be given the same meaning. As indicated above, both the Superior Court and the Court of Appeal held that freedom of expression includes the freedom to express oneself in the language of one's choice. After indicating the essential relationship between expression and language by reference to dictionary defintions of both, Boudreault J. in the Superior Court said that in the ordinary or general form of expression there cannot be expression without language. Bisson J.A. in the Court of Appeal said that he agreed with the reasons of Boudreault J. on this issue and expressed his own view in the form of the following question: "Is there a purer form of freedom of expression than the spoken language and written language?" He supported his conclusion by quotation of the following statement of this Court in Reference re Manitoba Language Rights, [1985] 1 S.C.R. 721, at p. 744: "The importance of language rights is grounded in the essential role that language plays in human existence, development and dignity. It is through language that we are able to form concepts; to structure and order the world around us. Language bridges the gap between isolation and community, allowing humans to delineate the rights and duties they hold in respect of one another, and thus to live in society."

The conclusion of the Superior Court and the Court of Appeal on this issue is correct. Language is so intimately related to the form and content of expression that there cannot be true freedom of expression by means of language if one is prohibited from using the language of one's choice. Language is not merely a means or medium of expression; it colours the content and meaning of expression. It is, as the preamble of the Charter of the French Language itself indicates, a means by which a people may express its cultural identity. It is also the means by which the individual expresses his or her personal identity and sense of individuality. That the concept of "expression" in s. 2(b) of the Canadian Charter and s. 3 of the Quebec Charter goes beyond mere content is indicated by the specific protection accorded to "freedom of thought, belief [and] opinion" in s. 2 and to "freedom of conscience" and "freedom of opinion" in s. 3. That suggests that "freedom of expression" is intended to extend to more than the content of expression in its narrow sense.

The Attorney General of Quebec made several submissions against the conclusion reached by the Superior Court and the Court of Appeal on this issue, the most important of which may be summarized as follows: (a) in determining the meaning of freedom of expression the Court should apply the distinction between the message and the medium which must have been known to the framers of the Canadian and Quebec Charters; (b) the express provision for the guarantee of language rights in ss. 16 to 23 of the Canadian Charter indicate that it was not intended that a language freedom should result incidentally from the guarantee of freedom of expression in s. 2(b); (c) the recognition of a freedom to express oneself in the language of one's choice under s. 2(b) of the Canadian Charter and s. 3 of the Quebec Charter would undermine the special and limited constitutional position of the specific guarantees of language rights in s. 133 of the Constitution Act, 1867 and ss. 16 to 23 of the Canadian Charter

that was emphasized by the Court in *MacDonald* v. *City of Montreal*, [1986] 1 S.C.R. 460, and *Société des Acadiens du Nouveau-Brunswick Inc.* v. *Association of Parents for Fairness in Education*, [1986] 1 S.C.R. 549; and (d) the recognition that freedom of expression includes the freedom to express oneself in the language of one's choice would be contrary to the views expressed on this issue by the European Commission of Human Rights and the European Court of Human Rights.

The distinction between the message and the medium was applied by Dugas J. of the Superior Court in *Devine* v. *Procureur général du Québec, supra*, in holding that freedom of expression does not include freedom to express oneself in the language of one's choice. It has already been indicated why that distinction is inappropriate as applied to language as a means of expression because of the intimate relationship between language and meaning. As one of the authorities on language quoted by the appellant Singer in the *Devine* appeal, J. Fishman, *The Sociology of Language* (1972), at p. 4, puts it: "language is not merely a means of interpersonal communication and influence. It is not merely a carrier of content, whether latent or manifest. Language itself is content, a reference for loyalties and animosities, an indicator of social statuses and personal relationships, a marker of situations and topics as well as of the societal goals and the large-scale value-laden arenas of interaction that typify every speech community.". . .

The second and third of the submissions of the Attorney General of Quebec which have been summarized above, with reference to the implications for this issue of the express or specific guarantees of language rights in s. 133 of the Constitution Act, 1867, and ss. 16 to 23 of the Canadian Charter of Rights and Freedoms, are closely related and may be addressed together. These special guarantees of language rights do not, by implication, preclude a construction of freedom of expression that includes the freedom to express oneself in the language of one's choice. . . . The central unifying feature of all of the language rights given explicit recognition in the Constitution of Canada is that they pertain to governmental institutions and for the most part they oblige the government to provide for, or at least tolerate, the use of both official languages. In this sense they are more akin to rights, properly understood, than freedoms. They grant entitlement to a specific benefit from the government or in relation to one's dealing with the government. Correspondingly, the government is obliged to provide certain services or benefits in both languages or at least permit use of either language by persons conducting certain affairs with the government. . . . In contrast, what the respondents seek in this case is a freedom as that term was explained by Dickson J. (as he then was) in *R.* v. *Big M Drug Mart Ltd.*, [1985] 1 S.C.R. 295, at p. 336: ''Freedom can primarily be characterized by the absence of coercion or constraint. If a person is compelled by the state or the will of another to a course of action or inaction which he would not otherwise have chosen, he is not acting of his own volition and he cannot be said to be truly free. One of the major purposes of the Charter is to protect, within reason, from compulsion or restraint.'' The respondents seek to be free of the state imposed requirement that their commercial signs and advertising be in French only, and seek the freedom, in the entirely private or non-governmental realm of commercial activity, to display signs and advertising in the language of their choice as well as that of French. Manifestly the respondents are not seeking to use the language of their choice in any form of direct relations with any branch of government and are not seeking to oblige government to provide them any services or other benefits in the language of their choice. In this sense the respondents are asserting a freedom, the freedom to express oneself in the language of one's choice in an area of non-governmental activity, as opposed to a language right of the kind guaranteed in

the Constitution. The recognition that freedom of expression includes the freedom to express oneself in the language of one's choice does not undermine or run counter to the special guarantees of official language rights in areas of governmental jurisdiction or responsibility. . . .

The decisions of the European Commission of Human Rights and the European Court of Human Rights on which the Attorney General of Quebec relied are all distinguishable on the same basis, apart from the fact that, as Bisson J.A. observed in the Court of Appeal, they arose in an entirely different constitutional context. They all involved claims to language rights in relations with government that would have imposed some obligation on government. . . .

Whether the Guarantee of Freedom of Expression Extends to Commercial Expression

In argument there arose a question whether the above issue is an issue in this appeal. The Attorney General of Quebec contended that if the guarantee of freedom of expression included the freedom to express oneself in the language of one's choice the respondents must still show that the guarantee extends to commercial expression. The respondents disputed this on the ground that the challenged provisions are directed to the language used and not to regulation of the substantive content of the expression. At the same time they made alternative submissions that the guarantee extended to commercial expression. The Attorney General of Quebec is correct on this issue: there cannot be a guaranteed freedom to express oneself in the language of one's choice in respect of a form or kind of expression that is not covered by the guarantee of freedom of expression. The question whether the guarantee of freedom of expression in s. 2(b) of the Canadian Charter and s. 3 of the Quebec Charter extends to the kind of expression contemplated by ss. 58 and 69 of the Charter of the French Language, which for convenience is referred to as commercial expression, is therefore an issue in this appeal. The submissions that were made on the question of commercial expression in the Devine and Irwin Toy appeals will be considered in determining that issue in this appeal.

It was not disputed that the public signs and posters, the commercial advertising, and the firm name referred to in ss. 58 and 69 of the Charter of the French Language are forms of expression, and it was also assumed or accepted in argument that the expression contemplated by these provisions may be conveniently characterized or referred to as commercial expression. Sections 58 and 69 appear in Chapter VII of the Charter of the French Language, entitled "The Language of Commerce and Business." It must be kept in mind, however, that while the words "commercial expression" are a convenient reference to the kind of expression contemplated by the provisions in issue, they do not have any particular meaning or significance in Canadian constitutional law, unlike the corresponding expression "commercial speech," which in the United States has been recognized as a particular category of speech entitled to First Amendment protection of a more limited character than that enjoyed by other kinds of speech. The issue in the appeal is not whether the guarantee of freedom of expression in s. 2(b) of the Canadian Charter and s. 3 of the Quebec Charter should be construed as extending to particular categories of expression, giving rise to difficult definitional problems, but whether there is any reason why the guarantee should not extend to a particular kind of expression, in this case the expression contemplated by ss. 58 and 69 of the Charter of the French Language. Because, however, the American experience with the First Amendment protection of "commercial speech" was invoked in argument, as it has been in other cases, both for and against the recognition in Canada that the guarantee of freedom of expression extends to the kinds of expression that may be described as commercial expression, it is convenient to make brief reference to it at this point.

In *Valentine* v. *Chrestensen*, 316 U.S. 52 (1942), the Supreme Court of the United States declined to afford First Amendment protection to speech which did no more than propose a commercial transaction. Some thirty-four years later, in *Virginia State Board of Pharmacy* v. *Virginia Citizens Consumer Council Inc.*, 425 U.S. 748 (1976), the Court affirmed a repudiation of the notion that commercial speech constituted an unprotected exception to the First Amendment guarantee. *Virginia Pharmacy* concerned a Virginia statute which prohibited pharmacists from advertising prices for prescription drugs. The statute was challenged by customers who asserted a First Amendment right to receive drug price information that the pharmacist wished to communicate. The speech at issue was purely commercial in that it simply proposed a commercial transaction. By holding that price advertising was not outside the First Amendment, the Court rejected the central premise of the commercial speech doctrine—that is, that business advertising which merely solicits a commercial transaction is susceptible to government regulation on the same terms as any other aspect of the market place. The reasons of Justice Blackmun, writing for the Court, focus on the informative function of the speech from the point of view of the listener whose interest, it was said, "may be as keen, if not keener by far, than his interest in the day's most urgent political debate" (p. 763). The rationale stated by the Court for a First Amendment protection of commercial speech was the interest of the individual consumer and the society generally in the free flow of commercial information as indispensable to informed economic choice. The reasons are careful to note, however, that although commercial speech is protected it is entitled to a lesser degree of protection than that afforded to other forms of speech. . . .

By 1980, when the Court decided *Central Hudson Gas and Electric Corp.* v. *Public Service Commission of New York*,

447 U.S. 557 (1980), it was apparent that some control of truthful advertising was legitimate as long as the regulation directly advanced a substantial state interest. Justice Powell, writing for the Court, formulated a four-part analysis for determining whether a particular regulation of commercial speech is consistent with the First Amendment, which he summed up as follows at p. 566:

In commercial speech cases, then, a four-part analysis has developed. At the outset, we must determine whether the expression is protected by the First Amendment. For commercial speech to come within that provision, it at least must concern lawful activity and not be misleading. Next, we ask whether the asserted governmental interest is substantial. In both inquiries yield positive answers, we must determine whether the regulation directly advances the governmental interest asserted, and whether it is not more extensive than is necessary to serve that interest.

. . . It has been observed that this test is very similar to the test that was adopted by this Court in *R*. v. *Oakes*, [1986] 1 S.C.R. 103, for justification under s. 1 of the Charter. The Central Hudson test has been described as "an uneasy compromise" between competing strains of commercial speech theory. It is an attempt to balance the legitimacy of government regulations intended to protect consumers from harmful commercial speech with the belief that a free market in ideas and information is necessary to an informed and autonomous consumer.

In *Posadas de Puerto Rico Associates* v. *Tourism Co. of Puerto Rico*, 106 S.Ct. 2968 (1986), the Court applied the Central Hudson test in a manner that attracted much criticism as reflecting, in the opinion of some commentators, an excessively deferential attitude to government regulation in the face of little or no demonstration by the state that the legislative means it had adopted either directly advanced the asserted substantial interest or minimally restricted first amendment

interests. See, for example, Philip B. Kurland, "*Posadas de Puerto Rico* v. *Tourism Company*: Twas Strange, Twas Passing Strange; Twas Pitiful, Twas Wondrous Pitiful," [1986] Sup. Ct. Rev. 1; and "The Supreme Court-Leading Cases" (1986), 100 Harv. L. Rev. 100, at p. 172. Posadas reflects how differences of view or emphasis in the application of the Central Hudson test can determine the effective extent of the protection of commercial speech from legislative limitation or restriction. It reveals the tension between two values: the value of the free circulation of commercial information and the value of consumer protection against harmful commercial speech. The American experience with the constitutional protection of commercial speech further indicates the difficulties inherent in its application, in particular the degree to which the courts are involved in the evaluation of regulatory policy in the field of consumer protection. The American jurisprudence with respect to commercial speech has been the subject of much scholarly analysis and criticism. There is an analysis of the American jurisprudence in the very helpful article on commercial expression by Professor Robert J. Sharpe, "Commercial Expression and the Charter" (1987), 37 U. of T.L.J. 229.

In the case at bar Boudreault J. in the Superior Court held that the guarantee of freedom of expression in s. 3 of the Quebec Charter extended to commercial expression. He relied particularly on the reasoning in the American decisions, quoting at length from the judgment of Justice Blackmun in *Virginia Pharmacy* for the rationale underlying the protection of commercial speech in the United States. He emphasized, as does that case, that it is not only the speaker but the listener who has an interest in freedom of expression. In the Court of Appeal, Bisson J.A. applied the judgment of the majority of the Court on this issue in *Irwin Toy Ltd.* v. *Procureur général du Québec*, [1986] R.J.Q. 2441, and quoted from the opinions of Jacques J.A. and Vallerand J.A. in that case. In Irwin Toy,

Jacques J.A. held that there was no basis on the face of s. 2(b) of the Canadian Charter for distinguishing, in respect of the guarantee of freedom of expression, between different kinds of expression, whether they be of a political, artistic, cultural or other nature. He held that commercial expression was as much entitled to protection as other kinds of expression because of the important role played by it in assisting persons to make informed economic choices. He added, however, that commercial expression might be subject to reasonable limits under s. 1 of the Canadian Charter of a kind that would not be reasonable in the case of political expression. . . .

In the course of argument reference was made to two other Canadian decisions which reflect the contrasting positions on the question whether freedom of expression should extend to commercial expression: the majority decision of the Ontario Divisional Court in *Re Klein and Law Society of Upper Canada* (1985), 16 D.L.R. (4th) 489, and the unanimous decision of the Alberta Court of Appeal in *Re Grier and Alberta Optometric Association* (1987), 42 D.L.R. (4th) 327. In *Klein*, on which the Attorney General of Quebec and those who supported his contention that freedom of expression should not extend to commercial expression placed particular reliance, the relevant issue was whether the Rules of Professional Conduct of the Law Society of Upper Canada prohibiting fee advertising by solicitors infringed the guarantee of freedom of expression in s. 2(b) of the Charter. After referring to the pre-Charter decisions on freedom of speech and the American jurisprudence on commercial speech, Callaghan J., with whom Eberle J. concurred, concluded that the guarantee of freedom of expression in s. 2(b) should not extend to commercial expression. He held that commercial expression was unrelated to political expression, which in his view was the principal if not exclusive object of the protection afforded by s. 2(b). He said at p. 532: "The Charter reflects a concern with the political

rights of the individual and does not, in my view, reflect a similar concern with the economic sphere nor with its incidents such as commercial speech" and "*Prima facie* then, the freedom of expression guaranteed by s. 2(b) of the Charter would appear to apply to the expression of ideas relating to the political and governmental domains of the country. (I leave aside the question of whether or not artistic expression falls within s. 2(b))." After a very full discussion of American jurisprudence and experience with respect to the First Amendment protection of commercial speech Callaghan J. expressed the view that there were good reasons for not following it, among them the extent to which such protection involved the courts in a difficult case-by-case review of regulatory policy. He concluded as follows at p. 539: "I would conclude that there is no reason to expand the meaning of the word "expression" in s. 2(b) of the Charter to cover pure commercial speech. Commercial speech contributes nothing to democratic government because it says nothing about how people are governed or how they should govern themselves. It does not relate to government policies or matters of public concern essential to a democratic process. It pertains to the economic realm and is a matter appropriate to regulation by the Legislature.". . .

In *Grier*, the Alberta Court of Appeal (Lieberman, Kerans and Irving JJ.A.) held that a brochure mailed by a licensed optometrist to patients and others quoting prices for various services was protected expression within the meaning of s. 2(b) of the Charter. It declined to follow *Klein* on the question of commercial expression and expressed agreement with the decision of the Quebec Court of Appeal in *Irwin Toy* on that question. . . .

The submissions of the Attorney General of Quebec and those who supported him on this issue may be summarized as follows. The scope of a guaranteed freedom must be determined, as required by *R. v. Big M Drug Mart Ltd., supra*, in the light of the character and larger objects of the Canadian Charter and the linguistic, philosophic and historical context of the particular freedom. There is no historical basis for a guarantee of freedom of commercial expression in pre-Charter jurisprudence, in which recognition was given, on the basis of the division of powers and the "implied bill of rights," to freedom of political expression. Freedom of expression appears in both the Canadian Charter and the Quebec Charter under the heading of "Fundamental Freedoms"; there is nothing fundamental about commercial expression. A guarantee of freedom of expression which embraces commercial advertising would be the protection of an economic right, when both the Canadian Charter and the Quebec Charter clearly indicate that they are not concerned with the protection of such rights. The American decisions recognizing a limited First Amendment protection for commercial speech must be seen in the context of a constitution that protects the right of property, whereas that right was deliberately omitted from the protection afforded by s. 7 of the Canadian Charter. This Court, in refusing to constitutionalize the right to strike, has recognized that the Canadian Charter does not extend to economic rights or freedoms. To extend freedom of expression beyond political expression, and possibly artistic and cultural expression, would trivialize that freedom and lead inevitably to the adoption of different justificatory standards under s. 1 according to the kind of expression involved. The terms of s. 1, as interpreted and applied by the courts, do not permit of such differential application. Freedom of commercial expression, and in particular commercial advertising, does not serve any of the values that would justify its constitutional protection. Commercial advertising is manipulative and seeks to condition or control economic choice rather than to provide the basis of a truly informed choice. As the American experience shows, the recognition of a limited protection for commercial expression involves an evaluation of regulatory policy that is better left to the legislature. Academic criticism of the American approach to commercial speech and judicial expression of misgivings concerning it provide sufficient reason for declining to follow it.

It is apparent to this Court that the guarantee of freedom of expression in s. 2(b) of the Canadian Charter and s. 3 of the Quebec Charter cannot be confined to political expression, important as that form of expression is in a free and democratic society. The pre-Charter jurisprudence emphasized the importance of political expression because it was a challenge to that form of expression that most often arose under the division of powers and the "implied bill of rights," where freedom of political expression could be related to the maintenance and operation of the institutions of democratic government. But political expression is only one form of the great range of expression that is deserving of constitutional protection because it serves individual and societal values in a free and democratic society.

The post-Charter jurisprudence of this Court has indicated that the guarantee of freedom of expression in s. 2(b) of the Charter is not to be confined to political expression. In holding, in *RWDSU* v. *Dolphin Delivery Ltd.*, [1986] 2 S.C.R. 573, that secondary picketing was a form of expression within the meaning of s. 2(b) the Court recognized that the constitutional guarantee of freedom of expression extended to expression that could not be characterized as political expression in the traditional sense but, if anything, was in the nature of expression having an economic purpose. . . .

Various attempts have been made to identify and formulate the values which justify the constitutional protection of freedom of expression. Probably the best known is that of Professor Thomas I. Emerson in his article, "Toward a General Theory of the First Amendment" (1963), 72 Yale L.J. 877, where he sums up these values as follows at p. 878:

The values sought by society in protecting the right to freedom of expression may be grouped into four broad categories.

Maintenance of a system of free expression is necessary (1) as assuring individual self-fulfillment, (2) as a means of attaining the truth, (3) as a method of securing participation by the members of the society in social, including political, decision-making, and (4) as maintaining the balance between stability and change in society.

The third and fourth of these values would appear to be closely related if not overlapping. Generally the values said to justify the constitutional protection of freedom of expression are stated as three-fold in nature, as appears from the article by Professor Sharpe referred to above on "Commercial Expression and the Charter," where he speaks of the three "rationales" for such protection as follows at p. 232:

The first is that freedom of expression is essential to intelligent and democratic self-government. . . . The second theory is that freedom of expression protects an open exchange of views, thereby creating a competitive market-place of ideas which will enhance the search for the truth. . . . The third theory values expression for its own sake. On this view, expression is seen as an aspect of individual autonomy. Expression is to be protected because it is essential to personal growth and self-realization.

While these attempts to identify and define the values which justify the constitutional protection of freedom of expression are helpful in emphasizing the most important of them, they tend to be formulated in a philosophical context which fuses the separate questions of whether a particular form or act of expression is within the ambit of the interests protected by the value of freedom of expression and the question whether that form or act of expression, in the final analysis, deserves protection from interference under the structure of the Canadian Charter and the Quebec Charter. These are two distinct questions and call for two distinct analytical processes. The first, at least for the

Canadian Charter, is to be determined by the purposive approach to interpretation set out by this Court in *Hunter* v. *Southam Inc.*, [1984] 2 S.C.R. 145, and *Big M Drug Mart Ltd.*, *supra*. The second, the question of the limitation on the protected values, is to be determined under s. 1 of the Charter as interpreted in *Oakes, supra*, and *R.* v. *Edwards Book and Art Ltd.*, [1986] 2 S.C.R. 713. The division between the two analytical processes has been established by this Court in the above decisions. First, consideration will be given to the interests and purposes that are meant to be protected by the particular right or freedom in order to determine whether the right or freedom has been infringed in the context presented to the court. If the particular right or freedom is found to have been infringed, the second step is to determine whether the infringement can be justified by the state within the constraints of s. 1. It is within the perimeters of s. 1 that courts will in most instances weigh competing values in order to determine which should prevail.

In order to address the issues presented by this case it is not necessary for the Court to delineate the boundaries of the broad range of expression deserving of protection under s. 2(b) of the Canadian Charter or s. 3 of the Quebec Charter. It is necessary only to decide if the respondents have a constitutionally protected right to use the English language in the signs they display, or more precisely, whether the fact that such signs have a commercial purpose removes the expression contained therein from the scope of protected freedom.

In our view, the commercial element does not have this effect. Given the earlier pronouncements of this Court to the effect that the rights and freedoms guaranteed in the Canadian Charter should be given a large and liberal interpretation, there is no sound basis on which commercial expression can be excluded from the protection of s. 2(b) of the Charter. It is worth noting that the courts below applied a similar generous and broad interpretation to include commercial expression within the protection of freedom of expression contained in s. 3 of the Quebec Charter. Over and above its intrinsic value as expression, commercial expression which, as has been pointed out, protects listeners as well as speakers plays a significant role in enabling individuals to make informed economic choices, an important aspect of individual self-fulfillment and personal autonomy. The Court accordingly rejects the view that commercial expression serves no individual or societal value in a free and democratic society and for this reason is undeserving of any constitutional protection.

Rather, the expression contemplated by ss. 58 and 69 of the Charter of the French Language is expression within the meaning of both s. 2(b) of the Canadian Charter and s. 3 of the Quebec Charter. This leads to the conclusion that s. 58 infringes the freedom of expression guaranteed by s. 3 of the Quebec Charter and s. 69 infringes the guaranteed freedom of expression under both s. 2(b) of the Canadian Charter and s. 3 of the Quebec Charter. Although the expression in this case has a commercial element, it should be noted that the focus here is on choice of language and on a law which prohibits the use of a language. We are not asked in this case to deal with the distinct issue of the permissible scope of regulation of advertising (for example to protect consumers) where different governmental interests come into play, particularly when assessing the reasonableness of limits on such commercial expression pursuant to s. 1 of the Canadian Charter or to s. 9.1 of the Quebec Charter. It remains to be considered whether the limit imposed on freedom of expression by ss. 58 and 69 is justified under either s. 1 of the Canadian Charter or s. 9.1 of the Quebec Charter, as the case may be.

Whether the limit imposed on freedom of expression by ss. 58 and 69 of the Charter of the French Language is justified under s. 9.1 of the Quebec Charter of the Human Rights and Freedoms and s. 1

of the Canadian Charter of Rights and Freedoms

The issues raised in this part are as follows: (a) the meaning of s. 9.1 of the Quebec Charter and whether its role and effect are essentially different from that of s. 1 of the Canadian Charter; (b) whether the requirement of the exclusive use of French by ss. 58 and 69 of the Charter of the French Language is a limit within the meaning of s. 9.1 and s. 1; (c) whether the material (hereinafter referred to as the s. 1 and s. 9.1 materials) relied on by the Attorney General of Quebec in justification of the limit is properly before the Court; and (d) whether the material justifies the prohibition of the use of any language other than French.

A. The meaning of s. 9.1 of the Quebec Charter of Human Rights and Freedoms

The issue here is whether s. 9.1 is a justificatory provision similar in its purpose and effect to s. 1 of the Canadian Charter and if so what is the test to be applied under it. Section 9.1 is worded differently from s. 1, and it is convenient to set out the two provisions again for comparison, as well as the test under s. 1. Section 9.1 of the Quebec Charter of Human Rights and Freedoms, which was added to the Charter by An Act to amend the Charter of Human Rights and Freedoms, S.Q. 1982, c. 61, s. 2 and entered into force by proclamation on October 1, 1983, reads as follows:

9.1. In exercising his fundamental freedoms and rights, a person shall maintain a proper regard for democratic values, public order and the general well-being of the citizens of Quebec.

In this respect, the scope of the freedoms and rights, and limits to their exercise, may be fixed by law.

Section 1 of the Canadian Charter provides:

1. The Canadian Charter of Rights

and Freedoms guarantees the rights and freedoms set out in it subject only to such reasonable limits prescribed by law as can be demonstrably justified in a free and democratic society.

The test under s. 1 of the Canadian Charter was laid down by this Court in *R. v. Oakes, supra,* and restated by the Chief Justice in *R. v. Edwards Books and Art Ltd., supra,* as follows at pp. 768-69:

Two requirements must be satisfied to establish that a limit is reasonable and demonstrably justified in a free and democratic society. First, the legislative objective which the limitation to promote must be of sufficient importance to warrant overriding a constitutional right. It must bear on a "pressing and substantial concern." Second, the means chosen to attain those objectives must be proportional or appropriate to the ends. The proportionality requirement, in turn, normally has three aspects: the limiting measures must be carefully designed, or rationally connected, to the objective; they must impair the right as little as possible; and their effects must not so severely trench on individual or group rights that the legislative objective, albeit important, is nevertheless outweighed by the abridgment of rights. The Court stated that the nature of the proportionality test would vary depending on the circumstances. Both in articulating the standard of proof and in describing the criteria comprising the proportionality requirement the Court has been careful to avoid rigid and inflexible standards.

It was suggested in argument that because of its quite different wording s. 9.1 was not a justificatory provision similar to s. 1 but merely a provision indicating that the fundamental freedoms and rights guaranteed by the Quebec Charter are not absolute but relative and must be construed and exercised in a manner consistent with the values, interests and considerations indicated in s. 9.1— "democratic values, public order and the general well-being of the citizens of Quebec." In the case at bar the Superior Court and the Court of Appeal held that s. 9.1 was a justificatory provision corresponding to s. 1 of the Canadian Charter and that it was subject, in its application, to a similar test of rational connection and proportionality. This Court agrees with that conclusion. . . .

B. Whether the prohibition of the use of any language other than French by ss. 58 and 69 of the Charter of the French Language is a "limit" on freedom of expression within the meaning of s. 1 of the Canadian Charter and s. 9.1 of the Quebec Charter

The respondents contended that ss. 58 and 69 of the Charter of the French Language were not subject to justification under s. 1 of the Canadian Charter of Rights and Freedoms because they prescribe a denial or negation of freedom of expression rather than a limit on it within the meaning of that provision. In support of this contention they referred to the opinion to this effect of Deschenes C.J.C. in the Superior Court and of a majority of the Court of Appeal in *Quebec Association of Protestant School Boards* v. *Procureur général du Québec,* [1982] C.S. 673, at pp. 689-693; [1983] C.A. 77, at p. 78. They submitted that while this Court did not rule on the general question whether a denial or negation of a guaranteed right or freedom could be a limit within s. 1, it did not expressly or implicitly disavow the opinion expressed by the Superior Court and the Court of Appeal (*Attorney General of Quebec* v. *Quebec Association of Protestant School Boards,* [1984] 2 S.C.R. 66, at p. 78). . . .

In the *Quebec Association of Protestant School Boards* case, the minority language educational rights created by s. 23 of the Canadian Charter were, as the Court observed, of a very specific, special and limited nature, unlike the fundamental rights and freedoms guaranteed by other provisions. They were well defined rights for specific classes of persons. In the opinion of the Court, the effect of ss. 72 and 73 of Bill 101 was to create an exception to s. 23 for Quebec, that is, to make it inapplicable as a whole in Quebec. There was thus what amounted to a complete denial in Quebec of the rights created by s. 23. The extent of the denial was co-extensive with the potential exercise of the very specific and limited rights created by s. 23. Such an exception to s. 23, as the Court characterized it, was tantamount to an impermissible attempt to override or amend s. 23. An exception of such effect could not be a limit within the meaning of s. 1 of the Charter. Thus insofar as the distinction between a complete denial of a right or freedom and a limitation of it is concerned, the *Quebec Association of Protestant School Boards* is a rather unique example of a truly complete denial of guaranteed rights—a denial that is co-extensive with the complete scope of the potential exercise of the rights. The decision is thus not authority for the proposition that where the effect of a legislative provision is to deny or prohibit the exercise of a guaranteed right or freedom in a limited area of its potential exercise that provision cannot be a limit on the right or freedom subject to justification under s. 1.

In the opinion of this Court, apart from the rare case of a truly complete denial of a guaranteed right or freedom in the sense indicated above, the distinction between the negation of a right or freedom and the limitation of it is not a sound basis for denying the application of s. 1 of the Charter. Many, if not most, legislative qualifications of a right or freedom in a particular area of its potential exercise will amount to a denial of the right or freedom to that limited extent. If this effect were to mean that s. 1 could have no application in such a case, the section could have little application in practice. . . .

C. The admissibility of the s. 1 and s. 9.1 materials submitted in justification of the limit imposed on free-

dom of expression by ss. 58 and 69 of the Charter of the French Language

In the Court of Appeal the Attorney General of Quebec attached to his factum certain material of a justificatory nature which Bisson J.A. referred to as linguistic and sociological studies from Quebec and elsewhere and which the respondents describe in their factum in this Court as "numerous sociological, demographic and linguistic studies." The respondents moved to have this material struck from the record as not being in conformity with art. 507 of the Code of Civil Procedure and art. 10 of the Rules of Practice of the Court of Appeal respecting the parts of the record that must be attached to or form part of a factum. The ground of attack was presumably that the material did not form part of the record before the trial judge. . . .

In view of the fact that the parties did not appear to be taken by surprise or placed at an unfair disadvantage by the submission of the s. 1 and 9.1 materials in this Court, but showed themselves fully prepared to argue the merits of the material, which they did, this Court is of the opinion that the material should be considered as properly before the Court and should be considered by it. The material is of the kind that has been invited and considered by the Court in other cases involving the application of s. 1 of the Charter, without having been subjected to the evidentiary testing of the adversary process. It is material that is treated similarly to treatises and articles in other judicial contexts. Due regard should be given, however, to the submissions of the appellant Singer in *Devine* concerning some of the statistical material.

D. Whether the s. 1 and s. 9.1 materials justify the prohibition of the use of any language other than French

The s. 1 and s. 9.1 materials consist of some fourteen items ranging in nature from the general theory of language policy and planning to statistical analysis of the position of the French language in Quebec and Canada. The material deals with two matters of particular relevance to the issue in the appeal: (a) the vulnerable position of the French language in Quebec and Canada, which is the reason for the language policy reflected in the Charter of the French Language; and (b) the importance attached by language planning theory to the role of language in the public domain, including the communication or expression by language contemplated by the challenged provisions of the Charter of the French Language. As to the first, the material amply establishes the importance of the legislative purpose reflected in the Charter of the French Language and that it is a response to a substantial and pressing need. Indeed, this was conceded by the respondents both in the Court of Appeal and in this Court. The vulnerable position of the French language in Quebec and Canada was described in a series of reports by commissions of inquiry beginning with the Report to the Royal Commission on Bilingualism and Biculturalism in 1969 and continuing with the Parent Commission and the Gendron Commission. It is reflected in statistics referred to in these reports and in later studies forming part of the materials, with due adjustment made in the light of the submissions of the appellant Singer in *Devine* with resect to some of the later statistical material. The causal factors for the threatened position of the French language that have generally been identified are: (a) the declining birth rate of Quebec francophones resulting in a decline in the Quebec francophone proportion of the Canadian population as a whole; (b) the decline of the francophone population outside Quebec as a result of assimilation; (c) the greater rate of assimilation of immigrants to Quebec by the anglophone community of Quebec; and (d) the continuing dominance of English at the higher levels of the economic sector. These factors have favoured the use of the English language despite the predominance in Quebec of a francophone popula-

tion. Thus, in the period prior to the enactment of the legislation at issue, the "visage linguistique" of Quebec often gave the impression that English had become as significant as French. This "visage linguistique" reinforced the concern among francophones that English was gaining in importance, that the French language was threatened and that it would ultimately disappear. It strongly suggested to young and ambitious francophones that the language of success was almost exclusively English. It confirmed to anglophones that there was no great need to learn the majority language. And it suggested to immigrants that the prudent course lay in joining the anglophone community. The aim of such provisions as ss. 58 and 69 of the Charter of the French Language was, in the words of its preamble, "to see the quality and influence of the French language assured." The threat to the French language demonstrated to the government that it should, in particular, take steps to assure that the "visage linguistique" of Quebec would reflect the predominance of the French language.

The s. 1 and s. 9.1 materials establish that the aim of the language policy underlying the Charter of the French Language was a serious and legitimate one. They indicate the concern about the survival of the French language and the perceived need for an adequate legislative response to the problem. Moreover, they indicate a rational connection between protecting the French language and assuring that the reality of Quebec society is communicated through the "visage linguistique." The s. 1 and s. 9.1 materials do not, however, demonstrate that the requirement of the use of French only is either necessary for the achievement of the legislative objective or proportionate to it. That specific question is simply not addressed by the materials. Indeed, in his factum and oral argument the Attorney General of Quebec did not attempt to justify the requirement of the exclusive use of French. He concentrated on the reasons for the adoption of the Charter of the French Language and the earlier language legislation, which, as was noted above, were conceded by the respondents. The Attorney General of Quebec relied on what he referred to as the general democratic legitimacy of Quebec language policy without referring explicitly to the requirement of the exclusive use of French. Insofar as proportionality is concerned, the Attorney General of Quebec referred to the American jurisprudence with respect to commercial speech, presumably as indicating the judicial deference that should be paid to the legislative choice of means to serve an admittedly legitimate legislative purpose, at least in the area of commercial expression. He did, however, refer in justification of the requirement of the exclusive use of French to the attenuation of this requirement reflected in ss. 59 to 62 of the Charter of the French Language and the regulations. He submitted that these exceptions to the requirement of the exclusive use of French indicate the concern for carefully designed measures and for interfering as little as possible with commercial expression. The qualifications of the requirement of the exclusive use of French in other provisions of the Charter of the French Language and the regulations do not make ss. 58 and 69 any less prohibitions of the use of any language other than French as applied to the respondents. The issue is whether any such prohibition is justified. In the opinion of this Court it has not been demonstrated that the prohibition of the use of any language other than French in ss. 58 and 69 of the Charter of the French Language is necessary to the defence and enhancement of the status of the French language in Quebec or that it is proportionate to that legislative purpose. Since the evidence put to us by the government showed that the predominance of the French language was not reflected in the "visage linguistique" of Quebec, the governmental response could well have been tailored to meet that specific problem and to impair freedom of expression minimally. Thus, whereas requiring the pre-

dominant display of the French language, even its marked predominance, would be proportional to the goal of promoting and maintaining a French "visage linguistique" in Quebec and therefore justified under s. 9.1 of the Quebec Charter and s. 1 of the Canadian Charter, requiring the exclusive use of French has not been so justified. French could be required in addition to any other language or it could be required to have greater visibility than that accorded to other languages. Such measures would ensure that the "visage linguistique" reflected the demography of Quebec: the predominant language is French. This reality should be communicated to all citizens and non-citizens alike, irrespective of their mother tongue. But exclusivity for the French language has not survived the scrutiny of a proportionality test and does not reflect the reality of Quebec society. Accordingly, we are of the view that the limit imposed on freedom of expression by s. 58 of the Charter of the French Language respecting the exclusive use of French on public signs and posters and in commercial advertising is not justified under s. 9.1 of the Quebec Charter. In like measure, the limit imposed on freedom of expression by s. 69 of the Charter of the French Language respecting the exclusive use of the French version of a firm name is not justified under either s. 9.1 of the Quebec Charter or s. 1 of the Canadian Charter.

Do ss. 58 and 69 of the Charter of the French Language infringe the guarantee against discrimination based on language in s. 10 of the Quebec Charter of Human Rights and Freedoms?

In view of the above conclusion it is not necessary to the disposition of the appeal that the Court should pronounce on the contention of the respondents that ss. 58 and 69 of the Charter of the French Language are inoperative as infringing the guarantee against discrimination based on language in s. 10 of the Quebec Charter of the Human Rights and Freedoms. In view, however, of the fact that this issue is also raised in the *Devine* appeal and the Superior Court and the Court of Appeal addressed it in both cases it is probably desirable that this Court should do so as well because of the general importance of the question.

For convenience s. 10 of the Quebec Charter is quoted again:

10. *Every person has a right to full and equal recognition and exercise of his human rights and freedoms, without distinction, exclusion or preference based on race, colour, sex, pregnancy, sexual orientation, civil status, age except as provided by law, religion, political convictions, language, ethnic or national origin, social condition, a handicap or the use of any means to palliate a handicap.*

Discrimination exists where such a distinction, exclusion or preference has the effect of nullifying or impairing such right.

. . .

In addressing the question whether s. 58 of the Charter of the French Language infringes the guarantee against discrimination based on language in s. 10 of the Quebec Charter of Human Rights and Freedoms we are obliged to consider the effect of s. 58, insofar as that may be ascertained. The second observation to be made here is that in order for a distinction based on a prohibited ground to constitute discrimination within the meaning of s. 10 it must have the effect of nullifying or impairing the right to full and equal recognition and exercise of a human right or freedom, which must mean a human right or freedom recognized by the Quebec Charter of Human Rights and Freedoms. With these observations in mind we turn to the question whether s. 58 infringes s. 10. It purports, as was said by the Superior Court and the Court of Appeal, to apply to everyone, regardless of their language of use, the requirement of the exclusive use of French. It has the effect, however, of impinging dif-

ferentially on different classes of persons according to their language of use. Francophones are permitted to use their language of use while anglophones and other non-francophones are prohibited from doing so. Does this differential effect constitute a distinction based on language within the meaning of s. 10 of the Quebec Charter? In this Court's opinion it does. Section 58 of the Charter of the French Language, because of its differential effect or impact on persons according to their language of use, creates a distinction between such persons based on language of use. It is then necessary to consider whether this distinction has the effect of nullifying or impairing the right to full and equal recognition and exercise of a human right or freedom recognized by the Quebec Charter. The human right or freedom in issue in this case is the freedom to express oneself in the language of one's choice, which has been held to be recognized by s. 3 of the Quebec Charter. In this case, the limit imposed on that right was not a justifiable one under s. 9.1 of the Quebec Charter. The distinction based on language of use created by s. 58 of the Charter of the French Language thus has the effect of nullifying the right to full and equal recognition and exercise of this freedom. Section 58 is therefore also of no force or effect as infringing s. 10 of the Quebec Charter. The same conclusion must apply to s. 69 of the Charter of the French Language. We note that since one of the appellants, Valerie Ford, is an individual and not a corporation, it is unnecessary in this case to decide whether corporations are entitled to claim the benefit of equality guarantees and we do not do so.

For these reasons the appeal is dismissed with costs and the constitutional questions are answered as follows:

1. *Are section 214 of the Charter of the French Language, R.S.Q. 1977, c. C-11, as enacted by S.Q. 1982, c. 21, s. 1, and section 52 of An Act to Amend the Charter of the French Language, S.Q. 1983, c. 56, inconsistent with section 33(1) of*

the Constitution Act, 1982 and therefore inoperative and of no force or effect under section 52(1) of the latter Act?

Answer: No, except in so far as section 214 is given retrospective effect by section 7 of An Act respecting the Constitution Act, 1982, S.Q. 1982, c. 21.

2. *If the answer to question 1 is affirmative, to the extent that they require the exclusive use of the French language, are sections 58 and 69, and sections 205 to 208 to the extent they apply thereto, of the Charter of the French Language, R.S.Q. 1977, c. C-11, as amended by S.Q. 1983, c. 56, inconsistent with the guarantee of freedom of expression under section 2(b) of the Canadian Charter of Rights and Freedoms?*

Answer: Insofar as section 214 of the Charter of the French Language has ceased to have effect but section 52 of An Act to Amend the Charter of the French Language remains in effect, section 58 of the Charter of the French Language is protected from the application of the Canadian Charter of Rights and Freedoms but it is inoperative as infringing the guarantee of freedom or expression in section 3 of the Quebec Charter of Human Rights and Freedoms and the guarantee against discrimination based on language in section 10 of the Quebec Charter. Insofar as section 214 of the Charter of the French Language has ceased to have effect, section 69 thereof is inconsistent with the guarantee of freedom of expression under section 2(b) of the Canadian Charter of Rights and Freedoms. Sections 205 to 208 of the Charter of the French Language to the extent they apply to section 69 thereof are inconsistent with the guarantee of freedom of expression under section 2(b) of the Canadian Charter of Rights and Freedoms. Section 69 of the Charter of the French Language, and sections 205 to 208 thereof, to the extent they apply to sections 58 and 69, are also inconsistent with the guarantee of freedom of expression under section 3 of the Quebec Charter of Human Rights and Freedoms.

3. *If the answer to question 2 is affirmative in whole or in part, are sections 58 and 69, and sections 205 to 208 to the extent they apply thereto, of the Charter of the French Language, R.S.Q. 1977, c. C-11, as amended by S.Q. 1983, c. 56 justified by the application of section 1 of the Canadian Charter of Rights and Freedoms and therefore not inconsistent with the Constitution Act, 1982?*

Answer: Section 58 of the Charter of the French Language is not justified under section 9.1 of the Quebec Charter of Human Rights and Freedoms. Section 69 of the Charter of the French Language, and sections 205 to 208 thereof, to the extent they apply to section 69, are not justified under section 1 of the Canadian Charter of Rights and Freedoms and are therefore inconsistent with the Constitution Act, 1982. Nor is section 69 of the Charter of the French Language, or sections 205 to 208 thereof, to the extent they apply to sections 58 and 69, justified under section 9.1 of the Quebec Charter of Human Rights and Freedoms.

52A. Andrews *v*. Law Society of British Columbia, *1989*

~ *Andrews* is the first case based exclusively on section 15 to be decided by the Supreme Court. The case arises out of circumstances identical to those of Skapinker, who took the first major Charter case to the Supreme Court, but who had to rely on section 6 "mobility rights" because section 15 had not yet come into effect.[1] Like *Skapinker, Andrews* will be remembered not so much for the precise legal issue it settled as for the interpretive orientation it established. Just as *Skapinker* provided the Court with the opportunity to indicate the general approach it would take to the Charter, so *Andrews* gave it the opportunity to establish the principles of section 15 jurisprudence. The Court's discussion of such terms as equality and discrimination, and of the overall structure of section 15 and its relationship to other parts of the Charter, will become the point of departure for subsequent debate (both in and out of court) about the section 15 equality rights. The pathbreaking importance of this case was recognized by several interest groups who, while not much concerned with the particulars of Andrew's claim, sought and received intervenor status in order to persuade the Court to lay a foundation for section 15 jurisprudence that was compatible with their section 15 litigation strategies.[2]

Andrews wished to practice law in British Columbia and had met all the standards for admission to the bar except for the requirement of Canadian citizenship contained in section 42(a) of the *Barristers and Solicitors Act.* He argued that this legislative discrimination against non-citizens infringed section 15 of the *Charter.* Since "citizenship" is not one of the prohibited grounds of discrimination explicitly enumerated by section 15, the case raised questions about the reach of that section's open-ended wording. The Court unanimously agreed that the citizenship requirement violated section 15 but divided on the question of whether it could be saved as a "reasonable limit" under section 1: five of the six-judge panel[3] concluded that it could not be so defended; Justice McIntyre, who wrote the controlling opinion on most other issues, dissented on this section 1 question.

The Court was obviously concerned about the potential for the open-ended wording of section 15 to force the judicial evaluation of almost all legislation. This would occur especially if the term "discrimination" were interpreted in a neutral fashion as meaning simply "distinction," and if the open-ended phraseology were taken literally to cover all distinctions. Most laws make

---

[1] See case 40 above.

[2] Intervening on the side of *Andrews* were the Women's Legal Education and Action Fund (LEAF), the Coalition of Provincial Organizations of the Handicapped, the Canadian Association of University Teachers, and the Ontario Confederation of University Faculty Associations. The Federation of Law Societies of Canada and several provincial Attorneys General intervened on the other side.

[3] Justice Le Dain was on the panel but took no part in the judgment.

distinctions and would, under such an interpretation, violate section 15;[4] they could thus be sustained only as "reasonable limits" under section 1. Although such an interpretation had been suggested by leading commentators, it was too daunting for the Court. Justice La Forest, for example, could not "accept that all legislative classifications must be rationally supportable before the courts" because this would involve the judicial assessment of "much economic and social policy-making [that] is simply beyond the institutional competence of the courts." The proper judicial role, he said, "is to protect against incursions on fundamental values, not to second guess policy decisions."

Writing for a unanimous court on this point, Justice McIntyre reduced the potential for violating section 15 by placing two limitations upon its scope. First, he held that "discrimination" did not mean merely "distinction" but required the showing of some harm or prejudice. Second, he restricted the reach of the open-ended wording to grounds "analogous" to the enumerated grounds. Both qualifications on the scope of section 15 were designed to ensure that many legislative distinctions will not violate the Charter's equality rights and will thus not have to defend themselves under section 1 as "reasonable limits . . . demonstrably justified in a free and democratic society."

Neither qualification applied in this case, however. Justice McIntyre found that non-citizens were harmed by the legislation and that citizenship was an analogous ground because non-citizens "are a good example of a 'discrete and insular minority' who come within the protection of s. 15." Justice Wilson added that discrete and insular minorities were groups "lacking in political power and as such vulnerable to having their interests overlooked and their rights to equal concern and respect violated. They are among 'those groups in society to whose needs and wishes elected officials have no apparent interest in attending.' " This emphasis on section 15's role in protecting groups that lack power and influence is consistent with Chief Justice Dickson's theory, enunciated in both *Edwards Books* and the *Alberta Labour Reference*, that an important purpose of the Charter is to help social and economic "underdogs."[5]

While the Court clearly intended to limit the scope of section 15 challenges, the limits are not terribly clear and are likely to generate considerable controversy. For example, the question of whether or not an unlisted group is an "underdog" deserving constitutional protection will not be easy to determine.[6] Nor is the question whether a legislative distinction causes harm likely to be free of difficulty. A further source of ambiguity is introduced by the way in which the Court chose to define the term "discrimination." It does not mean

---

[4] Justice McIntyre, following the court below, uses the example of laws forbidding children or drunk persons from driving.

[5] See the introductions to cases 48 and 49 above.

[6] Consider, for example, the disagreement between Justice Dickson and McIntyre about the power of the labour movement in the *Alberta Labour Reference*.

just direct, intentional discrimination against the enumerated or analogous groups but also the "disparate impact" on these groups of otherwise neutral policies. This means that classifications not based on an analogous ground will nevertheless be subject to section 15 challenge if they have an unintentional negative "effect" on a group defined by an enumerated or analogous group. For example, war veterans are overwhelmingly male. Does this mean that a "veterans preference," which does not appear to be based on an "analogous ground," is nevertheless open to challenge because its indirect effect is to deny "equal benefit of the law" to women? Justice McIntyre insists that "A complainant under s. 15(1) must show not only that he or she is not receiving equal treatment before and under the law or that the law has a differential impact on him or her in the protection or benefit accorded by law but, in addition, must show that the legislative impact of the law is discriminatory [i.e. harmful]." He intends this to be a formula for limiting the scope of section 15. In fact, it opens as many interpretive doors as it closes, and the precise scope of section 15 will remain an open question for some time to come. ~

ANDREWS v. LAW SOCIETY OF BRITISH COLUMBIA
In the Supreme Court of Canada (unreported at time of publication).

The judgment of Dickson C.J.C. and Wilson and L'Heureux-Dube JJ. was delivered by

WILSON J.: I have had the benefit of the reasons of my colleague, Justice McIntyre, and I am in complete agreement with him as to the way in which s. 15(1) of the Canadian Charter of Rights and Freedoms should be interpreted and applied. I also agree with my colleagues as to the way in which s. 15(1) and s. 1 of the Charter interact. I differ from him, however, on the application of s. 1 to this particular case. . . .

I agree with my colleague that a rule which bars an entire class of persons from certain forms of employment solely on the ground that they are not Canadian citizens violates the equality rights of that class. I agree with him also that it discriminates against them on the ground of their personal characteristics i.e., their non-citizen status. I believe, therefore, that they are entitled to the protection of s. 15.

Before turning to s. 1 I would like to add a brief comment to what my colleague has said concerning non-citizens perma-nently resident in Canada forming the kind of "discrete and insular minority" to which the Supreme Court of the United States referred in United States v. Carolene Products Co., 304 U.S. 144 (1938), at pp. 152-53, n. 4.

Relative to citizens, non-citizens are a group lacking in political power and as such vulnerable to having their interests overlooked and their rights to equal concern and respect violated. They are among "those groups in society to whose needs and wishes elected officials have no apparent interest in attending": see J. H. Ely, Democracy and Distrust (1980), at p. 151. Non-citizens, to take only the most obvious example, do not have the right to vote. Their vulnerability to becoming a disadvantaged group in our society is captured by John Stuart Mill's observation in Book III of Considerations of Representative Government that "in the absence of its natural defenders, the interests of the excluded is always in danger of being overlooked. . . ." I would conclude therefore that non-citizens fall into an analogous category to those specifically enumerated in s. 15. I emphasize, moreover, that this is a determination which is not to be made only in the context of the law which is subject to challenge but rather in the context of the place of the group in the entire social, political and legal fabric of our society. While legislatures must inevitably draw distinctions among the governed, such distinctions should not bring about or reinforce the disadvantage of certain groups and individuals by denying them the rights freely accorded to others.

I believe also that it is important to note that the range of discrete and insular minorities has changed and will continue to change with changing political and social circumstances. For example, Stone J. writing in 1938, was concerned with religious, national and racial minorities. In enumerating the specific grounds in s. 15, the framers of the Charter embraced these concerns in 1982 but also addressed themselves to the difficulties experienced by the disadvantaged on the grounds of ethnic origin, colour, sex, age and physical and mental disability. It can be anticipated that the discrete and insular minorities of tomorrow will include groups not recognized as such today. It is consistent with the constitutional status of s. 15 that it be interpreted with sufficient flexibility to ensure the "unremitting protection" of equality rights in the years to come.

While I have emphasized that non-citizens are, in my view, an analogous group to those specifically enumerated in s. 15 and, as such, are entitled to the protection of the section, I agree with my colleague that it is not necessary in this case to determine what limit, if any, there is on the grounds covered by s. 15 and I do not do so. . . .

Having found an infringement of s. 15 of the Charter, I turn now to the question whether the citizenship requirement for entry into the legal profession in British Columbia constitutes a reasonable limit which can be "demonstrably justified in a free and democratic society" under s. 1.

As my colleague has pointed out, the onus of justifying the infringement rests

upon those seeking to uphold the legislation, in this case the Attorney General of British Columbia and the Law Society of British Columbia, and the analysis to be conducted is that set forth by Chief Justice Dickson in *R. v. Oakes*, [1986] 1 S.C.R. 103.

The first hurdle to be crossed in order to override a right guaranteed in the Charter is that the objective sought to be achieved by the impugned law must relate to concerns which are "pressing and substantial" in a free and democratic society. . . . This, in my view, remains an appropriate standard when it is recognized that not every distinction between individuals and groups will violate s. 15. If every distinction between individuals and groups gave rise to a violation of s. 15, then this standard might well be too stringent for application in all cases and might deny the community at large the benefits associated with sound and desirable social and economic legislation. This is not a concern, however, once the position that every distinction drawn by law constitutes discrimination is rejected as indeed it is in the judgment of my colleague, McIntyre J. Given that s. 15 is designated to protect those groups who suffer social, political and legal disadvantage in our society, the burden resting on government to justify the type of discrimination against such groups is appropriately an onerous one.

The second step in a s. 1 inquiry involves the application of a proportionality test which requires the Court to balance a number of factors. . . .

I appreciate the desirability of lawyers being familiar with Canadian institutions and customs but I agree with McLachlin J.A. that the requirement of citizenship is not carefully tailored to achieve that objective and may not even be rationally connected to it. McDonald J. pointed out in *Re Dickson and Law Society of Alberta* (1978), 84 D.L.R. (3d) 189, at p. 195 that such a requirement affords no assurance that citizens who want to become lawyers are sufficiently familiar with Canadian institutions and "it could be better achieved by an examination of the particular qualifications of the applicant, whether he is a Canadian citizen, a British subject, or something else.''

The second justification advanced by the appellants in support of the citizenship requirement is that citizenship evidences a real attachment to Canada. Once again I find myself in agreement with the following observations of McLachlin J.A. at pp. 612-13:

The second reason for the distinction— that citizenship implies a commitment to Canadian society—fares little better upon close examination. Only those citizens who are not natural-born Canadians can be said to have made a conscious choice to establish themselves here permanently and to opt for full participation in the Canadian social process, including the right to vote and run for public office. While no doubt most citizens, natural- born or otherwise, are committed to Canadian society, citizenship does not ensure that that is the case. Conversely, non-citizens may be deeply committed to our country.

The third ground advanced to justify the requirement relates to the role lawyers are said to play in the governance of our country. McLachlin J.A. disputed the extent to which the practice of law involves the performance of a govern- mental function. She stated at p. 614:

While lawyers clearly play an impor- tant role in our society, it can not be contended that the practice of law involves performing a state or govern- ment function. In this respect, the role of lawyers may be distinguished from that of legislators, judges, civil servants and policemen. The practice of law is first and foremost a private profession. Some law- yers work in the courts, some do not. Those who work in the courts may repre- sent the Crown or act against it. It is true that all lawyers are officers of the court. That term, in my mind, implies allegiance and certain responsibilities to the institu- tion of the court. But it does not mean that lawyers are part of the process of government.

Although I am in general agreement with her characterization of the role of lawyers *qua* lawyers in our society, my problem with this basis of justification is more fundamental. To my mind, even if law- yers do perform a governmental function, I do not think the requirement that they be citizens provides any guarantee that they will honourably and conscientiously carry out their public duties. They will carry them out, I believe, because they are good lawyers and not becuase they are Cana- dian citizens.

In my view, the reasoning advanced in support of the citizenship requirement simply does not meet the tests in *Oakes* for overriding a constitutional right par- ticularly, as in this case, a right designed to protect "discrete and insular minor- ities" in our society. I would respectfully concur in the view expressed by McLachlin J.A. at p. 617 that the citizen- ship requirement does not "appear to relate closely to those ends, much less to have been carefully designed to achieve them with minimum impairment of indi- vidual rights." . . .

LA FOREST J.: . . . My colleague, Jus- tice McIntyre, has set forth the facts and the judicial history of this appeal and it is unnecessary for me to repeat them. Nor need I enter into an extensive examination of the law regarding the meaning of s. 15(1), because insofar as it is relevant to this appeal I am in substantial agree- ment with the views of my colleague. I hasten to add that the relevant question as I see it is restricted to whether the impugned provision amounts to discrimi- nation in the sense in which my colleague has defined it, i.e., on the basis of "irrele- vant personal differences" such as those listed in s. 15 and, traditionally, in human rights legislation.

I am not prepared to accept at this point that the only significance to be attached to the opening words that refer more gener- ally to equality is that the protection afforded by the section is restricted to discrimination through the application of law. It is possible to read s. 15 in this way and I have no doubt that on any view redress against that kind of discrimination will constitute the bulk of the courts' work under the provision. Moreover, from the manner in which it was drafted, I also have no doubt that it was so intended. However, it can reasonably be argued that the opening words, which take up half the section, seem somewhat excessive to accomplish the modest role attributed to them, particularly having regard to the fact that s. 32 already limits the application of the Charter to legislation and governmental activity. It may also be thought to be out of keeping with the broad and generous approach given to other Charter rights, not the least of which is s. 7, which like s. 15 is of a generalized character. In the case of s. 7, it will be remembered, the Court has been at pains to give real meaning to each word of the section so as to ensure that the rights to life, liberty and security of the person are separate, if closely related rights.

That having been said, I am convinced that it was never intended in enacting s. 15 that it become a tool for the wholesale subjection to judicial scrutiny of variegated legislative choices in no way infringing on values fundamental to a free and democratic society. Like my colleague, I am not prepared to accept that all legislative classifications must be rationally supportable before the courts. Much economic and social policy-making is simply beyond the institutional competence of the courts: their role is to protect against incursions on fundamental values, not to second guess policy decisions.

I realize that it is no easy task to distinguish between what is fundamental and what is not and that in this context this may demand consideration of abstruse theories of equality. For example, there may well be legislative or governmental differentiation between individuals or groups that is so grossly unfair to an individual or group and so devoid of any rational relationship to a legitimate state purpose as to offend against the principle of equality before and under the law as to merit intervention pursuant to s. 15. For

these reasons I would think it better at this stage of Charter development to leave the question open. I am aware that in the United States, where Holmes J. has referred to the equal protection clause there as the "last resort of constitutional arguments" (*Buck* v. *Bell*, 274 U.S. 200 (1927), at p. 208), the courts have been extremely reluctant to interfere with legislative judgment. Still, as I stated, there may be cases where it is indeed the last constitutional resort to protect the individual from fundamental unfairness. Assuming there is room under s. 15 for judicial intervention beyond the traditionally established and analogous policies against discrimination discussed by my colleague, it bears repeating that considerations of institutional functions and resources should make courts extremely wary about questioning legislative and governmental choices in such areas.

As I have indicated, however, this issue does not arise here. For we are concerned in this case with whether or not the legislation amounts to discrimination of a kind similar to those enumerated in s. 15. It was conceded that the impugned legislation does distinguish the respondents from other persons on the basis of a personal characteristic which shares many similarities with those enumerated in s. 15. The characteristic of citizenship is one typically not within the control of the individual and, in this sense, is immutable. Citizenship is, at least temporarily, a characteristic of personhood not alterable by conscious action and in some cases not alterable except on the basis of unacceptable costs.

Moreover, non-citizens are an example without parallel of a group of persons who are relatively powerless politically, and whose interests are likely to be compromised by legislative decisions. History reveals that Canada did not for many years resist the temptation of enacting legislation the animating rationale of which was to limit the number of persons entering into certain employment. Discrimination on the basis of nationality has from early times been an inseparable companion of discrimination on the basis of race and national or ethnic origin, which are listed in s. 15. . . .

There is no question that citizenship may, in some circumstances, be properly used as a defining characteristic for certain types of legitimate governmental objectives. I am sensitive to the fact that citizenship is a very special status that not only incorporates rights and duties but serves a highly important symbolic function as a badge identifying people as members of the Canadian polity. Nevertheless, it is, in general, irrelevant to the legitimate work of government in all but a limited number of areas. By and large, the use in legislation of citizenship as a basis for distinguishing between persons, here for the purpose of conditioning access to the practice of a profession, harbours the potential for undermining the essential or underlying values of a free and democratic society that are embodied in s. 15. Our nation has throughout its history drawn strength from the flow of people to our shores. Decisions unfairly premised on citizenship would be likely to "inhibit the sense of those who are discriminated against that Canadian society is not free or democratic as far as they are concerned and . . . such persons are likely not to have faith in social and political institutions which enhance the participation of individuals and groups in society, or to have confidence that they can freely and without obstruction by the state pursue their and their families' hopes and expectations of vocational and personal development" (*Kask* v. *Shimizu*, [1986] 4 W.W.R. 154, at p. 161, *per* McDonald J. (Alta. Q.B.)).

While it cannot be said that citizenship is a characteristic which "bears no relation to the individual's ability to perform or contribute to society" (*Fontiero* v. *Richardson*, 411 U.S. 677 (1973), at 686), it certainly typically bears an attenuated sense of relevance to these. That is not to say that no legislative conditioning of benefits (for example) on the basis of citizenship is acceptable in the free and democratic society that is Canada, merely

that legislation purporting to do so ought to be measured against the touchstone of our Constitution. It requires justification.

I turn then to a consideration of the justifiability, fairness or proportionality of the scheme. I agree with McIntyre J. that any such justification must be found under s. 1 of the Charter, essentially because, in matters involving infringements of fundamental rights, it is entirely appropriate that government sustain the constitutionality of its conduct. I am in general agreement with what he has to say about the manner in which legislation must be approached under the latter provision, in particular the need for a proportionality test involving a sensitive balancing of many factors in weighing the legislative objective. If I have any qualifications to make, it is that I prefer to think in terms of a single test for s. 1, but one that is to be applied to vastly differing situations with the flexibility and realism inherent in the word "reasonable" mandated by the Constitution.

The degree to which a free and democratic society such as Canada should tolerate differentiation based on personal characteristics cannot be ascertained by an easy calculus. There will rarely, if ever, be a perfect congruence between means and ends, save where legislation has discriminatory purposes. The matter must, as early cases have held, involve a test of proportionality. In cases of this kind, the test must be approached in a flexible manner. The analysis should be functional, focussing on the character of the classification in question, the constitutional and societal importance of the interests adversely affected, the relative importance to the individuals affected of the benefit of which they are deprived, and the importance of the state interest.

With deference, however, I am unable to agree with McIntyre J.'s application of these principles to the present case. I therefore turn to the task of balancing the objectives sought to be accomplished by the legislation against the means sought to achieve that objective. . . .

While there is no evidence on this

point, the Attorney General offers three purposes sought to be attained by the legislation. These are: 1) citizenship ensures a familiarity with Canadian institutions and customs; 2) citizenship implies a commitment to Canadian society; 3) lawyers play a fundamental role in the Canadian system of democratic government and as such should be citizens. . . .

~ Like Justice Wilson, Justice La Forest essentially follows the reasoning of McLachlin J.A. in the Court of Appeal on these points. ~

The third objective advanced by the Attorney General has more substance. It is that certain state activities should for both symbolic and practical reasons be confined to those who are full members of our political society. The Attorney General reduced his arguments regarding this objective to the following syllogism:

(a) persons who are involved in the processes or structure of government, broadly defined, should be citizens;
(b) lawyers are involved in the processes or structure of government;
(c) lawyers, therefore, should be citizens.

I do not quarrel with the first assertion as a general proposition. The Court of Appeal accepted it, noting that this rationale underlies the common requirement that legislators, voters, judges, police and senior public servants be citizens. However, it rejected the second proposition that lawyers play a vital role in the administration of law and justice and are themselves as much a part of the government processes as are judges, legislators and so on. It rejected the notion that the practice of law itself involved performing a state or government function. . . .

I agree. . . . It is only in the most unreal sense that it can be said that a lawyer working for a private client plays a role in the administration of justice that would require him or her to be a citizen in order to be allowed to participate therein. Obviously lawyers occupy a position of trust and responsibility in our society, but that is true of all professions, and the members of some of these, like that of chartered accountants, for instance, are privy to matters of the most serious import.

On a more mundane level, the essential purpose behind occupational licensing is to protect the public from unqualified practitioners. But as Lenoir points out (*supra*, at p. 547), citizenship has not been shown to bear any correlation to one's professional or vocational competency or qualification. Like him, I see no sufficient additional dimension to the lawyer's function to insist on citizenship as a qualification for admission to this profession.

It is not without significance that a requirement of citizenship has not been found to be necessary to the practice of law in either the United States (see *In Re re Griffiths*, 413 U.S. 717 (1973)), or England (see *Solicitors (Amendment) Act 1974* (U.K.) 1974, c. 26, s. 1); see also *Re Howard, supra*, at p. 647. The doc- . trine of privileged communications was pressed into service, but that doctrine exists for the protection of the client. I fail to see what this has to do with the requirement of citizenship.

A requirement of citizenship would be acceptable if limited to Crown Attorneys or lawyers directly employed by government and, therefore, involved in policy making or administration, so that it could be said that the lawyer was an architect or instrumentality of government policy; see *Reyners* v. *The Belgian State*, [1974] 2 Common Market Law R. 305. But ordinary lawyers are not privy to government information any more than, say, accountants, and there are rules to restrict lawyers from obtaining confidential governmental information.

I would conclude that although the governmental objectives, as stated, may be defensible, it is simply misplaced vis-à-vis the legal profession as a whole. However, even accepting the legitimacy and importance of the legislative objectives, the legislation exacts too high a price on persons wishing to practice law in that it may deprive them, albeit perhaps temporarily, of the "right" to pursue their calling. . . .

The judgment of McIntyre and Lamer JJ. was delivered by

McINTYRE J. (dissenting): This appeal raises only one question. Does the citizenship requirement for entry into the legal profession contained in s. 42 of the Barristers and Solicitors Act, R.S.B.C. 1979, c. 26, (the "Act") contravene s. 15(1) of the Canadian Charter of Rights and Freedoms? Section 42 provides:

> 42. The benchers may call to the Bar of the Province and admit as a solicitor of the Supreme Court
> (a) a Canadian citizen with respect to whom they are satisfied that he. . .

and s. 15 of the Charter states:

> 15. (1) Every individual is equal before and under the law and has the right to the equal protection and equal benefit of the law without discrimination and, in particular, without discrimination based on race, national or ethnic origin, colour, religion, sex, age or mental or physical disability.
> (2) Subsection (1) does not preclude any law, program or activity that has as its object the amelioration of conditions of disadvantaged individuals or groups including those that are disadvantaged because of race, national or ethnic origin, colour, religion, sex, age or mental or physical disability.

The respondent, Andrews, was a British subject permanently resident in Canada at the time these proceedings were commenced. He had taken law degrees at Oxford and had fulfilled all the requirements for admission to the practice of law in British Columbia, except that of Canadian citizenship. He commenced proceedings for a declaration that s. 42 of the Act violates the Charter. He also sought an order in the nature of mandamus requiring the benchers of the Law Society of British Columbia to consider his application for call to the Bar and admission as a solicitor. His action was dismissed at trial before Taylor J. in the Supreme Court of British Columbia in a judgment reported at (1985), 22 D.L.R. (4th) 9. An appeal was allowed in the Court of Appeal (Hinkson, Craig and McLachlin JJ.A., at (1986), 27 D.L.R. (4th) 600), and this appeal is taken by the Law Society of British Columbia, by leave granted November 27, 1986. Pursuant to an order of this Court on January 28, 1987, Gorel Elizabeth Kinersly, an American citizen who was at the time a permanent resident of Canada articling in the Province of British Columbia, was added as a co-respondent in this appeal. . . . Following the judgment in his favour, the respondent Andrews was called to the Bar and admitted as a solicitor in the Province of British Columbia and is now a Canadian citizen. The co-respondent, Kinersly, who had expressed an intention to become a Canadian citizen, became eligible to do so on March 15, 1988. . . .

THE CONCEPT OF EQUALITY

Section 15(1) of the Charter provides for every individual a guarantee of equality before and under the law, as well as the equal protection and equal benefit of the law without discrimination. This is not a general guarantee of equality; it does not provide for equality between individuals or groups within society in a general or abstract sense, nor does it impose on individuals or groups an obligation to accord equal treatment to others. It is concerned with the application of the law. No problem regarding the scope of the word "law," as employed in s. 15(1), can arise in this case because it is an Act of the Legislature which is under attack. Whether other governmental or quasi-governmental regulations, rules, or requirements may be termed laws under s. 15(1) should be left for cases in which the issue arises.

The concept of equality has long been a

feature of Western thought. As embodied in s. 15(1) of the Charter, it is an elusive concept and, more than any of the other rights and freedoms guaranteed in the Charter, it lacks precise definition. As has been stated by John H. Schaar, "Equality of Opportunity and Beyond," in *Nomos IX: Equality*, ed. J. Roland Pennock and John W. Chapman (1967), at p. 228:

Equality is a protean word. It is one of those political symbols—liberty and fraternity are others—into which men have poured the deepest urgings of their heart. Every strongly held theory or conception of equality is at once a psychology, an ethic, a theory of social relations, and a vision of the good society.

It is a comparative concept, the condition of which may only be attained or discerned by comparison with the condition of others in the social and political setting in which the question arises. It must be recognized at once, however, that every difference in treatment between individuals under the law will not necessarily result in inequality and, as well, that identical treatment may frequently produce serious inequality. . . . The same thought has been expressed in this Court in the context of s. 2(b) of the Charter in *R. v. Big M. Drug Mart Ltd.*, [1985] 1 S.C.R. 295, where Dickson C.J.C. said at p. 347:

The equality necessary to support religious freedom does not require identical treatment of all religions. In fact, the interests of true equality may well require differentiation in treatment.

In simple terms, then, it may be said that a law which treats all identically and which provides equality of treatment between "A" and "B" might well cause inequality for "C," depending on differences in personal characteristics and situations. To approach the ideal of full equality before and under the law and in human affairs an approach is all that can be expected—the main consideration must be the impact of the law on the individual or the group concerned.

Recognizing that there will always be an infinite variety of personal characteristics, capacities, entitlements and merits among those subjec to a law, there must be accorded, as nearly as may be possible, an equality of benefit and protection and no more of the restrictions, penalties or burdens imposed upon one than another. In other words, the admittedly unattainable ideal should be that a law expressed to bind all should not because of irrelevant personal differences have a more burdensome or less beneficial impact on one than another.

McLachlin J.A. in the Court of Appeal expressed the view, at p. 605, that:

. . . the essential meaning of the constitutional requirement of equal protection and equal benefit is that persons who are "similarly situated be similarly treated" and conversely, that persons who are "differently situated be differently treated." . . .

In this, she was adopting and applying as a test a proposition which seems to have been widely accepted with some modifications in both trial and appeal court decisions throughout the country on s. 15(1) of the Charter. . . . The similarly situated test is a reinstatement of the Aristotelian principle of formal equality—that "things that are alike should be treated alike, while things that are unalike should be treated unalike in proportion to their unalikeness" (*Ethica Nichomacea*, trans. W. Ross, Book V3, at p. 1131a-6 (1925)).

The test as stated, however, is seriously deficient in that it excludes any consideration of the nature of the law. If it were to be applied literally, it could be used to justify the Nuremberg laws of Adolf Hitler. Similar treatment was contemplated for all Jews. The similarly situated test would have justified the formalistic separate but equal doctrine of *Plessy* v. *Ferguson*, 163 U.S. 637 (1896). . . . The test, somewhat differently phrased, was applied in the British Columbia Court of Appeal in *R. v. Gonzales* (1962), 132

C.C.C. 237. The Court upheld, under s. 1(b) of the Canadian Bill of Rights, R.S.C. 1970, s. 1(b), a section of the Indian Act, R.S.C. 1970, c. I-6, which made it an offence for an Indian to have intoxicants in his possession off a reserve. In his locality there were no reserves. Tysoe J.A. said that equality before the law could not mean "the same laws for all persons," and defined the right in these words, at p. 243:

> ... in its context s. 1(b) means in a general sense that there has existed and there shall continue to exist in Canada a right in every person to whom a particular law relates or extends no matter what may be a person's race, national origin, colour, religion or sex to stand on an equal footing with every other person to whom that particular law relates or extends and a right to the protection of the law.

This approach was rejected in this Court by Ritchie J. in *R.* v. *Drybones*, [1970] S.C.R. 282, in a similar case involving a provision of the Indian Act making it an offence for an Indian to be intoxicated off a reserve. He said, at p. 297:

> ... I cannot agree with this interpretation pursuant to which it seems to me that the most glaring discriminatory legislation against a racial group would have to be construed as recognizing the right of each of its individual members "to equality before the law," so long as all the other members are being discriminated against in the same way.

Thus, mere equality of application to similarly situated groups or individuals does not afford a realistic test for a violation of equality rights. For, as has been said, a bad law will not be saved merely because it operates equally upon those to whom it has application. Nor will a law necessarily be bad because it makes distinctions.

A similarly situated test focussing on the equal application of the law to those to whom it has application could lead to results akin to those in *Bliss* v. *Attorney General of Canada*, [1979] 1 S.C.R. 183. In *Bliss*, a pregnant woman was denied unemployment benefits to which she would have been entitled had she not been pregnant. She claimed that the Unemployment Insurance Act violated the equality guarantees of the Canadian Bill of Rights because it discriminated against her on the basis of her sex. Her claim was dismissed by this Court on the grounds that there was no discrimination on the basis of sex, since the class into which she fell under the Act was that of pregnant persons, and within that class, all persons were treated equally. This case, of course, was decided before the advent of the Charter.

... For the reasons outlined above, the test cannot be accepted as a fixed rule or formula for the resolution of equality questions arising under the Charter. Consideration must be given to the content of the law, to its purpose, and its impact upon those to whom it applies, and also upon those whom it excludes from its application. The issues which will arise from case to case are such that it would be wrong to attempt to confine these considerations within such a fixed and limited formula.

It is not every distinction or differentiation in treatment at law which will transgress the equality guarantees of s. 15 of the Charter. It is, of course, obvious that legislatures may—and to govern effectively—must treat different individuals and groups in different ways. Indeed, such distinctions are one of the main preoccupations of legislatures. The classifying of individuals and groups, the making of different provisions respecting such groups, the application of different rules, regulations, requirements and qualifications to different persons is necessary for the governance of modern society. As noted above, for the accommodation of differences, which is the essence of true equality, it will frequently be necessary to make distinctions. What kinds of distinctions will be acceptable under s. 15(1) and what kinds will violate its provisions?

In seeking an answer to these questions, the provisions of the Charter must have their full effect. In *R. v. Big M. Drug Mart Ltd.*, this Court emphasized this point at p. 344, where Dickson C.J.C. stated:

This Court has already, in some measure, set out the basic approach to be taken in interpreting the Charter. In Hunter v. Southam Inc., *[1984] 2 S.C.R. 145, this Court expressed the view that the proper approach to the definition of the rights and freedoms guaranteed by the Charter was a purposive one. The meaning of a right or freedom guaranteed by the Charter was to be ascertained by an analysis of the purpose of such a guarantee; it was to be understood, in other words, in the light of the interests it was meant to protect.*

In my view this analysis is to be undertaken, and the purpose of the right or freedom in question is to be sought by reference to the character and the larger objects of the Charter itself, to the language chosen to articulate the specific right or freedom, to the historical origins of the concepts enshrined, and where applicable, to the meaning and purpose of the other specific rights and freedoms with which it is associated within the text of the Charter. The interpretation should be, as the judgment in Southam emphasizes, a generous rather than a legalistic one, aimed at fulfilling the purpose of the guarantee and securing for individuals the full benefit of the Charter's protection. At the same time it is important not to overshoot the actual purpose of the right or freedom in question, but to recall that the Charter was not enacted in a vacuum, and must therefore, as this Court's decision in Law Society of Upper Canada v. Skapinker, *[1984] 1 S.C.R. 357, illustrates, be placed in its proper linguistic, philosophic and historical contexts.*

These words are not inconsistent with the view I expressed in *References re Public Service Employee Relations Act (Alta.)*, [1987] 1 S.C.R. 313.

The principle of equality before the law

has long been recognized as a feature of our constitutional tradition and it found statutory recognition in the Canadian Bill of Rights. However, unlike the Canadian Bill of Rights, which spoke only of equality before the law, s. 15(1) of the Charter provides a much broader protection. Section 15 spells out four basic rights: (1) the right to equality before the law; (2) the right to equality under the law; (3) the right to equal protection of the law; and (4) the right to equal benefit of the law. The inclusion of these last three additional rights in s. 15 of the Charter was an attempt to remedy some of the shortcomings of the right to equality in the Canadian Bill of Rights. It also reflected the expanded concept of discrimination being developed under the various Human Rights Codes since the enactment of the Canadian Bill of Rights. The shortcomings of the Canadian Bill of Rights as far as the right to equality is concerned are well known. In *Attorney General of Canada* v. *Lavell*, [1974] S.C.R. 1349, for example, this Court upheld s. 12(1)(b) of the Indian Act which deprived women, but not men, of their membership in Indian Bands if they married non-Indians. The provision was held not to violate equality before the law although it might, the Court said, violate equality under the law if such were protected. In *Bliss, supra*, this Court held that the denial of unemployment insurance benefits to women because they were pregnant did not violate the guarantee of equality before the law, because any inequality in the protection and benefit of the law was ''not created by legislation but by nature'' (p. 190). The case was distinguished from the Court's earlier decision in *Drybones, supra*, as not involving (pp. 191-2) the imposition of a penalty on a racial group to which other citizens are not subjected, but as involving rather ''a definition of the qualifications required for entitlement to benefits.'' It is readily apparent that the language of s. 15 was deliberately chosen in order to remedy some of the perceived defects under the Canadian Bill of Rights. The antecedent statute is part of the ''linguistic, philosophic and historical context" of s. 15 of the Charter.

It is clear that the purpose of s. 15 is to ensure equality in the formulation and application of the law. The promotion of equality entails the promotion of a society in which all are secure in the knowledge that they are recognized at law as human beings equally deserving of concern, respect and consideration. It has a large remedial component. Chief Justice Howland (with Robins J.A. dissenting in the result but not with respect to this comment) in *Reference Re An Act to Amend the Education Act* 53 O.R. (2d) 513 1, attempts to articulate the broad range of values embraced by s. 15. He states at p. 554:

In our view, s. 15(1) read as a whole constitutes a compendious expression of a positive right to equality in both the substance and the administration of the law. It is an all-encompassing right governing all legislative action. Like the ideals of "equal justice" and "equal access to the law," the right to equal protection and equal benefit of the law now enshrined in the Charter rests on the moral and ethical principle fundamental to a truly free and democratic society that all persons should be treated by the law on a footing of equality with equal concern and respect.

It must be recognized, however, as well that the promotion of equality under s. 15 has a much more specific goal than the mere elimination of distinctions. If the Charter was intended to eliminate all distinctions, then there would be no place for sections such as 27 (multicultural heritage); 2(a) (freedom of conscience and religion); 25 (aboriginal rights and freedoms); and other such provisions designed to safeguard certain distinctions. Moreover, the fact that identical treatment may frequently produce serious inequality is recognized in s. 15(2), which states that the equality rights in s. 15(1) do "not preclude any law, program or activity that has as its object the amelioration of conditions of disadvantaged individuals or groups. . . ."

DISCRIMINATION

The right to equality before and under the law, and the rights to the equal protection and benefit of the law contained in s. 15, are granted with the direction contained in s. 15 itself that they be without discrimination. Discrimination is unacceptable in a democratic society because it epitomizes the worst effects of the denial of equality, and discrimination reinforced by law is particularly repugnant. The worst oppression will result from discriminatory measures having the force of law. It is against this evil that s. 15 provides a guarantee.

Discrimination as referred to in s. 15 of the Charter must be understood in the context of pre-Charter history. Prior to the enactment of s. 15(1), the Legislatures of the various provinces and the federal Parliament had passed during the previous fifty years what may be generally referred to as Human Rights Acts. . . .

What does discrimination mean? The question has arisen most commonly in a consideration of the Human Rights Acts and the general concept of discrimination under those enactments has been fairly well settled. There is little difficulty, drawing upon the cases in this Court, in isolating an acceptable definition. In *Ontario Human Rights Commission* v. *Simpsons-Sears and O'Malley*, [1985] 2 S.C.R. 536, at p. 551, discrimination (in that case adverse effect discrimination) was described in these terms: "It arises where an employer . . . adopts a rule or standard . . . which has a discriminatory effect upon a prohibited ground on one employee or group of employees in that it imposes, because of some special characteristic of the employees or group, obligations, penalties, or restrictive conditions not imposed on other members of the work force." It was held in that case, as well, that no intent was required as an element of discrimination, for it is in essence the impact of the discriminatory act or provision upon the person affected which is decisive in considering any complaint. At page 547, this proposition was expressed in these terms:

The Code aims at the removal of discrimination. This is to state the obvious. Its main approach, however, is not to punish the discriminator, but rather to provide relief for the victims of discrimination. It is the result or the effect of the action complained of which is significant. If it does, in fact, cause discrimination; if its effect is to impose on one person or group of persons obligations, penalties, or restrictive conditions not imposed on other members of the community, it is discriminatory.

In *Canadian National Railway* v. *Canada (Canadian Human Rights Commission)*, [1987] 1 S.C.R. 1114, better known as the *Action Travail des Femmes* case, where it was alleged that the Canadian National Railway was guilty of discriminatory hiring and promotion practices contrary to s. 10 of the Canadian Human Rights Code, S.C. 1976-77, c. 33, in denying employment to women in certain unskilled positions, Dickson C.J.C. in giving the judgment of the Court said, at pp. 1138-39:

A thorough study of "systemic discrimination" in Canada is to be found in the Abella Report *on equality in employment. The terms of reference of the Royal Commission instructed it "to inquire into the most efficient, effective and equitable means of promoting employment opportunities, eliminating systemic discrimination and assisting individuals to compete for employment opportunities on an equal basis." (Order in Council P.C. 1983-1924 of 24 June 1983). Although Judge Abella chose not to offer a precise definition of systemic discrimination, the essentials may be gleaned from the following comments, found at p. 2 of the* Abella Report.

Discrimination . . . means practices or attitudes that have, whether by design or impact, the effect of limiting an individual's or a group's right to the opportunities generally available because of attributed rather than actual characteristics. . . . It is not a question

of whether this discrimination is motivated by an intentional desire to obstruct someone's potential, or whether it is the accidental by-product of innocently motivated practices or systems. If the barrier is affecting certain groups in a disproportionately negative way, it is a signal that the practices that lead to this adverse impact may be discriminatory.

There are many other statements which have aimed at a short definition of the term discrimination. In general, they are in accord with the statements referred to above. I would say then that discrimination may be described as a distinction, whether intentional or not but based on grounds relating to personal characteristics of the individual or group, which has the effect of imposing burdens, obligations, or disadvantages on such individual or group not imposed upon others, or which withholds or limits access to opportunities, benefits, and advantages available to other members of society. Distinctions based on personal characteristics attributed to an individual solely on the basis of association with a group will rarely escape the charge of discrimination, while those based on an individual's merits and capacities will rarely be so classed.

The Court in the case at bar must address the issue of discrimination as the term is used in s. 15(1) of the Charter. In general, it may be said that the principles which have been applied under the Human Rights Acts are equally applicable in considering questions of discrimination under s. 15(1). Certain differences arising from the difference between the Charter and the Human Rights Acts must, however, be considered. To begin with, discrimination in s. 15(1) is limited to discrimination caused by the application or operation of law, whereas the Human Rights Acts apply also to private activities. Furthermore, and this is a distinction of more importance, all the Human Rights Acts passed in Canada specifically designate a certain limited number of grounds upon which discrimination is forbidden. Section 15(1) of the Charter is not so limited. The enumerated grounds in s. 15(1) are not exclusive and the limits, if any, on grounds for discrimination which may be established in future cases await definition. The enumerated grounds do, however, reflect the most common and probably the most socially destructive and historically practised bases of discrimination and must, in the words of s. 15(1), receive particular attention. Both the enumerated grounds themselves and other possible grounds of discrimination recognized under s. 15(1) must be interpreted in a broad and generous manner, reflecting the fact that they are constitutional provisions not easily repealed or amended but intended to provide a "continuing framework for the legitimate exercise of governmental power" and, at the same time, for "the unremitting protection" of equality rights: see *Hunter* v. *Southam Inc.*, [1984] 2 S.C.R. 145, at p. 155.

It should be noted as well that when the Human Rights Acts create exemptions or defences, such as a *bona fide* occupational requirement, an exemption for religious and political organizations, or definitional limits on age discrimination, these generally have the effect of completely removing the conduct complained of from the reach of the Act. See, for example, exemptions for special interest organizations contained in the Human Rights Code, R.S.B.C. 1979, c. 186, as am., s. 22; The Human Rights Act, S.M. 1974, c. 65, as am., s. 6(7); and the Human Rights Code, 1981, S.O. 1981, c. 53, s. 17. "Age" is often restrictively defined in the Human Rights Acts; in British Columbia, it is defined in s. 1 of the Code to mean an age between 45 and 65; in s. 38 of the Individual's Rights Protection Act, R.S.A. 1980, c. I-2, it is defined as eighteen and over. For an example of the application of a *bona fide* occupational requirement, see *Bhinder* v. *Canadian National Railway Co.*, [1985] 2 S.C.R. 561. Where discrimination is forbidden in the Human Rights Acts it is

done in absolute terms, and where a defence or exception is allowed it, too, speaks in absolute terms and the discrimination is excused. There is, in this sense, no middle ground. In the Charter, however, while s. 15(1), subject always to subs. (2), expresses its prohibition of discrimination in absolute terms, s. 1 makes allowance for a reasonable limit upon the operation of s. 15(1). A different approach under s. 15(1) is therefore required. While discrimination under s. 15(1) will be of the same nature and in descriptive terms will fit the concept of discrimination developed under the Human Rights Acts, a further step will be required in order to decide whether discriminatory laws can be justified under s. 1. The onus will be on the state to establish this. This is a distinct step called for under the Charter which is not found in most Human Rights Acts, because in those Acts justification for or defence to discrimination is generally found in specific exceptions to the substantive rights.

RELATIONSHIP BETWEEN S. 15(1) AND S. 1 OF THE CHARTER

In determining the extent of the guarantee of equality in s. 15(1) of the Charter, special consideration must be given to the relationship between s. 15(1) and s. 1. It is indeed the presence of s. 1 in the Charter and the interaction between these sections which has led to the differing approaches to a definition of the s. 15(1) right, and which has made necessary a judicial approach differing from that employed under the Canadian Bill of Rights. Under the Canadian Bill of Rights, a test was developed to distinguish between justified and unjustified legislative distinctions within the concept of equality before the law itself in the absence of anything equivalent to the s. 1 limit: see *MacKay* v. *The Queen*, [1980] 2 S.C.R. 370, where it was said, at p. 407:

. . . and whether it is a necessary departure from the general principle of universal application of the law for the attainment of some necessary and desir-

able social objective. Inequalities created for such purposes may well be acceptable under the Canadian Bill of Rights.

It may be noted as well that the 14th Amendment to the American Constitution, which provides that no State shall deny to any person within its jurisdiction the "equal protection of the laws," contains no limiting provisions similar to s. 1 of the Charter. As a result, judicial consideration has led to the development of varying standards of scrutiny of alleged violations of the equal protection provision which restrict or limit the equality guarantee within the concept of equal protection itself. Again, article 14 of the European Convention on Human Rights, 23 U.N.T.S. 222, which secures the rights guaranteed therein without discrimination, lacks a s. 1 or its equivalent and has also developed a limit within the concept itself. In the *Belgian Linguistic Case (No. 2)* (1968), 1 E.H.R.R. 252, at p. 284, the court enunciated the following test:

the principle of equality of treatment is violated if the distinction has no objective and reasonable justification. The existence of such a justification must be assessed in relation to the aim and effects of the measure under consideration, regard being had to principles which normally prevail in democratic societies. A difference in treatment in the exercise of a right laid down in the Convention must not only pursue a legitimate aim: article 14 is likewise violated when it is clearly established that there is no reasonable relationship of proportionality between the means employed and the aim sought to be realised.

The distinguishing feature of the Charter, unlike the other enactments is that consideration of such limiting factors is made under s. 1. This Court has described the analytical approach to the Charter in *R. v. Oakes*, [1986] 1 S.C.R. 103; *R. v. Edwards Books and Art Ltd.*, [1986] 2 S.C.R. 713, and other cases, the essential feature of which is that the right guaran-

teeing sections be kept analytically separate from s. 1. In other words, when confronted with a problem under the Charter, the first question which must be answered will be whether or not an infringement of a guaranteed right has occurred. Any justification of an infringement which is found to have occurred must be made, if at all, under the broad provisions of s. 1. It must be admitted at once that the relationship between these two sections may well be difficult to determine on a wholly satisfactory basis. It is, however, important to keep them analytically distinct if for no other reason that the different attribution of the burden of proof. It is for the citizen to establish that his or her Charter right has been infringed and for the state to justify the infringement.

APPROACHES TO S. 15(1)

Three main approaches have been adopted in determining the role of s. 15(1), the meaning of discrimination set out in that section, and the relationship of s. 15(1) and s. 1. The first one, which was advanced by Professor Peter Hogg in *Constitutional Law of Canada* (2nd ed.) would treat every distinction drawn by law as discrimination under s. 15(1). There would then follow a consideration of the distinction under the provisions of s. 1 of the Charter. He said, at pp. 800-1:

I conclude that s. 15 should be interpreted as providing for the universal application of every law. When a law draws a distinction between individuals, on any ground, that distinction is sufficient to constitute a breach of s. 15, and to move the constitutional issue to s. 1. The test of validity is that stipulated by s. 1, namely, whether the law comes within the phrase "such reasonable limits prescribed by law as can be demonstrably justified in a free and democratic society."

He reached this conclusion on the basis that, where the Charter right is expressed in unqualified terms, s. 1 supplies the standard of justification for any abridgement of the right. He argued that the word "discrimination" in s. 15(1) could be read as introducing a qualification in the section itself, but he preferred to read the word in a neutral sense because this reading would immediately send the matter to s. 1, which was included in the Charter for this purpose.

The second approach put forward by McLachlin J.A. in the Court of Appeal involved a consideration of the reasonableness and fairness of the impugned legislation under s. 15(1). She stated, as has been noted above, at p. 610:

The ultimate question is whether a fair-minded person, weighing the purposes of legislation against its effects on the individuals adversely affected, and giving due weight to the right of the Legislature to pass laws for the good of all, would conclude that the legislative means adopted are reasonable or unfair.

She assigned a very minor role to s. 1 which would, it appears, be limited to allowing in times of emergency, war, or other crises the passage of discriminatory legislation which would normally be impermissible.

A third approach, sometimes described as an "enumerated or analogous grounds" approach, adopts the concept that discrimination is generally expressed by the enumerated grounds. Section 15(1) is designed to prevent discrimination based on these and analogous grounds. The approach is similar to that found in human rights and civil rights statutes which have been enacted throughout Canada in recent times. . . .

The analysis of discrimination in this approach must take place within the context of the enumerated grounds and those analogous to them. The words "without discrimination" require more than a mere finding of distinction between the treatment of groups or individuals. Those words are a form of qualifier built into s. 15 itself and limit those distinctions which are forbidden by the section to those which involve prejudice or disadvantage.

I would accept the criticisms of the first approach made by McLachlin J.A. in the Court of Appeal. She noted that the labelling of every legislative distinction as an infringement of s. 15(1) trivializes the fundamental rights guaranteed by the Charter and, secondly, that to interpret "without discrimination" as "without distinction" deprives the notion of discrimination of content. She continued, at p. 607:

Third, it cannot have been the intention of Parliament that the government be put to the requirement of establishing under s. 1 that all laws which draw distinction between people are "demonstrably justified in a free and democratic society." If weighing of the justifiability of unequal treatment is neither required or permitted under s. 15, the result will be that such universally accepted and manifestly desirable legal distinctions as those prohibiting children or drunk persons from driving motor vehicles will be viewed as violations of fundamental rights and be required to run the gauntlet of s. 1.

Finally, it may further be contended that to define discrimination under s. 15 as synonymous with unequal treatment on the basis of personal classification will be to elevate s. 15 to the position of subsuming the other rights and freedoms defined by the Charter.

In rejecting the Hogg approach, I would say that it draws a straight line from the finding of a distinction to a determination of its validity under s. 1, but my objection would be that it virtually denies any role for s. 15(1).

I would reject, as well, the approach adopted by McLachlin J.A. She seeks to define discrimination under s. 15(1) as an unjustifiable or unreasonable distinction. In so doing she avoids the mere distinction test but also makes a radical departure from the analytical approach to the Charter which has been approved by this Court. In the result, the determination would be made under s. 15(1) and virtually no role would be left for s. 1.

The third or "unenumerated and analogous grounds" approach most closely accords with the purposes of s. 15 and the definition of discrimination outlined above and leaves questions of justification to s. 1. However, in assessing whether a complainant's rights have been infringed under s. 15(1), it is not enough to focus only on the alleged ground of discrimination and decide whether or not it is an enumerated or analogous ground. The effect of the impugned distinction or classification on the complainant must be considered. Once it is accepted that not all distinctions and differentiations created by law are discriminatory, then a role must be assigned to s. 15(1) which goes beyond the mere recognition of a legal distinction. A complainant under s. 15(1) must show not only that he or she is not receiving equal treatment before and under the law or that the law has a differential impact on him or her in the protection or benefit accorded by law but, in addition, must show that the legislative impact of the law is discriminatory.

Where discrimination is found a breach of s. 15(1) has occurred and—where s. 15(2) is not applicable—any justification, any consideration of the reasonableness of the enactment; indeed, any consideration of factors which could justify the discrimination and support the constitutionality of the impugned enactment would take place under s. 1. This approach would conform with the directions of this Court in earlier decisions concerning the application of s. 1 and at the same time would allow for the screening out of the obviously trivial and vexatious claim. In this, it would provide a workable approach to the problem.

It would seem to me apparent that a legislative distinction has been made by s. 42 of the Barristers and Solicitors Act between citizens and non-citizens with respect to the practice of law. The distinction would deny admission to the practice of law to non-citizens who in all other respects are qualified. Have the respondents because of s. 42 of the Act been denied equality before and under the law or the equal protection of the law? In practical terms it should be noted that the citizenship requirement affects only those non-citizens who are permanent residents. The permanent resident must wait for a minimum of three years from the date of establishing permanent residence status before citizenship may be acquired. The distinction therefore imposed a burden in the form of some delay on permanent residents who have acquired all or some of their legal training abroad and is, therefore, discriminatory.

The rights guaranteed in s. 15(1) apply to all persons whether citizens or not. A rule which bars an entire class of persons from certain forms of employment, solely on the grounds of a lack of citizenship status and without consideration of educational and professional qualifications or the other attributes or merits of individuals in the group, would, in my view, infringe s. 15 equality rights. Non-citizens, lawfully permanent residents of Canada, are—in the words of the U.S. Supreme Court in *United States* v. *Carolene Products Co.*, 304 U.S. 144 (1938), at pp. 152-53, n. 4, subsequently affirmed in *Graham* v. *Richardson*, 403 U.S. 365 (1971), at p. 372—a good example of a "discrete and insular minority" who come within the protection of s. 15.

SECTION 1

Having accepted the proposition that s. 42 has infringed the right to equality guaranteed in s. 15, it remains to consider whether, under the provisions of s. 1 of the Charter, the citizenship requirement which is clearly prescribed by law is a reasonable limit which can be "demonstrably justified in a free and democratic society."

The onus of justifying the infringement of a guaranteed Charter right must, of course, rest upon the parties seeking to uphold the limitation, in this case, the Attorney General of British Columbia and the Law Society of British Columbia. As is evident from the decisions of this Court, there are two steps involved in the s. 1 inquiry. First, the importance of the objective underlying the impugned law must be assessed. In *Oakes*, it was held that to override a Charter guaranteed right the objective must relate to concerns which are "pressing and substantial" in a free and democratic society. However, given the broad ambit of legislation which must be enacted to cover various aspects of the civil law dealing largely with administrative and regulatory matters and the necessity for the Legislature to make many distinctions between individuals and groups for such purposes, the standard of "pressing and substantial" may be too stringent for application in all cases. To hold otherwise would frequently deny the community-at-large the benefits associated with sound social and economic legislation. In my opinion, in approaching a case such as the one before us, the first question the Court should ask must relate to the nature and the purpose of the enactment, with a view to deciding whether the limitation represents a legitimate exercise of the legislative power for the attainment of a desirable social objective which would warrant overriding constitutionally protected rights. The second step in a s. 1 inquiry involves a proportionality test whereby the Court must attempt to balance a number of factors. The Court must examine the nature of the right, the extent of its infringement, and the degree to which the limitation furthers the attainment of the desirable goal embodied in the legislation. Also involved in the inquiry will be the importance of the right to the individual or group concerned, and the broader social impact of both the impugned law and its alternatives. As the Chief Justice has stated in *R. v. Edwards Books and Art Ltd., supra*, at pp. 768-69:

> Both in articulating the standard of proof and in describing the criteria comprising the proportionality requirement the Court has been careful to avoid rigid and inflexible standards.

I agree with this statement. There is no single test under s. 1; rather, the Court must carefully engage in the balancing of many factors in determining whether an infringement is reasonable and demonstrably justified.

The section 15(1) guarantee is the broadest of all guarantees. It applies to and supports all other rights guaranteed by the Charter. However, it must be recognized that Parliament and the Legislatures have a right and a duty to make laws for the whole community: in this process, they must make innumerable legislative distinctions and categorizations in the pursuit of the role of government. When making distinctions between groups and individuals to achieve desirable social goals, it will rarely be possible to say of any legislative distinction that it is clearly the right legislative choice or that it is clearly a wrong one. As stated by the Chief Justice in *R. v. Edwards Books and Art Ltd.*, at pp. 781-82:

> A *"reasonable limit"* is one which, having regard to the principles enunciated in Oakes, it was reasonable for the legislature to impose. The Courts are not called upon to substitute judicial opinions for legislative ones as to the place at which to draw a precise line.

In dealing with the many problems that arise legislatures must not be held to the standard of perfection, for in such matters perfection is unattainable. I would repeat the words of my colleague, La Forest J., in *R. v. Edwards Books and Art Ltd.*, at p. 795:

> By the foregoing, I do not mean to suggest that this Court should, as a general rule, defer to legislative judgments when those judgments trench upon rights considered fundamental in a free and democratic society. Quite the contrary, I would have thought the Charter established the opposite regime. On the other hand, having accepted the importance of the legislative objective, one must in the present context recognize that if the legis-

lative goal is to be achieved, it will inevitably be achieved to the detriment of some. Moreover, attempts to protect the rights of one group will also inevitably impose burdens on the rights of other groups. There is no perfect scenario in which the rights of all can be equally protected.

In seeking to achieve a goal that is demonstrably justified in a free and democratic society, therefore, a legislature must be given reasonable room to manoeuvre to meet these conflicting pressures.

DISPOSITION

. . . There is no difficulty in determining that in general terms the Barristers and Solicitors Act of British Columbia is a statute enacted for a valid and desirable social purpose, the creation and regulation of the legal profession and the practice of law. The narrower question, however, is whether the requirement that only citizens be admitted to the practice of law in British Columbia serves a desirable social purpose of sufficient importance to warrant overriding the equality guarantee. It is incontestable that the legal profession plays a very significant—in fact, a fundamentally important—role in the administration of justice, both in the criminal and the civil law. I would not attempt to answer the question arising from the judgments below as to whether the function of the profession may be termed judicial or quasijudicial, but I would observe that in the absence of an independent legal profession, skilled and qualified to play its part in the administration of justice and the judicial process, the whole legal system would be in a parlous state. In the performance of what may be called his private function, that is, in advising on legal matters and in representing clients before the courts and other tribunals, the lawyer is accorded great powers not permitted to other professionals. As pointed out by Taylor J. at first instance, by the use of the subpoena which he alone can procure on behalf of another, he can compel attendance upon examinations before

trial and at trial upon pain of legal sanction for refusal. He may, as well, require the production of documents and records for examination and use in the proceedings. He may in some cases require the summoning of jurors, the sittings of courts and, in addition, he may make the fullest inquiry into the matters before the court with a full privilege against actions for slander arising out of his conduct in the court. The solicitor is also bound by the solicitor and client privilege against the disclosure of communications with his client concerning legal matters. This is said to be the only absolute privilege known to the law. Not only may the solicitor decline to disclose solicitor and client communications, the courts will not permit him to do so. This is a privilege against all comers, including the Crown, save where the disclosure of a crime would be involved. The responsibilities involved in its maintenance and in its breach where crimes are concerned are such that citizenship with its commitment to the welfare of the whole community is not an unreasonable requirement for the practice of law. While it may be arguable whether the lawyer exercises a judicial, quasijudicial, or governmental role, it is clear that at his own discretion he can invoke the full force and authority of the State in procuring and enforcing judgments or other remedial measures which may be obtained. It is equally true that in defending an action he has the burden of protecting his client from the imposition of such state authority and power. By any standard, these powers and duties are vital to the maintenance of order in our society and the due administration of the law in the interest of the whole community.

The lawyer has, as well, what may be termed a public function. Governments at all levels, federal, provincial and municipal, rely extensively upon lawyers, both in technical and policy matters. In the drafting of legislation, regulations, treaties, agreements and other governmental documents and papers lawyers play a major role. In various aspects of this work they are called upon to advise upon legal and constitutional questions which frequently go to the very heart of the governmental role. To discharge these duties, familiarity is required with Canadian history, constitutional law, regional differences and concerns within the country and, in fact, with the whole Canadian governmental and political process. It is entirely reasonable, then, that legislators consider and adopt measures designed to maintain within the legal profession a body of qualified professionals with a commitment to the country and to the fulfillment of the important tasks which fall to it.

McLachlin J.A. was of the view that the citizenship requirement would not ensure familiarity with Canadian institutions and customs, nor would it ensure a commitment to Canada going beyond one involved in the concept of allegiance, as recognized by the taking of an oath of allegiance. I would agree with her that the desired results would not be insured by the citizenship requirement but I would observe, at the same time, that no law will ever ensure anything. To abolish the requirement of citizenship on the basis that it would fail to insure the attainment of its objectives would, in my view, be akin to abolishing the law against theft, for it has certainly not insured the elimination of that crime. Citizenship, however, which requires the taking on of obligations and commitments to the community, difficult sometimes to describe but felt and understood by most citizens, as well as the rejection of past loyalties may reasonably be said to conduce to the desired result.

I would observe, as well, that the comment of McLachlin J.A. that the citizenship requirement was first adopted in British Columbia in 1971 requires some explanation. I do not think that the historical argument should be pushed too far: things need not always remain as once they were although, as noted in *R.* v. *Big M. Drug Mart Ltd.* and *Reference re Public Service Employee Relations Act (Alta.), supra,* Charter construction should be consistent with the history, traditions and social philosophies of our society. The concept of citizenship has been a requirement for entry into the legal profession in British Columbia from its earliest days. When the Law Society was formed in 1874 the profession was open to British subjects. At that time, the idea of a separate Canadian citizenship, as distinct from the general classification of British subject which included Canadians, was scarcely known—though as early as 1910, Immigration Act, S.C. 1910, c. 27, the term "Canadian citizen" was defined for the purpose of the Immigration Act as a "British subject who has Canadian domicile." The concept of citizenship in those early days was embodied in the expression, British Subject, and thus it was recognized as a requirement for entry into the legal profession in British Columbia. As Canada moved away from its colonial past, a separate identity for Canadians emerged and in 1946 with the passage of The Canadian Citizenship Act, S.C. 1946, c. 15, the term, Canadian citizen, was formally recognized, giving effect to what had long been felt and accepted by most Canadians. In adopting the term as a qualification for entry into the legal profession in British Columbia, the Legislature was merely continuing its earlier requirement that the concept of citizenship, as then recognized in the term "British subject," be necessary for entry into the profession.

Public policy, of which the citizenship requirement in the Barristers and Solicitors Act is an element, is for the Legislature to establish. The role of the Charter, as applied by the courts, is to ensure that in applying public policy the Legislature does not adopt measures which are not sustainable under the Charter. It is not, however, for the courts to legislate or to substitute their views on public policy for those of the Legislature. I would repeat for ease of reference the words of the Chief Justice in *R.* v. *Edwards Books and Art, supra,* at pp. 781-82:

A *"reasonable limit"* is one which hav-

ing regard to the principles enunciated in Oakes, *it was reasonable for the Legislature to impose. The courts are not called upon to substitute judicial opinions for legislative ones as to the place at which to draw a precise line.*

The function of the Court is to measure the legislative enactment against the requirements of the Charter and where the enactment infringes the Charter, in this case the provisions of s. 15(1), and is not sustainable under s. 1, the remedial power of the Court is set out in s. 52 of the Constitution Act, 1982 ". . . any law that is inconsistent with the provisions of the Constitution is, to the extent of the inconsistency, of no force or effect."

The essence of s. 1 is found in the expression "reasonable" and it is for the Court to decide if s. 42 of the Barristers and Solicitors Act of British Columbia is a reasonable limit. In reaching the conclusion that it is, I would say that the legislative choice in this regard is not one between an answer that is clearly right and one that is clearly wrong. Either position may well be sustainable and, as noted by the Chief Justice, *supra*, the Court is not called upon to substitute its opinions as to where to draw the line. The Legislature in fixing public policy has chosen the cit-

izenship requirement and, unless the Court can find that choice unreasonable, it has no power under the Charter to strike it down or, as has been said, no power to invade the legislative field and substitute its views for that of the Legislature. In my view, the citizenship requirement is reasonable and sustainable under s. 1. It is chosen for the achievement of a desirable social goal: one aspect of the due regulation and qualification of the legal profession. This is an objective of importance and the measure is not disproportionate to the object to be attained. The maximum delay imposed upon the non-citizen from the date of acquisition of permanent resident status is three years. It will frequently be less. No impediment is put in the way of obtaining citizenship. In fact, the policy of the Canadian government is to encourage the newcomer to become a citizen. It is reasonable, in my view, to expect that the newcomer who seeks to gain the privileges and status within the land and the right to exercise the great powers that admission to the practice of law will give should accept citizenship and its obligations as well as its advantages and benefits. I would therefore allow the appeal and restore the judgment at trial. . . .

D. Language and Cultural Rights

53. Ottawa Separate Schools Trustees *v.* Mackell, *1917*

~ The B.N.A. Act contains only two sections explicitly recognizing constitutional rights of groups or individuals. These are sections 93 and 133. The rights enshrined in these sections do not take the form of abstract universal rights but are specific to the Canadian historical experience reflecting the accommodation of European cultures upon which Confederation was based. The two cases set out below display contrasting styles of constitutional interpretation. The *Mackell* case shows how the Privy Council gave the narrowest possible interpretation of the minority education right in section 93, whereas the Supreme Court in the *Blaikie* case expressed an intention to give the broadest possible construction of the minority language right in section 133.

Section 93 provided generally that no law should prejudicially affect rights to denominational schools enjoyed by any group at the time of Confederation and specifically that the Protestants in Quebec should have the same school rights as were enjoyed by Ontario Catholics at the time of union. This guarantee of denominational schools was varied slightly for the prairie provinces when they became part of Canada and a more extensive guarantee covering the post-secondary level was included in Newfoundland's Terms of Union in 1949. The Privy Council, not the Supreme Court, has played the decisive role in determining the scope of section 93.

Historically, the most important decisions on this section occurred in the *Barrett* case[1] in 1892 when the Privy Council reversed the Supreme Court of Canada and upheld Manitoba's Public Schools Act which replaced a denominational school system with a system of secular public schools. In the Privy Council's view the fact that Roman Catholics were still free to send their children to separate schools providing they were willing and able to pay for these schools in addition to contributing to the tax supported public school system was sufficient to satisfy the constitutional right to denominational education. The Privy Council opinion, written by Lord MacNaghten, expressed a preference for a national school system. In his view, such a system would be endangered if section 93 were extended to protect religious minorities from paying an economic penalty for denominational education.

Subsequently, in the *Brophy*[2] case, the Privy Council upheld the right of

---

[1] (1892) A.C. 445.
[2] (1895) A.C. 202.

Manitoba's disgruntled Catholic minority under section 93 to appeal to the federal cabinet for remedial legislation. The Conservative government introduced a Remedial Bill but before it could be enacted a general election took place which was won by the Laurier Liberals who, on provincial rights grounds, opposed federal intervention in education matters. This series of events, in which the Privy Council's decisions played a prominent part, was a major cause of the failure of Western Canada to develop along bicultural lines.

The *Mackell* case raised the important question of whether section 93 could provide any protection for minority language rights in education. In the early years of this century Ontario's English majority felt threatened by the growth of the province's French population and took steps to eliminate the use of French as a means of instruction in both public and separate schools. In Ottawa the trustees of the separate schools which served a largely French-speaking population refused to open the schools but were taken to court by English-speaking separate school supporters. In response, the Ottawa trustees claimed that the Ontario regulations restricting the use of French violated their right under section 93 to determine "the kind and description" of denominational schools. The Privy Council rejected the trustees' argument and upheld the Ontario regulations. The judgment categorically denied that section 93 had anything to do with language rights: "The only section in the British North America Act, 1867 which relates to the use of the English or French languages (s. 133) does not relate to education and is directed to an entirely different subject matter."

There was historical justice and legal continuity in the decision of Quebec's Superior Court some sixty years after Mackell upholding the education provisions of Quebec's Bill 22. Like the earlier Ontario regulations this legislation was based on fear for the survival of the majority culture in the province. However, it was not nearly as repressive of minority education rights as the Ontario regulations had been. Nonetheless, it was attacked in the courts on section 93 grounds. Quebec's Chief Justice Deschenes dismissed the constitutional challenge on the grounds that section 93 is concerned with religious education not the language of education.[3] His decision was not appealed.

Section 23 of the Charter of Rights and Freedoms for the first time, gave parents a constitutional right to educate their children in the official language of their choice. The right is extended to all citizens whose first language is English or French or who were educated in Canada in either language. It is available in all provinces wherever numbers warrant and includes the right to minority educational facilities provided out of public funds. This section of the Charter will fully apply to Quebec if and when Quebec's legislative assembly or government agrees to it.[4] In the meantime, English-speaking Canadians have a

---

[3] *Protestant School Board of Greater Montreal* v. *Minister of Education of Quebec* 83 D.L.R. (3d) 645 (1978).

[4] This is provided for in section 58 of the Constitutional Act, 1982.

constitutional right to place their children in that province's English schools, only if they or one of their children have attended English schools in Canada. In its second decision on the Charter, the Supreme Court struck down sections of Quebec's Bill 101 which violated this right.[5] ~

OTTAWA ROMAN CATHOLIC SEPARATE SCHOOL *v.* MACKELL
In the Privy Council. [1917] A.C. 62; II Olmsted.

The judgment of their Lordships was delivered by

LORD BUCKMASTER L.C. This appeal raises an important question as to the validity of a Circular of Instructions issued by the Department of Education for the Province of Ontario on August 17, 1913.

The primary schools within the province are for the purposes of this circular separated into two divisions, public schools and separate schools, the latter, with which alone this appeal is concerned, being denominational schools, established, supported, and managed under certain statutory provisions to which reference will be made. The population of the province is, and has always been, composed both of English and of French-speaking inhabitants, and each of the two classes of schools is attended by children who speak some one language, some the other, while some, again, have the good fortune to speak both, so that distinction in language does not and cannot be made to follow the distinction in the schools themselves. The circular in some of its clauses deals with all schools, but its heading refers only to English-French schools, which it defines as being those schools, whether separate or public, where French is a language of instruction or communication, which have been marked out by the Minister for inspection as provided by the circular.

The object of the circular is to restrict the use of French in these schools, and to this restriction the appellants, who are the Board of Trustees of the Roman Catholic Separate Schools of the city of Ottawa, assert that they are not obliged to submit. The respondents, who are supporters of the same Roman Catholic schools, desire to maintain the Circular of Instructions in its integrity, and upon the appellants' refusal to abide by its terms the respondents instituted against them the proceedings out of which this appeal has arisen, asking, among other things, a mandatory order enforcing against the appellants obedience to the circular.

The Supreme Court of Ontario granted the injunction that was sought, and their judgment was affirmed by the unanimous opinion of the judges of the Appellant Division of the Supreme Court.

The appellants' defence to the action rests in substance upon the contention that the instructions were, and are, wholly unauthorized and unwarranted and beyond the powers of the Minister of Education because they were contrary to, and in violation, of the British North America Act, 1867. The number of schools which are affected by the dispute is considerable, for of 192 Roman Catholic schools under the charge of the appellants 116 have been designated English-French schools.

The material sections in the British North America Act upon which the appellants rely are ss. 91, 92, and 93. Section 91 authorizes the Parliament of Canada to make laws for the peace, order and good government of Canada in relation to all matters not coming within the classes of subjects by the Act assigned

[5] See case 55 below.

exclusively to the Legislatures of the provinces. Section 92 enumerates the classes of subjects in relation to which the Legislatures of the provinces may exclusively make laws, and includes therein generally all matters of a merely local or private nature in the province. Section 93 deals specifically with education, and enacts that in and for each province the Legislature may exclusively make laws in relation to education, subject and according to the provisions therein contained. It appears, therefore, that the subject of education is excluded from the powers conferred on the Parliament of Canada, and is placed wholly within the competence of the provincial Legislatures, who again are subject to limitations expressed in four provisions. Provision 1 is in these terms: "Nothing in any such law shall prejudicially affect any right or privilege with respect to denominational schools which any class of persons have by law in the province at the Union."

Provision 3 contains an important safeguard, which gives an appeal to the Governor-General in Council from any act or decision of any provincial authority affecting any right or privilege of the Protestant or Roman Catholic minority of the King's subjects in relation to education. Provision 4 provides machinery for making the decision of the Governor-General in Council effective. If a provincial law which seems to the Governor-General in Council requisite for the due execution of the provisions of the section is not made, or any decision of the Governor-General in Council is not duly executed by the proper provincial authority, then and in every such case, and so far only as the circumstances of each case require, the Parliament of Canada may make remedial laws for the due execution of the provisions of this section, and of any decision of the Governor-General in Council under the section. . . .

There is no question that the English-French Roman Catholic separate schools in Ottawa are denominational schools to which the provision applies, and it has been decided by this Board that the right or privilege reserved in the provision is a legal right or privilege, and does not include any practice, instruction, or privilege of a voluntary character which at the date of the passing of the Act might be in operation: *City of Winnipeg* v. *Barrett.* Further, the class of persons to whom the right or privilege is reserved must, in their Lordships' opinion, be a class of persons determined according to religious belief, and not according to race or language. In relation to denominational teaching, Roman Catholics together form within the meaning of the section a class of persons, and that class cannot be subdivided into other classes by considerations of the language of the people by whom that faith is held. . . .

Now it appears that at the date of the passing of the British North America Act, 1867, a statute was in operation in Upper Canada by which certain legal rights and privileges were conferred on Roman Catholics in Upper Canada in respect to separate schools, and so far as the facts of this case are concerned this was the only source from which the rights and privileges could have proceeded.

This Act enabled any number of people, not less than five and being Roman Catholic, to convene a public meeting of persons who desire to establish a separate school for Roman Catholics, and for the election of trustees for the management of such schools; by s. 7 it is enacted that the trustees of such schools should form a body corporate under the statute, should have power to impose, levy, and collect school rates or subscriptions from persons sending children to, or subscribing towards the support of, such schools, and should have "all the powers in respect of separate schools that the trustees of common schools have and possess under the provisions of the Act relating to common schools." A special clause also related to the appointment of teachers, who, before the passing of this statute, had been arbitrarily appointed by boards of trustees, and this power was regulated and restricted by s. 13, which provided that the teachers of the separate schools should be subject to the same examinations and receive their certificate of qualification in the same manner as common school teachers; while s. 26 provided that the schools should be subject to inspection, and should be subject also "to such regulations as may be imposed from time to time by the Council of Public Instruction for Upper Canada."

In order, therefore, to ascertain the true extent and limit of the powers conferred by this statute it is necessary to see what were the powers enjoyed by trustees of the common schools. These are to be found in another statute of Upper Canada, 22 Vict. c. 64, known as the Common Schools Act, 1859. This statute conferred upon trustees for common schools (now called public schools) certain powers, the most important of which are to be found collected under several heads in s. 79. A mere glance at this section will show that such powers are undoubtedly wide. They include under sub-s. 7 power to acquire school sites and premises, and to do what may seem right for procuring textbooks and establishing school libraries, while sub-s. 8 places in the hands of the trustees the determination of "the kind and description of schools to be established," the teachers to be employed, and generally the terms of their employment. These powers are, however, to some extent limited by sub-ss. 15 and 16, the first of which in effect requires that the textbooks should be a uniform series of authorized textbooks, while the latter compels the trustees to see that all the schools under their charge are conducted according to the authorized regulations.

Counsel for the appellants naturally place great reliance upon these provisions, and in the wider aspect of their argument they contend that "the kind of school" that the trustees are authorized to provide is a school where education is to be given in such language as the trustees think fit. They urge that it was a right or privilege possessed with respect to denominational schools in 1867 in determining the number and kind of schools to

say within what limits the French language is to be used; for, according to their contention, "kind of school" means a school where the French language, under the direction of trustees, may be used as a medium of instruction on terms not less favourable than the use of English. Their Lordships are unable to agree with this view. The "kind" of school referred to in sub-s. 8 of s. 79 is, in their opinion, the grade or character of school, for example, "a girls' school," "a boys' school," or "an infants' school," and a "kind" of school, within the meaning of that subsection, is not a school where any special language is in common use.

The schools must be conducted in accordance with the regulations, and their Lordships can find nothing in the statute to take away from the authority that had power to issue regulations the power of directing in what language education is to be given. If, therefore, the trustees of the common schools would be bound to obey a regulation which directed that education should, subject to certain restrictions, be given in either English or French, the trustees of the separate schools would also be bound to obey a regulation of the same character affecting their school, provided that it does not interfere with a right or privilege reserved under the Act of 1867, i.e., a right or privilege attached to denominational teaching.

The objections to the instructions which were urged before their Lordships, however, were not chiefly based on the allegation that they prejudicially affected in any special manner denominational teaching, but on the wider ground. Their Lordships appreciate the affection which the French-speaking residents in Ottawa feel for the French language; but it must not be forgotten that, although a majority of the supporters of the English-French separate schools in Ottawa are of French origin, there are other supporters to whom French is not the natural language. This fact has no doubt caused great difficulty in adjusting fairly as between the different inhabitants the natural rivalry as to the languages to be used in the education of the children, and the care with which this difficulty has been considered is evidenced in the terms of a valuable report which is printed in the record and to which their Lordships would direct attention:

As was stated in our former report, while all classes of the French people are not willing but desirous that their children should learn the English language, they at the same time wish them to retain the use of their own language, and there is no reason why they should not do so. To possess the knowledge of both languages is an advantage to them. And the use of the English language instead of their own, if such a change should ever take place, must be brought about by the operation of the same influences which are making it all over this continent the language of other nationalities as tenacious of their native tongue as the French. It is a change that cannot be forced. To attempt to deprive a people of the use of their native tongue would be as unwise as it would be unjust, even if it were possible. In the British Empire there are people of many languages. The use of these does not affect the loyalty of the people to the Crown, and the English language remains the language of the Empire. The object of these schools is to make better scholars of the rising generation of French children, and to enable them to do better for themselves by teaching them English, while leaving them free to make such use of their own language as they please.

It therefore becomes necessary to examine closely the terms of the circular in order to ascertain the nature and extent of the restrictions it imposes. . . .

Clause 3 regulates the use of French as the language of instruction and communication, and it is against these provisions that the complaint of the appellants is mainly directed. The clause refers equally to public and separate schools, and directs that modifications shall be made in the course of study in both classes of schools, subject to the direction and approval of the chief inspector. In the case of French-speaking pupils, French, where necessary, may be used as the language of instruction and communication, but not beyond Form I, except on the approval of the chief inspector in the case of pupils beyond Form I who are unable to speak and understand the English language. There are further provisions for a special course in English for French-speaking pupils, and for French as a subject of study in public and separate schools.

Mr. Belcourt urged that so to regulate use of the French language in the separate Roman Catholic schools in Ottawa constituted an interference, and is in some way inconsistent with a natural right vested in the French-speaking population; but unless this right was one of those reserved by the Act of 1867, such interference could not be resisted, and their Lordships have already expressed the view that people joined together by the union of language and not by the ties of faith do not form a class of persons within the meaning of the Act. If the other opinion were adopted, there appears to be no reason why a similar claim should not be made on behalf of the English-speaking parents whose children are being educated in the Roman Catholic separate schools in Ottawa. In this connection it is worthy of notice that the only section in the British North America Act, 1867, which relates to the use of the English and French languages (s. 133), does not relate to education and is directed to an entirely different subject matter. It authorizes the use of either the English or French language in debates in the Houses of Parliament in Canada and the Houses of Legislature in Quebec, and by any person, or in any pleading or process in, or issuing from, any Court of Canada, and in and from all or any of the Courts of Quebec. If any inference is to be drawn from this section, it would not be in favour of the contention of the appellants.

Further objections that are taken to the circular depend upon these considerations, that it interferes with the right to manage which the trustees possess, and that it further infringes a right on the part of the trustees to appoint teachers whose certificates are provided by a board of whom the trustees can appoint one.

In their Lordships' view there is no substance in either of these contentions. The right to manage does not involve the right of determining the language to be used in the schools.

In the result, their Lordships are of opinion that, on the construction of the Acts and documents before them, the regulations impeached were duly made and approved under the authority of the Department of Education and became binding according to the terms of those provisions on the appellants and the schools under their control, and they will humbly advise His Majesty to dismiss this appeal.

54. Attorney General of Quebec v. Blaikie, *1979*

~ Section 133 of the B.N.A. Act established a limited bilingual regime at the federal level of government and for the Province of Quebec. It provided (a) that either English or French may be used in debates in the federal and Quebec legislatures; (b) that both languages shall be used in the records of these legislatures; (c) that either language may be used in courts established by the federal government or in the courts of Quebec; and (d) that Acts passed by the federal or Quebec legislature be printed and published in English and French. When Manitoba entered Confederation in 1870 it was made subject to the same bilingual requirements as section 133 applied to Quebec.

Section 133 has been the source of very little litigation. The Supreme Court dealt with it for the first time in 1975 in the *Jones*[1] case when it upheld the validity of the federal Official Languages Act. This legislation represented the major effort of the federal government to implement the recommendations of the Royal Commission on Bilingualism and Biculturalism. In providing for a much more thoroughly bilingual regime in the executive branch of the federal government it went beyond the constitutional requirements of section 133. It was on this basis that Mayor Jones of Moncton challenged the constitutional validity of the Act. The Supreme Court ruled against Mayor Jones, pointing out that section 133 set limits on the contraction of language rights but not on their enlargement. It based the constitutional validity of the Act on the residual use of Parliament's peace, order and good government power.

At issue in the *Blaikie* case was Chapter III of Title I of Quebec's Charter of the French Language. This part of the Charter dealing with the language of the legislature and the courts was much more vulnerable to constitutional challenge than were the education provisions of the Charter. However, it had been carefully drafted to minimize conflict with section 133. It declared French to be the official language of the legislature and the courts, but did not ban the use of English in these institutions. Statutes and regulations would continue to be printed in both languages, but only the French version would be official. Individuals could continue to plead their case in English, but corporate bodies would have to use French unless all the parties involved agreed to the use of English. If there was any conflict with section 133, the Quebec government hoped that the courts would find that section 133 so far as it pertains to Quebec was part of the province's constitution and therefore subject to provincial legislative jurisdiction under section 92(1).

The Quebec courts and, on appeal, the Supreme Court of Canada rejected the Quebec government's arguments and found the impugned provisions of Quebec's Language Charter *ultra vires*. The Supreme Court regarded section 133 as an entrenched provision of the B.N.A. Act which neither the federal Parliament nor the Quebec legislature could unilaterally modify. It thus clearly repudiated the exhaustion theory which holds that no power of self-government

[1] [1975] 2 S.C.R. 1982.

is withheld from both levels of government.

In finding conflict between the Quebec Charter and section 133 the Supreme Court gave a very broad interpretation of that section. It justified a broad and flexible approach to constitutional guarantees by citing some exceptional dicta from Privy Council opinions which emphasized the need to interpret the constitution so that it can be kept in tune with changing circumstances. The Court's interpretation of the rights protected in section 133 was expansive in four respects. First, it was not enough for statutes to be printed and published in both languages. Both versions had to have official status, otherwise laws would not be "enacted" in both languages. Secondly, not just Acts passed by the legislature but all of the regulations and subordinate legislation enacted under the authority of Acts must be in English and French. Thirdly, the right of a "person" to use English or French in the courts of Quebec extended to artificial persons, such as corporations. Finally, the "Courts of Quebec" was interpreted to mean administrative agencies exercising adjudicative responsibilities as well as the regular courts.

At the same time as the Court decided the *Blaikie* case it also decided the *Forest*[2] case which raised similar questions concerning the denial of minority language rights in Manitoba. Although the outcome of the *Forest* case was the same as *Blaikie*—the challenged sections of Manitoba's Official Language Act were found to be unconstitutional—the circumstances differed from those in *Blaikie* in several respects. The Manitoba legislation which, in effect, was a charter of the English language, was not recent. It had been in force since 1890 despite several successful court challenges at the lower court level. Also it was more extreme than Quebec's Charter in suppressing minority language rights: it forbad the use of French in the records and journals of the legislature and in court proceedings and provided that the Acts of the legislature be printed and published in English only.[3]

The Charter of Rights expands official language rights slightly beyond section 133. Section 16 declares English and French to be the official languages of Canada and of New Brunswick, and sections 17 to 19 in effect extend the constitutional guarantees of section 133 to New Brunswick. Section 20 is a significant addition in that it creates a constitutional right to use either of the official languages in dealing with the executive branch of government and in receiving government services. At the federal level this right applies only to communication with a "head or central office' and where either there is sufficient demand for services in both languages or the nature of the services makes bilingualism appropriate. While these limitations do not apply to the right in New Brunswick, still section 20 is a significant step in converting

---

[2] [1979] 2 S.C.R. 1032.

[3] See case 56 below for the Supreme Court's involvement in the problems which arose in securing Manitoba's compliance with this decision.

statutory rights under the Official Languages Act into constitutional rights.

The language rights which the Supreme Court has held to be entrenched in section 133 will continue to apply to Manitoba and Quebec. For the other provinces (with the exception, of course, of New Brunswick) there are no entrenched language of government rights. In its 1988 *Mercure* decision,[4] the Supreme Court ruled that Saskatchewan (and by implication, Alberta) were legally bound to abide by the language guarantees of section 110 of the Northwest Territories Act of 1886. Section 110 created the same kind of bilingual regime as s. 23 of the Manitoba Act (1870), except that it allowed for subsequent unilateral amendment or repeal by the provincial legislatures. Following the Court's ruling, both the Saskatchewan and Alberta governments enacted new legislation repealing their s. 110 obligations and affirming the validity of their English-only statutes. Saskatchewan did commit itself to translating some of its more important statutes into French, and the Federal government agreed to pay the costs. Alberta, however, made no such commitment. Both provinces did provide for increased use of French in the courts and legislative debates, but were still widely criticized for violating the "spirit" of the Meech Lake Accord. A notable exception was Quebec Premier Robert Bourrassa, who actually praised the Saskatchewan government's "go slow" approach to language rights. Eight months later the same Premier Bourassa invoked the section 33 override to avoid complying with the Supreme Court's decision in the *Ford* and *Devine* cases.[5]~

ATTORNEY GENERAL OF QUEBEC v. BLAIKIE
In the Supreme Court of Canada. [1979] 2 S.C.R. 1016.

THE COURT: In detailed and extensive reasons for judgment, delivered on January 23, 1978 ([1978] C.S. 37, 85 D.L.R. (3d) 252), Deschênes C.J. of the Quebec Superior Court granted a declaration sought by the plaintiffs Blaikie, Durand and Goldstein that Chapter III of Title I of the Charter of the French lanaguage, 1977 (Que.), c. 5, being ss. 7 to 13 of that Statute, was *ultra vires* the Legislature of Quebec. He held that the challenged statutory provisions were in direct violation of s. 133 of the British North America Act and that it was beyond the competence of the Quebec Legislature to modify unilaterally the prescriptions of that section. . .

A seven-Judge Quebec Court of Appeal unanimously affirmed the judgment of Deschênes C.J. . . . Leave was sought and given to the Attorney General of Quebec to argue the issue of constitutionality here, the following question being posed for determination:

Are the provisions of Chapter III of Title One of the Charter of the French language (L.Q. 1977, ch. 5) entitled "The Language of the Legislature and the Courts" unconstitutional, ultra vires or inoperative to the extent that they violate the provisions of Section 133 of the British North America Act (1867)?

[4] *Mercure* v. *A.G. Saskatchewan* [1988] 1 S.C.R. 234.
[5] See case 52, above.

The Attorney General of Canada had been an intervenor before the Quebec Superior Court and before the Quebec Court of Appeal, supporting the claim of the plaintiffs. He took the same position as intervenor here. In addition, the Attorney General of Manitoba intervened to support the appellant and the Attorney General of New Brunswick intervened in support of the respondents. A late intervention in support of the respondents was allowed to Georges Forest, who was the successful party in the Manitoba Court of Appeal in attacking the validity of The Official Language Act, 1890 (Man.). . .

Chapter III of Title I of the Charter of the French language, entitled "The Language of the Legislature and of the Courts," reads as follows:

7. French is the language of the legislature and the courts in Quebec.

8. Legislative bills shall be drafted in the official language. They shall also be tabled in the Assemblée nationale, passed and assented to in that language.

9. Only the French text of the statutes and regulations is official.

10. An English version of every legislative bill, statute and regulation shall be printed and published by the civil administration.

11. Artificial persons addressing themselves to the courts and to bodies discharging judicial or quasi-judicial functions shall do so in the official language, and shall use the official language in pleading before them unless all the parties to the action agree to their pleading in English.

12. Procedural documents issued by bodies discharging judicial or quasi-judicial functions or drawn up and sent by the advocates practising before them shall be drawn up in the official language. Such documents may, however, be drawn up in another language if the natural person for whose intention they are issued expressly consents thereto.

13. The judgments rendered in Quebec by the courts and by bodies discharging judicial or quasi-judicial functions must be drawn up in French or be accompanied with a duly authenticated French version. Only the French version of the judgment is official.

The competence of the Quebec Legislature to enact all or any part of the foregoing provisions, in the face of s. 133 of the British North America Act, was asserted by the appellant mainly in reliance upon s. 92(1) of the British North America Act, which was said to provide adequate authority for the challenged provisions. A subsidiary contention of the appellant was that the challenged provisions were not incompatible with s. 133. Section 133 and s. 92(1) are in the following terms:

133. Either the English or the French Language may be used by any Person in the Debates of the Houses of the Parliament of Canada and of the Houses of the Legislature of Quebec; and both those Languages shall be used in the respective Records and Journals of those Houses; and either of those Languages may be used by any Person or in any Pleading or Process in or issuing from any Court of Canada established under this Act, and in or from all or any of the Courts of Quebec.

The Acts of the Parliament of Canada and of the Legislature of Quebec shall be printed and published in both those Languages.

92. In each Province the Legislature may exclusively make Laws in relation to Matters coming within the Classes of Subjects next herein-after enumerated: that is to say,—

1. The Amendment from Time to Time, notwithstanding anything in this Act, of the Constitution of the Province, except as regards the Office of Lieutenant Governor.

Chapter III of Title I of the Charter of the French language is a particular projection of s. 1 of Chapter 1, Title I, of this statute which declares that "French is the official language of Quebec." This Court is concerned here only with the particular, and nothing in these reasons is to be taken as passing upon the validity of any other provisions of the enactment. . . .

Sections 8 and 9 of the Charter of the French language, reproduced above, are not easy to reconcile with s. 133 which not only provides but requires that official status be given to both French and English in respect of the printing and publication of the Statutes of the Legislature of Quebec. It was urged before this Court that there was no requirement of enactment in both languages, as contrasted with printing and publishing. However, if full weight is given to every word of s. 133 it becomes apparent that this requirement is implicit. What is required to be printed and published in both languages is described as "Acts" and texts do not become "Acts" without enactment. Statutes can only be known by being printed and published in connection with their enactment so that Bills be transformed into Acts. Moreover, it would be strange to have a requirement, as in s. 133, that both English and French "shall be used in the . . . Records and Journals" of the Houses (there were then two) of the Quebec Legislature and not to have this requirement extend to the enactment of legislation.

So, too, is there incompatibility when ss. 11 and 12 of the Charter would compel artificial persons to use French alone and make it the only official language of "procedural documents" in judicial or quasi-judicial proceedings, while section 133 gives persons involved in proceedings in the Courts of Quebec the option to use either French or English in any pleading or process. Whether s. 133 covers the process of "bodies discharging judicial or quasi-judicial functions," whether it covers the issuing and publication of judgments of the Courts and decisions of "judicial or quasi-judicial" tribunals, and also whether it embraces delegated legislation will be considered later.

The central issue in this case, reflected in the question posed for determination by this Court, is whether the Legislature of Quebec may unilaterally amend or modify the provisions of s. 133 in so far as they relate to the Legislature and Courts of Quebec. It was the contention of the appellant that the language of the Legislature and of the Courts of Quebec is part of the Constitution of the Province and hence is within the unilateral amending or modifying authority of the Legislature under s. 92(1). Emphasis was, understandably, placed on the words in s. 92(1) "notwithstanding anything in this Act."

What is meant by "the Constitution of the Province" is not defined or described in any enacting terms of the British North America Act. . . .

~ The Court then reviewed arguments which would limit "the Constitution of the Province" to Part V of the B.N.A. Act which is sub-titled "Provincial Constitutions" and includes ss. 58 to 90 of the Act. The Court then considered counter-arguments, pointing to sections outside of Part V, such as s. 128 (a section concerning oaths of allegiance before the Governor General or before the Lieutenant-Governor of a province by members of the federal or provincial legislatures) which could be part of the constitution of the province. ~

It does not seem necessary to come to a determination whether s. 128 is part of the Constitution of the Province and amendable as such under s. 92(1), so as to lend support to the appellant's contention of the amendability by unilateral action of s. 133. The reasons for this transcend even the widest operation of s. 92(1) and are cogently set out in the judgment of Deschênes C.J., followed by the Quebec Court of Appeal. He found that s. 133 is not part of the Constitution of the Province within s. 92(1) but is rather part of the Constitution of Canada and Quebec in an indivisible sense, giving official status to French and English in the Parliament and in the Courts of Canada as well as in the Legislature and Courts of Quebec. . . .

There is, moreover, another consideration noticed in the Courts below which should also be brought into account. In *Jones* v. *Attorney General of New*

Brunswick ([1975] 2 S.C.R. 182), which concerned the validity of the federal Official Languages Act, the Court had this to say about s. 133 (at pp. 192-3):

. . . Certainly, what s. 133 itself gives may not be diminished by the Parliament of Canada, but if its provisions are respected there is nothing in it or in any other parts of the British North America Act (reserving for later consideration s. 91(1)) that precludes the conferring of additional rights or privileges or the imposing of additional obligations respecting the use of English and French, if done in relation to matters within the competence of the enacting Legislature.

The words of s. 133 themselves point to its limited concern with language rights; and it is, in my view, correctly described as giving a constitutionally based right to any person to use English or French in legislative debates in the federal and Quebec Houses and in any pleading or process in or issuing from any federally established Court or any Court of Quebec, and as imposing an obligation of the use of English and French in the records and journals of the federal and Quebec legislative Houses and in the printing and publication of federal and Quebec legislation. There is no warrant for reading this provision, so limited to the federal and Quebec legislative chambers and their legislation, and to federal and Quebec Courts, as being in effect a final and legislatively unalterable determination for Canada, for Quebec and for all other Provinces, of the limits of the privileged or obligatory use of English and French in public proceedings, in public institutions and in public communications. On its face, s. 133 provides special protection in the use of English and French; there is no other provision of the British North America Act referable to the Parliament of Canada (apart from s. 91(1)) which deals with language as a legislative matter or otherwise. I am unable to appreciate the submission that to extend by legislation the privileged or required public use of English and French would be violative of s. 133 when there has been no interference with the special protection which it prescribed. . .

What the *Jones* case decided was that Parliament could enlarge the protection afforded to the use of French or English in agencies and institutions and programmes falling within federal legislative authority. There was no suggestion that it could unilaterally contract the guarantees or requirements of s. 133. Yet it is contraction not enlargement that is the object and subject of Chapter III, Title I of the Charter of the French language. But s. 133 is an entrenched provision, not only forbidding modification by unilateral action of Parliament or of the Quebec Legislature but also providing a guarantee to members of Parliament or of the Quebec Legislature and to litigants in the Courts of Canada or of Quebec that they are entitled to use either French or English in parliamentary or legislative assembly debates or in pleading (including oral argument) in the Courts of Canada or of Quebec.

Subject to consideration of the range of protection given by s. 133 in the use of either French or English, there does not appear any need to expand any further on the main issue in this case. On matters of detail and of history, we are content to adopt the reasons of Deschênes C.J. as fortified by the Quebec Court of Appeal.

Dealing now with the question whether "regulations" issued under the authority of acts of the Legislature of Quebec are "Acts" within the purview of s. 133, it is apparent that it would truncate the requirement of s. 133 if account were not taken of the growth of delegated legislation. This is a case where the greater must include the lesser. Section 9 of the impugned provisions, in giving official status only to the French text of regulations as well as of statutes and s. 10 in providing for the subordinate position of an English version of bills, statutes and regulations appear to put all these instruments on an equal footing with respect to language and, consequently, towards s. 133. . . .

. . . the reference in s. 133 to "any of

the Courts of Quebec'' ought to be considered broadly as including not only so-called s. 96 Courts but also Courts established by the Province and administered by provincially appointed Judges. It is not a long distance from this latter class of tribunal to those which exercise judicial power, although they are not in courts in the traditional sense. If they are statutory agencies which are adjudicative, applying legal principles to the assertion of claims under their constituent legislation, rather than settling issues on grounds of expediency or administrative policy, they are judicial bodies, however some of their procedures may differ not only from those of Courts but also from those of other adjudicative bodies. In the rudimentary state of administrative law in 1867, it is not surprising that there was no reference to non-curial adjudicative agencies. Today, they play a significant role in the control of a wide range of individual and corporate activities, subjecting them to various norms of conduct which are at the same time limitations on the jurisdiction of the agencies and on the legal position of those caught by them. The guarantee given for the use of French or English in Court proceedings should not be liable to curtailment by provincial substitution of adjudicative agencies for Courts to such extent as is compatible with s. 96 of the British North America Act.

Two judgments of the Privy Council, which wrestled with similar questions of principle in the construction of the British North America Act, are, to some degree, apposite here. In *Edwards* v. *Attorney General of Canada* ([1930] A.C. 124), the ''persons'' case (respecting the qualification of women for appointment to the Senate under s. 24), there are observations by Lord Sankey of the need to give the British North America Act a broad interpretation attuned to changing circumstances: "The British North America Act," he said, at p. 136, "planted in Canada a living tree capable of growth and expansion within its natural limits." Dealing, as this Court is here, with a constitutional guarantee, it would be overly-technical to ignore the modern development of non-curial adjudicative agencies which play so important a role in our society, and to refuse to extend to proceedings before them the guarantee of the right to use either French or English by those subject to their jurisdiction.

In *Attorney General of Ontario* v. *Attorney General of Canada* ([1947] A.C. 127), (the *Privy Council Appeals Reference*), Viscount Jowitt said in the course of his discussion of the issues, that "it is, as their Lordships think, irrelevant that the question is one that might have seemed unreal at the date of the British North America Act. To such an organic statute the flexible interpretation must be given which changing circumstances require" (at p. 154).

Although there are clear points of distinction between these two cases and the issue of the scope of s. 133, in its reference to the Courts of Quebec, they nonetheless lend support to what is to us the proper approach to an entrenched provision, that is, to make it effective through the range of institutions which exercise judicial power, be they called courts or adjudicative agencies. In our opinion, therefore, the guarantee and requirements of s. 133 extend to both.

It follows that the guarantee in s. 133 of the use of either French or English "by any person or in any pleading or process in or issuing from . . . all or any of the Courts of Quebec" applies to both ordinary Courts and other adjudicative tribunals. Hence, not only is the option to use either language given to any person involved in proceedings before the Courts of Quebec or its other adjudicative tribunals (and this covers both written and oral submissions) but documents emanating from such bodies or issued in their name or under their authority may be in either language, and this option extends to the issuing and publication of judgments or other orders.

In the result, the appeals are dismissed in both cases with costs to the plaintiffs as provided in the orders granting leave. There shall be no order as to costs either to or against any of the other parties.

55. Attorney-General of Quebec *v*. Association of Quebec Protestant School Boards, *1984*

~ This case dealt with two of the most divisive and longstanding issues in Canadian politics—language and education. It was a case that became inevitable the day the Charter of Rights was proclaimed. There was a direct, unavoidable, and intentional conflict between the "Quebec Clause" in sections 71 and 72 of Bill 101, and the "Canada Clause" in section 23(1)(b) of the Charter of Rights. Bill 101, also known as the Charter of the French Language, was the centrepiece of separatist Premier René Levesque's policy to preserve the "French fact" in Canada. Sections 72-73 effectively limited English-language instruction to the children of Anglophone families already living in Quebec. It was the Parti Quebecois' attempt to prevent the growth of the anglophone minority in Quebec by detering English-speaking Canadians from moving to Quebec and forcing new immigrants to integrate into the francophone majority.

The purpose of the "Canada clause" in section 23(1)(b) of the Charter was to override the "Quebec clause" by guaranteeing all English and French-speaking Canadians the right to have their children educated in their mother tongue despite their minority status in a province. This meant open access to English language education in Quebec just as it protected French-speaking communities outside of Quebec. Section 23 was central to Pierre Trudeau's vision of a thoroughly bilingual country, where both anglophones and francophones have equal access to all government services in their mother tongues.

The language rights sections (ss. 16-23) of the Charter of Rights represented the culmination of Trudeau's political career, his solution to Canada's national unity crisis. Trudeau's first major achievement as Prime Minister had been the Official Languages Act (1969). The language rights section of the Charter culminated this effort by extending and entrenching these rights in the constitution. For this very reason, section 23 was anathema to Premier Levesque, and the principal reason his government refused to support the constitutional Accord of November, 1981. "No self-respecting Quebec government," angrily declared Levesque, "could ever abandon the smallest fraction of this absolutely fundamental right to protect the only French island in the English-speaking sea of the North American continent."[1] In its broadest sense, this case represented nothing less than the final clash between the two old rivals, Trudeau and Levesque, and their two very different visions of the future of the French in Canada.[2]

Unlike some of its other Charter decisions,[3] the Court relied heavily on the legislative history or "original understanding" of the Charter to strengthen the

---

[1] 26 Journal des Débats 4 (Nov. 9, 1981)

[2] See Paul Weiler, "Rights and Judges in a Democracy: A New Canadian Version," *University of Michigan Journal of Law Reform* 18 (Fall, 1984), 51-92, at 88-92.

[3] See *Reference re British Columbia Motor Vehicle Act*, case 45.

authority of their judgement. Section 23 "was not enacted by the legislator in a vacuum," observed the Court. Its framers' "intention was to remedy the perceived defects of these regimes by uniform corrective measures, namely those contained in s. 23 of the Charter. . ." The Court hoped to send a message to its inevitable critics that their decision was not based simply on their "interpretation" of section 23, but on its clearly intended meaning.

This did not satisfy Quebec nationalists. The Levesque government conceded from the outset that the education provisions of Bill 101 clashed with section 23 of the Charter. Their defense was based on section 1 of the Charter—that the "Quebec Clause" was a "reasonable limitation" on the education language rights of the English minority. This argument was supported by several sophisticated demographic studies showing the decline in the percentage of French-speaking Quebeckers. There were also examples of similar language policies in other "free and democratic" societies—Belgium and Switzerland. The Quebec trial judge had accepted this extrinsic evidence as justifying the "purpose" of the law, but concluded that the "means" used were too sweeping to be reasonable.[4] The Supreme Court, however, sidestepped the demographic statistics. It declared that the Quebec Clause was not a "limitation" of language rights but a complete denial, so there could be no question of it being "reasonable." Critics have argued that the "denial-limitation" distinction is unconvincing, and was simply an easy way for the Court to avoid confronting the demographic, policy rationale behind Quebec's education policy.

The political background of the case is essential to understand many of its other unique aspects. It explains, for example, why the Trudeau government intervened in the case in support of the Quebec Protestant School Boards. It also explains why the Court handed down its decision as an unsigned, "per curiam" decision of the Court. When the Court knows that it is dealing with a politically explosive issue, the judges sometimes resort to this anonymous, united-front tactic to bolster the authority of their decision. Finally, it explains why Levesque could not use the section 33 legislative override to avoid complying with the decision. When the Trudeau government was cutting its final deal with the provincial opponents of his package of constitutional reforms in November, 1981, language rights were "non-negotiable." They were exempted from the section 33 legislative override demanded by the provincial premiers who feared the Charter. This preferred status indicates their pride of place in Trudeau's agenda. It was also the major reason Levesque refused to support the Constitution Act, 1982.

The defeat in the *Bill 101 Case* came on the heels of the *Quebec Constitu-*

---

[4] Dale Gibson, *The Law of the Charter: General Principles.* Carswell, 1986. pp. 145-146, 149-150.

tional Veto loss.[5] Together they further contributed to Quebec's sense of alienation from the rest of English Canada in the wake of the Constitution Act, 1982. It was generally recognized that no Quebec government would consent to the Constitution Act, 1982, until it regained control of the language of education within the province. The Meech Lake Accord of April, 1987, addressed these issues in an attempt to bring Quebec back within the constitutional fold. It proposed to partially restore Quebec's veto over certain constitutional amendments.[6] Education was not dealt with explicitly, but through what has come to be referred to as the "distinct society" clause:

> *The Constitution of Canada shall be interpreted in a manner consistent with*
> *(a) the recognition that the existence of French-speaking Canadians, centered in Quebec but also present elsewhere in Canada, and English-speaking Canadians, concentrated outside Quebec but also present in Quebec, constitutes a fundamental characteristic of Canada; and*
> *(b) the recognition that Quebec constitutes within Canada a distinct society.*

Quebec Premier Robert Bourassa and most Quebec nationalists think that the "distinct society" clause will restore Quebec's autonomy in educational policy matters. But this is hardly certain. A careful reading of Section 2 of the Meech Lake Accord shows that part of what is "distinctive" about Quebec is the English-speaking minority. If the Meech Lake Accord is adopted, and Quebec re-enacts the "Quebec Clause" in the education sections of Bill 101, would the Supreme Court reverse its 1984 precedent? Students can decide for themselves. ~

ATTORNEY-GENERAL OF QUEBEC *v.* QUEBEC ASSOCIATION OF PROTESTANT SCHOOL BOARDS
In the Supreme Court of Canada. [1984] 2 S.C.R. 66.

The judgment of Dickson C.J.C., Ritchie, Beetz, Estey, McIntyre, Lamer and Wilson JJ. was delivered by

THE COURT: The question is whether the provisions regarding instruction in English contained in Chapter VIII of the Charter of the French Language, R.S. Quebec, 1977, c. C-11, and in the regulations adopted thereunder, are inconsistent with the Canadian Charter of Rights and Freedoms and of no force or effect to the extent of the inconsistency.

The applicable legislative and constitutional provisions must first be considered. . . .

It is not in dispute that ss. 72 and 73 of Bill 101 and s. 23 of the Charter are inconsistent. Nevertheless, it is useful to indicate exactly the nature and extent of this inconsistency. The trial judge made a comparative study of the applicable legis-

---

[5] See the *Quebec Veto Reference*, case 63 below.
[6] For further discussion of the Meech Lake Accord, see the Introductions to case 63 and 52. The full text of the Meech Lake Accord is found in the Appendix.

lative and constitutional provisions, and described this inconsistency in language the accuracy of which, at least in general terms, does not appear to have been disputed. He said the following, at pp. 681 and 682 of his judgment:

~ The following are some excerpts from the decision of Chief Justice Deschênes of the Quebec Superior Court. ~

But under s. 73 the children of immigrants, even English-speaking immigrants from other parts of Canada or from foreign countries, are not to be admitted into English schools in Quebec.

Section 73 sets out what has come to be known, in constitutional jargon in the last few years, as the 'Quebec clause.'

Undoubtedly, the Minister, Mr. Laurin, had this clause in mind when he spoke, last May 5th, of the "authentically English-speaking minority of Quebec."

Without doubt, it was this clause which was contemplated by the White Paper of March, 1977, setting out 'La politique québecoise de la langue française' when it described English schooling as 'an exceptional system for the present minority in Quebec.'

On the other hand, s. 23 of the Charter, in s-ss. 1(b) and (2)—the only ones, along with s-s. (3) which are in force in Quebec—allows access to English schools to children whose parents being citizens of Canada resident in Quebec, have received primary instruction in English in Canada or those children of citizens of Canada having a brother or a sister who has received or is receiving primary or secondary instruction in English in Canada.

In the same constitutional jargon, s. 23 of the Charter sets out the 'Canada clause' in the general sense.

Section 23 of the Charter only applies to citizens of Canada: one must keep this premise constantly in mind.

Section 23(1)(b) opens English schooling in Quebec to children whose parents have received their primary instruction in English anywhere in Canada.

This general eligibility is prohibited in Quebec by the combined effect of ss. 72 and 73 of Bill 101.

Section 23(2) of the Charter opens English schooling in Quebec to children of citizens of Canada who have a brother or sister who has received or is receiving primary or secondary instruction in English anywhere in Canada.

This general eligibility is, again, denied by the effect of the same provisions of Bill 101.

The conclusion, then, is inevitable: Bill 101 and the Charter are incompatible. . . .

The arguments raised by the appellant may be summarized in three propositions: (1) section 1 of the Charter, which guarantees the rights and freedoms contained in that document, applies to all the rights so guaranteed, including that conferred by s. 23; (2) section 1 of the Charter does not distinguish between the limitation and denial of a right, and makes the reasonable and justifiable nature of the limit the true test of its constitutionality; (3) the provisions of Chapter VIII of Bill 101 place upon the right secured by s. 23 of the Charter reasonable limits that can be justified in a free and democratic society.

The first proposition was approved by the Court of Appeal and the Superior Court. We are disposed to take this proposition as established, but for the sake of discussion only and without deciding the point.

The second and third propositions, like the first, were supported by a thorough memorandum and argument in which, *inter alia,* s. 1 of the Charter, the requirements which it imposes, the presumption of constitutionality and the question of the burden of proof were analysed in light of judicial interpretation of similar clauses in other constitutional charters by the Judicial Committee of the Privy Council for the Commonwealth nations and by the Supreme Court of India, and in light of American precedents and decisions of the courts on the Canadian Bill of Rights. Counsel for the appellant further argued that not only have respondent applicants not succeeded in establishing that the provisions for access to English schooling in Quebec are unreasonable, but the latter are reasonable within the meaning of s. 1 of the Charter, in view of factors such as demographic patterns, the physical mobility (migration) and linguistic mobility ("assimilation") of individuals and the regional distribution of interprovincial migrants. It was further argued that other free and democratic societies such as Switzerland and Belgium, which have socio-linguistic situations comparable to that in Quebec, have adopted stricter linguistic measures than Bill 101, and these measures have been held to be reasonable and justified by the Swiss and European courts. Finally, it was argued that the collective right of the Anglophone minority in Quebec to cultural survival is not threatened by Bill 101, which establishes a system providing access to English schooling which is not unreasonable.

We do not think it necessary to go into these arguments. . . .

Section 23 of the Charter is not, like other provisions in that constitutional document, of the kind generally found in such charters and declarations. It is not a codification of essential, pre-existing and more or less universal rights that are being confirmed and perhaps clarified, extended or amended, and which, most importantly, are given a new primacy and inviolability, by entrenching them in the supreme law of the land. The provisions of s. 23 of the Charter make it a unique set of constitutional provisions, quite peculiar to Canada.

This set of constitutional provisions was not enacted by the legislator in a vacuum. When it was adopted, the legislator knew, and clearly had in mind the regimes governing the Anglophone and Francophone linguistic minorities in various provinces in Canada so far as the language of instruction was concerned. It also had in mind the history of these regimes, both earlier ones such as Regulation 17, which for a time limited instruction in French in the separate schools of

Ontario—*Ottawa Separate Schools Trustees* v. *MacKell*, [1917] A.C. 62—as well as more recent ones such as Bill 101 and the legislation which preceded it in Quebec. Rightly or wrongly—and it is not for the courts to decide—the framers of the Constitution manifestly regarded as inadequate some—and perhaps all—of the regimes in force at the time the Charter was enacted, and their intention was to remedy the perceived defects of these regimes by uniform corrective measures, namely those contained in s. 23 of the Charter, which were at the same time given the status of a constitutional guarantee. The framers of the Charter unquestionably intended by s. 23 to establish a general regime for the language of instruction, not a special regime for Quebec; but in view of the period when the Charter was enacted, and especially in light of the wording of s. 23 of the Charter as compared with ss. 72 and 73 of Bill 101, it is apparent that the combined effect of the latter two sections seemed to the drafter like an archetype of the regimes needing reform, or which at least had to be affected, and the remedy prescribed for all of Canada by s. 23 of the Charter was in large part a response to these sections.

Up to 1969, the laws of Quebec appear to have been silent on the language of instruction, but in fact the system operated so as to leave almost complete freedom to everyone at all educational levels. Following the conflict that occurred in 1968 at the Saint-Leonard school board, where an attempt had been made to impose instruction in French on children of Italian immigrants—see Joseph Eliot Magnet, "Minority-Language Educational Rights," (1982) 4 *The Supreme Court Law Review* 195, at p. 202—the Quebec legislator adopted the Act to promote the French language in Quebec, 1969 (Que.), c. 9, also known as Bill 63. Despite its title, this Act embodied in legislation the freedom of choice regarding language of instruction which had existed up to then. However, the Quebec legislator indicated a concern with immigration in s. 3, where he directed the Minister of Immigration to

> . . . in co-operation with the Minister of Education, take the measures necessary so that the person who settles in Quebec may acquire the knowledge of the French language upon arrival or even before they leave their country of origin, and may have their children instructed in educational institutions where the courses are given in the French language.

This Act was replaced in 1974 by the Official Language Act, 1974 (Que.), c. 6, also known as Bill 22. Title 1 of this Act stated in its single section that French is the official language of Quebec. Chapter V of Title III is titled "The Language of Instruction". Sections 40 and 41 gave French a certain degree of priority. The first paragraph of s. 40 provided that the language of instruction shall be French in the schools governed by the school boards, the regional school boards and corporations of trustees, and the second paragraph states that school boards, regional school boards and corporations of trustees "shall continue" to provide instruction in English. The third paragraph provided for control over increasing or reducing instruction in English by the Minister of Education, who would not give his authorization "unless he considers that the number of pupils whose mother tongue is English and who are under the jurisdiction of such body warrants it." Section 41 provided that pupils must have sufficient knowledge of the language of instruction to receive their instruction in that language, which had the practical effect of closing off French schooling to the majority of Anglophone pupils and English schooling to the majority of Francophone pupils. Section 41 also provided that pupils who do not have a sufficient knowledge of any of the languages of instruction must receive their instruction in French, a provision which, though it did not say so expressly, was directed at immigrants, unless they were French- or English-speaking.

These provisions of the Official Language Act were found to be *intra vires* by Deschenes C.J. of the Superior Court in *Bureau Metropolitan des ecoles protestantes de Montréal* v. *Ministre de l'education du Québec*, [1976] C.S. 430, (1976) 83 D.L.R. (3d) 645. . . .

Thus, at the time the Charter was adopted, there had for some years been legislation in Quebec which, apart from the Act adopted in 1969, tended to give preferred treatment to French as the language of instruction, and correspondingly to lessen the benefits given to English until then, in fact if not in law. The culmination of this legislation was Bill 101.

Although the fate reserved to the English language as a language of instruction had generally been more advantageous in Quebec than the fate reserved to the French language in other provinces, Quebec seems nevertheless to have been the only province where there was then such a tendency to limit the rights conferred on the minority language group. In other provinces at the time, either the earlier situation remained unchanged, at least so far as legislation was concerned, as in Newfoundland and British Columbia which have no legislation on the language of instruction, or else relatively recent statutes had been adopted improving the situation of a linguistic minority, as in New Brunswick, Nova Scotia and Prince Edward Island. . . .

It is therefore not surprising that Bill 101 was very much in the minds of the framers of the Constitution when they enacted s. 23 of the Charter, which guarantees "minority language educational rights." This is confirmed when the wording of this section is compared with that of ss. 72 and 73 of Bill 101, and with other provincial statutes on the language of instruction.

To begin with, the fact that Quebec is the only province in Canada in which, by virtue of s. 59(1) and (2) of the Constitutional Act, 1982, s. 23(1)(a) of the Charter is not yet in force and cannot be brought into force without the consent of

Quebec, indicates clearly that the framers of the Constitution had Quebec specially in mind when they enacted s. 23 of the Charter. It may be possible to suggest a reason for this exception: so far as Quebec is concerned, s. 23(1)(a) applies to Canadian citizens whose first language is English but who did not receive their primary school instruction in that language in Canada, that is, in practice, largely immigrants whose first language is English and who have become Canadian citizens. It can therefore be plausible to think that this particular provision of the Charter was suspended for Quebec in part so as to calm the concerns expressed in Quebec long before Bill 101 was adopted regarding immigration, because of the minority status of French in North America.

It is above all when we compare s. 23(1)(b) and (2) of the Charter with s. 73 of Bill 101 that it becomes most apparent that the latter is the type of regime on which the framers of the Constitution modelled s. 23. Both in the Charter and in Bill 101, the requirements to be considered in deciding as to the right to instruction in the minority language are the place where the parents received their instruction in the minority language. Both in the Charter and in Bill 101, that place is where the parents received their primary school instruction. Both in the Charter and in Bill 101, satisfying this requirement gives the right to primary and secondary school instruction in the minority language, and Bill 101 adds the right to education at the kindergarten level. Both in the Charter and in Bill 101, the requirements also include the language of instruction of a child's brothers and sisters, though Bill 101 specifies the younger brothers and sisters of children included in a category which is temporary by nature—limitations not found in the Charter.

By incorporating into the structure of s. 23 of the Charter the special structure of the rules in s. 73 of Bill 101, the framers of the Constitution identified the type of system they wished to correct and

on which they would base the remedy prescribed. The framer's objective appears simple, and may readily be inferred from the concrete method used by them: to adopt a general rule guaranteeing the Francophone and Anglophone minorities in Canada an important part of the rights which the Anglophone minority in Quebec had enjoyed, with respect to the language of instruction, before Bill 101 was adopted.

If, as is apparent, Chapter VIII of Bill 101 is the prototype of the regime which the framers of the Constitution wished to remedy by adopting s. 23 of the Charter, the limitations which this regime imposes on rights involving the language of instruction, so far as they are inconsistent with s. 23 of the Charter, cannot possibly have been regarded by the framers of the Constitution as coming within "such reasonable limits prescribed by law as can be demonstrably justified in a free and democratic society." Accordingly, the limits imposed by Chapter VIII of Bill 101 are not legitimate limits within the meaning of s. 1 of the Charter to the extent that the latter applies to s. 23. . . .

The real effect of s. 73 of Bill 101 is to make an exception to s. 23(1)(b) and (2) of the Charter in Quebec, whereas those subsections are not provisions to which exceptions can be made under s. 33(1) and (2) of the Charter. Additionally, s. 73 of Bill 101 directly alters the effect of s. 23 of the Charter for Quebec, without following the procedure laid down for amending the Constitution. . . .

The provisions of s. 73 of Bill 101 collide directly with those of s. 23 of the Charter, and are not limitations which can be legitimized by s. 1 of the Charter. Such limitations cannot be exceptions to the rights and freedoms guaranteed by the Charter or amount to amendments of the Charter. An Act of Parliament or a legislature which, for example, purported to impose the beliefs of a state religion would be in direct conflict with s. 2(a) of the Charter, which guarantees the freedom of conscience and religion, and would have to be ruled of no force or effect without even considering whether such legislation could be legitimized by s. 1. The same applies to Chapter VIII of Bill 101 in respect of s. 23 of the Charter.

This other method of interpretation, based on the true nature and effects of Chapter VIII of Bill 101 in light of the Charter provisions, takes an opposite route to that based on the purpose of the Charter, but leads to the same result: Chapter VIII is inoperative.

For these reasons, we would answer "yes" to the first constitutional question formulated by Chief Justice Laskin.

56. Reference Re Manitoba Language Rights, *1985*

~ The *Manitoba Language Reference* is a dramatic illustration of the statecraft the Supreme Court may be called upon to exercise in securing compliance with constitutional norms. In 1979 in *Forest*[1] the Supreme Court ruled that Manitoba's Official Language Act which had been in force since 1890 and which made English the official language of the province violated the constitutional requirement in section 23 of the Manitoba Act, 1870 (the Act creating Manitoba) that the province's laws be enacted in English and French. In the years immediately following this decision little was done to give effect to it. A few laws were translated but many were not and some new legislation was enacted in English only. Roger Bilodeau, a francophone charged with a traffic offence, challenged this inaction by arguing that Manitoba's Highway Traffic Act as well as its Summary Conviction Act were null and void because they were enacted only in English. In 1981, Manitoba's Court of Appeal ruled that even though these statutes failed to meet the constitutional requirement of bilingualism the courts must still give effect to them.[2]

The Supreme Court of Canada delayed hearing Bilodeau's appeal from this judgment while Manitoba's N.D.P. government and the Liberal government in Ottawa worked out the terms of a constitutional amendment which would secure the rights of Manitoba francophones but also provide a reasonable timetable for translating the province's laws into French. The amendment agreed to by the two governments made English and French the official languages of the province, extended French language rights to government services and established a ten year period for translating laws into French. Under the new rules governing constitutional amendments, agreement at the executive level was no longer enough. An amendment to language rights in a single province requires the approval of the legislature of the province concerned and the federal Parliament. There appeared to be no difficulty in securing legislative approval at the federal level but the proposal soon began to meet stiff resistance in Manitoba.

A referendum held in the fall of 1983 in the city of Winnipeg where over half of Manitoba's population resides produced a 4 to 1 majority against the proposed amendment and in favour of proceeding with the Bilodeau appeal. In the legislature the amendment was bitterly attacked by the Conservative opposition. Sensing widespread support throughout the province where other ethnic groups outnumbered the Francophone community (now just 6% of the population) and where bilingualism was associated with the unpopular Trudeau administration in Ottawa, the Conservatives dug in their heels. With the support of the Speaker they were able to bring the business of the legislature to a halt. Under this pressure, the N.D.P. government, although it had a majority in the legislature, withdrew the proposed amendment.

---

[1] Discussed at p. 613 above.
[2] *Bilodeau* v. *A.G. Manitoba* (1981) 5 W.W.R. 393.

With the failure of the politicians to work out a solution the ball was squarely returned to the judicial arena. In the spring of 1984 the federal government made an omnibus reference to the Supreme Court combining "legal and constitutional questions of the utmost subtlety and complexity with political questions of great sensitivity." The Court took over a year to hear the arguments and render judgment. Its opinion when it came, as might be expected, took the form of an institutional opinion of "The Court".

The Court faced a difficult dilemma. If, like Manitoba's Court of Appeal, it ruled that Manitoba's unilingual, English laws were valid, its decision in the *Forest* case could be completely ignored by the province. If, on the other hand, it ruled that these laws, which constituted nearly the entire provincial statute book, were null and void, Manitoba would be plunged into a condition of legal anarchy. Its solution was to find the unilingual laws unconstitutional but to declare that, while all new statutes must be enacted in both languages, old laws would be deemed to be valid "until the expiry of the minimum period necessary for translation, re-enactment, printing and publishing." The Court invited the Manitoba and federal governments to make submissions at a subsequent hearing on what the length of this minimum period should be. The Court's response to these submissions was rendered in November, 1985. It is printed below following the reference case opinion. As can be seen, Manitoba was given until the end of 1990 to meet the requirement of legislative bilingualism.

The Supreme Court's decision giving temporary effect to unconstitutional laws should not be dismissed as putting expediency ahead of law. The Court drew heavily upon international jurisprudence. It employed the *de facto* doctrine to maintain the validity of legal relationships entered into in the past by the people and government of the province under the mantle of what from 1890 on were unconstitutional laws. It found support for giving temporary effect to invalid laws in the doctrine of state necessity enunciated by courts dealing with laws sanctioned by insurrectionary governments. The fundamental principle underlying this jurisprudence is the Rule of Law. The Court considered that it would be an abdication of its role "as protector and preserver of the Constitution" to allow a condition of lawlessness to result from its constitutional rulings. This would be to defeat the most fundamental purpose of the Constitution in the process of enforcing one of its rules. "The Constitution," said the Court, "will not suffer a province without laws." The Court's decision in this case is the most important contribution it has made to a universal theory of constitutionalism.

But what about Roger Bilodeau, whose challenge to Manitoba's unilingualism began all of this? His appeal was finally heard after this reference and, of course, he was unsuccessful because the unilingual laws he challenged were now deemed to be valid for the temporary period established by the Supreme

Court.[3] His challenge to the issuing of his summons in English only failed for a different reason. In *MacDonald* v. *City of Montreal*,[4] a companion case involving a challenge to French only summons' in Quebec, the Court held that the right to use French and English in court proceedings, guaranteed in section 133 of the B.N.A. Act and section 23 of the Manitoba Act, did not mean that all court documents must be issued in both languages.[5] The Court now appeared to be moving away from the very expansive interpretation of language rights it had rendered in 1979 in *Blaikie* and *Forest*. ~

REFERENCE RE MANITOBA LANGUAGE RIGHTS
In the Supreme Court of Canada. [1985] 2 S.C.R. 347.

The Judgment of Dickson C.J.C., Beetz, Estey, McIntyre, Lamer, Wilson and Le Dain JJ. was delivered by

THE COURT: This Reference combines legal and constitutional questions of the utmost subtlety and complexity with political questions of great sensitivity. . . .

~ The Reference posed four questions. ~

1. Are the requirements of section 133 of the Constitution Act, 1867 and of section 23 of the Manitoba Act, 1870 respecting the use of both the English and French languages in (a) the Records and Journals of the Houses of the Parliament of Canada and of the Legislatures of Quebec and Manitoba, and (b) the Acts of the Parliament of Canada and of the Legislatures of Quebec and Manitoba, mandatory?

2. Are those statutes and regulations of the Province of Manitoba that were not printed and published in both the English and French languages invalid by reason of section 23 of the Manitoba Act, 1870?

3. If the answer to question 2 is affirmative, do those enactments that were not printed and published in English and French have any legal force and effect, and if so, to what extent and under what conditions?

4. Are any of the provisions of An Act Respecting the Operation of section 23 of the Manitoba Act in Regard to Statutes, enacted by S.M. 1980, Ch. 3, inconsistent with the provisions of section 23 of the Manitoba Act, 1870, and if so are such provisions, to the extent of such inconsistency, invalid and of no legal force and effect? . . .

Section 23 of the Manitoba Act, 1870 was the culmination of many years of co-existence and struggle between the English, the French and the Metis in Red River Colony, the predecessor to the present day Province of Manitoba. Though the region was originally claimed by the English Hudson's Bay Company in 1670 under its Royal Charter, for much of its preconfederation history, Red River Colony was inhabited by Anglophones and Francophones in roughly equal proportions. On November 19, 1869 the Hudson's Bay Company issued a deed of surrender to transfer the North-West Territories, which included the Red River Colony, to Canada. The transfer of title took effect on July 15, 1870.

Between November 19, 1869 and July 15, 1870, the provisional government of Red River Colony attempted to unite the various segments of the Red River colony and drew up a "Bill of Rights" to be used in negotiations with Canada. A Conven-

---

[3] *Bilodeau* v. *A.G. Manitoba* (1986) 1 S.C.R. 449.

[4] *MacDonald* v. *City of Montreal* (1988) 1 S.C.R. 460.

[5] These cases are discussed further below, at p. 644.

tion of Delegates was elected in January, 1870 to prepare the terms upon which Red River Colony would join the Confederation. The Convention was made up of equal numbers of anglophones and francophones elected from the various French and English parishes.

The final version of the Bill of Rights which was used by the Convention delegates in their negotiations with Ottawa, contained these provisions:

That the English and French languages be common in the Legislature, and in the courts, and that all public documents, as well as all Acts of the Legislature, be published in both languages.

That the Judge of the Superior Court speak the English and French languages.

These clauses were re-drafted by the Crown lawyers in Ottawa and included in a Bill to be introduced in Parliament. The Bill passed through Parliament with no opposition from either side of the House, resulting in s. 23 of the Manitoba Act, 1870. In 1871 this Act was entrenched in the British North America Act, 1871 (renamed Constitution Act, 1871 in the Constitution Act, 1982, s. 53). The Manitoba Act, 1870 is now entrenched in the Constitution of Canada by virtue of s. 52(2)(b) of the Constitution Act, 1982.

In 1890 the Official Language Act, S.M. 1890, c. 14 (hereafter "the Official Language Act") was enacted by the Manitoba Legislature. This Act provides:

1) Any statute or law to the contrary notwithstanding, the English language only shall be used in the records and journals of the House of Assembly for the Province of Manitoba, and in any pleadings or process in or issuing from any court in the Province of Manitoba. The Acts of the Legislature of the Province of Manitoba need only be printed and published in the English language.

2) This Act shall only apply so far as this Legislature has jurisdiction so to enact, and shall come into force on the day it is assented to.

Upon enactment of the Official Language Act, 1890 the Province of Manitoba ceased publication of the French version of Legislative Records, Journals and Acts.

The Official Language Act, 1890 was challenged before the Manitoba courts soon after it was enacted. It was ruled *ultra vires* in 1892 by Judge Prud'homme of the County Court of St. Boniface, who stated: "Je suis donc d'opinion que le c. 14, 53 Vict. est *ultra vires* de la legislature du Manitoba et que la clause 23, de l'Acte de Manitoba, ne peut pas être changée et encore moins abrogée par la législature de cette province": *Pellant* v. *Hebert*, first published in *Le Manitoba*, (a French language newspaper), 9 mars 1892, reported in (1981), 12 R.G.D. 242. This ruling was not followed by the legislature or the Government of Manitoba. The 1890 Act remained in successive revisions of the Statutes of Manitoba; the Government did not resume bilingual publication of Legislative Records, Journals or Acts.

In 1909, the 1890 Act was again challenged in Manitoba Courts and again ruled unconstitutional: *Bertrand* v. *Dussault*, Jan. 30, 1909, County Court of St. Boniface (unreported), reproduced in *Re Forest and Registrar of Court of Appeal of Manitoba*, (1977), 77 D.L.R. (3d) 445 (Man. C.A.), at pp. 458-62. According to Monnin J.A. in *Re Forest, supra,* at p. 458, "This latter decision, not reported, appears to have been unknown or ignored."

In 1976, a third attack was mounted against the 1890 Act and the Act was ruled unconstitutional: *R.* v. *Forest* (1976), 74 D.L.R. (3d) 704 (Man. Co. Ct.). Nonetheless, the 1890 Act remained on the Manitoba statute books; bilingual enactment, printing and publication of Acts of the Manitoba Legislature was not resumed.

In 1979, the constitutionality of the 1890 Act was tested before this Court. On December 13, 1979, in *Attorney General of Manitoba* v. *Forest*, [1979] 2 S.C.R. 1032, this Court, in unanimous reasons, held that the provisions of Manitoba's Official Language Act were in conflict with s. 23 of the Manitoba Act, 1870 and unconstitutional.

On July 9, 1980, after the decision of this Court in *Forest*, the Legislature of Manitoba enacted An Act Respecting the Operation of Section 23 of the Manitoba Act in Regard to Statutes, S.M. 1980, c. 3. The validity of this Act is the subject of question 4 of this Reference.

In the fourth session (1980) and the fifth session (1980-1981) of the thirty-first Legislature of Manitoba, the vast majority of the Acts of the Legislature of Manitoba were enacted, printed and published in English only.

Since the first session of the thirty-second Legislature of Manitoba (1982), the Acts of the Legislature of Manitoba have been enacted, printed and published in both English and French. However, those Acts that only amend Acts that were enacted, printed and published in English only, and private Acts, have in most instances been enacted in English only.

In *Bilodeau* v. *Attorney General of Manitoba*, [1981] 5 W.W.R. 393, the Manitoba Court of Appeal held that Manitoba's Highway Traffic Act, R.S.M. 1970, cap. H-60 and Summary Convictions Act, R.S.M. 1970, cap. S.230, although enacted in English only, were valid.

On July 4, 1983, the Attorney General of Manitoba introduced into the Legislative Assembly of Manitoba a resolution to initiate a constitutional amendment under s. 43 of the Constitution Act, 1982. The purpose of the resolution was to amend the language provisions of the Manitoba Act, 1870. The second session of the thirty-second Legislature was prorogued on February 27, 1984, without the resolution having been adopted.

It might also be mentioned that on December 13, 1979, in *Attorney General of Quebec* v. *Blaikie*, [1979] 2 S.C.R. 1016 (*Blaikie No. 1*), this Court held that the provisions of Quebec's Charter of the French Language (Bill 101), enacted in 1977, were in conflict with s. 133 of the

Constitution Act, 1867. The Charter purported to provide for the introduction of Bills in the legislature in French only, and for the enactment of statutes in French only. The day after the decision of this Court in *Blaikie No. 1*, the Legislature of Quebec re-enacted in both languages all those Quebec statutes that had been enacted in French only. See: *An Act respecting a judgment rendered in the Supreme Court of Canada on 13 December 1979 on the language of the legislature and the courts in Quebec*, S.Q. 1979, c. 61.

The implication of this Court's holdings in *Blaikie No. 1*, *supra* and *Forest*, *supra* was that provincial legislation passed in accordance with the *ultra vires* statutes, i.e. enacted in one language only, was itself in derogation of the constitutionality entrenched language provisions of the Constitution Act, 1867 and the Manitoba Act, 1870, and therefore invalid. In *Société Asbestos Limitée* v. *Société Nationale de l'Amiante*, [1979] C.A. 342, the Quebec Court of Appeal held, in a judgment also rendered December 13, 1979, that this was indeed the consequence of unilingual enactment and struck down two statutes that had not been enacted in English. . . .

QUESTION 1

. . . Section 23 of the Manitoba Act, 1870, provides that both English and French "*shall* be used in the . . . Records and Journals" of the Manitoba Legislature. It further provides that "[t]he Acts of the Legislature *shall* be printed and published in both those languages." Section 133 of the Constitution Act, 1867, is strikingly similar. It provides that both English and French "*shall* be used in the respective Records and Journals" of Parliament and the Legislature of Quebec. It also provides that "[t]he Acts of the Parliament of Canada and the Legislature of Quebec *shall* be printed and published in both those languages."

As used in its normal grammatical sense, the word "shall" is presumptively imperative. . . .

The conclusion seems inescapable that the drafters of the Constitution Act, 1867 deliberately selected the imperative term "shall" in preference to the permissive term "may" because they intended s. 133's language guarantees to be just that—*guarantees*. And the use by Parliament only three years later of nearly identical language in s. 23 of the Manitoba Act, 1870 is strong evidence of a similar intendment with regard to the language provisions of that Act. The requirements of s. 133 of the Constitution Act, 1867 and of s. 23 of the Manitoba Act, 1870 respecting the use of both English and French in the Records, Journals and Acts of Parliament and the Legislatures of Quebec and Manitoba are "mandatory" in the normally accepted sense of that term. That is, they are obligatory. They must be observed.

QUESTIONS 2 AND 3

Question 2 asks whether the unilingual statutes and regulations of Manitoba are invalid. Question 3 asks about the force and effect of these statutes and regulations if they are found to be invalid. Before addressing the consequences of the Manitoba Legislature's failure to enact its laws in both French and English, it will be necessary to determine what is encompassed by the words "Acts of the Legislature" in s. 23 of the Manitoba Act, 1870.

The requirements of s. 23 of the Manitoba Act, 1870 pertain to "Acts of the Legislature." These words are, in all material respects, identical to those found in s. 133 of the Constitution Act, 1867. As we have already indicated, in *Blaikie No. 2, supra*, this Court held that s. 133 applied to regulations enacted by the Government of Quebec, a Minister of the Government or a group of Ministers and to regulations of the civil administration and of semi-public agencies which required the approval of that Government, a Minister or group of Ministers for their legal effect. It was emphasized that only those regulations which could properly be called "delegated legislation" fell within the scope of s. 133; rules or directives of internal management did not. It was also held that s. 133 applied to rules of practice enacted by courts and quasi-judicial tribunals, but that it did not apply to the by-laws of municipal bodies or the regulations of school bodies.

Given the similarity of the provisions, the range of application of s. 23 of the Manitoba Act, 1870, should parallel that of s. 133 of the Constitution Act, 1867. All types of subordinate legislation that in Quebec would be subject to s. 133 of the Constitution Act, 1867, are, in Manitoba, subject to s. 23 of the Manitoba Act, 1870.

In this judgment, all references to "Acts of the Legislature" are intended to encompass all statutes, regulations and delegated legislation of the Manitoba Legislature, enacted since 1890, that are covered by this Court's judgments in *Blaikie No. 1* and *Blaikie No. 2*.

Section 23 of the Manitoba Act, 1870 entrenches a mandatory requirement to enact, print, and publish all Acts of the Legislature in both official languages (see *Blaikie No. 1, supra*). It establishes a constitutional duty on the Manitoba Legislature with respect to the manner and form of enactment of its legislation. This duty protects the substantive rights of all Manitobans to equal access to the law in either the French or the English language.

Section 23 of the Manitoba Act, 1870 is a specific manifestation of the general right of Franco-Manitobans to use their own language. The importance of language rights is grounded in the essential role that language plays in human existence, development and dignity. It is through language that we are able to form concepts: to structure and order the world around us. Language bridges the gap between isolation and community, allowing humans to delineate the rights and duties they hold in respect of one another, and thus to live in society.

The constitutional entrenchment of a duty on the Manitoba Legislature to enact, print and publish in both French and English in s. 23 of the Manitoba Act, 1870 confers upon the judiciary the responsibility of protecting the correlative language rights of all Manitobans including the Franco-Manitoban minority. The judiciary is the institution charged with the duty of ensuring that the government complies with the Constitution. We must protect those whose constitutional rights have been violated, whomever they may be, and whatever the reasons for the violation.

The Constitution of a country is a statement of the will of the people to be governed in accordance with certain principles held as fundamental and certain prescriptions restrictive of the powers of the legislature and government. It is, as s. 52 of the Constitution Act, 1982 declares, the "supreme law" of the nation, unalterable by the normal legislative process, and unsuffering of laws inconsistent with it. The duty of the judiciary is to interpret and apply the laws of Canada and each of the provinces, and it is thus our duty to ensure that the constitutional law prevails. . . .

Section 52 of the Constitution Act, 1982 does not alter the principles which have provided the foundation for judicial review over the years. In a case where constitutional manner and form requirements have not been complied with, the consequence of such non-compliance continues to be invalidity. The words "of no force or effect" mean that a law thus inconsistent with the Constitution has no force or effect because it is invalid.

Canadian courts have been unanimous in finding that failure to respect mandatory requirements to enact, print and publish statutes and regulations in both official languages leads to inconsistency and thus invalidity. See, *Société Asbestos Ltée. c. Société Nationale de l'Amiante, supra; Procureur général du Québec* v. *Linda Collier,* [1983] C.S. 366; *Procureur général du Québec* v. *Brunet,* J.E. 83-510, reversed on other grounds, J.E. 84-62 (Que. S.C.). . . .

In the present case the unilingual enactments of the Manitoba Legislature are inconsistent with s. 23 of the Manitoba Act, 1870 since the constitutionally

required manner and form for their enactment has not been followed. Thus they are invalid and of no force or effect.

THE RULE OF LAW

The difficulty with the fact that the unilingual Acts of the Legislature of Manitoba must be declared invalid and of no force or effect is that, without going further, a legal vacuum will be created with consequent legal chaos in the Province of Manitoba. The Manitoba Legislature has, since 1890, enacted nearly all of its laws in English only. Thus, to find that the unilingual laws of Manitoba are invalid and of no force or effect would mean that only laws enacted in both French and English *before 1890*, would continue to be valid, and would still be in force even if the law had purportedly been repealed or amended by a post-1890 unilingual statute; matters that were not regulated by laws enacted before 1890 would now be unregulated by law. . . .

The situation of the various institutions of provincial government would be as follows: the courts, administrative tribunals, public officials, municipal corporations, school boards, professional governing bodies, and all other bodies created by law, to the extent that they derive their existence from or purport to exercise powers conferred by Manitoba laws enacted since 1890 in English only, would be acting without legal authority.

Questions as to the validity of the present composition of the Manitoba Legislature might also be raised. Under the Manitoba Act, 1870, the Legislative Assembly was to be composed of 24 members (s. 14), and voters were to be male and over 21 (s. 17). By laws enacted after 1890 in English only, the size of the Legislative Assembly was increased to 57 , members, and all persons, both women and men, over 18 were granted the right to vote: see Act to Amend the Election Act, S.M. 1916, c. 36; Act to Amend the Election Act, S.M. 1969 (2nd Sess.), c. 7; The Legislative Assembly Act, R.S.M. 1970, c. L110, s. 4(1). If these laws are invalid and of no force or effect, the present composition of the Manitoba Legislature might be invalid. The invalidity of the post-1890 laws would not touch the existence of the Legislature or its powers since these are matters of federal constitutional law: Constitution Act, 1867, ss. 92, 92A, 93, 95; Manitoba Act, 1870, s. 2.

Finally, all legal rights, obligations and other effects which have purportedly arisen under all Acts of the Manitoba Legislature since 1890 would be open to challenge to the extent that their validity and enforceability depends upon a regime of unconstitutional unilingual laws.

In the present case, declaring the Acts of the Legislature of Manitoba invalid and of no force or effect would, without more, undermine the principle of the Rule of Law. The Rule of Law, a fundamental principle of our Constitution, must mean at least two things. First, that the law is supreme over officials of the government as well as private individuals, and thereby preclusive of the influence of arbitrary power. Indeed, it is because of the supremacy of law over the government, as established in s. 23 of the Manitoba Act, 1870 and s. 52 of the Constitution Act, 1982, that this Court must find the unconstitutional laws of Manitoba to be invalid and of no force and effect.

Second, the Rule of Law requires the creation and maintenance of an actual order of positive laws which preserves and embodies the more general principle of normative order. Law and order are indispensable elements of civilized life. "The Rule of Law in this sense implies . . . simply the existence of public order." (I. Jennings, The Law and the Constitution, 5th ed., 1959, at p. 43). As John Locke once said, "A government without laws is, I suppose, a mystery in politics, inconceivable to human capacity and inconsistent with human society." (quoted by Lord Wilberforce in *H.L. Carl Zeiss-Stiftung* v. *Rayner and Keeler Ltd. (No. 2)*, [1966] 2 All E.R. 536 (H.L.) at p. 577). . . .

It is this second aspect of the Rule of Law that is of concern in the present situation. The conclusion that the Acts of the Legislature of Manitoba are invalid and of no force or effect means that the positive legal order which has purportedly regulated the affairs of the citizens of Manitoba since 1890 will be destroyed and the rights, obligations and other effects arising under these laws will be invalid and unenforceable. As for the future, since it is reasonable to assume that it will be impossible for the Legislature of Manitoba to rectify *instantaneously* the constitutional defect, the Acts of the Manitoba Legislature will be invalid and of no force or effect until they are translated, re-enacted, printed and published in both languages. . . .

The constitutional status of the Rule of Law is beyond question. The preamble to the Constitution Act, 1982 states:

Whereas Canada is founded upon principles that recognize the supremacy of God and the rule of law.

This is explicit recognition that "the rule of law [is] a fundamental postulate of our constitutional structure." (Per Rand J. *Roncarelli* v. *Duplessis* [1959] S.C.R. 121, at p. 142). The Rule of Law has always been understood as the very basis of the English Constitution characterising the political institutions of England from the time of the Norman Conquest (A.V. Dicey, *The Law of the Constitution*, 10th ed., 1959, at p. 183). It becomes a postulate of our own Constitutional order by way of the preamble to the Constitution Act, 1982, and its implicit inclusion in the preamble to the Constitution Act, 1867 by virtue of the words "with a Constitution similar in principle to that of the United Kingdom."

Additional to the inclusion of the Rule of Law in the preambles of the Constitution Acts of 1867 and 1982, the principle is clearly implicit in the very nature of a Constitution. The Constitution, as the Supreme Law, must be understood as a purposive ordering of social relations providing a basis upon which an actual order of positive laws can be brought into existence. The founders of this nation must have intended, as one of the basic principles of nation building, that Canada be a society of legal order and normative structure: one governed by Rule of Law. While this is not set out in a specific provision, the principle of the Rule of Law is clearly a principle of our Constitution.

This Court cannot take a narrow and literal approach to constitutional interpretation. The jurisprudence of the Court evidences a willingness to supplement textual analysis, with historical, contextual and purposive interpretation in order to ascertain the intent of the makers of our Constitution.

The Court has in the past inferred constitutional principles from the preambles to the Constitution Acts and the general object and purpose of the Constitution. In the *Patriation Reference, supra*, the Court found the federal principle to be inherent in the Constitution in this way. . . .

In other words, in the process of Constitutional adjudication, the Court may have regard to unwritten postulates which form the very foundation of the Constitution of Canada. In the case of the *Patriation Reference, supra*, this unwritten postulate was the principle of federalism. In the present case it is the principle of Rule of Law.

It is clear from the above that: (i) the law as stated in s. 23 of the Manitoba Act, 1870 and s. 52 of the Constitution Act, 1982 requires that the unilingual Acts of the Manitoba Legislature be declared to be invalid and of no force or effect, and (ii) without more, such a result would violate the Rule of Law. The task the Court faces is to recognize the unconstitutionality of Manitoba's unilingual laws and the Legislature's duty to comply with the "supreme law" of this country, while avoiding a legal vacuum in Manitoba and ensuring the continuity of the Rule of Law.

A number of the parties and intervenors have suggested that the Court declare the unilingual Acts of the Manitoba legislature to be invalid and of no force or effect

and leave it at that, relying on the legislatures to work out a constitutional amendment. This approach because it would rely on a future and uncertain event, would be inappropriate. A declaration that the laws of Manitoba are invalid and of no legal force or effect would deprive Manitoba of its legal order and cause a transgression of the Rule of Law. For the Court to allow such a situation to arise and fail to resolve it would be an abdication of its responsibility as protector and preserver of the Constitution.

Other solutions suggested by the parties and intervenors are equally unsatisfactory. Counsel for the Attorney General of Manitoba argues that the linguistic rights guaranteed by s. 23 of the Manitoba Act, 1870 can be protected by the Lieutenant-Governor of the province, who can either withhold Royal Assent to a unilingual bill or reserve the bill for the signification of the Governor General's pleasure: Constitution Act, 1867, ss. 55, 57, 90. See also Manitoba Act, 1870 s. 2. Though this legal power continues to exist, it has not been exercised in recent years. See, *Reference re Disallowance and Reservation*, [1938] S.C.R. 71.

The fundamental difficulty with the Attorney General of Manitoba's suggestion is that it would make the executive branch of the federal government, rather than the courts, the guarantor of constitutionally entrenched language rights. It should be noted that a decision of a provincial Lieutenant Governor as to whether to withhold assent or reserve a bill is not reviewable by the courts. *Reference re Disallowance and Reservation, supra*, at p. 95. The overall effect of implementing the suggestion of the Attorney General of Manitoba would be to insulate the Legislature's failue to comply with s. 23 of the Manitoba Act, 1870 from judicial review. Such a result would be entirely inconsistent with the judiciary's duty to uphold the Constitution. . . .

The only appropriate resolution to this Reference is for the Court to fulfill its duty under s. 52 of the Constitution Act, 1982 and declare all the unilingual Acts of the

Legislature of Manitoba to be invalid and of no force and effect and then to take such steps as will ensure the Rule of Law in the Province of Manitoba.

There is no question that it would be impossible for all the Acts of the Manitoba Legislature to be translated, re-enacted, printed and published overnight. There will necessarily be a period of time during which it would not be possible for the Manitoba Legislature to comply with its constitutional duty under s. 23 of the Manitoba Act, 1870.

The vexing question, however, is what will be the legal situation in the Province of Manitoba for the duration of this period. The difficulties faced by the Province of Manitoba are two-fold: first, all of the rights, obligations and other effects which have arisen under the repealed, spent and current Acts of the Manitoba Legislature will be open to challenge, since the laws under which they purportedly arise are invalid and of no force or effect; and, second, the Province of Manitoba has an invalid and therefore ineffectual legal system until the Legislature is able to translate, re-enact, print and publish its current Acts.

With respect to the first of these problems, it was argued by a number of the parties and intervenors that the *de facto* doctrine might be used to uphold the rights, obligations and other effects which have purportedly arisen under the unilingual Acts of the Manitoba Legislature since 1890.

The *de facto* doctrine is defined by Judge Albert Constantineau in *The De Facto Doctrine* (1910), at pp. 3-4 as follows:

The de facto doctrine is a rule or principle of law which, in the first place, justifies the recognition of the authority of governments established and maintained by persons who have usurped the sovereign authority of the State, and assert themselves by force and arms against the lawful government; secondly, which recognizes the existence of, and protects from collateral attack, public or private
bodies corporate, which, though irregularly or illegally organized, yet, under color of law, openly exercise the powers and functions of regularly created bodies; and, thirdly, which imparts validity to the official acts of persons who, under color of right or authority, hold office under the aforementioned governments or bodies, or exercise lawfully existing offices of whatever nature, in which the public or third persons are interested, where the performance of such official acts is for the benefit of the public or third persons, and not for their own personal advantage.

. . . The *de facto* doctrine has long been accepted in Canada. In *O'Neil* v. *Attorney-General of Canada* (1896), 26 S.C.R. 122, at p. 130, Chief Justice Strong said: "The rule of law is that the acts of a person assuming to exercise the functions of an office to which he has no legal title are, as regards third persons, . . . legal and binding." . . .

The application of the *de facto* doctrine is, however, limited to validating acts which are taken under invalid authority: it does not validate the authority under which the acts took place. In other words, the doctrine does not give effect to unconstitutional laws. It recognizes and gives effect only to the justified expectations of those who have relied upon the acts of those administering the invalid laws and to the existence and efficacy of public and private bodies corporate, though irregularly or illegally organized. Thus, the *de facto* doctrine will save those rights, obligations and other effects which have arisen out of actions, performed pursuant to invalid Acts of the Manitoba Legislature by public and private bodies corporate, courts, judges, persons exercising statutory powers and public officials. Such rights, obligations and other effects are, and will always be, enforceable and unassailable.

The *de facto* doctrine will not by itself save all of the rights, obligations and other effects which have purportedly arisen under the repealed and current Acts of the Legislature of Manitoba from 1890 to the date of this judgment. Some of these rights, obligations and other effects did not arise as a consequence of reliance by the public on the acts of officials acting under colour of authority or on the assumed validity of public and private bodies corporate. Furthermore, the *de facto* authority of officials and entities acting under the invalid laws of the Manitoba Legislature will cease on the date of this judgment since all colour of authority ceases on that date. Thus, the *de facto* doctrine only provides a partial solution. . . .

The only appropriate solution for preserving the rights, obligations and other effects which have arisen under invalid Acts of the Legislature of Manitoba and which are not saved by the *de facto* or other doctrines is to declare that, in order to uphold the Rule of Law, these rights, obligations and other effects have, and will continue to have, the same force and effect they would have had if they had arisen under valid enactments, for that period of time during which it would be impossible for Manitoba to comply with its constitutional duty under s. 23 of the Manitoba Act, 1870. The Province of Manitoba would be faced with chaos and anarchy if the legal rights, obligations and other effects which have been relied upon by the people of Manitoba since 1890 were suddenly open to challenge. The constitutional guarantee of Rule of Law will not tolerate such chaos and anarchy.

Nor will the constitutional guarantee of Rule of Law tolerate the Province of Manitoba being without a valid and effectual legal system for the present and future. Thus, it will be necessary to deem temporarily valid and effective the unilingual Acts of the Legislature of Manitoba which would be currently in force, were it not for their constitutional defect, for the period of time during which it would be impossible for the Manitoba Legislature to fulfill its constitutional duty. Since this temporary validation will include the legislation under which the Manitoba Legislature is presently constituted, it will be legally able to re-enact, print and publish its laws

in conformity with the dictates of the Constitution once they have been translated.

Analogous support for the measures proposed can be found in cases which have arisen under the doctrine of state necessity. Necessity in the context of governmental action provides a justification for otherwise illegal conduct of a government during a public emergency. In order to ensure Rule of Law, the Courts will recognize as valid the constitutionally invalid Acts of the Legislature. According to Professor Stavsky, *The Doctrine of State Necessity in Pakistan* (1983), 16 Cornell Int. L.J. 341, at p. 344: "If narrowly and carefully applied, *the doctrine constitutes an affirmation of the rule of law.*"

The courts have applied the doctrine of necessity in a variety of circumstances. A number of cases have involved challenges to the laws of an illegal and insurrectionary government. In the aftermath of the American Civil War, the question arose as to the validity of laws passed by the Confederate States. The Courts in addressing this question were primarily concerned with ensuring that the Rule of Law be upheld. The principle which emerges from these cases can be summarized as follows: During a period of insurrection, when territory is under the control and dominance of an unlawful, hostile government and it is therefore impossible for the lawful authorities to legislate for the peace and good order of the area, the laws passed by the usurping government which are necessary to the maintenance of organized society and which are not in themselves unconstitutional will be given force and effect: see *Texas* v. *White* (1868) 74 U.S. 700; *Horn* v. *Lockhart* (1873) 84 U.S. 570; *United States* v. *Insurance Companies* (1874), 89 U.S. 99; *Baldy* v. *Hunter* (1898) 171 U.S. 388.

The doctrine of necessity was also applied with respect to an insurrectionary government in *Madzimbamuto* v. *Lardner-Burke*, [1969] 1 A.C. 645 (P.C.). This case dealt with the efficacy of official acts of the Smith regime shortly after Southern Rhodesia's unilateral declaration of independence from Britain in 1965. Lord Reid, writing for the majority, canvassed the American authorities discussed above, but found them distinguishable on the ground that in this case, Parliament had specifically provided that it would have legislative authority for the territory of Southern Rhodesia (in the *Southern Rhodesia Act* and Order in Council of 1965), and it thereby followed that there was no "legal vacuum" necessitating recognition by the Courts of the laws purportedly enacted by the insurrectionary Smith government.

Lord Pearce dissented from the majority view. He saw no merit in the distinction drawn by the majority, noting that while the lawful government had *formally* asserted its authority, it was in no position, *as a practical matter*, to actually govern. In his view, the American cases presented "a helpful analogy" and, in reliance on them, he formulated the "state necessity doctrine" as follows, at p. 732:

> *I accept the existence of the principle that acts done by those actually in control without lawful validity may be recognized as valid or acted upon by the courts, with certain limitations namely (a) so far as they are directed to and reasonably required for ordinary orderly running of the State, and (b) so far as they do not impair the rights of citizens under the lawful (1961) Constitution, and (c) so far as they are not intended to and do not in fact directly help the usurpation and do not run contrary to the policy of the lawful Sovereign. This last, i.e., (c), is tantamount to a test of public policy.*

Again, it is clear that the reasons for applying the state necessity doctrine pertain to a concern with the Rule of Law. At p. 740, Lord Pearce says:

> *If one disregards all illegal provision for the needs of the country, there is a vacuum and chaos. In my view, the principle of necessity or implied mandate applies to the present circumstances in Rhodesia.*

It should be noted that neither the American cases on necessity, nor the comments of Lord Pearce in *Madzimbamuto* can be applied directly to the present case. All of these cases are concerned with insurrectionary governments, the present case is not. But even more fundamental than this distinction is the fact that all of these cases require that the laws saved by the application of the doctrine not impair the rights of the citizens guaranteed by the Constitution. In the present case, the laws in question *do* impair these rights. Nonetheless, the necessity cases on insurrectionary governments illustrate the more general proposition that temporary effect can be given to invalid laws where this is necessary to preserve the Rule of Law.

The doctrine of state necessity has also been used to uphold laws enacted by a lawful government in contravention of express constitutional provisions under extraordinary circumstances which render it impossible for the government to comply with the Constitution. In the *Attorney General of the Republic* v. *Mustafa Ibrahim*, [1964] Cyprus Law Reports 195 the Court of Appeal of Cyprus invoked the doctrine of state necessity to hold valid a law passed in direct contravention of the express provisions of the Cypriot Constitution.

Cyprus is a dyarchy, power being shared between Greek and Turkish Cypriots. The 1960 Cypriot Constitution contained several entrenched provisions guaranteeing the equality of status of the two Cypriot communities. In particular, the Constitution established a High Court of Justice and a Supreme Constitutional Court, each staffed by judges from both communities and governed by a neutral (non-Cypriot) President. A Turkish Cypriot charged with an offence against a Greek Cypriot was given the right to be tried by such a "mixed" court. In addition, all laws were required to be enacted in both the Turkish and the Greek languages. These constitutional provisions, termed "basic articles," could not be amended.

In 1963, Turkish insurgents gained control over those parts of Cyprus inhabited by the Turkish community. This effectively prevented Turkish Cypriots from participating in the government of the country, including the Parliament of Cyprus and all courts located outside the Turkish areas. As a consequence, it became impossible to constitute "mixed" courts as required by the Constitution, to assemble the Supreme Constitutional Court, or to enact laws in Turkish, there being virtually no qualified translators available during this insurgency.

To deal with the emergency, the Parliament of Cyprus passed a temporary law abolishing the requirement of mixed courts for the duration of the insurrection and conferring on a new Court of Appeal, composed solely of Greek Cypriot Judges, the jurisdiction then vested by the Constitution in the Supreme Constitutional Court. This temporary measure, enacted in Greek only, was challenged as unconstitutional.

The Court of Appeal upheld the law on grounds of necessity. Josephides J. at p. 265 set forth four prerequisites which he said must be satisfied before the doctrine of state necessity could apply to validate such an unconstitutional law: (a) an imperative and inevitable necessity or exceptional circumstances; (b) no other remedy to apply; (c) the measure taken must be proportionate to the necessity; and (d) it must be of a temporary character limited to the duration of the exceptional circumstances.

Josephides J. added:

A law thus enacted is subject to the control of this court to decide whether the aforesaid prerequisites are satisfied, i.e. whether there exists such necessity and whether the measures taken were necessary to meet it.

All four conditions being satisfied, Josephides J. concluded (at p. 268) that the impugned law, while unconstitutional, was nevertheless effectual "for the duration of the necessity and no more."

The question in *Ibrahim, supra* was whether a temporary unconstitutional law, enacted in order to meet the exigencies of a state of emergency, could be valid. The question in the present Reference is quite different. Here, the Court is concerned with whether unconstitutional laws can be given temporary validity in order to avoid a state of emergency. . . .

The principle that can be deduced from the *Ibrahim* case with respect to the present context, however, is that a Court may temporarily treat as valid and effective laws which are constitutionally flawed in order to preserve the Rule of Law. The case stands for the proposition that under conditions of emergency, when it is impossible to comply with the Constitution, the Court may allow the government a temporary reprieve from such compliance in order to preserve society and maintain as nearly as possible, normal conditions. The overriding concern is the protection of the Rule of Law.

A third situation in which the doctrine of necessity has been applied is where the executive has taken emergency action to fill a legislative void created by a court ruling. In the Pakistani case of *Special Reference No. 1 of 1955*, P.L.R. 1956 W.P. 598, there was a challenge to emergency action taken by the Governor General of Pakistan in the face of an apparent legal vacuum. The Indian Independence Act, 1947, was the original Constitution for the newly created Dominions of India and Pakistan. As a step toward complete independence, the Act provided for a Constituent Assembly in each country, with power to amend the Act and enact new constitutional laws. Royal assent was required for the passage of all such constitutional legislation.

The Constituent Assembly of Pakistan set out immediately to forge its own Constitution. From 1947 to 1954 it enacted 44 constitutional amendments. The members of the Assembly, however, felt that it was important that the new Constitution have roots as independent of imperial authority as possible. They therefore deliberately failed to obtain Royal Assent to any of the amendments. Indeed, in 1948, the Assembly passed an amendment purportedly abolishing the requirement of Royal Assent. This amendment, like the other 43, was itself passed without royal assent.

In *Federation of Pakistan* v. *Tamizuddin Khan*, P.L.R. 1956 W.P. 306, the Federal Court of Pakistan held the constitutional amendments void. It followed that a great many statutes and regulations enacted pursuant to the invalid amendments were themselves nullities. The situation that obtained was in many respects similar to that now facing Manitoba.

The Governor General of Pakistan reacted to the emergency by summoning a Constituent Convention and issuing a proclamation assuming to himself, until the Convention could act, the power to validate and enforce all laws necessary to preserve the State and maintain the government of the country. This action was challenged, and in *Special Reference No. 1 of 1955*, *supra*, the Federal Court of Pakistan held that although the Governor General's action was not authorized by the Constitution, it nevertheless was valid under the doctrine of state necessity. . . .

The *Special Reference No. 1 of 1955*, *supra*, stands for the proposition that a situation of state necessity can arise as a consequence of judicial invalidation of unconstitutional laws, leaving a legal void. The difference between that case and the present is that in the present case it is the *judicial* branch of government that is retrospectively recognizing unconstitutional laws as temporarily valid and enforceable, while in the *Special Reference* case it was the *executive* branch of government which proclaimed that laws were retrospectively valid and enforceable, and the role of the judiciary was simply to condone the actions of the executive.

Thus, the *Special Reference No. 1 of 1955*, *supra*, case cannot be directly applied to the present set of circumstances. It is, however, illustrative of the broader principles which justify this Court's action in the present case: namely, that otherwise invalid acts may be recognized as temporarily valid in order to preserve normative order and the Rule of Law. . . .

The cases on the necessity doctrine in all three circumstances discussed above point to the same conclusion: the Courts will recognize unconstitutional enactments as valid where a failure to do so would lead to legal chaos and thus violate the constitutional requirement of the Rule of Law. This is well expressed by Mr. Justice Triantafyllides in *Ibrahim, supra*, at p. 237:

> If the position was that the administration of justice and the preservation of the rule of law and order in the State could no longer be secured in a manner which would not be inconsistent with the constitution, a constitution under which the sovereign will of the people could not be expressed so as to regulate through an amendment of the fundamental law such a situation, then the House of Representatives, elected by the people, should be empowered to take such necessary steps as are warranted, by the doctrine of necessity, in the exigencies of the situation. *Otherwise the absurd corollary would have been entailed viz, that a State, and the people, should be allowed to perish for the sake of the constitution; on the contrary, a constitution should exist for the preservation of the State and the welfare of the people.*

(Emphasis added)

The doctrine of necessity is not used in these cases to support some law which is above the Constitution; it is, instead used to ensure the unwritten but inherent principle of Rule of Law which must provide the foundation of any constitution.

In every case in which the doctrine of state necessity has been applied it has been either the executive or the legislative branch of government which has responded to the necessitous circumstances, later to have its actions tested in the courts. This fact does not, however, detract from the general relevance of these cases in demonstrating that the courts will not allow the Constitution to be used to create chaos and disorder.

Turning back to the present case, because of the Manitoba Legislature's persistent violation of the constitutional dictates of the Manitoba Act, 1870, the Province of Manitoba is in a state of emergency: all of the Acts of the Legislature of Manitoba, purportedly repealed, spent and current (with the exception of those recent laws which have been enacted, printed and published in both languages), are and always have been invalid and of no force or effect, and the legislature is unable to immediately re-enact these unilingual laws in both languages. The Constitution will not suffer a province without laws. Thus the Constitution requires that temporary validity and force and effect be given to the current Acts of the Manitoba Legislature from the date of this judgment, and that rights, obligations and other effects which have arisen under these laws and the repealed and spent laws of the Province prior to the date of this judgment, which are not saved by the *de facto* or some other doctrine, are deemed temporarily to have been and continue to be effective and beyond challenge. It is only in this way that legal chaos can be avoided and the Rule of Law preserved.

To summarize, the legal situation in the Province of Manitoba is as follows. All unilingually enacted Acts of the Manitoba Legislature are, and always have been, invalid and of no force or effect.

All Acts of the Manitoba Legislature which would currently be valid and of force and effect, were it not for their constitutional defect, are deemed temporarily valid and effective from the date of this judgment to the expiry of the minimum period necessary for translation, re-enactment, printing and publishing. . . .

All rights, obligations and any other effects which have arisen under Acts of the Manitoba Legislature which are purportedly repealed, spent, or would currently be in force were it not for their constitutional defect, and which are *not* saved by the *de facto* doctrine, or doctrines such as *res judicata* and mistake of law, are deemed temporarily to have

been, and to continue to be, enforceable and beyond challenge from the date of their creation to the expiry of the minimum period of time necessary for translation, re-enactment, printing and publishing of these laws. At the termination of the minimum period these rights, obligations and other effects will cease to have force and effect unless the Acts under which they arose have been translated, re-enacted, printed and published in both languages. . . .

As concerns the future, the Constitution requires that, from the date of this judgment, all new Acts of the Manitoba Legislature be enacted, printed and published in both French and English. Any Acts of the Legislature that do not meet this requirement will be invalid and of no force and effect.

THE DURATION OF THE TEMPORARY PERIOD

The difficult question, then, is what is the duration of the minimum period necessary for translation, re-enactment, printing and publishing of the unilingual Acts of the Manitoba Legislature?

It was argued by the Attorney General of Canada and by the Féderation Des Francophones Hors Quebec that this Court fix some arbitrary period such as a year or two years during which the Manitoba Legislature could re-enact its unilingual legislation in both languages.

This solution would not be satisfactory. We do not know how many of the Acts of the Legislature have already been translated. We know nothing as to the availability of translators or their daily output. We thus have no factual basis for determining a period during which compliance with s. 23 of the Manitoba Act, 1870 would not be possible.

As presently equipped the Court is incapable of determining the period of time during which it would not be possible for the Manitoba Legislature to comply with its constitutional duty. The Court will, however, at the request of either the Attorney General of Manitoba, made within one hundred and twenty days of the date of this judgment, make such a determination. The Attorney General of Canada was granted carriage of this *Reference* and the Attorney General of Manitoba represents the province whose laws are in issue in this case. Following such a request, a special hearing will be set and submissions will be accepted from the Attorney General of Canada and the Attorney General of Manitoba and the other intervenors.

The period of temporary validity will not apply to any unilingual Acts of the Legislature enacted after the date of the judgment. From the date of judgment, laws which are not enacted, printed and published in both languages will be invalid and of no force and effect *ab initio*.

QUESTION 4

Question No. 4 of this Reference asks whether any of the provisions of An Act Respecting the Operation of Section 23 of the Manitoba Act in Regard to Statutes, S.M. 1980, c. 3 are inconsistent with s. 23 of the Manitoba Act, 1870 and, if so, whether the inconsistent provisions are invalid and of no force or effect. . . .

There is a dispute among the parties . . . as to whether the 1980 Act itself was enacted, printed and published in both languages or whether it was enacted, printed and published in English only. . . .

On the record as it stands, it is difficult to say with certitude whether the 1980 Act was indeed passed in both languages or whether, even if passed in both languages, it ever received Royal assent, or whether, even if passed and assented to in both languages, it was ever actually published in French. It is unnecessary to resolve this factual question for the purposes of this Reference. It is enough to say that if the 1980 Act was not enacted, printed and published in both English and French, the entire Act, with the exception of new subs. 4(3), is invalid and of no force or effect under s. 23 of the Manitoba Act, 1870. Beyond this, several individual sections of the 1980 Act, including

new subs. 4(3), are, themselves, in substantive conflict with s. 23 of the Manitoba Act, 1870 and invalid.

In *Blaikie No. 1*, this Court held that Chapter III of Title I of the Charter of the French Language, L.Q. 1977, c. 5, ss. 7-13, were *ultra vires* the Legislature of Quebec by virtue of s. 133 of the Constitution Act, 1867. . . .

The teaching of *Blaikie No. 1* is threefold. First, s. 133 of the Constitution Act, 1867 demands not just bilingual printing and publication, but bilingual *enactment*. . . .

Second, the English and French texts of law must be equally authoritative. . . .

The third criterion which emerges from *Blaikie No. 1* is the requirement of simultaneity in the use of both languages in the enactment process. . . .

Nothing less would adequately preserve the linguistic guarantees of those sections or ensure that the law was equally accessible to francophones and anglophones alike.

As we have said, s. 23 of the Manitoba Act, 1870 and s. 133 of the Constitution Act, 1867 are coterminous. *Blaikie No. 1* is therefore controlling on the question of the effect of s. 23 of the Manitoba Act, 1870 on the similar legislation in issue here. Applying the criteria as laid down in *Blaikie No. 1* to the present case, it is clear that the 1980 Act does not meet the requirements of s. 23 of the Manitoba Act, 1870.

The heart of the 1980 Act is s. 4(1), which authorizes the bilingual promulgation of legislation in two stages: (i) the enactment of a statute in one official language only; and (ii) subsequent translation into the other official language. The translation, once certified and deposited with the Clerk of the House, is deemed "valid and of the same effect" as the formally enacted version.

This procedure is insufficient to satisfy s. 23 of the Manitoba Act, 1870. Bilingual enactment is required by s. 23 and unilingual enactment, followed by the later deposit of a translation, is not bilingual enactment. Moreover, s. 4(1) does not contemplate simultaneity in the use of English and French in the enactment process, *i.e.* in the Records and Journals of the legislature, as required by s. 23.

Beyond this, the provision for the deposit of a translation is entirely voluntary. There is no requirement that a translation be deposited. . . .

Finally, the effort to give legal force and effect to a mere translation of an Act through certification and deposit with a Clerk of the House must fail as an unconstitutional attempt to interfere with the powers of the Lieutenant-Governor. Royal assent is required of all enactments. Section 4(1) purports to do away with Royal assent for the translation of Acts, while giving the translation the full force of law. This scheme is clearly *ultra vires* the province under s. 41(a) of the Constitution Act, 1982. See *In re Initiative and Referendum Act*, [1919] A.C. 935 (P.C.).

For all these reasons, s. 4(1) of the 1980 Act is invalid. . . .

Additionally, ss. 2(a) and 5 violate *Blaikie No. 1*'s requirement that the English and French texts of statutes be equally authoritative. Section 2(a) provides that when one version conflicts with the other, the original enactment prevails over the subsequent translation. And s. 5 provides that for all laws enacted before January 1, 1981 any ambiguities or inconsistencies in cross-references to other laws are to be resolved by reference to the English text of such laws. These provisions cannot stand. . . .

Section 1, which provides simply that the term "official language" means either English or French, would be innocuous in any other context. It is clearly, however, ancillary to the invalid provisions of the 1980 Act. The term it defines, "official language," appears fourteen times in the four unconstitutional sections discussed above. In our view, s. 1, although unobjectionable in itself, is inseverable from the invalid provisions and falls with them. It would, in any event, be meaningless standing alone. . . .

To summarize, the entire Act, except for new subs. 4(3), may be invalid under s. 23 of the Manitoba Act, 1870, if it was not enacted, printed and published bilingually. The record is inconclusive on this point. Substantively, ss. 6, 7 and 8 are unobjectionable. Section 4(1), however, violates s. 23's requirement of simultaneous, bilingual enactment and ss. 2(a) and 5 violate s. 23's requirement that both language versions be equally authoritative. The remaining sections of the Act are inseverable from the constitutionally infirm provisions and fall with them. . . .

REFERENCE RE MANITOBA LANGUAGE RIGHTS (ESTABLISHMENT OF TRANSLATION PERIOD)

The opinion of Dickson, C.J.C., Beetz, McIntyre, Wilson and Le Dain JJ.:
. . .

THIS COURT: 1. Gives effect to the commitment of the Province of Manitoba that the Continuing Consolidation of the Statutes of Manitoba and Rules of Court and Administrative Tribunals will appear in bilingual, parallel column format when printed and published.

2. Orders that the period of temporary validity for the laws of Manitoba will continue as follows:

(a) to December 31, 1988 for (i) the Continuing Consolidation of the Statutes of Manitoba; and (ii) the Regulations of Manitoba; and (iii) Rules of Court and of Administrative Tribunals;

(b) to December 31, 1990 for all other laws of Manitoba.

3. Any of the parties hereto, may, in the case of necessity upon further application, supported by such evidence as may be required, return to this Court for such further determination as this Court may decide.

57. Société des Acadiens v. Association of Parents, *1986*

~ The expansion and extension of bilingualism had always been at the top of the Trudeau government's agenda. Shortly after his first election as Prime Minister in 1969, for example, Trudeau had Parliament enact the Official Languages Act, which extended bilingualism in federal government services beyond those required by section 133 of the B.N.A. Act. In 1982, the provisions of section 133 were reaffirmed, and the principles of the Official Languages Act were constitutionalized, in sections 16 to 22 of the Charter. Trudeau had also hoped that the provinces would agree to bind themselves by the same provisions. Only New Brunswick agreed to do so, and the language rights sections of the Charter thus apply to that province as well as to the federal sphere.

The *Acadiens* case grew out of a New Brunswick judicial proceeding and raised the question whether s. 19(2) of the Charter provided a right to be understood in court in either official language. Together with the *Macdonald* and *Bilodeau* parking-ticket cases, *Acadiens* occasioned one of the earliest and most dramatic disagreements among the judges about the issue of judicial activism versus restraint.

In *Macdonald* and *Bilodeau* the majority opinion, written by Justice Beetz and concurred in by all of the francophone judges on the panel, decided that section 133 of the B.N.A. Act and section 23 of the Manitoba Act protected the right of the issuer of a legal "process" (such as a parking ticket) to do so in either official language, but that there was no corresponding right of the addressee of such a process to receive it in the official language of his choice. Similarly, the majority in this case, again speaking through Justice Beetz and including all of his francophone colleagues, holds that the participants in court proceedings have a right to use either official language but not to be understood by those to whom they address themselves. The right to be understood does exist, according to Beetz, but it is based on the fair hearing principles embodied in the Charter's legal rights sections. For the majority, language rights serve a different and narrower purpose than fair hearing rights and should not be confused with the latter.

Chief Justice Dickson takes a broader view of the Charter's language provisions. "Though couched in individualistic terms," he says, "language rights, by their very nature, are intimately and profoundly social." They are communication rights and communication involves not only speaking but being heard and understood. In order for the right to communicate in either official language to be effective, he concludes, it must include the right to be understood. Justice Dickson concedes that this interpretation of language rights involves some overlap with fair hearing rights, but this does not concern him. Both kinds of rights are communication rights, and though they are conceptually distinct, they do not occupy "watertight compartments." Because he does not think it is necessary to dispose of the case, Justice Dickson does not investigate the nature and degree of the overlap—whether, for example, these two "communication" rights perform the same function or whether one of them imposes more demanding standards of understanding than the other.

Justice Wilson has the most sweeping understanding of language rights. Like Justice Dickson, she thinks language rights overlap with fair hearing rights, but she does not hesitate to assert that they require a level of comprehension that goes beyond fairness. Due process considerations, for example, might be satisfied by simultaneous translation during court proceedings, but the language rights of section 19(2), at least at the appellate level, require not only some degree of direct understanding of the language by the judge, but a "level of comprehension [that goes] beyond a mere literal understanding of the language used by counsel. It must be such that the full flavour of the argument can be appreciated."

Justice Wilson does not dwell on the significant changes this standard would require in the staffing of Canada's appellate courts. Appeals are usually heard by panels of at least three judges. Implementing Justice Wilson's test would thus mean that all provincial appellate courts would need three substantially bilingual judges. It is also worth considering the implications of this test for the Supreme Court of Canada, where five judges constitute the minimum panel.

In addition, Justice Wilson does not view the content of the Charter's language rights as constant. She believes that the language rights sections constitutionalize a "principle of growth" toward the fullest degree of bilingualism possible. This means that "What may be adequate to-day in terms of protection for the litigant's right under s. 19(2) may not be adequate tomorrow," and that the aforementioned standard of judicial bilingualism is not "static" but "must be subject to continuous scrutiny." Needless to say, she is thinking of continuous *judicial* scrutiny.

This is precisely the problem for Justice Beetz and the majority. Beetz agrees with Wilson that "s. 16 of the Charter does contain a principle of advancement or progress in the equality of status or use of the two official languages," but he believes that such advancement is the prerogative of the legislative process under s. 16(3). Indeed, he makes a distinction between rights rooted in principle, such as fair hearing rights, and rights rooted in historically specific political compromise, such as language rights. Some of the former may indeed "call for frequent judicial determination," but the legislative process is "particularly suited to the advancement of rights founded on political compromise." In further support of judicial restraint in the area of language rights, and in direct response to Justice Wilson, Justice Beetz (quite uncharacteristically) makes one of the most nakedly political arguments to be found in Supreme Court jurisprudence. It was hoped, he says, that other provinces would follow the lead of New Brunswick and opt into the language provisions of the Charter. These provinces would hesitate to do so, however, if they did not know in advance what they were committing themselves to—i.e. if they thought the rights in question were "inherently dynamic and progressive, apart from legislation and constitutional amendment, and that the speed of progress of this scheme was to be controlled mainly by the courts." ~

SOCIÉTÉ DES ACADIENS v. ASSOCIATION OF PARENTS
In the Supreme Court of Canada. [1986] 1 S.C.R. 549.

DICKSON C.J.C. (Concurring in the result but dissenting on the constitutional question): I agree with my colleagues, Beetz and Wilson JJ. in dismissing the appeal. I adopt the reasoning of Wilson J. on the issues relating to the inherent jurisdiction of the New Brunswick Court of Appeal and its exercise of discretion. On the constitutional question, I am of the view that an affirmative response should be given.

The constitutional question was stated as follows:

Does s. 19(2) of the Canadian Charter of Rights and Freedoms entitle a party in a court of New Brunswick to be heard by a court, the member or members of which are capable of understanding the proceedings, the evidence and the arguments, written and oral, regardless of the official language used by the parties?

I shall confine my review of the facts to those which are pertinent to the constitutional question. The appellants, the Société des Acadiens du Nouveau-Brunswick Inc. and the Association des conseillers scolaires francophones du Nouveau-Brunswick, allege that their constitutional language rights were infringed when Stratton J.A., whose comprehension of French is contested, heard an application for leave to appeal as part of a panel of three judges. The hearing took place in both French and English. The appellants contend that Stratton J.A. did not have sufficient French language abilities to sit on the case.

Initially, the application was scheduled to be heard by Stratton J.A. alone. At the outset of the hearing of the motion, the appellants requested that the matter be heard by a bilingual judge. Stratton J.A. acceded to this request and referred the matter to Angers J.A. When Angers J.A. decided that the matter should be heard by a panel of three judges, Stratton J.A. sat as one of the panel members along with Angers and La Forest JJ.A., despite his earlier decision not to hear the case alone. At the time of the hearing before the panel, the appellants did not object to Stratton J.A.'s appearance on the bench. . . .

The question we must answer is whether the right to choose which language to use in court includes the right to be understood by the judge or judges hearing the case. In the context of this appeal we need not resolve all of the ancillary issues which will arise under s. 19. In particular, we need not determine whether the assistance of interpreters or simultaneous translation would meet the requirement that a litigant be understood by the court. Stratton J.A. did not rely on the assistance of either. No evidence was adduced as to the effectiveness of interpreters or of simultaneous translation, in the context of s. 1 of the Charter or otherwise. No argument was addressed to this point and indeed counsel specifically requested that the Court refrain from deciding this issue in this case. Thus, we need only consider whether s. 19(2) gave the litigants in this case a right to be fully understood by the panel of three judges, including Stratton J.A.

In interpreting Charter provisions, this Court has firmly endorsed a purposive approach. . . . To give effect to a purposive approach in the language context, it is important to consider the constitutional antecedents of the Charter language protections, the cardinal values and purpose of the guarantees, the words chosen to articulate the rights, the character and larger objects of the Charter, and the purpose and meaning of other relevant Charter rights and freedoms. . . .

PRE-CHARTER LANGUAGE PROTECTIONS

It has been suggested that because of the similarity of the language in s. 133 of the Constitution Act, 1867 and s. 19(2) of the Charter the jurisprudence under the former will be influential in determining the outcome of Charter litigation. The actual wording of s. 19(2) parallels in part s. 133.

I wish to make three preliminary observations with respect to the usefulness of s. 133 case law in interpretation of the Charter language guarantees. First, the specific issue to be resolved in the case at bar has not been decided in the context of s. 133 and related provisions; there is considerable litigation in courts across Canada on this very question. . . . It is not within the scope of this case to give a definitive interpretation to s. 133 and related provisions vis-a-vis the language rights of litigants. I leave that debate to another day.

Secondly, despite the similarity between s. 133 and s. 19(2), we are dealing with different constitutional provisions enacted in different contexts. In my view, the interpretation of s. 133 of the Constitution Act, 1867 is not determinative of the interpretation of Charter provisions.

Finally, although the specific issue raised in this appeal has not been decided in a s. 133 context, there is much to be learned about the general approach adopted by this Court to constitutional language protections from a review of the jurisprudence under s. 133 and related provisions. The full 133 reads:

Either the English or the French Language may be used by any Person in the Debates of the Houses of the Parliament of Canada and of the Houses of the Legislature of Quebec; and both those Languages shall be used in the respective

Records and Journals of those Houses; and either of those Languages may be used by any Person or in any Pleading or Process in or issuing from any Court of Canada established under this Act, and in or from all or any of the Courts of Quebec.

The Acts of the Parliament of Canada and of the Legislature of Quebec shall be printed and published in both those Languages.

~ Dickson C.J.C. then discusses *Jones, Blaikie 1* and 2, and the *Reference Re Manitoba Language Rights*. His comments parallel those of Wilson J. below. ~

The final two decisions of this Court I wish to discuss are *MacDonald* v. *City of Montreal*, [1986] 1 S.C.R. 460, and *Bilodeau* v. *Attorney General of Manitoba*, [1986] 1 S.C.R. 449 which are being rendered concurrently with this judgment. Both raised the question of whether a unilingual summons for a traffic violation offended the constitutional language provisions. A majority of the Court held in each case that a unilingual summons did meet the constitutional requirements. In my opinion, the outcome in both *MacDonald* and *Bilodeau* was clearly required by the words ". . . either of those languages may be used . . . in any . . . Process . . . issuing from any Court."

The conclusion in each of these cases does not affect the present appeal. Nor would *MacDonald* and *Bilodeau* be determinative of the outcome of an appeal similar to the one at bar arising pursuant to s. 133. Section 133 states clearly that the issuance of process from any court may be in either French or English. In contrast, we are concerned in this case with interpreting the phrase "either of those languages may be used by any Person . . . in . . . any Court." This is something quite different from the language used in issuing documents. While s. 133 expressly limits the rights of recipients of court documents by empowering the court to issue documents in a language which the recipient may not understand, no such explicit limitation is to be found with respect to in-Court proceedings. In the absence of such a limitation, it is open for the Court to conclude that the litigant's right to use either language entails a right to be understood, just as in *Blaikie No. 2*, it entailed a right to bilingual rules of practice.

In summary, the jurisprudence of this Court under s. 133 of the Constitution Act, 1867 and s. 23 of the Manitoba Act, 1870 reveals for the most part a willingness to give constitutional language guarantees a liberal construction, while retaining an acceptance of certain limits on the scope of protection when required by the text of the provisions.

THE PURPOSE OF THE LANGUAGE RIGHTS PROTECTED IN THE CHARTER

Linguistic duality has been a longstanding concern in our nation. Canada is a country with both French and English solidly embedded in its history. The constitutional language protections reflect continued and renewed efforts in the direction of bilingualism. In my view, we must take special care to be faithful to the spirit and purpose of the guarantee of language rights enshrined in the Charter. In the words of André Tremblay, in his article "L'interpretation des dispositions constitutionnelles relatives aux droits linguistiques" (1983), 13 Man. L. J. 651 at p. 653:

[Translation] In short, a broad, liberal and dynamic interpretation of the language provisions of the Constitution would be in line with the exceptional importance of their function and would remedy the ills which the new Constitution was undoubtedly meant to address.

Sections 16 to 23 of the Charter entrench two official languages in Canada. They provide language protection in a broad spectrum of public life, including legislatures, courts, government offices and schools. . . . Despite academic debate about the precise significance of s. 16, at the very least it provides a strong indicator of the purpose of the language guarantees in the Charter. By adopting the special constitutional language protections in the Charter, the federal government of Canada and New Brunswick have demonstrated their commitment to official bilingualism within their respective jurisdictions. Whether s. 16 is visionary, declaratory or substantive in nature, it is an important interpretive aid in construing the other language provisions of the Charter, including s. 19(2).

In looking at the Charter it is worth observing that, unlike s. 133, the provisions go beyond general principles to specific modalities for the achievement of equality of status in language, and expressly provide in s. 16(3) for legislative measures to advance the equality of status of the two official languages. Undoubtedly the fact that the two languages are to be of equal status (s. 16(1) and (2)) encourages a generous application of such measures and of the Charter itself in achieving that goal.

I should add that the Charter was designed primarily to recognize the rights and freedoms of individuals vis-à-vis the State. When acting in their official capacities on behalf of the State, therefore, judges and court officials do not enjoy unconstrained language liberties. Rather, they are invested with certain duties and responsibilities in their service to the community. This extends to the duty to give a meaningful language choice to litigants appearing before them.

THE RIGHT TO USE THE OFFICIAL LANGUAGE OF ONE'S CHOICE

Section 19(2) provides to litigants the right to use the official language of their choice. The essence of this appeal, therefore, is whether this right to "use" French or English in the courts embraces the right to be understood by the court in the language of one's choice as well as the right to make oral and written submissions in that language.

There is no disagreement amongst members of this Court that the right embodies at a minimum the right to speak and make written submissions in the language of one's choice. Must this right, to be meaningful, extend to the right to be understood, either directly or possibly with the aid of an interpreter or simultaneous translation? In my opinion, the answer must be in the affirmative. What good is a right to use one's language if those to whom one speaks cannot understand? Though couched in individualistic terms, language rights, by their very nature, are intimately and profoundly social. We speak and write to communicate to others. In the courtroom, we speak to communicate to the judge or judges. It is fundamental, therefore, to any effective and coherent guarantee of language rights in the courtroom that the judge or judges understand, either directly or through other means, the language chosen by the individual coming before the court.

Both parties and the intervenors agreed on this point. . . .

LANGUAGE RIGHTS VS. PROCEDURAL FAIRNESS

Language rights in the courts are, in my opinion, conceptually distinct from fair hearing rights. While it is important to acknowledge this distinction, each category of rights does not occupy a watertight compartment. Just as fair hearing rights are, in part, intimately concerned with effective communication between adjudicator and litigant, so too are language rights in the court. There will therefore be a certain amount of overlap between the two. At the same time, each category of rights will continue to address concerns not touched by the other. For example, whether or not an individual is even entitled to an oral hearing comes under the exclusive rubric of natural justice, not language rights.

The existence of a certain amount of overlap between various rights and freedoms is not unusual. Rights and freedoms often relate to and supplement each other. For example, the freedom of religion in s. 2(a) of the Charter is closely related to the protection against discrimination on the basis of religion in s. 15 and the free-

dom of assembly and association of religious groups in subsections 2(c) and (d) respectively. In a similar vein, the protection afforded by common law natural justice requirements or by s. 7 of the Charter to be heard and understood by the adjudicator in an oral hearing does not undermine the importance of being understood by the adjudicator as an aspect of one's language rights in s. 19 of the Charter.

CONCLUSIONS REGARDING S. 19(2)

In my opinion, the right to use either French or English in court, guaranteed in s. 19(2), includes the right to be understood by the judge or judges hearing the case. I reiterate that the techniques or mechanisms which might aid in such understanding, such as the use of interpreters or simultaneous translation, are not before us in this appeal. I would answer the constitutional question in the affirmative. . . .

Having decided that s. 19(2) gives litigants the right to be understood by the judges hearing their case, we must determine whether Stratton J.A. had sufficient abilities in the French language to enable him to understand the submissions made by the appellants. The evidentiary basis for deciding this question is far from satisfactory. It consists of two affidavits and the procedural history of the case. . . .

In cases such as these, it is my view that we must presume good faith on the part of judges. In light of the lack of any objection at the time of the hearing and in the absence of convincing evidence, I think we must assume that Stratton J.A. had a sufficient knowledge of French to understand the submissions made by the appellants. . . .

Accordingly, I would dismiss the appeal with costs.

The Judgment of Beetz, Estey, Chouinard, Lamer and Le Dain JJ. was delivered by

BEETZ J: I have had the advantage of reading the reasons of the Chief Justice and those of Wilson J. . . . I respectfully disagree as to the answer which they would give to the constitutional question and as to their reasons for answering it as they propose. . . .

The issue raised by this question has to do with the content of the constitutional right to use either English or French in any court of New Brunswick: does this right comprise the right to be heard and understood by the court regardless of the official language used?

The issue was different in *MacDonald* v. *City of Montreal*, [1986] 1 S.C.R. 460, where what had to be decided was not the content of the right to choose English or French but in whom the right vested, the issuer or the recipient of a summons issued by a Quebec court. However, in *MacDonald*, submissions were made with respect to communication as a purpose of language rights and with respect to the right to understand judicial processes and proceedings as a requirement of natural justice. These submissions, which are closely related to the issue raised in the case at bar, were considered and discussed in the reasons for judgment. A certain degree of overlapping between the two cases is accordingly inevitable and therefore it will be necessary to quote in this case from the reasons in *MacDonald*.

The other difference between the two cases is that the *MacDonald* case dealt with s. 133 of the Constitution Act, 1867 whereas the relevant provision in the case at bar is s. 19(2) of the Canadian Charter of Rights and Freedoms. In my view however, given the similarities of the two provisions, this difference is only one of form, not of substance.

Section 19(2) of the Charter should be read in the context of that part of the Charter that is entitled "Official languages of Canada" and comprises ss. 16 to 22: . . .

Subject to minor variations of style, the language of s. 17, 18 and 19 of the Charter has clearly and deliberately been borrowed from that of the English version of s. 133 of the Constitution Act 1867 of which no French version has yet been proclaimed pursuant to s. 55 of the Con-

stitution Act, 1982. It would accordingly be incorrect in my view to decide this case without considering the interpretation of s. 133. . . .

The somewhat compressed and complicated statutory drafting exemplified in s. 133 has been shortened and simplified in ss. 17 to 19 of the Charter, as befits the style of a true constitutional instrument. The wording of the relevant part of s. 133 ("may be used by any Person or in any Pleading or Process in or issuing from . . . all or any of the Courts of") has been changed to "may be used by any person in, or in any pleading in or process issuing from, any court of". I do not think that anything turns on this change which is one of form only.

Furthermore, in my opinion, s. 19(2) of the Charter does not, anymore than s. 133 of the Constitution Act, 1867, provide two separate rules, one for the languages that may be used by any person with respect to in-court proceedings and the languages that may be used in any pleading or process. A proceeding as well as a process have to emanate from someone, that is from a person, whose language rights are thus protected in the same manner and to the same extent, as the right of a litigant or any other participant to speak the official language of his choice in court. Under both constitutional provisions, there is but one substantive rule for court processes and in-court proceedings and I am here simply paraphrasing what has been said on this point in the *MacDonald* case, in the reasons of the majority, at p. 484.

It is my view that the rights guaranteed by s. 19(2) of the Charter are of the same nature and scope as those guaranteed by s. 133 of the Constitution Act, 1867 with respect to the courts of Canada and the courts of Quebec. As was held by the majority at pp. 498 to 501 in *MacDonald*, these are essentially language rights unrelated to and not to be confused with the requirements of natural justice. These language rights are the same as those which are guaranteed by s. 17 of the Charter with respect to parliamentary debates.

They vest in the speaker or in the writer or issuer of court processes and give the speaker or the writer the constitutionally protected power to speak or to write in the official language of his choice. And there is no language guarantee, either under s. 133 of the Constitution Act, 1867, or s. 19 of the Charter, any more than under s. 17 of the Charter, that the speaker will be heard or understood, or that he has the right to be heard or understood in the language of his choice.

I am reinforced in this view by the contrasting wording of s. 20 of the Charter. Here, the Charter has expressly provided for the right to communicate in either official language with some offices of an institution of the Parliament or Government of Canada and with any office of an institution of the Legislature or Government of New Brunswick. The right to communicate in either language postulates the right to be heard or understood in either language.

I am further reinforced in this view by the fact that those who drafted the Charter had another explicit model they could have used had they been so inclined, namely s. 13(1) of the Official Languages of New Brunswick Act, R.S.N.B. 1973, c. 0-1:

13. (1) Subject to section 15, in any proceeding before a court, any person appearing or giving evidence may be heard in the official language of his choice and such choice is not to place that person at any disadvantage.

Here again, s. 13(1) of the Act, unlike the Charter, has expressly provided for the right to be heard in the official language of one's choice. Those who drafted s. 19(2) of the Charter and agreed to it could easily have followed the language of s. 13(1) of the Official Languages of New Brunswick Act instead of that of s. 133 of the Constitution Act, 1867. That they did not do so is a clear signal that they wanted to provide for a different effect, namely the effect of s. 133. If the people of the Province of New Brunswick

were agreeable to have a provision like s. 13(1) of the Official Languages of New Brunswick Act as part of their law, they did not agree to see it entrenched in the Constitution. I do not think it should be forced upon them under the guise of constitutional interpretation.

The only other provision, apart from s. 20, in that part of the Charter entitled "Official Languages of Canada," which ensures communication or understanding in both official languages is that of s. 18. It provides for bilingualism at the legislative level. In *MacDonald* one can read the following passage, in the reasons of the majority, at p. 496:

Section 133 has not introduced a comprehensive scheme or system of official bilingualism, even potentially, but a limited form of compulsory bilingualism at the legislative level, combined with an even more limited form of optional unilingualism at the option of the speaker in Parliamentary debates and at the option of the speaker, writer or issuer in judicial proceedings or processes. Such a limited scheme can perhaps be said to facilitate communication and understanding, up to a point, but only as far as it goes and it does not guarantee that the speaker, writer or issuer of proceedings or processes will be understood in the language of his choice by those he is addressing.

The scheme has now been made more comprehensive in the Charter with the addition of New Brunswick to Quebec—and Manitoba—and with new provisions such as s. 20. But where the scheme deliberately follows the model of s. 133 of the Constitution Act, 1867, as it does in s. 19(2), it should, in my opinion, be similarly construed.

I must again cite a passage of the reasons of the majority, at p. 500, in *MacDonald* relating to s. 133 of the Constitution Act, 1867 but which is equally applicable, *a fortiori*, to the official languages provisions of the Charter:

This is not to put the English and the French languages on the same footing as other languages. Not only are the English and the French languages placed in a position of equality, they are also given a preferential position over all other languages. And this equality as well as this preferential position are both constitutionally protected by s. 133 of the Constitution Act, 1867. Without the protection of this provision, one of the two official languages could, by simple legislative enactment, be given a degree of preference over the other as was attempted in Chapter III of Title 1 of the Charter of the French Language, invalidated in Blaikie No. 1. *English unilingualism, French unilingualism and, for that matter, unilingualism in any other language could also be imposed by simple legislative enactment. Thus it can be seen that, if s. 133 guarantees but a minimum, this minimum is far from being insubstantial.*

The common law right of the parties to be heard and understood by a court and the right to understand what is going on in court is not a language right but an aspect of the right to a fair hearing. It is a broader and more universal right than language rights. It extends to everyone including those who speak or understand neither official language. It belongs to the category of rights which in the Charter are designated as legal rights and indeed it is protected at least in part by provisions such as those of ss. 7 and 14 of the Charter: . . .

Unlike language rights which are based on political compromise, legal rights tend to be seminal in nature because they are rooted in principle. Some of them, such as the one expressed in s. 7 of the Charter, are so broad as to call for frequent judicial determination.

Language rights, on the other hand, although some of them have been enlarged and incorporated into the Charter, remain nonetheless founded on political compromise.

This essential difference between the two types of rights dictates a distinct judicial approach with respect to each. More particularly, the courts should pause before they decide to act as instruments of change with respect to language rights. This is not to say that language rights provisions are cast in stone and should remain immune altogether from judicial interpretation. But, in my opinion, the courts should approach them with more restraint than they would in construing legal rights.

Such an attitude of judicial restraint is in my view compatible with s. 16 of the Charter, the introductory section of the part entitled "Official Languages of Canada."

Section 19(2) being the substantive provision which governs the case at bar, we need not concern ourselves with the substantive content of s. 16, whatever it may be. But something should be said about the interpretative effect of s. 16 as well as the question of the equality of the two official languages.

I think it is accurate to say that s. 16 of the Charter does contain a principle of advancement or progress in the equality of status or use of the two official languages. I find it highly significant however that this principle of advancement is linked with the legislative process referred to in s. 16(3), which is a codification of the rule in *Jones* v. *Attorney General of New Brunswick*, [1975] 2 S.C.R. 182. The legislative process, unlike the judicial one, is a political process and hence particularly suited to the advancement of rights founded on political compromise.

One should also take into consideration the constitutional amending formula with respect to the use of official languages. Under s. 41(c) of the Constitution Act, 1982, the unanimous consent of the Senate and House of Commons and of the legislative assembly of each province is required for that purpose but "subject to section 43." Section 43 provides for the constitutional amendment of provisions relating to some but not all provinces and requires the "resolutions of the Senate and House of Commons and of the legislative assembly of each province to which the amendment applies." It is public knowledge that some provinces other than

New Brunswick—and apart from Quebec and Manitoba—were expected ultimately to opt into the constitutional scheme or part of the constitutional scheme prescribed by ss. 16 to 22 of the Charter, and a flexible form of constitutional amendment was provided to achieve such an advancement of language rights. But again, this is a form of advancement brought about through a political process, not a judicial one.

If however the provinces were told that the scheme provided by ss. 16 to 22 of the Charter was inherently dynamic and progressive, apart from legislation and constitutional amendment, and that the speed of progress of this scheme was to be controlled mainly by the courts, they would have no means to know with relative precision what it was that they were opting into. This would certainly increase their hesitation in so doing and would run contrary to the principle of advancement contained in s. 16(3).

In my opinion, s. 16 of the Charter confirms the rule that the courts should exercise restraint in their interpretation of language rights provisions.

I do not think the interpretation I adopt for s. 19(2) of the Charter offends the equality provision of s. 16. Either official language may be used by anyone in any court of New Brunswick or written by anyone in any pleading in or process issuing from any such court. The guarantee of language equality is not, however, a guarantee that the official language used will be understood by the person to whom the pleading or process is addressed.

Before I leave this question of equality however, I wish to indicate that if one should hold that the right to be understood in the official language used in court is a language right governed by the equality provision of s. 16, one would have gone a considerable distance towards the adoption of a constitutional requirement which could not be met except by a bilingual judiciary. Such a requirement would have far reaching consequences and would constitute a surprisingly roundabout and implicit way of amending the judicature

provisions of the Constitution of Canada.

I have no difficulty in holding that the principles of natural justice as well as s. 13(1) of the Official Languages of New Brunswick Act

entitle a party pleading in a court of New Brunswick to be heard by a court, the member or members of which are capable of understanding the proceedings, the evidence and the arguments, written and oral, regardless of the official language used by the parties.

But in my respectful opinion, no such entitlement can be derived from s. 19(2) of the Charter. . . .

I will leave for another day the question as to the reasonable means necessary to ensure that the member or members of a Court understand the proceedings, the evidence and the arguments, written or oral, regardless of the official language used by the parties.

It remains to be decided whether Stratton J.A. was disqualified on the ground that his command of the French language was allegedly inadequate. . . .

I agree with the following reasons given by Madame Wilson J. why, on the facts of this case, we cannot reach the conclusion that Stratton J.A. was disqualified:

1. In the absence of any system of testing, it is for the judge to assess in good faith and in as objective a manner as possible, his or her level of understanding of the language of the proceedings.

2. We cannot infer, from Stratton J.A.'s accession to counsel's request that he refer the applications to a bilingual judge, that he necessarily agreed with the appellants that his degree of understanding of the French language was inadequate.

3. We may infer from the conduct of Stratton J.A. that he considered that he had an adequate understanding of the French language to sit on the case in accordance with the requirements of natural justice and of s. 13(1) of the Official Languages of New Brunswick Act.

4. It is very significant that counsel did not raise the issue of Stratton J.A.'s competence to sit on the merits of the applications.

I would dismiss the appeal with costs. However, there will be no order as to costs for or against the interveners.

WILSON J. (Concurring in the result but dissenting on the constitutional question): . . . It has been suggested by a number of writers and by some courts also that the meaning to be given to the official languages sections of the Charter including s. 19(2) will be heavily influenced by the view that is taken of s. 16. I think this is probably correct and it might be useful therefore to see what the differing views of s. 16 are. . . .

Professor Tremblay discusses two possible approaches to s. 16 at p. 450:

There are two hypotheses. The declaration [in s. 16(1)] can be considered as purely platonic or abstract, like a preamble which sets forth a goal or a general rule whose scope would be determined by ss. 17 to 22. The aim of the declaration would not be to establish complete or absolute bilingualism, but only the level or forms of bilingualism specified in the subsequent sections. According to the second hypothesis, s. 16(1) would be seen as containing the fundamental and autonomous principle of language policy at the federal level, or what can be called the cornerstone or pivot of all language provisions at the federal level. Section 16(1) would have the effect of restricting the powers of the federal government, which would have the constitutional obligation to ensure equality of status and the equal rights and privileges of French and English. It would also have the effect of leading to extensive judicial control of the constitutionality of federal laws and rules which would be contrary to the principle of equality. This interpretation is feasible and we understand how the Supreme Court could arrive at it. . . .

In my view, the difficulty in characterizing s. 16 of the Charter stems in large part from the problems of construction inherent in s. 16(1). I would read the opening statement ''English and French are the official languages of Canada'' as declaratory and the balance of the section as identifying the main consequence in the federal context of the official status which has been declared, namely that the two languages have equality of status and have the same rights and privileges as to their use in all institutions of the Parliament and government of Canada. Subsection (3) of s. 16 makes it clear, however, that these consequences represent the goal rather than the present reality; they are something that has to be ''advanced'' by Parliament and the legislatures. This would seem to be in the spirit of *Jones* v. *Attorney General of New Brunswick*, [1975] 2 S.C.R. 182, namely that legislatures cannot derogate from already declared rights but they may add to them. Provided their legislation ''advances'' the cause of equality of status of the two official languages it will survive judicial scrutiny; otherwise not. I do not believe, however, that any falling short of the goal at any given point of time necessarily gives a right to relief. I agree with those who see a principle of growth or development in s. 16, a progression towards an ultimate goal. Accordingly the question, in my view, will always be—where are we currently on the road to bilingualism and is the impugned conduct in keeping with that stage of development? If it is, then even if it does not represent full equality of status and equal rights of usage, it will not be contrary to the spirit of s. 16.

One of the difficulties in interpreting s. 16 in the way I have suggested lies in s. 20(1) which confers a right to communicate in English or French with and receive available services from ''any head or central office of an institution of the Parliament or government of Canada'' but imports a limit on such right in dealing with ''any other office of any such institution.'' The narrowness of s. 20(1), although it may very well be appropriate in terms of present resources and capabilities, seems to directly contradict the spirit of s. 16(1). Any steps towards full accommodation of language rights endorsed by the courts under the growth principle in s. 16(1) would have to be consistent with s. 20(1), a provision which can only be changed by constitutional amendment requiring the consent of all the provinces. It is perhaps possible, however, to find latitude for growth by combining the message of s. 16(3) with the use in s. 20(1) of "significant demand for services and communications" and "reasonableness due to the nature of the office" as the determining factor in whether an individual has full rights under s. 20(1). If I am correct in my characterization of s. 16(1) as constitutionalizing a societal commitment to growth, then presumably our understanding of what is significant and what is reasonable under present conditions will evolve at a pace commensurate with social change. Under the aegis of s. 16(3) Parliament and the legislatures may legislate as to what is a "significant demand" and what is "reasonable" in a manner that reflects heightened social expectations. Accordingly, it is only judicial development of the right in s. 20(1) that is hampered by the section's limited scope.

I am inclined to accept this as a workable interpretation of the interplay between the provisions in the official languages part of the Charter and as a way around the difficulty posed by s. 20(1). I find it unlikely that the finite language employed in s. 20(1) was meant to inhibit the interpretive impact of s. 16(1) on the rest of the language provisions and to negate the principle of growth which has traditionally been associated with the interpretation of constitutional provisions. Such a finding would render s. 16(1) redundant or at best a formal embellishment and would run counter to the approach of this Court which has been to give full and purposive meaning to every word of the Charter. In addition to considering s. 16 of the Charter in relation to the interpretation to be given to s. 19(2) consideration also has to be given to ss. 27 and 14: . . .

It has been suggested that there may be some conflict between s. 27 and s. 16(3), particularly the French text of s. 16(3), if the phrase "favoriser la progression," in contradistinction to the word "advance" in the English text, is construed as involving an element of preferment to English and French over other languages: see Alain Gautron, "French/English Discrepancies in the Canadian Charter of Rights and Freedoms" (1982), 12 *Man. L.J.* 220. While I appreciate the point that is being made, I do not believe that s. 27 was intended to deter the movement towards the equality of status in English and French until such time as a similar status could be attained for all the other languages spoken in Canada. This would derogate from the special status conferred on English and French in s. 16.

As far as s. 14 is concerned it might be argued that it supports the view that translation or interpretation would be adequate under s. 19. But this is far from clear. The right to an interpreter has usually been identified with the right to be present at trial. For example, in *Attorney General of Ontario* v. *Reale*, [1975] 2 S.C.R. 624, this Court held that an accused, though physically present at his trial, was not present within the meaning of s. 577(1) of the Criminal Code because he was unable to understand the language in which the proceedings were being conducted. It seems to me that the right to the assistance of an interpreter would extend to all cases where the right to be heard was either expressly or impliedly provided for by law and also to all cases where the rules of natural justice required that a hearing take place. Indeed, this seems to be the effect of the existing Canadian jurisprudence. For example, in *Unterreiner* v. *The Queen* (1980), 51 C.C.C. (2d) 373, it was held that the absence of a competent interpreter amounted to a denial of natural justice serious enough to order a re-trial. These cases certainly indicate that the ability to understand and be understood is a minimal requirement of due process. They do not, however, assist in answering the question whether the assistance of an interpreter satisfies the requirements of

s. 19(2). Indeed, it may be significant that s. 14 is not included in the sections dealing with Canada's official languages.

It is interesting to note that in the "Final Report to the Council of the Barristers' Society of New Brunswick, Committee on Integration of the Two Official Languages in the Practice of Law, September 1981,'' strong views were expressed on the subject of interpreters and translation. The Report was particularly critical of the use of simultaneous translation. Quoting from p. 64:

The discussion focussed primarily on the problems resulting from the use of translation. The majority of lawyers felt that simultaneous translation would not work in a trial in New Brunswick. In their opinion there was no properly qualified interpreter in the province who possesses the necessary competence to do simultaneous translation in a trial because of the high standards required for this form of translation. They mentioned as examples, the difficulties resulting from fast exchanges between two and maybe more persons in a trial, and the highly technical and legal language unique to each trial. Experience shows that the interpreter has some difficulty in following the proceedings often rendering an incomplete translation which is unacceptable in "a profession of words." Only if properly qualified interpreters such as in the Federal Court of Canada were available, should this method be preferred.

The view was expressed in the Report, however, that simultaneous translation in its present state might be adequate in situations where there was very little cross-examination such as in the Court of Appeal and in some tribunals. The Committee also pointed out the limitations of consecutive translation where the testimony of witnesses is completely modified through the use of an interpreter and becomes for all practical purposes the testimony of the interpreter. The Report indicated that the lawyers thought the use of an interpreter reduced the effectiveness

of trial techniques. However, the Committee concluded "In spite of these problems, consecutive translation is preferred to simultaneous translation at the present time because the system offers the possibility of correcting the interpreter if he does not give the right interpretation" (p. 64).

If the views expressed in the Report are sound they would certainly seem to suggest that simultaneous translation and perhaps consecutive translation also would place a litigant at a disadvantage at least in trial proceedings and would therefore fall under the ban of s. 13(1) of the Official Languages of New Brunswick Act.

The striking similarity in language between ss. 17, 18 and 19 of the Charter and s. 133 of the Constitution Act, 1867 would appear to support the view expressed by Professor Tremblay that one of the characteristics of the Charter is constitutional continuity (p. 445). The jurisprudence developed under s. 133 would therefore apply to these sections. . . . The crucial difference, he points out, is that by virtue of the amending provisions in the Charter linguistic rights are "doubly entrenched," first by s. 33 which precludes "opting out" of these provisions and secondly by s. 41 which requires the unanimous consent of all the provinces to change them (pp. 445-46). The salient, and for purposes of these reasons most useful, feature of the jurisprudence under s. 133 is its expansive and purposive approach to the scope of linguistic rights at least at the level of this Court. . . .

In the two *Blaikies* the Court, reflecting the spirit of *Jones* that s. 133 did not establish a ceiling of linguistic rights protection but rather a base that could be built upon, found that the section contained an organic principle of growth capable of responding to changing social realities. In *Blaikie No. 1* by giving "full weight . . . to every word of s. 133" (p. 1022) the Court found that the requirement to enact legislation in both official languages was implicit in the section. Similarly, the Court found that the phrase "Courts of

Quebec' ought to be considered broadly'' (p. 1028) to include other adjudicative agencies and that 'Acts . . . of Quebec' ought to include delegated legislation in order not to ''truncate the requirement of s. 133'' (p. 1027). In both instances the Court demonstrated a willingness to enlarge the scope of the literal words so as to tailor the protection to the exigencies of contemporary structures of law-making and adjudication. The spirit of this approach is continued in *Blaikie No. 2* where the Court, taking account of ''the phenomenal growth of delegated legislation since 1867'' held that s. 133 applied to regulations made by certain boards and subordinate law-making agencies. It is in its treatment of Court rules of practice, however, that its expansive approach to the section is most visible. The Court found that the rules of practice were subject to s. 133 ''by necessary intendment.'' . . .

Finally, in *Reference re Manitoba Language Rights, supra*, the Court rejected the submission that the first part of s. 133 should be construed as merely ''directory'' in order to uphold the validity of legislation which did not comply with the section. . . . This spirit of vigilance in safeguarding a meaningful exercise of linguistic rights should also, in my view, inform our approach to ss. 16 and 19 of the Charter. . . .

As mentioned at the outset, many questions are subsumed in the constitutional question framed for the Court. On the most simplistic level it may be answered by a simple yes. On the broader question of how the litigant's right under s. 19(2) of the Charter may be given practical effect, some aspects of this question are left at counsels' request to another day. However, it seems to me that the appeal cannot be disposed of without answering at least two questions, namely: (a) what level of language comprehension must a judge sitting on an appellate process have? and (b) how is the question whether he or she has that level of comprehension to be determined?

In order to answer the first question it is, I believe, necessary to revert to a question already touched upon, namely whether s. 19(2) affords the litigant something more than the fair hearing rights accorded by ss. 7 and 14. I think that it does. . . . [E]ven if we assume that due process considerations in a language context lie at the heart of s. 19, the constitutional minimum required by the section must in some way reflect s. 16's commitment to the equal status of the two official languages. . . .

History, no doubt, will continue to add a dimension to the social and legal content of these rights. Indeed, the double entrenchment of language rights in the Charter and the commitment to linguistic duality in s. 16 would seem to support the view expressed by Professor Tremblay that in terms of importance linguistic rights now stand ''at the highest level of the constitutional hierarchy'': . . .

The difficulty lies in giving a precise formulation of what this qualitative difference means in terms of the court process above and beyond the fair hearing concern which the jurisprudence would seem to indicate can be satisfied by translation. Indeed, it is because of this difficulty that I am limiting my discussion to the requirements at the appellate level, leaving the more problematic issue of the requirements at the trial level to another day.

It seems to me that given the commitment to linguistic duality contained in s. 16 of the Charter and the principle of growth implied by that commitment, the Court's process cannot be perceived as static. What may be adequate to-day in terms of protection for the litigant's right under s. 19(2) may not be adequate tomorrow. The last few decades have witnessed a concentrated and broadly based effort to give practical effect to language rights. The passage of Official Languages Act has heightened the sensitivity of public officials and raised the expectations of the Canadian public with regard to the provision of government services in both official languages in the federal and in certain provincial jurisdictions. . . . We are looking at a process which will call for a progressively expansive interpretation of the litigant's right under s. 19(2) to meet gradually increasing social expectations. Clearly the courts cannot define *in futuro* what is going to be required from time to time to satisfy the litigant's language right but they can determine *ex post facto* whether or not it was satisfied in a particular case and this is what the Court must decide here. It must decide what, as a practical matter, the state was called upon to do at this point in time in order to accommodate the appellant's language right under s. 19(2) of the Charter. . . .

. . . [A]t the very least, the standard against which the judge's level of comprehension should be measured goes beyond that required by fairness. However, as pointed out by the Royal Commission on Bilingualism and Biculturalism (Report of the Royal Commission on Bilingualism and Biculturalism, Book I, The Official Languages, at pp. 6-8) individual bilingualism is a relative and not an absolute concept. The Commission states at pp. 6-7:

8. *One of the greatest obstacles to understanding the nature of bilingualism—and probably to accepting it—is the still commonly-held notion that, to be bilingual, a person must have an equal command of two languages. In fact, this phenomenon is so distinct as to have a special name, "equilingualism."*

9. *Insistence on an equal command of two languages as the criterion of bilingualism has long retarded research in this field. In recent years, however, the concept of bilingualism has become broader. It is now no longer identified with equilingualism, which some consider to be theoretically and practically impossible; for they believe that a bilingual's language learning experience would have to be identical in both languages in order to produce identical results.*

The Commission then goes on to differentiate "receptive bilinguals" i.e. those who can receive communications in both languages through the written and spoken word but can express themselves in only one language; those who can function in both languages but have a lower level of proficiency in one or in both from unilingual persons; and those who are bilingual only in the particular area of their life's experience. All may be described as bilingual in some contexts and for some purposes.

Accepting that the concept of bilingualism is relative and not absolute and that it must be related to function and purpose, I would conclude that the judge's level of comprehension must go beyond a mere literal understanding of the language used by counsel. It must be such that the full flavour of the argument can be appreciated. To the extent that this requires what Monnin C.J.M. describes as a comprehension of the nuances of the spoken word, I would agree with him that a judge must attain that level of sophistication in order to make the litigant's linguistic right meaningful in the context of the court's process. I do not think, however, that the content of s. 19(2) can be expanded beyond this at the present time. Furthermore, I believe that in the absence of evidence to the contrary, we must assume that Stratton J.A. applied this standard to himself and concluded that he met it. However, as mentioned earlier, because the content of the litigant's right is not static, the standard to be met by the judiciary must be subject to continuous scrutiny.

While there was little discussion in this case of the acceptability of either simultaneous translation or the practice . . . of taking a bilingual judge from the trial division to sit ad hoc on the appellate bench, it would seem to me that such mechanisms might, from the purely language point of view, provide a more satisfactory interim measure than reliance on a judge who cannot fully participate in the proceedings. However, there may be other disadvantages to the use of trial judges sitting ad hoc on appeal. Counsel and the public may be concerned over the fact that appellate adjudication is significantly different from trial adjudication.

They may also be under the misguided impression that trial judges will inevitably be disposed to favour the views of their colleagues in the courts below.

Simultaneous translation, which if conscientiously used allows some sort of interchange between the bench and counsel, may be a preferable solution to the need for a fully responsive bench. A judge in Stratton J.A.'s position could perhaps solve some of the problems arising from his or her inability to converse in the language by inviting counsel to use the translation service to receive questions in English to which he might respond in French. Ultimately, however, any such measures can only be viewed as inadequate substitutes for true equality. It is evident that linguistic duality has a crucial role to play in social and cultural development in New Brunswick and that heightened public expectations with regard to that role are reflected in the Charter as well as in provincial legislative attempts to expand and protect the exercise of language rights. Against this backdrop, the inequality of status of a litigant who must present his or her case to a bench that is not fully able to respond must eventually give way to the escalating standard in s. 16(1) and (2).

The appellant argued additionally that s. 13(1) of the Official Languages of New Brunswick Act supports their claim that French speaking litigants in New Brunswick have the right to be heard in the language of their choice and not to be disadvantaged by that choice. Again the same comments apply. Even if one assumes that "heard" and "disadvantage" in this context envision more than the requirements of fairness, I do not think that an examination of the statute as a whole supports the formulation of a standard higher than that found in s. 19(2) of the Charter. . . .

I would dismiss the appeal with costs. . . .

58. Reference Re Bill 30 (Funding of Ontario Catholic Schools), *1987*

~ In this reference we can see the principles of Canada's original Constitution colliding with more contemporary values in the new Charter of Rights. The denominational school rights enshrined in section 93 of the B.N.A. Act as part of the historic compromise of Confederation recognized the special position of the Protestant minority in Quebec and the Catholic minority in English Canada. Section 15, the equality clause in the Charter, expresses the modern egalitarian precept that the benefits of law should extend equally to all. But the Charter also contains section 29 stipulating that nothing in the Charter derogates from denominational school rights guaranteed "by or under" the Constitution. In this case, the Supreme Court, in upholding full funding of Ontario's Roman Catholic separate schools, gives clear priority to the Constitution's historic principles and it does this without relying on section 29 of the Charter.

In 1928, the Privy Council in the *Tiny Township* case[1] concluded that Ontario legislation prohibiting the separate schools from offering secondary (high school) education beyond grade 10 did not violate the minority school right guaranteed in section 93(1). Viscount Haldane's interpretation of the rights of Ontario Catholics under 93(1) was so narrow as to render them virtually meaningless: the right to denominational schools was subject to a broad regulatory power which could control the level of teaching and cut off public funds. Ontario's publicly funded separate school system was left to function on a truncated basis with the funding extending only to grade 10.

The situation changed dramatically in 1984 when William Davis, on the eve of his retirement as Premier and Leader of the Conservative Party, announced his intention to break with the province's long-standing policy and extend public funding of the schools administered by Separate School Boards to the full secondary school program (then to grade 13, now to grade 12). Although in many Ontario communities there was considerable opposition to the new policy, the Liberals and N.D.P. as well as the Conservatives supported it in the 1985 provincial election. The remarkable growth of Ontario's Roman Catholic population and the poor facilities available to senior students in the separate schools may well have been factors in generating this tri-partisan support. Following the election, the new Liberal government introduced Bill 30 to give effect to the full funding policy. Immediately Toronto's Public School Board engaged the services of one of Canada's leading constitutional lawyers, J.J. Robinette, and announced its intention to challenge Bill 30 on the grounds that it contravened the Charter of Rights. At this point the government referred the legislation to the Ontario Court of Appeal. Intervenor status was granted to 24 interest groups representing parents, religious organizations and teachers on both sides of the issue.

---

[1] *Tiny Township Catholic Separate Schools Trustees* v. *The Queen* (1928) A.C. 363.

The Ontario Court of Appeal, and on appeal, the Supreme Court of Canada both rejected the challenge to Bill 30—but for quite different reasons. The majority in the Ontario Court of Appeal viewed the extension of public funding to the end of high school not as part of the right guaranteed in section 93(1) but as a new right provided at the discretion of the provincial legislature under 93(3). Although such a right was not guaranteed "by" the Constitution, it was considered to be guaranteed "under" the Constitution and therefore to enjoy the protection from Charter review afforded by section 29.[2] For the Supreme Court section 29 was not crucial. The point common to Justice Wilson's and Justice Estey's opinions is that the plenary legislative power given to the provinces under the opening words of section 93 and section 93(3) to develop a system of denominational schools takes precedence over anything in the Charter—with or without section 29. The "new Constitution" is not to invalidate fundamental provisions of the "old Constitution".

Justice Wilson, characteristically, goes further and overrules the Judicial Committee's decision in *Tiny Township*. Three justices support her in this. On the basis of their understanding of the denominational school rights Ontario Roman Catholics had by law at the time of Confederation, they find that the right to public funding of the entire school program was entrenched in section 93(1). This means that the Ontario legislature is constitutionally barred from rescinding Bill 30.

In a number of Ontario cities with large Catholic populations, the new schools policy upheld in this reference case has led to an acrimonious process of transferring public secondary schools to Roman Catholic School Boards. A section added to Bill 30 after the reference case had commenced requires Catholic Boards, for ten years, to offer employment to teachers rendered redundant in the public school system. Whether this obligation to hire non-Catholics is consistent with the separate school rights guaranteed in section 93(1) may be a question that the courts will have to decide in the future. ~

REFERENCE RE BILL 30, AN ACT TO AMEND THE EDUCATION ACT
In the Supreme Court of Canada. [1987] 1 S.C.R. 1148.

The judgment of Dickson C.J.C., McIntyre, La Forest and Wilson JJ. was delivered by

WILSON J.: This is an appeal from the decision of the Court of Appeal for Ontario on a question referred for its consideration by the Lieutenant Governor by Order in Council 1774/85, dated July 3, 1985 pursuant to the Courts of Justice Act, 1984, S.O. 1984, c. 11, s. 19. The question reads as follows:

---

[2] The two dissenting judges in the Ontario Court of Appeal did not agree that denominational school rights created at the discretion of the legislature enjoyed the protection of section 29. In their view legislation creating special rights for Catholics violated section 15 of the Charter.

Is Bill 30, An Act to Amend the Education Act, *inconsistent with the provisions of the Constitution of Canada including the Canadian Charter of Rights and Freedoms and, if so, in what particular or particulars and in what respect?*

By order of the Chief Justice of Ontario dated July 4, 1985 the Attorney General for the Province of Ontario was given carriage of the Reference and notice of the Reference was duly published. A number of parties were given leave by the Court of Appeal to intervene in the hearings before that Court. On February 18, 1986 a majority of the Court of Appeal (Zuber, Cory and Tarnopolsky JJ.A.) answered the Reference question in the negative: see *Reference re an Act to Amend the Education Act* (1986), 53 O.R. (2d) 513. The Chief Justice of Ontario and Robins J.A. dissented.

The appellants have appealed to this Court pursuant to s. 37 of the Supreme Court of Canada Act, R.S.C. 1970, c. S-19, as amended, and s. 19(7) of the Courts of Justice Act, 1984, S.O. 1984, c. 11. Leave to intervene was granted by this Court to the Quebec Association of Protestant School Boards. Notices of intention to intervene in this Court were duly filed by the Attorney General for the Province of Alberta and the Attorney General for the Province of Quebec.

The preamble to Bill 30 indicates that its purpose is to implement a policy of full funding for Roman Catholic separate high schools in Ontario. The preamble reads as follows:

Whereas section 93 of the Constitution Act, 1867 embodies one of the essential conditions which facilitated the creation of a united Canada in 1867 by guaranteeing to Roman Catholics in Ontario certain rights and privileges with respect to denominational schools; and whereas the Roman Catholic separate schools have become a significant part of the schools system in Ontario; and whereas it has been public policy in Ontario since 1899 to provide for public funds to support

education in the Roman Catholic separate schools to the end of Grade 10; and whereas it is recognized that today a basic education requires a secondary as well as an elementary education; and whereas it is just and proper and in accordance with the spirit of the guarantees given in 1867 to bring the provisions of the law respecting Roman Catholic separate schools into harmony with the provisions of the law respecting public elementary and secondary schools, by providing legislative recognition of and funding for secondary education by Roman Catholic separate schools. . . .

The Bill permits a separate school board to elect by by-law to perform the duties of a secondary school board with the approval of the Minister (s. 136a). Once such an election has been made and approved by the Minister, the separate school board becomes a "Roman Catholic school board" (s. 46a) and, according to s. 136e(1), becomes "entitled to share in the legislative grants for secondary school purposes." Section 136j exempts separate school supporters within the jurisdiction of a Roman Catholic school board from the payment of rates or taxes for secondary school purposes. But, by section 136k, "[t]he provisions [of the Education Act, R.S.O. 1980, c. 129] . . . that apply to . . . the levying and collection of rates or taxes for separate school purposes apply with necessary modifications for secondary school purposes in respect of a Roman Catholic school board." Every public board of education is required by s. 136l to prepare a list of teaching and non-teaching staff whose services will not be required because of an election by a Roman Catholic school board to perform the duties of a secondary school board. During the ten years following its election the Roman Catholic school board must fill positions on its teaching staff by offering employment to those on that list who possess proper qualifications. There are other provisions concerning the functions of the Planning and Implementation Commission established in the Bill and transfers of use or ownership of real and personal property between public school boards and Roman Catholic school boards which are not central to the constitutional issues in this appeal.

The Ontario Court of Appeal, quite properly, considered the constitutional validity of Bill 30 as it stood at the date of the Reference. At that time Bill 30 had already been given first reading in the Ontario legislature. Subsequent to the decision of the Court of Appeal Bill 30 was passed into law, as An Act to Amend the Education Act, S.O. 1986, c. 21. This Act contains a number of sections which were not present in Bill 30 at the time of the Reference. In particular, s. 136.1a dealing with the hiring and promotion of teachers was not in the Bill. . . .

I want to emphasize, therefore, that in this case the Court is determining the Constitutionality of Bill 30 in the form referred to the Ontario Court of Appeal and not the constitutionality of the Act currently in force in Ontario. . . .

Before considering the merits of the appeal I want to stress, as did the Chief Justice of Ontario in the Court below, that it is not the role of the Court to determine whether as a policy matter a publicly funded Roman Catholic School system is or is not desirable. That is for the legislature. The sole issue before us is whether Bill 30 is consistent with the Constitution of Canada.

It is apparent from the reasons for judgment in the court below and from the submissions of the parties that there are three distinct questions which must be addressed on the Reference. First, is Bill 30 a valid exercise of the provincial power in relation to education under the opening words of s. 93 and s. 93(3) of the Constitution Act, 1867? Second, is Bill 30 a valid exercise of provincial power because it returns to Roman Catholic separate school supporters rights which were constitutionally guaranteed to them by s. 93(1) of the Constitution Act, 1867? We are urged to decide this question regardless of our answer to the first ques-

tion in order to obviate any further controversy concerning the rights and privileges of Roman Catholic separate school supporters in the Province of Ontario. The final question which must be examined if an affirmative answer is given to either or both of the above questions is whether the Constitution Act, 1982 and, in particular, the Canadian Charter of Rights and Freedoms is applicable to Bill 30 and, if so, to what extent and with what effect. I shall examine these issues in turn.

THE OPENING WORDS OF S. 93 AND S. 93(3)

. . . On their face these provisions would appear to support the view that Bill 30 is a valid exercise of legislative power by the provincial legislature. The opening words of s. 93 vest an exclusive plenary power over education in the Province "subject and according to" the provisions that follow. Section 93(3) does not appear to derogate in any way from that power. It seems rather to contemplate its exercise where a province has a separate or dissentient school system by law at the time of Union or establishes one at any time after Union. In either of these circumstances it provides that "any Act or Decision of any Provincial Authority" affecting the rights or privileges of the province's Protestant or Roman Catholic minority shall be subject to appeal to the Governor General in Council. The enactment of legislation would seem to be an "Act or Decision" and "Provincial Authority" has been interpreted by the Privy Council as including a provincial legislature: see *Brophy* v. *Attorney-General for Manitoba*, [1895] A.C. 202 at pp. 220-21 and see also the Privy Council's judgment in *Tiny* at p. 371. Section 93(3) would appear, therefore, to provide in express terms for an appeal to the Governor General in Council from legislation passed by a provincial legislature which affects the rights and privileges of denominational minorities. Counsel for the appellants submitted that s. 93 should be interpreted along the following lines. Section 93(1) permits a legal recourse if rights or privileges at law are prejudicially affected. For provinces where a denominational school system exists s. 93(3) adds a political recourse if rights or privileges not at law are prejudicially affected. So, the appellants submit, s. 93(3) has a different and more limited purpose than that contended for by the respondents; it provides a remedy for acts or decisions affecting rights or privileges not at law. I do not find this analysis of s. 93 persuasive. If the expression "by law" as used in s. 93(1) has the broad meaning adopted by Anglin, C.J.C. in *Tiny* i.e. as tantamount to "permitted by law," then it is hard to think of any right or privilege not "by law" in that sense. If the appellants' submissions were accepted s. 93(3) would effectively become otiose. It is also difficult to imagine why a constitutional right of appeal would have been conferred from the removal of a right or privilege which was never formally and legally granted by the legislature.

In my view, s. 93(3) in no way limits the exercise of the province's plenary power. Rather, it expressly contemplates that after Confederation a provincial legislature may, pursuant to its plenary power, pass legislation which augments the rights or privileges of denominational school supporters. It would be strange, indeed, if the system of separate schools in existence at Confederation were intended to be frozen in an 1867 mold.

Prior authority would seem to support this view of s. 93. . . .

The decisions of the Privy Council in *Barrett* and *Brophy* clearly indicate, although admittedly by way of obiter, that it is *intra vires* a province to pass denominational schools legislation after Union, the repeal of which may be subject to an appeal to the Governor General in Council. In my view, subject to the comments I shall make concerning s. 93(1) of the Constitution Act, 1867 and the Charter of Rights, Bill 30 stands in precisely the same constitutional position as the various Acts of the Manitoba legislature prior to 1890 which augmented the educational rights and privileges of the Roman Catholic minority in that province.

The purpose and history of s. 93 would seem to support this interpretation. The protection of minority religious rights was a major preoccupation during the negotiations leading to Confederation because of the perceived danger of leaving the religious minorities in both Canada East and Canada West at the mercy of overwhelming majorities. Given the importance of denominational educational rights at the time of Confederation, it seems unbelievable that the draftsmen of the section would not have made provision for future legislation conferring rights and privileges on religious minorities in response to new conditions. In his address to the British Parliament in which he proposed second reading of the British North America Act, see U.K., H.L., Parliamentary Debates, 3rd ser., vol. 185, col. 557, at p. 565, 19 February 1867, Lord Carnarvon explained the purpose of s. 93 in terms of a guarantee of equality:

[T]he object of the clause [s. 93] is to secure to the religious minority of one province the same rights, privileges and protection which the religious minority of another Province may enjoy. The Roman Catholic minority of Upper Canada, the Protestant minority of Lower Canada and the Roman Catholic minority of the Maritime Provinces, will thus stand on a footing of entire equality.

Some time after Confederation in the debate re 2nd reading of Bill No. 58, The Remedial Act (Manitoba), in Debates of the House of Commons, 6th Sess., 7th Parliament, 59 Vic. 1896, col. 2719, at 2724, 3 March 1896 Sir Charles Tupper confirmed that s. 93 was part of a solemn pact resulting from the bargaining which made Confederation possible:

. . . I say it within the knowledge of all these gentlemen . . . that but for the consent to the proposal of the Hon. Sir Alexander Galt, who represented especially the Protestants of the great province of Quebec on that occasion, but for the assent of that conference to the proposal

of Sir Alexander Galt, that in the Confederation Act should be embodied a clause which would protect the rights of minorities, whether Catholic or Protestant, in this country, there would have been no Confederation. . . . I say, therefore, it is important, it is significant that without this clause, without this guarantee for the rights of minorities being embodied in that new constitution, we should have been unable to obtain any confederation whatever. That is my reason for drawing attention to it at present.

Judicial authority affirms that religion was of fundamental importance. As the Privy Council stated in *Brophy, supra,* at p. 214:

There can be no doubt that the views of the Roman Catholic inhabitants of Quebec and Ontario with regard to education were shared by the members of the same communion in the territory which afterwards became the Province of Manitoba. They regarded it as essential that the education of their children should be in accordance with the teachings of their Church, and considered that such an education could not be obtained in public schools designed for all the members of the community alike, whatever their creed, but could only be secured in schools conducted under the influence and guidance of the authorities of their church.

The compromise or, as Duff C.J.C. in the *Reference Re Adoption Act,* [1938] S.C.R. 398 at p. 402 termed it, "the basic compact of Confederation," was that rights and privileges already acquired by law at the time of Confederation would be preserved and provincial legislatures could bestow additional new rights and privileges in response to changing conditions. As was said by Meredith C.J.C.P. in *Ottawa Separate School Trustees* v. *City of Ottawa* (1915), 34 O.L.R. 624 (reversed on other grounds) it was not intended that separate schools should be "left forever in the educational wilderness of the enactments in force in 1867"

(p. 630). Instead, he said, "[t]he machinery may be altered, the educational methods may be changed, from time to time, to keep pace with advanced educational systems." While these new rights and privileges could be legally repealed by the Legislature at a future date, a safeguard against their repeal as a result of local pressure insensitive to minority rights was provided by the inclusion of a right of appeal to the Governor General in Council under s. 93(3). This would appear to have also been the view of the Lord Chancellor in *Brophy.* He clearly believed that the purpose of s. 93(3) was to protect minorities in both Ontario and Quebec against the subsequent repeal of rights created after Confederation. He said at p. 223:

Bearing in mind the circumstances which existed in 1870, it does not appear to their Lordships an extravagant notion that in creating a Legislature for the province with limited powers it should have been thought expedient, in case either Catholics or Protestants became preponderant, and rights which had come into existence under different circumstances were interfered with, to give the Dominion Parliament power to legislate upon matters of education so far as was necessary to protect the Protestant or Catholic minority as the case might be.

I do not believe that the comments made by Beetz J. (for the majority) in *La Société des Acadiens* v. *Association of Parents,* [1986] 1 S.C.R. 549 foreclose a purposive approach to s. 93. In that case, Beetz, J. (Estey, Chouinard, Lamer and Le Dain JJ. concurring) stated at p. 578:

Unlike language rights which are based on political compromise, legal rights tend to be seminal in nature because they are rooted in principle. Some of them, such as the one expressed in s. 7 of the Charter, are so broad as to call for frequent judicial determination.

Language rights, on the other hand, although some of them have been enlarged and incorporated into the Char-

ter, remain nonetheless founded on political compromise.

This essential difference between the two types of rights dictates a distinct judicial approach with respect to each. More particularly, the courts should pause before they decide to act as instruments of change with respect to language rights. This is not to say that language rights provisions are cast in stone and should remain immune altogether from judicial interpretation. But in my opinion, the courts should approach them with more restraint than they would in construing legal rights.

While due regard must be paid not to give a provision which reflects a political compromise too wide an interpretation, it must still be open to the Court to breathe life into a compromise that is clearly expressed. The contextual background of s. 93 is being reviewed in these reasons not for the purpose of enlarging upon the compromise but in order to confirm its precise content. The contextual background suggests that part of the compromise was that future legislation on the part of the province with respect to separate denominational schools was permissible. The province was to be able to grant new rights and privileges to denominational schools after Union in response to new conditions but that subsequent repeal of those post-Union rights or privileges would be subject to an appeal to the Governor General in Council. This is apparent from the very text of s. 93. I would therefore conclude, subject to the comments that follow concerning the applicability of the Charter of Rights to Bill 30, that Bill 30 is a valid exercise of the provincial power to add to the rights and privileges of Roman Catholic separate school supporters under the combined effect of the opening words of s. 93 and s. 93(3) of the Constitution Act, 1867.

SECTION 93(1) OF THE CONSTITUTION ACT 1867

While, strictly speaking, it may be unnecessary in light of the above to consider whether the Roman Catholic separate schools in Ontario have a constitutionally guaranteed right to full funding by virtue of s. 93(1) of the Constitution Act, 1867, I shall address the issue since full argument was made on it during the lengthy hearing before the Court. It also has relevance to the submissions made by the parties on the applicability of the Charter. . . .

It is immediately apparent that the scope of the rights and privileges protected under the section must be determined by ascertaining the rights and privileges in existence at the time of the Union. Was there any right or privilege entitling denominational secondary schools to full funding by law at the time of Confederation? To answer this it is necessary to consider the history of pre-Confederation legislation pertaining to education in Upper Canada. It is also necessary to consider the decision of the Privy Council in *Tiny* in which the effect of such legislation was reviewed.

1. The situation prior to Confederation. Prior to Confederation there were three main classes of schools in Upper Canada—common schools, grammar schools and separate schools. There was no counterpart of today's secondary school. In fact the evidence discloses that the word "secondary" was not used to describe any portion of the school system in Ontario until the end of the nineteenth century. . . .

So by 1843 this tripartite system of education, consisting of common schools, grammar schools and separate schools, was firmly in place. A number of amending Acts which affected all three branches of the educational system were passed from 1843 on. But none of these statutes bears directly on the interpretation of s. 93(1) of the Constitution Act, 1867. The legislation which was in effect at the time of Union and which is therefore crucial to the proper interpretation of s. 93(1) of the Constitution Act, 1867 is found in four statutes: the Common Schools Act, C.S.U.C. 1859, c. 64; the Separate Schools Act, C.S.U.C. 1859, c. 65; the Separate Schools Act (Scott

Act), C.S.U.C. 1863, c. 5; and the Grammar Schools Act, C.S.U.C. 1865, c. 23.

The Common Schools Act, C.S.U.C. 1859, c. 64 passed in 1859 consolidated many of the provisions relating to common schools which had been in the earlier Acts. It is of particular interest for two reasons 1) it was the legislation which governed common schools at the time of Confederation and 2) the Separate Schools Act, C.S.U.C. 1859, c. 65 and later the Separate Schools Act (The Scott Act), C.S.U.C. 1863, c. 5 made the main provisions of the Common Schools Act of 1859 applicable to the separate schools. It is therefore necessary to examine the provisions of this Act quite closely.

. . . I would conclude, therefore, that the trustees of the common schools had by law the power, subject to regulation, to prescribe what branches of education were to be taught in a particular school and could, by law, prescribe any level of instruction which, in their view, the needs of the particular community warranted. This would include instruction at the second school level. . . .

The provisions of the 1859 Common Schools Act were generally made applicable to separate schools by the Separate Schools Act of 1859. . . .

The Separate Schools Act (The Scott Act), 1863 (U.C.), 26 Vic. c. 5 was the last statute pertaining to separate schools enacted prior to Confederation. It is entitled An Act to restore to Roman Catholics in Upper Canada certain rights in respect to Separate Schools. Its preamble reads:

WHEREAS it is just and proper to restore to Roman Catholics in Upper Canada certain rights which they formerly enjoyed in respect to separate Schools, and to bring the provisions of the Law respecting Separate Schools more in harmony with the provisions of the Law respecting Common Schools. . .

It repealed ss. 18 to 36 of the Separate Schools Act of 1859. It authorized Roman Catholics to establish separate schools

and elect trustees "for the management" of each school (ss. 2-6). The trustees were vested with "all the powers in respect of separate schools, that the Trustees of Common Schools have and possess under the provisions of the Act relating to Common Schools [C.S.U.C., 1859, c. 64]" (s. 7) and all "the same duties . . . as Trustees of the Common Schools" (s. 9). This meant the separate school trustees, like common school trustees, had a duty to permit residents between 5 and 21 years of age to attend school and a power, subject to regulation, to determine the subjects to be taught and the level of instruction. Separate school supporters were exempted from payment of municipal rates for common schools (s. 14) but were subject to pay school rates levied by the separate school trustees (s. 7). By virtue of s. 20 separate school supporters were also entitled to a share, proportionate to the numbers of pupils, in the fund annually granted by the legislature for the support of common schools. . . . Finally, separate schools were subject to inspection by the Chief Superintendent and were subject to "such regulations, as may be imposed from time to time, by the Council of Public Instruction for Upper Canada" (s. 26). Interestingly, the Council's control over the separate school curriculum was arguably weaker than that over common schools as the Separate Schools Act contained no provision similar to s. 119(5) of the Common Schools Act giving the Council supervision over textbooks used in the schools.

I turn now to a consideration of the *Tiny* case (1926), 59 O.L.R. 96; aff'd. 60 O.L.R. 15 (C.A.); aff'd. [1927] S.C.R. 637; aff'd. [1928] A.C. 363 in which the effect of these various pre-Confederation statutes was reviewed.

2. *The Tiny case.* In *Tiny* the board of trustees of the separate school in the Township of Tiny, on behalf of themselves and all other separate school trustees in the province, brought a petition of right challenging the validity of certain provincial legislation prohibiting the teaching of and funding for secondary

school subjects in separate schools. The challenged legislation also denied separate school supporters exemption from the rates levied in support of public secondary schools. The trustees submitted that this legislation offended s. 93(1) of the British North America Act because it prejudicially affected a right or privilege with respect to denominational education possessed by Roman Catholics at the date of Confederation. They also sought a proportionate share of public monies granted by the legislature "for common school purposes" computed in accordance with their statutory rights at the date of Confederation.

The plaintiffs failed at trial. Rose J. held that because the rights and privileges of the separate schools at Confederation concerning money grants depended upon legislation of the former Province of Canada and were expressly described as grants "of this province," the Province of Ontario was unaffected by any such obligation (p. 150). Accordingly separate school supporters had no legal right to share in any appropriations. He was upheld on this issue by the Court of Appeal. The effect of such an interpretation is that s. 93(1) which protects all rights and privileges which any class of persons had by law at the time of Union is an empty shell in Ontario because all rights and privileges were granted by the law of the Province of Canada. Such an interpretation seems patently unsound. I would adopt the views of Anglin C.J.C. in the Supreme Court of Canada on this point. In rejecting the position taken by Rose J. and the Ontario Court of Appeal on this issue he stated at p. 657:

This view is utterly at variance with the spirit and intent of s. 93(1) of the British North America Act. Unless the legislatures of Ontario and Quebec are debarred from prejudicially affecting the rights and privileges of the respective religious minorities in regard to maintenance and support which their denominational schools enjoyed at Confederation under legislation of the former Province of Canada, the protection of such rights and privileges afforded by ss. 1 of s. 93 becomes illusory and the purpose of the Imperial legislation is subverted.

The Judicial Committee of the Privy Council agreed with Anglin C.J.C.: see pp. 373-74.

Rose J. also held that pursuant to the Common Schools Act of 1859 the common schools and thus the separate schools were to be subject to such regulations as might be imposed from time to time by the Council of Public Instruction. As this was the relevant legislation in force at the time of Confederation Rose J. held that the right preserved by s. 93(1) of the Constitution Act, 1867 was merely the right to maintain separate schools subject to regulation by the Council. Rose J. also had in the alternative that even "if . . . the class of persons represented by the petitioners had by law at the Union a right to a share, ascertainable in a way fixed by statute, in such moneys as might be granted by the Ontario Legislature for common school purposes," there was "no proof that the legislation and regulations affect that right prejudicially" (p. 152). This was because in his view those rights had always been subject to a broad power of regulation in favour of the Council.

The Ontario Court of Appeal unanimously dismissed the appeal: (1926), 60 O.L.R. 15. A further appeal to the Supreme Court of Canada was dismissed because the justices were evenly divided: [1927] S.C.R. 637. Anglin C.J.C., with whom Rinfret J. concurred, Mignault J. concurring in separate reasons, would have allowed the appeal. Duff and Lamont JJ., Newcombe J. concurring in separate reasons, dismissed the appeal. Those Justices who would have dismissed the appeal held that the regulatory power of the Council of Public Instruction was sufficiently broad to have enabled it, had it so chosen, to prohibit secondary level instruction. The existence of such a broad power was sufficient to deny s. 93(1) protection.

The appeal was also dismissed by the

Privy Council: [1928] A.C. 363. The Privy Council shared the view that the broad power of regulation vested in the Council of Public Instruction, including the power to determine what courses of study could be offered, was sufficient to prevent the separate schools from providing secondary school education. Even though the broad power of regulation had never been used by the Council prior to Confederation, its very existence meant that separate secondary school education fell outside the protection of s. 93(1).

On the funding issue the Privy Council was required to interpret s. 120 of the Common Schools Act of 1859. This is the section which provided that out of the sum granted for common schools "and not otherwise expressly appropriated by law" the Governor in Council could authorize certain expenditures set out in the section in aid of the common schools. Section 20 of the Scott Act provided that separate schools were entitled "to a share in the fund annually granted by the Legislature . . . for the support of Common Schools." But since there was no limit on the sums that could be "otherwise appropriated" for the common schools, the Privy Council held that there was no guaranteed right in the separate schools to funding. Viscount Haldane held at p. 388:

. . . the question really turns on whether the authorities of the Province had power to make apportionments and payments out of the funds granted before the balance was arrived at which should be available for common school purposes. In their Lordships' opinion it is clear that there was such power. . . .

In their Lordships' view, in the face of the provisions referred to, it is impossible to contend successfully that it was ultra vires *after Confederation to make new appropriations out of the grants which would diminish what would otherwise have come to the appellants. Whether the case is looked at from the point of view of regulation, or whether it is regarded from that of discretion in power of appropriation, the result is the same.*

The appellants rely on *Tiny* and submit that at the date of Confederation separate school supporters, together with all other common school supporters, had the right to public funding of elementary school education for their children but no right to such funding for secondary school education. The appellants also submit that, since *Tiny* has stood for almost sixty years as an authoritative decision on this issue, it should not now be disturbed.

The Attorney General of Ontario, in asking this Court to review the Privy Council's decision in *Tiny*, submitted that the courts in *Tiny* were asked the wrong question. All of the judgments concentrated on the question whether the separate schools had an unfettered discretion to operate their schools free from any regulatory interference. The Attorney General submits that the real question, unsatisfactorily addressed by the various courts in *Tiny*, was what level of instruction were separate schools permitted by law to provide in 1867. I would agree with this submission. When the correct question is asked it is seen that every judge who participated in the *Tiny* decisions, with the exception of Duff J. in this Court, held that separate schools were permitted by law to offer any level of courses at the time of Confederation. For example, in the Privy Council Viscount Haldane stated at p. 376 that "[b]efore Confederation the common schools and with them the separate schools were left free, by statute . . . to educate pupils up to the age of 21, and some of them were in the habit of giving to the older pupils advanced teaching such as would fit them to enter the University."

The essence of the various *Tiny* decisions was that the presence in the statute of an apparently unfettered power of regulation in the Council made it impossible for the separate schools to have any rights or privileges by law capable of being protected by the guarantee in s. 93(1). Any "rights" they might otherwise have had were totally defeasible because they were subject to a statutory power of regulation "in the full sense": per Viscount Haldane at p. 386.

It is, however, well established today that a statutory power to make regulations is not unfettered. It is constrained by the policies and objectives inherent in the enabling statute. A power to regulate is not a power to prohibit. It cannot be used to frustrate the very legislative scheme under which the power is conferred. This principle was cogently expressed in *Padfield* v. *Minister of Agriculture, Fisheries and Food*, [1968] A.C. 997 and was recently approved by this Court in *Oakwood Development Ltd.* v. *Rural Municipality of St. Francois Xavier*, [1985] 2 S.C.R. 164. The roots of this principle stretch back beyond the date of Confederation. In considering the exercise of a power of expropriation or compulsory acquisition of property statutorily granted to a company Lord Cranworth L.C. in *Galloway* v. *The Mayor and Commonally Of London* (1866) L.R. 1 H.L. 34 stated at p. 43:

The principle is this, that when persons embarking on great undertakings, for the accomplishment of which those engaged in them have received authority from the Legislature to take compulsorily the lands of others, making to the latter proper compensation, the persons so authorized cannot be allowed to exercise the powers conferred on them for any collateral object; that is, for any purposes except those for which the Legislature has invested them with extraordinary powers.

The power of the Council of Public Instruction was to make regulations for explicitly stated purposes—''for the organization, government and discipline of common schools, for the classification of schools and teachers, and for school libraries throughout Upper Canada.'' Its power did not extend to prohibiting a secondary level of instruction if such was deemed necessary by the trustees in order to meet local educational needs. I would adopt what Mignault J. said in this Court in *Tiny* (p. 707) with respect to the scope of the Council's regulatory power:

It seems to me inconceivable that when

it granted to the Roman Catholics of Upper Canada the privilege of having their own separate schools, the Legislature could have intended to render this privilege valueless by allowing the Council of Public Instruction of that Province to restrict, by regulations, the scope of the education to be given in these schools.

I would also adopt the following comments of Anglin C.J.C. at p. 671:

The statutes which entitled pupils up to the age of 21 years to attend the common and separate schools were certainly not designed to enable the Council of Public Instruction, under the guise of regulation, so to restrict the courses of studies for which the trustees might provide that they would be suitable only for pupils up to the age of, say, 12 or even 16 years.

As was forcibly pointed out during the argument, that would be to prohibit, not to regulate. . . . If the power of regulation of the Council of Public Instruction could be so exercised, the work of the schools could be indefinitely cut down. . . . But that an emasculation of the courses of study which Catholic separate school trustees were at the Union entitled to provide in their denominational schools for pupils up to 21 years of age would prejudicially affect a right or privilege with respect to such schools legally enjoyed them is indisputable; . . . Legislation purporting to authorize such an injustice would contravene s. 93(1) of the British North America Act; and it is obvious that what the legislature cannot do by direct action its creature may not do by regulation.

In the Privy Council Viscount Haldane noted (without any elaboration) at p. 359 that ''[i]t is indeed true that power to regulate does not imply a power to abolish.'' But he did not go on to point out that a right subject to a power of regulation is nevertheless a right and that the power must be exercised in conformity with the objectives of the Act. He simply concluded that the existence of the regulatory power at the date of Confederation, even although it had never been exercised up to the time of Confederation, prevented the separate schools at the time of Confederation from having the right to provide a secondary level of education for their pupils. For the reasons I have expressed above, this conclusion does not appear to me to be sound.

The Privy Council's disposition of the funding issue is, in my respectful view, equally unsatisfactory. The Privy Council seems not to have fully appreciated the purpose of s. 20 of the Scott Act and its relationship to s. 120 of the Common Schools Act. The whole purpose of these two sections was to preserve the separate school system. The security afforded the Roman Catholic minority through the tying of funding for its schools to a proportion of the funding for the common schools was in the certainty that the legislature would never cut off funding for the common schools. There would therefore always be a grant in which the separate schools would be entitled to share. However, by interpreting "otherwise appropriated by law" as permitting appropriations to schools other than "common schools" serving the majority, the Privy Council created a result quite contrary to the one which seems to have been intended by the draftsmen of the Scott Act. It created a situation where the schools of the majority could be fully funded by the legislature but the separate schools' funding was dependent upon the grace, generosity and good will of the legislature. This hardly seems consonant with the purpose of the Scott Act, which, as stated in its preamble, was to:

> . . . *restore to Roman Catholics in Upper Canada certain rights which they formerly enjoyed in respect to Separate Schools and to bring the provisions of the Law respecting Separate Schools more in harmony with the provisions of the Law respecting Common Schools.*

The view expressed by Anglin C.J.C. in this Court's decision in *Tiny* at pp. 678-79 seems apposite:

> *To exclude from the additional monetary benefits in which the right to "a share" was conferred on the separate schools in 1863 grants "for a common school purpose" . . . would defeat the apparent intention of the Legislature in 1863 to put separate schools on a footing of absolute equality with common schools in regard to all grants, municipal or legislative, of public moneys. . . .*
>
> *If, therefore, a grant of public moneys is made by the Legislature or by a municipal authority to aid or assist in the carrying out of what would in 1867 have been deemed a common school purpose, either it must be so made that it is apportionable between the common schools (or their present day successors) and the separate schools, or compensation to the latter for their proportion of such grant must be provided for.*

A further reason why the rights of separate school supporters to a secondary level of instruction should not be dismissed as non-rights and why the phrase "otherwise appropriated by law" in s. 120 of the Common Schools Act of 1859 should not be interpreted so broadly as to allow the legislature to impair the funding of separate schools, is that s. 93(1) of the Constitution Act, 1867 was intended to give constitutional value to the rights and privileges conferred in the Scott Act and the Common Schools Act of 1859. Section 93(1) should, in my view, be interpreted in a way which implements its clear purpose which was to provide a firm protection for Roman Catholic education in the Province of Ontario and Protestant education in the Province of Quebec. To interpret the provisions of the Scott Act and the Common Schools Act in the way in which the Privy Council interpreted them in *Tiny* is to render this constitutionalized protection illusory and wholly undermine this historically important compromise.

I would therefore conclude that Roman Catholic separate school supporters had at Confederation a right or privilege, by law, to have their children receive an appropriate education which could include instruction at the secondary school level and that such right or privilege is therefore constitutionally guaranteed under s. 93(1) of the Constitution Act, 1867. My reasons in support of this conclusion may be briefly summarized. By s. 7 of the Scott Act separate school trustees were given the same powers and duties as common school trustees. They were subject to a duty to allow pupils between the ages of 5 and 21 to attend their schools and to provide them with a suitable education. As in the case of the common school trustees the separate school trustees had, by law, a right to manage and control their schools. They also had a broad power, subject to regulation by the Council of Public Instruction, to determine the courses to be taught and to prescribe the level of education required to meet the needs of the local community. As Anglin C.J.C. pointed out in *Tiny* this was not a mere practice tolerated by the educational authorities but was permitted by law. I believe the Privy Council was in error in holding that the existence of the Council's general regulatory power (which, in my view, had to be exercised in conformity with the provisions of the enabling statute) nullified the trustees' power to provide a secondary level of instruction in their schools if they deemed it appropriate.

It is clear that if the foregoing right was to be meaningful an adequate level of funding was required to support it. This Court held unanimously in *Attorney General of Quebec* v. *Greater Hull School Board et al*, [1984] 2 S.C.R. 575 that the right of dissentient schools in Quebec to a proportionate share of government funding was a right protected by s. 93 of the Constitution Act, 1867. Likewise, in my view, is the right of separate schools in Ontario. They were entitled to the proportionate funding provided for in s. 20 of the Scott Act. This conclusion, it seems to me, is fully consistent with the clear purpose of s. 93, namely that the denominational minority's interest in a separate but suitable education for its children be protected into the future. I would therefore conclude (subject to the comments that follow on the applicability of the Charter of Rights) that Bill 30, which returns rights constitutionally guaranteed to separate schools by s. 93(1) of the Constitution Act, 1867, is *intra vires* the Provincial Legislature.

THE APPLICABILITY OF THE CHARTER OF RIGHTS

The appellants urged upon the Court that Bill 30 contravened s. 15 and s. 2(a) of the Charter in that it provided full funding for Roman Catholic secondary schools but not for other secondary schools, denominational or non-denominational, in the Province. The respondents submit that s. 29 of the Charter is a complete answer to this allegation. . . . This section, the respondents argued, makes Bill 30 immune from Charter review because Bill 30 deals with ''rights or privileges guaranteed . . . under the Constitution of Canada.'' The respondents are no doubt correct if Bill 30 is supported under s. 93(1) of the Constitution Act, 1867. It would then fall fairly and squarely within the language of s. 29. The Charter cannot be applied so as to abrogate or derogate from rights or privileges guaranteed by or under the constitution. But does s. 29 provide immunity from Charter review if the Bill is supportable only under the plenary power and s. 93(3)?

The respondents submitted that post-Confederation legislation enacted under the legislature's plenary power in relation to education and s. 93(3), while it may not be guaranteed by the constitution, is guaranteed under the constitution and is therefore immune from Charter review under s. 29. I have some difficulty with this submission if what the respondents are saying is that rights or privileges acquired under legislation enacted by a province pursuant to its plenary power in relation to education in the opening words of s. 93 have the same protection as the rights and privileges protected by s. 93(1). This cannot be so. It is clear from the wording of s. 93(3) that post-

Confederation legislation referred to in that subsection may be subsequently amended or repealed by the legislature which passed it in a way which affects rights or privileges initially granted by it. The only recourse if such occurs is an appeal to the Governor General in Council. It cannot be concluded, therefore, that rights or privileges conferred by post-Confederation legislation under s. 93(3) are "guaranteed" within the meaning of s. 29 in the same way as rights or privileges under s. 93(1).

This does not mean, however, that such rights or privileges are vulnerable to attack under ss. 2(a) and 15 of the Charter. I have indicated that the rights or privileges protected by s. 93(1) are immune from Charter review under s. 29 of the Charter, I think this is clear. What is less clear is whether s. 29 of the Charter was required in order to achieve that result. In my view, it was not. I believe it was put there simply to emphasize that the special treatment guaranteed by the constitution to denominational, separate or dissentient schools, even if it sits uncomfortably with the concept of equality embodied in the Charter because not available to other schools, is nevertheless not impaired by the Charter. It was never intended, in my opinion, that the Charter could be used to invalidate other provisions of the constitution, particularly a provision such as s. 93 which represented a fundamental part of the Confederation compromise. Section 29, in my view, is present in the Charter only for greater certainty, at least insofar as the Province of Ontario is concerned.

To put it another way, s. 29 is there to render immune from Charter review rights or privileges which would otherwise i.e. but for s. 29 be subject to such review. The question then becomes: does s. 29 protect rights or privileges conferred by legislation passed under the province's plenary power in relation to education under the opening words of s. 93? In my view, it does although again I do not believe it is required for this purpose. The Confederation compromise in relation to

education is found in the whole of s. 93, not in its individual parts. The s. 93(3) rights and privileges are not guaranteed in the sense that the s. 93(1) rights and privileges are guaranteed i.e. in the sense that the legislature which gave them cannot later pass laws which prejudicially affect them. But they are insulated from Charter attack as legislation enacted pursuant to the plenary power in relation to education granted to the provincial legislatures as part of the Confederation compromise. Their protection from Charter review lies not in the guaranteed nature of the rights and privileges conferred by the legislation but in the guaranteed nature of the province's plenary power to enact that legislation. What the province gives pursuant to its plenary power the province can take away, subject only to the right of appeal to the Governor General in Council. But the province is master of its own house when it legislates under its plenary power in relation to denominational, separate or dissentient schools. This was the agreement at Confederation and, in my view, it was not displaced by the enactment of the Constitution Act, 1982. As the majority of the Court of Appeal concluded at pp. 575-76:

> These educational rights, granted specifically to the Protestants in Quebec and the Roman Catholics in Ontario, make it impossible to treat all Canadians equally. The country was founded upon the recognition of special or unequal educational rights for specific religious groups in Ontario and Quebec. The incorporation of the Charter into the Constitution Act, 1982 does not change the original Confederation bargain. A specific constitutional amendment would be required to accomplish that.

I would conclude, therefore, that even if Bill 30 is supportable only under the Province's plenary power and s. 93(3) it is insulated from Charter review. . . .

The judgment of Estey and Beetz JJ. was delivered by

ESTEY J.: (concurring with reasons) I have had the benefit of reading the reasons for judgment of my colleague Wilson J. and, with respect, I reach the same conclusion but by a different and shorter route. In the result, I conclude that Bill 30, An Act to Amend the Education Act, is not inconsistent with the provisions of the Constitution of Canada. Because Madame Justice Wilson has fully set out and reviewed the Bill which gave rise to these proceedings, the circumstances which led up to the appeal to this Court, and the judgments in the Court of Appeal, it is possible to proceed directly to the issues required to be settled in the disposition of this appeal.

The first question that must be addressed in this appeal is whether Bill 30 is a valid exercise of the provincial power in relation to education under the opening words of s. 93 and s. 93(3) of the Constitution Act, 1867. Like my colleague Wilson J., I conclude that Bill 30 is a valid exercise of this provincial power. The only remaining question is whether the exercise of this valid provincial power can be limited, or in this case entirely truncated, by the operation of the Charter. This judgment concludes that the Charter cannot operate to erase this provincial power under the Constitution. Bill 30 is therefore upheld. Unlike my colleague Wilson J., I conclude with respect that it is therefore unnecessary to consider the operation of s. 93(1) of the Constitution Act, 1867, to reexamine the scope of the rights guaranteed to Roman Catholics by the Constitution Act, 1867, or to reconsider the decision of the Privy Council on that issue in *Tiny Separate School Trustees* v. *The King*, [1928] A.C. 363. This judgment of the Privy Council supports and indeed relies upon the factual conclusions reached in all the courts below except the Supreme Court. It would be most inappropriate and indeed dangerous for this Court over half a century later to review and then reverse or revise findings of fact made at trial by Rose J., confirmed by a unanimous Court of Appeal and undisturbed by the even division of this Court. At the Supreme Court, Duff J., who had been both a student and a teacher in the school systems of Ontario there under examination, agreed with the factual findings of the courts below. Where it is not essential to the disposition of the issue here, it would be imprudent for an appellate court sitting almost 60 years distant from the scene to reassess a factual situation peculiarly within the experience of the members of the lower courts who were called upon to make their judgment of then recent history. For all these reasons, in my view, *Tiny, supra*, should not now be reopened. The state of separate school education in 1867 in Ontario is in my view therefore wholly irrelevant to the measurement of the constitutionality of Bill 30 in this appeal.

Before one can discuss the main point around which this appeal turns it is necessary to clear away some underbrush which, though argued at length, in truth only conceals the main point.

THE OPENING WORDS OF S. 93 AND S. 93(3)

. . . The opening words of s. 93 are a clear grant of legislative power to the province, providing the province with the authority to make laws in relation to education. As such, the opening words of s. 93 are similar to the various grants of provincial power found in s. 92 of the Constitution Act, 1867 and might well have been included in s. 92 along with the related federal responsibility under s. 93(3). This would have resulted in a sub-subsection of s. 92 in a form very similar to that of 92(10) (Local Works and Undertakings) which also acknowledges a related federal authority.

Section 93(3) provides for an appeal to the Governor General in Council when "any Act or Decision of any Provincial Authority" affects any right or privilege "of the Protestant or Roman Catholic Minority" that existed either: (a) at the time of Confederation, or (b) was "thereafter established by the Legislature." Subsection (3) thus contemplates that after Confederation the Legislature may establish a new system of separate schools or may enlarge an existing system of separate schools. Should this system of schools be later repealed or otherwise affected by the Legislature, an appeal to the Governor General in Council would lie, in addition to any right to appeal to the courts challenging legislative action prejudicially affecting the rights guaranteed under s. 93(1).

When read with the opening words of s. 93, which provide the province with a general plenary power to "exclusively make laws in relation to Education," it is clear that the province can make any laws with respect to education subject only to two limitations. First, any such laws may not violate the minimum constitutional guarantees found in s. 93(1), and second, the exercise of this provincial power may also face federal intervention under s. 93(4). Support for this general proposition can be found in both *Brophy* v. *A.G. of Manitoba*, [1895] A.C. 202 and *Tiny Separate School Trustees* v. *The King*, [1928] A.C. 363 (P.C.).

With respect to the operation s. 93(3), Lord Halsbury L.C., speaking for the Privy Council in *Brophy, supra*, stated at p. 220:

It is admitted that the 3rd and 4th subsections of sect. 93 (the latter of which is, as has been observed, identical with subsect. 3 of sect. 22 of the Manitoba Act) were not intended to have effect merely when a provincial Legislature had exceeded the limit imposed on its powers by sub-sect. 1, for sub-sect. 3 gives an appeal to the Governor-General, not only where a system of separate or dissentient schools existed in a province at the time of the Union, but also where in any province such a system was "thereafter established by the Legislature of the province." It is manifest that this relates to a state of things created by post-Union legislation.

The Privy Council in *Tiny, supra*, returned to the analysis of s. 93(3), when Viscount Haldane stated at pp. 369-70:

Sub-s. 3 contemplates that within the powers of the Provincial legislature Acts might be passed which did affect rights and privileges of religious minorities in relation to education, and gives a different kind of remedy, which appears, as has already been pointed out, to have been devised subsequently to the Quebec resolutions of 1864, and before the bill of 1867 was agreed on. Whenever an Act or decision of a Provincial authority affecting any right or privilege of the minority, Protestant or Roman Catholic, in relation to education is challenged, an appeal is to lie to the Governor-General in Council, as distinguished from the Courts of law. No doubt if what is challenged is challenged on the ground of its being ultra vires, the right of appeal to a Court of law remains for both parties unimpaired. But there is a further right not based on the principle of ultra vires. That this is so is shown by the extension of the power to challenge to any system of separate or dissentient schools established by law after Confederation, and which accordingly could not be confined to rights or privileges at the time of Confederation.

The following conclusions can be drawn from the above analysis. The appeal process established by s. 93(3) is primarily a political appeal; it is not the legal right to challenge constitutionality that is found in s. 93(1). It is clear that no right of appeal lies under s. 93(3) unless there has been an "Act or Decision of any Provincial Authority" which affects rights or privileges. Rights or privileges granted after Confederation can be protected by the political appeal process in s. 93(3); rights or privileges in place at the time of Confederation can be protected by either the political appeal process in s. 93(3) or a legal challenge in the courts pursuant to s. 93(1). It is therefore a basic premise or a binding assumption on the part of the authors of s. 93(3) that for a right of appeal to arise under s. 93(3), the province has by legislation established or enlarged, after Confederation, a separate school system and has thereafter abolished or affected the rights granted to the minority under that legislation.

The ultimate question posed in this appeal is whether Bill 30, which extends full funding for secondary education to separate schools already in existence, falls within the provincial power contemplated in s. 93(3). The dissent in the Court of Appeal was of the opinion that s. 93(3) did not expand the rights or privileges protected by s. 93(1) and that the reference to "thereafter established" in s. 93(3) ". . . would apply to a province such as Manitoba or Newfoundland which established a system of separate schools after Confederation." If this were so, these key words would have no application to Ontario. With all respect, I cannot accept the reasoning of the minority. It would in my view be quite incorrect to conclude that the words "thereafter established" in s. 93(3), and the appeal process found therein, only apply to provinces which at the time of union had no publicly funded separate school system. There is no compelling reason to interpret so restrictively the words in s. 93(3). In my respectful view, the plain meaning of the words "thereafter established" necessarily includes additional rights or privileges, such as full funding for secondary education in Ontario, that have been granted subsequent to Confederation and in addition to the minimum rights and privileges guaranteed in s. 93(1).

I conclude therefore that this post-Confederation legislative power of the province to legislate with respect to education includes the establishment of separate schools providing education at the secondary school level. Without this post-Confederation legislative sovereignty in the province, the right of appeal which is granted under s. 93(3) would be illusory and completely without any future use. It is also important to note that s. 93(4) provides for an extraordinary federal jurisdiction over education in the event that an appeal under s. 93(3) meets with the favour of the Governor General in Council. The Parliament of Canada may make any such remedial laws as are necessary for the implementation of any decision by the Governor General in Council in response to an appeal under s. 93(3). Indeed, the federal power to enact remedial laws under s. 93(4) does not appear to be limited only to situations where there has been an appeal to the Governor General in Council. The opening words of s. 93(4) contemplate that whenever it appears to the Governor General in Council that a provincial law is "requisite for the due execution of the provisions" of s. 93, Parliament may enact remedial legislation. It would appear, although it is not necessary to decide, that the remedial power of Parliament can be exercised either in the event of an appeal to the Governor General in Council or upon the initiative of the Governor General in Council should it be deemed necessary. Some counsel suggested that s. 93(4) has been effectively removed from the Constitution because it has never been used. While it is not necessary to decide whether the lack of exercise of this federal power under s. 93(4) has rendered this power obsolete or atrophic, the removal of the federal power in this matter would not reduce but could indeed strengthen the freedom of the province to exercise its unfettered power, apart from section 93(1) which is not here applicable, under the opening part of s. 93. In any event, it should be observed that s. 93(4) is a key provision in the delicate balance of interests found in s. 93, and it is a grant of federal power as vital as any found in s. 91 of the Constitution Act, 1867. Consequently it is difficult to understand how lack of exercise can operate as a repeal.

As a result, in order that life may be given to s. 93(3) and (4) it is fundamental that the province enjoy the power to create or add to a separate school system. The next question that must therefore be addressed is the application of the Charter to the exercise of this provincial power.

APPLICATION OF THE CHARTER OF RIGHTS

The appellants have argued that Bill 30 violates s. 2(a) and s. 15 of the Charter in that Bill 30 provides full funding for Roman Catholic secondary schools but not for other secondary schools, denominational or non-denominational, in the province. . . .

It is axiomatic (and many counsel before this Court conceded the point) that if the Charter has any application to Bill 30, this Bill would be found discriminatory and in violation of s. 2(a) and s. 15 of the Charter of Rights. Notwithstanding this conclusion, the real contest in this appeal is clearly between the operation of the Charter in its entirety and the integrity of s. 93. By s. 52 of the Constitution Act, 1982, s. 93 is a part of the Constitution of Canada. Section 93 is a fundamental constitutional provision because it is a part of the pattern of the sharing of sovereign power between the two plenary authorities created at Confederation. The importance of this provision is underlined by its separate existence outside the catalogue of powers in ss. 91 and 92.

Once s. 93 is examined as a grant of power to the province, similar to the heads of power found in s. 92, it is apparent that the purpose of this grant of power is to provide the province with the jurisdiction to legislate in a *prima facie* selective and distinguishing manner with respect to education whether or not some segments of the community might consider the result to be discriminatory. In this sense, s. 93 is a provincial counterpart of s. 91(24) (Indians and Indian land) which authorizes the Parliament of Canada to legislate for the benefit of the Indian population in a preferential, discriminatory, or distinctive fashion vis-à-vis others.

The role of the Charter is not envisaged in our jurisprudence as providing for the automatic repeal of any provisions of the Constitution of Canada which includes all of the documents enumerated in s. 52 of the Constitution Act, 1982. Action taken under the Constitution Act, 1867 is of course subject to Charter review. That is a far different thing from saying that a specific power to legislate as existing prior to April 1982 has been entirely removed by

the simple advent of the Charter. It is one thing to supervise and on a proper occasion curtail the exercise of a power to legislate; it is quite another thing to say that an entire power to legislate has been removed from the Constitution by the introduction of this judicial power of supervision. The power to establish or add to a system of Roman Catholic separate schools found in s. 93(3) expressly contemplates that the province may legislate with respect to a religiously-based school system funded from the public treasury. Although the Charter is intended to constrain the exercise of legislative power conferred under the Constitution Act, 1867 where the delineated rights of individual members of the community are adversely affected, it cannot be interpreted as rendering unconstitutional distinctions that are expressly permitted by the Constitution Act, 1867.

I therefore would conclude that s. 93(3) does indeed introduce a recognition of a legislative power granted in the opening words of s. 93 and surviving the operations of s. 93(1). This legislative power in the province is not subject to regulation by other parts of the Constitution in any way which would be tantamount to its repeal. The Charter would not be available to disallow the implementation of s. 93(1), or legislation for the protection of the rights embedded by s. 93(1), or legislation contemplated in s. 93(3).

This conclusion, that Bill 30 finds its validity in the exercise of provincial power under s. 93 and that the exercise of this power cannot be abolished or truncated by the Charter, is sufficient to dispose of this appeal. However, as there was much discussion before the Court regarding the operation of s. 29 of the Charter, it may be useful to make some comments in response to those arguments. The interpretation of s. 29 was also critical to the finding by the majority in the Ontario Court of Appeal that Bill 30 was not subject to review by the Charter. . . .

It was argued by the respondents that the "rights or privileges" which are protected from Charter review by s. 29 include the rights and privileges that have been granted by the passage of Bill 30 itself. Section 29 is thereby interpreted as applying to post-Confederation legislation because that legislation is considered by the terms of s. 29 to be a guarantee "by or under the Constitution" protecting rights or privileges of separate schools.

There are several approaches one could take when examining the ambiguous wording in s. 29. The majority below chose to focus on the words "or under" found in s. 29 and they concluded that these words were intended to cover guarantees in addition to those granted specifically by the Constitution itself. The words "under the Constitution" it was said should include rights or privileges granted by laws enacted under the authority of the Constitution. The majority held that this interpretation was supported by the French version of s. 29 which employs the single phrase "*en vertu de*" in the place of "by or under." Further, the respondent in this appeal argued that an interpretation of s. 29 which restricted the protection it provided to only those rights specifically guaranteed by the Constitution would render s. 29 redundant as the Charter cannot possibly operate so as to overrule any rights specifically granted in other parts of the Constitution.

The minority of the Court of Appeal was not persuaded by this interpretation of s. 29 and chose instead to focus on the operation of the word "guaranteed" in s. 29. To be protected by s. 29, the rights referred to therein must be constitutionally guaranteed and a constitutional guarantee does not attach to rights or privileges conferred by an ordinary provincial statute. The minority also expressed concern that to interpret s. 29 as protecting all statutory enactments with respect to separate schools from Charter review would additionally have the effect of transforming these additional privileges granted to

separate schools into guarantees under the Constitution and thus forever immune from legislative repeal or amendment.

I have concluded, with respect to those who have concluded otherwise, that it is unnecessary to resolve the meaning of "by" or "under" because the dominant word in s. 29 is "guaranteed." Statutes cannot by their very nature guarantee anything, susceptible as they are to legislative repeal. As the rights granted by Bill 30 are not "guaranteed" under the Constitution Act, 1867 (*Tiny, supra*, at p. 387), s. 29 cannot operate so as to protect these rights. I would therefore adopt the reasoning of the minority at the Court of Appeal with respect to the interpretation to be given to s. 29 of the Charter. I repeat however that Bill 30 cannot be struck down by the Charter because Bill 30 is a valid exercise of a specific power to legislate granted under s. 93; Bill 30 does not require the protection of s. 29 in order to be upheld.

I would dismiss the appeal and answer the reference question in the negative.

LAMER J. (concurring in part): I have had the benefit of reading the reasons for judgment prepared in this appeal by my colleagues, Wilson and Estey JJ. I agree with them that this appeal should be dismissed. However, I would dismiss the appeal only on the basis of the opening words of s. 93 and s. 93(3) of the Constitution Act, 1867, for the reasons given by Wilson J. I also agree with Wilson J. as to the effect of the Canadian Charter of Rights and Freedoms on s. 93 of the Constitution Act, 1867.

Given my decision on this first point, it is unnecessary for me to deal with the interpretation of s. 93(1) of the Constitution Act, 1867 and *Tiny Separate School Trustees* v. *The King*, [1928] A.C. 363.

I would therefore dismiss the appeal and answer the reference question in the negative.

PART THREE:
CONSTITUTIONAL CHANGE

A. Delegation

59. Nova Scotia Interdelegation Case, *1951*

~ Canadians are almost obsessed with changing their constitution. The Canadian constitutional myth is the opposite of the American: whereas Americans are apt to believe they have a perfect constitution if only the country could live up to it, Canadians are more apt to believe that they have a marvellous country if only they could find the ideal constitution.

One reason for the Canadian preoccupation is the strictness with which the courts have enforced the federal division of legislative powers. Whereas in the United States for nearly four decades following the Roosevelt court-packing threat of 1937 the Supreme Court has been inclined to let the national legislature set the limits of its own regulatory power, in Canada, as the cases in Part One of this book show, the Supreme Court (and the country) have continued to treat federalism seriously as a system of constitutionality divided and mutually exclusive powers. However, many of the social and economic problems which modern governments wish to tackle, because they have closely intertwined national and local dimensions, are not easily handled by a system of federalism based on a division of powers into exclusive watertight compartments. Thus there is an unending search for a satisfactory division of powers as well as for ways of transcending the constitutional division of powers.

One of the devices most often canvassed for overcoming rigidities in the division of powers has been the delegation of legislative powers from one level of government to the other. Such a mechanism was recommended in 1939 by the Rowell-Sirois Royal Commission on Dominion-Provincial Relations in order to overcome barriers to effective administration created by strict judicial enforcement of divided jurisdictions. Because of doubts as to whether it was constitutionally valid for the federal Parliament and provincial legislatures to transfer legislative functions to one another, the Royal Commission called for a constitutional amendment to establish such a power of delegation.

In was precisely this technique of voluntary interdelegation which was embodied in the Nova Scotia statute challenged before the Supreme Court in this case. This Bill would have authorized the provincial government to delegate to the federal Parliament the power to legislate with respect to employment in areas under provincial jurisdiction. Complete flexibility would be achieved by providing for delegation in the opposite direction: the Bill anticipated the Nova Scotia Legislature receiving from the national Parliament the power to make laws in relation to employment in industries under federal jurisdictions as well as legislative authority in the indirect tax field. Before proceeding with its enactment the government of Nova Scotia first submitted the question of the constitutional validity of this delegation procedure to the Supreme Court of Nova Scotia. A majority of the Court ruled that it was unconstitutional for either Parliament or the legislatures to employ the delegation device contemplated in the Nova Scotia legislation.

The appeal from this judgment was dismissed by the Supreme Court of Canada in a unanimous decision. The various members of the Court who wrote opinions insisted upon a fundamental distinction between delegations of power by Parliament or the legislatures to subordinate agencies, and delegations of power from one legislative level to the other. There was ample authority to justify the former type of delegation but the latter was, in their view, clearly unconstitutional. Interdelegation between the national and provincial legislatures would have the effect of altering the basic scheme of Canadian federalism and neither Parliament nor the legislatures were authorized by the B.N.A. Act to make what in the Court's opinion would be tantamount to *ad hoc* amendments to the division of legislative powers. Here the Supreme Court demonstrated how fully committed it was to federalism as a basic principle of the Canadian constitution.

Although the Supreme Court's decision in this case put the interdelegation of power between Parliament and the provincial legislatures beyond the pale of the constitution it left intact other possible forms of legislative collaboration. Referential and conditional legislation are two such techniques which have been frequently employed in the past and which, in principle, were not affected by this case. In referential legislation either Parliament or a provincial legislature referentially incorporates in a statute the valid enactments of the other; in conditional legislation a legislature makes the carrying out of the policy stated in a statute conditional upon the act of another governmental agency. But an additional and far more useful avenue for the advancement of co-operative federalism was to be opened up by the Supreme Court two years after this case in the Willis[1] case. ~

ATTORNEY GENERAL OF NOVA SCOTIA *v.* ATTORNEY GENERAL
OF CANADA
In the Supreme Court of Canada. [1951] S.C.R. 31.

RINFRET C.J.: This is a reference by the Lieutenant-Governor in Council of the Province of Nova Scotia, submitting to the Supreme Court of that Province the question of the constitutional validity of a Bill, Number 136, entitled "An Act respecting the delegation of jurisdiction from the Parliament of Canada to the Legislature of Nova Scotia and *vice versa*."

By virtue of this Bill, if it should come into force, by proclamation, as therein provided, the Lieutenant-Governor in Council, may from time to time delegate

[1] See case 60 below.

to and withdraw from the Parliament of Canada authority to make laws in relation to any matter relating to employment in any industry, work or undertaking in respect of which such matter, is by section 92 of the British North America Act, 1867, exclusively within the jurisdiction of the Legislature of Nova Scotia. It provides that any laws so made by the Parliament of Canada shall, while such delegation is in force, have the same effect as if enacted by the Legislature.

The Bill also provides that if and when the Parliament of Canada shall have delegated to the Legislature of the Province of Nova Scotia authority to make laws in relation to any matter relating to employment in any industry, work or undertaking in respect of which such matter is, under the provisions of the British North America Act, 1867, exclusively within the legislative jurisdiction of such Parliament, the Lieutenant-Governor in Council, while such delegation is in force, may, by proclamation, from time to time apply any or all of the provisions of any Act in relation to a matter relating to employment in force in the Province of Nova Scotia to any such industry, work, or undertaking.

Finally, the Bill enacts that if and when the Parliament of Canada shall have delegated to the Legislature of the Province of Nova Scotia authority to make laws in relation to the raising of a revenue for provincial purposes by the imposing of a retail sales tax of the nature of indirect taxation, the Lieutenant-Governor in Council, while such delegation is in force, may impose such a tax of such amount not exceeding 3 per cent of the retail price as he deems necessary, in respect of any commodity to which such delegation extends and may make regulations providing for the method of collecting any such tax.

The provisions of the Bill, therefore, deal with employment in industries, works, or undertakings, exclusively within the legislative jurisdiction in the one case of the Legislature of the Province of Nova Scotia and in the other case

within the exclusive legislative jurisdiction of the Parliament of Canada, and it also deals with the raising of revenue for provincial purposes by means of indirect taxation.

In each of the supposed cases either the Parliament of Canada, or the Legislature of Nova Scotia, would be adopting legislation concerning matters which have not been attributed to it but to the other by the constitution of the country.

The Supreme Court of Nova Scotia *en banc*, to which the matter was submitted, answered that such legislation was not within the competence of the Legislature of Nova Scotia, except that Doull J. dissented and expressed the opinion that the Bill was constitutionally valid, subject to the limitations stated in his answers. I agree with the answers given by the majority of the Judges in the Supreme Court *en banc*.

The Parliament of Canada and the Legislatures of the several Provinces are sovereign within their sphere defined by the British North America Act, but none of them has the unlimited capacity of an individual. They can exercise only the legislative powers respectively given to them by sections 91 and 92 of the Act, and these powers must be found in either of these sections.

The constitution of Canada does not belong either to Parliament, or to the Legislatures; it belongs to the country and it is there that the citizens of the country will find the protection of the rights to which they are entitled. It is part of the protection that Parliament can legislate only on the subject matters referred to it by section 91 and that each Province can legislate exclusively on the subject matters referred to it by section 92. The country is entitled to insist that legislation adopted under section 91 should be passed exclusively by the Parliament of Canada in the same way as the people of each Province are entitled to insist that legislation concerning the matters enumerated in section 92 should come exclusively from their respective Legislatures. In each case the Members elected to Parliament or to the

Legislatures are the only ones entrusted with the power and the duty to legislate concerning the subjects exclusively distributed by the constitutional Act to each of them.

No power of delegation is expressed either in section 91 or in section 92, nor, indeed, is there to be found the power of accepting delegation from one body to the other; and I have no doubt that if it had been the intention to give such powers it would have been expressed in clear and unequivocal language. Under the scheme of the British North America Act there were to be, in the words of Lord Atkin in *The Labour Conventions Reference* ([1937] A.C. 326), "water-tight compartments which are an essential part of the original structure."

Neither legislative bodies, federal or provincial, possess any portion of the powers respectively vested in the other and they cannot receive it by delegation. In that connection the word "exclusively" used both in section 91 and in section 92 indicates a settled line of demarcation and it does not belong to either Parliament, or the Legislatures, to confer powers upon the other. . . .

TASCHEREAU J.: These questions, although limited to indirect taxation and to laws in relation to employment matters, cover a much wider field. For if it is within the powers of Parliament and of the Legislatures to confer upon each other by consent, a legislative authority which they do not otherwise possess, to deal with the subject matters found in the questions submitted, the same powers would naturally exist to enact laws affecting all the classes of subjects enumerated in section 91 and 92 of the B.N.A. Act. I must say at the outset that I am of the opinion that the conclusion arrived at by the Supreme Court of Nova Scotia is right.

The British North America Act, 1867, and amendments has defined the powers that are to be exercised by the Dominion Parliament and by the Legislatures of the various provinces. There are fields where the Dominion has exclusive jurisdiction, while others are reserved to the provinces. This division of powers has received the sanction of the Imperial Parliament, which was then and is still the sole competent authority to make any alterations to its own laws. If Bill 136 were *intra vires*, the Dominion Parliament could delegate its powers to any or all the provinces, to legislate on commerce, banking, bankruptcy, militia and defence, issue of paper money, patents, copyrights, indirect taxation, and all other matters enumerated in section 91; and on the other hand, the Legislatures could authorize the Dominion to pass laws in relation to property and civil rights, municipal institutions, education, etc. etc., all matters outside the jurisdiction reserved to the Dominion Parliament. The powers of Parliament and of the Legislatures strictly limited by the B.N.A. Act, would thus be considerably enlarged, and I have no doubt that this cannot be done, even with the joint consent of Parliament and of the Legislatures.

It is a well settled proposition of law that jurisdiction cannot be conferred by consent. None of these bodies can be vested directly or indirectly with powers which have been denied them by the B.N.A. Act, and which therefore are not within their constitutional jurisdiction.

This question has often been the subject of comments by eminent text writers, and has also been definitely settled by numerous authoritative judicial pronouncements.

Lefroy's *Canada Federal System* (1913 at p. 70) cites the words of Lord Watson on the argument in *C.P.R.* v. *Bonsecours* ([1899] A.C. 367):

The Dominion cannot give jurisdiction, or leave jurisdiction, with the province. The provincial parliament cannot give legislative jurisdiction to the Dominion parliament. If they have it, either one or the other of them, they have it by virtue of the Act of 1867. I think we must get rid of the idea that either one or the other can enlarge the jurisdiction of the other or surrender jurisdiction. . . .

. . . Lefroy in *Legislative Power in Canada* at page 242, expresses the view with which I agree, that the federal Parliament cannot amend the British North America Act, nor either expressly or impliedly take away from, or give to, the provincial Legislatures a power which the Imperial Act does, or does not give them; and he adds that the same is the case, *mutatis mutandis*, with the Provincial Legislatures. At page 689, the same author adds that within the area and limits of subjects mentioned in section 92 of the British North American Act, the provincial Legislatures are supreme and have the same authority as the Imperial Parliament or the Dominion would have under like circumstances, to confide to a municipal institution or body of its own creation, authority to make by-laws or regulations as to subjects specified in the enactment and with the object of carrying the enactment into operation and effect. This proposition rests upon the language and decisions of the Judicial Committee of the Privy Council in *Hodge* v. *The Queen* (9 App. Cas. 117).

It will be seen therefore that as a result of all these authorities and pronouncements, Parliament or the Legislatures may delegate in certain cases their powers to subordinate agencies, but that it has never been held that the Parliament of Canada or any of the Legislatures can abdicate their powers and invest for the purpose of legislation, bodies which by the very terms of the B.N.A. Act are not empowered to accept such delegation, and to legislate on such matters.

It has been further argued that as a result of the delegation made by the federal government to the Provinces, the laws enacted by the Provinces as delegates would be federal laws and that they would, therefore, be constitutionally valid. With this proposition I cannot agree. These laws would not then be enacted "with the advice and consent of the Senate and House of Commons," and would not be assented to by the Governor General, but by the Lieutenant-Governor, who has no power to do so. Moreover, as already stated, such a right has been denied the Provinces by the B.N.A. Act.

If the proposed legislation were held to be valid, the whole scheme of the Canadian constitution would be entirely defeated. The framers of the B.N.A. Act thought wisely that Canada should not be a unitary state, but it would be converted into one, as Mr. Justice Hall says, if all the Provinces empowered Parliament to make laws with respect to *all matters* exclusively assigned to them. Moreover, it is clear that the delegation of legislative powes by Parliament to the ten Provinces on matters enumerated in section 91 of the B.N.A. Act could bring about different criminal laws, different banking and bankruptcy laws, different military laws, different postal laws, different currency laws, all subjects in relation to which it has been thought imperative that uniformity should prevail throughout Canada.

For the above reasons, I have come to the conclusion that this appeal should be dismissed.

~ Justices Kerwin, Rand, Kellock, Estey, and Fauteux all wrote opinions holding that Bill No. 136 was unconstitutional. ~

60. P.E.I. Potato Marketing Board *v.* H.B. Willis Inc., *1952*

~ In this case the Supreme Court was asked to determine the constitutional validity of a slightly modified version of the delegation device which the Court had ruled unconstitutional in the *Nova Scotia Interdelegation* case. Here it was a question of whether the federal Parliament could validly delegate legislative powers not to a provincial legislature but to an administrative board created by a provincial legislature. This question arose out of another joint effort by the legislature of a province and the Dominion to arm a single provincial marketing board with the power of regulating both intra-provincial and extra-provincial aspects of trade in natural produce. The Prince Edward Island Legislature had passed the Agricultural Products Marketing Act in 1940 authorizing the Lieutenant-Governor in Council to establish a board for regulating various aspects of trade in natural products within the province. The Act also provided that such a board could, with the approval of the Lieutenant-Governor in Council, perform any functions delegated to it by the Dominion. In September 1950, the government of P.E.I., exercising its power under this Act, established a Potato Marketing Board to administer a scheme for regulating local trade in potatoes. Meanwhile, at the federal level, Parliament had enacted in 1949 the Agricultural Products Marketing Act, the crucial section of which authorized the Governor in Council to delegate the Dominion's jurisdiction over interprovincial and export trade to a provincial board. Following this, the federal government by order-in-council in October 1950, delegated to the P.E.I. Potato Marketing Board the power to regulate the extra-provincial marketing of potatoes from the province.

The validity of this device of Dominion delegation to a provincial board was first challenged successfully before the Supreme Court of Prince Edward Island. The provincial Supreme Court simply followed the Supreme Court of Canada's earlier decision in the *Nova Scotia Interdelegation* case and reasoned that if the B.N.A. Act prohibited Parliament from delegating legislative power to a provincial legislature it must also prohibit Parliament from delegating power to a creature of such a legislature. But the federal Supreme Court was able to find a distinction of kind between the type of delegation at issue in this case and that which it had found invalid the year before. Delegation from Parliament to a provincial board did not, apparently, involve a transfer of power across the sacrosanct wall dividing provincial from federal powers. A provincial board, although it might be a thoroughly subordinate offspring of a provincial legislature could still exist, at least in thought, as an autonomous unit entirely distinct from the provincial legislature which created it. Justice Rand rationalized this point of view by suggesting that it could be regarded as simply a coincidence that both the Dominion and a province had decided to bestow their regulatory powers on the same group of men.

Devious as the Court's logic in this case might seem, its decision to uphold this form of delegation did, in large measure, reverse the consequences of its earlier decision. The power which Parliament could not delegate directly to a provincial legislature could be indirectly delegated to an agency established by such a legislature.

The first application of this valid form of delegation had the ironic purpose of reversing the Privy Council's last decision on the B.N.A. Act—a decision which had had an expansionary effect on the Dominion's powers. In the *Winner*[1] case the Privy Council had ruled that an interprovincial bus line, even though one phase of its operation was completed entirely within a province, was, for purposes of licensing regulations, entirely within the jurisdiction of the federal Parliament. Shortly after this decision was brought down, the Dominion agreed to enact legislation which would return to the individual provincial transport boards the power of licensing interprovincial carriers. Thus while the type of delegation validated in the *Willis* case might facilitate greater decentralization in the operation of Canadian federalism, it is doubtful whether it could work in the opposite direction to promote greater administrative uniformity or simplification. On this point it must be noted that the Supreme Court in the *Willis* case declined to determine whether the indirect delegation procedure could be validly reversed and the provinces delegate regulatory powers to federal agencies.

In 1968 the Supreme Court by a five-to-two majority turned back a challenge to the federal Motor Transport Vehicle Act which delegated regulatory power over extra-provincial carriers to provincial boards.[2] The legislation challenged in this case went even further than that at issue in the *Willis* case towards a delegation of legislative power from federal to provincial authorities. Here Parliament had delegated authority directly to the provincial boards, authorizing them to apply to extra-provincial carriers not simply existing provincial licensing regulations but also any subsequent changes provincial legislatures might make in provincial regulations. By validating this form of delegation the Supreme Court further reduced the impact of the *Nova Scotia Interdelegation* case and by the same token increased the opportunities for a more flexible working of the Canadian federal system.

The Supreme Court's decision in *Willis* undoubtedly contributed to the era of "co-operative federalism" which flourished in Canada in the 1950s and 1960s. Its approval of delegation to administrative agencies also reinforced an emphasis on "executive federalism." The establishment of the Canadian Egg Marketing Agency (C.E.M.A.)[3] in the 1970s shows that even when federal-provincial relations revert to a more combative style, co-operative interdelega-

---

[1] *A.-G. Ont.* v. *Winner* [1954] A.C. 541.

[2] *Coughlin* v. *Ontario Highway Transport Board et al.*, [1968] S.C.R. 569.

[3] For a discussion of the Supreme Court's decision in 1978 upholding C.E.M.A., see p. 154 above.

tion may still take place especially when important symbolic issues or economic resources are not at stake.

A proposal to reverse the *Nova Scotia Interdelegation* decision and permit direct delegation between legislatures was included in the "Fulton-Favreau" constitutional proposals which came close to adoption in 1964. However, delegation has not been a feature of the plethora of constitutional proposals considered since then.[4] This may reflect the efficacy of the administrative delegation validated in the *Willis* case and a diminution of interest in facilitating co-operative federalism. ~

P.E.I. POTATO MARKETING BOARD *v.* H.B. WILLIS INC.
In the Supreme Court of Canada. [1952] 2 S.C.R. 392.

RINFRET C.J.: In my opinion the appeal of the Prince Edward Island Potato Marketing Board should be upheld.

The judgment of the Supreme Court of Prince Edward Island *in banco* was delivered on the 31st of January, 1952. The Lieutenant-Governor in Council had referred to that Court for hearing and consideration the following questions:

(1) Is it within the jurisdiction and competence of the Parliament of Canada to enact The Agricultural Products Marketing Act, (1949) 13 George VI, (1st Session) c. 16?

(2) If the answer to question No. 1 is yes, is it within the jurisdiction and competence of the Governor-General in Council to pass P.C. 5159?

(3) Is it within the jurisdiction and competence of the Lieutenant-Governor in Council to establish the said Scheme and in particular s. 16 thereof?

(4) Is it within the jurisdiction and competence of the Prince Edward Island Potato Marketing Board to make the Orders made under the said Scheme any of the Orders so made?

Tweedy J. wrote the main judgment, in which the Chief Justice and MacGuigan J.

concurred, the Chief Justice simply adding a few additional reasons.

The main ground of the judgment of Tweedy J. appears to have been that the Supreme Court of Canada in *A.-G. of N.S.* v. *A.-G. of Can.* ([1951] S.C.R. 31) which held that the Parliament of Canada and each provincial legislature were not capable of delegating one to the other the powers with which it had been vested, nor of receiving from the other the powers with which the other has been vested. In the opinion of the Supreme Court *in banco* of Prince Edward Island that judgment was really decisive with respect to the first two questions in the reference under appeal.

With deference, such is not the effect of the judgment of this Court in the Nova Scotia reference. It was made quite clear in our reasons for judgment that they only applied to the questions as put and which had to deal only with an Act respecting the delegation from Parliament of Canada to the Legislature of Nova Scotia and *vice versa*. The unanimous opinion of this Court was that each legislature could only exercise the legislative powers respectively given to them by ss. 91 and 92 of the Act, that these sections indicated a settled line of demarcation and it did not

---

[4] A delegation device was included in the amending formula agreed to on April 16, 1981, by the eight provinces then opposing Ottawa. But this element of the "April accord" was dropped from the amending formula agreed to by the federal government and nine provinces on November 5, 1981 and was not included in the Constitution Act, 1982.

belong to the Parliament of Canada or the Legislatures to confer their powers upon the other. At the same time it was pointed out that *In re Gray* ((1918) 57 Can. S.R.C. 150) and *The Chemical Reference* ([1943] S.C.R. 1), the delegations there dealt with were delegations to a body subordinate to Parliament and were, therefore, of a character different from the delegation meant by the Bill submitted to the Court in the Nova Scotia reference.

But, on the other hand, the delegations passed upon by this Court *In re Gray* and *The Chemical Reference* were along the same lines as those with which we are concerned in the present appeal. It follows that our judgment in the Nova Scotia reference can be no authority for the decision which we have to give in the present instance. It may be added that at bar counsel did not rely upon that ground in this Court.

The first question submitted to the Supreme Court *in banco* of Prince Edward Island had to do with the jurisdiction and competence of the Parliament of Canada to enact the Agricultural Products Marketing Act (1949), 13 George VI, (1st Session) c. 16. That Act was assented to on the 30th of April, 1949. The preamble, among other things, stated that it was "desirable to co-operate with the provinces and to enact a measure respecting the marketing of agricultural products in interprovincial and export trade." S. (2) of the Act reads as follows:

2. (1) The Governor in Council may by order grant authority to any board or agency authorized under the law of any province to exercise powers of regulation in relation to the marketing of any agricultural product locally within the province, to regulate the marketing of such agricultural product outside the province in interprovincial and export trade and for such purposes to exercise all or any powers like the powers exercisable by such board or agency in relation to the marketing of such agricultural product locally within the province.

(2) The Governor in Council may by order revoke any authority granted under subsection one.

The effect of that enactment is for the Governor in Council to adopt as its own a board, or agency already authorized under the law of a province, to exercise powers of regulation outside the province in inter-provincial and export trade, and for such purposes to exercise all or any powers exercisable by such board, or agency, in relation to the marketing of such agricultural products locally within the province. I cannot see any objection to federal legislation of this nature. Ever since *Valin* v. *Langlois* ((1879) 5 App. Cas. 115), when the Privy Council refused leave to appeal from the decision of this Court ((1879) 3 Can. S.C.R. 1), the principle has been consistently admitted that it was competent for Parliament to "employ its own executive officers for the purpose of carrying out legislation which is within its constitutional authority, as it does regularly in the case of revenue officials and other matters which need not be enumerated." The latter are words of Lord Atkin, who delivered the judgment of the Judicial Committee in *Proprietary Articles Trade Association et al.* v. *A.-G. for Canada et al* ([1931] A.C. 310).

In the Agricultural Products Marketing Act of 1949 that is precisely what Parliament has done. Parliament has granted authority to the Governor in Council to employ as its own a board, or agency, for the purpose of carrying out its own legislation for the marketing of agricultural products outside the province in interprovincial and export trade, two subject-matters which are undoubtedly within its constitutional authority. Moreover, it may be added, that in doing so Parliament was following the advice of the Judicial Committee in the several judgments which it rendered on similar Acts and, more particularly, on the Reference concerning the Natural Products Marketing Act ([1937] 1 D.L.R. 691), adopted by Parliament in 1934 (S. of C. 24 and 25 George V, c. 57), (1937), that the proper way to carry out legislation of that character in Canada, in view of the distribution of legislative powers under the British North America Act, was for Parliament and the Legislatures to act by co-operation.

I would, therefore, answer question (1) in the affirmative. . . .

RAND J.: The validity of the provincial legislation generally was not impugned since its provisions are virtually identical with those of the Act of British Columbia which was approved by the Judicial Committee in *Shannon* v. *Lower Mainland Dairy Products Board* ([1938] A.C. 708. The Committee there construed the Act as a whole to be limited to transactions strictly within the field of local or provincial trade. The administration of the Act so circumscribed, apart from co-operative Dominion legislation, may encounter serious practical difficulties if not insuperable obstacles; but that cannot affect its constitutional validity nor its administration conjointly with Dominion powers.

The principal point of attack was the efficacy of the Dominion delegation. Mr. Farris argued that the province was incompetent to confer on the Board capacity to accept such powers from the Governor in Council. This question was not involved in Shannon, *supra*, as the administration there was provincial only and s. 7 of the Act was not expressly considered. The Potato Board is not, under the statute, a corporation, and the contention is this: the power to create such an entity and to clothe it with jural attributes and capacities is derived from head 13 of s. 92 of the Act of 1867 which deals with property and civil rights within the province; as the incorporation of companies under head 11 has its source in the prerogative, a body so created may have unlimited "capacities"; the prerogative is not drawn on for a body created under any other head than 11; a board created as here can have, then, only a capacity in relation to local law. From this it follows that the purported grant of authority from the Dominion is inoperative.

The central feature of this argument is the notion of the creation of an "entity." That a group of human beings acting jointly in a certain manner, with certain scope and authority and for certain objects, can be conceived as an entirety, different from that of the sum of the individuals and their actions in severalty, is undoubted; and it is the joint action so conceived that is primarily the external counterpart of the mental concept.

But to imagine that total counterpart is an organic creation fashioned after the nature of a human being with faculties called "capacities" and to pursue a development of it logically, can lead us into absurdities. We might just as logically conceive it as a split personality with co-ordinate creators investing it with two orders of capacities. These metaphors and symbolisms are convenient devices to enable us to aggregate incidents or characteristics but carried too far they may threaten common sense.

What the law in this case has done has been to give legal significance called incidents to certain group actions of five men. That to the same men, acting in the same formality, another co-ordinate jurisdiction in a federal constitution cannot give other legal incidents to other joint actions is negated by the admission that the Dominion by appropriate words could create a similar board, composed of the same persons, bearing the same name, and with a similar formal organization, to execute the same Dominion functions. Twin phantoms of this nature must, for practical purposes, give way to realistic necessities. As related to courts, the matter was disposed of in *Valin* v. *Langlois*. No question of disruption of constitutive provincial features or frustration of provincial powers arises: both legislatures have recognized the value of a single body to carry out one joint, though limited, administration of trade. At any time the Providence could withdraw the whole or any part of its authority. The delegation was, then, effective.

~ Justice Kerwin (Justice Fauteux concurring), Justices Taschereau, Kellock

(Justice Locke concurring) and Justice Estey (Justice Cartwright concurring) all wrote opinions in which they held that the Agricultural Products Marketing Act, 1949, was *intra vires*. The answers to the other questions in the reference are not included here as they were not directly concerned with the constitutional question of delegation. ∼

B. *Constitutional Amendment*

61. Reference Re Legislative Authority of Parliament to Alter or Replace the Senate, *1980*

~ As originally enacted in 1867 the B.N.A. Act did not include an amending clause. In those days of liberal imperialism it was accepted that as an Act of the Imperial Parliament it would be amended by that parliament in response to requests from Canada. In 1949, at the request of the federal Parliament, the United Kingdom Parliament amended the B.N.A. Act to give the federal Parliament a limited legislative power, section 91(1), to amend "the Constitution of Canada". Excluded from this power were the jurisdiction of provincial legislatures, the rights and privileges of provincial governments, education and language rights, and some of the requirements of parliamentary government at the federal level (annual sessions of Parliament and an election every five years). Section 91(1) paralleled the power which the provincial legislatures had enjoyed since Confederation to amend the constitution of the province. The federal Parliament exercised its constitution-amending power five times after 1949: three times to change representation in the House of Commons and twice to alter the Senate (compulsory retirement of senators at age 75 in 1965 and the representation of the Northwest Territories and the Yukon by one member each in 1974).

The *Senate Reference* of 1980 provided the only occasion for judicial scrutiny of the scope of the amending power obtained by the federal Parliament in 1949. The reference was provoked by the two-phase programme of constitutional reform initiated by Prime Minister Trudeau in June 1978. Phase I concerned changes which the federal government believed it could accomplish on its own using section 91(1). It included a codification of the position of Governor General, changes in the Supreme Court, a constitutional charter of rights applying only to the federal level (provinces could opt in) and replacing the Senate with a new upper house half of whose members would be chosen by the House of Commons and the other half by the provincial legislatures. The Constitution Amendment Bill (Bill C-60) embodying Phase I was referred to a special Joint Committee of the Senate and House of Commons. In response to a vote of the Committee to seek the Supreme Court's opinion on the constitutional validity of sections of the Bill dealing with the Governor General and the Senate, the federal government decided to submit questions to the Court on Parliament's power to abolish or alter the Senate.

The questions covered a wider range of upper house reforms than the proposals in Bill C-60. Reference was also made to the possibility of an elected upper house or a house composed of provincial government representatives (a proposal favoured by British Columbia, the Quebec Liberal party and the federal (Pepin/Robarts) Task Force on Canadian Unity). The Supreme Court's answers to these questions were essentially in the negative. It held that the federal Parliament could not under Section 91(1) change the essential character of the Senate. Although the Court refused to answer questions which were too broadly phrased, its opinion made it clear that the Senate's essential features were its capacity to represent the various regions of Canada and to function as a non-elected chamber of "sober second thought" in relation to the elected House of Commons.

A remarkable feature of the Court's opinion is the extent to which it goes beyond narrow textual interpretation of the B.N.A. Act. The Court's view of the Senate's essential features was based on its understanding of the historical background which led to the creation of the Senate. Its appreciation of the limits of the unilateral federal amending power under section 91(1) was expressed in terms of that power's relationship to the whole constitutional framework of federal government. It is also interesting to observe that this broad statesmanlike approach, as in the *Blaikie*[1] decision, was not associated with the authorship of a particular judge but was a decision of "The Court."

The Court's decision had no immediate practical consequences because by the time it was rendered the Trudeau Liberal government had been replaced by the Clark Conservative government. The new government gave a low priority to constitutional reform and did not wish to proceed with the Constitutional Amendment Bill. However, the decision pointed to possible important longer-term consequences insofar as it suggested that the Supreme Court might be a serious obstacle to unilateral federal restructuring of the Canadian constitution.

The new all-Canadian constitutional amending formula which came into effect in 1982 gives the provinces a substantial role in Senate reform. Constitutional amendments concerning the powers of the Senate, the method of selection and residential qualifications of Senators and the distribution of Senate positions among the provinces require the approval of the House of Commons and the legislatures of seven provinces containing 50% of the population. The Senate's role in all constitutional amendments (except those few which can still be effected unilaterally by the federal Parliament) has been reduced to a suspensory, six-month veto. If the Meech Lake proposals are adopted a reconstruction of the Senate will require the approval of all ten provincial legislatures. In the meantime, Senators while still appointed by the federal government will be chosen from names submitted by provincial governments. ~

[1] See above, case 54.

REFERENCE RE LEGISLATIVE AUTHORITY OF PARLIAMENT TO ALTER OR REPLACE THE SENATE
In the Supreme Court of Canada. [1980] 1 S.C.R. 54.

THE COURT: By Order in Council P.C. 1978-3581, dated November 23, 1978, the Governor-General in Council, pursuant to s. 55 of the Supreme Court Act, R.S.C. 1970, c. S-19, referred to this Court for hearing and consideration the following two questions:

1. Is it within the legislative authority of the Parliament of Canada to repeal sections 21 to 36 of the British North America Act, 1867, as amended, and to amend other sections thereof so as to delete any reference to an Upper House or the Senate? If not, in what particular or particulars and to what extent?

2. Is it within the legislative authority of the Parliament of Canada to enact legislation altering, or providing a replacement for, the Upper House of Parliament, so as to effect any or all of the following:

(a) to change the name of the Upper House;

(b) to change the numbers and proportions of members by whom provinces and territories are represented in that House

(c) to change the qualifications of members of that House;

(d) to change the tenure of members of that House;

(e) to change the method by which members of that House are chosen by

    (i) conferring authority on provincial legislative assemblies to select, on the nomination of the respective Lieutenant Governors in Council, some members of the Upper House, and, if a legislative assembly has not selected such members within the time permitted, authority on the House of Commons to select those

members on the nomination of the Governor General in Council, and

    (ii) conferring authority on the House of Commons to select, on the nomination of the Governor General in Council, some members of the Upper House from each province, and, if the House of Commons has not selected such members from a province within the time permitted, authority on the legislative assembly of the province to select those members on the nomination of the Lieutenant Governor in Council,

    (iii) conferring authority on the Lieutenant Governors in Council of the provinces or on some other body or bodies to select some or all of the members of the Upper House, or

    (iv) providing for the direct election of all or some of the members of the Upper House by the public; or

(f) to provide that Bills approved by the House of Commons could be given assent and the force of law after the passage of a certain period of time notwithstanding that the Upper House has not approved them?

If not, in what particular or particulars and to what extent?

Submissions in respect of these questions were made to the Court on behalf of the Attorney General of Canada and also on behalf of the Attorneys General of Ontario, Nova Scotia, New Brunswick, Prince Edward Island, Saskatchewan, Alberta and Newfoundland.

QUESTION 1

Sections 21 to 36 of the British North

America Act, 1867, hereinafter referred to as "the Act," referred to in Question 1, appear in the Act under the heading "The Senate" and deal with the constitution of that body, including the number of senators; the representation in the Senate of the four divisions, *i.e.*, Ontario, Quebec, the Maritime Provinces and the Western Provinces; the qualifications for appointment to the Senate; the appointment of senators; the age limit for senators; resignation and disqualification of senators. References to the Senate by name, or as a House of Parliament, and references to senators are also to be found in ss. 17, 18, 39, 51A, 55, 56, 57, 59, 73, 74, 91, 128, 133, 146 and 147.

It is clear that Question 1 in essence, although not in terms, asks whether the Parliament of Canada has legislative authority to abolish the Senate. The Attorney General of Canada contends that the question should be answered in the affirmative. All of the Attorneys General of the Provinces, represented on the hearing, contended that the question should be answered in the negative.

The Attorney General of Canada bases his submission upon the provisions of Class 1 of the subject matters enumerated in s. 91 of the Act. Section 91, which appears in Part VI of the Act, under the heading "Powers of the Parliament," defines the legislative authority of the Parliament of Canada. The opening words of this section are as follows:

91. It shall be lawful for the Queen, by and with the Advice and Consent of the Senate and House of Commons, to make Laws for the Peace, Order and good Government of Canada, in relation to all Matters not coming within the Classes of Subjects by this Act assigned exclusively to the Legislatures of the Provinces; and for greater Certainty, but not so as to restrict the Generality of the foregoing Terms of this Section, it is hereby declared that (notwithstanding anything in this Act) the exclusive Legislative Authority of the Parliament of Canada extends to all Matters coming within the

Classes of Subjects next herein-after enumerated. . . .

Class 1 of s. 91 was added to it by an amendment to the Act enacted by the British Parliament on December 16, 1949. Section 1 of the amending statute [1949 (U.K.), c. 81] provided as follows:

1. Section 91 of the British North America Act, 1867 is hereby amended by renumbering Class 1 thereof as Class 1A and by inserting therein immediately before that Class the following as Class 1:—

1. The amendment from time to time of the Constitution of Canada, except as regards matters coming within the classes of subjects by this Act assigned exclusively to the Legislatures of the provinces, or as regards rights or privileges by this or any other Constitutional Act granted or secured to the Legislature or the Government of a province, or to any class of persons with respect to schools or as regards the use of the English or the French language or as regards the requirements that there shall be a session of the Parliament of Canada at least once each year, and that no House of Commons shall continue for more than five years from the day of the return of the Writs for choosing the House: Provided, however, that a House of Commons may in time of real or apprehended war, invasion or insurrection be continued by the Parliament of Canada if such continuation is not opposed by the votes of more than one-third of the members of such House.

Prior to 1949, in most respects, the Act did not provide for its amendment by any legislative authority in Canada. Accordingly, as it was a statute enacted by the British Parliament, any changes in its content had to be made by way of an amending Act enacted by that Parliament. Many amendments have been made in that way. A brief account of them and of other statutes of a constitutional character is found in a White Paper published in 1965 under the authority of the Honourable Guy Favreau, then Minister of Justice for Canada, under the title of ''The Amendment of the Constitution of Canada'';

1. The Rupert's Land Act, 1868 authorized the acceptance by Canada of the rights of the Hudson's Bay Company over Rupert's Land and the North-Western Territory. It also provided that, on Address from the Houses of Parliament of Canada, the Crown could declare this territory part of Canada and the Parliament of Canada could make laws for its peace, order and good government.

2. The British North America Act of 1871 ratified the Manitoba Act passed by the Parliament of Canada in 1870, creating the province of Manitoba and giving it a provincial constitution similar to those of the other provinces. The British North America Act of 1871 also empowered the Parliament of Canada to establish new provinces out of any Canadian territory not then included in a province; to alter the boundaries of any province (with the consent of its legislature), and to provide for the administration, peace and good goverment of any territory not included in a province.

3. The Parliament of Canada Act of 1875 amended section 18 of the British North America Act, 1867, which set forth the privileges, immunities and powers of each of the Houses of Parliament.

4. The British North America Act of 1886 authorized the Parliament of Canada to provide for the representation in the Senate and the House of Commons of any territories not included in any province.

5. The Statute Law Revision Act, 1893 repealed some obsolete provisions of the British North America Act of 1867.

6. The Canadian Speaker (Appointment of Deputy) Act, 1895 confirmed an Act of the Parliament of Canada which provided for the appointment of a Deputy-Speaker for the Senate.

7. The British North America Act, 1907 established a new scale of financial subsidies to the provinces in lieu of those set forth in section 118 of the British North America Act of 1867. While not expressly repealing the original section, it made its provisions obsolete.

8. The British North America Act, 1915 re-defined the Senatorial Divisions of Canada to take into account the provinces of Manitoba, British Columbia, Saskatchewan and Alberta. Although this statute did not expressly amend the text of the original section 22, it did alter its effect.

9. The British North America Act, 1916 provided for the extension of the life of the current Parliament of Canada beyond the normal period of five years.

10. The Statute Law Revision Act, 1927 repealed additional spent or obsolete provisions in the United Kingdom statutes, including two provisions of the British North America Acts.

11. The British North America Act, 1930 confirmed the natural resources agreements between the Government of Canada and the Governments of Manitoba, British Columbia, Alberta and Saskatchewan, giving the agreements the force of law notwithstanding anything in the British North America Acts.

12. The Statute of Westminster, 1931, while not directly amending the British North America Acts, did alter some of their provisions. Thus, the Parliament of Canada was given the power to make laws having extra-territorial effect. Also, Parliament and the provincial legislatures were given the authority, within their powers under the British North America Acts, to repeal any United Kingdom statute that formed part of the law of Canada. This authority, however, expressly excluded the British North America Act itself.

13. The British North America Act, 1940 gave the Parliament of Canada the exclusive jurisdiction to make laws in relation to Unemployment Insurance.

14. The British North America Act, 1943 provided for the postponement of redistribution of the seats in the House of Commons until the first session of the Parliament after the cessation of hostilities.

15. The British North America Act, 1946 replaced section 51 of the British North America Act, 1867, and altered the provisions for the readjustment of representation in the House of Commons.

16. The British North America Act, 1949 confirmed the Terms of Union between Canada and Newfoundland.

17. The British North America Act (No. 2), 1949 gave the Parliament of Canada authority to amend the Constitution of Canada with certain exceptions.

18. The Statute Law Revision Act, 1950 repealed an obsolete section of the British North America Act, 1867.

19. The British North America Act, 1951 gave the Parliament of Canada concurrent jurisdiction with the provinces to make laws in relation to Old Age Pensions.

20. The British North America Act, 1960 amended section 99 and altered the tenure of office of superior court judges.

21. The British North America Act, 1964 amended the authority conferred upon the Parliament of Canada by the British North America Act, 1951, in relation to benefits supplementary to Old Age Pensions.

22. Amendment by Order in Council Section 146 of the British North America Act, 1867 provided for the admission of other British North American territories by Order in Council and stipulated that the provisions of any such Order in Council would have the same effect as if enacted by the Parliament of the United Kingdom. Under this section, Rupert's

Land and the North-Western Territory were admitted by Order in Council on June 23rd, 1870; British Columbia by Order in Council on May 16th, 1871; Prince Edward Island by Order in Council on June 26th, 1873. Because all of these Orders in Council contained provisions of a constitutional character— adopting the provisions of the British North America Act to the new provinces, but with some modifications in each case—they may therefore be regarded as constitutional amendments.

The practice, since 1875, has been to seek amendment of the Act by a joint address of both Houses of Parliament. Consultation with one or more of the provinces has occurred in some instances. The amendment in 1907 was based on resolutions passed at provincial conferences, although opposed by British Columbia. The 1930 amendment respecting the transfer of resources to the four western Provinces resulted from agreements with those Provinces. The 1949 amendment respecting Newfoundland becoming a Province was made after there had been an agreement with that Province. The amendments of 1940, 1951, 1960 and 1964, respecting unemployment insurance, old age pensions, the compulsory retirement of Judges and adding supplementary benefits to old age pensions all had the unanimous consent of the Provinces.

The White Paper, after reviewing the procedures followed in respect of amendments to the Act, went on to state four general principles, as follows:

The first general principle that emerges in the foregoing resume is that although an enactment of the United Kingdom is necessary to amend the British North America Act, such action is taken only upon formal request from Canada. No Act of the United Kingdom Parliament affecting Canada is therefore passed unless it is requested and consented to by Canada. Conversely, every amendment requested by Canada in the past has been enacted.

The second general principle *is that the sanction of Parliament is required for a request to the British Parliament for an amendment to the British North America Act. This principle was established early in the history of Canada's constitutional amendments, and has not been violated since 1895. The procedure invariably is to seek amendments by a joint Address of the Canadian House of Commons and Senate to the Crown.*

The third general principle *is that no amendment to Canada's Constitution will be made by the British Parliament merely upon the request of a Canadian province. A number of attempts to secure such amendments have been made, but none has been successful. The first such attempt was made as early as 1868, by a province which was at that time dissatisfied with the terms of Confederation. This was followed by other attempts in 1869, 1874 and 1887. The British Government refused in all cases to act on provincial government representations on the grounds that it should not intervene in the affairs of Canada except at the request of the federal government representing all of Canada.*

The fourth general principle *is that the Canadian Parliament will not request an amendment directly affecting federal-provincial relationships without prior consultation and agreement with the provinces. This principle did not emerge as early as others but since 1907, and particularly since 1930, has gained increasing recognition and acceptance. The nature and the degree of provincial participation in the amending process, however, have not lent themselves to easy definition.*

The apparent intention of the 1949 amendment to the Act which enacted s. 91(1) was to obviate the necessity for the enactment of a statute of the British Parliament to effect amendments to the Act which theretofore had been obtained though a joint resolution of both Houses of Parliament and without provincial con-

sent. Legislation enacted since 1949 pursuant to s. 91(1) has not, to quote the White Paper, "affected federal-provincial relationships." The following statutes have been enacted by the Parliament of Canada:

1. The British North America Act, 1952, effected a readjustment of representation in the House of Commons. The principle of representation by population was not affected by this legislation.

2. The British North America Act, 1965, provided for the compulsory retirement of senators, henceforth appointed, at age seventy-five.

3. The British North America Act (No. 2) 1974, repealed the provisions of the Act of 1952 and substituted a new readjustment of representation in the House of Commons. The principle of representation by population was maintained.

4. The British North America Act, 1975, increased the representation of the Northwest Territories in the House of Commons from one to two members.

5. The British North America Act (No. 2) 1975, increased the total number of senators from 102 to 104, and provided for representation in the Senate for the Yukon Territory and the Northwest Territories by one member each.

All of these measures dealt with what might be described as federal "housekeeping" matters which, according to the practice existing before 1949, would have been referred to the British Parliament by way of a joint resolution of both Houses of Parliament, and without the consent of the Provinces. The last two of these statutes were within the power of the Parliament of Canada to enact by virtue of s. 1 of the British North America Act, 1886. Like the others they did not in any substantial way affect federal-provincial relationships.

The legislation contemplated in the first question is of an entirely different character. While it does not directly affect federal-provincial relationships in the sense of changing federal and provincial legislative powers, it does envision the elimination of one of the two Houses of Parliament to which the federal power to legislate is entrusted under s. 91 of the Act.

The Senate has a vital role as an institution forming part of the federal system created by the Act. The recitals in the Act have some significance:

Whereas the Provinces of Canada, Nova Scotia, and New Brunswick have expressed their Desire to be federally united into One Dominion under the Crown of the United Kingdom of Great Britain and Ireland, with a Constitution similar in Principle to that of the United Kingdom:

And whereas such a Union would conduce to the Welfare of the Provinces and promote the Interests of the British Empire:

And whereas on the Establishment of the Union by Authority of Parliament it is expedient, not only that the Constitution of the Legislative Authority in the Dominion be provided for, but also that the Nature of the Executive Government therein be declared:

Under the constitution of the United Kingdom, to which reference is made in the first recital, legislative power was and is exercised by the Queen, by and with the advice and consent of the House of Lords and the House of Commons. The Upper House was not and is not an elected body, the Lower House was and is.

It is, we think, proper to consider the historical background which led to the provision which was made in the Act for the creation of the Senate as a part of the apparatus for the enactment of federal legislation. In the debates which occurred at the Quebec Conference in 1864, considerable time was occupied in discussing the provisions respecting the Senate. Its important purpose is stated in the following passages in speeches delivered in the debates on Confederation in the Parliament of the Provinces of Canada:

SIR JOHN A. MACDONALD:

In order to protect local interests and to prevent sectional jealousies, it was found requisite that the three great divisions into which British North America is separated, should be represented in the Upper House on the principle of equality. There are three great sections, having different interests, in this proposed Confederation. . . . To the Upper House is to be confided the protection of sectional interests: therefore it is that the three great divisions are there equally represented for the purpose of defending such interests against the combinations of majorities in the Assembly.

(Parliamentary Debates on the Subject of the Confederation of the British North American Provinces, Quebec, 1865, pages 35 and 38.)

THE HONOURABLE GEORGE BROWN:

But the very essence of our compact is that the union shall be federal and not legislative. Our Lower Canada friends have agreed to give us representation by population in the Lower House, on the express condition that they shall have equality in the Upper House. On no other condition could we have advanced a step; and, for my part, I am quite willing they should have it. In maintaining the existing sectional boundaries and handing over the control of local matters to local bodies, we recognize, to a certain extent, a diversity of interests; and it is quite natural that the protection for those interests, by equality in the Upper Chamber, should be demanded by the less numerous provinces.

(Parliamentary Debates on the Subject of the Confederation of the British North American Provinces, Quebec, 1865, p. 88.)

A primary purpose of the creation of the Senate, as a part of the federal legislative process, was, therefore, to afford protection to the various sectional interests in Canada in relation to the enactment of federal legislation. The Act, as originally enacted, provided, in s. 22, that, in relation to the constitution of the Senate, Canada should be deemed to consist of Three Divisions, to be equally represented, *i.e.*, Ontario, Quebec and the Maritime Provinces (Nova Scotia and New Brunswick). This provision was later amended [1915 (U.K.), c. 45] and s. 22 now provides for Four Divisions, the Western Provinces of Manitoba, British Columbia, Saskatchewan and Alberta being added as a Fourth Division. The Act now makes provision for representation of Prince Edward Island (as one of the Maritime Provinces), Newfoundland, the Yukon Territory and the Northwest Territories. Subsection 23(5) of the Act requires that a senator shall be resident in the Province for which he is appointed.

The place of the Senate in the exercise of federal legislative powers is determined by ss. 17 and 91 of the Act. The former section provides that:

17. There shall be One Parliament of Canada, consisting of the Queen, an Upper House styled the Senate, and the House of Commons.

The opening words of s. 91, the all-important section defining federal legislative powers, have already been quoted. Power to "make laws for the Peace, Order and Good Government of Canada in relation to all Matters not coming within the Classes of Subjects of this Act assigned exclusively to the Legislatures of the Provinces" was conferred by the British Parliament upon "the Queen, by and with the Advice and Consent of the Senate and the House of Commons."

The creation of a federal system in Canada involved the necessity of effecting a division of legislative powers. This division is made by the provisions of ss. 91 and 92 of the Act. The latter section empowered each provincial Legislature generally to make laws, effective within the Province, in respect of matters of a local or private nature. Fifteen specific classes of subjects were enumerated. Section 91 provided generally for the making of laws for the peace, order and good

government of Canada. Twenty-nine classes of subject matters were enumerated. Legislation dealing with those matters might affect local or private matters within a Province.

The power to enact federal legislation was given to the Queen by and with the advice and consent of the Senate and the House of Commons. Thus, the body which had been created as a means of protecting sectional and provincial interests was made a participant in this legislative process.

The amendment to the Act made in 1949 added an additional class of subject-matters to those which already existed. By that time the classes had been increased to thirty. The amendment was made on a joint resolution of both Houses of Parliament, but without the consent of the provinces. It gave power to the Queen, by and with the advice and consent of the Senate and the House of Commons to amend "the Constitution of Canada." This power was made subject to certain specific exceptions, as follows:

. . . except as regards matters coming within the classes of subjects by this Act assigned exclusively to the Legislatures of the provinces, or as regards rights or privileges by this or any other Constitutional Act granted or secured to the Legislature or the Government of a province, or to any class of persons with respect to schools or as regards the use of the English or the French language or as regards the requirements that there shall be a session of the Parliament of Canada at least once each year, and that no House of Commons shall continue for more than five years from the day of the return of the Writs for choosing the House: Provided, however, that a House of Commons may in time of real or apprehended war, invasion or insurrection be continued by the Parliament of Canada if such continuation is not opposed by the votes of more than one-third of the members of such House.

The phrase "Constitution of Canada" does not appear elsewhere in the Act. The word "constitution" appears in various places and in different contexts. The preamble to the Act refers to "a Constitution similar in principle to that of the United Kingdom" and, later, to "the constitution of Legislative Authority in the Dominion." Section 22 refers to "the Constitution of the Senate" as being deemed to consist of four divisions. Part V of the Act is entitled "Provincial Constitutions" and the sections in that Part, 58 to 90, deal with the exercise of executive power and legislative power in the Provinces. Section 92(1) refers to the amendment of "the Constitution of the Province." Section 147 refers to "Three Divisions into which Canada is, in relation to the Constitution of the Senate, divided by this Act."

The Attorney General of Canada submitted that the power conferred upon Parliament by s. 91(1) is limited only by the specific exceptions contained in it. He contended that the very specificity of these exceptions pointed to the wide powers being conferred. If this approach were adopted, it would mean that the federal Parliament, acting unilaterally, could amend any part of the Act, subject only to the exceptions specified in s. 91(1). But s. 91(1) does not give power to amend the Act. Instead, the phrase "Constitution of Canada" is used. In our opinion, the word "Canada" as used in s. 91(1) does not refer to Canada as a geographical unit but refers to the juristic federal unit. "Constitution of Canada" does not mean the whole of the British North America Act, 1867, but means the constitution of the federal government, as distinct from the provincial goverments. The power of amendment conferred by s. 91(1) is limited to matters of interest only to the federal government.

The word "Canada" is used with reference to the juristic federal unit in several sections of the Act, of which the following are examples:

Section 111 provided that "Canada shall be liable for the debts and Liabilities of each Province existing at the Union."

Section 125 provides that "No Lands or Property belonging to Canada or any Province shall be liable to Taxation."

Section 101 refers to "the Laws of Canada," the meaning of which phrase has recently been interpreted by this Court. The section reads as follows:

101. The Parliament of Canada may, notwithstanding anything in this Act, from Time to Time provide for the Constitution, Maintenance, and Organization of a General Court of Appeal for Canada, and for the Establishment of any additional Courts for the better Administration of the Laws of Canada.

In our opinion, the power of amendment given by s. 91(1) relates to the constitution of the federal government in matters of interest only to that government. The statutes enacted by the federal Parliament since 1949, to which we have previously referred, are illustrations of the exercise of that power.

The next question is whether, in that limited sense, s. 91(1) would permit the federal Parliament to abolish the Senate.

Bearing in mind the historical background in which the creation of the Senate as a part of the federal legislative process was conceived, the words of Lord Sankey, L.C., in *Re Aerial Navigation; A.-G. Can.* v. *A.-G. Ont. et al.*, [1932] 1 D.L.R. 58 at p. 65, [1932] A.C. 54 at p. 70, [1931] 3 W.W.R. 625, although they were written in relation to the Act as originally enacted, are apt:

Inasmuch as the Act embodies a compromise under which the original Provinces agreed to federate, it is important to keep in mind that the preservation of the rights of minorities was a condition on which such minorities entered into the federation, and the foundation upon which the whole structure was subsequently erected. The process of interpretation as the years go on ought not to be allowed to dim or to whittle down the provisions of the original contract upon which the federation was founded, nor is it legitimate that any judicial construction of the provisions of ss. 91 and 92 should impose a new and different contract upon the federating bodies.

In our opinion, the power given to the federal Parliament by s. 91(1) was not intended to enable it to alter in any way the provisions of ss. 91 and 92 governing the exercise of legislative authority by the Parliament of Canada and the Legislatures of the Provinces. Section 91(1) is a particularization of the general legislative power of the Parliament of Canada. That general power can be exercised only by the Queen by and with the advice and consent of the Senate and the House of Commons. Section 91(1) cannot be construed to confer power to supplant the whole of the rest of the section. It cannot be construed as permitting the transfer of the legislative powers enumerated in s. 91 to some body or bodies other than those specifically designated in it.

This Court, in *A.-G. N.S. et al.* v. *A.-G. Can. et al.* [1950] 4 D.L.R. 369, [1951] 31, determined that neither the Parliament of Canada nor a provincial Legislature could delegate to the other the legislative powers with which it has been vested nor receive from the other the powers with which the other has been vested. The elimination of the Senate would go much further in that it would involve a transfer by Parliament of all its legislative powers to a new legislative body of which the Senate would not be a member. . . .

The continued existence of the Senate as a part of the federal legislative process is implied in the exceptions provided in s. 91(1). One exception to the power conferred by s. 91(1) to amend the Constitution of Canada is "as regards the requirement that there shall be a session of the Parliament of Canada at least once each year." "Parliament" under s. 17 is to consist of the Queen, the Senate and the House of Commons. This exception contemplates that there shall continue to be sessions of the Senate and the House of Commons at least once each year.

The next exception requires that "no House of Commons shall continue for more than five years from the day of the return of the Writs for choosing the House" except in time of real or apprehended war, invasion or insurrection.

These two exceptions indicate that the power to amend "the Constitution of Canada" given by s. 91(1) was not intended to include the power to eliminate the Senate or the House of Commons.

The Attorney General of Canada contended that the power to amend given by s. 91(1) was the equivalent, in the federal field, of s. 92(1) in the provincial field.

He points out that, pursuant to that power, the Provinces of Manitoba, New Brunswick, Prince Edward Island, Nova Scotia and Quebec abolished their respective legislative councils.

The two sections are not, however, analogous. Section 92 does not, as does s. 91, particularize the participants in the law-making process. Section 91 confers the authority to legislate in respect of matters within that section upon the Queen, with the advice and consent of the Senate and the House of Commons. Section 92 confers the authority to legislate in respect of matters within that section upon "the Legislature."

More importantly, s. 92(1) gives a power to amend the constitution of a Province to the Legislature, except as regards the office of the Lieutenant-Governor, "notwithstanding anything in this Act." Section 91(1) confers a power of amendment subject to specified exceptions which, as we have already pointed out, contemplate the continued existence of both the Senate and the House of Commons.

For the foregoing reasons, we would answer the first question in the negative.

QUESTION 2

The Attorney General submits that this question, in all its aspects, should be answered in the affirmative. Differing views were expressed by the Attorneys General of the Provinces.

All of the provincial Attorneys General, other than the Attorney General of

Prince Edward Island, submitted that para. (f) of Question 2 should be answered in the negative. This paragraph raises the question of the power of Parliament, under s. 91(1), to provide that all bills be given assent and the force of law after a certain time period notwithstanding that they had not been approved by the Upper House. The only provision presently existing, which limits the power of the Senate as compared with the power of the House of Commons, is s. 53 which provides that bills for appropriating any part of the public revenue or for imposing any tax or impost shall originate in the House of Commons.

A provision of the kind contemplated would seriously impair the position of the Senate in the legislative process because it would permit legislation to be enacted under s. 91 without the consent of the Senate. For the reasons already given in the respect of Question 1, it is our view that Parliament cannot under s. 91(1) impair the role of the Senate in that process. We would answer this question in the negative.

With respect to the other portions of Question 2, the Attorney-General of Ontario and the Attorney General of Nova Scotia submit that these subquestions cannot be answered categorically in the form in which they are asked. As the Attorney General of Nova Scotia puts it, they cannot be answered "in the absence of a factual context or actual draft legislation." In our opinion there is merit in this contention. We will deal with the subquestions seriatim.

Subquestion (a) asks whether Parliament could change the name of the Upper House. We would assume that a change of name would be proposed only as a part of some scheme for the alteration of the Senate itself. If that scheme were to be held *ultra vires* of Parliament, then the change of name would probably go with it. We do not think the question can properly be answered in the absence of such a context.

Subquestion (b) involves changing the numbers and proportions of members by whom Provinces and Territories are represented in the Senate. None of the Provinces supported the federal submission on this point.

As previously noted, the system of regional representation in the Senate was one of the essential features of that body when it was created. Without it, the fundamental character of the Senate as part of the Canadian federal scheme would be eliminated. In the absence of a factual context, it is not possible to say whether a change contemplated by this question would be in keeping with that fundamental character.

Subquestion (c) deals with a change in the qualifications of senators. The difficulty here is that we have not been told what changes are contemplated. Some of the qualifications for senators prescribed in s. 23, such as the property qualifications, may not today have the importance which they did when the Act was enacted. On the other hand, the requirement that a senator should be resident in the Province for which he is appointed has relevance in relation to the sectional characteristic of the make-up of the Senate. In our opinion, the question cannot be answered categorically.

Subquestion (d) relates to the tenure of senators. At present, a senator, when appointed, has tenure until he attains the age of 75. At some point, a reduction of the term of office might impair the functioning of the Senate in providing what Sir John A. Macdonald described as "the sober second thought in legislation." The Act contemplated a constitution similar in principle to that of the United Kingdom, where members of the House of Lords hold office for life. The imposition of compulsory retirement at age 75 did not change the essential character of the Senate. However, to answer this question we need to know what change of tenure is proposed.

Subquestion (e), paras. (i), (ii) and (iii), contemplates changing the method of appointment of senators, presently the function of the Governor General, by having "some" members selected by provincial Legislatures, "some" members by the House of Commons, "some" members selected by the Lieutenant-Governor in Council for "some other body or bodies." The selection of senators by a provincial Legislature or by the Lieutenant-Governor of a Province would involve an indirect participation by the Provinces in the enactment of federal legislation and is contrary to the reasoning of this Court in the *A.-G. N.S.* v. *A.-G. Can.* case previously cited.

Again, we do not feel that we have a factual context in which to formulate a satisfactory answer.

Subquestion (e)(iv) deals with the possible selection of all or some members of the Senate by direct election by the public. The substitution of a system of election for a system of appointment would involve a radical change in the nature of one of the component parts of Parliament. As already noted, the preamble to the Act referred to "a constitution similar in principle to that of the United Kingdom," where the Upper House is not elected. In creating the Senate in the manner provided in the Act, it is clear that the intention was to make the Senate a thoroughly independent body which could canvass dispassionately the measures of the House of Commons. This was accomplished by providing for the appointment of members of the Senate with tenure for life. To make the Senate a wholly or partially elected body would affect a fundamental feature of that body. We would answer this subquestion in the negative.

Dealing generally with Question 2, it is our opinion that while s. 91(1) would permit some changes to be made by Parliament in respect of the Senate as now constituted, it is not open to Parliament to make alterations which would affect the fundamental features, or essential characteristics, given to the Senate as a means of ensuring regional and provincial representation in the federal legislative process. The character of the Senate was determined by the British Parliament in response to the proposals submitted by the three provinces in order to meet the requirement of the proposed federal system. It was that Senate, created by the Act, to which a legislative role was given by s. 91. In our opinion, its fundamental character cannot be altered by unilateral action by the Parliament of Canada and s. 91(1) does not give that power.

We answer Question 1 in the negative. We answer subquestions 2(b), 2(e)(iv) and 2(f) in the negative. In our opinion, the other subquestions in Question 2, in the absence of a factual background, cannot be answered categorically.

62. The Patriation Reference, *1981*

~ Under Pierre Trudeau's leadership the Liberals returned to power in February 1980. It did not take long for Trudeau to renew the momentum of constitutional reform. He and other representatives of the federal government played a prominent role in the Quebec referendum campaign which took place in the spring of 1980. To persuade Quebeckers not to give René Lévesque's government a mandate to negotiate Quebec independence, Trudeau and his colleagues promised to work towards a constitutional restructuring of Canadian federalism. Following the defeat of the independence option in the referendum, the Prime Minister convened a meeting with the provincial premiers. Twelve areas were agreed to as priority items on the agenda of constitutional reform: six concerned various aspects of the federal division of powers, two were directed toward restructuring federal institutions (the Supreme Court and the Senate) and the remaining four dealt with a new preamble, the principle of fiscal equalization, a formula for amending a patriated constitution entirely in Canada and a charter of fundamental rights and freedoms. A continuing committee of ministers representing the eleven governments was established to develop proposals in these areas. This process culminated in a Federal Provincial First Ministers Conference in September, 1980. After a week of discussion, the conference failed to produce a consensus on any combination of proposals in the twelve areas.

At this point the federal government took the initiative that led to this case. On October 2, 1980, Trudeau announced plans to proceed unilaterally with the federal government's reform priorities, the so-called "peoples' package" of patriation with an amending formula, a charter of rights and recognition of the principle of fiscal equalization. The Constitution Act, 1981 was drafted containing proposals on these items and a resolution was placed before the federal Parliament requesting the Queen to lay the Constitution Act before the United Kingdom Parliament.

Most of the provinces objected strongly to this departure from what they regarded as the well-established constitutional convention of obtaining the agreement of the provinces to amendments affecting provincial powers. Only Ontario and New Brunswick supported the Trudeau constitutional plan. The Prime Minister claimed that the long series of failures to reach a federal-provincial consensus on constitutional reform justified unilateral federal action, and that, in any event, the question of whether provincial consent was needed for federal requests to the U.K. Parliament to amend the B.N.A. Act was a matter of convention not law, to be settled in the political not the judicial arena. Accordingly he refused to submit a reference question to the Supreme Court on the validity of his procedure. Once Parliament (in which his party had a clear majority) passed the resolution, it was his intention to have the U.K. Parliament pass the Constitution Act forthwith. His government took the view that constitutional convention required the British Parliament automatically to pass any amendment to the Canadian constitution requested by the federal Parliament regardless of provincial objections.

Three of the dissident provinces decided to seek the judicial opinion which Trudeau spurned. The governments of Manitoba, Quebec[1] and Newfoundland submitted questions to their provincial Courts of Appeal on 1/ whether the Constitution Act, 1981 affects the federal-provincial relationship or provincial powers; 2/ whether there is a convention requiring provincial consent for such an amendment; and 3/whether provincial consent for such an amendment was a "constitutional requirement."[2] The provincial Courts of Appeal were divided in answering the crucial third question. While the Manitoba Court (three judges to two) and the Quebec Court (four to one) found that provincial consent was not a constitutional requirement, the Newfoundland courts held unanimously (three to zero) that it was. The Quebec Court, the last of the three to render a decision, released its decision in April 1981. Both sides then prepared to appeal these decisions to the Supreme Court of Canada.

Meanwhile the resolution continued to be debated by a Joint Parliamentary Committee and eventually in both houses of Parliament. The government was able to broaden the base of its parliamentary support by amending the constitutional proposals to accommodate the views of the small left-wing New Democratic Party: the Charter of Rights was strengthened (except for property rights, which were removed) and a section enhancing provincial jurisdiction over natural resources was added. These changes did not placate the Conservatives whose opposition focused on the extent to which Trudeau's constitutional plans violated both in substance and procedure the principles and practices of Canadian federalism. In terms of substance they were particularly concerned about the inclusion of a referendum method of amending the constitution which could be initiated only by the federal government and would therefore by-pass the provincial governments.

By April 1981, the Conservatives had resorted to filibuster tactics in the House of Commons as the only way of preventing the government from proceeding unilaterally with its request to the U.K. Parliament. The Conservatives agreed to stop their filibuster when the government agreed not to submit its constitutional package to Britain until the Supreme Court rendered its opinion on the appeals from the Manitoba, Quebec and Newfoundland courts. The Prime Minister indicated that his government would not proceed with its constitutional plans if the Supreme Court found the unilateral procedure unconstitutional. On the other hand, if the Supreme Court decided in his favour

---

[1] Quebec's questions were somewhat different from those of Manitoba and Newfoundland, see p. 712 below.

[2] A fourth question referred to the Newfoundland Court of Appeal asked whether Newfoundland's Terms of Union with Canada or section 3 of the B.N.A. Act of 1871 requiring a province's consent to changes in its boundaries could, if the Constitution Act, 1981 were enacted, be amended without the consent of Newfoundland's legislature or a majority of its people.

he would proceed after no more than two days of parliamentary debate. For their part, the opposition leaders agreed not to submit any additional amendments to the proposal. Thus, the fate of Trudeau's constitutional proposals rested, for the moment, with the nine judges of the Supreme Court.

On Monday, September 28, 1981, the Supreme Court of Canada released its decision. On the first question, all of the judges agreed that the federal government's constitutional package would affect federal-provincial relationships and the powers of the provincial legislatures. But on the second and third questions the Court gave a mixed verdict. The Court held (six to three) that there was a constitutional convention requiring "a substantial degree of provincial consent" for federal requests to the U.K. Parliament to amend the B.N.A. Act in matters affecting federal-provincial relationships or provincial powers. But the Court also held (seven to two) that although this convention was a "constitutional requirement," observance of the convention was not "legally required."

The key to understanding the internal consistency of this judgment is the position of the majority (Justices Martland, Ritchie, Dickson, Beetz, Chouinard and Lamer)[3] on the nature of constitutional conventions. The majority divided the constitution of Canada into two categories: conventions and constitutional law. The purpose of conventions "is to ensure that the legal framework of the Constitution will be operated in accordance with the prevailing constitutional values and principles." Because conventions are part of the constitution, and indeed "some conventions may be more important than some laws," the failure of politicians or officials to observe convention in the way they exercise their legal powers is unconstitutional. However, unlike violations of constitutional law, the remedy for breaches for convention does not lie with the courts. Conventions by their very nature are distinct from the legal system. Unlike common law, the precedents on which constitutional conventions are based are not judge-made rules but are established "by the institutions of government themselves." Courts may describe conventions and, as in this case, answer requests for advisory opinions about conventions, but they do not enforce conventions. The sanctions for enforcing conventions "rest with institutions of government other than courts, such as the Governor General or the Lieutenant-Governor, or the Houses of Parliament, or with public opinion and ultimately with the electorate. . . ." In this sense the remedies for breach of convention are political not legal.

The majority's finding that a constitutional convention exists requiring substantial provincial consent was based, in part, on an examination of earlier

---

[3] The judges are listed in order of seniority. No authorship is attributed. While some unanimous decisions have not attributed authorship (see cases 21, 40 and 43 above), this is the first time, of which this author is aware, that no authorship has been attributed to majority and dissenting opinions.

amendments. The majority regarded only five of the twenty-two amendments to the B.N.A. Act as meeting its criterion of amendments directly affecting provincial powers: the 1930 amendment confirming the transfer of natural resources to the western provinces; the Statute of Westminster; the 1940 unemployment insurance amendment; and the 1951 and 1964 amendments giving the federal Parliament jurisdiction over old age pensions and supplementary benefits. For the last four, the consent of all the provinces was obtained, while the 1930 amendment was based on explicit agreements with the provinces directly concerned and had received the general approval of all the provinces at a dominion-provincial conference. While these precedents might be thought to point to a convention of unanimity, the majority pointed to statements of political leaders and the wording of the fourth principle in the 1965 White Paper as evidence for the finding that the unanimity principle was not accepted "by all the actors in the precedents."

The majority did not rest their case solely on relevant precedents or the statements of politicians. They contended that a convention to be accepted as obligatory must be based on "principles of the period." The principle or reason for the rule requiring provincial consent for constitutional amendments to their powers was the principle of federalism. In their view, "The federal principle cannot be reconciled with a state of affairs where the modification of provincial legislative powers could be obtained by the unilateral action of the federal authorities."

The dissenting judges[4] on the convention part of the decision felt that the question submitted to the courts must be interpreted as asking only whether *unanimous* agreement was required. Also, they did not accept the majority's narrowing of the relevant precedents to those which altered the distribution of powers. In their view the real test was whether amendments sponsored by the federal government provoked a negative reaction from one or more of the provinces. Using this test, they had no difficulty in identifying a number of amendments which were made despite some strenuous provincial opposition: for instance, the 1943 amendment postponing a redistribution of seats in the House of Commons which would have favoured Quebec. This, they held, demonstrated that there was not a consistent practice of obtaining provincial consent. They could not understand how a convention could exist when the degree of provincial participation was a matter of continuing controversy and the requirements of the convention (i.e., exactly how many provinces must agree) could not be stated with precision. Finally, they rejected the majority's understanding of the federal principle. They took the position that the overriding powers which the B.N.A. Act bestows upon the central government deprives the federalism argument of its force.

---

[4] Chief Justice Laskin, Justices Estey and McIntyre (again listed in order of seniority with no authorship attributed).

Justices Dickson, Beetz, Chouinard and Lamer, who were in the majority on the question of convention, were joined by the three judges who dissented on that issue to form the majority on the question of law. Their opinion examined the English and Canadian cases cited by counsel for the provinces in which courts had referred to constitutional conventions but concluded that, while conventions may have been used as an aid to interpreting common law and statute law, no case constituted an instance of a convention crystallizing into a rule of law. The opinion of the two dissenting judges, Martland and Ritchie, was not based on this issue. These two judges contended that since the privileges and powers of the House of Commons and Senate, including their right to address resolutions concerning the constitution to the British Parliament, were limited by statute to activities "consistent with and not repugnant to" the B.N.A. Act, neither of the houses of the federal Parliament was legally authorized to pass a resolution striking at what, in their view, was a basic element of the B.N.A. Act—the federal system. The majority, on the other hand, held that the content of parliamentary resolutions, unlike legislation, was subject only to the "self-regulating authority of Houses of Parliament" and not subject to court-enforced legal constraints. The majority also rejected provincial arguments to the effect that events leading up to the Statute of Westminster and the language of the Statute itself provided a basis in law for requiring provincial agreement to amendments altering provincial powers. Generally the Court endeavoured to avoid ruling on the powers of the U.K. Parliament. The majority stated that ". . . the authority of the British Parliament and its practices and conventions are not matters upon which this Court would presume to pronounce."

Both the federal government and the eight provinces that opposed its unilateral approach found support in this decision. By undermining the legitimacy of the federal government's unilateralism, the Court's decisions greatly increased the political costs of proceeding without substantial provincial consent. On the other hand, provincial leaders realized now that there was no legal bar to the federal initiative. Consequently the decision had the immediate effect of renewing interest in reaching a federal-provincial agreement on the terms for patriating the Canadian constitution. The prospects for reaching an accord were now somewhat increased by virtue of the fact that the Supreme Court had declared that unanimous agreement was not necessariy required.

The effectiveness of the Supreme Court's decision in promoting a federal-provincial accommodation on the constitution was soon demonstrated. A federal-provincial conference was held five weeks after the decision in November 1981. At this conference the federal government agreed to replace the amending formula it had favoured with one originally put forward by eight of the provinces (including Quebec). In return, all of the provinces except Quebec agreed to accept a modified version of the Charter of Rights. The November Accord with some further amendments agreed to by the federal government and all the provinces except Quebec, served as the basis for the resolution adopted by the federal parliament on Dec. 9, 1981 requesting the Queen to submit to the United Kingdom Parliament a measure to patriate the Canadian Constitution. On March 25, 1982, the U.K. Parliament passed the Canada Act severing Canada's last remaining legal ties to Britain and making the Constitution Act, 1982 the law of Canada. The Constitution Act, 1982 contains an all-Canadian amending formula and the Charter of Rights. It was proclaimed in force by the Queen of Canada on April 17, 1982. ~

ATTORNEY GENERAL OF MANITOBA ET AL. *v.* ATTORNEY GENERAL OF CANADA ET AL.
In the Supreme Court of Canada. September 28, 1981

A. *THE QUESTION OF LAW*

Chief Justice Laskin and Dickson, Beetz, Estey, McIntyre, Chouinard and Lamer JJ.

I

Three appeals as of right are before this Court, concerning in the main common issues. They arise out of three References made, respectively, to the Manitoba Court of Appeal, to the Newfoundland Court of Appeal and to the Quebec Court of Appeal by the respective governments of the three provinces.

Three questions were posed in the Manitoba Reference, as follows:

1. If the amendments to the Constitution of Canada sought in the "Proposed Resolution for a Joint Address to Her Majesty the Queen respecting the Constitution of Canada," or any of them, were enacted, would federal-provincial relationships or the powers, rights or privileges granted or secured by the Constitution of Canada to the provinces, their legislatures or governments be affected and if so, in what respect or respects?

2. Is it a constitutional convention that the House of Commons and Senate of Canada will not request Her Majesty the Queen to lay before the Parliament of the United Kingdom of Great Britain and Northern Ireland a measure to amend the Constitution of Canada affecting federal-provincial relationships or the powers, rights or privileges granted or secured by the Constitution of Canada to the provinces, their legislatures or governments without first obtaining the agreement of the provinces?

3. Is the agreement of the provinces of Canada constitutionally required for amendment to the Constitution of Canada where such amendment affects federal-provincial relationships or alters the powers, rights or privileges granted or secured by the Constitution of Canada to the provinces, their legislatures or governments?

The same three questions were asked in the Newfoundland Reference and, in addition, a fourth question was put in these terms:

4. If Part V of the proposed resolution referred to in question 1 is enacted and proclaimed into force could

(a) the Terms of Union, including terms 2 and 17 thereof contained in the Schedule to the British North America Act 1949 (12-13 George VI, c. 22 (U.K.)), or

(b) section 3 of the British North America Act, 1871 (34-35 Victoria, c. 28 (U.K.))

be amended directly or indirectly pursuant to Part V without the consent of the Government, Legislature or a majority of the people of the Province of Newfoundland voting in a referendum held pursuant to Part V?

In the Quebec Reference there was a different formulation, two questions being asked which read:

TRANSLATION:

A. If the Canada Act and the Constitution Act 1981 should come into force and if they should be valid in all respects in Canada would they affect:
  (i) the legislative competence of the provincial legislatures in virtue of the Canadian Constitution?
  (ii) the status or role of the provincial legislatures or governments within the Canadian Federation?

B. Does the Canadian Constitution empower, whether by statute, convention or otherwise, the Senate and the House of Commons of Canada to cause the Canadian Constitution to be amended without the consent of the provinces and in spite of the objection of several of them, in such a manner as to affect:
  (i) the legislative competence of the provincial legislatures in virtue of the Canadian Constitution?
  (ii) the status or role of the provincial legislatures or governments within the Canadian Federation?

The answers given by the Judges of the Manitoba Court of Appeal, each of whom wrote reasons, are as follows:

FREEDMAN C.J.M.:
Question 1 - Not answered, because it is tentative and premature.
Question 2 - No
Question 3 - No

HALL, J.A.:
Question 1 - Not answered because it is not appropriate for judicial response, and, in any event, the question is speculative and premature.
Question 2 - Not answered because it is not appropriate for judicial response.
Question 3 - No, because there is no legal requirement of provincial agreement to amendment of the Constitution as asserted in the question.

MATAS, J.A.:
Question 1 - Not answered, because it is speculative and premature.
Question 2 - No
Question 3 - No

O'SULLIVAN, J.A.:
Question 1 - Yes, as set out in reasons.
Question 2 - The constitutional convention referred to has not been established as a matter simply of precedent; it is, however, a constitutional principle binding in law that the House of Commons and Senate of Canada should not request Her Majesty the Queen to lay before the Parliament of the United Kingdom of Great Britain and Northern Ireland any measure to amend the Constitution of Canada affecting federal-provincial relationships or the powers, rights or privileges granted or secured by the Constitution of Canada to the provinces, their legislatures or governments without first obtaining the agreement of the provinces.
Question 3 - Yes, as set out in reasons.

HUBAND, J.A.:
Question 1 - Yes.
Question 2 - No
Question 3 - Yes

The Newfoundland Court of Appeal, in reasons of the Court concurred in by all three Judges who sat on the Reference, answered all three questions common to the Manitoba Reference in the affirmative. The Court answered the fourth question in this way:

1. By Sec. 3 of the British North America Act, 1871, Term 2 of the Terms of Union cannot now be changed without

the consent of the Newfoundland Legislature.

2. By Sec. 43 of the "Constitution Act," as it now reads, none of the Terms of Union can be changed without the consent of the Newfoundland Legislative Assembly.

3. Both of these sections can be changed by the amending formulae prescribed in Sec. 41 and the Terms of Union could then be changed without the consent of the Newfoundland Legislature.

4. If the amending formula under Sec. 42 is utilized, both of these sections can be changed by a referendum held pursuant to the provisions of Sec. 42. In this event, the Terms of Union could then be changed without the consent of the Newfoundland Legislature, but not without the consent of the majority of the Newfoundland people voting in a referendum.

The Quebec Court of Appeal, in reasons delivered by each of the five Judges who sat on the Reference, answered the two questions submitted to it as follows:

(TRANSLATION)

Question A i) yes (unanimously)
     ii) yes (unanimously)
Question B i) yes (Bisson J.A. dissenting would answer no)
     ii) yes (Bisson J.A. dissenting would answer no)

II

The References in question here were prompted by the opposition of six provinces, later joined by two others, to a proposed Resolution which was published on October 2, 1980 and intended for submission to the House of Commons and as well to the Senate of Canada. It contained an address to be presented to Her Majesty the Queen in right of the United Kingdom respecting what may generally be referred to as the Constitution of Canada. The address laid before the House of Commons on October 6, 1980, was in these terms:

To the Queen's Most Excellent Majesty:
Most Gracious Sovereign:

We, Your Majesty's loyal subjects, the House of Commons of Canada in Parliament assembled, respectfully approach Your Majesty, requesting that you may graciously be pleased to cause to be laid before the Parliament of the United Kingdom a measure containing the recitals and clauses hereinafter set forth:

An Act to give effect to a request by the Senate and House of Commons of Canada

Whereas Canada has requested and consented to the enactment of an Act of the Parliament of the United Kingdom to give effect to the provisions hereinafter set forth and the Senate and the House of Commons of Canada in Parliament assembled have submitted an address to Her Majesty requesting that Her Majesty may graciously be pleased to cause a bill to be laid before the Parliament of the United Kingdom for that purpose.

Be it therefore enacted by the Queen's Most Excellent Majesty, by and with the advice and consent of the Lords Spiritual and Temporal, and Commons, in this present Parliament assembled, and by the authority of the same, as follows:

1. The Constitution Act, 1981 set out in Schedule B to this Act is hereby enacted for and shall have the force of law in Canada and shall come into force as provided in that Act.

2. No Act of Parliament of the United Kingdom passed after the Constitution Act, 1981 comes into force shall extend to Canada as part of its law.

3. So far as it is not contained in Schedule B, the French version of this Act is set out in Schedule A to this Act and has the same authority in Canada as the English version thereof.

4. This Act may be cited as the Canada Act.

It will be noticed that included in the terms of the address are the words "cause to be laid before the Parliament of the

United Kingdom'' and that they are reflected in question B put before the Quebec Court of Appeal. The proposed Resolution, as the terms of the address indicate, includes a statute which, in turn, has appended to it another statute providing for the patriation of the British North America Act (and a consequent change of name), with an amending procedure, and a Charter of Rights and Freedoms including a range of provisions (to be entrenched against legislative invasion) which it is unnecessary to enumerate. The proposed Resolution carried the approval of only two provinces, Ontario and New Brunswick, expressed by their respective governments. The opposition of the others, save Saskatchewan, was based on their assertion that both conventionally and legally the consent of all the provinces was required for the address to go forward to Her Majesty with the appended statutes. Although there was general agreement on the desirability of patriation with an amending procedure, agreement could not be reached at conferences preceding the introduction of the proposed Resolution into the House of Commons, either on the constituents of such a procedure or on the formula to be embodied therein, or on the inclusion of a Charter of Rights.

The References to the respective Courts of Appeal were made and the hearings on the questions asked were held before the proposed Resolution was adopted. This fact underlies the unwillingness of Judges in the Manitoba Court of Appeal to answer question 1; changes might be made to the proposed Resolution in the course of debate and hence the assertion of prematurity.

The proposed Resolution, as adopted by the House of Commons on April 23, 1981, and by the Senate on April 24, 1981, achieved its final form (there were but a few amendments to the original proposal) almost on the eve of the hearings in this Court on the three appeals. Indeed, the opinions of the Courts in all three References were given and certified before the ultimate adoption of the proposed Resolution. The result of its adoption by the Senate and by the House of Commons was to change the position of the Attorney General of Canada and of his two supporting intervenors on the propriety of answering question 1 in the Manitoba and Newfoundland References. He abandoned his initial contention that the question should not be answered.

III

The Reference legislation under which the various questions were put to the three Courts of Appeal is in wide terms. The Manitoba legislation, An Act for Expediting the Decision of Constitutional and other Provincial Questions, R.S.M. 1970, c. C-180 provides in s. 2 that the Lieutenant-Governor in Council may refer to the Court of Queen's Bench or a Judge thereof or to the Court of Appeal or a Judge thereof for hearing or consideration "any matter which he thinks fit to refer." The Newfoundland Judicature Act, R.S.Nfld. 1970, c. 187, s. 6, as amended, similarly provides for a reference by the Lieutenant-Governor in Council to the Court of Appeal of "any matter which he thinks fit to refer." The Court of Appeal Reference Act, R.S.Q. 1977, c. R-23, s. 1 authorizes the Government of Quebec to refer to the Court of Appeal for hearing and consideration "any question which it deems expedient." The scope of the authority in each case is wide enough to saddle the respective Courts with the determination of questions which may not be justifiable and there is no doubt that those Courts, and this Court on appeal, have a discretion to refuse to answer such questions. . . .

IV

A summary of the views expressed in the Courts below on the various questions before them may usefully be set out at this point. . . .

V

The reasons which now follow deal

with questions 1 and 3 in the Manitoba and Newfoundland References, with question 4 in the Newfoundland Reference, with question A in the Quebec Reference and with question B in that Reference in its legal aspect. Question 2 in the Manitoba and Newfoundland References and question B in the Quebec Reference in its comparable conventional aspect are dealt with in separate reasons.

VI

On the footing of the adopted Resolution, the Attorney General of Canada agrees that question 1 in the Manitoba and Newfoundland References and question A in the Quebec Reference should be answered in the affirmative as is asserted by the Attorneys General of Manitoba, Newfoundland and Quebec. Certainly, it is plain that under the terms of the enactments proposed in the Resolution, the legislative powers of the provincial legislatures would be affected, indeed, limited by the Charter of Rights and Freedoms. The limitations of the proposed Charter of Rights and Freedoms on legislative power apply both at the federal level and the provincial level. This does not, however, alter the fact that there is an intended suppression of provincial legislative power. Moreover, the enhancement of provincial legislative authority under some provisions of the proposed enactment, as for example, in respect of resource control, including interprovincial export (albeit subject to federal paramountcy), and in respect of taxing power, does not alter the fact that there is an effect on existing federal-provincial relationships under these and other provisions of the draft statute intended for submission to enactment by the Parliament of the United Kingdom.

The simple answer "yes" to question 1 and question A answers both of them sufficiently, even though question 1 asks also "in what respect or respects" would federal-provincial relationships and provincial powers, rights or privileges be affected. Counsel were agreed that it would carry them and the Court into considerable exposition of detail if this aspect of question 1 were to be explored; for the time being, an affirmative answer to the primary issue in the question would satisfy all concerned.

VII

Coming now to question 3 in the Manitoba and Newfoundland References and part B (on its legal side) in the Quebec Reference. By reason of the use of the words "constitutionally required" in question 3, the question imports both legal and conventional issues, and as the latter are dealt with in separate reasons, what follows is concerned only with the legal side of question 3 in the Manitoba and Newfoundland References and part B (on its legal side) in the Quebec Reference, which meets the submissions of all counsel on this issue.

There are two broad aspects to the matter under discussion which divide into a number of separate issues: (1) the authority of the two federal Houses to proceed by Resolution where provincial powers and federal-provincial relationships are thereby affected and (2) the role or authority of the Parliament of the United Kingdom to act on the Resolution. The first point concerns the need of legal power to initiate the process in Canada; the second concerns legal power or want of it in the Parliament of the United Kingdom to act on the Resolution when it does not carry the consent of the provinces.

The submission of the eight provinces which invites this Court to consider the position of the British Parliament is based on the Statute of Westminster, 1931 in its application to Canada. The submission is that the effect of the Statute is to qualify the authority of the British Parliament to act on the federal Resolution without previous provincial consent where provincial powers and interests are thereby affected, as they plainly are here. This issue will be examined later in these reasons.

Two observations are pertinent here. First, we have the anomaly that although

Canada has international recognition as an independent, autonomous and self-governing state, as, for example, a founding member of the United Nations, and through membership in other international associations of sovereign states, yet it suffers from an internal deficiency in the absence of legal power to alter or amend the essential distributive arrangements under which legal authority is exercised in the country, whether at the federal or provincial level. When a country has been in existence as an operating federal state for more than a century, the task of introducing a legal mechanism that will thereafter remove the anomaly undoubtedly raises a profound problem. Secondly, the authority of the British Parliament or its practices and conventions are not matters upon which this Court would presume to pronounce.

The proposition was advanced on behalf of the Attorney General of Manitoba that a convention may crystallize into law and that the requirement of provincial consent to the kind of Resolution that we have here, although in origin political, has become a rule of law. (No firm position was taken on whether the consent must be that of the Governments or that of the Legislatures.)

In our view, this is not so. No instance of an explicit recognition of a convention as having matured into a rule of law was produced. The very nature of a convention, as political in inception and as depending on a consistent course of political recognition by those for whose benefit and to whose detriment (if any) the convention developed over a considerable period to time, is inconsistent with its legal enforcement.

The attempted assimilation of the growth of a convention to the growth of the common law is misconceived. The latter is the product of judicial effort, based on justiciable issues which have attained legal formulation and are subject to modification and even reversal by the Courts which gave them birth when acting within their role in the State in obedience to statutes or constitutional directives. No parental role is played by the Courts with respect to conventions.

It was urged before us that a host of cases have given legal force to conventions. This is an overdrawn proposition. One case in which direct recognition and enforcement of a convention was sought is *Madzimbamuto* v. *Lardner-Burke*, [1969] 1 A.C. 645. There the Privy Council rejected the assertion that a convention formally recognized by the United Kingdom as established, namely, that it would not legislate for Southern Rhodesia on matters within the competence of the latter's legislature without its government's consent, could not be overriden by British legislation made applicable to Southern Rhodesia after the unilateral declaration of independence by the latter's government. Speaking for the Privy Council, Lord Reid pointed out that although the convention was a very important one, "it had no legal effect in limiting the legal power of Parliament" (at p. 723). And, again, (at the same page):

It is often said that it would be unconstitutional for the United Kingdom Parliament to do certain things, meaning that the moral, political and other reasons against doing them are so strong that most people would regard it as highly improper if Parliament did these things. But that does not mean that it is beyond the power of Parliament to do such things. If Parliament chose to do any of them the courts could not hold the Acts of Parliament invalid. . . .

Quite a number of cases were cited on which counsel for Manitoba relied to support his contention of conventions crystallizing into law. The chief support put forward for the "crystallization into law" proposition was the opinion of Duff C.J.C. in *Reference re Weekly Rest in Industrial Undertakings Act*, [1936] S.C.R. 461, better known as the *Labour Conventions* case. . . .

The following portion of the reasons of Sir Lyman Duff contains the passage relied on, but extends it for more accurate context (at pp. 476-8):

With reference to the Report of the Conference of 1926, which in explicit terms recognizes treaties in the form of agreements between governments (to which His Majesty is not, in form, a party), it is said that since an Imperial Conference possesses no legislative power, its declarations do not operate to effect changes in the law, and it is emphatically affirmed that, in point of strict law, neither the Governor General nor any other Canadian authority has received from the Crown power to exercise the prerogative.

The argument is founded on the distinction it draws between constitutional convention and legal rule; and it is necessary to examine the contention that, in point of legal rule, as distinct from constitutional convention, the Governor-General in Council had no authority to become party by ratification to the convention with which we are concerned.

There are various points of view from which this contention may be considered. First of all, constitutional law consists very largely of established constitutional usages recognized by the Courts as embodying a rule of law. An Imperial Conference, it is true, possesses no legislative authority. But there could hardly be more authoritative evidence as to constitutional usage than the declarations of such a Conference. The Conference of 1926 categorically recognizes treaties in the form of agreements between governments in which His Majesty does not formally appear, and in respect of which there has been no Royal intervention. It is the practice of the Dominion to conclude with foreign countries agreements in such form, and agreements even of a still more informal character—merely by an exchange of notes. Conventions under the auspices of the Labour Organization of the League of Nations invariably are ratified by the Government of the Dominion concerned. As a rule, the crystallization of constitutional usage into a rule of constitutional law to which the Courts will give effect is a slow process extending over a long period of time; but the Great War accelerated the pace of development in the region with which we are concerned, and it would seem that the usages to which I have referred, the practice, that is to say, under which Great Britain and the Dominion enter into agreements with foreign countries in the form of agreements between governments and of a still more informal character, must be recognized by the Courts as having the force of law.

Indeed, agreements between the Government of Canada and other governments in the form of an agreement between Governments, to which His Majesty is not a party, have been recognized by the Judicial Committee of the Privy Council as adequate in international law to create an international obligation binding upon Canada (Radio Reference, [1932] A.C. 304). . . .

Ratification was the effective act which gave binding force to the convention. It was, as respects Canada, the act of the Government of Canada alone, and the decision mentioned appears, therefore, to negative decisively the contention that, in point of strict law, the Government of Canada is incompetent to enter into an international engagement.

What the learned Chief Justice was dealing with was an evolution which is characteristic of customary international law: the attainment by the Canadian federal executive of full and independent power to enter into international agreements. (Indeed, in speaking of "convention" in the last quoted paragraph, he was referring to an international agreement and, similarly, in the use of the word in the second last line of the second paragraph of the quotation and again in the middle of the third paragraph.) International law perforce has had to develop, if it was to exist at all, through commonly recognized political practices of states, there being no governing constitution, no legislating authority, no executive enforcement authority and no generally accepted judicial organ through which international law could be developed. The situation is entirely different in domestic law, in the position of a state having its own governing legislative, executive and judicial organs and, in most cases, an overarching written constitution.

Chief Justice Duff indicated his view of convention as allegedly maturing into law in a domestic setting in *Reference re Disallowance and Reservation of Provincial Legislation*, [1938] S.C.R. 71. There it was urged that a certain portion of s. 90 of the British North America Act (incorporating, in respect of the provinces, ss. 56 and 57, with some modification) had by reason of convention become spent and was suspended by the alleged convention. As to this, the Chief Justice said (at p. 78):

We are not concerned with constitutional usage. We are concerned with questions of law which, we repeat, must be determined by reference to the enactments of the British North America Acts of 1867 to 1930, the Statute of Westminster, and, it might be, to relevant statutes of the Parliament of Canada if there were any.

Section 90 which, with the changes therein specified, re-enacts sections 55, 56 and 57 of the B.N.A. Act, is still subsisting. It has not been repealed or amended by the Imperial Parliament and it is quite clear that, by force of subsection 1 of section 7 of the Statute of Westminster, the Dominion Parliament did not acquire by that statute, any authority to repeal, amend or alter the British North America Acts. Whether or not, by force of section 91(29) and section 92(1) of the B.N.A. Act, the Dominion Parliament has authority to legislate in respect of reservation, it is not necessary to consider because no such legislation has been passed.

The powers are, therefore, subsisting. Are they subject to any limitation or restriction?

Once more, we are not concerned with constitutional usage or constitutional practice. . . .

There is nothing in the other judgments

delivered in the *Labour Conventions* case, either in the Supreme Court or in the Privy Council that takes the matter there beyond its international law setting or lends credence to the crystallization proposition urged by counsel for the Attorney General of Manitoba and, it should be said, supported by other provinces and observations in the reasons of the Newfoundland Court of Appeal. Other cases cited for the proposition turn out, on examination, to be instances where the Courts proceeded on firm statutory or other legal principles. This is as true . . . of the denial of injunctive relief in respect of disclosure of the Crossman diaries in *Attorney General* v. *Jonathon Cape Ltd.*, [1976] 1 Q.B. 752. The Court pointed out in the latter case that it had the power to restrain breaches of confidence where demanded in the public interest, although the confidence stemmed from a convention respecting Cabinet deliberations. However, the need for restraint had gone because of the passage of time. The Court was applying its own legal principles as it might to any question of confidence, however it arose.

A close look at some other cases and issues raised on so-called crystallization reveals no support for the contention. . . .

Finally, there was an appeal to the Senate Reference decision of this Court. It is baffling how it can be said that this Court recognized convention as having *per se* grown into law. What was involved was a proposed federal enactment sought to be justified mainly under s. 91(1) of the British North America Act. This Court held that the proposal, at least in its main features, was beyond federal competence. Although the Court referred to certain historical background for perspective on the position of the Senate as it was dealt with under the British North America Act, its fundamental duty was to examine the validity of a proposed federal measure sought to be justified under a grant of federal power under that Act.

As to all the cases cited, it must be said that there is no independent force to be found in selective quotations from a portion of the reasons unless regard is had to issues raised and the context in which the quotations are found.

We were invited to consider academic writings on the matter under discussion. There is no consensus among the author-scholars, but the better and prevailing view is that expressed in an article by Munro, "Laws and Conventions Distinguished" (1975), 91 *Law Quarterly Review* 218 where he says (at p. 228):

The validity of conventions cannot be the subject of proceedings in a court of law. Reparation for breach of such rules will not be effected by any legal sanction. There are no cases which contradict these propositions. In fact, the idea of a court enforcing a mere convention is so strange that the question hardly arises.

Another passage from this article deserves mention, as follows (at p. 224):

If in fact laws and conventions are different in kind, as is my argument, then an accurate and meaningful picture of the constitution may only be obtained if this distinction is made. If the distinction is blurred, analysis of the constitution is less complete; this is not only dangerous for the lawyer, but less than helpful to the political scientist. . . .

There is no difference in approach whether the issue arises in a unitary state or in a federal state: see Hogg, *Constitutional Law of Canada* (1977), at pp. 7-11.

A contrary view relied on by the provincial appellants is that expressed by Professor W.R. Lederman in two published articles, one entitled "Process of Constitutional Amendment in Canada" (1967), 12 *McGill Law Journal* 371 and the second entitled "Constitutional Amendment and Canadian Unity" (1978), *Law Society of Upper Canada Lectures*, 17. As a respected scholar, Professor Lederman's views deserve more than cursory consideration. He himself recognizes that there are contrary views, including those of an equally distinguished scholar, Professor F.R. Scott: see Scott, *Essays on the Constitution*

(1977), pp. 144, 169, 204-205, 245, 370-371, 402. There is also the contrary view of Professor Hogg, already cited.

Professor Lederman relies in part on a line of cases that has already been considered, especially the reasons of Sir Lyman Duff in the *Labour Conventions* case. The leap from convention to law is explained almost as if there was a common law of constitutional law, but originating in political practice. That is simply not so. What is desirable as a political limitation does not translate into a legal limitation, without expression in imperative constitutional text or statute. The position advocated is all the more unacceptable when substantial provincial compliance or consent is by him said to be sufficient. Although Professor Lederman would not give a veto to Prince Edward Island, he would to Ontario or Quebec or British Columbia or Alberta. This is an impossible position for a Court to manage. Further reference to this is made later in these reasons.

VIII

Turning now to the authority or power of the two federal Houses to proceed by Resolution to forward the address and appended draft statutes to Her Majesty the Queen for enactment by the Parliament of the United Kingdom. There is no limit anywhere in law, either in Canada or in the United Kingdom (having regard to s. 18 of the British North America Act, as enacted by 1875 (U.K.), c. 38, which ties the privileges, immunities and powers of the federal Houses to those of the British House of Commons) to the power of the Houses to pass resolutions. Under s. 18 aforesaid, the federal Parliament may by statute define those privileges, immunities and powers, so long as they do not exceed those held and enjoyed by the British House of Commons at the time of the passing of the federal statute. . . .

How Houses of Parliament proceed, how a provincial Legislative Assembly proceeds, is in either case a matter of self-definition, subject to any overriding constitutional or self-imposed statutory or indoor prescription. It is unnecessary here to embark on any historical review of the "court" aspect of Parliament and the immunity of its procedures from judicial review. . . . Reference may appropriately be made to article 9 of the Bill of Rights of 1689, undoubtedly in force as part of the law of Canada, which provides that "proceedings in Parliament ought not to be impeached or questioned in any Court or place out of Parliament."

It is said, however, that where the Resolution touches provincial powers, as the one in question here does, there is a limitation on federal authority to pass it on to Her Majesty the Queen unless there is provincial consent. If there is such a limitation, it arises not from any limitation on the power to adopt Resolutions but from an external limitation based on other considerations which will shortly be considered.

Although the British North America Act itself is silent on the question of the power of the federal Houses to proceed by Resolution to procure an amendment to the Act by an address to Her Majesty, its silence gives positive support as much as it may reflect the negative. Quebec question B suggests in its formulation that there is the necessity of affirmative proof of the power asserted, but it would be equally consistent with constitutional precedent to require disproof. Moreover, if the two federal Houses had the power to proceed by Resolution, how is it that they have lost it?

For the moment, it is relevant to point out that even if those cases where an amendment to the British North America Act was founded on a Resolution of the federal Houses, after having received provincial consent, there is no instance, save in the British North America Act 1930 where such consent was recited in the Resolution. The matter remained, in short, a conventional one within Canada, without effect on the validity of the Resolution in respect of United Kingdom action. The point is underscored in relation to the very first amendment directly

affecting provincial legislative power, that in 1940 which added "Unemployment Insurance" to the catalogue of exclusive federal powers. Sir William Jowitt, then Solicitor General and later Lord Chancellor, was asked in the British House of Commons about provincial consent when the amendment was in course of passage. The question put to him and his answer are as follows (see 362 U.K. Parliamentary Debates 5th Series, H.C. 1177-1181):

Mr. Mander . . . In this bill we are concerned only with the Parliament of Canada, but, as a matter of interest, I would be obliged if the Solicitor General would say whether the Provincial Canadian Parliaments are in agreement with the proposals submitted by the Dominion Parliament. . . .

Sir William Jowitt . . . One might think that the Canadian Parliament was in some way subservient to ours, which is not the fact. The true position is that at the request of Canada this old machinery still survives until something better is thought of, but we square the legal with the constitutional position by passing these Acts only in the form that the Canadian Parliament require and at the request of the Canadian Parliament.

My justification to the House for this Bill—and it is important to observe this— is not on the merits of the proposal, which is a matter for the Canadian Parliament; if we were to embark upon that, we might trespass on what I conceive to be their constitutional position. The sole justification for this enactment is that we are doing in this way what the Parliament of Canada desires to do. . . .

In reply to the hon. Member for East Wolverhampton (Mr. Mander), I do not know what the view of the Provincial Parliaments is. I know, however, that when the matter was before the Privy Council some of the Provincial Parliaments supported the Dominion Parliament. It is a sufficient justification for the Bill that we are morally bound to act on the ground that we have here the request of the Dominion Parliament and that we must operate the old machinery which has been left over at their request in accordance with their wishes.

IX

This Court is being asked, in effect, to enshrine as a legal imperative a principle of unanimity for constitutional amendment to overcome the anomaly—more of an anomaly today than it was in 1867—that the British North America Act contained no provision for effecting amendments by Canadian action alone. Although Saskatchewan has, alone of the eight provinces opposing the federal package embodied in the Resolution, taken a less stringent position, eschewing unanimity but without quantifying the substantial support that it advocates, the provinces, parties to the References and to the appeals here, are entitled to have this Court's primary consideration of their views.

An important question was raised by the Saskatchewan position which invited this Court to take a severable view of the substance of the Resolution, namely, to hive off the Charter of Rights and Freedoms and perhaps other elements, save the amending formula and the patriation feature. This was not the position of the Attorney General of Canada nor of any of the other provincial Attorneys General; they were all of the view that it was the whole package that was involved in the legal issue posed by question 3 and question B. Indeed, the legal arguments pro and con do not engage the contents of the package, and it is impossible to qualify the issue of legality by considerations of fairness or equity or political acceptability or even judicial desirability.

The stark legal question is whether this Court can enact by what would be judicial legislation a formula of unanimity to initiate the amending process which would be binding not only in Canada but also on the Parliament of the United Kingdom with which amending authority would still remain. It would be anomalous indeed,

overshadowing the anomaly of a Constitution which contains no provision for its amendment, for this Court to say retroactively that in law we have had an amending formula all along, even if we have not hitherto known it; or, to say, that we have had in law one amending formula, say from 1867 to 1931, and a second amending formula that has emerged after 1931. No one can gainsay the desirability of federal-provincial accord of acceptable compromise. That does not, however, go to legality. As Sir William Jowitt said, and quoted earlier, we must operate the old machinery perhaps one more time.

X

The provincial contentions asserted a legal incapacity in the federal Houses to proceed with the Resolution which is the subject of the References and of the appeals here. Joined to this assertion was a claim that the United Kingdom Parliament had, in effect, relinquished its legal power to act on a Resolution such as the one before this Court, and that it could only act in relation to Canada if a request was made by "the proper authorities." The federal Houses would be such authorities if provincial powers or interests would not be affected; if they would be, then the proper authorities would include the Provinces. It is not that the provinces must be joined in the federal address to Her Majesty the Queen; that was not argued. Rather their consent (or, as in the Saskatchewan submission, substantial provincial compliance or approval) was required as a condition of the validity of the process by address and Resolution and, equally, as a condition of valid action thereon by the United Kingdom Parliament.

XI

The Court was invited to regard the Balfour Declaration of 1926 as embracing the Provinces of Canada (and, presumably, the states of the sister Dominion of Australia) in its reference to "autonomous communities.'' That well-known statement of principle, a political statement in the context of evolving independence of the Dominions in their relations with the United Kingdom, is as follows:

They are autonomous Communities within the British Empire, equal in status, in no way subordinate one to another in any aspect of their domestic or external affairs, though united by a common allegiance to the Crown, and freely associated as members of the British Commonwealth of Nations.

It is impossible to seek nourishment for the provincial position in these appeals in this Declaration. The Provinces did not come into the picture in the march to the Statute of Westminster, 1931 until after the 1929 Conference on the Operation of Dominion Legislation, although to a degree before the Imperial Conference of 1930. They then made their views known on certain aspects of the looming statute, views which were canvassed in a Dominion-Provincial Conference in 1931. The main concern touched the proposed repeal of the Colonial Laws Validity Act (U.K.), c. 63 and the effect that this might have on the amendment of the British North America Act, a matter to be considered later in these reasons.

Although the Balfour Declaration cannot, of itself, support the assertion of provincial autonomy in the wide sense contended for, it seems to have been regarded as retroactively having that effect by reason of the ultimate enactment of the Statute of Westminster. That statute is put forward not only as signifying an equality of status as between the Dominion and the provinces *vis-à-vis* the United Kingdom Parliament, but also as attenuating the theretofore untrammelled legislative authority of that Parliament in relation to Canada where provincial interests are involved. . . .

~ The relevant provisions of the Statute of Westminster were then set out. ~

There is nothing in the preamble that

relates to the provinces other than the reference to the Report of the Imperial Conference of 1930. What emerged prior to this Conference was an understandable provincial concern that the effect of the proposed repeal of the Colonial Laws Validity Act in favour of the Parliament of a Dominion and, in addition, the effect of what became s. 2(2) of the Statute might enlarge federal power to alter, by its own legislation, provisions of the British North America Act. Thus it was that the Conference of 1930 placed on record (Cmd. 3717, pp. 17-18):

that the sections of the Statute relating to the Colonial Laws Validity Act should be so drafted as not to extend to Canada unless the Statute was enacted in response to such requests as are appropriate to an amendment of the British North America Act. It also seemed desirable to place on record the view that the sections should not subsequently be extended to Canada except by an Act of the Parliament of the United Kingdom enacted in response to such requests as are appropriate to an amendment of the British North America Act.

The Colonial Laws Validity Act was intended to be a liberating statute, releasing colonial legislatures from subservience to British common law (subject to Privy Council authority) and from subservience to British statute law unless such statute law applied expressly or by necessary implication to the colony. In the evolution of independence of the Dominions, it came to be recognized that the United Kingdom should no longer legislate at its own instance for any Dominion; and that the latter should be free to repeal any British legislation that was or would be made applicable to it. . . . Following the Imperial Conference of 1930 and as a result of the Dominion-Provincial Conference of 1931, the provinces obtained an assurance that they too would benefit by the repeal of the Colonial Laws Validity Act and by being empowered to repeal any British legislation made applicable to them. This was achieved by s. 7(2) of the Statute of Westminster. . . .

The most important issue was, however, the position of the Dominion *vis-à-vis* the British North America Act. What s. 7(1), reinforced by s. 7(3), appeared to do was to maintain the *status quo ante*; that is, to leave any changes in the British North America Act (that is, such changes which, under its terms, could not be carried out by legislation of the provinces or of the Dominion) to the prevailing situation, namely, with the legislative authority of the United Kingdom Parliament being left untouched. . . .

The argument on the Statute of Westminster is untenable, but it leaves for more anxious consideration the effect of the removal of the British North America Act from the Statute of Westminster and the preservation of s. 7(3) of the existing distribution of legislative powers under the British North America Act.

XII

This leads to the submissions made on the sovereignty of the provinces in respect of their powers under the British North America Act, the term "sovereignty" being modified in the course of argument to "supremacy." Allied to this was the contention that Canada cannot do indirectly what it cannot do directly; it could not by an enactment of its own accomplish that which is proposed by the Resolution. Such an enactment would be clearly *ultra vires* as to most of the provisions put forward by the Resolution, and it should not be able to improve its position in law by invoking the aid of the United Kingdom Parliament. Moreover, even if the Parliament of the United Kingdom retained its formal legal authority over the British North America Act, as one of its enactments, it was in the words used by the late and at the time, former Justice Rand, "a bare legislative trustee," subject as a matter of law to the direction of the beneficiaries, namely, the Dominion and the Provinces, in respect of the Resolution.

. . . The direct-indirect contention, taken by itself, amounts to this: that whether or not the federal Houses can seek to obtain enactment of the draft statute appended to the Resolution, it would, in any event, be illegal to invoke United Kingdom authority to do for Canada what it cannot do itself. The maxim "you cannot do indirectly what you cannot do directly" is a much abused one. . . .

However, it does not preclude a limited legislature from achieving directly under one head of legislative power what it could not do directly under another head. The question, of course, remains whether the two federal Houses may alone initiate and carry through the process to invoke the competence of the United Kingdom Parliament.

At least with regard to the amending formula the process in question here concerns not the amendment of a complete constitution but rather the completion of an incomplete constitution.

We are involved here with a finishing operation, with fitting a piece into the constitutional edifice; it is idle to expect to find anything in the British North America Act that regulates the process that has been initiated in this case. Were it otherwise, there would be no need to resort to the Resolution procedure invoked here, a procedure which takes account of the intergovernmental and international link between Canada and Great Britain. There is no comparable link that engages the provinces with Great Britain. Moreover, it is to confuse the issue of process, which is the basic question here, with the legal competence of the British Parliament when resort is had to the direct-indirect argument. The legal competence of that Parliament, for the reasons already given, remains unimpaired, and it is for it alone to determine if and how it will act.

The late Justice Rand used the words "a bare legislative trustee" in the Holmes Lecture delivered at Harvard Law School under the title "Some Aspects of Canadian Constitutionalism" and reproduced in (1960), 38 *Canadian Bar Review* 135. His use of the phrase came in the course of his discussion of the effect of the Statute of Westminster. He said this (at p. 145):

Legislatively, a unique situation has been created. The British Parliament has in effect become a bare legislative trustee for the Dominion; the constitutional organ for altering the provisions of the Canadian constitution contained in the Act of 1867 remains so far the British Parliament; but the political direction resides in the Parliament of the Dominion; the former has conceded its residue of legislative power vis-à-vis Canada, to be no more than means for effecting the will of Canada. . . .

The Newfoundland Court of Appeal adopted the phrase but decided that Justice Rand should not have limited the suggested trusteeship as being for the Dominion of Canada alone. Moreover, the Court overlooked a central point in the Rand lecture that ''the political direction resides in the Parliament of the Dominion.'' Thus the Court said:

We adopt that statement fully with the important addition that the Parliament of Great Britain is a ''bare legislative trustee'' for both the Federal Parliament and the Provincial Legislatures in relation to the matters within their respective legislative competence. Any amendment enacted by the Parliament of Great Britain affecting the legislative competence of either of the parties, without that party's consent, would not only be contrary to the intendment of the Statute of Westminster, but it could defeat the whole scheme of the Canadian Federal constitution.

It is enough to counter this assessment of the Newfoundland Court of Appeal by referring to what Gérin-Lajoie said in his seminal text, *Constitutional Amendment in Canada* (1950), at p. 138:

While the Parliament of the United Kingdom is precluded from enacting any constitutional amendment without a proper request from Canada the only competent voice of Canada for this pur- *pose is that of the federal power. The provincial authorities—either executive or legislative—have no locus standi to move the British Parliament or Government with a view to securing an amendment to the federal Constitution. . . .*

XIII

At bottom, the challenge to the competency in law of the federal Houses to seek enactment by the Parliament of the United Kingdom of the statutes embodied in the Resolution is based on the recognized supremacy of provincial legislatures in relation to the powers conferred upon them under the British North America Act, a supremacy *vis-à-vis* the federal Parliament. Reinforcement, or perhaps the foundation of this supremacy is said to lie in the nature or character of Canadian federalism.

The supremacy position, taken alone, needs no further justification than that found in the respective formulations of the powers of Parliament and the provincial Legislatures in ss. 91 and 92 of the British North America Act. Federal paramountcy is, however, the general rule in the actual exercise of these powers. This notwithstanding, the exclusiveness of the provincial powers (another way of expressing supremacy and more consonant with the terms of the British North America Act) cannot be gainsaid. The long list of judicial decisions, beginning with *Hodge* v. *The Queen* (1883), 9 App. Cas. 117 and carrying through such cases as *Liquidators of the Maritime Bank* v. *Receiver General of New Brunswick*, [1892] A.C. 437 and the *Labour Conventions* case where the Privy Council expressed its ''watertight compartment view'' of legislative power (see [1937] A.C. 326, at p. 354) provide adequate support for the principle of exclusiveness or supremacy but, of course, within the limits of the British North America Act.

Although there are what have been called unitary features in the British North America Act, involving overriding powers (to be distinguished from paramountcy of legislation) in the federal Parliament and Government, their modification of exclusive provincial authority does not detract from that authority to any substantial degree. Thus, the federal declaratory power under s. 92(10)(c) has a limited operation; reservation and disallowance of provincial legislation, although in law still open, have, to all intents and purposes, fallen into disuse. The fact of appointment of the Lieutenant-Governors of the provinces by the central government does not, as a practical matter, have any significance for provincial powers when, under the law, the Lieutenant-Governor is as much the personal representative of the Crown as is the Governor General. In each case, the representation is, of course, in respect of the powers respectively assigned to Parliament and the legislatures. Moreover, since there is an international, a foreign relations aspect involved in the relationship of Canada and Great Britain, any formal communication between a province and its Lieutenant-Governor with the United Kingdom Government or with the Queen, must be through the federal government or through the Governor General.

It is important in this connection to emphasize that the Government of Canada had, by 1923, obtained recognition internationally of its independent power to enter into external obligations when it negotiated the Halibut Treaty with the United States. Great Britain understood this by that time as did the United States. The subsequent Imperial Conferences added confirmation, sanctified by the Statute of Westminster which also put internal independence from Great Britain on a legal foundation. The remaining badge of subservience, the need to resort to the British Parliament to amend the British North America Act, although preserved by the Statute of Westminster, did not carry any diminution of Canada's legal right in international law, and as a matter of Canadian constitutional law, to assert its independence in external relations, be they with Great Britain or other

countries. The matter is emphasized by the judgment of this Court in *Reference re Offshore Mineral Rights*, [1967] S.C.R. 792, at p. 816. This is a relevant consideration in the appeals which are before this Court.

What is put forward by the provinces which oppose the forwarding of the address without provincial consent is that external relations with Great Britain in this respect must take account of the nature and character of Canadian federalism. It is contended that a legal underpinning of their position is to be found in the Canadian federal system as reflected in historical antecedents, in the pronouncements of leading political figures and in the preamble to the British North America Act.

The arguments from history do not lead to any consistent view or any single view of the nature of the British North America Act. . . So, too, with pronouncements by political figures or persons in other branches of public life. There is little profit in parading them.

Support for a legal requirement of provincial consent to the Resolution that is before this Court, consent which is also alleged to condition United Kingdom response to the Resolution, is, finally, asserted to lie in the preamble of the British North America Act itself, and in the reflection, in the substantive terms of the Act, of what are said to be fundamental presuppositions in the preamble as to the nature of Canadian federalism. The preamble recites . . . the following:

WHEREAS the Provinces of Canada, Nova Scotia and New Brunswick have expressed their Desire to be federally united into One Dominion under the Crown of the United Kingdom of Great Britain and Ireland, with a Constitution similar in Principle to that of the United Kingdom:

What is stressed is the desire of the named provinces "to be federally united . . . with a Constitution similar in principle to that of the United Kingdom." The preamble speaks also of union into "one Dominion" and of the establishment of the Union "by authority of Parliament," that is the United Kingdom Parliament. What, then, is to be drawn from the preamble as a matter of law? A preamble, needless to say, has no enacting force, but, certainly, it can be called in aid to illuminate provisions of the statute in which it appears. Federal union "with a constitution similar in principle to that of the United Kingdom" may well embrace responsible government and some common law aspects of the United Kingdom's unitary constitutionalism, such as the rule of law and Crown prerogatives and immunities. The "rule of law" is a highly textured expression, importing many things which are beyond the need of these reasons to explore but conveying, for example, a sense of orderliness, of subjection to known legal rules and of executive accountability to legal authority. Legislative changes may alter common law prescriptions, as has happened with respect to Crown prerogatives and immunities. There is also an internal contradiction in speaking of federalism in the light of the invariable principle of British parliamentary supremacy. Of course, the resolution of this contradiction lies in the scheme of distribution of legislative power, but this owes nothing to the preamble, resting rather on its own exposition in the substantive terms of the British North America Act.

There is not and cannot be any standardized federal system for which particular conclusions must necessarily be drawn. Reference was made earlier to what were called unitary features of Canadian federalism and they operate to distinguish Canadian federalism from that of Australia and that of the United States. Allocations of legislative power differ as do the institutional arrangements through which power is exercised. This Court is being asked by the provinces which object to the so-called federal "package" to say that the internal distribution of legislative power must be projected externally, as a matter of law, although there is no legal warrant for this assertion. . . .

At bottom, it is this distribution, it is the allocation of legislative power as between the central Parliament and the provincial Legislatures that the provinces rely on as precluding unilateral federal action to seek amendments to the British North America Act that affect, whether by limitation or extension, provincial legislative authority. The Attorney General of Canada was pushed to the extreme by being forced to answer affirmatively the theoretical question whether in law the federal government could procure an amendment to the British North America Act that would turn Canada into a unitary state. That is not what the present Resolution envisages because the essential federal character of the country is preserved under the enactments proposed by the Resolution.

That, it is argued, is no reason for conceding unilateral federal authority to accomplish, through invocation of legislation by the United Kingdom Parliament, the purposes of the Resolution. There is here, an unprecedented situation in which the one constant since the enactment of the British North America Act in 1867 has been the legal authority of the United Kingdom Parliament to amend it. The law knows nothing of any requirement of provincial consent, either to a resolution of the federal Houses or as a condition of the exercise of United Kingdom legislative power.

In the result, the third question in the Manitoba and Newfoundland cases should, as a matter of law, be answered in the negative and question B should, in its legal aspect, be answered in the affirmative.

XIV

There remains for consideration question 4 in the Newfoundland Reference. . . .

~ The Newfoundland Court of Appeal's answer to question 4 is upheld except for the correction which follows. ~

. . . It was wrong to say that in a referendum under s. 42 (as it then was) of the proposed statute (now s. 46) the approval of the majority of the people in each province was required. The proper view was that only the approval of the majority of the people voting in a referendum in those provinces, the approval of whose legislatures would be required under the general amending formula, would be necessary. . . .

In summary, the answers to question 1 and 3 common to the Manitoba and Newfoundland References, should be as follows:

Question 1: Yes.
Question 3: As a matter of law, no.

The answer to question 4 in the Newfoundland Reference should be as expressed in the reasons of the Newfoundland Court of Appeal, subject to the correction made in the reasons herein.

The answers to the questions in the Quebec Reference should be as follows:

Question A (i): Yes.
       (ii): Yes.

Question B (i): As a matter of law, yes.
      (ii): As a matter of law, yes.

There will be, of course, no order as to costs.

MARTLAND and RITCHIE JJ. (dissenting): . . . The third question in the Newfoundland References asks whether the agreement of the provinces of Canada is "constitutionally required" for amendment to the Constitution of Canada where such amendment affects federal provincial relationships or alters the powers, rights or privileges granted or secured by the Constitution of Canada to the provinces, their legislatures or governments. If the second question is answered in the affirmative, then it is recognized that a constitutional convention exists that the House of Commons and the Senate will not request an amendment of the B.N.A. Act of the kind contemplated in

question 2 without first obtaining the agreement of the provinces. If that is so, then the agreement of the provinces is constitutionally required for such an amendment and the answer to question 3 should be in the affirmative and, in our opinion, that answer should be given.

However, there is a further issue which requires consideration in that in the Courts below and in the arguments submitted by counsel before this Court, the answer to question 3 was debated as though the words "constitutionally required" were to be considered as meaning "legally required."

In the Quebec Reference the question is phrased differently in question B. What is asked is whether the Senate and the House of Commons are empowered by the Canadian Constitution, whether by statute, convention or otherwise, to cause the Canadian Constitution to be amended without the consent of the provinces, and in spite of the objection of several of them, in such a manner as to affect the legislative competence of provincial legislatures, or the status or role of provincial legislatures or governments within the Canadian federation.

We were not referred to any statute which confers such a power. The answer to question 2, if answered in the affirmative, denies that such a power exists by convention. The remaining issue is whether such a power has been conferred on the two Houses otherwise than by statute or convention.

We think Question B of the Quebec Reference more clearly raises the legal issue than does question 3 in the other two References and we shall deal with that issue in these reasons.

At the outset, we would point out that we are not concerned with the matter of legality or illegality in the sense of determining whether or not the passage of the resolution under consideration involves a breach of the law. The issue is as to the existence of a power to do that which is proposed to be done. The question is whether it is *intra vires* of the Senate and the House of Commons to cause the proposed amendments to the B.N.A. Act to be made by the Imperial Parliament by means of the resolution now before the Court, in the absence of provincial agreement.

This issue is unique because in the 114 years since Confederation the Senate and House of Commons of Canada have never sought, without the consent of the provinces, to obtain such an amendment nor, apparently, has that possibility ever been contemplated.

The British North America Act, 1867 (herein the B.N.A. Act) commences with the following significant recitals:

WHEREAS the Provinces of Canada, Nova Scotia and New Brunswick have expressed their Desire to be federally united into One Dominion under the Crown of the United Kingdom of Great Britain and Ireland, with a Constitution similar in Principle to that of the United Kingdom: . . .

. . . The first recital makes it clear that this statute was passed at the behest of the named provinces and that what was sought was a federal union. . . .

. . . This Act became the Constitution of Canada. It created a federal union of provinces and it carefully defined the respective spheres of the Canadian Parliament and the provincial legislatures in matters of legislative jurisdiction and property rights.

The status of the provinces under the Constitution was determined by the Privy Council in two important cases which arose not long after the enactment of the B.N.A. Act.

It was contended in *Hodge v. The Queen*, ([1883-84] 9 A.C. 117) that a provincial legislature could not delegate its legislative powers to License Commissioners, for it was itself merely a delegate of the Imperial Parliament. The Judicial Committee of the Privy Council rejected this argument in the following terms, at p. 132:

It appears to their Lordships, however, that the objection thus raised by the appellants is founded on an entire misconception of the true character and position of the provincial legislatures. They are in no sense delegates of or acting under any mandate from the Imperial Parliament. When the British North America Act enacted that there should be a legislature for Ontario, and that its legislative assembly should have exclusive authority to make laws for the Province and for provincial purposes in relation to the matters enumerated in sect. 92, it conferred powers not in any sense to be exercised by delegation from or as agents of the Imperial Parliament, but authority as plenary and as ample within the limits prescribed by sect. 92 as the Imperial Parliament in the plenitude of its power possessed and could bestow. Within these limits of subjects and area the local legislature is supreme, and has the same authority as the Imperial Parliament, or the Parliament of the Dominion, would have had under like circumstances to confide to a municipal institution or body of its own creation authority to make by-laws or resolutions as to subjects specified in the enactment, and with the object of carrying the enactment into operation and effect.

In *Liquidators of the Maritime Bank of Canada* v. *Receiver General of New Brunswick*, ([1892] A.C. 437) it was argued that the province enjoyed no part of the Crown prerogative, and accordingly the Province of New Brunswick could not claim priority in respect of the Bank's assets for a debt owed to the province. The argument also involved the proposition that the federal government did not share this constitutional incompetence. . . .

Lord Watson spoke for the Judicial Committee and, at p. 441, had this to say:

. . . Their Lordships do not think it necessary to examine, in minute detail, the provisions of the Act of 1867, which nowhere profess to curtail in any respect the rights and privileges of the Crown, or to disturb the relations then subsisting between the Sovereign and the provinces.

The object of the Act was neither to weld the provinces into one, nor to subordinate provincial governments to a central authority, but to create a federal government in which they should all be represented, entrusted with the exclusive administration of affairs in which they had a common interest, each province retaining its independence and autonomy.

. . . The assignment of powers by the Act to the Parliament of Canada and to the provincial legislatures covered the whole area of self government. This was recognized by the Privy Council in *Attorney General for Ontario* v. *Attorney General for Canada*, [1912] A.C. 571 at 581. . . .

. . . The foregoing review shows that the enactment of the B.N.A. Act created a federal constitution of Canada which confided the whole area of self-government within Canada to the Parliament of Canada and the provincial legislatures each being supreme within its own defined sphere and area. It can fairly be said, therefore, that the dominant principle of Canadian constitutional law is federalism. The implications of that principle are clear. Each level of government should not be permitted to encroach on the other, either directly or indirectly. The political compromise achieved as a result of the Quebec and London Conferences preceding the passage of the B.N.A. Act would be dissolved unless there were substantive and effective limits on unconstitutional action.

The B.N.A. Act did not make any specific provision as to the means of determining the constitutionality of any federal or provincial legislation. That task has been assumed and performed by the courts, with supreme authority initially resting with the Judicial Committee of the Privy Council and, since 1949, with this Court.

In performing this function, the courts, in addition to dealing with cases involving alleged excesses of legislative jurisdiction, have had occasion to develop legal principles based on the necessity of preserving the integrity of the federal structure. We will be dealing with these later in this judgment. We will, however, at this point cite one instance of the performance of this task in the following case by the Privy Council.

In *Attorney General of Canada* v. *Attorney General of Ontario*, [1937] A.C. 326 (the *Labour Conventions* case) the issue was as to the constitutional validity of three federal statutes enacted in 1935 dealing with labour matters, such as weekly rest in industrial undertakings, hours of work and minimum wages. In substance, they gave effect to draft conventions adopted by the International Labour Organization of the League of Nations in accordance with the Labour Pact of the Treaty of Versailles, 1919, ratified by Canada. For the Attorney General of Canada it was argued that the legislation was valid because it was for the purpose of performing Canadian treaty obligations. . . .

There are several features of the *Labour Conventions* case which require emphasis. The federal government was in that case asserting the right to enact legislation which was within provincial authority in order to carry out the treaty obligations which it had assumed. No question was raised as to the validity of the federal government's authority to negotiate and ratify international treaties. What was held unconstitutional by the Privy Council was the use of that lawful procedure to legislate indirectly beyond the powers invested in the federal Parliament by s. 91 of the B.N.A. Act.

In these appeals this Court is equally concerned with the exercise of a valid power, namely, the power of the federal Houses of Parliament to pass resolutions requesting amendments to the B.N.A. Act. That power has historic foundations, but we note that it has never before been exercised for the purpose of curtailing provincial legislative authority without provincial consent. In the context of the *Labour Conventions* case, the issue in these appeals is whether the established incompetence of the federal government to encroach on provincial powers can be avoided through the use of the resolution procedure to effect a constitutional amendment passed at the behest of the federal government by the Parliament of the United Kingdom.

The only provisions of the B.N.A. Act dealing with amendments to the constitution are as follows. Head 1 of s. 92 empowered a provincial legislature to make laws in relation to:

1. The Amendment from Time to Time, notwithstanding anything in this Act, of the Constitution of the Province, except as regards the Office of Lieutenant-Governor.

Section 146, already cited, made provision for the admission of other colonies and territories into the Union.

By an amendment made in 1949 to s. 91 of the B.N.A. Act, a limited power of amendment was given to the federal Parliament. Head 1 of s. 91 enabled it to legislate in relation to:

1. The amendment from time to time of the Constitution of Canada, except as regards matters coming within the classes of subjects by this Act assigned exclusively to the Legislatures of the provinces, or as regards rights or privileges by this or any other Constitutional Act granted or secured to the Legislature or the Government of a province, or to any class of persons with respect to schools or as regards the use of the English or the French language or as regards the requirements that there shall be a session of the Parliament of Canada at least once each year, and that no House of Commons shall continue for more than five years from the day of the return of the Writs for choosing the House: provided, however, that a House of Commons may in time of real or apprehended war, invasion or insurrection be continued by the Parliament of Canada if such continuation is not opposed by the votes of more than one-third of the members of such House.

This provision specifically excepted from its operation, *inter alia*, matters coming within the classes of subjects assigned exclusively to the provinces. The scope of s. 91.1 was considered by this Court in *Re Authority of Parliament in Relation to the Upper House*, [1980] 1 S.C.R. 54 (herein the Senate Reference). In that case, this Court unanimously held that the federal government could not, acting under s. 91.1, abolish the Senate. The term "Constitution of Canada" found in s. 91.1 was held in its context to refer only to the federal juristic unit. It is significant that when, as recently as 1949, the Houses of Parliament sought and obtained a provision permitting the federal Parliament to amend the Constitution by legislation, specific provision was made to ensure that this power was not capable of implying any right to interfere with those powers assigned to the provinces by the B.N.A. Act.

Because the Canadian Constitution was created by the B.N.A. Act in the form of an Imperial statute, it followed that in the absence of a provision for amendment within it, its amendment could only be effected by the enactment of an Imperial statute. Over the years many amendments have occurred in this way. The practice had developed, since 1895, to have the formal approach to the Imperial Parliament made by means of a joint address of both Houses of Parliament. . . .

~ Justices Martland and Ritchie then set out statements from the 1965 White Paper describing the procedure followed with respect to the fourteen important amendments to the B.N.A. Act passed by the Imperial Parliament since 1867. ~

In no instance has an amendment to the B.N.A. Act been enacted which directly affected federal-provincial relationships in the sense of changing provincial legislative powers, in the absence of federal consultation with and the consent of all the provinces. Notably, this procedure continued to be followed in the four instances which occurred after the enactment of the Statute of Westminster.

This history of amendments reveals the operation of constitutional constraints.

While the choice of the resolution procedure is itself a matter of internal parliamentary responsibility, the making of the addresses to the Sovereign falls into two areas. Resolutions concerning the federal juristic unit and federal powers were made without reference to any but the members of the federal Houses. Resolutions abridging provincial authority have never been passed without the concurrence of the provinces. In other words, the normal constitutional principles recognizing the inviolability of separate and exclusive legislative powers were carried into and considered an integral part of the operation of the resolution procedure.

The history of constitutional amendments also parallels the development of Canadian sovereignty. The B.N.A. Act did not have among its purposes the severance of Canada from the British Commonwealth. However, the vital role of Canadian consent as an expression of Canadian sovereignty is revealed in the fact that no constitutional amendment has been passed without that consent. . . .

. . . The Statute of Westminster was passed on December 11, 1931. Earlier that year, Mr. Louis St. Laurent, then President of the Canadian Bar Association, and a distinguished constitutional lawyer, referred in his presidential address, reported in 9 *Canadian Bar Review*, p. 525, to the resolutions of the Houses of Commons and the Senate requesting the enactment of the Statute. This speech was not delivered in a political context. At that time he did not hold any political office. It was some years later that he became a Member of the House of Commons and a Minister of the Crown. The following passage from that speech is relevant to the issue now before the Court:

Now, it may be that while both the Dominion and the Provinces remained subject to the legislative jurisdiction of His Majesty's Parliament of the United Kingdom, that Parliament had, in theory, full power to vary the distribution of legislative jurisdiction between them. But after *the declaration of 1926 that both the United Kingdom and the Dominions are autonomous communities equal in status, in no way subordinate one to another in any aspect of their domestic or external affairs, it would hardly seem probable that the Parliament of the United Kingdom would undertake to legislate for the territory of any one of those Dominions, unless it be expressly declared in the Act that the Dominion had requested and consented to the enactment for the proposed legislation. And if the United Kingdom and the Dominions are equal in status and in no way subordinate one to another in any aspect of their domestic or external affairs, does not the provision of section 92 of the Act of 1867, that in each province the legislature may exclusively make laws in relation to the amendment from time to time of its constitution, except as regards the office of Lieutenant-Governor, seem to indicate that the Houses of the Dominion Parliament would have no jurisdiction to request or to consent to enactments that might extend or abridge Provincial legislative autonomy? . . .*

The Statute of Westminster gave statutory recognition to the independent sovereign status of Canada as a nation. However, while Canada, as a nation, was recognized as being sovereign, the government of the nation remained federal in character and the federal Parliament did not acquire sole control of the exercise of that sovereignty. Section 2 of the Statute of Westminster, standing alone, could be construed as giving that control to the federal Parliament, but the enactment of s. 7, at the instance of the provinces, was intended to preclude that exercise of power by the Federal Parliament. Subsection 7(3) in particular gave explicit recognition to the continuation of the division of powers created by the B.N.A. Act. The powers conferred on the Parliament of Canada by the Statute of Westminster were restricted to the enactment of laws in relation to matters within the competence of the Parliament of Canada.

The effect of s. 7(1) was to preserve the Imperial Parliament as the legal instrument for enacting amendments to the B.N.A. Acts, 1867-1930. This clearly had no effect on the existing procedure which had been used to obtain the amendment of the B.N.A. Act. The resolution procedure, which, after 1896, had produced all the constitutional amendments until 1931, has been followed in respect of all the constitutional amendments passed since 1931.

The Attorney General of Canada presented a deceptively simple argument in support of the legality of the Resolution at issue in these appeals. It was argued that the Resolution is not a law, and therefore not a proper subject for judicial consideration and, further, that the two Houses can legally pass any resolution which they desire. The Imperial Parliament has full legal authority to amend the B.N.A. Act by enacting a statute, and its power to do so cannot be questioned. If, therefore, the Imperial Parliament enacts such a statute in response to a resolution of the Senate and the House of Commons, there can be no question of illegality.

However, it was also submitted that while the Imperial Parliament has full legal authority to amend the B.N.A. Act, there exists a "firm and unbending" convention that such an amendment will only be enacted in response to a resolution of the two Houses requesting it, and, further, that it will enact any amendment to the B.N.A. Act which is so requested.

In the result, if this process is examined from the point of view of substance rather than of form, what is being asserted is the existence of a power in the Senate and the House of Commons to cause any amendment to the B.N.A. Act which they desire to be enacted, even though that amendment subtracts, without provincial consent, from the legislative powers of the provinces granted to them by the B.N.A. Act. . . .

The power of the Senate and the House of Commons to pass resolutions of any kind, and to use such resolutions for any purpose, was stated by the Attorney General to have been recognized in s. 18 of the B.N.A. Act and s. 4 of the Senate and House of Commons Act, R.S.C. 1970, c. S-8. Section 18 of the B.N.A. Act provides:

> *18. The privileges, immunities, and powers to be held, enjoyed, and exercised by the Senate and by the House of Commons, and by the Members thereof respectively, shall be such as are from time to time defined by Act of the Parliament of Canada, but so that any Act of the Parliament of Canada defining such privileges, immunities, and powers shall not confer any privileges, immunities, or powers exceeding those at the passing of such Act held, enjoyed, and exercised by the Commons House of Parliament of the United Kingdom of Great Britain and Ireland, and by the Members thereof.*

. . . Section 18 did not, in itself, create or recognize the existence of the privileges, immunities and powers of the Senate and the House of Commons. It provided that their privileges, immunities and powers should be such as are, from time to time, defined by Act of the Parliament of Canada, subject to the limitation that Parliament could not, by statute, give to the Senate or the House of Commons any privileges, immunities or powers which exceeded those enjoyed by the House of Commons of the United Kingdom Parliament. Parliament could not grant legislative powers to its two Houses. Furthermore, because, unlike the Parliament of the United Kingdom, Parliament's power to legislate was limited in extent, it could not grant to the Senate and the House of Commons powers which it did not itself possess.

In the exercise of the power granted to it by s. 18 of the B.N.A. Act, the Parliament of Canada, in 1868, passed an Act to define the privileges, immunities and powers of the Senate and House of Commons, S.C. 1868, c. 23. . . .

The essential provisions . . . now appear in sections 4 and 5 of the Senate and House of Commons Act, R.S.C. 1970, c. S-8, as follows:

4. The Senate and the Houses of Commons respectively, and the members thereof respectively, hold, enjoy and exercise,

    (a) such and the like privileges, immunities and powers as, at the time of the passing of the British North America Act, 1867, were held, enjoyed and exercised by the Commons House of Parliament of the United Kingdom, and by the members thereof, so far as the same are consistent with and not repugnant to that Act; and

    (b) such privileges, immunities and powers as are from time to time defined by Act of the Parliament of Canada, not exceeding those at the time of the passing of such Act held, enjoyed and exercised by the Commons House of Parliament of the United Kingdom and by the members thereof respectively.

5. Such privileges, immunities and powers are part of the general and public law of Canada, and it is not necessary to plead the same, but the same shall, in all courts in Canada, and by and before all judges, be taken notice of judicially.

Parliament did not confer upon the Senate and the House of Commons all of the privileges, immunities and powers held, enjoyed and exercised by the House of Commons of the United Kingdom, but only conferred them "so far as the same are consistent with and not repugnant to that Act," i.e. the B.N.A. Act, 1867. It thus recognized that some powers enjoyed by the House of Commons of the United Kingdom might not be consistent with the provisions of the B.N.A. Act.

In our opinion this very important proviso took into account the fact that, whereas the House of Commons in the United Kingdom was one of the Houses in the Parliament of a unitary state, the Canadian Senate and House of Commons were Houses in a Parliament in a federal state, whose powers were not all-embracing, but were specifically limited to the Act which created it.

In order to pass the Resolution now under consideration the Senate and the House of Commons must purport to exercise a power. The source of that power must be found in paragraph 4(a) of the Senate and House of Commons Act, since there has been no legislation enacted to date, other than paragraph 4(a) which actually defines the privileges, immunities and powers upon the two Houses of Parliament. The Resolution now before us was passed for the purpose of obtaining an amendment to the B.N.A. Act, the admitted effect of which is to curtail provincial legislative powers under s. 92 of the B.N.A. Act. In our opinion that power is not consistent with the B.N.A. Act but is repugnant to it. It is a power which is out of harmony with the very basis of the B.N.A. Act. Therefore paragraph (a) of s. 4, because of the limitations which it contains, does not confer that power. The Senate and the House of Commons are purporting to exercise a power which they do not possess.

The effect of the position taken by the Attorney General of Canada is that the two Houses of Parliament have unfettered control of a triggering mechanism by means of which they can cause the B.N.A. Act to be amended in any way they desire. It was frankly conceded in argument that there were no limits of any kind upon the type of amendment that could be made in this fashion. In our opinion, this argument in essence maintains that the provinces have since, at the latest 1931, owed their continued existence not to their constitutional powers expressed in the B.N.A. Act, but to the federal parliament's sufferance. While the federal Parliament was throughout this period incompetent to legislate in respect of matters assigned to the provinces by s. 92, its two Houses could at any time have done so by means of a resolution to the Imperial Parliament, procuring an amendment to the B.N.A. Act.

The Attorney General of Canada, in substance, is asserting the existence of a power in the two Houses of Parliament to obtain amendments to the B.N.A. Act which could disturb and even destroy the federal system of constitutional government in Canada. We are not aware of any possible legal source for such a power. . . .

. . . In our opinion, the two Houses lack legal authority, of their own motion, to obtain constitutional amendments which would strike at the very basis of the Canadian federal system, i.e., the complete division of legislative powers between the Parliament of Canada and the provincial legislatures. It is the duty of this Court to consider this assertion of rights with a view to the presentation of the Constitution.

This Court, since its inception, has been active in reviewing the constitutionality of both federal and provincial legislation. This role has generally been concerned with the interpretation of the express terms of the B.N.A. Act. However, on occasions, this Court has had to consider issues for which the B.N.A. Act offered no answer. In each case, this Court has denied the assertion of any power which would offend against the basic principles of the Constitution.

In *Amax Potash Limited et al v. The Government of Saskatchewan*, [1977] 2 S.C.R. 576 the plaintiff sued for a declaration that certain sections of The Mineral Taxation Act, R.S.S. 1965, c. 64, and certain regulations made pursuant to that Act, were *ultra vires* and sought the recovery of moneys paid by way of tax under the regulations. The Government of Saskatchewan disputed the contention that these provisions were *ultra vires*, but also contended that no cause of action was disclosed because subs. 5(7) of The Proceedings against the Crown Act, R.S.S. 1965, c. 87, was a bar to the recovery of moneys paid to the Crown. . . .

. . . In the course of his reasons, Dickson J., who delivered the judgment of the Court, said at p. 590:

A state, it is said, is sovereign and it is not for the Courts to pass upon the policy or wisdom of legislative will. As a broad statement of principle that is undoubtedly correct, but the general principle must yield to the requisites of the constitution in a federal state. By it the bounds of sovereignty are defined and supremacy circumscribed. . .

In *British Columbia Power Corporation Limited* v. *British Columbia Electric Company Limited*, [1962] S.C.R. 642 this Court had to decide whether a receivership order could be made to preserve assets pending a decision as to the constitutionality of certain legislation in British Columbia which litigation would determine whether the Crown had title to the common shares of British Columbia Electric Company Limited which the legislation gave to the Crown.

It was contended that a receivership order could not be made by virtue of the Crown's prerogative of immunity. Chief Justice Kerwin, who delivered the judgment of the Court, said at pp. 644-45:

. . . In a federal system, where legislative authority is divided, as are also the prerogatives of the Crown, as between the Dominion and the Provinces, it is my view that it is not open to the Crown, either in right of Canada or of a Province, to claim a Crown immunity based upon an interest in certain property, where its very interest in that property depends completely and solely on the validity of the legislation which it has itself passed, if there is a reasonable doubt as to whether such legislation is constitutionally valid. To permit it to do so would be to enable it, by the assertion of rights claimed under legislation which is beyond its powers to achieve the same results as if the legislation were valid. In a federal system it appears to me that, in such circumstances, the Court has the same jurisdiction to preserve assets whose title is dependent on the validity of the legislation as it has to determine the validity of the legislation itself.

In *The Attorney General of Nova Scotia* v. *The Attorney General of Canada*, [1951] S.C.R. 31 the Court had to consider the validity of legislation which contemplated a delegation of legislative powers by the provincial legislature to the Parliament of Canada, and by Parliament to the provincial legislature. Chief Justice Rinfret said, at p. 34:

The constitution of Canada does not belong either to Parliament, or to the Legislatures; it belongs to the country and it is there that the citizens of the country will find the protection of the rights to which they are entitled. It is part of that protection that Parliament can legislate only on the subject matters referred to it by section 91 and that each Province can legislate exclusively on the subject matters referred to it by section 92. . . .

In *Reference re Alberta Statutes*, [1938] S.C.R. 100 the Court considered, *inter alia*, the constitutional validity of the Accurate News and Information Act which imposed certain duties of publication upon newspapers published in Alberta. Chief Justice Duff (Davis J. concurring) referred to the right of public discussion and the authority of Parliament to protect that right and said at pp. 133-134:

. . . That authority rests upon the principle that the powers requisite for the protection of the constitution itself arise by necessary implication from The British North America Act as a whole (Fort Frances Pulp & Paper Co. Ltd. v. Manitoba Free Press Co. Ltd. [1923] A.C. 695); and since the subject-matter in relation to which the power is exercised is not exclusively a provincial matter, it is necessarily vested in Parliament.

It may be noted that the above instances of judicially developed legal principles and doctrines share several characteristics. *First*, none is to be found in express provisions of the British North America Acts or other constitutional enactments. *Second*, all have been perceived to represent constitutional requirements that are derived from the federal character of Canada's constitution. *Third*, they have been accorded full legal force in the sense of

being employed to strike down legislative enactments. *Fourth*, each was judicially developed in response to a particular legislative initiative in respect of which it might have been observed, as it was by Dickson J. in the *Amax (supra)* case at p. 591, that: "There are no Canadian constitutional law precedents addressed directly to the present issue. . . ."

In our opinion the accession of Canada to sovereign international status did not enable the federal Parliament, whose legislative authority is limited to the matters defined in s. 91 of the B.N.A. Act unilaterally by means of a resolution of its two Houses, to effect an amendment to the B.N.A. Act which would offend against the basic principle of the division of powers created by that Act. The assertion of such a right, which has never before been attempted, is not only contrary to the federal system created by the B.N.A. Act, but also runs counter to the objective sought to be achieved by s. 7 of the Statute of Westminster.

The federal position in these appeals can be summarized in these terms. While the federal Parliament lacks legal authority to achieve the objectives set out in the Resolution by the enactment of its own legislation, that limitation upon its authority can be evaded by having the legislation enacted by the Imperial Parliament at the behest of a resolution of the two Houses of the federal Parliament. This is an attempt by the federal Parliament to accomplish indirectly that which is it legally precluded from doing directly by perverting the recognized resolution method of obtaining constitutional amendments by the Imperial Parliament for an improper purpose. In our opinion, since it is beyond the power of the federal Parliament to enact such an amendment, it is equally beyond the power of its two Houses to effect such an amendment through the agency of the Imperial Parliament.

CONCLUSIONS:

. . . The fact that the status of Canada became recognized as a sovereign state did not alter its federal nature. It is a sovereign state, but its government is federal in character with a clear division of legislative powers. The Resolution at issue in these appeals could only be an effective expression of Canadian sovereignty if it had the support of both levels of government.

The two Houses of the Canadian Parliament claim the power unilaterally to effect an amendment to the B.N.A. Act which they desire, including the curtailment of provincial legislative powers. This strikes at the basis of the whole federal system. It asserts a right by one part of the Canadian governmental system to curtail, without agreement, the powers of the other part.

There is no statutory basis for the exercise of such a power. On the contrary, the powers of the Senate and the House of Commons, given to them by paragraph 4(a) of the Senate and House of Commons Act, excluded the power to do anything inconsistent with the B.N.A. Act. The exercise of such a power has no support in constitutional convention. The constitutional convention is entirely to the contrary. We see no other basis for the recognition of the existence of such a power. This being so, it is the proper function of this Court, in its role of protecting and preserving the Canadian Constitution, to declare that no such power exists. We are, therefore, of the opinion that the Canadian Constitution does not empower the Senate and the House of Commons to cause the Canadian Constitution to be amended in respect of provincial legislative powers without the consent of the provinces.

Question B in the Quebec Reference raises the issue as to the power of the Senate and the House of Commons of Canada to cause the Canadian Constitution to be amended "without the consent of the provinces and in spite of the objection of several of them." The Attorney General of Saskatchewan when dealing with question 3 in the Manitoba and Newfoundland References submitted that it was not necessary in these proceedings for the Court to pronounce on the necessity

for the unanimous consent of all the provinces to the constitutional amendments proposed in the Resolution. It was sufficient, in order to answer the question, to note the opposition of eight of the provinces which contained a majority of the population of Canada.

We would answer question B in the negative. We would answer question 3 of the Manitoba and Newfoundland References in the affirmative without deciding, at this time, whether the agreement referred to in that question must be unanimous.

B. THE QUESTION OF CONVENTION

MARTLAND, RITCHIE, DICKSON, BEETZ, CHOUINARD and LAMER JJ.:

The second question in the Manitoba Reference and Newfoundland Reference is the same:

> 2. Is it a constitutional convention that the House of Commons and Senate of Canada will not request Her Majesty the Queen to lay before the Parliament of the United Kingdom of Great Britain and Northern Ireland a measure to amend the Constitution of Canada affecting federal-provincial relationships or the powers, rights or privileges granted or secured by the Constitution of Canada to the provinces, their legislatures or governments without first obtaining the agreement of the provinces?

As for question B in the Quebec Reference, it reads in part as follows:

(TRANSLATION)
> B. Does the Canadian Constitution empower . . . by . . . convention . . . the Senate and the House of Commons of Canada to cause the Canadian Constitution to be amended without the consent of the provinces and in spite of the objection of several of them, in such a manner as to affect:
>   (i) the legislative competence of the provincial legislatures in virture of the Canadian Constitution?
>   (ii) the status or role of the provincial legislatures or governments within the Canadian Federation?

In these questions, the phrases "Constitution of Canada" and "Canadian Constitution" do not refer to matters of interest only to the federal government or federal juristic unit. They are clearly meant in a broader sense and embrace the global system of rules and principles which govern the exercise of constitutional authority in the whole and in the same broad sense in these reasons.

The meaning of the second question in the Manitoba and Newfoundland Reference calls for further observations.

As will be seen later, counsel for several provinces strenuously argued that the convention exists and requires the agreement of all the provinces. However, we did not understand any of them to have taken the position that the second question of the Manitoba and Newfoundland References should be dealt with and answered as if the last part of the question read

. . . without obtaining the agreement of all the provinces?

By that as it may, the question should not in our view be so read.

It would have been easy to insert the word "all" into the question had it been intended to narrow its meaning. But we do not think it was so intended. The issue raised by the question is essentially whether there is a constitutional convention that the House of Commons and Senate of Canada will not proceed alone. The thrust of the question is accordingly on whether or not there is a conventional requirement for provincial agreement, not on whether the agreement should be unanimous assuming that it is required. Furthermore, this manner of reading the question is more in keeping with the wording of question B in the Quebec Reference which refers to something less than unanimity when it says:

. . . without the consent of the provinces and in spite of the objection of several of them . . .

I THE NATURE OF CONSTITUTIONAL
  CONVENTIONS

A substantial part of the rules of the Canadian Constitution are written. They are contained not in a single document called a Constitution but in a great variety of statutes some of which have been enacted by the Parliament of Westminster, such as the British North America Act 1867, (the B.N.A. Act) or by the Parliament of Canada, such as the Alberta Act, the Saskatchewan Act, the Senate and House of Commons Act, or by the provincial legislatures, such as the provincial electoral acts. They are also to be found in orders in council like the Imperial Order in Council of May 16, 1871 admitting British Columbia into the Union, and the Imperial Order in Council of June 26, 1873, admitting Prince Edward Island into the Union.

Another part of the Constitution of Canada consists of the rules of the common law. These are rules which the courts have developed over the centuries in the discharge of their judicial duties. An important portion of these rules concerns the prerogative of the Crown. Sections 9 and 15 of the B.N.A. Act provide:

9. The Executive Government and authority of and over Canada is hereby declared to continue and be vested in the Queen.

15. The Commander-in-Chief of the land and Naval Militia, and of all Naval and Military Forces, of and in Canada, is hereby declared to continue and be vested in the Queen.

But the Act does not otherwise say very much with respect to the elements of "Executive Government and authority" and one must look at the common law to find out what they are, apart from authority delegated to the Executive by statute.

The common law provides that the authority of the Crown includes for instance the prerogative of mercy or clemency and the power to incorporate by charter. . . .

Those parts of the Constitution of Canada which are composed of statutory rules and common law rules are generically referred to as the law of the Constitution.

In cases of doubt or dispute, it is the function of the courts to declare what the law is and since the law is sometimes breached, it is generally the function of the courts to ascertain whether it has in fact been breached in specific instances and, if so, to apply such sanctions as are contemplated by the law, whether they be punitive sanctions or civil sanctions such as a declaration of nullity. Thus, when a federal or a provincial statute is found by the courts to be in excess of the legislative competence of the legislature which has enacted it, it is declared null and void and the courts refuse to give effect to it. In this sense it can be said that the law of the Constitution is administered or enforced by the courts.

But many Canadians would perhaps be surprised to learn that important parts of the Constitution of Canada, with which they are the most familiar because they are directly involved when they exercise their right to vote at federal and provincial elections, are nowhere to be found in the law of the Constitution. For instance it is a fundamental requirement of the Constitution that if the Opposition obtains the majority at the polls, the Government must tender its resignation forthwith. But fundamental as it is, this requirement of the Constitution does not form part of the law of the Constitution.

It is also a constitutional requirement that the person who is appointed Prime Minister or Premier by the Crown and who is the effective head of the government should have the support of the elected branch of the legislature; in practice this means in most cases the leader of the political party which has won a majority of seats at a general election. Other ministers are appointed by the Crown on the advice of the Prime Minister or Premier when he forms or reshuffles his cabinet. Ministers must continuously have the confidence of the elected branch of the legislature, individually and collectively. Should they lose it, they must either resign or ask the Crown for a dissolution of the legislature and the holding of a general election. Most of the powers of the Crown under the prerogative are exercised only upon the advice of the Prime Minister or the cabinet which means that they are effectively exercised by the latter, together with the innumerable statutory powers delegated to the Crown in council.

Yet none of these essential rules of the Constitution can be said to be a law of the Constitution. It was apparently Dicey who, in the first edition of his *Law of the Constitution*, in 1885, called them ''the conventions of the constitution,'' an expression which quickly became current. What Dicey described under these terms are the principles and rules of responsible government, several of which are stated above and which regulate the relations between the Crown, the Prime Minister, the Cabinet and the two Houses of Parliament. These rules developed in Great Britain by way of custom and precedent during the nineteenth century and were exported to such British colonies as were granted self-government.

Dicey first gave the impression that constitutional conventions are a peculiarly British and modern phenomenon. But he recognized in later editions that different conventions are found in other constitutions. As Sir William Holdsworth wrote:

In fact conventions must grow up at all times and in all places where the powers of government are vested in different persons or bodies—where in other words there is a mixed constitution. ''The constituent parts of a state,'' said Burke, [French Revolution, 28] ''are we obliged to hold their public faith with each other, and with all those who derive any serious interest under their engagements, as much as the whole state is bound to keep its faith with separate communities.'' Necessarily conventional rules spring up to regulate the working of the various parts of the constitution, their relations to one another, and to the subject.

(W.S. Holdsworth, ''The conventions of the eighteenth century constitution,''

(1932), 17 Iowa Law Review, 161 at p. 162.)

Within the British Empire, powers of government were vested in different bodies which provided a fertile ground for the growth of new constitutional conventions unknown to Dicey whereby self-governing colonies acquired equal and independent status within the Commonwealth. Many of these culminated in the Statute of Westminster, 1931.

A federal constitution provides for the distribution of powers between various legislatures and governments and may also constitute a fertile ground for the growth of constitutional conventions between those legislatures and governments. It is conceivable for instance that usage and practice might give birth to conventions in Canada relating to the holding of federal-provincial conferences, the appointment of lieutenant-governors, the reservation and disallowance of provincial legislation. . . .

The main purpose of constitutional conventions is to ensure that the legal framework of the Constitution will be operated in accordance with the prevailing constitutional values or principles of the period. For example, the constitutional value which is the pivot of the conventions stated above and relating to responsible government is the democratic principle: the powers of the state must be exercised in accordance with the wishes of the electorate; and the constitutional value or principle which anchors the conventions regulating the relationship between the members of the Commonwealth is the independence of the former British colonies.

Being based on custom and precedent, constitutional conventions are usually unwritten rules. Some of them however may be reduced to writing and expressed in the proceedings and documents of imperial conferences, or in the preamble of statutes such as the Statute of Westminster, 1931, or in the proceedings and documents of federal-provincial conferences. They are often referred to and recognized in statements made by members of governments.

The conventional rules of the Constitution present one striking peculiarity. In contradistinction to the laws of the Constitution, they are not enforced by the courts. One reason for this situation is that, unlike common law rules, conventions are not judge-made rules. They are not based on judicial precedents but on precedents established by the institutions of government themselves. Nor are they in the nature of statutory commands which it is the function and duty of the courts to obey and enforce. Furthermore, to enforce them would mean to administer some formal sanction when they are breached. But the legal system from which they are distinct does not contemplate formal sanctions for their breach.

Perhaps the main reason why conventional rules cannot be enforced by the courts is that they are generally in conflict with the legal rules which they postulate and the courts are bound to enforce the legal rules. The conflict is not of a type which would entail the commission of any illegality. It results from the fact that legal rules create wide powers, discretions and rights which conventions prescribe should be exercised only in a certain limited manner, if at all.

Some examples will illustrate this point.

As a matter of law, the Queen, or the Governor General or the Lieutenant-Governor could refuse assent to every bill passed by both Houses of Parliament or by a Legislative Assembly as the case may be. But by convention they cannot of their own motion refuse to assent to any such bill on any ground, for instance because they disapprove of the policy of the bill. We have here a conflict between a legal rule which creates a complete discretion and a conventional rule which completely neutralizes it. But conventions, like laws, are sometimes violated. And if this particular convention were violated and assent were improperly withheld, the courts would be bound to enforce the law, not the convention. They would refuse to recognize the validity of a vetoed bill. This is what happened in *Gallant* v. *The King* ([1949] 2 D.L.R. 425) a case in keeping with the classic case of *Stockdale* v. *Hansard* ([1839] 9 Ad. and E.1) where the English Court of Queen's Bench held that only the Queen and both Houses of Parliament could make or unmake laws. The Lieutenant-Governor who had withheld assent in *Gallant* apparently did so towards the end of his term of office. Had it been otherwise, it is not inconceivable that his withholding of assent might have produced a political crisis leading to his removal from office which shows that if the remedy for a breach of a convention does not lie with the courts, still the breach is not necessarily without a remedy. The remedy lies with some other institutions of government; furthermore it is not a formal remedy and it may be administered with less certainty or regularity than it would be by a court.

Another example of the conflict between law and convention is provided by a fundamental convention already stated above: if after a general election where the Opposition obtained the majority at the polls the Government refused to resign and clung to office, it would thereby commit a fundamental breach of conventions, one so serious indeed that it could be regarded as tantamount to a coup d'état. The remedy in this case would lie with the Governor General or the Lieutenant-Governor as the case might be who would be justified in dismissing the Ministry and in calling on the Opposition to form the Government. But should the Crown be slow in taking this course, there is nothing the courts could do about it except at the risk of creating a state of legal discontinuity, that is a form of revolution. An order or a regulation passed by a Minister under statutory authority and otherwise valid could not be invalidated on the ground that, by convention, the Minister ought no longer to be a Minister. A writ of *quo warranto* aimed at Ministers, assuming that *quo warranto* lies against a Minister of the Crown, which is very doubtful, would be of no avail to remove them from office. Required to say by what warrant they occupy their ministerial office, they would answer that they occupy it by the pleasure of the Crown under a commission issued by the Crown and this answer would be a complete one at law, for at law the Government is in office by the pleasure of the Crown although by convention it is there by the will of the people.

This conflict between convention and law which prevents the courts from enforcing conventions also prevents conventions from crystallizing into laws, unless it be by statutory adoption.

It is because the sanctions of convention rest with institutions of government other than courts, such as the Governor General or the Lieutenant-Governor, or the Houses of Parliament, or with public opinion and, ultimately, with the electorate that it is generally said that they are political.

We respectfully adopt the definition of a convention given by the learned Chief Justice of Manitoba, Freedman C.J.M. in the Manitoba Reference at pp. 13 and 14:

What is a constitutional convention? There is a fairly lengthy literature on the subject. Although there may be shades of difference among the constitutional lawyers, political scientists, and judges who have contributed to that literature, the essential features of a convention may be set forth with some degree of confidence. Thus there is general agreement that a convention occupies a position somewhere in between a usage or custom on the one hand and a constitutional law on the other. There is general agreement that if one sought to fix that position with greater precision he would place convention nearer to law than to usage or custom. There is also general agreement that "a convention is a rule which is regarded as obligatory by the officials to whom it applies." (Hogg, "Constitutional Law of Canada," (1977), p. 9.) There is, if not general agreement, at least weighty authority, that the sanction for breach of a convention will be political rather than legal.

It should be borne in mind however that, while they are not laws, some conventions may be more important than some laws. Their importance depends on that of the value or principle which they are meant to safeguard. Also they form an integral part of the Constitution and of the constitutional system. They come within the meaning of the word "Constitution" in the preamble of the British North America Act, 1867:

Whereas the Provinces of Canada, Nova Scotia and New Brunswick have expressed their Desire to be federally united . . . with a Constitution similar in principle to that of the United Kingdom:

That is why it is perfectly appropriate to say that to violate a convention is to do something which is unconstitutional although it entails no direct legal consequence. But the words "constitutional" and "unconstitutional" may also be used in a strict legal sense, for instance with respect to a statute which is found *ultra vires* or unconstitutional. The foregoing may perhaps be summarized in an equation: constitutional conventions plus constitutional law equal the total Constitution of the country.

II WHETHER THE QUESTIONS SHOULD BE ANSWERED

It was submitted by counsel for Canada and for Ontario that the second question in the Manitoba and Newfoundland References and the conventional part of question B in the Quebec Reference ought not to be answered because they do not raise a justiciable issue and are accordingly not appropriate for a court. It was contended that the issue whether a particular convention exists or not is a purely political one. The existence of a definite convention is always unclear and a matter of debate. Furthermore, conventions are flexible, somewhat imprecise and unsuitable for judicial determination.

The same submission was made in sub-stance to the three courts below and, in our respectful opinion, rightfully dismissed by all three of them, Hall J.A. dissenting in the Manitoba Court of Appeal.

We agree with what Freedman C.J.M. wrote on this subject in the Manitoba Reference at p. 13:

In my view this submission goes too far. Its characterization of Question 2 as "purely political" overstates the case. That there is a political element embodied in the question, arising from the contents of the Joint Address, may well be the case. But that does not end the matter. If Question 2, even if in part political, possesses a constitutional feature, it would legitimately call for our reply.

In my view the request for a decision by this Court on whether there is a constitutional convention, in the circumstances described, that the Dominion will not act without the agreement of the Provinces poses a question that is, at least in part, constitutional in character. It therefore calls for an answer, and I propose to answer it.

Question 2 is not confined to an issue of pure legality but it has to do with a fundamental issue of constitutionality and legitimacy. Given the broad statutory basis upon which the Governments of Manitoba, Newfoundland and Quebec are empowered to put questions to their three respective Courts of Appeal, they are in our view, entitled to an answer to a question of this type.

Finally, we are not asked to hold that a convention has in effect repealed a provision of the B.N.A. Act, as was the case in the *Reference re Disallowance (supra)*. Nor are we asked to enforce a convention. We are asked to recognize it if it exists. Courts have done this very thing many times in England and the Commonwealth to provide aid for and background to constitutional or statutory construction. Several such cases are mentioned in the reasons of the majority of this Court relating to the question whether constitutional conventions are capable of crystallizing into law. There are many others. . . . This court did the same in the recent case of *Arseneau* v. *The Queen* ([1979] 2 S.C.R. 136 at p. 149) and in the still unreported judgment rendered on April 6, 1981 after the re-hearing of *Attorney General of Quebec* v. *Peter Blaikie et al.*

In so recognizing conventional rules, the courts have described them, sometimes commented upon them and given them such precision as is derived from the written form of a judgment. They did not shrink from doing so on account of the political aspects of conventions, nor because of their supposed vagueness, uncertainty or flexibility.

In our view, we should not, in a constitutional reference, decline to accomplish a type of exercise that courts have been doing of their own motion for years.

III WHETHER THE CONVENTION EXISTS

It was submitted by counsel for Canada, Ontario and New Brunswick that there is no constitutional convention that the House of Commons and Senate of Canada will not request Her Majesty the Queen to lay before the Parliament of Westminster a measure to amend the Constitution of Canada affecting federal-provincial relationships, etc., without first obtaining the agreement of the provinces.

It was submitted by counsel for Manitoba, Newfoundland, Quebec, Nova Scotia, British Columbia, Prince Edward Island and Alberta that the convention does exist, that it requires the agreement of all the provinces and that the second question in the Manitoba and Newfoundland References should accordingly be answered in the affirmative.

Counsel for Saskatchewan agreed that the question be answered in the affirmative but on a different basis. He submitted that the convention does exist and requires a measure of provincial agreement. Counsel for Saskatchewan further submitted that the resolution before the Court has not received a sufficient measure of provincial consent.

We wish to indicate at the outset that we find ourselves in agreement with the submissions made on this issue by counsel for Saskatchewan.

1. The class of constitutional amendments contemplated by the question

Constitutional amendments fall into three categories: (1) amendments which may be made by a provincial legislature acting alone under s. 92.1 of the B.N.A. Act; (2) amendments which may be made by the Parliament of Canada acting alone under s. 91.1 of the B.N.A. Act; (3) all other amendments.

The first two categories are irrelevant for the purposes of these References. While the wording of the second and third questions of the Manitoba and Newfoundland References may be broad enough to embrace all amendments in the third category, it is not necessary for us to consider those amendments which affect federal-provincial relationships only indirectly. In a sense, most amendments of the third category are susceptible of affecting federal-provincial relationships to some extent. But we should restrict ourselves to the consideration of amendments which

. . . *directly affect federal-provincial relationships in the sense of changing federal and provincial legislative powers* . . . (*The* Senate Reference *at p. 65.*)

The reason for this is that the second and third questions of the Manitoba and Newfoundland References must be read in the light of the first question. They must be meant to contemplate the same specific class of constitutional amendments as the ones which are sought in the ''Proposed Resolution for a Joint Address to Her Majesty the Queen respecting the Constitution of Canada.'' More particularly, they must be meant to address the same type of amendments as the Charter of Rights, which abridges federal and provincial legislative powers, and the amending formula, which would provide for the amendment of the Constitution including the distribution of legislative powers.

These proposed amendments present one essential characteristic: they directly affect federal-provincial relationships in changing legislative powers and in providing for a formula to effect such change.

Therefore, in essence although not in terms, the issue raised by the second question in the Manitoba and Newfoundland References is whether there is a constitutional convention for agreement of the provinces to amendments which change legislative powers and provide for a method of effecting such change. The same issue is raised by question B of the Quebec Reference, above quoted in part.

2. *Requirements for establishing a convention*

The requirements for establishing a convention bear some resemblance with those which apply to customary law. Precedents and usage are necessary but do not suffice. They must be normative. We adopt the following passage of Sir W. Ivor Jennings in *The Law and the Constitution* (5th ed. 1959, p. 136):

We have to ask ourselves three questions: first, what are the precedents; secondly, did the actors in the precedents believe that they were bound by a rule; and thirdly, is there a reason for the rule? A single precedent with a good reason may be enough to establish the rule. A whole string of precedents without such a reason will be of no avail, unless it is perfectly certain that the persons concerned regarded them as bound by it.

i) The precedents

An account of the statutes enacted by the Parliament of Westminster to modify the Constitution of Canada is found in a White Paper published in 1965 under the authority of the Honourable Guy Favreau, then Minister of Justice for Canada, under the title of "The Amendment of the Con-stitution of Canada." This account is quoted in the *Senate Reference (supra)* but we find it necessary to reproduce it here for convenience: . . .*

Of these twenty-two amendments or groups of amendments, five directly affected federal-provincial relationships in the sense of changing provincial legislative powers: they are the amendment of 1930, the Statute of Westminster, 1931, and the amendments of 1940, 1951 and 1964.

Under the agreements confirmed by the 1930 amendment, the Western provinces were granted ownership and administrative control of their natural resources so as to place these provinces in the same position *vis-à-vis* natural resources as the original confederating colonies. The Western provinces, however, received these natural resources subject to some limits on their power to make laws relating to hunting and fishing rights of Indians. Furthermore, the agreements did provide a very substantial object for the provincial power to make laws relating to "The Management and Sale of Public Lands belonging to the Province and of the Timber and Wood thereon" under s. 92.5 of the B.N.A. Act. . . . The preamble of the Act recites that "each of the said agreements has been duly approved by the Parliament of Canada and the Legislature of the Province to which it relates." The other provinces lost no power, right or privilege in consequence. In any event, the proposed transfer of natural resources to the Western provinces had been discussed at the 1927 Dominion-Provincial Conference and had met with general approval (Paul-Gérin Lajoie, *Constitutional Amendment in Canada*, pp. 91 and 92).

All the provinces agreed to the passing of the Statute of Westminster, 1931. It changed legislative powers: Parliament and the legislatures were given the authority, within their powers, to repeal any United Kingdom statute that formed

---

*This list of amendments can be found in case 43 above, pp. 697-98.

part of the law of Canada; Parliament was also given the power to make laws having extra-territorial effect.

The 1940 amendment is of special interest in that it transferred an exclusive legislative power from the provincial legislatures to the Parliament of Canada.

In 1938, the Speech from the Throne stated:

The co-operation of the provinces has been sought with a view to an amendment of the British North America Act, which would empower the parliament of Canada to enact forthwith a national scheme of unemployment insurance. My ministers hope the proposal may meet with early approval, in order that unemployment insurance legislation may be enacted during the present session of parliament. (Common Debates, *1938, p. 2.*)

In November 1937, the Government of Canada had communicated with the provinces and asked for their views in principle. A draft amendment was later circulated. By March 1938, five of the nine provinces had approved the draft amendment. Ontario had agreed in principle, but Alberta, New Brunswick and Quebec had declined to join in. The proposed amendment was not proceeded with until June 1940 when Prime Minister King announced to the House of Commons that all nine provinces had assented to the proposed amendment.

The 1951 and 1964 amendments changed the legislative powers: areas of exclusive provincial competence became areas of concurrent legislative competence. They were agreed upon by all the provinces.

These five amendments are the only ones which can be viewed as positive precedents whereby federal-provincial relationships were directly affected in the sense of changing legislative powers.

Every one of these five amendments was agreed upon by each province whose legislative authority was affected.

In negative terms, no amendment changing provincial legislative powers has been made since Confederation when agreement of a province whose legislative powers would have been changed was withheld.

There are no exceptions.

Furthermore, in even more telling negative terms, in 1951, an amendment was proposed to give the provinces a limited power of indirect taxation. Ontario and Quebec did not agree and the amendment was not proceeded with. (*Commons Debates*, 1951 pp. 2682 and 2726 to 2743.)

The Constitutional Conference of 1960 devised a formula for the amendment of the Constitution of Canada. Under this formula, the distribution of legislative powers could have been modified. The great majority of the participants found the formula acceptable but some differences remained and the proposed amendment was not proceeded with.

In 1964, a conference of first ministers unanimously agreed on an amending formula that would have permitted the modification of legislative powers. Quebec subsequently withdrew its agreement and the proposed amendment was not proceeded with.

Finally, in 1971, proposed amendments which included an amending formula were agreed upon by the federal government and eight of the ten provincial governments. Quebec disagreed and Saskatchewan which had a new government did not take a position because it was believed the disagreement of Quebec rendered the question academic. The proposed amendments were not proceeded with.

The accumulation of these precedents, positive and negative, concurrent and without exception, does not of itself suffice in establishing the existence of the convention; and it unmistakedly points in its direction. Indeed, if the precedents stood alone, it might be argued that unanimity is required. . . .

We do not think it is necessary to deal with classes of constitutional amendments other than those which change legislative powers or provide for a method to effect such change. But we will briefly comment on two amendments about which much has been made to support the argument against the existence of the convention. These are the amendment of 1907 increasing the scale of financial subsidies to the provinces and the amendment of 1949 confirming the Terms of Union between Canada and Newfoundland.

It was contended that British Columbia objected to the 1907 amendment which had been agreed upon by all the other provinces.

Even if it were so, this precedent would at best constitute an argument against the unanimity rule.

But the fact is that British Columbia did agree in principle with the increase of financial subsidies to the provinces. It wanted more and objected to the proposed finality of the increase. The finality aspect was deleted from the amendment by the United Kingdom authorities. Mr. Winston Churchill, Under Secretary of State for the Colonies made the following comment in the House of Commons:

In deference to the representations of British Columbia the words "final and unalterable" applying to the revised scale, have been omitted from the Bill.
Common Debates *(U.K.)*
June 13, 1907 p. 1617

In the end, the Premier of British Columbia did not refuse to agree to the Act being passed.

With respect to the 1949 amendment, it was observed by Turgeon J.A. in the Quebec Reference that, without Quebec's consent, this amendment confirmed the Quebec-Labrador Boundary as delimited in the report delivered by the Judicial Committee of the Privy Council on March 1, 1927.

The entry of Newfoundland into Confederation was contemplated from the beginning by s. 146 of the B.N.A. Act. It was at the request of Quebec in 1904 that the dispute relating to the boundary was ultimately submitted to the Judicial Committee. Quebec participated in the litiga-

tion, being represented by counsel appointed and paid by the province, although the province did not intervene separately from Canada. When the 1949 amendment was passed, the Premier of Quebec is reported to have stated at a press conference simply that the province should have been "consulted" or "advised" as a matter of "courtesy." He is not reported as having said that the consent of the province was required. (See Luce Patenaude, *Le Labrador à l'heure de la contestation.*) The Premier of Nova Scotia spoke to the same effect. Neither Premier made any formal demand or protest.

We fail to see how this precedent can affect the convention.

It was also observed by Turgeon J.A. in the Quebec Reference that the Charter of Rights annexed to the proposed Resolution for a Joint Address does not alter the distribution of powers between the Parliament of Canada and the provincial legislatures.

This observation may be meant as an argument to the effect that the five positive precedents mentioned above should be distinguished and ought not to govern the situation before the Court since in those five cases the distribution of legislative powers was altered.

To this argument we should reply that if provincial consent was required in those five cases, it would be *a fortiori* required in the case at bar.

Each of those five constitutional amendments effected a limited change in legislative powers, affecting one head of legislative competence such as unemployment insurance. Whereas if the proposed Charter of Rights became law, every head of provincial (and federal) legislative authority could be affected. Furthermore, the Charter of Rights would operate retrospectively as well as prospectively with the result that laws enacted in the future as well as in the past, even before Confederation, would be exposed to attack if inconsistent with the provisions of the Charter of Rights. This Charter would thus abridge provincial legislative authority on a scale exceeding the effect of any previous constitutional amendment for which provincial consent was sought and obtained.

Finally, it was noted in the course of argument that in the case of four or five amendments mentioned above where provincial consent effectively had been obtained, the statutes enacted by the Parliament of Westminster did not refer to this consent. This does not alter the fact that consent was obtained.

ii) The actors treating the rule as binding

In the White Paper, one finds this passage at pages 10 and 11:

> *Procedures Followed in the Past in Securing Amendments to the British North America Act*
>
> *The procedures for amending a constitution are normally a fundamental part of the laws and conventions by which a country is governed. This is particularly true if the constitution is embodied in a formal document as is the case in such federal states as Australia, the United States and Switzerland. In these countries, the amending process forms an important part of their constitutional law.*
>
> *In this respect, Canada has been in a unique constitutional position. Not only did the British North America Act not provide for its amendment by Canadian legislative authority, except to the extent outlined in the beginning of this chapter, but it also left Canada without any clearly defined procedure for securing constitutional amendments from the British Parliament. As a result, procedures have varied from time to time, with recurring controversies and doubts over the conditions under which various provisions of the Constitution should be amended.*
>
> *Certain rules and principles relating to amending procedures have nevertheless developed over the years. They have emerged from the practices and procedures employed in securing various amendments to the British North America Act since 1867. Though not constitutionally binding in any strict sense, they have come to be recognized and accepted in practice as part of the amendment process in Canada.*
>
> *In order to trace and describe the manner in which these rules and principles have developed, the approaches used to secure amendments through the Parliament of the United Kingdom over the past 97 years are described in the following paragraphs. Not all the amendments are included in this review, but only those that have contributed to the development of accepted constitutional rules and principles.*

There follows a list of fourteen constitutional amendments thought to ''have contributed to the development of accepted constitutional rules and principles.'' The White Paper then goes on to state these principles, at p. 15:

> *The first general principle that emerges in the foregoing resumé is that although an enactment by the United Kingdom is necessary to amend the British North America Act, such action is taken only upon formal request from Canada. No Act of the United Kingdom Parliament affecting Canada is therefore passed unless it is requested and consented to by Canada. Conversely, every amendment requested by Canada in the past has been enacted.*
>
> *The second general principle is that the sanction of Parliament is required for a request to the British Parliament for an amendment to the British North America Act. This principle was established early in the history of Canada's constitutional amendments, and has not been violated since 1895. The procedure invariably is to seek amendments by a joint Address of the Canadian House of Commons and Senate to the Crown.*
>
> *The third general principle is that no amendment to Canada's Constitution will be made by the British Parliament merely upon the request of a Canadian province. A number of attempts to secure such amendments have been made, but none*

has been successful. The first such attempt was made as early as 1868, by a province which was at that time dissatisfied with the terms of Confederation. This was followed by other attempts in 1869, 1874 and 1887. The British Government refused in all cases to act on provincial government representations on the grounds that it should not intervene in the affairs of Canada except at the request of the federal government representing all of Canada.

The fourth general principle is that the Canadian Parliament will not request an amendment directly affecting federal-provincial relationships without prior consultation and agreement with the provinces. This principle did not emerge as early as others but since 1907, and particularly since 1930, has gained increasing recognition and acceptance. The nature and the degree of provincial participation in the amending process, however, have not lent themselves to easy definition.

The text which precedes the four general principles make it clear that it deals with conventions. It refers to the laws and conventions by which a country is governed and to constitutional rules which are not binding in any strict sense (that is in a legal sense) but which have come to be recognized and accepted in practice as part of the amendment process in Canada. The first three general principles are statements of well-known constitutional conventions governing the relationships between Canada and the United Kingdom with respect to constitutional amendments.

In our view, the fourth general principle equally and unmistakedly states and recognizes as a rule of the Canadian Constitution the convention referred to in the second question of the Manitoba and Newfoundland References as well as in question B of the Quebec Reference, namely that there is a requirement for provincial agreement to amendments which change provincial legislative powers.

This statement is not a casual utterance. It is contained in a carefully drafted document which had been circulated to all the provinces prior to its publication and been found satisfactory by all of them (*Commons Debates*, 1965, p. 1157). It was published as a White Paper, that is an official statement of government policy, under the authority of the federal Minister of Justice as member of a government responsible to Parliament neither House of which, so far as we know, has taken issue with it. This statement is a recognition by all the actors in the precedents that the requirement of provincial agreement is a constitutional rule.

In the Manitoba Reference, Freedman C.J.M. took the view that the third sentence in the fourth general principle stated in the White Paper contradicted, and therefore negated, the first sentence.

With the greatest respect, this interpretation is erroneous. The first sentence is concerned with the existence of the convention, and the third sentence, not with its existence, but with the measure of provincial agreement which is necessary with respect to this class of constitutional amendment. It seems clear that while the precedents taken alone point at unanimity, the unanimity principle cannot be said to have been accepted by all the actors in the precedents.

This distinction is illustrated by statements made by Prime Minister King in the House of Commons in 1938 and 1940 with respect to the unemployment insurance amendment.

In 1938, some provinces had not yet assented to the unemployment insurance amendment and one finds the following exchange in the Commons Debates:

Right Hon. R.B. BENNETT (Leader of the Opposition): Perhaps the Prime Minister would not object to a supplementary question: Does he conceive it necessary or desirable that all the provinces should agree before action is taken?

Mr. MACKENZIE KING: I do not think this is the moment to answer that ques-

tion. *We had better wait and see what replies we get in the first instance.*
(Commons Debates, *1938, p. 1747)*

In 1940, Mr. J.T. Thorson, not then a member of the Government, took issue with the contention that it was necessary to obtain the consent of the provinces before an application is made to amend the B.N.A. Act. Mr. Lapointe replied:

May I tell my hon. friend that neither the Prime Minister nor I have said it is necessary, but it may be desirable.
(Commons Debates, *1940, p. 1122.*)

But what the Prime Minister had said in fact was this:

We have avoided anything in the nature of coercion of any of the provinces. Moreover we have avoided the raising of a very critical constitutional question, namely, whether or not in amending the British North America Act it is absolutely necessary to secure the consent of all the provinces, or whether the consent of a certain number of provinces would of itself by sufficient. That question may come up by not in reference to unemployment insurance at some time later on.
(Commons Debates, *1940, p. 1117.*)

This statement expressed some uncertainty as to whether unanimity is a necessity, but none as to whether substantial provincial support is required.

As for Mr. Lapointe's reply, it is noncommittal and must be qualified by several other statements he made indicating the necessity of provincial consent. . . .

Most declarations made by statesmen favour the conventional requirement of provincial consent. We will quote only two such declarations.

In discussing the 1943 amendment, Mr. St. Laurent argued that the amendment did not alter the allocation of federal and provincial powers. He said:

I would readily concede to hon. members that if there were to be any suggested amendment to change the allocation of legislative or administrative jurisdiction as between the provinces, on the one hand, and the federal parliament, on the other, it could not properly be done without the consent of the organism that was set up by the constitution to have powers that would assumably be taken from that organism. . .

I submit that it would have been quite improper to take away from the provinces without their consent anything that they had by the constitution.
(Commons Debates, *1943, p. 4366)*

The statement is addressed at constitutional propriety which is the terminology ordinarily used for conventions.

In 1960, it was suggested to Prime Minister Diefenbaker that his proposed Canadian Bill of Rights be entrenched in the Constitution and made binding on the provinces as would be the Charter of Rights annexed to the proposed Resolution for a Joint Address. Here is how he dealt with this suggestion:

They say, if you want to make this effective it has to cover the provinces too. Any one advocating that must realize the fact that there is no chance of securing the consent of all the provinces. . . .

As far as constitutional amendment is concerned, it is impossible of attainment at this time.

Mr. Winch: Why?

Mr. Diefenbaker: Simply because of the fact that the consent of the provinces to any interference with property and civil rights cannot be secured. . . .

I also want to add that if at any time the provinces are prepared to give their consent to a constitutional amendment embodying a bill of rights comprising these freedoms, there will be immediate co-operation from this government. We will forthwith introduce a constitutional amendment covering not only the federal, but the provincial jurisdictions when and if there is consent to the provinces everywhere in this country.
(Common Debates, *1960, pp. 5648 and 5649)*

Prime Minister Diefenbaker was clearly of the view that the Canadian Bill of Rights could not be entrenched in the Constitution and made to apply to the provinces without the consent of all of them. We have also indicated that while the precedents point at unanimity, it does not appear that all the actors in the precedents have accepted the unanimity rule as a binding one.

In 1965, the White Paper had stated that

The nature and the degree of provincial participation in the amending process . . . have not lent themselves to easy definition.

Nothing has occurred since then which would permit us to conclude in a more precise manner.

Nor can it be said that this lack of precision is such as to prevent the principle from acquiring the constitutional status of a conventional rule. If a consensus had emerged on the measure of provincial agreement, an amending formula would quickly have been enacted and we would no longer be in the realm of conventions. To demand as much precision as if this were the case and as if the rule were a legal one is tantamount to denying that this area of the Canadian Constitution is capable of being governed by conventional rules.

Furthermore, the Government of Canada and the governments of the provinces have attempted to reach a consensus on a constitutional amending formula in the course of ten federal-provincial conferences held in 1927, 1931, 1935, 1950, 1960, 1964, 1971, 1978, 1979 and 1980. A major issue at these conferences was the quantification of provincial consent. No consensus was reached on this issue. But the discussion of this very issue for more than fifty years postulates a clear recognition by all the governments concerned of the principle that a substantial degree of provincial consent is required.

It would not be appropriate for the Court to devise in the abstract a specific formula which would indicate in positive terms what measure of provincial agreement is required for the convention to be complied with. Conventions by their nature develop in the political field and it will be for the political actors, not this Court, to determine the degree of provincial consent required.

It is sufficient for the Court to decide that at least a substantial measure of provincial consent is required and to decide further whether the situation before the Court meets with this requirement. The situation is one where Ontario and New Brunswick agree with the proposed amendments whereas the eight other provinces oppose it. By no conceivable standard could this situation be thought to pass muster. It clearly does not disclose a sufficient measure of provincial agreement. Nothing more should be said about this.

iii) A reason for the rule

The reason for the rule is the federal principle. Canada is a federal union. The preamble of the *B.N.A. Act* states that

the Provinces of Canada, Nova Scotia, and New Brunswick have expressed their Desire to be federally united . . .

The federal character of the Canadian Constitution was recognized in innumerable judicial pronouncements. We will quote only one, that of Lord Watson in *Liquidators of the Maritime Bank of New Brunswick (supra)* at pp. 441, 442:

The object of the Act was neither to weld the provinces into one, nor to subordinate provincial governments to a central authority, but to create a federal government in which they should all be represented, entrusted with the exclusive administration of affairs in which they had a common interest, each province retaining its independence and autonomy.

The federal principle cannot be reconciled with a state of affairs where the modification of provincial legislative powers could be obtained by the unilateral action of the federal authorities. It would indeed offend the federal principle that "a radical change to [the] constitution [be] taken at the request of a bare majority of the members of the Canadian House of Commons and Senate." (Report of Dominion-Provincial Conference 1931, p. 3).

This is an essential requirement of the federal principle which was clearly recognized by the Dominion-Provincial Conference of 1931. . . .

Furthermore, as was stated in the fourth general principle of the White Paper, the requirement of provincial consent did not emerge as early as other principles, but it has gained increasing recognition and acceptance since 1907 and particularly since 1930. This is clearly demonstrated by the proceedings of the Dominion-Provincial Conference of 1931.

Then followed the positive precedents of 1940, 1951 and 1964 as well as the abortive ones of 1951, 1960 and 1964, all discussed above. By 1965, the rule had become recognized as a binding constitutional one formulated in the fourth general principle of the White Paper already quoted reading in part as follows:

The fourth general principle is that the Canadian Parliament will not request an amendment directly affecting federal-provincial relationships without prior consultation and agreement with the provinces.

The purpose of this conventional rule is to protect the federal character of the Canadian Constitution and prevent the anomaly that the House of Commons and Senate could obtain by simple resolutions what they could not validly accomplish by statute.

It was contended by counsel for Canada, Ontario and New Brunswick that the proposed amendments would not offend the federal principle and that, if they became law, Canada would remain a federation. The federal principle would even be reinforced, it was said, since the provinces would as a matter of law be given an important role in the amending formula.

It is true that Canada would remain a federation if the proposed amendments became law. But it would be a different federation made different at the instance of a majority in the Houses of the federal Parliament acting alone. It is this process itself which offends the federal principle.

It was suggested by counsel of Saskatchewan that the proposed amendments were perhaps severable; that the proposed Charter of Rights offended the federal principle in that it would unilaterally alter legislative powers whereas the proposed amending formula did not offend the federal principle.

To this suggestion we cannot accede. Counsel for Canada (as well as counsel for other parties and all intervenors) took the firm position that the proposed amendment formed an unseverable package. Furthermore, and to repeat, whatever the result, the process offends the federal principle. It was to guard against this process that the constitutional convention came about.

IV CONCLUSION

We have reached the conclusion that the agreement of the provinces of Canada, no views being expressed as to its quantification, is constitutionally required for the passing of the "Proposed Resolution for a joint Address to Her Majesty respecting the Constitution of Canada" and that the passing of this Resolution without such agreement would be unconstitutional in the conventional sense.

We would, subject to these reasons, answer question 2 of the Manitoba and Newfoundland References and that part of question B in the Quebec Reference which relates to conventions as follows:

2. Is it a constitutional convention that the House of Commons and Senate of Canada will not request Her Majesty the Queen to lay before the Parliament of the United Kingdom of Great Britain and Northern Ireland a measure to amend the Constitution of Canada affecting federal-provincial relationships or the powers,

rights or privileges granted or secured by the Constitution of Canada to the provinces, their legislatures or governments without first obtaining the agreement of the provinces?
YES

B. *Does the Canadian Constitution empower . . . by . . . convention . . . the Senate and the House of Commons of Canada to cause the Canadian Constitution to be amended without the consent of the provinces and in spite of the objection of several of them, in such a manner as to affect:*

(i) *the legislative competence of the provincial legislatures in virtue of the Canadian Constitution?*
(ii) *the status or role of the provincial legislatures or governments within the Canadian Federation?*

NO

THE CHIEF JUSTICE and ESTEY and McINTYRE JJ. (*dissenting*):

These reasons are addressed solely to question 2 in the Manitoba and Newfoundland References and the conventional segment of question B in the Quebec Reference. Our views upon the other questions raised in the three References are expressed in another judgment. As will be pointed out later, no legal question is raised in the questions under consideration in these reasons and, ordinarily, the Court would not undertake to answer them for it is not the function of the Court to go beyond legal determinations. Because of the unusual nature of these References and because the issues raised in the questions now before us were argued at some length before the Court and have become the subject of the reasons of the majority, with which, with the utmost deference, we cannot agree, we feel obliged to answer the questions notwithstanding their extra-legal nature.

At the outset it should be observed that the convention referred to in the above questions, and contended for by all objecting provinces except Saskatchewan, is a constitutional convention which requires that before the two

Houses of the Canadian Parliament will request Her Majesty the Queen to lay before the Parliament of the United Kingdom a measure to amend the Constitution of Canada, affecting federal-provincial relationships, it will obtain agreement thereto from the provinces. From the wording of the questions and from the course of argument it is clear that the questions mean the consent of *all* the provinces. This then is the question which must be answered on this part of the References. An affirmative answer would involve a declaration that such a convention, requiring the consent of *all* the provinces, exists while a negative answer would, of course, deny its existence. No other answers can be open to the Court for, on a reference of this nature, the Court may answer only the questions put and may not conjure up questions of its own. . . .

. . . Where there is ambiguity, or where questions are phrased in such general terms that a precise answer is difficult or impossible to give, the Court may qualify the answers, answer in general terms, or refuse to answer: see *Reference re Waters and Water-Powers* ([1929] S.C.R. 200). No such considerations apply here. There is no ambiguity in the questions before the Court. Question 2 in the Manitoba and Newfoundland References refers without qualification to the "agreement of the provinces." Question B in the Quebec Reference uses the words "the consent of the provinces," also without qualification. The expressions "of the provinces" or "of the provinces of Canada" in this context and in general usage mean in plain English *all* of the provinces of Canada, and our consideration of the questions must be upon this basis. . . .

What are conventions and, particularly, what are constitutional conventions? While our answers to question 2 in the Manitoba and Newfoundland References and the conventional segment of question B in the Quebec Reference will differ from those of the majority of the Court, we are in agreement with much of what has been said as to the general nature of constitutional conventions in the reasons for judgment by the majority, which we have had the advantage of reading. We are in agreement, as well, with the words of Freedman C.J.M. in his reasons for judgment in the Manitoba Reference, referred to with approval and quoted by the majority. We cannot, however, agree with any suggestion that the non-observance of a convention can properly be termed unconstitutional in any strict or legal sense, or that its observance could be, in any sense, a constitutional requirement within the meaning of question 3 of the Manitoba and Newfoundland References. In a federal state where the essential feature of the Constitution must be the distribution of powers between the two levels of government, each supreme in its own legislative sphere, constitutionality and legality must be synonymous, and conventional rules will be accorded less significance than they may have in a unitary state such as the United Kingdom. . . . Constitutionalism in a unitary state and practices in the national and regional political units of a federal state must be differentiated from constitutional law in a federal state. Such law cannot be ascribed to informal or customary origins, but must be found in a formal document which is the source of authority, legal authority, through which the central and regional units function and exercise their powers.

The Constitution of Canada, as has been pointed out by the majority, is only in part written, i.e., contained in statutes which have the force of law and which include, in addition to the British North America Act (hereinafter called the BNA Act), the various other enactments which are listed in the reasons of the majority. Another, and indeed highly important, part of the Constitution has taken the form of custom and usage adopting in large part the practices of the Parliament of the United Kingdom and adapting them to the federal nature of this country. These have evolved with time to form with the statutes referred to above and certain rules of

the common law a constitution for Canada. This Constitution depends then on statutes and common law rules which declare the law and have the force of law, and upon customs, usages and conventions developed in political science which, while not having the force of law in the sense that there is a legal enforcement process or sanction available for their breach, form a vital part of the Constitution without which it would be incomplete and unable to serve its purpose.

As has been pointed out by the majority, a fundamental difference between the legal, that is the statutory and common law rules of the Constitution, and the conventional rules is that, while a breach of the legal rules, whether of statutory or common law nature, has a legal consequence in that it will be restrained by the courts, no such sanction exists for breach or non-observance of the conventional rules. The observance of constitutional conventions depends upon the acceptance of the obligation of conformance by the actors deemed to be found thereby. When this consideration is insufficient to compel observance no court may enforce the convention by legal action. The sanction for non-observance of a convention is political in that disregard of a convention may lead to political defeat, to loss of office, or to other political consequences, but it will not engage the attention of the courts which are limited to matters of law alone. Courts, however, may recognize the existence of conventions and that is what is asked of us in answering the questions. The answer, whether affirmative or negative however, can have no legal effect, and acts performed or done in conformance with the law, even though in direct contradiction of well-established conventions, will not be enjoined or set aside by the courts. . . .

There are different kinds of conventions and usages, but we are concerned here with what may be termed "constitutional" conventions or rules of the Constitution. They were described by Professor

Dicey in the tenth edition of his *Law of the Constitution*, at pp. 23-24, in the following passage:

> The one set of rules are in the strictest sense "laws", since they are rules which (whether written or unwritten, whether enacted by statute or derived from the mass of custom, tradition, or judge-made maxims known as the common law) are enforced by the courts; these rules constitute "constitutional law" in the proper sense of that term, and may for the sake of distinction be called collectively "the law of the constitution".
>
> The other set of rules consist of conventions, understandings, habits, or practices which, though they may regulate the conduct of the several members of the sovereign power, of the Ministry, or of other officials, are not in reality laws at all since they are not enforced by the courts. This portion of constitutional law may, for the sake of distinction, be termed the "conventions of the constitution", or constitutional morality.

Later, at page 27, after discussing examples from English practice, he said:

> . . . Under the English constitution they have one point in common: they are none of them "laws" in the true sense of that word, for if any or all of them were broken, no court would take notice of their violation. . . .

This view has been adopted by Canadian writers, e.g., Professor Peter W. Hogg in *Constitutional Law of Canada* dealt with the matter in these terms, at page 7:

> Conventions are rules of the constitution which are not enforced by the law courts. Because they are not enforced by the law courts they are best regarded as non-legal rules, but because they do in fact regulate the working of the constitution they are an important concern of the constitutional lawyer. What conventions do is to prescribe the way in which legal powers shall be exercised. Some conventions have the effect of transferring effective power from the legal holder to another official or institution. Other conventions limit an apparently broad legal power, or even prescribe that a legal power shall not be exercised at all.

At page 8, he said:

> If a convention is disobeyed by an official, then it is common, especially in the United Kingdom, to describe the official's act or omission as "unconstitutional". But this use of the term unconstitutional must be carefully distinguished from the case where a legal rule of the constitution has been disobeyed. Where unconstitutionality springs from a breach of law, the purported act is normally a nullity and there is a remedy available in the courts. But where "unconstitutionality" springs merely from a breach of convention, no breach of the law has occurred and no legal remedy will be available. If a court did give a remedy for a breach of convention, for example, by declaring invalid a statute enacted for Canada by the United Kingdom Parliament without Canada's request or consent, or by ordering an unwilling Governor General to give his assent to a bill enacted by both houses of Parliament, then we would have to change our language and describe the rule which used to be thought of as a convention as a rule of the common law. In other words a judicial decision could have the effect of transforming a conventional rule into a legal rule. A convention may also be transformed into law by being enacted as a statute.

It will be noted that Professor Hogg, in the quotation immediately above, has expressed the view that a judicial decision could have the effect of transforming a conventional rule into a legal rule, as could the enactment of a convention in statutory form. There can be no doubt that a statute, by enacting the terms of a convention, could create positive law, but it is our view that it is not for the courts to raise a convention to the status of a legal principle. As pointed out above, courts may recognize the existence of conventions in their proper sphere. That is all that may be properly sought from the Court in answering question 2 in the Manitoba and Newfoundland References and the conventional part of question B in the Quebec Reference: an answer by the Court recognizing the existence of the convention or denying its existence. For the Court to postulate some other convention requiring less than unanimous provincial consent to constitutional amendments would be to go beyond the terms of the References and in so doing to answer a question not posed in the References. It would amount, in effect, to an attempt by judicial pronouncement to create an amending formula for the Canadian Constitution which, in addition to being beyond the Court's power to declare, not being raised in a question posed in any of the References before the Court, would be incomplete for failure to specify the degree or percentage of provincial consent required. Furthermore, all the provinces, with the exception of Saskatchewan, oppose such a step. Those favouring the position of the federal Parliament, Ontario and New Brunswick do so because they say no convention exists and those attacking the federal position, Quebec, Nova Scotia, Prince Edward Island, Manitoba, Alberta and British Columbia, do so because they say provincial participation is already fixed by what may be called "the rule of unanimity."

Conventions, while frequently unwritten, may nonetheless be reduced to writing. They may be reached by specific agreement between the parties to be bound, or they may more commonly arise from practice and usage. It is true, as well, that conventions can become law but this, in our view, would require some formal legal step such as enactment in statutory form. The Statute of Westminster of 1931 affords an example of the enactment of conventions concerning constitutional relations between the United Kingdom and the various Dominions. However a convention may arise or be created, the essential condition for its recognition must be that the parties concerned regard it as binding upon them. While a convention, by its very nature,

will often lack the precision and clearness of expression of a law, it must be recognized, known and understood with sufficient clarity that conformance is possible and a breach of conformance immediately discernible. It must play as well a necessary constitutional role.

There are many such conventions of the Canadian Constitution and while at different periods they may have taken different forms, and while change and development have been observable and are, no doubt, continuing processes, they have been recognized nonetheless as rules or conventions of the Canadian Constitution, known and observed at any given time in Canadian affairs. As the reasons of the majority point out, there are many examples. The general rule that the Governor General will act only according to the advice of the Prime Minister is purely conventional and is not to be found in any legal enactment. In the same category is the rule that after a general election the Governor General will call upon the leader of the party with the greater number of seats to form a government. The rule of responsible government that a government losing the confidence of the House of Commons must itself resign, or obtain a dissolution, the general principles of majority rule and responsible government underlying the daily workings of the institutions of the executive and legislative branches of each level of government, and a variety of other such conventional arrangements, serve as further illustrations. These rules have an historical origin and bind, and have bound, the actors in constitutional matters in Canada for generations. No one can doubt their operative force or the reality of their existence as an effective part of the Canadian Constitution. They are, nonetheless, conventional and, therefore, distinct from purely legal rules. . . .

These then are recognized conventions, they are definite, understandable and understood. They have the unquestioned acceptance not only of the actors in political affairs but of the public at large. Can it be said that any convention having such clear definition and acceptance concerning provincial participation in the amendment of the Canadian Constitution has developed? It is in the light of this comparison that the existence of any supposed constitutional convention must be considered. It is abundantly clear, in our view, that the answer must be No. The degree of provincial participation in constitutional amendments has been a subject of lasting controversy in Canadian political life for generations. It cannot be asserted, in our opinion, that any view on this subject has become so clear and so broadly accepted as to constitute a constitutional convention. It should be observed that there is a fundamental difference between the convention in the Dicey concept and the convention for which some of the provinces here contend. The Dicey convention relates to the functioning of individuals and institutions within a parliamentary democracy in unitary form. It does not qualify or limit the authority or sovereignty of Parliament or the Crown. The convention sought to be advanced here would truncate the functioning of the executive and legislative branches at the federal level. This would impose a limitation on the sovereign body itself within the Constitution. Surely such a convention would require for its recognition, even in the non-legal, political sphere, the clearest signal from the plenary unit intended to be bound, and not simply a plea from the majority of the beneficiaries of such a convention, the provincial plenary units.

An examination of the Canadian experience since Confederation will, bearing in mind the considerations above described, serve to support our conclusion on this question. It may be observed here that it was not suggested in argument before this Court that there was any procedure for amendment now available other than by the addresses of both Houses of Parliament to Her Majesty the Queen. It was argued, however, that this was a procedural step only and that before it could be undertaken by Parliament the consent of the provinces would be required. It is with the frequency with which provincial consents were obtained or omitted, with the circumstances under which consent was or was not sought, with the nature of the amendments involved, and with provincial attitudes towards them that we must concern ourselves. As has been pointed out in other judgments on these References, here and in the other courts, there have been since Confederation some twenty-two amendments to the BNA Act. . . .

In examining these amendments it must be borne in mind that all do not possess the same relevance or force for the purpose of this inquiry. Question 2 of the Manitoba and Newfoundland References and the conventional segment of question B in the Quebec Reference raise the issue of the propriety of non-consensual amendments which affect federal-provincial relationships and the powers, rights and privileges of the provinces. The questions do not limit consideration to those amendments which affected the distribution of legislative powers between the federal Parliament and the provincial legislatures. Since the distribution of powers is the very essence of a federal system, amendments affecting such distribution will be of especial concern to the provinces. Precedents found in such amendments will be entitled to serious consideration. It does not follow, however, that other amendments which affected federal-provincial relationships without altering the distribution of powers should be disregarded in this inquiry. Consideration must be given in according weight to the various amendments, to the reaction they provoked from the provinces. This is surely the real test of relevance in this discussion. On many occasions provinces considered that amendments not affecting the distribution of legislative power were sufficiently undesirable to call for strenuous opposition. The test of whether the convention exists, or has existed, is to be found by examining the results of such opposition. . . .

Prior to the amendment effected by the

BNA Act of 1930 there were at least three amendments, those of 1886, 1907 and 1915, which substantially affected the provinces and which were procured without the consent of all the provinces. The amendment of 1886 gave power to Parliament to provide for parliamentary representation in the Senate and House of Commons for territories not forming part of any province, and therefore altered the provincial balance of representation. That of 1907 changed the basis of federal subsidies payable to the provinces and thus directly affected the provincial interests. That of 1915 redefined territorial divisions for senatorial representation, and therefore had a potential for altering the provincial balance. Those of 1886 and 1915 were passed without provincial consultation or consent, and that of 1907 had the consent of all provinces save British Columbia, which actively opposed its passage both in Canada and in the United Kingdom. The amendment was passed with minor changes. These precedents, it may be said, should by themselves have only a modest influence in the consideration of the question before the Court. It is clear, however, that no support whatever for the convention may be found on an examination of the amendments made up to 1930. None had full provincial approval.

The BNA Act of 1930 provided for the transfer of natural resources within the provincial territories to the provinces of Manitoba, Saskatchewan and Alberta. It also provided for the re-conveyance of certain railway lands to British Columbia. In effecting this amendment the consent of the provinces directly concerned, *i.e.* the four western provinces only, was obtained, although the arrangement had received the general approval of the other provinces as expressed at a conference in 1927. This is a precedent of modest weight, but it is worthy of note that despite that fact that the interests of all non-involved provinces were affected by the alienation of the assets formerly under federal control, it was not considered necessary to procure any formal consent

from them. It is of more than passing interest to note that in the amending procedure provided for in the 1930 British North America Act Amendment there is no requirement for consent or participation by any of the other five provinces (as they then were) although their indirect interest in federal resources might be affected.

The amendments of 1943, 1946, 1949, 1949(2), 1950 and 1960 were not considered of great significance on this issue by the parties and little comment was made upon them but all, save that of 1960, were achieved without full provincial consent. This, subject to what is later said concerning the 1943 amendment, leaves for consideration the Statute of Westminster of 1931 and the amendments of 1940, 1951 and 1964. The Statute of Westminster and the amendments of 1940, 1951 and 1964 affected the provinces directly. Canadian participation in the settlement of the provisions of the Statute and the said amendments had the consent of all provinces. These examples were heavily relied upon by the objecting provinces to support an affirmative answer to question 2 of the Manitoba and Newfoundland References and the negative answer to the conventional part of question B of the Quebec Reference. As to the Statute of Westminster, it freed federal and provincial legislation from the restrictions imposed by the Colonial Laws Validity Act of 1865 and gave statutory recognition to certain conventions which had grown up with the development of self-government in the former colonies. The pre-existing division of legislative power between federal and provincial legislatures in Canada was not, however, in any way affected and it did not recognize or give statutory form to any convention requiring provincial consent to the amendment of the BNA Act. . . .

The amendment of 1940 transferring legislative power over unemployment insurance to the federal Parliament also had full provincial consent. It must be observed here, however, that when questioned in the House of Commons on this point Mr. Mackenzie King, then Prime Minister, while acknowledging that consents had been obtained, specifically stated that this course had been followed to avoid any constitutional issue on this point and he disclaimed any necessity for such consent. . . . It is clear, we suggest, that he procured the consent of the provinces on that occasion in order to avoid raising any question on the subject and as a measure of good politics rather than as a constitutional requirement. It is surely obvious that the federal government would always prefer to have, as a political matter, provincial approval, but the position of the federal authorities as expressed in the foregoing parliamentary exchange does not support the proposition that they considered that they were bound by any convention.

We are aware, of course, that other declarations have been made upon this subject by persons of high political rank as well as academics of high standing. Many such pronouncements were cited in argument before us. We do not propose to deal with them in detail. It is sufficient to say that many favour the existence of the convention; many deny its existence. . . . The continuation of controversy on the subject among political and academic figures only adds additional weight to the contention that no convention of provincial consent has achieved constitutional recognition to this day.

The amendment of 1951 had full approval from the provinces, as did that of 1964. The 1951 amendment gave power relating to old age pensions to the federal Parliament and the 1964 amendment was merely a supplementary tidying-up of the original 1951 provisions. In our view, they dealt with the same matter and can stand as only one precedent favouring the existence of the convention.

After examining the amendments made since Confederation, and after observing that out of the twenty-two amendments listed above only in the case of four was unanimous provincial consent sought or obtained and, even after according special weight to those amendments relied on by the provinces, we cannot agree that history justifies a conclusion that the convention contended for by the provinces has emerged.

Great weight was put upon the 1940 Unemployment Insurance Act amendment as a precedent favouring the existence of the convention. Despite the obtaining of provincial consent for the 1940 amendment, the federal government proceeded three years later to the completion of the amendment of 1943 without provincial consent and in the face of the strong protests of the Province of Quebec. This amendment did not touch provincial powers. It dealt with the postponement of redistribution of seats in the House of Commons. Nevertheless, it was deemed of sufficient importance by Quebec because its interest was particularly affected to arouse active opposition which was overborne by the federal government in procuring the amendment. . . .

In summary, we observe that in the 114 years since Confederation Canada has grown from a group of four somewhat hesitant colonies into a modern, independent state, vastly increased in size, power and wealth, and having a social and governmental structure unimagined in 1867. It cannot be denied that vast change has occurred in dominion-provincial relations over that period. Many factors have influenced this process and the amendments to the BNA Act—all the amendments— have played a significant part and all must receive consideration in resolving this question. Only in four cases has full provincial consent been obtained and in many cases the federal government has proceeded with amendments in the face of active provincial opposition. In our view, it is unrealistic in the extreme to say that the convention has emerged.

As a further support for the convention argument, the White Paper referred to above was cited and relied upon. . . . It is the fourth principle which is stressed by the objecting provinces. In our view, they have attributed too much significance to this statement of the four principles. The author of the White Paper was at pains to say, at page 11:

Certain rules and principles relating to amending procedures have nevertheless developed over the years. They have emerged from the practices and procedures employed in securing various amendments to the British North America Act since 1867. Though not constitutionally binding in any strict sense, *they have come to be recognized and accepted in practice as part of the amendment process in Canada (emphasis added).*

It would appear that he was satisfied that the principles had become so well established that they had acquired strict constitutional force. Furthermore, we are unable to accord to the fourth principle the significance given to it by the objecting provinces. The first sentence pronounces strongly in favour of the existence of the convention. If it stopped there, subject to what the author had said earlier, it would constitute a statement of great weight. However, the third sentence contradicts the first and, in fact, cancels it out. By suggesting the possibility of a requirement of partial provincial consent it answers question 2 in the Manitoba and Newfoundland References and the conventional segment of question B in the Quebec Reference against the provinces. "Increasing recognition," that is 'partial' but not 'complete' recognition, is all that is claimed by the author of the White Paper. A convention requires universal recognition by the actors in a scheme and this is certainly so where, as here, acceptance of a convention involves the surrender of a power by a sovereign body said to be a party to the convention. Furthermore, in recognizing uncertainty in specifying the degree of provincial participation, it denies the existence of any convention including that suggested by the Province of Saskatchewan. If there is difficulty in defining the degree of provincial participation, which there surely is, it cannot be said that any convention on the subject has been settled and recognized as

a constitutional condition for the making of an amendment. It is the very difficulty of fixing the degree of provincial participation which, while it remains unresolved, prevents any formation or recognition of any convention. It robs any supposed convention of that degree of definition which is necessary to allow for its operation. . .

It was also argued that Canada was formed as a federal union and that the existence of a legal power of the central government to unilaterally change the Constitution was inimical to the concept of federalism. The convention then, it was argued, arose out of the necessity to restrain such unilateral conduct and preserve the federal nature of Canada. In this connection, it must be acknowledged at once that, in a federal union, the powers and rights of each of the two levels of government must be protected from the assault of the other. The whole history of constitutional law and constitutional litigation in Canada since Confederation has been concerned with this vital question. We are asked to say whether the need for the preservation of the principles of Canadian federalism dictates the necessity for a convention, requiring consent from the provinces as a condition of the exercise by the federal government of its legal powers, to procure amendment to the Canadian Constitution. If the convention requires only partial consent, as is contended by Saskatchewan, it is difficult to see how the federal concept is thereby protected for, while those provinces favouring amendment would be pleased, those refusing consent could claim coercion. If unanimous consent is required (as contended by the other objecting provinces), while it may be said that in general terms the concept of federalism would be protected it would only be by overlooking the special nature of Canadian federalism that this protection would be achieved. The BNA Act has not created a perfect or ideal federal state. Its provisions have accorded a measure of paramountcy to the federal Parliament. Certainly this has been done in a more marked degree in Canada than in many other federal states. For example, one need only look to the power of reservation and disallowance of provincial enactments; the power to declare works in a province to be for the benefit of all Canada and to place them under federal regulatory control; the wide powers to legislate generally for the peace, order and good government of Canada as a whole; the power to enact the criminal law of the entire country; the power to create and admit provinces out of existing territories and, as well, the paramountcy accorded federal legislation. It is this special nature of Canadian federalism which deprives the federalism argument described above of its force. This is particularly true when it involves the final settlement of Canadian constitutional affairs with an external, government, the federal authority being the sole conduit for communication between Canada and the Sovereign and Canada alone having the power to deal in external matters. We therefore reject the argument that the preservation of the principles of Canadian federalism requires the recognition of the convention asserted before us.

While it may not be necessary to do so in dealing with question 2, we feel obliged to make a further comment related to the federalism argument. It was argued that the federal authorities were assuming a power to act without restraint in disregard of provincial wishes which could go so far as to convert Canada into a unitary state by means of a majority vote in the Houses of Parliament. A few words will suffice to lay that argument at rest. What is before the Court is the task of answering the questions posed in three references. As has been pointed out, the Court can do no more than that. The questions all deal with the constitutional validity of precise proposals for constitutional amendment and they form the complete subject matter of the Court's inquiry and our comments must be made with reference to them. It is not for the Court to express views on the wisdom or lack of wisdom of these proposals. We are concerned solely with their constitutionality. In view of the fact that the unitary argument has been raised, however, it should be noted, in our view, that the federal constitutional proposals, which preserve a federal state without disturbing the distribution or balance of power, would create an amending formula which would enshrine provincial rights on the question of amendments on a secure, legal and constitutional footing, and would extinguish, as well, any presently existing power on the part of the federal Parliament to act unilaterally in constitutional matters. In so doing, it may be said that the Parliamentary resolution here under examination does not, save for the enactment of the Charter of Rights, which circumscribes the legislative powers of both the federal and provincial Legislatures, truly amend the Canadian Constitution. Its effect is to complete the formation of an incomplete constitution by supplying its present deficiency, i.e., an amending formula, which will enable the Constitution to be amended in Canada as befits a sovereign state. We are not here faced with an action which in any way has the effect of transforming this federal union into a unitary state. The *in terrorem* argument raising the spectre of a unitary state has no validity.

For the above reasons we answer the questions posed in the three References as follows:

Manitoba and Newfoundland References:
Question 2: No

Quebec Reference
Question B (i): Yes
              (ii): Yes

63. Re: Objection to a Resolution to Amend the Constitution (Quebec *Veto Reference*), 1982

~ On November 25, 1981, just three weeks after Prime Minister Trudeau and the premiers of all the provinces except Quebec reached an accord on the terms of patriation, the Quebec National Assembly passed a resolution objecting to making these changes in Canada's Constitution without Quebec's consent. At that time the government of Quebec also referred to Quebec's Court of Appeal the question of whether proceeding with these amendments without Quebec's consent was "unconstitutional in the conventional sense". On April 7, 1982, the Quebec Court of Appeal brought down its decision, holding unanimously that as a matter of constitutional convention Quebec's consent was not required. On April 13, 1982, just four days before the changes to which Quebec objected were proclaimed in force in Canada, this decision was appealed to the Supreme Court of Canada. On December 6, 1982, the Supreme Court of Canada rendered its decision upholding the verdict of the Quebec Court of Appeal.

In dealing with this reference case, the Supreme Court was in a peculiar position. Since the question at issue was entirely one of convention, the Court's answer could have no legal consequences. But it would have been a political bombshell for the Supreme Court to find that Canada's so-called "new constitution" had been obtained in a manner that violates a convention of the Canadian constitution. Such a ruling would certainly detract from the "new Constitution's" legitimacy and bolster the political fortunes of René Lévesque's Parti Québecois government. To nobody's great surprise, the Supreme Court did not render such a decision.

It was easy for the Court to reject Quebec's argument that under the unpatriated constitution a convention had developed requiring the unanimous consent of the provinces for requests to amend the constitution in matters effecting the powers or status of the provinces. A year earlier the entire Court had rejected the claim that there existed a conventional rule of unanimity and the majority had found that only "a substantial degree of provincial consent" was required. The Court composed of the same nine judges who had participated in the *Patriation Reference* simply invoked that ruling here. Quebec, however, had a second argument that virtually contradicted the first: namely that Quebec was not a province like the others but as the home province of one of the country's two founding peoples it forms a "distinct society within the Canadian federation" and under the principle of "Canadian duality" it had a power of veto over constitutional changes affecting its position in Confederation.

The Court through an anonymous and unanimous decision managed to reject this second argument without addressing the principle on which it rests. It did so by concentrating on one of Sir Ivor Jennings' three tests for the existence of a constitutional convention: recognition of the convention by the political actors involved in the precedents. The Court took the view that such recognition must be explicit and rejected Quebec's argument because it had not been presented with any evidence that politicians outside Quebec had explicitly acknowledged such a convention. This may not have been an entirely convincing performance but was perhaps the best the Court could do under the circumstances.[1]

The subsequent course of constitutional politics demonstrated widespread recognition among leading politicians throughout Canada of the need to secure Quebec's support for the changes made to the Constitution in 1982. With the Mulroney Conservatives replacing the Trudeau Liberals in Ottawa in 1984 and the Bourassa Liberals taking over from the Parti Québecois in Quebec City a year later, the prospects improved of working out terms on which Quebec could accept the 1982 changes. On April 30, 1987 at a federal government retreat on Meech Lake, Prime Minister Mulroney and the premiers of all ten provinces reached an agreement in principle on a package of proposed constitutional amendments. The Meech Lake Accord was based on proposals brought forward by Premier Bourassa as Quebec's minimal conditions for accepting the Constitution Act, 1982.[2] The first and, as it has turned out, the most controversial of these proposals is constitutional recognition of Quebec as a "distinct society"—the very principle on which Quebec based its challenge to the earlier constitutional process.

Under the new amending system which came into effect in 1982, constitutional changes do not flow automatically from agreement at the executive level. Formal approval of the federal and provincial legislatures must be obtained. For the Meech Lake package all of the provincial legislatures and the federal House of Commons must approve the amendments. At the time of writing the necessary approvals had been obtained from all except Manitoba and New Brunswick. If the approval of these legislatures is not obtained by June 1990, the Meech Lake proposals will die. Thus, in the end, the question of whether Quebec's approval of the 1982 constitutional changes was and is necessary will be decided not by the Supreme Court but in the arena of constitutional politics. ~

---

[1] For a critical appraisal of the Court's argument see Marc E. Gold, "The Mask of Objectivity: Politics and Rhetoric in the Supreme Court of Canada," (1985) 7 *Supreme Court Review*, 455.

[2] For an account and analysis of the accord, see Peter W. Hogg, *Meech Lake Constitutional Accord Annotated* (Toronto, 1988). The Accord is reproduced below as Appendix 3.

RE: OBJECTION TO A RESOLUTION TO AMEND THE CONSTITUTION
(QUEBEC VETO REFERENCE)
In the Supreme Court of Canada. (1982) 2 S.C.R. 793.

THE COURT

I—The facts

This is an appeal from the opinion pronounced on April 7, 1982, by the Quebec
Court of Appeal on a question referred to
it by the Government of Quebec regarding
the Resolution to amend the
Constitution. . . .

The reference is the second one on this
subject. The first reference also gave rise
to an appeal to this Court in which judgment was delivered on September 28,
1981 at the same time as in two other
appeals arising from a reference by the
Government of Manitoba and a reference
by the Government of Newfoundland: *Re:
Resolution to amend the Constitution*,
[1981] 1 S.C.R. 753, hereinafter referred
to as the *First Reference*.

Following the judgment in the *First
Reference*, the Government of Canada
and the governments of the ten provinces
held a Constitutional Conference, on
November 2 to 5, 1981, to seek agreement on the patriation of the Constitution
together with a charter of rights and an
amending formula. On November 5, 1981
Canada and nine of the ten provinces
signed an agreement to this effect.
Quebec was the dissenting province. . . .

On November 18, 1981 the Minister of
Justice of Canada laid before the House of
Commons a resolution which contained a
joint address of the Senate and the House
of Commons to be presented to Her Majesty the Queen in right of the United
Kingdom. While in substance the joint
address reflected the agreement of
November 5, 1981 it was similar in form
to the one quoted in the *First Reference*, at
p. 766. It included a draft United Kingdom statute the short title of which was
the *Canada Act* which, in turn, had
appended to it another draft statute
entitled the *Constitution Act, 1981*, later
designated as the *Constitution Act, 1982*.
The latter statute provided for the

entrenchment of a *Canadian Charter of
Rights and Freedoms* and it contained the
new procedure for amending the Constitution of Canada. The *Constitution Act,
1982* also contained a range of other
provisions which it is unnecessary to
enumerate. . . .

On November 25, 1981 the Government of Quebec expressed its formal
opposition to the proposed Resolution in
Decree No. 3214-81:

[TRANSLATION]

DECREE

GOVERNMENT OF QUEBEC

CONCERNING the objection by
Quebec to the proposed patriation
and amendment of the Constitution
of Canada

· · ·

WHEREAS on November 18, 1981 the
federal government tabled in the House of
Commons a motion regarding the patriation and amendment of the Constitution of
Canada;

WHEREAS if implemented, this
motion would have the effect of substantially reducing the powers and rights of
Quebec and of its National Assembly
without its consent;

WHEREAS it has always been recognized that no change of this kind could be
made without the consent of Quebec.

BE IT RESOLVED, on the motion of
the Premier:

THAT Quebec formally vetoes the
Resolution tabled in the House of Commons on November 18, 1981 by the
federal Minister of Justice.

THAT this objection be officially communicated to the federal government and
the governments of the other provinces.

AUTHENTIC COPY
DEPUTY CLERK OF THE
EXECUTIVE COUNCIL
Jean-Pierre Vaillancourt

On the same date, the Government of Quebec ordered the present reference in Decree No. 3215-81. . . .

The joint address was adopted by the House of Commons on Decmeber 2, 1981 and by the Senate on December 8, 1981. It included further amendments agreed upon by Canada and all the provinces except Quebec.

On December 8, 1981 the Governor General of Canada received the text of the joint address and, pursuant to the advice of Her Majesty's Privy Council for Canada, transmitted it to Her Majesty on December 9, 1981.

On the same date, the Government of Quebec re-ordered the present reference in Decree No. 3367-81:

[TRANSLATION] WHEREAS the Senate and House of Commons of Canada adopted a Resolution regarding the Constitution of Canada;

WHEREAS this Resolution requests the introduction in the Parliament of the United Kingdom of a bill entitled the Canada Act which, if adopted by the Parliament of the United Kingdom, will most notably have the effect of enacting for Canada the Constitution Act, 1981;

WHEREAS the proposed legislation has the effect of making significant changes in the status and role of Quebec within the Canadian federal system;

WHEREAS Quebec forms a distinct society within the Canadian federation;

WHEREAS the Supreme Court of Canada stated on September 28, 1981 that the consent of the provinces is constitutionally necessary for the adoption of this proposal;

WHEREAS Quebec has not agreed and has objected to the proposed changes;

WHEREAS no change of a similar significance to that proposed in this Resolution has to date been made without the consent and over the objection of Quebec;

WHEREAS it is expedient to submit to the Court of Appeal for hearing and consideration, pursuant to the Court of Appeal Reference Act the question herein below set out.

ACCORDINGLY, it is ordered, upon the proposal of the Minister of Justice, that the following question be submitted to the Court of Appeal for hearing and consideration:

Is the consent of the Province of Quebec constitutionally required, by convention, for the adoption by the Senate and the House of Commons of Canada of a resolution the purpose of which is to cause the Canadian Constitution to be amended in such a manner as to affect:

  i) the legislative competence of the Legislature of the Province of Quebec in virtue of the Canadian Constitution;

  ii) the status or role of the Legislature or Government of the Province of Quebec within the Canadian federation;

and, does the objection of the Province of Quebec render the adoption of such resolution unconstitutional in the conventional sense?

On December 22, 1981 the Government of the United Kingdom introduced in the Parliament of Westminster a bill known as "A Bill to Give Effect to a Request of the Senate and House of Commons of Canada" which was to become the *Canada Act 1982.*

The Quebec Court of Appeal heard counsel in argument on the reference on March 15, 16 and 17, 1982.

The bill introduced at Westminster was passed on March 25, 1982 and received royal assent on March 29, 1982. The *Canada Act 1982* came into force on this date.

On April 7, 1982 the Quebec Court of Appeal rendered its unanimous opinion answering in the negative the question referred to it.

On April 13, 1982 the Attorney General of Quebec appealed to this Court and on April 15, 1982 at the request of the appellant, Lamer J. stated a constitutional question pursuant to Rule 17 of this Court. The terms of this question are identical to those of the question referred to the Quebec Court of Appeal.

On April 17, 1982 the Constitution Act, 1982 was proclaimed in force by the Queen under the Great Seal of Canada and has been in force since that date.

II—The opinion of the Court of Appeal

The unanimous opinion of the Quebec Court of Appeal, answering the question in the negative, is a collective one. It has been signed as a multiple-author opinion by the five judges who participated in the reference, Crête, C.J.Q., and Montgomery, Turgeon, Monet and Jacques JJ.A.

The Court of Appeal first observed that at the time of the hearing, on March 15, 16 and 17, 1982 the process of constitutional amendment had not yet been completed. Although it had been conceded by counsel for the Attorney General for Quebec that an affirmative answer to the question could have politicial consequences but no legal ones, the Court of Appeal took the view that, given the broad terms of the Court of Appeal Reference Act, R.S.Q. 1977, c. R-23, it should answer a question which had to do with the "legitimacy" if not the "legality" of the patriation process.

The Court of Appeal was asked by the Attorney General of Quebec to answer the question in the affirmative on the basis of two alternative submissions. According to the first submission, there was a convention requiring the unanimous consent of the ten provinces to any constitutional amendment of the type in issue. According to the second submission, because of the principle of duality, Quebec had by convention a power of veto over any constitutional amendment affecting the legislative competence of the Province or the status or role of its legislature or government within the Canadian federation.

The Court of Appeal rejected the first submission as it found that this Court had already ruled it out in the *First Reference*. It rejected the second submission on the following grounds: at law, all the provinces are fundamentally equal and the Attorney General of Quebec had failed to establish that either the Government of Canada or the other provinces had conventionally recognized in Quebec any special power of veto over constitutional amendment not possessed by the other provinces. . . .

III—The position of the parties

Before coming to the submissions made by the parties, it should be said at the outset that the Attorney General of Canada conceded that the Canadian Charter of Rights and Freedoms contained in the Constitution Act, 1982 affects the legislative competence of all the provinces including Quebec.

To the question whether the status or role of the Legislature or Government of the Province of Quebec within the Canadian federation is affected by the Constitution Act, 1982 the factum of the Attorney General of Canada makes the following answer:

As for the role and status of Quebec within the Canadian federation, this Act provides Quebec a constitutionally guaranteed right to participate in the amendment of the constitution and to opt out of amendments that derogate from its legislative powers, its proprietary rights or any other rights or privileges of its legislature or government (section 38(2)) under reserve of its constitutionally guaranteed right to financial compensation when the amendment involves a transfer of provincial legislative competence to Parliament in relation to education or other cultural matters (section 40).

This answer is a qualified admission, but an admission nonetheless, that the role and status of Quebec within the Canadian federation are modified by the procedure for amending the Constitution. . . .

The position of the appellant was that the appeal should be allowed and the constitutional question answered in the affirmative on the basis of the same two submissions which he had made to the Court of Appeal, the first relating to a conventional rule of unanimity and the second to a conventional power of veto said to have been held by Quebec. (Actually, the submission relating to unanimity was made in the second place, but it will be dealt with first, as was done in the Court of Appeal).

While both submissions seek the same answer to the constitutional question, they are alternative ones, as they have to be, for not only are they quite distinct from each other, they actually contradict one another: the rule of unanimity is predicated on the fundamental equality of all the provinces as it would give a power of veto to each of them whereas an exclusive power of veto for Quebec negates the rule of unanimity as well as the principle of fundamental equality. Also, and as will be seen below, the reason which is said to anchor the conventional rule is a different one in each submission. . . .

At page 888 of the *First Reference*, the majority opinion adopted the following passage of Sir W. Ivor Jennings, *The Law and the Constitution* (5th ed., 1959), at p. 136:

We have to ask ourselves three questions: first, what are the precedents; secondly, did the actors in the precedents believe that they were bound by a rule; and thirdly, is there a reason for the rule? A single precedent with a good reason may be enough to establish the rule. A whole string of precedents without such a reason will be of no avail, unless it is perfectly certain that the persons concerned regarded them as bound by it.

The main purpose of constitutional conventions is to ensure that the legal framework of the constitution will be operated in accordance with generally accepted principles. It should be borne in mind however that conventional rules, although quite distinct from legal ones, are nevertheless to be distinguished from rules of morality, rules of expediency and subjective rules. Like legal rules, they are positive rules the existence of which has to be ascertained by reference to objective standards. In being asked to answer the question whether the convention did or did not exist, we are called upon to say

whether or not the objective requirements for establishing a convention had been met. But we are in no way called upon to say whether it was desirable that the convention should or should not exist and no view is expressed on the matter.

Subject to an important qualification which will be dealt with in due course, appellant accepted the above stated requirements for establishing conventions and made his two submissions within the framework defined by this Court in the *First Reference*.

With respect to the precedents, positive and negative, the appellant invoked for the purposes of his two submissions the same precedents as had been relied upon by the majority opinion in the *First Reference*, at pp. 891 to 894.

The positive precedents are the constitutional amendments leading to the Constitution Act, 1930, the Statute of Westminster, 1931, the Constitution Act, 1940, the British North America Act, 1951 and the Constitution Act, 1964, all of which directly affected federal-provincial relationships in the sense of changing legislative powers and each of which was agreed upon by each province whose legislative authority was affected.

The negative precedents are the failure of a proposed amendment relating to indirect taxation in 1951 and the failure of the Constitutional Conferences of 1960, 1964 and 1971. The precedents also comprise, in negative terms, the fact that no amendment changing provincial legislative powers had been made when agreement of a province whose legislative power would have been changed was withheld.

It was further pointed out by the appellant that no relevant constitutional amendment had been passed without the consent of Quebec and that with respect to one of them, the Constitution Act, 1964 Quebec alone had delayed the amendment already agreed upon by the nine other provinces as early as 1962. Quebec finally gave its consent in 1964 and the amendment was passed.

The appellant also underlined that the Constitution Act, 1940 had been delayed because three provinces, Quebec, New-Brunswick and Alberta had not yet consented to it; that the lack of agreement of two provinces, Ontario and Quebec, had prevented a proposed constitutional amendment relating to indirect taxation in 1951; and that the lack of agreement of the sole Province of Quebec had caused the failure of the Constitutional Conference of 1964, relating to the Fulton-Favreau formula as well, in practice, as the failure of the Constitutional Conference of 1971 relating to the Victoria Charter, although in the latter case, Saskatchewan did not make its position known.

It was recognized by the appellant that there must be a reason for the alleged conventional rule.

The reason for the unanimity rule, he argued, was the federal principle within the meaning given to this principle by the majority opinion in the *First Reference*.

The reason for the conventional rule giving to Quebec a power of veto was said to be the principle of duality, the meaning and nature of which will be discussed in more detail below.

Finally, as to the requirement that the actors in the precedents believe that they were bound by the rule, the appellant submitted that it had been met. But his counsel substantially qualified this submission by pleading in his factum and in oral argument that the precedents and the reason for the rule suffice to establish a constitutional convention and, accordingly that the recognition of the actors in the precedents is not required or alternatively that recognition can be tacit and inferred from the precedents.

The respondent submitted that the Court should refuse to answer the question. He also submitted that if the Court should answer the question it should answer in the negative on the basis of the *First Reference*. He submitted alternatively that, if the Court should answer the question, it should answer that the political leaders had complied with the convention recognized by this Court in the *First Reference*.

The interveners generally supported the position of the appellant.

IV—Whether the question should be answered

The respondent advanced two reasons why the Court should refuse to answer the question: it was a purely political question and it had become academic.

The first objection had also been raised in the *First Reference* and dismissed in the majority opinion as well as in the dissenting opinion. The majority opinion adopted the view of Freedman C.J.M. on this point, at p. 884:

In my view, this submission goes too far. Its characterization of Question 2 as "purely political" overstates the case. That there is a political element embodied in the question, arising from the contents of the joint address, may well be the case. But that does not end the matter. If Question 2, even if in part political, possesses a constitutional feature, it would legitimately call for our reply.

In my view, the request for a decision by this Court on whether there is a constitution convention, in the circumstances described, that the Dominion will not act without the agreement of the Provinces poses a question that it, [sic], at least in part, constitutional in character. It therefore calls for an answer, and I propose to answer it.

This view is still valid and ought to prevail in the case at bar.

On the other hand, counsel for the respondent is right in asserting that the constitutional question has become moot. The Constitution Act, 1982 is now in force. Its legality is neither challenged nor assailable. It contains a new procedure for amending the Constitution of Canada which entirely replaces the old one in its legal as well as in its conventional aspects. Even assuming therefore that there was a conventional requirement for the consent of Quebec under the old system, it would no longer have any object or force.

However, when the reference was ordered, when it was argued before the Court of Appeal and when the Court of Appeal delivered its certified opinion on April 7, 1982 it could not be said that the question was moot since the process of constitutional amendment had not been completed, the Constitution Act, 1982 having not yet been proclaimed. . . .

While this Court retains its discretion to entertain or not to entertain an appeal as of right where the issue has become moot, it may, in the exercise of its discretion, take into consideration the importance of the constitutional issue determined by a court of appeal judgment which would remain unreviewed by this Court.

In the circumstances of this case, it appears desirable that the constitutional question be answered in order to dispel any doubt over it and it accordingly will be answered.

V—Whether there exists a convention rule of unanimity

It was the appellant's contention that the majority opinion in the *First Reference* has left open the question whether there existed a conventional rule of unanimity. His main argument for so contending was that the majority opinion did not limit the meaning of the questions relating to convention solely to determining whether there existed a convention which required the unanimous consent of the provinces.

It is quite true that the majority opinion in the *First Reference* gave to the constitutional questions a wider scope than did the dissenting opinion, but this enabled the majority to consider all arguments, including the one relating to unanimity, which it clearly rejected. . . .

At page 905 of the *First Reference*, the majority decided that "a substantial degree of provincial consent" was required. A "substantial degree of provincial consent" means less than unanimity. This is what the dissenting judges understood that the majority was deciding: the dissenting opinion contains the following statement at p. 856:

For the Court to postulate some other convention requiring less than unanimous provincial consent to constitutional amendments would be to go beyond the terms of the References and in so doing to answer a question not posed in the References.

The dissenting opinion was based on the understanding of the dissenting judges that the constitutional questions relating to conventions meant the consent of all the provinces. The dissenting judges held that there existed no convention requiring any such consent.

This Court was therefore unanimous in the *First Reference* in rejecting the conventional rule of unanimity.

The appellant advanced no compelling reason why this unanimous opinion should be modified. . . .

VI—Whether Quebec has a conventional power of veto

It has already been indicated, with respect to the precedents which are said to establish the conventional rule of a power of veto for Quebec, that the appellant relied upon those which had been invoked by the majority opinion in the *First Reference*, at pp. 891 to 894.

The reason advanced by the appellant for the existence of a conventional rule of a power of veto for Quebec is the principle of duality, this principle being however understood in a special sense.

The expression "Canadian duality" is frequently used to refer to the two larger linguistic groups in Canada and to the constitutional protection afforded to the official languages by provisions such as s. 133 of the Constitution Act, 1867 and s. 23 of the Manitoba Act, 1870.

Counsel for the appellant characterized this aspect of the Canadian duality as the "federal" aspect and recognized that the central government had a role to play in this respect within the framework of federal institutions as well as outside Quebec. But he also made it clear that what he meant by the principle of duality embraced much more than linguistic or cultural differences. What was meant by the principle of duality was what counsel called its "Quebec" aspect which he defined more precisely in his factum at pp. 8 and 16:

[TRANSLATION] *In the context of this reference, the word "duality" covers all the circumstances that have contributed to making Quebec a distinct society, since the foundation of Canada and long before, and the range of guarantees that were made to Quebec in 1867, as a province which the Task Force on Canadian Unity has described as "the stronghold of the French-Canadian people" and the "living heart of the French presence in North America"*. *These circumstances and these guarantees extend far beyond matters of language and culture alone: the protection of the British North America Act was extended to all aspects of Quebec society—language, certainly, but also the society's values, its law, religion, education, territory, natural resources, government and the sovereignty of its legislative assembly over everything which was at the time of a "local" nature.*

. . .

In 1867, the French Canadian minority became a majority within the Quebec Legislature. This is what accounts for the special nature of this province, and it is the reason underlying the convention that the powers of its Legislature cannot be reduced without consent.

One finds another expression of the principle of duality understood in this sense in the preamble of the above quoted Decree No. 3367-81, dated December 9, 1981, the fourth paragraph of which states in concise terms:

[TRANSLATION] *WHEREAS Quebec forms a distinct society within the Canadian federation;*

Another more elaborate expression of the principle of duality understood in the special sense urged by counsel for the appellant is to be found in a resolution passed by the Quebec National Assembly on December 1, 1981, and more particularly in condition no. 1 of the Resolution:

[TRANSLATION] *. . . that the National Assembly of Quebec, having in mind the right of the people of Quebec to self-determination and exercising its historical right to be a party to and approve any change in the Constitution of Canada which might affect the rights and powers of Quebec, states that it cannot approve the proposal to patriate the constitution unless it includes the following conditions:*

"1. It shall be recognized that the two founding people of Canada are fundamentally equal, and that within the Canadian federation Quebec forms a society distinct by its language, culture and institutions, one which possesses all the attributes of a distinct national community;

"2. The constitutional amending formula:

a) *shall either preserve Quebec's right of veto, or*

b) *shall be the one approved in the constitutional agreement signed by Quebec on April 16, 1981, affirming the right of Quebec not to have imposed on it any change which would reduce its powers or rights, and if such a reduction were to take place, to be given reasonable compensation as a matter of right; . . .*

These then are the precedents and the reason for the rule, according to counsel for the appellant.

It will not be necessary in our view to look further into these matters because this submission must in any event be rejected, the appellant having failed completely to demonstrate compliance with the most important requirement for establishing a convention that is, acceptance or recognition by the actors in the precedents.

We have been referred to an abundance

of material, speeches made in the course of parliamentary debates, reports of royal commissions, opinions of historians, political scientists, constitutional experts which endorse in one way or another the principle of duality within the meaning assigned to it by the appellant, and there can be no doubt that many Canadian statesmen, politicians and experts favoured this principle.

But neither in his factum nor in oral argument did counsel for the appellant quote a single statement made by any representative of the federal authorities recognizing either explicitly or by necessary implication that Quebec had a conventional power of veto over certain types of constitutional amendments. The statement made by Minister Favreau on November 20, 1964, and the passage to be found at pp. 46 and 47 of the White Paper have been quoted twice in the appellant's factum, as if they supported the veto rule as well as the unanimity one, but they refer only to unanimity and have been above dealt with in this respect.

Furthermore, a convention such as the one now asserted by Quebec would have to be recognized by other provinces. We have not been referred to and we are not aware of any statement by the actors in any of the other provinces acknowledging such a convention. Not only have we not been given any evidence of the acquiescence of other provinces but in the *First Reference*, three of them, Manitoba, Prince Edward Island and Alberta, explicitly pleaded in favour of the unanimity rule in their factums, a position compatible only with the principle of equality among the provinces and incompatible with a special power of veto for Quebec. It should also be noted that in the *First Reference*, Ontario and New Brunswick had taken the position that the constitutional amending process was not regulated by conventions involving provinces.

In order to make up for these fundamental flaws in his submission, counsel for the appellant argued as follows in his factum:

[TRANSLATION] *In the opinion of the Attorney General, custom and a reason suffice by themselves to establish the normative nature of the rule.*

Counsel for the appellant also referred to Sir Ivor Jennings' test, adopted by this Court in the *First Reference*, and more particularly to the last part of this test:

A single precedent with a good reason may be enough to establish the rule. A whole string of precedents without such a reason will be of no avail, unless it is perfectly certain that the persons concerned regarded them as bound by it.

As we understand it, the contention was that recognition by the actors in the precedents is not an absolutelyessential requirement for establishing a convention and that the last part of Jennings' test is an authority for that proposition.

This contention is based on two sentences taken out of context and is an oversimplified and erroneous view of Jennings' test. In these two sentences, Jennings is merely expanding on what he said in the sentence immediately preceding them about the three requirements and illustrating the interrelation between them. He is not doing away with the requirement that the actors in the precedents believe that they were bound by a rule. Indeed Jennnings insists in several passages of his book, *The Law and the Constitution*, that recognition or acquiescence is an essential ingredient of constitutional conventions. Thus he writes, at p. 81:

"Convention" implies some form of agreement, whether expressed or implied. . . .

And at page 117:

The conventions are like most fundamental rules of any constitution in that they rest essentially upon general acquiescence.

And at page 135:

. . . if the authority itself and those connected with it believe that they ought to do

so, then the convention does exist. This is the ordinary rule applied to customary law. Practice alone is not enough. It must be normative.

In the *First Reference*, at pp. 852, 857 and 883, these views were approved by all the members of this Court who adopted the definition of convention given by Freedman, C.J.M. in the Manitoba Reference, including, at p. 883, the following quotation of Hogg, *Constitutional Law of Canada* (1977), at p. 9:

a convention is a rule which is regarded as obligatory by the officials to whom it applies.

Recognition by the actors in the precedents is not only an essential element of conventions. In our opinion, it is the most important element since it is the normative one, the formal one which enables us unmistakably to distinguish a constitutional rule from a rule of convenience or from political expediency.

Counsel for the appellant also contended in reply that recognition by the actors in the precedents need not be explicit, and this contention appears to be supported by the following statement of Jennings already quoted above:

"Convention" implies some form of agreement, whether expressed or implied. . . .

Again, Jennings' assertion must be qualified. Some conventions have been formulated in writing, for instance in the Reports of Imperial Conferences or in the preamble of the *Statute of Westminster, 1931*. Such conventions can be said to have been expressly agreed upon in authoritative or official form.

The majority of constitutional conventions however have not so been reduced to writing. Does this mean that they are based on implied agreements strictly so-called in that they have never been the object of any form of utterance? We do not think so.

Conventions are commonly asserted or claimed by some political actors in more or less informal statements, while the other actors similarly acknowledge them in principle if not always in their application to particular facts. Conventions are analysed, dissected, commented upon and sometimes criticized albeit not to the point of rejection. But, in our view, a convention could not have remained wholly inarticulate, except perhaps at the inchoate stage when it has not yet been accepted as a binding rule. We know of no example of a convention being born while remaining completely unspoken, and none was cited to us. . . .

In our view, the Quebec Court of Appeal was correct in holding that the appellant had failed to establish that Quebec had a conventional power of veto over constitutional amendments such as those in issue in the present Reference.

VII—Conclusion

For these reasons, we would answer "No" to the constitutional question, and we would dismiss the appeal. There should be no order as to costs.

Appendix 1:

Constitution Act, 1867

VI.—DISTRIBUTION OF LEGISLATIVE POWERS.

Powers of the Parliament.

91. It shall be lawful for the Queen, by and with the Advice and Consent of the Senate and House of Commons, to make Laws for the Peace, Order, and good Government of Canada, in relation to all Matters not coming within the Classes of Subjects by this Act assigned exclusively to the Legislatures of the Provinces; and for greater Certainty, but not so as to restrict the Generality of the foregoing Terms of this Section, it is hereby declared that (notwithstanding anything in this Act) the exclusive Legislative Authority of the Parliament of Canada extends to all Matters coming within the Classes of Subjects next hereinafter enumerated; that is to say,— *Legislative Authority of Parliament of Canada.*

1. Repealed.

1A. The Public Debt and Property.

2. The Regulation of Trade and Commerce.

2A. Unemployment insurance.

3. The raising of Money by any Mode or System of Taxation.

4. The borrowing of Money on the Public Credit.

5. Postal Service.

6. The Census and Statistics.

7. Militia, Military and Naval Service, and Defence.

8. The fixing of and providing for the Salaries and Allowances of Civil and other Officers of the Government of Canada.

9. Beacons, Buoys, Lighthouses, and Sable Island.

10. Navigation and Shipping.

11. Quarantine and the Establishment and Maintenance of Marine Hospitals.

12. Sea Coast and Inland Fisheries.

13. Ferries between a Province and any British or Foreign Country or between Two Provinces.

14. Currency and Coinage.

15. Banking, Incorporation of Banks, and the Issue of Paper Money.

16. Savings Banks.

17. Weights and Measures.

18. Bills of Exchange and Promissory Notes.

19. Interest.

20. Legal Tender.

21. Bankruptcy and Insolvency.

22. Patents of Invention and Discovery.

23. Copyrights.

24. Indians, and Lands reserved for the Indians.

25. Naturalization and Aliens.

26. Marriage and Divorce.

27. The Criminal Law, except the Constitution of Courts of Criminal Jurisdiction, but including the Procedure in Criminal Matters.

28. The Establishment, Maintenance, and Management of Penitentiaries.

29. Such Classes of Subjects as are expressly excepted in the Enumeration of the Classes of Subjects by this Act assigned exclusively to the Legislatures of the Provinces.

And any Matter coming within any of the Classes of Subjects enumerated in this Section shall not be deemed to come within the Class of Matters of a local or private Nature comprised in the Enumeration of the Classes of Subjects by this Act assigned exclusively to the Legislatures of the Provinces.

Exclusive Powers of Provincial Legislatures

Subjects of exclusive Provincial Legislation.

92. In each Province the Legislature may exclusively make Laws in relation to Matters coming within the Classes of Subject next hereinafter enumerated; that is to say,—

1. Repealed.

2. Direct Taxation within the Province in order to the raising of a Revenue for Provincial Purposes.

3. The borrowing of Money on the sole Credit of the Province.

4. The Establishment and Tenure of Provincial Offices and the Appointment and Payment of Provincial Officers.

5. The Management and Sale of the Public Lands belonging to the Province and of the Timber and Wood thereon.

6. The Establishment, Maintenance, and Management of Public and Reformatory Prisons in and for the Province.

7. The Establishment, Maintenance, and Management of Hospitals, Asylums, Charities, and Eleemosynary Institutions in and for the Province, other than Marine Hospitals.

8. Municipal Institutions in the Province.

9. Shop, Saloon, Tavern, Auctioneer, and other Licences in order to the raising of a Revenue for Provincial, Local, or Municipal Purposes.

10. Local Works and Undertakings other than such as are of the following Classes:—

    (*a*) Lines of Steam or other Ships, Railways, Canals, Telegraphs, and other Works and Undertakings connecting the Province with any other or others of the Provinces, or extending beyond the Limits of the Province;

    (*b*) Lines of Steam Ships between the Province and any British or Foreign Country;

    (*c*) Such Works as, although wholly situate within the Province, are before or after their Execution declared by the Parliament of Canada to be for the general Advantage of Canada or for the Advantage of Two or more of the Provinces.

11. The Incorporation of Companies with Provincial Objects.

12. The Solemnization of Marriage in the Province.

13. Property and Civil Rights in the Province.

14. The Administration of Justice in the Province, including the Constitution, Maintenance, and Organization of Provincial Courts, both of Civil and of Criminal Jurisdiction, and including Procedure in Civil Matters in those Courts.

15. The Imposition of Punishment by Fine, Penalty, or Imprisonment for enforcing any Law of the Province made in relation to any Matter coming within any of the Classes of Subjects enumerated in this Section.

16. Generally all Matters of a merely local or private Nature in the Province.

*Non-Renewable Natural Resources, Forestry Resources and
Electrical Energy*

Laws respecting
non-renewable
natural
resources,
forestry
resources and
electrical energy

92A. (1) In each province, the legislature may exclusively make laws in relation to

(*a*) exploration for non-renewable natural resources in the province;

(*b*) development, conservation and management of non-renewable natural resources and forestry resources in the province, including laws in relation to the rate of primary production therefrom; and

(*c*) development, conservation and management of sites and facilities in the province for the generation and production of electrical energy.

Export from
provinces of
resources

(2) In each province, the legislature may make laws in relation to the export from the province to another part of Canada of the primary production from non-renewable natural resources and forestry resources in the province and the production from facilities in the province for the generation of electrical energy, but such laws may not authorize or provide for discrimination in prices or in supplies exported to another part of Canada.

Authority of
Parliament

(3) Nothing in subsection (2) derogates from the authority of Parliament to enact laws in relation to the matters referred to in that subsection and, where such a law of Parliament and a law of a province conflict, the law of Parliament prevails to the extent of the conflict.

Taxation of
resources

(4) In each province, the legislature may make laws in relation to the raising of money by any mode or system of taxation in respect of

(*a*) non-renewable natural resources and forestry resources in the province and the primary production therefrom, and

(*b*) sites and facilities in the province for the generation of electrical energy and the production therefrom,

whether or not such production is exported in whole or in part from the province, but such laws may not authorize or provide for taxation that differentiates between production exported to another part of Canada and production not exported from the province.

"Primary
production"

(5) The expression "primary production" has the meaning assigned by the Sixth Schedule.

(6) Nothing in subsections (1) to (5) derogates from any powers or rights that a legislature or government of a province had immediately before the coming into force of this section.

Existing powers or rights

Education.

93. In and for each Province the Legislature may exclusively make Laws in relation to Education, subject and according to the following Provisions:—

Legislation respecting Education.

(1) Nothing in any such Law shall prejudicially affect any Right or Privilege with respect to Denominational Schools which any Class of Persons have by Law in the Province at the Union:

(2) All the Powers, Privileges, and Duties at the Union by Law conferred and imposed in Upper Canada on the Separate Schools and School Trustees of the Queen's Roman Catholic Subjects shall be and the same are hereby extended to the Dissentient Schools of the Queen's Protestant and Roman Catholic Subjects in Quebec:

(3) Where in any Province a System of Separate or Dissentient Schools exists by Law at the Union or is thereafter established by the Legislature of the Province, an Appeal shall lie to the Governor General in Council from any Act or Decision of any Provincial Authority affecting any Right or Privilege of the Protestant or Roman Catholic Minority of the Queen's Subjects in relation to Education:

(4) In case any such Provincial Law as from Time to Time seems to the Governor General in Council requisite for the due Execution of the Provisions of this Section is not made, or in case any Decision of the Governor General in Council on any Appeal under this Section is not duly executed by the proper Provincial Authority in that Behalf, then and in every such Case, and as far only as the Circumstances of each Case require, the Parliament of Canada may make remedial Laws for the due Execution of the Provisions of this Section and of any Decision of the Governor General in Council under this Section.

Uniformity of Laws in Ontario, Nova Scotia and New Brunswick.

94. Notwithstanding anything in this Act, the Parliament of Canada may make Provision for the Uniformity of all or any of

Legislation for Uniformity of Laws in Three Provinces.

the Laws relative to Property and Civil Rights in Ontario, Nova Scotia, and New Brunswick, and of the Procedure of all or any of the Courts in Those Three Provinces, and from and after the passing of any Act in that Behalf the Power of the Parliament of Canada to make Laws in relation to any Matter comprised in any such Act shall, notwithstanding anything in this Act, be unrestricted; but any Act of the Parliament of Canada making Provision for such Uniformity shall not have effect in any Province unless and until it is adopted and enacted as Law by the Legislature thereof.

Old Age Pensions.

Legislation respecting old age pensions and supplementary benefits.

94A. The Parliament of Canada may make laws in relation to old age pensions and supplementary benefits, including survivors, and disability benefits irrespective of age, but no such law shall affect the operation of any law present or future of a provincial legislature in relation to any such matter.

Agriculture and Immigration.

Concurrent Powers of Legislation respecting Agriculture, etc.

95. In each Province the Legislature may make Laws in relation to Agriculture in the Province, and to Immigration into the Province; and it is hereby declared that the Parliament of Canada may from Time to Time make Laws in relation to Agriculture in all or any of the Provinces, and to Immigration into all or any of the Provinces; and any Law of the Legislature of a Province relative to Agriculture or to Immigration shall have effect in and for the Province as long and as far only as it is not repugnant to any Act of the Parliament of Canada.

VII.—JUDICATURE.

Appointment of Judges.

96. The Governor General shall appoint the Judges of the Superior, District, and County Courts in each Province, except those of the Courts of Probate in Nova Scotia and New Brunswick.

Selection of Judges in Ontario, etc.

97. Until the laws relative to Property and Civil Rights in Ontario, Nova Scotia, and New Brunswick, and the Procedure of the Courts in those Provinces, are made uniform, the Judges of the Courts of those Provinces appointed by the Governor General shall be selected from the respective Bars of those Provinces.

Selection of Judges in Quebec.

98. The Judges of the Courts of Quebec shall be selected from the Bar of that Province.

99. (1) Subject to subsection two of this section, the Judges of the Superior Courts shall hold office during good behaviour, but shall be removable by the Governor General on Address of the Senate and House of Commons. Tenure of office of Judges.

(2) A Judge of a Superior Court, whether appointed before or after the coming into force of this section, shall cease to hold office upon attaining the age of seventy-five years, or upon the coming into force of this section if at that time he has already attained that age. Termination at age 75.

100. The Salaries, Allowances, and Pensions of the Judges of the Superior, District, and County Courts (except the Courts of Probate in Nova Scotia and New Brunswick), and of the Admiralty Courts in Cases where the Judges thereof are for the Time being paid by Salary, shall be fixed and provided by the Parliament of Canada. Salaries etc., of Judges.

101. The Parliament of Canada may, notwithstanding anything in this Act, from Time to Time provide for the Constitution, Maintenance, and Organization of a General Court of Appeal for Canada, and for the Establishment of any additional Courts for the better Administration of the Laws of Canada. General Court of Appeal, etc.

132. The Parliament and Government of Canada shall have all Powers necessary or proper for performing the Obligations of Canada or of any Province thereof, as Part of the British Empire, towards Foreign Countries, arising under Treaties between the Empire and such Foreign Countries. Treaty Obligations.

133. Either the English or the French Language may be used by any Person in the Debates of the Houses of the Parliament of Canada and of the Houses of the Legislature of Quebec; and both those Languages shall be used in the respective Records and Journals of those Houses; and either of those Languages may be used by any Person or in any Pleading or Process in or issuing from any Court of Canada established under this Act, and in or from all or any of the Courts of Quebec. Use of English and French Languages.

The Acts of the Parliament of Canada and of the Legislature of Quebec shall be printed and published in both those Languages.

Appendix 2:

Constitution Act, 1982

CONSTITUTION ACT, 1982

SCHEDULE B

CONSTITUTION ACT, 1982

PART I

CANADIAN CHARTER OF RIGHTS AND FREEDOMS

Whereas Canada is founded upon principles that recognize the supremacy of God and the rule of law:

Guarantee of Rights and Freedoms

Rights and freedoms in Canada

1. The *Canadian Charter of Rights and Freedoms* guarantees the rights and freedoms set out in its subject only to such reasonable limits prescribed by law as can be demonstrably justified in a free and democratic society.

Fundamental Freedoms

Fundamental freedoms·

2. Everyone has the following fundamental freedoms:

(*a*) freedom of conscience and religion;

(*b*) freedom of thought, belief, opinion and expression, including freedom of the press and other media of communication;

(*c*) freedom of peaceful assembly; and

(*d*) freedom of association.

Democratic Rights

Democratic rights of citizens

3. Every citizen of Canada has the right to vote in an election of members of the House of Commons or of a legislative assembly and to be qualified for membership therein.

Maximum duration of legislative bodies

4. (1) No House of Commons and no legislative assembly shall continue for longer than five years from the date fixed for the return of the writs of a general election of its members.

Continuation in special circumstances

(2) In time of real or apprehended war, invasion or insurrection, a House of Commons may be continued by Parliament and a legislative assembly may be continued by the legislature beyond

five years if such continuation is not opposed by the votes of more than one-third of the members of the House of Commons or the legislative assembly, as the case may be.

5. There shall be a sitting of Parliament and of each legislature at least once every twelve months.

Annual sitting of legislative bodies

Mobility Rights

6. (1) Every citizen of Canada has the right to enter, remain in and leave Canada.

Mobility of citizens

(2) Every citizen of Canada and every person who has the status of a permanent resident of Canada has the right

Rights to move and gain livelihood

(*a*) to move to and take up residence in any province; and

(*b*) to pursue the gaining of a livelihood in any province.

(3) The rights specified in subsection (2) are subject to

Limitation

(*a*) any laws or practices of general application in force in a province other than those that discriminate among persons primarily on the basis of province of present or previous residence; and

(*b*) any laws providing for reasonable residency requirements as a qualification for the receipt of publicly provided social services.

(4) Subsections (2) and (3) do not preclude any law, program or activity that has as its object the amelioration in a province of conditions of individuals in that province who are socially or economically disadvantaged if the rate of employment in that province is below the rate of employment in Canada.

Affirmative action programs

Legal Rights

7. Everyone has the right to life, liberty and security of the person and the right not to be deprived thereof except in accordance with the principles of fundamental justice.

Life, liberty and security of person

8. Everyone has the right to be secure against unreasonable search or seizure.

Search or seizure

9. Everyone has the right not to be arbitrarily detained or imprisoned.

Detention or imprisonment

10. Everyone has the right on arrest or detention

Arrest or detention

(*a*) to be informed promptly of the reasons therefor;

(*b*) to retain and instruct counsel without delay and to be informed of that right; and

(*c*) to have the validity of the detention determined by way of *habeas corpus* and to be released if the detention is not lawful.

Proceedings in criminal and penal matters

11. Any person charged with an offence has the right

(*a*) to be informed without unreasonable delay of the specific offence;

(*b*) to be tried within a reasonable time;

(*c*) not to be compelled to be a witness in proceedings against that person in respect of the offence;

(*d*) to be presumed innocent until proven guilty according to law in a fair and public hearing by an independent and impartial tribunal;

(*e*) not to be denied reasonable bail without just cause;

(*f*) except in the case of an offence under military law tried before a military tribunal, to the benefit of trial by jury where the maximum punishment for the offence is imprisonment for five years or a more severe punishment;

(*g*) not to be found guilty on account of any act or omission unless, at the time of the act or omission, it constituted an offence under Canadian or international law or was criminal according to the general principles of law recognized by the community of nations;

(*h*) if finally acquitted of the offence, not to be tried for it again and, if finally found guilty and punished for the offence, not to be tried or punished for it again; and

(*i*) if found guilty of the offence and if the punishment for the offence has been varied between the time of commission and the time of sentencing, to the benefit of the lesser punishment.

Treatment or punishment

12. Everyone has the right not to be subjected to any cruel and unusual treatment or punishment.

Self-crimination

13. A witness who testifies in any proceedings has the right not to have any incriminating evidence so given used to incriminate that witness in any other proceedings, except in a prosecution for perjury or for the giving of contradictory evidence.

Interpreter

14. A party or witness in any proceedings who does not understand or speak the language in which the proceedings are conducted or who is deaf has the right to the assistance of an interpreter.

Equality Rights

15. (1) Every individual is equal before and under the law and has the right to the equal protection and equal benefit of the law without discrimination and, in particular, without discrimination based on race, national or ethnic origin, colour, religion, sex, age or mental or physical disability.

Equality before and under law and equal protection and benefit of law

(2) Subsection (1) does not preclude any law, program or activity that has as its object the amelioration of conditions of disadvantaged individuals or groups including those that are disadvantaged because of race, national or ethnic origin, colour, religion, sex, age or mental or physical disability.

Affirmative action programs

Official Languages of Canada

16. (1) English and French are the official languages of Canada and have equality of status and equal rights and privileges as to their use in all institutions of the Parliament and government of Canada.

Official languages of Canada

(2) English and French are the official languages of New Brunswick and have equality of status and equal rights and privileges as to their use in all institutions of the legislature and government of New Brunswick.

Official languages of New Brunswick

(3) Nothing in this Charter limits the authority of Parliament or a legislature to advance the equality of status or use of English and French.

Advancement of status and use

17. (1) Everyone has the right to use English or French in any debates and other proceedings of Parliament.

Proceedings of Parliament

(2) Everyone has the right to use English or French in any debates and other proceedings of the legislature of New Brunswick.

Proceedings of New Brunswick legislature

18. (1) The statutes, records and journals of Parliament shall be printed and published in English and French and both language versions are equally authoritative.

Parliamentary statutes and records

(2) The statutes, records and journals of the legislature of New Brunswick shall be printed and published in English and French and both language versions are equally authoritative.

New Brunswick Statutes and Records

Proceedings in courts established by Parliament

19. (1) Either English or French may be used by any person in, or in any pleading in or process issuing from, any court established by Parliament.

Proceedings in New Brunswick courts

(2) Either English or French may be used by any person in, or in any pleading in or process issuing from, any court of New Brunswick.

Communications by public with federal institutions

20. (1) Any member of the public in Canada has the right to communicate with, and to receive available services from, any head or central office of an institution of the Parliament or government of Canada in English or French, and has the same right with respect to any other office of any such institution where

(*a*) there is a significant demand for communications with and services from that office in such language; or

(*b*) due to the nature of the office, it is reasonable that communications with and services from that office be available to both English and French.

Communications by public with New Brunswick institutions

(2) Any member of the public in New Brunswick has the right to communicate with, and to receive available services from, any office of an institution of the legislature or government of New Brunswick in English or French.

Continuation of existing constitutional provisions

21. Nothing in sections 16 to 20 abrogates or derogates from any right, privilege or obligation with respect to the English and French languages, or either of them, that exists or is continued by virtue of any other provision of the Constitution of Canada.

Rights and privileges preserved

22. Nothing in sections 16 to 20 abrogates or derogates from any legal or customary right or privilege acquired or enjoyed either before or after the coming into force of this Charter with respect to any language that is not English or French.

Minority Language Educational Rights

Language of instruction

23. (1) Citizens of Canada

(*a*) whose first language learned and still understood is that of the English or French linguistic minority population of the province in which they reside, or

(*b*) who have received their primary school instruction in Canada in English or French and reside in a province where the language in which they received that instruction is the language of the English or French linguistic minority population of the province, have the right to have their children receive primary and secondary school instruction in that language in that province.

(2) Citizens of Canada of whom any child has received or is receiving primary or secondary school instruction in English or French in Canada, have the right to have all their children receive primary and secondary school instruction in the same language.

Continuity of language instruction

(3) The right of citizens of Canada under subsections (1) and (2) to have their children receive primary and secondary school instruction in the language of the English or French linguistic minority population of a province

Application where numbers warrant

(a) applies wherever in the province the number of children of citizens who have such a right is sufficient to warrant the provision to them out of public funds of minority language instruction; and

(b) includes, where the number of those children so warrants, the right to have them receive that instruction in minority language educational facilities provided out of public funds.

Enforcement

24. (1) Anyone whose rights or freedoms, as guaranteed by this Charter, have been infringed or denied may apply to a court of competent jurisdiction to obtain such remedy as the court considers appropriate and just in the circumstances.

Enforcement of guaranteed rights and freedoms

(2) Where, in proceedings under subsection (1), a court concludes that evidence was obtained in a manner that infringed or denied any rights or freedoms guaranteed by this Charter, the evidence shall be excluded if it is established that, having regard to all the circumstances, the admission of it in the proceedings would bring the administration of justice into disrepute.

Exclusion of evidence bringing administration of justice into disrepute

General

25. The guarantee in this Charter of certain rights and freedoms shall not be construed so as to abrogate or derogate from any aboriginal, treaty or other rights or freedoms that pertain to the aboriginal peoples of Canada including

Aboriginal rights and freedoms not affected by Charter

(a) any rights or freedoms that have been recognized by the Royal Proclamation of October 7, 1763; and

(b) any rights or freedoms that may be acquired by the aboriginal peoples of Canada by way of land claims settlement.

Other rights and freedoms not affected by Charter

26. The guarantee in this Charter of certain rights and freedoms shall not be construed as denying the existence of any other rights or freedoms that exist in Canada.

Multicultural heritage

27. This Charter shall be interpreted in a manner consistent with the preservation and enhancement of the multicultural heritage of Canadians.

Rights guaranteed equally to both sexes

28. Notwithstanding anything in this Charter, the rights and freedoms referred to in it are guaranteed equally to male and female persons.

Rights respecting certain schools preserved

29. Nothing in this Charter abrogates or derogates from any rights or privileges guaranteed by or under the Constitution of Canada in respect of denominational, separate or dissentient schools.

Application to territories and territorial authorities

30. A reference in this Charter to a Province or to the legislative assembly or legislature of a province shall be deemed to include a reference to the Yukon Territory and the Northwest Territories, or to the appropriate legislative authority thereof, as the case may be.

Legislative powers not extended

31. Nothing in this Charter extends the legislative powers of any body or authority.

Application of Charter

Application of Charter

32. (1) This Charter applies

(*a*) to the Parliament and government of Canada in respect of all matters within the authority of Parliament including all matters relating to the Yukon Territory and Northwest Territories; and

(*b*) to the legislature and government of each province in respect of all matters within the authority of the legislature of each province.

Exception

(2) Notwithstanding subsection (1), section 15 shall not have effect until three years after this section comes into force.

Exception where express declaration

33. (1) Parliament or the legislature of a province may expressly declare in an Act of Parliament or of the legislature, as the case may be, that the Act or a provision thereof shall operate notwithstanding a provision included in section 2 or sections 7 to 15 of this Charter.

Operation of exception

(2) An Act or a provision of an Act in respect of which a declaration made under this section is in effect shall have such

operation as it would have but for the provision of this Charter referred to in the declaration.

(3) A declaration made under subsection (1) shall cease to have effect five years after it comes into force or on such earlier date as may be specified in the declaration.

Five year limitation

(4) Parliament or the legislature of a province may re-enact a declaration made under subsection (1).

Re-enactment

(5) Subsection (3) applies in respect of a re-enactment made under subsection (4).

Five year limitation

Citation

34. This Part may be cited as the *Canadian Charter of Rights and Freedoms*.

Citation

PART II

RIGHTS OF THE ABORIGINAL PEOPLES OF CANADA

35. (1) The existing aboriginal and treaty rights of the aboriginal peoples of Canada are hereby recognized and affirmed.

Recognition of existing aboriginal and treaty rights

(2) In this Act, "aboriginal peoples of Canada" includes the Indian, Inuit and Métis peoples of Canada.

Definition of "aboriginal peoples of Canada"

(3) For greater certainty, in subsection (1) "treaty rights" includes rights that now exist by way of land claims agreements or may be so acquired.

(4) Notwithstanding any other provision of this Act, the aboriginal and treaty rights referred to in subsection (1) are guaranteed equally to male and female persons.''

PART III

EQUALIZATION AND REGIONAL DISPARITIES

36. (1) Without altering the legislative authority of Parliament or of the provincial legislatures, or the rights of any of them with respect to the exercise of their legislative authority, Parliament and the legislatures, together with the government of Canada and the provincial governments, are committed to

Commitment to promote equal opportunities

(a) promoting equal opportunities for the well-being of Canadians;

(b) furthering economic development to reduce disparity in opportunities; and (*c*) providing essential public services of reasonable quality to all Canadians.

Commitment respecting public services

(2) Parliament and the government of Canada are committed to the principle of making equalization payments to ensure that provincial governments have sufficient revenues to provide reasonably comparable levels of public services at reasonably comparable levels of taxation.

PART IV

CONSTITUTIONAL CONFERENCE

Constitutional conference

37. (1) A constitutional conference composed of the Prime Minister of Canada and the first ministers of the provinces shall be convened by the Prime Minister of Canada within one year after this Part comes into force.

Participation of aboriginal peoples

(2) The conference convened under subsection (1) shall have included in its agenda an item respecting constitutional matters that directly affect the aboriginal peoples of Canada, including the identification and definition of the rights of those peoples to be included in the Constitution of Canada, and the Prime Minister of Canada shall invite representatives of those peoples to participate in the discussions on that item.

Participation of territories

(3) The Prime Minister of Canada shall invite elected representatives of the governments of the Yukon Territory and the Northwest Territories to participate in the discussions on any item on the agenda of the conference convened under subsection (1) that, in the opinion of the Prime Minister, directly affects the Yukon Territory and the Northwest Territories.

PART V

PROCEDURE FOR AMENDING CONSTITUTION OF CANADA

General procedure for amending Constitution of Canada

38. (1) An amendment to the Constitution of Canada may be made by proclamation issued by the Governor General under the Great Seal of Canada where so authorized by

(*a*) resolutions of the Senate and House of Commons; and

(*b*) resolutions of the legislative assemblies of at least two-thirds of the provinces that have, in the aggregate, according to the then latest general census, at least fifty per cent of the population of all the provinces.

(2) An amendment made under subsection (1) that derogates from the legislative powers, the proprietary rights or any other rights or privileges of the legislature or government of a province shall require a resolution supported by a majority of the members of each of the Senate, the House of Commons and the legislative assemblies required under subsection (1). *Majority of members*

(3) An amendment referred to in subsection (2) shall not have effect in a province the legislative assembly of which has expressed its dissent thereto by resolution supported by a majority of its members prior to the issue of the proclamation to which the amendment relates unless that legislative assembly, subsequently, by resolution supported by a majority of its members, revokes its dissent and authorizes the amendment. *Expression of dissent*

(4) A resolution of dissent made for the purposes of subsection (3) may be revoked at any time before or after the issue of the proclamation to which it relates. *Revocation of dissent*

39. (1) A proclamation shall not be issued under subsection 38(1) before the expiration of one year from the adoption of the resolution initiating the amendment procedure thereunder, unless the legislative assembly of each province has previously adopted a resolution of assent or dissent. *Restriction on proclamation*

(2) A proclamation shall not be issued under subsection 38(1) after the expiration of three years from the adoption of the resolution initiating the amendment procedure thereunder. *Idem*

40. Where an amendment is made under subsection 38(1) that transfers provincial legislative powers relating to education or other cultural matters from provincial legislatures to Parliament, Canada shall provide reasonable compensation to any province to which the amendment does not apply. *Compensation*

41. An amendment to the Constitution of Canada in relation to the following matters may be made by proclamation issued by the Governor General under the Great Seal of Canada only where authorized by resolutions of the Senate and House of Commons and of the legislative assembly of each province: *Amendment by unanimous consent*

- (*a*) the office of the Queen, the Governor General and the Lieutenant Governor of a province;
- (*b*) the right of a province to a number of members in the House of Commons not less than the number of Senators by which the province is entitled to be represented at the time this Part comes into force;

(*c*) subject to section 43, the use of the English or the French language;

(*d*) the composition of the Supreme Court of Canada; and

(*e*) an amendment to this Part.

Amendment by general procedure

42. (1) An Amendment to the Constitution of Canada in relation to the following matters may be made only in accordance with subsection 38(1):

(*a*) the principle of proportionate representation of the provinces in the House of Commons prescribed by the Constitution of Canada;

(*b*) the powers of the Senate and the method of selecting Senators;

(*c*) the number of members by which a province is entitled to be represented in the Senate and the residence qualifications of Senators;

(*d*) subject to paragraph 41(*d*), the Supreme Court of Canada;

(*e*) the extension of existing provinces into the territories; and

(*f*) notwithstanding any other law or practice, the establishment of new provinces.

Exception

(2) Subsections 38(2) to (4) do not apply in respect of amendments in relation to matters referred to in subsection (1).

Amendment of provisions relating to some but not all provinces

43. An amendment to the Constitution of Canada in relation to any provision that applies to one or more, but not all, provinces, including

(*a*) any alteration to boundaries between provinces, and

(*b*) any amendment to any provision that relates to the use of the English or the French language within a province,

may be made by proclamation issued by the Governor General under the Great Seal of Canada only where so authorized by resolutions of the Senate and House of Commons and of the legislative assembly of each province to which the amendment applies.

Amendments by Parliament

44. Subject to sections 41 and 42, Parliament may exclusively make laws amending the Constitution of Canada in relation to the executive government of Canada or the Senate and House of Commons.

Amendments by provincial legislatures

45. Subject to section 41, the legislature of each province may exclusively make laws amending the constitution of the province.

46. (1) The procedures for amendment under sections 38, 41, 42 and 43 may be initiated either by the Senate or the House of Commons or by the legisative assembly of a province.

Initiation of amendment procedures

(2) A resolution of assent made for the purposes of this Part may be revoked at any time before the issue of a proclamation authorized by it.

Revocation of authorization

47. (1) An amendment to the Constitution of Canada made by proclamation under section 38, 41, 42 or 43 may be made without a resolution of the Senate authorizing the issue of the proclamation if, within one hundred and eighty days after the adoption by the House of Commons of a resolution authorizing its issue, the Senate has not adopted such a resolution and if, at any time after the expiration of that period, the House of Commons again adopts the resolution.

Amendments without Senate resolution

(2) Any period when Parliament is prorogued or dissolved shall not be counted in computing the one hundred and eighty day period referred to in subsection (1).

Computation of period

48. The Queen's Privy Council for Canada shall advise the Governor General to issue a proclamation under this Part forthwith on the adoption of the resolutions required for an amendment made by proclamation under this Part.

Advice to issue proclamation

49. A constitutional conference composed of the Prime Minister of Canada and the first ministers of the provinces shall be convened by the Prime Minister of Canada within fifteen years after this Part comes into force to review the provisions of this Part.

Constitutional conference

PART VI

AMENDMENT TO THE CONSTITUTION ACT, 1867

50. [See section 92A of the Constitution Act, 1867]

51. (Schedule to section 92A).

PART VII

GENERAL

52. (1) The Constitution of Canada is the supreme law of Canada, and any law that is inconsistent with the provisions of the Constitution is, to the extent of the inconsistency, of no force or effect.

Primacy of Constitution of Canada

Constitution of
Canada

(2) The Constitution of Canada includes

(*a*) the *Canada Act 1982*, including this Act;

(*b*) the Acts and orders referred to in the schedule; and

(*c*) any amendment to any Act or order referred to in para-. graph (*a*) or (*b*).

Amendments to
Constitution of
Canada

(3) Amendments to the Constitution of Canada shall be made only in accordance with the authority contained in the Constitution of Canada.

Repeals and new
names

53. (1) The enactments referred to in Column I of the schedule are hereby repealed or amended to the extent indicated in Column II thereof and, unless repealed, shall continue as law in Canada under the names set out in Column III thereof.

Consequential
amendments

(2) Every enactment, except the *Canada Act 1982*, that refers to an enactment referred to in the schedule by the name in Column I thereof is hereby amended by substituting for that name the corresponding name in Column III thereof, and any British North America Act not referred to in the schedule may be cited as the *Constitution Act* followed by the year and number, if any, of its enactment.

Repeal and
consequential
amendments

54. Part IV is repealed on the day that is one year after this Part comes into force and this section may be repealed and this Act renumbered, consequentially upon the repeal of Part IV and this section, by proclamation issued by the Governor General under the Great Seal of Canada.

French version
of Constitution
of Canada

55. A French version of the portions of the Constitution of Canada referred to in the schedule shall be prepared by the Minister of Justice of Canada as expeditiously as possible and, when any portion thereof sufficient to warrant action being taken has been so prepared, it shall be put forward for enactment by proclamation issued by the Governor General under the Great Seal of Canada pursuant to the procedure then applicable to an amendment of the same provisions of the Constitution of Canada.

English and
French versions
of certain
constitutional
texts

56. Where any portion of the Constitution of Canada has been or is enacted in English and French or where a French version of any portion of the Constitution is enacted pursuant to section 55, the English and French versions of that portion of the Constitution are equally authoritative.

English and
French versions
of this Act

57. The English and French versions of this Act are equally authoritative.

58. Subject to section 59, this Act shall come into force on a day to be fixed by proclamation issued by the Queen or the Governor General under the Great Seal of Canada.

Commencement

59. (1) Paragraph 23(1)(*a*) shall come into force in respect of Quebec on a day to be fixed by proclamation issued by the Queen or the Governor General under the Great Seal of Canada.

Commencement of paragraph 23(1)(*a*) in respect of Quebec

(2) A proclamation under subsection (1) shall be issued only where authorized by the legislative assembly or government of Quebec.

Authorization of Quebec

(3) This section may be repealed on the day paragraph 23(1)(*a*) comes into force in respect of Quebec and this Act amended and renumbered, consequentially upon the repeal of this section, by proclamation issued by the Queen or the Governor General under the Great Seal of Canada.

Repeal of this section

60. This Act may be cited as the *Constitution Act, 1982*, and the Constitution Acts 1867 to 1975 (No. 2) and this Act may be cited together as the *Constitution Acts, 1867 to 1982*.

Short title and citations

Appendix 3:

The Meech Lake Accord

Appendix IV

SCHEDULE

CONSTITUTION AMENDMENT, 1987

Constitution Act, 1867

1. The *Constitution Act, 1867* is amended by adding thereto, immediately after section 1 thereof, the following section:

Interpretation

2. (1) The Constitution of Canada shall be interpreted in a manner consistent with

(*a*) the recognition that the existence of French-speaking Canadians, centred in Quebec but also present elsewhere in Canada, and English-speaking Canadians, concentrated outside Quebec but also present in Quebec, constitutes a fundamental characteristic of Canada; and

(*b*) the recognition that Quebec constitutes within Canada a distinct society.

Role of Parliament and legislatures

(2) The role of the Parliament of Canada and the provincial legislatures to preserve the fundamental characteristics of Canada referred to in paragraph (1)(*a*) is affirmed.

Role of legislature and Government of Quebec

(3) The role of the legislature and Government of Quebec to preserve and promote the distinct identity of Quebec referred to in paragraph (1)(*b*) is affirmed.

Rights of legislatures and governments preserved

(4) Nothing in this section derogates from the powers, rights or privileges of Parliament or the Government of Canada, or of the legislatures or governments of the provinces, including any powers, rights or privileges relating to language.

2. The said Act is further amended by adding thereto, immediately after section 24 thereof, the following section:

Names to be submitted

25. (1) Where a vacancy occurs in the Senate, the government of the province to which the vacancy relates may, in relation to that vacancy, submit to the Queen's Privy Council for Canada the names of persons who may be summoned to the Senate.

(2) Until an amendment to the Constitution of Canada is made in relation to the Senate pursuant to section 41 of the *Constitution Act, 1982*, the person summoned to fill a vacancy in the Senate shall be chosen from among persons whose names have been submitted under subsection (1) by the government of the province to which the vacancy relates and must be acceptable to the Queen's Privy Council for Canada. Choice of Senators from names submitted

3. The said Act is further amended by adding thereto, immediately after section 95 thereof, the following heading and sections:

Agreements on Immigration and Aliens

95A. The Government of Canada shall, at the request of the government of any province, negotiate with the government of that province for the purpose of concluding an agreement relating to immigration or the temporary admission of aliens into that province that is appropriate to the needs and circumstances of that province. Commitment to negotiate

95B. (1) Any agreement concluded between Canada and a province in relation to immigration or the temporary admission of aliens into that province has the force of law from the time it is declared to do so in accordance with subsection 95C(1) and shall from that time have effect notwithstanding class 25 of section 91 or section 95. Agreements

(2) An agreement that has the force of law under subsection (1) shall have effect only so long and so far as it is not repugnant to any provision of an Act of the Parliament of Canada that sets national standards and objectives relating to immigration or aliens, including any provision that establishes general classes of immigrants or relates to levels of immigration for Canada or that prescribes classes of individuals who are inadmissible into Canada. Limitation

(3) The *Canadian Charter of Rights and Freedoms* applies in respect of any agreement that has the force of law under subsection (1) and in respect of anything done by the Parliament or Government of Canada, or the legislature or government of a province, pursuant to any such agreement. Application of Charter

Proclamation relating to agreements

95C. (1) A declaration that an agreement referred to in subsection 95B(1) has the force of law may be made by proclamation issued by the Governor General under the Great Seal of Canada only where so authorized by resolutions of the Senate and House of Commons and of the legislative assembly of the province that is a party to the agreement.

Amendment of agreements

(2) An amendment to an agreement referred to in subsection 95B(1) may be made by proclamation issued by the Governor General under the Great Seal of Canada only where so authorized

(*a*) by resolutions of the Senate and House of Commons and of the legislative assembly of the province that is a party to the agreement; or

(*b*) in such other manner as is set out in the agreement.

Application of sections 46 to 48 of *Constitution Act, 1982*

95D. Sections 46 to 48 of the *Constitution Act, 1982* apply, with such modifications as the circumstances require, in respect of any declaration made pursuant to subsection 95C(1), any amendment to an agreement made pursuant to subsection 95C(2) or any amendment made pursuant to section 95E.

Amendments to sections 95A to 95D or this section

95E. An amendment to sections 95A to 95D or this section may be made in accordance with the procedure set out in subsection 38(1) of the *Constitution Act, 1982*, but only if the amendment is authorized by resolutions of the legislative assemblies of all the provinces that are, at the time of the amendment, parties to an agreement that has the force of law under subsection 95B(1).

4. The said Act is further amended by adding thereto, immediately preceding section 96 thereof, the following heading:

General

5. The said Act is further amended by adding thereto, immediately preceding section 101 thereof, the following heading:

Courts Established by the Parliament of Canada

6. The said Act is further amended by adding thereto, immediately after section 101 thereof, the following heading and sections:

Supreme Court of Canada

Supreme Court continued

101A. (1) The court existing under the name of the Supreme Court of Canada is hereby continued as the general court of appeal for Canada, and as an additional court for the better administration of the laws of Canada, and shall continue to be a superior court of record.

(2) The Supreme Court of Canada shall consist of a chief justice to be called the Chief Justice of Canada and eight other judges, who shall be appointed by the Governor General in Council by letters patent under the Great Seal.

Constitution of court

101B. (1) Any person may be appointed a judge of the Supreme Court of Canada who, after being admitted to the bar of any province or territory, has, for a total of at least ten years, been a judge of any court in Canada or a member of the bar of any province or territory.

Who may be appointed judges

(2) At least three judges of the Supreme Court of Canada shall be appointed from among persons who, after having been admitted to the bar of Quebec, have, for a total of at least ten years, been judges of any court of Quebec or of any court established by the Parliament of Canada, or members of the bar of Quebec.

Three judges from Quebec

101C. (1) Where a vacancy occurs in the Supreme Court of Canada, the government of each province may, in relation to that vacancy, submit to the Minister of Justice of Canada the names of any of the persons who have been admitted to the bar of that province and are qualified under section 101B for appointment to that court.

Names may be submitted

(2) Where an appointment is made to the Supreme Court of Canada, the Governor General in Council shall, except where the Chief Justice is appointed from among members of the Court, appoint a person whose name has been submitted under subsection (1) and who is acceptable to the Queen's Privy Council for Canada.

Appointment from names submitted

(3) Where an appointment is made in accordance with subsection (2) of any of the three judges necessary to meet the requirements as set out in subsection 101B(2), the Governor General in Council shall appoint a person whose name has been submitted by the Government of Quebec.

Appointment from Quebec

Appointment from other provinces

(4) Where an appointment is made in accordance with subsection (2) otherwise than is required under subsection (3), the Governor General in Council shall appoint a person whose name has been submitted by the government of a province other than Quebec.

Tenure, salaries, etc., of judges

101D. Sections 99 and 100 apply in respect of the judges of the Supreme Court of Canada.

Relationship to section 101

101E. (1) Sections 101A to 101D shall be construed as abrogating or derogating from the powers of the Parliament of Canada to make laws under section 101 except to the extent that such laws are inconsistent with those sections.

References to the Supreme Court of Canada

(2) For greater certainty, section 101A shall not be construed as abrogating or derogating from the powers of the Parliament of Canada to make laws relating to the reference of questions of law or fact, or any other matters, to the Supreme Court of Canada.

7. The said Act is further amended by adding thereto, immediately after section 106 thereof, the following section:

Shared-cost program

106A. (1) The Government of Canada shall provide reasonable compensation to the government of a province that chooses not to participate in a national shared-cost program that is established by the Government of Canada after the coming into force of this section in an area of exclusive provincial jurisdiction, if the province carries on a program or initiative that is compatible with the national objectives.

Legislative power not extended

(2) Nothing in this section extends the legislative powers of the Parliament of Canada or of the legislatures of the provinces.

8. The said Act is further amended by adding thereto the following heading and sections:

XII—CONFERENCES ON THE ECONOMY AND OTHER MATTERS

Conferences on the economy and other matters

148. A conference composed of the Prime Minister of Canada and the first ministers of the provinces shall be convened by the Prime Minister of Canada at least once each year to discuss the state of the Canadian economy and such other matters as may be appropriate.

XIII—References

149. A reference to this Act shall be deemed to include a reference to any amendments thereto.

Reference includes amendments

Constitution Act, 1982

9. Sections 40 to 42 of the *Constitution Act, 1982* are repealed and the following substituted therefor:

40. Where an amendment is made under subsection 38(1) that transfers legislative powers from provincial legislatures to Parliament, Canada shall provide reasonable compensation to any province to which the amendment does not apply.

Compensation

41. An amendment to the Constitution of Canada in relation to the following matters may be made by proclamation issued by the Governor General under the Great Seal of Canada only where authorized by resolutions of the Senate and House of Commons and of the legislative assembly of each province:

Amendment by unanimous consent

(*a*) the office of the Queen, the Governor General and the Lieutenant Governor of a province;

(*b*) the powers of the Senate and the method of selecting Senators;

(*c*) the number of members by which a province is entitled to be represented in the Senate and the residence qualifications of Senators;

(*d*) the right of a province to a number of members in the House of Commons not less than the number of Senators by which the province was entitled to be represented on April 17, 1982;

(*e*) the principle of proportionate representation of the provinces in the House of Commons prescribed by the Constitution of Canada;

(*f*) subject to section 43, the use of the English or the French language;

(*g*) the Supreme Court of Canada;

(*h*) the extension of existing provinces into the territories;

(*i*) notwithstanding any other law or practice, the establishment of new provinces; and (*j*) an amendment to this Part.

10. Section 44 of the said Act is repealed and the following substituted therefor:

Amendments by
Parliament

44. Subject to section 41, Parliament may exclusively make laws amending the Constitution of Canada in relation to the executive government of Canada or the Senate and House of Commons.

11. Subsection 46(1) of the said Act is repealed and the following substituted therefor:

Initiation of
amendment
procedures

46. (1) The procedures for amendment under sections 38, 41 and 43 may be initiated either by the Senate or the House of Commons or by the legislative assembly of a province.

12. Subsection 47(1) of the said Act is repealed and the following substituted therefor:

Amendments
without Senate
resolution

47. (1) An amendment to the Constitution of Canada made by proclamation under section 38, 41 or 43 may be made without a resolution of the Senate authorizing the issue of the proclamation if, within one hundred and eighty days after the adoption by the House of Commons of a resolution authorizing its issue, the Senate has not adopted such a resolution and if, at any time after the expiration of that period, the House of Commons again adopts the resolution.

13. Part VI of the said Act is repealed and the following substituted therefor:

PART VI

CONSTITUTIONAL CONFERENCES

Constitutional
conference

50. (1) A constitutional conference composed of the Prime Minister of Canada and the first ministers of the provinces shall be convened by the Prime Minister of Canada at least once each year, commencing in 1988.

Agenda

(2) The conferences convened under subsection (1) shall have included on their agenda the following matters:

(*a*) Senate reform, including the role and functions of the Senate, its powers, the method of selecting Senators and representation in the Senate;

(*b*) roles and responsibilities in relation to fisheries; and (*c*) such other matters as are agreed upon.

14. Subsection 52(2) of the said Act is amended by striking out the word ''and'' at the end of paragraph (*b*) thereof, by adding the word ''and'' at the end of paragraph (*c*) thereof and by adding thereto the following paragraph:

(*d*) any other amendment to the Constitution of Canada.

15. Section 61 of the said Act is repealed and the following substituted therefor:

61. A reference to the *Constitution Act, 1982*, or a reference to the *Constitution Acts 1867 to 1982*, shall be deemed to include a reference to any amendments thereto.

References

General

16. Nothing in section 2 of the *Constitution Act, 1867* affects section 25 or 27 of the *Canadian Charter of Rights and Freedoms*, section 35 of the *Constitution Act, 1982* or class 24 of section 91 of the *Constitution Act, 1867*.

Multicultural heritage and aboriginal peoples

CITATION

17. This amendment may be cited as the *Constitution Amendment, 1987*.

Citation

Suggestions for Further Reading

General:

CHEFFINS, R.I. and JOHNSON, P.A. *The Revised Canadian Constitution: Politics As Law.* Toronto: McGraw-Hill Ryerson, 1986.

HOGG, PETER W. *Constitutional Law of Canada* (2nd ed.). Toronto: Carswell, 1985.

LASKIN, BORA. "Tests for the Validity of Legislation: What is the Matter?" (1955-56) 11 *University of Toronto Law Journal*, 298.

LEDERMAN, W.R. (ed.) *The Courts and the Canadian Constitution.* Toronto: The Carleton Library, McClelland and Stewart, 1964.

MCCONNELL, W.H. *Commentary on the British North America Act.* Toronto: Macmillan, 1977.

MCWHINNEY, EDWARD. *Judicial Review in the English-Speaking World* (4th ed.) Toronto: University of Toronto Press, 1968.

MURPHY, WALTER F. and TANENHAUS, JOSEPH. *Comparative Constitutional Law, Cases and Commentaries.* New York: St. Martin's Press, 1977.

RUSSELL, PETER H. *The Judiciary in Canada: The Third Branch of Government.* Toronto: McGraw-Hill Ryerson, 1987.

SMITH, JENNIFER. "The Origins of Judicial Review in Canada." (1983) 16 *Canadian Journal of Political Science*, 115.

STRAYER, BARRY L. *The Canadian Constitution and the Courts* (2nd ed.). Toronto: Butterworths, 1983.

The Judicial Committee of the Privy Council:

BROWNE, G.P. *The Judicial Committee and the British North America Act.* Toronto: University of Toronto Press, 1967.

CAIRNS, ALAN C. "The Judicial Committee and Its Critics," (1971) 3 *Canadian Journal of Political Science*, 301.

GREENWOOD, F. MURRAY. "Lord Watson, Institutional Self-Interest and the Decentralization of Canadian Federalism in the 1890's," (1974) 9 *University of British Columbia Law Review*, 244.

HALDANE, VISCOUNT. "The Work for the Empire of the Judicial Committee of the Privy Council," (1922) 1 *Cambridge Law Journal*, 143.

JENNINGS, W. IVOR. "Constitutional Interpretation—The Experience of Canada," (1937) 51 *Harvard Law Review* 1.

KENNEDY, W.P.M. "Interpretation of the British North America Act," (1943) 8 *Cambridge Law Journal*, 146.

MACDONALD, V.C. "The Privy Council and the Canadian Constitution," (1951) 29 *Canadian Bar Review*, 1024.

SCOTT, F.R. "The Consequences of the Privy Council Decisions," (1937) 15 *Canadian Bar Review*, 485.

THE SENATE OF CANADA. *Report to the Honourable the Speaker Relating to the Enactment of the B.N.A. Act, 1867.* (O'Connor Report) Ottawa: Queen's Printer, 1939.

VAUGHAN, FREDERICK. "Critics of The Judicial Committee: The New Orthodoxy and an Alternative Explanation," and Replies by Alan Cairns and Peter Russell. (1986) 19 *Canadian Journal of Political Science*, 495.

VIPOND, ROBERT C. "Constitutional Politics and The Legacy of The Provincial Rights Movement in Canada," (1985) 18 *Canadian Journal of Political Science*, 271.

The Supreme Court of Canada:

BEAUDOIN, GERALD-A (eds.). *The Supreme Court of Canada*. Cowansville: Yvon Blais, 1985.

BROSSARD, J. *La Cour suprême et la constitution*. Montréal: Les Presses de l'Université de Montréal, 1968.

CAIRNS, ALAN and WILLIAMS, CYNTHIA (eds). *Constitutionalism, Citizenship and Society in Canada*. Toronto: University of Toronto Press, 1985.

FOUTS, DONALD E. "Policy-Making in the Supreme Court of Canada, 1950-1960" in GLENDON SCHUBERT and DAVID J. DANELSKI (eds.), *Comparative Judicial Behaviour*. Toronto: Oxford University Press, 1969.

LASKIN, BORA. "The Supreme Court of Canada: a Final Court of and for Canadians," (1951) 29 *Canadian Bar Review*, 1038. Also in W.R. LEDERMAN (ed.), *The Courts and the Canadian Constitution*, 125.

MACKINNON, FRANK. "The Establishment of the Supreme Court of Canada," (1946) 27 *Canadian Historical Review*, 258. Also in W.R. LEDERMAN (ed.), *The Courts and the Canadian Constitution*, 106.

MONAHAN, PATRICK. *Politics and The Constitution: The Charter, Federalism and The Supreme Court of Canada*. Toronto: Carswell/Methuen, 1987.

PECK, SIDNEY R. "A Scalogram Analysis of the Supreme Court of Canada, 1958-67," in GLENDON SCHUBERT and DAVID J. DANELSKI (eds.), *Comparative Judicial Behaviour*.

RUSSELL, PETER H. *The Supreme Court of Canada as a Bilingual and Bicultural Institution*. Ottawa: Queen's Printer, 1969.

_____ "The Supreme Court Proposals in the Meech Lake Accord," (1988) 14 *Canadian Public Policy*, S81.

SNELL, JAMES and VAUGHAN, FREDERICK. *The Supreme Court of Canada: History of the Institution*. Toronto: University of Toronto Press, 1985.

WEILER, PAUL C. *In The Last Resort*. Toronto: Carswell/Methuen, 1974.

The Division of Powers:

CHANDLER, MARSHA. "Constitutional Change and Public Policy: The Impact of the Resource Amendment," (1986) 19 *Canadian Journal of Political Science*, 103.

FLETCHER, MARTHA. "Judicial Review and the Division of Powers," in J. PETER MEEKISON (ed.), *Canadian Federalism: Myth or Reality*. Toronto: Methuen, 1968.

HEAD, IVAN L. "The Canadian Offshore Mineral Rights Reference: The Application of International Law to a Federal Constitution," (1968) 18 *University of Toronto Law Journal*, 131.

HOGG, PETER W. "Is the Supreme Court of Canada Biased in Constitutional Cases?" (1979) 57 *Canadian Bar Review*, 721.

LASKIN, BORA. " 'Peace, Order and Good Government' Re-examined," (1947) 25 *Canadian Bar Review*, 1054. Also in W.R. LEDERMAN (ed.), *The Courts and the Canadian Constitution*, 66.

L'ECUYER, GILBERT. *La Cour Suprême du Canada et la Partage des Compétences, 1949-78*. Québec: Gouvernement du Québec, 1978.

LEDERMAN, W.R. "Unity and Diversity in Canadian Federalism: Ideals and Methods of Moderation," (1975) 53 *Canadian Bar Review*, 597.

LYSYK, K. "Constitutional Reform and the Introductory Clause of Section 91: Residual and Emergency Law-Making Authority," (1979) 57 *Canadian Bar Review*, 687.

MACPHERSON, JAMES C. "Developments in Constitutional Law: The 1978-79 Term," (1979) 1 *Supreme Court Review*, 77.

MALLORY, J.R. *Social Credit and the Federal Power in Canada*. Toronto: University of Toronto Press, 1954.

MCCONNELL, W.H. "The Judicial Review of Prime Minister Bennett's 'New Deal'," (1968) 6 *Osgoode Hall Law Review*, 39.

MCWHINNEY, EDWARD. *Comparative Federalism*. Toronto: University Press, 1962.

MOULL, W.D. "Natural Resources: The Other Crisis in Canadian Federalism," (1980) 18 *Osgoode Hall Law Journal*, 2.

PIGEON, LOUIS-PHILIPPE. "The Meaning of Provincial Autonomy," (1951) 29 *Canadian Bar Review*, 1126. Also in W.R. LEDERMAN (ed.) *The Courts and the Canadian Constitution*, 35.

REMILLARD, GIL. *Fédéralisme Canadien*. Montreal: Québec/Amérique, 1980.

RUSSELL, PETER H. "The *Anti-Inflation* Case: The Anatomy of a Constitutional Decision," (1977) 20 *Canadian Public Administration*, 632.

_____ "The Supreme Court and Federal-Provincial Relations: The Political Use of Legal Resources," (1985) 11 *Canadian Public Policy*, 161.

SMITH, ALEXANDER. *The Commerce Power in Canada and the United States*. Toronto: Butterworth, 1963.

TREMBLAY, ANDRE. *Les Compétences législatives au Canada et les Pouvoirs provinciaux en Matière de Propriété et de Droits civils*. Ottawa: Editions de Université d'Ottawa, 1967.

TREMBLAY, GUY. "The Supreme Court of Canada: Final Arbiter of Political Disputes," in IVAN BERNIER and ANDREE LAJOIE (eds.), *The Supreme Court of Canada as an Instrument of Political Change*. Toronto: University of Toronto Press, 1985.

WILKIE, J.S. "The Radio Reference and Onward: Exclusive Federal Jurisdiction over General Content in Broadcasting," (1980) 18 *Osgoode Hall Law Journal*, 49.

Rights and Freedoms:

BAYEFSKY, ANNE F. and EBERTS, MARY (eds.). *Equality Rights and the Canadian Charter of Rights and Freedoms*. Toronto: Carswell, 1985.

BEATTY, DAVID. *Putting the Charter to Work: Designing a Constitutional Labour Code*. Kingston & Montreal: McGill-Queen's University Press, 1987.

BECKTON, CLARE F. and MACKAY, A. WAYNE. *The Courts and The Charter*. Toronto: University of Toronto Press, 1985.

CAVALLUZZO, PAUL. "Judicial Review and the Bill of Rights: Drybones and Its Aftermath," (1971) 9 *Osgoode Hall Law Journal*, 511.

GIBSON, DALE. *The Law of The Charter: General Principles*. Toronto: Carswell, 1986.

GOLD, M.E. "Equality Before the Law in the Supreme Court of Canada: A Case Study," (1980) 18 *Osgoode Hall Law Journal*, 336.

KNOPFF, RAINER. "What Do Constitutional Equality Rights Protect Canadians Against?" (1987) 20 *Canadian Journal of Political Science*, 265.

LASKIN, BORA. "Our Civil Liberties—The Role of the Supreme Court," (1955) 41 *Queen's Quarterly*, 445.

MORTON, F.L. "The Political Impact of the Canadian Charter of Rights and Freedoms," (1987) 20 *Canadian Journal of Political Science*, 31.

_____ "The Politics of Rights: What Canadians Should Know About the American Bill of Rights," (1988) 1 *Windsor Review of Legal and Social Issues*.

PETTER, ANDREW. "The Politics of the Charter," (1986) 8 *Supreme Court Review*, 473.

RUSSELL, PETER H. "The Political Purposes of the Canadian Charter of Rights and Freedoms," (1983) 61 *Canadian Bar Review*, 30.

_____ "Canada's Charter: A Political Report," (1988) *Public Law*, 385.

SCHMEISER, D.A. *Civil Liberties in Canada*. Toronto: Oxford University Press, 1964.

SCOTT, F.R. *Civil Liberties and Canadian Federalism*. Toronto: University of Toronto Press, 1959.

_____ "The Privy Council and Minority Rights," (1930) *Queen's Quarterly*, 668.

SHARPE, ROBERT J. *Charter Litigation*. Toronto: Butterworths, 1987.

SMILEY, DONALD. "Courts, Legislatures and the Protection of Human Rights," in M.L. FRIEDLAND (ed.), *Courts and Trials*. Toronto: University of Toronto Press, 1975.

STRAYER, BARRY. "Life Under the Charter: Adjusting the Balance Between Legislatures and Courts," (1988) *Public Law*, 347.

TARNOPOLSKY, W.S. *The Canadian Bill of Rights*. Toronto: The Carleton Library, McClelland and Stewart Limited, 1975.

TARNOPOLSKY, WALTER F. and BEAUDOIN, GERALD-A. (eds.). *The Canadian Charter of Rights and Freedoms: Commentary*. Toronto: Carswell, 1982.

WEILER, PAUL. "Rights and Judges in a Democracy: A New Canadian Version," (1984) 18 *University of Michigan Journal of Law Reform*, 51.

WILSON, BERTHA. "The Making of a Constitution: Approaches to Judicial Interpretation," (1988) *Public Law*, 370.

Constitutional Change:

BANTING, KEITH and SIMEON, RICHARD (eds.). *And No One Cheered: Federalism, Democracy and the Constitution Act*. Toronto: Methuen, 1983.

CORRY, J.A. "Difficulties of Divided Jurisdiction; Appendix: The Delegation of Power by Dominion to Province or by Province to Dominion," *Appendix 7 to Report of Royal Commission on Dominion-Provincial Relations*. Ottawa: Queen's Printer, 1940.

FAVREAU, GUY. *The Amendment of the Constitution of Canada*. Ottawa: Queen's Printer, 1965.

GERIN-LAJOIE, PAUL. *Constitutional Amendment in Canada*. Toronto: University of Toronto Press, 1950.

HOGG, PETER. *Meech Lake Constitutional Accord Annotated*. Toronto: Carswell, 1988.

KNOPFF, RAINER. "Legal Theory and the "Patriation" Debate." (1981) 7 *Queen's Law Journal*, 41.

LEDERMAN, W.R. *Continuing Constitutional Dilemmas*. Toronto: Butterworth, 1981.

LYSYK, K. "Constitutional Law—The Inter-Delegation Doctrine: A Constitutional Paper Tiger?" (1969) 47 *Canadian Bar Review*, 271.

MILNE, DAVID. *The New Canadian Constitution*. Toronto: James Lorimer, 1982.

ROMANOW, ROY, WHYTE, JOHN and LEESON, HOWARD. *Canada Notwithstanding: The Making of the Constitution, 1976-1982*. Toronto: Carswell/Methuen, 1984.

RUSSELL, PETER H., ROBERT DECARY ET AL. *The Court and the Constitution*. Kingston: Institute of Intergovernmental Relations. Queen's University, 1982.

SMILEY, DONALD. *Canada in Question: Federalism in the Eighties* (3rd ed.) Toronto: McGraw-Hill/Ryerson, 1980.